New Dictionary of Scientific Biography

Published by special arrangement with the American Council of Learned Societies

The American Council of Learned Societies, organized in 1919 for the purpose of advancing the study of the humanities and of the humanistic aspects of the social sciences, is a nonprofit federation comprising thirty-three national scholarly groups. The Council represents the humanities in the United States in the International Union of Academies, provides fellowships and grants-in-aid, supports research-and-planning conferences and symposia, and sponsers special projects and scholarly publications.

MEMBER ORGANIZATIONS

American Philosophical Society, 1743
American Academy of Arts and Sciences, 1780
American Antiquarian Society, 1812
American Oriental Society, 1842
American Numismatic Society, 1858
American Philological Association, 1869
Archaeological Institute of America, 1879
Society of Biblical Literature, 1880
Modern Language Association of America, 1883
American Historical Association, 1884
American Economic Association, 1885
American Folklore Society, 1888
American Society of Church History, 1888
American Dialect Society, 1889
American Psychological Association, 1892
Association of American Law Schools, 1900
American Philosophical Association, 1900
American Schools of Oriental Research, 1900
American Anthropological Association, 1902
American Political Science Association, 1903
Bibliographical Society of America, 1904
Association of American Geographers, 1904
Hispanic Society of America, 1904
American Sociological Association, 1905
American Society of International Law, 1906
Organization of American Historians, 1907
American Academy of Religion, 1909
College Forum of the National Council of Teachers of English, 1911
Society for the Advancement of Scandinavian Study, 1911
College Art Association, 1912
National Communication Association, 1914
History of Science Society, 1924
Linguistic Society of America, 1924
Medieval Academy of America, 1925
American Association for the History of Medicine, 1925
American Musicological Society, 1934
Economic History Association, 1940

Society of Architectural Historians, 1940
Association for Asian Studies, 1941
American Society for Aesthetics, 1942
American Association for the Advancement of Slavic Studies, 1948
American Studies Association, 1950
Metaphysical Society of America, 1950
North American Conference on British Studies, 1950
American Society of Comparative Law, 1951
Renaissance Society of America, 1954
Society for Ethnomusicology, 1955
Society for French Historical Studies, 1956
International Center of Medieval Art, 1956
American Society for Legal History, 1956
American Society for Theatre Research, 1956
African Studies Association, 1957
Society for the History of Technology, 1958
Society for Cinema and Media Studies, 1959
American Comparative Literature Association, 1960
Law and Society Association, 1964
Middle East Studies Association of North America, 1966
Latin American Studies Association, 1966
Association for the Advancement of Baltic Studies, 1968
American Society for Eighteenth Century Studies, 1969
Association for Jewish Studies, 1969
Sixteenth Century Society and Conference, 1970
Society for American Music, 1975
Dictionary Society of North America, 1975
German Studies Association, 1976
American Society for Environmental History, 1976
Society for Music Theory, 1977
National Council on Public History, 1979
Society of Dance History Scholars, 1979

New Dictionary of Scientific Biography

VOLUME 6
PACHYMERES–SZILARD

Noretta Koertge
EDITOR IN CHIEF

CHARLES SCRIBNER'S SONS
An imprint of Thomson Gale, a part of The Thomson Corporation

THOMSON
GALE

Detroit • New York • San Francisco • New Haven, Conn. • Waterville, Maine • London

New Dictionary of Scientific Biography

Noretta Koertge

LIBRARY OF CONGRESS CATALOGING-IN-PUBLICATION DATA

New dictionary of scientific biography / Noretta Koertge, editor in chief.
    p. cm.
    Includes bibliographical references and index.
    ISBN 978-0-684-31320-7 (set : alk. paper)—ISBN 978-0-684-31321-4 (vol. 1 : alk. paper)—ISBN 978-0-684-31322-1 (vol. 2 : alk. paper)—ISBN 978-0-684-31323-8 (vol. 3 : alk. paper)—ISBN 978-0-684-31324-5 (vol. 4 : alk. paper)—ISBN 978-0-684-31325-2 (vol. 5 : alk. paper)—ISBN 978-0-684-31326-9 (vol. 6 : alk. paper)—ISBN 978-0-684-31327-6 (vol. 7 : alk. paper)—ISBN 978-0-684-31328-3 (vol. 8 : alk. paper)
    1. Scientists—Biography—Dictionaries. I. Koertge, Noretta.

Q141.N45 2008
509.2'2—dc22
[B]
    2007031384

Editorial Board

P

PACHYMERES, GEORGES (OR GEORGE) (*b.* Nicaea, 1242; *d.* 1310), *history, mathematics*).

Of a Constantinopolitan family, Pachymeres was born in 1242 at Nicaea, where the Byzantine court and government had taken refuge under the Latin occupation following on the capture of Constantinople under the Fourth Crusade in 1204. At the time of the restoration in 1261, he returned to Constantinople, where higher education would soon be restored under the direction of George Acropolites. Georges Pachymeres followed his courses and became deacon. He then followed a brilliant career in the hierarchy of the church and palace. He assumed the high offices of *Protekdikos* (director of the inspectors of churches and monasteries) and of *Dikaiophylax* (guardian of the seals), and was *Didascalos tôn apostolôn* (professor of New Testament exegesis) at the Patriarchal School. One supposes that he was responsible for teaching in many fields, such as rhetoric, philosophy, the sciences. His *History* stopped in 1307. His death occurred around 1310.

Historical Works. Pachymeres's output can be divided into two parts. On the one hand, there are his *Historical Accounts* in thirteen books, which retraced the reign of Michael Palaeologus (Michael VIII, 1259–1282) and a part of the reign of Andronicus III, from 1282 to 1307. On the other hand, he composed several works devoted to his teaching, both religious and secular: scholia on the Psalms, a paraphrase of the works of Denys the Areopagite, a summary of the *Logic* of Aristotle, exercises in rhetoric, and a *Quadrivium* of the sciences. To this were to be added a *Treatise on the Holy Spirit* devoted to affirming the orthodoxy of doctrine after the Union of the Churches after the Council of Lyon (1274), letters to the patriarch of Alexandria, Athanasius II, and several short poems in a prologue to these works. His handwriting can be identified in several manuscripts, namely those of philosophical texts, and the autograph of his *Quadrivium* is preserved in the *Angelicus gr.* 38 (C.3.7).

***Quadrivium* Treatise.** The *Quadrivium* (or *Treatise of the Four Sciences*) was intended for his teaching of the sciences at the Patriarchal School, restored after the reconquest of Constantinople in 1261. The Patriarchal School was the foundation for advance teaching controlled by the church, and patronized by the emperor, intended for the training of both clerics and seculars. It has been said that the division of scientific teaching into four sciences was due to Western influence, but that is not at all the case. This classification, already mentioned by Nicomachus of Gerasa (second century CE), is regularly found in Byzantine teaching. For example, there exists an anonymous *quadrivium,* written around 1007 or 1008.

The *Quadrivium* of Georges Pachymeres began with a short poem presenting the author and his treatise, and with a prologue to the glory of science, impregnated with Platonism, where the author commented on a sentence of Favorinus of Arles (second century CE): science is natural to the human mind and brings it pleasure. Next he defined science, its aims, and divisions drawing heavily on Nicomachus: Arithmetic and Harmony are sciences of the discontinous (*to diôrismenon*); Geometry and Astronomy, sciences of the continuous (*to synekhes*).

The first of sciences is therefore Arithmetic, to which is devoted Book 1. The *Arithmetic* of Pachymeres draws mainly on Nicomachus, Diophantus, who was paraphrased in many passages, and Euclid (*Elements* 7–9). The second book was devoted to *Harmony* (or *Music*), and consisted of a compilation from different authors, such as Nicomachus, Ptolemy, and Aristoxenus. The third book, the *Geometry* (and *Stereometry*) was based on Euclid, as expected. Finally the fourth book was devoted to *Astronomy*. This fourth book, very ill-assorted, began with a long account of arithmetic, devoted to sexagesimal operations and to the multiplication and division of ratios. Then followed long explanations of general astronomy (celestial sphere, shape of Earth, dimensions of Earth, the principal circle of the celestial sphere, the Sun, the Moon, the planets, phases of the Moon, eclipses, etc.). They are followed by a description of the constellations, mainly their simultaneous risings and settings. The author returned once again to operations in the sexagesimal system and to the calculation of the table of chords in the *Almagest*.

Pachymeres gave, in passing, some notions of astrological theories even though he condemns the astrologers who link the destinies of men to such configurations. In his *Astronomy*, Plato, Aristotle, Archimedes, Hipparchus, Aratus, Theon of Smyrna, Theon of Alexandria, Cleomedes, and Ptolemy were heavily drawn upon. However, he nowhere put Ptolemy's astronomy into practice to calculate the positions of Sun, Moon, or planets, the syzygies, or eclipses. He never departed from parameters given by Ptolemy or his predecessors, but one does find a brief notice (chapter 21) of the rate of precession of 1° per sixty-six years, in contrast to Ptolemy's value, 1° per 100 years—but this passage may not be authentic.

The *Quadrivium* of Georges Pachymeres has been published, but not translated or commentated. According to Paul Tannery, who had prepared its edition, the work of Pachymeres is only a compilation of classical works, but it shows precisely how the Byzantines used the classical heritage for the teaching of mathematics (citation from Stephanou, *Quadrivium*, p. 6, note 2). It is also astonishing that the work met with so little success in its time—most of the manuscripts indeed are from the sixteenth century. In reality, a number of Byzantine scholars, such as Theodore Metochites or Theodore Meliteniotes, made full use of it, even plagiarized it, for arithmetic. But in line with the custom of Byzantines, who cited only the ancients, and never their contemporaries, the latter never mentioned his name. One does not know the relation between the *Harmonic* of Georges Pachymeres and the voluminous treatise on the same subject by Manuel Bryennius, his contemporary, but it is likely that the latter also used it.

If he brought nothing new, Pachymeres proved to have a vast erudition, and in this writer's opinion, his influence on his contemporaries and successors was important. This is a major source regarding the language and practice of arithmetic of Byzantine scholars. One must not forget that it was a teaching manual and that the length of certain explanations was doubtless in proportion to the difficulties met by the students!

BIBLIOGRAPHY

WORKS BY PACHYMERES

Tannery, Paul ed. *Quadrivium de Georges Pachymère*. Texte révisé et établi par le R. P. E. Stephanou, *Studi e Testi* 94, Città del Vaticano, 1940.

OTHER SOURCES

Lampakis, Stylianos. *Georgios Pachymeris, Protekdikos and Dikaiophylax: An Introductory Essay*. Monograph 5. Athens: National Hellenic Research Foundation, Institute for Byzantine Research, 2004.

Anne Tihon

PALMÉN, ERIK HERBERT (*b.* Vaasa, Russia [Finland], 31 August 1898; *d.* Helsinki, Finland, 19 March 1985), *synoptic and dynamic meteorology, aerology, oceanography.*

Palmén's major contributions to meteorology were studies of the hemispheric character of the jet stream, the existence of a separate subtropical jet stream and the necessary condition for the formation of tropical cyclones. His scientific breakthrough came when he was approaching his fifties and had left his country with the intention of possibly staying away.

Education. The son of a judge, Eskil Herbert Palmén, and Sally Maria Skog, Palmén grew up in an intellectual setting and went to the University of Helsinki, where he studied astronomy and was awarded a master of science degree in 1921. The mathematical formalism of celestial mechanics bored him, so he turned to meteorology, in which he had been interested since childhood.

At this time there was, as yet, no academic faculty for meteorology in Finland, so Palmén had to earn his living at the Institute for Marine Research, while, in his spare time, he studied meteorology and lectured in geophysics at the University of Helsinki. During his time at the Marine Institute, which lasted until 1946, he came to acquire a deep knowledge of problems related to the interaction between the atmosphere and the sea. Notable among his oceanographic works are the determination of interactions between wind stress and water-level changes and stratification, an explanation of the equatorial countercurrent, and analysis of the momentum balance of the Antarctic circumpolar current. But it was in meteorology that Palmén would make his greatest contributions, based on his oceanographic work and his independent education, which made him as a meteorologist "a self-made man" (Holopainen, 1985).

Early Meteorological Work. Erik Palmén's scientific career coincided with the era during which theory and observations were increasingly brought together in a coherent conception of the global atmosphere. In the 1920s Scandinavian meteorologists working for Professor Vilhelm Bjerknes in Bergen, Norway ("the Bergen School") explored new ideas about the general circulation of the atmosphere, in particular with respect to storm developments. The new ideas were introduced to Palmén by one of its leading teachers, Tor Bergeron, who visited Finland in 1922. Palmén's interest in the new theory is apparent in his 1926 doctoral dissertation on the movement of extratropical cyclones. In 1928 Palmén made a three-month journey in Europe to meet leading meteorologists. After a one month's stay at the Geophysical Institute in Bergen he began a long working association with Jacob Bjerknes on the three-dimensional structure of atmospheric disturbances.

While the new cyclone theories were received with enthusiasm in the Soviet Union, and with a positive curiosity by the Anglo American meteorological world, the attitude of the Austrian-German meteorologists was hostile. In opposition to the Bergen School they stressed the importance of the redistribution of air of different densities in the upper atmospheric layers, in particular the stratosphere, for controlling lower-level pressure changes. The debate was at first forwarded by theoretical arguments, because observations from the upper atmosphere by kites, airplanes, and balloonborne self-reregistering meteographs were sparse and infrequent.

Together with Jacob Bjerknes, Palmén championed the Bergen School notion that storms developed in the troposphere, in particular in the border zones (frontal zones) of major air masses of different densities. It was true that the Bergen School at first had little to say about the role of the higher atmospheric layers. However, during the mid- and late 1930s they organized or took part in several coordinated releases by means of the serial release of balloons equipped with registering instruments, which resulted in the first comprehensive aerological analyses over an entire extratropical cyclone (J. Bjerknes and Palmén, 1937). In many of these pioneer studies Palmén showed his intuitive ability to distinguish important aspects of problems from minor ones and to derive from a small amount of data results that later research, based on a much larger body of data, has shown to be essentially correct.

While the Bergen School extended their perspective upward in the troposphere, the German school began to move downward, gradually appreciating the role of the troposphere. A consensus that the main "steering level" of atmospheric motion was in the middle troposphere had to wait until after World War II.

The War Years. At the outbreak of the war Palmén became director of the Marine Research Institute after the previous director, Rolf Witting, had become a leading member of the Finnish government. The war and administrative obligations limited any scientific productivity but Palmén found time to help his Swedish colleague and student Alf Nyberg to construct three-dimensional images of the atmosphere based on aerological material collected during two experiments in 1935 and 1939.

The war over and approaching his fifties one would have expected that Palmén would have passed his zenith of scientific achievements. Instead he left Finland with his family in June 1946 for the United States, for a period that turned out to be the most fruitful of his scientific life. In his pocket he carried an immigration visa; he arrived in the New World with the intention of possibly staying there.

Most of his life Palmén had difficulty getting a meteorology position in Finland. The 1930s was a time of political tension in Finland. The small Swedish-speaking minority was regarded by ultranationalistic Finns as alien subjects, reminiscent of a colonial upper class. Though the Swedish minority socially did not differ significantly from their Finnish compatriots, this could not be said about Erik Palmén, who indeed was a baron (Swedish *friherre*). In 1931, Palmén was refused permission to apply for the post as director of the Meteorological Institute on the grounds that he had not passed a formal test in Finnish.

During the "Finnish Winter War" (1939–1940) the Finnish military was not content with the weather forecasts. They insisted that, in spite of his lack of formal linguistic qualifications, Palmén should replace the head of the forecast office as soon as the ice service work at the marine institute permitted. Before the ice season was over the war ended, in March 1940.

There was another, less political reason why Palmén could not easily make an academic career in Finland. At this time this relatively small country housed another of the world's leading meteorologists, Vilho Väisälä, the creator of the well-known high-quality radiosondes. Neither Väisälä nor Palmén held a chair at Helsinki University, but were both given the title of professor in 1940. When the existing professor retired in 1943 the chair was left vacant since the university could not choose between the two.

Palmén's departure was partly a reaction to his difficulty in being recognized as a scientific meteorologist in his home country, and partly because of promising perspectives offered by the Swedish American Carl-Gustaf Rossby, the leading meteorologist at the time. Palmén had met Rossby, then professor at the Massachusetts Institute of Technology, in 1930 on a visit to Bergen. They immediately struck up a lasting friendship sharing common scientific interests, the same (Swedish) mother tongue, a taste for the good things in life, and a nonbureaucratic attitude to work.

Already in February 1941 Rossby had tried to bring Palmén to Chicago as assistant professor in the newly organized Department of Meteorology at the University of Chicago. The wartime conditions had prevented that, but now Palmén accepted Rossby's renewed invitation and with his family crossed the Atlantic in a weeklong journey in June 1946. Within a couple of years Palmén would make several important contributions to dynamic meteorology which made his name famous in the meteorological world.

Palmén and the "Chicago School." World War II had established a huge increase in the meteorological observational network, in particular of the upper atmosphere. To investigate the atmosphere's general circulation from this extensive network Rossby had organized a project with a large group of young American and foreign meteorologists. As the deputy leader of the project he chose Erik Palmén.

Erik Palmén's scientific contributions in this "Chicago School" project, like almost all of his work, were observational studies where the core always was the physical interpretation of the observations or the diagnostic results derived from them. He wanted to counteract a tendency to regard the general circulation as nothing but "the statistical manifestation of currents as they appear in the actual atmosphere" and to treat the atmospheric flow as large-scale turbulence, as a substitute for "real knowledge" (Palmén, 1951b). The physical nature of the actual atmosphere could only be understood through detailed analyses of characteristic disturbances. Palmén is one of the few meteorologists who attempted (in 1951) to outline a physical portrait of the general circulation (the others incidentally being his close colleagues Bergeron in 1928 and Rossby in 1941). Prominent in this portrait are the dominant upper-air wind bands, in whose discovery and analysis Palmén played a major role.

It was known already in the 1930s that the wind increased with height, often to speeds of 50–70 meters per second. But it was not until the late 1940s that it was recognized that these strong winds were organized into long, narrow bands, jet streams. Using the technique of vertical cross sections, the same as he had done in the 1930s, Palmén elucidated the nature and dynamics of the midlatitude jet streams and their relation to the Bergen School concept of air-mass fronts. These investigations led Palmén to further studies of energy conversions in the atmosphere.

Existence of what came to be known as the subtropical jet stream had for long been evident in scattered high-level observations of very strong winds at low latitudes. Using a simplified model based on angular momentum conservation Palmén argued that a strong accumulation of momentum ought to be found around 30° latitude. This is where the air, which has been heated in the equatorial belt and then risen to about 10 kilometers' height, starts to accelerate away from the tropics, starts to be deflected eastward due to Earth's rotation and is thus barred from further progress poleward. Of special importance was the important distinction he made between this subtropical jet stream and the midlatitude jet streams that were caused by local thermal contrast along the border zones of neighboring air masses.

It was remarkable that Palmén, a meteorologist raised and educated at northern latitudes, made fundamental contributions to the dynamics of tropical cyclones. Through investigations of a hurricane crossing Florida in autumn 1947 Palmén reached the conclusion that tropical cyclones can form only if the ocean surface temperature exceeds 27 degrees Celsius. On a visit to the United States in October 1954 Palmén observed Hurricane Hazel and was able to calculate the internal release of kinetic energy.

Half a year after Palmén had left Finland the Helsinki University authorities decided to appoint Palmén to the chair. But Palmén had by now settled well in the United States and would need more to convince him to come home. He was in particular not happy with the lack of recognition of general sciences in Finland. Just before his departure, he had published an article in a journal on "the economic plight of science in Finland" (Palmén, 1946). There he gave voice to Finnish scientists, who did not see any future for scientific research in their home country. Many of them had already emigrated.

The article stirred a nationwide debate that two years later resulted in the revival of the old project about a Finnish academy. Among those elected was Erik Palmén, then still in Chicago. These signs of recognition acted strongly to make him return home. It meant the possibility of continuing research and maintaining international contacts in the field of dynamic meteorology. It also paid off well for Finland: in the early 1960s, thanks to Palmén's wide international outlook and travel funds, some of his students started to work on problems in the new and promising field of numerical weather prediction.

Palmén's sixtieth birthday was marked by an international celebration. In 1956 he was awarded the Symons Memorial Gold Medal by the Royal Meteorological Society and in 1960, together with Jacob Bjerknes, the AMS Rossby Prize for "their pioneering and distinguished research contributions and synoptic aerology which had given a unified picture of the general circulation of the atmosphere." He was awarded the Swedish Rossby Prize in 1966 and in 1968 the Silver Medal of the Finnish Geophysical Society (in 1988 renamed the Erik Palmén medal). After his retirement in 1963 Palmén began work with his student Chester W. Newton on a comprehensive textbook on circulation processes in the atmosphere from the large-scale weather patterns covering most of continents down to thundery squall-lines.

Palmén's Personality. In 1923 Erik Palmén married Synnöve Maria von Hellens, a teacher of mathematics. They had two children: Ann Marie (Mrs. Walter Hackman) and Lars Johan.

The common image of Palmén, conveyed by the traditional photo, shows the formal stern side of his person. His friends and colleagues knew him as an enthusiastic and open-minded scientist, never hesitating to enter into any discussion, whether it was about meteorology, nature, or world affairs. Journalists who interviewed him noted his preference for "counter-opposing views," and provocative statements, the reaction to which he awaited with "jubilant wrinkles around the sunken brown eyes" (Marcella, 1955).

Among those "provocative statements" was his often expressed opinion that anything more than four to five years of basic university education led only to being conformist. "The scientific mind withers away, bored and tired of reading too much." Like other members of the Bergen School, most notably Vilhelm Bjerknes himself, Palmén credited his own success partly because he was himself "merely an amateur" in this special field: "I was, obviously, unburdened by prejudicial opinions and theories. It is often good not to have too much knowledge" (Marcella, 1968).

BIBLIOGRAPHY

WORKS BY PALMÉN

With Jacob Bjerknes. "Investigations of Selected European Cyclones by Means of Serial Ascents. Case 4: February 15–17 1935." *Geophysiske Publikasjoner* 12, no. 2 (1937): 1–62.

Vetenskapens Ekonomiska Nödläge I Finland (The economic plight of science in Finland), Nya Argus, March 1946.

With Staff Members of the Department of Meteorology of the University of Chicago. "On the General Circulation of the Atmosphere in Middle Latitudes." *Bulletin of the American Meteorological Society* 28 (1947): 255–280.

"The Aerology of Extratropical Disturbances." *Compendium of Meteorology*, edited by Thomas F. Malone. Boston: American Meteorological Society, 1951a.

"The Role of Atmospheric Disturbances in the General Circulation." *Quarterly Journal of the Royal Meteorological Society* 77 (1951b): 337–354. Symons Memorial Lecture.

With Chester W. Newton. *Atmospheric Circulation Systems: Their Structure and Physical Interpretation*. New York: Academic Press, 1969.

"Personal Recollections about the Bergen School." Translated and edited from a lecture given in Finnish at the Department of Meteorology, University of Helsinki, 21 February 1979. Available from the Department of Meteorology, University of Helsinki.

"Muistelmia Bergenin ja Chicagon koulukunnan ajoilta." Lecture given in Finnish at the Department of Meteorology, University of Helsinki, 1979. Available from the Department of Meteorology, University of Helsinki.

"In My Opinion…." *Geophysica* 21, no. 1 (1985): 5–18. Autobiographical notes and bibliography.

OTHER SOURCES

Holopainen, Eero. "Erik Herbert Palmén." *Geophysica* 21 (1985): 1–3.

Marcella [Margareta Normeen]. 1955, Interview with Erik Palmén. *Hufudstadsbladet*, Helsinki, 29 July 1955.

———. 1968, Interview with Erik Palmén. *Hufudstadsbladet*, Helsinki, 30 August 1968.

Newton, Chester W. "Erik Palmén: Synthesizer of the Atmospheric General Circulation." *Bulletin of the American Meteorological Society* 67, no. 3 (1986): 282–293.

———, and Eero O. Holopainen, eds. "The Life Cycle of Extratropical Cyclones." *The Erik Palmén Memorial Volume*. American Meteorological Society, 1990. Contains scientific articles on atmospheric dynamics by friends and colleagues of Erik Palmén, who in 1988, three years after his death and on the ninetieth anniversary of his birth, had organized an international symposium in Helsinki.

Riehl, Herbert. "Erik Palmén 1898–1985." *Quarterly Journal of the Royal Meteorological Society* 111 (1985): 1142–1143. Obituary.

Taba, H. "The Bulletin Interviews: Professor E. H. Palmén." *WMO Bulletin* 30 (1981): 92–100.

Anders Persson

PANETH, FRIEDRICH ADOLF (*b.* Vienna, Austria, 31 August 1887; *d.* Mainz, Germany, 17 September 1958), *radiochemistry, inorganic chemistry, philosophy of science.* For the original article on Paneth see *DSB*, vol. 10.

Unlike many chemists, Paneth was deeply interested in the historical roots and philosophical foundations of science in general and of chemistry in particular throughout his entire scientific life. This postscript will concentrate on his historical and philosophical contributions. He read primary sources from antiquity (pre-Socratics, Aristotle), the Renaissance (Robert Boyle), classical (Benedict Spinoza, Immanuel Kant, John Stuart Mill) and contemporary authors (Heinrich Rickert, Moritz Schlick, Emile Meyerson, Gaston Bachelard), and was well aware of the main achievements and developments of philosophy. His epistemological point of view can be considered as Kantian, and his philosophical writings as highly influential to modern philosophy of chemistry.

The discovery of isotopes and radioactivity meant that it was no longer strictly the case that all atoms of the elements as listed in the Periodic Table were identical. (Consider, for example, carbon-12 versus carbon-14.) In addition, in the process of radioactive decay, one element was destroyed and a new element was created. Paneth was the first to grapple with the implications of these discoveries for the most fundamental concepts in chemistry. In 1914 Paneth had published on general problems of isotopy, and in 1916 he produced a systematic survey on the concepts of *element* and *atom* in which he referred critically to the "law of substance" (*Stoffgesetz*). With this law, Wilhelm Ostwald had claimed that two chemical substances are identical with respect to all properties if they are identical in a few of these. Paneth explicitly denied the validity of this expression because isotopy, strictly taken, had made it invalid. However, Paneth conceded that a strict interpretation of this denial would lead to a devaluation of the concept of the element within chemistry: similar to uncreatability and indestructibility, it would also be necessary to abandon the idea that there was a limited number of basic chemical substances (1916, p. 182). Because of this dilemma, Paneth suggested the following definition of an element: Two elements are assigned with the same name if a mixture of these cannot be separated by chemical operations (1916, p. 183). It is noteworthy that this definition is operational and phenomenological. It is operational because it delivers a kind of recipe on how to treat two substance samples in order to differentiate or identify them. It is phenomenological because it uses real, macroscopic materials only, rather than an atomistic vocabulary.

Sixteen years later, however, there no longer was consensus regarding strictly phenomenological, non-atomistic approaches to the foundations of chemistry. Referring to ancient atomists and their reception, and more particularly to the theoretical work of František Wald (1861–1930) and Ostwald, Paneth said in 1931: "We wholly disregard here the deliberations of Wald and Ostwald, who depart from the usual notion of element and follow their own anti-atomistic lines of thought" (1962, p. 9). The source of this quotation, a lecture presented in Königsberg titled "Die erkenntnistheoretische Stellung des chemischen Elementbegriffs" (The epistemological status of the chemical concept of element), was his main philosophical contribution. In his introduction, Paneth discussed the question of why chemistry has been of only minor interest to philosophers. He came to the conclusion that the deficient chemical knowledge of philosophers is primarily responsible for the neglect of chemistry in the humanities.

The two main topics of the Königsberg lecture were the question of persistence of elements in compounds and the problem of reduction of chemistry to physics. Referring to the former topic, Paneth suggested a dualist interpretation of the notion *element*. This distinction marks clearly the difference between two traditional conceptions of element that are often conflated. If one says, as did Boyle, that elements are the last products of analysis, then one is using the concept of simple substances (*einfache Stoffe*). However, if one thinks of elements as the ultimate constituents of matter that are invariant during chemical reactions, one is dealing with the concept of basic substances (*Grundstoffe*). In modern philosophical terms, simple substances are *observables*, basic substances are *non-observables*. Here is seen a hint of the Kantian *phenomena* (the observables) and *noumena* (the non-observables). Paneth claimed: "to understand the change of properties of substances we require transcendental hypotheses" (1962, p. 14). Hence, he expanded his former merely phenomenological point of view and added the realm of transcendental ideas to his philosophy of chemistry.

Referring to reductionism, Paneth said: "Even if the essential character of chemistry should change in the future as the result of the expansion of mathematical-physical methods, its history during the nineteenth century, when it achieved such successes without mathematics, must never be ignored in its philosophic evaluation" (1962, p. 8). Thus, as the result of his Kantian philosophy of science, he rejected the reduction of chemistry to physics (or mathematics) with the argument that chemistry never will lose contact to the realm of observables.

SUPPLEMENTARY BIBLIOGRAPHY

WORKS BY PANETH

"Über den Element- und Atombegriff in Chemie und Radiologie." *Zeitschrift für Physikalische Chemie* 91 (1916): 171–198.

Über die erkenntnistheoretische Stellung des chemischen Elementbegriffs. Halle/Saale: Niemeyer, 1931. Published as "The Epistemological Status of the Chemical Concept." *The British Journal for the Philosophy of Science* 13 (1962): 1–14, 144–160. Translated into English by Paneth's son.

OTHER SOURCES

Ruthenberg, Klaus. "Friedrich Adolf Paneth (1887–1958)." *Hyle* 3 (1997): 103–106.

Scerri, Eric. "Editorial 14." *Foundations of Chemistry* 5 (2003) 107–111.

Schummer, Joachim. *Realismus und Chemie*. Würzburg: Königshausen und Neumann, 1996.

Van Brakel, Jaap. *Philosophy of Chemistry: Between the Manifest and the Scientific Image.* Leuven: Leuven University Press, 2000.

Klaus Ruthenberg

PANOFSKY, HANS ARNOLD (*b.* Kassel, Germany, 18 September 1917; *d.* San Diego, California, 28 February 1988), *aerology, air pollution, atmospheric dynamics, boundary layers, diffusion, planetary atmospheres, similarity theory, turbulence and turbulence spectrum.*

Panofsky contributed to a wide range of scientific and engineering disciplines over the span of his illustrious forty-seven-year professional career, including astronomy, planetary and atmospheric sciences, climate, oceanography, air pollution, and most notably, the characteristics, spectrum, and statistical nature of turbulence. A recipient of several distinguishing awards, author of more than 150 papers and several books, supervisor of more than seventy master's theses and thirty doctoral dissertations, Panofsky contributed a monumental and enduring legacy.

The Early Years. In 1916 Dora Mosse married Erwin Panofsky; they had two sons, Hans in 1917 and Wolfgang ("Pief") two years later. As a scholar of art history, Erwin published his first significant work in 1924 on the history of the Neoplatonic theory of art, and he began to develop his "iconological" approach to art history while at the universities of Berlin, Munich, and Hamburg. When Hans was seventeen years old, the Panofsky family was forced to flee Germany as the Nazis came to power. In 1934 they immigrated to the United States, where Erwin took on joint appointments at New York University and at Princeton. In 1935 Erwin was invited to join the faculty at the Institute for Advanced Study at Princeton University, and there he remained until his death in 1968. As a teenager, Hans found himself immersed in the stimulating intellectual company of some of the most outstanding scientists and humanists of the twentieth century at a time when science and society were in a profound state of flux. The Panofskys' neighbor, Albert Einstein, would frequently spend leisure time with Hans's father. Because Erwin did not drive, he would ask Hans to drive them around Princeton while Einstein and the elder Panofsky, speaking German, would converse in the back seat. One can only imagine the rich conversations that Hans was party to during these outings.

Hans earned a BS in astronomy from Princeton in 1938, graduating summa cum laude. He then left for the West Coast to continue his education at the University of California at Berkeley, where he completed his PhD in astronomy in 1941. Along the way, Panofsky gained notoriety for breaking instruments; he would have others operate a telescope while he gathered his data. His first job after completing his PhD took him to Wilson College, a small women's liberal arts college in Chambersburg, Pennsylvania, as an instructor in mathematics and astronomy. It was there that Panofsky met and married Margaret Ann (Nancy) Riker, also originally from Princeton.

Upon leaving Wilson College, he joined the faculty at New York University where, in addition to his regular assignments, he taught wartime courses in meteorology for the Air Force. It was during the 1940s while at NYU that Panofsky became involved in air quality and boundary layer research and other geophysical subjects such as climate theory, oceanography, and the nature of atmospheric turbulence. His range of interests is exemplified by his published work in the *Journal of Meteorology* and the *Bulletin of the American Meteorological Society* between 1944 and 1950, on topics that included computing vertical motion in the atmosphere, pressure systems, vertical velocities and changes in cloudiness, radiative cooling, the significance of meteorological correlation coefficients, objective weather map analysis, a zonal index for Jupiter's Red Spot, and the stability and meandering of the Gulf Stream.

During this period he held research associate positions at Princeton, Woods Hole Oceanographic Institution, the University of California at Los Angeles (UCLA), and Lowell Observatory. By 1950 Panofsky had developed a reputation as a highly regarded scientist and outstanding teacher at NYU. He continued his ties with Princeton and Brookhaven National Laboratory into the early 1950s, collaborating with John von Neumann at Princeton during the early days of numerical weather prediction (they were among the first to apply computer analysis to weather prediction) and working with the meteorology group at Brookhaven. It was during this time that Hans's brother Wolfgang became an esteemed professor of physics at Stanford University and director of the Stanford High Energy Physics Laboratory; he was later appointed director of the Stanford Linear Accelerator Center, a position he held from 1961 to 1984.

The Penn State Years: 1951–1982. In 1951 Panofsky left NYU and joined the fledgling meteorology program at Pennsylvania State College as associate professor of meteorology at a time when meteorology was a division of the Department of Earth Sciences under the chairmanship of Hans Neuberger. Panofsky was promoted to the rank of professor in 1953, the same year that the name of the institution was changed to Pennsylvania State University (PSU) under President Milton Eisenhower. HAP, as he signed his name and many affectionately called him, played a key role in strengthening and expanding the meteorological program, and he served as acting head during Neuberger's sabbatical, at a critical time when the Division of Meteorology became the Department of Meteorology. A 1960 visiting committee to evaluate the department identified Panofsky as the most prolific faculty member (Harry Wexler Papers, Library of Congress).

Panofsky's scientific contribution to the understanding of the atmospheric boundary layer and the spectrum of turbulence stands at the pinnacle of his lifetime scholarly achievements. Panofsky's interest in boundary layers and turbulence actually began at NYU with an air quality study sponsored by Consolidated Edison Company of New York. Shortly after moving to PSU, he collaborated with Brookhaven National Laboratory (BNL) to study the diffusion of plumes released from tall towers. From 1958 through 1962, he was prolific in groundbreaking research on turbulence, including the derivation of wind profiles under diabatic conditions, meteorological and aeronautical aspects of atmospheric turbulence, turbulent energy budget, scale analysis of atmospheric turbulence, and the effects of wind loads on structures. Many of these topics were new areas of study at the time, and Panofsky led the way with insight and enthusiasm. In the early twenty-first century scientists continued to expand on his early work to better understand the conditions that lead to turbulence under varying atmospheric conditions.

In 1960 Panofsky was named a John Simon Guggenheim Memorial Fellow, and he spent a year at Cambridge University to study the basic theory of turbulence under G. K. Batchelor, publishing two short papers. It was during this period that Panofsky invited John Lumley to join him in writing the milestone monograph *The Structure of Atmospheric Turbulence* (1964). Panofsky's interest in Monin-Obukhov similarity theory (to use a set of nondimensional parameters to describe surface later fluxes), Kolmogorov scaling (to describe the smallest scales of turbulences) , and the spectrum of turbulence (describes the relationship between the energy of a turbulent eddy and the eddy size (wavelength or wave number) is evident in the monograph, and served as the impetus for his research efforts for the rest of his career.

Panofsky's boundless curiosity sustained his multifaceted interests across a range of subjects throughout this period, as demonstrated by his publications on TIROS measurements of tropospheric conditions, estimates of stratospheric flow from satellite 15-micron radiation, relationships between synoptic variables and satellite radiation data, and climate. Panofsky was at the forefront of a growing number of scientists whose research sparked concern about threats to the ozone layer; this at a time when CFCs in spray cans were being banned by Oregon (1975) and by the United States (1978), and the United States

was considering building a fleet of stratospheric commercial jetliners, and seven years before British investigators discovered the "ozone hole." This led to his appointment to a National Academy of Sciences (NAS) committee to evaluate the Department of Transportation's Climatic Impact Assessment Program. The committee focused on the ramification of large-scale use of the supersonic transport (SST) on stratospheric ozone, and went on to show that "while high-level flights can diminish ozone concentrations, their impact is felt to be small in comparison to the problems these flights create in the form of sonic booms and high costs" (NAS, 1975).

In addition, Panofsky coauthored publications with his students and colleagues on mesoscale variations and phenomena, radiation fluxes, and large-scale vertical motion. In 1965 he received the American Meteorological Society's Clarence Leroy Meisinger Award in recognition of his research achievements in aerology and atmospheric motions on all scales. Panofsky spent the spring of 1966 as visiting professor at the University of Washington. Upon his return, university president Eric Walker appointed him the Evan Pugh Professor of Atmospheric Science on 1 July 1966, the highest distinction PSU bestows on a faculty member.

Panofsky's interest in turbulence in the free atmosphere above the planetary boundary layer developed in conjunction with the ability of aircraft to reach greater altitudes. Clear air turbulence (CAT) became a hazard to be reckoned with, and Panofsky focused his interest in upper tropospheric and stratospheric dynamics and turbulence to address the problem, publishing with coauthors two manuscripts on CAT: the first on case studies of the distribution of CAT in 1968, and the second in 1976 on temperature gradients and CAT probabilities. His work continued through the 1970s on surface similarity, scale analysis of atmospheric turbulence, spectra and cospectra of turbulence, heat and momentum fluxes, and spectral gaps, and led to significant progress in the areas of boundary layers, turbulence, and the meteorology of air pollution events. Instrumented towers provided him with the necessary measurements to characterize turbulence under a variety of stability conditions and to assess the integrity of structures to wind loading, a topic that had sparked his interest since his early work with BNL.

In addition to the Lumley-Panofsky monograph on *The Structure of Atmospheric Turbulence* (1964), Panofsky published *An Introduction to Dynamic Meteorology* in 1956, *Some Applications of Statistics to Meteorology* with Glenn Briar in 1958, and a general undergraduate textbook, *The Atmosphere,* with Richard A. Anthes, John J. Cahir, and Albert Rango in 1975.

The Panofsky Legacy. The atmospheric sciences community was not remiss in acknowledging Panofsky's contributions. Most notably, in 1976 Panofsky received the American Meteorological Society's Carl-Gustaf Rossby Research Medal "for his many fundamental contributions to the understanding of turbulent processes and the links between small-scale and large-scale dynamics in the atmosphere." The Rossby Medal represents the highest honor that the Society can bestow upon an atmospheric scientist, and Panofsky described the receipt of this medal as "the culmination of my career." In addition, he was a Fellow of the American Meteorological Society, American Geophysical Union, and the American Association for the Advancement of Science, for which he served as chairman for the Atmospheric and Hydrological Sciences. He held memberships in the Royal Meteorological Society, Sigma Xi, and Phi Beta Kappa.

For all the fundamental contributions that Panofsky made to the subjects of atmospheric turbulence, satellite meteorology, planetary atmospheres, and climate, it was his students, colleagues, and friends that meant the most to him, according to Alfred Blackadar. In later years, when asked to describe his career, Panfosky said, "My principal interest as a university professor has always been teaching, at all levels. It is a great pleasure to share one's limited knowledge and understanding with students, and occasionally see them develop an enthusiasm for the subject" (http://www.met.psu.edu/dept/aboutus/his.html#recollections). Threading through the testimonies of former students and colleagues in a dedication to Panofsky by John Wyngaard in *Boundary Layer Meteorology* (1989) are attributes such as generosity, modesty, warmth, humility, enthusiasm, curiosity, and boundless imagination. Many of his contemporary professional associates have come to be considered some of the most influential leaders in the atmospheric sciences, and many of his students have occupied key positions in universities, national laboratories and agencies, and private enterprises.

Panofsky retired from PSU in 1982 but remained actively involved in research and publication. In 1983 he was named the Erskine Fellow at the University of Canterbury in Christchurch, New Zealand. The same year he published an article with coauthors on a refinement to an explicit eddy exchange coefficient formulation while at Colorado State University as a visiting professor, and the following year he took a position as research associate at the Scripps Institution of Oceanography. Still trying to shape the thinking of generations of students, in 1984, two years after his retirement, Panofsky and John Dutton produced a text, *Atmospheric Turbulence: Models and Methods for Engineering Applications,* that continued to serve as a valuable reference in the early twenty-first century. Also in 1984, Panofsky was honored by his undergraduate alma mater when Princeton University presented him with the Class of 1938 Distinguished Service Award.

Panofsky's insatiable curiosity never waned. John Dutton, Dean Emeritus, College of Earth and Mineral Sciences at PSU, recalls last seeing HAP in March 1986, age sixty-eight, at the American Meteorological Society Short Course of Air Pollution Modeling in San Diego, "enrolled as a student, taking a front-row seat and keeping the lecturer alert." His youthful inquisitiveness remained a hallmark of his character until his death in 1988. Alfred Blackadar, professor emeritus of Meteorology at PSU, described Panofsky as a "brilliant mind, interested in everything, and unfailingly observant," and his research across the broad panorama of geophysical and atmospheric sciences bears this out.

While Panofsky's contributions are many and varied, he is most likely to be remembered for his work on the spectrum of turbulence. His publications on clear-air turbulence, diabatic wind profiles, scale analysis of turbulence, spectra and co-spectra of atmospheric turbulence, similarity theory, and the turbulent energy budget were mileposts in a fledgling discipline into which a generation of students would venture.

BIBLIOGRAPHY

See the Pennsylvania State University Special Archives on Hans A. Panofsky. Reminiscences are available from http://www.met.psu.edu/dept/aboutus/his.html#recollections.

WORKS BY PANOFSKY

An Introduction to Dynamic Meteorology. University Park: Pennsylvania State University Press, 1956.

With G. Briar. *Some Applications of Statistics to Meteorology.* University Park: Pennsylvania State University Press, 1958.

With Alfred K. Blackadar and G. E. McVehil. "The Diabatic Wind Profile." *Quarterly Journal of the Royal Meteorological Society* 86 (January 1960): 390–398.

"The Budget of Turbulent Energy in the Lowest 100 Meters." *Journal of Geophysical Research* 67 (July 1962): 3161–3165.

With John L. Lumley. *The Structure of Atmospheric Turbulence, Monographs and Texts in Physics and Astronomy.* Vol. XII. New York: Wiley and Sons, 1964.

"Analyzing Atmospheric Behavior." *Physics Today* 23 (December 1970): 32–35.

With John A. Dutton. "Clear Air Turbulence." *The Physics Teacher* 8 (December 1970): 489–498.

With Richard Anthes, John J. Cahir, and Albert Rango. *The Atmosphere.* Columbus, OH: Charles E. Merrill, 1975.

With John A. Dutton. *Atmospheric Turbulence: Models and Methods for Engineering Applications.* New York: Wiley and Sons, 1984.

OTHER SOURCES

National Academy of Sciences (NAS). *Environmental Impact of Stratospheric Flight.* Washington, DC: NAS, 1975.

Wyngaard, John C. "Hans Panofsky, 1917–1988." *Boundary Layer Meteorology* 47 (1989): 1–14.

Richard D. Clark

PAPEZ, JAMES WENCESLAS (*b.* Glencoe, Minnesota, 18 August 1883; *d.* Columbus, Ohio, 13 April 1958), *neuroanatomy, emotion and feeling, limbic system, amygdala, hippocampus, thalamus, cingulated cortex.*

Papez was one the greatest twentieth-century explorers of brain anatomy. In an effort to explain emotions in the brain, he proposed the existence of a complex set of circuits. Some of the connections proposed were purely speculative because the techniques available at the time were not capable of revealing the detailed connectivity of the brain. The Papez circuit, as it came to be called, was one of the first examples of a network or systems-level explanation of a complex mental function. His speculations about brain wiring, when evaluated with modern techniques, have turned out to be amazingly accurate. Although his theory of the emotional functions of the circuit turned out to not be correct, it was of great heuristic value and led to much research. All subsequent approaches to the emotional brain build upon the Papez circuit theory.

Early Development. James Wenceslas Papez was born in the small town of Glencoe, Minnesota, to an American family of Czech descent. His ancestors were members of the Moravian Church, which was based on the teachings of Jan Huss, a Czech reformer of Christianity accused of heresy and burned at the stake. Their religious tradition, as noted by Paul MacLean, a colleague and a collaborator, might have contributed to Papez's extreme caution in publicly challenging dominant views. According to MacLean there were occasions when Papez even used to whisper when he was about to question prevailing theories.

After completing his undergraduate education, Papez entered the University of Minnesota College of Medicine and Surgery, where he received his MD in 1911. Under the influence of a comparative neuroanatomist, John Black Johnston, Papez began his training in neuroanatomy. The book on comparative anatomy that Johnston had published in 1906, which was accompanied by beautiful illustrations, was an inspiration for Papez when writing his own text more than two decades later.

In 1912 Papez married (Bessie) Pearl Sowden, an artist, with whom he later had three children: James Pitney, Julia, and Loyd. From 1914 to 1920, Papez served as a faculty member at University of Atlanta (now a part of Emory University). In 1920 he joined the Ithaca Division of Cornell University Medical College as assistant professor of anatomy. Burt Green Wilder, the Cornell professor of zoology and a founder of the famous brain collection named after him, was instrumental in bringing Papez to Cornell.

Time in Ithaca: Theory of Emotions. Papez spent the most productive years of his professional career at Cornell. There he conducted comparative studies of brain anatomy, which resulted in numerous publications. His research on the diencephalon (thalamus and hypothalamus), which he carried out with Lester Aronson, his student and collaborator, was especially well received, and even admired, among fellow anatomists. In addition, Papez served as a curator of the Wilder Brain Collection. This collection consisted of numerous human brains, including those of famous people. Many of these brains, including the one of the collection's founder, were examined by Papez himself.

During his time at Cornell, Papez was very active in teaching courses in anatomy, anthropology, and human development. His celebrated lectures, which revealed his skills as an actor and showman, were loved and admired by students: "Dr. Papez's clinicoanatomical viewpoint and his unforgettable pantomimes of individuals afflicted with neurological disorders of every conceivable kind had great appeal" (Angevine, 1978, p. 23). However, as one of his younger collaborators noted:

> the real excitement came during informal discussions after lectures. In conversation it was almost as important to watch the play of expression of his face as it was to hear his words—his squinting skepticism, his lips pursed in puzzlement. On the few occasions I saw Papez I must have been so intent on listening to his words and trying to catch the meaning of his expression that, in retrospect, I retain only the image of his face and his moving hands. (MacLean, 1978, p. 3)

In 1929 James Papez published his *Comparative Neurology.* This notable textbook, which was based on his famous lectures and which was accompanied by his wife's intricate illustrations, served later generations of anatomists for some time. However, the greatest acclaim Papez received was for proposing his neural theory of emotions.

For centuries, it was thought that feelings trigger bodily responses such as shaking, sweating, changes in heart rate, and respiration. This traditional view was questioned in the 1890s by the James-Lange theory. William James in his 1884 paper titled "What Is an Emotion?" suggested a reverse order, namely that feelings arise from the bodily expression of emotions, the commotion in inner organs and in behavior. A similar view was independently formulated in 1885 by a Danish anatomist, Carl G. Lange, who studied physiological responses accompanying emotions. The James-Lange "peripheral" theory of emotions, while appealing to many psychologists, was not supported by much experimental data. On the contrary, anatomical and clinical findings were suggesting the opposite. Observations of patients with severed spinal cord, as well as experiments on animals with disrupted major sensory pathways, indicated the presence of emotional reactions despite the apparent disconnection between the brain and periphery. Such findings led to severe criticism of the James-Lange theory. Among the critics were Walter B. Cannon and Charles L. Dana.

Cannon in particular proposed that the James-Lange theory could not be correct because bodily responses, especially of the autonomic nervous system, would be too slow and would lack the specificity needed to distinguish fear from anger from joy and so on. From his own research with Philip Bard, Cannon proposed that the hypothalamus plays a key role in emotions. It receives sensory information about external stimuli and then sends signals to the body to control emotional responses and sends signals to the cortex to define feelings. Another line of argument against the James-Lange theory came from Dana, a neurologist who based on his observations of the symptoms accompanying brain damage in humans, emphasizing the importance of the cortex itself, as opposed to body feedback to the cortex, in generating conscious feelings.

Although Papez never did research on emotions, he was fascinated with the topic and was aware of Cannon's critique of the James-Lange theory as well as of the Cannon-Bard alternative. Rumor has it that when Papez learned that a prominent private foundation in the United States had donated a large sum of money to a British laboratory for the purpose of studying the nature of emotions, Papez became annoyed: "I was mad, because the English proposal seemed to ignore what was already known about this subject" (quoted in MacLean, 1978, p. 5). In particular, it seemed to ignore the research that had been done in the United States. In a fit of national pride, Papez wrote, in few days, his famous paper "A Proposed Mechanism of Emotion," which was published in *Archives of Neurology and Psychiatry* in 1937.

This influential review article largely was a product of speculative thinking. He took the classic findings about brain organization and function from animal research by Cannon, Bard, C. Judson Herrick, and others, and synthesized them with observations about the consequences of brain damage in humans. The result was a proposal about the organization of neural circuitry involved in emotional processing, starting at the point of sensory input up to the level of subjective feeling. According to Papez, this plausible emotional circuit involved sensory areas of the thalamus and cortex, the hypothalamus, anterior thalamus, cingulate cortex, hippocampus, and mammillary bodies.

Why did he include these brain regions? Some were included because of experimental findings. The hypothalamus was on his list because of Bard's research in Cannon's laboratory at Harvard, which showed that the hypothalamus was essential for the expression of emotional responses. The sensory thalamus was included for two reasons. First, the standard view held that the sensory thalamus transfers information to the cortex for perception, thought, and memory. But Cannon had noted that sensory pathways diverge in the thalamus, with a second component going directly to the hypothalamus. This component was viewed as important in activating the emotional functions of the hypothalamus. The key area of the hypothalamus was thought to be the mammillary bodies (breastlike protrusions at the ventral part of the brain). These were pinpointed in part because Papez knew about a report of monkeys with damage in the area. The behavior of these animals was characterized by a lack of emotional responsiveness. The anterior thalamus was included because it connected the mammillary bodies to the cingulate cortex.

The cingulate cortex, a region located in the medial wall of the brain, had a long and interesting history in studies of the brain. The great French anatomist Pierre-Paul Broca had in the nineteenth century named this area the limbic cortex, because a significant part of it is situated at the edge dividing the medial and the dorsal parts of each hemisphere (in Latin, *limbus* means "rim" or "edge"). Herrick, an anatomist who specialized in brain evolution and who was working during the same period as Papez, distinguished between the medial and the lateral cortices. Herrick proposed that the medial cortex, which in lower animals is responsible for processing olfactory information, in the course of evolution gave rise to the lateral cortex, a part of the brain that subserves higher intellectual functions. Papez utilized Herrick's distinction, as well as clinical observations reporting that brain tumors compressing limbic cortex, as well as occlusion of arteries supplying this region, were accompanied by several emotional disturbances, such as easy irritability, euphoria, and depression.

Finally, the hippocampus, a structure sitting mostly inside the medial temporal lobe, was justified by observations of people suffering from rabies. Papez observed that negri bodies, microscopic changes in the brain tissue which accompany rabies, are localized mainly in the hippocampus. He linked these anatomical findings to the clinical picture of rabies, which involves enhanced repsonsiveness to various stimuli, irritability, and sleeplessness, as well as intense emotions, such as fear and rage. Based on this evidence, Papez hypothesized that the hippocampus plays a crucial role in the production of emotional states (1995, p. 107).

Putting all this information together, Papez proposed three streams of processing that start with the receptor organs and then split at the level of the thalamus into the "stream of movement," the "stream of thought," and the "stream of feeling." The stream of movement projects to the subcortical areas involved in movement control; the stream of thought conducts information from the thalamus to the lateral cerebral cortex and allows sensations to be transformed into perceptions, thoughts, and memories. The stream of feeling transmits sensory information from the ventral thalamus directly to the hypothalamus. Based on available anatomical data, Papez hypothesized that a part of the hypothalamus-mammillary bodies receives the thalamic projections and connects to the cingulate cortex via the anterior thalamus. Thus, the cingulate cortex may be excited either directly by the sensory pathways coming through the hypothalamus or by interconnections with the lateral cortex.

Papez proposed that the cingulate cortex is the site where emotions are experienced. This happens when the impulses coming from the hypothalamus reach the cingulate cortex. In turn, widespread projections from the cingulate cortex to other cortical regions add emotional coloring to various psychological processes. This may explain, thought Papez, two ways, in which emotions arise: (1) a consequence of hypothalamic stimulation and/or (2) a result of mental activity (1995, pp. 104–105).

Papez posited that the cingulate cortex influences emotional processing in the hypothalamus through its outputs to the hippocampus, which via the fornix sends messages to the posterior region of hypothalamus, thus completing the circle of emotion. In Papez's model, the key role in emotions was assigned to the hippocampus.

The hippocampus and the associated areas were supposed to be a place where original emotive processes arise, and from where they are transferred for further processing to the mammillary bodies, the anterior thalamic nuclei, and the cingulate cortex (1995, p. 104).

Papez's paper did not receive much interest until 1949, when Paul MacClean published his article revising the organization of emotional circuits proposed by the anatomist from Cornell. Interestingly, even if not yet identified at the time, most of the pathways that Papez posited do exist. Unfortunately, the hippocampus and

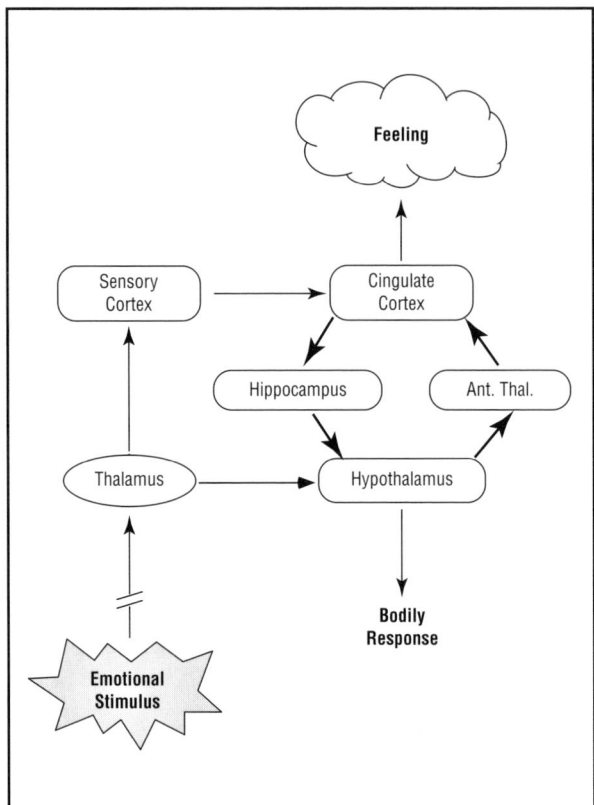

The Papez Circuit Theory.

other components of Papez's circuit appear to have very little involvement in emotion. If Papez had waited a bit, he would have learned about the findings of Heinrich Klüver and Paul Bucy from the University of Chicago. In 1939 Klüver and Paul published their observations of emotional changes in monkeys following lesions of the temporal lobe. Later studies by Lawrence Weiskrantz in 1956 showed that the amygdala was the culprit. While for Papez, the amygdala was merely playing an unspecified role in visceral and gustatory functions, the new findings demonstrated a crucial role of this structure in emotions.

Papez never specified what he meant by "emotion." He was an anatomist, not a psychologist. Emotion, for him, was a tool for thinking about how brain pathways are organized. His very specific suggestion led to much research on both the connections involved and their role in emotion. Though his ideas concerning their role in emotion have not held up, his speculations about connection were remarkably accurate. Papez was aware of the limitations of his emotional hypothesis: "The new interpretation which I propose can be supported by much more data at present available in the literature, but it is evident that any such doctrine will have to stand the test of experimental and clinical experience if it is to be useful in science" (1995, p. 111).

Even if his emotional model did not stand the scrutiny of empirical verification, the conceptual framework of his theory is still commonly applied. Papez's intuitions that brain structures are anatomically and functionally interrelated, such that a disturbance in one area also affects other brain regions became a common way of thinking in neuroscience. The metaphors "stream of thought," "stream of movement," "stream of feeling," or "emotional coloring," originally introduced by the neuroanatomy professor, took on a life of their own (Neylan, 1995, p. 102).

After the Cornell Medical School moved from Ithaca to New York City in the 1940s, Papez remained on the Ithaca campus as professor of anatomy in the Department of Zoology. He began to spend more time on other interests: anthropology and development. However, in 1941, he published another remarkable article, a synthesis of his observations on the basal ganglia and their connections. In this review, Papez described neural pathways linking basal ganglia with each other and with other brain areas.

Late Work and Retirement. In 1951, after thirty-one years at Cornell, Papez retired and left Ithaca. He and Pearl moved to Ohio to take the position of director of the newly established Laboratory for Biological Research in the Department of Mental Hygiene and Corrections at the Columbus State Hospital. He was involved there in studying slowly developing degenerative changes in the brains of people suffering from chronic neurological and psychiatric disorders. He developed a special method to detect inclusion-like bodies.

He collaborated, as during his entire career, with Pearl, who did the drawings of changes observed using the microscope. Papez's findings led him to suspect that the changes had been caused by viruses or other microbial organisms. However, neuropathologists who used conventional methods of staining strongly rejected Papez's hypothesis. His research was considered controversial, and Papez was even very close to losing his job. Yet, it is possible that Papez might have been partially correct; a few decades later, stronger evidence was presented to support the hypothesis of parasitic causation of degenerative changes in the brain.

During his time in Ohio, Papez dedicated himself to his other passion: poetry. In 1957 he published his volume of poems *Fragments of Verse*. One of the poems, "My Girl on Broad Street," describes his loneliness at their house on Broad Street, while Pearl was away:

It's Pearl, my girl on Broad Street

That I miss.

(MacLean, 1978, p. 7)

On Sunday, 13 April 1958, while having breakfast with his wife, Papez felt sudden chest pain. He said, "This is it," and went to lie down on the couch. Soon after, he died. James Wenceslas Papez was one of greatest anatomists of the twentieth century, but he was also remembered as a husband, father, scholar, and poet.

BIBLIOGRAPHY

For the collection of James Wenceslas Papez's papers, contact: Archives and Modern Manuscripts Program, History of Medicine Division, U.S. National Library of Medicine, 8600 Rockville Pike, Bethesda, MD 20894; http://www.nlm.nih.gov/hmd/manuscripts/ead/papez.html.

WORKS BY PAPEZ

"Reticulo-Spinal Tracts in the Cat: Marchi Method." *Journal of Comparative Neurology* 41 (1926): 365–399.

"The Brain of Helen H. Gardner (Alice Chenoweth Day)." *American Journal of Physical Anthropology* 11 (1927): 29–79.

"Subdivisions of the Facial Nucleus." *Journal of Comparative Neurology* 43 (1927): 159–191.

"The Brain of Burt Green Wilder (1841–1925)." *Journal of Comparative Neurology* 47 (1929): 285–341.

Comparative Neurology. New York: Thomas Y. Crowell, 1929.

"The Brain of Sutherland Simpson, 1863–1926." *Journal of Comparative Neurology* 51 (1930): 165–196.

"The Thalamic Nuclei of the Nine-Banded Armadillo (*Tatusia novemcincta*)." *Journal of Comparative Neurology* 56 (1932): 49–103.

With Lester R. Aronson. "Thalamic Nuclei of Pithecus (Macacus) Rhesus I. Ventral Thalamus." *Archives of Neurology and Psychiatry* 32 (1934): 1–26.

———. "Thalamic Nuclei of Pithecus (Macacus) Rhesus II. Dorsal Thalamus." *Archives of Neurology and Psychiatry* 32 (1934): 27–44.

"Thalamus of Turtles and Thalamic Evolution." *Journal of Comparative Neurology* 61 (1935): 433–475.

"Evolution of the Medial Geniculate Body." *Journal of Comparative Neurology* 64 (1936): 41–61.

"A Proposed Mechanism of Emotion." *Archives of Neurology and Psychiatry* 38 (1937): 725–743. This work was reprinted by the *Journal of Neuropsychiatry and Clinical Neurosciences* 7 (1995): 103–112.

"Connections of the Pulvinar." *Archives of Neurology and Psychiatry* 41 (1939): 277–289.

"A Summary of Fiber Connections of the Basal Ganglia with Each Other and with Other Portions of the Brain." *Research Publications, the Association for Research in Nervous and Mental Disease* 21 (1941): 21–68.

"Neuronal Disease Associated with Intracytoplasmic Inclusion Bodies." *Archives of Neurology and Psychiatry* 52 (1944): 217–229.

"Fiber Tracts of the Amygdaloid Region in the Human Brain, from a Graphic Reconstruction of Fiber Connections and Nuclear Masses." *Anatomical Record* 91 (1945): 294.

With J. F. Bateman. "Cytological Changes in Nerve Cells in Dementia Preacox." *Journal of Nervous and Mental Disease* 110 (1949): 425–437.

"Changes in Nerve Cells and Hypophysis in Old Psychotic Patients: A Review of 90 Cases." *Journal of Gerontology* 9 (1954): 363.

Fragments of Verse. Los Angeles: New Age Publishing, 1957.

With Pearl Papez. "Mycotic Nature of Brain-Damage in Mental Deficiency." *American Journal of Psychology* 70 (1957): 333–346.

"Visceral Brain, Its Component Parts and Their Connections." *Journal of Nervous and Mental Disease* 126 (1958): 40–56.

OTHER SOURCES

Angevine, Jay B., Jr. "Embryogenesis and Phylogenesis in the Limbic System." In *Limbic Mechanisms: The Continuing Evolution of the Limbic System Concept,* edited by Kenneth E. Livingston and Oleh Hornykiewicz. New York and London: Plenum Press, 1978.

Finger, Stanley. "Defining and Controlling the Circuits of Emotion." In *Origins of Neuroscience: A History of Explorations into Brain Function.* New York and Oxford: Oxford University Press, 1994.

Haymaker, Webb, and Francis Schiller. *The Founders of Neurology.* Springfield, IL: Charles C. Thomas, 1970.

LeDoux, Joseph E. *Emotional Brain: The Mysterious Underpinnings of Emotional Life.* New York: Simon & Schuster, 1996. See especially Chapter 4, "The Holy Grail."

MacLean, Paul D. "Challenges to the Papez Heritage." In *Limbic Mechanisms: The Continuing Evolution of the Limbic System Concept,* edited by K. E. Livingston and O. Hornykiewicz. New York and London: Plenum Press, 1978.

Mettler, Fred. "James Wenceslas Papez: August 18, 1883–April 13, 1958." *Anatomical Record* (1958): 279–282.

Neylan, Thomas C. "Classic Articles in Neuropsychiatry: Introduction to the Series." *Journal of Neuropsychiatry and Clinical Neurosciences* 7 (1995): 102–103.

Yakovlev, Paul I. (as told to Ken Livingston). "Recollections of James Papez and Comments on the Evolution of the Limbic System Concept." In *Limbic Mechanisms: The Continuing Evolution of the Limbic System Concept,* edited by K. E. Livingston and O. Hornykiewicz. New York and London: Plenum Press, 1978.

Jacek Dębiec
Joseph E. LeDoux

PARACELSUS, THEOPHRASTUS PHILIPPUS AUREOLUS BOMBASTUS VON HOHENHEIM (*b.* near Einsiedeln, Switzerland, 1493 or 1494; *d.* Salzburg, Austria, 24 September 1541), *alchemy/chymistry, medicine, natural philosophy, cosmology, theology, natural magic, astrology/prognostication, folklore, philosophy/ethics, iatro-*

chemistry. For the original article on Paracelsus see *DSB,* vol. 10.

In the few decades following Walter Pagel's trailblazing research on Paracelsus, which is brilliantly and succinctly presented in Pagel's *DSB* article, Paracelsus studies have experienced dynamic activity, including a host of fresh interpretations and newly available primary sources. The trend to ground interpretations of Paracelsus's biography and concepts in documentary evidence exclusively—and an increasing sensitivity to the demarcation between Paracelsus's own works and those of dubious authenticity that bear his name—is a welcome development. For example, such spurious and/or dubious works as *Philosophy to the Athenians* and *De natura rerum* require more cautious use and indication of questionable nature in citations. There is also an increasing interest in Paracelsus's explicitly theological works and concepts, as well as the dating of his writings, and thus the development of his thought.

Biographical Information. Scholars no longer take for granted that the nickname "Paracelsus," dating from circa 1529, either denotes "surpassing Celsus" (for Paracelsus first used the name in prognosticative rather than medical writings and—more importantly—never once referred to Celsus) or corresponds to a Latinization of "Hohenheim" (although it may be a Greek version of "Hohenheim": "para" for the German *bei,* and "celsus" for *hoch*). However, as Pagel suggests, perhaps it is related to his confrontation of authority in his "para [doxical]" writings. In his rigorously documented biography of Paracelsus (1997), Udo Benzenhöfer discusses the subject at length, adding that there seems to be a relationship between "Paracelsus" and Paracelsus's frequent use of the prefix "para," which surfaces in the titles of some of his important works, for example, *Opus Paragranum* and *Opus Paramirum.* Benzenhöfer shows that Paracelsus usually referred to himself as "Theophrastus von Hohenheim," but also occasionally as "Theophrastus Bombast von Hohenheim" and—especially in his last several years— "Aureolus." When evoking the family name of "Bombast," which points to his roots in old Swabian nobility, Paracelsus never used the Latinized form "Bombastus." "Philippus" is first seen on Paracelsus's tombstone and may refer to his Christian name (*Taufname*) (Benzenhöfer, 1997).

During his perennial itinerancy—well discussed by Pagel—Paracelsus often clashed with authority, but this does not necessarily include an involvement with the German Peasant's War. Paracelsus recalls in the *De Septem Punctis* of his mature years that in 1525 the authorities complained stridently when he turned the farmers against them in Salzburg. He could have been referring to one of the uprisings of the Peasant's War; however, it is also

14

possible that he meant another agitation in Salzburg, namely, a revolt by tradesmen and mining squires in the silver-gold industry in Gastein and Rauris. In this latter case, Melchior Spach—who was later among the list of witnesses on Paracelsus's Testament—was the top field captain in the armed uprising in Hallein against Salzburg's Prince-Archbishop and Cardinal Matthäus Lang (Dopsch, 1993).

In his *DSB* article Pagel has highlighted most of the essential aspects of Paracelsus's biography, but requiring further explication are those points related to his theology. During the tumultuous years of his unbroken peregrination, Paracelsus had begun writing at length about not only alchemy and medical theory, but also such theological topics as Mariology and the idolatries of the church—nearly half of his prodigious oeuvre would be explicitly theological, including multifarious biblical exegeses.

He never officially left the Catholic Church, but became deeply involved in the Reformation fervor. George Huntston Williams, in his *The Radical Reformation,* ranked Paracelsus alongside Caspar Schwenckfeld and Sebastian Franck as one of the spiritualists of the Radical Reformation (Williams, 1992, pp. 721–722). In his heterodox religious works Paracelsus criticized institutionalized Christendom, which he called a church in walls, a *Mauerkirche.* True Christianity, Paracelsus wrote, does not require rituals and denominations. Rather, there is one spiritual church of all true believers. In the 1530s, his theology would increase in its distinctiveness and in many respects become integrated with his Eucharistic theology, that is the *philosophia de limbo aeterno* associated with the "spiritual body" and "new Adam" of 1 Corinthians 15. Kurt Goldammer and Hartmut Rudolph have written about the topic extensively. This philosophy—which forwarded the idea that Christians receive their subtle resurrection body at baptism and then nourish it with the Eucharist—would be echoed in Book II of Paracelsus's magnum opus, the *Astronomia Magna* (1537/38). Paracelsus believed that medical and natural "miracles" could be performed via the enlargement and employment of the immortal body, and he evokes this Christian magic to explain many biblical miracles.

Cosmological Views. When one reads the "religious writings" in coordination with the "medical-scientific writings"—a dichotomy problematically forced upon Paracelsus's oeuvre by the dean of Paracelsus studies, Karl Sudhoff—one can grasp far more easily his division of the cosmos and human being—a partition at the heart of his medical, scientific, and magical mechanisms. In fact, one sees that Paracelsus's works subsequent to the mid-1520s tended to feature a quadripartite (and not a tripartite) view of the components of the world and human being.

Paracelsus. HULTON ARCHIVE/GETTY IMAGES.

Actually, given his propensity for analogous dichotomies, it is perhaps preferable to refer to his cosmology/ anthropology as a body-spirit dichotomy at the immortal level and a body-spirit dichotomy at the mortal level— thus, Paracelsus's division consists of mortal spirit (sidereal body), mortal body (elemental body), immortal spirit (soul), and immortal body (resurrection body). Paracelsus writes that the first three of these components—which can be termed spirit, body, and soul—first came together in the human in Genesis 2:7: "And the Lord God formed man of the dust of the ground, and breathed into his nostrils the breath of life; and man became a living soul." According to Paracelsus, Adam's spirit and body, which are mortal, came from this *limus terrae* (dust of the ground) while the immortal soul was drawn from God's breath. When discussing the dust, Paracelsus says it contained both "sidereal" and "elemental" components. God thus formed Adam, the first human, out of the matter of the stars and the matter of the earthly realm—the immortal spirit (soul) came into Adam when God breathed into this combination of "spirit" (sidereal component) and "body" (earthly component).

Paracelsus adds that the *limus terrae* was a "quintessence" that possessed the essences of all being in the world within it. (One should note here that in his mature works Paracelsus employed the term *quintessence,* discussed in Pagel's *DSB* article, in a much different manner than in his formative chemical work of the mid-1520s, the *Archidoxis.*) Thus Adam became a microcosm, possessing all things within him that exist in the greater world (macrocosm), from herbs and minerals to heavenly constellations. His elemental body (consisting of "fruits" born in the invisible elemental matrices—or universal spheres—of water, earth, air, and fire) was made out of seeds (which give form) and the *tria prima* of sulfur, salt, and mercury (principles that provide tangibility). Adam's sidereal body was composed of the subtle matter of the firmament (born from "the stars," and present within the *limus terrae*)—it was through this sidereal body/mortal spirit that he received his mental faculties and talents. Paracelsus adds that through mastery of the sidereal body, a subtle "dust," the natural magician can perform amazing feats, such as simultaneous long-distance communication. To Adam's elemental and sidereal bodies was added God's very breath—the divine image—that is, the soul. The immortal body—of which Christ's body, the resurrection body, and the Eucharist consist—was a distinct creation by God the Son (Christ) rather than God the Father.

As the above discussion indicates, the progression of Paracelsus's thought is receiving more marked attention; scholars point to, for example, how his religious development sheds light on the dating of his works. C. Andrew Weeks, who often stresses Paracelsus's affinity with Martin Luther and other Reformers, argues that "[T]he epoch in which [Paracelsus's] theories were forged … occurred under the decisive impact of the early Reformation, to which the thirty-year-old Theophrastus responded with radical polemical writings during his early, stormy sojourn in Salzburg" (Weeks, 1997, p. 36). Weeks, seeking to approximate better the precise years in which Paracelsus's individual works were produced, demonstrates that Paracelsus' earliest works were often theological—and that "the naturalism of Paracelsus turns on a religious center from the very beginning" (Weeks, 1997, pp. 43, 162).

Clearly, given Paracelsus's extensive reliance on scripture and Genesis cosmogony in the formation of his thought, one should be careful not to overemphasize his adherence to Renaissance Neoplatonism (even if clear ties do exist). Especially problematic are such notions as "uncreated seeds" and Neoplatonic and/or Gnostic emanation theory. Such concepts—which tend to arise more often in spurious works—do not map on well to Paracelsus's interpretation of Genesis 2:7.

SUPPLEMENTARY BIBLIOGRAPHY

Benzenhöfer, Udo. *Paracelsus.* Reinbek bei Hamburg, Germany: Rowohlt Taschenbuch Verlag, 1997. Although a rather quick read, this is a book crafted from meticulous attention to primary sources. It is probably the most accurate account of Paracelsus.

———, ed. *Studien zum Frühwerk des Paracelsis im Bereich Medizin und Naturkunde.* Münster, Germany: Klemm & Oelschläger, 2005.

Biegger, Katharina. *De Invocatione Beatae Mariae Virginis. Paracelsus und die Marienverehrung.* Stuttgart, Germany: Franz Steiner, 1990. See this text for a bibliography and discussion of Paracelsus's explicitly theological writings, including those on Mariology and the idolatries of the church; half of his *theologica* exist only in manuscript form.

Daniel, Dane T. "Invisible Wombs: Rethinking Paracelsus's Concept of Body and Matter." *Ambix* 53, no. 2 (July 2006): 129–142.

Debus, Allen G., and Michael T. Walton. *Reading the Book of Nature: The Other Side of the Scientific Revolution.* Kirksville, MO: Sixteenth Century Journal Publishers, 1998.

Dopsch, Heinz. "Paracelsus, die Reformation und der Bauernkrieg." In *Paracelsus (1493–1541). "Keines andern Knecht …,"* edited by Heinz Dopsch, Kurt Goldammer, and Peter Kramml, 201–215. Salzburg, Austria: Pustet, 1993.

———. "Paracelsus, Salzburg und der Bauernkrieg." In *Paracelsus (1493–1541). "Keines andern Knecht …,"* edited by Heinz Dopsch, Kurt Goldammer, and Peter Kramml, 299–308. Salzburg, Austria: Pustet, 1993.

Goldammer, Kurt. *Paracelsus in Neuen Horizonten: Gesammelte aufsätze.* Vienna, Austria: Verband der wissenschaftlichen Gesellschaften Österreichs, Verlag, 1986. Goldammer, who edited a number of Paracelsus's religious writings, was the authority on Paracelsus's *theologica,* and this collection—too often overlooked in Anglo-American circles—provides adroit insight into Paracelsus's worldview.

Grell, Ole Peter, ed. *Paracelsus: The Man and His Reputation, His Ideas and Their Transformation.* Leiden, Netherlands: Brill, 1998.

Kühlmann, Wilhelm, and Joachim Telle, eds. and comm. *Corpus Paracelsisticum.* Vol. 1, *Der Frühparacelsismus,* Part I. Tübingen, Germany: Max Niemeyer Verlag, 2001.

———, and Joachim Telle, eds. and comm. *Corpus Paracelsisticum.* Vol. 2, *Der Frühparacelsismus,* Part II. Tübingen, Germany: Max Niemeyer Verlag, 2004. Kühlmann and Telle have brought rich new insight into the Paracelsians with the *Corpus Paracelsisticum,* in which dozens of early modern German and Latin texts by significant Paracelsians are presented with the highest standard of philology and erudite commentary.

Newman, William R. *Promethean Ambitions: Alchemy and the Quest to Perfect Nature.* Chicago: University of Chicago Press, 2004. This work is good on Paracelsus's views on monsters and androgyny.

———, and Lawrence M. Principe. *Alchemy Tried in the Fire: Starkey, Boyle, and the Fate of Helmontian Chymistry.* Chicago: University of Chicago Press, 2002. This is good on historical alchemy and "chymistry," including some discussion of the place of Paracelsus therein.

Paulus, Julian. *Paracelsus-Bibliographie 1961–1996.* Heidelberg, Germany: Palatina Verlag, 1997. This is the definitive bibliography for works in Paracelsus studies from 1961 to 1996.

Rudolph, Hartmut. "Hohenheim's Anthropology in the Light of His Writings on the Eucharist." In *Paracelsus: The Man and His Reputation, His Ideas and Their Transformation,* edited by Ole Peter Grell, 187–206. Leiden, Netherlands: Brill, 1998.

Schott, Heinz, and Ilana Zinguer, eds. *Paracelsus und seine Internationale Rezeption in der Frühen Neuzeit. Beiträge zur Geschichte des Paracelsismus.* Leiden, Netherlands, Boston, Cologne, Germany: Brill, 1998.

Weeks, C. Andrew. *Paracelsus: Speculative Theory and the Crisis of the Early Reformation.* Albany: State University of New York Press, 1997.

Williams, George Huntston. *The Radical Reformation.* 3rd ed. Kirksville, MO: Sixteenth Century Journal Publishers, 1992.

Williams, Gerhild Scholz, and Charles D. Gunnoe Jr., eds. *Paracelsian Moments: Science, Medicine, and Astrology in Early Modern Europe.* Kirksville, MO: Sixteenth Century Journal Publishers, 2002.

Dane T. Daniel

PARETO, VILFREDO (*b.* Paris, France, 15 July 1848; *d.* Céligny, Switzerland, 19 August 1923), *economics, sociology.*

Pareto, economist and sociologist, contributed to the development of general equilibrium theory and defined the criterium of optimality known as Pareto optimum. He studied income distribution defining the Pareto's law of distribution and advanced the application of statistical methods in the social sciences. In sociology he underlined the distinction of logical and non logical actions and proposed a dynamic theory of the circulation of elites.

Life. Vilfredo Pareto, the son of a marquis, Raffaele Pareto, graduated in mathematics and engineering from the Polytechnic University of Turin in Italy. Beginning in 1875, he was technical director of an iron and steel company, based in the Tuscany region and subsequently was the company's general manager. In contact with the cultural elite of Florence, Tuscany's main city, he cultivated history, sociology, and the classics and was a militant upholder of free trade. He twice stood, unsuccessfully, as a candidate in the legislative elections of the young Kingdom of Italy. In the late 1880s and early 1890s, Pareto wrote articles opposing policies of protectionism and militarism in Italy. His intransigent criticism of the Italian government had some international resonance. Meanwhile, the financial situation of the Italian Ironworks Company, of which he was director general, seriously deteriorated, and Pareto finally had to resign in 1890. He broke away from active politics and business to turn to scholarship but continued participating in sharp political and economic controversies. The Italian economist Maf-

feo Pantaleoni recommended him as a possible successor to the French economist Léon Walras, who held the chair of political economy at the University of Lausanne in Switzerland. Pareto was eventually appointed in 1893 after having become personally acquainted with Walras, whose general equilibrium approach Pareto appreciated while scoffing at his utopian visions of social justice.

Pareto taught economics and sociology at the University of Lausanne until his retirement in 1911. Having inherited a fortune in 1899, he bought a villa at Céligny, on Lake Geneva in Switzerland. After his marriage broke down in 1901, Pareto lived at Céligny with a much younger companion, Jeanne Regis, whom he married just two months before his death in 1923. In his maturity, Pareto departed entirely from the liberal and pacifist creed of his youth. During Europe's post–World War I crisis, he heralded the downfall of the parliamentary system. In Italy, he was initially diffident toward the fascist movement, but he then approved of Benito Mussolini's rise to power in 1922 and placed his trust in the emerging authoritarian regime, although fearing despotism and the suppression of free speech. At the end of his life, in some notes on the constitutional reform, he recommended the shift of power into the hands of a strong governing elite and some executive committees, but maintaining the parliament and free press. In 1923 Pareto accepted quite reluctantly the honor of being named senator by Mussolini's government, but he eventually refused to submit the required documents to validate the act.

Economic Equilibrium and Optimal Allocations. Pareto published his first theoretical contributions to economics in 1892, having read Walras and the leading economists in the so-called marginalist revolution. In the essay "Considerazioni sui principi fondamentali dell'economia politica pura" (1892–1893; Considerations on the fundamental principles of pure political economy), he studied consumer equilibrium and made a resolute defense of the theory of relative prices based on marginal utility. He still assumed cardinally measurable utility functions and tried to prove rigorously that the demand curve for each good is negatively sloped with respect to price.

In his first treatise, the *Cours d'économie politique* (2 vols., 1896–1897; A course in political economy), Pareto aimed at applying the "experimental method," according to the principle of "successive approximations," in the scientific study of economic and social phenomena. He meant "to offer an outline of economic science considered as a natural science and founded solely on facts" (Pareto 1896–1897 [1964, p. iii]). Scientists have to single out broad uniformities of phenomena, based on empirical evidence, to identify scientific laws. To move on from theory to the analysis of each concrete phenomenon, scientists

Vilfredo Pareto. THE LIBRARY OF CONGRESS.

must take into account, through successive approximations, the richer interdependences disregarded in pure theory. According to the principle of successive approximations, economic science, which Pareto called the science of ophelimity, is the abstract theory, in mathematical language, of the ideal conditions of exchange by optimizing agents. Pareto stressed that the utility dealt with in pure economics (ophelimity) has the sole function of expressing the subjective preferences of the economic agent, whom he identified with the fictitious "homo oeconomicus."

Together with Irving Fisher and Philip Wicksteed, Pareto championed the interpretation of market equilibrium theory as a theory of compatible optimal choices based on the ranking of individual preferences. In his second treatise, the *Manuale di economia politica* (1906), he criticized the notion of cardinal utility and the hazy philosophical background underlying ideas of measurable utility in economics. He suggested the plotting of consumers' subjective preferences solely with indifference curves and argued that, given indifference curves, it was possible to index each consumer's preferences with infinite utility functions. In the crude language of mechanical analogies that he extensively adopted, Pareto accounted for choices

as paths along which economic agents move like material points, drawn on by forces of attraction (tastes) or constrained by obstacles (technology and resource constraints). Pareto built his economic theory on the frame of Walras's general equilibrium model. He offered an updated version of economic equilibrium equations in the extended mathematical appendix added to the French edition of his *Manuale di economia politica* (*Manuel d'économie politique*, 1909) and in the entry "Economie mathématique" (Mathematical economics) for the *Encyclopédie des Sciences Mathématiques* (1911). Pareto differentiated "statics," or the study of isolated equilibria from the "dynamics of successive equilibria," the sequence of equilibria over time, and he considered long-term trends and cyclical fluctuations. He conjectured that, in principle, equilibrium prices and quantities might be calculated if all the data and parameters could be known in advance; he emphasized, however, the extraordinary complexity of the problem, concluding that actual computation of equilibrium would remain a mirage.

Pareto was far from consistent in the ordinalist approach, and the inconsistencies were pointed out in later economic literature. Pareto did not totally reject the assessment of social utility, which he identified with the rational evaluation of social well-being, a difficult task because of its dependence on the cultural context and the modest scientific scope it offered. To deal with a well-defined notion of social optimum, "the greatest possible welfare to the individuals of the collectivity," he introduced the principle later associated with his name in the term *Pareto optimality* or *Pareto efficiency.* An optimum allocation of resources is reached, it stated, if the allocation is feasible and no individual agent's well-being may be improved except by reducing the well-being reached by some other agent. Pareto defined "the position of maximum ophelimity" to be an allocation from which it is impossible to move—given the available resources—in such a way that the ophelimities of the agents, except for some which remain constant, all increase. The principle made it possible to clearly single out suboptimal allocations, where at least one agent could improve its well-being with none of the other agents being worse off.

> Given certain rules of distribution, we can seek the position which gives, always in conformance with these rules, the greatest possible welfare to the individuals of the collectivity. Consider any position, and assume that we move away from it by a very small amount, consistent with the restrictions. If in so doing the welfare of all the individuals of the collectivity is increased, it is obvious that the new position is more advantageous to each one of them; and vice versa, it is less so if the welfare of all the individuals is decreased. Moreover, the welfare of some of them

can remain the same, without changing these conclusions. But on the other hand, if this small movement increases the welfare of certain individuals and decreases that of others, we can no longer state positively that it is advantageous to the entire collectivity to carry out that movement. (Pareto, 1909 [1971, p. 451])

Optimal allocations are contingent on the initial distribution of wealth, and Pareto argued that pure economics did not offer criteria that might prove decisive in the choice between a system based on private property and a socialist system. Although a collectivist state could achieve, in principle, the same productive efficiency as a free market economy and obtain the maximum ophelimity for the economic agents—according to some chosen distributive criteria—by appropriate transfers, the computation of the optimum solution would be impracticable. Moreover, state employees would prove less efficient than the entrepreneurs of a market economy because of the former's lack of incentives.

According to his vision of scientific research, which was modeled on physics, Pareto looked at empirical verification as the ultimate criterion of truth. He contributed to the development of econometrics and applied economics, employing time series techniques for the analysis of economic and social data (income distribution, demography, wages, exchange rates) and investigating the best interpolation methods (especially Cauchy's method and least squares). Beginning in his early years in Lausanne, he studied the distribution of incomes on available statistical evidence. Pareto identified a remarkably stable pattern of income distribution, expressed by an equation known in later literature as Pareto's law or Pareto's distribution. The unequal income distribution that Pareto held to be quite invariant throughout history was to form the basis of his theory of the circulation of elites or "aristocracies"—social groups in a dominant position that succeed one upon another in the course of history.

Later Ideas: Nonlogical Actions. The early years of the new century saw Pareto abandoning the ideology of his youth to stress the role that primary impulses and deceptive ideologies play in human history. In *Les systèmes socialistes* (2 vols., 1902–1903), he critically examined both collectivist organization and socialist ideas from antiquity to his own time. He explained the powerful appeal of socialist ideologies with the theory of elites, or the alternation in power, amidst social and political conflict, of emerging and declining aristocracies. Pareto saw the socialist ideologies as offering a rational semblance to the urge driving new social groups to assert themselves as an emerging aristocracy. In *Les systèmes socialistes,* he moved away from liberal ideals to study, with professed

scientific detachment, the power struggle concealed in the clash of ideologies.

In Pareto's sociological thought, nonlogical actions play a central role. Pareto classified as nonlogical an array of human actions, from simply stupid or purely conventional behavior up to the higher forms of symbolic thinking. In his sociology he argued that although humans most often act to achieve a subjective end—namely, the conscious aim that frames the action—it may prove to be totally different from the objective end, the real effect that the action achieves.

In his *Trattato di sociologia generale* (2nd ed., 3 vols., 1923; *The Mind and Society: A Treatise on General Sociology,* 4 vols., 1963), Pareto dealt primarily with human action in history and nonlogical actions, already explored in the *Manuale di economia politica,* as the main focus of his studies. Logical actions are only those that logically connect means and ends, being directed to a conscious finality and being inspired by a correct perception of the relevant causal nexuses. Nonlogical actions are either those not moved by a conscious finality (such as instinctual behavior or settled habits) or those that are aimed at an end that does not correspond to the effects produced. Logical actions have vast scope in society (as in rational scientific enquiry), but nonlogical actions play a predominant part. According to Pareto, men tend to give a logical veneer to their behavior, justifying it with deceptive motivations. At the source of all human action are universal primary impulses; Pareto named the sentiments and beliefs that arise from such primary impulses *residues* and classified them into basic types. Humans act under the drive of the residues and under the cover of false rationalizations—that self-deception which Pareto termed *derivations.* The derivations are the complex web of fictitious rational motivations that both express and conceal the basic sentiments and beliefs at the root of acting. In Pareto's sociology, the sphere of rationalized feelings (such as myth, religion, ethics, and ideology) is essential for social life and historical evolution. Misconceived emotional motives, concealed under the disguise of religion, myth, or ideologies, bind together people in sociality and drive them to act, forging the history of nations through the alternation of aristocracies.

Turning to Political Science. In his sociology, Pareto had extensively dealt with political power in societies. From 1920 onward he devoted more and more papers to political developments, commenting on contemporary events in Italy or in the international scene. In the book *Trasformazione della democrazia* (1921; *The Transformation of Democracy,* 1984), he evoked the crisis of the parliamentary democracies, the parliaments' loss of effective sovereignty, the progressive predominance of coalitions of interests suffocating free competition, and the escalating antagonism on the international scene. Democracy, he held, was an unstable system, and he regarded the democracies of his time as being undermined by irreversible crisis. Pareto analyzed the European conflict as generated by a clash between peoples—Germans, Slavs, and Britons—lusting for supremacy and germinating from conflict between the aristocratic and military bureaucracies of Germany and Austria, on one side, and the "demagogic plutocracy" prevailing in most countries among the Entente Powers, especially in Great Britain, France, and the United States. The cure Pareto prescribed for the ailing state of Europe's political system after the Great War was not a reform of institutions to consolidate the democracies, but rather the emergence of an authoritarian state to guarantee the survival of a much-enfeebled parliamentary democracy. Pareto, never a militant fascist and until the end of his life an independent thinker, contributed to the decline of liberal culture in crucial years of European history, in the aftermath of World War I.

BIBLIOGRAPHY

WORKS BY PARETO

"Considerazioni sui principi fondamentali dell'economia politica pura." *Giornale degli Economisti* May 1892: 389–420; June 1892: 485–512; August 1892: 119–157; January 1893: 1–37; October 1893: 279–321. Reprinted in *Oeuvres complètes de Vilfredo Pareto,* edited by Giovanni Busino. Vol. 26, *Ecrits d'économie politique pure.* Geneva, Switzerland: Librairie Droz, 1982.

La courbe de la répartition de la richesse. Lausanne, Switzerland: Charles Viret-Genton, 1896. Reprinted in *Oeuvres complètes de Vilfredo Pareto,* edited by Giovanni Busino. Vol. 3, *Écrits sur la courbe de la répartition de la richesse.* Geneva, Switzerland: Librairie Droz, 1965.

Cours d'économie politique professé à l'Université de Lausanne. 2 vols. Lausanne, Switzerland: F. Rouge, 1896–1897. Reprinted in *Oeuvres complètes de Vilfredo Pareto,* edited by Giovanni Busino. Vol. 1, *Cours d'économie politique.* Geneva, Switzerland: Librairie Droz, 1964.

Les systèmes socialistes. 2 vols. Paris: V. Giard & E. Brière, 1902–1903. Reprinted in *Oeuvres complètes de Vilfredo Pareto,* edited by Giovanni Busino. Vol. 5, *Les systèmes socialistes.* Geneva, Switzerland: Librairie Droz, 1978.

Manuale di economia politica. Milan, Italy: Società Editrice Libraria, 1906. Translated by Alfred Bonnet as *Manuel d'économie politique,* Paris: V. Giard & E. Brière 1909. Reprinted in *Oeuvres complètes de Vilfredo Pareto,* edited by Giovanni Busino. Vol. 7, *Manuel d'économie politique.* Geneva, Switzerland: Librairie Droz, 1981. Translated by Ann S. Schwier as *Manual of Political Economy,* edited by Ann S. Schwier and Alfred N. Page. New York: A. M. Kelley, 1971.

"Economie mathématique." In *Encyclopédie des Sciences Mathématiques Pures et Appliquées, Publié sous les Auspices des Académies des Sciences de Gottingue, de Leipzig, de Munich et*

de Vienne avec la collaboration de nombreux savants. Paris: Gauthiers-Villar, Tome 1, Vol. IV, issue 4, edited by Jules Monk, 1911. Reprinted in *Oeuvres complètes de Vilfredo Pareto,* edited by Giovanni Busino. Vol. 8, *Statistique économie et mathématique.* Geneva, Switzerland: Librairie Droz, 1966.

Trattato di sociologia generale. 2nd ed. 3 vols. Florence, Italy: G. Barbera, 1923. Translated by Pierre Boven and revised by the author as *Traité de sociologie génerale* (2 vols., Lausanne, Switzerland; Paris: Payot, 1917–1919). Reprinted in *Oeuvres complètes de Vilfredo Pareto,* edited by Giovanni Busino. Vol. 12, *Traité de sociologie générale.* Geneva, Switzerland: Librairie Droz, 1968. Translated by Andrew Bongiorno and Arthur Livingston, with the advice and active cooperation of James Harvey Rogers, as *The Mind and Society: A Treatise on General Sociology,* edited by Arthur Livingston. 4 vols. New York: Dover, 1963.

Fatti e teorie. Florence, Italy: Vallecchi, 1920. Reprinted in *Oeuvres complètes de Vilfredo Pareto,* edited by Giovanni Busino. Vol. 21, *Faits et théories,* translated by Micheline Tripet. Geneva, Switzerland: Librairie Droz, 1976.

Trasformazione della democrazia. Milan, Italy: Corbaccio, 1921. Reprinted in *Oeuvres complètes de Vilfredo Pareto,* edited by Giovanni Busino. Vol. 13, *La transformation de la démocratie,* translated by Corinne Beutler-Real. Geneva, Switzerland: Librairie Droz, 1970. Translated by Renata Girola as *The Transformation of Democracy,* edited by Charles H. Powers. New Brunswick, NJ: Transaction Books, 1984.

Oeuvres complètes de Vilfredo Pareto. Edited by Giovanni Busino. 32 vols. Geneva, Switzerland: Librairie Droz, 1964–2005.

OTHER WORKS

Aron, Raymond. "Le machiavélisme, doctrine des tyrannies modernes." In *L'homme contre les tyrans,* by Raymond Aron. 4th ed. Paris: Gallimard, 1946. Reprinted in *Chroniques de guerre: La France libre, 1940–1945,* by Raymond Aron. Paris: Gallimard, 1990.

Blaug, Mark, ed. *Vilfredo Pareto (1848–1923).* Pioneers in Economics series 35. Brookfield, VT; Aldershot, U.K.: Edward Elgar, 2002.

Bruni, Luigino. *Vilfredo Pareto and the Birth of Modern Microeconomics.* Northampton, MA; Cheltenham, U.K.: Edward Elgar, 2002.

Chipman, J. S. "The Paretian Heritage." *Revue Européenne des sciences sociales* 14, no. 37 (1976): 65–171.

Kirman, Alan. "Pareto as an Economist." In *The New Palgrave: A Dictionary of Economics,* edited by John Eatwell, Murray Milgate and Peter Newman. Vol. 4. London: Macmillan, 1987.

McLure, Michael. *Pareto, Economics and Society: The Mechanical Analogy.* London; New York: Routledge, 2001.

———, and John Cunningham Wood. *Vilfredo Pareto: Critical Assessments of Leading Economists.* 4 vols. London: Routledge, 1999.

Schumpeter, Joseph A. "Vilfredo Pareto. 1848–1923." *Quarterly Journal of Economics* 63, no. 2 (May 1949): 147–173. Reprinted in *Ten Great Economists, from Marx to Keynes,* by Joseph A. Schumpeter. New York: Oxford University Press, 1951.

Weber, Christian E. "Pareto and the 53 Percent Ordinal Theory of Utility." *History of Political Economy* 33 (2001): 541–576.

Bruna Ingrao

PASTEUR, LOUIS (*b.* Dole, Jura, France, 27 December 1822; *d.* Villeneuve-l'Étang, near Paris, France, 28 September 1895), *crystallography, organic chemistry, microbiology, immunology.* For the original article on Pasteur see *DSB,* vol. 10.

By the end of the nineteenth century, Pasteur had no equal as a symbol of heroic and beneficent modern Western science. His theoretical and practical achievements in diverse areas of chemistry, biology, agriculture, industry, and medicine, combined with a pugnacious personality eager for fame, and an exceptional ability to stage and perform public controversies demonstrating his own claims, gave him an unrivaled public status. A vivid and suggestive account of Pasteur's central role as a pioneer in the hygienic movement in the second half of the nineteenth century has been given by Bruno Latour (1988), and later balanced and filled in by other scholars (Löwy, 1995; Contrepois, 2002). It was not by accident that Pasteur's work on fermentation and spontaneous generation were picked as two out of the three biological examples in the celebrated *Harvard Case Histories in Experimental Science* (Conant and Nash, 1957). His serious and somewhat pompous and fanatic personality also made Pasteur a natural object for the efforts to bring science down from the pedestal that started a decade later. This article will not attempt to replace the extensive and comprehensive overview provided by the original *DSB* article, but rather will concentrate on certain aspects of Pasteur historiography that have emerged since the 1970s.

The seven-volume *Œuvres de Pasteur* published by his grandson Pasteur Vallery-Radot from 1922 to 1939 is a representative and highly accessible selection of his main contributions, from the early work on molecular structure, through basic microbiology, to practical industrial, agricultural, and medical science. In breadth and significance Pasteur's contributions were massive. His ability to move between basic theoretical and applied research and make the one stimulate the other is almost unique. Modern science policy is often torn by the dilemma of choosing between applied and basic theoretical research. Pasteur has inspired a tempting solution: instead of assessing projects either as applied (symbolized by Thomas Edison) or theoretical (symbolized by Niels Bohr) one should strive for the combination, namely Pasteur (Stokes, 1997). Whether this makes good sense in terms of evaluating individual research proposals is another question.

The Organismic Principle. Despite its breadth, Pasteur's science displays the quality of a coherent research program—a life project. His efforts were connected by a common idea sufficiently fundamental and sufficiently flexible to constitute a continuous and fruitful source of theoretical intuitions. Pasteur believed a special kind of physicochemical force to be responsible for the distinction between living and nonliving things.

Friedrich Wöhler's synthesis of urea from ammonium cyanate in 1828 signaled the development of a chemistry of organic compounds based on the same methods and theories as that of mineral substances. But the idea that a special force or principle was responsible for the processes that distinguished living from nonliving things was not completely given up. The ability of substances in solution to rotate the plane of polarized light, for instance, had been found only in products of living organisms. The physicist Jean-Baptiste Biot, one of Pasteur's teachers, was among those who thought this optical activity might point toward such a fundamental force of life (Dagognet, 1967).

Pasteur made his first major discovery in 1848, well before he was thirty. Among the crystals of the sodium ammonium salt of the optically inactive organic compound racemic acid, he distinguished two types of asymmetric crystals whose shapes were exact mirror images, like a right and a left hand. When dissolved in water, one type turned out to rotate polarized light to the right, precisely like the well-known isomer of racemic acid, tartaric acid. The other type rotated light the same number of degrees in the opposite direction, to the left. Pasteur's discovery of this new "levoracemic acid," as he called it (*Œuvres,* vol. 1, p. 83), amounted to the discovery of a new kind of isomerism. The process has been analyzed in great detail by Gerald Geison and James A. Secord (1988).

The production of the left-rotating tartaric acid from the optically inactive racemic acid inspired Pasteur to speculate on fundamental questions about the physical basis of life. His idea of a radical difference between living and nonliving, his organismic principle or "vegetalism" as it has been called (Dagognet, 1967), did not imply that there was no bridge between biological and physical science. It meant only that the construction of such a bridge needed physical principles of a new kind.

A Research Program in Organic Chemistry. In organic chemistry Pasteur's organismic principle was expressed in two basic ideas: chemical molecules can have either a symmetric or an asymmetric structure, and asymmetric structures have their origin in living organisms. This suggested the existence of four isomers of tartaric acids: the first two were the natural tartaric and the new left-rotating tartaric, which he had discovered. The third was inactive "by nature" (*Œuvres,* vol. 1, p. 346), while the fourth was inactive by internal compensation: each molecule had two asymmetric but opposite components, which resulted in overall molecular symmetry and hence no external effect on light. This last case was the racemic (or paratartaric) acid from which Pasteur had produced his new l-tartaric acid.

Pasteur explicitly stated this classification in a short note in 1861 (*Œuvres,* vol. 1, p. 346). But it is consistent with the way he discusses the relationship between racemic and tartaric acids in his 1850 account of the discovery. The sodium ammonium paratartrate was a special case. It was here, and a little later with the sodium potassium salt, that he was able to find and separate the two kinds of asymmetric crystals (*Œuvres,* vol. 1, pp. 86–120). In reporting this paper to the academy of sciences Pasteur's mentor, Biot, explicitly described the racemic as a compound molecule and not as a mixture (*Œuvres,* vol. 1, p. 427).

Pasteur saw his twofold organismic principle as part of a general theory of organic chemistry. His idea was that the same four categories existing in tartaric acids would recur in other similar substances. Some early successes reinforced Pasteur's belief in this scheme.

For instance, in 1850, Victor Dessaignes claimed that he had transformed maleic and fumaric acids into aspartic acid by purely traditional chemical means. Because fumaric and maleic acids were known to be inactive and Pasteur had recently shown naturally-occurring aspartic acid to be active, he immediately predicted that the synthesized aspartic acid must be optically inactive. After obtaining a sample he could proudly confirm that this was the case. At the same time he investigated the optical activity of malic acid regularly found together with tartaric. He speculated that these three acids, tartaric, malic, and aspartic, had similar molecular structures. It was a new, striking confirmation of his general theory when in 1853 he was able to produce the predicted tartaric acid that was inactive "by nature."

The nature and origin of racemic acid intrigued Pasteur. In 1853 he was able to transform tartaric into racemic acid by heating a compound of tartaric acid with an optically active organic base. He also found a new way of transforming (splitting) racemic into the two tartaric acids by reacting it with optically active organic bases (Debré, 1998, pp. 72–73).

Pasteur's clearest statement of this research program in organic chemistry was given in two lectures to the Société Chimique of Paris in 1860. He assumed the general existence of four isomers for organic compounds of similar nature to tartaric acid, for instance, succinic, malic, and aspartic acids. But by then Pasteur's research program in organic chemistry was starting to degenerate.

William Henry Perkin and B. F. Duppa had produced a tartaric acid from inactive succinic acid. Pasteur first suggested that the product must be the internally compensated, inactive "by nature" tartaric acid. But it turned out to be the racemic variety, and Pasteur fell back on the ad hoc suggestion that either the succinic acid starting material was so weakly active that the activity had not been discovered, or it was, despite appearances, a racemic isomer (*Œuvres,* vol. 1, p. 347). He reacted to new, troublesome facts with ad hoc modifications of his own organismic theory, adjusting its basic principles without being able to produce any new discoveries himself.

The development of Pasteur's research in structural organic chemistry supports Imre Lakatos's theory of scientific research programs (Lakatos, 1970): after a first progressive phase of discoveries it degenerated to mere ad hoc modifications. But Pasteur was already deep into research on fermentation and spontaneous generation. The fundamental organismic idea, the "metaphysical hard core" in Lakatos's terminology, was revitalized in new highly productive research programs in fermentation and various branches of microbiology, basic as well as applied (Dagognet, 1967; Roll-Hansen, 1972, 1974).

In the interpretation of Pasteur's organic chemistry it is essential to take into account the difference between his ideas on molecular constitutions and present conceptions based on the tetrahedral carbon atom, which was introduced in the 1870s. In 1860 he considered various molecular possibilities, a right- or left-handed helix, a "fixed dissymmetric structure," or an "irregular tetrahedron" (Kottler, 1978, p. 70; *Œuvres,* vol. 1, p. 327). It appears that he saw the production of the two tartaric acids from racemic acid as a transformation of the whole molecule, and not as a separation of a mixture of already existing mirror-image molecules, as is often assumed in historical accounts (e.g., Dubos, 1950, p. 105; Debré, 1998, p. 49). As the theory of the tetrahedral carbon atom became generally accepted and the structure of these acids well defined, Pasteur's theorizing on molecular structure was made obsolete: there were only two malic and two aspartic acids, only one succinic acid (inactive "by nature" to use Pasteur's terminology), and only three tartaric acids. The racemic no more existed as a separate molecular kind but became a mixture of the right and left rotating tartaric acids. Thus Pasteur's organismic principle after a while failed in structural organic chemistry, but it continued to inspire his great successes in research on fermentation and microbiology.

Fermentation. Amyl alcohol, an optically active by-product of ordinary alcoholic fermentation, provided a link between Pasteur's early research on molecular dissymmetry and the research on fermentation starting in the

Louis Pasteur. *Louis Pasteur in his laboratory, circa 1870.* HULTON ARCHIVE/GETTY IMAGES.

1850s. In 1849 Biot had told him of the optical activity of amyl alcohol and Pasteur had tried to make crystals, hoping to confirm the correspondence between crystal form, molecular structure, and optical activity. This project failed. But after he had given up the idea that asymmetric crystal form was closely correlated to asymmetric molecular structure, he continued research on amyl alcohol. In 1855 he claimed to have revealed the existence of two isomers, an optically active and an optically inactive amyl alcohol. The production of these alcohols by fermentation became an important starting point for his research in this area (*Œuvres*, vol. 2, pp. 3–4, 25–28; Geison, 1995, pp. 95–103).

In the early 1850s Pasteur was obsessed by the ideas of an asymmetric physical force, molecular asymmetry, and optical activity as the basis of life. He even constructed elaborate experiments to test the possibility that asymmetric "cosmic" forces due to the revolution of Earth could create dissymmetric molecules. His loyal wife described Pasteur's romantic hubris in private letters: if Louis succeeds, the world will have "a Newton or a Galileo" (Dubos, 1950, pp. 40–41). Depression followed when these hopes did not materialize. Colleagues did their best to dissuade him from these pursuits, which many considered ill-advised (Debré, 1998, pp. 76–80).

In December 1854, Pasteur became professor of chemistry and dean of the new faculty of sciences at Lille, an industrial center in the north of France. Contacts with the brewing industry stimulated his interest in fermentation. In August 1857 he published a paper on lactic acid fermentation sketching his new organismic research program in fermentation. His idea was that the different kinds of fermentation were caused by the growth of specific microorganisms, for example, lactic fermentation by a specific lactic "yeast" that he was able to isolate and cultivate in a precisely defined chemical medium. Pasteur formulated his theory explicitly in opposition to the widely accepted "chemical" theory of fermentation, namely that "ferments" and well-defined chemical substances, although produced by living organisms, could be isolated and made to work without their presence.

The idea that specific kinds of organisms cause specific kinds of effects was connected to the problem of "diseases" in brewing and wine making. When beer or wine went bad, Pasteur argued, it was due to the presence of unwanted kinds of microbes. The remedy for such a disease was to prevent the intrusion of the specific microbes responsible. Thus Pasteur's organismic principle of fermentation opposed currently popular views of microorganisms as highly pleomorphic and variable, without stable species like higher organisms. From the start of his work on fermentation Pasteur was interested in the origin and propagation of microbes. The organismic principle set him on a collision course with scientists claiming to have observed the spontaneous origin of microbes under various conditions.

Status of Spontaneous Generation. As cytology developed, the question of spontaneous generation of microscopic organisms became accessible in a new way. Introduction of effective achromatic lenses for microscopes during the 1830s paved the way for cell theory, pioneered by Matthias Schleiden and Theodor Schwann around 1840. Within a period of about seventy years the detailed mapping of cell structures and processes—life cycles, fertilization, cell divisions, structure and behavior of cell organelles such as chromosomes, and so forth—would lay the foundations for a deeper understanding of the nature of living organisms, culminating with the founding of genetics.

Cytology was still in its beginnings when Pasteur first entered the debates over spontaneous generation at the end of the 1850s, but important discoveries were made at a rapid pace. The discovery of new structures and processes quickly made earlier theories about fertilization and sexual and asexual propagation obsolete. Cryptogamic plants, internal parasitic worms, and infusoria were areas of intensive research. The French Académie des Sciences announced a number of prizes in these fields between 1837 and 1862 (Gálvez, 1988).

Pasteur's main opponent in the debates about spontaneous generation, Félix-Archimède Pouchet, received a prestigious physiology prize in 1845 for his work on ovulation in animals, demonstrating that egg cells were produced in females independently of contact with males. According to Pouchet's theory of "spontaneous ovulation"

the ova (egg cells) developed in the ovary because of a "plastic force." In 1849 he was elected corresponding member of the academy. Pouchet's ideas about the interaction of sperm and ova were contradicted by the discovery in the early 1850s that sperm entered the ova as part of the fertilization process. By this time Pouchet was more interested in the study of medieval science than in empirical cytological investigations.

He did not give up his theory of spontaneous ovulation, however, but developed it into a general theory of "spontaneous generation." In 1864 he argued that the opponents of this theory had lagged behind in the development of "philosophical sciences." Pouchet's disregard of empirical developments in cytology and embryology produced a highly critical attitude in the academy (Gálvez, 1988, pp. 358–361). His theory of spontaneous generation conflicted with the most recent discoveries in the field.

Pasteur did not take part in the first confrontation over spontaneous generation between Pouchet and the academy. In December 1858 Pouchet claimed to have repeated a classical experiment by Schwann with the opposite result. Oxygen was often thought to have a crucial role. Organic matter could be kept sterile indefinitely by heating it in a closed vessel, but microbes quickly appeared when fresh air was let in. Schwann had shown in 1836 that heating of the introduced air prevents this. His result indicated that something in the air was destroyed by heating, probably "germs" of microbes. Pouchet consistently got the opposite result and argued that germs in the air could not be the source of microbes. But his claims met strong and unanimous criticism from members of the academy. They found his theory incompatible with general biological knowledge, and his experiments technically unconvincing (Roll-Hansen, 1979, pp. 281–282).

The Pouchet-Pasteur Controversy. Pouchet's *Hétérogénie ou traité de la génération spontanée* was published in October 1859, and in January 1860 the academy announced a prize for the best experimental contribution to "throw light on the question of spontaneous generation." It was the wish of the commission named by the academy that "candidates focus on the effects of heat and other physical factors on the vitality and development of germs and lower animals and plants" (Gálvez, 1988, p. 349). Already at the following meeting Pasteur presented his first results. He clearly had been working on the problem for some time. Between February 1860 and January 1861 Pasteur made altogether five short presentations.

In a series of experiments Pasteur demonstrated how germs could have entered Pouchet's experiments, and how any organic matter could be kept indefinitely sterile in contact with fresh air in a swan-necked flask. Most significant perhaps were his experiments of opening and closing a series of sterile flasks in different locations, thus taking small samples of fresh air and observing the effect on the sterile organic medium. The result was systematic statistical differences in the proportion of flasks containing microbial growths. The more polluted the air with dust particles the greater the chance of microbial growth: high in the streets of Paris and lower in a quiet basement room, relatively high in country fields, and decreasing in ascending high mountains. Of twenty flasks opened on a glacier 2,000 meters above sea level, only one was fertile (Roll-Hansen, 1979, pp. 283–284). Pasteur had thus invented a method of measuring the density of germs in the air.

During the same period, Pouchet also made a series of presentations to the members of the academy, which demonstrated at the same time that he was not well updated. For instance, he assumed that "all physiologists unanimously agree that no egg, no animal, no plant can resist a humid temperature of 100 degrees" Celsius, while Pasteur had shown a month before that heating milk to 100 degrees did not kill all microbes. Pouchet also described how alcoholic yeast developed into a mold, *Aspergillus,* and claimed that yeast globules never propagated by budding (Roll-Hansen, 1979, pp. 285–287). In the early 1860s, however, medical and biological scientists generally thought microorganisms to be highly polymorphic and changeable. The belief in specific and stable kinds of microbes was still a minority view that Pasteur shared with other pioneers such as the German botanist Ferdinand Cohn. Only with the foundation of bacteriology in the following two decades did it become the generally accepted view (Mazumdar, 1995, Gradmann, 2000).

In November 1862 Pouchet withdrew from the competition, and on 29 December Pasteur was awarded the prize. But in September 1863 Pouchet, together with two colleagues, challenged Pasteur's key experiment of sampling fresh air with sterile flasks. At more than 2,000 meters altitude in the Pyrenees they opened four flasks in a glacier crevice and four in a nearby village. Their paper to the academy described how two flasks from each location had given rise to an abundance of microorganisms.

Pasteur was not impressed. He found the argument poor and doubted the technical quality of the experiment as a repetition and challenge to his own: Four flasks at each location was insufficient for statistical analysis, and the report described only half of them, showing that Pouchet and the others had not grasped the point of the experiment. That Pouchet after consulting with his collaborators confirmed growth in all flasks did not invalidate this methodological criticism.

Pasteur now used his opponents' claim to have disproved *his* experiment for all it was worth, for they were now obliged to accept his challenge to a careful and precise repetition under closely controlled circumstances.

Pasteur had a penchant for staging such crucial experiments, or "duels" as he called them, with his opponents. He had a typically nineteenth-century excessive faith in the possibility of reaching a final verdict in this way. Nevertheless, this sort of adversarial procedure could stimulate focused and fruitful research.

Pouchet's two collaborators picked up "the gauntlet" and promised

> to conform even more scrupulously than before to all the minute details which he points to as absolutely indispensable. If a single one of our flasks remains unaltered in contact with air taken at Toulouse, we will loyally concede our defeat. If all are populated with infusoria and mould, what will Mr. Pasteur answer and do? (Joly and Musset, 1863, p. 845 [translated by author]).

Two weeks later Pouchet assented to their proposal that the academy name a commission to oversee and judge the experimental claims. He defiantly proclaimed that a decimeter of air taken anywhere on Earth will always be able to generate living organisms from organic matter (Roll-Hansen, 1979, p. 289).

But Pouchet and the others resigned before the "duel" was consummated. The commission asked that both parties carry out an experiment opening about twenty flasks prepared according to Pasteur's method in each of three different locations. Pouchet's party would use hay infusion and Pasteur's yeast extract. This was the experiment that Pouchet had challenged and that needed testing. However, Pouchet's party asked to start with other investigations, such as a microscopic analysis of the air in the room or of a liter of beer. The commission believed such investigations were doomed to be inconclusive and insisted that first the experiment of opening sterile flasks had to be repeated. Pouchet's party then withdrew and left Pasteur to carry out his part with the same result as before. Thus Pouchet's party had produced no evidence that Pasteur's experiment was faulty, reported the commission. But it was careful not to reject Pouchet's claim with respect to hay infusion, and said it ventured to repeat his experiment (Flourens et al., 1865).

The difference in their preferred growth mediums, yeast extract for Pasteur and hay infusion for Pouchet, is widely presented as a crucial point. The hay bacillus produces spores that can survive heating to 100 degrees Celsius, a fact that was only discovered some years later. Thus growth in all flasks with hay infusion would probably have occurred even following the strict procedures of Pasteur. So if Pouchet and the others had not lost their nerve they might well have won their point (Duclaux, 1896, p. 141; Geison, 1995, pp. 131–132). However, both the commission and Pasteur were well aware of this possibility, and there is no reason not to assume that such a result would have been followed up quickly by Pasteur, introducing more rigorously sterile methods.

In hindsight the descriptions that Pouchet and his collaborators give of the content of the flasks indicate serious weaknesses in their experimental techniques. The presence of "touffes de Mycelium," "Mucédinées articulées," "bacteries," "amibes," and so forth (Pouchet et al., 1863, p. 560) is clear evidence that not only spores of the hay bacillus were at work. Because a belief in the strong polymorphy of microorganisms was still dominant among biologists, Pasteur's belief in a high degree of specificity was not in itself a passable argument. But it could fruitfully guide his own investigations. By forcing Pouchet and others to repeat their experiments under controlled circumstances, and in strict parallel to the experiments they claimed to contradict, Pasteur assumed that he would be able to spot the holes in their presumed disproof of his claims. That is, he would be able to show where the specific organisms that grew up in their flasks had come from, whether they were due to germs introduced through careless techniques in opening and closing the flasks or whether the broth contained some kind of heat-resistant stage of the organism in question (Roll-Hansen, 1998).

An Alternative Interpretation. The preceding is a rough outline of the scientific issues and institutional framework of the Pasteur-Pouchet debate of 1859 to 1864. In traditional rationalist accounts it is a paradigmatic example of how experimental science can reveal superstitions and advance human understanding of the world (Duclaux, 1896; Bulloch, 1938; Dubos, 1950; Debré, 1998). The scientifically superior quality of Pasteur's experiments, it is said, established facts and supported principles that pointed toward conclusions that would be generally accepted within a few decades.

However, in a 1974 paper John Farley and Gerald Geison claimed that Pasteur's victory in the controversy with Pouchet was due to external factors—to cultural, political, and institutional power—rather than to sound scientific evidence and argument. They claimed to have revealed the "very real significance of the extra-scientific, political aspects of the debate" (p. 162) and they were "persuaded that external factors influenced Pasteur's research and scientific judgment more powerfully than they did the defeated Pouchet" (p. 197). With the Académie des Sciences as the judge, Farley and Geison said that the outcome was more or less inevitable given the cultural and political ideologies that the academy shared with ruling groups.

Farley and Geison argued that the outcome was in harmony with the interests of cultural and political conservative elites who feared the influence of radical materialist views about the nature of human beings, where the

demonstration of spontaneous generation could be taken as further supporting evidence. But as both men were confessional Christians, Pasteur a Catholic and Pouchet a Protestant, and neither had a radical political profile, a clear effect of such factors appears hard to substantiate. Farley and Geison also point out that Pasteur was an insider in the academy, while Pouchet was a minor figure in the French scientific establishment, but suggestions concerning the effects of social loyalty or elite networks on the knowledge claims of scientist need to be scrutinized carefully. In the Pouchet-Pasteur case the conclusions of the French academy's commission were carefully limited to rather uncontroversial statements on the experimental results, not stating any further generalizations on the possibility or impossibility of spontaneous generation. Leading members of the commission had expressed a clear preference for the germ hypothesis but took care to proceed in a reliably objective manner. They can be understood as genuinely interested in pinpointing clear evidence in conflict with the germ hypothesis.

Pasteur's Scientific Method. However, the salient point in the argument of Farley and Geison was a critique of Pasteur's scientific method. By claiming that Pasteur's method had serious weaknesses and was no better than Pouchet's, they depicted a situation where it appears more likely that "extrascientific" factors were decisive. According to Farley and Geison, Pasteur violated fundamental precepts of experimental method, for instance, failing to repeat and falsify Pouchet's experiment in the Pyrenees. However, as shown above, that experiment was modeled on an earlier set of experiments by Pasteur in which Pouchet claimed to have shown that the conclusion Pasteur had drawn from them was mistaken. Thus Pouchet had taken on a burden of proving Pasteur wrong on the experimental level. If the modified experiment of Pouchet and others, with hay infusion instead of yeast extract, had been verified under strictly controlled and analogous experimental circumstances it would have been Pasteur's challenge to explain the difference in terms of his own germ theory. But his opponents withdrew and Pasteur had a walkover.

Farley and Geison further argued that there was a basic methodological asymmetry in the debate based on the logical difference between proving and disproving a universal claim. While a universal claim can be disproved by a single counterinstance, it can never be conclusively proved however large a number of positive instances are found. Farley and Geison argued that the proponents of a spontaneous generation theory such as that of Pouchet "needed only to show that the feat was possible" while opponents had to demonstrate the general claim that it never happens (1974, p. 192; Farley, 1978, p. 144). But, as shown, there was hardly any difference in the level of generality in their claims. Pasteur held that it was always possible to draw a sample of air that would not provoke growth of microorganisms—with his methods. Likewise, Pouchet claimed it was always possible to draw a sample that would provoke growth—with *his* methods.

Implications of the pervasive dependence of observation on theory was perceived by thoughtful methodologists long before twentieth-century philosophers of science began to develop more explicit ideas about competing theories, paradigms, and research programs. Pasteur explicitly promoted a sophisticated hypothetico-deductive method where both sides in a controversy have an obligation both to substantiate their generalizations and to undermine their opponent's interpretation of specific experimental and observational results (Latour, 1992). Pasteur was more successful than Pouchet in both respects, in producing new striking experimental phenomena and in showing that his opponent's experiments on closer examination did not show what Pouchet claimed. Even in his famous public lecture on spontaneous generation at the Sorbonne in April 1864, at the height of the controversy with Pouchet, Pasteur was very circumspect in his conclusion, avoiding any dogmatic universal claim about the impossibility of the phenomenon: "there are no circumstances known today in which one can affirm that microscopic organisms come into the world without germs, without parents similar to themselves" (*Œuvres,* vol. 2, p. 346). Nevertheless, the assumption of a deep asymmetry between proponents and opponents of spontaneous generation has continued in historical accounts of the Pasteur-Pouchet debate (Geison, 1995, p. 131).

Scientific Misconduct? Geison's 1995 analysis of Pasteur's "private science" emphasized his tendency toward secrecy about his intentions and technical methods. In publicly staged experiments in particular he was often reticent to reveal details. Geison suggested that sometimes Pasteur consciously created a false public impression, and Geison found some of the accusations of plagiarism plausible. For instance, in the famous anthrax experiment at Pouilly-le-Fort in 1881 Pasteur did not inform the public that the vaccine used was not the type that he had been developing, but rather had been made according to different principles by one of his collaborators, Charles Chamberland. Pasteur thus took the honor that really belonged to another person. His spectacular vaccinations against rabies also met with strong contemporary criticisms and were replete with ethical dilemmas (Geison, 1995, pp. 171, 218–223). Though customary norms of scientific behavior were different in the late nineteenth century from what they are in the early twenty-first century, there may indeed be reasons to be critical of Pasteur. Geison's analysis in connection with the approaching centennial of

Pasteur's death in 1995 triggered a public debate with a spirited French defense against Anglo-American hints at "fraud" (Debré, 1998, pp. xiiv, 537).

Bacteria, Specificity, and Vaccination. Together with his German rival Robert Koch, Pasteur has a secure standing as a founder of bacteriology. In continuation of the work on fermentation and spontaneous generation Pasteur developed general ideas about bacteria and their various roles. And it was in particular his work on vaccination and immunology, both practical and theoretical, that made him world famous. Pasteur and Koch have traditionally been depicted as champions of the germ theory of disease against those who thought that microbes were too variable to be important explanations of specific diseases and looked instead to environmental conditions.

This picture has recently been further developed and nuanced by tracing how Pasteur and Koch interacted in shaping more precise ideas about the specificity and limits of variation in bacteria during the 1880s (Mazumdar, 1995, pp. 68–97; Mendelsohn, 2003). In accordance with his organismic principle Pasteur emphasized specificity, but in his fermentation studies he had also discovered how environmental conditions radically affected microbial processes, such as in his theory about fermentation as life without oxygen. When Pasteur announced his theory of "attenuation," a way of making pathogens fit for vaccination, Koch was at first skeptical. But Pasteur would soon confirm the claims with own experiments.

Pasteur and his pupils were not as one-sided in their support of the germ theory as is often thought. Studies of diphtheria and tuberculosis showed how epidemics needed to be explained by complex causes. Differences in onset and course were due to many factors, from variation in environmental conditions like nutrition, to changes in virulence of the bacteria, to differences in the immunity of host populations. Bacteriology was a leading discipline in the trend toward laboratory-based experimental biology, and contributed importantly to the general concepts of "identity and stability of biological species" (Mendelsohn 2002, p. 27). There is remarkable continuity from the bacteriological and immunological studies of the 1880s to the identification of DNA as a "transforming principle" in the 1940s (Mendelsohn, 2002, pp. 29–30).

Experimental Method. One merit of externalist criticism is to demonstrate more clearly the limited force and fragile nature of scientific rationality, how easily it can be invoked in favor of loose speculation and how dependent it is on the existence of stable institutions and actors with adequate understanding of scientific methods and their limitations. It took decades before the ideas that guided Pasteur in the controversy with Pouchet won general acceptance among scientists, and crucial general questions about the origin of life remain open in the early 2000s. For instance, it is still beyond the reach of empirical science to decide whether life originated on Earth in a distant past or whether the first germs came with meteorites from space (Fry, 2000).

Pasteur and the French Académie des Sciences were concerned with a more limited question of heterogenesis, whether microscopic living organisms can arise from dead organic matter. They were well aware that general claims about natural phenomena are never proven in a strict sense, but only tested and supported. The academy asked for experiments that would illuminate the question. Under public scrutiny, Pasteur undermined Pouchet's purported results by analyzing his experiment and repeating modified versions, while Pouchet was unable to do the same to Pasteur's main experiment. This outcome of experimental efforts was what the academy proclaimed as a fact in February 1865, neither more nor less.

When a young British medical scientist, Henry Charlton Bastian, claimed experimental demonstration of heterogenesis a decade later, the debate took a similar course. In the summer of 1870 he published a long paper in *Nature* describing various kinds of microorganisms that had grown up in hay infusion and other media under vacuum in flasks similar to Pasteur's. Throughout the paper he argued against Pasteur and in favor of Pouchet, invoking a methodological asymmetry similar to that claimed by Farley and Geison (Bastian, 1870, p. 228). Bastian set up experiments in which it appeared that a much more severe treatment than the usual boiling was insufficient to prevent bacterial growth. He argued that it was generally agreed that no "fungus-spore" could survive these conditions, and thus the result was strong evidence for de novo origin of life (Bastian, 1870, p. 219).

Thomas Henry Huxley had warned Bastian against publishing these claims because of weaknesses in experimental methodology and argumentation, and a protracted controversy ensued (Strick, 2000, pp. 84–91). Bastian was able to set up experiments that only later found a clear explanation, as the existence of highly resistant fungal spores was definitively demonstrated by Ferdinand Cohn in 1876. In the final phase of the controversy (1876–1877) when the physicist John Tyndall was Bastian's main opponent, Pasteur also entered the fray (Strick, 2000, pp. 157–182); in his familiar incisive way he pointed to a neglected entry route for microbes in one of Bastian's main experiments.

In July 1876 Bastian announced that by adding potash solution to sterile urine he could produce living bacteria. Pasteur quickly responded to this direct challenge from Bastian. Urine was a medium that Pasteur was familiar with and the reagent was a well-defined chemical substance. In other words, here was an experiment that promised an unequivocal answer. Pasteur repeated Bastian's experiment and found that by making sure that the added potash did not contain living germs either by strongly heating the solid potash or heating the solution to 110 degrees the urine remained sterile (*Nature* 15, 8 February 1877, p. 314). But Bastian refused to accept Pasteur's explanation, that germs were introduced with the potash. In Bastian's own experiments the potash solution was just as potent after having been heated to 110 degrees. However, his reasoning appears in part unconvincing: "[I]t is to me incredible that a fluid so caustic as the strong liquor potassæ which I have employed could contain living germs after it has been raised to 100 degrees C." He also suggested that Pasteur's flask had remained sterile because of too much potash that made the urine alkaline instead of just neutralizing it (*Nature* 15, 8 February 1877, p. 314).

At a meeting of the French Académie des Sciences in January 1877, Pasteur pointed out that the issue was the effect of chemically "pure potash" and challenged Bastian to demonstrate this "in the presence of competent judges" (*Nature* 15, 1 March 1877, p. 380; *Œuvres*, vol. 1, p. 467). Bastian quickly accepted the challenge, adding that even heating to 110 degrees for 60 minutes or 20 hours made no difference. Once more the French Académie des Sciences set up a commission who clearly favored the germ theory (*Nature* 15, 1 March 1877, pp. 380–381).

As had happened a decade earlier with Pouchet, the commission and Bastian could not agree on the precise terms of the inquiry. Bastian insisted that the commission limited itself to report on "the mere question of fact" of the generative power of "liquor potassæ" (*Nature* 16, 2 August 1877, p. 277). The commission was reluctant to preclude a follow-up with further experiments. It apparently did not share Bastian's implicit belief in a sharp separation of fact from interpretation. Bastian met with the commission and Pasteur in Paris in July 1877, but negotiations quickly broke down and Bastian returned to London without performing his experiment (Bastian, 1877). Pasteur then carefully repeated Bastian's experiment under control of the commission and concluded that there were three sources of germs: the urine, the potash, and the glassware. Insufficient sterilization of the glassware had not been prominent in the earlier written exchange. When sufficient care was taken with all three sources the result was continued sterility in 100 percent of the flasks (*Œuvres*, vol. 2, pp. 471–473). After this Bastian soon withdrew from the public debate and the controversy between him and Tyndall petered out in a brief exchange in 1878 (Farley, 1977, p. 141). By then spontaneous generation had lost most of its support in the British medical community (Thomson, 1877, pp. 303–304).

What characterizes Pasteur's unique ability with the experimental method is not only an exceptional technical performance in the laboratory but also a superior ability to focus experiments on theoretically crucial questions. Such experiments were crucial, not in determining the absolute truth of certain claims, but in their impact on the course of theoretical debate. Pasteur did not see Bastian's challenge as trivial, but he waited for the right occasion, until an effective "crucial experiment" presented itself, before he entered the controversy. The Pasteur camp acknowledged Bastian had made an important contribution to scientific progress by forcing them to develop more effective techniques of sterilization (Duclaux, 1896, pp. 146–152).

Besides presenting an overview of some recent contributions to the historical understanding of Pasteur's role in the history of science, the thrust of this article has been to suggest that internal aspects must be taken into consideration to achieve an adequate comprehensive understanding in the longer run. The controversies over spontaneous generation are given extensive treatment because they have been so widely appealed to in critiques of scientific rationalism. Following the well-justified insistence that "external" cultural, ideological, and political factors are important, there is a need to investigate more effectively how they interact with "internal" factors, such as experimental evidence and theoretical reasoning. It is problematic even to formulate clear and precise externalist claims without close attention to the questions that scientists posed and tried to solve. In particular, misunderstandings have resulted from simple assumptions that some historians have made with respect to scientific method.

SUPPLEMENTARY BIBLIOGRAPHY

Within the very large literature on Pasteur, the extensive and comprehensive article of Gerald Geison (1974) in the old DSB *remains the most accessible and comprehensive overview.*

WORKS BY PASTEUR

Œuvres de Pasteur. Edited by Pasteur Vallery-Radot. 7 vols. Paris: Masson, 1922–1939.

OTHER SOURCES

Bastian, H. Charlton. "Facts and Reasonings concerning the Heterogeneous Evolution of Living Things." *Nature* (1870, 30 June, 7 and 14 July): 170–177, 192–201, 219–228.

———. "The Commission of the French Academy and the Pasteur-Bastian Experiments." *Nature* 16 (2 August 1877): 276–279.

Bulloch, William. *The History of Bacteriology.* London: Oxford University Press, 1938.

Conant, James B., and Leonard Nash. *Harvard Case Histories in Experimental Science.* 2 vols. Cambridge, MA: Harvard University Press, 1957.

Contrepois, Alain. "The Clinician, Germs and Infectious Diseases: The Example of Charles Bouchard in Paris." *Medical History* 46 (2002): 197–220.

Dagognet, François. *Méthodes et doctrine dans l'œuvre de Pasteur.* Paris: Presses universitaires de France, 1967.

Debré, Patrice. *Louis Pasteur.* Baltimore, MD: Johns Hopkins University Press, 1998. Translation from French, Paris: Flammarion, 1994.

Dubos, René. *Louis Pasteur: Free Lance of Science.* New York: Charles Scribner, 1950.

Duclaux, Émile. *Pasteur: Histoire d'un esprit.* Paris: Sceaux, 1896. Translated by Erwin F. Smith and Florence Hedges as *Pasteur: The History of a Mind.* Philadelphia: W.B. Saunders, 1920.

Farley, John. *The Spontaneous Generation Controversy from Descartes to Oparin.* Baltimore, MD: Johns Hopkins University Press, 1977.

———. "The Social, Political and Religious Background to the Work of Louis Pasteur." *Annual Review of Microbiology* 32 (1978): 143–154.

———, and Gerald L. Geison. "Science, Politics and Spontaneous Generation in Nineteenth-Century France: The Pasteur-Pouchet Debate." *Bulletin of the History of Medicine* 48 (1974): 161–198.

Flourens, Pierre, et al., and Jerôme Balard rapporteur. "Rapport sur les experiénces relative à la géneration spontanée." *Comptes Rendus de l'Academie des Sciences* 60 (20 February 1865): 385–397.

Fry, Iris. *The Emergence of Life on Earth: A Historical and Scientific Overview.* New Brunswick, NJ: Rutgers University Press, 2000.

Gálvez, Antonio. "The Role of the French Academy of Sciences in the Clarification of the Issue of Spontaneous Generation in the Mid-nineteenth Century." *Annals of Science* 45 (1988): 345–365.

Geison, Gerald L. *The Private Science of Louis Pasteur.* Princeton, NJ: Princeton University Press, 1995.

———, and James A. Secord. "Pasteur and the Process of Discovery: The Case of Optical Isomerism." *Isis* 79 (1988): 6–36.

Gradmann, Christoph. "Isolation, Contamination, and Pure Culture: Monomorphism and Polymorphism of Pathogenic Micro-Organisms as Research Problem 1860–1880." *Perspectives on Science* 9 (2000): 147–172.

Joly, N., and Ch. Musset. "Réponse aux observations critiques de M. Pasteur, relatives aux expériences exécutées dans les glaciers de la Maladetta." *Comptes rendus hebdomadaires des séances de l'Académie des sciences* 57 (1863): 842–845.

Kottler, Dorian. "Louis Pasteur and Molecular Dissymmetry, 1844–1857." *Studies in the History of Biology* 2 (1978): 57–98.

Lakatos, Imre. "Falsification and the Methodology of Scientific Research Programmes." In *Criticism and the Growth of Knowledge,* edited by Imre Lakatos and Alan Musgrave. Cambridge, U.K.: Cambridge University Press, 1970.

Latour, Bruno. *The Pasteurization of France.* Cambridge, MA: Harvard University Press, 1988.

———. "Pasteur on Lactic Acid Yeast: A Partial Semiotic Analysis." *Configurations* 1 (1992): 129–145.

Löwy, Ilana. "Disciplines: The Pasteur Institute and the Development of Microbiology in France." *Studies in the History and Philosophy of Science* 25 (1995): 655–688.

Mauskopf, Seymour H. "Crystals and Compounds: Molecular Structure and Composition in Nineteenth-Century French Science." *Transactions of the American Philosophical Society,* n.s., 66, part 3 (1976): 1–82.

Mazumdar, Pauline M. H. *Species and Specificity: An Interpretation of the History of Immunology.* Cambridge, U.K.: Cambridge University Press, 1995.

Mendelsohn, Everett. "The Political Anatomy of Controversy in the Sciences." *Scientific Controversies: Case Studies in the Resolution and Closure of Disputes in Science and Technology,* edited by H. Tristram Engelhardt Jr. and Arthur Caplan. Cambridge, U.K.: Cambridge University Press, 1987.

Mendelsohn, J. Andrew. "'Like All That Lives': Biology, Medicine and Bacteria in the Age of Pasteur and Koch." *History and Philosophy of the Life Sciences* 24 (2002): 3–36.

———. "The Microscopist of Modern Life." *Osiris* 18 (2003): 150–170.

Moreau, Richard. "Les expériences de Pasteur sur les générations spontanées. Le point de vue d'un microbiologiste." *La Vie des Sciences. Comptes rendus,* série générale, 9 (1992): no. 3, pp. 231–226, and no. 4, pp. 287–321.

Pouchet, Félix-Archimède. *Hétérogénie ou traité de la génération spontanée.* Paris: J.B. Baillière et fils, 1859.

———, N. Joly, and Ch. Musset. "Expériences sur l'hétérogénie exécutés dans l'intérieure des glaciers de la Maladetta (Pyrénées d'Espagne)." *Comptes rendus hebdomadaires des séances de l'Académie des sciences* 57 (1863): 558–561.

Roll-Hansen, Nils. "Louis Pasteur: A Case against Reductionist Historiography." *British Journal for the Philosophy of Science* 23 (1972): 347–361.

———. *Forskningens Frihet og Nødvendighet. Pasteurs teorier I vekst og forfall* [The freedom and necessity of research: Growth and decline of Pasteur's theories]. Oslo: Gyldendal, 1974.

———. "Experimental Method and Spontaneous Generation: The Controversy between Pasteur and Pouchet, 1859–64." *Journal of the History of Medicine and Allied Sciences* 34 (1979): 273–292.

———. "Pasteur: An Underestimated Hero of Science." Review of *The Private Science of Pasteur* by Gerald Geison. *Centaurus* 40 (1998): 81–93.

Stokes, Donald. *Pasteur's Quadrant: Basic Science and Technological Innovation.* Washington, DC: Brookings Institution Press, 1997.

Strick, James. *Sparks of Life: Darwinism and the Victorian Debates over Spontaneous Generation.* Cambridge, MA: Harvard University Press, 2000.

Thomson, Allen. "Inaugural address," as newly elected president of the British Association for the Advancement of Science. *Nature* 16 (16 August 1877): 302–311.

Nils Roll-Hansen

PATTERSON, COLIN (*b.* Hammersmith, London, United Kingdom, 13 October 1933; *d.* Chelsea, London, 9 March 1998), *zoology, ichthyology, paleontology, systematics, evolution, cladistics.*

Patterson was the major player in the cladistic reform of paleontology of the 1970s. From his perspective in 1997, the process "began in the late 1960s, accelerated in the 1970s, and was virtually complete by the eighties" (p. 4). This was the period in which the traditional method in paleontology, the search for ancestors, was abandoned in favor of the search for the sister group—for evidence of the nearest relative, either fossilized and extinct, or currently alive in the geological Recent. It was a period of controversy over basic principles, over different paradigms, and scientific revolution, in the sense of Thomas Kuhn. Patterson's success in this endeavor stemmed from his empirical studies of fossil and Recent fishes, his employment in the British Museum (Natural History) with its human and material resources, and his open nature, curiosity, and lack of pretension—his "intellectual honesty" as Niels Bonde put it in 1999 (p. 258).

Career. Patterson was born in London in 1933, the only child of Maurice William Patterson (1908–1991), branch manager of the Midland Bank, and Norah Joan Elliott (1907–1984), a secretary. In 1942 wartime evacuation put him in the Hill Place School, Stow-on-the-Wold, Gloucester. In 1947 he attended Tonbridge School, Kent. After national service in the Royal Engineers, he attended Imperial College, London, on a state scholarship (1955–1957), obtained first-class honors in zoology, and received the Forbes Medal for the best performance in final examinations in biology. On 9 April 1955 he married Rachel Caridwen Richards (b. 1932), artist and elder daughter of artists Ceri Giraldus Richards CBE, D Litt, F.R.C.A., and Frances Clayton ARCA. Two daughters were born, Sarah and Jane.

In 1957 Patterson was appointed assistant lecturer at Guy's Hospital Medical School, and following his friend Brian Gardiner began PhD study at University College with Kenneth A. Kermack. His research was on Mesozoic fishes, specimens of which he borrowed from the British Museum and from the Geological Survey Museum, and prepared and studied in the laboratory of George Eric Howard Foxon, head of the Biology Department of the Medical School. After three years he received the PhD from London University in 1961, and in June 1962 was appointed senior scientific officer in the Department of Palaeontology of the British Museum (Natural History), where he remained, nominally retiring in October 1993, continuing as honorary research fellow until his death.

He was regularly promoted, and shortly before retirement was elected Fellow of the Royal Society of London in March 1993. He was active in the Linnean Society of London, serving terms as councilor (1970–1973, 1979–1984), zoological editor (1977–1982), vice president (1980–1981), and editorial secretary (1982–1985); posthumously in 1998 he received the Annual Medal for Zoology (the society's highest award), accepted by daughter Sarah Patterson.

Other honors and awards came from the Zoological Society of London (Scientific Medal, 1972, to a zoologist of forty years or younger, in recognition of scientific merit), the American Society of Ichthyologists and Herpetologists (Honorary Foreign Member, 1985), the Willi Hennig Society (Fellow Honoris Causa), and the Society of Vertebrate Paleontology (Romer-Simpson Medal, 1997, for sustained and outstanding scholarly excellence). He was research associate in ichthyology of the American Museum of Natural History from 1968; Agassiz Visiting Lecturer, Museum of Comparative Zoology at Harvard University in 1970; visiting scientist, University of Michigan, in 1987. He served on advisory panels on biology in Sweden (Swedish Natural Sciences Research Council) and France (Ministry of Education). His final official appointment, in 1997, was to the Science Board of the National Museum of Natural History, Smithsonian Institution, Washington, D.C.

His research continued in retirement, and he was mortally stricken by a heart attack while bicycling from home to the Natural History Museum—the new name, use of which he resisted, dating from the Museums and Galleries Act of 1992. He was survived by his wife and daughters.

Fishes. Critical to his PhD study were methods developed by Harry Ashley Toombs, technical assistant to Errol Ivor White, keeper of palaeontology at the British Museum (Natural History) and future examiner of Patterson's thesis. To Patterson, Toombs "revolutionized the study of small fossil vertebrates" (1987b, p. 192). The material assigned by White for Patterson's PhD—fossil fishes of the English Chalk—proved ideal for Toombs's methods of acid preparation. In Patterson's words:

> I spent months dunking lumps of chalk in and out of 2% acetic acid, and soon discovered that once you had dissolved the chalk away you got something almost like a Recent skeleton: I could find all the details of the braincase …, same thing with the jaws, palate, paired fin girdles…. I could describe these things in such excruciating detail. (1995, p. 4)

This rich source of information naturally led to detailed comparison with Recent fishes, those alive today, and collaboration with Peter Humphry Greenwood of the Department of Zoology of the museum. In September

1963 Greenwood, with Donn Eric Rosen (American Museum of Natural History, New York) and Stanley H. Weitzman (National Museum of Natural History, Smithsonian Institution, Washington, D.C.), were recruited by George Sprague Myers, Stanford University, to rework the classification of Recent teleostean fishes, including some twenty thousand species, with "provisional" results published in 1966. Patterson was drawn into this wide-ranging project and began extensive "Recent-fossil" collaborations with Rosen, and later with G. David Johnson (National Museum of Natural History), resulting in significant publications dealing with the whole range of teleostean diversity—roughly equivalent to that of the assemblage of land vertebrates, including birds, and its extensive fossil record. His informative reviews and overviews of his various research projects were models of clarity, highly appreciated by the scientific community.

A colleague close to Patterson commented on

> his prodigious memory.… From 1962 onwards he would once a week peruse all the individual libraries in the Natural History Museum—combing the journals and new books as they appeared and reading every paper he considered relevant. This ever-increasing memory bank, coupled with his innate curiosity, not only provided him with the information for his own inductive reasoning but also allowed him to advise his colleagues on their numerous scientific problems. (Gardiner, 1998)

Cladistics. In 1966 appeared a publication by the senior entomologist of the Swedish Museum of Natural History, Stockholm (Naturhistoriska Riksmuseet), that upset and recast Patterson's basic frame of reference. Patterson wrote in 1995:

> the week … I got back from New York, … I [was told] that there was something new in the Library that might interest me. It was this, … Lars Brundin's 500-page monograph on chironomid midges, at first sight an unlikely place to find enlightenment. The Museum date stamp—17th April 1967—fixes the week when I first saw it. I don't know if anyone reads Brundin these days, but he was my first introduction to [Willi] Hennig and phylogenetic systematics, what we now call cladistics. The first fifty pages of this are still a wonderfully clear and strong statement of Hennig's ideas. I was bowled over by it and became an instant convert. (p. 9)

Thus began the long and convoluted discussion about cladistics, which continues into the early twenty-first century in new dimensions provided by amino-acid sequences of proteins, and nucleotide sequences of nucleic acids, DNA and RNA. Patterson likened the whole to an underground rabbit-warren with a single exit. This metaphor reflects his own perception of the general problem and its solution, which begins and ends with Hennig's concept of paraphyly and its reflection in the traditional literature of paleontology and evolution.

An Internet search on the term *paraphyly* returns some hundreds of thousands of items. The term was invented by the entomologist Hennig in 1962, and was used first with reference to the relationships between certain insects. He meant it to apply to an artifactual, or mistaken, assemblage of organisms (Zygoptera, or damselflies) whose only characters in common he thought primitive relative to those of a related group (Anisozygoptera-Anisoptera, or dragonflies). A simpler example would be nonvertebrate animals (invertebrates), or nonhuman anthropoids (apes), or non-Greek-speaking humans ("barbarians" in the classical sense). Patterson's insight is that the ancestral groups of traditional paleontology are all paraphyletic and therefore artifactual, both in theory and in practice:

> Evolutionary relationship includes an additional type, ancestor-descendant relationship. And it is this type that fossils are expected to document. When viewed as relationship between two groups, descent means that one (the ancestral group) is paraphyletic—characterized only by lack of homologies rather than their presence. Most fossil-based theories of relationship concern such groups. The superficial attraction of these stories, apparent illumination of the history of life, has bolstered the belief that fossils determine evolutionary relationships. Yet extinct paraphyletic groups seem to me to obscure rather than illuminate relationships, for they exist not in nature but in the minds of evolutionists. Such groups lead to a sterile inversion of problems of relationships, which come to depend not on comparative analysis of what is accessible—the Recent biota—but on juggling what is inaccessible—uncharacterizable abstractions from the fossil record. (1981, pp. 218–219)

In its simplicity, Patterson's is a logical argument: to state that vertebrates evolved from invertebrates (or humans from apes, or Greeks from barbarians) means only that vertebrates evolved from nonvertebrates (or humans from nonhumans, or Greeks from non-Greeks)—a truism empty of meaning because it specifies no recognizable entity among nonvertebrates (or among nonhumans or non-Greeks). In its complexity, Patterson's is an empirical claim that the traditional literature of paleontology and evolution actually conforms to this logical simplicity devoid of meaning. Can the claim really be true? Apparently it was true enough to power a wave of

change within paleontology, which effectively gave up the search for ancestors, replacing it with "the search for the sister group" as shown by shared characters actually present, not primitive ones such as absences (no vertebrae, no language, no knowledge of Greek). Extinct relatives (sister-groups) of birds, for example, some dinosaurs, are recognized by the presence of feathers. The call for this more general search Patterson saw as the "heart of Brundin's paper," such that "much of the hundreds of pages on systematic theory and method published by morphologists during the last 20 years is embroidery on and exploration of Brundin's message" (1989, p. 472).

This insight did not arise, fully formed, all at once. Initially, Brundin was invited to lecture to the participants in Nobel Symposium 4, "Current Problems of Lower Vertebrate Phylogeny" (June 1967, Stockholm), with Greenwood, Patterson, and Roger Miles in attendance. Eventually this trio from the British Museum organized their own symposium, in the Linnean Society of London, on "Interrelationships of Fishes." According to Patterson:

> our hidden agenda was cladistics, to get as many groups of fishes as possible worked over in the new cladistics framework. The symposium volume came out in 1973 [Patterson et al.]. We didn't manage to raise a complete cast of cladists but I think this was the first multi-author volume, anywhere in biology, in which the overall message is cladistics. It has a certain historical significance. (1995, pp. 11–12)

A flood of literature followed throughout the world, and established cladistics as the "traditional" method of the early 2000s, replacing what is often termed the school of "evolutionary systematics" with its ancestor-descendant sequences of groups, such as fishes-amphibians-reptiles-mammals, all but the last, like invertebrates, paraphyletic in Hennig's terms.

Controversies. Two peripheral controversies may be mentioned. The first followed Patterson's evening lecture in November 1981 to the Systematics Discussion Group of the American Museum of Natural History, titled "Evolutionism and Creationism," the text of which was published posthumously in 2002. Previously inspired by Louis Agassiz, Patterson attempted to look at systematics from a nonevolutionary standpoint so as to put in relief the meaning, if any, of evolutionary theory. A creationist in the audience recorded Patterson's lecture, an inaccurate transcript of which, over Patterson's objection and to his dismay, was then used to promote creationism in the United States, with reverberations to the present day. Patterson stated:

> One of the reasons I started taking a nonevolutionary view was my sudden realization after

working, as I thought, on evolution for 20 years, that I knew nothing whatever about it. (2002, p. 15)

The second was provoked in the mid-1970s by Lambert Beverly Halstead Tarlo, chronicled by Steven Schafersman in 1985, and for which Patterson had a kindly last word (1991). It began with Halstead's (1978) criticism, published in *Nature* (London), of new British Museum exhibits with explicit cladistic content. This meant, among other things, that although fossils were on display, none was identified as ancestral to humans. Patterson remarked at the time: "Fossils may tell us many things, but one thing they can never disclose is whether they were ancestors of anything else" (1978, p. 133; 1998 reprint, p. 109.

As it developed, cladistics spawned various computer implementations, relying upon data, whether morphological or molecular, organized in the form of a two-way matrix of groups × characters, with entries consisting basically of zeros and ones—the matrix taken from the "numerical taxonomy" of an earlier time. Program output is in the form of one or more tree diagrams of the groups, showing some related more closely than to others—the sister-group relationships of the early cladists. An informative output tree depends upon an optimization criterion and procedure, whereby data can be said to fit one tree better than all other possible trees. For example, birds and their extinct (dinosaur) relatives emerge as a group marked by feathers because a (parsimony) program would minimize the number of origins of feathers.

With experience in his own analyses, both of morphological and molecular data, Patterson was ever skeptical of optimization, of procedure, and of theory in general. In his 1981 lecture he remarked that resulting trees

> don't pop out of the data [matrix], so I suppose they come from massaging the data with a theory—or with a computer programme based on a theory; and the theory is evolutionary theory, descent with modification. So what does the tree tell us about—is it telling us something about nature, or something about evolutionary theory—I'll leave you to decide. (2002, p. 27)

And in a final summary much later in 1997 (p. 9), Patterson remarked in retrospect, on behalf of his scientific community, that "we managed to get rid of one pernicious black box—evolutionary systematics—but we've replaced it with another black box—the [data] matrix."

Before his election to the Royal Society, delayed apparently by controversy for a time damaging to his reputation, Patterson was asked to prepare a biographical memoir of a deceased foreign member, paleontologist Erik Stensiö, of the Swedish Museum of Natural History, for

whom Patterson always had the highest regard. He praised Stensiö's "style," but his words apply equally to himself and his personal standards—perhaps the only matters of science beyond the motto of the Royal Society—that he held dear and indispensable: "First, encyclopaedic knowledge of the literature in geology, palaeontology, and anatomy; second, minute attention to detail in description; third, and most important, his readiness to treat the fossil not as an object, but as an anatomical specimen which one might dissect in as much detail as a cadaver" (1990, p. 366).

BIBLIOGRAPHY

The Natural History Museum in London is in process of organizing an archive with a number for each item. At this time it is not certain whether the archive will remain where it is at present in the Palaeontology Department, or be transferred to a central archive elsewhere in the museum.

WORKS BY PATTERSON

"A Review of Mesozoic Acanthopterygian Fishes with Special Reference to Those of the English Chalk." *Philosophical Transactions of the Royal Society of London, Series B, Biological Sciences* 247, no. 739 (2 July 1964): 213–482. PhD thesis.

"Are the Teleosts a Polyphyletic Group?" In *Problèmes Actuels de Paléontologie (Évolution des Vertébrés)*. Colloques Internationaux du Centre National de la Recherche Scientifique no. 163. Paris: Éditions du Centre National de la Recherche Scientifique, 1967. First overview by Patterson, reemphasizes systematic value of caudal skeleton in definition of teleost fishes.

With P. Humphry Greenwood and Roger S. Miles, eds. *Interrelationships of Fishes.* Suppl. no. 1 to the *Zoological Journal of the Linnean Society* 53. London: Academic Press, 1973. Cladistics is the "hidden agenda."

Evolution. London: British Museum (Natural History); Ithaca, NY: Cornell University Press; Brisbane: University of Queensland Press, 1978. Subsequent editions in Danish, Dutch, and Japanese; revised in 1998.

"Cladistics. Pattern versus Process in Nature: A Personal View of a Method and a Controversy." *Biologist* 27, no. 5 (1980): 234–240. Emphasizes phylogenetic and geographic patterns of cladistics. Reprinted in *Evolution Now*, edited by John Maynard Smith. London: Macmillan, 1981.

"Significance of Fossils in Determining Evolutionary Relationships." *Annual Review of Ecology and Systematics,* edited by Richard F. Johnston, Peter W. Frank, and Charles D. Michener, 12 (1981): 195–223. A cladistic overview, resonating with Louis Agassiz's view of the relation between paleontology and systematics, and specifically that "Agassiz's is compatible with a hierarchy of natural (monophyletic) groups" (p. 201).

"Morphological Characters and Homology." In *Problems of Phylogenetic Reconstruction,* edited by Kenneth A. Joysey and Adrian E. Friday. Systematics Association Special Volume no.

21. London: Academic Press, 1982. Widely cited paper on homology.

Editor. *Molecules and Morphology in Evolution: Conflict or Compromise?* Cambridge, U.K.: Cambridge University Press, 1987a. Proceedings from Third International Congress of Systematic and Evolutionary Biology, University of Sussex, 4–11 July 1985, organized by Patterson. Eight contributions from thirteen contributors of the United Kingdom and United States.

"Harry Ashley Toombs, 1909–1987." *London Naturalist* 66 (1987b): 191–193. With list of twenty-three publications.

"Phylogenetic Relations of Major Groups: Conclusions and Prospects." In *The Hierarchy of Life: Molecules and Morphology in Phylogenetic Analysis, Proceedings from Nobel Symposium 70 Held at Alfred Nobel's Björkborn, Karlskoga, Sweden, August 29–September 2, 1988,* edited by Bo Fernholm, Kåre Bremer, and Hans Jörnvall. Amsterdam: Excerpta Medica, 1989. Closes Nobel Symposium, which (p. 486) "summarises the progress we have made towards a tree of life, encompassing the whole in a single hierarchy, a goal hardly attempted since [Ernst] Haeckel."

"Erik Helge Osvald Stensiö 2 October 1891–11 January 1984." *Biographical Memoirs of Fellows of the Royal Society* 35 (1990): 363–380. Praise for Stensiö's "style."

"Beverly Halstead." *Independent,* 3 May 1991. Obituary of colleague and old friend from university.

"Adventures in the Fish Trade." Unpublished address to the Systematics Association. Palaeontology Department archives. Natural History Museum, London, 1995.

"Molecules and Morphology, Ten Years On." Unpublished address to conference on Molecules and Morphology in Systematics, Paris. Palaeontology Department archives. Natural History Museum, London, 1997.

"Evolutionism and Creationism, American Museum of Natural History, 11/81 (from the script)." *Linnean* 18 (2002): 15–33. Text used by Patterson for evening lecture at Systematics Discussion Group of AMNH, with editorial comment by Brian G. Gardiner (p. 3), and by Peter L. Forey ("Systematics and Creationism," pp. 13–14).

OTHER SOURCES

Bonde, Niels. "Colin Patterson (1933–1998): A Major Vertebrate Palaeontologist of This Century." *Geologie en Mijnbouw* 78 (1999): 255–260. Headings include: An Exceptional Career; Interest in Phylogeny, Classification, and Cladistics; The Cladistics Struggle; and Intellectual Honesty.

Brundin, Lars. "Transantarctic Relationships and Their Significance, as Evidenced by Chironomid Midges." *Kungliga Svenska Vetenskapsakademiens Handlingar,* Fjärde Serien, 11, no. 1 (1966). With a fifty-page account of Hennig's principles, and original critiques of vertebrate paleontology and biogeography that decisively influenced Patterson and colleagues.

Forey, Peter. "Patterson, Colin (1933–1998)." In *Oxford Dictionary of National Biography, from the Earliest Times to the Year 2000, in Association with the British Academy,* edited by H. C. G. Matthew and Brian Harrison. Oxford: Oxford University Press, 2004. Informative account with list of newspaper notices: *Guardian* (26 March 1998, p. 16),

Independent (24 March, p. 22), *Times* (London) (8 April, p. 19).

———, Brian G. Gardiner, and Christopher J. Humphries. *Colin Patterson (1933–1998): A Celebration of His Life: An Edited Volume Arising from Addresses Presented at the Linnean Society of London during the Afternoon of 17 July 1998 with Additional Contributions. Linnean* Special Issue no. 2. London: Academic Press, 2000. Memorial volume with seventeen contributors from five countries.

Fortey, Richard A. "Colin Patterson. 13 October 1933–9 March 1998." *Biographical Memoirs of Fellows of the Royal Society* 45 (1999): 367–377. With four-page bibliography of 137 items on microfiche.

Gardiner, Brian. "Colin Patterson." *Independent,* 24 March 1998.

Halstead, L. Beverly. "Whither the Natural History Museum?" *Nature* 275, no. 5682 (26 October 1978): 683. Beginning of controversy over Natural History Museum exhibits.

Ørvig, Tor, ed. *Current Problems of Lower Vertebrate Phylogeny: Proceedings of the Fourth Nobel Symposium held in June 1967 at the Swedish Museum of Natural History (Naturhistoriska Riksmuseet) in Stockholm.* Stockholm: Almqvist & Wiksell, 1968. Contains paper by Lars Brundin: "Application of Phylogenetic Principles in Systematics and Evolutionary Theory."

Schaeffer, Bobb, and Brian G. Gardiner. "An Annotated Bibliography of the Work of Colin Patterson." In *Interrelationships of Fishes,* edited by Melanie L. J. Stiassny, Lynne R. Parenti, and G. David Johnson. San Diego: Academic Press, 1996. With list of 135 items through 1995; volume dedicated to Patterson's "remarkable and enduring influence on the field of fish systematics" (p. xii) of thirty-one contributors from seven countries.

Schafersman, Steven D. "Anatomy of a Controversy: Halstead vs. the British Museum (Natural History)." In *What Darwin Began: Modern Darwinian and Non-Darwinian Perspectives on Evolution,* edited by Laurie Rohde Godfrey. Boston: Allyn and Bacon, 1985. History of controversy provoked by L. B. Halstead Tarlo.

Gareth Nelson

PAULI, WOLFGANG

(*b.* Vienna, Austria, 25 April 1900; *d.* Zurich, Switzerland, 14 December 1958), *physics.* For the original article on Pauli see *DSB,* vol. 10.

Pauli was a leading figure of modern physics from the 1920s through the 1950s. His Nobel Prize, awarded in 1945, recognized the 1924 discovery of the exclusion (or Pauli) principle in atomic physics. Pauli made crucial contributions to quantum mechanics, quantum statistics, and the quantum theory of fields, and he set a broadly recognized standard for critical analyses of those domains. Beginning with the 1921 survey of Albert Einstein's relativity theory that announced him to the scientific world,

Wolfgang Pauli. LIBRARY OF CONGRESS.

his review articles were widely consulted synthetic accounts. The excellent edition of his correspondence has made it possible to trace his influence in important domains of physics. Since his death, the interest he had in Jungian psychoanalysis has attracted attention as well.

Pauli as scientist and human being is well-described in Markus Fierz's sympathetic entry in the original *DSB*. Scholars since Fierz have done much work filling out Pauli's intellectual context. In particular, historical studies of quantum physics have made plain how powerfully Pauli shaped the trajectory from the old (Bohr-Sommerfeld) quantum theory of atomic structure to the new quantum mechanics. John Hendry has examined the exchanges between Pauli and Niels Bohr, and other studies have illuminated Pauli's influence on Werner Heisenberg from the 1920s onward. Pauli's work leading to the exclusion principle has been taken up by several historians and followed out to the spin-statistics theorem in Michela Massimi's philosophical account.

Most attention to Pauli has concentrated on the 1920s, though his role in quantum field theory in the 1930s and beyond was no less significant. His 1932 pro-

posal of the neutrino was one important intervention. Pauli's greatest contribution to quantum field theory, however, was his systematic and critical exploration of its formalism. Pauli's extraordinary scientific correspondence, edited by Karl von Meyenn, has many insights, while Charles P. Enz's scientific biography analyzes Pauli's publications across his full career. Enz's biography also provides many personal details. A very valuable set of reflections by colleagues (*Wolfgang Pauli: Das Gewissen der Physik,* 1988) likewise carries the story up to Pauli's early death.

One feature of Pauli's life that has come to prominence is his interest in dreams, archetypes, and the unconscious. Pauli's correspondence with Carl Gustav Jung has been published, and their relationship has been analyzed in several books. More broadly, Pauli's collected philosophical writings (published in English and German) have made this side of his thought accessible. A full synthetic treatment is as of 2007 still outstanding.

SUPPLEMENTARY BIBLIOGRAPHY

WORKS BY PAULI

With Carl Gustav Jung. *Naturerklärung und Psyche: Synchronizität als ein Prinzip akausaler Zusammenhänge.* Zurich: Rascher, 1952. Published as *The Interpretation of Nature and the Psyche.* New York: Pantheon, 1955.

Aufsätze und Vorträge über Physik und Erkenntnistheorie. Braunschweig: Vieweg, 1961.

Collected Scientific Papers. Edited by R. Kronig and V. F. Weisskopf. New York: Interscience, 1964.

Wissenschaftlicher Briefwechsel mit Bohr, Einstein, Heisenberg u.a. 6 vols. Edited by Karl von Meyenn et al. New York: Springer, 1979–2005.

With Carl Gustav Jung. *Wolfgang Pauli and C. G. Jung: Ein Briefwechsel, 1932–1958.* Edited by C. A. Meier. Berlin: Springer, 1992. Translated by David Roscoe as *Atom and Archetype: The Pauli-Jung Letters, 1932–1958.* Princeton, NJ: Princeton University Press, 2001.

Writings on Physics and Philosophy. Edited by Charles P. Enz and Karl von Meyenn, translated by Robert Schlapp. Berlin: Springer, 1994.

OTHER SOURCES

Atmanspacher, H., H. Primas, and E. Wertenschlag-Birkenhäuser, eds. *Der Pauli-Jung-Dialog und seine Bedeutung für die moderne Wissenschaft.* Berlin: Springer, 1995.

Enz, Charles P. *No Time to be Brief: A Scientific Biography of Wolfgang Pauli.* Oxford: Oxford University Press, 2002. Mostly technical, but much personal information.

———, and Karl von Meyenn, eds. *Wolfgang Pauli: Das Gewissen der Physik.* Braunschweig: Vieweg, 1988. Recollections and original documents.

Hendry, John. *The Creation of Quantum Mechanics and the Bohr-Pauli Dialogue.* Dordrecht: D. Reidel, 1984.

Laurikainen, Kalervo V. *The Message of the Atoms: Essays on Wolfgang Pauli and the Unspeakable.* Berlin: Springer, 1997.

Massimi, Michela. *Pauli's Exclusion Principle: The Origin and Validation of a Scientific Principle.* Cambridge, U.K.: Cambridge University Press, 2005. Includes citations to earlier historical literature.

Cathryn Carson

PAULING, LINUS CARL (*b.* Portland, Oregon, 28 February 1901; *d.* Big Sur, California, 19 August 1994), *chemistry, quantum chemistry, nature of the chemical bond, x-ray crystallography and molecular structure, biochemistry and molecular biology, molecular medicine.*

Often called the Einstein of chemistry, Pauling is widely regarded as the most important chemist of the twentieth century. Best known for his foundational work in theoretical chemistry, and in biochemistry and molecular biology, he played a formative role in at least five major developments in twentieth-century science: the application of quantum physics to chemistry; the use of theories of chemical structure in biology; the construction of molecular models that became a characteristic tool of modern chemistry; the study of diseases as a product of molecular processes; and the role of scientist as public citizen and political activist. Pauling received the Nobel Prize in Chemistry for 1954 and the Nobel Peace Prize for 1962. He is the only individual to receive two unshared Nobel awards.

Early Life and Education. Pauling was born in Portland, Oregon. His father, Herman Henry William Pauling, was a pharmacist who moved to Condon in eastern Oregon, and young Linus watched his father make extracts and salves, measure and mix powders, and test solutions with litmus papers. Among the boy's early reading were his father's pharmacopoeia and dispensatory, along with the Bible and Charles Darwin's *Origin of Species.* His father died suddenly of a perforated stomach ulcer in June 1910, and Pauling's mother Lucy Isabelle moved Linus and his two younger sisters back to Portland, where Belle took boarders into their house. Linus attended Washington High School, where his coursework included general sciences, chemistry, and physics. He failed to complete the American history requirement because of a scheduling conflict, and he entered Oregon Agricultural College (later Oregon State University) in Corvallis without a diploma in 1917.

At that time the college in Corvallis was one of the nation's largest land-grant institutions, with four thousand students and two hundred instructors. Pauling quickly attracted the attention of his teachers in his chemical engineering major, and they enlisted him to teach freshman-

and sophomore-level chemistry courses while he was still a student. As he prepared his chemistry lectures in 1920, Pauling ran across Irving Langmuir's articles in the 1919 *Journal of American Chemistry* on the structure of atoms and the electron theory of the valence bond. Langmuir's publications led Pauling back to the 1916 paper of Gilbert Newton Lewis, whom he revered for the rest of his life. In this paper Lewis proposed the electron pair as the fundamental chemical bond, with the loss or capture of electrons accounting for chemical reactivity when an atom tends to achieve the two-electron or eight-electron structure of an inert gas. From 1920 on, Pauling rarely had the chemical bond far from his mind. Nor did he relinquish the fascination with molecular form and structure that first engaged him in a course in Corvallis with Samuel Graf on the crystallography of metals. The chemical bond and molecular structure became permanent leitmotifs for Pauling's chemical career.

Pauling was ambitious early on. He applied unsuccessfully for a Rhodes Scholarship and, like others of his twelve classmates in chemical engineering, he applied to graduate school. Six of the twelve completed their PhDs, including Paul Emmett, who married Pauling's sister Pauline. In the fall of 1922 Pauling and Emmett both entered the California Institute of Technology (Caltech), where Arthur Amos Noyes headed the chemistry department.

During the summer before graduate school, Pauling worked for the Oregon Highway Department near Astoria. By then, he had proposed marriage to Ava Helen Miller (1903–1981), a student in Chemistry for Home Economics Majors, a class he had taught the previous spring. Pauling's summer letters to Ava Helen give insights into his aims and ambitions, which, he wrote, included not only a PhD but also a Nobel Prize. Ava Helen and Linus were the closest of companions following their marriage in June 1923, and she played an important role in his later political activism. It was her influence that led him to change his registration in 1934 from the Republican to the Democratic Party, and they worked closely together in the campaign of the 1950s for a ban on nuclear testing. The first of their four children, Linus Carl Pauling Jr., was born in 1925, followed by Peter Jeffress Pauling (b. 1931), Linda Helen Pauling (b. 1932), and Edward Crellin Pauling (1937–1997).

After arriving at Caltech in fall 1922, Pauling's coursework included thermodynamic chemistry with Noyes, statistical mechanics and atomic structure with Richard Chace Tolman, kinetic theory with Robert Millikan, advanced dynamics with Arnold Sommerfeld's student Paul Epstein, and statistical mechanics and quantum theory with the visiting Austrian theoretical physicist Paul Ehrenfest. Pauling's first paper, on the structure of the mineral molybdenite (MoS_2), appeared in 1923. It was coauthored with Roscoe G. Dickinson, his research supervisor in x-ray crystallography. In the next three years, Pauling authored or coauthored a dozen crystal-structure publications, completing his PhD in 1925 with the dissertation "The Determination with X-Rays of the Structure of Crystals." In 1928 Pauling developed systematic rules governing the geometry of the coordination polyhedron of negative ions around a positive ion in an ionic crystal, enabling him to solve the structures of silicates such as mica, talc, and topaz. The work on silicates gained him his first international recognition.

Pauling's 1926 application for a Guggenheim Foundation Fellowship focused on something different, however. Pauling expressed the aim to take up the programmatic goal expressed by Sommerfeld for working out a topology of the interior of the atom and a system of mathematical chemistry that would detail the exact position of electrons and explain the formation of molecules and chemical compounds. Embarking on a physicist-inspired reductionist program for chemistry during his first trip to Europe, Pauling spent a year with Sommerfeld in Munich, a month in Copenhagen with Niels Bohr, and six months in Zürich with Erwin Schrödinger, whose electron wave theory and equation had just appeared in 1926.

While in Zürich, Pauling met Fritz London and Walter Heitler, who were working out a valence bond (atomic orbital or AO) treatment of the electron bond in the hydrogen molecule, which they published in 1927 using Werner Heisenberg's new notion of exchange or resonance energy arising from the interchange of two electrons with opposite spin. About the same time, in Göttingen, Friedrich Hund was developing a molecular orbital approach (MO), generalizing recent work by the Danish physicist Oyvind Burrau. The AO approach treats the hydrogen molecule as two hydrogen nuclei with the wave function of each electron centered on one of the nuclei and electrons tending to aggregate in the region between the two protons. In contrast, the MO theory assumes that any one electron moves in a potential field that results from all the nuclei and other electrons together. The AO method exaggerates the covalent character of chemical bonds, and the MO method the ionic character. In the long run, Pauling was to become a champion of the AO theory, and Robert S. Mulliken, who met Hund in Göttingen, became an outspoken advocate in the United States of the MO theory.

Pauling became an assistant professor of theoretical chemistry when he returned to Caltech in late 1927. He corresponded and collaborated with Samuel Goudsmit, whom he had met in Copenhagen, on an expansion and English translation of Goudsmit's Leiden doctoral thesis under Ehrenfest, into a book *The Structure of Line Spectra*, which appeared in 1930. While working on the structure of silicates, Pauling also published an explanation in *Chemical Reviews* of the AO and MO theories that he had learned in Germany, and he began to sketch out his own ideas for a theoretical treatment of the chemical bonds in methane, which, as a chemist, he considered the most crucial molecule after hydrogen.

The Chemical Bond and Quantum Chemistry. Methane is composed of one atom of carbon and four atoms of hydrogen. The carbon atom has six electrons, which should be distributed on the basis of quantum principles into energy states of $1s^2$, $2s^2$, $2p^2$. Carbon has four valence electrons, however, and they are identical in their energy states. Pauling's notion was to do away with a distinction between 2s and 2p energy sublevels in favor of four mixed levels or orbitals of the same energy value. From 1929 to 1934 Pauling presented these ideas to advanced students and faculty in Lewis's chemistry department at Berkeley, where he shared his time in teaching with Caltech. In these lectures Pauling presented his notion of mixed or "changed quantization" (later called hybridization) of electron energy levels, setting up quantum wave functions to represent valence, or electron-pair, bonds, in carbon compounds. In 1931 Pauling (and, independently, John Slater at Harvard University) demonstrated that wave functions project out in characteristic directions: p-level energy waves, for example, are represented by three dumbbell-shaped distributions or contour-lines at right angles to one another, whereas the s-level wave is a spherically shaped distribution. Pauling extended this treatment to other kinds of bonds, for example, double and triple bonds using trigonal and digonal mixed orbitals. Energy data from thermochemistry and from spectroscopy provided solutions to calculations of the bond energies, while information from x-ray crystallography about bond angles and interatomic distances further grounded the theory in chemical and physical facts. Pauling also developed a scale or table of atomic electronegativities for the chemical elements that predicted the energy and electric dipole moment, or ionic character, of any type of bond.

Among the most puzzling molecular structures that had been studied since the nineteenth century were conjugated molecules of alternating single and double bonds, including aromatic compounds such as benzene. Benzene resisted representation by any one structural formula, and its conflicting structures came to be identified with the names of August Kekulé and James Dewar in the late nineteenth century. In the 1920s and 1930s Pauling's Caltech colleague Howard J. Lucas, along with the British chemist Christopher Ingold and the German chemist Fritz Arndt, were among those who proposed that the real structure for a conjugated molecule such as benzene may be one single structure that is different from any of the familiar valence-bond structures that had been used simultaneously and interchangeably. Arndt used the term *Zwischenstufe* for this nonvisualizable real structure and Ingold coined the word *mesomer*.

Collaborating with George Willard Wheland, Pauling explained aromatic structure as another instance of resonance or the behavior of wave functions in quantum mechanical exchange phenomena. Their paper was one of a series of seven papers written or coauthored by Pauling (with Wheland or Albert Sherman) that appeared from 1931 to 1933 under the title "The Nature of the Chemical Bond" in the *Journal of the American Chemical Society* and the *Journal of Chemical Physics*. Pauling followed up these papers by enlisting Edgar Bright Wilson Jr. to help write the rigorously mathematical *Introduction to Quantum Mechanics, with Applications to Chemistry*. The 1935 book's claims are modest but profound: All the chemical properties of atoms and molecules are explicable in terms of the laws and equations governing the motions of the electrons and nuclei composing them.

In 1939 Pauling revised the earlier papers on the chemical bond into a series of lectures at Cornell University. The manuscript became his classic textbook, *The Nature of the Chemical Bond and the Structure of Molecules and Crystals*. It was a textbook that changed the way scientists thought about chemistry, presenting chemistry as a discipline unified by an underlying theory. By demonstrating how the characteristics of the chemical bond determine the structure of molecules and how the structure of molecules determine their properties, Pauling showed for the first time, as the Austrian-born British biochemist Max Perutz later said, that chemistry could be understood rather than simply memorized. Fifty years later, in 1989, *The Nature of the Chemical Bond* still ranked among the top five most-cited books in the Institute for Scientific Information database.

The valence-bond atomic-orbital theory shared theoretical territory with an increasingly powerful MO theory in the long run. Pauling's AO approach, well-grounded in traditional chemical theory of the nineteenth century and in Lewis's hypothesis of the electron-valence bond, earned most chemists' allegiance until the 1950s and 1960s, when MO methods became more widespread, partly as the result of developments in molecular spectroscopy and in electronic computers, and partly through the influence of English theoretical chemist Charles Alfred Coulson, whose book championing MO theory, *Valence,* first appeared in 1952. Pauling himself always preferred the valence-bond AO approach, but quantitatively-minded quantum chemists came to prefer the convenience of calculation of the MO approach, especially for large molecules.

Molecular Structure, Biology, and Medicine. Pauling became professor at Caltech in 1931, the year that he received the American Chemical Society's first Langmuir Prize for the most promising young chemist in the country. In 1933 Pauling became the youngest member ever elected to the National Academy of Sciences. He was appointed director of the Gates Laboratory and chairman of the Division of Chemistry and Chemical Engineering at Caltech in 1937, following the death of Noyes. Like many chemists in the 1930s, Pauling found himself in a university-level institution in which biology and medicine increasingly were gaining prominence in teaching and research. After Thomas Hunt Morgan organized a biology division at Caltech in 1928, Pauling began to participate in biology seminars on campus, and in 1931 some of the Caltech biologists invited Pauling to give a seminar on a German article about a mathematical theory of crossing over in chromosomes. His reading in biology began to affect his thinking about chemistry, including his adoption of the term *hybridization* to describe the "changed quantization" of the chemical bond.

Biologically significant compounds such as urea, oxamide, and oxamic acid were among the compounds that Pauling and his associates investigated in the 1930s from the standpoint of thermodynamics, bond configurations, and resonance structure in the amide group. The nucleic acid bases guanine and purine were among the compounds for which Sherman and Pauling calculated resonance energy in 1933. Pauling's visit to Hermann Mark's Berlin laboratory in 1930 familiarized Pauling with Mark's use of x-ray diffraction data in the study of proteins and with Mark's and Kurt Meyer's ideas on the structure of proteins whereby long and flexible polypeptide chains are attracted to one another by forces between the $C=O$ groups and the NH groups on adjunct chains. Pauling himself turned in 1932 to the structures of proteins, including hemoglobin and other molecules of medical interest.

A shift in emphasis toward a biological program at the Rockefeller Foundation, which had been funding Pauling's work in chemistry, offered support for his investigations in biochemistry. This biologically oriented research included a 1935 paper on the shape of the oxygen equilibrium curve for the protein hemoglobin and an investigation in 1936 with Charles Coryell of the magnetic properties of a hemoglobin molecule. In another paper, written with Alfred Mirsky from the Rockefeller Institute, Pauling proposed a coiled, or folded, structure for the protein keratin, arguing, like Mark and Meyer, for the molecular structure of proteins at a time when the colloidal theory of proteins was not yet dead. In 1939 Pauling wrote a controversial paper with Carl Niemann discrediting Dorothy Wrinch's cyclol theory of a symmetrical geometry in protein structure.

Correlating his interest in molecular structure or shape with an emerging focus on biological function, Pauling tried to answer a question posed to him by Karl Landsteiner at the Rockefeller Institute in 1936: could the properties of antibodies and antigens be a result of molecular structure? In 1940 Pauling proposed that polypeptide chains might fold and wind around the exterior of an antigen structure, creating an antibody that is complementary in structure to the invading antigen, similar to a lock-and-key (a metaphor used by the German protein chemist Emil Fischer in 1894 for an enzyme and its substrate). After discussing with his Caltech colleague Max Delbrück the need to explain the duplication of the antibody form, they collaborated in a note to *Science* on a speculation that biological replication likely is a matter of complementary shapes.

Another example of the usefulness of the hypothesis of complementary molecular shapes came in Pauling's work with Harvey Itano on sickle-cell anemia in the late 1940s. Using electrophoresis, Itano discovered in 1949 that a sickle-cell individual's hemoglobin has more positive charge on its surface than normal hemoglobin. Pauling proposed that this alteration in surface charge created an area complementary in shape to neighboring hemoglobin, like antigen and antibody. The molecules stick together, twisting the red blood cells out of shape into sickles rather than flat disks and clogging small blood vessels in the body. Pauling coined the term *molecular disease*.

During the early 1940s, Pauling's systematic research program was interrupted by two events: illness and war. In 1941 he fell ill with a serious form of Bright's disease, an often fatal kidney disease. His grandfather Linus Darling had died of kidney disease. For the next fifteen years Pauling followed a diet advocated by Dr. Thomas Addis of Stanford University, which stressed a low protein, salt-free diet with lots of water, and he improved remarkably after only six months.

At this time he already was at work at Caltech on military-related projects following a meeting in Washington, D.C., in October 1940, at which military officers presented chemical researchers with a list of needed breakthroughs in medicines, explosives, and monitoring and detection devices. Pauling immediately went to work on an oxygen meter for monitoring the air in submarines, and he arranged its production with Arnold Beckman, who had left teaching chemistry at Caltech to establish a scientific instruments business. Money flowed to Caltech during the war, and Pauling traveled once per month to Washington for meetings, making a three-day train trip each way. Pauling directed research projects at Caltech on rocket propellants and explosives powders. He headed a team for the synthesis of artificial plasmas that enlisted the expertise of Addis and the immunology expert Dan Campbell. Pauling also continued work, which had begun

before the war with Campbell, on the synthesis of artificial antibodies. When J. Robert Oppenheimer asked Pauling in early 1943 to join the Manhattan Project at Los Alamos as head of the chemistry division, Pauling declined, preferring to remain at Caltech. In 1948 he received the Presidential Medal for Merit for his war-related work.

Pauling's government and Rockefeller Foundation–sponsored research during the war years kept him focused on hemoglobin, immunology, and proteins along with other projects. Protein research was one of the major areas of study in x-ray crystallography and biochemistry, with British x-ray crystallographers such as John Desmond Bernal, Dorothy Hodgkin, and William Astbury among the pioneers in the field. While visiting Oxford in 1948 and confined with the flu, Pauling started building protein models, constructing a three-dimensional model of keratin as a spiral molecular structure using paper, ruler, and pencil to sketch out a chain of amino acids, and drawing the atomic-bond lengths and angles from memory. He realized, however, that an x-ray pattern produced from his model would not match the x-ray patterns that Astbury had published. After his return to Caltech, Pauling set to work with Herman Branson and Robert Corey to come up with an accurate model. In 1950 he and Corey published two structures for keratin, using hydrogen bonding for a coiled peptide chain. Their alpha-helix model had 3.7 amino acid residues per turn and called for a diffraction pattern showing about 5.4 angstroms between each turn, not quite on target with Astbury's value of 5.1 angstroms. The fiber manufacturing firm of Courtaulds in London soon confirmed the alpha-helix in its commercial synthesis of artificial fiber similar to natural keratin, as did Perutz in later studies of natural keratin in the form of horsehair. In May 1951 Pauling and his coworkers published seven papers on protein structures in one issue of the *Proceedings of the National Academy of Sciences* (*PNAS*), including the alpha helix, parallel and antiparallel pleated sheets, and a winding three-helix model for the protein collagen.

Pauling's method of modeling structures employed not only paper and pencil but wooden and plastic models constructed in Caltech's chemistry shop. In the fall of 1938 Pauling had initiated correspondence with Joseph Hirschfelder at the University of Wisconsin about the usefulness of three-dimensional molecular models for teaching and research. The German chemist Herbert Arthur Stuart had designed "space-filling" models in 1934. In this type of model, spherical atom units are brought into contact with each other in diameters roughly proportional to van der Waals radii (the estimated atomic radius for a hard atom sphere). By 1939 the Fisher Scientific Company was selling kits of the space-filling models, while technicians at Caltech continued making models locally that were designed by Pauling, Verner Schomaker, and James Holmes Sturdivant. In the late 1940s the design and combination of atoms in these molecules used data about atomic sizes and interatomic distances and bond angles from x-ray spectrography, electron diffraction, and an electrical Fourier synthesizer.

Following his success with protein, Pauling began to apply his methods for uncovering molecular architecture to deoxyribonucleic acid (DNA), the molecule that the Rockefeller Institute bacteriologist Oswald Avery identified in 1944 as the transforming principle or material that transferred genetic traits between *Pneumococcus* bacteria. Most biochemists and biologists had assumed that protein is the principal material of the gene, but because DNA is the most common form of nucleic acid in chromosomes, Avery's findings directed attention to the possible significance of DNA. A protein is a more complex molecule than DNA, and protein seemed the most likely candidate for the complexity of a genetic carrier. Protein consists of polypeptide chains of amino acids, of which twenty different ones are available for combinations within protein. In contrast, DNA contains only four nucleotides, each consisting of a sugar attached to a phosphate group and to one of four organic nitrogenous bases.

In February 1953 Pauling and Corey published a paper modeling DNA with three polynucleotide intertwined chains and with negatively charged phosphates at the core and nitrogenous bases on the outside. They based their structure on what turned out to be a misleading photograph made by Astbury in 1947 of what in fact was a mixture of two forms of DNA. The Astbury photograph resulted in calculation of an inaccurate figure for the density of the DNA molecule. Pauling did not try to make x-ray photographs himself, nor did he build a three-dimensional model before publishing his three-chain structure in 1953, nor did he focus on DNA as the possible genetic material. At the time, Pauling knew that Maurice Wilkins was working on DNA at King's College and that Wilkins had some unpublished DNA photographs, but Wilkins had declined to share them when Pauling wrote him in the summer of 1951. Pauling did not contact Wilkins again when Pauling was in England in the summer of 1952.

In April 1953, Wilkins's laboratory had new photographs of the dry and hydrated forms of DNA that had been made by Rosalind Franklin. Wilkins showed Franklin's picture of the pure beta (extended and hydrated) DNA to James Watson and Francis Crick, who were working in the Cavendish Laboratory of William Lawrence Bragg, one of the founders and masters of x-ray crystallography. Watson and Crick immediately published a structure for DNA: two helical chains, each coiled round the same axis, with bases on the inside of the helix and phosphates on the outside. Franklin herself earlier had told them, when they were toying with a three-strand model, that the phosphates must be on the outside. All this was detailed by Watson himself in his popular but controversial book *The Double Helix,* published in 1968.

Watson, a young microbiologist, had worked with Delbrück for a few months in 1949 in Pasadena and stayed in touch with him. More significantly, Pauling's son Peter, who was sharing an office at the Cavendish Laboratory with Watson and Crick in 1953, showed them a copy of his father and Corey's prepublication paper with the three-strand model of DNA, precipitating what Watson and Crick later described as their mad pursuit to beat Pauling to the prize. In their work Watson and Crick self-consciously and successfully used Pauling's method of model building. Their paper in *Nature* explicitly contrasted their double helix model with Pauling's triple helix model and noted the implications of the two-strand model for genetic replication. Pauling was gracious about his missed discovery, later expressing puzzlement that he had ignored his earlier idea published with Delbrück in 1940 that genetic material might consist of two complementary molecules.

Nuclear Weapons and Political Activism. In 1954 Pauling received the Nobel Prize in Chemistry for his research into the nature of the chemical bond and its application to the elucidation of the structure of complex substances. The award came at a time when his work on proteins and DNA was getting much welcome attention, in contrast to the unwelcome attention paid his political activities. Following the war, Pauling joined several organizations concerned with atomic-science issues, including the Emergency Committee of Atomic Scientists, chaired by Albert Einstein, whom Pauling had first met in Pasadena in 1932. Pauling's criticism of U.S. nuclear policy included worries about the Truman administration's talk of a first nuclear strike against the Soviet Union. Pauling and Ava Helen joined the Independent Citizens' Committee for the Arts, Sciences, and Professions (ICCASP), a left-wing organization of Los Angeles–area artists and intellectuals, which came under scrutiny from the House Un-American Activities Committee in 1947. In 1948 Federal Bureau of Investigation agents investigated Pauling for Communist sympathies, and in November 1950 he was called to testify before the California Senate Investigating Committee on Education, where he defended his objection to loyalty oaths. Under criticism for his political views from Caltech trustees, he began losing consulting contracts, committee appointments, and speaking engagements, and he was denied a passport in early 1952, preventing him from attending a spring Royal Society discussion on proteins. Ironically, Pauling was an object of denunciation by the Chemists' Division in the Soviet

Linus Carl Pauling. OMIKRON/PHOTO RESEARCHERS, INC.

Academy of Sciences in the summer of 1951 on the grounds that his chemical resonance theory was an idealistic, antimaterialistic, and bourgeois invention.

Following his trip to Stockholm to receive the Nobel chemistry prize in December 1954, Linus and Ava Helen Pauling visited Israel, India, Thailand, and Japan, arriving in Japan in February 1955, when the crew of the *Lucky Dragon* still was under observation following the U.S. explosion of thermonuclear devices over Bikini Atoll the previous spring. In July 1955 he joined more than fifty other Nobel laureates in issuing the Mainau Declaration, which called for an end to all war, especially nuclear war. Pauling also entered a long-running scientific debate over the biological effects of chronic, low-level radiation from atmospheric nuclear tests, connecting the problem of possible genetic damage to his knowledge of DNA and nucleic acids as carriers of inherited characteristics.

In 1958 and 1959 Pauling wrote papers, one of them with his future son-in-law Barclay Kamb, on the probabilities of genetic mutations from radionuclides in atmospheric fallout, concentrating on ^{90}Sr, which the U.S. Atomic Energy Commission (AEC) had previously been studying, and ^{14}C, which had not been considered to pose a possible hazard. In opposition to optimistic reports from the AEC and scientists such as Willard Frank Libby,

Edward Teller, and Miriam Finkel that radioactive isotopes in fallout were unlikely to cause genetic or somatic effects, Pauling adopted the linear hypothesis of Edward B. Lewis, his Caltech colleague in genetics, that even minimum levels of radiation are cumulative in effect and can cause cell damage. A live debate between Teller and Pauling aired on public television in San Francisco in February 1958.

In May 1957, following a visit to Washington University in St. Louis, Pauling joined with the biologist Barry Commoner and the physicist Edward Condon in writing an appeal for a ban on the testing of nuclear weapons. By late 1957 he and Ava Helen had circulated letters that garnered more than nine thousand signatures from scientists in forty-nine countries on a petition that they presented to United Nations (UN) Secretary-General Dag Hammarskjöld at the UN in January 1958, supplemented by an additional two thousand signatures received shortly afterward. In the same year Pauling's book *No More War!* appeared. At this time President Dwight D. Eisenhower and Secretary of State John Foster Dulles tended to support a test ban, while the Department of Defense and the AEC opposed it. At the end of 1958 the United States, United Kingdom, and Soviet Union agreed to a moratorium on nuclear weapons testing, but the

Soviet leader Nikita Khrushchev announced the end of the moratorium after the French government tested their first atomic bomb in the Sahara Desert in 1960. By this time Pauling had been subpoenaed by the U.S. Senate Internal Security Subcommittee to explain possible Communist involvement in the nuclear-test ban movement and refused, under threat of being held in contempt, to reveal the names of those who helped circulate the UN petition. The Cuban missile crisis of 1962 moved the United States and Soviet Union to a focused effort on achieving in August 1963 a Limited Test Ban Treaty, which allowed only underground nuclear testing.

In December 1963 Pauling received the deferred 1962 Nobel Peace Prize. The reaction from his colleagues and the public was a divided one because many people had come to identify Pauling with radical or suspect political actions considered unfitting for a responsible scientist. Caltech's president Lee DuBridge had asked Pauling in 1958 to resign as chairman of the chemistry and chemical engineering division on the grounds that Pauling's attention was insufficiently focused on his laboratory and his department. When DuBridge made a public statement acknowledging the difference of opinion among Pauling's colleagues about Pauling's campaign against nuclear war, Pauling announced in October 1963 that he was leaving the institution with which he had been associated since 1922. After the *Journal of the American Chemical Society* mentioned the peace prize only in a single paragraph in the back pages of an issue, Pauling resigned from the American Chemical Society, whose presidency he had held in 1949.

Vitamin C and Molecular Medicine. Pauling's next years were spent in several institutions: 1963 to 1967 as a research professor at the Center for the Study of Democratic Institutions in Santa Barbara; 1967 to 1969 as professor of chemistry at the University of California at San Diego; 1969 to 1972 as professor of chemistry at Stanford University; and 1973 to 1992 as chairman of the board of trustees for the Laboratory of Orthomolecular Medicine, which he founded and which in 1974 became the Linus Pauling Institute of Science and Medicine in Palo Alto. Two new research interests emerged in the 1960s from some of his earlier work: the use of the hemoglobin protein molecule as an evolutionary clock and the application of vitamin therapy in molecular medicine.

Pauling proposed investigation of the idea of an evolutionary clock to Emile Zuckerkandl, who arrived as a postdoctoral fellow at Caltech in 1959. The project began as one to track the evolution, or mutations, of the molecule hemoglobin by comparing its size and structure in different animals. A study of horse hemoglobin, for example, showed that it differs from human hemoglobin by

approximately eighteen amino-acid substitutions in each of its four chains. When this information was compared with paleontologists' estimates of the divergence of horse and human lines, Pauling and Zuckerkandl arrived at a value of one evolutionary mutation every 14.5 million years in hemoglobin. They found that there was a closer relationship between the hemoglobin of humans and apes than between humans and orangutans, and they estimated that human and apes diverged more than 11 million years ago after their hemoglobin had stabilized. Pauling and Zuckerkandl's work was pathbreaking in founding a new research specialty, with DNA soon replacing hemoglobin in the role of evolutionary clock. Zuckerkandl served as director of the Linus Pauling Institute from 1980 to 1991.

Pauling continued to think about sickle-cell anemia as a molecular disease and to consider how abnormal hemoglobin might have evolved as a mutagenic mistake that turned out to be helpful in preventing malaria. Pauling's long bout with Bright's disease, which is a disease linked to protein metabolism, likely contributed to his preoccupation with how diseases are caused and cured by molecules. In 1962 it occurred to Pauling that the human need for vitamins might be the result of molecular diseases contracted millions of years earlier. Not surprisingly he found attractive the hypothesis of the biochemist Irwin Stone that vitamin C in large doses is effective in treating viral diseases, heart disease, and cancer, and that humans' inability to synthesize their own vitamin C is an evolutionary condition shared with other primates and only a few other mammals. Pauling also was intrigued with psychiatrists' use of niacin in the treatment of schizophrenia as another instance of vitamin therapy, and he enlisted Arthur Robinson, who had completed a PhD with the chemist Martin Kamen at the University of California at San Diego, to head studies of mental diseases and therapies at Pauling's institute.

In 1970 Pauling published a paper in *PNAS* on evolution and the need for ascorbic acid. The same year he published the best seller *Vitamin C and the Common Cold,* in which he surveyed the results of scientific trials on the preventive and therapeutic effects of doses of vitamin C ranging from 0.25 to 4.0 grams per day. In 1971 Dr. Ewan Cameron informed Pauling of his work near Glasgow in treating cancer patients with large doses daily of 10 grams of vitamin C. *PNAS* rejected a paper they coauthored, presaging the controversies that would follow in the next decade with members of the Mayo Clinic and the broader medical community over the merits of vitamins in the treatment of cancer. Pauling's personal commitment to vitamin C became only more pronounced with the diagnosis in 1976 of Ava Helen Pauling's stomach cancer, which led to her death in December 1981 after five years of good health following surgery and vitamin C therapy. In 1991, at the age of ninety, Pauling was diagnosed with rectal and prostate cancer, which was treated with surgeries and megadoses of vitamin C. He died at his ranch in Big Sur in August 1994.

Before his death, Pauling had the pleasure of seeing a change in attitude toward vitamin C therapies. In the fall of 1990 the National Cancer Institute (NCI) sponsored an international conference on "Ascorbic Acid: Biological Functions in Relation to Cancer," to which he was invited as a speaker. In early 1992 the New York Academy of Sciences held a meeting that emphasized, like the NCI conference, the importance of vitamin C in enzymatic and nonenzymatic reactions, its effect in delaying tumor growth and prolonging survival times, and its action as an antioxidant that quenches free radicals implicated in the onset of cancer. After his death, the Linus Pauling Institute moved in 1996 to Oregon State University, where Pauling and Ava Helen had graduated. The institute continues to focus on the role of vitamins and essential minerals and plant chemicals in human health and disease.

Although Pauling's public crusades in politics and medicine discredited him in some professional and public circles in the 1970s and early 1980s, the rancor had abated by the time of his death. On his eighty-fifth birthday, in 1986, Caltech declared an academic holiday and hosted a banquet where Pauling received praise as the greatest chemist of the twentieth century, a man deserving of a third Nobel Prize for his work on sickle-cell hemoglobin, and the true father of molecular biology. Pauling's scientific work ranged broadly across physics, chemistry, biology, and medicine. His textbook *General Chemistry*, first published in 1947, defined a new chemistry just as *The Chemical Bond* had done in 1939. The 1947 textbook and its later editions emphasized both the dissimilarity and the similarity of chemistry and physics, and it taught chemistry on a firm theoretical foundation of electrons, atoms, and molecules with dimensions and images captured by three-dimensional models and by data from both physical instruments and chemical reactions. The high school chemistry curriculum in the United States in the 1960s was based in Pauling's chemical bond approach, and Corey-Pauling Space Filling Models with Improved Koltun Connectors became as common in chemistry classrooms as the periodic table of the elements.

Pauling's role as brilliant scientist and charismatic personality was not unlike Einstein's in the twentieth century. Pauling was a legendary speaker and performer in lectures and public appearances, as well as a media star. Like Einstein, Pauling took delight in crossing boundaries and frontiers, and in confounding and even scandalizing his peers and colleagues. Neither Einstein nor Pauling lived tranquil lives, but they chose to become and remain public figures. Pauling was one of the great revolutionary scientists of the twentieth century, and few chemists doubt his place as the greatest of twentieth-century chemists.

BIBLIOGRAPHY

For a listing of all of Pauling's publications, manuscripts, correspondence, and other materials, with commentary and illustrations, see The Pauling Catalogue: Ava Helen and Linus Pauling Papers at Oregon State University. *6 vols. Edited by Chris Petersen and Cliff Mead. Corvallis: Valley Library Special Collections, Corvallis, Oregon State University Libraries, 2006. The most detailed and comprehensive source for references to Pauling's published and unpublished papers, details of his life, honors and degrees that he received, and essays and articles on his life and work with accompanying photographs, illustrations, and documents is the Web site at Oregon State University for the Ava Helen and Linus Pauling Papers in Special Collections at the Valley Library: http://osulibrary.oregonstate.edu/specialcollections/.*

WORKS BY PAULING

With Samuel Goudsmit. *The Structure of Line Spectra.* New York: McGraw-Hill, 1930.

"The Nature of the Chemical Bond." Parts I and II. *Journal of the American Chemical Society* 53 (1931): 1367–1400, 3225–3237.

"The Nature of the Chemical Bond." Parts III and IV. *Journal of the American Chemical Society* 54 (1932): 988–1003, 3570–3582.

With George W. Wheland. "The Nature of the Chemical Bond." Part V. *Journal of Chemical Physics* 1 (1933a): 362–374.

With Jack Albert Sherman. "The Nature of the Chemical Bond." Parts VI and VII. *Journal of Chemical Physics* 1 (1933b): 606–617, 679–686.

With E. Bright Wilson. *Introduction to Quantum Mechanics, with Applications to Chemistry.* New York: McGraw-Hill, 1935.

The Nature of the Chemical Bond and the Structure of Molecules and Crystals: An Introduction to Modern Structural Chemistry. Ithaca, NY: Cornell University Press; London: Oxford University Press, 1939.

General Chemistry: An Introduction to Descriptive Chemistry and Modern Chemical Theory. San Francisco: W.H. Freeman, 1947.

With Robert B. Corey and Herman R. Branson. "The Structure of Proteins: Two Hydrogen-Bonded Helical Configurations of the Polypeptide Chain." *Proceedings of the National Academy of Sciences of the United States of America* 37 (1951): 205–210.

With Robert B. Corey. "A Proposed Structure for the Nucleic Acids." *Proceedings of the National Academy of Sciences of the United States of America* 39 (1953): 84–97.

No More War! New York: Dodd, Mead, 1958.

Vitamin C and the Common Cold. San Francisco: W.H. Freeman, 1970.

How to Live Longer and Feel Better. New York: W.H. Freeman, 1986. A reprint in paperback, with an introduction by

Melinda Gormley, was published by Oregon State University Press in 2006.

Linus Pauling on Peace: A Scientist Speaks Out on Humanism and World Survival; Writings and Talks by Linus Pauling. Selected and edited by Barbara Marinacci and Ramesh Krishnamurthy. Los Altos, CA: Rising Star, 1998.

Linus Pauling: Selected Scientific Papers. 2 vols. Edited by Barclay Kamb et al. River Edge, NJ: World Scientific, 2001.

OTHER SOURCES

Dunitz, Jack D. "Linus Carl Pauling: February 28, 1901–August 19, 1994." *Biographical Memoirs of the National Academy of Sciences* 71 (1997): 220–261. Available from http://www.nap.edu/readingroom/books/biomems/lpauling.html.

Francoeur, Eric. "Molecular Models and the Articulation of Structural Constraints in Chemistry." In *Communicating Chemistry: Textbooks and Their Audiences, 1789–1939,* edited by Anders Lundgren and Bernadette Bensaude-Vincent. Canton, MA: Science History Publications, 2000.

Gavroglu, Kostas, and Ana I. Simões. "The Americans, the Germans, and the Beginnings of Quantum Chemistry." *Historical Studies in the Physical and Biological Sciences* 25 (1994): 47–110.

Goertzel, Ted, and Ben Goertzel. *Linus Pauling: A Life in Science and Politics.* New York: Basic, 1995.

Hager, Thomas. *Force of Nature: The Life of Linus Pauling.* New York: Simon and Schuster, 1995.

Jolly, J. Christopher. "Linus Pauling and the Scientific Debate over Fallout Hazards." *Endeavour* 26 (2002): 149–153.

Krishnamurthy, Ramesh, et al., eds. *The Pauling Symposium: A Discourse on the Art of Biography.* Corvallis: Oregon State University Libraries, 1996.

Mason, Stephen F. "The Science and Humanism of Linus Pauling (1901–1994)." *Chemical Society Reviews* 26 (1997): 29–39.

Nye, Mary Jo. "What Price Politics? Scientists and Political Controversy." *Endeavour* 23 (1999): 148–154.

———. "Physical and Biological Modes of Thought in the Chemistry of Linus Pauling." *Studies in the History and Philosophy of Modern Physics* 31B (2000): 475–492.

Richards, Evelleen. *Vitamin C and Cancer: Medicine or Politics?* New York: St. Martin's Press, 1991.

                                        Mary Jo Nye

PAULZE-LAVOISIER, MARIE-ANNE-PIERETTE (*b.* Montbrison, France, 20 January 1758; *d.* Paris, France, 10 February 1836), *chemistry, botany, economics, social reform.*

Marie-Anne Paulze-Lavoisier was the wife of Antoine-Laurent Lavoisier (1743–1794), the figure known as the father of the chemical revolution. She was an active collaborator across the full range of her husband's encyclopedic activities as chemist, financial admin-

istrator, and social reformer, but she especially exerted herself to help bring about the success and widespread diffusion of the chemical revolution.

Paulze-Lavoisier was born into the wealthy bourgeois class in 1758. As was customary at that time, she received her elementary education at a boarding school attached to a convent and was not given any education in science. Her father was a colleague of Lavoisier in the Ferme Général. Paulze-Lavoisier's apprenticeship in science began in December 1771, after she had married Lavoisier. The occasion that first led her to embark on this goal is not known, but it is apparent that this young woman wanted to become a suitable wife for her husband, the great scholar, and it is also apparent that this is what her husband wanted. She learned the basics of chemistry from Lavoisier's colleagues, particularly Jean-Baptiste Michel Bucquet (1746–1780). She learned Latin from a private tutor and her older brother and studied drawing with Jacques-Louis David (1748–1825). She also learned Italian and English (which Lavoisier found difficult) and even mastered the technique of print engraving. Paulze-Lavoisier was present at scientific experiments as well, and many volumes of laboratory notes that she took are in the archives of the French Academy of Sciences in Paris. The thirteen copperplate illustrations included in Lavoisier's *Traité élémentaire de chimie,* in particular, and the drawings of the laboratory in their residence in the Paris Arsenal were works by Paulze-Lavoisier. These provide precious concrete documentation of her role in Lavoisier's chemical experiments as well as illustrations of the advanced nature of Lavoisier's experimental techniques.

Paulze-Lavoisier also contributed to the Chemical Revolution through her translations. She translated into French *An Essay on Phlogiston* (1787) and *Of the Strength of Acids* (1791), both written by Richard Kirwan, who opposed Lavoisier's theory of oxygen. Her translations of these works were published in 1788 and 1792, respectively, the former with her preface and both with her translator's notes containing brief refutations of Kirwan's arguments. In the manuscript of the later work, however, the notes are written in Lavoisier's hand. The manuscript of the earlier work has not been found. The identity of the true author of these notes remains a mystery. What is certain is that the Republic of Letters treated Paulze-Lavoisier as an intellectual who was worthy of having authored the notes. The savants received by Paulze-Lavoisier in her own salon were dazzled by the brilliance of this woman's clear exposition of the theories of her husband.

After Lavoisier and her father were executed as farmers-general in 1794 during the Terror, Paulze-Lavoisier edited and published his posthumous writings as the *Mémoires de physique et de chimie* (1805), with a preface praising her late husband. That same year, Paulze-Lavoisier remarried. Her new husband was the American expatriate Benjamin Thompson, Count Rumford, a proponent of an early dynamical theory of heat. She thereby acquired the title of countess, but her relationship with her new husband quickly broke down, and her scientific activity came to an end in 1805. The Countess Lavoisier de Rumford thereafter devoted herself to social life, holding salons reminiscent of the period before the Revolution, when she had planned elegant intellectual events, such as those that emblematized the overturning of phlogiston, and basked in the acclamation of the savants. She is said to have kept this eighteenth-century salon style alive until her death in 1836 at age seventy-eight.

BIBLIOGRAPHY

Some manuscripts of translations are held in the Fonds Lavoisier, Archives de l'Académie des Sciences, Paris.

WORKS BY PAULZE-LAVOISIER

Translation, preface, and three translator's notes to Richard Kirwan, *Essai sur le phlogistique et sur la constitution des acides, traduit de l'anglais, avec des notes de MM. de Morveau, Lavoisier, de la Place, Monge, Berthollet et de Fourcroy.* Paris, 1788.

Copperplate illustrations to Antoine-Laurent Lavoisier, *Traité élémentaire de chimie.* Paris, 1789.

Translation and four translator's notes to Richard Kirwan, "De la force des acides et de la proportion des substances qui composent les sels neutres." "Suite du Mémoire sur la force des acides et sur la proportion des substances qui composent les sels neutres." *Annales de Chimie* 14 (July 1792): 152–211, 238–286.

Dénonciation présentée au Comité de législation de la Convention nationale, contre le représentant du Peuple Dupin; par les Veuves et Enfans soussignés des ci-devant Fermiers Généraux. Paris: Chez Du Pont, l'An III de la République (22 messidor), 1795. Written with George Montcloux *fils,* Pignon, *veuve* de La Haye & Papillon-Sannois, *fils* de Papillon-Autroche.

Addition à la Dénonciation présentée au Comité de législation; contre le représentant du Peuple Dupin; par les Veuves et Enfans soussignés des ci-devant Fermiers Généraux. Paris: Chez Du Pont, l'An III de la République (7 thermidor), 1795. Written with George Montcloux *fils,* Pignon, *veuve* de La Haye & Papillon-Sannois, *fils* de Papillon-Autroche.

Seconde addition à la Dénonciation présentée au Comité de législation; contre le représentant du Peuple Dupin; par les Veuves et Enfans soussignés des ci-devant Fermiers Généraux. Paris: Chez Du Pont, l'An III de la République (7 thermidor), 1795. Written with George Montcloux *fils,* Pignon, *veuve* de La Haye & Papillon-Sannois, *fils* de Papillon-Autroche.

Editor and preface to Antoine-Laurent Lavoisier, *Mémoires de physique et de chimie.* 2 vols. Paris, 1805.

OTHER SOURCES

Beretta, Marco. "Lavoisier and His Last Printed Work: The *Mémoire de physique et de chimie* (1805)." *Annals of Science* 58, no. 4 (2001): 327–356.

Blatin, Suzanne. "Un amour physique et chimique." *Historia* 356 (July 1976): 98–107.

Dujarric de la Rivière, René. *Dames de la Revolution.* Pérgueux, France: Fanlac, 1963.

Duveen, Denis I. "Madame Lavoisier." *Chymia* 4 (1953): 13–29.

———, and Lucien Scheler. "Des illustrations inédites pour les *Mémoires de chimie,* ouvrage postume de Lavoiser." *Revue d'Histoire des Sciences* 12 (1959): 345–353.

Gillispie, Charles Coulston. "Notice biographique de Lavoisier par Madame Lavoisier." *Revue d'Histoire des Sciences et Leur Applications* 9 (1956): 52–61.

Goupil, Michelle. "Madame Lavoisier." In *Oeuvres de Lavoisier, Correspondance.* Vol. 5, edited by Michelle Goupil. Paris: Académie des Sciences, 1997.

Guizot, François. *Madame de Rumford.* Paris: Crapelet, 1841.

Kawashima, Keiko. "Madame Lavoisier: Assistante invisible d'une communauté scientifique." *Bulletin of Nagoya Institute of Technology* 47 (1995): 249–259. Written in French.

———. "Madame du Châtelet et Madame Lavoisier, deux femmes de science." *La Revue, Musée des Arts et Métiers* (March 1998): 22–29.

———. "Madame Lavoisier et la traduction française de l'*Essay on phlogiston* de Kirwan." *Revue d'Histoire des Sciences* 53, no. 2 (2000): 253–263.

———. "Madame Lavoisier et l'*Essai sur le phlogistiquei.*" *Bulletin of Nagoya Institute of Technology* 55 (2003): 159–161. Written in French.

———. "Madame Lavoisier: Participation of a *salonière* in the Chemical Revolution." In *Lavoisier in Perspective,* edited by Marco Beretta. Munich, Germany: Deutsches Museum, 2005.

Perrin, Carleton. "The Lavoisier-Bucquet Collaboration: A Conjecture." *Ambix* 36, no. 1 (1989): 5–13.

Pinault-Sørensen, Madeleine. "Madame Lavoisier, dessinatrice et peintre." *La Revue, Musée des Arts et Métiers* 6 (March 1994): 23–25.

Poirier, Jean-Pierre. "Madame Lavoisier." *Actualité Chimique* 2 (March–April 1994): 44–47.

———. "Madame Lavoisier." In his *Histoire des femmes de science en France.* Paris: Pygmalion, 2002.

———. *La science et l'amour, Madame Lavoisier.* Paris: Pygmalion, 2004.

Scheler, Lucien. "Deux lettres inédites de Madame Lavoisier." *Revue d'Histoire des Sciences et Leurs Applications* 38 (1985): 121–130.

Keiko Kawashima

PAVLOV, IVAN PETROVICH (*b.* Ryazan, Russia, 27 September 1849; *d.* Leningrad, U.S.S.R., 27 February 1936), *physiology, psychology.* For the original article on Pavlov see *DSB,* vol. 10.

Near the end of his long productive career, Pavlov mused that the life's work of a scientist consisted in the writing of "only a single book," by which he meant the development of a single set of basic themes through a consistent set of scientific practices. That was certainly true of Pavlov himself: an unvarying scientific style united his Nobel Prize-winning research on digestion with his renowned investigations of higher nervous activity. This research prospered under czarism and then gained fulsome levels of support from Russia's Communist leaders despite Pavlov's frequent bitter criticism of their policies.

Research Style. Pavlov's scientific style represented a layering of experiences and attitudes from his youth in Ryazan in the 1860s, his studies at St. Petersburg University in the 1870s, his stay in the laboratories of Rudolf Heidenhain and Carl Ludwig in the 1880s, and the institutional circumstances from the 1890s through the 1930s that allowed him to refine and practice his conception of good science. That conception and those practices remained remarkably consistent during more than fifty years of scientific work.

As a teenage seminarian Pavlov fell under the spell of Russia's "men of the sixties" and their vision of curing Russia's backwardness through the ideological clarity and technological progress resulting from the practice and popularization of materialist natural science. As a student at St. Petersburg University (1870–1875), however, his beloved mentor in physiology was the politically conservative Ilya Tsion. Tsion taught him a Bernardian style of physiology and the surgical skills to practice it. According to this style, the physiologist sought determined, purposive patterns in the activity of organ systems (which were "high" enough to capture the vital qualities the physiologist studied, while "low" enough to establish the determined relations governing their activity). In one respect, Pavlov would go Claude Bernard one better: From the 1880s onward, he insisted upon studying intact, "normal" organisms in order to examine physiological processes in an undistorted state. As a visitor in Ludwig's lab in Leipzig and Heidenhain's in Breslau (1884–1886), Pavlov appreciated Ludwig's insistence upon quantitative results but preferred Heidenhain's more supple and specifically physiological interpretive style. These various experiences framed what Pavlov would call "physiological thinking." For him, good physiology must both study the intact normal organism (in which, Pavlov knew, uncontrolled variables always abounded) and also establish the precise, determined, repeatable results that characterized any true science.

Pavlov's tenure with Heidenhain and Ludwig also impressed upon Pavlov the advantages of the larger lab enterprise that was beginning to replace the Bernardian-style single investigator and led him to reflect upon the spiritual and organizational attributes of a scientific manager. He was able to put these into effect only in 1890–1891 when, at age forty-one, a set of unlikely circumstances transformed him from a floundering, part-time lecturer and lab assistant into the master of Russia's largest physiological laboratory at Prince Ol'denburgskii's new Imperial Institute of Experimental Medicine in St. Petersburg. Here Pavlov coordinated the labors of about twelve co-workers annually, the great majority of whom were physicians untrained in physiology and seeking a quick doctorate. During the last decade of czarist rule, women entered this laboratory work force. Pavlov's lab featured an authoritarian structure and cooperative ethos that allowed him to use co-workers as extensions of his sensory reach while enabling him constantly to monitor the work process, to control the interpretive moments in experiments, and to incorporate results into his developing ideas. His laboratory enterprise expanded in pre-revolutionary years to include also smaller labs at St. Petersburg's Military Medical Academy and Academy of Sciences.

Scientific Research. In the years 1891–1903, Pavlov concentrated on the studies of the digestive system that were systematized in his *Lectures on the Work of the Main Gastric Glands* (1897) and won him a Nobel Prize in Physiology or Medicine (1904). In this research, Pavlov's "physiological thinking" was embodied in the "chronic experiment," and his analysis of data was structured by his metaphor of the digestive system as a precise and purposive "chemical factory." For the chronic experiment, experimental dogs were prepared surgically with an operation designed to give the experimenter access to a digestive gland. Experiments began only after the dog had recovered and regained a "normal" state. These operations included the esophagotomy, which separated the cavities of the mouth and stomach, allowing Pavlov to use sham-feeding experiments to demonstrate the centrality of a psychic actor, appetite, in the first phase of digestive secretion. To study the second, nervous-chemical phase of digestion, he developed an innervated version of Heidenhain's "isolated stomach." In Pavlov's isolated sac, the main stomach remained continuous with the digestive tract, but a smaller pouch, isolated from food by a mucous membrane, maintained its nervous connections to the larger stomach. For Pavlov, as a nervist, the innervation of the isolated sac assured that its glandular reactions would mirror those in the main stomach. Inserting a fistula in this small stomach, Pavlov and his co-workers measured the quantity and quality of its glandular secretions, which Pavlov analyzed in his "characteristic secretory curves." For Pavlov, these curves reflected the precise and purposive action of the glands as they processed different foods.

Pavlov constantly sought to link his laboratory findings to clinical concerns. The results of his digestive research ranged from specific discoveries (for example, the central role of the vagus nerve) to clinical innovations (for example, the use of the "natural gastric juice" drawn from lab animals as a scientific remedy for dyspepsia) to an all-encompassing nervist analysis of the factorylike functioning of the digestive glands.

By the time Pavlov received the Nobel Prize for this research, he was moving his lab group on to the use of conditional reflexes as a method to investigate the principal actor in the first phase of digestion, the psyche. The dogs used in chronic experiments often lived for years in the lab, and experimenters were familiar with their differing moods and personalities (which Pavlov often invoked to explain discrepancies in experimental results). Now that psyche itself, under the rubric of "higher nervous activity," became Pavlov's investigative target. Here, too, Pavlov relied on chronic experiments with intact dogs (usually fitted with a salivary fistula) to produce quantitative data (saliva drops); and here, too, he attempted to reason from that data to the determined physiological processes that had produced them.

Like Darwin, Pavlov assumed that dogs were conscious beings with thoughts and emotions, and unlike the behaviorists of his day, he considered the explanation of such subjective states the proper province of science. The iconic image of a Pavlovian dog salivating to the sound of the buzzer captures not the end point, but rather the point of departure for Pavlov's investigations. Lay observers, animal trainers, and physiologists had long noticed that a hungry dog salivates at the sight of food, its food bowl, or the person who usually fed it. Pavlov always viewed his particular achievement as the transformation of this familiar "psychic secretion" into a reliable laboratory phenomenon and its use as a method for understanding the unseen processes in the brain that produce thoughts, emotions, and behaviors.

His research strategy from 1903 to 1936 involved three basic, and constantly interacting, steps: (1) establish experimentally the fully determined regularities in the salivation elicited by highly varied experiments on conditional reflexes; (2) use these regularities to develop a model of the unseen processes in the brain that might have produced them; and (3) use this model to explain the behavior, affect and personality of his experimental animals.

From 1903 to 1936 Pavlov employed conditional reflex experiments in elegant analyses of the sensory abilities of the dog (for example, its ability to distinguish between colors, shapes, and time intervals) and to develop a schematic map of higher nervous processes that featured the interplay of the two basic processes of inhibition and excitation and their movement and complex interaction in the cerebral cortex. His determination that a balance between excitation and inhibition was necessary to a dog's ability to perceive accurately and respond to its environment—and his awareness that identical experiments produced varying results in different dogs—encouraged his interest in "nervous types" among dogs, people, and peoples. In keeping with his lifelong determination to link laboratory studies to the clinic, research on nervous types generated a line of investigation on "the pathology and therapeutics of higher nervous activity"—involving the creation and treatment of "experimental neurosis" in lab animals—and then on psychiatry.

By the late 1920s Pavlov concluded that the explanation of a dog's performance in experiments required not just an understanding of its inborn nervous type, but also of the influence upon its nervous system of upbringing, training, and the "social exciter." In the late 1920s and 1930s these became research subjects at his rural science village in Koltushi, some twelve miles (twenty kilometers) outside of Leningrad. At this Institute of the Experimental Genetics of Higher Nervous Activity, Pavlov and his co-workers also studied the chimpanzees Roza and Rafael and launched an attempt to develop an "improved nervous type" through selective breeding. Long concerned about the weaknesses of the "Russian type"—which he believed to be badly imbalanced toward excitation—Pavlov announced that this eugenics project was "for the use and glory, most of all, of my homeland."

Political and Cultural Figure. The construction of Koltushi—which began in earnest as an eightieth birthday present from the Communist Party—represented the culmination of a long process of struggle and accommodation between Pavlov and the Bolsheviks. Pavlov's political views had always revolved around his scientism and contradictory patriotism (on the one hand, concern about the "Russian type," on the other, a deep cultural pride and identification with the power and prestige of the Russian state). Before 1917 he had supported Russia's gradual evolution toward a constitutional monarchy and stood unsuccessfully for the Duma in 1907 as a candidate of the center-right Octobrist Party. Appalled by the Bolshevik seizure of power, he seriously considered emigration before reaching an uneasy accommodation with the Communist Party in 1921. He received virtual carte blanche from the state, and his scientific enterprise expanded far beyond that of czarist days; in his final years he was coordinating the scientific work of about fifty co-workers annually. With the booming support for science of the Soviet state, the new

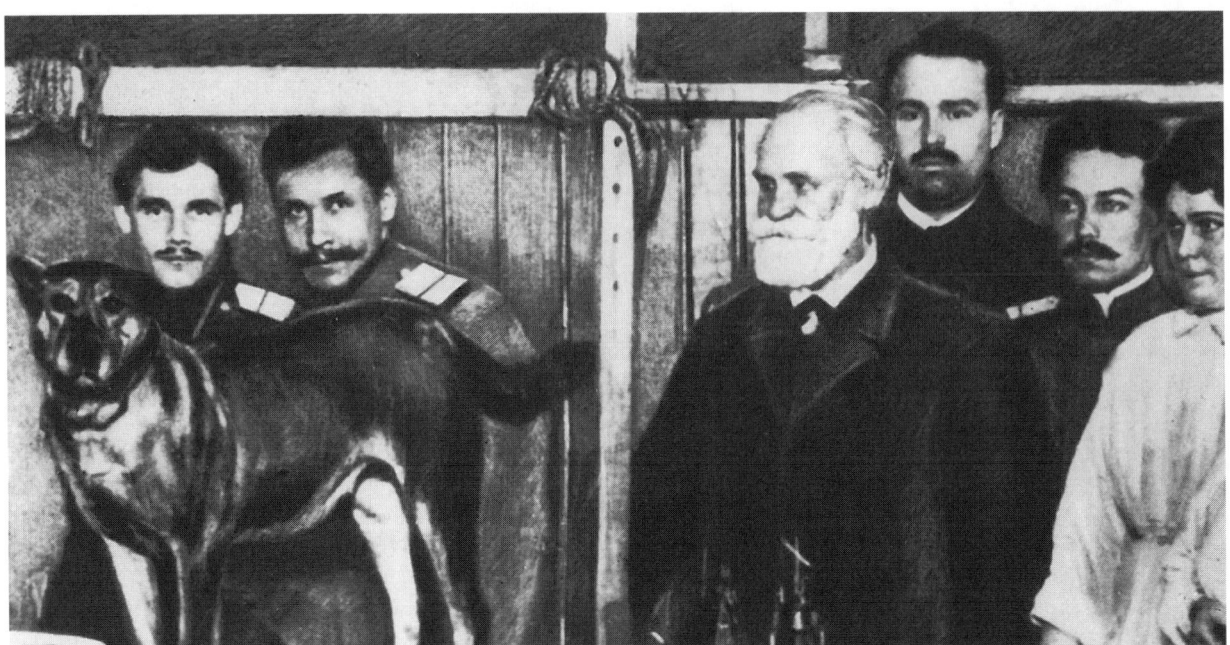

Ivan Pavlov. *Pavlov with dog.* © BETTMANN/CORBIS.

generation of co-workers in his labs were no longer the mere "skilled hands" of czarist days, but rather professional physiologists who often remained in the lab long enough to contribute research ideas of their own.

Pavlov excoriated the Communist Party throughout the 1920s, when he became a rare public voice of dissent. Yet he enjoyed good working relations with Communists in his lab and the state apparatus. By the 1930s he had been successfully cultivated by several national Communist leaders, most notably Nikolai Bukharin. Pavlov continued to denounce the regime's incompetence, dishonesty, suppression of dissent, ideological dogmatism, and persecution of religion. (This latter position encouraged the erroneous rumor that he was himself a believer.) Yet he also praised Soviet achievements, most importantly the support for and popularization of science. As a lifelong adherent of scientism, Pavlov believed the development of Russian science would eventually moderate and improve the regime itself. In addition, the Nazi seizure of power encouraged him to close ranks behind his country's leadership. In 1935 he rewarded the Bolsheviks by using his influence to bring the Fifteenth International Congress of Physiologists to Russia and by toasting his country's "great experimenters" before the audience there. At that meeting and elsewhere he used his access to high state officials to save co-workers and acquaintances from the gulag.

Merely famous as a Nobelist in the early twentieth century, Pavlov achieved iconic status in the late 1920s as an international symbol of the power of experimental biology to understand and control human nature. Yet he was disappointed by the failure of scientists, particularly in the west, to adopt his approach and methodologies.

Western studies of Pavlov were long hampered by Soviet state control of Pavlov's rich archival legacy and by the language barrier. The standard English translations of his works do not capture the metaphorical resonance of his language and are sometimes misleading—for example, in their rendering of the Russian *uslovnyi refleks* as "conditioned reflex" rather than "conditional reflex."

Furthermore, because Pavlov's reports and publications synthesized his co-workers' experiments, his reasoning can be understood only by reading his works (and lab notebooks) alongside their dissertations and articles. In Russia, Pavlov scholarship was initially dominated by his admiring disciples and then, until the fall of Communism, by physiologist-historians constrained by the official image of this national hero and trained in the combination of positivism and wooden Whig Marxism (teleological interpretations of the past from the perspective of the present) that dominated the history of science during the Soviet era.

SUPPLEMENTARY BIBLIOGRAPHY

Gray, Jeffrey. *Ivan Pavlov.* New York: Viking Press, 1979.

Joravsky, David. *Russian Psychology: A Critical History.* Oxford; Cambridge, MA: Basil Blackwell, 1989.

Nozdrachev, Aleksandr Danilovich, Poliakov, E. L., Kosmachevskaia, E. A., et al., eds. *I. P. Pavlov: Pervyi Nobelevskii Laureat Rossii.* 3 vols. St. Petersburg, Russia: Gumnistika, 2004.

Rütting, Torsten. *Pavlov und der Neue Mensch: Diskuse uber Disziplinierung in Sowjetrussland.* Munich, Germany: R. Oldenbourg, 2002.

Todes, Daniel. "Pavlov and the Bolsheviks." *History and Philosophy of the Life Sciences* 17, no. 3 (1995): 379–418.

——. *Pavlov's Physiology Factory: Experiment, Interpretation, Laboratory Enterprise.* Baltimore, MD: Johns Hopkins University Press, 2002.

Daniel P. Todes

PAYNE, CECILIA

SEE **Payne-Gaposchkin, Cecilia Helena**.

PAYNE-GAPOSCHKIN, CECILIA HELENA (*b.* Wendover, Buckinghamshire, United Kingdom, 10 May 1900; *d.* Cambridge, Massachusetts, 7 December 1979), *astrophysics.*

Payne was born to a family with genealogical and intellectual connections to the intelligentsia of England. A box of letters she had inherited from her family included the autographs of Charles Darwin and the geologist Charles Lyell. Her father, Edward Payne, a lawyer, musician, and scholar, died when she was four, so she was essentially raised by her mother, Emma Pertz Payne. Her educational trajectory took her in 1919 to Newnham College in the English Cambridge, where she was allowed the unusual combination of botany, physics, and chemistry. Though she was soon disillusioned by botany, her love of taxonomy found a natural niche in her ultimate pursuit of astronomy, where she eventually became a relentless classifier of variable stars, although her reputation as the most eminent woman astrophysicist of all time began with her doctoral dissertation on stellar spectra.

In Cambridge her interests turned more strongly to physics and then, inspired by a lecture on relativity by Arthur Eddington, to astronomy. In May 1922 Harlow Shapley, the newly appointed director of Harvard College Observatory, visited England and spoke at the Royal Astronomical Society. Payne, in the audience, was captivated, and after the lecture expressed to him her desire to study astronomy at Harvard. Shapley encouraged her dream and, after receiving recommendations that praised her energy, enthusiasm, and originality, arranged for a fellowship at Harvard.

Her contemporaries at Harvard would later describe her as an extraordinary figure and a stormy personality. Payne arrived in America in September 1923, for what was to become her lifelong home; she knew that in Eng-

land astronomical research opportunities for women were extremely limited (and, for example, women were not ordinarily made members of the Royal Astronomical Society). Though she found the atmosphere in the American Cambridge "intoxicating," she later described New England as a "stony-hearted stepmother," a literary allusion from Thomas De Quincey's *Confessions of an English Opium Eater* typical of her humanistic erudition (Haramundanis, p. 129). By June 1924 she had already taken a preliminary general examination for a PhD (arranged by Shapley and Theodore Lyman, chairman of the Harvard Physics Department) and the academic year 1924–1925 was spent researching and writing her doctoral thesis.

Although Shapley had originally suggested that she should take up a topic in stellar photometry, her undergraduate background in England with luminaries such as Eddington and Ernest Rutherford led her inexorably toward astrophysics, and in particular to the great collection of photographic stellar spectra in the plate stacks at Harvard Observatory. Throughout the nineteenth century, the temperatures of stars were seen as a central unsolved astrophysical problem. By the early 1920s, especially following the pioneering work of Meghnad Saha in 1920–1921, the first tables that correlated spectral type with surface temperature were published. There was much disparity between them, and when Payne began to work on this problem, it was indeed a hot problem in astrophysics.

Her solution was so ingenious and satisfactory that it essentially turned the temperature scale into a nonproblem, with the result that astronomers have tended to forget the significance of this achievement and its consequences. What she did was to use the new quantum mechanical understanding of atomic structure, that is, the energy levels and how they are populated, to examine the temperature where a given atomic level would reach its maximum population. Employing these concepts not only for hydrogen but for the other major elements with conspicuous lines in the visible region of the stellar spectra, she established that despite the varied appearance of these spectra, their differences resulted essentially from the physical conditions and not from abundance variations. This chemical homogeneity of the starry universe was the essential point of her thesis, and it is this result that Otto Struve highlighted when he called her book, *Stellar Atmospheres,* "undoubtedly the most brilliant PhD thesis ever written in astronomy" (Struve and Zebergs, 1962, p. 220). It was a stunning insight into the uniformity of nature in the chemical construction of the universe.

But there was more. Following Part II, called "Theory of Thermal Ionization," comes Part III, "Additional Deductions from Ionization Theory," and in a short chapter titled "The Relative Abundance of the Elements" there

Cecilia Helena Payne-Gaposchkin. © BETTMANN/CORBIS.

is a ticking time bomb. This finding was the extremely high abundance of hydrogen and helium that had emerged under certain assumptions in the analysis. To the astronomers of the day, such a result was as ludicrous as the heliocentric cosmology had seemed to Nicolas Copernicus's contemporaries. All the experts believed that iron had to be the most abundant element. The density of Earth could be understood only if our planet had a heavy iron core. Meteorites from outer space confirmed that iron was widely abundant. And the Sun's spectrum showed vastly more iron lines than any other element. When Eddington demonstrated that stars were gaseous throughout and that they shone because of an energy source concentrated in their hellishly hot cores, he did so assuming that the Sun was made of iron.

Unexpectedly, Payne's calculations, made with meticulous thoroughness, showed something different. They indicated that hydrogen (as well as helium, which ran a distant second) were overwhelmingly abundant compared to iron, which seemed a mere whiff in the cosmic composition. However, even Payne was persuaded (largely by Shapley's mentor, Princeton astrophysicist Henry Norris Russell), incorrectly as it turned out, that something was amiss in the physics of these two lightest elements. Nevertheless, before the decade was out, other observations convinced astronomers (led by Russell) that Earth was not,

after all, typical of the cosmos as a whole, and that iron seemed only a minor contaminant in the larger world of stars and galaxies. Payne was delighted when Eddington, in his magisterial book *The Internal Constitution of the Stars* (1926), included a sentence to say that her original deductions were "not so wild as we might suppose," but she had forfeited the opportunity to be the one who convinced astronomers that hydrogen was so abundant in the universe (p. 369).

By the time Payne had completed her doctorate she had already finished a total of six papers. Her thesis clearly played a seminal role in the development of astrophysics. In 1926 she became the youngest astronomer ever starred in *American Men of Science*, and two years later she became a member of the International Astronomical Union and was appointed to the Commission on Spectral Classification. The astrophysicist Jesse Greenstein, who first met her when he was a Harvard undergraduate in 1927, recalled that, "it was not uncommon to find her personally upset or tense, but willing to talk for hours about literature, or science.... Her intuition as to what was important in astronomy was truly deep" (Haramundanis, 1984, p. 8).

Payne subsequently researched the intrinsically brightest stars, and first described many of their peculiarities and identified numerous exotic ions in their spectra. Her second Harvard College Observatory monograph, *The Stars of High Luminosity*, appeared in 1930, followed by additional papers on these rare and unusual stars. Her studies provided the foundation for later work in which she used these brilliant beacons to probe the distant structure of our Milky Way system. Between 1923 and 1942, she was author or coauthor of seventy-eight papers dealing with the analysis of stellar spectra.

But it was a man's world and when Shapley began to assemble teachers for an astronomy graduate department at Harvard, he looked elsewhere. Thus the astrophysics appointment went to the Canadian astronomer Harry Plaskett, and when he left for Oxford, the position fell to Donald Menzel, a doctoral student of Russell's who had originally come to exploit Harvard's collection of spectra at the same time as Payne (thereby creating for Shapley an awkward duplication of competing interests). As a consequence of these appointments, Payne was shunted aside from her beloved spectra and astrophysics, and to maintain a research position, she was obliged to work on stellar photometry, which she did with more competence than enthusiasm. When in 1934 Princeton's president inquired with Henry Norris Russell about a possible staff member to groom as his replacement, Russell wrote that the best candidate in America "alas, is a woman!—not at present on our staff," an obvious reference to Payne (DeVorkin, 2000, p. 341).

In 1933 Payne toured the observatories of northern Europe, going as far as Leningrad. At the Astronomisches Gesellschaft meeting in Göttingen she met a young Russian-born astronomer, Sergei I. Gaposchkin, who was trying to escape Nazi persecution. Back in the United States, she went to Washington, D.C., to expedite a visa for this stateless man, she persuaded Shapley to offer him a position at Harvard Observatory, and in March 1934 she became Cecilia Payne-Gaposchkin. Theirs was a tempestuous but enduring relationship; the couple became the parents of a daughter and two sons, all of whom have scientific careers.

From 1928 through 1942 Payne-Gaposchkin was author or coauthor of fifty-eight papers dealing with photometry. But, she later reported in her autobiography, her efforts to establish standards photographically for red and yellow magnitudes "was labor thrown away" (Haramundanis, 1984, p. 184); photoelectric standards were coming, and the day of absolute photographic photometry was over. However, building on her researches on stellar photometry, the Gaposchkins began an ambitious systematic investigation of all known variable stars brighter than the tenth magnitude. "The time was ripe for such a survey," she later wrote. "Twenty years earlier the data would have been too sparse.… Thirty years later, they would be unmanageable" (p. 199). Her astonishing encyclopedic memory made these stars her personal friends and provided a constant source of amazement to her colleagues. The Gaposchkins' 1938 monograph *Variable Stars* quickly became the standard reference. Subsequently, during the late 1930s and 1940s, with the help over time of twenty-nine assistants, they made more than 1,250,000 measurements of variable stars on the Harvard photographic plates.

In 1939 they were invited to a select international conference in Paris on novae and white dwarf stars, indicative of their stature in the variable star field. The meeting took place on the very brink of World War II. When the United States entered the war, the Gaposchkins purchased and equipped a poultry farm in central Massachusetts, from which they sent thousands of eggs and hundreds of turkeys to the market, but their intentions to provide employment for a refugee family went unfulfilled. They also organized a Forum for International Problems, which met at the observatory and which attempted to represent each side of the issues, but which earned for Payne-Gaposchkin the reputation of being a dangerous radical.

Early in her career Payne wrote that "observations must make the way for theory," (Payne-Gaposchkin, 1925, p. 200) and from her storehouse of information she put together empirical patterns that helped define the structure of our galaxy and the paths of stellar evolution. Her boldly titled popular book of 1952, *Stars in the Mak-*

ing, came when most astronomers assumed that the age of the Sun was essentially the age of the universe, and when they were only just starting to appreciate the vast quantities of hydrogen in interstellar space. There she wrote, "We can even toy with the idea that stars are being born continuously, and the places where the young stars are found suggest very definitely that they are born in the interstellar dust" (p. 118), ideas that soon became commonplace. Her monographs *Variable Stars and Galactic Structure* (1954) and *The Galactic Novae* (1957), and her final book *Stars and Clusters* (1979), published shortly before her death, helped link more closely the connection of star births with the structure of the Milky Way. However, her patient posthumous editing of Walter Baade's 1958 Harvard lectures, *Evolution of Stars and Galaxies* (1963), may have been her most influential contribution toward the general understanding of the evolutionary significance of the population of hot, young supergiants and Cepheid variables in the spiral arms of galaxies, in contrast to the population of older stars and the RR Lyrae variables in the globular clusters and galactic nuclei.

Much as Payne-Gaposchkin might have wished to obtain her own observations, particularly high-dispersion spectra of stars, to fuel her astrophysical interests, she was in a singularly poor position to procure these. Harvard Observatory at that time did not have adequate spectrographic facilities for herself or her students. The large telescopes in the American West were entirely male dominated during those years, and at best she could beg spectra of secondary interest from her western colleagues.

But she continued to make use of the plates acquired by Harvard, particularly from the southern stations. In the 1960s the Gaposchkins undertook a systematic reanalysis of the variable stars in the Magellanic Clouds, based on the photographic plates in the Harvard collection. Sergei Gaposchkin and eighteen assistants made more than a million visual estimates of magnitudes for variable stars in the Magellanic Clouds and Payne-Gaposchkin derived the periods for 3,100 of them. Later (in 1974) she noted that the Cepheid variables with the longest periods (and therefore the youngest stars) were concentrated at the northern end of the Large Magellanic Cloud's well-known and conspicuous bar. She outlined the broad history of the relatively recent burst of star formation in this nearby galaxy, which about 100 million years ago swept from the southeast to the northwest ends of the bar, with a duration of about 20 million years.

In 1936 Payne-Gaposchkin became a member of the American Philosophical Society (America's oldest scientific academy), and shortly thereafter of the American Academy of Arts and Sciences, but academic advancement at Harvard was long denied to women. Though she lectured at the observatory and advised doctoral dissertations, her classes were not listed in the course catalog until 1945. In 1956 she became the first woman professor to have received tenure at Harvard, although she was not the first tenured woman professor at Harvard. The basis of this curious distinction is that she was tenured by the Harvard Corporation in 1938 as Phillips Astronomer, but she did not become a professor until 1956, by which time three other women had become professors in the arts and sciences. When Payne-Gaposchkin became Phillips Professor, she was simultaneously appointed department chairman, the first woman to achieve this distinction at Harvard. At a party celebrating her appointment, she described herself as "cast in the unlikely role of a thin wedge" (Haramundanis, 1984, p. 29), which brought down the house because she was, in fact, of imposing stature. In 1977 she received the highest honor of the American Astronomical Society, the Henry Norris Russell lectureship.

At the end of her life Payne-Gaposchkin wrote her autobiography, taking her title, *The Dyer's Hand,* from William Shakespeare's "Sonnet 111":

> And almost thence my nature is subdued
> To what it works in, like the dyer's hand

but never mentioning the source. Well-versed in classics both early and modern, as well as music and art, it may never have occurred to her that many readers would not recognize the context of the title or of dozens of other literary allusions that peppered her text. Long a dedicated chain smoker for whom a single match sufficed for an entire class lecture, she eventually succumbed to cancer a few months before her eightieth birthday.

BIBLIOGRAPHY

Payne-Gaposchkin never systematically retained her correspondence, so her papers in the Harvard University Archives are sparse. Some early letters are found among Harlow Shapley's Director's files there, and a few others are in the Margaret Harwood archives in the Schlesinger Library of the Radcliffe Institute in Cambridge, Massachusetts. There is an oral history interview by Owen Gingerich in the American Institute of Physics, Niels Bohr Library.

WORKS BY PAYNE-GAPOSCHKIN

Stellar Atmospheres: A Contribution to the Observational Study of High Temperature in the Reversing Layers of Stars. Harvard Observatory Monographs, no. 1. Cambridge, MA: Observatory, 1925. Her dissertation.

The Stars of High Luminosity. Harvard Observatory Monographs, no. 3. New York: McGraw-Hill, 1930.

With Sergei Gaposchkin. *Variable Stars.* Cambridge, MA: Observatory, 1938.

Stars in the Making. Cambridge, MA: Harvard University Press, 1952.

Variable Stars and Galactic Structure. London: University of London, Athlone Press, 1954.

The Galactic Novae. Amsterdam: North-Holland; New York: Interscience Publishers, 1957.

As editor. *Evolution of Stars and Galaxies,* by Walter Baade. Cambridge, MA: Harvard University Press, 1963.

Distribution and Ages of Magellanic Cepheids. Washington, DC: Smithsonian Institution Press, 1974.

Stars and Clusters. Cambridge, MA: Harvard University Press, 1979.

Cecilia Payne-Gaposchkin: An Autobiography and Other Recollections. Edited by Katherine Haramundanis. 2nd ed. Cambridge, U.K.: Cambridge University Press, 1984. Note especially "An Introduction to 'The Dyer's Hand'" by Jesse Greenstein, "An Historical Introduction to 'The Dyer's Hand'" by Peggy A. Kidwell, and "A Personal Recollection" by her daughter, Katherine Haramundanis.

OTHER SOURCES

DeVorkin, David. *Henry Norris Russell, Dean of American Astronomers.* Princeton, NJ: Princeton University Press, 2000.

Eddington, Arthur Stanley. *The Internal Constitution of the Stars.* Cambridge, U.K.: Cambridge University Press, 1926.

Gingerich, Owen. "Cecilia Payne-Gaposchkin." *Quarterly Journal of the Royal Astronomical Society* 23 (1982): 450–451.

Philip, A. G. Davis, and Rebecca A. Koopmann, eds. *The Starry Universe: The Cecilia Payne-Gaposchkin Centenary; Proceedings of a Symposium Held at the Harvard-Smithsonian Center for Astrophysics, Cambridge, Massachusetts, October 26–27, 2000.* Schenectady, NY: L. Davis Press, 2001. Note especially "'The Most Brilliant Ph.D. Thesis Ever Written in Astronomy'" by Owen Gingerich, and "Cecilia and Her World" (including an extensive photographic section) by Katherine Haramundanis.

Struve, Otto, and Velta Zebergs. *Astronomy of the 20th Century.* New York: Macmillan, 1962.

Owen Gingerich

PEARSON, KARL
(b. London, England, 27 March 1857; d. Coldharbour, Surrey, England, 27 April 1936), *applied mathematics, biometry, statistics, philosophy and social role of science, eugenics.* For the original article on Pearson see *DSB,* vol. 10.

Pearson largely founded statistics as a mathematical field, and Churchill Eisenhart's excellent entry on Pearson for the original *Dictionary of Scientific Biography* reasserts his importance as a giant of the field. Eisenhart was in a way defending Pearson against the critique of Ronald Aylmer Fisher and his followers, for whom Pearson, having made the way crooked, was not even a worthy precursor. Pearson and Fisher were embattled for almost two decades, from the late 1910s to Pearson's death in 1936 and beyond. The historical memory of statisticians was shaped in part by this controversy and in particular by a somewhat technical disagreement over the number of degrees of freedom that are appropriate for a chi-square test. Fisher convinced many that Pearson, by getting it wrong, revealed profound mathematical incapacities. With this dispute clearly in mind, Eisenhart develops at some length a more charitable view of Pearson's contribution, and Stephen Stigler (1999) has shown more recently that Pearson's formulation reflected a subtly different understanding of a tricky problem rather than a mere mathematical howler.

Indeed, an important difference of perspective lay behind the battles between these founding statisticians. While Pearson was a visionary in his claims for the historical and social significance of this new mathematical science, his methods were somewhat makeshift, while Fisher's mathematical approach was more systematic and coherent. Perhaps the most fundamental difference of approach between the two men is that Fisher was committed to an alliance of statistics and experimentation, while Pearson, who emphasized curve-fitting, did not distinguish systematically between observation and experiment. Pearson regarded Fisher's mature work as the misguided deployment of mathematical virtuosity to conjure bold conclusions from scanty data, and Fisher, who saw Pearson mainly as an obstacle to statistics rather than a new point of departure, preferred to trace his own lineage to others such as William Sealey Gosset, who had learned statistics in Pearson's biometric laboratory. Fisher's insistence on his own originality was largely accepted by the next generation of statisticians. Under other circumstances, Fisher's highly original and mathematically elegant program of statistical inference, which, like Pearson's, focused on biological measures, might have been viewed as the fulfillment of Pearson's vision rather than its rejection.

Pearson's Road to Statistics. Pearson began working in earnest on statistics in about 1892, and scholars have been greatly interested in how he got there. Pearson himself was acutely conscious of what he owed to Francis Galton's work on statistics, evolution, and eugenics (a field of study concerned with improving hereditary qualities of a race or breed), and his four-volume *Life, Letters, and Labours of Francis Galton* attests massively to this sense of obligation. But he had been somewhat skeptical of Galton's attempt to subject biology and the human sciences to quantitative reason when he reported on *Natural Inheritance* to his "Men and Women's Club" in 1889. His faith that statistics was the proper method for the study of evolution owed, in the first instance, to discussions and then collaboration with his biological colleague at University College London, Walter Frank Raphael Weldon. Eileen Magnello (1996) particularly emphasizes Weldon's responsibility for

Karl Pearson. *Portrait of Karl Pearson seated at his desk.* SPL/ PHOTO RESEARCHERS, INC.

Pearson's change of direction, and discusses at length the role of his quantitative ambitions in their shared program for the statistical study of evolution. Weldon, however, had himself found in Galton's work a convincing alternative to the morphological perspective within which he had been trained, and a key aspect of Weldon's role was indeed to persuade Pearson of Galton's fundamental importance. Weldon and Galton communicated frequently about Pearson's mathematical program, and while they were enthusiastic they also worried that his scheme of quantitative description tended to suppress the biology.

Stigler (1986) has called attention to Pearson's interactions in the early 1890s with the economist and utilitarian philosopher Francis Ysidro Edgeworth, who had been writing on statistical mathematics since 1883. In his 1892 Newmarch Lectures, which Pearson may have attended, Edgeworth included a discussion of graphical methods of statistics. This work informed Pearson's own important lectures on graphical statistics, delivered at Gresham

College from 1891 to 1894. In fact, in the years just before 1890, Pearson was already growing more and more committed to graphical geometry, which he was then teaching to engineering students at University College London. He saw graphs as a means not only to represent scientific problems but also to solve them and he spoke euphorically of the dawn of a new mathematical epoch. Whereas René Descartes (1596–1650), with his analytic geometry, had made algebra the proper foundation for geometry, now Pearson imagined that a graphical form of geometry could become the master science, providing visually satisfying solutions even to problems of algebra. This program of graphical description lived on through the 1890s and beyond in a statistical method based first of all on fitting curves to data and of comparing these curves with other data (though often algebraically rather than visually). His chi-square test of goodness of fit, introduced in 1900, was a way of assessing probabilistically the fit of data points to a frequency distribution. He used this test, for example, to determine if some newly discovered skulls could be from the same population (or race) as others that had been excavated nearby, or if the death rate of a vaccinated population diverged significantly from that of an unvaccinated one.

Pearson's statistical enthusiasm was about science and not primarily a matter of mathematics. He was thrilled to discover, through his exchanges with Weldon, that he possessed the tools to work out a new, quantitative basis for Charles Darwin's theory of evolution, which he already had come to regard as the great scientific advance of the nineteenth century. The statistical journal Pearson and Weldon began to publish in 1901 was titled, significantly, *Biometrika,* and in the first decade of the twentieth century these biometricians were virtually the only prominent scientific supporters of Darwinian evolution by natural selection. Given the proto-eugenic aspect of Pearson's essays on the "woman's question" beginning in the mid-1880s, it is plausible that Pearson's program of statistical biology had from the outset an important eugenic aspect. In alliance with Galton, whose studies of evolution had been motivated by eugenic ambitions since the time of his first paper on heredity in 1865, Pearson took up eugenics in earnest at the beginning of the new century. Within a decade, it would become an international movement of sociobiological politics. Not all of Pearson's statistical work was biometrical, and much even of the biometry was not directly linked to eugenics. Conversely, eugenic study was often distinct from Pearsonian statistics, and Pearson himself presided over an important project of nonstatistical eugenic study within the eugenics laboratory that Galton had established earlier. Still, as Donald MacKenzie argued in 1981, eugenic ambitions pervaded the new statistics. From craniometry to public health to education and intelligence testing, they were never far below the sur-

face. Pearson's somewhat alarmist public lectures on the eugenic threat of national deterioration were unfailingly expressed in the statistical idiom of differential fertility and high heritability.

The Controversialist. While Pearson was especially devoted to biometry, statistics for him was a field of applied mathematics that stood above every particular scientific discipline. The task of building up his new field involved both the development of appropriate technical tools and the training of people, and Pearson worked at both. Almost from the beginning, he set about creating a standard technical language for statistics, fixing or coining such terms as *normal law* and *standard deviation.* He worked out a formula, actually a family of formulas, for the coefficient of correlation, which Galton had estimated loosely using graphical methods, and he undertook to systematize the analysis of frequency distributions. He fit curves using a method of moments, which meant choosing the parameters of a distribution formula to match the average (first moment), the standard deviation (second moment), and so on, of the data points. Pearson's goal was to work out methods of statistics that could be applied to any field whatsoever and that would raise the standard of statistical practice throughout the sciences.

It was a Herculean task—of cleaning stables more often than killing lions—since every field had its own distinctive problems and since many did not welcome the imperious if well-meaning interventions of this acerbic outsider. In some cases, as in the emerging science of heredity, there was sharp resistance to the effort to conceive the field as fundamentally statistical. For William Bateson and other pioneers of genetics, science meant experimentation laboratories and experimental interventions, designed to reveal underlying causes acting at the level of individuals. Pearson and Weldon, by contrast, conceived the study of heredity as fundamental to Darwin's theory of evolution by natural selection, and they announced in the introduction to the first volume of *Biometrika* that evolution is a science of mass phenomena to be investigated through the study of populations rather than of individuals. Although modern scholarship has made it clear that Pearson never rejected the possible reality of Mendelian genes, and even took on occasion a positive interest in them, the Weldon-Pearson program involved a refashioning of biology that many biologists found unacceptable.

Others, however, welcomed statistics, and even viewed the biometric program with great favor. The American biologist Raymond Pearl, who was interested in population dynamics, traveled from Baltimore, Maryland, to spend a term in Pearson's laboratory. The Danish botanist Wilhelm Johannsen also came to London to meet the biometricians, though Pearson rebuffed him, and he regarded statistics as at least equal in importance to Mendelism for the study of heredity. The botanist Hugo de Vries, from the Netherlands, was a great admirer of Adolphe Quetelet and of statistics. Still, Pearson fought with all of them, including his student Pearl. Pearson's problem was not that they rejected statistics, but that they failed to practice statistics at the level of his expectations or in accordance with his dogmas. In later life, Pearson liked to think of himself as struggling heroically against a conception of science that was indifferent or hostile to statistics, but in fact statistics was springing up in science everywhere. Most of Pearson's battles were provoked not by a rejection of statistics, but by rival statistical practices, dissenters from the church biometric. Many of his opponents were far less skilled in mathematics than Pearson, but some, including Fisher, were capable or even superb mathematicians. Probably Pearson's most distinguished statistical pupils were George Udny Yule and Major Greenwood, and for a time they were very tight personally as well as scientifically, but later he fought with each of them. His dispute with Yule over measures of association culminated in a 150-page rebuttal and in Yule's expulsion for a time from the community over which Pearson, in effect, presided.

Other controversies included a sharp exchange and what seem to have been bad or nonexistent personal relations with Pearson's colleague at University College, the psychologist Charles Spearman, who used correlations among school tests to define a unitary measure of intelligence. Spearman is known to history as an important statistical psychologist, but Pearson thought his methods inadequate and was forthright about saying so. Many of Pearson's disputes involved medicine, and again this was a case of denouncing what he saw as incorrect statistical methods rather than pushing the need for statistics where it was not being used. Often in these cases his discontent reflected also a conviction that the environmental causes emphasized by physicians were less important than hereditary ones. One of the best known of these environmental claims concerned the presumed effects of parental alcoholism on the health and ability of the child. Pearson (with Ethel Elderton, a worker in his laboratory), procured and analyzed data from two institutions for children to show statistically that the apparent effects of alcohol on the offspring were all nonexistent or small. Such effects as appeared in the statistics, they proposed, might well be due to hereditary correlations with other mental characteristics of the parents. In this case, the economist John Maynard Keynes joined in to defend the temperance reformers against Pearson's eugenic doubts. Pearson crossed swords with the public health official Arthur Newsholme over the causes of infant mortality, which he preferred to attribute to hereditary weakness rather than to an unhealthy environment, and with the pathologist Almoth Wright over the effectiveness of antityphoid inoculation. In most of these cases Pearson objected that the doctors were taking superficial associations at face value rather than employing the more advanced methods that might allow a deeper understanding of the effective causes.

Statistics and the Social Role of Science. Deeper understanding, at least in the form of causal knowledge, is what Pearson the positivist is supposed to have rejected, and indeed he often argued that science can only describe rather than explain or that causation is merely the limit of correlation. But he used such rhetoric opportunistically, and his philosophy did not keep him from trying to cut through meaningless correlations or from giving explanations in terms of entities that are wholly inaccessible to the senses. The most striking of these is the "ether squirts" whose hydrodynamics, Pearson suggested in *The Grammar of Science,* might explain the phenomena of physics and chemistry. Pearson's philosophy owed less to the Austrian positivist Ernst Mach than to post-Kantian idealists such as Johann Gottlieb Fichte. The phenomenal world, he supposed, is not an external reality, but is created by the human mind. Yet if the mind can spin our visible world out of itself, it can also conceive, and in this sense create, genes and ether squirts.

Pearson typically invoked philosophical considerations to challenge the supposed limits of knowledge rather than to assert them. Science, he insisted, is a method, applicable to any topic whatsoever. It applies just as well to social life as to the motions of the planets. Although in his maturity he spoke of statistics as paradigmatic of scientific method, he did not undertake to codify that method. Instead, he presented science as a moral virtue. For Pearson, scientific method meant honest, disinterested investigation, so that opinion could be grounded in facts rather than in prejudice or self-interest. Science makes us citizens, he continued, by teaching us to accept as valid for ourselves only what is valid for everyone. It is tantamount to socialism, a naturalistic basis for knowledge that must sever any tie between religion and rationality. Science involves, in several senses, renunciation: of beliefs grounded in prejudice or selfish interest; of the quest for higher meanings; and of the possibility of direct sensuous contact with a world outside us. However, these sacrifices, which are simultaneously moral and epistemological, can provide the foundation of an efficient social life based on genuine knowledge.

As a young man, Pearson was fascinated by history, especially of the German Reformation, and of what could be gleaned from it about the historical situation of his own time. The crucial factors of history, he thought, were property and relations of sex, represented in modern times by movements of workers and of women, and he expected that the era of selfish capitalism would soon give way to a new socialism. The bigotry and ignorance of the German religious reformer Martin Luther (1483–1546), he argued, had made the rise of individualistic capitalism as painful and inefficient as it could have been, and he looked to science rather than class violence to ease the birth of modern collectivism. He took the lead in forming a "Men and Women's Club" to investigate the historical conditions and modern possibilities of relations between the sexes, and he became for a time an important intellectual authority for the women's movement. His growing concern with statistics and biological evolution were linked to his sense of large historical changes calling for new forms of science. Pearson was concerned equally with the content of the science and with the character and roles of the scientist. His ambition to recover some features of the medieval university, especially the intense personal relationship of master to student, crystallized in the form of biometric and eugenic laboratories, where textbooks were eschewed in favor of closely supervised research. He wanted to avoid reducing statistics, or science generally, to something formulaic, stressing instead that the progress of science depends on cultivated individuality. But it was no easy matter to fuse individuality with impersonal objectivity or to ground wisdom in quantitative methods, and Pearson, whose habit was always to set himself against the conventions of his time, spoke often with regret in later life over the reduction of science to a mere profession.

SUPPLEMENTARY BIBLIOGRAPHY

Aldrich, John. "The Language of the English Biometric School." *International Statistical Review* 71 (2003): 109–131.

Eyler, John. *Sir Arthur Newsholme and State Medicine, 1885–1935.* Cambridge, U.K.: Cambridge University Press, 1997.

Gayon, Jean. *Darwin et l'après-Darwin: Une histoire de l'hypothèse de sélection naturelle.* Paris: Editions Kimé, 1992.

Kevles, Daniel J. *In the Name of Eugenics: Genetics and the Uses of Human Heredity.* New York: Knopf, 1985.

Kingsland, Sharon. *Modeling Nature: Episodes in the History of Population Ecology.* Chicago: University of Chicago Press, 1985.

MacKenzie, Donald. *Statistics in Britain, 1865–1930: The Social Construction of Scientific Knowledge.* Edinburgh, U.K.: Edinburgh University Press, 1981.

Magnello, Eileen. "Karl Pearson's Gresham Lectures: W. F. R. Weldon, Speciation, and the Origins of Pearsonian Statistics." *British Journal for the History of Science* 29 (1996): 43–63.

———. "Karl Pearson's Mathematization of Inheritance: From Ancestral Heredity to Mendelian Genetics (1895–1909)." *Annals of Science* 55 (1998): 35–94.

———. "The Non-Correlation of Biometrics and Eugenics: Rival Forms of Laboratory Work in Karl Pearson's Career at University College London." *History of Science* 37, pts. 1 and 2 (1999): 79–106, 123–150.

Matthews, J. Rosser. *Quantification and the Quest for Medical Certainty.* Princeton, NJ: Princeton University Press, 1995.

Norton, Bernard J. "Metaphysics and Population Genetics: Karl Pearson and the Background to Fisher's Multi-Factorial Theory of Inheritance." *Annals of Science* 32 (1975): 537–553.

———. "Karl Pearson and Statistics: The Social Origins of Scientific Innovation." *Social Studies of Science* 8 (1978): 3–34.

Porter, Theodore M. *The Rise of Statistical Thinking, 1820–1900.* Princeton, NJ: Princeton University Press, 1986.

———. *Trust in Numbers: The Pursuit of Objectivity in Science and Public Life.* Princeton, NJ: Princeton University Press, 1995.

———. *Karl Pearson: The Scientific Life in a Statistical Age.* Princeton, NJ: Princeton University Press, 2004.

Provine, William B. *The Origins of Theoretical Population Genetics.* Chicago: University of Chicago Press, 1971.

Roll-Hansen, Nils. "The Crucial Experiment of Wilhelm Johannsen." *Biology and Philosophy* 4 (1989): 303–329.

Stamhuis, Ida. "The Reaction on Hugo de Vries's *Intracellular Pangenesis:* The Discussion with August Weismann." *Journal of the History of Biology* 36 (2003): 119–152.

Stigler, Stephen. *The History of Statistics: The Measurement of Uncertainty before 1900.* Cambridge, MA: Belknap Press of Harvard University Press, 1986.

———. *Statistics on the Table: The History of Statistical Concepts and Methods.* Cambridge, MA: Harvard University Press, 1999.

Szreter, Simon. *Fertility, Class, and Gender in Britain, 1860–1940.* Cambridge, U.K.: Cambridge University Press, 1996.

Walkowitz, Judith R. *City of Dreadful Delight: Narratives of Sexual Danger in Late-Victorian London.* Chicago: University of Chicago Press, 1992.

Theodore M. Porter

PEI WENZHONG (Pei Wen-Chung, Pei Wen-Jung) (*b.* Luanxian, Zhili, China, Lunar date 19 January 1904/Gregorian date 5 March 1904; *d.* Beijing, 18 September 1982), *paleoanthropology, vertebrate paleontology.*

Pei is considered a pioneer of Chinese paleoanthropology, archaeology, and vertebrate paleontology. He is best known for the 1929 discovery of the first complete calvarium (skull cap) of "Peking Man" (*Sinanthropus; Homo erectus*) from the famous archaeological site of Zhoukoudian, 50 kilometers southwest of central Beijing. His career spanned almost half a century, during which he excavated at archaeological localities all over China and became a recognized expert in identifying fossil animal bones. Pei understood and promoted the *science* of archaeology at least four decades before it became standard procedure to apply quantitative analytical methodologies to excavation and analysis of fossil and artifactual materials. Perhaps most extraordinary was Pei's consideration of the complex processes of site formation long before the formal terminology of *taphonomy* was a part of the archaeologists' vocabulary.

Early Life. Pei Wenzhong was born seven years before the overthrow of the Qing dynasty, in Lauxian, Zhili (now Fengnan, Hebei). He was the youngest son of Pei Tingying, a school teacher. Pei began formal schooling in a county elementary school at the age of eight; and in 1916, lacking the financial resources to attend middle school, he enrolled in the government-funded provincial teacher-training school. Several historical and biographical sources recount Pei's early participation in patriotic demonstrations in 1915 and again in 1919 during the May Fourth Movement. The latter led to a short suspension from the teachers school during this unsettled period as China struggled to establish its first republic.

Unable to secure a teaching position after completing his training in 1921, Pei went to Beijing (formerly known as Peking) and was admitted to the preparatory class for Peking University. Two years later he began his formal study in the Department of Geology. His motivation for choosing geology is unclear since he exhibited a keen interest in literature and would often audit literature classes while at the university. To support himself, Pei substituted in local schools and earned money by submitting articles to newspapers. Nonetheless, Pei's training in geology was the beginning of a lifelong focus on interpreting the biocultural evolution of humans in China and resulted in an eminent career. After his graduation in 1927, Pei struggled to make ends meet by working part-time teaching geology and biology at a high school. Desperate for a full time position, he sent a letter to Weng Wenhao, director of the Geological Survey of China. To Pei's surprise, Weng responded promptly, offering him a project-based research assignment studying trilobite fossils from Shandong Province. Coincidentally, the Geological Survey had just formed a collaboration with Peking Union Medical College to investigate the tertiary and quaternary deposits of northern China after fossil human teeth were discovered at Zhoukoudian, a small village southwest of Beijing. When Pei finished the trilobite project the following spring, he was recommended to Yang Zhongjian (C. C. Young), a young paleontologist who had earned his PhD from the University of Munich in Germany. Yang was the new representative of the Geological Survey on the Zhoukoudian exploration team. In April 1928, Pei became an assistant to Yang and began his intensive field training and the excavations that would shape the rest of his professional life.

Zhoukoudian. In the first two decades of the 1900s, western scientists including Johan Gunnar Andersson, Birger Bohlin, Otto Zdansky, and Fathers Pierre Teilhard de Chardin and Emile Licent began systematic prospecting of China's paleontological and archaeological localities. Large expeditions were undertaken to the remote Ordos Desert region of Inner Mongolia and farther west into Gansu Province. Sporadic discoveries of stone artifacts in association with Pleistocene animal fossils hinted at the great antiquity of humans in Asia. Mammalian fauna excavated from Zhoukoudian in 1921 and 1923 yielded the first indication of human fossils in the form of two isolated teeth. This was enough incentive to stimulate the newly formed Cenozoic Research Laboratory of the Geological Survey of China to apply for fieldwork funds from the Rockefeller Foundation (Jia and Huang, 1990). The respected Canadian anatomist Davidson Black was instrumental in obtaining this support. His prominence in the Anatomy Department of Peking Union Medical College developed in the years between 1919, when he first arrived in China, and 1925 when he publicly promoted the idea that Asia was the cradle of humankind. It was Black who first assigned the taxonomic designation, *Sinanthropus pekinensis,* to the precious fossil teeth that foreshadowed Pei's dramatic discovery several years later. In 1927 the Zhoukoudian project began a collaboration between foreign and Chinese scientists that would continue until the Chinese Liberation (the creation of the People's Republic of China) in 1949.

Pei's long and productive career is intimately tied to this most famous archaeological locality in northern China. Long recognized as a source of "dragon bones," the fossiliferous deposits of Zhoukoudian had been explored and exploited by the local people as a valuable resource of vertebrate fossils to be ground up and used for medicinal purposes. The productivity of the deposits became clear during the first two years of formal excavation when thousands of animal fossils were recovered from the quaternary layers at the site. As a new graduate of Peking University in 1928, the twenty-four-year-old geologist was recruited along with Yang Zhongjian to join the field team. Just one year later Pei was given the position of leading the Zhoukoudian Project when Yang and Birger Bohlin (the field advisor) were both involved with other expeditions. As often happens on field projects, harsh winter weather that threatens to bring an end to excavation instead brings unexpected luck. Pei relates the story of finding the first *Sinanthropus* (now called *Homo erectus*) skull as the sun was setting on a chilly December day in 1929. He was supervising a group of four workers in a narrow pit that was especially productive with fossil specimens when he recognized a round object in the dirt that he suspected was a human skull. In the dim candle light that illuminated the cramped excavation pit of Locality 1, he worked tirelessly to remove the fossil. The thought of leaving it in place, even one more night after perhaps 500,000 years, was too hard for him to imagine! Late into the evening he prepared the precious fossil for transport back to the Cenozoic Laboratory in Beijing. The next morning Pei dispatched a man to deliver a letter to Weng Wenhao, and, worried that the letter would arrive late in the day, he also sent a telegram to Davidson Black. On 6 December, Pei personally delivered the skullcap to Black, who began on the reconstruction and in the true spirit of collegiality, praised Pei for his skill and diligence in excavating and transporting the specimen.

Through the 1930s new fossil localities were unearthed at Zhoukoudian. Pei's versatility as an excavator and growing expertise in fossil identification and stone tool analysis made him invaluable to the project. Excavations at the newly discovered Localities 3, 5, 13, and 15 provided Pei with a wealth of material to study and interpret. He was a prolific scholar with more than twenty publications in the years between 1929 and 1939, including extensive treatises on the mammalian fauna and a study of the abundant stone artifacts from Locality 15. Pei recognized that chronological context was of primary importance in the analysis and interpretation of the human fossil record and he published an important comparison in 1931 of the Zhoukoudian fauna with two other well-known faunal collections; the Yanjinggou fauna of Sichuan and the animal fossils from the Nihewan Beds in Hebei. He concluded that the antiquity of the deposits was perhaps as great as the early part of the Ice Age (Lower Pleistocene). Recent geochemical dating techniques have reassessed these deposits as later in time, Middle Pleistocene (500,000–300,000 years ago), but Pei's comparative faunal studies were a landmark in the initial attempts to understand the early human occupation of China.

This early phase of investigations at Zhoukoudian came to a close in July 1937 shortly before the outbreak of the Sino-Japanese War. The fossil inventory from these excavations was astounding. Several fine skull specimens, numerous cranial fragments, hundreds of human teeth and jaw fragments, thousands of animal fossils, and a diverse collection of stone tools were among the specimens curated by the Cenozoic Laboratory in Beijing when Pei followed Yang Zhongjian as laboratory director. Ironically, these first Peking Man fossils became notorious for the mysterious circumstances surrounding their disappearance in 1941 at the start of World War II. Pei's commitment to their careful study and timely analysis make his publications all the more valuable given the subsequent loss of the original materials. His familiarity with the animal fossils, especially his study of the carnivores

represented in the Locality 1 deposits, initiated a research emphasis that continues as a primary focus in paleoanthropology under the rubric of *taphonomy*: that is, investigating what agents collect and modify bone and archaeological assemblages.

In the prewar years, the renowned German osteologist, Franz Weidenreich (1873–1948), was selected by the China Medical Board of the Rockefeller Foundation to resume the work that had abruptly ended with Black's untimely death in 1934. Fortunately, Weidenreich had the foresight to fashion a superb set of fossil casts from the original Peking Man specimens. As war seemed imminent, Pei actively petitioned the U.S. Embassy to ensure the safety of the fossil collection. He was subject to several episodes of intense interrogation by the Japanese as they tried in vain to determine the location of the cache of specimens.

French Years and Sino-Japanese War. It is not difficult to imagine the initial shock generated by the news that a complete *Sinanthropus* skull was unearthed by the relatively inexperienced geologist Pei Wenzhong. As Jia Lanpo and Huang Weiwen state in *The Story of Peking Man: From Archaeology to Mystery*, "The skeptics either doubted Pei's ability to correctly identify the specimen or simply refused to believe in such good luck" (1990, p. 65). When Pei was hired a year and a half before the discovery, his main jobs were bookkeeping, dealing with workers, and miscellaneous organizational tasks. Birger Bohlin, the field advisor, appreciated this young assistant and Pei soon took a more active role in the excavation. Pei must have also impressed Abbé Henri Breuil, the famous French archaeologist who visited Zhoukoudian twice in 1931 and was one of the first foreign scholars to publish extensive treatises on Chinese Paleolithic materials. Breuil encouraged Pei to continue his studies in France where comparative collections of the French Paleolithic would provide an excellent basis for understanding and interpreting the Chinese fossil record. In July 1935, Pei set off from Shanghai for Paris, and for the next two years Breuil devised an intensive study plan for Pei. In the first few months, his days began with a four-hour French lesson followed by another four hours of research at the Institute de Paléontologie Humaine (Institute of human paleontology). Pei remarked that the months from October 1935 to June 1936 were the most diligent academic experiences of his life. In June 1937, Pei completed a dissertation on the challenges of distinguishing humanly produced stone artifacts in archaeological context and received a doctoral degree as the culmination of his studies in France.

Hostilities between Japan and China had been intensifying since 1931 and Pei's trip home from Europe was detoured by the 7 July Lugouqiao incident that marked full-scale resistance to the Japanese. By the time Pei arrived in Nanjing in October, China was at war. Weng Wenhao welcomed Pei in Nanjing and urged him to return to Beijing (called Beiping at the time). The capital city was already under Japanese control and Pei planned to gather his family and then move to Changsha with the Geological Survey of China. While Pei was in France, a bright young archaeologist, Jia Lanpo, had joined the Zhoukoudian team as excavation leader. When Pei got to Beijing in November, however, a letter from Weng instructed him to stay and oversee the Geological Survey and the Cenozoic Laboratory. Thus Pei never left Beijing throughout the Sino-Japanese War and served as director of the Cenozoic Laboratory from November 1937 until December 1941. Shortly after the attack on Pearl Harbor, the laboratory was closed. Through the war years, Pei taught at Yanjing University, Beijing Normal University, and Zhongfa University.

People's Republic of China and Cultural Revolution. When the war was over in 1945, the Beijing office of the Geological Survey was again under Chinese governmental supervision and the Cenozoic Research Laboratory reopened. The next few years, however, saw little activity at the Zhoukoudian site since funding from the Rockefeller Foundation was no longer available. Pei continued to lecture at several universities, including Peking University, and in subsequent years devoted much of his research attention to newly discovered Neolithic localities in the Gansu region. Some biographical commentaries suggest that Pei was disheartened by the lack of academic and financial support from the Nationalist government for archaeological research during the postwar years. This may have prompted his allegiance to the Communist Party in the hope that they would be receptive to an archaeology that "made the past serve the present"—a popular slogan reflecting communist ideology toward societal structure. In any case, Pei chose to stay in Beijing as the Communist Party took over China in 1949.

If Zhoukoudian was a factor for Pei's remaining in Beijing, he must have been reassured when the new government approved the resumption of excavation work at the site, under the direction of Jia Lanpo and Liu Xianting. Although Pei continued to serve as director of the Cenozoic Laboratory, he was officially working for the Ministry of Culture from December 1949 to December 1953. Much of his work involved the curation and exhibition of antiquities and administrative duties associated with museum operation. It was not until 1953, when the Vertebrate Paleontology Research Laboratory of the Chinese Academy of Sciences was established, that Pei was permitted to go back to his devout dedication to archaeological research. The Vertebrate Paleontology Research Laboratory was an informal successor to the Cenozoic

Laboratory and the predecessor of the Institute of Vertebrate Paleontology and Paleoanthropology (IVPP). Pei began to oversee the IVPP Research Laboratory when it was established in 1956, and was appointed director in 1963 and served that institute until his death in 1982.

Other than the unfortunate pause during the Cultural Revolution, Pei's professional life after 1949 was active and productive. He held a number of scientific posts in the People's Republic of China and participated in numerous archaeological surveys and excavations, working literally until the end of his life. Pei surveyed Paleolithic sites in Nihewan, Hebei Province, and Datong, Shanxi Province, in 1950. In 1951, he led the excavation effort in Ziyang, Sichuan Province, where an Upper Paleolithic *Homo sapiens* skull was found by railroad workers. After 1949, the emphasis on Paleolithic and Neolithic archaeology reflected the political dogma to serve the workers, farmers, and soldiers. For example, Marxist theorists held that the archaeological evidence could be interpreted to support the communal social structure of early agricultural villages in Neolithic China. The research focus was directed toward supporting the in situ antiquity of humans in China and the inevitable struggle for existence through labor (cf. Engel's theory that "labor created man"; Tong 1995). From 1952 to 1955, Pei was charged with training new archaeologists, a joint effort of the Ministry of Culture, the Institute of Archaeology, and Peking University. This marked the establishment of archaeology as a formal field of study at the prestigious university. In 1954 Pei directed the Dingcun excavations at Xiangfen county, Shanxi, where stone tools and several *Homo sapiens* teeth of late Middle Pleistocene age were found. One of Pei's most prolific years was 1957, when he published seventeen articles in Chinese, English, and French. Archaeological surveys from 1959 to 1965 took Pei to Hebei, Guangxi, Yunnan, Shanxi, and Hetao.

Like most of his contemporaries and many other intellectuals, Pei bore his share of painful experiences during the Cultural Revolution. As a teacher and scholar, Pei was labeled a "reactionary academic authority," sent to the "cowshed" (*niupeng*), investigated, and criticized. He was confined in isolation from May 1968 to January 1969, and according to recollections of his friends and students, he suffered physical punishments when a verse in his private journal was interpreted as expressing contempt toward the propaganda campaign of the government. Pei was seen sweeping the courtyard and street near the crowded house his family shared with several others. Then in 1974, as the Cultural Revolution was nearing an end, he was formally photographed by the *Chinese Pictorial* (*Renmin Huabao*) presumably to demonstrate to the outside world that the famous paleoanthropologist was alive and well.

Teacher-Scholar. When Pei first arrived at Zhoukoudian, he had very little experience in excavation techniques or in identifying fossils and assigning taxonomic designation. The practical knowledge of a valued field-worker made Pei realize the importance of hands-on experience and motivated him to develop expertise in field methodologies. Pei was credited for introducing high standards at Zhoukoudian. In particular he revised and refined the excavation techniques to include systematic trenching that added a level of precision and stratigraphic control (Jia and Huang, 1990). Pei's students recalled their teacher's "four wheels" and "four means of diligence" philosophy. To become well-rounded archaeologists, Pei advised his students to run on "four wheels," that is to master the subject areas of geology, paleontology, paleoanthropology, and Paleolithic archaeology. He taught that diligent study made use of the brain, the hands, the eyes, and the mouth, and so he urged his students to think more, work more, observe more, and inquire more.

In the 1940s Pei became embroiled in an interesting controversy. The renowned anatomist Franz Weidenreich, who had intensively studied the fossil humans from Zhoukoudian, argued that the scarcity of postcranial remains and the characteristic breakage pattern of the calvaria could be interpreted as support for the idea that Peking Man practiced cannibalism. Pei disagreed and instead suggested that Peking Man was the prey of other carnivorous animals that shared the Pleistocene landscape. More than sixty years later, scholars still argue about the relative roles of carnivores and humans in the formation of archaeological deposits. It remains an integral part of paleoanthropological work in every region of the world.

In 1956 Pei, along with Jia Lanpo, led an expedition to southern China in search of the fossil remains of *Gigantopithecus,* a species of giant ape. Isolated fossils of this rare primate had been surfacing in provincial museums near the spectacular karst tower mountains of Guangxi. Pei enlisted the help of a local peasant to investigate the cave site of Liucheng, near Liuzhou City. The precipitous karst towers riddled with fossil-rich caverns were irresistible to Pei and his team of excavators, even though it was an extreme physical feat to climb up and into these caves. Their perseverance paid off and over a seven-year period, the team recovered the largest collection of *Gigantopithecus* fossils to date: three mandibles, more than a thousand fossil teeth, and an associated collection of mammalian fauna documenting a unique environmental context. Qing recalls that Pei was generous with both his knowledge and in rewarding his hardworking field crew. He held a number of public lectures in Liucheng and offered remuneration to his workers (Ciochon, Olsen, and James, 1990).

Pei earned a reputation as a meticulous and innovative scholar. His colleagues recall the extraordinary care he took with the recovery of a rare rhinoceros fossil specimen. Pei's reconstruction was so exceptional that the complete skeleton was placed on display in the exhibition hall of the China Geological Survey. He recognized the complexities in distinguishing humanly produced stone artifacts and bone flakes at early Paleolithic sites and this led to the formulation of his PhD dissertation research. His work marked one of the first exercises in experimental archaeology (Lu, 2002) and stimulated an interest in understanding the technological aspects of the toolmaking process. This focus on tool technology and manufacture influenced the interpretation of discoveries at important sites such as Dingcun, the Nihewan Basin localities, and the southern Chinese cave site of Guanyindong. The large, heavy-duty Dingcun stone tools suggested that the Chinese Paleolithic was technologically diverse and the idea of regional differences among Paleolithic assemblages became a focus of archaeological studies after the discovery of thousands of Lower Paleolithic artifacts at Guanyindong (Wu and Olsen, 1985).

Private Life and Later Years. When the Cultural Revolution was finally over in 1976, Pei was seventy-two years old and in declining health. He was hospitalized in 1975, suffered from lower-limb thrombosis in 1980, then had a stroke the following year. Though ailing since the end of the Cultural Revolution, Pei continued to take part in archaeological surveys and was invited to give a presentation in Japan two years before his death. As a young scholar, the now-eminent archaeologist Zhang Senshui worked as Pei's assistant through his final years. With Zhang's assistance, Pei completed his last book *Zhongguo yuan ren shi qi yan jiu* (A study on the lithic artifacts of *Sinanthropus*), although he did not live to see it published. A second posthumous publication, *Liucheng Juyuan dong ji Guangxi qi ta shan dong zhi shi rou lei, chang bi lei he nie chi lei hua shi* (A study of Carnivora, Proboscidea, and Rodentia fossils from Liucheng *Gigantopithecus* cave and other caves in Guangxi), documented the fossil mammals from the *Gigantopithecus* cave, establishing a date for those materials at about one million years.

Pei earned his fame early in his career with an extraordinary fortuitous discovery but retained a sense of humility through his long career. He is remembered as a teacher who cared about students both personally and professionally. During the Cultural Revolution years he walked miles to visit a sick student even though he himself was suffering from abusive treatment at the hands of the Red Guard. He took time to tutor students in the English language, for he believed that mastering foreign languages was essential to quality scholarship. He maintained that his accomplishments in archaeology were simply part of his professional duties, and he was a devoted scholar who worked until the end of his life.

Pei was married to Shu Lingyi in 1932. Pei was a friend of Shu's uncle and a generation older when they met in 1928. According to the traditional Chinese view, this was not an ideal match but their courtship took place despite the disapproval of Shu's family. Pei and Shu proved themselves to be a loving couple who supported and took care of each other during good and bad times. Shu taught high school before the Cultural Revolution and she outlived Pei by a few years. They had three sons, Pei Duan, Pei Run, and Pei Shen, and two daughters, Pei Gui and Pei Li. Pei Duan remembers that his father spent most of the family savings on books and educational expenses for the children. He expected them to study hard and urged them to be extremely inquisitive in the pursuit of knowledge. Pei Wenzhong died on 18 September 1982 and is buried alongside Yang Zhongjian and Jia Lanpo at Zhoukoudian.

BIBLIOGRAPHY

A detailed bibliography of Pei's works is included in Bu xiu de ren ge yu ye ji: ji nian Pei Wenzhong xian sheng dan chen 100 zhou nian *[Commemorate the 100th birthday of Pei Wenzhong]. Beijing: Ke xue chu ban she, 2004.*

WORKS BY PEI

"An Account of the Discovery of an Adult *Sinanthropus* Skull in the Choukoutien Deposit." *Bulletin of the Geological Society of China* 8, no. 3 (1929): 203–205.

"The Age of Choukoutien Fossiliferous Deposit: A Tentative Determination by Comparison with Other Later Cenozoic (Phychozoic) Deposits in China." *Bulletin of the Geological Society of China* 10 (1931): 165–178.

"Mammalian Remains from Locality 5 at Choukoutien." *Palaeontologia sinica*, series C, 7, no. 2 (1931): 1–18.

"Notice of the Discovery of Quartz and Other Stone Artifacts in the Lower Pleistocene Hominid-Bearing Sediments of the Choukoutien Cave Deposit." *Bulletin of the Geological Society of China* 11, no. 2 (1931): 109–146.

With Pierre Teilhard de Chardin. "The Lithic Industry of the *Sinanthropus* Deposits in Choukoutien." *Bulletin of the Geological Society of China* 11, no. 4 (1932): 317–358.

With Davidson Black, Pierre Teilhard de Chardin, and C. C. Young. "Fossil Man in China." *Geological Memoirs, Geological Survey of China*, series A, 11 (1933): 1–174.

"On the Carnivora from Locality 1 of Choukoutien." *Palaeontologia sinica*, series C, 8, no. 1 (1934): 1–216.

"Report on the Excavation of the Locality 13 in Choukoutien." *Bulletin of the Geological Society of China* 13, no. 3 (1934): 359–367.

"On the Mammalian Remains from Locality 3 at Choukoutien." *Palaeontologia sinica*, series C, 7, no. 5 (1936): 1–120.

"Le role des animaux et des causes naturelles dans la cassure des os." *Palaeontologia sinica*, new series D, 7 (1938): 1–60.

"New Fossil Material and Artifacts Collection from the Choukoutien Region during the Years 1937–1939." *Bulletin of the Geological Society of China* 19, no. 3 (1939): 207–234.

"A Preliminary Study on a New Palaeolithic Station Known as Locality 15 within the Choukoutien Region." *Bulletin of the Geological Society of China* 19, no. 2 (1939): 147–187.

With Pierre Teilhard de Chardin. "The Fossil Mammals of Locality 13 in Choukoutien." *Palaeontologia sinica*, n.s., C, 11 (1941): 1–118.

"Archaeological Research in Kansu." *Peking Natural History Bulletin* 16, nos. 3–4 (1947–1948): 231–238.

"New Light on Peking Man." *China Reconstructs* 3, no. 4 (1954): 133–136.

"Discovery of *Gigantopithecus* Mandibles and Other Material in Liu-Cheng District of Central Kwangsi in South China." *Vertebrate Palasiatica* 1, no. 2 (1957): 65–72.

"Discovery of Lower Jaws on Giant Ape in Kwangsi, South China." *Science Record*, n.s., 1, no. 3 (1957): 49–52.

"Giant Ape's Jaw Bone Discovered in China." *American Anthropologist*, n.s., 59, no. 5 (1957): 834–838.

"On the Problem of the 'Bone Implements' of the Choukoutien *Sinanthropus* Site." *Acta archaeologia sinica* 2 (1960): 1–9. Pages 1–7 in Chinese and 8–9 in English.

"Reflections on the 'Pseudo-Tool' Question—Discussions on a Few Problems in *Sinanthropus* Culture." *Xinjianshe* 8 (1961): 12–23.

"Quaternary Mammals from the Liucheng *Gigantopithecus* Cave and Other Caves of Kuangsi." *Scientia sinica* 12 (1963): 221–229.

With Zhang Senshui. *Zhongguo yuan ren shi qi yan jiu* [A study on the lithic artifacts of *Sinanthropus*]. Beijing: Ke xue chu ban she, 1985.

Liucheng Juyuan dong ji Guangxi qi ta shan dong zhi shi rou lei, chang bi lei he nie chi lei hua shi [A study of Carnivora, Proboscidea and Rodentia fossils from Liucheng *Gigantopithecus* cave and other caves in Guangxi]. Beijing: Ke xue chu ban she, 1987.

Pei Wenzhong ke xue lun wen ji [Selected works of Pei Wenzhong]. Beijing: Ke xue chu ban she, 1990.

OTHER SOURCES

Chang, K. C. "Obituary: W. C. Pei (1904–1982)." *American Anthropologist*, n.s., 86, no. 1 (1984): 115–118.

Ciochon, Russell, John Olsen, and Jamie James. *Other Origins: The Search for the Giant Ape in Human Prehistory.* New York: Bantam Books, 1990.

Gao Xing and Pei Shen, eds. *Bu xiu de ren ge yu ye ji: ji nian Pei Wenzhong xian sheng dan chen 100 zhou nian* [Commemorate the 100th birthday of Pei Wenzhong]. Beijing: Ke xue chu ban she, 2004.

Jia Lanpo and Huang Weiwen. *The Story of Peking Man: From Archaeology to Mystery.* Translated by Yin Zhiqi. Beijing: Foreign Languages Press, 1990.

Liu Houyi and Liu Qiusheng. *Fa xian Zhongguo yuan ren de ren: Pei Wenzhong* [The man who discovered Peking Man]. Kunming: Yunnan ren min chu ban she, 1980.

Lu, Tracey Lie-dan. "The Transformation of Academic Culture in Mainland Chinese Archaeology." *Asian Anthropology* 1 (2002): 117–152.

Olsen, John W. "Pei Wenzhong 1904–1982." In *Encyclopedia of Archaeology: The Great Archaeologists*, edited by Tim Murray. Santa Barbara, CA: ABC-CLIO, 1999.

Tong Enzheng. "Thirty Years of Chinese Archaeology (1949–1979)." In *Nationalism, Politics, and the Practice of Archaeology,* edited by Philip L. Kohl and Clare Fawcett. Cambridge, U.K.: Cambridge University Press, 1995.

Wu, Rukang, and John W. Olsen. *Palaeoanthropology and Palaeolithic Archaeology in the People's Republic of China.* Orlando, FL: Academic Press, 1985.

Annie Y. Hor
Sari Miller-Antonio

PEIERLS, RUDOLF ERNST

(*b.* Ober-schöneweide, Berlin, Germany, 5 June 1907; *d.* Oxford, United Kingdom, 19 September 1995), *solid-state physics, nuclear physics, nuclear fission, nuclear weapons, education, nuclear weapon control.*

Peierls is known for his profound contributions to the theory of condensed matter, nuclear structure, and elementary particles, including his pioneering work on the quantum-mechanical theory of solids and the electronic band theory. His demonstration with Otto Frisch of the feasibility of an atomic fission weapon gave rise to the British and American efforts to build the first atomic bombs at Los Alamos, New Mexico, where Peierls led the implosion theory program.

Early Years. Peierls was the third child in his immediate family. His father, Heinrich, an electrical engineer from Breslau, had become the managing director of Allgemeine Elektrizitäts-Gesellschaft (AEG) by the time Peierls was born; his mother, Elisabeth, died when he was fourteen. In 1925 after schooling in the local *Gymnasium* (Humboldtschule) Peierls passed the *Abiturium*, the high-school graduation examination, and that same year he began his university studies. Some experience in AEG underlined his interests in mathematics rather than engineering, so from 1925, when he began his studies in the Humboldt University, Berlin, he concentrated on theoretical physics.

Peierls joined a higher education system that valued academic freedom and to which anyone who had passed the *Abiturium* had access. Lectures were not compulsory and there were neither a set of courses that a physics student had to follow nor examinations to pass unless teaching was considered. Often the first examination would be that for a doctorate. An aspiring physicist would expect to choose courses where noted professors worked; it was normal for students to go to various universities during their

Sir Rudolf Ernst Peierls. *Peierls, September 1962.* HULTON ARCHIVE/GETTY IMAGES.

studies. There was no real separation between graduates and undergraduates; after eight or twelve semesters a student could finish with a vocational diploma or with a "Staatsexamen" for work in the state service. Promising students could begin their doctorate work after six or seven semesters. This is the course that Peierls took. Courses given by Walther Nernst and Max Planck introduced him to the quantum theory, which interested him very much. After two semesters at Berlin, Peierls moved to Munich, where he remained from 1926 to 1928.

Atomic physics had only recently been transformed by Werner Heisenberg's invention in 1925 of the matrix formulation of quantum mechanics, and in the following year by Erwin Schrödinger's introduction of his wave formulation of quantum mechanics. Arnold Sommerfeld, during the 1910s and early 1920s, extended Niels Bohr's theory of the hydrogen atom so it could deal with complex atoms, but enthusiastically adopted wave mechanics into lectures and research. Sommerfeld introduced quantum mechanics to Peierls, who quickly mastered the formalism. While in Munich Peierls met Hans Bethe, who became a lifelong friend and colleague.

In 1927 Peierls moved to Leipzig, where Heisenberg had founded a school of theoretical physics with which

Peierls wished to associate himself. Heisenberg suggested that Peierls should examine the electrical conductivity in metals and should develop further the pathbreaking quantum-mechanical electron theory of metals that Heisenberg's student Felix Bloch had recently developed. Bloch had approximated a lattice as a three-dimensional periodic potential, ignored the forces between electrons, and effectively had applied the existing theories of hydrogen molecule and formed the basis of the quantum-mechanical theory of solids. From this framework Peierls wrote several influential papers in 1929 and 1930 out of which the modern theory of electronic bands would emerge. Peierls realized that Bloch's work was flawed by his assumption of the independence of the electrons, and began to seek a theory that would extend the theory to the many-electrons. The application of Bloch's insights to the anomalous Hall effect suggested that there existed "holes" in nearly filled bands in some solids; and Marcel-Louis Brillouin extended Peierls's idea to real solids in 1930. Now all the important parts of band theory were available: Bloch's tight binding, Peierls's weak binding, general and exact examples, and a fuzzy concept of holes still to be described clearly. In 1931 Alan Wilson drew on the work of Peierls and others to develop a simpler formulation of the band theory, widely used by experimentalists, that offered the first clear explanation of the difference between metals and insulators and for the behavior and nature of semiconductors.

While Heisenberg was away from Leipzig in the spring of 1929, Peierls worked as a research student and later as the *Assistent* of Wolfgang Pauli, who was the professor of theoretical physics at the Eidgenössische Technische Hochschule in Zürich. During this time Peierls developed a fundamental theory of thermal conductivity in crystals, in which he pointed out how the Umklapp-processes keep the lattice vibrations of solids in equilibrium and limit the electrical and thermal conductivity at low temperatures. For this work he received a PhD from Leipzig in 1929. In 1932, as Peierls's student days came to an end, he published a major review article that helped to establish the new quantum-mechanical electron theory of metals. In 1932 he gained his *Habilitation* from the Eidgenössische Technische Hochschule with a paper titled "Zur Theorie der Absorptionsspektren fester Körper."

During his student years, he traveled to many of the leading universities in Europe, interacting with leaders in the physics community, and finding friends and colleagues with whom he would work and correspond throughout his life. An All-Union Physical Congress held in Odessa in August 1930 was particularly memorable. Not only did he meet Yacov Frenkel and Igor Tamm, but he was introduced to Eugenia Kannegiser, a physics graduate from the University of Leningrad (now Saint Petersburg State University) and a contemporary of Peierls's

friend Lev Landau. The wedding in the spring of 1931 of Eugenia and Rudolf Peierls began their long, close, and very happy marriage. Wherever they lived their household would be open to colleagues and friends. Four children were born to them; Gaby Ellen, Ronald Frank, Catherine (Kitty), and Joanna.

Academic Appointments, 1932–1937. The award of a Rockefeller traveling scholarship in 1932 made it possible for Rudolf and Eugenia Peierls to spend the winter and spring of 1932 in Rome and the summer of 1933 in Cambridge, U.K.: in his own account of his time in Italy and England there are no clear reasons given for his decision to go to these centers of physics research. The impression is given that he wanted to interact with leading workers, not to work with particular men and women. In Rome, despite Enrico Fermi's interest in nuclear physics, Peierls continued his theoretical work on solids. While in Munich Peierls and others had shown that the complex nature of solids could be understood; hence, while in Rome Peierls developed a quantum-mechanical description of diamagnetism. In Cambridge Peierls met Nevill Mott, who was to contribute notably to solid-state physics. Peierls remained in close touch with Mott for the rest of his life. In the late 1930s, for example, the two corresponded extensively about the theory of rectification that Mott developed with Harry Jones in Bristol.

Toward the end of his Rockefeller Fellowship Peierls had been offered an appointment in Hamburg. However, the political situation in Germany was becoming difficult for Jewish scientists. Although Peierls had been christened as a Lutheran, he was Jewish in background, and with political discrimination beginning he considered that returning to work in Germany would be an error. So during 1933 Peierls sought employment in Britain. Fortunately Manchester University appointed Peierls as an honorary research fellow from 1933 to 1935, using a fund administered by a Senate-Council's Joint Committee on Assistance to Foreign Scholars, which liaised with the Academic Assistance Council in London. Peierls was granted a third year but resigned during 1935 in order to take up a post with the Mond Laboratory in Cambridge. While in Manchester Peierls collaborated with Bethe and they published several papers in nuclear physics: two on neutrinos, deuterium (they used the name "diplon") and on the scattering of neutrons by protons. Just before leaving Manchester, Peierls was awarded a honorary DSc.

Between 1935 and the end of 1937 Peierls continued his theoretical work in solid-state physics in Cambridge, as much of the work in the Mond Laboratory was concerned with the physics of solids. Peierls continued on order-disorder problems that fitted in with the interests in the laboratory. In Cambridge he forged links with

Maurice Goldhaber, Leo Szilard, and Marcus Oliphant, and continued with his studies of solids. In this he enlarged his superlattice theory of metals, which had stemmed from the researches of William L. Bragg and which had been begun by Evan J. Williams of Manchester, and which Peierls and Bethe had developed further.

Birmingham: 1937–1940. By the spring of 1937 Peierls had published some forty papers, had studied and worked in many of the most significant universities in Europe and had met with and had made friends of many men and women who were or who were about to become leading physicists. In 1936 Marcus Oliphant was appointed to the chair of physics at the University of Birmingham, and shortly afterward asked Peierls if he would be interested in a professorship at that university. As Peierls was interested in the offer from Birmingham, the university founded a chair in applied mathematics and appointed Peierls to it. The post was in the Mathematics Department, for in England theoretical physics was then typically judged as part of mathematics. He was professor of applied mathematics in Birmingham University until 1963.

In Birmingham he found himself the lone theoretician, and, furthermore, there were only a few research students in mathematics, and none in theoretical physics. However, two students, P. L. Kapur and Fred Hoyle, who had started their research in Cambridge, continued to work with him in Birmingham. Kapur coauthored two papers in 1937–1938, before he returned home to India. One of the papers, "The Dispersion Formula for Nuclear Reactions," became well known, but in a few years was displaced by a method proposed by Eugene Wigner and Leonard Eisenbud. Peierls's teaching load was not onerous, although he was required to teach a course in hydrodynamics for which some study was necessary.

During his first three years as a professor in Birmingham, Peierls turned increasingly toward the rapidly developing fields of nuclear and elementary particle physics; the majority of his academic papers concerned discoveries made in these fields. He worked on problems on B-particles (1937, 1939), mesons (1939), neutrons (1939), and nuclear forces (1940).

The Second World War: 1940–1945. Peierls had completed two years as a professor in Birmingham when World War II directed many scientists to war work, bringing rapid change to academic work in science. As a German, Peierls was initially considered an enemy alien and thus could not be brought into sensitive war work. He was joined in Birmingham by the Austrian experimental physicist Otto Robert Frisch, also Jewish. Frisch had been trapped in England at the outbreak of the war in late 1939. Roughly a year earlier, during the Christmas holi-

days of December 1938, Frisch visited his aunt Lise Meitner, also a physicist, who had fled to Stockholm after the German annexation of Austria in March 1938. Together Frisch and Meitner conceived of the notion of nuclear fission, announcing it publicly in early 1939.

In Birmingham, Frisch worked with Peierls to sort out theoretically the question of separating out the ^{235}U fissionable isotope from ^{238}U, the more abundant isotope in natural uranium, and making enriched uranium for an atomic bomb. He was also barred from sensitive employment in England because of his enemy alien status. At this point Frisch was living in Birmingham with Rudolf and Eugenia Peierls, in their small flat. Frisch and Rudolf Peierls, perhaps unaware that British scientists had dismissed an atomic bomb, prepared the first thorough analysis of the possibility of building a fission bomb in a March 1940 memorandum. In it they not only suggested that such a bomb was feasible, but also calculated the critical mass of uranium needed for a chain reaction, and found that it might be possible to separate in just a few weeks the few kilograms they computed would be needed to make a bomb. They also suggested a means to control the process and outlined a means of separating the ^{235}U isotope to form enriched uranium. And they warned of the radiation dangers after the use of such a bomb.

At a point when winning the war against the Nazis did not look hopeful to these refugees, the 1940 memorandum that Frisch and Peierls wrote on this problem was forwarded, via Peierls's friend and colleague Marc Oliphant, to James Chadwick and then George P. Thomson, then in charge of uranium research and thus in a position to take action. As the Peierls and Frisch memorandum led directly to the establishment of the projects in Britain and later America to build the atomic bomb, it can be argued that it is one of the most significant scientific papers of the twentieth century. The memorandum led to the organization of the committee, code-named MAUD.

Frisch and Peierls, as enemy aliens, were initially not allowed to take part in the committee's meetings, but after Peierls pointed out the pointlessness of this exclusion, they were allowed to join part of the discussions. On 26 March 1940 the undersecretary of state at the Home Office signed Peierls's certificate of naturalization as a British citizen, and his naturalization was registered on 12 April 1940. Now the government was prepared to use the expertise of men and women from enemy nations. In this way Frisch and Peierls were conscripted into the project to explore the possibility of developing an atomic bomb, but they were never included in the main MAUD committee.

Thirty-one of the thirty-four papers that Peierls wrote in 1940 were related to the atomic bomb. A few of his papers were coauthored by his assistant, Klaus Fuchs, who would later became notorious when it was learned that as a member of the theoretical division at Los Alamos, he passed classified secrets to the Soviet Union about the design of the implosion bomb.

During 1940 and most of 1941 Peierls worked on behalf of the Tube Alloys project, the front for the British development of the atomic bomb. Technical matters were the purview of a committee of which Peierls was a member. The preferred method of enriching uranium with ^{235}U was gaseous diffusion using uranium hexafluoride. It was, however, clear that Britain would not be able to build or run a gas diffusion plant. For this and other reasons, it was important for Britain to join with the United States to develop and produce an atomic bomb. In December 1941 the MAUD committee was disbanded, giving some aggravation to some of its members as Tube Alloys was constructed without them being consulted. According to Margaret Gowing in *Britain and Atomic Energy* (1964, p. 111), the slights were eased and "leisurely research" continued.

Peierls and other British-based physicists had been in contact with American workers throughout 1941. Some Americans had visited Britain. But coordinated work on building the atomic bomb was not yet being pursued. After the Japanese attack on Pearl Harbor on 7 December 1941 brought the United States into the war, cooperation was more actively pursued. The Americans could draw on their industrial strength in this development. But, as Gowing has discussed, there were political difficulties, particularly concerning problems about secrecy. Cooperation between Britain and the United States on the atomic bomb effort was impossible to carry out across the Atlantic Ocean. Eventually in August 1943, British Prime Minister Winston Churchill and American President Franklin D. Roosevelt made an agreement in Quebec to allow a number of senior British scientist to join the Manhattan Project; they would work in Los Alamos as the "British Mission," a group that included Peierls, Frisch, and in time nineteen others, including Chadwick and Niels Bohr.

Peierls initially spent some time in New York studying problems related to the diffusion separation method, but he soon moved to Los Alamos, where he took on the important responsibility of leading the Implosion Theory Group, replacing in this role Edward Teller, who had antagonized J. Robert Oppenheimer, the director of the Los Alamos laboratory, as well as Bethe, the head of the Theory Division, by focusing on the problem of the hydrogen bomb rather than the higher priority problem of building an implosion bomb. Among the top-priority problems Peierls coordinated at Los Alamos during the war was finding a realistic description of neutron diffraction through the core of the implosion weapon and developing a theory for the explosive lenses used in assembling

the implosion bomb. Peierls was among the many Los Alamos scientists who watched the Trinity test of the first implosion bomb on 16 July 1945 in the Alamogordo desert of New Mexico.

Birmingham: 1945–1963. When Peierls returned to England in the summer of 1945, he had a problem, for he had been offered several professorships in Britain including in Cambridge. He was attracted to Cambridge, but in the end decided to remain in Birmingham, where his title was changed to professor of mathematical physics. His goal was to place the theoretical physics program in his independent department in Birmingham among the world's leaders. He proved foundational in the growth of his department. His wide experience of physics, his acquaintanceships with contemporaries, his knowledge of many centers, and his inspiring and forthright character enabled him to construct and maintain the high quality of the physics department in Birmingham. His style of working with research students was critical, encouraging, helpful, and generous, and he had a great capacity for work. From the department that Peierls built in Birmingham came a number of physicists who became scientific leaders, for example, Richard Dalitz, Sam Edwards, and Brian Flowers.

By the end of the 1940s, the department was able to attract international scholars of the caliber of Freeman Dyson to Birmingham. In 1948 and 1953 the physics and mathematical physics departments joined forces to organize two international conferences in nuclear physics, which further widened Birmingham's reputation as a leading center for physics. Peierls's published papers in the years after the war reflect the wide range of research then being undertaken in theoretical physics. His published books include the textbook, *The Quantum Theory of Solids* (1955), and the popular book, *Atomic Energy* (1950).

In the years when Peierls worked in Birmingham he consulted for the Atomic Energy Research Establishment (AERE) in Harwell, United Kingdom, which had been founded 1945. He was particularly valuable to Harwell because of his knowledge and experience in the separation of uranium-235. By 1950 Harwell had become a general research establishment with weapon developments concentrated in Aldermaston, and with its production organization centered around Risley in the north of England. Peierls eventually became more interested in power reactors than in nuclear weapons.

In 1950 Klaus Fuchs, who had worked as an assistant to Peierls at Los Alamos during the war, was unmasked as a spy. At the time he was arrested Fuchs was the head of Harwell's theoretical physics division. Because Fuchs and Peierls had worked closely together for years, the British secret service carefully investigated Peierls's interests and background. As the files held in the Public Record Office show, nothing against him was found. He remained as a consultant to the AERE for power reactors.

From 1954, Peierls also consulted with the English Electric Company. By this time, Britain had begun building civil nuclear reactors. For Peierls, contacts with industry had a significance over and above the pure technical and scientific. As he later wrote in his autobiography, "I was always convinced that the experience of thinking physicists could be useful in more practical fields, and … my contact with English Electric [seemed] to confirm this. I enjoyed these problems and [the] contacts [demonstrated] to my students that their talents could be put to good use outside the narrow academic field" (*Bird of Passage*, 1985, pp. 279–280). His consulting for the English Electric Company continued until 1969, when the structure of the nuclear industry changed.

Five years later he arranged a second international conference. Conferences and international contacts were important to Peierls. After all, before the war he had moved around Europe from one center of physics to another and began attending conferences from the early years of his researches, and links between Britain and the United States were to the mutual benefit of the participants. By the end of the 1950s theoretical physics in Birmingham was truly world class.

Oxford: 1963–1974. Nevertheless, in 1963 Peierls accepted a professorship in Oxford, where he was named the Wykeham Professor in Theoretical Physics. By this time, theoretical physics was thriving, but it was somewhat diffused at Oxford. Peierls insisted that a department of theoretical physics should be gathered into a suitable, single building. The department quickly became bigger than the one that Peierls had left in Birmingham, and he was not able to operate in the same way that he had previously. In Birmingham because he was the first professor of theoretical physics he was able to control the growth and development from the beginning. In Oxford many structures and interests were already in place. In particular there were fewer social situations available in Oxford in which members of the department, senior and postdoctoral, could meet. Believing frequent intercourse was essential for making good progress in physics, Peierls created a number of initiatives that would help the work of the department become more coherent, for instance, a weekly lunch for senior researchers and postdoctoral visitors. He encouraged and attended most of the more general seminars and colloquia in order to cement a coherence between the researchers. His student Richard Dalitz believed that the increase in coherence may possibly be Peierls's most important contribution to Oxford during his time there.

When Peierls retired from full-time work in 1974, he accepted a part-time professorship at the University of Washington, Seattle, thereby continuing his association with an institution he first visited in 1962.

Political Activities. Peierls played an active role in a number of political organizations relating to the peaceful use of atomic energy. In 1945 he was a founding member of the Atomic Scientists' Association and served as its first acting president. The aim of the association was to inform the public about matters nuclear, particularly about the hazards of nuclear power. In 1958, when this association wound up its work, it was not clear to what extent it had been successful. Peierls also participated in the Pugwash Movement, which stemmed from a manifesto published in 1955 aimed at nuclear disarmament. He attended Pugwash conferences in the period 1960–1992 and served as chairman from 1970 to 1972. Peierls's commitment to nuclear disarmament was also demonstrated by his patronage of FREEZE, the U.K. Coalition for a Nuclear Weapon Freeze. For nearly ten years Peierls was a member of the Advisory Panel on Arms Control and Disarmament, which began its work in 1964 in the Labour government of 1964. By 1974, however, Peierls had grown disillusioned with the work of this panel, as he indicated in a letter to the Conservative government, and he resigned from the panel.

Retirement and Honors. After Peierls retired from full-time teaching, he continued a full program of research, lecturing, writing, and traveling, but in the 1980s his health started to decline. He died in Oxford on 19 September 1995, after a productive physics career of more than sixty-five years. Between 1929 and 1995 Peierls authored or coauthored some 378 papers, letters, and books, of which the vast majority were concerned with physics. In the year of his death he published five works.

Peierls received many honors and held numerous visiting posts around the world. There are too many to list here in full, but R. H. Dalitz and Peierls's *Selected Papers* (1997) contain a full chronology of Peierls's life and work. Among his honors were fellow of the Royal Society in 1945, the Royal Society's Royal Medal in 1959 and its Copley Medal in 1986, CBE in 1946, knighthood in 1968, honorary fellow of the Institute of Physics in 1973, the Guthrie medal in 1968, and the Dirac medal in 1991.

BIBLIOGRAPHY

For archival material, see list in Dalitz (2004), to which should be added files related to Peierls in the Public Record Office, the National Archives, Kew, Richmond, Surrey, TW9 4DU, and some sources in the AIP oral history collection, American

Institute of Physics, One Physics Ellipse, College Park, Maryland 20740-3843 (http://www.aip.org/history).

WORKS BY PEIERLS

"On the Kinetic Theory of Thermal Conduction in Crystals." *Annalen der Physik* 3 (1929): 1055–1101.

"On the Theory of Galvanomagnetic Effects." *Zeitschrift für Physiks* 53 (1929): 255–266.

"On the Theory of the Hall Effect." *Physiks Zeitschrift* 30 (1929): 273–274.

"On the Theory of Electric and Thermal Conductivity of Metals." *Annalen der Physik* 4 (1930): 121–148.

"Elektronentheorie der Metalle." *Ergebnisse der Exakten Naturwissenschaften* 11 (1932): 264–322.

"Zur Theorie de Absorptionsspektren fest Körper." *Annalen der Physik* 13 (1932): 905–952.

"Statistical Theory of Superlattices with Unequal Concentrations of the Components." *Proceedings of the Royal Society*, Series A, 154 (1936): 207–222.

Atomic Energy. London: Penguin, 1950.

The Laws of Nature. London: Allen and Unwin, 1955.

The Quantum Theory of Solids. Oxford: Clarendon, 1955.

"The Development of Quantum Theory. Part 1. Formulation and Interpretation." *Contemporary Physics* 6 (1964): 129–139.

The Frisch-Peierls memorandum (in two parts): Part I. "On the Construction of a 'Super-Bomb,' Based on a Nuclear Chain Reaction in Uranium." In Appendix 1, *Britain and Atomic Energy, 1939–1945*, by M. Gowing. London: Macmillan, 1964. Part II. "The Properties of a Radioactive 'Super-Bomb.'" In *Tizard*, by R. W. Clark. London: Methuen, 1965.

"The Development of Quantum Theory. Part 2. Consolidation and Extension." *Contemporary Physics* 6 (1965): 192–205.

Surprises in Theoretical Physics. Princeton, NJ: Princeton University Press, 1979.

Bird of Passage. Princeton, NJ: Princeton University Press, 1985.

More Surprises in Theoretical Physics. Princeton, NJ: Princeton University Press, 1991.

Atomic Histories. Woodbury, NY: American Institute of Physics Press, 1997.

With R. H. Dalitz. *Selected Scientific Papers of Sir Rudolf Peierls: With Commentary.* London: Imperial College Press, 1997. Contains a complete bibliography, together with a chronology of Peierls's life.

OTHER SOURCES

Clark, Ronald William. *Tizard.* London: Methuen, 1965.

Dahl, Per F. *Superconductivity: Its Historical Roots and Development from Mercury to the Ceramic Oxides.* New York: American Institute of Physics Press, 1992.

Dalitz, R. H. "Sir Rudolf Ernst Peierls." In *Oxford Dictionary of National Biography*, edited by H. C. G. Matthew and Brian Harrison. Oxford: Oxford University Press, 2004. Contains a list of archival information.

Edwards, S. "Rudolph E. Peierls." [*sic*] *Physics Today* (February 1996): 75–77.

Gowing, Margaret. *Britain and Atomic Energy, 1939–1945.* London: Macmillan, 1964.

Hendry, John. *Cambridge Physics in the Thirties.* Bristol, U.K.: Adam Hilger, 1984. Contains essays written by physicists working in Cambridge in the thirties. These, and the introductions, include comments on the relationships between mathematics, theoretical and experimental physics, and the institutional contexts in Cambridge.

Hoddeson, Lillian, Ernest Braun, Jürgen Teichmann, et al., eds. *Out of the Crystal Maze: Chapters from the History of Solid-State Physics.* New York: Oxford University Press, 1991.

———, Paul W. Henriksen, Roger Meade, et al. *Critical Assembly: A Technical History of Los Alamos during the Oppenheimer Years, 1943–1945.* New York: Cambridge University Press, 1993.

Kapur, P. L. "The Dispersion Formula for Nuclear Reactions." *Proceedings of the Royal Society*, Series A, 166 (1938): 277–295.

Mott, N. "Rudolf Peierls (1907–95)." *Nature* 377 (1995): 577.

Colin Hempstead

PELLICIER, GUILLAUME (*b.* Mauguio [near Montpellier], France, probably late 1490s, likely 1498 or 1499; *d.* Montferrand [later Saint-Mathieu-de-Tréviers], 1568), *diplomat, classical scholar, patron of natural sciences and medicine.*

A diplomat, a book collector, and a protector of the University of Montpellier, Pellicier was interested in medicine and natural sciences, the renewal of which he fostered in Montpellier. Born at an unknown date, probably in the late 1490s (1498 or 1499), in Mauguio (east of Montpellier), Pellicier studied philosophy and canon law at the nearby University of Montpellier, and was a protégé of his uncle Guillaume Pellicier, the bishop of the diocese of Maguelone (south of Montpellier, later Villeneuve-lès-Maguelonne). Appointed a canon of the cathedral of Maguelone by his uncle, he then succeeded him after his uncle resigned as bishop in 1527. A classical scholar, Pellicier drew the attention of King Francis I (r. 1515–1547) and his sister Marguerite de Navarre (1492–1549), the most educated and literate woman known from this time. The king and his sister entrusted Pellicier with several delicate diplomatic missions: the conclusion of the war with Austrian Emperor Charles V in 1529 (Treaty of Cambrai); the marriage of the king's son (the Duc d'Orléans) with Catherine de Medici in 1533; and a mission to Pope Paul III, from whom Pellicier obtained the transfer of the See of Maguelone to Montpellier in 1536.

In 1539 Pellicier became the ambassador of France to Venice, where he was in a good position to collect information and convey instructions between Paris and Constantinople in the continued conflict between France and the German Empire. Caught for his activity as a spy by the Venetian authority, he was recalled to France in 1542. After Francis I's death in 1547 and a brief stint the same year at a session of the Trent Council held in Bologna, he stayed in Montpellier and exerted his functions of bishop, particularly the patronage of the university, as his predecessors had done. Accused of sympathy to the Reformers and other criminal charges, he was jailed (1551), put on trial, and eventually exonerated (1557). In 1559 a first Protestant church was built in Montpellier and, in 1561–1562, the city was controlled by the Reformers. After the Amboise Pacification (1563), Pellicier regained Montpellier, but could not oppose the sack of the cathedral in 1567. He then retired in the castle of Montferrand (later Saint-Mathieu-de-Tréviers), where he died in 1568.

Promotion of Science and Medicine. Early in his life Pellicier was interested in the natural sciences and medicine. Before his diplomatic mission in Venice he was in contact with François Rabelais (1494–1553), who studied medicine at the University of Montpellier and taught there in 1531, commenting on Hippocrates's *Aphorisms* and Galen's *Ars parva*. Both were in Rome in 1535, and Rabelais wrote some letters to Pellicier (1540 and 1541) while the latter stayed in Venice. Pellicier is not known, however, to have left any original scientific work, although at one time he was credited with the authorship of a book on fishes (*Libri De piscibus marinis,* 1554–1555) published under the name of Guillaume Rondelet. Pellicier did write notes of commentary on Pliny's *Natural History*, which were praised and used by later editors of Pliny's Latin text from Adrien Turnèbe (1512–1565) to Jean Hardouin (1646–1729); these notes remain unpublished as of 2007.

Pellicier's main scientific endeavor was the renewal of interest in medicine and natural sciences at the University of Montpellier. Because Pellicier was classically educated, Francis I entrusted him with the task of collecting manuscripts for the Bibliothèque royale while in Venice. Pellicier secured the purchase of many manuscripts and printed versions of classical texts (particularly in Greek) on the Venetian marketplace; he also employed several Greek copyists to construct a personal collection of manuscripts. Simultaneously, Pellicier purchased many of the available printed versions of ancient scientific texts, some through his personal contacts with the heirs of Aldo Manuzio, who founded the Aldine Press. Significantly, he acquired for his personal collection one or more copies of many of the Greek texts available at that time in the fields of medicine and natural sciences, including works by Hip-

pocrates and Galen, encyclopedias and compendia of the mid- and late-Byzantine periods, and fourteenth-century Byzantine translations of Arabo-Persian treatises.

In a 1534 reform made under Pellicier's supervision, the University of Montpellier limited the teaching of Arabic authors. After his return from Venice in 1542, the availability of these materials was further reduced. The works of Persian physician Avicenna (Ibn Sina), which were taught every year during the 1530s, seem to have been taught for the last time in 1545 (with one exception in 1565). Simultaneously, the work of ancient Greek physician Dioscorides appears in the program from 1545 on, together with *herborisations* (collecting plants in the field). Rabelais probably collected plants in nature during his years in Montpellier, as he credited his character Gargantua with such training; Pellicier also is believed to have personally done so, with Rondelet. This new orientation was confirmed in the so-called *Grands Jours de Béziers* of 1550, which transformed the teaching activity of the university. Supposedly inspired by Pellicier, but more probably authored by the university chancellor Antoine Saporta, this new program divided the academic year into two major terms: the study of botany (in the field) from Easter to Feast of Saint Luke (October 18), and the study of anatomy during the rest of the year—that is, during winter. Rondelet, who was instrumental in the construction of the first theater of anatomy at the University of Montpellier in 1556, has also been credited (without clear evidence, however) with the creation of a botanic garden, antedating that of Pierre Richer de Belleval (created in 1593).

By this new organization of medical studies, Pellicier concretized the epistemological program promoted by Nicolao Leoniceno, which had started to be realized in Germany with the publication of such works as *Herbarum vivae eicones* (Strasbourg, 1530) by Otto Brunfels and, even more, by the *Historia Stirpium* (Basel, 1542) of Leonhart Fuchs. It was in Italy, however, that the program was fully realized, exactly during the period of Pellicier's diplomatic mission in Venice, with the creation of botanic gardens in Pisa and Padua, and the anatomical demonstrations of André Vésale (1514–1564) and the publication of the *De humani corporis fabrica libri* (Basel, 1543). The similarity between the new organization of teaching at Montpellier and the innovations in north Italy is too strong to be casual and suggests that Pellicier exported from Venice not only books and their knowledge, but also the practice of science. In this, Pellicier anticipated in a certain sense the Republic of Botanists best represented somewhat later by the Italian physician Pietro Andrea Mattioli (1501–1577) in his translation of and commentaries on Dioscorides's *De materia medica* (first published in 1544, with many revised editions).

Pellicier was a man deeply involved in the transformations of his time. In politics, he was on the forefront of the reshaping of Europe with the war between France and the Holy Roman Empire, and the relatively new presence of the Ottoman Empire in the Mediterranean. In culture, he encouraged the return to the classical heritage, thus minimizing the contribution of both the Arabic world and the Latin Middle Ages. Contributing to the diffusion of knowledge, he purchased ancient manuscripts (so as to recollect the heritage of the past) and, at the same time, frequented the world of printing, acquiring an important collection that he used as a tool for the production of a new knowledge. In promoting the scientific method, Pellicier fostered a shift from the medieval comment on canonical texts to direct observation, be it in the field (botany) or in an ad hoc demonstration room (the theater of anatomy). Under Pellicier's guidance, the University of Montpellier quickly attracted students in medicine and the natural sciences from across Europe, from Charles de l'Ecluse (1526–1609) to Felix Platter (1536–1614) to Johann Bauhin (1541–1613).

BIBLIOGRAPHY

Bonnet, Hubert. *La Faculté de médecine de Montpellier: Huit siècles d'histoire et d'éclat.* Montpellier: Sauramps médical, 1992.

Cataldi Palau, Annaclara. "Manoscritti greci della collezione di Guillaume Pellicier, Vescovo di Montepellier (c. 1490–1568): Disiecta membra." *Studi Italiani di Filologia Classica* III, no. 3 (1985): 103–115.

———. "Les vicissitudes de la collection de manuscrits grecs de Guillaume Pellicier." *Scriptorium* 40 (1986): 32–53.

———. *Gian Francesco d'Asola e la tipografia aldina. La vita, le edizioni, la biblioteca dell'Asolano.* Genova: SAGEP, 1998.

Dulieu, Louis. *La médecine à Montpellier.* Vol. 2: *La Renaissance.* Avignon: Les Presses Universelles, 1979.

Foerster, Richard. "Zur Handschriftenkunde und Geschichte der Philologie, III. Die griechische Handschriften von Guillaume Pellicier." *Rheinisches Museum für Philologie,* NF 40 (1885): 453–461.

Guiraud, Louise. *Le procès de Guillaume Pellicier, évêque de Maguelone-Montpellier de 1527 à 1567.* Paris: Picard, 1907.

Irigoin, Jean. "Les ambassadeurs à Venise et le commerce des manuscrits grecs dans les années 1540–1550." In *Venezia centro di mediazione tra Oriente e Occidente, Secoli XV–XVI, Aspetti e problemi. Atti del II Convegno Internazionale di Storia della Civiltà Veneziana promosso e organizzato dalla Fondazione Giorgio Cini, dal Centro Tedesco di Studi Veneziani (Venezia, 3–6 ottobre 1973),* vol. II, edited by Hans-Gorg Beck, Manoussos Manoussacas, and Agostino Pertusi. Florence: Leo S. Olschki.

Nauert, Charles G., Jr. "Caius Plinius Secundus." *Catalogus Translationum et Commentariorum,* vol. 4, edited by Paul Oskar Kristeller. Washington, DC: Catholic University of America Press, 1980.

Omont, Henri. "Catalogue des manuscrits grecs de Guillaume Pelicier." *Bibliothèque de l'Ecole des Chartes* 6 (1885): 45–83, 594–624.

———. *Catalogue des manuscrits grecs de Fontainebleau sous François Ier et Henri II.* Paris: Imprimerie Nationale, 1889.

———. "Inventaire de la bibliothèque de Guillaume Pelicier évêque de Montpellier (1529–1568)." *Revue des Bibliothèques* 1 (1891): 161–172.

Palau, Annaclara. "Les copistes de Guillaume Pellicier, évêque de Montpellier." *Scrittura e Civiltà* 10 (1986): 199–237.

von Rath, Ulrich. "The Function and Architecture of the Botanic Garden of the University of Montpellier (1593–1622)." In *Studies in Renaissance Botany,* edited by Zbigniew Mirek and Alicja Zemanek. Crakow: W. Szafer Institute of Botany, Polish Academy of Sciences, 1998.

Reeds, Karen Meier. *Botany in Medieval and Renaissance Universities.* New York: Garland, 1991.

Taussera-Radel, Alexandre. *Correpondance politique de Guillaume Pellicier, Ambassadeur de France à Venise, 1540–1542. Publiée sous les auspices de la Commission des Archives Diplomatiques.* Paris: Alcan, 1899.

Walter, Hermann. "Il commentario Pliniano di Guillaume Pellicer, vescovo di Montpellier, e l'incunabolo N 614 della Biblioteca Palatina di Parma." *Studi Piceni* 18 (1998): 187–196.

———. "Tre commentatori della Storia naturale di Plinio il Vecchio: Guillaume Pellicier, Filippo Strozzi il Giovane e Jean Hardouin." *Rapporti e scambi tra umanesimo italiano ed umanesimo europeo,* edited by Luisa Rotondo Secchi Tarugi. Milan: Nuovi Orizzonti, 2001.

Zeller, Jean. *La diplomatie française d'après la correspondance de G. Pellicier.* Paris: Hachette, 1880.

Alain Touwaide

PENFIELD, WILDER GRAVES (*b.* Spokane, Washington, 26 January 1891; *d.* Montreal, Canada, 5 April 1976), *neurosurgery, neurology, epilepsy.*

Penfield helped develop an important surgical treatment for epilepsy and used the results to investigate the functional organization of the brain. He was instrumental in founding, funding, and staffing the Montreal Neurological Institute (MNI) at McGill University, which he directed from 1934 to 1960. Penfield, according to his autobiography *No Man Alone* (1977), valued his fund-raising and administrative work at MNI, perhaps as much as his research and clinical practice. Penfield devotes more than a chapter of *No Man Alone* to an unprecedented and dangerous operation to relieve a patient's debilitating epileptic seizures. Penfield says its success was important to him not only because he hoped it would open the way to new surgical treatments of epilepsies caused by circulatory defects, but also because the patient's parents decided to make a generous financial contribution to MNI.

Wilder Graves Penfield was born in Spokane, Washington, in 1891, while Hughlings Jackson was treating and observing epileptics in London. Crucial components of Penfield's research program were later to develop from Jackson's clinical studies. At the time of Penfield's death in 1976, technicians and statisticians were developing brain imaging techniques that would help neuroscientists pursue Penfield's goal of mapping the functional geography of the brain.

Becoming a Surgeon. Penfield's father, Charles Samuel Penfield, was an unsuccessful, financially distressed physician. He abandoned the family when Penfield was eight. His mother, Jean (Jefferson) Penfield, moved him with his brother and sister to Hudson, Wisconsin, where they lived for some time with her father. She founded the Galahad School for Boys, where Penfield received his high school education. When he was thirteen a friend told his mother about the Rhodes Scholarship. "This … is just the thing for you, Wide," she said. He went to Princeton University because that seemed a good place to apply for a Rhodes. There he became interested in human physiology and chose medicine for a profession. He played football (Rhodes applicants were judged partly on athletic prowess). After graduation he coached to earn money while he waited for his Rhodes. He married Helen Kermott, and as World War I began, they left for Oxford University, where he studied clinical medicine with William Osler and neurology with Charles Sherrington. During a spring vacation the Germans torpedoed the ferry on which he was trying to cross the English Channel to volunteer at a Red Cross hospital. Osler invited Penfield to stay in his home while he recuperated from the injuries he sustained.

After Oxford, Penfield completed his MD at Johns Hopkins University. He interned under Harvey Cushing in Boston at Peter Brent Brigham Hospital. After his internship he practiced surgery for seven years at New York Presbyterian Hospital. During a leave he traveled to Spain to learn nerve cell staining techniques from Santiago Ramón y Cajal and Pio del Rio-Hortega. Penfield also went to Germany, where he watched Ottfrid Foerster employ surgical techniques he would use later to treat his own patients. He also investigated microscopic details of brain healing and scarring in tissue samples that Foerster provided.

Clinical Research and the MNI. Penfield became convinced that the best way to investigate the brain would be for clinicians, neurologists, anatomists, pathologists, and psychologists to collaborate. He left New York for Montreal in 1928, hoping to practice surgery in an environment that fostered interdisciplinary brain research. His

Wilder Graves Penfield, pictured with his wife.
THE LIBRARY OF CONGRESS.

efforts made it possible for MNI to open six years later; it continues to be a leading center for neurological research and the treatment of brain diseases. In 1954 Penfield and Herbert Jasper published *Epilepsy and the Functional Anatomy of the Human Brain,* an exemplary product of the interdisciplinary research that MNI was designed to facilitate. It contains Penfield's most influential contributions to the surgical treatment of epilepsy, along with discussions of what he and his multidisciplinary collaborators learned about the brain from 750 patients Penfield treated between 1928 and 1953.

In 1874 the servant of a surgeon named Barthalow had an accident that left a hole in her skull. Although she was conscious, Barthalow found he could manipulate the top of her brain without causing her additional pain. (The brain contains no pain sensors.) Mechanical irritation had no effect, but weak electrical stimulation caused muscle contractions. Strong shocks caused convulsions, followed by coma. Some years before Penfield's internship, Harvey

Cushing had elicited sensations in a patient by introducing a weak electric current behind the Rolandic fissure. In the operations Penfield observed in Germany, Foerster stimulated different points on the surface of a conscious patient's brain and used the resulting motor and verbal responses as clues to the location of tissues he could ablate to prevent or relieve their seizures. Like Cushing, he applied local anesthetics to the scalp and the inner lining of the skull to keep the patient relatively comfortable without general anesthetic. Penfield realized that, besides helping patients, this technique could provide valuable data for neurologists, physiologists, and anatomists. He left for Montreal looking forward to "operating, under local anesthesia, on a long series of patients." During his career he performed 1,132 such operations and used the results to investigate the following four issues. The first two are clinical. The third has to do with functional anatomy. The last is philosophical.

1. Locating Seizure Sources. Many epileptic seizures begin with abnormal activity in a relatively small brain region. Motor and cognitive functions are disrupted as this activity spreads to other parts of the brain. Before it does so, it may produce distinctive motor symptoms (e.g., weakness or twitching) or experiential states called auras. If the fits are severe enough to warrant the risk, and if they cannot be controlled with drugs, the surgeon may treat the patient by destroying the brain region where the seizures begin. To this end, Penfield and his colleagues adapted Foerster's techniques to develop what came to be called the Montreal procedure. The surgeon peels back flaps of skull and brain covering, passes an electrical current into one cortical bulge and crevasse after another, placing small numbered squares of paper on locations whose stimulation produces interesting results. The clinically significant tissue is in and near places where stimulation causes responses that mimic the aura or the motor activities that signal the start of a fit. Recording electrodes can also be inserted to detect abnormal electrical effects. The surgeon then destroys brain tissue judged to be responsible for seizures on the basis of the electrical recordings, responses to stimulation, and other evidence, including preoperative electroencephalograms (EEGs).

Although this technique benefited many patients, Penfield once said that brain surgery was such a terrible profession that he would hate it if he did not think it would change during his lifetime. A case in point was his removal of a great deal of frontal lobe tissue in a futile attempt to cure his older sister. She had been epileptic for so long that Penfield could remember being frightened by her seizures as a child. The surgery revealed an untreatable tumor that eventually killed her.

2. Locating Tissue the Surgeon Must Spare. To avoid doing more harm than good, surgeons must spare brain regions whose destruction would cause unacceptably severe deficits. Some psychological functions required for acceptably decent quality of life depend upon structures whose location varies from brain to brain. For example, right hemisphere lesions impair speech in some patients, but not in many others. Penfield and his colleagues exploited the fact that cortical regions do not function normally under weak electrical stimulation to locate brain regions they should spare. To find speech areas, they stimulated various cortical regions while the patient performed naming and other simple language tasks. For example, when he was shown a picture of a foot, one patiently easily produced the word *foot* until a current was passed into the left side of his brain. As long as the stimulation continued, his best effort on the naming task was to say "that is what you put in your shoes." Such results, together with his successful performances during right brain stimulation, indicated that his speech areas were in the left rather than the right hemisphere. By contrast, left brain tissue could be ablated in patients whose linguistic performance was impaired by right hemisphere stimulation only.

3. Localizing Brain Functions. Penfield studied the effects of stimulation and surgical ablation to learn about the functional anatomy of the brain. In doing so, he said he was applying to humans the techniques of stimulating and surgically destroying small brain regions that Sherrington had used to study the organization of the primate nervous system. When Sherrington was in his nineties, he remarked to

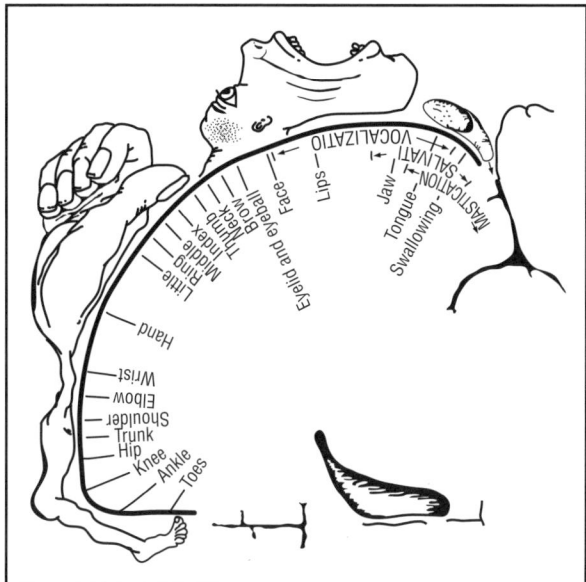

Figure 1. *Motor homunculus.*

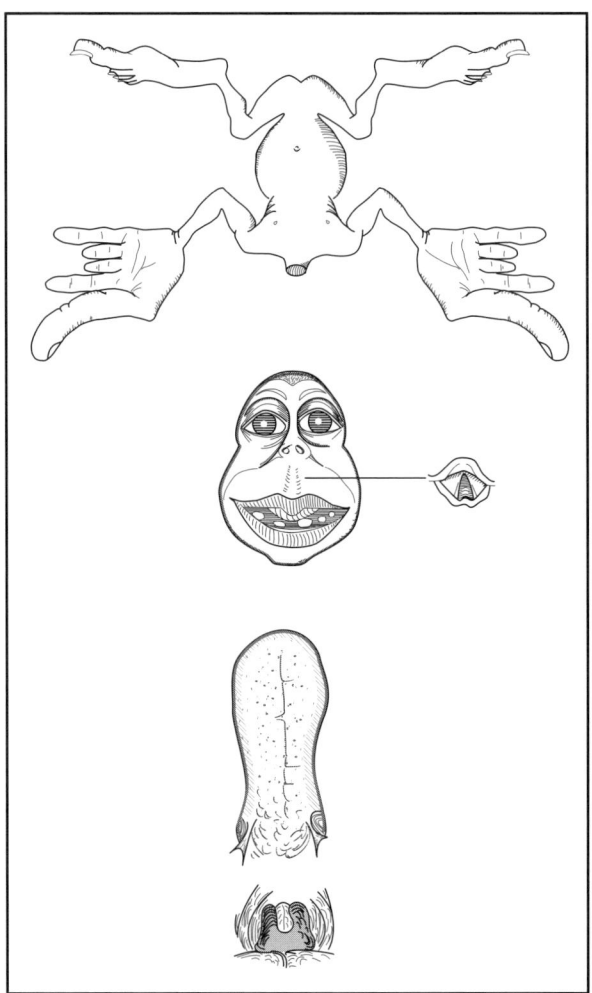

Figure 2. *Sensory and motor homunculus. The general order of representation and relative extent occupied in the sensorimotor strip are indicated.*

Penfield that it must be great fun to speak to an experimental preparation and have it answer you. The ability of a conscious patient to describe what he or she experienced during surgery enabled Penfield to study psychological responses that Sherrington's simian subjects could not reveal.

First-year neural anatomy students are familiar with one of the fruits of this research—the homuncular diagrams drawn by a Mrs. Cantlie. Penfield published the original diagram in 1937 and a revised version in 1950. Mrs. Cantlie's homunculi are grotesquely distorted outlines of a body superimposed on a sketch of the top of the brain. They depict regions on either side of the Rolandic fissure whose stimulation produces sensory or motor effects. The shapes' relative sizes, and relative positions of the homunculus's head, hand, foot, and so on, indicate the relative sizes of the brain regions whose stimulation influenced the corresponding parts of the body. Thus, the

homuncular hands are much larger than the homuncular chest because the regions where stimulation produces responses in the former are much larger than those whose stimulation produces responses in the latter. Homuncular genitals are drawn next to homuncular feet to indicate the relative positions of their cortical regions.

The best-known result of Penfield's stimulation studies was his discovery that temporal lobe stimulation could produce vivid experiential effects. Some patients reported experiencing things they had experienced in the past. One said he saw a 7-Up bottling company, and then a bakery he had seen years before. Another heard the theme song of a radio program he used to listen to. Another heard an orchestra playing "Marching along Together." When Penfield ran a weak current into a boy's frontal lobe he said he could hear his mother telling his brother he had his coat on wrong. Stimulation a short distance away elicited the experience of listening to his mother talking on the phone to an aunt. In some cases. Penfield obtained independent evidence that the electrically induced sights and sounds were very similar to experiences from the patient's past. He concluded that in such cases the stimulation activated memory records through a process that differed from normal recollection.

In other cases, electrical stimulation evoked simple hallucinatory experiences of flashes of light, colored triangles, banging noises, noxious smells, the feeling of something stroking the back of the hand, and so forth. Some electrical stimulations altered the patient's experience of what was actually happening, producing feelings of strangeness, loneliness, fear, déjà vu, and so on. Penfield argued that such results could bring sensation, perception, memory, emotion, one's interpretation of one's own ongoing experience, along with other "psychical phenomena … into the field of physiology." (An online video of Penfield at work stimulating patients' brains and interviewing the woman who heard "Marching along Together" is available from http://www.virtualmuseum.ca/Exhibitions/Medicentre/en/penf_video.htm.)

Penfield originally thought memory records of past experiences were stored in the cortex. But the evidence he accumulated between 1950 and 1958 inclined him to a more complicated theory. He knew that during electrically induced auditory or visual experiences the patient cannot hear or see normally. During electrically induced motor activity, the patient cannot voluntarily control the affected body part. Penfield concluded that electrical stimulation disables the region into which the current passes at the same time that it produces an experiential or motor effect. If a bit of cortical tissue is disabled by electrical stimulation, it is plausible that it contributes to the production of a motor or sensory response by transmitting electrical impulses to brain regions that can still function normally enough to produce it.

Penfield decided that cortical stimulation produces its effects via impulses that travel from the cortex to subcortical ganglia too far from the stimulating current to be disabled. By analogy, if cortical stimulation activates memory records, those records must be stored below rather than in the cortex. The profusion of nerve fibers that connect the cortex to subcortical ganglia in and near the top of the brain stem suggests that nerve signals can easily pass back and forth between these regions. Furthermore, it was well-known that memory deficits result from hippocampal lesions. Penfield proposed (in his last scientific book, *The Mystery of the Mind,* 1975) that the hippocampi contain "keys-of-access" to records of past experiences. In an early work, he had characterized memory records as pathways "of synaptic and ganglionic facilitations which linger on after present experience is passed." Accordingly, he concluded that cortical stimulation can make a patient relive an old experience by initiating a current that turns the key to the pathway which constitutes its memory record.

Penfield told roughly the same story about other responses to brain stimulation. The keys to pathways whose activation produces different sensory and motor effects occupy different positions in and around the top of the brain stem. When different cortical regions are stimulated, they transmit electrical impulses to different keys. Which effect is produced depends upon which ganglionic pathway is opened by the key that the current reaches. Furthermore, when a given cortical region is disabled temporarily by stimulation or permanently by ablation, the brain loses its normal access to one or more subcortical pathways. That would explain, for example, why patients cannot voluntarily lift an arm while it moves in response to brain stimulation, pronounce words correctly during stimulation that elicits vocal responses, and why stimulation effects involving memory do not mimic normal recollection.

Penfield and Jasper argued for the existence of what they called a "centrencephalic system" consisting of structures that receive and integrate inputs from opposite sides of the brain. Without such a system, the fact that visual stimuli for objects on opposite sides of the nose do not register on the same side of the brain would prevent us from experiencing the visual field as a single, well-unified whole. Without such a system, electrical activity in one hemisphere could not initiate motor activity in response to commands whose understanding depends on activity in the other hemisphere. In general, both reflex and purposeful responses to environmental stimuli would seem to depend upon the integration of inputs from anatomically discrete brain regions. Penfield tentatively proposed that centrencephalic integration is accomplished in the region in and around the top of the brain stem where he had located the keys to memory, motor, and sensory pathways.

(For reasons he did not explain, Penfield ignored the corpus callosum—a massive bundle of nerve fibers that run between the hemispheres.)

Penfield made significant, if controversial, contributions to long-standing disputes over locationism. Locationists follow Franz Gall in supposing that each basic sensory, motor, or other psychological function is uniquely supported by its own anatomically discrete brain structure. Antilocationists, such as Marie-Jean-Pierre Flourens and Karl Lashley, believe that some important functions can be supported equally well by different parcels of brain tissue. Penfield's findings favored the locationists with regard to relatively simple motor and sensory functions. For example, motor regions whose stimulation elicits movements in the fingers of the left hand stand in the same positions relative to one another and to the Rolandic fissure on the right side of every normal brain, even though their sizes and the distances between them vary.

Things are not so clear with regard to more complicated functions. For example, the standard aphasia literature purports to identify a fairly large number of sharply distinguishable language deficits, each of which results from damage to a different anatomical structure. In right-handed subjects, damage to Broca's area in the left hemisphere is said to cause a distinctive inability to produce words, while damage to Wernicke's area is supposed to cause an independent and very different deficit involving an inability to understand words. Damage to counterpart regions in the right brain is said produce the same deficits in left-handers. Locationists think that Broca's and Wernicke's areas operate more or less independently to support different language functions.

In their 1959 *Speech and Brain Mechanisms,* Penfield and Roberts reviewed 569 of their case histories, together with some others reported in the standard literature. They concluded, contrary to received doctrine, that "the left hemisphere is usually dominant for speech, regardless of handedness" but that it is not dominant for speech in every right-handed subject. Only 46 of 52 right-handers exhibited symptoms of Broca's aphasia during left hemisphere stimulation near Broca's area. Five left-handed patients did not exhibit language difficulties during right hemisphere stimulation near Broca's area. The literature included one (controversial) report of surgical destruction of Broca's area that did not produce permanent symptoms of Broca's aphasia.

Another remarkable finding was that although language task performances were impaired by stimulation within a relatively large parieto-temporal region and a smaller frontal region, no more than half of Penfield's patients exhibited the same (or any) temporary deficits during the stimulation at exactly the same location in either region. Penfield and Roberts could say the posterior tempero-parietal region and Broca's area were the first and second most important areas for speech. A locationist might find that congenial in spite of the anatomical variations among different brains. But Penfield and Roberts rejected the locationist idea that language and other basic functions are executed by relatively small, anatomically discrete brain structures functioning in relative independence from one another. Believing as they did that these functions involve activities on both sides of the brain, the locations they proposed were complex networks of cortical and subcortical structures with many anatomical and physiological interconnections.

In this way, Penfield could square his locationist sympathies with another finding. Contrary to the locationist picture of sharply distinguishable, mutually independent language functions, Penfield found that surgical interventions typically did not produce pure examples of the allegedly independent language deficits that the locationists described. Instead, simulating or ablating a single cortical region produced combinations of symptoms of varying severity associated with a number (in some cases, a large number) of different language deficits. This was in keeping with Jackson's idea that motor and sensory functions are carried out by hierarchically arranged networks of interconnected structures in various places between the top of the spinal cord and the outer surface of the brain. But Penfield allows for more extensive and different kinds of anatomical variation over different brains than Jackson recognized.

4. Mind and Brain. What do brain and mental functions have to do with one another? Although he considered this a philosophical question, Penfield thought putative answers should be tested against anatomical, physiological, and clinical evidence. Following Sherrington, he assumed that unless our mental lives can be satisfactorily explained just by appeal to brain functions, we must think that mind and brain are different entities that interact somehow.

Penfield characterized consciousness as the mental state that distinguishes wakefulness from dreamless sleep, and normal self-aware purposeful activity from the aimless, stereotypical, perseverative behavior of epileptics who have lost both awareness of and control over what they are doing, and who cannot adjust their behavior to what goes on around them. Consciousness and the ability to plan and direct behavior and to adjust it to changing circumstances vanish when a seizure spreads to the top of the brain stem and neighboring structures. It returns when this mechanism resumes its normal functions. It follows that consciousness depends upon the centrencephalic system.

But are the functions of this or any other part of the brain sufficient for conscious mental activity? Penfield

says he cannot prove they are not sufficient, but that the available evidence provides no good reason to think they are. He was struck by his inability to stimulate the cortex to make patients think that they were responsible for the movements his manipulations evoked. Nor could he make patients think the things they experienced during brain stimulations were actually happening. Accordingly, he thought, if the centrencephalic system is fully active during cortical stimulation, it is plausible that it cannot account for consciousness. That is why Penfield thought his research had produced "no good evidence that the brain alone can carry out the work the mind does." But he warns us not to "pretend to draw a final scientific conclusion" about whether mind and brain are separate entities until the energy that the mind uses to act on the brain is discovered (as he expected would happen eventually).

Later Life. Penfield retired from the McGill medical faculty in 1954, and gave up his directorship of MNI six years later. During his retirement he continued his application of clinical findings to questions about mind and brain, delivering the lectures incorporated into *Speech and Brain Mechanisms* in 1956, and completing the final draft of *Mystery of the Mind* two years before he died. And there were other interests. Before his mother died, Penfield promised to complete a novel she had been writing based on the biblical story of Sarah. He rewrote the book and published it under the title *No Other Gods*. In addition to traveling and lecturing in Russia, China, and India, he also found time to publish *The Torch*, a novel about Hippocrates; *The Difficult Art of Giving*, a tribute to the Rockefeller Foundation administrator who helped fund the MNI; and *The Second Career*, a collection of essays on education and other topics. He completed his autobiography the year he died of stomach cancer in Montreal, survived by two daughters—Priscilla and Ruth Mary—two sons, Wilder Jr. and Amos Jefferson, and many grandchildren.

BIBLIOGRAPHY

WORKS BY PENFIELD

Editor. *Cytology and Cellular Pathology of the Nervous System.* New York: Paul B. Hoeber, 1932.

With J. Evans. "The Frontal Lobe in Man: A Clinical Study of Maximum Removals." *Brain* 58 (1935): 115–138.

With E. Boldery. "Somatic, Motor, and Sensory Representation in the Cerebral Cortex of Man as Studied by Electrical Stimulation." *Brain* 60 (1937): 389–443.

"Epileptic Automatism and the Centrencephalic Integrating System." *Association for Research in Nervous and Mental Disorders* 30 (1950): 513–538.

With Theodore B. Rasmussen. *The Cerebral Cortex of Man.* New York: Macmillan, 1950.

With Kristian Kristiansen. *Epileptic Seizure Patterns.* Springfield, IL: Charles Thomas, 1951.

No Other Gods. Boston: Little Brown, 1954.

With Herbert Jasper. *Epilepsy and the Functional Anatomy of the Human Brain.* Boston: Little Brown, 1954.

"The Permanent Record of the Stream of Consciousness." *Proceedings XIV International Congress on Psychology: Acta Psychologica* 11 (1955): 47–69.

The Excitable Cortex in Conscious Man. Fifth Sherrington Lecture. Liverpool, U.K.: University of Liverpool Press, 1958.

With Lamar Roberts. *Speech and Brain Mechanisms.* Princeton, NJ: Princeton University Press, 1959.

The Torch. Boston: Little Brown, 1960.

The Mystery of the Mind: A Critical Study of Consciousness and the Human Brain. Princeton, NJ: Princeton University Press, 1975.

No Man Alone: A Neurosurgeon's Life. Boston: Little Brown, 1977. Penfield's autobiography.

With Phanor Perot. "The Brain's Record of Auditory and Visual Experiences: A Final Summary and Discussion." *Brain* 86 (1963): 595–696.

The Second Career with Other Essays and Addresses. Boston: Little Brown, 1963.

The Difficult Art of Giving: The Epic of Alan Gregg. Boston: Little Brown, 1967.

OTHER SOURCES

Feindel, William, and Richard Leblanc. "History of the Surgical Treatment of Epilepsy." In *A History of Neurosurgery, in Its Scientific and Professional Contexts,* edited by Samuel H. Greenblatt, T. Forcht Dagi, and Mel Epstein, 465–488. Park Ridge, IL: American Association of Neurological Surgeons, 1997.

Rasmussen, Theodore. "Wilder Penfield, 1891–1976." *Journal of Neurosurgery* 45, no. 3 (1976): 248–250.

Ruelland, J. G. "Wilder G. Penfield (1891–1976), Neurosurgeon and Scientist." *Versalius: Acta Internationales Historiae Medicinae* 11, no. 2 (December 2005): 64–69.

Jim Bogen

PEREY, MARGUERITE CATHERINE

(*b.* Villemomble, France, 19 October 1909; *d.* Louveciennes, France, 13 May 1975), *radioactivity, radiochemistry, nuclear sciences.*

Perey is an important figure in nuclear chemistry. Trained by Marie Curie, she discovered in 1939 the last natural radioactive element predicted by Dmitrii Mendeleev's periodic table, francium. In 1962 she was the first woman to be elected a correspondent member to the French Académie des sciences since its founding in 1666. Neither Marie Curie nor her daughter, Irène Joliot-Curie,

in spite of their respective Nobel Prizes, managed to join the institution.

Training and First Steps in Scientific Research. Marguerite Catherine Perey was born on 19 October 1909 in Villemomble, near Paris. She came from a middle-class Protestant family. Her father, Louis Émile Perey, was a bank employee. He died in 1914, leaving his wife, Anne Ruissel, with their five children. For financial reasons, Marguerite, the youngest, could not attend a university but instead had to work early in her life. She studied at a private but state-recognized school for technicians, the École d'enseignement technique féminine (school for female technicians). She was first in her class upon completing her studies in 1929. As she was applying for jobs, she was given the opportunity to work at the Institut du Radium (Radium Institute) of Paris, the prestigious institution directed by Marie Curie. She started there as a chemical assistant on 1 October 1929 with a grant from the Union Minière du Haut-Katanga (Mining Union of Upper Katanga), a Belgian multinational company that controlled, during the interwar period, the market for radioactive elements and closely collaborated with Curie's laboratory.

Perey began her career in one of the most dynamic scientific fields of the time—radioactivity—and furthermore, worked alongside one of the founders of the field. Indeed, the word *radioactive* had been coined by Curie in 1898 to characterize chemical substances that emitted rays similar to those of uranium. Shortly thereafter, the word was used to qualify the physical phenomena, as well as the field of research of radioactive elements and their emitted rays. A community of scientists quickly formed a network of several laboratories all over Europe that was dominated during the 1920s by four major centers: the Institut du Radium of Paris, the Cavendish Laboratory in Cambridge directed by Ernest Rutherford, the Institut für Radiumforschung (Vienna Radium Institute) at the University of Vienna directed by Stefan Meyer, and the Kaiser Wilhelm Institut für Chemie (Kaiser Wilhelm Institute of Chemistry) in Berlin, under the direction of Otto Hahn and Lise Meitner. Different ideas, concepts, and experimental practices existed regarding the application of radioactive elements, and each institution had its own approach. For instance, Rutherford's collaborators had at first primarily concentrated on the study of physical radioactive changes and on mechanisms of disintegration of radioactive elements and their daughter products. Then, they progressively started to study atomic structure. In Berlin, researchers specialized in the identification of new radioactive elements and in the physical study of their emissions. At Curie's laboratory, part of the work was devoted to the study of the physical and chemical properties of radioactive elements, with particular interest in the development of

Marguerite Catherine Perey. *Portrait of Marguerite Catherine Perey.* **AIP/PHOTO RESEARCHERS, INC.**

different applications of radioactive elements, for example, in medical use and industrial production.

At the beginning of the 1930s, the field was transformed. A new generation of researchers included James Chadwick, Walther Bothe, and Irène and Frédéric Joliot-Curie and others. They began to get new and interesting results, such as those of Enrico Fermi in Rome and of Ernest Lawrence in Berkeley, California. New research questions oriented toward the structure of atoms and particles emerged. This led to the development and the use of new laboratory techniques such as the Geiger-Müller counter in 1928—the first model was conceived before World War I—and bubble chambers such as the Wilson chamber and later particle accelerators.

Work in radioactivity, and particularly the discovery of isotopes, opened the door to a significant change in the definition of a chemical element and in the interpretation of the periodic table. Nevertheless, the traditional methods of chemistry, especially analytical methods to isolate and purify radioactive elements, still played an important role in scientists' daily activities. When Perey arrived at

Marie Curie's laboratory, Curie was working on an element called actinium, which had been discovered in 1899 by one of her earliest collaborators, the chemist André Debierne. It was a difficult element to isolate, in part because its properties were close to those of the rare earth family of elements. Most of the chemists' work dealt with the preparation of pure sources of the products of the disintegration of actinium, which took months, and with the magnetic spectroscopy of these daughter products' α-radiations. Perey was in charge of the preparation of solutions containing actinium, which required patience and a great deal of precision. Under the supervision of Curie herself, she developed a great talent for the preparation of radioactive sources, and she quickly became Curie's personal assistant. In 1934 the scientist, placing her confidence in Perey, asked her to prepare the most concentrated actiniferous sample ever prepared and to study the spectrum of actinium with Pieter Zeeman, a specialist in optical spectroscopy in Amsterdam. This was the last task Curie requested from her before her death caused by the ill effects of radiation on 4 July 1934. Perey spent four months in the Netherlands working with W. A. Lub, a chemist in Zeeman's laboratory, measuring the spectrum of actinium for the very first time.

Discovering the Missing Element. When she came back to the Institut du Radium, Perey worked under the direction of André Debierne, Curie's successor there. She studied the spectrum of two other radioactive elements, barium and strontium, and also continued preparing sources of actinium, notably for Salomon Rosenblum, who was interested in α-spectroscopy. He was a well-known physicist working in Bellevue, near Paris, at the Laboratoire du Grand Électro-aimant (The Big Electromagnet Laboratory) with a large electromagnet and had discovered the emission of long-range α-particles by radioactive elements in 1929. Perey first published as a contributor to his work.

At the Institut du Radium, Perey was regarded as a specialist in the preparation of actinium sources. Thus, when Debierne and Irène Joliot-Curie both decided to study the actinium family, albeit for different reasons, they independently asked Perey for actinium samples. After long and repetitive work, the young technician managed to get a sample as pure as possible, about ten micrograms of actinium in a few milligrams of lanthanum solution. But during the fractional crystallizations phase, she noticed anomalies in the B-emission of actinium's daughter products. At the end of 1938, she realized that this was due to an unknown radioactive substance formed from actinium by an α-decay. The half-life of this new element was about twenty-one minutes.

As Perey tried to study more precisely the chemical properties of this new element, she found that they perfectly matched the description of the element 87 predicted by Mendeleyev. She first called this element actinium K. It was one isotope of the only natural radioactive element not yet observed. All other elements still missing in Mendeleyev's table happened to be artificial radioactive elements. But Perey was merely a technician without a reputation as a scientist, and so it was the French Nobel Prize–winner Jean Perrin who announced this discovery to the French Académie des sciences on 9 January 1939. This was an important event in the field of radioactivity, as several physicists in Europe and in the United States had been looking for this element for years.

A Successful Scientific Career. The discovery of the new element changed Perey's status at the Institut du Radium. She was from then on regarded as an independent researcher, free to do her own work. From 1939 to 1941 she was mobilized by the French Ministre de la défense (Ministry of Defense) to study artificial radioactivity, which had been discovered by Irène and Frédéric Joliot-Curie in 1934. She worked more precisely on B-radiations of artificial elements. Perey also continued her work on actinium and actinium K. She collaborated with Marcel Lecoin, a French researcher at the Institut du Radium, and together they showed how actinium disintegrated into actinium K.

During World War II, Perey also carried on with her university studies. André Debierne and Irène Joliot-Curie encouraged her to pass certificates in general chemistry, general physiology, and general biology at the Faculté des sciences in Paris, which enabled her to prepare a PhD thesis and to obtain a grant from the France's Centre national de la recherche scientifique (National Center for Scientific Research). She presented her thesis at the Faculté des sciences in Paris on 21 March 1946. It dealt with the discovery of element 87. Debierne was the foreman of the jury. Irène Joliot-Curie and Pierre-Paul Grassé, a professor of zoology, were members of the board of examiners. At the end of her thesis, Perey suggested calling this element catium or francium in honor of her country, France. The name of the element was not determined until July 1947, when, in London, the International Commission of Chemistry finally adopted the latter, francium, and the symbol "Fr" for element 87.

From 1946 to 1949, Perey worked as a *maître de recherche* (research assistant) for the Centre national de la recherche scientifique, pursuing her research on physical and chemical properties of actinium and its daughter products. She also taught spectroscopy to researchers of the center. From then on, she was well-known and respected as a scientist and was invited to give lectures throughout Europe in Aarau, Lausanne, and Zürich, Switzerland; Liège, Belgium; and Amsterdam in the Netherlands in 1949, during the Congress of the International Commission of Chemistry. In 1950, she won the Wilde Prize of the French Académie des sciences for the discovery of francium.

On 10 March 1949, Perey was assigned a chair in nuclear chemistry at the Université de Strasbourg, France, with the charge to create a nuclear chemistry laboratory. At that time Strasbourg, being located next to the German border, was in a unique situation. During the war, it had been annexed to the German Reich and most of the researchers had taken refuge in the unoccupied part of France. The Germans had moved into the university and had created a Reichuniversität (state university) as a symbol of the Nazi's supremacy over the rest of Europe. In particular, they had set up an Institute of Medical Research (Medizinisches Forschungsinstitut) located within the public hospital, dedicated to nuclear medical research through the collaboration with biologists, physicists, and chemists. This institute had been well financed by the Nazis. The Germans had built a Cockroft & Walton accelerator, one of the most efficient instruments used at that time in nuclear physics. For technical reasons, the Germans could not use this machine before the end of the war. As they were forced to leave Strasbourg in a hurry, they abandoned all the technical installations, including the precious accelerator.

The French medical staff, having returned to Strasbourg in 1945, discovered what the Germans had built. Some physicists, biologists, chemists, and physicians quickly realized that it might be helpful to use the accelerator to produce artificial radioactive elements for biological research. The Centre national de la recherche scientifique, directed by Frédéric Joliot-Curie, was also very interested in this accelerator; it was a promising machine at a time when French nuclear research needed significant upgrading. After long and vehement discussions between the Université de Strasbourg and the Centre national de la recherche scientifique, they formed a committee composed of members from the Faculté de médecine, the Faculté de pharmacologie and the Faculté des sciences, as well as from the Centre national de la recherche scientifique and from the Commissariat à l'énergie atomique (Atomic Energy Commission), the new French institution in charge of nuclear energy. This commission then created an interdisciplinary institute, the Institut de recherches nucléaires (Institute of Nuclear Research), at the beginning of 1948, which marked the beginning of nuclear research in Strasbourg.

The researchers from Strasbourg also decided to call upon important individuals to direct the laboratories of the institute. Thus, a chair in nuclear chemistry was offered to Perey, as she had been working on the use of radioactive labels in biology in the Parisian scientific community. With the help of her colleague, André Coche, also of the Institut du Radium of Paris, she began teaching nuclear chemistry at the Faculté des sciences of the Université de Strasbourg in September 1950, and she set up her laboratory in a building that was renovated with subsidies from the French Ministry of National Education (Ministère de l'éducation nationale). Perey's laboratory expanded very quickly. In 1951 two young researchers joined her staff, composed of only few technicians, but a few years afterward about ten students, researchers, and lecturers were working together in the laboratory. In 1955 the number of students doubled in one year, a rise due, in part, to a teaching reform in French universities.

The research in the laboratory took two main directions. Perey studied actinium and francium's properties and worked with biologists on biological applications of nuclear chemistry. For instance, they used radioactive elements produced by the accelerator for a series of experiences on rats, seeking to compare the way the francium and other radioactive isotopes could fix on cancerous cells to be used a radioactive tracer. Concurrently, Coche was in charge of an electronic group and was responsible for the electronic system of the laboratory. He elaborated particle detectors and studied nuclear physics such as spectroscopy. The needs of the research group continued to grow. A new research centre, made up of four laboratories—a department of nuclear physics; a department of corpuscular physics; the department of nuclear chemistry, still directed by Perey; and a department of nuclear biology—was built in the suburbs of Strasbourg and opened on 20 May 1960. Perey played an important role in the establishment of this center.

Victim of Radiation. Unfortunately, Perey had to stop working a few months after the inauguration of the new center. She had been quite sick for years. Her body had been irradiated at the Institut du Radium, and she found it increasingly difficult to pursue her research because of frequent attacks of neuralgia. In 1951 she was deeply affected by the death of her mother, who was living with her in Strasbourg. From 1955 to 1957, her state improved and she was able to develop her laboratory. At the end of 1957, she had a particularly bad attack and complained about her head and shoulders. Physicians in Strasbourg did not know the cause of the attack and were not able to treat her. She, however, was persuaded that her illness was due to the effects of radiation. Her suspicions were confirmed in 1958 by Dr. Shields Warren, a physician from Boston she met at a congress in Geneva, Switzerland, on the peaceful applications of the nuclear sciences in Geneva. He had treated the Japanese victims of Hiroshima and Nagasaki and was able to measure the quantity of radioactivity in her

bones. After this meeting she went to Paris for treatment and then to a health clinic in Nice.

Her medical treatments were very costly and Perey faced financial problems. She attempted in vain to have her disease recognized as an occupational one, but she did not manage to obtain an extended sick leave. Perey had first a bone cancer (which then became generalized) and the symptoms she had were less known and could be attributed to other pathologies. The physicians could clearly identify her disease only when she got a body scan in 1958 by Dr. Warren in Switzerland (this was a very recent technology and not used yet in France). They realized then that her body was completely contaminated by actinium. She remained the head of the laboratory in Strasbourg until her death. In December 1959, Gabriel Foëx, a professor at the Université de Strasbourg and a member of the French Académie des sciences, asked the academy to allocate a prize to Perey in honor of her work on francium, arguing that she had served the state and that the state was indebted to her. In 1960, Perey received the Prix Leconte (Leconte Prize) of the academy, which helped her financially for a time.

The media were greatly interested in Perey's life. Some French popular magazines, as well as the European press, wanted to interview her and visit her new laboratory. They presented her as a new Marie Curie, as a heroine of science and victim of her research at the same time. At one point, the media coverage was so intense that Perey began refusing interviews. Although she had ceased her scientific activity, she continued to be awarded professional and public honors, such as the great medal of Paris in 1964 and the silver medal of the Université de Nice in 1969. She stayed in Nice for more than ten years, growing continually weaker, before dying of widespread cancer in a hospital in Louveciennes, near Paris, on 13 May 1975.

BIBLIOGRAPHY

A complete bibliography of Perey is available at the Université Louis Pasteur of Strasbourg, France, where some professional and personal archives of Perey have been collected. The inventory of these papers and instruments is in "Fonds Marguerite Perey, répertoire numérique détaillé, 1929–1998," available from http://www.hp-physique.org.

WORKS BY PEREY

"Sur un élément 87 dérivé de l'actinium." *Comptes-rendus Hebdomadaires des Séances de l'Académie des Sciences* 208 (1939): 97–99.

"Méthodes chimiques et physiques de marquage en biologie." *Année Biologique* 24 (1948): 1–14.

"Nouvelle méthode de fractionnement des terres rares." *Journal de Chimie Physique* 46 (1949): 485–493.

"Le francium: élément 87." *Bulletin de la Société Chimique de France* 18 (1951): 779–785.

With André Chevallier and Charles Lausecker. "Sur la fixation, comparée de l'actinium K, du césium 134 et du rubidium 86 dans les sarcomes et les granulomes expérimentaux chez le rat." *Comptes-rendus des Séances de la Société de Biologie de France* 146 (1952): 1141–1152.

OTHER SOURCES

Adloff, Jean-Pierre, and George B. Kauffman. "Marguerite Perey (1909–1975): A Personal Retrospective Tribute on the 30th Anniversary of Her Death." *Chemical Educator* 10 (2005): 378–386.

———, and George B. Kauffman. "Francium (Atomic Number 87), the Last Discovered Natural Element." *Chemical Educator* 10 (2005): 387–394.

———, and George B. Kauffman. "Triumph over Prejudice: The Election of Radiochemist Marguerite Perey (1909–1975) to the French Académie des Sciences." *Chemical Educator* 10 (2005): 395–399.

Kastler, Alfred. "Notice nécrologique sur Marguerite Perey (1909–1975)." *Comptes-rendus Hebdomadaires des Séances de l'Académie des Sciences, Vie Académique* 280 (21 May 1975): 4–6.

Anne Fellinger
Soraya Boudia

PERUTZ, MAX FERDINAND (*b.* Vienna, Austria, 19 May 1914; *d.* Cambridge, United Kingdom, 6 February 2002), *x-ray crystallography, molecular biology, hemoglobin.*

Perutz dedicated a large part of his long scientific career to unraveling the molecular structure and function of hemoglobin, the protein of red blood cells. In this work he made pioneering use of x-ray crystallography. He was a co-recipient of the 1962 Nobel Prize for Chemistry and the founder and first chairman of the Medical Research Council Laboratory of Molecular Biology in Cambridge, which produced a string of Nobel Prize winners.

Education and Early Career. Born into an affluent Viennese family of textile industrialists, Perutz soon resolved not to step into the family business and instead pursue a career in science. He studied chemistry in his hometown. In 1936, after graduation, he joined John Desmond Bernal's Crystallographic Department at the Cavendish laboratory in Cambridge following an introduction by his teacher Hermann Mark. Perutz had to learn x-ray crystallography from scratch by working on some silicate mineral fragments. Yet from the beginning his aspiration was to work on biological material.

A few years before Perutz joined the laboratory, Bernal, together with Dorothy Crowfoot (later Hodgkin), had obtained the first sharp x-ray diffraction images of a protein using crystals in their mother liquid instead of the usual dry crystals. In principle, this observation opened the way to the determination of the atomic structure of proteins. Proteins were considered to hold the key to all life processes, including inheritance; knowing their structure promised to provide clues to their function. Yet by the time Perutz joined the laboratory, Bernal, a key exponent of the scientific Left, was increasingly taken up with political activities connected to the rising threat of a Fascist war. When he moved to London in 1938 to take up a chair at Birkbeck College, Perutz stayed on at the Cavendish. By that time he had settled on a diffraction analysis of hemoglobin as the topic for his PhD thesis. The suggestion had come from the Prague biochemist Felix Haurowitz whom Perutz had asked for advice. Haurowitz had observed that hemoglobin showed a change in crystal form under the microscope when moving from the oxygenated to the deoxygenated form. Gilbert Adair from the Physiology Department in Cambridge supplied the first crystals.

Fortunately for Perutz, Bernal's departure coincided with Lawrence Bragg's appointment as Ernest Rutherford's successor to the Cavendish Chair in Cambridge. Bragg became excited at the prospect of extending the method he himself had first applied to propose a structure for common salt some twenty-five years before, to the fantastically complex structure of proteins. When later in 1938 Adolf Hitler annexed Austria and Perutz became an émigré, Bragg obtained a grant from the Rockefeller Foundation that supported Perutz until the end of the war. It also enabled Perutz to have his Jewish parents, Hugo and Adele Perutz, come to Britain and thus escape deportation.

Perutz was to dedicate most of his scientific career to the study of the structure and function of the hemoglobin molecule, but he had certainly not anticipated this at the time. The original aims were rather modest, although the hopes to achieve a significant result ran high. To prepare and mount the hemoglobin crystals, determine the dimensions and hydration of the crystals, and study the effects of denaturation was enough to acquire a PhD. Perutz's dissertation also included the discussion of a two-dimensional vector analysis (also known as Patterson analysis) of a hemoglobin derivative calculated by Dennis Riley of Dorothy Hodgkin's group in Oxford.

Comparison with Hodgkin's Patterson analysis of insulin led Perutz to confirm that protein molecules were composed of small subunits, arranged in a regular manner. This was a common assumption at the time. It also led crystallographers to believe that the knowledge of the structure of one protein would provide decisive clues for the structure of all proteins. Although these expectations proved wrong, they provided the motivation for researchers including

Max Ferdinand Perutz. AP IMAGES.

Perutz to approach the problem; without those expectations they might have been discouraged.

Internment and Secret War Work. Perutz submitted his doctoral dissertation on the structure of hemoglobin in the spring of 1940. A few months later, with mounting fears of a German invasion, he was rounded up with other "enemy aliens." After prolonged stays in various remote parts of Britain, twelve hundred internees including Perutz were herded on a large troopship that eventually brought them to an internment camp in Canada (while still at sea they learned that another troopship crammed with internees had been sunk by a German U-boat; more than six hundred of the fifteen hundred people on board lost their lives). The humiliating and uncomfortable conditions did not lead to complete despair. With his freshly gained PhD Perutz found himself the doyen of the camp's scholars and set out to organize a camp university. The staff included several future fellows of the Royal Society, among them the mathematician and cosmologist Hermann Bondi, who was to become chief scientific adviser to the Ministry of Defence, the astronomer Thomas Gold; and Klaus Fuchs, who was to join the Manhattan Project and became an "atom spy," a role to which he was led not as a German but as a communist.

Unknown to Perutz, in the meantime his British colleagues were agitating for his and other internees' release. He was offered the choice to return to England or take up a professorship at the New School for Social Research in New York, organized as part of a rescue campaign by the Rockefeller Foundation for its grantees. Undeterred by the perils of the transatlantic passage, Perutz opted to return to England. The whole adventure had lasted about eight months.

Perutz resumed his research at the Cavendish, but before long was called to participate at a secret wartime project code-named Habakkuk. The plan, conceived by the maverick Geoffrey Pyke, scientific advisor of General Mountbatten, chief of Combined Operations, consisted in building an airplane base made of reinforced ice in the Atlantic. Perutz, who before the war had combined his (lifelong) passion for the mountains and for science by participating in a scientific expedition to the Alps to study the crystalline structure of ice in glaciers, was called to the project as an expert. Working for several months in a cold room at minus 20 degrees Celsius beneath Smithfield Market in London (the rooms were normally used for meat storage), Perutz and his team managed to develop a mixture of ice and wood pulp as strong as concrete; the reinforced ice became known as pykrete.

After a successful demonstration of the qualities of pykrete to Franklin Roosevelt and Winston Churchill at their meeting in Quebec in August 1943, Habakkuk gained top priority. The British team was ordered to continue work in Washington. For the overseas mission Perutz was rapidly naturalized and received a British passport. Yet by the time he reached America, Mountbatten had been ordered to Southeast Asia. Having lost its strongest supporter, Habakkuk slid down the priority list and eventually was abandoned. A further reason for the demise of the project was that the rapidly increasing range of aircraft made artificial landing strips in the Atlantic superfluous.

In January 1944, Perutz once more returned to his research in the Cavendish. Later he gave a detailed and humorous account of his wartime experience as enemy alien and as scientist on a secret wartime project. "Enemy Alien" first appeared in the *New Yorker* in August 1985 and established his fame as a writer. It has since been reprinted several times.

Structure and Function of Hemoglobin. In the last years of the war, Perutz's work on the structure of hemoglobin was the only piece of pure research still pursued in the Cavendish. Blood and its products, however, were intensively studied in other laboratories because of their relevance to wartime medicine, and Perutz was part of an active network of Cambridge researchers working on different aspects of hemoglobin. The informal group was held together by the physiologist Joseph Barcroft, a pioneer in the field and an inspired teacher.

After the war, John Kendrew, a physical chemist who had occupied high offices in operational research during the war and, while on a common mission in Ceylon, had been convinced by Bernal of the promises of protein crystallography, joined Perutz to do a PhD. (Although working closely with Perutz, Kendrew was officially supervised by William T. Taylor, head of the crystallography division at the Cavendish; like most professional crystallographers Taylor regarded protein crystallography as a hopeless undertaking, but still accepted the formal agreement.) Kendrew first embarked on a comparative analysis of fetal and adult hemoglobin, but later switched to the simpler protein myoglobin, the oxygen carrier in muscle.

Although Perutz now had a collaborator, his own future was still uncertain. With the end of the war, the Rockefeller grant had run out. Bragg had obtained a two-year Imperial Chemical Industries fellowship for Perutz, but his aim to secure a university post for his protégé looked increasingly bleak. At this critical juncture, the Cambridge parasitologist and biochemist David Keilin, a strong supporter of Perutz's work, suggested to Bragg to apply to the Medical Research Council (MRC) for funding. The successful application led to the establishment of the MRC Unit for the Study of Molecular Structure of Biological Systems with Perutz as its director. Among the first recruits were Hugh Huxley, Francis Crick, James Watson (who joined as a visitor) and, somewhat later, Sydney Brenner.

In 1949 Perutz published a paper in which he proposed the "pill box" or "hat-box" model of hemoglobin. It featured the polypeptide chains running in parallel bundles. Crick, although still a newcomer in the field, forcefully criticized the model and the assumption of a regular arrangement on which it was based. Crick's attack produced some turmoil, but Perutz recognized the force of his argument. He developed a strong respect for Crick's sharp judgment and, on several occasions, defended him against the grudge of the Cavendish head who resented his irreverent behavior.

The turning point in Perutz's endeavor to unravel the structure of the complex hemoglobin model came in 1953, when he found a solution to the so-called phase problem. To derive the structure of a molecule from its diffraction pattern both the intensity as well as the phase of each spot were required. Yet while the intensities could be directly measured on the diffraction pictures (up to the mid-1950s this was done by eye), the phases had to be established by other methods. To circumvent the phase problem, Perutz and his colleagues used the Patterson function. It allowed them to calculate the distances between atoms on the basis of the intensities alone, but it left ample space for interpretation regarding the actual position of the atoms in space. The infamous hat-box model still relied on that method.

Perutz now managed to attach a heavy atom (mercury) to the hemoglobin molecule. From the difference produced in the diffraction pattern he was able to deduce the phase of the reflections. The method had been known since the 1930s, but it had only been used for small molecules. Although the suggestion to apply the method to proteins dated from the same period, its applicability had not been proved. The problem consisted, firstly, in finding a heavy metal compound that could be attached to a specific site without altering the arrangement of the other atoms in the molecule and, secondly, in estimating with sufficient accuracy the overall changes in intensity produced by the heavy atoms. In Bragg's judgment, Perutz's skill in this last respect was "probably unique" at the time (Bragg, 1965, p. 12). To this day, the isomorphous replacement method is considered the key method to determine the crystal structure of proteins.

Kendrew, working on the smaller myoglobin molecule, was the first to take full advantage of the new method. In 1958, he presented the first model ever of a globular protein derived by direct structure determination. The model showed the general outline of the

Max Perutz. *Max Perutz (left) with fellow Nobel Prize winner Paul Kendrew, 1962.* © **HULTON-DEUTSCH COLLECTION/CORBIS.**

molecule; a second model at atomic resolution followed two years later. In the same year Perutz presented the first model of hemoglobin at 5.5 Ångstrøm. Its four subunits proved to be closely related to the myoglobin molecule. The white-and-black disk model built of thermosetting plastic is still widely reproduced.

The determination of any of these protein structures could not have been contemplated without the use of ever more powerful electronic computers. Perutz initially distrusted the new calculating devices and resisted resorting to the experimental digital computers developed at the nearby Mathematical Laboratory. Eventually he came around to recognize their usefulness, but he freely admitted that he was always hopeless at computing. He never made use of the machine himself and rather left this part of the work to the younger people in his group.

Perutz and Kendrew shared the 1962 Nobel Prize for Chemistry for their work on the structure of proteins.

However, for Perutz the challenge posed by hemoglobin continued. He realized that to understand the oxygen-binding function of hemoglobin, including its cooperative effect, he needed an atomic model of both the oxygenated and deoxygenated forms of hemoglobin. This immense task involved measuring several hundred thousand reflections, stretching even the patience of a crystallographer. Perutz and his collaborators completed it in 1970, well thirty-three years after Perutz had taken the first x-ray picture of the molecule. Close examination of the two models led Perutz and his colleagues to propose a cooperative mechanism that saw the different parts of the model clicking back and forth between the two forms. The proposed mechanism included relative movement of the four subunits as well as conformational change of the subunits when oxygen was bound. It beautifully illustrated, and refined, the mechanism of conformational change (or allostery) postulated by the French biochemist Jacques

Monod a few years earlier. For his argument, intended to explain regulatory functions in enzymes, Monod had used hemoglobin as a model. As a result, and to Perutz's delight, hemoglobin was elevated to the status of an "honorary enzyme."

Another important resource for Perutz's work was the extensive clinical and biochemical knowledge of abnormal hemoglobins gathered by Hermann Lehmann, professor of clinical biochemistry at Cambridge. By building the known amino acid substitutions into the hemoglobin model, clinical symptoms could be explained in molecular terms; at the same time the functional knowledge of the clinic provided decisive clues for deriving the working mechanism of the molecule. The two researchers published a paper (1968) announcing the new field of molecular pathology. Perutz was deeply satisfied that his research was becoming medically important. Although details of Perutz's proposed mechanism of the hemoglobin model were contested, the model as a whole stood the test of time.

Laboratory of Molecular Biology. Besides remaining deeply committed to work at the bench, Perutz was an effective institute builder. Throughout the 1950s the MRC Unit at the Cavendish under his direction grew in size and importance. Apart from the protein work that was attracting more researchers, Watson's arrival in 1951 stirred Crick into a collaboration on the structure of DNA that led to the proposal of the complementary double helical structure of the molecule in 1953. Although only time would confer on it the iconic place it later gained, the DNA model was regarded early on as an important achievement that confirmed the power of structure-function analysis.

Watson's later account of the discovery in the best-selling *The Double Helix* (1968) put Perutz in the awkward position of appearing as the person who passed on decisive data gained by the London crystallographer Rosalind Franklin contained in a report on her unit's work to an MRC committee of which he was a member. In a letter to *Science* Perutz made clear that the report was not confidential and the data had been presented at talks before, although he acknowledged that as a matter of courtesy he should have asked the London unit for permission. Watson responded by apologizing for having misrepresented the incident.

The double-helix work gave rise to further research in the Cambridge unit on the mechanism by which DNA is translated into proteins. With the work and the number of researchers it attracted expanding, the unit outgrew its place in the physics laboratory. At this critical juncture Perutz, joining forces with the Cambridge protein biochemist Fred Sanger, applied to the MRC for a new Laboratory of Molecular Biology (known as the LMB). The

laboratory opened on the outskirts of Cambridge in 1962. Perutz became its first chair and for seventeen years light-handedly guided the institution, which quickly established itself as a key center of the burgeoning new field of molecular biology. The memorandum written to argue for the new laboratory became the basis for a series of lectures and finally a book on *Proteins and Nucleic Acids: Structure and Function* (1962), which Perutz liked to regard as the first textbook of the new discipline.

Perutz's approach in leading the laboratory consisted in keeping administration and formal paperwork at a minimum. Asked for the recipe for a successful laboratory such as the LMB, Perutz's usual answer was that the key lay in picking good people and helping them get what they needed to develop their work and for the rest let them follow their own interests. He also believed that seeing the leading people of a lab doing work at the bench helped boost working morale.

Despite disliking committee work, Perutz agreed to act as first chair of the European Molecular Biology Organization, founded in 1963. The main aim of the organization, formed by molecular biologists, was to fund a European fellowship, training, and travel program. However, Perutz remained critical of the plan to found a European molecular biology laboratory, which he thought would become too much a bureaucratic structure and would divert capable people away from existing laboratories. At times Perutz was disappointed that he missed out on a university career, but in later years he increasingly saw the advantages of being able to dedicate all his time to research and to building up the LMB.

Active Retirement. Perutz retired as chair of the LMB in 1979, but his research work continued. Initially hemoglobin remained at the heart of the problems he tackled. One project concerned the adaptation of hemoglobin in different species. Another, in the end unsuccessful, project aimed at identifying drugs that would improve the solubility of sickle cell hemoglobin. However, the work on ligand binding to hemoglobin led to other clinical investigations. Aged eighty, Perutz for the first time strayed away from hemoglobin and, with several collaborators, started a series of original studies on glutamine repeats in proteins connected to neurodegenerative conditions such as Huntington disease. They showed that proteins carrying the repeats form aggregates that lead to neural cell death. In a paper published shortly before his death, Perutz and his coauthor linked the onset of Huntington's disease to the length of the glutamine repeat.

In his later years Perutz became a regular contributor to the *London Review of Books* and the *New York Review of Books*. Scientific biographies fascinated him most. He also wrote autobiographical pieces and personal vignettes of scientists he knew, and engaged with political and moral issues, including the organization and freedom of science, population politics, food production, nuclear energy, and human rights. Many of these topics he addressed in public speeches. In all his writings he emphasized the passionate and heroic aspects of scientific research as well as the humanizing influence of science in society. His essays were collected in two volumes, *Is Science Necessary?* (1989) and *I Wish I'd Made You Angry Earlier* (1998), edited by himself. In 1997 he was awarded the Lewis Thomas Prize of the Rockefeller University, which honors the scientist as poet.

This was the last in a long series of awards and honors. He was elected a fellow of the Royal Society in 1954 and received the Royal Medal of the Royal Society in 1971 and the Copley Medal of the Royal Society in 1979. He was made a Companion of the British Empire in 1963 and a Companion of Honour in 1975, and was appointed to the Order of Merit in 1988. Among others he was a member of the U.S. National Academy of Sciences and a foreign member of the Pontifical Academy of Sciences.

He married Gisela Peiser in 1942 and had a daughter (Vivien) and a son (Robin). He died of cancer.

BIBLIOGRAPHY

The memoir of the Royal Society (see below) includes a full bibliography.

WORKS BY PERUTZ

The Crystal Structure of Methaemoglobin. PhD diss., University of Cambridge, 1940.

"Recent Developments in the X-Ray Study of Haemoglobin." In *Haemoglobin: A Symposium Based on a Conference Held at Cambridge in June 1948 in Memory of Sir Joseph Barcroft,* edited by Francis J. Roughton and John C. Kendrew London: Butterworths Scientific Publications, 1949.

With Michael G. Rossmann, Ann F. Cullis, Hilary Muirhead, et al. "Structure of Haemoglobin: A Three-Dimensional Fourier Synthesis at 5.5 Å. Resolution, Obtained by X-Ray Analysis." *Nature* 185 (1960): 416–422.

Proteins and Nucleic Acids: Structure and Function. Amsterdam: Elsevier, 1962.

With Hermann Lehmann. "Molecular Pathology of Human Haemoglobin." *Nature* 219 (1968): 402–409.

With Maurice H. F. Wilkins and James D. Watson. "DNA Helix." *Science* 164 (1969): 1537–1539.

"Stereochemistry of Cooperative Effects in Haemoglobin." *Nature* 228 (1970): 726–739.

Haemoglobin: Mr Max Perutz Interviewed by Mr H. Judson, 13 November 1987. Video interview. Biochemical Society. Available from http://www.filmandsound.ac.uk/.

Is Science Necessary? Essays on Science and Scientists. New York: E.P. Dutton, 1989. Includes the autobiographical essay "Enemy Alien."

Science Is No Quiet Life. Videotape of a lecture on his scientific career held at the Kelvin Club in Peterhouse, Cambridge, 12 November 1996. Available from Peterhouse College.

Science Is Not a Quiet Life: Unravelling the Atomic Mechanism of Haemoglobin. London: Imperial College Press, 1997. A collection of all Perutz's major scientific papers, with introduction.

I Wish I'd Made You Angry Earlier: Essays on Science, Scientists, and Humanity. Cold Spring Harbor, NY: Cold Spring Harbor Press, 1998. A collection of his major reviews.

"Interview with Max Perutz: Discoverer of the Structure of Haemoglobin." Vega Science Trust interviews with Max Perutz, 2001. Video excerpts available from http://www.vega.org.uk/video/programme/1.

With Alan H. Windle. "Cause of Neural Death in Neurodegenerative Disease Attributable to Expansion of Glutamine Repeats." *Nature* 412 (2001): 143–144.

OTHER SOURCES

Blow, David M. "Max Ferdinand Perutz OM CH CBE 19 May 1914–6 February 2002." *Biographical Memoirs of Fellows of the Royal Society* 50 (2004): 227–256. Includes a microfiche with a full bibliography of Max Perutz's publications. A photocopy is available from the Royal Society Library.

Bragg, William Lawrence. "First Stages in the X-Ray Analysis of Proteins." *Reports on Progress in Physics* 28 (1965): 1–16.

Ferry, Georgina. *Max Perutz and the Secret of Life.* London: Chatto & Windus, 2007.

Kendrew, John C., Gerhard Bodo, Howard M. Dintzis, et al. "A Three-Dimensional Model of the Myoglobin Molecule Obtained by X-Ray Analysis." *Nature* 181 (1958): 662–666.

———, Richard E. Dickerson, Bror E. Strandberg, et al. "Structure of Myoglobin: A Three-Dimensional Fourier Synthesis at 2 Å. Resolution." *Nature* 185 (1960): 422–427.

Olby, Robert. "Perutz, Max Ferdinand (1914–2002)." In *Oxford Dictionary of National Biography.* Online ed., edited by Lawrence Goldman. Oxford: Oxford University Press, 2006. Available from http://www.oxforddnb.com.

Watson, James D. *The Double Helix: A Personal Account of the Discovery of the Structure of DNA.* New York: Atheneum, 1968.

———, and Francis H. C. Crick. "Molecular Structure of Nucleic Acids: A Structure for Deoxyribose Nucleic Acid." *Nature* 171 (1953): 737–738.

Soraya de Chadarevian

PETTERSSEN, SVERRE (*b.* Hadsel, Norway, 19 February 1898; *d.* London, United Kingdom, 31 December 1974), *synoptic and dynamic meteorology, weather forecasting, aerology, wartime meteorology.*

While theoretical meteorologists looked at Petterssen as a practical weather man, practitioners looked at him as a theoretician with some practical capability. But in reality he was both, which qualified him for important meteorological tasks during World War II, most notably the preparation of the weather forecast for the D-day landing 6 June 1944. Petterssen's main achievement, however, was his teaching and a renowned textbook, which aimed at building a bridge between theory and practice in weather forecasting.

Education and Inspiration. Petterssen was born to Edward H. Petterssen and Petronella Olava. He grew up in a fishing community in the Lofoten islands in northernmost Norway. Life was hard, opportunities meager, but challenging. As a young boy he followed the adult fishermen in open boats out to the fishing banks. He would have continued in his forefathers' paths, had it not been for his gift and interest in the mathematical sciences.

In 1911 the family moved to Trondheim in central Norway, one of the major cities with its own university and high schools. His intellect earned him a scholarship to support his high school studies in physical sciences. To help him further economically in his education he attended an army school from 1915 to 1918 and earned the rank of sergeant before entering the University of Oslo.

In the summer of 1923 Petterssen, upon the advice of his geography professor, took part in a four-week international meteorological seminar in Bergen. It was organized by professor Vilhelm Bjerknes who had found that storms develop in the border zones (frontal zones) of major air masses of different densities. Now he was interested in attracting young talents to his meteorology group, which was working on guidelines that would help to predict storms more accurately.

Weather forecasting was a thankless job, mostly performed by poorly educated civil servants relying on experience, intuition, and luck. For Bjerknes and his collaborators it was a science in which methods could be taught, experience accumulated, and physically based causes and effects derived. The defining moment for Petterssen during the course came when one of the teachers, Tor Bergeron, introduced him to maps of a dramatic weather event, a rapid storm development in October 1921, which Vilhelm Bjerknes's methods had managed to forecast. Bergeron's discussion inspired Petterssen to become a meteorologist, to work on the problem of quantified weather predictions, and to explore the limits of predictability.

Work as a Weather Forecaster. After a brief interlude as a forecaster in Oslo (1924–1926) where he took his BSc in 1924 and MSc in 1926, he moved to the Geophysical Institute in Tromsø in northernmost Norway. There he was instrumental in the successful forecast for the airship *Norge* crossing the North Pole from Spitsbergen to Alaska

with the famous Danish explorer Roald Amundsen and the equally famous, but also adventurous, Italian explorer Umberto Nobile.

Two years later tragedy struck when Nobile, in a partly politically motivated expedition, reached the North Pole in an Italian-built airship, but did not follow Petterssen's advice on the return trip, and ran into adverse weather. The highly publicized rescue efforts resulted in the death of Amundsen and others.

When the Tromsø bureau split into the Weather Forecasting Center for Northern Norway and the Northern Light observatory in 1928, Petterssen moved back to Bergen. There he replaced his old teacher Bergeron, who had begun some international engagements. In 1931 Petterssen was promoted to regional director for west Norway after Jacob Bjerknes.

The culture at Vilhelm Bjerknes's weather service in Bergen encouraged cross-fertilization, to actively bridge the demarcation line between practical and academic meteorologists. The experiences the forecasters accumulated during a day's shift were discussed from a scientific point of view; and new scientific ideas were examined to see if they could be included in the forecast routines.

Petterssen became the champion teacher with his ability to formulate working methods and principles that could be assimilated by other forecasters. Petterssen developed a series of simple mathematical expressions for the velocity, acceleration, and rate of development of weather fronts and pressure centers both at surface and upper levels. They did not necessarily increase the knowledge or understanding of atmospheric motion, but supplied the forecasters with workable tools to compute the movement and rate of development of storms. His work on the kinematics of the pressure field, summarized in his 1933 PhD thesis at Oslo University, was to see application in forecast offices in the coming years. As the amount and quality of observations from the atmosphere increased, it would become possible to make more extensive atmospheric maps, even in three dimensions.

Many prominent foreign meteorologists came to Bergen in the 1930s, several from the United States and Canada. In 1935 Sverre Petterssen was invited to spend almost a year in North America to give nationwide courses. When he returned in March 1936 he started to work on a professional textbook that would be published in 1940 with the title *Weather Analysis and Forecasting*, together with a more elementary *Introduction to Meteorology* (1941).

During a 1939 meeting in Berlin, where he was elected president of the Committee for Maritime Meteorology, he learned that Germany had educated 2,700 meteorologists, ten times more than the rest of Europe and the United States together, most of them with a doctoral degree.

Just before the war broke out Petterssen left Bergen and went to the Massachusetts Institute of Technology in Cambridge, where he replaced Carl-Gustaf Rossby as professor of meteorology. His warning about the mobilization of thousands of German meteorologists at first fell on deaf ears, until early in 1940 when thanks to Captain Arthur Merewether, the head of the U.S. Army Air Corps Weather Service, Petterssen was encouraged to start comprehensive weather courses. In 1941 he had 96 student forecasters, with 155 planned to come the following year. Pearl Harbor would accelerate this educational development but by then Petterssen had gone to the United Kingdom.

The War Years. In August 1941 Petterssen was asked by the exiled Norwegian government in London to come to England to the Central Forecasting Office (CFO) located at the United Kingdom Meteorological Office in Dunstable, to help in the weather forecasting for the war effort. Petterssen, formally an officer in the Norwegian Air Force, but in effect a civilian, made secret arrangements for getting certain Norwegian meteorologists into England. Many eventually crossed over both from Norway and Sweden. Petterssen soon became a reinforcement to the team at the CFO and was a driving force in the initiation and elaboration of novel techniques of upper-air analysis and forecasting which were vital for the operations of the air forces.

Petterssen issued the forecast for the successful air attack against the German destroyer *Tirpitz* in 1942, which had sought shelter in a Norwegian fjord near Trondheim. Relying on his childhood acquaintance with the area and some scattered reconnaissance photos he was able to infer that a light breeze would develop and blow away *Tirpitz*'s fog cover and pave the way for a successful attack. An attempt by Norwegian commandos and British marines to destroy the German heavy-water facility near Vemork, Norway, in November 1942 failed disastrously because the group had ignored Petterssen's warning about adverse weather.

The U.S. Army asked for his advice on vehicle traction in snow (he conducted field experiments on this) and the U.S. Navy on marine forecasting problems. In 1944 he was called to the Mediterranean to forecast for the successful invasion at the Anzio beachhead on April 22. In June the same year Petterssen was in the team of British and American meteorologists who successfully advised General Dwight D. Eisenhower on the D-day landing in Normandy.

A major bombing mission in the Balkans in early 1944 turned into a disaster because of unexpected strong upper winds. Petterssen taught pilots and meteorologists, mainly from theoretical viewpoints, to watch out for very strong upper-level winds above anticyclones of a specific internal thermal structure. When the war effort became more concentrated in the Pacific, Petterssen was sent there. During a course in Hawaii, he again warned about strong upper-level westerly winds of possibly 100 meters per second over Japan. He was not quite believed by the audience, some of whom would soon experience exactly this phenomenon on their air missions during winter 1945.

Administrator and Teacher. During their occupation of Norway from 1940 to 1945, the Germans had established an effective telecommunication system for meteorology, a rather good network of radiosonde (weather balloon) stations and airport observation stations. When the war was over Petterssen returned to Norway to reorganize, direct, and expand the Norwegian Weather Service, in particular to meet the demands of aviation. The task offered lots of responsibilities and good pay but he was afraid that he would end up with too much administrative work.

After a short period as advisor to the Indian government early in 1948, he at first planned to accept a new chair in meteorology at Copenhagen University. This was abandoned when the Cold War convinced him to take up a renewed career in America, first as director of science services of the U.S. Air Force Weather Service in the period 1948–1952. From 1946 to 1951 Petterssen was president of the International Aerological Commission.

The arduous task of organization and administration did not leave as much time as he would have liked to study and write. His love for research and teaching again became too strong and he accepted an invitation in 1953 to become a professor at the University of Chicago, where he served as chair of the Department of Meteorology from 1959 to 1961, and then the Department of Geophysical Sciences until his retirement in 1963. He continued over the years to serve as an interim consultant to the U.S. armed services.

At the University of Chicago he founded a Weather Forecasting Research Center and set up a program to investigate the general question of storm development: its dynamics, energetics, and synoptic manifestations. In his later work he combined physical, dynamical, and kinematical principles with analysis of particular cases to obtain new results on the general circulation, propagation, and growth of jet-stream waves in relation to intensifications of cyclones. Inspired by similar work done by the British meteorologist R. C. Sutcliffe, Petterssen (1955) presented a development equation which in four terms expressed different dynamical-physical characteristics or processes crucial for the cyclone development.

Petterssen's greatest fame rests with his major work *Weather Analysis and Forecasting*, a revised and updated version of his 1940 textbook expanded into two volumes. Issued in 1956, it is unique in its combination of basic science and technical application to give a coherent, although perhaps not complete, picture of meteorology and weather forecasting, presented in language and style of great clarity and almost artistic quality.

In hindsight it could be said that his textbook came too late. The work on computer-based forecasts had just started. Maturing into the postwar period of mathematical models and high-speed computers he might readily have entered this field; he was well qualified to do so, but characteristically he preferred to make his own approaches. As a part of the celebration of the Vilhelm Bjerknes centenary he presented an investigation of cyclone developments over the North Atlantic, inspired by the Bergen School (Petterssen et al., 1962). His work led ultimately (Petterssen and Smebye, 1971) to the recognition of two distinct types of extratropical cyclone development processes, one due to local influences, the other due to forcing from upstream influences. A planned investigation into the mechanism of indirect circulation, where sinking warm air and rising cold air, in discord with the schoolbook scenario, sharpens the thermal contrast during the intensification of cyclone, was never completed.

His Last Years. Petterssen was president of the American Metrological Society (1958–1959) and in 1962 became a panelist member of President John F. Kennedy's Scientific Advisory Committee for the atmospheric sciences. After his retirement he served as scientific attaché to the Scandinavian countries at the U.S. Embassy to Sweden in Stockholm from 1963 to 1965. Although he moved in October 1965 with his wife to live his last years in London, he still kept up his American connections and was up to 1971 an invited lecturer to several universities.

Numerous awards were bestowed on Petterssen: in 1948 the Buys Ballot Gold Medal and in 1951 the USAF Distinguished Service Award. In 1965 he was honored with the World Meteorological Organization Gold Medal and in 1969 with the Symons Gold Medal by the Royal Meteorological Society for "his outstanding contributions to the science of meteorology and weather forecasting" (*Quarterly Journal of the Royal Meteorological Society,* 1969).

Petterssen was a man of vitality, a lively philosopher, a bon vivant and a friendly humorous companion with an intriguing air of deep understanding and a neat turn of irony. He was "fun to be with." Students looked forward to his classes because they were spiked with bons mots and other commentary on men and affairs. Petterssen said at the end of his life that he certainly had not got where he was by being methodical. He was not the type of scholar who pursues knowledge for its own sake. Knowledge had to have application, purpose, and fit into a scheme.

Maybe he felt like many other progressive meteorologists of his generation: they had much interest in the new ideas, but, at the same time, felt an undercurrent of regret. With the arrival of the computer, days of the meteorological maestro were drawing to a close, along with a sort of subliminal fear that the fun was over and forecasting would never be the same again.

He was married three times. The first marriage, which was dissolved in 1939, resulted in two children, one son who moved to Boston and one daughter who remained in Norway. His second marriage was a short wartime marriage from September 1941 to October 1942 but the divorce was granted only in April 1947. By then Petterssen had already married his last wife, Grace, in June 1946.

Petterssen became a U.S. citizen in March 1955. During the Vietnam War and the Watergate scandal he gradually became alienated and disillusioned with the White House administration and in 1973 relinquished his U.S. citizenship, without reactivating his Norwegian citizenship. During his later years Petterssen suffered from heart problems after a heart attack in 1957. He died suddenly in London on 31 December 1974.

BIBLIOGRAPHY

WORKS BY PETTERSSEN

Weather Analysis and Forecasting: A Textbook on Synoptic Meteorology. New York: McGraw-Hill, 1940.

Introduction to Meteorology. New York: McGraw-Hill, 1941. 2nd ed. 1958. 3rd ed. 1969.

"A General Survey of Factors Influencing Development at Sea Level." *Journal of Meteorology* 12 (1955): 36–42.

Weather Analysis and Forecasting. 2 vols. New York: McGraw-Hill, 1956. Revised and expanded edition of the 1940 textbook.

With D. L. Bradbury and K. Pedersen. "The Norwegian Cyclone Models in Relation to Heat and Cold Sources." *Geofysiske Publikasjoner* 24 (1962): 243–280.

With S. J. Smebye. "On the Development of Extratropical Cyclones." *Quarterly Journal of the Royal Meteorological Society* 97 (1971): 457–482.

Kuling fra nord: En værvarslers erindringer. [Gale from the north: a weather forecaster's reminiscences]. Oslo: Aschehoug, 1974. Translated from the original English to Norwegian, he sums up the experiences and philosophy of an extremely active, exciting, and fruitful life. He told his friends that he originally intended to make the title *Tales of a Maverick in Science,* later to be changed to *Of Storms and Men.*

Weathering the Storm: Sverre Petterssen, the D-Day Forecast and the Rise of Modern Meteorology, edited by James R. Fleming. Boston: American Meteorological Society, 2001. The original English autobiography with added footnotes and a selected bibliography.

OTHER SOURCES

Bundgaard, R. C. "Sverre Petterssen, Weather Forecaster." *Bulletin of the American Meteorological Society* 60, no. 3 (1979): 182–195. A summary of Petterssen's 1974 autobiography.

Fleming, James R. "Sverre Petterssen, the Bergen School, and the Forecasts for D-Day." *History of Meteorology* 1 (2004): 75–83. Available from http://www.meteohistory.org.

Johannessen, K. R. "Sverre Petterssen 1898–1974." *Bulletin of the American Meteorological Society* 56, no. 8 (1975): 892–893.

Mason, B. J., and J. S. Sawyer. "Professor Sverre Petterssen." *Meteorological Magazine* 104 (1975): 93–94.

Sutcliffe, R. C. "Professor Sverre Petterssen, C.B.E." *Quarterly Journal of the Royal Meteorological Society* 101 (1975): 703–704.

Anders Persson

PETTERSSON, SVEN OTTO (*b.* Gothenburg, Sweden, 12 February 1848; *d.* 16 January 1941), *chemistry, physical chemistry, oceanography.*

Pettersson is mostly remembered for his organizational capacity, especially in the founding and running of the International Council for the Exploration of the Sea (ICES). But Pettersson's scientific interests and executive skills embraced a wide range of fields. In addition to the physics of the ocean, he contributed in chemistry, especially physical chemistry, and he was a skilled inventor of scientific instruments.

Otto Pettersson was born in Gothenburg on the western coast of Sweden. He was the son of wealthy merchant Johan Fredrik Pettersson and Emelie Leontine Borgman, who both came from villages in the county of Bohuslän. The wealth of the paternal family partly originated from the herring-fisheries in Bohuslän. Pettersson grew up in Gothenburg and spent his summers on the coast of Bohuslän, a landscape that remained beloved to him. In 1875 Pettersson married Agnes Irgens, daughter of the Norwegian Major General and cabinet minister Nils C. Irgens and Louise F. Linaae. They had two daughters and three sons. Pettersson was eager to educate his sons in oceanography, and he had success in so far as the youngest son, Hans Pettersson, became a physicist and professor in oceanography at the University of Gothenburg.

Academic Career. From 1866 to 1872 Pettersson studied chemistry at the University of Uppsala. After having earned a doctoral degree with a thesis on selenium alums, Pettersson spent two years (1872–1874) in the laboratory of Carl Remigus Fresenius in Wiesbaden, Germany, specializing in analytical chemistry. He returned to Sweden and obtained a post as assistant professor (docent) in physical chemistry at the University of Uppsala from 1874 to 1884.

Pettersson grew critical of what he considered insufficient and old-fashioned training in the disciplines of chemistry and physics, and so he shifted to the newly founded Stockholms høgskola as a temporary teacher. Høgskola was a non-degree-granting private, polytechnic institution established in 1878; the training was primarily oriented toward pursuit of scientific knowledge rather than teaching and examinations for civil services. In 1884 he got the first chair in chemistry at the institution and kept the professorship until his retirement in 1909. In the years 1893–1896 Pettersson served as the rector of the school, and in this function sought to secure its financial basis by private donations and to restructure Stockholms høgskola into a degree-giving institution after the model of the universities. At the school Pettersson was eager to foster the career of outstanding natural researchers like the young Norwegian physicist and founder of modern meteorology Vilhelm Bjerknes, and the physicist and chemist Svante Arrhenius, best known for the molecular dissociation theory. From 1900 to 1912 Pettersson was the chairman of the Nobel Committee in Chemistry.

In 1909, at the age of sixty-one, Pettersson moved back to Bohuslän and settled down at the Fiord of Gullmarn. Already in 1892 he had bought an estate, Holma Manor, not far from the town of Lysekil. His family moved to the manor and ran the farm. In 1902 on the small island of Bornö, which belong to the estate, Pettersson had built a private marine research station for oceanographic investigations.

Beside the work and duties at Stockholms högskola, Pettersson was, from its founding in 1896, one of three members of the board of the Svenska Hydrografiska Kommissionen (the Swedish Hydrographic Commission) and its successor Svenska Hydrografisk-Biologiska Kommission (the Swedish Hydrographic-Biological Commission) from 1901 to 1930. The commission was set up by the Royal Academy of Sweden and was submitted to the Ministry of Agriculture by reorganization in 1901. The commission was primarily set up to investigate physical and chemical aspects of the waters around Sweden, but soon biological oceanography and fisheries biology investigations were added. From 1902 Pettersson's professional life was largely devoted to building and securing the existence of ICES. He served as a member of its board (the Bureau) from 1902 to his death in 1941 and acted as vice president from 1902 to 1915. As it became vital to save the existence of ICES during World War I, Pettersson (from neutral Sweden) became president in March 1915 and guided the council until March 1920 when he was released from the duty.

Chemistry and Oceanography. In chemistry Pettersson wrote numerous works mainly on inorganic elements and compounds; several of the works dealt with the chemical compositions of rare metals. He often worked with a colleague at the University of Uppsala, Lars F. Nilsson, with whom he also published in 1878 his probably best-known article in chemistry, titled "Über die Darstellung und Valenz des Berylliums." The research of Nilsson and Pettersson helped to clarify and define the placement of the element beryllium in the periodic table.

In the same year, 1878, Pettersson published the first of numerous works on chemical aspects of the ocean, namely on the properties of water and ice. That the inorganic constituents of sea water were in constant proportion relative to one another had been confirmed around 1860; Pettersson now investigated whether the constituents of sea water behaved likewise in sea ice. In the first article he discussed the latent heat of water at temperatures below 0 degrees Celsius, and also included comments on the formation of ice in the sea. He enlarged his interest in ice and ice-melting in broader views, and around 1900 they were gradually developed into a hypothesis that melting ice forms oceanic deep water. Pettersson held that water from melting ice in polar regions provided the motive forces for the manner in which deep and bottom water is formed. The Norwegian oceanographer Fridtjof Nansen contested Pettersson's ice-melting mechanism, claiming that that cooling of the atmosphere and/or ice formation are the primary forces. In the dispute Nansen formulated one of his lasting contributions to oceanography.

Pettersson's publication on the properties on ice and water from 1878 led the polar explorer Adolf Erik Nordenskiöld, and led him to invite Pettersson to report on the oceanographic observations made during the *Vega* expedition north of Europe and Asia from 1878 to 1880. In the early 1880s at the time he worked up the report from the *Vega* expedition, Pettersson became aware of a possible connection between the sudden occurrence of herring (*Clupea harengus*) on the coast of Bohuslän and the salinity in the waters in Skagerrak. A fellow chemist and friend Gustaf Ekman had late in 1877 discovered that herring seemed to prefer layers of water with high salinity and a certain temperature. Ekman was a distant relative of a pioneer in Swedish oceanography (named hydrography at the time), Fredrik Laurentz Ekman. Following the death of F. L. Ekman, Pettersson was asked to finalize the report of the first overall investigations of waters around Sweden's coast in 1877. The efforts to complete F. L. Ekman's investigations of physics of the ocean and the search for an explanation of the particular and periodical phenomena of appearance of winter herring at the coast of Bohuslän encouraged Pettersson's interest in oceanography. Gustaf Ekman became Pettersson's faithful partner

and accomplished many of the practical tasks linked to seagoing and working up material. Around 1890 the two of them began making systematic observations in the strait of Kattegat and in the strait of Skagerrak, which connects the Baltic Sea to the North Sea. Pettersson decided to undertake temperature and current observations from different vessels at the same time. Ekman and Pettersson aimed to establish a plan for a network of fixed stations that would operate at virtually the same time, with observations made at a number of standard depths. Pettersson's investigations were small-scale studies of delimited areas with the aim to enable the establishment of synoptic charts. In 1891 nearby Denmark adopted the Swedish method and Pettersson's program. In 1892 following the meeting of Scandinavian natural researchers (the *skandinaviske naturforskermøter*) he proposed formally inviting scientists from Denmark, Norway, Germany, England, and Scotland to join cooperative surveys to take place in 1893 and 1894. The cooperation enlarged the areas of investigations to the North Sea and sections of the North Atlantic. In his 1894 article "A Review of Swedish Hydrographic Research in the Baltic and the North Seas," Pettersson summed up the investigations so far, and he advocated continuing his program and furthering oceanography as an international field of science. Another important hallmark of Pettersson's investigations as well as other Scandinavian natural researchers was an understanding of relationships between the chemistry and the physics of the ocean and the biology of fishes including the significance of biological oceanography.

During the 1890s Pettersson stood in the forefront of a small group of Scandinavians who committed themselves to found an international body for scientific fisheries investigations in the North Sea, the Baltic Sea, and Atlantic waters. In the group were many of the scientists who constituted the modern field of oceanography: zoologist, oceanographer, polar explorer Fridtjof Nansen, zoologist Johan Hjort, physical oceanographer Bjørn Helland-Hansen, biological oceanographer Haaken Hasberg Gran, and physicist Martin Knudsen. With his organizational skills Pettersson led the move from informal arrangements to the formally organized ICES in 1902. The council was a leading force in Europe and in North American fisheries biology and adjacent fields until World War II. In ICES the Swedish style of intensive area studies was continued. Pettersson embraced Bjerknes's hydrodynamic circulation theorem in 1897 as a possible theoretical breakthrough for the ocean. He had Helland-Hansen invited to Stockholm to learn to apply Bjerknes's model on the ocean. Helland-Hansen in cooperation with Nansen and the renowned oceanographer Vagn Walfrid Ekman (son of F. L. Ekman) formulated the foundation for today's understanding of the physical structure and dynamics of the ocean.

A common standard for measurements and reliable instruments were important factors in Pettersson's contributions to establishing the field of oceanography. He himself was a competent inventor of instruments and constructed in the 1890s an insulated water bottle and a current meter. This sampler was used by Nansen during his *Fram* expedition (1893–1896); after the return Nansen suggested improvements to Pettersson, the most important being to mount a thermometer into the water bottle. V. W. Ekman at ICES's Central Laboratory around 1905 constructed a current meter and a new reversing water bottle, devices that were superior to Pettersson's constructions.

Pettersson pursued several lines in his research. After 1909 he concentrated on tidal movements in the deeper water layers and the relationship between oceanographic and meteorological phenomena. Pettersson was considered an esteemed chemist and researcher even though some of the late publications contained hypotheses that have been superseded. Pettersson stimulated scientific discussions, and in a formative period of Scandinavian science and modern international oceanography from 1880 to 1910, the amiable, pragmatic, and energetic Pettersson played a crucial role with his large intellectual capacity and desire for scientific entrepreneurship.

BIBLIOGRAPHY

WORKS BY PETTERSSON

"Bidrag til kännedom om de selen-syrade alunarterne." PhD diss., University of Uppsala, Sweden, 1872.

With L. F. Nilson. "Über die Darstellung und Valenz des Berylliums." *Annalen der Physik und Chemie* 4 (1878): 554–585.

"Om vattens latenta värme vid temperaturer under O° jemte några anmärkningar om isbildningen i hafvet." *Öfversigt af KVA* [Kunglega Vetenskapsakademiens] *förhandlingar*, N:03 (1878): 53–61 and fig. III.

"Striden om undervisningen i naturvetenskap vid Uppsala Universitet." *Stockholms Dagblad*, several articles in April and May 1881.

"On the Properties of Water and Ice." In *Vega-expeditionens vetenskapliga iakttagelser. Bearbetade af deltagere i resan och andre forskare*, vol. 2, edited by Adolf Erik Nordenskiöld. Stockholm: Beijer, 1883.

"Contributions to the Hydrography of the Siberian Sea." In *Vega-expeditionens vetenskapliga iakttagelser. Bearbetade af deltagere i resan och andre forskare*, vol. 2, edited by Adolf Erik Nordenskiöld. Stockholm: Beijer, 1883.

With Gustaf Ekman. "Grunddragen af Skageracks och Kattegats hydrografi enligt den svenska vinterexpeditionens 1890 iakttagelser samt föregående arbeten." *KVA Handlingar* 24, no. 1 (1891): 1–162.

"Några allmänna drag af Nord- och Östersjöens hydrografi." *Forhandlingerne ved de skandinaviske naturforskeres 14. møde* (København 4–9 July 1892): 78–87.

With F. L. Ekman. "Den svenska hydrografiska expeditionen år 1877 under ledning af FLE." *KVA Handlingar* 25, no. 1 (1893): 1–163. Pettersson wrote the second part of the report beginning on page 73.

"A Review of Swedish Hydrographic Research in the Baltic and the North Seas." *Scottish Geographical Magazine* 10 (1894): part I 281–302, part II 352–359, part III 414–427, part IV 449–462, part V 525–539, part VI 617–624, part VII 623–634, part VIII 631–635.

"The International Conference for Marine Research in Stockholm 1899." *Scottish Geographical Magazine* (1900): 299–312.

"On the Influence of Ice-Melting upon Oceanic Circulation." *Geographical Journal* 24 (1904): 285–333.

"On the Influence of Ice-Melting upon Oceanic Circulation." *Geographical Journal* 27 (1907): 273–295.

En självbiografi. Göteborg: Göteborgslitografen, 1938.

OTHER SOURCES

Department of Foreign Affairs, Ministerial Cabinet Meetings. UD:0–6. Swedish National Archive.

Gustaf Ekman's Archive Box 15 and 16 and Archival Files from the Station at Bornö. A360. Regional Archives in Gothenburg.

Ekman, Vagn Walfrid. "Otto Pettersson 12/2 1848–17/1 1941." *Svensk Geografisk årsbok* (1941): 85–92.

Johan Hjort's Archive. Ms. 29911. Norwegian National Library in Oslo, Department of Manuscripts.

ICES Archive. 10.649. Danish National Archive.

Letters to Otto Pettersson. AccH 1985:25 and AccH1993:12. University Library in Gothenburg, Sweden.

Fridtjof Nansen's Archive. Ms. 48 and Ms. Fol. 1924. Norwegian National Library in Oslo, Department of Manuscripts.

Rozwadowski, Helen M. *The Sea Knows No Boundaries: A Century of Marine Science under ICES*. Copenhagen and Seattle: University of Washington Press, 2002. The most extensive study in English about Pettersson and founding of ICES.

Skottsberg, Carl. "Minnesteckning Sven Otto Pettersson." In *Minnestal hållna i Kungl. Vetenskaps- och vitterhetssamhället i Göteborg*, edited by J. V. Johansson. Göteborg, 1942.

Svansson, Artur. "Otto Pettersson." In *Svenskt biografisk leksikon*, no. 142, edited by Göran Nilzén. Stockholm: A. Bonnier, 1995. The article includes an extensive bibliography.

———, and Elisabeth Crawford, eds. *Neptun och Mammon. Brev från Otto Pettersson til Gustaf Ekman 1884–1929*. Göteborg: Tre Böcker, 2003.

Vera Schwach

PIAGET, JEAN (*b.* Neuchâtel, Switzerland, 9 August 1896; *d.* Geneva, Switzerland, 16 September 1980), *psychology, epistemology, biology.*

Piaget is best known for his studies on the development of human intelligence from infancy to adolescence. He contributed crucially to the shaping of twentieth-century child psychology, cognitive psychology, and educational theory and practice. Nevertheless, he always considered that his specific domain was that of "genetic" (in the sense of "developmental") epistemology, and he saw psychology as an instrument for developing a theory of scientific knowledge, specifically for understanding the growth of knowledge and the emergence of the concepts and cognitive mechanisms that make science possible. The idea of "intelligence," as he used it, encompassed the capacities (such as that for abstraction and logical thinking) and notions (such as time, space, and substance) that are constitutive of scientific thought. His oeuvre includes more than fifty books and hundreds of articles.

Piaget's entire professional life took place in Switzerland. After a dissertation in the natural sciences (1918) at the University of Neuchâtel, and studies in psychology and philosophy in Zürich and Paris, Piaget joined the Jean-Jacques Rousseau Institute of Geneva in 1921. Founded by the Genevan psychologist Édouard Claparède as a center for research on child development and education, the institute evolved into the Department of Psychology and Education of the University of Geneva. In the course of his long academic career, Piaget taught experimental and developmental psychology, sociology, and history of scientific thought, mostly at the University of Geneva. From 1929 to 1967 he also directed the International Bureau of Education, originally established to coordinate educational information and research, and to promote peace and international understanding through education. In 1955, with support from the Rockefeller Foundation, he created the interdisciplinary International Center for Genetic Epistemology (which closed in 1984). Piaget received numerous honorary doctorates (the first one from Harvard University in 1936), as well as such prestigious international awards as the Erasmus (1971) and Balzan (1979) prizes.

Early Development. Piaget was born in 1896 in the French-speaking Swiss city of Neuchâtel to Rebecca-Suzanne Jackson, a religious mother with socialist leanings, and Arthur Piaget, an agnostic medievalist who was professor at the University of Neuchâtel and director of the local State Archives. In his 1952 autobiography, Piaget described his early commitment to "serious work" as a way of escaping the difficult family situation created by his mother's mental instability. From 1910 to 1915 Piaget was active in the Club des Amis de la Nature (Club of the friends of nature), an amateur naturalist society for high-school students, supported by parents and local naturalists and academics. Shortly after an early initiation to malacological taxonomy with Paul Godet, director of the

Jean Piaget. © FARRELL GREHAN/CORBIS.

Neuchâtel Museum of Natural History (Musée d'histoire naturelle), he immersed himself in mollusk classification; by the time he finished his doctoral thesis on the taxonomy of Alpine mollusks (1918), he had published numerous articles in specialized journals. He later traced his "biological" view of intelligence as an adaptive function to this early scientific activity, which (in his 1952 autobiography) he also thanked for having protected him against the "demon of philosophy." Piaget's turn from classificatory natural history to problems of adaptation and evolution, however, were largely due to his adolescent philosophical outlook.

Piaget became interested in the nature of life and evolution in 1912, after reading *Creative Evolution* (1907) by the French philosopher Henri Bergson. Inspired by this celebrated work, he rejected the Darwinian theory of natural selection (to which he would always prefer a form of Lamarckism), and he adopted the basic postulate of his later thought: the idea that the theory of knowledge and the theory of life are inseparable. He nevertheless stayed with classificatory natural history until his 1918 thesis; later, at a time when he was already involved in psychological research, he undertook a years-long "biometrical and genetic" study of the freshwater snail *Limnaea stagnalis*'s adaptation to natural lake environments. In 1929 he published a major monograph on the topic, thus giving closure to his empirical work in the natural sciences.

During his high school studies (1912–1915), Piaget began a lifelong friendship with his philosophy teacher and mentor Arnold Reymond. (After graduating in theology in 1900 with an essay on "subjectivism and the problem of religious knowledge," Reymond served as a Protestant minister for three years before turning to philosophy and the history of science, specializing, at the time he was Piaget's teacher, in the history of logic and mathematics in Greco-Roman antiquity.) During World War I, Piaget joined socialist and Christian youth groups, and he spent time at a sanatorium in Leysin, in the Swiss Alpine canton of Vaud, a place reminiscent (in some literature of the time) of Thomas Mann's "magic mountain."

In ways that are also reminiscent of Mann's characters, the young Piaget went through deep crises in which issues of personal identity merged with religious and political questions, a revolt against bourgeois conservatism and the official churches, and the aspiration to work for the "new birth of Christianity." Combining Bergson's doctrine of the élan vital and the philosophy of religion "based on psychology and history" of the French theologian Auguste Sabatier, Piaget sketched a "Bergsonian Protestantism" in which the evolution of dogmas was a part of "creative evolution." In March 1914 he published a comparison of Bergson and Sabatier, his first article outside the domain of natural history. Piaget obliterated these experiences and ideas from his later autobiographical writings, but left abundant traces of them in such youthful writings as the prose poem *The Mission of the Idea* (1915); a "prayer" titled "Les mystères de la douleur divine" (The Mysteries of Divine Suffering, 1916), in which a desperate man discovers God's fraternity with humanity; and the 1918 article "Biology and War," in which he asserts that to struggle against war is to follow the "logic of life." He also described his youthful crises and their solution in *Recherche* (1918; Quest), an autobiographical *Bildungsroman* and philosophical essay that was severely criticized by Reymond. (Piaget, 1977c, includes a partial translation of *Mission,* a complete translation of "Biology and War," and a chapter-by-chapter summary of *Recherche.* The full text of *Recherche* is available at the site of the Jean Piaget Foundation; see Bibliography below.)

In *Recherche,* Piaget elaborated a theory of organic, psychological, and social phenomena based on the idea of equilibrium between parts and wholes. While real-life disequilibria (between individual and collective interests, for example) tend toward equilibrium, disequilibria can lead to such events as war. Piaget's ultimate goal was the new birth of Christianity and the reconstruction of postwar humanity. Much of his later thinking built directly on these youthful speculations and values, but its empirical

impetus derived from a reaction against the metaphysical and mystical inclinations of his adolescence.

The Child's "Mentality." After spending the winter semester of 1918–1919 in Zürich, where he enrolled at the university but mainly attended lectures on psychoanalysis (a field he knew since 1916), Piaget left for Paris, where he went to classes and lectures in psychiatry, logic, and philosophy of science. In the fall of 1919, he gave a lecture on psychoanalysis and child psychology (a special Swiss interest), which was one of the first psychoanalytic presentations on French soil. In Zürich he tried out psychoanalysis, both as a practitioner and as a patient. Thanks to a recommendation from Pierre Bovet (a friend of Piaget's family and director of the Rousseau Institute), Théodore Simon, who had collaborated with Alfred Binet in developing intelligence tests, asked Piaget to standardize Cyril Burt's tests for Parisian children. Rather than adhere to the task, Piaget focused on how children proceeded and then justified their answers.

In the early 1920s Piaget combined the use of items from intelligence tests, new problem-solving situations, and open-ended conversations with school-age children into what he called the "clinical method." His first five books (1923–1932) use this method to examine the development of the child's language, reasoning, conceptions of the world, theories of causality, and moral judgment. Piaget found that children are at first "egocentric" (i.e., cannot take another person's point of view) and attached to concrete appearances, but that they gradually move away from egocentrism and become capable of reciprocity and of thinking abstractly and logically. Earlier child study had focused on the contents of the children's minds and inventoried age-related behaviors; Piaget concentrated on the main features of children's "mentality." In so doing, he drew inspiration from work by the French ethnologist Lucien Lévy-Bruhl, who described "primitive mentality" as prelogical and mystical. Piaget's first books also bear the traces of his psychoanalytic interests, and they reveal various influences, especially that of Zürich psychiatrist Eugen Bleuler, who coined the term *schizophrenia* and described the "autistic thinking" to which Piaget compared egocentric thought; that of two of his Paris teachers, the psychiatrist Pierre Janet and the philosopher Léon Brunschvicg; and that of James Mark Baldwin, the American pioneer of "genetic" psychology and epistemology.

In his first books, Piaget sometimes presented the development of intelligence as a process of socialization of thought that is largely driven by social interactions; in *The Moral Judgment of the Child,* for example, he argued that children leave egocentrism behind as the result of the practice of cooperation among peers. In the 1920s Piaget rapidly gained an international reputation, and within the progressive education movement his work seemed to provide scientific support for pedagogical methods based on children's interests, activity, and "self-government." He described development as moving from egocentrism (which manifested itself as children's dependence on perceptual appearances and acceptance of external authority) toward logical thinking and moral autonomy. He also pursued research on mollusk adaptation, and he wrote about epistemological, sociological, and religious topics.

The totality of Piaget's writings at the time shows that, for him, development in ontogeny went in the same direction as historical progress: from the child and the primitive to the adult and the modern, from heteronomy to autonomy in the cognitive and moral domains, from authoritarian regimes to parliamentary democracy, and from dogmatic religions to liberal Protestantism. *The Moral Judgment of the Child,* a book of great personal significance that is connected to Piaget's political ideals and to his defense of "immanence" in religion, closes the first phase of his work.

Infancy, Logic, and Stages. Starting in the mid-1920s, with the help of his wife (and former student) Valentine Châtenay, Piaget studied his three children, born in 1925, 1927, and 1931, and recorded his observations in three major classics. *The Origins of Intelligence* and *The Construction of Reality* (1936–1937) describe how basic forms

of intentionality and of the categories of object, space, causality, and time evolve between the newborn's reflex activities and the emergence of language at about eighteenth months. *Play, Dreams, and Imitation,* originally titled *La formation du symbole chez l'enfant. Imitation, jeu et rêve, image et représentation,* appeared in 1945, but was largely composed earlier; it deals with the development of mental representation up to the age of six. Piaget was criticized for drawing general conclusions from the observation of a very small number of subjects, who were in addition his own children. At the time, however, studying few subjects—and one's children—was current and legitimate within psychology.

In *The Origins of Intelligence,* Piaget linked biological, epistemological, and psychological theories. He characterized human intelligence as a form of adaptation that prolongs organic adaptation and employs the same mechanisms of "assimilation" and "accommodation" (which he also termed the "functional invariants" of development). He asserted the primary role of activity, and he criticized both nativism and empiricism. He later called his approach *constructivist,* meaning by this term that the concepts and structures of intelligence are constructed and reconstructed by means of the physical and mental activities whereby the organism adapts to the external world. The books Piaget derived from observing his children constitute a second group of works, after which Piaget turned to the study of logical thinking, adopting formal logical and mathematical models to characterize mental "structures" and "operations."

In the 1930s Piaget and his former student Bärbel Inhelder began a remarkable instance of scientific collaboration that lasted until Piaget's death. By the 1940s, Inhelder recalled in her autobiography, Piaget said he needed her "to counter his tendency toward becoming a totally abstract thinker." In 1948 Inhelder became professor at the University of Geneva. While Piaget never lost sight of his epistemological goals, Inhelder was more of a psychologist, devising many of the problem-solving situations that have become the distinguishing feature of Piagetian research. Their first collaborative work, on the child's understanding of quantity conservation, appeared in 1941; in her dissertation, published in 1943, Inhelder made pioneering use of conservation tests as diagnostic tools. Together, they wrote books on the development of logic and the conceptions of movement, speed, time, space, geometry, chance, and probability.

Together with *The Origins of Intelligence* and *The Construction of Reality,* these books describe a sequence of four developmental stages from birth through adolescence. Piaget, who has often been reduced to a "stage theorist," maintained that the stages appear in an invariable order, but recognized that they do so at somewhat different ages

COMMUNICATION MILESTONES	
Age	**Milestone**
0–12 months	• Responds to speech by looking at the speaker; responds differently to aspects of speakers voice (such as friendly or angry, male or female). • Turns head in direction of sound. • Responds with gestures to greetings such as "hi," "bye-bye," and "up" when these words are accompanied by appropriate gestures by speaker. • Stops ongoing activity when told "no," when speaker uses appropriate gesture and tone. • May say two or three words by around 12 months of age, although probably not clearly. • Repeats some vowel and consonant sounds (babbles) when alone or spoken to; attempts to imitate sounds.
12–24 months	• Responds correctly when asked "where?" • Understands prepositions *on, in,* and *under;* and understands simple phrases (such as "Get the ball.") • Says 8–10 words by around age 18 months; by age two, vocabulary will include 20–50 words, mostly describing people, common objects, and events (such as "more" and "all gone"). • Uses single word plus a gesture to ask for objects. • Refers to self by name; uses "my" or "mine."
24–36 months	• Points to pictures of common objects when they are named. • Can identify objects when told their use. • Understands questions with "what" and "where" and negatives "no," "not," "can't," and don't." • Responds to simple directions. • Selects and looks at picture books; enjoys listening to simple stories, and asks for them to be read aloud again. • Joins two vocabulary words together to make a phrase. • Can say first and last name. • Shows frustration at not being understood.
36–48 months	• Begins to understand time concepts, such as "today," "later," "tomorrow," and "yesterday." • Understands comparisons, such as "big" and "bigger." • Forms sentences with three or more words. • Speech is understandable to most strangers, but some sound errors may persists (such as "t" sound for "k" sound).
48–60 months	• By 48 months, has a vocabulary of over 200 words. • Follows two or three unrelated commands in proper order. • Understands sequencing of events, for example, "First we have to go to the grocery store, and then we can go to the playground." • Ask questions using "when," "how," and "why." Talks about causes for things using "because."

Jean Piaget's Communication Milestone Table.
Communication milestone table, ages birth through five years.

in different individuals, cultures, and settings. The stages are named sensorimotor (from birth to about two years), preoperational (until about age seven, sometimes defined as an initial substage of the following one), concrete operational (until about age eleven), and formal operational. This sequence highlights "operational" thought as the point toward which development tends. For Piaget, "operations" are interiorized actions that have become reversible and coordinated with other interiorized actions into a totality; cognitive development therefore consists of the emergence of such operations. It begins with the transformation of innate reflexes into action "schemes," whereby the subject initially assimilates the world and accommodates to it, through the child's "operational" activities (e.g., classification and seriation of concrete objects), to the adolescent's capacity for hypothetico-deductive thinking.

The Growth of Logical Thinking from Childhood to Adolescence: An Essay on the Construction of Formal Operational Structures (1953) and *The Early Growth of Logic in the Child* (1959), which are among the most influential works coauthored by Piaget and Inhelder, define the stage of "formal operations." Piaget argued that adolescents actually (though intuitively) employ the operations of propositional logic. In his view, because logic represents the axiomatization of the internal structures of thought, and because thought derives from biological mechanisms and is an adaptive function, logico-mathematical structures are "biological" and developmentally "constructed." This would explain their power to describe reality. Parallel to empirical investigations, Piaget published (in 1942, 1949, and 1952) elaborate studies in "logistic" (a term to be understood as the elaboration of abstract models for describing the logico-mathematical operations that manifest themselves behaviorally or psychologically). These untranslated books have been variously criticized by philosophers, logicians, and psychologists as psychologistic, logicistic, or conceptually and formally flawed.

Biology, History of Science, and Piagetian Tasks. In addition to the topics already mentioned, Piaget, Inhelder, and their numerous collaborators investigated the mechanisms of perception, the relations between memory and intelligence, mental image, causal and physical explanations, number, the grasp of consciousness, contradiction, generalization, possibility, and necessity. Thirty-seven volumes of the collaborative *Études d'épistémologie génétique* (Studies of genetic epistemology) were published between 1957 and 1980. Starting in the 1960s, Piaget also published several theoretical books, including: *Insights and Illusions of Philosophy* (1965, with an autobiographical first chapter); *Biology and Knowledge: An Essay on the Relations between Organic Regulations and Cognitive Processes* (1967); *Structuralism* (1968); *Genetic Epistemology* (1970); *Adaptation*

and Intelligence (1974, originally titled *Adaptation vitale et psychologie de l'intelligence: Sélection organique et phénocopie*); *The Equilibration of Cognitive Structures* (1975); and *Behavior and Evolution* (1976, originally titled *Le comportement, moteur de l'évolution*). Piaget's three-volume *Introduction à l'épistémologie génétique* (1950; Introduction to genetic epistemology, 1: mathematical thought, 2: physical thought, 3: biological, psychological and sociological thoughts) remains untranslated.

Piaget was driven by the goal of elaborating a theory of knowledge that would demonstrate empirically, rather than philosophically, the conditions of possibility of scientific thought. Psychologizing the Kantian categories, he chose to ask how they develop. As illustrated by his objects of research and by the tasks he used to pursue them (see below), he identified "science" mainly with the physico-mathematical disciplines—hence, too, his steady interest in the history of science. In the general terms he used later in life, Piaget saw mental development and the history of science as a process of "equilibration" toward an ever-increasing capacity to assimilate the world. In the posthumous book *Psychogenesis and the History of Science* (1983, with Rolando García), Piaget established parallelisms between the two processes, thus elaborating on a postulate of his entire intellectual enterprise. He nevertheless focused on knowledge mechanisms rather than contents, thus distancing himself, in his own view, from the classical formulation of the biogenetic law "ontogeny recapitulates phylogeny."

Piaget's work prior to the infancy books was rapidly translated. A hiatus followed until the 1950s, when the critique of behaviorism stimulated a renewed interest and turned Piaget into a major inspiration for the "cognitive revolution." His rediscovery in the 1960s began in the Americas, and was promoted by such presentations as John Flavell's *The Developmental Psychology of Jean Piaget* (1963) in the United States and Antonio Battro's *Diccionario de epistemología genética* (1966) and *El pensamiento de Jean Piaget* (1969) in Argentina. His work launched empirical investigations throughout the world. Although these investigations prolonged mainly the infancy books and especially the later studies, Piaget's early work, *The Moral Judgment of the Child* (1932), in which he confronted children with moral dilemmas and observed them play games, was a major source of inspiration for the American student of moral development Lawrence Kohlberg, whose work has been immensely influential in the field.

The technically accessible nature of Piagetian tasks facilitated their adoption as research paradigms. In one famous instance, children are shown a scale model of three mountains and are asked to choose from a series of pictures the one that represents the mountains as seen by a doll at other positions. "Egocentric" younger subjects identify the doll's viewpoint with their own. In research on the conservation of substance, the child faces two identical balls of clay; the shape of one is modified, and the experimenter investigates whether and why the child believes the amount, weight, or volume of clay has changed. Other situations involve manipulating blocks or pouring identical quantities of liquid in differently shaped containers (children begin by saying there is more or less depending on whether they pay attention to height or width, and only later attain "reversibility").

What Piaget described as the "triumph" of operation over perceptual intuition is further illustrated in a task from *The Child's Conception of Number* (1941), coauthored with Alina Szeminska: two lines of beads, including the same number of items, are placed parallel to each other; the beads on one row are then set further apart or brought closer together, and children are asked about the transformation. The younger children believe that quantity has changed; the older ones, in contrast, use one-to-one correspondence (which conflicts with perception) to conclude it has been conserved. In one study of inductive reasoning, subjects were asked to discover the factors (such as length or thickness) that make metal rods more or less flexible. First discussed in *The Origins of Intelligence,* the study of the "object concept" or "permanent object" by observing infants' reactions after an object disappears from their view has, like many other Piagetian tasks, given rise to numerous variations, validation research (including intercultural studies), and theoretical discussions.

Critique and Assessment. Much work of Piagetian inspiration has questioned Piaget's conclusions, suggesting that children's competencies appear earlier than he believed, that subjects "fail" the tests because they cannot make sense of them, that both the tasks and the results should be understood in a framework that includes not only cognitive, but also social, cultural, and affective factors, or that the structure of intelligence is domain-specific rather than homogeneous. Piaget devoted his 1953–1954 Sorbonne lectures to *Intelligence and Affectivity: Their Relationship during Child Development* (published in English in 1981). Nevertheless, his view that affect has a motivational and regulatory function (and may thus accelerate or delay development), while cognition provides the structures of thought, has not satisfied his critics. In the 1980s and 1990s, it became fashionable to contrast his viewpoint to the cultural-historical approach of the Soviet psychologist Lev Vygotsky.

Most "Piagetian" research is actually disconnected from the theoretical goals of genetic epistemology. Piaget's overall views and goals, as well as his descriptions of the stages, mechanisms, and structures involved in the development of intelligence, have inspired research programs in various fields outside psychology, including the history of art, religion, and science. More than anything, however, it is Piaget's investigative approach and empirical findings, his formulation of new problems, and his emphasis on cognitive development that contributed to shape child and cognitive psychology in the second half of the twentieth century. His work also had a significant impact on pedagogy, giving new impetus to the belief that instruction must adapt to children's developmental levels and must involve their interests and activity. Its effect on teaching methods (especially in mathematics) was much more concrete and successful during the postwar period than in the interwar years. Nevertheless, even in the second half of the 1930s, when he published most of his reflections about education, Piaget distanced himself from professional pedagogues.

Similarly, Piaget gave psychology a preeminent place among the sciences, because, in his view, only psychology studies the development of the logico-mathematical operations that make science possible. But he insisted that he was not a psychologist, and explained that he studied the "epistemic" rather than the "psychological" subject. This claim provides the clue to a historical examination and assessment of Piaget's contribution. Equally important for this purpose are the diversity and temporal dimension of his oeuvre, which evolved over more than six decades and includes not only psychology, but also sociology, philosophy of science and religion, theory of knowledge, education, and biology.

BIBLIOGRAPHY

WORKS BY PIAGET

"Bergson et Sabatier." *Revue chrétienne* 61 (1914): 192–200. Piaget's first article outside natural history.

"Les mystères de la douleur divine (1916)." In Fernando Vidal, "'Les mystères de la douleur divine.' Une 'prière' du jeune Jean Piaget pour l'année 1916" ["The mysteries of divine suffering": A "prayer" for the year 1916 by the young Jean Piaget]. *Revue de théologie et de philosophie* 126 (1994): 97–118.

"L'adaptation de la *Limnaea stagnalis* aux milieux lacustres de la Suisse romande. Étude biométrique et génétique" [The adaptation of the *Limnaea stagnalis* to the lake environments of French-speaking Switzerland. A biometric and genetic study]. *Revue suisse de zoologie* 36 (1929): 263–531.

Immanentisme et foi religieuse [Immanentism and religious faith]. Geneva: Groupe romand des anciens membres de l'Association chrétienne d'étudiants, 1930. Piaget's final statement on religion.

The Psychology of Intelligence (1947). Translated by Malcolm Piercy and D. E. Berlyne. Totowa, NJ: Littlefield, Adams, 1972. Together with Piaget and Inhelder (1966) and Piaget

(1970a), one of Piaget's somewhat difficult presentations of his thinking.

"Autobiography." In *A History of Psychology in Autobiography.* Vol. 4, edited by Edwin G. Boring, et al. Worcester, MA: Clark University Press, 1952. Widely used, but biased and incomplete in its narrative of Piaget's youth.

Logic and Psychology. Translated by Wolfe Mays. Manchester, U.K.: Manchester University Press, 1953.

Six Psychological Studies (1964). Translated by Anita Tenzer. New York: Vintage, 1968. Together with 1969, 1970b, 1972a, 1972b, and 1977a, one of Piaget's several useful collection of articles from the 1940s through the 1960s.

With Bärbel Inhelder. *The Psychology of the Child* (1966). Translated by H. Weaver. New York: Basic Books, 1969.

Science of Education and the Psychology of the Child (1969). Translated by Derek Coltman. New York: Viking Press, 1971.

Psychology and Epistemology: Towards a Theory of Knowledge (1970b). Translated by P. A. Wells. Harmondsworth, U.K.: Penguin, 1972.

The Child and Reality: Problems of Genetic Psychology (1972a). Translated by Arnold Rosin. New York: Grossman, 1973.

To Understand Is to Invent: The Future of Education (1972b). Translated by George-Anne Roberts. New York: Grossman, 1973.

With Richard I. Evans. *Jean Piaget: The Man and His Ideas.* New York: Dutton, 1973. Together with 1977b, useful informal introduction to Piaget.

"Autobiographie" [Autobiography]. *Revue européenne des sciences sociales (Cahiers Vilfredo Pareto)* 14 (1976): 1–43.

Sociological Studies (1977a). Translated by Terry Brown, et al. Introduction by L. Smith. London and New York: Blackwell, 1995. Translates the second, expanded edition of *Études sociologiques* (first ed., 1965).

With Jean-Claude Bringuier. *Conversations with Jean Piaget* (1977b). Translated by Basia Miller-Gulati. Chicago: University of Chicago Press, 1989.

The Essential Piaget: An Interpretive Reference and Guide (1977c). Edited by Howard E. Gruber and Jacques Vonèche. New York: Basic Books, 1996. A valuable anthology with comments and introductions.

Studies in Reflecting Abstraction (1977d). Edited and translated by Robert L. Campbell. Hove, U.K.: Psychology Press, 2000. Empirical and theoretical studies on a process (*abstraction réfléchissante*, also rendered as "reflective abstraction") to which Piaget attributed a central role in the growth of knowledge.

Genetic Epistemology. Translated by Eleanor Duckworth. New York: Norton, 1979.

L'éducation morale à l'école: De l'éducation du citoyen à l'éducation internationale [Moral education in the school: From the education of the citizen to international education]. Edited by Constantin Xypas. Paris: Anthropos, 1997a. Selection of texts, 1928–1944. Overlaps with 1997b and 1998.

Piaget et l'éducation [Piaget and education]. Edited by Constantin Xypas. Paris: Presses universitaires de France, 1997b. Selection of texts, 1930–1966. Overlaps with 1997a and 1998.

De la pédagogie [On pedagogy]. Edited by Silvia Parrat-Dayan and Anastasia Tryphon. Paris: Odile Jacob, 1998. Selection of texts, 1930–1976. Overlaps with 1997a and 1997b.

"La vanité de la nomenclature" et autres écrits de jeunesse de Jean Piaget ["The vanity of nomenclature" and other early writings by Jean Piaget], edited by Fernando Vidal, 1999. Available from http://www.piaget.org/piaget/. Manuscripts and other materials from the Club des Amis de la Nature, 1910–1915.

OTHER SOURCES

Barrelet, Jean-Marc, and Anne-Nelly Perret-Clermont, eds. *Jean Piaget et Neuchâte: L'apprenti et le savant* [Piaget and Neuchâtel: The apprentice and the scholar]. Lausanne, Switzerland: Payot, 1996.

Battro, Antonio. *Piaget: Dictionary of Terms* (1966). Translated by Elizabeth Rütschi-Hermann and Sarah F. Campbell. New York: Pergamon, 1973.

Boden, Margaret. *Jean Piaget.* Harmondsworth, U.K.: Penguin, 1979. Excellent short introduction.

Catalogue annuel des Archives Jean Piaget (previously *Catalogue des Archives Jean Piaget*). Geneva: Fondation Archives Jean Piaget. Annual bibliographies of Piaget-related publications.

Chapman, Michael. *Constructive Evolution: Origins and Development of Piaget's Thought.* New York: Cambridge University Press, 1988. Like Kitchener, but more comprehensive and biographical, a complex analysis of Piaget's work.

Ducret, Jean-Jacques. *Jean Piaget: Biographie et parcours intellectuel* [Jean Piaget: Biography and intellectual itinerary]. Neuchâtel, Switzerland: Delachaux et Niestlé, 1990. Illustrated.

Inhelder, Bärbel. "Autobiography." In *A History of Psychology in Autobiography,* vol. 8, edited by Gardner Lindzey. Stanford, CA: Stanford University Press, 1989.

Kitchener, Richard F. *Piaget's Theory of Knowledge: Genetic Epistemology and Scientific Reason.* New Haven, CT: Yale University Press, 1986.

Montangero, Jacques, and Danielle Maurice-Naville. *Piaget, or, The Advance of Knowledge.* Translated by Angela Cornu-Wells. Mahwah, NJ: Erlbaum, 1977. Like Battro, a glossary (this one limited to Piaget's psychological work).

Smith, Leslie, ed. *Jean Piaget. Critical Assessments.* 4 vols. London and New York: Routledge, 1992.

Vidal, Fernando. *Piaget before Piaget.* Cambridge, MA: Harvard University Press, 1994. A historical and contextual biography focused on Piaget's youth.

———. *Piaget neuchâtelois.* Neuchâtel, Switzerland: Bibliothèque publique et universitaire, 1996. An illustrated exhibition catalog.

———. "Immanence, affectivité et démocratie dans *Le jugement moral chez l'enfant*" [Immanece, affectivity and democracy in *The Moral Judgment of the Child*]. *Bulletin de psychologie* 51, no. 437 (1998): 585–597. Discusses the origins and significance of *The Moral Judgment,* as well as Piaget's religious writings of the 1920s.

Fernando Vidal

PICARDET, CLAUDINE (*b.* Dijon, France, 7 August 1735; *d.* Paris, France, 4 October 1820), *chemistry, mineralogy, meteorology, translation.*

Picardet was one of the few women who was notably active in science in late-eighteenth-century France. With the translation of dozens of scientific papers and three volumes into French from several foreign languages to her credit, she was one of the primary translators of chemistry and mineralogy at the time of the chemical revolution. Her scientific work also included meteorological observations made for the great chemist Antoine-Laurent Lavoisier.

Early Life. Claudine was the first child of a wealthy royal notary who had bought a fief and aspired to nobility, François Poulet de Champlevey. At twenty, she married Claude Picardet, a barrister and councillor at the Table de marbre (Marble table)—one of the high judicial courts of Burgundy—who soon thereafter became a member of the Académie royale des sciences, arts, et belles-lettres de Dijon (Dijon academy of sciences, arts, and literature) and later the director of its botanical garden. Picardet thus became a learned woman and received the bourgeoisie and high society of the provincial capital town in her. Her only son died in 1776 at age nineteen, soon after being called to the bar; he had been a promising student at both François Devosges's school of drawing and in Louis Bernard Guyton de Morveau's chemistry courses at the Dijon Academy.

Picardet's Translations. A close friend of Guyton de Morveau, Picardet also attended his famous courses and their replications of foreign chemical experiments. In 1782, with the help of Jacques Magnien, a barrister and an amateur linguist, and under Guyton de Morveau's scientific supervision, she entered the small group he had created around the local academy to disseminate foreign chemistry works in France. Most participants in the group were members of the Dijon Academy, including Jacques-Pierre Champy, Jean Lemulier de Bressey, Claude Varenne de Béost, Charles André Hector Grossart de Virly, and the Spanish mineralogist Francisco Javier de Angulo, later the director general of the Mines in Spain. In nine years, Picardet translated into French from four foreign languages some eight hundred pages on chemistry or mineralogy and one paper on astronomical observations by Thomas Bugge. Six of her authors were Swedish (primarily Carl Wilhelm Scheele and Torbern Olof Bergman), six were German (including Johann Christian Wiegleb, Johann Friedrich Westrumb, Johann Carl Friedrich Meyer, and Martin Heinrich Klaproth), two were English (Richard Kirwan and William Fordyce), and one was Italian (Marsilio Landriani). After signing only as "Mme P.***

de Dijon" in her first few years as a translator, she claimed her full identity in July 1786. By this time, her name was already known among scientists, and Joseph Jérôme Lefrançois de Lalande published it in the *Journal des savants* (Journal of scholars) in reviewing her edition of Scheele's collected papers.

One-half of the papers that she translated were published in the leading scientific journal, *Observations sur la physique* (Observations on physics) run by Abbé François Rozier, Abbé Jean-André Mongez, and Jean-Claude de la Métherie. A few were given to the *Journal des savants*, to the *Nouvelles de la république des lettres et des arts* (News of the republic of letters and arts) before 1789, then to the *Annales de chimie* (Annals of chemistry) until a last paper translated from Klaproth appeared in 1797. Lastly, one-third of her translations were gathered and published in the two volumes of Scheele's *Mémoires de chymie* (1795; Memoirs of chemistry), a model for later editions in other languages, notably Thomas Beddoes's English edition of 1786. Picardet added footnotes or long endnotes, most of them by Guyton but probably including some she had written herself. She also provided the first translation of a book published in 1774 by Abraham Gottlob Werner; her edition of his *Traité des caractères extérieurs des fossiles* (1790; Treatise on the external characteristics of fossils) was actually a second edition, with additions by the author and comments by the translator, together with an introductory methodological note about her translation—published fifteen years before Thomas Weaver's translation into English in 1805. She received congratulations from the Dijon Academy for both these publications.

Two other important translations of the 1780s are sometimes ascribed to Picardet: James R. Partington states that she translated the greater part of Guyton's edition of Bergman's *Opuscula physica et chemica* from Latin into French as *Opuscules chymiques et physique* (2 vols., 1780–1785; Physical and chemical essays). She is also believed to have helped Marie Anne Paulze, wife of Antoine-Laurent Lavoisier, in translating Kirwan's *An Essay on Phlogiston* (*Essai sur le Phlogistique*, 1788). It may have been, however, that Picardet merely assisted Guyton in his work, while Paulze-Lavoisier may simply have been encouraged to follow her model.

From 1785, Picardet belonged to Lavoisier's network for meteorological data—the other members of which were professors and correspondents of the Royal Academy of Science. She made daily observations on the barometer that Lavoisier had given to the academy. Her results were read and published in part by her husband at the academy and sent to Lavoisier.

After her first husband's death in 1796, she moved to Paris and in 1798 married Guyton de Morveau, then a deputy in the lower chamber of the national legislature, the Conseil des Cinq-Cents (Council of five hundred) and a professor of chemistry at, and the director of, the École polytechnique (Polytechnic institute) in Paris. During Napoleon's reign, as Baroness Guyton-Morveau, she entertained the scientific elite.

Praise for Her Work. A number of French scientists (Georges-Louis de Buffon, Antoine-Laurent Lavoisier, Claude-Louis Berthollet, Antoine-François de Fourcroy, Joseph-Jérôme de Lalande, René-Just Haüy, and others) spoke of her in the most laudatory terms, as did foreign scholars such as Kirwan, Landriani, and Arthur Young. Visiting Guyton in the summer of 1789, Young wrote: "Madame Picardet is as agreeable in conversation as she is learned in the closet; a very pleasing unaffected woman; … a treasure to M. de Morveau, for she is able and willing to converse with him on chymical subjects, and on any others that tend either to instruct or please" (Young, 1909, 4.66 [2]).

Significance of Her Work. Although Picardet neither performed any original work in chemistry nor contributed to the chemical revolution by preparing a major translation, she played an important role as an eighteenth-century woman in science. She published twice as much as Marie Anne Paulze-Lavoisier, who merely followed her model. Nor did any male translator in chemistry publish as much as she did in the 1780s, with the exception of Dr. Jacques Gibelin. Thus, her work notably contributed to the dissemination of chemistry at a crucial time, especially regarding the chemistry of salts and minerals; it also contributed to the birth of new specialized scientific journals and to the definition of certain editorial features (including dates of first publication), and to the recognition of scientific translators as authors. Finally, thanks to her work and Guyton's activity, a mere provincial academy received international recognition.

BIBLIOGRAPHY

WORKS BY PICARDET

Translator. *Mémoires de chymie de M.* By Carl Wilhelm Scheele. 2 vols. Dijon, France: L'éditeur, 1785; Paris: Théophile Barrois Jr., 1785.

Translator. *Traité des caractères extérieurs des fossiles.* By Abraham Gottlob Werner. Dijon, France: L. N. Frantin and Mailly, 1790; Paris: Onfroy, 1790.

OTHER SOURCES

Bret, Patrice. *Mme P*** de Dijon: Sociabilités savantes, traduction scientifique et presse spécialisée à la fin du XVIIIᵉ siècle.* Paris: CNRS Éditions, 2007.

Poirier, Jean-Pierre. *Histoire des femmes de science en France: Du Moyen Âge à la Révolution.* Paris: Pygmalion-Gérard Watelet, 2002.

Rayner-Canham, Marelene, and Geoffrey Rayner-Canham. *Women in Chemistry: Their Changing Roles from Alchemical Times to the Mid-Twentieth Century.* Washington, DC: American Chemical Society and Chemical Heritage Foundation, 1998.

Young, Arthur. *Travels in France during the Years 1787, 1788, 1789.* Edited by Matilda Bentham-Edwards. London: George Bell and Sons, 1909.

Patrice Bret

PICKERING, WILLIAM HAYWARD

(*b.* Wellington, New Zealand, 24 December 1910; *d.* La Canada, California, 15 March 2004), *physics, cosmic rays, guided missiles, space-age technology, space science, solar system exploration, renewable energy.*

A seminal figure of the age of space, New Zealand–born Pickering was recognized internationally for his significant contributions to the founding of the space age, and for the first robotic explorations of the Moon, Venus, and Mars. Lauding him at an award ceremony in 1993, a former president of the California Institute of Technology observed, "More than any other individual, Bill Pickering was responsible for America's success in exploring the planets—an endeavor that demanded vision, courage dedication, expertise and the ability to inspire two generations of scientists and engineers at the Jet Propulsion Laboratory." William Pickering was director of the world-famous Jet Propulsion Laboratory in Pasadena, California, from 1954 until he retired in 1976.

Origin and Education. Born in the city of Wellington, New Zealand, in 1910, William Pickering spent his early childhood and primary school days in Havelock, a small country town in the South Island of that country. Returning to Wellington for his secondary education at Wellington College, he excelled in mathematics and science and discovered an intense interest in the (then new) techniques of amateur radio communication. In later years, he often recalled that it was his experience at Wellington College that sparked his abiding interest in science and technology, an interest that would ultimately carry him to a career beyond his wildest dreams.

After spending one year studying electrical engineering at Canterbury (University) College in Christchurch, he moved to Pasadena, California, to complete his education at the prestigious California Institute of Technology (Caltech). He earned a BS (1932), MS (1933), and in 1936 a PhD (physics) cum laude. He became a member of the Caltech faculty in 1936, and professor of electrical engineering in 1944.

In 1932, William Pickering married the former Muriel Bowler of Texas, and eventually made his home near the Jet Propulsion Laboratory in the Pasadena area of Southern California. A son and daughter were added to the family in 1939 and 1943 respectively. William Pickering became a naturalized American citizen in February 1941. Following the death from natural causes of his first wife in 1992, Pickering married the former Inez Chapman, a longtime family friend with origins in North Carolina, in 1994.

Cosmic-Ray Research. At Caltech he worked as a researcher under the famous physicist Robert Millikan on cosmic-ray experiments, a relatively new field of physics at the time. In the course of this work he refined existing techniques for producing rugged Geiger-Müller tubes for cosmic-ray detection, and developed electronic counters for detecting the simultaneous incidence of cosmic ray particles upon two or more Geiger tubes. The so-called coincidence counters were used, in conjunction with a suitable array of Geiger tubes, to determine the directional characteristics of cosmic radiation. With three Geiger tubes arranged in an array and a suitable arrangement of coincidence-counting apparatus and lead plates, he constructed a cosmic-ray telescope to investigate the directional and penetrating characteristics of cosmic-ray showers, and the processes involved in producing the showers. Among his key findings were:

> a. Shower particles have a penetrating power that on the average is less than that required to penetrate 5 cm. of lead plate, b. Showers are caused by groups of shower-producing photons rather than single photons that give rise to a series of showers, c. Showers observed under large thicknesses of lead are caused by photons that are produced in the lead by high energy incoming radiation. (1936, p. 57)

Pickering then extended his research to investigate the effect of Earth's magnetic field on the shower-producing radiation. At the time, the diminished intensity of cosmic radiation observed in the equatorial regions was thought to be caused by Earth's magnetic field deflecting the incoming particles away from the equator. If this was correct, Pickering reasoned, it should be possible to observe a "latitude effect" on the number of "showers" produced by this primary radiation passing through a lead plate (1936, p. 66).

To determine this effect across a wide range of latitude, he constructed suitable detection equipment and carried out a series of observations on a sea voyage from California to New Zealand, and back. Due to numerous practical difficulties, however, the results were inconclusive. Nevertheless, as part of his thesis the work was very

highly regarded, and earned him the doctor of philosophy cum laude degree at Caltech in 1936.

After graduation, Pickering continued his cosmic ray work, now as a faculty member of Robert Millikan's cosmic-ray research team at Caltech in company with Victor Neher and Carl Anderson. Stimulated by Millikan's interest in the use of high-altitude balloons to measure cosmic rays beyond the dense regions of the atmosphere, Pickering developed light-weight instrument packages that employed new electronic techniques for returning the cosmic-ray data to Earth. This technology came to be called "telemetry," and eventually established him as leader in that field. Together with Millikan and Neher, another pioneer in early cosmic-ray research, he carried out extensive observations in India, Canada, and Mexico searching for the "latitude effect" in cosmic-ray intensity at high altitudes. A succession of papers published in *Physical Review, Review of Scientific Instruments,* and *Reviews of Modern Physics* are testament to his productivity at this period of his life.

Guided Missile Development. During World War II Pickering served as an electrical engineering educator and advisor to the U.S. Navy at Caltech. In 1944, when Caltech's Jet Propulsion Laboratory (JPL) was developing rocket propulsion systems for the U.S. Army, Pickering joined the workforce as a technical manager. At war's end he toured Germany and Japan with Theodor von Kármán's technical assessment team to evaluate the state of rocket technology in those countries. Ten years later, at the height of the Cold War with the U.S.S.R., Caltech named him to the position of director of JPL.

As director of JPL, Pickering oversaw the development and test of the U.S. Army's first two Intermediate Range Ballistic Missile weapon systems, the Corporal and Sergeant. From this body of work emerged the basic technology for the precision guidance systems on which all such weapons depend for their ultimate target accuracy. During this period he met, and eventually became a close friend of, Wernher von Braun, the scientist who directed rocket research in Germany during World War II. Von Braun, along with many other German scientists, had been brought to the United States after the war to assist with the United States's long-range rocket development program.

Following the appearance of the first Soviet Sputnik in October 1957, Pickering led the JPL effort that, together with a team led by von Braun from the Army Ballistic Missile Agency and by scientist James Van Allen of the University of Iowa, astonished the world with America's prompt response to the Soviet challenge. The Pickering–von Braun–Van Allen teams launched *Explorer 1,* America's first satellite into Earth orbit, just eighty-three days after receiving the president's order to go ahead. It was a new era—the space age had begun.

Deep Space Exploration. Toward the end of 1958, the U.S. government established the National Aeronautics and Space Administration (NASA); JPL, although it remained a part of Caltech, severed its connection with the military and became a private contractor for NASA. From a choice of three NASA space programs, human space flight, Earth satellites, and exploration of the solar system, Pickering opted for the latter. He would take JPL where none had gone before—into deep space to carry out NASA's ambitious program for the exploration of the solar system and its planets.

Under Pickering's inspiring, but often controversial, direction JPL went from success to success, in an amazing succession of challenging programs to explore the Moon and near planets and to beat the Russians to it. Supported by JPL's global network of tracking stations, JPL-built spacecraft sent back the first close-up photographs of the lunar surface, others journeyed far beyond the Moon to examine Venus, and later still others returned the first close-up views of the surface of Mars. On each occasion, Venus (March 1963) and Mars (July 1965), *Time* magazine honored him with a cover picture. Later in his tenure at JPL, NASA's programs called for even more complex space missions to carry out soft landings on the Moon and on Mars to gather a plethora of new science about the surface features of those bodies.

In all, during the period of Pickering's directorship of the laboratory, NASA charged JPL with responsibility for designing and conducting nine lunar missions using Ranger spacecraft, seven lunar landing missions using Surveyor spacecraft, and ten planetary missions to Venus and Mars using Mariner spacecraft. All of these missions represented humanity's first attempts to overcome the confines and constraints of Earth, and reach for the Moon and the planets that lay beyond, in deep space. All, particularly the early Ranger missions, were conducted in the glare of public attention and anxiety associated with the race with the Soviets for preeminence in space. As with any attempts to go where none has gone before, not all were successful. But three Ranger missions, five Surveyors, and seven of the Mariner missions succeeded in achieving their full mission objectives.

The detail in the pictures of the lunar surface sent back from the Rangers just before they impacted the Moon represented a thousandfold improvement over existing telescopic images. Viewing the granular structure of the soil and the texture of the nearby rocks from the lunar surface itself, Surveyor's close-up television images afforded an additional improvement in detail of similar magnitude. Mariner spacecraft revealed details of the sur-

William Hayward Pickering. *Willliam Hayward Pickering standing with mock-up of Army satellite.* **J.R. EYERMAN/TIME LIFE PICTURES/GETTY IMAGES.**

face features of distant Mercury and the surface and atmosphere of clouded Venus that were unobservable by other means at the time. Mariner's television data replaced the indistinct markings on Mars, observed for centuries past by astronomers using the best telescopes, with detailed images of craters and chasms, volcanoes and sand dunes, liquid flow channels and icecaps. Remote sensing instruments operating in the infrared and ultraviolet returned data on surface temperature and atmospheric temperatures, pressure and composition. This wealth of new data, said Homer Newell, "completely revitalized the field of planetary studies, which had long been quiescent for lack of new data" (Newell, 1980, p. 343). Referring to this period of space exploration, he further observed, "the most revolutionary aspect of space science contributions to the earth and planetary sciences was probably in helping to develop an integrated picture of the moon and near planets" (p. 354).

The outcome of Pickering's effort at JPL was regarded as a major contribution to regaining America's technological dominance in the field of deep space exploration. His pioneering leadership in this field also laid the technological basis for even more ambitious, and more successful, missions to the Moon and the outer planets in subsequent years.

Technology Transfer. The new initiatives that Pickering espoused in his public discourses in the mid-1960s began to take shape in the laboratories at JPL in the late 1960s and early 1970s driven, in part, by his need to find viable alternatives for JPL's unique technical resources in light of the dwindling Congressional support for major unmanned space projects. His interest in the application of space-age technology to the solution of prevalent problems in the civil sector, found expression in many new, non-space-related projects at JPL, which were conducted in parallel with the ongoing NASA programs. These projects were funded, with NASA concurrence, by independent agencies in response to JPL's unsolicited proposals for solutions to recognized problems in appropriate areas of the civil sector.

The largest of these civil sector projects, known as the "Personal Rapid Transit" project, was an experiment in urban mass transportation using small, computer-controlled vehicles to move large numbers of students around the campus of the University of West Virginia at Morgantown. The "Four Cities" program was an experiment in which the principles of space-age management were applied to the problems of city government administration involving four major cities in California. JPL also found applications for its special expertise in the field of education (student career planning and classroom safety), and law enforcement (criminalistics and police surveillance), and in the biomedical field (hospital administration, patient record keeping and mobility, arterial blood flow, clean-room technology, heat sterilization). These were all examples of space-related technology applied to problems in fields other than space or, as Pickering called it, "technology transfer."

Pickering's concern with technology transfer, the encouragement and the disillusionment, was reflected in his publications and his public speeches of the time. "Technology in the Waning Century," an Institute of Electrical and Electronics Engineers address given in California in 1973 and a statement prepared for a Senate subcommittee on Science, Technology, and Commerce in 1973, are examples. In the latter statement Pickering described the growth of his laboratory's interest in transferring its intrinsic skills in space technology to the civil sector and gave examples of where this approach had produced positive results, and where it had not. Based on the problems he had encountered with technology transfer to the public sector over several years, Pickering observed that it was a slow process. It took a long time to understand the social, legal, and economic aspects of a techno-

logical solution to a civil-sector problem, and existing funding was not commensurate with that fact. Diffusion of responsibility and decision making authority (for introducing new technology into the existing systems) and distrust between public officials and technologists regarding the advantages of introducing new technology into existing systems made it difficult to define objectives. Finally, there was no mechanism to make civil-sector technology that had been developed in federally funded laboratories available to industry and commerce.

These difficulties, Pickering proposed, could be overcome by setting up interconnected regional technology application centers. Although this idea flourished for a while it eventually faded as the laboratory's interest in civil systems wound down and was eventually superseded by a growing interest in alternative energy conversion systems.

Management Approach. From the beginning of its association with NASA in 1958 to the end of William Pickering's tenure as director in 1976, JPL's relaxed, university-like, management style came into conflict with the more rigid civil service-like mode of management demanded by the government agency that now controlled JPL. JPL's preeminent expertise in missiles and rocketry engendered an attitude of arrogance in its director and staff that irritated the officials at NASA charged with the task of managing the new member of the NASA family. A top NASA official described JPL as "bright and undisciplined" (Koppes, 1982, p. 110).

Pickering was determined to establish JPL as a dominant force in the NASA space program and lost no time in presenting NASA with a plan for exploring the solar system with JPL as the leading agency. By contrast, NASA's more measured approach called for a program of lunar exploration that would eventually phase into the deep space phases of the program. The conflict of interest over the pace of the space program, was further exacerbated when the first several Ranger lunar missions, assigned by NASA to JPL, failed for various reasons, not all of them attributable to JPL.

In the investigations that followed, Pickering's management philosophy came under attack. It was perceived to be more suited to a pure research-oriented organization rather than the project-type organization that NASA believed was necessary to achieve its immediate goal of landing on the Moon. Nevertheless, Pickering believed his role was best served by setting broad policy and viable goals backed with commensurate resources and leaving the implementation of his objectives to his top-level management staff with minimal interference from his office. As he saw it, his responsibility was to "protect" his staff from direct NASA interference, to allow them full freedom to pursue their JPL-assigned tasks. Among his employees, his management style engendered loyalty and dedication of the highest order.

To attract the very best scientific and engineering staff, Pickering established a campuslike environment at JPL, and depended upon a matrix-based, organizational agreement between the specialized technical divisions and the individual space project managers to provide the engineering expertise to build, test and launch their spacecraft. He insisted that an environment of freedom such as this not only allowed him to attract and retain highly motivated staff, but encouraged the innovative and creative processes that the new space enterprises required for success. Pride in these unique achievements engendered the hubris that so aggravated NASA.

Thus, when the sixth Ranger mission failed for reasons clearly attributable to JPL, NASA blamed the loss on the lack of discipline and management attention prevailing at JPL. Subsequently, a Congressional inquiry resulted in severe criticism of JPL's attitude, its organization, its director and its relationship to NASA. It called for the installation of a general manager at JPL to bring its administrative and accounting procedures into line with NASA's directives, and a reorganization of the laboratory technical resources to create a strong project office for each space project with commensurate authority to draw upon the technical divisions for engineering and scientific support. Pickering implemented the recommended organizational changes, but resisted changes in the laboratory's top-level management (Koppes, 1982, pp. 156–160).

Eventually though, Caltech compelled him to accept, and cede the appropriate authority to, a general manager. Pickering could not accept the diminution of his authority easily, and it was not until the closing years of his tenure that he made the personal adjustments to resolve the conflicts in his office. By then, the Ranger and Surveyor lunar missions had been completed successfully and he had received worldwide acclaim for the first missions to Venus and Mars. Under Pickering's leadership, JPL had diversified its interests to include the civil sector and was engaged in several, even more-ambitious planetary missions for NASA.

Despite their initially turbulent beginnings, Pickering had forged an enduring and remarkably productive relationship between JPL and NASA. As associate administrator Homer Newell observed years later, "Men of goodwill made it work" (Newell, 1980, p. 273).

Public Recognition. Throughout his career, William Pickering received military, civilian, and academic awards and citations, too numerous to list in detail, from the United States, Great Britain, Italy, France, Germany, Japan, and New Zealand. President Gerald Ford awarded

him the National Medal of Science, America's highest award for science, in 1975, and in 1994 he was presented with Japan's highest scientific honor, the Japan Prize, in the presence of the emperor of Japan. The queen of England made him an Honorary Knight Commander of the Most Excellent Order of the British Empire (KBE) in 1975, and he received New Zealand's highest public honor, the Order of New Zealand (ONZ) in 2003. The Royal Society of New Zealand also honored Dr. Pickering in 2003 by striking the Pickering Medal to recognize excellence and innovation in the practical applications of technology in that country. In 1965, NASA recognized his service to the nation with the award of the Distinguished Service Medal, and the following year the Republic of Italy bestowed its Order of Merit upon him for his contribution to aerospace technology.

William Pickering was elected as a member to the National Academy of Sciences in 1962. The following year, as then president of the American Rocket Society, in collaboration with the president of the Institute of Aerospace Science, Pickering effected the merger of these two professional societies to create the prestigious American Institute of Aeronautics and Astronautics in February 1963. He was elected its first president, delivered the inaugural address on "The Exploration of Deep Space" in Pittsburgh in November 1963, and remained a powerful influence in expanding the international affiliation of that organization for the rest of his active life. In January 1965 he was inducted as a founding member into the newly formed, fourth element of the National Academies, the National Academy of Engineering.

As director of a world-class establishment of more than 5,000 engineers and scientists constantly in the media spotlight, Pickering became the voice, and the face, of JPL. In the United States and internationally, Pickering was in constant demand for speeches, addresses, interviews, and lectures to institutes of higher learning, scientific bodies, and organizations of all kinds. To his great credit he accepted them all—it seemed that he could not refuse an offer to speak about the space program and its influence on various aspects of modern life. He was very articulate and had the knack of making the most complex ideas on rocket propulsion or the latest scientific findings about Venus or Mars readily comprehensible to his audiences.

Several recurrent themes appeared in all of his public utterances. These lines of thought reflected the breadth of his interests and the depth of his concerns for the future well-being of his adopted country. He held no doubt that the United States could, and would, reestablish its preeminence over the Soviet Union in the field of space exploration, and he dedicated his outstanding talents to that end. He insisted that a measured approach to solving seemingly insurmountable problems, such as scientific exploration of distant planets, was the ultimate guarantee of success. He planned for success and would not accept failure. He believed that education, technology, and scientific curiosity were necessary underpinnings of a viable society.

Business and Philanthropy. Following his retirement in 1976, Pickering spent several years assisting the government of Saudi Arabia to establish an institute of advanced technology in that country. Later, back in the United States, he set up a short-lived business venture that involved commercial applications of technology associated with Earth satellite observing systems.

In later years his concern with environmental issues led to the founding of a small company to manufacture an alternative fuel for environmentally friendly, domestic heating systems in remote areas. The product, wood pellets created from heat and pressure-treated sawdust, was the antithesis of the high-tech projects that had dominated his early professional life, but he was content. Always a very public-spirited man, Pickering lent his support, and reputation, to many educational and historical projects in the local Pasadena community.

Despite the fact that he built his career and reputation in the United States, Pickering never lost touch with his New Zealand roots. Over the years he made many return visits to New Zealand, and was greeted with enthusiasm and reverence on each occasion. In the main street of Havelock, a beautiful plaza pays tribute to the brilliant careers of two world-renowned New Zealand scientists, William Pickering and Ernest Rutherford, both of whom received their primary education at the Havelock Primary School. His attendance at the memorial dedication ceremony on 15 March 2003 marked his final appearance in his beloved homeland. He died exactly one year later.

In public, he created a personality and an image for JPL that was embraced by the public and professional communities alike. In his professional life at JPL he engendered loyalty, dedication, and above all the pursuit of excellence, in all who came within his sphere of influence. His passing in March 2004 was noted in the media throughout the world. Alluding to his vision and remarkable passion for exploring space, an official of NASA said that his pioneering work formed the foundation upon which the current program for exploring our solar system was built. The director of JPL described him as, "One of the titans of our Nation's space program" (Whalen, 2004).

BIBLIOGRAPHY

A comprehensive compilation of publications written by William H. Pickering can be found in, "William H. Pickering; Bibliography 1934–1975," Jet Propulsion Laboratory, 1976: See

JPL Library Catalog under Pickering, William Hayward; Call No. Z8689.C153. Online: http://beacon.jpl.nasa.gov. For archival material, see Pickering, (William H.) Collection: 1958–1976. JPL 214, Jet Propulsion Laboratory. Other JPL collections listed at http://beacon.jpl.nasa.gov/Find/ FindHistorical/archlist.htm. The California Institute of Technology Archives holds papers of William Pickering. Finding aid "Guide to the Papers of William H. Pickering, 1941–1970" available from http://www.oac.cdlib.org/findaid/ark:/13030/ kt067n97n6.

WORKS BY PICKERING

"A Note on the Production of Cosmic-Ray Showers." *Physical Review* 47 (1 March 1935): 425.

"A Geiger Counter Study of the Cosmic Radiation." PhD diss., California Institute of Technology, Pasadena, 1936.

With H. Victor Neher. "The Latitude Effect for Cosmic-Ray Showers." *Physical Review* 53 (15 January 1938): 111–116.

———. "Modified High Speed Geiger Counter Circuit." Letter. *Physical Review* 53, no. 4 (15 February 1938): 316.

———. "Results of a High Altitude Cosmic-Ray Survey near the Magnetic Equator." *Physical Review* 61, nos. 7 and 8 (1 April 1942): 407–413.

———. "A Cosmic Ray Radio Sonde." *Review of Scientific Instruments* 13 (April 1942): 143–147.

With H. Victor Neher and Robert A. Millikan. "Hypothesis as to the Origin of Cosmic Rays and Its Experimental Testing in India and Elsewhere." *Physical Review* 61, nos. 7 and 8 (1 April 1942): 397–407.

"Electronics in a Postwar World." *Engineering and Science Monthly* 6 (November 1943): 11–14.

"The United States Satellite Tracking Program." In *Geophysics and the IGY: Proceedings of the Symposium at the Opening of the International Geophysical Year,* edited by Hugh Odishaw and Stanley Ruttenberg. American Geophysical Union Geophysical Monograph no. 2. Washington, DC: American Geophysical Union of the National Academy of Sciences, National Research Council, 1958.

"Missiles, Rockets and Space Flight." In 75th Anniversary Issue, *Electrical Engineering* 78 (May 1959): 449–459.

"Communications throughout the Solar System." In 15th Anniversary Issue, *Proceedings of the Institute of Radio Engineers* 50 (May 1962): 594–595.

"Man at the Threshold of Space." *Engineering and Science* 27, no. 1 (October 1963): 7–14.

"The Exploration of Deep Space." American Institute of Aeronautics and Astronautics, Presidential Address, Pittsburgh, PA, 13 November 1963. See Pickering, (William H.) Collection: 1958–1976. JPL 181, Fld 95, Jet Propulsion Laboratory Archives.

"Some New Methods for Planetary Exploration." *Proceedings of the National Academy of Sciences of the United States of America* 54 (December 1965): 1471–1479.

"The Selection of Space Experiments." *American Scientist* 54 (March 1966): 103–109.

"The Grand Tour." *American Scientist* 58 (March–April 1970): 48–155.

Interviews by James H. Wilson. 1972. Archives, Oral History Program. Jet Propulsion Laboratory, California Institute of Technology, Pasadena, CA.

"Some Practical Considerations in Technology Transfer." AAS 72-033. In *Space Technology Transfer to Community and Industry: Proceedings of the AAS Eighteenth Annual Meeting and the Tenth Goddard Memorial Symposium, Held March 13–14, 1972, in Washington, D.C.*, edited by Ralph H. Tripp and John K. Stotz Jr. American Astronautical Society Science and Technology series, vol. 29. Tarzana, CA: Distributed by the AAS Publications Office, 1972.

Statement of William H. Pickering, Director, Jet Propulsion Laboratory, California Institute of Technology. Prepared for Senate Commerce Committee, Sub-committee on Science, Technology and Commerce, September 4, 1973. JPL Archives History Collection HC 3-778. Master Index page 273 online at http://beacon.jpl.nasa.gov/pdf/hcmasterindex.pdf.

"Technology in the Waning Century." *Engineering and Science* 37, no. 1 (October 1973): 15–18.

"Proposal for an International Solar System Decade." *Astronautics and Aeronautics* 12 (September 1974): 22–23.

With James H. Wilson. "Countdown to Space Exploration: A Memoir of the Jet Propulsion Laboratory, 1944–1958." Volume 2. *History of Rocketry and Astronautics: Proceedings of the Third through the Sixth History Symposia of the International Academy of Astronautics History Symposium of the International Academy of Astronautics,* edited by R. Cargill. Hall. AAS History Series vol. 7, part 2, pp. 385–421, 1977. Originally published as *Essays on the History of Rocketry and Astronautics.* NASA Conference publication CP-2014. Washington, DC: NASA, 1977.

OTHER SOURCES

American Institute of Aeronautics and Astronautics. *The AIAA at 50.* New York: AIAA, 1981.

Campbell, John. *Rutherford: Scientist Supreme.* Christchurch, New Zealand: AAS Publications, 1999.

Hall, R. Cargill. *Lunar Impact: A History of Project Ranger.* NASA Special Publication 4210. NASA History Series. Washington, DC: Scientific and Technical Information Office, National Aeronautics and Space Administration, 1977.

Kluger, Jeffrey. *Journey beyond Selene: Remarkable Expeditions past Our Moon and to the Ends of the Solar System.* New York: Simon and Schuster, 1999.

Koppes, Clayton R. *JPL and the American Space Program: A History of the Jet Propulsion Laboratory.* New Haven, CT, and London: Yale University Press, 1982.

Logsdon, John M., ed. *Exploring the Unknown: Selected Documents in the History of the U.S. Civil Space Program.* 2 vols. NASA Special Publication 4407. NASA History Series. Washington, DC: National Aeronautics and Space Administration, 2001.

Mudgway, Douglas J. "Obituary: William Hayward Pickering, 1910–2004." *2004 Annual Report Incorporating the 2004 Academy Yearbook.* Wellington, New Zealand: Royal Society of New Zealand, 2004.

———. *Big Dish: Building America's Deep Space Connection to the Planets.* Gainesville: University Press of Florida, 2005.

Newell, Homer E. *Beyond the Atmosphere: Early Years of Space Science.* NASA Special Publication 4211. NASA History Series. Washington, DC: Scientific and Technical Information Branch, National Aeronautics and Space Administration, 1980.

Thomas, Shirley. *Men of Space*, vol. 2, *William H. Pickering.* Philadelphia: Chilton Co., 1961.

Whalen, Mark, ed. "Dr. William Pickering, 1910–2004." *Universe*, 4, no. 6, (March 2004): 1.

Douglas J. Mudgway

PIERO DELLA FRANCESCA (*b.* Borgo San-Sepolcro [now Sansepolcro], Italy, in the 1410s, *d.* Borgo San-Sepolcro, 12 October 1492), *mathematics, perspective, painting.* For the original article on Piero della Francesca see *DSB*, vol. 5.

Piero is one of the few persons who figures prominently both in the history of mathematics and art. While he has received much attention as a painter, his contributions to mathematics are not so well known and will be the main topic of this addendum (for Piero and mathematics in general, see the 2005 book by J.V. Field and its references; for Piero and perspective, see also the 2007 book by Kirsti Andersen and its references).

Although many scholars have worked on Piero during the decades since the original *DSB* article and thrown much light on his work, basic knowledge about him is still lacking. Thus, his exact year of birth is unknown, just as it is unclear how and where he learned mathematics and painting. Likewise, scholars have no dates for when he composed his three books on mathematics. Of these, his *Trattato d'abaco* (referred to as *Trattato*) is supposed to be the earliest. It belongs to the so-called abacus books, which, despite their name, presented not the abacus but mathematics on an elementary level for future merchants, bank clerks, artisans, and artists. The books dealt primarily with arithmetic, but often included some algebra and practical geometry as well—which is also true of Piero's *Trattato*. In addition, Piero treated some more advanced geometrical objects, such as the regular polyhedra. He returned to these solids in the last of his books *Libellus de quinque corporibus regularibus* (referred to as *Libellus*), in which he also included five semi-regular, also called Archimedean, polyhedra (Field, 1997). These solids are called Archimedean because Pappus of Alexandria in his *Collection* stated that Archimedes had found thirteen convex polyhedra that have regular polygons of more than one kind as faces. It is unlikely that Piero knew about Pappus's claim, and he may actually himself have rediscovered

Piero della Francesca. *Piero della Francesca, 1446.* HULTON
ARCHIVE/GETTY IMAGES.

some of the Archimedean polyhedra. In *Trattato* he
described two of these, one—later called a cuboctahe-
dron—having eight equilateral triangles and six squares as
faces, obtained by cutting off the corners of a cube
through the midpoints of the edges. The second was a
truncated tetrahedron that Piero constructed by cutting
off the vertices of a tetrahedron through points situated
one third of the edge length from the corners. In *Libellus*
he came back to the truncated tetrahedron and then
added the truncated versions of the remaining four regular polyhedra.

As to the rest of the contents of *Trattato* and *Libellus,*
Piero benefited a great deal from earlier treatises—the
material for which mainly dates back to Euclid, al-
Khwārizmī, and Leonardo da Pisa (also called Fibonacci)
(on Piero and Euclid, see Folkerts, 1996; and Piero and
the algebra tradition, see Giusti, 1993).

While able to draw on a tradition for the themes of
the *Trattato* and *Libellus,* Piero was pioneering new
ground when he composed his third book *De prospectiva
pingendi* (On the perspective of painting, referred to as *De
prospectiva*), which is the first work devoted entirely to
perspective. Most of the book consists of descriptions of
various constructions in a style that tends to become

tedious, but is useful because it guides the reader through
the entire construction. Piero not only wanted to explain
the *how* of perspective constructions, but the *why* as well.
In other words, he aimed to provide a scientific foundation for his subject. This was a task that he had to start
from scratch, and he did get started. Taken stepwise,
Piero's mathematical reasoning was sound, but he did not
always provide all the arguments that were needed for his
conclusions. For instance, in his "proof" of theorem 24 in
the first book, he proved with great accuracy that some triangles are similar, but overlooked the fact that the similarity in itself did not prove his original statement.

De prospectiva is divided into three parts; in the first
Piero discussed the problem of constructing perspective
images of figures situated in a horizontal plane applying a
total of three different methods. In the second part, Piero
threw some three-dimensional figures into perspective.
The third part of *De prospectiva* is devoted to a method
that applies to both plane and solid figures. This method
is based on making a plan and an elevation of a configuration consisting of the eye point, the picture plane, and
an object to be drawn in perspective. The method then
provides what corresponds to the horizontal and vertical
coordinates of the perspective images of special selected
points in the object. There are no traces of Piero's predecessors having applied this method, but still he takes it for
granted that his readers knew the technique of constructing plans and elevations of objects. The essential novelty
was that Piero applied this technique to perspective, and
he may well have been the first to do so. He himself stated
that he found this perspective method less abstract and at
the same time more powerful than the constructions presented in the two first parts of the book. In his own words,
it was "easy to demonstrate and understand" and advantageous to apply "to more difficult solids" (Piero, 1974, p.
129). And he did present impressive examples, among
them how to construct the perspective image of a tilted
cube in which none of the edges are horizontal or parallel
to the picture plane, and a trompe l'oeil giving the impression that a bowl pops up from a table when seen from the
intended eye point. What made the example with the
tilted cube difficult was to construct its plan and elevation; for this Piero applied a plan, an elevation, and a third
projection perpendicular to the two others to describe a
rotation of a cube having its sides parallel to the plans of
reference.

De prospectiva did in general not receive the appreciation it deserved. Presumably, its mathematical arguments
were too difficult for practitioners to follow and its long
and detailed descriptions of how to perform constructions
deterred mathematicians from studying it carefully.

Piero was admired by Luca Pacioli and Giorgio Vasari,
but by the end of the sixteenth century he seems to have

been forgotten both as a mathematician and as a painter. Thus, it took four hundred years after his death before his name appeared as the author of a printed book. Although his work was not mentioned often, Piero was not completely without influence. Presumably through Pacioli's praise of *De prospectiva*, Daniele Barbaro became aware of the work and copied longer passages from it almost verbatim without revealing his source. Before Barbaro, he himself had behaved similarly by including an Italian version of *Libellus* as a third section of his own *De divina proportione* (1509) with out referring to Piero. Through these publications, and presumably also through manuscripts that applied Piero's material, some of his ideas became part of textbooks. For instance, it is striking that in his books on geometry and proportions, the German painter and mathematician Albrecht Dürer applied methods that are similar to Piero's, including the technique of involving a plan and an elevation to describe movements of bodies in space.

SUPPLEMENTARY BIBLIOGRAPHY

WORKS BY PIERO DELLA FRANCESCA

Trattato d'abaco. Biblioteca Medicea Laurenziana, Florence, Codex Ashburnham 280, ed. Gino Arrighi, Pisa: Domus Galilæana, 1970.

De prospectiva pingendi, Biblioteca Palatina, Parma, Ms. no. 1576, ed. Giusta Nicco Fasola. Florence: Sansoni, 1942. Later editions 1974 and 1984. Written presumably before 1482 in Italian—but with the Latin title. Also published in German, French, and Latin translations.

Libellus de quinque corporibus regularibus, Biblioteca apostolica Vaticana, Codex Urbinas 632. In "L'opera de corporibus regularibus … usurpati da fra Luca Pacioli," ed. Girolamo Mancini. *Atti della Reale Accademia dei Lincei, Memorie della classe di scienze morali, storiche e filologiche* 5 (14, 1916): 441–580. Published as *Libellus de quinque corporibus regularibus*. Rome: Accademia dei Lincei, 1915. Also edited as *Libellus de quinque corporibus regularibus; corredato della versione volgare di Luca Pacioli*, 3 vols. Florence: Giunti, 1995. Latin version of a manuscript that Piero presumably composed in Italian and is now lost.

OTHER SOURCES

Andersen, Kirsti. *The Geometry of an Art: The History of the Mathematical Theory of Perspective From Alberti to Monge*. New York: Springer, 2007.

Banker, James R. *The Culture of San Sepolcro during the Youth of Piero della Francesca*. Ann Arbor: University of Michigan Press, 2003.

———. "Contributi alla cronologia della vita e delle opere di Piero della Francesca." *Arte Cristiana* 92 (2004): 248–258.

Dabell, Frank, and J. V. Field. "Piero della Francesca." In *The Dictionary of Art*, edited by Jane Turner. New York: Grove, 1996.

Davis, Magaret Daly. *Piero della Francesca's Mathematical Treatises*. Ravenna: Longo, 1977.

Field, J. V. "Rediscovering the Archimedean Polyhedra: Piero della Francesca, Luca Pacioli, Leonardo da Vinci, Albrecht Dürer, Daniele Barbaro, and Johannes Kepler." *Archive for History of Exact Sciences* 50 (1997): 241–289.

———. *Piero della Francesca. A Mathematician's Art*. New Haven, CT: Yale University Press, 2005.

Folkerts, Menso, "Piero della Francesca and Euclid." In *Piero della Francesca tra arte e scienza*, edited by Marisa Dalai Emiliani & Valter Curzi, Venice: Marsilio, 1996.

Giusti, Enrico. "Fonti medievali dell'*Algebra* di Piero della Francesca." *Bollettino di Storia delle Scienze Matematiche* 13 (1993): 199–250.

Jayawardene, S. A. "The *Trattato d'abaco* of Piero della Francesca." In *Cultural Aspects of the Italian Renaissance: Essays in Honour of Paul Oskar Kristeller*, edited by Cecil H. Clough. Manchester, U.K.: Manchester University Press, 1976.

                                        Kirsti Andersen

PIVETEAU, JEAN (*b.* Rouillac, Charente, France, 23 September 1899; *d.* Paris, France, 7 March 1991), *vertebrate paleontology, paleoanthropology.*

Piveteau was the best-known French paleontologist of the mid-twentieth century because he edited *Traité de Paléontologie* (Treatise on paleontology; seven volumes in ten tomes, 1952–1969). At that time, the only similar treatise was the Soviet *Osnovy Paleontologii* (Fundamentals of paleontology; thirteen volumes, 1958–1964), edited by Uri Orlov, whereas Raymond C. Moore's twenty-four-volume *Treatise on Invertebrate Paleontology* (1953–1981) had a more restricted scope. Piveteau was also an excellent anatomist who brought to light significant features of Triassic actinopterygian fish and of mammal neurocrania. He described and interpreted the evolutionary significance of an exceptional Triassic amphibian that partly bridges the gap between stegocephalians and anurans, and he studied the origin and evolution of humans, for which he proposed a spiritualist interpretation deeply inspired by Pierre Teilhard de Chardin's view of life.

Early Life. Jean Piveteau was a quiet, rather reserved, and distinguished man who enjoyed the silence of his work space. His father was Gaston Piveteau, a merchant established at Rouillac, a small city of the Charente department, near Cognac, and his mother was Marie Barbotteaud. After studying in the lycée (high school) of Angoulême, where he graduated in 1917, he immediately entered the French army. After World War I he settled in Paris to study at the Sorbonne while working for a Parisian publisher to fund his studies. At that time, he frequently visited the Institut catholique of Paris, where he met Teilhard de Chardin, who introduced him to Marcellin Boule, the holder of the chair of paleontology in the Muséum national d'histoire naturelle (French National Museum of Natural History). Just after his marriage to Marcelle Janet, the daughter of a renowned physicist and member of the French Académie des Sciences, he was sent in 1924 by Boule to southwest Madagascar to collect Permian amphibians and reptiles. Piveteau studied this material for his doctoral thesis, which he defended in 1926.

Studies in Fossil Vertebrate Anatomy. The same year, Piveteau was appointed a scientist in the National Museum of Natural History and turned his interest in part to fossil mammals. In 1929 he described fossil mammals from the Upper Miocene in collaboration with Camille Arambourg, who had collected them near Thessaloniki, Greece, during World War I. In "Les mammifères de Nihowan" (1930), he and Teilhard de Chardin described the Plio-Pleistocene fossil mammals of Nihowan, China. Piveteau had been appointed *chef de travaux* (director of applied studies) in 1928 at the National School of Mines, where he was in charge of the practical paleontological studies, especially those devoted to invertebrate fossils. In 1931 the Caisse nationale des sciences (a national scientific funding agency which was the ancestor of the French Centre national de la recherche scientifique supported his research work as *chargé de recherches* in the National Museum of Natural History, although Piveteau continued teaching at the National School of Mines.

Boule then convinced Piveteau to study the cranial anatomy of fossil creodonts and carnivores from the Quercy phosphorites in southwestern France. The remarkable quality of preservation of the fossil mammals found in these Upper Eocene and Oligocene karstic deposits allowed him to make precise anatomical investigations, especially concerning the position of foramens in the basal part of the skull and the disposition of the nerves and blood vessels. He was thus able in 1931 to document an evolutionary parallelism in two families of carnivores, Nimravidae and Felidae, and to reconstruct the evolution of the cephalic vascular system of several genera of mammals, especially among creodonts in 1931 and carnivores in 1935. Additionally, Piveteau began to study casts of mammal endocrania, thereby introducing himself into the field of paleoneurology, a relatively new branch of anatomy created by Tilly Edinger. This led him to show that archaic placental mammals like creodonts differ from theriodont reptiles by an increase in the size of the cerebellum and of the cerebral hemispheres and by a reduction of the olfactive region. He published his results in "Études sur quelques Créodontes des phosphorites du Quercy" (1935).

Piveteau also studied fossil fish preserved as negative casts in the Triassic from northwestern Madagascar, dedicating an important monograph, "Paléontologie de Madagascar. XXI. Les poissons du Trias inférieur" (1934), to them. The remarkable preservation of these fish gave him the opportunity to study the structure of the neurocrania of some primitive actinopterygians and to confirm the validity of the segmental theory of the skull. He also proposed an attempt to reconstruct the cephalo-branchial circulatory system. Additionally, Piveteau noted that the evolutionary history of the lower vertebrates was accompanied by a regression of the bony tissue. Another aspect of his research was the demonstration of the bipolar paleogeographical distribution of the Triassic fish fauna, as a great similarity exists between that from Madagascar and those from Svalbard and Greenland, described earlier by Erik Stensiö.

In addition to the fish from northwestern Madagascar, an exceptional fossil was described by Piveteau, who immediately recognized that it was an ancestral type of anuran frogs, which he named Protobatrachus in 1937. This name, already in use, was later replaced by Triadobatrachus. This unique fossil appeared to him as a transitional type, filling the gap between stegocephalians and anurans. Moreover, the fact that this fossil exhibits a skull already similar to that of a frog, but a vertebral column devoid of urostyle and forearms and legs with two separate bones instead of fused bones as in modern frogs, convinced him that heterochronic processes had taken place in the evolutionary development of frogs. Going further, Piveteau thought that two different processes might explain the evolutionary modifications of living beings, one based on extrinsic factors resulting from influences exerted by the environment and the other deriving from intrinsic factors corresponding to "the intimate nature of the organism." He was convinced that the occurrence of heterochrony in the development of such an organism is an argument for the predominance of intrinsic factors over environmental ones, as well as the existence of parallel trends in the evolution of different groups of amphibians, such as labyrinthodonts, phyllospondyles, and lepospondyles, a fact that he had commented one year earlier in "L'évolution parallèle et son mécanisme" (1936).

When Marcellin Boule retired in 1936, the position of professor of paleontology in the National Museum of Natural History opened up. Piveteau, supported by Boule, was the obvious favorite to succeed him, but behind-the-scenes machinations prevented his election, so that Camille Arambourg was eventually appointed.

Soon after his failed attempt to succeed Boule as head of the paleontological laboratory of the National Museum, Piveteau obtained the position of *maître de recherches* at the Caisse nationale des sciences in 1937. Thanks to the high level of his research on both lower vertebrates and the skull and brain of mammals, he was appointed *maître de conférences* in 1938 at the Sorbonne in Paris, a position equivalent to the first grade of professor. He was promoted to *professeur sans chaire* (full professor) in 1942 and finally obtained a chair of paleontology for himself at the Sorbonne in 1953. He occupied this chair until his retirement in 1970. Meanwhile Piveteau had been elected to the French Académie des Sciences in 1956 and to L'Académie Royale des Sciences of Belgium in 1962. He was also elected in the 1980s to the Accademia Nazionale dei Lincei (National Academy of Lincei) in Italy.

As a professor, Piveteau had an incomparable talent for explaining with great clarity his conception of the evolutionary history of vertebrates and the origin of humanity. He is remembered as a brilliant teacher whose lectures were highly appreciated by his students. His *Des premiers vertébrés à l'homme* (1963; From the first vertebrates to humankind), is a reliable indicator of the course that he taught at the Sorbonne in the early 1960s. His purpose was to describe the main stages of the anatomical evolution of vertebrates: from the armoured Agnatha to the Gnathostomata, first represented by fish and then by amphibians through the development of air breathing organs (lungs) and of paired limbs instead of fins; the development of reptiles, characterized by their amniotic eggs; and, finally, the appearance of mammals, with their more complex ear because of the transformation of the articulation of the jaw with the skull. Piveteau then focused on primates and finally on human origins, with special reference to Teilhard de Chardin's metaphysical model. Another successful book, demonstrative of Piveteau's great ability as a scientific writer, was *Images des mondes disparus* (1951; Images of bygone worlds), in which he described a series of paleontological scenes from the appearance of life to human paleontology in his native region of Charente.

The *Traité de Paléontologie*. Having developed successful anatomical research programs on fossil vertebrates, Piveteau engaged in a new and important project, the publication of a French-language *Traité de paléontologie* (seven volumes in ten tomes, 1952–1969; Treatise on paleontology). It was probably inspired by the successful handbook, *Les fossiles: Éléments de paléontologie* (1935), on which he had collaborated with Boule. The last-published paleontological treatise was the four-volume *Handbuch der Palaeontologie* (1876–1893), edited by Karl Zittel (1839–1904), which had been translated into French and English. The important progress of paleontological knowledge since then required a more ambitious project. For this reason, instead of the four volumes of paleozoology written by Zittel, Piveteau planned a seven-volume collective treatise, a project that soon grew as it rapidly

appeared that the sixth volume—devoted to fossil mammals—had to be divided into two tomes. It later became necessary to split volume four, which had been planned for fishlike vertebrates (Agnatha) and fish, into three parts. The publication of the treatise, which required the collaboration of fifty-one scientists, sixteen of them foreigners, was rapid except for one volume. From 1952 to 1961, six of the seven planned volumes appeared, but volume four appeared later because the best international expert for ostracoderms and placoderms, Stensiö, needed several years for his two long contributions. These parts of the fourth volume finally appeared in 1964 and 1969. Piveteau personally wrote several important chapters: for example, the ones on birds; on the origin and systematics of Mesozoic mammals, Prototheria, and Metatheria; on carnivores; and also on primates and human paleontology, to which the entire volume seven is dedicated.

The publication of the *Traité de paléontologie* was a great success, both for the fame of the French-speaking paleontological community and for the French publishers, Masson et Cie. Additionally, it provided Piveteau with international scientific status, and he was soon recognized in his own country as the highest paleontological authority, as illustrated by his election in 1956 to the Academy of Sciences.

Human Origins and Evolution. Piveteau's interest in the study of primate evolution began in 1948 with his anatomical study of the skull and brain cast of the subfossil Lemurian genus Archaeolemur from Madagascar. This convinced him that lemuriforms and lorisiforms were not involved in the origin of upper primates, because the design of their arterial cerebral system differs from that of simians and anthropomorphs.

Later, Piveteau introduced himself carefully into the "elite" field of paleoanthropology and prepared the anatomical description of the Neanderthalian skeleton found at Regourdou, near Montignac, Dordogne, a task he worked on from 1963 to 1966 but never completed. In 1967 he studied the Rissian parietal found in the Lazaret cave, on the outskirts of Nice, and finally, in 1970, the Rissian human remains found in "abri Suard" (Suard rock shelter) at La Chaise, Charente.

As demonstrated by the titles of several of his books on the topic, the origin and evolution of *Homo sapiens* rapidly became Piveteau's first intellectual concern during the last thirty years of his life: *L'origine de l'homme* (1962), *Origine et destinée de l'homme* (1973), *L'apparition de l'homme* (1986), and finally *La main et l'hominisation* (1991), which was printed a few weeks before his death. In the first three books, Piveteau described human evolution as a succession of stages. First, he emphasized the importance of the acquisition of verticality by transformation of the posterior limb and pelvis. Piveteau considered bipedalism a decisive step because as a result, the hands became free for making and using lithic tools. Progressively, modifications appeared in the hand structure, making it possible to oppose the thumb to the other fingers, which increased the possibility of prehension, or grasping. This process was accompanied by a correlative increase in the size of the cerebral cortex. The area devoted to the hand became progressively larger than the one corresponding to the foot. Piveteau also believed that the interaction between hand and brain was responsible for the development of a reflective way of thinking that, finally, opened the way to the appearance of a structured language when the larynx became able to produce articulated sounds. Spirituality appeared later, as evidenced by the funerary rites that are already well-documented for Neanderthals and, still better, by the development of art (parietal paintings, engravings, and sculptures) during Upper Paleolithic times.

Being a disciple of Teilhard de Chardin, Piveteau was evidently a deeply convinced transformist. However, his view of biological evolution was completely unrelated to Charles Darwin's, and he considered the recent progress of paleoanthropology as being totally independent of the Darwinian and Lamarckian theories. In this field he can be considered a spiritualist evolutionist who tried to avoid precise explanations concerning the mechanisms and modalities of biological transformations. He was convinced that "intrinsic" factors are predominate in the evolutionary process. In fact, being also influenced by Henri Bergson's *Évolution créatrice* (1907; Creative evolution) and Édouard Le Roy's *Les origines humaines et l'évolution de l'intelligence* (1928), Piveteau, who was interested in a scientific approach of finality, distinguished an internal finality, corresponding to the conditions making possible the existence of living beings, and an external one, which may be defined as an adaptation to environmental conditions. Moreover, as he stated in "Aspects du problème de la finalité dans les sciences de la nature" (1949), Piveteau considered that paleontological evolution can be understood as the expression of tendencies, without predetermined design.

Although his views concerning biological evolution were obviously Christian, as he was a convinced follower of Teilhard de Chardin's philosophy, Piveteau was an open-minded, tolerant scientist, respectful of divergent points of view. He demonstrated this by his decision to organize an international meeting in Paris in April 1947 (sponsored by the Rockefeller Foundation), to which he invited several important foreign scientists. Among them were the English (later Indian) geneticist John B. S. Haldane and the American paleontologist George Gaylord Simpson, two theoreticians of the neo-Darwinian New Synthesis. Haldane lectured on "The Mechanisms of Evolution" and Simpson on "Orthogenesis and the Synthetic Theory of Evolution" and also on "Micro-evolution, Macro-evolution, and Mega-evolution." This meeting, the proceedings of which were edited by Piveteau in a book, *Paléontologie et Transformisme* (1950), provided an excellent opportunity for the confrontation of different approaches to evolution; the French paleontologists and biologists were at that time generally more inclined to consider evolution as depending on internal tendencies leading to a final purpose, whereas English and American scientists considered natural selection to be the major evolutionary mechanism. It is significant that Piveteau, who convened the meeting, never intervened or objected to any argument opposed to his own conceptions. Nevertheless, Piveteau, who was little inclined to modify his own opinions, was not at all influenced by the new evolutionary synthesis and remained faithful to his previous conceptions.

History of Natural Sciences. Piveteau, finally, also contributed to the history of natural science and was sometimes asked to give lectures on this topic at the Sorbonne. Although he rarely published historical studies, his acute analysis of the 1830 debate between Étienne Geoffroy Saint-Hilaire and Georges Cuvier, in "Le débat entre Cuvier et Geoffroy Saint-Hilaire sur l'unité de plan et de composition" (The debate between Cuvier and Geoffroy Saint-Hilaire over unity of design and composition), appeared in 1950. Cuvier had strongly criticized the "théorie des analogues" of Geoffroy, who considered that all animal groups are designed according to the same organizational plan. Another major contribution by Piveteau to the history of science was the extensive *Oeuvres philosophiques de Buffon* (1954), which he edited. In it Piveteau reprinted significant excerpts from Comte Georges-Louis Leclerc de Buffon's works, especially from his *Théorie de la Terre* (1749) and *Époques de la Nature* (1778), and he provided an introduction to the volume.

BIBLIOGRAPHY

WORKS BY PIVETEAU

"Paléontologie de Madagascar. XIII. Amphibiens et reptiles permiens." *Annales de Paléontologie* 15 (1926): 53–179.

With Camille Arambourg. "Les vertébrés du Pontien de Salonique." *Annales de Paléontologie* 18 (1929): 59–138.

With Pierre Teilhard de Chardin. "Les mammifères fossiles de Nihowan." *Annales de Paléontologie* 19 (1930): 1–134.

"Les chats des phosphorites du Quercy." *Annales de Paléontologie* 20 (1931): 105–163.

"Paléontologie de Madagascar. XXI. Les poissons du Trias inférieur: Contribution à l'étude des Actinoptérygiens." *Annales de Paléontologie* 23 (1934): 81–183.

"Études sur quelques Créodontes des phosphorites du Quercy." *Annales de Paléontologie* 24 (1935): 73–95.

With Marcellin Boule. *Les fossiles: Éléments de paléontologie.* Paris: Masson, 1935.

"L'évolution parallèle et son mécanisme." *La terre et la vie* 6 (1936): 30–36.

"Paléontologie de Madagascar. XXIII. Un amphibien du Trias inférieur: Essai sur l'origine et l'évolution des amphibiens anoures." *Annales de Paléontologie* 26 (1937): 135–178.

"Recherches anatomiques sur les Lémuriens disparus: Le genre *Archaeolemur*." *Annales de Paléontologie* 34 (1948): 125–172.

"Aspects du problème de la finalité dans les sciences de la nature." *Annales Hébert et Haug* 7 (1949): 333–343.

"Le débat entre Cuvier et Geoffroy Saint-Hilaire sur l'unité de plan et de composition." *Revue d'Histoire des Sciences* 3 (1950): 343–363.

Editor. *Paléontologie et transformisme.* Paris: Albin Michel, 1950.

Images des mondes disparus. Paris: Masson, 1951.

Editor. *Traité de paléontologie.* 7 vols. Paris: Masson, 1952–1969.

Editor. *Oeuvres philosophiques de Buffon.* Paris: Presses universitaires de France, 1954.

L'origine de l'homme: L'homme et son passé. Paris: Hachette, 1962.

Des premiers vertébrés à l'homme. Paris: Albin Michel, 1963.

"La grotte de Regourdou (Dordogne): Paléontologie humaine." *Annales de Paléontologie* 49 (1963): 283–304; 50 (1964): 155–194; 52 (1966): 163–194.

"Un pariétal humain de la grotte du Lazaret (Alpes-Maritimes)." *Annales de Paléontologie* (Vertébrés) 53 (1967): 165–199.

"Les grottes de La Chaise (Charente): Paléontologie humaine. I. L'homme de l'abri Suard." *Annales de Paléontologie* (Vertébrés) 56 (1970): 173–325.

Origine et destinée de l'homme. 2nd ed. Paris: Masson, 1983.

L'apparition de l'homme—Le point de vue scientifique. Paris: O.E.I.L., 1986.

La main et l'hominisation. Paris: Masson, 1991.

OTHER SOURCES

Coppens, Yves. "La vie et l'œuvre de Jean Piveteau." *Comptes Rendus de l'Académie des sciences, Paris,* La vie des sciences, série générale, 9, no. 5 (1992): 445–451.

Gaudant, Jean. "Hommage à Jean Piveteau (1899–1991) pour le centenaire de sa naissance." *Travaux du Comité français d'Histoire de la Géologie,* 3rd series, 13, no. 3 (1999): 29–38.

Taquet, Philippe, ed. "Hommage au Professeur Jean Piveteau." *Annales de Paléontologie* 77, no. 4 (1991): 227–283.

Jean Gaudant

PLANCIUS, PETRUS (*b.* Dranouter, West-Vlaanderen, Southern Netherlands [now Belgium], 1552; *d.* Amsterdam, Netherlands, 15 May 1622), *cartography, cosmography, navigation, preaching.*

Born as Peter Platevoet in Flanders, Petrus Plancius studied abroad and became a theologian and a mapmaker.

He produced some globes and maps, including a well-known world map in 1592. He had a great influence on the Dutch Asian expeditions.

Early Years. Peter Platevoet was born in 1552 in the Flanders village of Dranouter. Little is known about his childhood, but it seems that his parents became Protestants. Platevoet studied theology, history, and languages in Germany and England. In England he probably learned about mathematics, astronomy, and geography. When he was older, Platevoet Latinized his name, as was the custom among savants at that time.

In 1576 he became a preacher in West-Flanders, a province in Belgium, and later that year he went to Mechelen, Brussels, and Louvain. In the 1580s he stayed in Brussels for a long time, but when the city surrendered to the duke of Parma, King Philip II of Spain's governor-general in the Netherlands, in 1585 Petrus Plancius fled to the north. He lived in Amsterdam and became a pastor of the Dutch Reformed Church. From December 1585 until his death on 15 May 1622, he fulfilled his job as preacher. Plancius was a fervent Contra-Remonstrant and discussed many theological issues.

In addition to his thorough knowledge of the Holy Bible, he was well-grounded in the study of cosmography, geography, and cartography. He was not only one of the most talked-about preachers in the Dutch republic, but also one of the important mapmakers of his time.

Early Publications. Petrus Plancius was the first *caertsnyder* (map cutter) in the Dutch republic to produce waxed grid maps. Therefore, on 12 September 1594 he received a patent for the publication and distribution of the world map for twelve years from the States-General. He was, together with the Flemish engraver and mapmaker Jodocus Hondius and the brothers Van Langren, one of the first makers of celestial globes in the Netherlands. His first globe was produced in 1589, a revision of an earlier celestial globe. Among his revisions were four additions to the southern sky: the two Magellanic Clouds (they were unnamed on the globe) and two new constellations, Crux and Triangulus Antarcticus. Their positions were taken from reports of explorers.

In 1590 Petrus Plancius made five terrestrial maps for a Dutch edition of the Holy Bible. Two years later he made a well-known world map: *Nova et exacta terrarum orbis tabula geographica ac hydrographica.* New and exact geographical and hydrographical map of the world). This map contained celestial planispheres in the upper corners on which he added two additional constellations.

Asian Expeditions. Petrus Plancius was one of the driving forces behind the first Dutch expeditions to Asia, assisting with preparations and providing instruction. To avoid encounters with Spain and Portugal, which were already sailing to the East Indies around southern Africa, Plancius decided to try a northeast route around Asia. He supplied maps for the voyage and advised the fleet commander, Willem Barents, in celestial navigation. The northeast voyages of 1594 and 1595 were failures, but a third attempt was made in 1596. It was on that last expedition that Barents's ship got stuck in the polar ice, and the crew had to spend the winter in Nova Zembla, an island northwest above Russia, in what came to be called the Barents Sea. Late in the spring of the next year, the crew was able to sail south in two small boats. Barents died on the return voyage; the survivors arrived at Amsterdam in November 1597, not having found a northeast passageway.

In 1595, together with Barents, Plancius published a book titled *Nieuwe Beschrijvinghe ende Caertboeck van de Middelandtsche Zee* (New description and map book of the Mediterranean Sea). In this work he designed a map that was engraved by the well-known globe- and mapmaker Hondius.

Because the northeast sea route around Asia did not seem very promising, even before the third voyage a group of Dutch merchants had financed a southern expedition. Plancius again helped with the planning and used the opportunity to conduct scientific research. A theory in the late sixteenth century claimed that a compass needle's variation from north (its declination) would enable one to determine longitude. Plancius developed his own theory to ascertain longitude at sea by means of magnetic variation. To test that theory during the southern voyage, Plancius taught junior merchant Frederik de Houtman how to measure and record compass declinations. It is known that the method developed by Plancius was used from 1596 onward by mariners.

Plancius also used the voyage to discover southern stars that were not visible from Europe. He taught navigators, especially Pieter Dircksz Keyser, but also other sailors, how to measure star positions with an astrolabe and instructed them to chart the southern sky. From ship records of 1596 it is known that the astrolabe was used to measure the declination of the southern stars.

The Dutch southern expedition, known as the Eerste Shipvaart, or First Voyage, set sail from the port of Texel in April 1595. It reached the East Indies in 1596 and returned to Texel in August 1597. Plancius asked Keyser, the chief pilot on the *Hollandia,* to make observations to fill in the blank area around the south celestial pole on European maps of the southern sky. Keyser died in Java the following year, but his catalog included 135 new stars arranged in twelve new constellations. Most of them were invented to honor discoveries by sixteenth-century

explorers. They were first published on a 1598 celestial globe made by Hondius.

After the foundation of the VOC (Verenigde Oostindische Compagnie, or East India Company) in 1602, Plancius became its first mapmaker. During the first quarter of the seventeenth century, he seemed more interested in preaching than in cartography and cosmography. But still, some of his maps were published during that time. In 1607 he produced a large revised world map. In 1612 he created a celestial globe, and later he designed an Earth and another celestial globe (1614 and 1615), both brought out by the well-known publisher Petrus Kaerius. His contemporaries described him as one of the greatest geographers of his time.

BIBLIOGRAPHY

A complete bibliography of Plancius's work, with descriptions of much of his maps and publications, is Günter Schilder, Monumenta Cartographica Neerlandica, *Vol. VII,* Cornelis Claesz (c. 1551–1609): Stimulator and Driving Force of Dutch Cartography, *Alphen aan den Rijn, Netherlands: Canaletto/Repro-Holland, 2003.*

WORK BY PLANCIUS

With Willem Barents. *Nieuwe Beschrijvinghe ende Caertboeck van de Middelandtsche Zee.* 1595. Amsterdam: C. Claesz, 1595.

OTHER SOURCES

Blondeau, Roger A. *Petrus Plancius (1552–1622) van Dranouter.* Roesbrugge, Belgium: Schoonaert, 1985.

Enckel, Carl. "The Representation of the North of Europe in the World Map of Petrus Plancius of 1592." *Imago Mundi* 10 (1952): 55–69.

Keuning, Johannes. *Petrus Plancius: Theoloog en Geograaf, 1555–1622.* Amsterdam: Van Kampen, 1946.

Ortroy, Fernand van. *Un précieux globe terrestre en cuivre jaune construit par Pierre Plancius.* Antwerp, Belgium: De Backer, 1899.

Parmentier, Jan. *Peper, Plancius en Porselein: De reis van het schip Swarte Leeuw naar Atjeh en Bantam.* Zutphen, Netherlands: Walburg Pers, 2003.

Wieder, Frederik C. *Petrus Plancius: Novus et exacta terrarium. …* Gravenhage, Netherlands: Martinus Kijhoff, 1927. The text is in English.

Steve Philips

PLANCK, MAX

(*b.* Kiel, Germany, 23 April 1858; *d.* Göttingen, Germany, 4 October 1947), *physics.* For the original article on Planck see *DSB,* vol. 10.

Taking advantage of scholarship that has appeared subsequent to the original *DSB* article, the author of this postscript offers a more critical assessment of the meaning of the "energy elements," or quanta, that Max Planck introduced in his black-body theory of 1900, and gives a more nuanced description of Planck's activities in science policy and public life in general, particularly Planck's behavior during the Third Reich.

Planck's Quantum Concept. The evolution of Planck's black-body theory and how he introduced his energy elements is clearly described in Hans Kangro's original *DSB* article. Nevertheless, over the thirty years following that publication historians have come to disagree about how Planck thought about his energy elements in 1900, and consequently, about the starting point of the quantum revolution. The origin of this disagreement came with the publication of Thomas S. Kuhn's book Black-*Body Theory and the Quantum Discontinuity* (1978). Kuhn argued forcefully that Planck did not intend his energy elements to express a quantum discontinuity. Instead, according to Kuhn, Einstein's 1905 hypothesis of light quanta, and his and Paul Ehrenfest's critical analyses of Planck's radiation formula in 1905–1906 mark the beginning of the modern understanding of quantum discontinuity. Only with Einstein's and Ehrenfest's analyses did it become clear that Planck's model of resonators in equilibrium with radiation did not behave according to classical physics and that the energy exchange mediated by these resonators had to exhibit some discontinuity.

In contrast, many physicists and textbooks still hold that Planck's resonators (or oscillators) were indeed quantized—that is, Planck unambiguously restricted their energies to integral multiples of h, Planck's constant multiplied by the resonator frequency. Such an unequivocal statement is difficult to defend on any understanding of Planck, and historians have almost invariably been more nuanced. Nevertheless, Martin J. Klein, whose papers from the 1960s paved the way for understanding Planck, argued that Planck took his energy quanta very seriously, though he also emphasized how little Planck said about them in 1900, and how uncertain he seemed for many years about their physical interpretation.

Kuhn, by contrast, argued that Planck could not possibly have intended to quantize his resonators. His central argument involves Planck's adoption of Boltzmann's use of combinatorials in 1877 to relate entropy to probability as a path to understanding the behavior of an ideal gas. Although Boltzmann began with finite energy elements as an illustrative if unphysical way of describing his new approach, his final result involved the partition of gas molecules with continuous energies among cells in phase space. Kuhn found clear indications in Planck's original papers that in adopting Boltzmann's general approach, Planck likewise had continuous resonator energies in

mind. Not until 1908, according to Kuhn, did Planck adopt the idea of discontinuous resonator energies.

Today, many though not all historian of physics follow the Kuhnian arguments, at least in broad outline. Nevertheless, Planck scholarship has not stood still. Allan Needell (1980) has shown that as early as 1899, Planck was expecting new and interesting physics to result from a better understanding of microscopic resonators in equilibrium with a Maxwellian radiation field, and has argued that Planck looked on his new law in just that light. Needell has also argued strongly that in focusing on the issue of "quantum discontinuity," historians are asking the wrong question: It is more fruitful to take Planck on his own terms, and trace the development of his ideas in the early years of the twentieth century, rather than focus too exclusively on a question that would have had little meaning in 1900. Olivier Darrigol, in a series of detailed and closely argued studies (1991, 1992, 2000), has likewise argued that Planck realized his work entailed significant new physics, though Darrigol also supported many of Kuhn's arguments, and noted in addition that Planck worked within a Helmholzian tradition of deemphasizing detailed microscopic models. Significantly, both Needell and Darrigol have shown, independently, building on a theme first pointed out by Klein, that in spite of his adoption of Boltzmann's relation of entropy to probability, Planck retained until 1914 or so his absolute interpretation of the second law of thermodynamics, in which spontaneous decreases in entropy were not merely improbable, but forbidden. Subsequently, Gearhart (2002) argued that Planck understood Boltzmann's 1877 derivation very well, and would surely have understood the significant and puzzling differences between Boltzmann's derivation and his own. Gearhart also notes that in Planck's 1906 *Lectures*, Planck pointedly declined to speculate on the physical significance of his new "action element" h, even as he emphasized its central importance. He suggests that by 1906, and possibly earlier, Planck understood that he had discovered something very new, but thought it premature to speculate on its physical significance. All of this work has led to a much deeper understanding of Planck's achievement and to a considerable measure of agreement, even if historians have not yet arrived at a consensus on how Planck regarded his energy elements and action element h in the early years of the twentieth century.

Planck and Policy Matters. Around 1910 Planck stepped more and more into the role of a representative of Berlin's scientific community and later of Germany in general—assuming the place which had been occupied by his mentor Hermann von Helmholtz during the last quarter of nineteenth century. This was brought about not only by Planck's extraordinary scientific rank and excellence, but also by his rising international prestige and the fact that he

Max Planck. © BETTMANN/CORBIS.

was always ready to take on administrative and political functions for his field. Such activity agreed not only with his professional ethos and his sense of duty, but also with his conviction that modern science functions optimally only when the researchers themselves do not shy away from such responsibilities. Therefore Planck was not an unworldly or secluded scientist—although he was very cautious about politics in his public statements. He made only a few explicit expressions of such opinions. But he nevertheless declared in various publications—in particular during the second part of his life—his views on philosophical, epistemological, and ideological issues of physics and modern science in general. This stemmed from his basic convictions about the cultural value of science for mankind—a typical attitude for Planck's generation. Public lectures became his preferred forum for these views, but he also wrote articles for daily newspapers and popular science magazines, gave interviews, and broadcast speeches on radio.

Planck's caution in political statements stands in a remarkable contrast to the broad spectrum of official and scientific-political functions he was willing to assume. He served the board of the German Physical Society for more than three decades—as treasurer, committee member, and between 1905 and 1908 and 1915–1916 as the society's chairman. Additionally, at the behest of the society he was one of the editors of the reputable *Annalen der Physik* for decades. He was also head of the Gesellschaft Deutscher Naturforscher und Ärzte (Society of German Naturalists and Physicians) and the dean and rector (1914–1915) of the University of Berlin. For more than a quarter of a century—from 1912 through 1938—Planck held the position of a permanent secretary of the Prussian Academy of Sciences. He was thus vested in one of the most powerful offices of science policy that a scientist could assume without changing completely to state service. In 1930 he also became president of the Kaiser Wilhelm Society for the Advancement of the Sciences, a position he held until 1937. In these capacities or within the framework of the funding institution Notgemeinschaft der Wissenschaft (later the Deutsche Forschungsgemeinschaft), as well as as member of several boards of other scientific institutions, Planck was able to foster and represent the high international reputation that German science had required during the first decades of the twentieth century.

Planck's social and political views as well as his self-image had their roots in Wilhelmian times and the German Kaiserreich. They were characterized by a conservative, patriotic attitude; the Prussian sense of duty (preußisches Pflichtgefühl); the acceptance of state order (Staatsgläubigkeit); and the German ideal of order and justice, along with a naive understanding of politics.

This attitude was behind Planck's glorification of World War I in the summer of 1914; he was likewise among the signers of the infamous "Appeal to the Civilized World" in which the intellectual elite of Germany legitimized German militarism as a safeguard for German culture. Subsequently Planck became more discriminate in his opinions and advocated that the war and political intolerance not inflict irreparable harm on international relations between scientists.

Like most of his academic colleagues, Planck had no understanding of the revolution of 1918, and he experienced a conflicted relationship with the Weimar Republic. He was a "republican of reason," although his activities in science policy had helped to stabilize the unloved Republic in this area. His dilemma became even bigger during the Third Reich. His behavior is characterized on the one hand by compromises with the Nazi authorities, and on the other hand by acts of moral courage. As secretary of the Prussian Academy and in particular as president of the Kaiser Wilhelm Society he did not put up a serious resistance against the "self-coordination" (Gleichschaltung) of these institutions and accepted without public protest the Nazi policy of dismissals for racist reasons. However, he took pains to find individual solutions for some of his expelled colleagues and to act behind the scenes, trying to preserve the autonomy and freedom of action of science. In 1935, for instance, he succeeded in holding a commemorative event in honor of the deceased emigré Fritz Haber despite the expressed opposition of the Ministry of Education, which had forbidden attendance at the meeting by civil servants. His personal fame and integrity helped to soften arbitrary measures of the Nazi government, but both these qualities were also taken and used for the political purposes of the Third Reich.

Last Years. The last years of Planck's life were darkened by the complicated conditions of wartime and its aftermath as well by personal blows of fortune. In February 1944 his home in the Berlin suburb Grunewald was totally gutted in a fire after an air raid and he lost almost all his possessions, including his irreplaceable notebooks, diaries, correspondence and other papers. He was hit even harder by the arrest and murder of his son Erwin, who had been involved in the attempt on Hitler's life on 20 July 1944. Erwin had become his father's closest friend and most trusted advisor, particularly during the period of the Nazi dictatorship.

With his scientific reputation and moral integrity as well as his enormous international prestige, Planck readily served after the war as a doyen in the reconstruction of German science. In the spring of 1946, for example, he endured the rigors of travel to England to take part in the Newton celebration of the Royal Society in London and to apply his personal integrity and influence toward promoting an "improved" Germany. Planck also came to the rescue of the Kaiser Wilhelm Society and assumed the presidency again during a vulnerable transitional period, which helped to preserve the society from liquidation by the occupation authorities and to save it as what became the Max Planck Society. Thus was the "Max Planck myth" born.

SUPPLEMENTARY BIBLIOGRAPHY

WORKS BY PLANCK

The Theory of Heat Radiation. American Institute of Physics, 1988. With an introduction by Allan Needell. This book contains the 1914 second edition in English, and the 1906 first edition in German.

Brieftagebuch zwischen Max Planck, Carl Runge, Bernhard Karsten und Adolf Leopold, introduced and annotated by Klaus Hentschel and Renate Tobies. Berlin: ERS-Verlag, 1999.

OTHER SOURCES

Albrecht, Helmuth. "Max Planck: Mein Besuch bei Adolf Hitler. Anmerkungen zum Wert einer historischen Quelle." In *Naturwissenschaft und Technik in der Geschichte.* Stuttgart: GNT-Verlag, 1993.

Büttner, Jochen, Jürgen Renn, and Matthias Schemmel. "Exploring the Limits of Classical Physics: Planck, Einstein, and the Structure of a Scientific Revolution." *Studies in History and Philosophy of Modern Physics* 34 (2003): 37–59.

Darrigol, Olivier. "Statistics and Combinatorics in Early Quantum Theory." *Historical Studies in the Physical Sciences* 19 (1988) 17–80; 21 (1991): 237–298.

———. *From c-numbers to q-numbers: The Classical Analogy in the History of Quantum Theory.* Berkeley: University of California Press, 1992.

———. "The Historians' Disagreement over the Meaning of Planck's Quantum." *Centaurus* 43 (2001): 219–239.

Gearhart, Clayton A. "Planck, the Quantum, and the Historians." *Physics in Perspective* 4 (2002) 170–215.

Hauke, Petra. *Max-Planck-Bibliographie.* Berichte und Mitteilungen der Max-Planck-Gesellschaft, Heft 4, 1997.

Heilbron, John L. *The Dilemmas of an Upright Man: Max Planck as Spokesman of German Science.* Berkeley: University of California Press, 1986. Second edition with a new afterword, 2000.

Hoffmann, Dieter. "Das Verhältnis der Akademie zu Republik und Diktatur. Max Planck als Sekretar." In *Die Preußische Akademie der Wissenschaften zu Berlin 1914–1945*, edited by Wolfram Fischer, et al. Berlin: Akademie-Verlag 2000.

———. "On the Experimental Context of Planck's Foundation of Quantum Theory." *Centaurus* 43 (2001) 240–259.

Kohl, Ulrike. *Die Präsidenten der Kaiser-Wilhelm-Gesellschaft im Nationalsozialismus: Max Planck, Carl Bosch und Albert Vögler zwischen Wissenschaft und Macht.* Stuttgart: Franz Steiner Verlag, 2002.

Kuhn, Thomas S. *Black-Body Theory and the Quantum Discontinuity, 1894–1912.* New York: Oxford University Press, 1978.

———. "Revisiting Planck." *Historical Studies in the Physical Sciences* 14 (1984): 232–252.

Künzel, Friedrich. *Max Plancks Wirken an der Berliner Akademie der Wissenschaften als Ordentliches Mitglied und Sekretar zwischen 1894 und 1947.* PhD diss., Humboldt-Universität Berlin, 1984.

Liesenfeld, Cornelia. *Philosophische Weltbilder des 20. Jahrhunderts: Eine interdisziplinäre Studie zu Max Planck und Werner Heisenberg.* Würzburg, Germany: Verlag Königshausen & Neumann, 1992.

Lowood, Henry. *Planck, Max: A Bibliography of His Non-Technical Writings.* Berkeley: University of California, 1977.

Max-Planck-Sonderheft [Special edition], *Physikalische Blätter* 51 (1997): 10.

Mehra, Jagish, and Helmut Rechenberg. *The Quantum Theory of Planck, Einstein, Bohr and Sommerfeld: Its Foundation and the Rise of ist Difficulties, 1900–1925.* The Historical Development of Quantum Theory, Volume 1, Parts 1 and 2. New York, Heidelberg, Berlin: Springer Verlag, 1982.

Needell, Allan A. *Irreversibility and the Failure of Classical Dynamics: Max Planck's Work on the Quantum Theory 1900–1915.* PhD diss., Yale University, 1980. See also his Introduction to Planck 1988, cited above.

Pufendorf, Astrid von. *Die Plancks: eine Familie zwischen Patriotismus und Widerstand.* Berlin: Prophyläen-Verlag, 2006.

Renn, Jürgen, G. Castagnetti, and S. Rieger. "Adolf Harnack und Max Planck." In *Adolf von Harnack. Theologe, Historiker, Wissenschaftspolitiker,* edited by Kurt Nowak and Otto Gerhard Oexle. Göttingen, Germany: Vandenhoeck & Ruprecht, 2001.

Schirrmacher, Arne. "Experimenting Theory: The Proofs of Kirchhoff's Radiation Law before and after Planck." *Historical Studies in the Physical and Biological Sciences* 33 (2003): 299–335.

Schöpf, Hans-Georg. "Von Kirchhoff bis Planck." *Theorie der Wärmestrahlung in historisch-kritischer Darstellung.* Berlin: Akademie-Verlag, 1978.

Seth, Suman. "Allgemeine Physik? Max Planck und die Gemeinschaft der theoretischen Physik 1906–1914." In *Der Hochsitz des Wissens,* edited by Michael Hagner und Manfred D. Laubichler. Zürich and Berlin: Diaphanes Verlag, 2006.

Stern, Fritz. "Max Planck. Größe des Menschen und Gewalt der Geschichte." In *Max Planck. Vorträge und Ausstellung zum 50. Todestag.* Munich: Max-Planck-Gesellschaft, 1997.

Ullman, Dirk. *Quelleninventar Max Planck.* Veröffentlichungen aus dem Archiv der Max-Planck-Gesellschaft 8, 1996.

Dieter Hoffman

Bust of Plato. THE LIBRARY OF CONGRESS.

PLATO (*b.* Athens, *c.* 427 BCE.; *d.* Athens, 348/347 BCE), *physics, cosmology, mathematical education; organization of research.* For the original article on Plato see *DSB,* vol. 11.

One task (although emphatically not the only one) of the *DSB* original entry was to help the reader judge Plato's contribution to scientific thought, with a concentration on the mathematical sciences and their strategic role in the philosophical curriculum. In this context, the account of the physical world that Plato offers in the *Timaeus* is relegated to a subordinate role. This postscript focuses on this account and its contribution to the development of scientific thought.

Plato describes the account of the physical world in the *Timaeus* as an *eikôs muthos* or an *eikôs logos*—that is to say, a likely account, a likely story, or even a myth. What exactly Plato means by this description is open to more than one interpretation. On all interpretations, however, there are distinctively human limitations to what can be said on the topic of the creation of the universe, the nature of the physical world, and the place of humans within it. In other words, one can improve on the account offered in the *Timaeus,* but one's account will always remain at best likely. Clearly the limitations that Plato has in mind are not contingent upon historical facts that can eventually be overcome; rather, they have to do with human nature as well as the nature of the object to be studied, the physical world. Once these limits are acknowledged, the reader is encouraged to engage in the study of the world around us and to produce the best possible account of it.

It is important to situate the *Timaeus* in the context of the ancient debate on the possibility of the study of nature. In antiquity, there was a philosophical tradition that regarded this study as a vain curiosity, if not a distraction from the care of the soul and the ethical life. In the *Memorabilia,* for example, Xenophon offers a powerful portrait of Socrates as a champion of this position. This attitude toward the study of nature is often found in the Socratic tradition. In this tradition, the reorientation of philosophy toward ethics is coupled with the emphasis on the limits of human knowledge. This emphasis can be found also in the *Timaeus.* In this case, however, it does not entail hostility to, or even a rejection of, the empirical sciences. On the contrary, this dialogue offers an account of the physical world, including an account of time, space, matter, and the four elements, as well as human physiology and pathology.

It is mildly surprising to find cosmology and medicine offered as parts of one and the same account. This can be explained by reflecting on the theoretical framework that Plato chose for this account. Plato borrowed this framework from an earlier tradition of writing about the nature of things (the *peri physeōs* tradition of the sixth and fifth century BCE). In this tradition, the study of the nature of humanity was an essential part of the study of the physical world. Moreover, this study had a narrative character. It did not simply state and explain why the physical world is the way it is; it narrated how the physical world in its present order came into existence. By choosing the narrative method, Plato placed himself in continuity with a tradition going back, ultimately, to early Greek philosophy. This does not necessarily mean that the cosmogonic account offered in the *Timaeus* has to be taken literally. It is significant that, from very early on, this account was subject to literal as well as non-literal interpretations. On all interpretations, however, the physical world was regarded as the product of a divine craftsman. The task of this divine craftsman was to introduce order into what lacked it. The creation of the physical world was regarded as the result of imposing order on a preexisting matter on the basis of an intelligible model.

The *Timaeus* can be usefully regarded as Plato's attempt to reconcile the early investigation of nature with the practical reorientation of philosophy urged by Socrates. But this requires prior clarity about a crucial feature of ancient thought that is no longer shared. The physical world as Plato conceived it is not a value-free world. On the contrary, values are for him part of the furniture of the physical world. The task of the scientist is to attain an understanding of the perfection and goodness of the natural world on the crucial assumption that one can objectively make value judgments about the physical world. In this context, the study of the physical world can provide objective grounds for the view that reason rules over necessity. In light of this conviction, dismissing the study of nature would make it difficult, if not even impossible, to achieve the Socratic goal of caring about the soul.

SUPPLEMENTARY BIBLIOGRAPHY

WORK BY PLATO

Complete Works. Edited by John M. Cooper and Douglas S. Hutchinson. Indianapolis, IN: Hackett Publishing, 1997.

OTHER SOURCES

Baltes, Matthias. *Die Weltenstehung des platonischen "Timaios" nach den antiken Interpreten*. 2 vols. Leiden: Brill, 1976–1978.

Brisson, Luc. *Le Même et l'Autre dans la Structure Ontologique du "Timée" de Platon*. Sankt Augustin, Germany: Academia Verlag, 1994.

Burnyeat, Myles. "Eikôs Muthos." *Rhizai: A Journal for Ancient Philosophy and Science* 2, no. 2 (2005): 143–165.

Carone, Gabriela Roxana. *Plato's Cosmology and its Ethical Dimensions*. Cambridge, U.K.: Cambridge University Press, 2005.

Cornford, Francis MacDonald. *Plato's Cosmology*. London: Routledge & Kegan Paul, 1937.

Hadot, Pierre. *The Veil of Isis: An Essay on the History of the Idea of Nature*. Translated by Michael Chase. Cambridge, MA: The Belknap Press of Harvard University Press, 2006.

Johansen, Thomas. *Plato's Natural Philosophy: A Study of the Timaeus-Critias*. Cambridge, U.K.: Cambridge University Press 2004.

Mohr, Richard. *The Platonic Cosmology*. Leiden: Brill, 1985.

Reydams-Schils, Gretchen. *Plato's Timaeus as Cultural Icon*. Notre Dame, IN: Notre Dame University Press, 2003.

Vlastos, Gregory. *Plato's Universe*. Seattle: University of Washington Press, 1975.

Andrea Falcon

PLINY THE ELDER (GAIUS PLINIUS SECUNDUS) (*b*. Como, Italy, 23/24 CE; *d*. near Pompeii, Italy, 79 CE), *natural history*. For the original article on Pliny see *DSB*, see vol. 11.

Pliny's *Natural History* is an extraordinarily important document in the history of Western science. From antiquity through the Middle Ages and into the Renaissance, Pliny's massive compilation of knowledge remained a valued source of practical information on medicine and on the natural world. Pliny's reputation as a scholar plummeted, however, as his science was overtaken and new mistakes were revealed in his use of his sources. Most nineteenth- and twentieth-century scholarship on the *Natural History* emphasized Pliny's errors and his pedantry in compiling an encyclopedia based on his reading of the original research of earlier authors. Since the original *DSB* article, however, Pliny's standing has risen again, as a result of new approaches to the text.

Although a great deal of useful work is still being done on specific subjects within the *Natural History*, work on the text in the original *DSB* entry has been animated by the desire to examine the broader strategies of the work, dealing with it as a cohesive narrative rather than focusing solely on its information. Two important strands of Pliny's thought have been isolated for exploration: the underlying concept of nature that runs through the *Natural History*, and the central importance of the Roman Empire and Roman traditional morality to the rationale of the text. The insights produced by these approaches will be discussed below.

Pliny's influence in postclassical periods has also come under renewed scrutiny: the *Natural History* is important not just for the information it provides on Roman scientific and cultural knowledge, but also for its influence on later European thinkers in a range of fields. Work on the *Natural History* has begun to explore the text's place in later scientific discourse, and also in the development of the disciplines of philology and art history, and the genre of encyclopedia. Some key aspects of Pliny's diffusion in later periods will be discussed in the final section.

Concept of Natural History. In the preface to the *Natural History*, Pliny explained that his subject matter would be "nature, that is life." Despite this, the *Natural History* presents very little overt theorizing about nature. Unlike his fellow Romans, Seneca and Lucretius, Pliny rarely presented sustained philosophical arguments in the *Natural History*. However, the work as a whole is informed by Stoic natural philosophy, as Mary Beagon demonstrated in her groundbreaking book, *Roman Nature: The Thought of Pliny the Elder* (1992). For Pliny, "*Natura* is the world, both as a whole and as its separate components; she is both the creator and the creation" (Beagon, 2005, p. 26). Pliny drew on the Stoic conception of a divine power permeating the universe, a directing force or spirit present in the world and in everything in the world. The whole of nature is animated by a providential presence that directs it, and this divine power can be identified both with nature and with the world itself. Of particular importance to Pliny was the Stoic idea of Nature the Creator/Artist (*Natura artifex*), which makes nature a conscious, creative power, who deliberately organizes the world with the needs of humanity in mind. Nature, then, can be the natural world itself, the intrinsic nature of an object, or a personified, divine Nature who designed the world with human beings at its center: all three concepts are in play within the *Natural History*. But although Pliny made use of such concepts, he offered his readers little in the way of original philosophical speculation, and was often contradictory and eclectic in his adoption of elements from different philosophical systems to suit his needs. As Beagon argues, Stoic cosmology was the well-assimilated underpinning of Pliny's thought, rather than an object of inquiry in its own right within the *Natural History*.

This absence of an explicit and overarching philosophical agenda is perhaps the most remarkable aspect of Pliny's account of the natural world in the context of surviving work from antiquity. It brings with it what appears to be a new approach to what knowing about nature entails. In the *Natural History*, nature is broken down into series of discrete places, animals, plants, medicines, and minerals, each discussed in its proper place in the comprehensive catalogs that Pliny assembled. For Pliny it was possible not just to know all of nature, but to itemize and count that knowledge: in the preface, Pliny advertises the twenty thousand facts he has assembled, a symbolically

colossal number, and goes on to quantify the number of "remedies, researches and observations" for each book in the list of contents he provided in Book 1. It is this radical segmentation of knowledge and drive for comprehensiveness, along with the absence of a strong theoretical framework, which makes the *Natural History*'s treatment of nature unique among other ancient accounts. For Pliny, discussing nature did not mean propounding the merits of a Stoic or Epicurean worldview, it meant: knowing that six European trees produce pitch, that there are three kinds of lettuce, that the best kind of emeralds come from Scythia, and that rocket is an excellent aphrodisiac (Pitch trees: bk. 16, sec. 38; lettuce: bk. 19, sec. 125; emeralds: bk. 37, sec. 65; rocket: bk. 19, sec. 154, bk. 20, sec. 19). In this version of natural history, nature becomes very much the sum of its parts and knowing these detailed elements has become an end in itself.

This conceptualization of natural knowledge as a comprehensive series of facts led to a curious openness in the structure of Pliny's text. Individual facts, whether quirky or useful, were the building blocks of Pliny's narrative, taken from his one hundred authorities and arranged into hierarchical lists. The overarching structure moves from the heavens (Book 2), to the earth and terrestrial geography (Books 3–6), to animals (starting with humans in Book 7 and proceeding through land animals in 8, sea creatures in 9, birds in 10, and insects in Book 11), to plants (Books 12–19), to medicines from plants (Books 20–27), to medicines from animals (Books 28–32), and finally metals and minerals (Books 33–37). The neat top-down structure is disturbed a little by the fact that a third of the work is devoted to *materia medica*. Within the books, the organizing principle changes frequently: it may be size (the elephant begins the account of land animals in Book 8 because it is the biggest and closest to humans in intelligence). It may be degree of usefulness (as with the vine in Book 14). It may be price (as with gemstones at the start of Book 37). The list is an essentially open structure. In the absence of a strong overarching argument, it allows facts to be easily excerpted from the *Natural History*. But within the text, facts are linked and held in place by the hierarchies that Pliny created with them. Pliny's lists are not just practical, however: they are also entertaining. Quite apart from the pleasure of learning that the text offers, the frequent changes in mode of hierarchy, the discursive openings to most of the books, the bizarre or miraculous stories that stud the drier lists of facts, all attest to Pliny's desire to entertain as well as instruct his reader.

Pliny's organizational strategy, his dependence on earlier sources, and his drive for comprehensiveness led later scholars to recognize his work as one of the first encyclopedias. Attempts have been made to create an ancient genre of encyclopedia by drawing parallels between Pliny's *Natural History* and the works of Cato, Varro, and Celsus;

Pliny the Elder. © BETTMANN/CORBIS.

but very little of these works survives, not enough to do more than surmise that these authors attempted to cover all the liberal arts. This is a very different project from Pliny's discussion of nature, but the authors have been linked because of their comprehensive ambitions and, more importantly, because of an etymological link between the Greek name for liberal arts or comprehensive education, *encyclios paideia,* and the modern term *encyclopedia.* Pliny's *Natural History* is the only "encyclopedia" of its kind that survives from antiquity, and its recognition as an encyclopedia depends on knowledge of a modern category of text which would have been unfamiliar to Pliny and to his first audience. Nevertheless, this modern identification of Pliny's work as an encyclopedia has had important implications for how scholars approached the work. It provides an implicit intellectual justification for the practice of extracting decontextualized facts from the text, or treating it in segments rather than as a coherent whole; more dynamically, Pliny's encyclopedism has become an important factor in unraveling the politics of his text.

Empire and the Encyclopedia. Pliny's underlying Stoic beliefs have implications not just for his view of nature, but also for his attitudes toward humans. Andrew Wallace-Hadrill (1990) and Roger French (1994) joined with Beagon in exploring nature and humanity's place in it as the central theme of the *Natural History,* discussing the role of luxury as a key element in Pliny's prescriptions about what is and what is not natural. Pliny's universe is organized with the concerns of humanity at its center, and although Nature can at times appear more wicked stepmother than loving parent (bk. 7, sec. 1), the *Natural History* ultimately presents an image of a world thoughtfully designed for humans to use. Pliny's descriptions of natural objects emphasize their human context: their availability at Rome, how much they cost, and, especially, their uses in medicine. It is also possible for humans to misuse nature, however, by perverting her providential purpose by wasteful indulgence in luxurious living. Pliny's view of nature as a providential divinity goes hand in hand with a particular moral worldview that both privileges humanity's place in nature and criticizes what he sees as abuse of that position. As Sandra Citroni Marchetti discussed (1991), the *Natural History*'s rhetoric can be read in the context of a wider Roman tradition of moral writing that compares a decadent, urban present with the self-sufficient simplicity of a rural past. In this view of history, Rome's empire holds an ambiguous position. Pliny was proud of Rome's greatness, and generally viewed the empire as a civilizing enterprise, but lamented the luxurious consumerism that it had made possible, and the decline in respect for learning that attended this (most notably, perhaps, in the opening of Book 14).

In the *Natural History,* the humans for whom nature has obligingly designed the natural world are not just any humans: they are Romans. As Gian Biagio Conte pointed out (1994), Pliny put the interests and needs of his Roman reader at the heart of his text, and chose which information to include or exclude based on the desires and competencies of his envisaged audience. Sorcha Carey, Trevor Murphy (2004), and Valérie Naas (2002) further politicized the Roman worldview at the heart of the *Natural History:* Pliny's information was gathered as a result of Roman imperial expansion and as a tool for further expansion, laying bare the contents of the empire and its usefulness for Rome. This codependency of knowledge and empire is perhaps most evident in the geographical sections of the *Natural History,* Books 3–6. Throughout these books, towns within the empire are generally described in terms of their tax-paying status and ordered by administrative district, and towns' major exports or links to Rome are emphasized. But one also finds more overt traces of Roman military power over conquered populations: an inscription from a triumphal arch was used as the source for the conquered peoples of the Alps (bk. 3, secs. 136–137); places with barbarian place names were explicitly excluded because of their unpleasantness to a Roman ear and their lack of importance (bk. 3, secs. 7, 28, 139); knowledge of Southern Cyrene comes from the military expedition of Cornelius Balbus, or, more exactly, from the triumphal procession following his victories there (bk. 5, secs. 36–37). Knowledge about the world was derived from Rome's military dominance and this knowledge is placed at the service of continuing that dominance.

On a symbolic level too, the *Natural History*'s encyclopedism can be seen as an imperial enterprise: just as empire represents the pursuit of power, so encyclopedism represents a desire to annex and organize knowledge. On this model, Pliny's encyclopedism became easily assimilated to the nationalistic encyclopedias of the late nineteenth and early twentieth centuries. As Murphy explained in the introduction to his important book on this aspect of the text,

> I shall argue for a reading of Pliny's encyclopedia as a political document, a cultural artifact of the Roman empire just as much as the *Encyclopedia Britannica* was an artifact of the British Empire. I shall demonstrate how the structure and content of the *Natural History* entwined with Roman political *imperium* in a relationship of mutual benefit, in that one of the functions of an encyclopedia is to embody how much is known and to demarcate it all from the perspective of central authority. (2004, p. 2. Cf. Carey p. 17)

Although the imperial perspective and comprehensive ambitions provide a clear parallel with these later works, it is important to bear in mind that the encyclopedia is a modern, not an ancient category, and encyclopedias have taken many forms, both in terms of their ideologies and their physical appearance over the years. The centralizing rhetoric of Pliny's opening table of contents is unlikely to have been lived up to by all copies of his text in an age of manuscripts. Tailor-made copies that included only the books on a particular set of subjects, for example, medicine or astronomy, must have been common right from the start of the text's long history of use. Although the rhetoric of the *Natural History* claims to cover everything, and links backward and forward with cross-references to other parts of the text, its massive bulk was always ripe for deconstruction, facts always easily removed for redeployment elsewhere. If the text provided an image of the empire, it was of an empire always open to expansion, but always, perhaps, on the verge of disintegration.

Pliny after Antiquity. Although Pliny's text may have been modeled on the interests of a Roman reader and deeply imbued with Roman imperialism, its importance did not end with the collapse of the Roman Empire. Pliny's information was widely disseminated throughout Europe in late antiquity and the Middle Ages. Arno Borst (1995) traced the range of approaches that could be applied to the *Natural History* by prominent scholars from antiquity to the fifteenth century, including St. Jerome, St. Augustine, John Scotus Eriugena, Hugh de Saint Victor, Albertus Magnus, and Petrarch. As Borst demonstrated, the text was used as a vital source of useful scientific knowledge, but it was also read for pleasure, and as a source of knowledge from ancient past that could be used to address contemporary problems. The entirety of the *Natural History* continued to be copied, but information was also excerpted and reused by other authors, notably Isidore of Seville and Vincent de Beauvais, in their own compendia of useful knowledge. Individual stories, recipes, and facts from the *Natural History* entered into the repertoire of scholarly knowledge so that it is often difficult to determine whether a later writer has gathered the information from reading Pliny directly or found the fact in a bestiary or recipe book or medical compilation that had long since naturalized the information as its own.

Specialist handbooks were also created by selectively editing the *Natural History* to meet the needs of new markets. As Bruce S. Eastwood has shown (1986), an influential series of astronomical excerpts, some with purpose-made figures, circulated separately for use in *computus* (determining the date of Easter). The medical sections of the *Natural History* were edited to produce the *Medicina Plinii* (Pliny's medicine), perhaps the most significant of these specialist collections of extracts. It seems to have first appeared in the fourth century CE, at a time when the institutions that had upheld complex theoretical medicine were beginning to collapse in the western half of the Roman Empire. It offered a selection of medical recipes, mostly culled from Pliny; but where Pliny had largely organized his medical information according to the type of substance rather than the type of illness, the *Medicina Plinii* organized its remedies by ailment, following a commonly used top-down structure, so that afflictions of the head were dealt with first. This compilation continued to grow and mutate with the addition of more information. A separate recension that substantially expanded the *Medicina* from other sources, known as the *Physica Plinii*, is also adduced for the sixth century. The collection was still in use in the early sixteenth century, when three separate editions were published, the most authoritative of which was edited by Alban Thorer, professor of medicine at the University of Basel from 1537 to 1545.

The *Natural History* continued to be used as a practical source of medical and scientific knowledge right into the sixteenth century. Despite its usefulness, or perhaps because of it, Pliny's text posed particular problems for readers: generations of copyists misunderstood and amended Pliny's technical and often obscure Latin. Others made additions or altered the text to suit their particular purposes. In the late fifteenth and early sixteenth centuries, the task of producing an accurate text of Pliny's

Natural History engaged the cream of humanist scholarship in competition and disputation, as figures such as Angelo Poliziano, Ermolao Barbaro, Beatus Rhenanus, and Desiderius Erasmus commented on the text. Before 1500, in the first fifty years of printing alone, there were fifteen editions of six separate recensions of the text published, as well as two Italian translations. One particular scholarly controversy has been singled out for its importance in signaling the gradual decline of Pliny's importance as a practical source of scientific information: a debate over the accuracy of Pliny's medicine, initiated by the professor of medicine at Ferrara, Niccolò Leoniceno in 1492 with the publication of his *De Plinii et plurium aliorum in medicina erroribus* (On the mistakes in medicine made by Pliny and several others). By comparing Pliny's text with that of Pedanius Dioscorides and Theophrastus, Leoniceno uncovered mistakes that Pliny made in his understanding of his Greek sources—mistakes that, he pointed out, could have disastrous consequences for those who followed his prescriptions. Pandolfo Colennuccio, a protégé of Poliziano, leapt to Pliny's defense, and the debate continued in pamphlet form for several years. As Charles Nauert (1979), among others, has discussed, although neither Leoniceno nor Colennuccio made much use of empirical evidence in their attempts to prove their point, this apparent attack on Pliny marked an important moment in the movement away from scholasticism toward early modern scientific inquiry and the eventual end of Pliny's importance as a practical guide to "nature, that is life."

SUPPLEMENTARY BIBLIOGRAPHY

In addition to the editions listed by David E. Eichholz in the original DSB article, the Latin text of Karl Mayhoff's 1909 Teubner edition (on which the Loeb edition is based) is available online from the Perseus Project, http://www.perseus.tufts.edu, together with an English translation by John Bostock and H.T. Riley (1855). There are also new Italian, German, and Spanish editions.

WORKS BY PLINY THE ELDER

Naturkunde. Naturalis historiae libri XXXVII. Edited by Gerhard Winkler, Barchiesi Roderich König, Karl Bayer, et al. Munich, Germany: Heimeran Verlag, 1973.

Storia naturale/Gaio Plinio Secondo. Edited by Gian B. Conte, Alessandro Barchiesi, Chiara Frugoni, et al. Turin, Italy: Einaudi, 1982.

Historia natural/Plinio el Viejo, Biblioteca clasica Gredos; 206, 308, etc. Edited by Guy Serbat, Antonio Fontán, and Ana María Moure Casas. Madrid: Gredos, 1995.

OTHER SOURCES

Barkan, Leonard. *Unearthing the Past: Archaeology and Aesthetics in the Making of Renaissance Culture.* New Haven, CT;

London: Yale University Press, 1999. Discusses the use of Pliny in Renaissance art criticism and archaeology.

Beagon, Mary. *Roman Nature: The Thought of Pliny the Elder.* Oxford: Oxford University Press, 1992.

———. *The Elder Pliny on the Human Animal: Natural History, Book 7, Clarendon Ancient History Series.* Oxford: Clarendon Press, 2005.

Bona, Isabella. *Natura terrestrium: (Plin. nat. hist. VIII).* Pubblicazioni del D.Ar.Fi.Cl.eT.; nuova serie, 138. Genoa, Italy: Universita di Genova, Facolta di lettere, Dipartimento di archeologia, filologia classica e loro tradizioni, 1991.

Borst, Arno. *Das Buch der Naturgeschichte. Plinius und seine Leser im Zeitalter des Pergaments.* Heidelberg, Germany: C. Winter, 1995.

Capponi, Filippo. *Natura aquatilium (Plin. nat. hist. IX).* Pubblicazioni del D.AR.FI.CL.ET; nuova serie, 131. Genoa, Italy: Universita di Genova, Facolta di lettere, Dipartimento di archeologia, filologia classica e loro tradizioni, 1990.

———. *Entomologia pliniana (N.H. XI, 1-120).* Pubblicazioni del D.AR.FI.CL.ET; nuova ser., n. 154. Genoa, Italy: Universita di Genova, Facolta di lettere, Dipartimento di archeologia, filologia classica e loro tradizioni, 1994.

———. *L'anatomia e la fisiologia di Plinio.* Pubblicazioni del D.AR.FI.CL.ET; n.s., n. 158. Genoa, Italy: Universita di Genova, Facolta di lettere, Dipartimento di archeologia, filologia classica e loro tradizioni, 1995.

Chibnall, Marjorie. "Pliny's Natural History and the Middle Ages." In *Empire and Aftermath,* edited by Thomas A. Dorey, 57–78. London: Routledge and Kegan Paul, 1975.

Citroni Marchetti, Sandra. *Plinio il Vecchio e la tradizione del moralismo romano.* Pisa, Italy: Giardini, 1991.

Conte, Gian Biagio. "The Inventory of the World: Form of Nature and the Encyclopedic Project in the Work of Pliny the Elder." In *Genres and Readers,* edited by Gian Biagio Conte. Baltimore, MD: Johns Hopkins University Press, 1994. English translation of Conte's introduction to the Einaudi Pliny.

Eastwood, Bruce S. "Plinian Astronomy in the Middle Ages and Renaissance." In *Science in the Early Roman Empire: Pliny the Elder, His Sources and Influence,* edited by Frank Greenaway and Roger K. French, 197–251. London: Croom Helm, 1986.

French, Roger K. "Pliny and Renaissance Medicine." In *Science in the Early Roman Empire: Pliny the Elder, His Sources and Influence,* edited by Roger K. French and Frank Greenaway, 252–281. London: Croom Helm, 1986.

———, and Frank Greenaway, eds. *Science in the Early Roman Empire: Pliny the Elder, His Sources and Influence.* London: Croom Helm, 1986. Important collection of papers that isolate particular subjects within the *Natural History:* for example, botany, pharmacology, zoology.

———. *Ancient Natural History: Histories of Nature.* London: Routledge, 1994.

Healy, John F. *Pliny the Elder on Science and Technology.* Oxford: Oxford University Press, 1999.

Murphy, Trevor. *Pliny the Elder's Natural History: The Empire in the Encyclopaedia.* Oxford: Oxford University Press, 2004.

Naas, Valérie. *Le projet encyclopédique de Pline l'Ancien*. Rome: École française de Rome, 2002.

Nauert, Charles G. "Humanists, Scientists and Pliny: Changing Approaches to a Classical Author." *American Historical Revue* 84 (1979): 72–85.

Roncoroni, Angelo, ed. *Plinio e la natura: Atti del ciclo di conferenze sugli aspetti naturalistici dell' opera pliniana, Como 1979*. Como: Camera di commercio, industria, artigianato e agricoltura di Como, 1982.

Wallace-Hadrill, Andrew. "Pliny the Elder and Man's Unnatural History." *Greece and Rome* 1 (1990): 80–96.

Aude Doody

POINCARÉ, JULES HENRI

(*b.* Nancy, France, 29 April 1854; *d.* Paris, France, 17 July 1912), *mathematics, celestial mechanics, theoretical physics, philosophy of science*. For the original article on Poincaré see *DSB*, vol. 11.

Historical studies of Henri Poincaré's life and science turned a corner two years after the publication of Jean Dieudonné's original *DSB* article, when Poincaré's papers were microfilmed and made available to scholars. This and other primary sources engaged historical interest in Poincaré's approach to mathematics, his contributions to pure and applied physics, his philosophy, and his influence on scientific institutions and policy. The result of these new sources and updated historiography is a new Poincaré: If Poincaré's outstanding achievements in mathematics ensure his prominent position in the history of this subject, his corpus and intellectual legacy are known to extend well beyond mathematics proper, touching the core methods of theoretical physics and central tenets of the philosophy of science. Increased recognition of the breadth of Poincaré's activity, from geodesy and electrical engineering to algebraic topology and the philosophy of space and time, is itself a prime result of Poincaré studies. A brief summary follows of the ways these studies have revised or enriched historical understanding of Poincaré's life and work.

Early Career. Consider, to begin with, Jean Dieudonné's evaluation of the young Poincaré's spotty education in higher mathematics, gleaned from Poincaré's published correspondence with Lazarus Fuchs and Felix Klein and since then confirmed, on one hand, by studies of Poincaré's qualitative theory of differential equations, and on the other hand, by analyses of the manuscripts submitted by Poincaré for the Grand Prix des Sciences Mathématiques in 1880 and discovered by Jeremy Gray a century later. These manuscripts, written between 28 June and 20 December 1880, show in detail how Poincaré exploited a

series of insights to arrive at his first major contribution to mathematics: the discovery of the automorphic functions of one complex variable (called "Fuchsian" and "Kleinian" functions by Poincaré). In particular, the manuscripts corroborate Poincaré's introspective account of this discovery (1908), in which the real key to his discovery is given to be the recognition that the transformations he had used to define Fuchsian functions are identical with those of non-Euclidean geometry.

The manuscripts of 1880 also shed light on the origins of Poincaré's conventionalist philosophy of geometry. Even at this early point in his career, Poincaré understood geometry to be the study of groups of transformations. Such a view recalls Klein's Erlangen program (1872), but where Klein's approach was projective and hierarchical, that employed by Poincaré in 1880 was entirely metrical and free of hierarchy, rendering unlikely any direct influence of Klein's program. The influence of Eugenio Beltrami, however, is apparent in Poincaré's disk model of hyperbolic geometry, a model he later employed in the service of his conventionalist philosophy of geometry.

Foundations of Geometry. Poincaré was elected to the geometry section of the Paris Academy of Sciences on 31 January 1887 (at age thirty-two) and that same year published his first paper on the foundations of geometry. Impressed with the writings of Sophus Lie and Hermann Helmholtz on the so-called Riemann-Helmholtz-Lie-Poincaré problem of space, Poincaré characterized plane geometries by considering intersections of a plane with a certain quadric and formulating a common set of axioms. In this way, straights and circumferences of hyperbolic geometry are made to correspond, for example, to straights and circumferences (circles) of Euclidean geometry, and the available theorems depend on the chosen quadric. (He later popularized this insight in terms of a translation dictionary for Euclidean and non-Euclidean geometry.) Extending his purview to the geometry of space, Poincaré held hyperbolic geometry and Euclidean geometry both to be adequate to the task of describing physical phenomena. Darwinian evolution had provided humans only with the general notion of a group; consequently, if humans regularly employed Euclidean geometry instead of hyperbolic geometry, this was by virtue of the simplicity and convenience of the former, the motion of solids corresponding roughly to the Euclidean group. Experience provided the occasion for this choice to be made in that employment of Euclidean geometry was an outcome contingent upon the behavior of light rays and solids on Earth.

A few years later Poincaré explained further that the choice of hyperbolic geometry entailed nonstandard laws of physics, thereby rendering his view equivalent in

Henri Poincaré. © HULTON-DEUTSCH COLLECTION/BETTMANN/CORBIS.

essentials to that of Helmholtz (1876). For Poincaré, the empirical equivalence of the two possible points of view—Euclidean geometry plus ordinary physics, or hyperbolic geometry plus some unspecified, alternative physics—ruled out an empirical foundation of the geometry of physical space. He regretted that Helmholtz—the champion of methodological empiricism—had not made this point clear. Few scientists found compelling Poincaré's extreme view of the geometry of physical space, but philosophers (including Paul Natorp, Aloys Müller, Moritz Schlick, and Rudolf Carnap) were swayed by the clever arguments advanced in its favor, which shaped later debates on the conventionality of the space-time metric in general relativity.

Poincaré's contributions to relativity theory have given rise to priority claims on his behalf because he presented a theory mathematically indistinguishable from that of Albert Einstein four weeks earlier than Einstein. In fact, Poincaré made a crucial step in 1900 toward Einstein's 1905 redefinition of physical time and space when he realized that the validity of the principle of relativity for electromagnetic phenomena depended on a certain definition of the time coordinate in uniformly moving systems (H. A. Lorentz's local time), realized by an exchange of light signals between co-moving observers relatively at rest. Like Einstein, Poincaré elevated the principle of relativity to a postulate in 1905; unlike Einstein, he retained the notion of a luminiferous ether (thus obviating the need for Einstein's light postulate). In addition, he characterized the Lie algebra of the Lorentz group and derived the first two Lorentz-covariant laws of gravitation. Along the way, Poincaré provided the four-vectors for Hermann Minkowski's four-dimensional space-time theory (1908) but deplored the latter's Einsteinian view of space and time coordinates, advocating in its place an interpretative convention equivalent to the postulation of Galilean space-time.

In practice Poincaré applied the principle of relativity as one prong of a two-pronged method for the discovery of relativistic laws: Whatever laws happen to describe the behavior of natural phenomena, these laws are required to be covariant with respect to a certain group of transformations. The first prong left him with an infinite number of candidate laws, all covariant with respect to the Lorentz group. The second prong placed a constraint on the search domain: For velocities that are small with respect to that of light, the relativistic law should correspond to that of classical physics. While Poincaré applied his covariance-plus-correspondence method only to the case of Lorentz-covariant laws of gravitation, his approach is applicable to any group of transformations and any principle of correspondence. Upon further formal elaborations from Minkowski and Arnold Sommerfeld, Poincaré's method became a touchstone of theoretical physics.

Work on Trajectories. Interest in Poincaré's innovative contributions to the theory of dynamical systems expanded with the rise of chaos theory in the 1970s and the archival discovery of the first version of Poincaré's submission for the King Oscar II of Sweden competition to solve the *n*-body problem in celestial mechanics (1889). The published version of Poincaré's paper on the restricted three-body problem (1890) contains the first mathematical description of a chaotic trajectory in a dynamical system, or what Poincaré referred to as a doubly-asymptotic (and later, homoclinic) trajectory, but this extraordinary result is absent from the original, prize-winning version of the paper. In its place is a hastily written corollary concerning unstable periodic solutions of differential equations, the flaw in which Poincaré discovered while preparing his manuscript for publication. In a moment of inattention Poincaré convinced himself of the convergence of the power series expansion of certain periodic solutions, which pointed to well-behaved asymptotic trajectories. In fact, the published version shows that the series in question belongs to the class of asymptotic series he had defined in 1886 (known later as a Poincaré expansion), and that in light of his recurrence theorem, the behavior of the corresponding trajectories becomes quite complicated (or in modern terms, chaotic). The significance of these doubly asymptotic trajectories was not generally recognized at first, perhaps in part because Poincaré soft-pedaled his discovery, the child of an oversight in the original submission that was a huge embarrassment both for him and for those who awarded him the prize (Karl Weierstrass, Charles Hermite, and Gösta Mittag-Leffler).

While the fate of doubly asymptotic trajectories, neglected for decades, is extreme, relative neglect befell other results obtained by Poincaré in algebraic topology and mathematical physics. There were several reasons for this, including an allusive writing style and a lack of follow-through. As his former student Émile Borel put it in 1909, Poincaré was "more a conqueror than a colonist." A self-made mathematician in the French style, Poincaré took on no doctoral students, formed no school, and delivered lectures incomprehensible to all but a handful of auditors. With the aid of student note takers, however, he published a complete series of lectures on mathematical physics and celestial mechanics, the technical sophistication and logical coherence of which were much admired; they effectively disseminated Poincaré's mathematical methods and problem-solving style.

Physics and Philosophy. Significantly for the historical development of electrodynamics, Poincaré's 1890 lectures on James Clerk Maxwell's theory of electromagnetism were the first to appear in German and the second to appear in French (other than translations of Maxwell's 1873 *Treatise*). Poincaré emphasized the Scottish physicist's abstract and powerful Lagrangian approach and proved his remark that if a phenomenon admits of one mechanical explanation, it admits of an infinity of such explanations. He also transformed Maxwell's single-fluid theory into a two-fluid theory, to the irritation of certain Maxwellians, and misrepresented its notions of charge and current. Nonetheless, his streamlined, inductive approach appealed to physicists in Britain as on the Continent and furthered the cause of Maxwell's theory and British abstract dynamics.

For the general reader, Poincaré explained the cosmic consequences of his discoveries in the dynamics of systems, for the foundations of the second law of thermodynamics, the question of determinism, and the stability of the Solar System. Starting in the 1890s Poincaré laid out in dozens of popular articles a coherent scientific worldview informed by contemporary research in mathematics and physics, and a familiarity with the writings of the leading physicist-philosophers: Maxwell, Helmholtz, Ernst Mach, and Heinrich Hertz. To Poincaré's surprise his epistemological reflections were enrolled by Catholic intellectuals in an effort to undermine scientific authority. This placed him in the delicate position of having to explain the value of a science whose pretension to absolute truth he had systematically destroyed.

Technological advances issuing from fundamental discoveries in physics were readily apparent in Poincaré's time, some of which he celebrated (including wireless telegraphy and the use of x-ray images in medical diagnostics). Nonetheless, he located the value of science not in its utility, or even in its power to relieve human suffering, but in its capacity to awaken the intellect: "to see," or at least, someday, "to let others see." The unity and progress of science were linked for Poincaré; the unity derived not from any shared method of investigation, a wholly illusory notion, but from the shared mathematical structures of the physical world. Progress, by contrast, was realized by overcoming the obstacles inherent in the methodological disunity of science. In practice, overcoming such obstacles meant adopting the most general point of view possible of the problem at hand, an approach he employed regularly himself.

While scientific progress in Poincaré's sense is possible, it is by no means inevitable, nor does it lead to absolute truth in the long run. Objectivity itself is a social construct for Poincaré: Without discourse, he wrote, there can be no objectivity. All science is not discourse, although some of Poincaré's contemporaries understood him to be a nominalist. Laws describing natural phenomena are elaborated pragmatically in the sense that scientists' choices remain free but are guided by experience. Mathematics is a science apart for Poincaré because the structure of the natural numbers is intuitively given (in a non-Kantian sense), while the natural sciences depend on a theory of measurement requiring the real numbers and arithmetical operations. Progress in mathematics is itself possible due to the principle of induction, which Poincaré understood to be a synthetic a priori judgment. Attempts to provide a logical foundation for mathematics by Bertrand Russell and Alfred North Whitehead were doomed to failure, Poincaré argued, because their constructions necessarily involved circular reasoning.

Reputation. The brilliance of Poincaré's contributions to mathematics, celestial mechanics, and mathematical physics was recognized by scientific academies across Europe and in the United States, most of which counted Poincaré as a foreign member by the end of the nineteenth century. The mathematical community was unanimous in its recognition of his accomplishments, the combined depth and breadth of which none could reasonably hope to emulate. This intellectual ascendancy had no counterpart in the French institutional domain, where Poincaré was visibly less skilled than some of his peers in securing his objectives. At the height of his scientific authority in 1907, he stood for the position of perpetual secretary for the physical sciences at the Paris Academy of Sciences, with the backing of members of the physics section. Faced with opposition from the chemistry and mineralogy sections, he withdrew his candidacy in order to avoid the humiliation of a loss or a narrow win. In return for his retreat, Poincaré's opponents endorsed his candidacy to join the Académie Française, where he was elected in 1908.

A second setback occurred in 1910. Following a highly concerted campaign, Poincaré garnered a record number of nominations for the Nobel Prize in Physics, for the most part in view of his advances in partial differential equations of mathematical physics. Support for his candidacy issued largely from France and Italy, with the British holding back, partly out of concern over a second de facto extension of the prize domain, this time to cover work in mathematical physics, only one year after it had been awarded for applied physics (wireless telegraphy). In the end the Royal Swedish Academy chose to recognize the work of another theorist, Johannes Diderik van der Waals.

While he did not win the Nobel Prize, Poincaré cut an authoritative figure among physicists, even in areas of physics he had ignored, such as the theory of black-body radiation. In the fall of 1911, he took an active part in the First Solvay Council, dedicated to the discussion of prob-

lems in molecular and kinetic theory, along with twenty of Europe's leading experimental and theoretical physicists. A few weeks after the meeting, inspired by what he had learned, he proved the quantum hypothesis to be a sufficient and necessary condition for Planck's law.

SUPPLEMENTARY BIBLIOGRAPHY

For a complete bibliography of Poincaré's writings, a calendar of his correspondence (with annotated transcriptions and digitized images), and a list of secondary sources, consult Archives Henri Poincaré, Laboratoire de Philosophie et d'Histoire des Sciences, Centre National de la Recherche Scientifique, Nancy-Université, available from www.univ-nancy2.fr/poincare/.

WORKS BY POINCARÉ

Papers on Fuchsian Functions. Translated by John Stillwell. Berlin: Springer, 1985.

Poincaré, Russell, Zermelo et Peano; Textes de la discussion (1906–1912) sur les fondements des mathématiques: Des antinomies à la prédicativité. Edited by Gerhard Heinzmann. Paris: Blanchard, 1986.

L'Analyse et la recherche. Edited by Girolamo Ramunni. Paris: Hermann, 1991.

New Methods of Celestial Mechanics. Edited by Daniel L. Goroff. Woodbury, NY: American Institute of Physics, 1993.

Trois suppléments sur la découverte des fonctions fuchsiennes. Edited by Jeremy Gray and Scott Walter. Berlin: Akademie Verlag, 1997.

La Correspondance entre Henri Poincaré et Gösta Mittag-Leffler. Edited by Philippe Nabonnand. Basel: Birkhäuser, 1999.

The Value of Science: Essential Writings of Henri Poincaré. New York: Random House, 2001.

L'Opportunisme scientifique. Edited by Laurent Rollet. Basel: Birkhäuser, 2002.

La Correspondance entre Henri Poincaré et ldes physiciens, chimistes, et ingénieurs. Edited by Scott Walter, Etienne Bolmont, and André Coret. Basel: Birkhäuser, 2007.

OTHER SOURCES

Barrow-Green, June. *Poincaré and the Three Body Problem.* Providence, RI: American Mathematical Society, 1997.

Ben-Menahem, Yemima. "Convention: Poincaré and Some of His Critics." *British Journal for the Philosophy of Science* 52 (2001): 471–513.

Darrigol, Olivier. "Henri Poincaré's Criticism of Fin-de-siècle Electrodynamics." *Studies in History and Philosophy of Modern Physics* 26 (1995): 1–44.

Folina, Janet. *Poincaré and the Philosophy of Mathematics.* London: Macmillan, 1992.

Galison, Peter. *Einstein's Clocks and Poincaré's Maps: Empires of Time.* New York: Norton, 2003.

Giedymin, Jerzy. *Science and Convention: Essays on Henri Poincaré's Philosophy of Science and the Conventionalist Tradition.* Oxford: Pergamon, 1982.

Gilain, Christian. "La théorie qualitative de Poincaré et le problème de l'intégration des équations difféntielles." *Cahiers d'Histoire et de Philosophie des Sciences* 34 (1991): 215–242.

Gray, Jeremy. *Linear Differential Equations and Group Theory from Riemann to Poincaré.* 2nd ed. Boston: Birkhäuser, 2000.

Greffe, Jean-Louis, Gerhard Heinzmann, and Kuno Lorenz, eds. *Henri Poincaré: Science et philosophie: Congrès international, Nancy, France, 1994.* Berlin: Akademie Verlag, 1996.

Heinzmann, Gerhard. *Zwischen Objektkonstruktion und Strukturanalyse: Zur Philosophie der Mathematik bei Jules Henri Poincaré.* Göttingen: Vandenhoeck & Ruprecht, 1995.

Paty, Michel. *Einstein philosophe: La physique comme pratique philosophique.* Paris: Presses Universitaires de France, 1993. Despite its title, this volume contains a perceptive discussion of Poincaré's view of relativity theory.

Prentis, Jeffrey J. "Poincaré's Proof of the Quantum Discontinuity of Nature." *American Journal of Physics* 63 (1995): 339–350.

Rollet, Laurent. *Henri Poincaré: Des mathématiques à la philosophie.* Lille: Éditions du Septentrion, 2001.

Sheynin, Oscar B. "H. Poincaré's Work on Probability." *Archive for History of Exact Sciences* 42 (1991): 137–171.

Torretti, Roberto. *Philosophy of Geometry from Riemann to Poincaré.* 2nd ed. Dordrecht: Reidel, 1984.

Volkert, Klaus. *Das Homöomorphismusproblem insbesondere der 3-Mannigfaltigkeiten in der Topologie 1892–1935.* Paris: Kimé, 2002.

Walter, Scott. "Breaking in the 4-Vectors: The Four-Dimensional Movement in Gravitation, 1905–1910." In *The Genesis of General Relativity,* vol. 3, edited by Jürgen Renn and Matthias Schemmel. Berlin: Springer, 2007.

Zahar, Elie. *Poincaré's Philosophy from Conventionalism to Phenomenology.* Chicago: Open Court, 2001.

Scott Walter

POLÁNYI, MIHÁLY (MICHAEL) (*b.* Budapest, Hungary, 11 March 1891; *d.* Northampton, England, 22 February 1976), *physical chemistry, x-ray crystallography, solid-state chemistry.* For the original article on Polányi see *DSB,* vol. 18, Supplement II.

During the last two decades of the twentieth century, many sociologists and historians of science adopted some of the key ideas of Polányi's writings in philosophy and sociology of science, and new studies appeared on his life and his scientific work.

Influence. Among the most important of Polanyi's philosophical and sociological ideas was his emphasis on the transmission of tradition and tacit knowledge in the material and bodily practices of science. By the end of the twentieth century Polanyi's name achieved iconic status among scholars in the field of the social construction of science (as well as among economists, who emphasize the role of tacit knowledge in innovation processes) who regularly cite Polányi's *Personal Knowledge: Towards a Post-Critical Philosophy* (1958) and *The Tacit Dimension* (1966) as pivotal writings for the analysis of science as a system of social practices rather than as a system of rational ideas. Scholars who have analyzed the impact of Thomas S. Kuhn's work in the history and philosophy of science, especially his book *The Structure of Scientific Revolutions* (1962), have remarked on Kuhn's possible debts to Polányi's early essays, their similar preoccupations with undercutting the philosophy of logical positivism, and their insistence on the dominant role of established beliefs or dogmas in scientific communities rather than of skepticism and impulses toward revolutionary change.

An important aspect of Polányi's philosophical writings on science was his attempt to develop an epistemological position that questioned the positivist definition of science as objective knowledge, while avoiding the relativist implications of a subjectivist perspective. His answer was the notion of science as personal knowledge, which is rooted in passion rather than in detachment and which is grounded in faith that there is a reality and a truth to be known. Polányi's notion of personal knowledge has remained a problematic one for many philosophers of science, as has the religious tone of some of his philosophical writings. What distinguishes the writings of Polányi on scientific life from those of many other philosophers is the fact that he drew upon the experiences of a long and distinguished career in physical science, mainly in the scientific center of Berlin.

Polányi's emphasis on faith, along with his interest in biological evolution as an emergent process, partly helps explain the appropriation of Polányi's name by William Dembski, a leader in the intelligent design movement in the United States, who established a short-lived Michael Polányi Center for Complexity, Information and Design (1999–2000) at Baylor University in Texas, although Polányi himself would not have endorsed intelligent design. Since the 1970s three societies have taken Polányi's work as their core interest. The Michael Polányi Liberal Philosophical Association in Budapest publishes the journal *Polányianna.* The Polányi Society, which is headquartered in the United States, publishes the journal *Tradition and Discovery* and meets annually with the American Academy of Religion and the Society for Biblical Literature. The Society for Post-Critical and Personalist Studies was founded in Great Britain in 2004 for the purpose of promoting interest in Polányi and publishes the journal *Appraisal.*

Biographical Studies. The broad scope of Polányi's political, philosophical, and scientific preoccupations throughout his life is captured in William T. Scott and Martin X. Moleski's *Michael Polányi: Scientist and Philosopher* (2005), which is the only major biography of Polányi other than Eugene P. Wigner and R. A. Hodgkin's obituary in *Biographical Memoirs of Fellows of the Royal Society* (1977). Scott and Moleski give a full account of Polányi's life, including attention to his early years in Budapest and his ongoing skepticism about political and economic changes taking place in Russia following the Bolshevik Revolution of 1917. Michael and his brother Karl Polányi, the economic historian who wrote *The Great Transformation* (1944), talked and argued about economic systems from their youth. Michael Polányi devoted considerable time in the 1930s and 1940s to making a film on liberal economics and the free market, and he developed a critique of central planning of all kinds, including in scientific research and technology.

Because of the shift in Polányi's main work away from physical chemistry by the late 1930s, the University of Manchester created a personal chair in social studies for him in 1948. He frequently visited the United States and accepted a position in social philosophy at the University of Chicago in 1951. He was unable to take up the position, however, because the U.S. State Department delayed a visa for several years on the grounds that he had spoken to a communist-controlled German refugee society in London in 1942. Polányi's impeccable credentials as an anticommunist and the fact that his 1942 lecture had discussed the suppression of genetics in the USSR and the need for scientific freedom from state control were ignored by State Department bureaucrats.

Polányi's older son, George Polányi, studied and published in economics, collaborating with his father in the 1950s in the work of the Committee on Science and Freedom in Oxford, which was associated with the international Congress of Cultural Freedom.

Scientific Work. Scott and Moleski describe at some length Polányi's work in physical chemistry, x-ray crystallography, and solid-state chemistry, as do other authors in new studies of Polányi's scientific work. A consistent focus in Polányi's research was the dynamics of simple chemical reactions involving three-atom and four-atom systems such as $H + Br_2 \rightarrow HBr + Br$ (schematized as $Y + XZ \rightarrow YX + Z$). Like some other chemists and physicists in the 1920s and 1930s, Polányi favored the hypothesis of a transition state in order to explain simple gas reactions as a step-by-step process.

When the young American chemist Henry Eyring arrived to work with Polányi in Berlin in 1929, Polányi encouraged Eyring to assist him in applying Fritz London's current work extending the use of quantum mechanics from the static 2-atom hydrogen molecule to the treatment of chemical combination in 2-, 3-, and 4-atom systems. London had suggested that it should be possible to construct a potential-energy surface giving variation of potential energy for all possible interatomic distances in a 3-atom system.

As noted by Jeffry Ramsey, Eyring and Polányi arrived at a unique procedure for mixing theoretical results and experimental results in order to arrive at a value for energy of formation of a transition complex by what they called a semiempirical method (*halbempirisches Verfahren*). After he left Berlin and had moved to Princeton, Eyring developed his theory of absolute reaction rates and activated complexes, while Polányi, working with Meredith G. Evans in Manchester, characterized the approach as the transition-state method. As discussed in recent scholarship, both Eyring and Polányi's methods were met with strong criticism for the next thirty years by chemists and physicists who disparaged the approximative character of the semiempirical approach and doubted the existence of transition-state structures. In contrast Polányi stressed the reality of the transition state and the value of a theory that could give a reasonable picture of the mechanism of chemical reaction. By the late 1950s computers made calculations of potential energy surfaces easy and by the 1960s new experimental methods using molecular beams and other methods corroborated the soundness of the principles of Eyring and Polányi. Polányi's younger son John, a student of Meredith Evans and Ernest Warhurst, was among those who confirmed the existence of the transition state.

In 1986 John Polányi, Dudley R. Herschbach, and Yuan T. Lee shared the Nobel Prize in Chemistry for their individual contributions to chemical dynamics in a fitting tribute to the work of Michael Polányi himself.

SUPPLEMENTARY BIBLIOGRAPHY

WORKS BY POLÁNYI

The Contempt of Freedom: The Russian Experiment and After. London: Watts, 1940; report, New York: Arno Press, 1975.

Society, Economics and Philosophy: Selected Papers. Edited by R. T. Allen. New Brunswick, NJ: Transaction, 1997.

OTHER SOURCES

Holton, Gerald. "Michael Polányi and the History of Science." *Tradition and Discovery* 19, no. 1 (1992–1993): 16–30. Republished in his *Einstein, History and Other Passions.* Woodbury, NY: American Institute of Physics Press, 1995.

Jacobs, Struan, and R. T. Allen, eds. *Emotion, Reason and Tradition: Essays on the Social, Political and Economic Thought of Michael Polányi.* Burlington, VT: Ashgate Publishing, 2005.

Jha, Stefania Ruzsits. *Reconsidering Michael Polányi's Philosophy.* Pittsburgh: University of Pittsburgh Press, 2002.

Nye, Mary Jo. "Laboratory Practice and the Physical Chemistry of Michael Polányi." In *Instruments and Experimentation in the History of Chemistry,* edited by Frederic L. Holmes and Trevor H. Levere. Cambridge, MA: MIT Press, 2000.

———. "Michael Polányi (1891–1976)." *Hyle: International Journal for Philosophy of Chemistry* 8, no. 2 (2002): 123–127.

———. "Working Tools for Theoretical Chemistry: Polányi, Eyring, and Debates over the 'Semi-Empirical Method,' " *Journal of Computational Chemistry* 28 (2007), 98 Polányi, Mihály (Michael) 108.

Palló, Gábor. "Michael Polányi's Early Years in Science." *Bulletin for the History of Chemistry* 21 (1998): 39–43.

Polányi, John C. "Michael Polányi, the Scientist." *Chemical Heritage* 23 (Spring 2005): 10–13.

Ramsey, Jeffry L. "Between the Fundamental and the Phenomenological: The Challenge of 'Semi-Empirical' Methods." *Philosophy of Science* 64 (1997): 627–653.

Scott, William Taussig, and Martin X. Moleski. *Michael Polányi: Scientist and Philosopher.* Oxford: Oxford University Press, 2005.

Thorpe, Charles. "Science against Modernism: The Relevance of the Social Theory of Michael Polányi." *British Journal of Sociology* 52, no. 1 (2001): 19–35.

Mary Jo Nye

PONTRYAGIN, LEV SEMION-OVICH (*b.* Moscow, Russia, 3 September 1908; *d.* Moscow, Russia, 3 May 1988), *topology, algebra, theory of differential equations, game theory.*

Pontryagin was born into an ordinary family; his father, Semen Akimovich Pontryagin, was a ledger clerk, his mother Tatyana Andreevna (maiden name Petrova) a dressmaker. Because his family's income was very small, he could not enter a gymnasium but only an ordinary municipal school. When he was fourteen years old, a stove explosion left him blind. His mother became his eyes and provided everything for his future education: She helped him to do lessons, read his books out loud (including the mathematical books in Russian and also in German), and later she inserted the formulas in his papers, which he typed himself. He had already become interested in mathematics at school, and in 1925 he entered the Mathematics and Physics Faculty of Moscow University. Among his professors were such scientists as Dmitri F. Egorov, Nikolai N. Luzin, Dmitri D. Men'shov, Aleksandr Y. Khinchin, and Pavel S. Aleksandrov. As early as his second year at the university Pontryagin began to participate in Aleksandrov's topological seminar, study combinatorial topology, and obtain his first important results on the Alexander duality theorem. He graduated from Moscow University in 1929 and was awarded a scholarship, with Aleksandrov

acting as his supervisor. Beginning in 1930 he worked in Moscow University, becoming a professor there in 1935. In 1934 the Steklov Institute moved from Leningrad to Moscow, and soon Pontryagin was invited to work there; he became head of the Department of Topology and Geometry at the institute in 1935. He combined this work with his responsibilities as a professor of the Mechanics and Mathematics Faculty of the Moscow University.

Topology. The first series of Pontryagin's topological works was completed by his demonstration of a duality law that connected the homology groups of bounded polyhedrons in Euclidean space and the homology groups of the complement of the space. Pontryagin's duality law was the beginning of a new direction in topological research—the theory of topological duality. Using it, Pontryagin elaborated the general theory of characters for commutative topological groups—the first distinguished achievement in topological algebra, a new branch of mathematics. Pontryagin went on to demonstrate that there are only three examples of locally compact connected division rings—the field of real numbers, the field of complex numbers, and the ring of quaternions. He found results that reveal the structure of compact and locally compact topological groups and resolved Hilbert's fifth problem for commutative locally bicompact groups in 1934. He published these findings in 1938 in his classic book, *Nepreryvnye gruppy,* which was immediately translated into English as *Topological Groups.*

In 1934 Elie Cartan proposed the problem of calculating the homology groups of the classical compact Lie groups in his lecture in Moscow University. Pontryagin played a very important role in solving this problem in 1935.

In the 1930s Pontryagin published work on the theory of dimension. He studied homotopy theory and the theory of fiber bundles. He introduced the notion of framed manifolds, which gave rise to the development of cobordism theory. He took the first steps in the theory of cohomology operations. His most famous achievement was the discovery of characteristic classes (Pontryagin characteristic classes). These studies prepared the way for the subsequent rise of algebraic topology.

Theory Oscillation; Theory of Automatic Control. In the early 1930s Pontryagin became acquainted with the physicist Alexander A. Andronov. At this time Pontryagin was beginning his studies in the theory of oscillation and the theory of automatic control. The first results of these studies were the works of Pontryagin and Andronov on dynamical systems ("O statisticheskom rassmotrenii dinamicheskikh system, 1933) and on structurally stable systems ("Systèmes grossiers," 1937). In these works Pontryagin showed a lively interest in questions about natural science and technology and demonstrated how to derive very productive mathematical problems from them.

But the sharpest turn in the direction of his research occurred in 1952. In the autumn of that year he organized a seminar at the Steklov Institute on mathematical questions in the theories of oscillation and automatic control. He drew Vladimir G. Boltyanskii, Revaz V. Gamkrelidze, and Evgenii F. Mishchenko into his work in these areas, and they became his active collaborators. One of the main directions of the work of this seminar became the elaboration of the theory of equations with a small parameter in the higher derivatives. The numerically rich results they obtained allowed them to obtain new outcomes in different physical phenomena.

Theory of Optimal Processes. Another direction of the seminar's activity was the theory of optimal control, which is the development of the classical calculus of variations. Results obtained by Pontryagin and his disciples Boltyanskii, Gamkrelidze, and Mishchenko, in this direction received recognition and found extensive technical applications. Pontryagin found a necessary optimality condition—the famous Pontryagin's maximum principle. He and his collaborators explored the existence and uniqueness of the optimal control in the linear case, the sliding modes in the nonlinear case, and other situations. Their results made up the contents of their famous book, *Matematicheskaia teoriia optimalnykh protsessov* (1961; *The Mathematical Theory of Optimal Processes,* 1962), which was awarded the Lenin Prize in 1962. In the years following, Pontryagin actively developed the theory of differential games.

Pontryagin combined research activity and pedagogical work. In 1954 he began to lecture in the Mechanics and Mathematics Faculty of Moscow University on ordinary differential equations. A considerable proportion of these lectures was devoted to important technical applications: the Vyshnegradskii theory of the Watt regulator, the Andronov theory of the valve generator, and so on. These lectures formed the basis of his well-known textbook, *Obyknovennye differentcial'nye uravneniya* (1961; *Ordinary Differential Equations,* 1962). In 1975 he received the State Prize for this book. In his final years, Pontryagin taught in the Computer Science and Cybernetics Faculty of Moscow University (from 1970 as the head of the department of the optimal control). An excellent teacher, he trained an entire galaxy of pupils, among whom are such famous scientists as Vladimir A. Rokhlin, E. F. Mishchenko, Vladimir G. Boltyanskii, R. V. Gamkrelidze, Mikhail M. Postnikov, and Dmitrii V. Anosov.

Pontryagin combined his strenuous research and pedagogical work with intensive activity within Soviet and international mathematics institutions. He was on the boards of various mathematical journals at home and abroad. For example, from 1958 to 1975 he was a board member of the mathematical series of the *Izvestiya Akademii Nauk SSSR* (*Proceedings of the Academy of Sciences of the USSR*). From 1969 to 1983, Pontryagin was the vice president of the Bureau of the National Committee of Soviet Mathematicians. In 1970–1974 he was the vice president and in 1974–1978 a member of the executive committee of the International Mathematical Union. In 1975–1987 he was the editor-in-chief of the *Matematicheskii Sbornik* (*Sbornik: Mathematics*). From 1982 to 1988 he was the president of the Commission on Mathematical Education in the Schools of the Komissiya po Shkol'nomu Matematicheskomu Obrazovaniyu Otdeleniya Matematiki Akademii Nauk SSSR (Mathematical class of the Academy of Sciences of the USSR). In the 1980s, he actively participated in the successful campaign against the Soviet government's plan to redirect the northern European and Siberian rivers, which could have had dangerous ecological consequences as well as damaging the economy and culture of the country.

Overcoming Disability. The most striking thing about all of Pontryagin's achievements is that they were done by a man who was blind. He had to make complicated calculations mentally and store enormous amounts of information in his memory. In addition to his work in mathematics, he participated in sports—in particular, skiing, which he did with the help of a person in front of him who made the ski track for those behind him to use. To some, Pontryagin resembled the heroes of the Renaissance. He liked Benvenuto Cellini's memoir, and in imitation of Cellini, Pontryagin wrote his own memoir, *Zhizneopisanie L'va Semionovicha Pontryagina, matematika, sostavlennoe im samim* (1998; Biography of Lev Semionovich Pontryagin, mathematician, composed by himself).

Honors and Awards. Pontryagin's scientific achievements brought him recognition at home and abroad. He was elected a corresponding member of the Akademii Nauk SSSR (Academy of Sciences of the USSR) in 1939 and became a full member in 1958. He received many other Soviet honors for his activities, including Hero of Socialist Labor (1969), the Order of Lenin on three occasions (1967, 1969, 1978), the Order of the October Revolution (1975), and the Order of the Labor Red Banner (1945). He also received the Stalin Prize (1941), the Lenin Prize (1962), and State Prize of the USSR (1975). For his series of works on the differentiable manifolds, the Academy of Sciences of the USSR gave him the N. I. Lobachevskii Prize in 1966.

He lectured in the United States (1964, 1972), Great Britain (1969), and France (1973). He never retired; up to his death he was the member of Steklov Institute and the director of his department in the university.

BIBLIOGRAPHY

Pontryagin's autobiography, Zhizneopisanie L'va Semionovicha Pontryagina, matematika, sostavlennoe im samim *(Moscow: IChP "Prima V," 1998), includes a bibliography of his works. The Archive of Russian Academy of Sciences has a significant quantity of unpublished documents related to Pontryagin.*

WORKS BY PONTRYAGIN

With Alexander Andronov and Alexander Vitt. "O statisticheskom rassmotrenii dinamicheskikh sistem." *Zhurnal eksperimental'noi i teoreticheskoi fiziki* 3, no. 3 (1933): 165–180.

"Systèmes grossiers." *Doklady Academii Nauk SSSR* 14, no. 5 (1937): 247–251.

Foundations of Combinatorial Topology. Translated by Frederick Bagemihl and Horace Komm. Rochester, NY: Graylock Press, 1952.

"Smooth Manifolds and Their Applications in Homotopy Theory." *American Mathematical Society Translations,* series 2, 11 (1959): 1–114.

Ordinary Differential Equations. Translated by Leonas Kacinskas and Walter B. Counts. Reading, MA: Addison-Wesley, 1962.

With Vladimir G. Boltyanskii, Revaz V. Gamkrelidze, and Evgenii F. Mishchenko. *The Mathematical Theory of Optimal Processes.* Translated by D. E. Brown. New York: Pergamon Press, 1964.

Topological Groups. 2nd ed. Translated by Arlen Brown. New York: Gordon and Breach, 1966.

Selected Works. Translated by P. S. V. Naidu. 4 vols. New York: Gordon and Breach, 1986.

Izbrannye nauchnye trudy. 3 vols. Moscow: Nauka, 1988. The Soviet edition of Pontryagin's *Selected Works.*

Zhizneopisanie L'va Semionovicha Pontryagina, matematika, sostavlennoe im samim. Moscow: IChP "Prima V," 1998. Pontryagin's memoir.

OTHER SOURCES

Aleksandrov, Pavel S., and Evgenii F. Mishchenko. "Lev Semionovich Pontryagin: K 50-letiyu so dnya rozhdeniya" (Lev Semionovich Pontryagin: For his 50th anniversary). *Uspekhi matematicheskikh* 14, no. 3 (1959): 195–199.

———, Vladimir G. Boltyanskii, Revaz V. Gamkrelidz, et al. "Lev Semionovich Pontryagin: K 60-letiyu so dnya rozhdeniya" (Lev Semionovich Pontryagin: For his 60th anniversary). *Uspekhi matematicheskikh nauk* 23, no. 6 (1968): 187–196.

Sergei S. Demidov

POPLE, JOHN ANTHONY (*b.* Burnham-on-Sea, United Kingdom, 31 October 1925, *d.* Wilmette, Illinois, 15 March 2004), *chemistry, computational quantum chemistry.*

Pople revolutionized the way that chemistry is practiced by making it possible to perform chemistry in the computer as a complement to the conventional chemistry of the laboratory. He was a giant in his chosen field of computational quantum chemistry, for which he was awarded the Nobel Prize in Chemistry in 1998. Pople was the person most responsible for making computational quantum chemistry usable by the community of chemists at large, and he dominated the scene in this area for five decades. By the time of his death in 2004, it would have been difficult to imagine any significant chemistry establishment in the world that did not make use of one or other of the Pople procedures.

Family Background and Early Education. John Pople was born in Burnham-on-Sea in southwest England in 1925. His paternal great-grandfather had been a successful businessman, and one of these businesses, a clothing shop, was inherited by John's grandfather and subsequently by his father. John's mother came from a farming background and, although most of her relatives remained in farming, she became a tutor and a librarian. John's parents were ambitious for their children and sent John and his brother to Bristol Grammar School, some thirty miles away. This provided a challenging experience during the war years, with the occurrence of heavy air raids in the vicinity of Bristol, but it was an excellent school that led to an excellent education.

John's intense interest and talents in mathematics were apparent at an early age. However, he describes in his Nobel autobiography how he introduced deliberate errors into his mathematics exercises at Bristol Grammar School so as not to appear too smart. It was not until a new mathematics teacher arrived on the scene and created a particularly challenging test that John succumbed to temptation and turned in a perfect paper, including multiple solutions to several of the problems. Despite the remarkable achievements that were to follow, Pople always retained his modest manner.

Once his talents were recognized, Pople was encouraged to apply for a scholarship to study at Cambridge University. Ironically, during his last two years at Bristol Grammar School, he abandoned chemistry to concentrate on mathematics and physics. Many years later, in the 1960s, this was to lead to an amusing situation where his initial application to join the American Chemical Society was rejected because he had not completed the requisite number of courses! Pople entered Cambridge in 1943 and completed his undergraduate education in May 1945.

John Anthony Pople. © EPA/CORBIS.

Cambridge and the National Physics Laboratory. Pople began life as a research student in theoretical chemistry at Cambridge University with Sir John Lennard-Jones in July 1948. His interest in pure mathematics had begun to wane by that time, so he decided to apply his mathematical skills to chemistry. He worked on the structure of liquid water and was awarded a PhD in 1952. During this early period in Cambridge, Pople was also learning to play the piano. His teacher was Joy Bowers, and they were subsequently married in 1952, a partnership that would continue for almost fifty years. Pople was appointed a Research Fellow at Trinity College in Cambridge in 1951 and a lecturer on the mathematics faculty in 1954. The germs of the ideas that were to provide the focus for the central theme of his life's work, namely, developing mathematical models that would be capable of describing all of chemistry, were sown during this period. However, there were two significant digressions along the way.

In 1955 Pople developed an interest in the then-emerging technique of nuclear magnetic resonance (NMR) spectroscopy, a forerunner to the magnetic resonance imaging of the early twenty-first century. He spent two summers at the National Research Council of Canada working on the theoretical basis of NMR. This work led to seminal contributions, including a landmark mono-

graph on the subject, and constituted Pople's main research activity during his final years in Cambridge.

The second digression arose because Pople had become dissatisfied with his mathematics teaching post and therefore sought a position with greater scientific content. He eventually accepted an appointment as head of the Basic Physics Division of the National Physical Laboratory in Teddington, near London. However, this also proved unsatisfactory, as he found the administrative load interfered too much with his research activities. Pople described the time in the National Physical Laboratory as a fallow period in his scientific life.

Carnegie Mellon University and the Brain Drain. In 1961 Pople was invited by Robert Parr, himself a leading international quantum chemist, to be the Ford Visiting Professor at the Carnegie Institute of Technology in Pittsburgh for the 1961–1962 academic year. This appointment was a thoroughly enjoyable experience for Pople and his family; it also made him aware of the opportunities for scientific advancement in the American environment. When Parr decided to leave for Johns Hopkins University in 1963, his position at Carnegie Tech was offered to Pople, who accepted it. In soliciting Parr's advice on this matter, Pople had written: "Like most of the academic community, I am looking for a lively scientific environment, a good salary, a tolerable place to live in, and freedom from administrative chores." This is a realistic summary of Pople's priorities (particularly his disdain for administration) and his relatively undemanding requirements throughout his academic life. The decision in favor of Carnegie Tech ahead of competing offers from Chicago and Princeton was probably decided by his enjoyable earlier experience in Pittsburgh. The departure from the United Kingdom of someone of Pople's stature was decried in the U.K. press with the headline "Another Brain down the Drain," but it was welcomed in the *Pittsburgh Press* with the headline "'Drain' Flows Our Way: Top British Brain Coming to Tech." Leaving the United Kingdom was a painful decision for the Poples, and they attempted to compensate in some respects with annual summer visits "back home." The appointment in 1964 marked the beginning of a thirty-year relationship (1964–1993) with Carnegie Tech (subsequently to become Carnegie Mellon University after a merger with Mellon Institute). Virtually all of Pople's prize-winning work was carried out while he was a professor at Carnegie Mellon from 1964 to 1993.

By 1981 all the Pople children had left home, and John and Joy set up house in Chicago, to be close to their daughter Hilary. John initially commuted from Pittsburgh, while also holding an adjunct appointment at Northwestern University. When he retired from Carnegie

Mellon in 1993, he completed the move to Chicago, taking up a full faculty position at Northwestern University. Pople also had close connections with the Australian National University in Canberra, which he described as his "second academic home—a great place for relaxed contemplation," and which he visited on nine occasions during the 1980s and 1990s. He also had close ties with Israel and Germany.

Pople's Main Research. Pople's long-term goal was the creation of theoretical models for studying chemistry. It was known a long time previously, and enunciated by Paul Dirac in 1929 with an often-quoted statement, that the laws of quantum mechanics could *in principle* be used to predict all of chemistry: "The fundamental laws necessary for the mathematical treatment of a large part of physics and the whole of chemistry are thus completely known, and the difficulty lies only in the fact that application of these laws leads to equations that are too complex to be solved" ("P. A. M. Dirac," 1929, p. 714). What Pople did was to convert the *principle* to a practical reality. His aim was to enable chemists at large to be able to straightforwardly predict the properties of molecules, such as molecular structures and the way that molecules reacted with one another, by using a computer rather than by carrying out experiments.

Pople went about this task by first formulating the essential characteristics of an acceptable theoretical model. For example, such a model should be unique, well-defined, unbiased, objective, and widely applicable, and it should also satisfy some more technical requirements (e.g., be "size-consistent"). If the model performs satisfactorily in systematic comparisons with available experimental data, it may then be used with confidence to make predictions in cases where experimental data are not available.

Pople then proceeded to design a series of theoretical procedures that could be used as the basis for the model. His first attempt in this direction in 1953 paralleled studies by Rudolph Pariser and Robert Parr in the United States, and was known collectively as "PPP theory." This was not a complete model because it could only be satisfactorily applied to conjugated organic molecules. However, in the precomputer age, that was the limit of what was feasible.

Pople resumed his work on implementing model chemistries when he moved to Pittsburgh in 1964. His next step was the introduction of a series of methods that were termed semiempirical. These simplified the quantum chemistry calculations by introducing approximations, while attempting to compensate for the approximations by including empirical parameters based on experimental data. Examples of these procedures include the complete neglect of differential overlap (CNDO) and intermediate neglect of differential overlap (INDO) methods. They represented genuine chemical models in that they could treat a wide variety of molecules and provide predictions of properties such as molecular structures and energies. However, they were of limited predictive value because of uncertainties regarding the consequences of the approximations made in their formulation.

By this time, the explosive growth of high-speed computers had begun, and Pople recognized that the use of computers would be the basis for the future of quantum chemistry calculations. He also recognized that the theoretical developments needed to move hand in hand with efficient computer code, and he mastered this new skill quickly and with enthusiasm. The initial university computer purchased after Pople joined Carnegie Mellon University was a Control Data Corporation (CDC) 1604 in 1966. It is of interest to note that the CDC 1604 had a delivered speed of 0.03 MFlops and a memory of 0.2 Mbytes; it was approximately 100,000 times slower and had 5,000 times less memory than an average laptop computer in 2006—making Pople's achievements in those early days all the more remarkable. Subsequently, a Univac 1108 was purchased in 1971, and in 1978 Pople was able to acquire the first VAX/780 minicomputer from Digital Equipment Corporation.

Pople felt that it would be desirable to implement molecular orbital theory procedures that did not require experimental data in their formulation, and he set about moving from semiempirical to ab initio methods. The term *ab initio* literally means "from the beginning" and in this context refers to the fact that the methods are based solely on the laws of quantum mechanics (in particular the Schrödinger equation) without recourse to any experimental information other than the values of fundamental constants such as the speed of light and the charge on the electron. Ab initio procedures had been in existence for many years, but the available general programs were very slow and thus severely limited the range of chemical systems to which they could be applied. In comparison to these ab initio programs, Pople's CNDO procedure was faster by a factor of approximately 1,000.

Pople's entry into the field and his contributions in the late 1960s and early 1970s changed the face of ab initio quantum chemistry. He designed highly efficient computer codes, involving features such as much faster routines for evaluation of the integrals that are required for the calculations. He created efficient purpose-built basis sets, a necessary input into the ab initio molecular orbital theory calculations. When the code (named Gaussian 70) was first completed in 1970, it was approximately 100 times faster than the most popular of the existing programs. Pople's development and release of the Gaussian 70 program marked a turning point in the field. Broad theoretical studies could now be carried out on real chemical problems on a scale that had not been previously possible.

The developments by Pople from 1968 to 1972 laid the foundations for the widespread use of ab initio calculations by the chemical community, as Gaussian 70 rapidly gained acceptance in chemical laboratories around the globe. Some of the reasons for this immediate popularity were that Gaussian 70 was fast and easy to use; the performance of the internal basis sets, with names such as STO-3G, 4-31G, and 6-31G* had been thoroughly tested and could therefore be employed where appropriate with confidence; a wide selection of fundamental examples of the types of problems that could be tackled and some of the important strategies that might be used in tackling them had been published; and through John Pople's generosity, the program was made available at minimal cost for general use via the Quantum Chemistry Program Exchange. These foundations were strengthened and expanded in subsequent years.

The initial molecular orbital procedures that had been coded into Gaussian involved the Hartree-Fock method. This method does not allow for so-called correlation in the motion of electrons. In the late 1970s, Pople formulated an efficient method for including such electron correlation in the calculations, based on the perturbation theory of Møller-Plesset, dating back to 1934. Electron correlation was certainly not a new concept, but it had previously been the province of specialized theoreticians. Pople had found a way to incorporate it straightforwardly and at low cost, thus making it readily usable by the nonspecialist. Simplicity and efficiency were two of the ever-present hallmarks of the Pople approach.

Even in the more recently popularized density functional theory, in which he was formally only a minor player (the dominant contributor being Walter Kohn, with whom Pople shared the 1998 Nobel Prize in Chemistry), Pople systematized the way in which such calculations were carried out and incorporated them into the Gaussian program. This undoubtedly helped significantly in accelerating the widespread acceptance and use of density functional theory in chemistry.

Pople made continuing innovative contributions to the development and application of ab initio quantum chemistry throughout his research career. In the final decade, he focused on formulating model theories that could provide thermochemical information of high accuracy at modest computational expense. These models were named *Gaussian n* (*Gn*) and had reached G3 at the time of his death. They were able to predict thermochemistry with an accuracy that rivaled that of experimental work.

Computational quantum chemistry has become used by myriad chemists across a variety of fields. It has become a viable adjunct to experiment in the pursuit of chemistry, and it is used to help solve problems of a fundamental nature. It is also being used increasingly by industrial companies in more practical situations, such as in the design of new drugs and of new materials. The computational approach to chemistry allows the study of substances that might be difficult to examine experimentally, for example, because they have a very short lifetime or because they are dangerously toxic or explosive. The computer is oblivious to such hazards, and the increasing applicability of the computational approach to chemistry has been helped by massive and continuing increases in computer power. The individual most responsible for bringing about this change in the way chemistry is practiced was John Pople.

Apart from being a brilliant researcher, Pople was also a great communicator, as anyone who ever heard him lecture would attest. Some people have the knack of making simple things complicated; Pople had the ability to keep simple material simple and the gift of making complicated material appear simple as well.

Pople's achievements received widespread recognition. He was elected a Fellow of the Royal Society in 1961, and was a founding member of the International Academy of Quantum Molecular Science in 1964, serving as president from 1977 to 2000. He was elected to the U.S. National Academy of Sciences in 1977. He received the Schrödinger Medal of the World Association of Theoretical and Computational Chemists in 1987. In 1992 he received Israel's premier prize, the Wolf Prize, and in 1993 he was elected a Corresponding Member of the Australian Academy of Science. He shared the 1998 Nobel Prize in Chemistry with Walter Kohn in 1998, and was awarded the Copley Medal of the Royal Society in 2002. In 2003 he was knighted by Queen Elizabeth II, becoming Knight Commander of the Order of the British Empire.

BIBLIOGRAPHY

WORKS BY POPLE

With William G. Schneider and Harold J. Bernstein. *High Resolution Nuclear Magnetic Resonance Spectroscopy*. New York: McGraw-Hill, 1959. A significant early monograph on NMR.

With David L. Beveridge. *Approximate Molecular Orbital Theory*. New York: McGraw-Hill, 1970. The first major book on semiempirical theory.

With Warren J. Hehre, Leo Radom, and Paul von R. Schleyer. *Ab Initio Molecular Orbital Theory*. New York: John Wiley, 1986. The classic text in the field.

"John Pople: Autobiography." In *Les Prix Nobel*, 187–193. Royal Swedish Academy of Sciences, 1998. Pople's life story, written with his renowned clarity. A major source for this article.

"Quantum Chemical Models." *Angewandte Chemie, International Edition* 38 (1999): 1894–1902. Pople's Nobel lecture.

OTHER SOURCES

Buckingham, A. David. "John Anthony Pople, KBE." *Biographical Memoirs of Fellows of the Royal Society* 52 (December 2006). A detailed biographical memoir written by Pople's first PhD student and longtime friend.

Frenking, Gernot, Paul von R. Schleyer, Norman L. Allinger, et al. "Publishers Note: Sir John A. Pople." *Journal of Computational Chemistry* 9 (2004): v–viii. Personal reflections on Pople.

Mangravite, Andrew. "The Flight of the Boffin." *Chemical Heritage* (Summer 2004): 27–29. This article gives an interesting account of Pople's move to the United States.

"P. A. M. Dirac." *Proceedings of the Royal Society* (London) 123 (1929): 714.

Radom, Leo. "John A. Pople: The Early Days." *Journal of Physical Chemistry* 94 (1990): 5439–5444. A detailed account of the critical developments leading up to the release of Gaussian 70.

———. "John A. Pople (1925–2004)." *Nature* 428 (2004): 816. An obituary that was a major source for the present article.

Leo Radom

POPPER, KARL RAIMUND (*b.* Vienna, Austria, 28 July 1902; *d.* London, United Kingdom, 17 September 1994), *philosophy, probability, logic, quantum theory, social theory, Darwinism.*

One of the twentieth century's leading philosophers of science, Popper is renowned for his contention that scientific theories are characterized by their falsifiability by evidence and for his rejection of inductivism in favor of an account of scientific progress through conjecture and refutation. In political philosophy Popper is remembered for his critique of historicism, which he saw present in the ideologies of both fascism and Soviet communism. Of wide-ranging intellectual interests, he also contributed to the axiomatization and interpretation of probability, the interpretation of quantum mechanics, the philosophy of logic, and the interpretation and application of Darwinian ideas.

Popper was born into a well-to-do Viennese family of Jewish descent, Lutheran practice, liberal sympathies, and cultured sensibilities. He left school at sixteen amid troubled times with the collapse of the Austro-Hungarian Empire. He worked as a manual laborer, was active in left-wing politics, undertook social work with deprived children, and worked with the psychoanalyst Alfred Adler. Initially as a nonmatriculated student, he took classes in history, literature, psychology, and philosophy, but mainly in mathematics and physics, at the University of Vienna. During this period he was apprenticed to a cabinetmaker, finishing that apprenticeship in 1924, not long after he had qualified as a primary school teacher. Always interested in music, Popper took piano lessons and was for a while a member of Schoenberg's Verein für musikalische Privataufführungen, his sympathies lying fundamentally with an earlier period; on the strength of a fugue for organ he had composed, he was admitted to the Department of Church Music of the Vienna Konservatorium, but left, having decided he did not have the talent to be a musician.

In 1925 Popper enrolled in the newly founded Pedagogic Institute in Vienna, an institution, loosely connected to the university, whose purpose was to support education reforms then underway in Viennese schools. Popper undertook research in the psychology of thinking (Denkpsychologie), including some experimental work, submitting a dissertation on this work in 1927. In the following year he submitted a doctoral thesis, of a more methodological orientation, to the University of Vienna. In 1929 he qualified as a teacher of science in secondary schools with a third thesis on geometry. At the institute he met his future wife, Josefine Anna Henninger (known as "Hennie"). They married in 1930, the year Popper obtained his first teaching appointment.

In the period of his doctoral research Popper was influenced by the psychologist Karl Bühler, his supervisor, and the theories of the Würzburg school that Bühler represented, but he grew increasingly convinced that, rather than the psychology of thinking and intellectual discovery, the topic that concerned him was a logical issue—objective methodology, not the study of subjective thinking processes. By his own account, as far back as 1919 he had been impressed by Albert Einstein's stated readiness to give up the theory of relativity should it fail certain experimental or observational tests. This Popper saw as in marked contrast to the psychoanalysts and vulgar Marxists who held it to be a virtue of their theories that there could be no conceivable counterevidence.

These issues came together in a long, and long unpublished, work, *Die beiden Grundprobleme der Erkenntnistheorie* (The two basic problems of the theory of knowledge). It was written at the instigation of Herbert Feigl, a member of the Vienna Circle of logical positivist philosophers, a group with whom Popper had begun to have contacts in 1929. The two basic problems dealt with the problem of induction and the problem of the demarcation of science. Popper proposed a single answer to both: scientific hypotheses are neither generated nor confirmed by any inductive process, rather they are tested with a view to falsifying them. It is the falsifiability of their hypotheses that distinguishes the sciences, and, contrary to David Hume, induction is not a logically indefensible

Karl Raimund Popper. HULTON ARCHIVE/GETTY IMAGES.

but psychologically necessary process. Rather, inductive reasoning has no part to play in learning from experience: What one learns is whether one's currently entertained hypothesis has survived a test. Falsifiability is the cornerstone of Popper's account of the methodology of the sciences and the growth of human knowledge. With that in place, a great deal remains to be elaborated, a task Popper took up in *Die beiden Grundprobleme* and in many subsequent publications.

In typescript, *Die beiden Grundprobleme* was much discussed by the members of the Vienna Circle. Rudolf Carnap in particular championed some of Popper's views, although by and large the positivists failed to realize how strongly Popper was opposed to their central contentions such as their verifiability theory of meaning according to which metaphysics is meaningless. Popper was encouraged to publish a shorter work in part extracted from the typescript. This was *Logik der Forschung*, published in 1934. In addition to problems of induction and demarcation, it included discussions of quantum mechanics and of probability.

Popper proposed a statistical interpretation of quantum mechanics, arguing at length against Werner Heisen-

berg's account of the uncertainty principle. He advanced a frequentist account of probability. The novelty of his version was his development of a testable notion of randomness, a topic on which he lectured to Karl Menger's Mathematical Colloquium, prompting Abraham Wald to his work on the consistency of Richard von Mises's notion of a collective.

As pointed out in one of the closing sections of the book, *Logik der Forschung* does not need the notions of truth and falsity. "Falsification" of a hypothesis occurs when consequences of the hypothesis are inconsistent with conventionally accepted basic statements (reports of experimental findings agreed by the scientific community). At the time of writing, philosophers were, by and large, suspicious of the notion of truth. In 1935 the Polish logician Alfred Tarski explained to Popper the essentials of his semantic conception of truth. In Popper's view, Tarski's work rehabilitated the correspondence theory of truth; subsequently Popper did not hesitate to use the notions truth and falsity and promoted Tarski's ideas.

Popper remained a schoolteacher through the early and mid-1930s. As his star rose in philosophical circles, he took time off to travel to Britain, where he gave lectures and met, among others, Bertrand Russell, Erwin Schrödinger, and Friedrich von Hayek, and to Copenhagen, where he had discussions with Niels Bohr. With no prospect of a university position in Austria and the political situation worsening, Popper applied for and was appointed to a lectureship at Canterbury University College, Christchurch, a component college of the federal University of New Zealand. The Poppers set sail in early 1937.

In New Zealand Popper had to shoulder a heavy burden of university teaching. Additionally, he lectured for the WEA (Workers Educational Association) and to other groups. His teaching was popular and he came to stand out in quiet Christchurch. There being no other philosopher in the college, Popper's closest academic acquaintances were mostly from the sciences.

Popper's research in New Zealand initially focused on the axiomatization of the probability calculus, a topic to which he would return throughout the rest of his life. He was to propose axiomatizations that take conditional probability as fundamental, not as a derived notion as in the familiar Kolmogorov axiomatization. A remarkable feature of Popper's axiomatization is that it does not presuppose any particular logico-algebraic structure on the domain of the probability function. Rather, one recovers a Boolean algebra from structure induced by a relation of probabilistic equivalence imposed by the probability function. (See *The Logic of Scientific Discovery*, Appendix *v.) Later, in work published in the years immediately after World War II, he turned to formal logic, developing his own natural deduction calculus, investigating classical and intuitionist logics in that framework, and exploring its philosophical implications.

At the same time, Popper's work turned in quite another direction, toward what he would describe as his "war effort": *The Poverty of Historicism* and the two-volume *The Open Society and Its Enemies* (whose bogeymen are Plato, G. W. F. Hegel, and Karl Marx). Popper labeled "historicist" any theory that discerns inexorable laws of historical development and took fascism and Marxism as exemplars: He believed historicist doctrines lead to totalitarianism. The fallibilism inherent in his general stand on knowledge encouraged him to reject any claim to knowledge of any such laws, and a commitment to indeterminism encouraged him to believe that there are no such laws. Popper saw the aim of social policy to be the reduction of suffering (negative utilitarianism) and thought this is best achieved through piecemeal social engineering in an "open society" that permits free and critical discussion. With its emphasis on criticism, Popper's political philosophy was of a piece with his account of science and the demarcation criterion.

With Hayek's assistance, "The Poverty of Historicism" was published as an article in three parts in *Economica* in 1944 and 1945. *The Open Society* was published in Britain in 1945 to some considerable success. Hayek had been instrumental in securing for Popper an invitation to take up a readership at the London School of Economics (LSE). He arrived in January 1946. In 1949 he was promoted to a professorship. Again his teaching proved popular. But over time he withdrew from active involvement with the school; he and Hennie moved from London to a rural retreat in Penn, Buckinghamshire, and Popper reduced to a minimum the occasions on which he had to be present at the LSE.

These years, the 1950s, were the years in which Popper's reputation was to grow, albeit that he was at odds in doctrine and method with the Wittgensteinians and ordinary language philosophers in Oxford and Cambridge. He began to draw to him students who would identify themselves as Popperians. In 1959 *The Logic of Scientific Discovery*, a much expanded English translation of *Logik der Forschung*, was published. It was intended to publish alongside a volume referred to as the *Postscript after Twenty Years* that would detail the results of further work on the topics of *Logik der Forschung*. Edited by William W. Bartley III, the *Postscript* finally emerged in three volumes in 1982 and 1983.

Popper had turned back to problems in the philosophy of physics and to probability. He campaigned against (the early Heisenberg's version of) the Copenhagen interpretation of quantum mechanics, developing the propensity interpretation of probability, an objective, dispositional understanding of probabilities that pertain to single instances. Popper maintained that all the mysteries of quantum mechanics stem from muddles about probability, a claim which, it has to be said, has gained few adherents and one that Popper himself was to weaken in the light of the Aspect experiments testing Bell's Inequality.

Many of the lectures and essays that were collected in *Conjectures and Refutations* (1963) were first delivered or written at this time. While largely concerned with matters methodological, the topics vary widely from the pre-Socratics to political philosophy. One methodological topic that began to feature more prominently was verisimilitude, the truthlikeness of false theories. Scientific knowledge grows, according to Popper, by the severe, critical testing of boldly conjectured hypotheses which are discarded when refuted in experiment. To uphold a conception of scientific progress, one must be able to make sense of one false theory being closer to the truth than another (even if one cannot know when this is the case). To this end Popper gave formal definitions of verisimilitude. Unhappily, in the 1970s these definitions were shown to fail: No false theory could, by their lights, be any nearer the truth than another—and there was no quick fix for the definitions, as Popper acknowledged. Before then, verisimilitude had been one of the elements in Popper's most public bust-up with a former colleague.

Imre Lakatos, who fled Hungary in 1956, had come to the LSE from Cambridge, where, in his *Proofs and Refutations*, he had applied Popperian ideas to mathematics. He was welcomed as a leading light among the Popperians but as he became more engaged in the philosophy of science tensions emerged. These came to a head in Lakatos's contribution to the volume in the Library of Living Philosophers series dedicated to Popper, *The Philosophy of Karl Popper*. A theory that has survived severe attempts at refutation is said, in Popperian jargon, to be well corroborated. What link, if any, is there between corroboration and verisimilitude? Any claim to a strong link smacks of an inductive inference, yet exactly this is what Lakatos urged upon Popper. (Popper himself said that the degree of corroboration of a theory at a time is an indicator of its verisimilitude as it appears at that time and this, if it says anything significant, has struck many as dangerously close to an inductive principle.) Lakatos was an outcast from the Popperian fold; no reconciliation had occurred by the time of Lakatos's death in 1974. The issue at stake between them here sometimes arises in the guise of the viability of a strictly noninductivist, falsificationist account of the technological application of scientific theories.

The 1960s saw Popper involved in a number of controversies. Firstly there was the so-called Positivismusstreit in German sociology in which Popper engaged with Theodor Adorno and Jürgen Habermas (among others) over the nature of social-scientific theorizing. Then there were disputes with Carnap over the form and function of inductive logic and with Thomas Kuhn over the nature of scientific revolutions.

Another strand to emerge in Popper's thinking during the 1960s concerned Darwinism. His views on it changed, so that, for example, in *Unended Quest*, his intellectual biography from the 1970s, he is at pains to argue that Darwinism is metaphysical, because unfalsifiable—but metaphysical ideas can be important for the development of a science, and they can be subject to criticism. He recanted this view in 1977's First Darwin Lecture, "Natural Selection and the Emergence of Mind," given at Darwin College, Cambridge. Popper developed an evolutionary epistemology: He offered a somewhat speculative, gene-based account of problem-solving activity, and even spoke of the universe as a whole as being creative. It is the role of trial-and-error behavior that connects his evolutionary epistemology with his falsificationist methodology and political philosophy.

Popper retired from the LSE in 1969. Throughout his retirement he continued to publish across the wide range of topics already mentioned. He received many prizes and honors. He was elected a fellow of both the British Academy (1958) and the Royal Society (1976); knighted in 1965, he was appointed a Companion of Honour in 1982. Popper lived long enough to know of the fall of the Berlin Wall and to have the significance of *The Open Society* for those struggling against oppression in Eastern Europe acknowledged time and again.

BIBLIOGRAPHY

Popper's papers, correspondence, and other materials are archived at the Hoover Institution, Stanford University. His library is housed in the Karl-Popper-Sammlung at the Alpen-Adria-Universität Klagenfurt, Austria. The majority of Popper's books in English have gone through a number of editions and impressions, often with significant changes. Mohr-Siebeck began publishing Popper's collected works (in German) in 2001. A comprehensive list of works to 1974, compiled by Troels Eggers Hansen, is to be found in The Philosophy of Karl Popper, *edited by Paul A. Schilpp. Manfred Lube has published a bibliography of Popper's writings and writings on Popper to 2004.*

WORKS BY POPPER

Logik der Forschung. Vienna: Julius Springer, 1934 [dated 1935].

"The Poverty of Historicism." *Economica* 11 (1944): 86–103, 119–137; 12 (1945): 69–89. In book form: *The Poverty of Historicism.* London: Routledge and Kegan Paul, 1957.

The Open Society and Its Enemies. London: George Routledge & Sons, 1945.

"New Foundations for Logic." *Mind* 56 (1947): 193–235.

"The Propensity Interpretation of the Calculus of Probability and the Quantum Theory." In *Observation and Interpretation,* edited by Stephan Körner. London: Butterworth, 1957.

The Logic of Scientific Discovery. London: Hutchinson, 1959.

Conjectures and Refutations. London: Routledge and Kegan Paul, 1963.

Objective Knowledge: An Evolutionary Approach. Oxford: Clarendon Press, 1972.

Unended Quest. Glasgow: Collins/Fontana, 1976.

"Natural Selection and the Emergence of Mind." *Dialectica* 32 (1978): 339–355.

Die beiden Grundprobleme der Erkenntnistheorie. Tübingen, Germany: J. C. B. Mohr (Paul Siebeck), 1979.

The Open Universe: An Argument for Indeterminism: From the Postscript to The Logic of Scientific Discovery. Edited by W. W. Bartley III. London: Hutchinson, 1982.

Quantum Theory and the Schism in Physics: From the Postscript to The Logic of Scientific Discovery. Edited by W. W. Bartley III. London: Hutchinson, 1982.

Realism and the Aim of Science: From the Postscript to The Logic of Scientific Discovery. Edited by W. W. Bartley III. London: Hutchinson, 1983.

A World of Propensities. Bristol, U.K.: Thoemmes, 1990.

OTHER SOURCES

Hacohen, Malachi Haim. *Karl Popper: The Formative Years, 1902–1945.* Cambridge, U.K.: Cambridge University Press, 2000.

Hark, Michel Ter. *Popper, Otto Selz, and the Rise of Evolutionary Epistemology.* Cambridge, U.K.: Cambridge University Press, 2004.

Jarvie, Ian, Karl Milford, and David Miller, eds. *Karl Popper: A Centenary Assessment.* Vol. I, *Life and Times, and Values in a World of Facts.* Aldershot, U.K.: Ashgate, 2007.

———, Karl Milford, and David Miller, eds. *Karl Popper: A Centenary Assessment.* Vol. II, *Metaphysics and Epistemology.* Aldershot, U.K.: Ashgate, 2007.

———, Karl Milford, and David Miller, eds. *Karl Popper: A Centenary Assessment.* Vol. III, *Science.* Aldershot, U.K.: Ashgate, 2007.

Keuth, Herbert. *The Philosophy of Karl Popper.* Cambridge, U.K.: Cambridge University Press, 2005.

Lakatos, Imre. "Proofs and Refutations." *British Journal for the Philosophy of Science* 14 (1963–1964): 1–25, 120–139, 221–245, 296–342. In book form: *Proofs and Refutations: The Logic of Mathematical Discovery,* edited by John Worrall and Elie G. Zahar. Cambridge, U.K.: Cambridge University Press, 1976.

Lube, Manfred. *Karl R. Popper: Bibliographie 1925–2004: Wissenschaftstheorie, Sozialphilosophie, Logik, Wahrscheinlichkeitstheorie, Naturwissenschaften* (Schriftenreihe der Karl Popper Foundation Klagenfurt, vol. 3). Frankfurt am Main, Germany, and New York: Peter Lang, 2005.

Miller, David. *Critical Rationalism: A Restatement and Defence,* Chicago and La Salle, IL: Open Court, 1994.

———. "Sir Karl Raimund Popper, CH, FBA." *Biographical Memoirs of Fellows of the Royal Society* 43 (1997): 367–409.

In book form as Chapter 1 of Miller, *Out of Error.* London: Ashgate, 2006.

O'Hear, Anthony, ed. *Karl Popper: Philosophy and Problems.* Cambridge, U.K.: Cambridge University Press, 1995.

Qureshi, Tabish. "Understanding Popper's Experiment." *American Journal of Physics* 73 (2005): 541–544.

Schilpp, Paul A., ed. *The Philosophy of Karl Popper.* La Salle, IL: Open Court, 1974. Two volumes with intellectual biography and replies by Popper.

Schroeder-Heister, Peter. "Popper's Theory of Deductive Inference and the Concept of a Logical Constant." *History and Philosophy of Logic* 5 (1984): 79–110.

Shih, Yanhua, and Yoon-Ho Kim. "Experimental Realization of Popper's Experiment—Violation of the Uncertainty Principle?" *Fortschritte der Physik* 48 (2000): 463–471.

Watkins, John. "Karl Raimund Popper, 1902–1994." *Proceedings of the British Academy* 94 (1997): 645–684.

Wettersten, John. "New Insights on Young Popper." *Journal of the History of Ideas* 66 (2005): 603–631.

Peter Milne

PORPHYRY (*b.* Tyre, 232–234 CE; *d.* 304), *ancient philosophy, musical theory.*

A Greek philosopher, Porphyry was pupil of the Neoplatonist Plotinus in Rome and popularizer of his master's doctrines. In the last part of his life he edited and published Plotinian writings. He was author of a massive quantity of philosophical, religious, historical, rhetorical, and philological books, most of which are lost. In his philosophical writings are found a synthesis of Platonic and Aristotelian elements, on which (despite his lack of originality) medieval thought drew mainly. Within the scope of his scientific activity, his main attention was directed to Ptolemy, on whose *Harmonic* he wrote a commentary.

Born in Tyre between 232 and 234 CE, his real name was Malchus, which in Semitic language means "king," but he became famous as "Porphyry" (an allusion to his place of origin, the city of purple), a nickname attributed to him by his teacher in Athens, the rhetorician and philosopher Cassius Longinus. In 263 he went to Rome and began to attend Plotinus's lectures, gradually becoming one of his closest assistants and helping the master in revising and correcting his writings. Overloaded with this work, he fell into depression, which culminated in an attempted suicide. After this, on Plotinus's advice, in 268 he left Rome for Sicily, where he stayed for some time even after his master's death in 270. On his return he took the direction of the Neoplatonic school and worked on the edition of Plotinus's writings, dividing them into six books of nine treatises each (hence the name *Enneads*) on the basis of a mystical numerology according to which "six" was the perfect number, prefacing them with a biography of the master. Scholars are not very well informed on the last part of his life: it is known that he married the widow of a friend, Marcella, to whom he dedicated one of his extant writings, the *Letter to Marcella,* in which his ethical conception, concerning the relations between the human and the divine world according to the Neoplatonic view, is displayed.

Notwithstanding the numerous works on which there is information, few of them survived (and not all complete): the *Introduction* to Aristotelian *Categories,* a commentary that combines the Aristotelian logic with Platonic theories; the *Starting-Points Leading to the Intelligibles,* a synthesis of Neoplatonic ideas; a *Commentary on Plato's Parmenides,* handed down as anonymous, but by Pierre Hadot (1968) attributed (even if not unanimously) to the Tyrian philosopher; the *Life of Plotinus,* where Porphyry depicts his master as a charismatic character, dwelling upon the story of his mystical union with the One, or the first cause of everything (by Plotinus experienced four times and by Porphyry himself once). The treatise *On Abstinence from Eating Food from Animals* observes in animals the presence of a soul similar to ours (although less rational). The work *To Gaurus* is erroneously attributed to Galen, once again on the conception of the soul. *Against the Christians,* perhaps one of his best-known titles, is a treatise in fifteen books in which he refuses the Christian idea of creation (despite the assertion of Socrates, the ecclesiastical historian, and Augustine, that Porphyry was once a Christian). A *Life of Pythagoras* (probably part of the first book of a history of philosophy) has affinities with the work by Iamblichus, affinities that can be explained by their dependence on the same source. Finally there is the previously mentioned *Letter to Marcella* and the allegoric interpretation of Homer displayed by the treatise *On the Cave of the Nymphs,* where he considers the Homeric texts to have a hidden and philosophical meaning behind the literal one are also included.

The cosmological vision according to which the universe was regulated by exact laws and correspondences led Porphyry to take a scientific interest in astronomy, mathematics, and music. As a consequence, he wrote commentaries on the Euclidean *Elements* and on some of Ptolemy's works, such as the astrological treatise known as *Tetrabiblos* and the *Harmonics.* The *Commentary on the Harmonics,* addressed to a certain Eudoxius, is particularly interesting not especially for the originality of its critical analysis (it is mainly a paraphrase of Ptolemy's first two books, which breaks off at the beginning of book two), but for the inclusion of quotations drawn from earlier literature, in many cases otherwise unknown. The primary intent of Porphyry really seems to have been the identification of Ptolemy's sources or opponents, whom the great scientist had avoided mentioning, and their excerpts are given in order to provide a basis for further digressions, which, however, do not lead to any substantial remarks.

He mainly discusses the basic conceptions of the harmonics, the science that grasps the distinctions related to high and low pitch in sounds, and its criteria, hearing and reason; but he does not investigate thoroughly the complex technical analysis of Ptolemy's himself, skimming over the surface of the topic. Furthermore, as it stands, the commentary does not represent a finished or complete work, because it is much more detailed on the first four chapters of *Harmonics,* book one, than on the part that goes from chapter five of book one to chapter seven of book two, where it suddenly stops.

The most important quotations preserved in Porphyry's work are the Peripatetic *De audibilibus,* which includes many pieces of information on the nature of sounds and the causes of their qualities' modifications; a fragment of a treatise *On music* by Theophrastus, whose bulk seems to be the polemic against the quantitative interpretation of sounds; extended fragments of works by Ptolemais of Cyrene (*Pythagorean Elements of Music*), Didymus (*On the Difference between the Aristoxenians and the Pythagoreans*), Aelian (*Commentary of the Timaeus*), and Panaetius (*Concerning the Ratios and Intervals in Geometry and Music*)—perhaps the philosopher of Rhodes—all of which are otherwise unknown.

Also the other commentary work on Ptolemy, the *Eisagoge Eis Ten Apotelesmatiken Tou Ptolemaiou* (where is found a succinct explanation of elementary concepts of Greek astrology), gets its importance especially for its valuable references to some astrological texts otherwise lost. Porphyry's interest in this science led him to write also an *Introduction to Astronomy,* where he supports the thesis according to which each soul receives particular features from different planets (such as the imagination from the Sun or the impulsiveness from Mars).

BIBLIOGRAPHY

The original Greek text of Porphyry's works and fragments, based on the best available editions, can now be found in an electronic version in the Thesaurus Linguae Graece *collection. For the text of* The Commentary on the Harmonics *see, in particular, Düring, Ingemar:* Porphyrios Kommentar zur Harmonielehre des Ptolemaios; *Göteborg, Sweden: Elanders, 1932. Reprint, New York: Garland, 1980. For the* Tetrabiblos *commentary see Boer, Aemilia, and Stephanus Weinstock,* Introductio in Tetrabiblum Ptolemaei, *in* Catalogus Codicum Astrologorum Graecorum 5, 4. *Brussels: Academia, 1940, pp. 190–228. Below is a list of some translations of Porphyry's work into English.*

WORKS BY PORPHYRY

The Cave of the Nymphs in the Odyssey. A revised text with translation by Seminar Classics 609. State University of New York at Buffalo, Arethusa Monograph 1. Buffalo: Dept. of Classics, State University of New York at Buffalo, 1969.

To Marcella. Text and translation with introduction and notes by Kathleen O'Brien Wicker. Atlanta: Scholars Press, 1987.

Greek Musical Writings. Vol. 2, *Harmonic and Acoustic Theory.* Edited by Andrew Barker. Cambridge, U.K.: Cambridge University Press, 1989. Translation of some excerpts of Porphyry's *Commentary on the Harmonics.*

Porphyry's Against the Christians: The Literary Remains. Edited and translated with an introduction and epilogue by R. Joseph Hoffmann. Amherst, MA: Prometheus, 1994.

Neoplatonic Saints: The Lives of Plotinus and Proclus. Translated Texts for Historians 35. Liverpool, U.K.: Liverpool University Press, 2000.

On Abstinence from Killing Animals. Translated by Gillian Clark. Ithaca, NY: Cornell University Press, 2000.

Porphyry's Introduction. Translated with a commentary by J. Barnes. Oxford: Clarendon Press, 2006.

OTHER SOURCES

Barker, Andrew. "Porphyry. Porphyry's Music Theory." In *The Oxford Classical Dictionary,* edited by Simon Hornblower and Antony Spawforth. Oxford: Oxford University Press, 1996.

Bidez, Joseph. *Vie de Porphyre: Le philosophe neo-platonicien, avec les fragments des traites Peri Agalmaton et De regressu animae.* Leipzig, Germany: Teubner, 1913. Reprint, Hildesheim, Germany: Olm, 1964.

Deuse, Werner. *Untersuchungen zur mittelplatonischen und neuplatonischen Seelenlehre.* Wiesbaden, Germany: Steiner, 1983.

Düring, Ingemar. *Ptolemaios uns Porphyrios über die Musik.* Göteborg, Sweden: Elanders, 1934. Reprint, New York: Garland, 1980.

Edwards, Mark J. "Porphyry and the Intelligible Triad." *Journal of Hellenic Studies* 110 (1990): 14–24.

Evangeliou, Christos. *Aristotle's Categories and Porphyry.* Leiden, Netherlands: Brill, 1988.

Girgenti, Giuseppe. *Porfirio negli ultimi cinquant'anni: bibliografia sistematica e ragionata della letteratura primaria e secondaria.* Milan, Italy: Vita e Pensiero, 1994.

Hadot, Pierre. *Porphyre et Victorinus.* Paris: Études augustiniennes, 1968.

———. *Plotin, Porphyre—études néoplatoniciennes.* Paris: Les belles lettres, 1999.

Smith, Andrew. *Porphyry's Place in the Neoplatonic Tradition: A Study in Post-Plotinian Neoplatonism.* The Hague: Nijhoff, 1974.

———. "Porphyrian Studies since 1913." *Aufstieg und Niedergang der Römischen Welt* 2, 36, 2 (1987): 717–773.

Strange, Steven K. "Plotinus, Porphyry and the Neoplatonic Interpretation of the 'Categories.'" *Aufstieg und Niedergang der Römischen Welt* 2, 36, 2 (1987): 955–974.

Eleonora Rocconi

PORTER, GEORGE

PORTER, GEORGE (*b.* Stainforth, Yorkshire, England, 6 December 1920; *d.* Canterbury, Kent, England, 31 August 2002), *chemistry, scientific administration, public understanding of science.*

George Porter was one of the leading English scientists of the post–1945 period. He invented and developed the method of flash photolysis, for which he was awarded jointly the Nobel Prize in Chemistry in 1967. He was director of the Royal Institution for nearly twenty years (1966–1985) and president of the Royal Society for five (1985–1990). In these roles he emerged as a major spokesperson for science, seeking to promote it to wide publics, and as a stern critic of government cuts in the science budget.

Early Life. Porter's father, John Smith Porter, was a builder and Methodist lay preacher and was also active in local politics. His mother, Alice Ann Porter, née Roebuck, had been a matron in a local poor law institution. They married in 1918 and George was their only child. He attended the local primary school from 1925 until 1931 and later recollected that he had been interested in chemistry since the age of eight. He won a county minor scholarship to Thorne Grammar School where he studied from 1931 until 1938. As a reward for winning the scholarship, his father bought him a chemistry set and an old bus where he could undertake experiments away from the house. Porter would reflect years later that he was "still very fond of explosions."

After leaving school he studied chemistry at the University of Leeds as an Ackroyd Scholar, developing his interest in physical chemistry, which had been inspired at Leeds by Meredith Evans. With the outbreak of war in 1939, Porter joined the Officer Training Corps and was commissioned as a second lieutenant in the Royal Fusiliers. At Leeds he became involved with a plan devised in the office of the chancellor of the Duchy of Lancaster. Under Maurice Hankey the duchy, responsible for many of the secret, scientifically based weapons programs of those years, wanted to ensure that science graduates learned something useful for the war effort. Thus, in his final year at Leeds, Porter was directed, without being told the reason, to study radiophysics. One suspects here the hand of Charles Snow (better known as C. P. Snow), who worked for Hankey at this time and was specifically concerned with radar development. After graduating in May 1941, Porter continued studying radiophysics at the University of Aberdeen. In August of that year he transferred to the Royal Naval Volunteer Reserve, being commissioned a sublieutenant radar officer aboard HMS *Rochester* based in Londonderry. The first part of his war service involved convoy protection. He sometimes went as far south as Freetown on the west coast of Africa and took part in sinking at least three U-boats. He also took part in the Operation Torch landings at Oran and Algiers on the coast of North Africa in late 1942. Promoted to lieutenant in 1944, he was the officer in charge of the Royal Navy's radar school in Belfast. The following year he was appointed to Joint Command Operations in Whitehall for the projected invasion of Japan, but as he commented, "I was too late!" (RI MS GP A1-7).

Serving at sea, even in wartime, gives sailors large amounts of time to think, and this is what Porter did. He later recollected:

> I read a lot outside science—classics, poetry, philosophy and religion—which I more or less left, although my father was a lay preacher. Lying in my hammock, I convinced myself that science was the true philosophy and that the search for knowledge is the highest aim of mankind. (RI MS GP A1-7)

> The Navy was a turning point in the sense that I had time to think deeply and when I came out I was absolutely clear what I wanted to do: research in the natural sciences, and that is all I would ever want to do. (Porter, *Chemistry in Britain,* 1975, p. 398)

Cambridge Years. Thus, following demobilization, he went in 1945 to Emmanuel College at the University of Cambridge where he became a research student with the photochemist Ronald Norrish in the Physical Chemistry Laboratory. In the 1940s Norrish was quite notorious for his drinking, and Fred Dainton, who had worked with him, commented that Norrish was "bad tempered and autocratic [in his] treatment of juniors" and Porter would experience problems with him. At Norrish's direction, Porter was put to work to find out more about the CH_2 radical. Until this time Norrish had undertaken his photochemical work using a continuous beam of light produced by an army searchlight, which could not be used to study reactions lasting even a millisecond; he and Porter were aware that much of interest must happen within that space of time—the problem was to make it somehow accessible to experimental investigation.

Porter's breakthrough came in 1947, when he visited the electrical engineering company Siemens in Preston, Lancashire, to collect a new bulb for the searchlight. There he saw the flash lamps made by Siemens and, in his own words, "immediately all the pulse techniques of radio clicked into place, and it was obvious that this was the way to tackle the problem" (Porter, *Chemistry in Britain,* 1975, p. 398). All the knowledge of radar that he had accumulated in the military context of his naval service could now be put to use in tackling the problem of how to study short-lived, transient chemical phenomena. Porter realized that the way to identify short-lived intermediates in such reactions was to use highly intense short pulses of light to excite a reaction, rather than the weaker continuous beam, as Norrish and he had done hitherto. The intermediates thus created could be detected by either a second continuous weak beam of light or a second pulse of light delayed in time with respect to the exciting flash. The latter method was the first "pump-and-probe" technique—a technique also transferred from radar. It should also be added that as a radar officer, Porter had additionally acquired considerable practical knowledge of electronics, which put him in good stead in overcoming the "rather severe experimental difficulties" of flash photolysis, as it was called (RI MS GP A1-7).

This method was to prove immensely fruitful in understanding short-lived transient molecules and molecular fragments. For instance his early studies of the free radical chlorine oxide (ClO) later became important in understanding the cause of the ozone hole. After completing his PhD in 1949 (the same year that he married Stella Brooke), he was appointed demonstrator in physical chemistry at Cambridge and began building up his first research group to explore the scientific terrain that his 1947 insight had opened up. By 1950 the members were studying reactions approaching a microsecond.

In 1952 Porter was appointed assistant director of research in physical chemistry and at the same time elected a Fellow of Emmanuel College. Two years later, for reasons that seem have coincided with a period of particular tension with Norrish, Porter left Cambridge and was appointed deputy director of the British Rayon Research Association in Manchester, which he later admitted may have been a mistake. Research associations had been established in the interwar period in an attempt to bring together academic science and industry. At the Rayon Research Association, Porter applied his science to understanding the essentially photochemical problems surrounding the fading of fabric dyes. But, as he fully appreciated, his employers needed practical results. Therefore, this was not a suitable environment for him to pursue his own research interests, and he left in 1955 to become the first professor of physical chemistry at the University of Sheffield.

Research at Sheffield. At Sheffield, Porter and his colleagues took advantage of the expansion of the English university system to build up the department of which he became head in 1963, the same year he was appointed Firth Professor. Porter developed a large research group that, in addition to working purely on photochemistry, diversified into biochemistry, biology, and so on to illustrate how useful the photochemical techniques developed by them could be. Thus far, he and his group had not been

able to study reactions lasting less than a microsecond. The invention of the laser in 1960 potentially gave Porter and his group the opportunity to get down to these much shorter time intervals. It was not a straightforward matter, however, as most lasers were then made in America and had to be sent from there, but gradually at Sheffield, laser flashes became of shorter and shorter duration and this work reached its climax after Porter and his group had moved to the Royal Institution in 1966, when they reached the nanosecond and then the picosecond level.

It was at Sheffield that Porter became interested in what for want of a better term can be called science communication to a broad audience. He later recollected that this stemmed from his inaugural lecture at Sheffield, when the university's vice-chancellor advised that it be filled with experimental demonstrations. An interest in making science accessible to the public at large manifested itself in his 1962 book, *Chemistry for the Modern World,* and a television program on his flash photolysis work. The latter in turn led to a television series in 1965–1966 titled *The Laws of Disorder,* in which he was able to present thermodynamics in an interesting way. With his reputation for scientific research and his interest in popularizing science, it is little wonder that he became interested in the long established work of the Royal Institution in both these areas and vice versa.

The Royal Institution. Porter's work at the Royal Institution to which he moved in 1966 as its director cannot be understood without an appreciation of the history of the Royal Institution during the previous fifteen years. In 1950 Edward Andrade was appointed Fullerian Professor of Chemistry and director of the Davy-Faraday Research Laboratory in the Royal Institution, the two key staff positions in Royal Institution. Andrade, not the most diplomatic of people, came with a strong reforming agenda that was opposed by the more conservative groups in the Royal Institution, which were led by the secretary, Alexander Rankine. During 1950 and 1951, Andrade and Rankine fought each other with every means available for control of the institution. In mid-1952, the members of the Royal Institution passed a vote of no confidence in Andrade, who resigned, but only after it was agreed that the terms of his settlement would go to independent arbitration, which eventually awarded him the substantial sum of seven thousand pounds.

In addition to the internal problems created by these developments, further difficulties were caused by Andrade's receiving support from a powerful group, mostly chemists, within the Royal Society, including Cyril Hinshelwood, who would become president of the society in 1955. Whatever the reasons for such support, it would put Andrade's eventual successor in a very difficult position indeed. In the end, after much agonizing, Lawrence Bragg, director of the Cavendish Laboratory at Cambridge University, accepted the position that his father had held in the interwar years. Bragg took over at the beginning of 1954 and in effect put himself and the Royal Institution in scientific purdah, at least for a few years.

Despite this, Bragg managed to turn the Royal Institution around from what had been the nadir of its fortunes. He reinvigorated the Davy-Faraday Research Laboratory, where scientists such as Max Perutz, John Kendrew, and David, later Lord, Phillips carried out much of their work on determining the structures of hemoglobin, myoglobin, and lysozyme in the 1950s and 1960s. Bragg also turned the public program around most effectively in founding the Schools' Programme.

It was in this context that Porter seems first to have become acquainted with the Royal Institution. In 1960 Bragg invited him to deliver the Salters' lectures for sixth formers on the subject of chemical reactions, which he did that year and the following one. Then, in 1963, Porter was appointed part-time professor of chemistry at the institution on Bragg's recommendation. Although Bragg, with his patience, tact, and diplomatic skills, had achieved a considerable degree of administrative reform since 1954, Porter's appointment to this position illustrates just how much more needed to be done. After the initial proposal, the managing committee at the institution agreed to determine whether such a position as professor of chemistry was vacant and, if not, to arrange for one to be declared vacant. At their next meeting a month later, the managers were informed that the professorship of chemistry had been vacated just under a century earlier by Edward Frankland. Porter was immediately appointed. One cannot but think that the title of Porter's 1965 Friday evening discourse, "The Chemical Bond since Frankland," was a slight dig at this process.

Toward the end of 1964, the officers (that is the president, secretary and treasurer) of the Royal Institution were giving thought as to who should succeed Bragg, who would become seventy the following year. Although there were other possibilities, it is clear that from a very early stage that Bragg had been grooming Porter as his successor. According to Porter, Bragg had told him about all the difficulties that had occurred at the Royal Institution. A key issue was Porter's title there in addition to that of Fullerian Professor and director of the Davy-Faraday Research Laboratory. He insisted that he also be called director of the Royal Institution, and to this the managing group somewhat reluctantly agreed. The sensitivity of such issues can be gauged from the Royal Institution's press release announcing Porter's appointment, in which it was stated that since the time of Thomas Young and Humphry Davy, the resident professors had directed the

George Porter. SINCLAIR STAMMERS/PHOTO RESEARCHERS, INC.

work of the Royal Institution. By referring to people more than a century and a half previously, the Royal Institution sought to place its difficulties in the long dead past.

At the Royal Institution, Porter reestablished his research group, which changed for the first time in over forty years the research direction of the Davy-Faraday Research Laboratory. There, Porter and his groups in 1967 (the year he won the Nobel Prize) were finally able to study reactions lasting for a nanosecond, and by 1975 they had reached the picosecond level. This level of investigation opened the way for the study of photosynthesis and for potentially replicating that natural process. Despite considerable effort in that direction, Porter was never quite able to get there. Throughout his time at the Royal Institution, Porter expanded the number of his research groups, especially with the appointment of David Phillips (no relation to Lord Phillips) from the University of Southampton in 1980 to be Wolfson Professor of Natural Philosophy and, in effect, Porter's deputy.

So far as running the Royal Institution was concerned, Porter addressed some of the issues relating to the basic infrastructure of the building, which had been neglected due to a want of resources following the Andrade affair. As early as June 1965 he envisaged the construction of a modern purpose-built laboratory next to the Royal Institution to allow further expansion of research. To secure the substantial funding needed, Porter in his early years oversaw a fund-raising campaign built around the centenary of the death of Michael Faraday. This campaign did not generate sufficient resources for the major new laboratory, but it did produce enough to permit the refurbishment of some existing laboratories. In addition, he also raised funds to construct a small lecture theater as well as the Faraday Museum (opened by the queen in 1973) and Archives Room.

Porter, acutely aware of the heritage of the Royal Institution and its contemporary resonances, not least the possession of a remarkable collection of iconic scientific apparatus and an archive, took a strong interest in the history of science. With Bragg he edited the ten volumes of the physical sciences section of *Library of Science,* which reprinted papers from the *Proceedings of the Royal Institution,* founded in 1851. With Jim Friday, he edited *Advice to Lecturers,* an anthology of writings by Faraday and Bragg about lecturing—a little volume that remains ever popular. Frank Greenway was appointed part-time reader in the history of science, while the award to the institution of a substantial Leverhulme Foundation grant allowed detailed study of the history of the Royal Institution during in the nineteenth century. This resulted in Sophie Forgan's thesis, Morris Berman's thesis and book (which had a mixed reception), the publication of the managers' nineteenth-century minutes, the establishment of a number of discussion series, and ultimately in the early 1980s the Royal Institution Centre for the History of Science and Technology. Such historical work had contemporary significance in that Porter was able to use it to bury the causes of problems that had taken on such vituperative form in the early 1950s, for example by referring entirely ahistorically to Faraday being director of the Royal Institution, Porter removed the problems surrounding his own use of that title. Furthermore, he used alleged reforms in the past, for instance, for instance Davy's supposed abolition of the proprietors in 1810, as justification for continuing Bragg's program of reforming and modernizing the Royal Institution's administration. In this Porter was assisted by H. J. V. Tyrrell who had been a colleague of his at Sheffield and had come to London in 1964 to be professor of chemistry at Chelsea College. He was secretary of the Royal Institution from 1978 to 1984, in which capacity he oversaw with Porter the merging of the managers and visitors (a sort of audit committee that had existed since the early nineteenth century) of the Royal Institu-

tion to form the council in 1984. Porter also abolished a large number of the smaller committees that in his view had outlived their usefulness. By the 1980s, therefore, the structures of the Royal Institution had been deliberately reformed in such a way as to make the recurrence of anything like the Andrade affair impossible.

Although Porter regarded the Royal Institution primarily as a research institute, under his direction the Schools' Lectures program was expanded, and in science communication, Porter was responsible for establishing the annual televising of the Royal Institution's Christmas Lectures (of which he gave two highly successful series himself). He was also the driving force behind the BBC's *Young Scientists of the Year,* in which school science projects were judged by panels of eminent scientists.

The Royal Society. In 1985 Porter was elected president of the Royal Society, which illustrates that the problems that had existed between the Royal Institution and Royal Society following the Andrade affair were no longer relevant. Because of his election he decided to retire, with a brief overlap, from the directorship of the Royal Institution—although, interestingly, neither William Bragg nor Henry Dale had, earlier in the twentieth century, felt the same need. Most of Porter's research groups moved to the Centre for Photomolecular Sciences, newly created for him at Imperial College. By this time, the femtosecond timescale had become accessible.

At the Royal Society, Porter's main task was to act as a spokesman for science at a time when the science budget was being drastically cut by the Conservative government led by Prime Minister Margaret Thatcher. He used his position as president to criticize sharply government science policy and delivered his most trenchant comments on the occasion of his final presidential address in 1990:

> It is difficult for ministers, some with little or no secondary education in science, to appreciate the anger and frustration that scientists have long felt at a system which is controlled and guided by those who have little understanding of what makes scientists tick or appreciation of what science has done and will do for mankind.

Porter, however, welcomed the decision by the government in 1988 to include science in the National Curriculum.

Another strategy that Porter developed in the 1980s to cope with the perceived crisis of confidence in science was to initiate a major program to promote the public understanding of science. In 1985, the Royal Society issued a report titled *The Public Understanding of Science.* Porter, who was then simultaneously and uniquely director of the Royal Institution, president of the Royal

Society, and president of the British Association for the Advancement of Science, used the opportunity to establish a joint Committee on the Public Understanding of Science (COPUS), representing the three organizations. He chaired COPUS himself for the first four years, thus giving it a high initial profile that it otherwise might not have enjoyed.

Following the end of his term of office at the Royal Society in 1990, Porter continued performing his research at Imperial College and promoting science. He did the latter particularly through his position in the House of Lords after he had been created a life peer as Baron Porter of Luddenham, in 1990, having been appointed to the Order of Merit the previous year and knighted in 1972. In the House of Lords he continued his criticisms of government science policy, particularly in the levels of funding accorded to the Research Councils. He was also scornful of their tendency to support "positively managed coherent programmes of research," as Aaron Klug recollected him ironically phrasing it in his address at Porter's memorial service at St Margaret's, Westminster (typescript copy in author's papers).

Porter can be viewed, in some sense, as a representative transitional figure in the development of science in the second half of the twentieth century. Moving from a time when a single individual could still make a fundamental experimental discovery to an era of large research groups, Porter was clearly adept at handling various approaches to scientific inquiry. Furthermore, for all the problems it created, Porter realized that science needed to be part of general culture (as it had been in the nineteenth century) rather than something separated from society at-large. For Porter, science as research and science as culture probably went together very closely. We have in Porter, as in his hero Faraday, a top scientist who was fully committed to communicating his science and that of others to a wide audience.

BIBLIOGRAPHY

The largest collection of Porter's papers is in the Royal Institution in London, while there are also significant collections in the Royal Society and at Imperial College, both in London. There is a selected bibliography in Fleming and Phillips cited below.

WORKS BY PORTER

Chemistry for the Modern World. London: George G. Harrap and Co., 1962.

"Quick as a Flash: An Interview with Sir George Porter." *Chemistry in Britain* 11 (1975): 398–401.

Chemistry in Microtime: Selected Writings on Flash Photolysis, Free Radicals, and the Excited State. London: Imperial College Press, 1997. Contains reprints of Porter's major papers.

OTHER SOURCES

Fleming, Graham R., and David Phillips. "George Porter KT OM, Lord Porter of Luddenham 6 December 1920–31 August 2002." *Biographical Memoirs of Fellows of the Royal Society* 50 (2004): 257–283. Very good on Porter's science.

James, Frank A. J. L., and David Phillips. "Obituaries: George Porter." *Physics Today* 53, no. 3 (2003): 94–96.

Phillips, David, and James Barber, eds. *The Life and Scientific Legacy of George Porter.* London: Imperial College Press, 2006. Contains essays and reprinted papers by colleagues and students of Porter, illustrating their personal and scientific relationships with him.

Frank A. J. L. James

PORTER, KEITH ROBERTS (*b.* Yarmouth, Nova Scotia, Canada, 11 June 1912; *d.* Bryn Mawr, Pennsylvania, 2 May 1997), *cell biology, electron microscopy, tissue culture*

Porter was a pioneer in the modern field of cell biology, playing important roles in the development of electron microscopy as a technique for studying cell structures, in creating new knowledge of structure-function relations in cell cytoplasm, and in establishing professional institutions for cell biology in North America.

Education Porter's father was a cabinetmaker and his earlier ancestors had been farmers. His interest in biology was kindled in high school where he and other students were given access to laboratory space after school to experiment on their own. Porter remained in Nova Scotia to attend college at Acadia University, graduating in 1934. He then moved to Harvard University for graduate training in experimental embryology, during which time he developed techniques for manipulating nuclei in frog eggs. By removing the nucleus from the egg before it was inseminated, he created embryos with a single set of chromosomes derived from the sperm, whose development he could then study. After finishing his PhD in 1938, Porter spent a year on a National Research Council postdoctoral fellowship in zoology at Princeton University, where he began to transplant the haploid nucleus of a frog of one geographically isolated race or subspecies into enucleated frog embryos of different races so as to evaluate the relative contributions of the nucleus and cytoplasm to development. The results indicated a genetic effect of the cytoplasm as well as of the nucleus (Porter, 1941).

Pioneering Electron Microscopy with Cultured Cells. In 1939, James Murphy recruited Porter to the Rockefeller Institute for Medical Research, where he directed a cancer research laboratory. In Murphy's laboratory Albert Claude had been employing high-speed centrifuges to isolate what he thought might be particles responsible for chicken tumors. Porter's facility with micromanipulation of cell nuclei suggested to Murphy that Porter might be able to develop procedures for transplanting the hypothesized tumor particles from an infected cell to other cells. When he came into the laboratory, Porter initially continued the transplant studies on which he had been engaged. Given the focus of the laboratory on cancer, though, Porter also began to investigate the inhibition of growth from carcinogenic agents such as x-rays and chemicals such as methylcholanthrene. He examined both the effects of different dosages on tail regeneration in the newt and the character of the tissue reaction induced.

During this period Porter also began teaching himself techniques for culturing cells in anticipation that it would be possible to incorporate the particles Claude was isolating into growing tissues so as to ascertain their effects on developing tissues. The benefits of this endeavor were, however, to be realized in an unexpected way. During this period Claude found particles similar to those he found in tumor cells in normal cells, and he began to expand his focus to the different fractions that could be isolated by centrifugation and what they revealed about the structure of normal eukaryote cells.

The increased resolution provided by the recently developed electron microscope drew the attention of numerous investigators in the biological sciences, including Claude, who found that the objects of interest to them were too small to be resolved with the light microscope. But there were a host of problems that needed to be resolved before the electron microscope could be utilized on biological specimens. For example, both whole cells and slices of the sort prepared for light microscopy were too thick to be penetrated by the relatively weak (50 KV) electron beam of the RCA EM-B microscope, the only model then available in the United States. Porter recognized, however, that because tissue-cultured cells spread thinly, they were sufficiently thin to be imaged with these microscopes. Reflecting back on this work, he commented: "Although not a peer among the microscopists at the time, I was experienced enough to perceive that such diaphanous cells might be suitable for electron microscopy, at least in their thinner margins" (Porter, 1987, p. 59).

During World War II electron microscopes were generally only available for military-related uses, but Claude developed a collaboration with Ernest Fullam, a pioneering electron microscopist at Interchemical Corporation, where he was able to examine his specimens at night. In 1944, Claude brought Porter along to attempt to prepare micrographs of tissue-cultured cells. The technique was demanding: Porter grew cells directly on Formar-coated coverslips, selected cells using a light microscope, and marked out an area slightly larger than the mesh disc. He described the rest of the procedure:

> This area of film is then cut from the surrounding film with a fine sharp instrument or a pair of watchmaker's forceps. Thus freed the bit of film with cultured cells is gently peeled away from the glass until only a small corner remains attached. Kept under water in this way the thin sheet of plastic retains its smooth extended form so that adhering cells are not distorted. The small wire mesh disc, immersed beforehand in the washing bath, is now slipped under the film and the two are so manipulated that the film is spread over the screen's surface. They are then lifted from the bath, drained of water, and placed to dry over phosphorus pentoxide. (Porter, Claude, and Fullam, 1945, p. 236)

Porter and his collaborators claimed that they had developed a "relatively simple means" to make micrographs of cultured cells, but in fact the procedure was extremely delicate and not widely adopted. Even with Porter's dexterity, he reported that he was successful in preparing a useable image of a specimen only about half the time. Widespread use of the electron microscope to examine cell specimens occurred only in the early 1950s after the development of microtomes for slicing preparations sufficiently thinly, as well as improved procedures for embedding and mounting specimens.

But in their 1945 paper, Porter and his collaborators published a micrograph showing a whole chicken embryo cell (the published micrograph was actually a composite of several pieces of the cell imaged separately). Although the nucleus was too dense to observe anything but the nucleolus, parts of the cytoplasm, especially at the periphery, generated an image with well-delineated detail. They interpreted the filamentous elements as mitochondria, the small dense elements around the nucleus as Golgi bodies, and identified a previously unknown "delicate lace-work extending throughout the cytoplasm" (p. 246).

The lacework or lacelike reticulum was to become a central focus of Porter's research in subsequent years. At first he interpreted the structure as providing a cell skeleton such as had been proposed by a number of biologists of the time to account for the ability of cells to maintain three-dimensional shape. In the micrographs of tissue-cultured cells the reticulum appeared to be fractured in various ways, which suggested to Porter that it was incapable of stretching as much as the structure it which it was embedded. A feature of the lacelike reticulum noted by Porter and his collaborators in the first micrograph was the occurrence adjacent to it of "vesicle-like bodies, *i.e.* elements presenting a center of less density, and ranging in size from 100 to 150 mμ" (p. 238). They suggested that this might be related to particles estimated to average about 70 millimicron in diameter that Claude had sedimented out of the cytoplasm through ultracentrifugation and initially identified as tumor particles before finding them also in normal cells and labeling them *microsomes*.

In the second half of the 1940s, Porter also performed electron microscopic investigations related to what was supposedly the prime focus of the laboratory—cancer. Together with visiting fellow Helen Thompson, he examined cultured cells from three different rat sarcomas. These cells, they claimed, exhibited a much greater density of endoplasmic granules located on shorter strands (Porter and Thompson, 1947). A second study involved mammary carcinoma in mice, which was known to be transmitted through their mother's milk. With Thompson, Porter used the electron microscope to examine mouse mammary gland tumor cells grown in tissue culture. They identified within them distinctive particles about 130 mμ in diameter with a dark, well-defined central core. Although the evidence was only circumstantial, they proposed "tentatively" that the particles were the viral agent in the milk (Porter and Thompson, 1948).

In 1949, the laboratory in which Porter had worked for ten years underwent a major transformation. Murphy reached the mandatory retirement age. Although he had not been involved in the investigations of cells on which Claude and Porter had been engaged, he was the director of the laboratory and member of the institute. Typically when the member left the institute or retired, the laboratory itself was dismantled. Anticipating that outcome, Claude accepted an invitation to direct the Jules Bordet Institute at the Université Libre de Bruxelles and left Rockefeller.

However, Herbert Gasser, then director of the Rockefeller Institute, took the unusual step of retaining Porter as well as George Palade. Palade had joined the laboratory a few years earlier and had collaborated in pioneering biochemical analyses of another fraction Claude had isolated through centrifugation and eventually identified as consisting of mitochondria. These biochemical studies proved pivotal in establishing the role of mitochondria in cellular respiration. The promise of this research and of Porter's work in electron microscopy apparently convinced Gasser that the duo were pioneers in the new study of cell structure and function and promoted Porter to associate member and director of a new Laboratory of Cytology. The laboratory also moved to new quarters where both the RCA EMU microscope that had been purchased a couple years earlier by the Rockefeller Foundation and a new RCA EMU-2A microscope were installed.

Preparing Thin-sections and Discovering the Endoplasmic Reticulum. One thread in Porter's research in the early 1950s continued the electron micrograph studies of the lacelike reticulum in whole cultured cells. In studies he carried out with Frances Kallman, a postdoctoral fellow of the National Cancer Institute, he increased the period of fixation in osmium vapors that digested some of the diffuse material in the cytoplasm, yielding micrographs showing a more sharply delineated membrane skeleton of the cell (Porter and Kallman, 1952, p. 883). Porter and Kallman renamed what they described as a structure consisting of vesicular or canalicular elements that sometimes formed a complex reticulum the *endoplasmic reticulum*.

They then turned their attention to the particles Porter and Thompson had observed in tumor cells (a result by then confirmed by other laboratories) and established that Porter and Thompson had been misled into thinking that these particles were distinctive of tumor cells by comparing the tumor cells to cells that were not engaged in active growth. When they looked at actively growing cells they found comparable particles, and concluded that they might be *growth particles*. They speculated that these particles might be

> centers of synthesis of all cytoplasmic components. There is some preliminary evidence from the micrographs that mitochondria may begin their development in this form, but elements of the endoplasmic reticulum, the lipid granules, and inclusions, the distinctive features of differentiated cells, may be similarly derived. If such is the case, we are led to postulate that there are several subspecies among this class of cytoplasmic particles and that the complement of these in any cell would determine the type of differentiation to some extent. (p. 890)

Although Porter was the master of electron microscopy of tissue-cultured cells, he recognized that much greater progress could be made if a means could be developed to slice cells sufficiently thinly that micrographs could be made of slices. (This was an approach widely used in studies with the light microscope, but the microtomes that had been developed for light microscopes could not cut slices sufficiently thinly for electron microscopy.) Before leaving the Rockefeller Institute, Claude had been involved in several failed efforts to develop a microtome adequate for electron microscopy.

In the early 1950s, Porter took up this quest together with Joseph Blum, an engineer and instrument maker at the Rockefeller Institute. Together they developed a microtome that was both reliable and easy to use (Porter and Blum, 1953). In it the specimen was held at the end of a bar that was mechanically advanced to the cutting edge, and a mechanism was incorporated to insure that the cutting edge was avoided on the return stroke. Many other investigators were pursuing the attempt to build a suitable microtome so that at a 1954 workshop sponsored by the New York Academy of Sciences about a dozen models were on display. But when Ivan Sorvall, Inc. of Norwalk, Connecticut, began to produce commercially the Porter-Blum model a year later, its dominance in the United States was established.

When researchers began to make micrographs of thin-sliced cells, they started reporting on filamentous elements that were clustered in parts of the cytoplasm and which appeared in reduced numbers in fasting cells. Other researchers did not link these with the endoplasmic reticulum reported by Porter, but in the paper introducing their new microtome, Porter and Blum reported on elongated elements and granules which they maintained were "*easily recognized* as the equivalent of the endoplasmic reticulum indicated previously in cultured cells" (p. 699). Although Porter and Blum claimed the recognition was easy, they nonetheless reported on a series of four serial sections in which they could demonstrate the continuity of many of the pieces appearing in different slices. Porter's identification of the structures in slices with the endoplasmic reticulum he claimed to have identified in micrographs of tissue-cultured cells proved contentious.

In collaboration with Palade (Palade and Porter, 1954), Porter adopted the strategy of preparing thin sections of tissue-cultured cells to see how these would look and comparing series of them to the usual whole mounts of such cells. Taking Porter's interpretation of the results with tissue-cultured cells as their guide, they inferred how such a structure would appear in slices and argued that this inference accounted for the results seen in slices. They presented micrographs of a sectioned chicken monocyte (white blood cell) as well as a whole-mounted and sectioned macrophage grown from monocytes in tissue culture to establish the correspondences in appearance between whole mounts and thin slices. Experience with whole tissue-cultured cells thus provided Porter with a perspective for interpreting sliced preparations which other investigators lacked.

But he and Palade also used to the micrographs of sliced cells to advance their understanding of the structure they had identified in cultured cells. For example, they concluded from the images from slices that the endoplasmic reticulum consisted of large, flattened vesicles of irregular outline and relatively constant shallow depth.

During this period Palade put considerable effort into investigating the effects of different fixatives and with a buffered osmium stain he developed (which soon became widely adopted) he discovered small particles 10 to 30 millimicron in size that frequently lined the wall of the endoplasmic reticulum. Palade's particles were almost an order of magnitude smaller than the particles that had been described by Porter, which likely included pieces of the endoplasmic reticulum. Porter (1954) attributed the long-noted tendency of areas of the cytoplasm to absorb basic stains to these particles and identified them with particles of the same size that had been determined by other investigators to have a large RNA content. He also identified similar particles in the nucleolus of the cell. Although Porter continued to speculate about the function of the endoplasmic reticulum and the particles attached to it, he did not contribute further to the experimental work that revealed how the particles, subsequently christened *ribosomes,* figured in protein synthesis. (An important aspect of that work was carried out in the Rockefeller laboratory after biochemist Philip Siekevitz was recruited and with Palade executed an integrated morphological and biochemical study of microsomes and their relation to the endoplasmic reticulum.)

Discovering More Structure, Especially Microtubules. During this period Porter directed his attention to applying electron microscopy to various structures in cells. In striated muscle he designated the structural equivalent of the endoplasmic reticulum in muscle cells, the sarcoplasmic reticulum, and demonstrated how it adapted to the demands of muscle tissue. With George Pappas he revealed the periodicity of isolated collagen fibrils, thereby providing one of the earliest demonstrations of the internal structure in a protein polymer. Don Fawcett, already a faculty member at Harvard, collaborated with Porter in a major study examining mollusk, amphibian, mouse, and human cilia from epithelial cells, demonstrating a common internal structure consisting of a bundle of eleven filaments arranged longitudinally in a column of protoplasm surrounded by a membrane. They established that the eleven filaments consisted of nine double filaments forming a ring and two single filaments in the center. They discussed not just the structural findings but their significance for cilia motion.

In the mid-1950s, the structure of the Rockefeller Institute underwent a dramatic transformation. Previously a research institute consisting of investigators from the postdoctoral level to senior scientists, it was transformed into Rockefeller University and took on the mission of training graduate students. Although initially not enthusiastic about training students, Porter soon acquired a number of talented graduate students who responded enthusiastically to his mentoring. Among these were Lee Peachey, who followed up on the investigation of the sarcoplasmic reticulum, and Peter Satir and Myron Ledbetter, who carried on the investigations of cilia.

In 1961, Porter accepted an offer to leave Rockefeller and return to Harvard University. With a number of his

Rockefeller graduate students accompanying him on the move to Harvard, Porter continued research on themes he had been pursuing at Rockefeller, and soon announced another major finding of previously unknown structure in cells. With Ledbetter, he was engaged in a detailed examination of plant cells in hopes of finding fine structure that could explain patterns of wall deposition that figured in cell differentiation. David Sabatini had introduced various aldehydes as fixatives for electron microscopy; Ledbetter and Porter adopted glutaraldehyde for their electron microscopy of plant cells and identified, in the cortical zone that had previously seemed empty, slender tubules of indeterminate length that were between 230 to 270 angstroms in diameter. They named these structures *microtubules* and advanced the hypothesis that they figured in wall depositions, because their location mirrored that of microfibrils of cellulose that were being deposited in the walls (Ledbetter and Porter, 1963).

The exploration of microtubules became one of the major foci of Porter's research at Harvard. He speculated on their potential significance not only for maintaining cell shape but also for cell motility and cell division. With Lewis Tilney, he explored their sensitivity to temperature and pressure. Adopting pigment cells in fish scales as an experimental system, he explored the role of microtubules in controlling the distribution of pigment granules.

Porter served as chair of the Biology Department at Harvard from 1965 to 1967, during which time he oversaw a major revision of the undergraduate curriculum that included the introduction of new courses in cell biology (a course Porter himself taught) and biochemistry. During this period he also produced two major atlases of electron micrographs: *An Introduction to the Fine Structure of Cells and Tissues*, prepared with Mary A. Bonneville and published in 1963, and *Introduction to the Fine Structure of Plant Cells*, prepared with Myron Ledbetter and published in 1970.

Studies with the High-Voltage Microscope and the Microtrabecular Lattice. Although he was apparently well-situated at Harvard, the University of Colorado tempted Porter with an offer to establish a laboratory for cell biology of his own design. Thus, in 1968, he moved to Boulder, where he served as chair of the new Department of Molecular, Cellular, and Developmental Biology. As part of the equipment for this new laboratory, Porter procured a scanning electron microscope, which had not yet been much used in biology, and applied it to imaging the morphology of cell surfaces (differentiating malignant and normal cells through the stages of the cell cycle). Doing this successfully required development of new fixation techniques that would not generate surface tension that would distort the structures. When applied to tissue-cultured cells or cells extracted from plant or animal tissues chemically, the technique facilitated images that revealed the structure of cell surfaces.

Porter's interest in structural organization of cells drew him back to a focus on whole cells, which he had used in his earliest micrographs. However, due to their thickness, such examination required higher voltages than available in conventional electron microscopes. High-voltage (1,000 KV) electron microscopes had been developed for other purposes such as metallurgy, and Porter first used one at the U.S. Steel Laboratories and then convinced the NIH to buy three such instruments for biological research in regional laboratories, including Porter's at Colorado.

With the high-voltage microscope Porter could examine the cytoplasm without interference resulting from embedding resins, and he turned his attention again to the ground substance of the cytoplasm and identified what he characterized as a *microtrabecular lattice*. Together with postdoctoral fellow John Wolosewick, he characterized it as a scaffold or spongework that encased the known structures in the cytoplasm except for the mitochondria (Wolosewick and Porter, 1976). To illustrate the three-dimensional character of the lattice, Porter presented images of it in talks using dual slide projectors with crossed-Polaroid filters while audience members wore crossed-Polaroid glasses. Porter began immediately to theorize about the significance of this structure, suggesting that in addition to providing a scaffold, it could serve to direct intercellular movements and provide information directing cellular organization (Porter and Tucker, 1981).

Critics, however, soon charged that the microtrabecular lattice was an artifact resulting from condensing of soluble components of the cytosol and an extensive controversy ensued. Porter drew upon a variety of fixation techniques including freeze drying and freeze substitution as well as chemical fixation to argue for the reality of the structure. Subsequent investigations showed that the microtrabecular lattice as described by Porter, which some cell biologists have referred to as *Porterplasm* (Heuser, 2002), represents an artifact of deposits of soluble, hydrophilic proteins that glom onto cytoskeletal filaments. Yet, the fundamental question of what sort of cytoskeleton underlies structure and function in the cytoplasmic matrix remains unanswered.

Porter retired from Colorado in 1983, and accepted a position as Wilson Elkins Distinguished Professor and chair of the Department of Biological Sciences at the University of Maryland, Baltimore County. There he continued research on microtubules and the movement of granules in chromatophores. Four years later, he was appointed Research Professor of Biology at the University of Pennsylvania, where his first graduate student, Lee

Peachey, had developed a laboratory using intermediate-voltage electron microscopes to study cell structure.

Creating a Society and Journal for Cell Biology. In addition to developing new techniques and pioneering findings about cell structures, Porter also played a central role in creating institutions that helped transform cell biology into a distinctive biological discipline. In part he was spurred to action by the rejection of a paper with Don Fawcett on the structure of cilia by two journals published by Rockefeller University Press, the *Journal of Experimental Medicine* and *The Journal of General Physiology*. The basis for rejection was, in large part, reluctance by these journals to publish too many anatomical studies based on electron microscopy. Although that paper subsequently was published in the *Journal of Morphology*, Gasser, who had stepped down as director of the Rockefeller Institute, but who was on the editorial board of two journals that had rejected the paper, encouraged Porter to consider creating a new journal that would emphasize such research. Porter made a proposal to President Detlev Bronk, that Rockefeller University should start yet another journal. Others whom Bronk consulted supported the idea but urged that the journal have a broad focus on cell structure and function, and so the journal began publication as the *Journal of Biophysical and Biochemical Cytology* in 1955.

Although eight editors shared decision-making responsibility, Porter became the de facto editor in chief, recognized by his fellow editors as such when they insisted on retaining him when, by lot, he was selected for replacement. Porter did eventually step down from the editorial board in December 1963, but during his tenure on the board he played an active role in determining the scope and direction of the journal. The original name of the journal was selected and editors were appointed by Bronk with the hopes of recruiting submissions from biochemistry and biophysics as well as electron microscopy, but electron microscope studies dominated the journal. Porter had never been a keen supporter of the title and in 1961 led an effort that succeeded in changing the name to the *Journal of Cell Biology*.

One of the arguments Porter used in advocating the name change was that a new society, the American Society for Cell Biology, had been created and within it there were advocates for a new journal focused on cell biology. In fact, Porter was a—if not the—leader in establishing of the new society. The initial inspiration for the new society appears to have derived from a resolution by the U.S. National Committee for the International Union of Biological Sciences within the U.S. National Academy of Sciences to have representation to the newly constituted International Society for Cell Biology.

The resolution was transmitted to Morgan Harris, president of the Tissue Culture Association (TCA), a technique-based society devoted to fostering use of tissue culture as a research tool within biology and medicine, of which Porter had been founding chairman. Harris and others within the TCA sought to transform that organization from one focused on technique to a society directed on a biological subject and he secured funding from the National Institutes of Health in the United States, which already had a study section devoted to cell biology, to fund a committee to "improve working relations among cell biologists." Harris assigned to Porter the responsibility of selecting representatives and hosting a meeting, which Porter held at the Rockefeller Institute on 9 January 1960. Despite the fact that the TCA and several other professional societies were considering explicitly adding cell biology to their domain, the committee voted to establish a new society, the American Society for Cell Biology, with Porter as chair of the provisional council.

Under Porter's leadership, the new society set out to establish itself with a broad base that would include "biochemists, biophysicists, cytologists, histologists, microbiologists, physiologists, and others having a common interest in the cell" (from the proposal to NIH to fund the first society meeting). The first scientific meeting of the society was held in Chicago in November 1961, attracting 844 scientists, of which 744 applied for membership in the society. Porter declined to run to be the first official president of the society (his collaborator, Don Fawcett, was elected) but remained on the council and was subsequently elected president in 1977.

Personal Life and Honors. In 1938, Porter married Elizabeth Lingley, with whom he had one son. In 1940 he, his wife, and his son all developed tuberculosis, from which his son died. Porter died on 2 May 1997 in Bryn Mawr, four years after Elizabeth. As befits a scientist who played such a guiding role in the development of a discipline, he received numerous professional tributes. In 1982, upon his retirement from the University of Colorado, that university named the Porter Bioscience Building after him. The imaging center at the University of Maryland, Baltimore County, is also named for him. In 1983, the Keith R. Porter Endowment for Cell Biology was established. It supports the annual Keith Porter Lecture, presented annually at the meetings of the American Society for Cell Biology since 1982, as well as two junior fellows selected each year and visits by major cell biologists and fellows to smaller colleges and schools. In 1977, Porter received the National Medal of Science from President Carter. Also in that year, the *Journal of Cell Biology* dedicated a volume to his career.

BIBLIOGRAPHY

The largest collection of Porter's papers are housed in the Archives Department in the University Libraries of the University of Colorado at Boulder. Additional materials are available at the Maryland Porter Archive at the Library of the University of Maryland in Baltimore County, which also houses the archives of the American Society for Cell Biology and at the Rockefeller Archive Center, which also houses archival material on the founding of the Journal of Biophysical and Biochemical Cytology.

WORKS BY PORTER

"Developmental Variations Resulting from the Androgenetic Hybridization of Four Forms of *Rana pipiens*." *Science* 93 (1941): 439.

With Albert Claude and Ernest F. Fullam. "A Study of Tissue Culture Cells by Electron Microscopy." *Journal of Experimental Medicine* 81 (1945): 233–246.

With Helen P. Thompson. "Some Morphological Features of Cultured Rat Sarcoma Cells as Revealed by the Electron Microscope." *Cancer Research* 7 (1947): 431–438.

With Helen P. Thompson. "A Particulate Body Associated with Epithelial Cells Cultured from Mammary Carcinomas of Mice of a Milk-Factor Strain." *Journal of Experimental Medicine* 88 (1948): 15–23.

With Frances L. Kallman. "Significance of Cell Particulates as Seen by Electron Microscopy. *Annals of the New York Academy of Sciences* 54 (1952): 882–891.

With Joseph Blum. "A Study in Microtomy for Electron Microscopy." *Anatomical Record* 117 (1953): 685–707.

With Don W. Fawcett. "A Study of the Fine Structure of Ciliated Epithelia." *Journal of Morophology* 94 (1953): 221–264.

"Electron Microscopy of Basophilic Components of Cytoplasm." *Journal of Histochemistry and Cytochemistry* 2 (1954): 346–375.

With George E. Palade. "Studies on Endoplasmic Reticulum: I. Its Identification in Cells *in Situ.*" *Journal of Experimental Medicine* 100 (1954): 641–656.

"The Certification of Commercial Culture Media." *Annals of the New York Academy of Sciences* 58 (1954): 1029–1038.

"The Submicroscopic Morphology of Protoplasm." *Harvey Lectures* 51 (1955–1956): 175–228.

With Mary A. Bonneville. *An Introduction to the Fine Structure of Cells and Tissues.* Philadelphia: Lea and Febiger, 1963.

With Myron C. Ledbetter. "A 'Microtubule' in Plant Cell Fine Structure." *Journal of Cell Biology* 19 (1963): 239–250.

With Myron C. Ledbetter. *Introduction to the Fine Structure of Plant Cells.* Berlin: Springer-Verlag, 1970.

With John Wolosewick. "Stereo High-Voltage Electron Microscopy of Whole Cells of the Human Diploid Line, WI-38." *American Journal of Anatomy* 147 (1976): 303–323.

With J. B. Tucker. "The Ground Substance of the Living Cell." *Scientific American* 244, no. 3 (1981): 56–67.

"Electron Microscopy of Cultured Cells." In *The American Association of Anatomists, 1888-1987: Essays on the History of Anatomy in America and a Report on the Membership—Past*

and Present, edited by J. E. Pauly. Baltimore: Williams and Wilkins, 1987.

OTHER SOURCES

Bechtel, William. *Discovering Cell Mechanisms: The Creation of Modern Cell Biology.* Cambridge, U.K.: Cambridge University Press, 2006.

Heuser, J. "Whatever Happened to the 'Microtrabecular Concept'?" *Biology of the Cell* 94 (2003): 561–596.

Palade, G. E. "Keith Robert Porter and the Development of Contemporary Cell Biology." *Journal of Cell Biology* 75 (1977): D3–D19.

Satir, P. "Keith Roberts Porter: 1912–1997." *Journal of Cell Biology* 138 (1997): 222–224

Wolosewick, J. J. "Joining the Trek with Keith up the Serpentine Road—the Lattice from another Perspective." *Biology of the Cell* 94 (2003): 557–559.

William Bechtel

POWELL, JOHN WESLEY (*b.* Mount Morris, New York, 24 March 1834; *d.* Haven, Maine, 23 September 1902), *geology, ethnology, federal science and mapping administration.* For the original article on Powell see *DSB,* vol. 11.

In 1889 John Powell reached the apex of his power and influence as the manager of the U.S. Geological Survey (USGS), its Irrigation Survey (IS), and the Smithsonian Institution's Bureau of Ethnology (BE), but his nadir followed in less than five years. Since 1950 evaluations in three significant book-length biographies, sections in related volumes, many articles, several film and television presentations, and an on-stage impersonator's portrayal ascribe the causes for and results of Powell's rapid decline to persons and circumstances beyond his control.

Expeditions. Powell served as an officer of Union artillery in combat during the Civil War and led a daring exploration of the Green and Colorado Rivers in 1869. Then he made significant contributions to geology and ethnology as he managed the organization that became the Interior Department's U.S. Geographical and Geological Survey of the Rocky Mountain Region. In partnership with Clarence Dutton and G. K. Gilbert, Powell advanced the understanding of how uplift and running water shape mountain and valley landforms. Powell also urged a more rational use of the West's arid lands and limited waters and a wiser, more humane policy toward its native peoples.

Powell, who insisted on being called "Major," proved himself brave, intelligent, and resourceful, but he also was aggressive, egotistical, and obstinate. During the 1869 voyage three men died after Powell failed to prevent their

John Wesley Powell. COURTESY OF U.S. GEOLOGICAL SOCIETY LIBRARY.

quiet mutiny and departure from the river. In later years he ignored the expedition's other participants, one of whom had saved his life in the Grand Canyon.

In the effort to reform federal mapping and science surveys during 1878 to 1879 Ferdinand Hayden, Clarence King, and Powell favored consolidating survey functions under civilian control within the Interior Department. King, not Powell, helped to write the plan presented by Yale's O. C. Marsh and his National Academy of Sciences (NAS) committee. When, at Interior Secretary Carl Schurz's request, Powell drafted unacceptable legislation from the NAS plan, Schurz asked King to co-write a new and the enacted version.

Powell, not yet in the NAS, co-founded with Dutton and others Washington's Cosmos Club to expand his social-scientific circle in the capital and also to support his brief quest to lead the new USGS. To defeat Hayden, Powell then backed King's stronger and successful candidacy for USGS director. Powell also knew that King intended (for reasons personal and professional) to remain with the USGS only long enough to get the fledgling agency up and running. When the reform-minded Schurz left office in

1881, King resigned and recommended Powell as his replacement to manage the mission-oriented USGS.

Director of the USGS. As USGS director Powell blended the staffs and work of the USGS and the BE. Powell's goals and methods in science and its administration, however, differed widely from those of the Yale-trained King. Powell represented an older, less-specialized, and often self-taught tradition in science in America. Everything possible, Powell believed, must be learned about a subject before applying the information gained to solving problems. His looser managerial style often allowed the USGS staff to choose their own subjects for study. Dutton and others in the USGS respected Powell as they had King, but Powell, unlike King, did not earn their affection.

By 1882 Congress had not yet founded the separate agency for surveys of measurement and position that King sought to secure a more reliable national geological map and to advance other USGS work. King and Powell's friends in Congress convinced their colleagues and President Chester Arthur to authorize the USGS to continue that map's preparation, by which Powell officially extended agency activities nationwide. To King's dismay Powell quickly remade the USGS into a national bureau for topographic mapping and basic geology but at the expense of the agency's mandated studies in mineral resources and other applied geology vital to the nation's economic health.

Under Powell's leadership USGS direct appropriations increased steadily through the 1880s and the agency's staff and activities grew proportionally to include, as full- or part-time employees, NAS president Marsh and almost all of Powell's other actual or potential critics. Congress, however, grew increasingly dissatisfied with the agency's paucity of products useful to meeting national needs, its unauthorized investigations and publications, and its alleged mismanagement. In 1886 Powell emerged relatively unscathed from hearings by the joint congressional commission headed by Senator William Allison and held to improve economy and efficiency in federal science bureaus. After the minority report trumpeted some of Powell's shortcomings, Congress asked the USGS to specify the funds it required for publications and then required the agency to itemize its entire budget.

Faced with the results of arid summers and harsh winters in the West, Congress and President Grover Cleveland enabled Powell to pursue his long-standing goal of improving the region's land- and water-use practices. In 1888 they authorized and funded the IS within the USGS to help redeem arid lands in the West by irrigation. Powell merged USGS and IS topographic work to advance the former's ongoing small-scale mapping of the West. Dutton, who led the IS engineers and hydrographers, told

Powell that the combination was illegal and then testified before Congress that his work required larger-scale maps of specific areas for which the smaller-scale regional maps were useless.

The attorney general's ruling on the 1888 statute closed the public lands to entry until the IS segregated the lands and locations for the dams, reservoirs, and canals required for successful irrigation, flood-control, and reclamation. When Powell refused to recommend promptly all the sites whose selection would have reopened the public lands and released federal dowry lands to the six states admitted to the Union during 1889 to 1890, Congress turned hostile and some members (especially in the Senate) grilled Powell severely (and a few even savagely). In 1890 Congress and President Benjamin Harrison repealed the land restrictions and terminated the IS. After a fifteen-year detail to Interior's surveys Dutton returned at his request to the Army Ordnance Corps. Congress turned to the Agriculture Department for aid in reaching a better understanding of the West's surface and underground water supplies.

When a new national monetary crisis began in 1890, Powell and the USGS did not respond as effectively during the next two years as King and the agency had done in 1879. In 1892 Congress and Harrison carefully and selectively slashed the agency's statutory staff (by fifty percent) and its operating expenses (by thirty-three percent), keeping the vital work on mineral resources and their statistics but eliminating unauthorized efforts and the general investigations in geology and paleontology they felt were less useful. Powell had to live within the new law but he responded to it by dismissing, transferring, or retiring fifteen percent of the agency's whole staff. His cuts, however, fell most heavily on the USGS geologic unit, which lost seventy percent of its funds and some of its staff. Powell fired Marsh, economic geologists Franklin Emmons and George Becker (the latter almost Gilbert's equal in geophysics), and other staffers. Emmons and Becker already had demonstrated to the mining industry the value of geology in discovering and developing mineral districts.

Powell also failed to heed useful advice from King, other scientists, and politicians concerned about the welfare of the USGS and the quality of its public service. Ignoring a new congressional investigation Powell refused to reform or resign, instead heeding those in his internal clique who advised him to die in office. Powell then spent most of his time away from Washington, continuing to promote before national, state, and territorial organizations his agrarian-populist ideas for public ownership of water supplies and organizing new states' counties by drainage-basin boundaries. In 1893 interior secretary Hoke Smith, advised by King, advanced chief paleontologist Charles Walcott (King's appointee in 1879) to replace

Gilbert as geologist-in-charge of Geology and Paleontology. Walcott rehired Emmons and Becker, restored much of the USGS efforts in economic geology, and returned Gilbert to field work.

When Powell schemed to have the USGS transferred to the Smithsonian (to join the BE) or to the Department of Agriculture (to emphasize USGS work on soils and surficial geology), Congress, Smith, and President Cleveland rang a decisive alarm bell. In 1894, adopting a time-honored method, they reduced Powell's salary by $1,000, to take effect when the new fiscal year began on 1 July. Powell resigned as director in May and underwent a needed operation on the stump of the arm he lost at Shiloh.

King could not, as many wished, resume the directorship. Instead he recommended Walcott to Smith and Cleveland. Director Walcott promptly returned the USGS to its earlier efforts on behalf of the country's significant economic and educational interests. From 1894 to 1896 Walcott began continuously funded and successful national studies of water resources (including artesian sources, whose importance Powell had decried), sent Becker and William Dall to study Alaska's gold and coal resources, and professionalized topographic mapping by introducing improved field procedures and records and placing topographers under civil-service rules.

As a measure of Walcott's success Powell's principal critics in Congress, especially those in the Senate, changed their opinion about the USGS. Those legislators supported the USGS strongly—increasing the agency's funding (including restoring the director's salary) and gave it new missions in topographic surveys (forest reserves, Indian reservations, and other federal lands), reclamation, and fuels and structural-materials testing. USGS direct and transferred appropriations quickly climbed to totals beyond any reached during Powell's years. They topped one million dollars in fiscal 1898 and rose steadily above that total after fiscal 1900.

Past views of Powell as victim are false. Powell, like all managers, was responsible for his actions and their results. Concluding otherwise absolves Powell of accountability. Some historians see Powell as the conservationists' Cassandra. Unfortunately he did not have all the answers to the West's problems in the 1880s and 1890s. To suggest that if congresses and presidents had merely followed Powell's policies all would have been well then (and now) in land and water issues in the West is historically untenable. Many in Congress and industry opposed Powell and his ideas, most of these persons with good reasons although some did so with ill grace. Powell's hubris and his unwillingness to compromise or to consider conflicting opinion or advice largely contributed to his failures.

Powell, as explorer and scholar, significantly advanced mapping and science during America's Gilded Age. As

USGS director, however, he also had opportunities, made choices, received repeated warnings, refused to change, and nearly brought the agency down with him. The principal managerial lesson from Powell's USGS directorate, especially after 1886, is how not to run a federal agency.

SUPPLEMENTARY BIBLIOGRAPHY

WORKS BY POWELL

Lands of the Arid Region of the United States. Boston: Harvard Common Press, 1983. Facsimile of the second (1879) edition, with an introduction by T. H. Watkins.

The Exploration of the Colorado River and Its Canyons. Washington, DC: National Geographic, 2002. Reprint of the 1895 edition of *Canyons of the Colorado*, with an introduction by Anthony Brandt.

OTHER SOURCES

Bartlett, Richard. *Great Surveys of the American West.* Norman: University of Oklahoma Press, 1962.

———. "Scientific Exploration of the American West, 1865–1900." In *American Exploration,* vol. 3, *A Continent Comprehended,* edited by John Allen. Lincoln: University of Nebraska Press, 1997. Chapter 22 summarizes the section on Powell's pre-USGS organization in Bartlett's 1962 volume.

Darrah, William. *Powell of the Colorado.* Princeton, NJ: Princeton University Press, 1951.

DeBuys, William. *Seeing Things Whole: The Essential John Wesley Powell.* Washington, DC: Island Press/Shearwater Books, 2001. DeBuys reprints and comments on a number of Powell's publications.

Dolnick, Edward. *Down the Great Unknown: John Wesley Powell's Journey of Discovery and Tragedy through the Grand Canyon.* New York: HarperCollins, 2001.

Flack, James. *Desideratum in Washington: The Intellectual Community in the Capital City, 1870–1900.* Cambridge, MA: Schenkman Publishing, 1975. Flack emphasizes the social context of Powell's work during these years.

Fowler, Don. "Powell, John Wesley." In *American National Biography,* edited by John Garrity and Mark Carnes. New York: Oxford University Press, 1999.

Hinsley, Curtis. *Savages and Scientists: The Smithsonian Institution and the Development of American Anthropology, 1846–1910.* Washington, DC: Smithsonian Institution Press, 1981. Hinsley assesses Powell's contributions to ethnology as a scientist-manager.

Lee, Lawrence. "Powell, John Wesley." In *Biographical Dictionary of American and Canadian Naturalists and Environmentalists,* edited by Kier Sterling. Westport, CT: Greenwood Press, 1997.

Nelson, Clifford. "Toward a Reliable Geologic Map of the United States, 1803–1893." In "Surveying the Record: North American Scientific Exploration to 1930," edited by Edward Carter II. *American Philosophical Society Memoir* 231 (1999): 51–74. Nelson evaluates Powell's contributions to this improving cartography.

———. "Powell, John Wesley." In *The Development of the Industrial United States, 1870–1899,* edited by Ari Hoogenboom. New York: Facts on File, 2003.

Pisani, Donald. *To Reclaim a Divided West: Water, Law, and Public Policy, 1848–1902.* Albuquerque: University of New Mexico Press, 1992. Pisani's evaluation of Powell's role in the development of land- and water-use policies and practices in the American West is the best of several assessments to date.

Rabbitt, Mary. "John Wesley Powell: Pioneer Statesman of Federal Science." In *The Colorado River Region and John Wesley Powell: A Collection of Papers Honoring Powell on the 100th Anniversary of His Exploration of the Colorado River, 1869–1969.* Washington, DC: USGS Professional Paper 669, 1969. Rabbitt revised this earlier and far less critical work in three later works.

———. *Minerals, Lands, and Geology for the Common Defense and General Welfare: A History of Public Lands, Federal Science and Mapping Policy, and Development of Mineral Resources in the United States,* vol. 1, *Before 1879.* Washington, DC: U.S. Geological Survey, 1979. Vol. 2, *1879–1904.* Washington, DC: U.S. Geological Survey, 1980. Rabbitt appraises Powell's role as a participant in and leader of federal mapping and science agencies.

———. *The United States Geological Survey 1879–1989.* Washington, DC: U.S. Geological Survey, 1989. Available from the Publications Warehouse at www.usgs.gov. Rabbitt briefly summarizes her two volumes cited above. Vol. 3 (*1904-1939*) appeared in 1986; Nelson is completing Vol. 4 (*1939–1979*).

Reisner, Marc. *Cadillac Desert: The American West and Its Disappearing Water.* New York: Viking, 1986.

Stegner, Wallace. *Beyond the Hundredth Meridian: John Wesley Powell and the Second Opening of the West.* Boston: Houghton, Mifflin, 1954.

Worster, Donald. *Rivers of Empire: Water, Aridity and the Growth of the American West.* New York: Pantheon Books, 1985.

———. "The Legacy of John Wesley Powell." In *An Unsettled Country: Changing Landscapes of the American West,* edited by Donald Worster. Albuquerque: University of New Mexico Press, 1994.

———. *A River Running West: The Life of John Wesley Powell.* New York: Oxford University Press, 2001. The first chapter extends the portrayals of Powell in William Darrah and Wallace Stegner. Like Darrah and Stegner, however, Worster does not adequately explain the cartographic, economic, engineering, managerial, political, and scientific reasons for the failure of the IS and Powell's demise as head of the USGS.

Zernel, John. "Powell, John Wesley." In *The History of Science in the United States: An Encyclopedia,* edited by Marc Rothenberg. New York: Garland Publishing, 2001.

Clifford M. Nelson

PRACHATICZ, CRISTANNUS DE (*b.* Prachatice, Bohemia, after 1360; *d.* Prague, 4 September 1439), *astronomy, mathematics, medicine, theology, education.*

Cristannus (Křišťan z Prachatic) was a master of Charles University in Prague. He is the author of the first printed treatises on the astrolabe, the ancient astronomical instrument that came into wide use during the Middle Ages.

Cristannus left his native town of Prachatice in southern Bohemia to study at Prague's Charles University, where he achieved his bachelor of arts in 1388 and master of arts in 1390. He then studied medicine and theology. As a master he spent his entire career at the university in different capacities: he was dean of the Faculty of Arts (1403–1404), rector (1405, 1412–1413, 1434, and 1437), and simultaneously was an important clergyman who also was involved in political affairs.

Cristannus supported his younger countryman and friend, the religious reformer John (Jan) Hus, during Hus's student years. The two men remained friends. Cristannus eventually became a representative of the conservative Calixtins, and he suffered at the hands of both the Catholics and the radical Hussites. He was known for his theological tracts on holy communion, but among his contemporaries he was especially renowned for his works in medicine and natural sciences and was widely praised as an astronomer.

Medical Treatises. Cristannus wrote several important medical works, including the *Lékařské knížky* (Medical books) and *Rozličná lékařství* (Diverse medicine), written in Czech and published several times throughout the sixteenth century, as well as the Latin texts *Collecta per magistrum Cristannum de Prachaticz de sanguinis minucione* (Exposition on bloodletting by Master Cristannus de Prachaticz), *Tabula minucionum sanguinis et lunacionum* (Lunation table for bloodletting), and *Herbarius*, on the medicinal use of plants. Apparently Cristannus's medical treatises derived from his own practice. Cristannus also wrote mathematical treatises, *Algorismus prosaycus* and *Computus chirometralis*, based on medieval textbooks by Johannes de Sacrobosco, Alexander de Villa Dei, Johannes de Erfordia, and others.

Works on the Astrolabe. Except for some minor works and astronomical excursions in his medical tracts, only two of Cristannus's major astronomical treatises are extant. They deal with the astrolabe, a universal astronomical and geodesic instrument that was used from antiquity into modern times. In European universities of the Middle Ages, the astrolabe was a fundamental focus of the astronomy curriculum. Theory of the astrolabe was based on Ptolemy's Greek treatise *Planisphaerium* (second century AD). Arabs were instrumental in bringing the astrolabe to Spain, from where the instrument and its descriptions in Latin translations and adaptations spread to Christian Europe in the tenth and eleventh centuries. One of the best-known treatises on the astrolabe was by Pseudo-Messahalla (no reliable edition has as of 2007 been published). The influence of this treatise is apparent in many Latin texts, and it was also gradually translated into other languages. A French translation of Pseudo-Messahalla was made in 1362 by Pèlerin de Prusse (an English translation of his *Practique de astralabe* is *Pèlerin de Prusse on the Astrolabe,* edited by Edgar Laird and Robert Fisher, 1995). Geoffrey Chaucer translated Pseudo-Messahalla's text in 1391 as *A Treatise on the Astrolabe* (subsequently edited by W. W. Skeat [London, 1872; reprinted 1968] and by R. T. Gunther as *Chaucer and Messahalla on the Astrolabe* [Oxford, 1929; reprinted 1968]). Cristannus's writings show some traces of Pseudo-Messahalla, but his work is essentially autonomous and much more elaborated, with a great deal of originality.

Cristannus wrote his *Composition* (incipit: "Quamvis de astrolabii composicione tam modernorum quam veterum dicta habentur pulcherrima") and *Use of the astrolabe* (incipit: "Quia plurimi ob nimiam quandoque accurtacionem") in 1407 as the basis of his university lectures. Although neither section of the original manuscript of the treatise has been preserved, the earliest copies were made within a year after it was written. Owing to its high quality, many copies of it were produced; some eighty manuscripts are known, the most recent of which date from the mid-sixteenth century. Cristannus's influence also can be traced in some treatises of late sixteenth century.

In the 1420s or 1430s a version of Cristannus's treatise on the astrolabe was written by a master of the University of Vienna, Johannes von Gmunden, who borrowed it in its entirety and developed some of its passages. He, together with the prior of Klosterneuburg monastery, Georg Müstinger, and a master of Charles University, Johannes Andreae dictus Schindel (Jan Ondřejův known as Šindel), helped to establish the first Viennese school of mathematics, astronomy, and cartography. Jan Šindel was Cristannus's contemporary and university colleague; he is known as the originator of the Prague astronomical clock, which dates to as early as 1410, the period when Cristannus was lecturing on the astrolabe at Charles University and when he wrote his two treatises on the subject. Together Cristannus de Prachaticz and Jan Šindel demonstrate the high level of astronomy at the medieval Prague university.

Cristannus's treatises became the first printed text on the astrolabe, in the well-known Perugia incunabulum printed by Petrus Petri de Colonia, Fridericus Ebert, and Johannes Conradi in 1477–1479 (*Gesamtkatalog der Wiegendrucke* [*GW*], Berlin, Staatsbibliothek, no. M38333; *The Illustrated Incunabula Short-Title Catalogue* [*IISTC*], London, British Library, no. ir00203000). The author of the foreword to this edition, Ulyxes Lanciarinus, praises the text for its high level of didacticism and clarity of exposition. However, Lanciarinus attributes its authorship to Robertus Anglicus. Cristannus's treatises subsequently were reprinted several times: Cologne, 1478; Venice, 1497–1498 (1494?); Venice, 1512; Venice, 1521 (this version was incorrectly attributed to Prosdocimo de Beldomandi); and Padua, 1549. These incorrect attributions gained acceptance in subsequent literature and have survived into the twenty-first century (Robertus Anglicus in *IISTC* and Prosdocimo de Beldomandi in the database *In principio*). However, arguments in favor of Cristannus's authorship and the text's Prague origin are provided by the interrelatedness of different manuscripts and by a number of references to Bohemia in the text and later interpolations about other localities. Cristannus's role in the Hussite revolution made him a heretical figure in the eyes of Catholic Europe. This explains why the Cristanus's authorship of both his favorably accepted treatises on astrolabe was generally concealed and eventually forgotten, and why subsequently it was wrongly attributed to other authors.

BIBLIOGRAPHY

WORKS BY PRACHATICZ

Lékařské knížky Mistra Křišťana z Prachatic z mnohých vybrané. Edited by Zdeňka Tichá. Prague: Avicenum, 1975. Edition of a Czech medical treatise.

Cristannus de Prachaticz, Algorismus prosaycus (*Základy aritmetiky*). Edited by Zuzana Silagiová. Prague: Oikumene, 1999. Edition of a Latin mathematical treatise with a Czech translation.

Cristannus de Prachaticz, De sanguinis minucione (*O pouštění krve*). Edited by Hana Florianová-Miškovská. Prague: Oikumene, 1999. Edition of a Latin medical treatise with a Czech translation.

"Replika M. Křišťana z Prachatic k proroctví M. Jana Pařížského [The reply of M. Cristannus of Prachatice to the prophecy of M. Iohannes Parisiensis]." Edited by Alena Hadravová, Alena M. Černá, Milada Homolková, and Petr Hadrava. *Listy filologické* (*Folia philologica*) 123 (2000): 40–51. Cristannus opposed by (imprecise) astronomical arguments to an apocalyptic astrological prophecy (with an anti-Hussite motivation) connected with incorrectly predicted lunar occultation and disregards astrology as unfair interfering with God's will.

Křišťan z Prachatic, Stavba a Užití astrolábu [Cristannus de Prachaticz: Composition and use of the astrolabe]. Edited by

Alena Hadravová and Petr Hadrava. Prague: Filosofia, 2001. The critical edition of main Latin astronomical treatises proving the Cristannus's authorship, with an annotated Czech translation, computer-simulated drawings, appendices, and an English summary, supplemented with an edition of a version by Johannes von Gmunden.

Staročeské knihy lékařské. Edited by Alena M. Černá. Brno: Host, 2006. Edition of a Czech medical treatise thought to have been written by Cristannus.

OTHER SOURCES

Hadravová, Alena, and Petr Hadrava. "Magister Cristannus de Prachaticz and His Astronomical Work." In *Acta historiae rerum naturalium necnon technicarum.* New series, vol. 3, edited by Jaroslav Folta. Prague: NTM, 1999. Short review with an English translation of Cristannus's "Reply to the Prophecy of Johannes Parisiensis."

———, and Petr Hadrava. "Johannes von Gmunden und seine Version des Astrolabtraktats des Christian von Prachatitz." In *Johannes von Gmunden (ca. 1384–1442), Astronom und Mathematiker*, edited by Rudolf Simek and Kathrin Chlench. Vienna: Fassbaender, 2006. On the relationship between Cristannus's and Johannes von Gmunden's treatises on the astrolabe; in German.

Alena Hadravová
Petr Hadrava

PRELOG, VLADIMIR

PRELOG, VLADIMIR (*b.* Sarajevo, Austria [later Bosnia], 23 July 1906; *d.* Zürich, Switzerland, 7 January 1998), *chemistry, stereochemistry, structure of natural products.*

Prelog is rightly considered the premier stereochemist of the second half of the twentieth century. In 1975 he received the Nobel Prize in Chemistry "for his work on the stereochemistry of organic molecules and reactions." The word *stereochemistry* is derived from the Greek στερεόσ (stereos) meaning "solid" and refers to the three-dimensional chemical properties of molecules. While the perception of the three-dimensional aspect goes back to Louis Pasteur (1848), and the concept of a tetrahedral carbon atom to Joseph Achille Le Bel and Jacobus Henricus van't Hoff (1874), even in the early twentieth century molecules were still commonly depicted as if they were planar. Such representations conceal important aspects of the mutual interaction of molecules, such as that of a drug with its biological receptor or that of an enzyme with its substrate.

Stereochemistry, among other aspects, conveys the concept of handedness (called chirality on the molecular scale): a right glove fits a right hand whereas its mirror

Vladimir Prelog with Leopold Ruzicka. AP IMAGES.

image (a left glove) does not. In an analogous way, a molecule of a given handedness may be effective as a drug, but its mirror image may not (Figure 1 A, B). This principle of *fit or misfit* plays an important role in chemistry.

Early History. In 1906 Prelog's birthplace, Sarajevo, was the capital of Bosnia-Herzegovina, a province of the Austro-Hungarian empire which later became part of Yugoslavia and was an independent country after 1992.

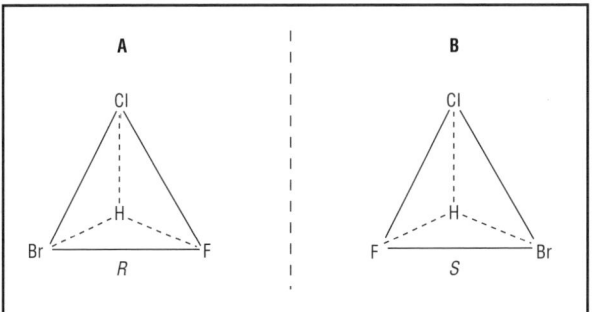

Figure 1. *Tetrahedrally substituted Carbon Atoms. The carbon atom—not shown—is at the center of the tetrahedron.*

The region has a long history of ethnic, religious, and political strife. In June 1914, when the Austrian crown prince, Archduke Franz Ferdinand, and his wife visited Sarajevo, young Prelog was delegated to strew flowers in front of their carriage. Just after the procession had passed him, he heard the fatal shots that killed the crown prince and his wife and ushered in World War I. The assassin was a Serbian student, and violent demonstrations against the Serbian minority in Bosnia ensued, resulting in the burning and looting of Serbian-owned shops. This incident left Prelog with a life-long aversion to all violent mass demonstrations, even if undertaken for just causes.

Prelog's Croatian parents, Milan and Mara (née Costello) separated in 1915 and Vladimir moved in with his paternal aunt in Zagreb, the capital of Croatia, where he completed three years of high school (Realgymnasium). At the age of twelve he had already started some chemical experiments with supplies and equipment he bought, and resolved to become a chemist. In 1918 he rejoined his father in Osijek, Croatia, where his interest in chemistry was encouraged by a good high school teacher, Ivan Kuria, who supervised the writing of Prelog's first scientific paper (1921) . That year he moved back to Zagreb, and upon graduating from high school (1924) he enrolled in a chemical engineering curriculum at the Czech Institute of Technology in Prague.

In his study of organic chemistry Prelog encountered Rudolf Lukeš, an enthusiastic young assistant professor, who engaged him as his research assistant. Lukeš worked on alkaloids, and taught Prelog both the theoretical and practical aspects of organic chemistry. Prelog spent most of his undergraduate days doing research and finished his diploma with distinction in three years. Subsequent doctoral studies with Emil Votoček, the professor of organic chemistry, involved the aglycone of the newly discovered glycoside rhamnoconvolvuline. Within a year Prelog found the compound to be 3,12-dihydroxypalmitic acid and obtained his doctoral degree in 1929.

Chemical Research in Prague and Zagreb. Jobs were scarce in 1929 and Prelog was fortunate to meet a schoolmate of Lukeš, Gothard J. Dříza, a young entrepreneur who was setting up a laboratory for the preparation of fine chemicals and simultaneously wanted to carry out a doctoral project. Dříza offered Prelog the job of assisting in the laboratory, with the opportunity to do some research of his own and the additional duty of supervising Dříza's PhD work (officially under Votoček). Prelog chose the antimalarial alkaloid quinine for his study, a subject he continued to pursue later in Zagreb and in Zürich. In 1932 he spent nine difficult months in the Royal Yugoslav Navy. On his return to Prague in 1933, he married Kamila Vítek, whom he had met six years earlier. Their son Jan was born in 1949.

In 1933 Prelog became a candidate for the chair of organic chemistry at the University of Zagreb, but, after long negotiation, he was offered instead an appointment (in 1935) as a docent (a poorly paid instructor with large teaching duties). Moreover, the Zagreb laboratory was not equipped for organic synthesis and the budget was insufficient for supplies and the support of coworkers and technicians.

Fortunately, Prelog was again able to make contact with a small but prospering commercial pharmaceutical enterprise, Kaštel, Ltd. (later Pliva). Eugen Ladany, an owner of the firm, decided to expand its scope from fabrication of pills, tablets, and injectables to the manufacture of medicinal products not available locally. Prelog accepted a consultancy with the firm, which involved his devoting part of his university work to the synthesis of pharmaceuticals, in return for support of his laboratory and a personal stipend. Thus one of Prelog's first doctoral students devised an inexpensive synthesis of the just-discovered antibacterial drug sulfanilamide. This led to financial success for both the company and Prelog and his laboratory and enabled him to spend several months in the laboratory of a fellow Croatian, Leopold Ruzicka, at

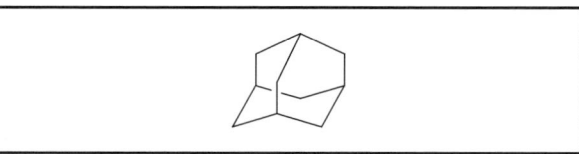

Figure 2. Adamantane.

the ETH (Federal Polytechnic Institute) in Zürich, Switzerland.

Back in Zagreb, Prelog tackled two exciting chemical problems: the synthesis of adamantane and the synthesis of quinine and related alkaloids. Adamantane ($C_{10}H_{16}$), isolated from Moravian petroleum by Stanislav Landa in 1933 has a melting point of 266 degrees Celsius, unusually high for a compound with only ten carbon atoms. Landa brought a sample to Lukeš's laboratory for advice; Lukeš, noting the tetrahedral crystals, immediately suggested (in Prelog's presence) that the substance had a highly symmetrical tetrahedral molecular architecture (Figure 2). In Zagreb, Prelog proved this structure by a "rational synthesis," that is, a synthesis in which each step was sufficiently clear to allow the resulting connectivity of the atoms to be inferred unequivocally. In publishing adamantane's unusual molecular architecture, he gave credit to his teacher Lukeš for his prediction. Prelog also pursued the synthesis of the antimalarial quinine ($C_{20}H_{24}N_2O_2$, Figure 3, isolated from cinchona bark in the early nineteenth century) with some success (1943), but this project was not complete at the time he left Zagreb and was later finished by others (Woodward and Doering, 1944 and 1945; see also Stork et al., 2001; summarized by Rúveda, 2005; Seeman, 2007).

The atmosphere for work in Zagreb became increasingly unfavorable with the outbreak of World War II (1939) and the occupation of Croatia by the Germans in 1941. Through his earlier stay in Zürich, Prelog was known to Ruzicka, who had given several German and Austrian Jewish refugees positions in his laboratory. But by 1941, most of them, concerned about the safety of Switzerland as a haven, had emigrated to the United States, leaving Ruzicka with few coworkers; thus his eyes fell on Prelog. Fortuitously, Prelog's work had also come to the attention of Richard Kuhn, who invited him to Heidelberg for a lecture.

With this invitation, Prelog and his wife were able to receive passports. Ruzicka then arranged for them to receive Swiss visas and once in Italy in transit, the Prelogs proceeded to Zürich rather than to Germany. There Prelog became an assistant in Ruzicka's laboratory; he was promoted to Privatdozent (roughly equivalent to assistant professor) in 1942 and to titular professor in 1945. In

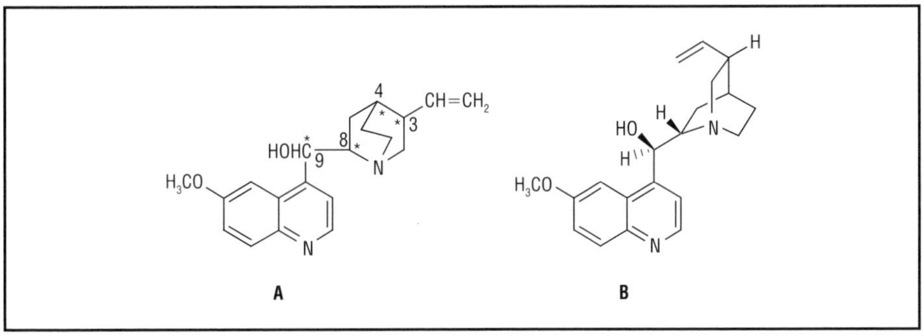

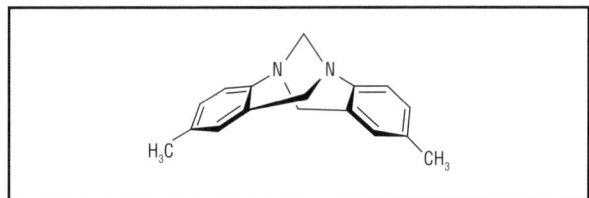

Figure 3. *Quinine. A: Connectivity. B: 3-D Structure (after Prelog).*

1943 he became a consultant for CIBA, which supported his research and also augmented his stipend.

Zürich: Natural Products. The tradition of the ETH laboratory under Ruzicka was elucidation of the structure of natural products. Thus Prelog's first project involved isolation of pure chemical compounds from pig testes extracts. Two of these products proved to be related to the known class of steroids but had a pronounced musk odor, and one was found to be a sex attractant for pigs. Interestingly, the same compound was later found to occur in truffles, which explains why pigs are expert in finding truffles in the ground! After some further successful work on steroids as well as terpenes, Prelog, independent of Ruzicka now, switched his interest to alkaloids, impelled perhaps by his long-standing interest in quinine.

Prelog's first structural target (1942) was the steroidal alkaloid solanidine, readily available locally from potato sprouts. The war-imposed scarcity, not only of chemicals but also of current foreign chemical journals, left him the leisure to read and think about prewar publications. In the process he found an error in the strychnine formula of Sir Robert Robinson—the formula that Prelog suggested in 1945 was not correct either but led Robinson to suggest the correct structure, which was confirmed at the same time by Woodward (1947). Another widely cited achievement of this period was the resolution of Tröger's base (Figure 4) into two mirror-image forms (Figure 1) (1944). Normally 3-coordinated nitrogen, RR'R"N:, where the fourth corner of the tetrahedron is occupied only by non-bonded electrons, does not sustain chirality because of facile nitrogen inversion, but in Tröger's base the nitrogen atoms are stereochemically locked and the two enantiomers (mirror-image forms) cannot interconvert. This is also one of the early instances where resolution was effected by column chromatography on an optically active support (specially prepared lactose hydrate).

Prelog then returned to his old love, quinine, but switched from its attempted synthesis to the elucidation of its configuration (3-dimensional architecture). Its constitution and connectivity (Figure 3, A) had been determined in 1908. Each of the four starred carbon atoms bears four different attached neighbors (Figure 1), so there are two possible mirror-image arrangements (A, B) for each starred carbon, making possible 2^4 or 16 configurational isomers in all. In spectacular studies, Prelog's group determined the configuration of these four carbon atoms in quinine (1944, 1950), thus completing the determination of its molecular structure (Figure 3, B).

By 1945 partly as a result of his work on adamantane, on Tröger's base, and on the configuration of the cinchona alkaloids, Prelog had developed a profound understanding of stereochemistry, a subject that would engage him for much of the rest of his life. He also continued working on the structures of natural products, but the war-imposed isolation slowed further progress. This situation changed dramatically in 1946. Renowned colleagues from Britain, France, and the United States visited Zürich to find out about work done there during the war. Thus Prelog met such luminaries as Robert Woodward (Harvard), Robert Robinson (Oxford), Derek H. R. Barton (London), and Maurice Janot (Gif-sur-Yvette, France). Some of these meetings gave rise to collaboration on natural products: on corynantheine and cinchonamine with Janot; and on cevine with Woodward, Barton, and Prelog's local colleague Oskar Jeger. The visitors also came to appreciate Prelog both as a scientist and as a human being. As a chemist, he was original, quick-minded, focused,

Figure 4. *Tröger's Base.*

well-read and informed, had an excellent memory, and could constructively discuss many scientific problems. As an individual he was personable, cultured, communicative, self-confident without being overbearing, witty, and collaborative (he preferred collaboration to competition).

In 1947 Prelog decided to present the then-new electronic theory of organic reactions in advanced chemistry lectures, which, he writes, led him to an experimental investigation of medium-sized (8 to 11–membered) ring compounds. These compounds were hard to come by. Prelog—simultaneously with his industrial colleague Max Stoll—found a way to obtain them in good yield by a modified acyloin synthesis. He found their properties to deviate substantially from those of analogous smaller or larger ring compounds, which Prelog ascribed to the unusual shape of these rings, which he called their "constellation." Because of the potential angle strain in a medium-sized ring, atoms some five or six positions apart tend to buckle into the ring and thus get close together. This gives rise to "transannular" interactions, both chemical and physical, of atoms that would otherwise be too far apart to interact, which had several unusual consequences. The initiation of studies of "medium rings" is one of Prelog's major achievements. At the same time, however, D. H. R. Barton had been studying and interpreting the chemical and physical behavior of 6-membered rings attributable to their chairlike shape, and coined the term *conformation* to describe their shape. This term has since been generally accepted in place of "constellation."

In 1950 Prelog occupied the Reilly lectureship at the University of Notre Dame (South Bend, Indiana) over a six-week period. In addition to presenting twelve lectures there, he visited most of the major Midwestern universities, stopping on the way home in the northeastern United States; in all he gave twenty-five talks. Prelog's visit to Harvard brought him an offer of a tenured professorship. To counter this offer, Ruzicka persuaded the ETH president to create a second full professorship in the Organic Chemistry Institute, something very unusual then in Europe. While attending the 75-year anniversary meeting of the American Chemical Society in 1951, Prelog was offered the research directorship of Hoffmann–La Roche, but turned it down despite its financial attractiveness—administration was not his métier. He used his stay in the United States to visit several West Coast universities and spent two stimulating months as Falk-Plaut lecturer at Columbia University in New York. By the time he returned to Zürich, chemistry was in a period of rapid change (and increasing cost!), thanks to the development of new instrumentation—infrared and nuclear magnetic resonance spectroscopy, readily accessible x-ray crystallography—that greatly facilitated the heretofore tedious determination of the structure of natural products by degradation.

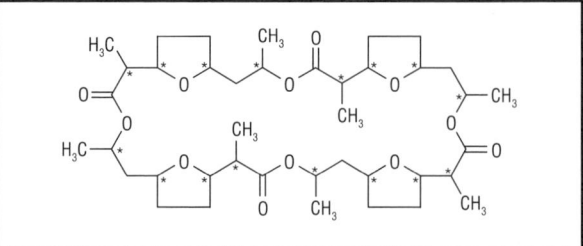

Figure 5. *Nonactin.*

In this area Prelog turned his attention to the structure of microbial metabolites and antibiotics, made notable by the earlier discovery of penicillin by Alexander Fleming. CIBA in Basel was working on such compounds and enlisted Prelog's help. The first representative, narbomycin, proved to have a large (14-membered) lactone ring, as did several other antibiotics (macrolides) discovered then and since. Degradation of narbomycin (1956) produced a lactone, also obtained by Carl Djerassi—later called, in view of its importance in synthesis, the Prelog-Djerassi lactone. Another interesting macrolide is nonactin, with a 32-membered ring (1962). The molecule has 16 stereogenic (chiral) centers but shows no optical activity, being made up of four subunits, two of which are mirror images of the other two. Thus the combination is superposable with its mirror image (Figure 5). Other interesting antibiotics studied were echinomycin (1959), the iron-containing ferrioxamines, the antitubercular rifamycin, and the boron containing boromycin.

Prelog's Rule. In 1950 Prelog came upon a 1936 review by the British stereochemist Alexander McKenzie concerning the reactions of esters of phenylpyruvic acid and chiral alcohols with Grignard reagents. The chiral alcohol moiety induces chirality in the atrolactic acid obtained after final saponification (Figure 6) but the correlation between the sign of rotation of the resulting acid and the configuration of the chiral alcohol was not clear. Reasoning on the basis of molecular models, Prelog concluded that alcohol A (Figure 6) would give rise to the known (*R*)-(-)-atrolactic acid and B to the (*S*)-(+) enantiomer. This hypothesis—now called Prelog's Rule—agreed with the configuration of those alcohols that had been independently established and allowed predictions for other alcohols of hitherto unknown configuration. This remarkably reliable though empirical rule pointed the way for similar configurational correlations for other types of compounds.

CIP System of Stereochemical Nomenclature. Up to 1951, the configuration of chemical compounds had

Figure 6. *Prelog's Rule. L, large, M, medium, S, small group.*

been denoted based on their two-dimensional projection formulas, but since there are different ways of projecting a three-dimensional molecule onto a plane, the notation was often not unequivocal and hence confusing. In 1951, Robert S. Cahn, editor of the British *Journal of the Chemical Society,* and Christopher K. Ingold of University College London devised a notation based on the actual (three-dimensional) disposition of a molecule's chiral center or centers, and specified the array by means of a prefix to the name of the compound. The system works as follows. Order the substituents a, b, c, and d about the chiral center shown in Figure 1 according to their atomic numbers (a > b > c > d, for example, Br > Cl > F > H; the so-called sequence rule) and orient the tetrahedra such that d is in the back. Then if a-b-c represents a clockwise array, the compound is given a descriptor (prefix) now called *R* (for Latin *rectus*); for the counterclockwise array the descriptor is *S* (for Latin *sinister*).

Prelog tells the story that, in an evening reception at a meeting of the British Chemical Society, he sat together with Cahn and Ingold (then president of the Chemical Society) drinking beer. Prelog vigorously criticized some aspects of the 1951 sequence rule, with the unexpected result that the two Englishmen asked him to join them in further developing their ideas. The eventual result was an improved paper in 1956 and a further extended one in 1966. This CIP (Cahn-Ingold-Prelog) stereochemical nomenclature is now used in hundreds of thousands of scientific papers all over the world. Some additional changes were suggested in 1982 (with G. Helmchen); Prelog also published a system to describe conformation (with W. Klyne, 1960) and a general system to describe the steric course of asymmetric reactions (with Seebach, 1982).

Institute Headship and Later Work. Ruzicka retired in 1957 and Prelog became head of the Organic Chemical Institute of the ETH. One of his tasks was to attract and retain top-notch faculty. Prelog realized that his institute already had a number of outstanding Privatdozenten: Edgar Heilbronner, Albert Eschenmoser, Duilio Arigoni, and Wilhelm Simon. He succeeded in gradually obtaining full professorships for all of them, as well as for associate professors Jack Dunitz, Oskar Jeger, and Emil Hardegger. Having more than one full professor in one European institute was still quite unusual in the early 1960s. In 1965 Prelog further decided to adopt the U.S. departmental model: he stepped down as department head and installed a rotating chairmanship, with all full professors participating in important decisions. In the process he created a remarkable collegial spirit in the institute that extended, beyond administration, to scientific interaction and personal friendship. Although most of the faculty members promoted under Prelog became widely recognized and sought after (several became foreign associates of the U.S. National Academy of Sciences); only one of them, Heilbronner, ever left the ETH.

Prelog was now at the peak of his scientific career. In 1960 he was elected to the governing board of the large Swiss pharmaceutical company CIBA. He presented lectures all over the world (at 150 locations, by his estimate), including many named lectureships, such as the Baker lectureship at Cornell University. During this period and in subsequent years he received many honorary degrees (eleven in all, including doctorates from Cambridge, Paris, and the Weizmann Institute) and numerous honorary or foreign memberships in national academies, including the Leopoldina, the Pontifical Academy, the National Academy of Sciences (USA), the (British) Royal Society, and the American Philosophical Society. His many medals and awards (nineteen in all) include the 1969 Roger Adams Award, then the top award in organic chemistry of the American Chemical Society. Perhaps significantly, the last sentence of the nomination for that award (following a description of Prelog's science) reads: "He has many friends and few enemies."

As Prelog's reputation spread in the 1950s, excellent PhD candidates joined his group; several of these later attained professorships at major universities, mainly in German-speaking Europe. He also attracted many postdoctoral fellows and senior visiting chemists from all over the world, especially Prelog's native Yugoslavia. He was a good academic host, ever ready to talk and interact with his visitors even when they did not work on joint problems with him.

The 1960s saw a renaissance in the understanding of stereochemistry, in part prompted by Prelog's work in the previous decade. In 1965, Professor Andre Dreiding (at the University of Zürich) organized a EUCHEM Conference on Stereochemistry, which took place in some very elegant hotels on the Bürgenstock, a steep bluff near the southwestern end of Lake Lucerne, and thereafter (it recurs annually) was known as the Bürgenstock Conference. As he explained later (1989), Prelog was at first unenthusiastic—he felt there were already too many meetings and thought the stereochemical viewpoint might be too narrow to sustain yearly conferences. On both points he quickly changed his mind: The conferences gave him an opportunity to discuss many aspects of the field with colleagues (mainly European ones), and it turned out that the stereochemical point of view easily covers many aspects of the increasingly cross-disciplinary chemical sciences. Prelog became a regular attendee at subsequent Bürgenstock conferences.

Although most of Prelog's research was basic, both his background and his industrial connection kept him in touch with applications, especially in drug development. One of these problems was the synthesis of compounds in enantiomerically pure form, for, as explained earlier, often only one of the two enantiomers of a chiral compound is pharmacologically active. Nature solves this problem with enzymes, which either produce or separate out single enantiomers. Prelog, in the 1950s, initiated a study of such enzymes, isolated from microorganisms, for use in vitro. The reactions chosen were reductions of cyclic ketones to alcohols, and by utilizing a large number of different ketones as well as three different enzymes, his group developed so-called *diamond lattice models* to depict the active sites of the enzymes by determining which compounds were reduced stereoselectively. The work continued for some fifteen years (1956–1977, including a review, 1964; see also 1976).

Although the enzymes studied were not accessible enough for commercial use, the work provided impetus for later studies by others. A later approach to the separation problem involved chiral ionophores (1975–1986). Ionophores (ion carriers) make salts that are ordinarily

water-soluble. When a chiral moiety is part of, or attached to, the ionophore (see e.g. Figure 7), the solubilization may be selective for a single enantiomer and may thus be used for separation of individual enantiomers (resolution). The actual separation may be effected by partition between a fat-soluble and a water-soluble phase by single or countercurrent extraction, by partition chromatography, by transport across fat-soluble membranes, or by migration between enantioselective electrodes.

The Later Years. Prelog's first involvement with nomenclature had been from 1951 to 1954, as a member of the international (IUPAC) Nomenclature Commission. It is there that he first met Robert S. Cahn and interacted with Friedrich Richter and Oskar Weissbach, editors of *Beilsteins Handbuch der organischen Chemie,* a compendium of all known organic compounds. It was those editors' acceptance, after extensive trials, of the CIP system for listings of chiral compounds in the *Handbuch* that secured worldwide acceptance of the system. There were compounds whose chirality was different from that depicted in Figure 1, such as appropriately substituted allenes (abC=C=Cab), spiranes, biphenyls, helical structures, and several other types (such as Tröger's base, Figure 4) and ad hoc rules had been added to the CIP system (1965, 1982) to include these types. Indeed, a new type of stereoisomerism, cyclostereoisomerism, discovered by Prelog with Hans Gerlach and Yuri Ovchinnikov (1962, 1964), is exemplified in Figure 8: Of the various sequences in which two enantiomeric monomers a and b, can be arranged in a cyclic oligomer (e.g., a cyclic oligopeptide), there are two that differ from each other by having clockwise or counterclockwise arrangements of the a-a-b-a-b-b sequence.

As a result of the diversity of chiral molecules, Prelog began to look for a system (presumably mathematically based) that would cover all such compounds and preferably even predict their existence. His group first synthesized a number of molecules with novel combinations of chiral centers, axes, and planes (1969–1982). All these

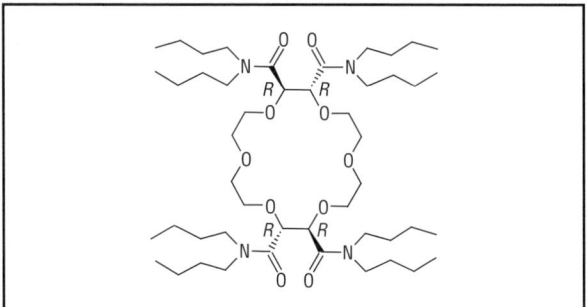

Figure 7. *Chiral Ionophore.*

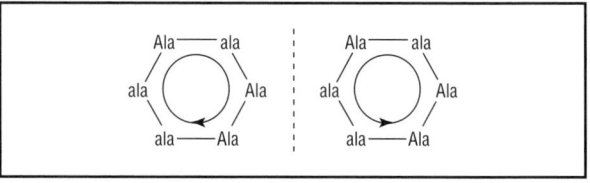

Figure 8. *Cyclostereoisomerism. Individual alanyl units, -NH-C*HMe-CO- are denoted Ala or ala depending on whether the configuration at the chiral carbon (C*) is S or R. The cyclic arrow in the center of the circle indicates if the unit as written above points in a clockwise or counterclockwise direction.*

molecules proved to be either chiral or achiral, according to prediction. However, the more general conceptual work, carried out in collaboration with Andre Dreiding until Prelog's death, did not lead to a final conclusion; a fragment of this work has been published in Prelog's Nobel lecture (1976).

In 1975 Prelog received the Nobel Prize in Chemistry jointly with John W. Cornforth (U.K.). Both prizes were for stereochemistry; Cornforth's for his ingenious work on biochemical applications, Prelog's for his leading role in the contemporary development of the subject. The following year Prelog , now seventy, had to retire, there being no emeritus status at the ETH. In order to retain an office and workplace, Prelog became the equivalent of a post-doctoral fellow, formally associated with one of his younger colleagues, and was able to continue his work, mostly with Croatian coworkers whom he paid with personal funds. In 1986 there was a grand celebration of his eightieth birthday, attended by many friends and colleagues from all over the world, which also involved the endowment of an annual Prelog Medal and lecture. (The first lecturer was the distinguished U.S. stereochemist Kurt Mislow.)

Prelog was a cultured individual with broad interests in music, art, and literature, but he rarely bared his innermost thoughts and feelings. Thus it is particularly significant that, on the occasion of the birthday celebration, an earlier response of Prelog's to a letter concerning religion emerged: "Dear … , Nobel prize winners are not more competent about God, religion, or life after death than other people but some of them, like myself, are agnostics. They just don't know and therefore they are tolerant to religious people, atheists, and others. What they dislike are militant zealots of any kind" (Arigoni, Dunits, and Eschenmoser, p. 459).

In 1996 *Croatica Chemica Acta* published a Festschrift in honor of Prelog's ninetieth birthday with several articles reminiscing about his work in Prague, Zagreb, and his early days in Zürich. Prelog was generally in good health, though late in life afflicted with pernicious anemia kept under control with vitamin B-12. He was an ardent skier well into his sixties. He died at the age of ninety-one after a short illness. Many extensive obituaries and memoirs by colleagues, friends and historians (1998–2000) were published all over the world.

BIBLIOGRAPHY

WORKS BY PRELOG

"Chirality in Chemistry." *Science* 193 (1976): 17–24. Nobel lecture. Also available from http://nobelprize.org/nobel_prizes/chemistry/laureates/1975/.

"Why Natural Products?" *Croatica Chemica Acta* 58 (1985): 349–351. Concerning the continuing value of investigating natural products.

"Fons et Origo." In *Euchem Conference on Stereochemistry Bürgenstock, Switzerland, 1965–1989,* edited by Monica and Rolf Scheffold. Aarau, Switzerland: Sauerländer, 1989. Concerning the Bürgenstock Conference.

My 132 Semesters of Chemistry Studies. Translated from the German by Otto Theodor Benfey and David Ginsburg. Washington, DC: American Chemical Society, 1991. A 120-page scientific autobiography with 114+ references, covering most of the work described above. The author is indebted to Prelog's book for much of the information contained in this article.

"My 'Nomenclature Years.'" In *Organic Chemistry: Its Language and Its State of the Art,* edited by M. Volkan Kisakürek. Weinheim, Germany: VCH, 1993.

OTHER SOURCES

Arigoni, Duilio; Jack D. Dunitz; and Albert Eschenmoser. "Vladimir Prelog." *Biographical Memoirs of Fellows of the Royal Society* 46 (2000): 443–464.

"In Memoriam Vlado Prelog." *Chimia* 53 (1999): 123–162. Includes a tribute by Albert Eschenmoser, a transcript of a 1988 German TV interview, and a complete list of Prelog's 423 references.

"Inauguration der Prelog Vorlesung" [Inauguration of the Prelog Lectureship]. *Chimia* 40 (1986): 389–393.

Jones, J. Bryan, and John F. Beck. "Asymmetric Syntheses and Resolutions Using Enzymes." In *Applications of Biochemical Systems in Organic Chemistry. Part I,* edited by J. Bryan Jones, Charles J. Sih, and David Perlman. New York: Wiley, 1976. See pp. 287–355 for the work of Prelog and collaborators.

Kauffman, George B. "In Memoriam Vladimir Prelog (1906–1998): Some Personal Reminiscences." *The Chemical Educator* 3, no. 2 (1998): 9 pp.

Kaufman, Teodoro S., and Edmundo A. Rúveda. "The Quest for Quinine: Those Who Won the Battles and Those Who Won the War." *Angewandte Chemie International Edition* 44 (2005): 854–885.

Mislow, Kurt. "Vladimir Prelog." *Proceedings of the American Philosophical Society* 144 (2000): 106–111.

Seeman, Jeffrey I. "The Woodward-Doering/Rabe-Kindler Total Synthesis of Quinine: Setting the Record Straight." *Angewandte Chemie International Edition* 46 (2007): 1378–1413.

"Surprise Festschrift in Honor of Professor Vladimir Prelog." *Croatica Chemica Acta* 69, no. 2 (1996): 379–739.

Woodward, Robert B. "Strychnine." *Journal of the American Chemical Society* 69 (1944): 2250.

———, and William E. Doering. "The Total Synthesis of Quinine." *Journal of the American Chemical Society* 66 (1944): 849; 67 (1945): 860–874.

Ernest L. Eliel

PRICE, DEREK JOHN DESOLLA (*b.*
Leyton [a London suburb], United Kingdom, 22 January 1922; *d.* London, 3 September 1983) *history of science, science of science, science policy.*

A prolific and influential writer and thinker of the 1960s and 1970s, Price made pioneering contributions to the history of science and scientific instruments, the sociology of science and the science of science, and science policy. His two PhDs, one in physics, one in the history of science, gave his work added authority in both scientific and nonscientific circles.

Early Years. Derek Price was the son of Philip Price, a tailor, and Fanny Price (née deSolla), a singer. As a youth, Derek delighted in making models and studying mathematics. He was particularly captivated by clockwork mechanisms and by all kinds of gear-train-driven machines. After secondary school he became a laboratory assistant in physics at South West Essex Technical College, Essex, Greater London, during which time he became thoroughly familiar with the construction of scientific instruments. When World War II broke out, he taught physics classes eight hours each day in South West Essex Technical College and studied part time, obtaining a BSc in physics and mathematics from the University of London (External) in 1942. (An "external" degree is one offered to students who did not attend the university but participated under its external program.) As a research assistant and part-time lecturer, he continued his studies, receiving his PhD in physics, again from the University of London (External), in 1946. He pursued mathematical physics at Princeton University as a Commonwealth Fund Fellow in 1946–1947. From 1947 to 1950 he was a lecturer in applied mathematics at Raffles College of the University of Malaya in Singapore (later the University of Singapore).

In Singapore, Price made a serendipitous discovery that led him to formulate the idea that scientific knowledge grows exponentially, a finding he announced at the Sixth International Congress of the History of Science at Amsterdam in 1950. Price had taken the university's recently obtained volumes of the *Philosophical Transactions* of the Royal Society into custody for safekeeping, but in later perusing them, he noticed that when the volumes were in chronological order, they grew in size so rapidly as to suggest that science grew exponentially. His perusal of the volumes also stimulated a deep interest in the history of science, and from 1950 to 1954 he studied that subject at Cambridge University in England, receiving a PhD in 1954. He published his first book in 1953, an edition of a medieval manuscript, titled *An Old Palmistry*, and also worked on instruments at the Whipple Museum of the History of Science. During his thesis research he found a

manuscript that proved to be *Equatorium of the Planetis*, written by Geoffrey Chaucer in the fourteenth century. In 1955 Price published an edition of the work with scholarly commentary. In 1955 and 1956 he prepared a catalog of the scientific instruments of the British Museum.

Move to America. In 1957 Price was invited to the United States as a consultant for planning what became the Smithsonian's National Museum of American History in Washington, D.C. After two years as a visiting fellow at the Institute for Advanced Study at Princeton University in New Jersey during 1958–1959, where he studied theoretical physics and the history of ancient astronomy, Price went to Yale University in the fall of 1959 as a visiting professor. In 1960 he was made professor in the newly created Department of the History of Science and Medicine. His book *Science since Babylon* followed in 1961, and he obtained the endowed Avalon Chair for the History of Science in 1962. Price remained at Yale for the rest of his life, the bulk of his more than two hundred articles and reviews and fourteen books being published during his tenure there. From the late 1950s to the early 1970s, the history of science and technology research field enormously, stimulated by new discoveries and technologies and by the Cold War and the space race. That period of unparalleled growth and interest constituted an optimistic context for Price's research.

Work in Science Studies. Price's approach to studies of the epiphenomena of scientific activity was largely quantitative, but his contributions to the sociology of science, science policy, and the interrelations between science and technology were broadly social-historical in orientation. His passion for scientific instruments fueled his interests in the history and nature of technology and his desire to create a theory of just how technology and science related to each other.

Price's quantitative approach led him to fundamental contributions in scientometrics, helping him to create, shape, and direct studies in that field, which he termed the science of science. His book *Little Science, Big Science* (1963) is a classic foundational work in the field. It summarized his quantitative researches and detailed the exponential growth of scientific papers, journals, and review journals; the mathematical distribution of scientific papers among authors (the number of authors publishing more than n papers is proportional to $1/n$); and the negative effects of world wars on scientific (but not technological) productivity. He went on to create what he called the immediacy factor and to investigate the half-life of citations, helping to distinguish "hard" from "soft" science and "hot" from "cold" research.

Price's early use of data listing journal-to-journal citations led to preliminary maps of the structure of scientific fields. His classic "Networks of Scientific Papers" (1965) graphically depicted the research front of science and demonstrated the existence, by citation analysis, of "classic" and "review" papers, whose functions were, respectively, to identify key contributions and to serve as surrogate citations for blocks of research papers. "Collaboration in an Invisible College" (1966), coauthored with Donald deB. Beaver, showed that many collaborative authors never contributed more than a fraction of a paper's worth of research in their careers and suggested that collaboration could in part be an ad hoc response to a researcher shortage. It also traced the developing collaborative structures of a subfield of science over five years and illustrated its gradual evolution into two distinct research traditions.

One of Price's later provocative researches showed that the rank order of a country's share of global wealth correlated highly with its rank ordered shares of the world literature in physics and chemistry, suggesting that pure research in science had tangible economic benefits. That work led to analyses of national research and development expenditures, showing that an increasing threshold for supporting internationally competitive research existed, a threshold that few countries could afford across the whole range of scientific research. In that connection he developed a technique for estimating the cost of production of one scientific paper, enabling comparisons among different scientific fields.

Not all was theory. For example, Price advised and encouraged Eugene Garfield in the creation of the Science Citation Index of the Institute of Scientific Information (ISI)—now part of the widely used and influential ISI Web of Knowledge of Thomson Scientific—not only in the natural sciences, but also the social sciences, art, and the humanities. Furthermore, in the early 1970s, Price testified at hearings before congressional committees on matters of science and technology policy.

Nearly all of Price's quantitative measures and patterns were relevant to the sociology of science, in particular to the influential functionalist and meritocratic version developed by the then-leading sociologist of science, Robert K. Merton of Columbia University. For example, Price's and others' work on cumulative advantage related closely to Merton's classic paper on "The Matthew Effect" (1966). That is, the more research a scientist has done that is recognized to be significant, the more visibility and recognition accrues, which improves the researcher's access to funding and collaborators.

Price's work on patterns of scientific collaboration outlined a normal pattern of creation, growth, and splitting apart of collaborative groups of researchers. Based on

his studies of scientific productivity, Price also developed a model of types of contributors to the formal scientific literature—continuants, intermittents, and transients—their proportions, and the sizes of their contributions. He also suggested the significance of a continuing tradition of informal "invisible colleges" of researchers for helping to communicate ideas and structure research projects.

Instruments and Technology. Price's most significant contributions to the history of science came in his studies related to scientific instruments, beginning with his collaborative work with Joseph Needham and Wang Ling on *Heavenly Clockwork: The Great Astronomical Clocks of Medieval China* (1960). Then came his reconstruction of the Tower of the Winds in "The Tower of the Winds—Piecing Together an Ancient Puzzle" (1967) and his astrolabe catalog with Sharon Gibbs and Janice Henderson (1973). The Tower of the Winds is a 12-meter tall octagonal building built between the mid-second and mid-first centuries BCE and located on the Roman agora in Athens. Each of its eight faces represents a wind, and has a sundial; originally there was a water clock inside.

Price's *Gears from the Greeks* (1974) elucidated the Antikythera mechanism, a compact, gear-driven, astronomical computing device from about 90 BCE. This work helped change views about the technological sophistication and prowess of the classical world. Throughout Price's career he remained fascinated with clockwork, and he published nearly annually on various types of clocks from different historical periods and nations. His interest extended naturally from clocks to automata, which he characterized as attempts to model the universe (inorganic nature, via astronomical clocks and gear-train computers) and to model life (organic nature, via gear-work figures). He suggested that the recurrent drive to create automata provoked technical improvements in clock making and gear-train design.

Again and again Price returned to the puzzle of the natures of science and technology and the relationship between them. He began to develop a theory challenging the conventional model that science led to technology, which thus impacted society. Instead, he stressed the counterflow of ideas from technology to science, arguing that, in particular, scientific instruments drive science's development just as significantly as science affects technology's. Price was convinced that the personal and ideational links between scientific and technological development were relatively few but extremely strong, and he used as examples of connecting links sixteenth- and seventeenth-century instrument makers and peripatetic nineteenth-century mechanics and engineers.

One of the more important articulations of his ideas came in his "Ups and Downs in the Pulse of Science and

Technology" (1978), in which he argued that the real Scientific Revolution, and the sustained exponential growth of fundamental research, did not take place in the seventeenth century, as commonly held, but was instead a nineteenth-century phenomenon, related to the burgeoning Industrial Revolution. Another was his last exposition of his theory, in a speech titled "Of Sealing Wax and String," delivered as the George B. Sarton Memorial Lecture of the American Association for the Advancement of Science in May 1983.

Later Career. Price's eclectic diversity and critical approaches to conventional wisdom were hallmarks of his career, leading some members of the Society for Social Studies of Science to suggest, in contemplation of creating an annual award in his name, that it be given to the author of outstanding "maverick" contributions. Price's substantial body of scholarship continues to influence science studies, as witnessed annually by the *Social Sciences Citation Index.*

In the 1970s Price began to receive formal recognition of his scholarship. Prominent among his awards were the Leonardo da Vinci Medal from the Society for the History of Technology (1976) and the John Desmond Bernal Award from the Society for Social Studies of Science (1981). Price was especially pleased with his election as a foreign member to the Royal Swedish Academy of Sciences, because he hoped that at last he would get to know how the Nobel Prizes winners are really determined—but unfortunately his death, the result of a heart attack, intervened.

BIBLIOGRAPHY

The Webster Institute for the History of Astronomy at the Adler Planetarium and Astronomy Museum, 1300 South Lakeshore Drive, Chicago, IL 60605, has nine boxes of papers by or relating to Price; collected papers and other documents are also to be found at the Centre de Recherche en histoire des sciences et des techniques, cité des sciences et de l'industrie, 75930 Paris, cedex 18, France. Silvio Bedini, "Eloge," Annali dell'Istituo e Museo di Storia della Scienza 9 (1984): 95–115, contains a bibliography of Price's publications.

WORKS BY PRICE

An Old Palmistry. Cambridge, U.K.: Heffer, 1953.

The Equatorie of the Planetis. Cambridge, U.K.: Cambridge University Press, 1955.

With Joseph Needham and Wang Ling. *Heavenly Clockwork: The Great Astronomical Clocks of Medieval China.* Cambridge, U.K.: Cambridge University Press, 1960.

Science since Babylon. New Haven, CT: Yale University Press, 1961.

Little Science, Big Science. New York: Columbia University Press, 1963.

"Networks of Scientific Papers." *Science* 149 (1965): 510–515.

With D. deB. Beaver. "Collaboration in an Invisible College." *American Psychologist* 21, no. 11 (November 1966): 1011–1018.

"The Tower of the Winds—Piecing Together an Ancient Puzzle." *National Geographic Magazine* 131 (1967): 586–596.

The Difference between Science and Technology. Detroit, MI: Thomas Alvin Edison Foundation, 1968.

"Citation Measures of Hard Science, Soft Science, Technology, and Nonscience." In *Communication among Scientists and Engineers,* edited by Carnot E. Nelson and Donald K. Pollock. Lexington, MA: Heath Lexington Books, 1970.

With Sharon L. Gibbs and Janice Henderson. "A Computerized Checklist of Astrolabe." Distributed privately by the Department of History of Science and Medicine, Yale University, New Haven, CT, 1973.

Gears from the Greeks: The Antikythera Mechanism, a Calendar Computer from ca. 80 BC. Philadelphia: American Philosophical Society, 1974.

With Ina Spiegel-Rösing, eds. *Science, Technology, and Society: A Cross-Disciplinary Perspective.* London: Sage Publications, 1977.

"Ups and Downs in the Pulse of Science and Technology." *Sociological Inquiry* 48 (1978) 162–171.

"Of Sealing Wax and String." *Natural History* 93 (January 1984): 48–56.

OTHER SOURCES

Beaver, Donald deB. "Eloge: Derek John deSolla Price (22 January 1922–3 September 1983)." *Isis* 76, no. 3 (September 1985): 371–374.

Bedini, Silvio, "Eloge." *Annali dell'Istituo e Museo di Storia della Scienza* 9 (1984): 95–115.

Merton, Robert K. "The Matthew Effect in Science." *Science* 159 (5 January 1968): 56–63.

Yagi, Eri, Lawrence Badash, Donald deB. Beaver. "Derek J. De S. Price (1922–1983): Historian of Science and Herald of Scientometrics." *Interdisciplinary Science Reviews* 21, no. 1 (1996): 64–84.

Donald deB. Beaver

PRIGOGINE, ILYA (*b.* Moscow, Russia, 25 January 1917, *d.* Brussels, Belgium, 28 May 2003), *chemistry, irreversible thermodynamics.*

Prigogine was awarded the 1977 Nobel Prize "for his contributions to non-equilibrium thermodynamics, particularly the theory of dissipative structures." His investigations into the origins of irreversibility in nature laid the groundwork for many important advances in nonlinear dynamics and complexity in the second half of the twentieth century.

Early Development. Prigogine, whose childhood years were marked by a spatial odyssey across Europe, occasioned by the Russian Revolution, was to spend most of his adult life probing the nature of motion through time. The son of Roman Prigogine, a chemical engineer, and Julia Wichman Prigogine, a conservatory student, the young Prigogine, accompanied by his parents and his older brother Alexander, arrived in Belgium by way of Lithuania and Berlin at the age of twelve and soon became fascinated by history, literature, archaeology, and particularly music. His skills at the keyboard were to provide a source of satisfaction and relaxation throughout his life. After much hesitation, he finally enrolled as an undergraduate in the chemistry curriculum at the Université Libre de Bruxelles, but his wide-ranging intellectual interests, notably in philosophy, continued to influence his scientific trajectory.

Inspired by his mentor at the university, Théophile de Donder, Prigogine became obsessed with understanding the nature of irreversible processes, or what he was later to refer to as "the arrow of time," a term apparently coined by Arthur Eddington (*The Nature of the Physical World*, 1929, p. 68). Classical thermodynamics, from the time of Rudolf Julius Emanuel Clausius, focused on the properties of systems at, or at least very near to, equilibrium, where the entropy is a maximum and is therefore constant. Prigogine and de Donder characterized this limited view as "thermostatics," and noted that in order to comprehend real, as opposed to ideal, natural processes, one has to deal with the entropy-producing phenomena that occur far away from equilibrium and that had been shunned by most physicists, chemists, and engineers as "parasitic," "transitory" phenomena of marginal importance. In any actual process, Prigogine and de Donder argued, what is significant and interesting is what is changing in time and cannot be undone. In 1945, four years after receiving his doctoral degree from the Université Libre, Prigogine formulated the theorem of minimum entropy production, which describes nonequilibrium stationary states, and noted its significance in relation to the most important far-from-equilibrium systems: living organisms.

Dissipative Structures. Prigogine recognized the limitations of his theory of minimum entropy production, particularly for chemical kinetics. Minimum entropy production holds only for the linear branch of irreversible phenomena, that is, for systems not too far from equilibrium, where the Onsager reciprocal relations are valid. In many reacting systems of interest this is not the case, because they are so far from equilibrium that only the forward reaction is relevant; the reverse reaction is negligible. To deal with such systems, Prigogine, with the aid of his colleague Paul Glansdorff, formulated the notion of "dissipative structures," stable ordered states that can emerge

Ilya Prigogine. © PIERRE VAUTHEY/CORBIS SYGMA.

from less ordered states when a system is sufficiently far from equilibrium. By virtue of their distance from equilibrium, these states are able to maintain their order by dissipating energy to the environment. Such states typically develop via fluctuations of increasingly larger magnitude, and fluctuations played a major role in Prigogine's thinking about temporal evolution. In his Nobel Lecture, he characterized the formation of a dissipative structure in the following terms: "A new supermolecular order appears that corresponds basically to a giant fluctuation stabilized by exchanges of energy with the outside world."

Although Prigogine and Glansdorff first considered dissipative structures in the context of hydrodynamics, the years during which they developed the approach, 1947 to 1967, saw some remarkable developments in the study of reaction-diffusion systems, and these eventually provided the most important applications of the theory. In 1952 Alan Turing wrote a seminal paper titled "The Chemical Basis of Morphogenesis," in which he showed that in an appropriate set of chemical reactions whose components diffuse with the proper rates, stable, stationary, spatially periodic structures can arise spontaneously from an initially homogeneous steady state. These dissipative structures, now known as Turing patterns, spawned a cottage industry of theoretical biologists and others in fields from chemistry to geology to economics, who formulated models for pattern formation of various kinds using Turing's approach and, implicitly, Prigogine's dissipative structure idea. The existence of Turing patterns was not demonstrated experimentally until 1990, when Patrick De Kepper and collaborators carried out a study of the reaction of chlorite, iodide, and malonic acid in a gel. Nonetheless, in the intervening four decades, scientists were confident of the scientific basis for Turing structures in large measure because of the power of Prigogine's theory.

A second instance of the application of dissipative structures involves the discovery of oscillating chemical reactions. While it is obvious that any living system contains chemicals whose concentrations increase and decrease periodically, the accidental discovery in 1921 by William Bray of a reaction between hydrogen peroxide and iodide, in which the concentration of iodine undergoes regular increases and decreases, did little to convince a skeptical chemical community that such behavior could occur in a beaker. The vast majority of chemists, perhaps driven by a kind of vitalism, were convinced that the second law of thermodynamics forbade concentration oscillations in a chemical reaction. In fact, the majority of papers written about the Bray reaction until the 1960s are devoted to attempts to discredit Bray's result. When Boris Belousov serendipitously found a second chemical oscillator in 1958, he was unable to publish his experimental results in a peer-reviewed journal because the referees insisted that his observations contradicted the second law of thermodynamics. Over the following decade, the combination of further experimental work by Anatol Zhabotinsky and the theoretical underpinning provided by the theories of nonequilibrium thermodynamics and dissipative structures convinced the scientific community that the phenomenon was indeed genuine. In the early twenty-first century, the Belousov-Zhabotinsky oscillating reaction serves as the prototype system for a field known as nonlinear chemical kinetics, and the spatiotemporal structures the reaction generates provide insights into a variety of chemical and biological pattern formation phenomena. Prigogine and his student René Lefever also formulated a simple model, now referred to as the Brusselator, which gives rise to a striking wealth of spatial and temporal dissipative structures, including periodic concentration oscillations and Turing patterns.

The Brusselator model consists of four elementary reactions:

$$A \rightarrow X$$
$$B + X \rightarrow Y + D$$
$$2X + Y \rightarrow 3X$$
$$X \rightarrow E$$

where A and B are usually considered to be reactants whose concentrations are maintained constant, and the system is maintained far from equilibrium either by removing D and E as soon as they are produced or by neglecting all reverse reactions. The beauty of this model, whose complexity arises from the trimolecular, autocatalytic third step, is that with the above assumptions it has only two variable concentrations, X and Y, and can therefore be analyzed in great detail using a variety of powerful mathematical tools. The trimolecular step as written is unlikely to arise as a result of simple molecular collisions, but, as Prigogine and his star pupil, Grégoire Nicolis, pointed out, the same kinetics can arise as the result of a sequence of, for example, enzymatic reactions (Nicolis and Prigogine, 1977, p. 94).

Prigogine saw the variety of the universe, and particularly of life, as arising from irreversibility and dissipative structures far from equilibrium. Perhaps in the spirit of Lev Tolstoy's observation that all happy families resemble one another, while each unhappy family is unhappy in its own way, he wrote, "The laws of equilibrium are universal. However, far from equilibrium the behavior may become very specific. This is of course a welcome circumstance, because it permits us to introduce a distinction in the behavior of physical systems which would be incomprehensible in an equilibrium world" (Frängsmyr, 1993, p. 270). The classical view of irreversible processes is that they increase entropy and hence lead to disorder. The concept of dissipative structures reveals that irreversible processes can, in fact, create order. Irreversible processes make life possible.

Further Contributions. Prigogine was a prolific author, not only of research papers, but also of books. His early works were written as textbooks or scientific monographs, focused on such subjects as irreversible thermodynamics and statistical mechanics. He addressed traditional problems in physical chemistry, such as developing theoretical models for liquids, although even as early as 1971 he applied his ideas to more complex, human problems in *Kinetic Theory of Vehicular Traffic*, written with Robert Herman. The two-fluid theory, adapted from the kinetic theory of gases, which Prigogine and Herman proposed, remains one of the three main approaches to modeling traffic flow.

In 1977 Prigogine and Nicolis wrote their chef d'oeuvre, *Self-Organization in Nonequilibrium Systems,* in which they laid out how systems could spontaneously self-organize without violating the second law of thermodynamics. The work was important primarily because it created an intellectual framework for understanding how temporal and spatial patterns could arise. Ironically, few scientists have employed Prigogine's approach to nonequilibrium thermodynamics directly in addressing real systems, but his work provided a solid theoretical foundation that made the study of such systems a respectable scientific enterprise.

As is often the case with major figures in science, in his later years Prigogine turned his attention increasingly to more global questions. In 1986 he published a quasi-popular book with Isabelle Stengers called *La Nouvelle alliance*, which was published in English as *Order Out of Chaos*. A more technical work, *From Being to Becoming*, had appeared in 1980. In these volumes Prigogine sought to come to terms with the question that had vexed him all his life—how can we understand the arrow of time? He was fond of saying, "We do not grow young!" But systems, as he had shown, can do more than decay as they approach equilibrium. He once said to one of the authors of this article, "Rome did not just decline—it also rose." He had demonstrated that increases in order and complexity do not contradict thermodynamics, as many before him had thought.

What bothered him was that the arrow of time was not to be found in classical theories. The fundamental laws of physics—Newtonian mechanics, Maxwell's equations of electrodynamics, quantum mechanics—are all time-reversible, meaning that one can substitute $-t$ for t and the equations remain unchanged. If these laws were all that governed nature, the arrow of time would be an illusion, as many scientists, including Einstein, believed. However, consistent with human experience, the phenomenological laws that describe irreversible processes such as heat and mass diffusion do not remain unchanged by a substitution of $-t$ for t. If one puts a drop of red ink into a beaker of water, one ends up with a beaker of pink water; the reverse transition never occurs. In his lectures at the University of Texas at Austin, where he spent three months a year in his Center for Studies in Statistical Mechanics, Prigogine would explain how a movie showing a temperature gradient being spontaneously created (without any chemical reactions) would tell the viewer that the movie was being played backwards. An observer can tell which way the video should be played because there is an intrinsic arrow of time. The arrow of time, Prigogine believed, is as fundamental as the existence of time itself, and he sought to reconcile this idea with the underlying laws of physics, even if it meant turning traditional theories on their head and thinking of mechanics as an approximation in a world that is ultimately irreversible.

In his later years, Prigogine became increasingly concerned with the role of time in quantum mechanics and with the related issue of the interplay between dynamics and thermodynamics. He saw a kind of complementarity between dynamics, based on knowledge of individual trajectories, which are reversible, and thermodynamics, where entropy, which can only increase in time, plays the key role. He argued that the key lay in recasting some of the fundamental equations describing mechanical systems in such a way that key operators, in particular the Liouville operator, are no longer represented by unitary transformations. In this way, the time reversal symmetry is broken, and a single trajectory for a system is no longer an observable. Irreversibility and the second law then emerge in a much more fundamental way. Whether Prigogine's reformulation of some of the most basic laws of physics will ultimately be accepted as successfully reconciling the apparent inconsistencies between dynamics and thermodynamics remains a matter of some controversy, much as the first expositions of his earlier ideas about the importance of irreversible processes were met with considerable skepticism.

Prigogine's Milieu. Prigogine was a true citizen of the world, and his contributions were recognized time and again. He was a member of more than a dozen national academies and received more than forty honorary degrees. In addition to the 1977 Nobel Prize, he received the Solvay Prize in 1955, the Rumford Gold Medal of the Royal Society in 1976, and the Honda Prize in 1983, along with many other international awards. He was a major figure in the development of an integrated approach to scientific research in Europe during the 1980s, stressing the need to encourage unconventional ideas and approaches, which he referred to as "hopeful fluctuations." He was keenly interested in the phenomenon of globalization, seeing it as an analog of long distance communication in nonliving systems, about which he wrote, "matter in equilibrium is blind, and it communicates over short distances over a short time. Matter out of equilibrium begins to see" (1989, p. 399). In addition to his professorship at the Université Libre in Brussels, he directed the International Solvay Institutes of Physics and Chemistry from 1959 to 2003 and was a professor in the Physics Department at the University of Texas in Austin, where he spent increasing portions of his time at his Ilya Prigogine Center for Studies in Statistical Mechanics, Thermodynamics and Complex Systems after his mandatory retirement from Brussels in 1987. For many years, his department in Brussels attracted those seeking to understand complex behavior in physical and biological systems, and some of the brightest minds in the world were drawn to the department, both as students and as visitors.

Prigogine's ideas provided a framework for many of the key developments in late-twentieth-century science, from chaos theory to self-organization, but his views were by no means universally accepted. Perhaps because it challenged some of the most revered figures in science, perhaps because he attempted to apply it so widely (another scientist once condescendingly remarked about the work coming out of Brussels, "A theory of everything is a theory of nothing"), Prigogine's vision often evoked heated controversy, and he knew it. He once told a prospective postdoctoral student to consider working on a safer topic, because "Research is like horse betting, interesting return is with the outsiders, but there is high risk to lose everything."

Prigogine and his first wife, Helene Jofé, had a son, Yves, in 1945. His second marriage, to Marina Prokopowicz in 1961, produced a son, Pascal, in 1970. In 1981 he was awarded hereditary nobility and the title of viscount by the king of Belgium. What drove Prigogine throughout his extraordinary life and scientific career is perhaps best summed up in these lines from the poet Kahlil Gibran: "Time has been transformed, and we have changed; it has advanced and set us in motion; it has unveiled its face, inspiring us with bewilderment and exhilaration" (Gibran, *The Vision*, London: Penguin, 2004, p. 29).

BIBLIOGRAPHY

A complete bibliography can be found in Ilya Prigogine's Is Future Given?*, cited below.*

WORKS BY PRIGOGINE

Structure, Dissipation and Life. Amsterdam: North-Holland, 1969.

With Paul Glansdorff. *Thermodynamic Theory of Structure, Stability and Fluctuations.* New York: John Wiley and Sons, 1971.

With Grégoire Nicolis. *Self-Organization in Nonequilibrium Systems: From Dissipative Structures to Order through Fluctuations.* New York: Wiley Interscience, 1977.

Autobiographie. Brussels: Florilège des Sciences en Belgique II, 1980.

From Being to Becoming. San Francisco: W. H. Freeman, 1980.

"The Philosophy of Instability." *Futures* 21 (1989): 396–400.

With Isabelle Stengers. *The End of Certainty—Time, Chaos, and the New Laws of Nature.* New York: Free Press, 1997.

With Dilip Kondepudi. *Modern Thermodynamics, from Heat Engines to Dissipative Structures.* Chichester, U.K.: John Wiley and Sons, 1998.

Is Future Given? River Edge, NJ: World Scientific Press, 2003.

OTHER SOURCES

Castets, Vincent, Etienette Dulos, Jacques Boissonade, et al. "Experimental Evidence of a Sustained Standing Turing-Type Nonequilibrium Chemical-Pattern." *Physical Review Letters* 64 (1990): 2953–2956.

Frängsmyr, Tore, ed. *Nobel Lectures in Chemistry, 1971–1980.* Singapore: World Scientific, 1993.

Kovac, Jeffrey. "Ilya Prigogine, 1977 Nobel Laureate." In *Nobel Laureates in Chemistry 1901–1992,* edited by Laylin K. James. Washington, DC: American Chemical Society and Chemical Heritage Foundation, 1993.

Turing, Alan M. "The Chemical Basis of Morphogenesis." *Philosophical Transactions of the Royal Society of London Series B-Biological Sciences* 237 (1952): 37–72.

Irving R. Epstein
John A. Pojman

PRIMAKOFF, HENRY (*b.* Odessa, Russia, 12 February 1914; *d.* Penn Valley, Pennsylvania, 25 July 1983), *condensed matter physics, nuclear physics, high-energy physics.*

Primakoff made major contributions to the theoretical physics of condesnsed matter and to nuclear and high energy physics. The so-called Primakoff effect deals with a method for determining the short lifespan of the meson from photoproduction. His name is also associated with topics as varied as spin waves in ferromagnetism, and the underwater propagation of shock waves. In addition, Primakoff was an expert on the manifestations of weak interaction phenomena in nuclei, such as double beta decay, muon capture, and neutrino scattering.

Youth. Henry Primakoff was born in Odessa in 1914. Through his mother, Primakoff was descended from a large, assimilated Jewish family of merchants who had lived in Odessa for several generations. Through his father, Henry came from a Greek Orthodox family of wealth and prestige, who banished Henry's paternal grandfather and father from the family estate for marrying Jews.

Primakoff's father, a doctor, was wounded while serving in the Russian army in World War I and died in 1919. About two years later, Henry's mother and her parents decided to leave Russia and join an uncle who had settled in New York. This required escaping across the nearest border into Romania, trudging for long night hours through woods, and hiding by day in remote farmhouses. After a long and difficult odyssey, including a long wait in Bremen before obtaining passage to the United States, they finally arrived in New York in 1922. Henry became a U.S. citizen in 1930.

The family settled in the Bronx where Primakoff learned English. He also learned, the hard way, that some four-letter words should be used with discretion. He excelled in high school where he took an active interest in politics and journalism, becoming editor of the school paper one year and class president another. He was offered scholarships to Harvard and Columbia; he chose to begin his freshman year at the latter, in the fall of 1931.

Education. His initial interests at Columbia were writing and philosophy. Primakoff's focus did not shift to science until he was a junior and to physics only in the middle of that year. He was one of a handful of students who constituted an informal club to study special relativity from Richard Tolman's *Relativity, Thermodynamics and Cosmology* (1934). Club members who went on to distinguished careers in physics include Norman Ramsey, Nobel laureate; Herbert Anderson, student and longtime collaborator of Enrico Fermi and codiscoverer of the (3,3) resonance in meson-nucleon scattering; Robert Marshak, coinventor of the universal (V-A) form of weak interactions and founder of the Rochester conferences in high energy physics; and Arthur Kantrowitz, former director of the Avco Everett Research Laboratory. Primakoff spent his senior year at Columbia taking graduate courses; in one laboratory course he met his future wife Mildred Cohn. Pursuing her own career in science, she would become a very distinguished chemist, particularly known for the application of nuclear magnetic resonance to biochemistry.

Primakoff's graduate studies began at Princeton. In those days there was little financial aid. With help from his family and money either saved from his undergraduate scholarships, or earned from various odd jobs, Primakoff managed to pay Princeton's tuition (about $100) and support himself for a year. Then he obtained a fellowship at New York University, where he earned his PhD in 1938. He married Mildred Cohn in May of that year.

Overview of Career. Despite the Depression, they both found jobs, Cohn in the Biochemistry Department of Cornell Medical School in New York and Primakoff first at Brooklyn Polytechnic Institute and then at Queens College. After Pearl Harbor he began to work on a navy project concerned with sonar and submarines. When asked by J. Robert Oppenheimer, Primakoff declined to join the Manhattan Project on the grounds that he wanted to work on projects for the present war and not the next one. He thought an atomic bomb could not be built in time, and was greatly surprised by the news of Hiroshima.

At the end of World War II, Primakoff took a joint physics and mathematics position at NYU, but a year later Arthur Hughes and Eugene Feenberg persuaded Primakoff to join the physics faculty of Washington University in Saint Louis. Cohn found work in Carl Cori's department at the medical school, so in 1946 they moved to Saint Louis, Missouri.

In 1959 Primakoff and Cohn, by now equally established scientists, were offered appointments at the University of Pennsylvania. Before that job offers had been to one with the promise of something for the other; then Penn offered appointments to both Primakoff and Cohn. They accepted, Primakoff becoming the first Donner Professor of physics at Penn and Cohn eventually receiving a chair in biochemistry. They were both elected to the National Academy of Sciences, Primakoff in 1968 and Cohn in 1971. Primakoff remained active in teaching and research at Penn until his death from cancer in 1983.

Early Research with Holstein. Primakoff's first published research paper (1937) was on the force between protons and neutrons due to the exchange of neutrino-electron pairs in the then new Fermi theory of beta decay. It was a prophetic choice of topic because after the war Primakoff, as already mentioned, devoted a great deal of attention to weak interactions in nuclei.

While still a graduate student, he began possibly the best known paper that he wrote, certainly the best known in what is now called condensed matter physics. While he and fellow student Theodore Holstein investigated the field dependence of the intrinsic magnetization of a ferromagnet at low temperatures, they had the ingenious idea of expressing the spin operators that appear in the Heisenberg exchange interaction model in terms of boson creation and annihilation operators. With appropriate approximations, which turned out to be equivalent to approximations used by Felix Bloch and by C. Møller in a very different and less complete treatment of the problem, they were able to diagonalize the Hamiltonian, including magnetic interactions as well as the exchange and dipole-dipole interactions.

Their essential idea was that, though the magnetic moments of most of the atoms in the ferromagnet line up with the external magnetic field, temperature agitation will always cause a few to deviate from complete alignment. Holstein and Primakoff used the boson transformation to demonstrate that the spin deviations were not localized on a particular atom, but propagated through the crystal as spin waves. Spin waves, originally proposed by Bloch, are now regarded as the principal modes of excitation of ferromagnets, and in recent years they have even entered nuclear theory.

Although this paper has become a classic, scientists did not recognize its importance until several years after the end of the war. Its impact began to be felt when in 1945 Oxford physicist James H. E. Griffiths discovered ferromagnetic resonance effects of unusually large frequency compared with the Larmor precession of electron spin in a magnetic field. Charles Kittel, then at MIT, gave a classical interpretation of the anomaly in 1947 and a year later Dirk Polder, of Bristol, derived the Kittel formula using quantum mechanics. Polder's derivation used the Holstein-Primakoff method for describing the quantum mechanical states of a ferromagnet and the corresponding energy eigenvalues. Subsequently, Kittel and Joaquin Luttinger used an "ingenious but somewhat devious method" (quoted by Rosen, 1995, p. 273) to calculate directly the ferromagnetic resonance frequencies from one term in the appropriate Hamiltonian. Holstein and Primakoff's paper received its due recognition once the relevance of quantum mechanics to ferromagnetism became firmly established.

Even though the Holstein-Primakoff transformation was a seminal contribution to theories of ferromagnetism and anti-ferromagnetism in the 1950s, and remained famous, it is interesting to note that neither Holstein nor Primakoff ever worked on this subject again.

War Research. Although Primakoff did not participate in the Manhattan Project, he did do some research relevant to the Bikini underwater tests of nuclear weapons. There was concern at the time that the test could set off a powerful tidal wave that would cause serious destruction in the Pacific basin. Applying methods Geoffrey I. Taylor had used for shock waves in air, Primakoff found a simple, exact solution for the problem in water at high energy and showed that the properties of a shock wave, including its height, are all determined solely by its energy. Known by some authors as the Primakoff wave, the result was never published in the open literature, but Richard Courant and Kurt O. Friedrichs (1948) describe and attribute it to Primakoff.

With his Washington University colleague Eugene Feenberg Primakoff coauthored a paper on collapsed nuclei; it anticipated ideas developed many years later by Tsung-Dao Lee and Gian Carlo Wick to study superdense matter. They also wrote on the interaction of cosmic-ray primaries with starlight and sunlight, showing that cosmic ray primaries should consist mainly of protons because energetic electrons would undergo too much scattering from photons in intergalactic space (through the inverse Compton effect) to reach the vicinity of the Earth. Primakoff's publications on muon decay, muon capture, and hypernuclei also evoked considerable interest. In a seminal paper, in collaboration with Sergio DeBenedetti, C. E. Cowan, and Wilfred R. Konneker, Primakoff derived the basic formulas for the angular distribution of photons from positron annihilation in solids; it is still quoted today. During this period he also first wrote on the so-called Primakoff effect and on double beta decay.

Double Beta Decay. Double beta decay takes place extremely slowly, being in a certain sense a succession of two ordinary nuclear beta decays, but it is important for fundamental questions regarding the neutrino. If the neutrino has a mass, and if it is its own antiparticle, then it is possible for double beta decay to take place without the emission of neutrinos in the final state; the neutrino emitted in the first ordinary beta decay is reabsorbed in the second. With the advent of the standard model for particle physics, the study of neutrino properties has become important for the new physics.

In the 1930s Maria Goeppert-Mayer, Ettore Majorana, Giulio Racah, and Wendell Furry had studied double beta decay. In 1959 Primakoff and Peter Rosen published a significant review article that formed a bridge between the earlier work and the important developments brought about by the discovery of parity nonconservation and the two-component neutrino in the late 1950s. For many years it was a standard reference as well as providing a useful starting point for the modern developments in double beta decay of the 1980s.

Primakoff Effect. At Penn Primakoff extended his work from 1951 on the photoproduction of the neutral pion in the electric field of the nucleus. The essential point of this paper, which has come to be known as the Primakoff effect, is that, under certain well-defined kinematic conditions, the photoproduction of neutral pions is controlled by exactly the same interaction as the decay of the pion into two photons. As a consequence the lifetime of the meson, which is difficult to measure directly, can be deduced from measurements of photoproduction, an easier task. With C. M. Andersen and Arthur Halprin, he applied this approach to the lifetime of the newly discovered eta meson, a pseudoscalar meson such as the neutral pion, and to the production of vector mesons. The Primakoff effect is now the standard method of measuring neutral meson lifetimes, of use as well for obtaining limits on the existence of conjectured but still undiscovered neutral mesons such as the axion. It also features prominently in astrophysics, providing a means of estimating some non-trivial stellar cooling mechanisms.

Muon Capture. At Penn, Primakoff continued to work on weak interactions. With the introduction of the universal V-A interaction for all four-fermion weak interactions in 1958, Primakoff had realized that the rate for muon capture in nuclei (the second leg in the Puppi triangle connecting different weak phenomena) would be sensitive to the hyperfine splitting of the parent atom. Jeremy Bernstein, T. D. Lee, and Chen Ning Yang had independently made the same discovery and they invited Primakoff to be a coauthor. Afterwards he developed an extensive theory of muon capture in nuclei, which culminated in the elementary particle treatment put forward by C. W. Kim and himself, relying upon the use of the Goldberger-Treiman relation in complex nuclei. At the same time Primakoff examined with P. Dennery and Joseph Dreitlein rare decays of the muon, the relationship between the decays of charged and neutral Sigma hyperons, and semileptonic decays of K-mesons. With Ephraim Fischbach and other students he investigated parity-violating nuclear forces, a topic that reached back to his very first paper.

In 1969 Primakoff and Rosen returned to the problem of double beta decay. When Primakoff was asked by colleagues at the time whether the smallness of the observed neutrino masses implied or at least strongly suggested their masses were zero, he would calmly reply one should not prejudge the result; experiment would settle the matter. He wisely pointed out that what seemed natural today might not appear so in a few years. Primakoff and Halprin went on to realize that heavy Majorana neutrinos could also give rise to no-neutrino double beta decay, and in collaboration with Peter Minkowski, showed that the existing limits on the process gave rise to a lower bound on the masses of such heavy neutrinos of several times the proton mass. This is entirely consistent with the seesaw model proposed by Murray Gell-Mann, Pierre Ramond and Richard Slansky and by Tsutomu Yanagida.

Later Research Interests. While always keeping a close eye on the experimental results of the day, Primakoff was also interested in broader and fundamental questions in many areas that touch physics. Toward the end of his life he wrote a review of baryon number and lepton number conservation with Rosen, a speculative paper on the chirality of electrons from beta decay and the origin of left-handed asymmetry of proteins with Alfred K. Mann and a note on testing the Pauli principle with R. D. Amado.

Primakoff was much loved as a teacher and colleague. He was encyclopedic in his knowledge and lavish in giving his time to the most senior colleague or the most junior student. For many years he taught at Penn a unique course that helped prepare graduate students for the PhD preliminary exam. Its central feature was that students would ask him questions on any subject; he would then patiently and systematically provide the answer, exploring its ramifications and extensions as he calmly worked out the solution.

Primakoff was very careful and complete in what he said and what he wrote. His lecture style and research notes were remarkable for their rococo notation and their aesthetic sense. A page would be filled with equations moving in all directions, sometimes moving back on themselves, with side remarks carefully annotating the symbols and arrows elegantly indicating the sequence in which they should be studied. At Penn pages of these handwritten research notes were the centerpieces of an art show and many colleagues still have these notes framed on their walls.

BIBLIOGRAPHY

WORKS BY PRIMAKOFF

With M. H. Johnson. "Relations between the Second and Higher Order Processes in the Neutrino-Electron Field Theory." *Physical Review* 51 (1937): 612–619.

With T. Holstein. "Field Dependence of the Intrinsic Domain Magnetization of a Ferromagnet." *Physical Review* 58 (1940): 1098–1113.

With E. Feenberg. "Possibility of 'Conditional' Saturation in Nuclei." *Physical Review* 70 (1946): 980–981.

With E. Feenberg. "Interaction of Cosmic-Ray Primaries with Sunlight and Starlight." *Physical Review* 73 (1948): 449–469.

With S. DeBenedetti, C. E. Cowan, and W. R. Konneker. "On the Angular Distribution of Two-Photon Annihilation Radiation." *Physical Review* 77 (1950): 205–212.

"Photo-Production of Neutral Mesons in Nuclear Electric Fields and the Mean life of the Neutral Meson." *Physical Review* 81 (1951): 899.

"Angular Correlation of Electrons in Double Beta-Decay." *Physical Review* 85 (1952): 888–890.

With W. Cheston. "'Nonmesonic' Bound *V*-Particle Decay." *Physical Review* 92 (1953): 1537–1541.

With J. Bernstein, T. D. Lee, and C. N. Yang. "Effect of the Hyperfine Splitting of a μ-Mesonic Atom on Its Lifetime." *Physical Review* 111 (1958): 313–315.

With S. P. Rosen. "Double Beta Decay." *Reports on Progress in Physics* 22 (1959): 121–166.

"Theory of Muon Capture." *Reviews of Modern Physics* 31 (1959): 802–822.

With A. Sher. "Approach to Equilibrium in Quantal Systems: Magnetic Resonance." *Physical Review* 119 (1960): 178–207.

With C. M. Andersen and A. Halprin. "Determination of the Two-Photon Decay Rate of the η Meson." *Physical Review Letters* 9 (1962): 512–516.

With A. Sher. "Approach to Equilibrium in Quantal Systems. II. Time-Dependent Temperatures and Magnetic Resonance." *Physical Review* 130 (1963): 1267–1282.

With C. W. Kim. "Application of the Goldberger-Treiman Relation to the Beta Decay of Complex Nuclei." *Physical Review* 139 (1965): B1447–B1463.

With C. W. Kim. "Theory of Muon Capture with Initial and Final Nuclei Treated as 'Elementary' Particles." *Physical Review* 140 (1965): B566–B575.

With A. Halprin and C. M. Andersen. "Photonic Decay Rates and Nuclear-Coulomb-Field Coherent Production Processes." *Physical Review* 152 (1966): 1295–1303.

With S. P. Rosen. "Nuclear Double-Beta Decay and a New Limit on Lepton Nonconservation." *Physical Review* 184 (1969): 1925–1933.

With Wen-Kwei Cheng, Ephraim Fischbach, Dubravko Tadić, and Kenneth Trabert. "Experimental Evidence from Parity-Forbidden α Decay for the Presence of Noncanceling Seagull and Schwinger Terms in Weak (Nucleon → Nucleon + Vector-Meson) Amplitudes." *Physical Review D* 3 (1971): 2289–2292.

With B. Goulard. "Relation between the Energy-Weighted Sum Rules for Nuclear Photoabsorption and Nuclear Muon Capture." *Physical Review C* 11 (1975): 1894–1898.

With A. Halprin, P. Minkowski, and S. Rosen. "Double-Beta Decay and a Massive Majorana Neutrino." *Physical Review D* 13 (1976): 2567–2571.

With A. K. Mann. "Neutrino Oscillations and the Number of Neutrino Types." *Physical Review D* 15 (1977): 655–665.

With John N. Bahcall. "Neutrino-Antineutrino Oscillations." *Physical Review D* 18 (1978): 3463–3466.

With H.-Y. P. Hwang. "Theory of Radiative Muon Capture with Applications to Nuclear Spin and Isospin Doublets." *Physical Review C* 18 (1978): 414–444.

With C. W. Kim. "Nuclei as Elementary Particles in Weak and Electromagnetic Processes." In *Mesons in Nuclei*, edited by Mannque Rho and Denys Wilkinson, vol. 1. Amsterdam: North-Holland Publishing Company, 1979.

With R. D. Amado. "Comments on Testing the Pauli Principle." *Physical Review C* 22 (1980): 1338–1340.

With A. K. Mann. "Weak Neutral Currents." In *Encyclopedia of Physics*, edited by Rita G. Lerner and George L. Trigg. Reading, MA: Addison-Wesley Pub. Co., 1981.

With A. K. Mann. "Chirality of Electrons from Beta-Decay and the Left-Handed Asymmetry of Proteins." *Origins of Life and Evolution of the Biosphere* 11, no. 3 (1981): 255–265.

With S. P. Rosen. "Baryon Number and Lepton Number Conservation-Laws." *Annual Review of Nuclear and Particle Scien*ce 31 (1981): 145–192.

OTHER SOURCES

Courant, Richard, and Kurt O. Friedrichs. *Supersonic Flow and Shock Waves.* New York: Springer-Verlag, 1976.

"Henry Primakoff Dead at 69; Professor of Science at Penn." *New York Times,* 28 July 1983.

Rosen, S. P. "Henry Primakoff: February 12, 1914–July 25, 1983." *Biographical Memoirs,* vol. 66. Washington, DC: National Academy of Sciences, 1995. This *DSB* entry relies heavily on this memoir.

Tolman, Richard. *Relativity, Thermodynamics and Cosmology.* Oxford: Clarendon Press, 1934.

R. D. Amado
Gino Segrè

PROSCHOLDT, HILDE

SEE **Mangold, Hilde**.

PTOLEMAIS OF CYRENE (*fl.* between the third century BCE and the first century CE), *history of science, musical theory, musical education.*

Ptolemais, whose biographical data are completely unknown to scholars, was the author of a handbook on musical theory titled *Pythagorean Elements of Music,* of which only few fragments—quoted by Porphyry of Tyre in his *Commentary on the Harmonics of Ptolemy*—survive. She is the only female musicologist known from classical antiquity and despite the title of her work it seems not to be a manifesto of the Pythagorean doctrine, but to refer to the various traditions of inquiry in harmonic science with no polemic intention.

On her life there is no information at all, except for her place of origin (thanks to the ethnic adjective *Kyrenaia* quoted by Porphyry). Porphyry neither remarked on her being a woman, nor about her activity or cultural context, but from her name it can be inferred that she was not active before the Ptolemaic era (that is, at the beginning of the Hellenistic period, when this sort of name became popular). A *terminus ante quem* may be deduced from what is known about another musical theorist quoted in the same passage of the *Commentary,* Didymus, who lived in the first century CE and was presumably Porphyry's source for quoting Ptolemais. He may have come across her writings thanks to his connections with the scholars of Alexandria. Because of the title of her treatise and because of the quite common presence of women philosophers among Pythagoreans (even if her name is not included in the list of Pythagorean women drawn up by Iamblichus in his *Life of Pythagoras*), scholars identified Ptolemais as a follower of neo-Pythagoreanism, whose culmination can be dated in the first imperial age. Therefore a dating around the early first century CE is the most reasonable for her chronological setting, although it cannot be given for certain.

Ptolemais's treatise was written in the form of question and answer (like another similar work, the *Introduction to the Art of Music* by Bacchius), therefore perhaps intended as a typical school text of the imperial age. However, its destination is unknown. According to the fragments quoted by Porphyry, her main interest was to draw an outline of the various traditions of inquiry in harmonic science (the study of the elements out of which melody is built) comparing them by reference to their methodologies. The most striking contrast among them was the preference given to perception (*aisthesis*) or reason (*logos*) as starting points of musical investigation. The practice of comparing schools of harmonic theory by reference to the status assigned by each to perception and to reason was quite common in Hellenistic and later times. In contrast to what is known from other sources—which describe a sharp division between these two approaches known as the empirical and the Pythagorean—Ptolemais described several shades between these two extremes.

Among Pythagoreans, for instance, she distinguished the *kanonikoi* and the *mathematikoi*. The *kanonikoi* (who, according to her, did not derive their name from the instrument called the *kanon,* as some people think, but from "straightness," the science through which reason discovers what is correct) agree to accept perception as a guide for reason at the outset. The *mathematikoi,* instead, from the very beginning of their musical inquiry adopt theoretical principles such as the fact that intervals are in ratios of numbers (hence the definition of the postulates of *kanonike* as lying both within the science concerned with music and within that concerned with numbers and geometry. Among empiricists, she separated the *mousikoi,* that is the harmonic theorists who, despite beginning from perception, applied themselves to a theoretical science based in thought, from the *organikoi,* who gave no thought at all to theory. It is interesting to notice Ptolemais's use of the word *harmonikoi,* which simply came to mean a theorist who has something to do with the harmonic science (instead of being the technical name to mean the empiricists, as it is in most of Greek theoretical sources), and the unusual usage of the term *mousikoi* intending the empiricists, this is sign of a lexical unlikeness among the different traditions in musical theory.

One of the most interesting passages among her fragments is the one in which she depicted the intellectual figure of Aristoxenus of Tarentum, the greatest musical authority of the ancient world, an Aristotelian pupil who studied the musical phenomena trying to infer the theoretical principles and laws governing them. According to Ptolemais, in his musical inquiry he "accepted both perception and reason in the same way, as being of equal power [...] for what is perceived cannot be constituted by itself apart from reason, and neither reason is strong enough to establish anything without taking its starting points (*archai*) from perception, and delivering the conclusion of its theorising (*theorema*) in agreement with perception once again" (Ptolemais, third extract, transl. Barker, 1989, p. 241). Despite the Pythagorean orientation of her handbook, it is clear that she described Aristoxenus in an honest and historically reliable way without the distortions typical of some limited followers who transformed him into a pure champion of scientific empiricism (while his real purpose was that of creating a theoretical science, *theoretike episteme,* concerning audible *melos*). Thus Ptolemais's work, despite its form of simple school handbook, displays a quite remarkable critical insight, at least in the part that survives.

A further passage in Porphyry's treatise includes Ptolemais among those theorists who did not make any distinction between the notions of *isotonia* (uniformity of pitch) and *homophonia* (unison). These ideas were later on differentiated by Ptolemy in his *Harmonics.*

BIBLIOGRAPHY

WORKS BY PTOLEMAIS OF CYRENE

Porphyrios Kommentar zur Harmonielehre des Ptolemaios. Edited by Ingemar Düring. Göteborg, Sweden: Elanders, 1932. Reprint, New York: Garland, 1980. The most recent critical edition of Porphyry's Greek text that includes Ptolemais's fragments.

Greek Musical Writings. Vol. 2, *Harmonic and Acoustic Theory.* Edited by Andrew Barker. Cambridge, U.K.: Cambridge University Press, 1989. It includes the English translation of Ptolemais's fragments.

OTHER SOURCES

Barker, Andrew. "Greek Musicologists in the Roman Empire." In *The Sciences in Greco-Roman Society,* edited by Timothy D. Barnes, 53–74. Edmonton, Canada: Academic Printing and Publishing, 1994.

———. "Ptolemaïs." In *The Oxford Classical Dictionary,* edited by Simon Hornblower and Antony Spawforth. Oxford: Oxford University Press, 1996.

Düring, Ingemar. *Ptolemaios uns Porphyrios über die Musik.* Göteborg, Sweden: Elanders, 1934. Reprint, New York: Garland, 1980.

Harmon, Roger. "Ptolemais [2] aus Kyrene." In *Der Neue Pauly. Enzyclopadie der Antike* 10, edited by Hubert Cancik and Helmuth Schneider. Stuttgart, Germany: Metzler, 2001.

Moretti, Gabriella. "Tolomeide di Cirene. Musicologa dell'antichità." *Kleos* 9 (2004): 123–152.

Rocconi, Eleonora. "Un manuale al femminile: l'*Introduzione Pitagorica alla musica* di Tolemaide di Cirene." In *Ars/Techne. Il manuale tecnico nelle civiltà greca e romana,* edited by Maria Silvana Celentano. Alessandria, Italy: Edizioni dell'Orso, 2003.

Thesleff, Holger. *The Pythagorean Texts of the Hellenistic Period.* Abo, Finland: Abo Akademi, 1965.

Ziegler, Konrat. "Ptolemais [3]." In *Real-Enzyklopädie der klassischen Altertumswissenschaft* 23, no. 2 (1959): 1867–1868.

Eleonora Rocconi

PTOLEMY (OR CLAUDIUS PTOLEMAEUS) (*b. c.* 100 CE; *d. c.* 170 CE), *mathematical sciences, especially astronomy.* For the original article on Ptolemy see *DSB,* vol. 11.

Doubts were raised in the original *DSB* article about Ptolemy's authorship of two works attributed to him in the manuscript tradition: the *Canobic Inscription,* which purports to be a transcription of a list of astronomical parameters that Ptolemy had erected at Canopus in Egypt in 146/147 CE (not 147/148 as stated in *DSB*), and *On the Criterion* (or "On the Faculties of Judgment and Command"). Subsequently, N. T. Hamilton brilliantly vindicated the authenticity of the *Canobic Inscription* and showed that the version of Ptolemy's parameters that it presents preceded the *Almagest* (Hamilton, Noel Swerdlow, and Gerald Toomer). Thus the *Almagest* must have been completed more than five years after the latest dated observation (2 February 141) that it reports.

The demonstration rests on a passage in Book Four of the *Almagest* in which Ptolemy described a method that he said he had formerly used to derive a correction to the Babylonian period relation for the Moon's motion in latitude that he had inherited from Hipparchus. Hamilton showed that by applying this repudiated method to two eclipse observations that Ptolemy used for other purposes in the *Almagest*, one obtains exactly the latitudinal periodicity in the *Canobic Inscription*. Ptolemy made several other changes in his system between the *Canobic Inscription* and the *Almagest*, including the eccentricity of Mercury, the epicycle radius of Saturn, and the latitudinal models and visibility criteria for the planets. It is noteworthy that Ptolemy continued to tinker with the Mercury model and the theories of planetary latitude and visibility in the later *Handy Tables* and *Planetary Hypotheses*, whereas in most other matters the *Almagest* had the last word. The final section of the *Canobic Inscription* lists the fixed stars, planets, Sun, Moon, and the four terrestrial elements (fire and air, water and earth) in descending order of distance from the center, and associates with each a whole number representing a musical pitch. This scheme, which had more to do with supposed astrological than with astronomical relations among the heavenly bodies, was apparently the one set out in the lost final three chapters of Book III of the *Harmonics*, a fact that suggests that the *Harmonics* may well have been an early work in Ptolemy's career.

The philosophical monograph *On the Criterion* has been dismissed by some competent scholars as a slight and probably spurious work, but it shares many stylistic habits with Ptolemy's accredited writings, and most decisively contains vocabulary that occurs practically nowhere else in the surviving corpus of Greek literature. Its basic argument (leaving aside some strikingly materialistic speculations about the interaction of the soul and body in its final section) is that the soul grasps truth about existing things using two of its faculties: sense perception, which communicates perceived attributes of things to the intellect, and reason, which through comparison and generalization yields knowledge of the essence of the things. Sense perception is thus necessary but not sufficient for scientific knowledge. Each faculty is reliable when operating in isolation on its proper objects, but they lose trustworthiness when they combine to make more complex judgments. Nevertheless, empirically grounded and appropriately generalized apprehensions of the reason constitute reliable knowledge. Surprisingly, in the light of Ptolemy's other

works, the *Criterion* does not discuss this epistemological model in the light of specific scientific problems, nor is there any serious discussion of the perception and analysis of the quantitative relations, which are fundamental to his approaches to astronomy, harmonic theory, and (to a lesser extent) optics. It is tempting to see the work as a juvenile exercise.

Scientific Epistemology in the *Harmonics*. Although its project, the mathematical modeling of the numerous systems of pitches employed by Greco-Roman musicians, may in the early twenty-first century appear parochial and even wrong-headed, the *Harmonics* deserves a prominent rank in Ptolemy's oeuvre because of its philosophically assured articulation of approaches to scientific epistemology that he applied with less overt rationalization elsewhere, especially in the *Almagest*. As in the *Criterion*, he started by accepting that reason and sense perception—in the present case, hearing—are necessary means of judging truth. But in place of a simplistic one-way relationship between the sense faculties and the intellect, the opening chapters of the *Harmonics* argue for the necessity of applying recursive strategies in which reason, initially informed by simple and "manifest" facts reported by the senses, guides sense perception by setting up the conditions of observation to minimize or eliminate errors of judgment resulting from the imperfect capacity of the senses to perceive quantities.

Thus without invoking any measurements or precise observations, Ptolemy argued on the basis of a wide range of broad empirical facts that musical pitches are essentially fixed magnitudes, and hence intervals between pitches have to be modeled as ratios, indeed ratios of whole numbers as in the Pythagorean harmonic theory. The theorist's problem, then, is to determine what ratios correspond to what intervals, taking into account certain universal perceptions. These perceptions are that pitches separated by certain intervals (e.g. the octave, fifth, and fourth) are "concordant," that is, have a high degree of likeness, and that a wider variety of smaller intervals are "melodic," that is, heard as appropriate, esthetically acceptable, steps in the scales in which musicians sing or tune their instruments. Recognizing that the senses are *par excellence* reliable in identifying the phenomenon of concordance, reason devises an experimental apparatus, the single-stringed *kanôn*, or monochord, in which a tensed string can be divided accurately by a bridge into sections in simple whole number ratios such as $1:2$, $2:3$, and $3:4$. All that is required of the hearing is to confirm that the pitches produced by these divisions are in concordant intervals. This leads to the next stage of modeling, in which rules governing the kinds of ratios producing concordance are devised according to criteria that are partly aprioristic. But the rules *must* be consistent with the elementary and uncontroversial facts about concordant intervals, and it is in this respect that the Pythagorean harmonic theory was methodologically unsound.

Ptolemy continued in this vein, progressively refining the models in the light of simple empirical judgments that are themselves only meaningful when interpreted according to the constraints that the models impose. A landmark stage along the way is the end of Book I, the point at which Ptolemy worked out a set of rules constituting a model for the acceptable ways in which the *tetrachord* (interval of a fourth) can be subdivided into melodic intervals. This model finds its empirical confirmation in the opening chapter of Book II. Here Ptolemy described a *tour de force* experiment in which pairs of tetrachords are tuned in specified ways by a musician, so that the scientist-auditor can logically deduce all the constituent ratios on the basis of hearing whether a particular note of one tetrachord is higher, lower, or indistinguishable from a particular note of the other tetrachord. Through this experiment Ptolemy showed that the set of distinct tetrachords conforming to his model can be matched roughly one to one to the set of tunings actually employed by musicians. Subsequently, he constructed systems of ratios comprising complete scales of tuning from these building blocks, and again he invited the reader to see a close correspondence between these theoretically predicted scales and the ones in actual use.

In the *Almagest* Ptolemy applied this same strategy of progressive refinements and confirmations to the problem of establishing models for the motions of the heavenly bodies, though without explaining or defending the epistemological approach. The basic model structure appropriate for each body is justified in terms of simple, minimally quantitative empirical assertions. For example, the fact that the Sun takes a longer time to go from minimum apparent speed to mean speed than from mean to maximum speed determines that the Sun's model involves either an eccenter or an epicycle such that the Sun revolves on the epicycle in the reverse direction to the epicycle's revolution around the Earth. The model is then quantified in stages by a mathematical analysis of specific observations that are chosen to isolate elements of the model and render them reliably perceptible.

Almagest Observations and Calculations.

Much of the *Almagest*'s impressiveness as a work of scientific writing consists in its presentation of a systematic route of deduction of practically all the elements of the mathematical models of the heavenly bodies, with generalized empirical phenomena, and, above all, specific dated observations appearing to provide the starting points for an ostensibly rigorous mathematical analysis. This logical structure turns out to be largely artificial, in that some of the reports

Ptolemy. *Engraving of Ptolemy.* DR. JEREMY BURGESS/PHOTO RESEARCHERS, INC.

of observations can be shown to have been tampered with, if not simply fabricated, and some of the calculations based on observations incorporate significant arithmetical inaccuracies, in both cases for the purpose of obtaining a preconceived result with apparent exactitude.

The longest recognized, and still the most irrefutable, instances of falsified observations in the *Almagest* are the four dates and times of equinoxes and solstices that Ptolemy says that he determined "with the greatest accuracy" by means of measurements of the Sun's altitude at its meridian crossings (*Almagest* I 1, 4, and 7), and on which his solar theory ostensibly depends. Ptolemy reported these times with implausible precision to the nearest hour, and they are all about a day too late. And yet they agree within a fraction of an hour with the times one would predict by using Ptolemy's tropical year to extrapolate from the older observations of Hipparchus and Meton that Ptolemy paired with them to establish his tropical year. Either Ptolemy simply fabricated these observations or, after making observations, he altered the times to obtain more exact correspondence between the empirical evidence and the theory. No one has found a plausible systematic cause for observing both kinds of equinox as well as summer solstices consistently a day late. (Incidentally, the large error in Ptolemy's times implies that in his time there was no extensive body of accurate solar observations.)

It has become more and more manifest that many others among the observations that Ptolemy claimed to have made are at the least adjusted to eliminate discrepancies between them and the theoretical parameters that Ptolemy derived from them. For example, if one repeats Ptolemy's iterative method of finding the eccentricities of the equant models for Mars, Jupiter, and Saturn (Book X, 7 and Book XI, 1 and 5) using exact calculations on Ptolemy's reported mean oppositions, one finds that they converge, within a minuscule fraction of a unit, on the round numbers that Ptolemy adopted (e.g., for Mars the procedure converges on an eccentricity of 12;0,0 sixtieths of the deferent's radius) (Duke, 2005, pp. 169–187). Again, the symmetries in the alleged observations of greatest elongations of Mercury and Venus from the mean Sun, from which Ptolemy derives the parameters of their models (Book IX 7–9, Book X 1–3), are much too exact to be genuine (Swerdlow, 1989). In one instance Ptolemy went so far as to present the reader, within a space of two pages, with two observations twenty-seven days apart that are *both* supposed to have Venus at greatest elongation as evening star, and for both observations the stated locations of Venus relative to nearby stars are about a degree further east than the planet really was on these dates. In general Ptolemy's practice was to determine each model relying on arguments or authorities that are *not* reported in the *Almagest*, and thereafter to construct a set of observation reports and a deductive argument from which the model can be proved logically on the hypothesis that these observations are true. It goes without saying that this practice, unhinted at in the text, makes the epistemological status of the *Almagest*'s demonstrations much less straightforward than they appear on the surface.

When deducing parameters on the basis of observation reports dating from before his time, Ptolemy often made arbitrary inferences from ambiguities in the reports, and discrepancies in the arithmetic of the mathematical analyses seem to be designed to force out a preordained result, facts that imply that he did not tamper with the wording of the reports themselves as he found them in his sources. He seems in fact to have extracted many of these reports from the theoretical works of his more immediate predecessors rather than from ancient collections of unanalyzed observations. It was to be expected that later astronomers would draw in the same way on the *Almagest* as a source of observations. Thus Ptolemy's introduction of factitious observation reports in company with genuine ones is open to severe criticism according to the standards of his own scientific practice.

Ptolemy's works in fields other than astronomy are less open to the kind of analysis that might reveal analogous manipulations of data. He quite openly used contrived calculations to obtain a figure of almost exactly 180° for the longitudinal extent of the known world in

Book I of the *Geography*. The tables of ostensibly observed angles of refraction corresponding to angles of incidence at ten degree intervals in *Optics* Book V are patently extrapolated from a very small genuine data set, because they exhibit constant second differences that are always precisely a small multiple of half a degree.

Context of Ptolemy's Astronomy. The demonstrable artificiality of many of Ptolemy's empirical deductions of his astronomical models means that one cannot take it for granted that the structures and parameters of the models were originally arrived at in the same way that Ptolemy proves them in the *Almagest*. Some elements of the models, in particular as the length of the tropical year and the size and direction of the solar eccentricity, are explicitly ascribed to Hipparchus, whereas Ptolemy said clearly that he himself found a few others by a stated route, among them the Moon's second anomaly, some of the mean motions of the Moon, and all the mean motions of the planets. There remain many elements for the discovery of which Ptolemy did not take credit unambiguously. Unfortunately the medieval manuscript tradition of Greco-Roman literature preserved no texts at all comparable to Ptolemy's, so that one is dependent on fragmentary and indirect sources for what is known of the background to his work and the extent to which the *Almagest* is the product of Ptolemy's own research.

One such source is the fragments of astronomical tables and texts in papyri from Greco-Roman Egypt, which are largely though not entirely an offshoot of the intense interest in astrology in the first four centuries of the common era. From them one learns that the most common means of making astronomical calculations for horoscopes and other astrological applications in Ptolemy's time were arithmetical methods descending from Babylonian astronomy, not at all resembling Ptolemy's tables with their geometrical and trigonometrical foundations. But non-Ptolemaic tables relating to geometrical models were also in current use, and it is particularly interesting to see tables reflecting solar models different from Hipparchus's, for example assuming a moving apogee and a latitudinal wobble. Ptolemy's adoption of Hipparchus's solar theory was not a simple matter of acquiescing in the only theory available.

The testimony of Indian astronomical texts is even more important, though not always easy to interpret. Extant Sanskrit writings on astronomy dating from the period after about 500 CE manifestly derive much of their contents from a transmission of Greek astronomy into India that must have taken place during the preceding three centuries. Part of this transmission consisted of the same arithmetical astronomy that is so well represented in the papyri, but the predominant part was based on geometrical modeling involving eccenters and epicycles, similar in general terms to Ptolemy's models but apparently showing no influences from his works. The numerical parameters of the Indian models are almost invariably different from Ptolemy's, and generally inferior in accuracy. Structurally the models reflect an understanding of astronomical phenomena and methods of computation that are not radically different from Ptolemy's. Most remarkably, algorithms for computing planetary positions are found in Indian texts that closely approximate the behavior of the equant model that Ptolemy assumed for all the planets except Mercury, a fact that casts some doubt on the widely held supposition that Ptolemy devised the equant model itself or that he discovered the inadequacy of a straightforward epicycle-and-eccenter model for the planets (Duke, 2005). Indian models for planetary latitude are nearer to the simpler (and more nearly correct) models that Ptolemy adopted in the *Planetary Hypotheses* than to those of Book Thirteen of the *Almagest*.

The existence of the *Canobic Inscription* proves that Ptolemy took a degree of personal credit for the parameters of his celestial system, taken as a whole, and the inscription, like the *Almagest*, was originally seen by contemporaries who had access to the astronomical literature that subsequently perished. With few exceptions these parameters are the most accurate examples from antiquity, and it is reasonable to maintain that part of Ptolemy's achievement as an astronomer consisted in the refinement of methods of calibrating geometrical models. His claim to have discovered the Moon's second anomaly is not contradicted by any evidence known as of 2007, but broadly speaking it would be a mistake to attribute to him every fundamental innovation in astronomical modeling that had been made since Hipparchus. For his own part, Ptolemy seems to have set more value in establishing a tight logical structure connecting theory with observation, and his complaint about his predecessors is not primarily that their hypotheses were incorrect but that they failed to prove them.

SUPPLEMENTARY BIBLIOGRAPHY

WORKS BY PTOLEMY

Berggren, J. Lennart, and Alexander Jones. *Ptolemy's Geography: An Annotated Translation of the Theoretical Chapters.* Princeton, NJ: Princeton University Press, 2000.

Hübner, Wolfgang. *Claudii Ptolemaei Opera quae exstant omnia,* III, 1, *ΑΠΟΤΕΛΕΣΜΑΤΙΚΑ.* Leipzig: Teubner, 1998. Supersedes the previous editions of Boll and Boer and of Robbins.

Lejeune, Albert. *L'Optique de Claude Ptolémée.* Leiden, Germany: Brill, 1989. Includes a French translation of the work.

Liverpool-Manchester Seminar on Ancient Greek Philosophy. "On the Kriterion and the Hegemonikon." In *The Criterion of Truth,* edited by P. Huby and G. Neal. Liverpool, U.K.:

Liverpool University Press, 1989. Revision of Lammert's edition of the *Criterion* with numerous textual improvements and an English translation.

Morelon, Regis. "La Version arabe du *Livre des hypothèses* de Ptolémée." *Mélanges de l'Institut dominicain d'études orientales* 21 (1993): 7–85. Critical edition and French translation of the Arabic text of the whole of Book One of the *Planetary Hypotheses.*

Solomon, Jon. *Ptolemy: Harmonics.* Leiden, Germany: Brill, 2002.

Stückelberger, Alfred, Gerd Grasshoff, et al., *Klaudios Ptolemaios: Handbuch der Geographie.* Basel: Schwabe, 2006. The first edition of the entire work since Nobbe's inadequate 1843–1845 text.

Toomer, James Gerald, trans. *Ptolemy's Almagest.* London: Duckworth, 1984. Reprinted with errata, Princeton, NJ: Princeton University Press, 1998. Annotated translation based on Heiberg's edition but incorporating numerous textual improvements derived from the Greek and Arabic manuscript traditions.

OTHER SOURCES

Anagnostakis, Christopher. *The Arabic Version of Ptolemy's Planisphaerium.* PhD diss., Yale University, 1984.

Aujac, Germaine. *Claude Ptolémée astronome, astrologue, géographe.* Paris: Comité des travaux historiques et scientifiques (CTHS), 1993.

Barker, Andrew. *Greek Musical Writings,* 2 vols. Cambridge, U.K.: Cambridge University Press, 1984–1989. Vol. 2 (pp. 270–391) contains an English translation of the *Harmonics.*

———. *Scientific Method in Ptolemy's Harmonics.* Cambridge, U.K.: Cambridge University Press, 2001.

Britton, John P. *Models and Precision: The Quality of Ptolemy's Observations and Parameters.* New York: Garland, 1992. A careful and judicious analysis of Ptolemy's solar and lunar observation reports and their relation to his models.

Duke, Dennis. "Ptolemy's Treatment of the Outer Planets." *Archive for the History of Exact Sciences* 59 (2005): 169–187.

Grasshoff, Gerd. *The History of Ptolemy's Star Catalogue.* New York: Springer, 1990. Refutes Vogt's often-cited statistical argument that the *Almagest's* star catalogue is independent of Hipparchus' positional data as represented by his *Commentary on Aratus and Eudoxus.*

Hamilton, Norman T., Noel M. Swerdlow, and Gerald J. Toomer. "The Canobic Inscription: Ptolemy's Earliest Work." In *From Ancient Omens to Statistical Mechanics: Essays on the Exact Sciences Presented to Asger Aaboe,* edited by J. Lennart Berggren and Bernard R. Goldstein. Copenhagen: University Library, 1987.

Jones, Alexander. *Ptolemy's First Commentator, Transactions of the American Philosophical Society,* 80 Part 7. Philadelphia: American Philosophical Society, 1990. A fragment of an early third century CE commentary on the *Handy Tables.*

———. *Astronomical Papyri from Oxyrhynchus,* 2 vols. in 1. Philadelphia: American Philosophical Society, Philadelphia, 1999. Papyrological evidence for the early reception of the *Handy Tables* among astrologers in Roman Egypt.

———. "A Likely Source of an Observation Report in Ptolemy's *Almagest.*" *Archive for History of Exact Sciences* 54 (1999): 255–258.

———. "Ptolemy's Canobic Inscription and Heliodorus' Observation Reports." *SCIAMVS: Sources and Commentaries in Exact Sciences* 6 (2005): 53–98.

———. "Ptolemy's Ancient Planetary Observations." *Annals of Science* 63 (2006): 255–290.

Kunitzsch, Paul. *Claudius Ptolemäus: Der Sternkatalog des Almagest*, 3 vols. Wiesbaden, Germany: Harrassowitz, 1986–1991. A fundamental contribution to knowledge of the catalogue's medieval transmission and influence.

Mogenet, Joseph, and Anne Tihon. *Le "Grand Commentaire" de Théon d'Alexandrie aux Tables Faciles de Ptolémée*, 3 vols. Vatican: Biblioteca Apostolica Vaticana, Vatican, 1985–1999.

Murschel, Andrea. "The Structure and Function of Ptolemy's Physical Hypotheses." *Journal for the History of Astronomy* 26 (1995): 33–61.

Neugebauer, Otto. *A History of Ancient Mathematical Astronomy*, 3 vols. Berlin: Springer, 1975. Book 1 is a detailed and penetrating mathematical commentary on the *Almagest.*

Newton, Robert R. *The Crime of Claudius Ptolemy.* Baltimore: Johns Hopkins University Press, 1975. A sustained attack on the veracity and originality of the *Almagest*, vitiated in part by uneven grasp of historical conditions and oversimplified probabilistic arguments, but the first work to show how pervasively the *Almagest* conceals the origins of its data.

Pedersen, Olaf. *A Survey of the Almagest.* Odense, Denmark: Odense University Press, 1974.

Simon, Gerard. *Le regard, l'être et l'apparence dans l'optique de l'Antiquité.* Paris: Seuil, 1988.

Smith, A. Mark. *Ptolemy's Theory of Visual Perception, Transactions of the American Philosophical Society* 86, Part 2. Philadelphia: American Philosophical Society, 1986.

———. *Ptolemy and the Foundations of Ancient Mathematical Optics, Transactions of the American Philosophical Society*, 89 Part 3. Philadelphia: American Philosophical Society, 1999.

Steele, John M. *Observations and Predictions of Eclipse Times by Early Astronomers.* Dordrecht, Netherlands: Kluwer, 2000.

———. "Ptolemy, Babylon and the Rotation of the Earth." *Astronomy and Geophysics* 46 (2005), 5.11–5.15.

Swerdlow, Noel. "Ptolemy's *Harmonics* and the 'Tones of the Universe' in the *Canobic Inscription.*" In *Studies in the History of the Exact Sciences in Honour of David Pingree*, edited by Charles Burnett, Jan P. Hogendijk, Kim Plofker, et al. Leiden, Germany: Brill, 2004.

———. "Ptolemy's Theories of the Latitude of the Planets in the *Almagest, Handy Tables*, and *Planetary Hypotheses.*" In *Wrong for the Right Reasons*, edited by Jed Z. Buchwald and Allan Franklin. Dordrecht, Netherlands: Springer, 2005.

Tihon, Anne. *Le "Petit Commentaire" de Théon d'Alexandrie aux Tables Faciles de Ptolémée.* Vatican: Biblioteca Apostolica Vaticana, Vatican, 1978.

———. "Théon d'Alexandrie et les *Tables Faciles* de Ptolémée." *Archives Internationales d'Histoire des Sciences* 35 (1985): 106–123. Demonstrates that Theon did not reedit the *Handy Tables.*

Alexander Jones

PURCELL, EDWARD MILLS (*b.* Taylorville, Illinois, 30 August 1912; *d.* Cambridge, Massachusetts, 7 March 1997), *physics, nuclear magnetism, radio astronomy, astrophysics, biological physics, physics education.*

Purcell was a complete physics professor. Through his research he helped originate nuclear magnetic resonance and radio astronomy. He won the Nobel Prize for Physics in 1952 for his magnetic resonance work. He was a gifted teacher, and throughout his professional career he devoted large blocks of time to his teaching responsibilities. He was active on his campus, in the physics community, and he served his nation in a variety of high-level advisory positions. He was a rare kind of man: he had no enemies, but an abundance of friends and admirers.

Early Influences. Purcell was born in the small farming town of Taylorville located in the middle of Illinois. His father, Edward A. Purcell, was raised on a farm and his education was limited. He was the manager of the independent local telephone company, and his son had access to the backroom of the telephone office where technical equipment was kept, as well as to the basement where discarded equipment was available. This treasure trove provided Purcell a ready source of wire, magnets, and other electrical components. His mother, Elizabeth Mills Purcell, a Vassar graduate with a Master of Arts degree in classics, taught high school Latin. Purcell's mother brought many books into the home and Edward took advantage of their presence. Literature and books were a familiar part of his childhood.

When Purcell was fifteen, his family moved sixty miles east to the small town of Mattoon where his father became the general manager of the Illinois Southeastern Telephone Company. The Illinois Southeastern, although not part of the Bell system, received the *Bell System Technical Journal*—which, because no one read it, Purcell's father brought home. This provided young Purcell, as he said in an interview with Katherine Sopka of the American Institute of Physics, "a glimpse into some kind of wonderful world where electricity and mathematics and engineering and nice diagrams all came together."

Purcell's future as an experimental physicist was portended in his high school physics class. He was given a problem: a rope ran from a seat up over a pulley at the top of a flagpole and back down to the seat. How hard would a man have to pull in order to move himself up the flagpole? Purcell and a classmate solved the problem and got the answer that he would have to pull with half his weight. The physics teacher, on the authority of the textbook, said since the pulley was fixed, the person would have to exert a pull equal to his weight. Purcell and his friend went home, hooked up a system of rope, pulley, and spring scales. Purcell, who weighed 120 pounds, started the experiment by pulling on the rope. When the scales reached 60 pounds, he started moving up. They ran back to the school to tell their teacher of their triumph.

Education. Upon completion of high school in 1929, Purcell went to Purdue University where he majored in electrical engineering. During his student days at Purdue, Karl Lark-Horovitz, a Viennese physicist with an international reputation, became head of the Purdue Physics Department and ultimately transformed a nondescript physics program into a respected department. In his junior year, Purcell signed up for an independent laboratory course offered in physics. Isador Walerstein assigned Purcell the task of examining some atomic spectra. To do this, Purcell had to assemble a spectrometer based on a long-unused Rowland grating. Following this project, Purcell built an electrometer to measure the half-life of a radioactive sample.

As a senior, Purcell continued independent research with a graduate student, H. J. Yearian. Purcell did an electron diffraction experiment and in the first photographic emulsion he developed, he saw Debye-Scherrer rings formed by the diffracting electrons. These independent projects gave Purcell a decisive push towards physics.

Purcell graduated from Purdue in 1933 with a degree in electrical engineering. He remained at Purdue the summer following graduation, continued his electron-diffraction research and wrote his first two papers based on the this work. Then, with the advice and the help of Lark-Horovitz, Purcell received an exchange-student fellowship to the Technische Hochschule in Karlesruhe, Germany. During his year in Germany, Purcell took physics courses and a range of other courses simply to improve his German.

On board ship en route for Germany, Purcell met Beth C. Busser, who was also an exchange student. She was headed to Munich to study German literature. Four years later, Beth and Edward were married in Cambridge, Massachusetts.

Purcell entered Harvard in the fall of 1934 as a graduate student in physics. In addition to courses in physics, Purcell took a complex variable course in the Mathematics Department and a course in cosmology taught by Alfred North Whitehead. It was a physics course in electric and magnetic susceptibilities taught by J. H. Van Vleck, however, that represented a turning point for Purcell. As a term problem, Van Vleck asked Purcell and the only other student in the course, Malcolm Hebb, to do a theoretical analysis of cooling by adiabatic demagnetization. Purcell and Hebb co-authored a paper that was the first significant paper on magnetic cooling, and it became a highly cited paper in the physics literature. Purcell has acknowledged that he came back again and again to the physics he learned in this term problem.

After Purcell "talked himself out of" his first thesis project, and demonstrated that his second thesis project was "hopeless," he then successfully completed a thesis under the direction of Kenneth T. Bainbridge. Bainbridge, a mass spectroscopist, was interested in focusing charged particles by means of electric and magnetic fields, and he suggested that Purcell consider the focusing properties of a spherical condenser (now called a capacitor). For his dissertation, Purcell studied this system experimentally and also analyzed it theoretically; he published his results in 1938.

When Purcell completed his dissertation, he moved seamlessly into the lowest-ranked faculty position at Harvard: instructor. In 1938, the cyclotron, first developed by Ernest O. Lawrence at the University of California seven years earlier, had become an important tool in the most prominent frontier of physics in the 1930s—nuclear physics. Bainbridge was building a cyclotron at Harvard and Purcell joined this effort; he developed methods to improve the homogeneity of the cyclotron magnets.

Wartime Work. The Harvard cyclotron became operational in 1939, but its future was not destined to be an academic research tool. Two dire situations changed everything. First, war had started in Europe and the Germans were conducting bombing raids over England. This put a stop to Purcell's Harvard research. Second, nuclear fission was discovered in 1939 in Germany, and it was quickly recognized that the nucleus held the potential for weapons of unprecedented destructive power. This ended the cyclotron's stay at Harvard, as it was needed for wartime research. Purcell went to the Massachusetts Institute of Technology (MIT) Radiation Laboratory; the Harvard cyclotron was disassembled, packed up, and shipped to a new location: Los Alamos, New Mexico.

The Radiation Laboratory at MIT began in October 1940 with the initial mission to develop microwave radar systems based on the magnetron, which had been developed in England. At the invitation of Isidor Isaac Rabi and Bainbridge, Purcell joined the Rad Lab, as it came to be called, in early 1941. Purcell quickly proved himself and became the leader of Group 41, the Advanced Development Group.

The magnetron, once called the most valuable cargo ever brought to the shores of the United States, emitted relatively high power microwaves with a wavelength of 10 centimeters. This wavelength made possible radar systems with sizes appropriate for mounting in aircraft. However, the immediate goal of Rad Lab leaders was to push to shorter wavelengths so that radar systems could become even more compact. Purcell's group was responsible for developing sources that emitted 3-centimeter microwaves and, later, 1.25-centimeter radiation.

In the testing phase of the newly developed 1.25-centimeter microwave sources in the spring of 1943, a curious and troubling thing happened. In a somewhat unpredictable fashion, the effective range of the 1.25-centimeter radar systems decreased considerably. It was soon recognized that the range of the radar beams decreased when the moisture content of the air was high. The explanation followed that water had two rotational quantum states separated perfectly to absorb the 1.25-centimeter radiation. Purcell did not know it at the time, but this experience would have a lasting influence on his future research.

The MIT Radiation Laboratory was closed when World War II ended in 1945; however, the work did not end for Purcell and a few others. Many electronic devices were invented and refined by the Rad Lab scientists during the war years. There were a few select industries, such as Bell Labs, that participated in the development. These microwave circuits were new and had the potential for many practical applications. Rabi, the associate director of the laboratory, ordered a book-writing program to put all the details of the government-sponsored radar work in the public domain so that everyone could have access to the information. Purcell, along with C. G. Montgomery and R. H. Dicke wrote Volume 8, *Principles of Microwave Circuits* (1948), of this twenty-seven-volume series. These books, "the Rad Lab series," became valuable references after the war, published by several different publishers over the years. Reprints of the Rad Lab books continued to sell into the 1990s—an amazing life of at least fifty years.

Academic Research. Purcell officially returned to Harvard in the fall of 1946. He returned as an associate professor of physics and was promoted to full professor in 1949. Purcell spent his entire professional academic career at Harvard University.

In his writing for the Rad Lab series, Purcell described the water absorption problem that he had encountered in 1943. As already stated, the radar beam was attenuated in moist air because two quantum states of water absorbed energy from the radar beam. Purcell liked this two-state quantum system, which he first encountered in his graduate work and again with the water-absorption problem. Purcell had also learned about Rabi's prewar molecular beam work and his discovery of magnetic resonance.

As the postwar writing period progressed, Purcell and two other physicists writing Rad Lab books, Henry C. Torrey and Robert V. Pound, went to lunch together. On the way to lunch, Purcell asked Torrey, a former Rabi student, about doing a Rabi-type resonance experiment—only in a solid instead of a gas. Torrey was skeptical, but upon reflection thought it might be possible.

During the evenings and on weekends in the fall of 1945, preparations were made at Harvard for doing an experiment designed to detect nuclear magnetic resonance in bulk matter. Pound, an electronic genius, designed the basic electronic equipment. A magnet was borrowed from Harvard physicist J. C. Street—the same magnet Street had used to obtain a photograph of a cloud-chamber track of a muon, which provided powerful early evidence for this new elementary particle. With this illustrious magnet and relatively simple electronic equipment, the experiment was ready to go in December.

Purcell bought paraffin wax at a local grocery store on his way to the laboratory where the experiment was set up. The paraffin, rich in hydrogen, was the sample they decided to use. Calculations were done by Torrey to determine the combination of radio-frequency radiation and magnetic field strength at which a nuclear resonance might occur. The resonant cavity, filled with paraffin, was designed to resonate at 30 megahertz. With the radio frequency fixed at 30 megahertz, a member of the Purcell team slowly varied the magnet current over the range from 65 to 80 amperes, which bracketed Torrey's calculated value. All the time they watched the output meter for evidence of a nuclear resonance absorption.

The experiment almost failed. On Thursday evening, December 13, Purcell, Pound, and Torrey swept back and forth through the magnetic field strength they had predicted would yield a resonance. They saw nothing. Early Friday morning, they stopped and planned to try again on Saturday afternoon.

When the Purcell team did their experiment, it was generally believed that the nuclear spin relaxation times would be very long. As Purcell said in his Nobel address, "this question [relaxation time] gave us much concern."

The nuclear relaxation time is the time required for the nuclear spins to come to thermal equilibrium with their environment. If this time is very long, it could make the nuclear magnetic resonance absorption impossible to observe, because the two nuclear spin states would have equal populations and there would be no net absorption. This long relaxation time was how they explained the failure of their first experiment. So Purcell arrived at the laboratory very early Saturday morning in order to turn on the magnet and allow many hours for the sample to come to equilibrium in the magnetic field.

By late Saturday afternoon, after many attempts to see the evidence of absorption, they were about to admit defeat and go home. Before shutting down, however, Pound suggested that they crank the magnet up to full strength and slowly decrease the current through the magnet and thereby decrease the magnetic field strength. In Pound's laboratory notebook, in Torrey's writing, are the words, "Dec. 15, 1945, proton resonance found at 83 amperes...." This magnet current was about 10 amperes larger than the expected resonance value of 73 amperes. In a letter dated 24 December 1946, they sent their results to the editor of *Physical Review*.

One month later, Felix Bloch and his group at Stanford, by a completely different experimental method, observed the proton resonance in a sample of water. Their methods were so conceptually different that when William Hansen, a member of Bloch's group, visited Purcell at Harvard, Purcell recalled that they talked for some time before they realized they were essentially doing the same thing.

After Purcell's discovery, a scientist from the DuPont chemical company visited Purcell and asked him if he saw any practical applications of his discovery. Purcell responded that he could see nothing practical coming from nuclear magnetic resonance. Later, he laughed about his response as his work was quickly followed by nuclear magnetic resonance (NMR), a powerful tool for chemists, and later, magnetic imaging became a powerful diagnostic tool for physicians.

For their discovery of nuclear magnetic resonance in bulk matter, Purcell and Bloch shared the Nobel Prize in Physics in 1952.

As already noted, the uncertainty that faced the Purcell team when they started the magnetic resonance experiment was the nuclear spin relaxation time. With their discovery, however, it was clear that the relaxation time was much shorter than had been predicted. (Purcell recalled later that when he had sat all Saturday morning hoping the spin system would equilibrate, he had the magnet on 10^8 seconds longer than necessary.) Nicolaas Bloembergen, a graduate student of Purcell, joined Pound and Purcell in experimental and theoretical work that resulted in the famous paper, "Relaxation Effects in Nuclear Magnetic Resonance Absorption" (1948), which explained the relaxation of nuclear spins. This paper, known as the BPP paper, established a record for the number of its citations.

The two-state system was the basis for Purcell's nuclear magnetic resonance experiment and still another two-state system awaited Purcell's attention. The transition between two hyperfine states of the ground state of the hydrogen atom has a wavelength of 21 centimeters. Purcell suggested to his graduate student, Harold I. Ewen,

Movement of spinning electrons. *Edward M. Purcell built this gyroscopic "bowling ball" to illustrate the complex movements of spinning electrons within an atom.* AP IMAGES.

that he look for radiation from this transition emitted by hydrogen atoms in interstellar space. With a horn antenna (mounted outside the window of Ewen's laboratory) as a detector, this transition was detected on 25 March 1951, and became the basis for mapping the Milky Way and other galaxies. After this discovery, radio frequency astronomy became an active area of research. The horn antenna that Purcell and Ewen used to detect the hydrogen 21-centimeter signal was later mounted on a pedestal as a monument in Green Bank, West Virginia, where the National Radio Astronomy Observatory is located.

It happened that two other groups, one from the Netherlands and one from Australia, had previously tried to detect this transition and failed. Purcell submitted a manuscript to the journal *Nature* but told the editors not to publish it. Purcell communicated his results to the two other groups and gave them the details of his and Ewen's experiment. The two groups were able to confirm Purcell's results and he asked them to write it up and send it to *Nature*. He then asked the editors of *Nature* to publish the three articles sequentially in the same issue. In an act of rare generosity, Purcell shared this important discovery with the two other research groups.

With another graduate student, James H. Smith, Purcell discovered what became known as the Smith-Purcell Effect. In 1953, they passed a beam of energetic electrons close to and parallel with the surface of an optical diffraction grating. They observed that this produced visible light. The Smith-Purcell Effect has been applied to generate radiation in various frequency domains and free electron lasers have been proposed based on this effect.

Purcell had a total of eighteen PhD students—sixteen of them before 1960. After the NMR period, Purcell mostly worked alone. As Purcell acknowledged in the Sopka interview, he did not "develop a kind of coherent ongoing self-perpetuating program of research. So I was dabbling really in different things in kind of an opportunistic way, which is not particularly good for graduate students, and I just sort of slipped into the role of not taking graduate students." In addition, membership on government committees consumed much of his time.

During the 1960s, Purcell turned his attention to astrophysics, which appealed to his interest in theoretical modeling. He examined the problem of light propagating through interstellar dust. Later, he became active in biophysics. Howard Berg, a Harvard Junior Fellow, showed that *E. coli* bacteria propel themselves by continuously rotating their corkscrew-like flagella. Purcell became interested in this and was able to describe *E. coli* hydrodynamically. For this work, Purcell and Berg were awarded the Biological Physics Prize in 1984 by the American Physical Society.

Academic Instruction. Purcell was a devoted teacher, devoted in a broad sense. His interest was mostly at the undergraduate level, where he created several new courses for the Physics Department. He was the author or co-author of two introductory-level textbooks: *Physics for Science and Engineering Students*, (1960, with W. H. Furry and J. C. Street) and *Electricity and Magnetism: Berkeley Physics Course, Volume 2* (1963). The latter textbook was part of a curriculum reform effort in the early 1960s organized by the Commission on College Physics, of which Purcell was a member. Of the original five-volume textbook, Purcell's book was the only one still in print in 2007.

Purcell was a senior fellow of the prestigious Harvard Society of Fellows. In this capacity, he helped select new junior fellows and for twenty years he had dinner with the junior fellows every Monday evening. Over these years, Purcell was an informal teacher to the junior fellows.

He was also a teacher of his colleagues. For twenty months, Purcell had a column in the *American Journal of Physics* called "Back of the Envelope," in which he presented problems that could be solved in a few steps on the back of an envelope.

Government Advisor. With the dawning of the nuclear age in 1945, leading physicists became public figures and Purcell was in demand as an advisor and a consultant. Purcell was a charter member of the President's Science Advisory Committee (PSAC), which was created by President Dwight D. Eisenhower in 1957 following the orbiting of *Sputnik I* by the Soviet Union. This advisory committee, with leading scientists as members and MIT president James R. Killian, Jr. as chairman, had direct access to the U.S. president. Purcell had great influence on the members of PSAC. Robert Kreidler of the Sloan Foundation, who worked with Killian, said of Purcell: "Ed Purcell did not speak often, but when he did, there would be enormous silence in the room because everybody knew that whatever he said was going to be worth listening to with careful attention" (Killian, 1977, p. 123).

In 1958, Killian named Purcell to head a subcommittee of PSAC whose assignment was to define a space program for the United States. The drafting of their report was done by Purcell, Edwin Land (president, Polaroid Corporation), Herbert York (director, Livermore Laboratory), and Francis Bello (future editor of *Scientific American*). This report was disseminated throughout the United States and the world. Purcell was proud of this report, as its projections proved accurate as the space program developed and the Moon landings occurred. This report exerted an important influence on both the forming of the National Aeronautics and Space Administration (NASA) and on the Apollo Mission.

Purcell received many honors. In addition to the 1952 Nobel Prize, he was named the Gerhard Gale University Professor at Harvard. He was a also a member of the National Academy of Sciences (1951), a member of the American Academy of Arts and Sciences, a fellow of the American Physical Society and its president in 1970, and a foreign member of the Royal Society. He was awarded the National Medal of Science in 1979 for his service to the nation, and won the Oersted Medal in 1968, given by the American Association of Physics Teachers for his contribution to physics education.

BIBLIOGRAPHY

WORKS BY PURCELL

With H. C. Torrey and R. V. Pound. "Resonance Absorption by Nuclear Magnetic Moments in a Solid." *Physical Review* 69 (1946): 37–38.

With Nicholaas Bloembergen and Robert V. Pound. "Relaxation Effects in Nuclear Magnetic Resonance Absorption." *Physical Review* 73, no. 7 (1948): 679–712.

With H. I. Ewen. "Observations of a Line in the Galactic Radio Spectrum." *Nature* 168 (1951): 356.

With W. H. Furry and J. C. Street. *Physics for Science and Engineering Students.* New York: Blakiston, 1952.

"Research in Nuclear Magnetism." *Science* 118 (1953): 431–36.

With S. J. Smith. "Visible Light from Localized Surface Charges Moving Across a Grating." *Physical Review* 92 (1953): 1069.

Electricity and Magnetism. New York: McGraw-Hill, 1963.

"On Alignment of Interstellar Dust." *Physica* 41 (1969): 100–127.

"Life at Low Reynolds Numbers." *American Journal of Physics* 45 (1977): 3–11.

OTHER SOURCES

Killian, James R., Jr. *Sputnik, Scientists, and Eisenhower: A Memoir of the First Special Assistant to the President for Science and Technology.* Cambridge, MA: MIT Press, 1977.

Pound, Robert V. "Edward Mills Purcell." *Biographical Memoirs,* Volume 78. Washington, DC: National Academy Press, 2000.

Rigden, John S. "Quantum States and Precession: The Two Discoveries of NMR." *Reviews of Modern Physics* 58 (1986): 433–448.

———. *Hydrogen: The Essential Element.* Cambridge: Harvard University Press, 2002.

Sopka, Katherine R. Interview. 8 June 1977. Oral Histories, Center for History of Physics, American Institute of Physics, College Park, MD.

John S. Rigden

Q

QŪHĪ (OR AL-KŪHĪ), ABŪ SAHL WAYJAN IBN RUSTAM AL-

(*fl.* Baghdad, c. 970–1000), *mathematics, astronomy.* For the original article on al-Qūhī see *DSB,* vol. 11.

Abū Sahl Wayjan, born Rustam al-Qūhī (in many manuscripts "al-Kūhī"), has come to be recognized by modern scholarship as one of the great geometers of tenth-century Islam. He was the only geometer in medieval Islam to obtain exact results on centers of gravity, and he also gave an elegant method for finding the side of a regular heptagon and the volume of a segment of a paraboloid. One of a number of geometers who worked in eastern Iraq and Iran, he enjoyed the patronage of three Būyid rulers: 'Adud al-Daulah, Samsam al-Daulah, and Sharaf al-Daulah, whose combined reigns cover the period 962–989. His contemporaries regarded his work highly, Ibn al-Haytham referring to al-Qūhī's *On the Measurement of the Paraboloid* and al-Bīrūnī citing his *On the Complete Compass.* In the twelfth century, 'Umar al-Khayyāmī cited him as one of the "distinguished mathematicians of Iraq," and al-Khāzinī summarized some of al-Qūhī's work on centers of gravity in the former's *Balance of Wisdom.*

Work in Geometry. Al-Qūhī's more than thirty extant treatises reveal him as primarily a geometer, a subject he described in the preface to his treatise on the regular heptagon as "the leader who is to be followed when it comes to honesty." In his correspondence with Abū Ishāq al-Sābī, he praised mathematics as a demonstrative science, whose goal was to seek the truth—not numerical approximations.

In his treatise *On Rising Times,* he wrote that he had also investigated astronomy as well as centers of gravity and optics. His *Perfect Compass,* for example, represented a step beyond Ibn Sinān's pointwise constructions of conic sections and described an instrument al-Qūhī characterized as useful for drawing these sections on sundials and astrolabes.

Yet these areas appealed to him primarily as sources for geometrical problems. His lengthy *Treatise on the Construction of the Astrolabe with Proofs* was principally devoted to the problem of completing the lines of an astrolabe, given certain of its circles and points. His *On the Distance from the Center of the Earth to the Shooting Stars* set out a method that is mathematically correct, though impractical at the time, for finding the distance and size of these objects. In his *Rising Times,* al-Qūhī took a conservative stance vis-à-vis the new trigonometrical theorems he had heard about, and he showed how the classical Menelaus's theorem might be used to solve a sequence of standard problems in spherical astronomy. (He emphasized that he had not devoted much attention to studying methods for constructing astronomical tables.)

Al-Qūhī took special interest in problems stemming from the works of Euclid, Apollonius, and Archimedes. In his *Revision* of Euclid's *Elements,* I, he reorganized the latter by eliminating all of its constructions, using the parallel postulate much earlier, devising a new proof of the Pythagorean theorem, and giving an ostensible proof of the fourth postulate on the equality of right angles.

Al-Qūhī's studies of *Elements,* II, provide twelve new propositions, very much in the spirit of the first ten propositions of that work, as well as a short *Lemmas to the Conics,* whose introduction describes it as "necessary in the second and third books of *The Conics."*

Archimedean Tradition. Unique in medieval Islam are al-Qūhī's results on centers of gravity of plane and solid figures, results very much in the tradition of Archimedes. This research, he said in the preface to *On the Volume of the Paraboloid,* motivated his work on that question. Although al-Khāzinī's *Balance of Wisdom* summarizes some of his work on centers of gravity, scholars have only al-Qūhī's correspondence with al-Sābi on the subject, in which he correctly located the centers of gravity of triangles (and cones) and segments of parabolas (and paraboloids), as well as of hemispheres (a result not found in Archimedes's works). He conjectured, on the basis of these results, that the center of gravity of a semicircle divides the radius perpendicular to its diameter into two parts, so that the part nearer the diameter has to the radius the ratio of 3:7. He was fully aware, and defended the implication, of this result, namely that the ratio of the circumference of a circle to its diameter is 28/9, an insistence that earned him the incredulity of his correspondent and the severe censure of Abū al-Futūh al-Sārī in his *Falsification of the Premises of the Discourse of Abū Sahl al-Qūhī.*

Also closely related to the medieval Islamic tradition of Archimedes's work is Al-Qūhī's *Construction of a Regular Heptagon in the Circle.* By the mid-tenth century, geometers such as al-Sijzī had become dissatisfied with Greek verging constructions, calling them "moving geometry." (Verging constructions demanded that one insert a line segment of given length so that its endpoints rest on two given curves and so that it points [or "verges"] towards a given point.) Archimedes's construction of the regular heptagon went beyond the usual verging construction in demanding not that the line inserted between two straight lines have a certain length but that the two triangles created thereby have equal areas. (One of al-Qūhī's contemporaries, Abū al-Jūd, described this particularly opaque auxiliary construction as "perhaps more difficult than the task itself.") It was in the context of this discussion of the limits of a proper construction that al-Qūhī wrote, in his preface to the work, that he had done what Archimedes had been unable to do. By this he meant that his construction used not verging but the intersection of conic sections.

Influence of Apollonius. Al-Qūhī's *On Tangent Circles* deals with constructing circles tangent to two given circles or straight lines (or passing through two given points) and having their centers on a given line. This is reminiscent of Apollonius's famous three-circles problem. Al-Qūhī also considered the case when the line is not just straight or a conic section but any curved line (though what he meant by that is not specified).

Al-Qūhī used freely the classical method of analysis and synthesis, familiar from his study of the works of Apollonius. One example is his *Drawing Two Lines from a Known Point,* a work probably motivated by his *Treatise on the Astrolabe,* in which he cited two results from *Drawing Two Lines.* Among the dozen problems he considers in *Drawing Two Lines,* the following is a typical one: Point *A* and line (not necessarily straight) *BG* are given; assuming this, draw two straight line segments from *A* to BG, containing a given angle, so that the two segments *AB* and *AG* have to each other a given ratio.

Al-Qūhī's analysis of each problem reduces it to a previously analyzed problem, but no synthesis is ever given. Work like this on analysis was likely the motivation for his treatise, *Additions to the Data,* which adds a number of new propositions and a new notion to Euclid's *Data.*

SUPPLEMENTARY BIBLIOGRAPHY

WORKS BY AL-QŪHĪ

Berggren, J. L. "The Correspondence of Abū Sahl al-Kūhī and Abū Ishaq al-Sābī: A Translation with Commentaries." *Journal for the History of Arabic Science* 7 (1983): 39–124.

Hogendijk, Jan P. "Al-Kūhī's Construction of an Equilateral Pentagon in a Given Square." *Zeitschrift für Geschichte der Arabisch-Islamischen Wissenschaften* 1 (1984): 100-144.

———. "Corrections and Supplements: 'Al-Kūhī's Construction of an Equilateral Pentagon in a Given Square.'" *Zeitschrift für Geschichte der Arabisch-Islamischen Wissenschaften* 4 (1987–1988): 267.

Young, Gregg de. "Abū Sahl's Additions to Book II of Euclid's 'Elements.'" *Zeitschrift für Geschichte der Arabisch-Islamischen Wissenschaften* 7 (1991–1992): 73–135.

Berggren, J. L. "Abū Sahl al-Kūhī's Treatise on the Construction of the Astrolabe with Proof: Text, Translation, and Commentary." *Physis* 31 (1994): 141–252.

Rashed, Roshdi. *Les mathématiques infinitésimales du IXe au XIe siècle.* Vol. I. *Fondateurs et commentateurs: Banū Mūsā, Ibn Qurra, Ibn Sinān, al-Khāzin, al-Qūhī, Ibn al-Samh, Ibn Hūd.* London: Al-Furqan Islamic Heritage Foundation, 1996. Contains Arabic text and translation of both versions of al-Kūhī's treatise on the measurement of the paraboloid.

Berggren, J. L. "Al-Kūhī's 'Filling a Lacuna in Book II of Archimedes' in the Version of Nasir al-Din al-Tusi." *Centaurus* 38 (1996): 140–207.

Rashed, Roshi. "Al-Qūhī vs. Aristotle: On Motion." *Arabic Sciences and Philosophy* 9 (1999): 7–24.

Berggren, J. L., and Glen Van Brummelen. "Abū Sahl al-Kūhī on 'Two Geometrical Questions.'" *Zeitschrift für Geschichte der Arabisch-Islamischen Wissenschaften* 13 (1999–2000): 165–187.

———. "Abū Sahl al-Kūhī's 'On the Ratio of the Segments of a Single Line that Falls on Three Lines.'" *Suhayl* 1 (2000): 11–56.

Rashed, Roshdi. "Al-Qūhī: From Meteorology to Astronomy." *Arabic Sciences and Philosophy* 11, no. 2 (2001): 157–204.

Van Brummelen, Glen, and J. L. Berggren. "Abū Sahl al-Kūhī on the Distance to the Shooting Stars." *Journal for the History of Astronomy* 32, no. 2 (2001): 137–151.

Berggren, J. L., and Glen Van Brummelen. "Abū Sahl al-Kūhī on Drawing Two Lines from a Point with a Known Angle." *Suhayl* 2 (2001): 161–198.

———, and Glen Van Brummelen. "Abū Sahl al-Kūhī on Rising Times." *SCIAMVS* 2 (2001): 31–46.

———, and Glen Van Brummelen. "From Euclid to Apollonius: Al-Kūhī's Lemmas to the *Conics.*" *Zeitschrift für Geschichte der Arabisch-Islamischen Wissenschaften* 15 (2002–2003): 165–174.

———, with Jan P. Hogendijk. "The Fragments of Abū Sahl al-Kūhī's Lost Geometrical Works in the Writings of al-Sijzī." In *Studies in the History of the Exact Sciences in Honour of David Pingree,* edited by Charles Burnett, Jan P. Hogendijk, Kim Plofker, et al. Leiden: Brill, 2003.

Abgrall, Philippe. *Le développement de la géométrie aux IXe–XIe Siècles: Al-Qūhī.* Paris: Albert Blanchard, 2004.

OTHER SOURCES

Berggren, J. L. "Tenth-century Mathematics through the Eyes of Abū Sahl al-Kūhī." In *The Enterprise of Science in Medieval Islam,* edited by Jan P. Hogendijk and Abdelhamid I. Sabra. Cambridge, MA, and London, England: MIT Press, 2003.

Hogendijk, Jan P. "Greek and Arabic Constructions of the Regular Heptagon." *Archive for History of Exact Sciences* 30 (1984): 197–330.

Sesiano, Jacques. "Note sur trois théorèmes de Mécanique d'al-Qūhī et leur conséquence." *Centaurus* 22, no. 4 (1978–1979): 281–297.

Sezgin, Fuat. *Geschichte des Arabischen Schrifttums.* Vol. 5, *Mathematik.* Leiden, Netherlands: E. J. Brill, 1974.

J. L. Berggren

QUIGNET, MICHIEL
SEE **Coignet, Michiel**.

QUINNIET, MICHIEL
SEE **Coignet, Michiel**.

QUṬB AL-DĪN MAḤMŪD IBN MASʿŪD IBN AL-MUṢLIḤ AL-SHĪRĀZĪ
(*b.* Shīrāz, Persia, October/November, 1236; *d.* Tabrīz, Persia, February 1311), *astronomy, medi-*

cine, philosophy. For the original article on Quṭb al-Dīn al-Shīrāzī see *DSB,* vol. 11.

Since the original *DSB* article first appeared, scholars have learned a bit more about Shīrāzī's astronomical work, and there have been some new interpretations regarding his overall philosophical positions. As for his astronomy, it has been determined that several models previously attributed to him are actually by an older contemporary, Muʾayyad al-Dīn al-ʿUrḍī. However, there is still no comprehensive study of his several astronomical books or of his actual contributions. His philosophical works, previously seen as unproblematically mystical or theosophical, have been subjected to a more rigorous analysis that has revealed an interesting and nuanced philosophical outlook. One of the things that awaits study is how this "mystical philosophy" helped shape and was shaped by the mathematical and empirical sciences. Because of the prominent position occupied by Shīrāzī, whose positions were debated for many centuries, studies of his work promise to reveal a great deal about the intellectual history of post-classical Islam.

Life and Philosophy. For an extended and detailed account of Quṭb al-Dīn's career that provides intellectual, social, and political context, see John Walbridge (pp. 7–26), which is based upon a close reading of the primary bio-bibliographical sources. In his study, Walbridge clarifies the meaning of Shīrāzī's intellectual Sufism, "the philosophy of illumination," removing it from a "theosophical" framework and placing it squarely within a more straightforward philosophical tradition.

Mathematics. It is not entirely clear what it means to ascribe to Quṭb al-Dīn Pythagorean tendencies. At present it can be said, based admittedly on limited research, that he seems to subscribe to the Ptolemaic view that the mathematical sciences can provide more insight into physics and metaphysics than the philosophical/a priori approach of Aristotle (see his *Nihāya,* preface). How this might fit in with Shīrāzī's illuminationist views that give priority to what Walbridge has called (p. 46) the "primacy of the concrete" (as opposed to Aristotelian metaphysical substrates) has yet to be explored.

Optics. There is little to recommend the opinion in the original article that Quṭb al-Dīn al-Shīrāzī was the first to have explained the rainbow correctly. This seems to be based on a series of misunderstandings in the secondary literature, beginning with Eilhard Wiedemann (see Roshdi Rashed, p. 213). It is true that Kamāl al-Dīn al-Fārisī, who did provide a reasonably accurate account of the rainbow phenomenon based upon experiments, was inspired by his teacher Quṭb al-Dīn to pursue his optical researches. And Shīrāzī did obtain a copy of Ibn al-Haytham's great work on optics for his eager student "from a distant land." But there is little evidence in the *Nihāya*, the *Tuḥfa*, or any other work by Shīrāzī of any great understanding of the type of advances made by Ibn al-Haytham or Kamāl al-Dīn in optics or visual theory (A. I. Sabra, pp. lxix–lxxi, esp. nn. 110–111).

Astronomy. Thanks to the work of George Saliba and Robert Morrison, considerably more is known about Shīrāzī's astronomical models, though much more needs to be done before a proper assessment can be arrived at. The model for the upper planets and Venus that E. S. Kennedy attributed to Shīrāzī turns out to be that of an older contemporary, Mu'ayyad al-Dīn al-'Urḍī. However, models for the Moon and Mercury from the *Tuḥfa* are his own (Saliba [1996], pp. 96–100, 104–108, 118–120). There Shīrāzī creatively used what are now known as the 'Urḍī lemma and the Ṭūsī couple to achieve combinations of uniform, circular motions (as required by ancient physics for motions in the heavens) that resolve the irregular motions resulting from Ptolemy's equant for Mercury and from his choice of the center of the universe as the reference point of motion for the Moon's eccentric orb. For a valuable study of Shīrāzī's hypotheses (basic models) for celestial motion, and an edition and translation of the relevant section of the *Tuḥfa* (Bk. II, Chap. 8), see Robert Morrison.

There is also a better understanding of Shīrāzī's attitude toward cosmological issues emerging. He gave high praise to astronomy in his introduction to the *Nihāya* and echoed Ptolemy who, in his introduction to the *Almagest*, referred to physics and theology as guesswork as opposed to the true knowledge offered by the mathematical sciences. Indeed, it would seem that Shīrāzī somewhat disagreed with his mentor Ṭūsī on this point. This manifested itself in the question of the Earth's motion: Ṭūsī had held that the matter had to be left to the natural philosophers because there was no decisive observational or mathematical proof, whereas Shīrāzī, not wishing to leave such an important matter to guesswork, insisted that there could be devised an observational test. This test took the form of two rocks of different weights thrown straight up in the air; Ṭūsī had said that in such a case a rotating Earth could carry the air and whatever was in it at the same speed, but Shīrāzī thought that objects of different weights would be carried with different speeds. Because one does not observe such an effect, the Earth must be at rest (Ragep, pp. 152–153, 155–157).

Physics. For an extended discussion of Quṭb al-Dīn's metaphysics of light, see Walbridge.

The following supplements and corrects the list of Shīrāzī's scientific and philosophical works found in the original article. For longer inventories of works attributed to Shīrāzī, including spurious ones, see Walbridge, pp. 175–191 and Rosenfeld/Ihsanoğlu, pp. 233–235.

1. *Tarjamah-i taḥrīr-i uṣūl-i Uqlīdis*: translation from Arabic into Persian of Naṣīr al-Dīn al-Ṭūsī's 15-part "Recension" of Euclid's *Elements*; completed in November/December 1282 and dedicated to the vizier Amīr Shāh ibn Tāj al-Dīn Mu'tazz ibn Ṭāhir, to whom Shīrāzī's *al-Tuḥfa al-Shāhiyya* was also dedicated.

2. *Risāla fī ḥarakat al-dahraja wa-' l-nisba bayn al-mustawī wa-' l-munḥanī* (Treatise on rolling motion and the relation between the straight and the curved), in Arabic. This work has been translated into German (partially) and Russian, and subject to several studies; see Rosenfeld/Ihsanoğlu, p. 234 (M5).

3. *Nihāyat al-idrāk fī dirāyat al-aflāk* (The highest attainment in comprehending the orbs), in Arabic; dedicated to the vizier Shams al-Dīn al-Juwaynī and completed in November 1281.

4. *Ikhtiyārāt-i muẓaffarī* (Selections for Muẓaffar al-Dīn), in Persian; dedicated to Muẓaffar al-Dīn Yūluq Arslān, the Chūpānid ruler of Kastamonu, who died in 1304 or 1305.

5. *al-Tuḥfa al-shāhiyya fī al-hay'a* (The royal gift on astronomy), in Arabic; dedicated to the same vizier, Amīr Shāh ibn Tāj al-Dīn, to whom (1) is dedicated, in Sivas in July/August 1285.

6. *Fa' alta fa-lā talum* (You've done it so don't blame [me]), in Arabic; a supercommentary on the *Tibyān maqāṣid al-Tadhkira* (Exposition on the intent of the *Tadhkira*) by Muḥammad ibn 'Alī ibn al-Ḥusayn al-Munajjim al-Ḥimādhī, which itself is a commentary on the *Tadhkira fī 'ilm al-hay'a* by Naṣīr al-Dīn al-Ṭūsī. Shīrāzī, who according to Walbridge completed the work in Tabrīz in 1304 or 1305, severely criticized Ḥimādhī and accused him of having plagiarized the *Tuḥfa*.

7. *Kitāb al-tabṣira fī al-hay'a*. Erroneously attributed to Shīrāzī; actually by Shams al-Dīn Abū Bakr Muḥammad ibn Aḥmad al-Kharaqī (*d.* 1138 or 1139).

8. *Sharḥ al-Tadhkira*: actually the *Fa' alta*, no. 6.

9. *Kharīdat al-'ajā' ib*: most likely not authentic.

10. *Khulāṣat iṣlāḥ al-majisṭī*: unable to ascertain whether this is authentic.

11. *Ḥall mushkilāt al-majisṭī*: most likely not authentic.

12. *Taḥrīr al-zīj al-jadīd al-riḍwānī:* most likely not authentic.

13. *al-Zīj al-sulṭānī:* most likely not authentic.

14. *Kitāb nuzhat al-ḥukamāʾ wa-rawḍat al-aṭibbāʾ*, in Arabic; according to Walbridge, there were three editions of this major work. The first two, published in 1283 and in 1294 or 1295, most likely went under the title *Sharḥ kulliyyāt al-qānūn*. The third and last edition, published 23 November 1310 just before his death, carried the title *al-Tuḥfa al-saʿdiyya fī al-ṭibb* to indicate its dedication to Saʿd al-Dīn Muḥammad Sāwujī.

15. *Risāla fī al-baraṣ,* in Arabic; according to Walbridge it is a short work in four folios.

16. *Sharḥ al-Urjūza:* unable to ascertain whether this is authentic.

17. *Risāla fī bayān al-ḥāja ila al-ṭibb…:* unable to ascertain whether this is authentic.

18. *Durrat al-tāj li-ghurrat al-dubāj* (The pearly crown for Dubāj's brow)*,* in Persian; completed 18 January 1306; cf. Walbridge, pp. 175–178.

19. *Sharḥ Ḥikmat al-ishrāq,* in Arabic; completed April 1295 and dedicated to the Grand Vizier Jamāl al-Dīn ʿAlī ibn Muḥammad al-Dastjirdānī.

20-26. Many of these may not be authentic; see Walbridge, pp. 179–181. In addition, there is another philosophical work by Shīrāzī entitled *Risāla fī taḥqīq ʿālam al-mithāl wa-ajwibat asʾilat baʿḍ al-fuḍalāʾ* (A treatise ascertaining the reality of the world of image and answers to the questions of a certain scholar), in Arabic; completed after 1295; edited and translated by Walbridge, pp. 196–271.

SUPPLEMENTARY BIBLIOGRAPHY

WORKS BY QUṬB AL-DĪN AL-SHĪRĀZĪ

Walbridge, John. *The Science of Mystic Lights: Quṭb al-Dīn Shīrāzī and the Illuminationist Tradition in Islamic Philosophy.* Cambridge, MA: Harvard Center for Middle Eastern Studies, 1992. Contains an edition and translation of *Risāla fī taḥqīq ʿālam al-mithāl wa-ajwibat asʾilat baʿḍ al-fuḍalāʾ*.

Bayān al-ḥājah ilā al-ṭibb wa-ʾl-aṭibbāʾ wa-ādābihim wa-waṣāyāhum. Edited and commented on by Aḥmad Farīd al-Mazyadī. Beirut, Lebanon: Dār al-Kutub al-ʿIlmiyya, 2003.

Morrison, Robert. "Quṭb al-Dīn al-Shīrāzī's Hypotheses for Celestial Motions." *Journal for the History of Arabic Science* 13 (2005): 21–140. Contains an edition and translation of Book II, Chap. 8 of *al-Tuḥfa al-shāhiyya.*

OTHER SOURCES

Bakar, Osman. *Classification of Knowledge in Islam: A Study in Islamic Philosophies of Science.* Cambridge, U.K.: The Islamic Texts Society, 1998. On Shīrāzī's classification of knowledge, see pp. 229–262.

Pourjavady, Reza, and Sabine Schmidtke. "Quṭb al-Dīn al-Shīrāzī's (634/1236 – 710/1311) Durrat al-Tāj and Its Sources (Studies on Quṭb al-Dīn al-Shīrāzī I)." *Journal Asiatique* 292 (2004): 311–330.

Ragep, F. Jamil. "Ṭūsī and Copernicus: The Earth's Motion in Context." *Science in Context* 14, nos. 1-2 (2001): 145–163.

Rashed, Roshdi. "Kamāl al-Dīn Abu'l Ḥasan Muḥammad ibn al-Ḥasan al-Fārisī." In *Dictionary of Scientific Biography,* edited by Charles Coulston Gillispie, vol. 7, 212–219. New York: Charles Scribner's Sons, 1973.

Rosenfeld, B. A., and Ekmeleddin Ihsanoğlu. *Mathematicians, Astronomers, and Other Scholars of Islamic Civilization and Their Works (7ᵗʰ–19ᵗʰ c.).* Istanbul: IRCICA, 2003. pp. 233–235.

Sabra, A. I. *The Optics of Ibn al-Haytham.* 2 vols. London: The Warburg Institute, 1989.

Saliba, George. "The Original Source of Quṭb al-Dīn al-Shīrāzī's Planetary Model." *Journal for the History of Arabic Science* 3 (1979): 3–18.

———. "The Height of the Atmosphere according to Muʾayyad al-Dīn al-ʿUrḍī, Quṭb al-Dīn al-Shīrāzī, and Ibn Muʿādh." In *From Deferent to Equant: Studies in Honor of E. S. Kennedy,* edited by David King and George Saliba. Vol. 500 of *The Annals of the New York Academy of Sciences,* 1987, pp. 445–465.

———. "Arabic Planetary Theories after the Eleventh Century AD." In *Encyclopedia of the History of Arabic Science,* edited by Roshdi Rashed. 3 vols. London: Routledge, 1996. Vol. 1, pp. 58–127.

F. Jamil Ragep

R

RABI, ISIDOR ISAAC (*b.* Rymanow, Austria-Hungary [later Poland], 29 July 1898; *d.* New York, New York, 11 January 1988), *physics, molecular beams, nuclear physics, physics statesman.*

When I. I. Rabi died at age eighty-nine, many of the world's leading physicists called him the "dean of world physics." All physicists recognized in Rabi the mark of an unusual man; he brought together that rare combination of a physicist par excellence, a statesman of science with many tangible accomplishments, an advocate for science with direct links to people in high places, and a savant with uncommon wisdom. In 1938 Rabi discovered the magnetic resonance method and for this he was awarded the Nobel Prize in 1944. Rabi could be tough, and his toughness sometimes made people angry; however, even at such times, he was universally admired.

Early Life. Rabi grew up in an environment dominated by religion, and the powerful influences of his thorough religious upbringing stayed with him throughout his life. His father, David, came to the United States in late 1898 or early 1899, shortly after his only son was born, and within a few months, he sent for Rabi and his mother, Sheindel.

When Rabi was about one year old, the family was reunited in New York City. Rabi had one sister, Gertrude, who was five years younger. Rabi's father was uneducated and unskilled; he supported his family through a variety of menial tasks. The family was poor. They lived in a Jewish ghetto on the Lower East Side of Manhattan; more specifically, they lived in a small cultural enclave dominated by other immigrants from their native town, Rymanow, which was in Galicia, the northeastern most

province of the old Austro-Hungarian Empire. Rabi spoke English on the streets and Yiddish in his home. When he was nine years old, his family moved to the Jewish community of Brownsville, in Brooklyn.

Rabi's parents never learned to read or write in English. His given name was Israel Isaac, and in his Yiddish-speaking home he was called Izzy. When Rabi's mother enrolled him in school, she gave his name as "Izzy" and the teacher wrote down "Isidor"; thus, he became Isidor Rabi. Later, in high school, Rabi brought back the second I. and from then on he was Isidor Isaac Rabi, or more simply, I. I. Rabi. To his family, his associates, and his friends he was always called "Rabi" (pronounced to rhyme with Bobby) or "Rab."

His parents were devoted to their orthodox Jewish religion both in their temple and their home. Throughout his childhood, Rabi said, "Even in casual conversation, God entered, not every paragraph, more like every sentence" (Rigden, 1987, p. 19). A defining moment came, however, when Rabi, at about age twelve, discovered the public library. He began his exploration of the library shelves in the science section, starting with "A" for astronomy. In one book he encountered the Copernican model of the solar system and quickly grasped its three-dimensional significance. He arrived home on that momentous day and said to his mother, "Who needs God?"

Education After he completed elementary school, Rabi's parents wanted him to go into Hebrew studies at a yeshiva, but Rabi refused. Nor did he wish to go to Boys High, where all the smart Jewish boys typically went. Rabi, immersed since birth in the Jewish community of his parents, wanted to get into a more typical American environment, so he elected to go to Manual Training High School in Brooklyn. At Manual Training, Rabi started a practice that became a pattern throughout his education: He concentrated and listened carefully while he was in his classes but pursued his own interests outside of class, reading four or five books per week. History was one subject of interest, and during his senior year he got the highest grade in the state on the New York Regents history exam.

Rabi entered Cornell University at Ithaca, New York, in 1916 not only with advanced standing, but also with a scholarship. He was an electrical engineering major until a chemistry course, qualitative analysis, unpopular with most students but an adventure for him, prompted him to switch to chemistry. His extensive reading, outside of class, about the history of science gave him a valuable overview that other students lacked. He graduated in 1919 with a major in chemistry, but chemistry did not satisfy him intellectually, and he decided to get a job rather than continue on to graduate school. For three years Rabi floundered, literally "bumming around" with three friends and reading in the New York Public Library.

In the summer of 1922, one of his friends said to him, "It is time to quit horsing around" (Rigden, 2000, p. 34). Rabi returned to Cornell and began a graduate program in chemistry. Still unhappy in that field, he applied for a fellowship in physics but failed to get it. He decided to leave both Cornell and chemistry. Rabi considered applying to Harvard University in Cambridge, Massachusetts, but this decision was altered by the appearance of Helen Newmark, from New York City, who arrived in Ithaca to take a summer course. Helen was an art student at Hunter College. Helen was a New Yorker, Rabi was a New Yorker, and Rabi wanted to be near Helen. In 1923 he entered Columbia University in Manhattan as a graduate student in physics.

Rabi's real interest was the quantum theory being developed in Europe. No physics professor at Columbia was sufficiently conversant with the new quantum theory to provide guidance, so he had to settle for a dissertation topic that involved measuring the magnetic susceptibility of a series of crystalline salts. The topic bored him, and he procrastinated. He organized a group of students to study quantum theory. Rabi was skeptical about quantum theory; however, the 1922 experiment of Otto Stern and Walther Gerlach that empirically demonstrated what was then called "space quantization" completely contradicted the tenets of classical physics, and Rabi recognized that quantum ideas were needed.

Months passed while Rabi grew crystals and avoided the hard work that his dissertation measurements would require. Then one day, back in the library, Rabi was reading—for pleasure—John Clerk Maxwell's *Treatise on Elec-*

tricity and Magnetism (1873), and as he read, Rabi recognized a new and simple way to make his measurements. In Rabi's method the crystal, whose susceptibility was to be determined, was suspended in a solution whose susceptibility could be matched exactly with the suspended crystal, then the solution's susceptibility was determined by a comparison with water—a simple two-step procedure. In six weeks he not only finished his dissertation, but did so with results of unexcelled accuracy.

On 16 July 1926, Rabi submitted his dissertation to the journal *Physical Review*. The next day Rabi married Helen Newmark. Three years later their first daughter, Nancy Elizabeth, was born, and in 1934 Helen gave birth to their second daughter, Margaret Joella.

Rabi in Europe. From mid-1927 to the fall of 1929, Rabi learned the new physics in Europe. He spent a short amount of time with Arnold Sommerfeld, Erwin Schrödinger, Niels Bohr, and Wolfgang Pauli. However, it was in Hamburg, Germany, that Rabi's career was determined. At Bohr's suggestion, Rabi went to Hamburg to work with Pauli. Also at Hamburg was Otto Stern, whose earlier experiment had so impressed Rabi. One day Rabi visited Stern's molecular-beam laboratory, where two English-speaking physicists worked. As Rabi talked with them, he suggested a different way to do their experiments. Stern invited him to do it. Rabi believed it was an honor to be asked by Stern and felt he could not refuse. Rabi carried out the experiment successfully, and the magnetic field configuration he designed to deflect the beam particles became known as the Rabi field.

After Hamburg, Rabi went to Leipzig to work with Werner Heisenberg. This turned out to be a fortunate decision for Rabi. In 1929 Jewish scholars had great difficulty finding positions as university professors, and because of this, Rabi did not expect to get a faculty position. Heisenberg, who began an extended lecture tour in the United States while Rabi was in Leipzig, began his tour in New York City at the Physics Department of Columbia University. The department was seeking a theoretical physicist who could teach the new quantum physics. Heisenberg strongly recommended Rabi. On 26 March 1929, Rabi received a cable from Columbia University offering him the position of lecturer. Rabi accepted immediately, and the future course of his career was established.

Columbia Professor. Rabi came to Columbia University in the fall of 1929 as a theoretical physicist. He taught statistical mechanics and quantum mechanics. Meanwhile, he spent over two years doing theoretical research in solid-state physics. All the time, however, thoughts of molecular beams kept asserting themselves in his mind. He wrote letters to experimentalists raising questions about some of

I. I. Rabi. © CORBIS.

the troublesome aspects associated with molecular-beam research, asking, for example, about detecting the particles that make up the beam.

In 1931 Harold Urey, Rabi's Columbia colleague, attempted to determine the nuclear spin of sodium by an analysis of its spectrum. Urey's results were inconclusive. Rabi was bored with his theoretical solid-state research, so little encouragement was needed for him to change direction. The uncertainty in the nuclear spin of sodium was the challenge, and the experimental method of molecular beams was Rabi's response.

Molecular beams satisfied Rabi because they enabled him to investigate nature at a fundamental level. Rabi's approach to physics was strongly influenced by his religious upbringing. Rabi said:

> To choose physics in the first place requires a certain direction of interest. In my case it was something that goes to my background, and that is religious in origin … religion as the inspirer of a way of looking at things. Choosing physics means, in some way, you're not going to choose

trivialities. The whole idea of God, that's real class … real drama. (Rigden, 2000, p. 79)

To determine a basic nuclear property of sodium, element number 11, was for Rabi at the level of the fundamental, or as Rabi expressed it, his molecular-beam experiments measuring basic nuclear properties was "walking the path of God."

Rabi and his first graduate student, Victor W. Cohen, built the first molecular-beam apparatus in Rabi's Columbia laboratory and began their investigation of sodium. In this process, Rabi's personal characteristics had a direct impact on his approach to physics. Rabi's father had always accused his son of being lazy, and Rabi acknowledged the validity of his father's accusation. Rabi had been unable to motivate himself to do his dissertation research in the standard labor-intensive way, and so he procrastinated until he found a fast, easy, and accurate way to measure magnetic susceptibilities. In a similar fashion, Rabi and Cohen collected quantities of data, subjected that data to statistical analyses, calculated standard deviations, and so on. Rabi hated it. "This was not for me," Rabi said. "I'm going to know my answer by the end of the day" (Rigden, 2000, p. 82).

In the molecular-beam method, beam particles are deflected by an inhomogeneous magnetic field. In the Cohen-Rabi experiment, Rabi varied the deflecting fields along the path traversed by the sodium atoms in such a way that the beam of atoms was teased apart into individual beamlets in each of which the sodium atoms were in the same nuclear quantum state. The total number of beamlets depended on the nuclear spin of sodium; therefore, all Rabi had to do was count—count the number of beamlets observed at the detector. In 1933 Cohen and Rabi detected four distinct beamlets reaching the detector, and from this they could infer unequivocally that the nuclear spin of sodium is 3/2. "Count them! It was wonderful. Each one, I suppose, seeks God in his own way" (Rigden, 2000, p. 88). This experimental result was published in 1933 in the *Physical Review* as "The Nuclear Spin of Sodium"—Rabi's first experimental result as a molecular-beam physicist.

The series of experiments that dominated the attention of Rabi and his students throughout most of the 1930s was the series on the first two isotopes of the hydrogen atom: hydrogen and deuterium. These experiments began in 1933. Once again, the experiments satisfied something deep within Rabi. The hydrogen atom has the most fundamental nucleus—the single proton—while the nucleus of deuterium, called the deuteron, has the simplest compound nucleus consisting of a single proton and one neutron. "Here you have a system that you could understand," said Rabi. "Anything I couldn't understand was because there was something to be discovered" (Rigden, 2000, p. 99).

The experiments on the hydrogens actually began in Hamburg in Otto Stern's laboratory. Stern's measured result for the magnetic moment of the proton, published in 1933, was a great surprise: It was three times larger than Paul Dirac's 1928 theory seemed to predict. Stern's result raised the question of whether the proton is truly an elementary particle in the sense that an electron is an elementary particle. Stern's unexpected result, plus the importance of understanding the proton, prompted Rabi to initiate his own attempt to measure the proton's magnetic moment; importantly, he would use a method very different than Stern's. Stern used a beam of molecular hydrogen, while Rabi would use atomic hydrogen. Stern used a strong magnetic field to deflect the hydrogen molecule beam particles, an approach that posed the difficult problem of the accurate calibration of the field strength. Rabi would use a weak magnetic field, whose strength could be directly calculated. Rabi's experiment avoided many of the difficulties that had complicated Stern's approach.

Rabi and his students carried out three distinct experiments on the hydrogens during the 1930s. Improved apparatus was designed for each experiment, with accuracy and precision steadily improving. As Rabi had suggested, there were surprises of great significance.

The results of Rabi's first experiment, published in 1934 ("The Magnetic Moment of the Proton"), indicated an even larger value for the magnetic moment of the proton than had Stern's surprising result. Furthermore, the two results did not agree within their cited experimental errors. For the proton, there was a 10 percent uncertainty in Rabi's result and for the deuteron the uncertainty was 26 percent. While there were several sources of error in this first experiment, the largest source of experimental uncertainty was determining exactly how much the hydrogen atoms were deflected by the magnetic field.

In 1936 the second experiment utilized a new method, the refocusing method, which dramatically improved the experimental results and, more importantly, set the stage for the discovery of the magnetic resonance method. Instead of one deflecting magnet, there were two deflecting fields that each beam particle passed sequentially. Between the two deflecting magnets was the new static, T-shaped field. The effect of this new arrangement was threefold. First, no assumption had to be made about the distribution of particle velocities in the beam as all beam particles, independent of their velocity, reached the detector. Second, because the two deflecting magnets acted in tandem to bring all beam particles to the detector, no measurement of the deflection due to a single magnet had to be made. Third, and finally, the static T-shaped

magnetic field allowed, for the first time, the signs—positive or negative—of the magnetic moments of the proton and deuteron to be made. In this second experiment, the uncertainty in the measured value of the proton's magnetic moment was reduced from 19 percent to 5 percent, while that of the deuteron was reduced from 26 percent to 4 percent.

During the planning for the third experiment in 1939, Rabi invented the magnetic resonance method, which provided a greater improvement in the experimental outcome. The experimental apparatus designed for this experiment was similar to that used in the preceding one. The powerful refocusing method was used again, but in a somewhat modified form. The two deflecting magnets were set up to deflect beam particles in opposite directions, and the field strength of the second magnet was set to exactly undo what the first magnet did, that is, refocus the beam particles into the detector. The new feature of this experiment was that the static T-field was replaced by a weak field that oscillated at an adjustable radio frequency. As particles coursed through the apparatus, the frequency of the oscillatory field was slowly varied. Particles entered the oscillatory magnetic field in a particular quantum state. As beam particles traversed the oscillatory field that was oscillating at a particular frequency, they could undergo a quantum transition to a new state and, in this new state, they would not be refocused into the detector and the observed signal at the detector would decrease. From knowledge of the frequency at which the signal at the detector decreased, magnetic moments could be determined. With this third experiment, Rabi obtained what Hans Bethe called "unprecedented accuracy" (Rigden, 1983, p. 355). The uncertainty in the measured values of both the proton's and deuteron's magnetic moments was 0.7 percent.

The sharpness of the signals available with the new resonance method revealed fundamental information that had been hidden to Rabi and his students in the less precise results of the earlier experiments. The signals from the deuteron resonances were disturbingly broad, and one of Rabi's students, Norman F. Ramsey Jr.—a Nobel Prize winner in physics in 1989—began an investigation. When he refined the experimental procedures by lowering the power level of the radio frequency field, he discovered that the broad signal was actually a series of overlapping signals. The analysis of the deuterium data revealed that the deuteron had, in addition to the known magnetic moment, an unknown electric quadrupole moment. This was a momentous discovery, as it negated the central forces assumed to be acting in the atomic nucleus and revealed a new type of nuclear force, a tensor force, that was needed to account for the new nuclear property.

The high point of Rabi's physical research came in 1939 with the discovery of the nuclear quadrupole moment. During the period 1939–1941, Rabi and his students applied the magnetic resonance method to a range of other atoms and succeeded in measuring nuclear properties to new levels of accuracy and precision. During these years, however, Rabi's attention became increasingly diverted from his research.

Wartime In 1933 Otto Stern, a Jew, was ordered by the German authorities to leave his faculty position at the University of Hamburg. This troubled Rabi. As Rabi's experiments continued to improve, conditions in Europe continued to deteriorate. In 1939 Germany invaded Poland; in 1940 France fell to the Germans. In 1940 Rabi was desperate to do something to counter the powerful German military. Adding to his anxiety was the discovery in 1939 of nuclear fission, coupled with his great respect for German physicists who, he thought, might exploit fission for military purposes. Rabi's opportunity came in October 1940.

In the fall of 1940, England was being bombed by the German air force. To obtain advanced warning of approaching bombers, a radar system using ten-meter radio waves was employed; however, ten-meter waves required very large equipment, which made them impractical for most military applications. Then, however, the magnetron, a high-power source of ten-centimeter microwaves, arrived in the United States from Britain in September 1940. The British magnetron represented a technical breakthrough because of its power level and short wavelength. While the equipment needed to generate and detect ten-meter radio waves was large, the ten-centimeter magnetron opened the door to radar systems small enough to mount in fighter planes as well as naval ships.

On 6 October 1940 the magnetron was taken to the Bell Telephone Laboratory, in Murray Hill, New Jersey, where it was demonstrated. The potential of the magnetron for radar purposes was recognized immediately, and key events quickly followed. On the weekend of 12–13 October, the Microwave Committee, a committee of the National Defense Research Committee formed by President Roosevelt, decided to establish a central laboratory; on 18 October, the Massachusetts Institute of Technology (MIT) was selected as the site for the laboratory; an earlier planned conference, supposedly on nuclear physics, had been scheduled at MIT for 28–31 October, to which a group of physicists were invited for purposes other than nuclear physics. At a luncheon at the Algonquin Club of Boston, plans for the microwave radar laboratory were revealed. Rabi was in this group. Seven days later, he left his Columbia laboratory, left his students, left his home, and left his beloved New York City to join the MIT Radiation Laboratory in Cambridge, Massachusetts. He did not return home for five years.

Rabi immediately went on a lecture tour to recruit physicists for the Radiation Laboratory. And they came. Rabi, the head of the Research Division, initiated the efforts to develop three-centimeter and one-centimeter magnetrons so that smaller radar systems could be designed. He quickly gained the reputation as being able to anticipate military needs, and Lee DuBridge, the laboratory's director, appointed him associate director.

On 4 January 1941, less than two months after the formation of the laboratory, a radar beam was bounced off a Boston building across the Charles River from MIT. On 7 February, a plane taking off from East Boston Airport (later Logan International Airport) was detected by a Radiation Laboratory radar system.

Rabi, who became a prominent voice of the Radiation Laboratory, worked directly with military leaders. At first, the military officers were unwilling to reveal how the devices they requested were to be used. Rabi, a tough negotiator, refused to work on that basis because he linked the design of apparatus to its use. Soon a trust was developed and mutual respect opened the door to significant discussions.

A new complication entered Rabi's life in early 1943. J. Robert Oppenheimer, Rabi's close friend, had been named the director of the Manhattan Project, located in Los Alamos, New Mexico. Oppenheimer needed first-rate talent, and the Radiation Laboratory was one place to get talented physicists. Oppenheimer first asked Rabi to join him at Los Alamos as the associate director of the Manhattan Project, but Rabi refused: he had doubts that the development of the atomic bomb could be concluded in time to affect the outcome of the war. More significantly, by 1943 Rabi was involved at the policy level with officials in Washington, D.C., and he knew that radar was having a direct impact on the conduct of the war, so he maintained his primary focus on that field. However, Rabi did agree to become an advisor to Oppenheimer, and in the summer of 1944, he and Niels Bohr were named senior consultants to him.

In 1944 Rabi won the Nobel Prize in Physics for his development of the magnetic resonance method. This method became the basis for nuclear magnetic resonance (NMR), discovered independently by Edward Purcell and Felix Bloch in 1945 and 1946. NMR quickly became an indispensable tool for chemists. Later, Rabi's prize-winning work was the basis for magnetic resonance imaging (MRI), which became an indispensable tool for physicians.

In the fall of 1944, Rabi organized a vast writing project at the Radiation Laboratory. Physicists were assigned topics and were told to write a book that fully described the development work they had done during the war years. The result of this effort was the twenty-eight-volume MIT Radiation Laboratory Series. Published from 1947 to 1953, these books on microwave electronics became primary reference sources after the war and enabled scientists to apply new instrumental techniques in their research. More than sixty years later, some of these books were still used. Rabi described the Radiation Laboratory Series as the "biggest thing since the Septuagint" (Rigden, 2000, p. 164).

When the war ended in 1945, the MIT Radiation Laboratory, unlike the Los Alamos Laboratory, closed down immediately. As the physicists returned to their home laboratories, many of them discovered that the world had changed. Many acknowledged that the atomic bomb ended the war; however, many recognized that radar had actually won the war. Both radar and the nuclear bomb were the handiwork of physicists, and after the war physicists were the darlings of society.

The Postwar Years. Rabi returned to Columbia University as chairman of the Physics Department. Administrative duties coupled with an increasing number of invitations to serve as an advisor in Washington, D.C., meant that Rabi's postwar research never achieved the intensity of his earlier research. His most important research result came soon after the war and was one of two experimental results that dominated the discussions at the Shelter Island Conference on Long Island, New York. This conference, held on 2–4 June 1947, brought together twenty-four physicists. It has been described by many of the participants as the most important conference they ever attended. Two experiments were reported at the conference: one by Rabi and one by Willis Lamb. Both experiments revealed subtle disparities in the spectrum of hydrogen. These experiments brought the theory of quantum electrodynamics to its current state of refinement, and Rabi's experimental results led directly to the discovery of the anomalous magnetic moment of the electron.

When the war ended, a new age began: the nuclear age. New policies were needed to guide U.S. leaders as they considered the implications of the awesome power of the nucleus. The General Advisory Committee (GAC), consisting of prominent physicists, was formed by the Atomic Energy Commission (AEC) to advise the federal government. Oppenheimer served as the chairman of the GAC, and Rabi was a member. When the Russians detonated their first atomic bomb on 29 August 1949, David Lilienthal, chairman of the Atomic Energy Commission (AEC), called for a meeting of the GAC, which gathered on 29–30 October.

The principal topic of the GAC meeting was what the U. S. response to the Russian nuclear success should be. One subject dominated the discussions: whether to start a crash program to build a fusion (hydrogen) bomb. The committee, for persuasive reasons, unanimously recommended against developing a hydrogen-fusion bomb. Rabi and Enrico Fermi wrote a minority report in which they opposed the fusion weapon on ethical grounds: They argued that "such a weapon cannot be justified on any ethical ground" and argued further that it was "an evil thing considered in any light" (Rigden, 2000, pp. 205–207.) President Harry S. Truman, however, ignored the advice of the GAC.

The opposition of the GAC to the hydrogen bomb in 1949 was linked directly to Oppenheimer, and this opposition was taken as evidence that Oppenheimer had connections with the Communist Party. In the 1954 hearing that revoked Oppenheimer's security clearance, this opposition was used by the "prosecution." In the hearing, instigated by Lewis Strauss, chairman, Atomic Energy Commission, Rabi was one of the most effective witnesses on Oppenheimer's behalf, but the outcome was foreordained. Rabi's friend, J. Robert Oppenheimer, had made enemies and these enemies brought him down.

Rabi is the "father" of two major laboratories. The first, the Brookhaven National Laboratory on Long Island, was established in 1947. Rabi was particularly proud that Brookhaven was a national laboratory that any qualified physicists could use provided they had an idea worthy of investigation.

In 1950 Rabi was named a U.S. delegate to the Fifth General Assembly of UNESCO held in Florence, Italy. After carefully laying the appropriate groundwork, Rabi presented a resolution stating that "to keep the light of science burning brightly in Europe" (Laws and Thompson, 1957, p. 194), a high-energy accelerator laboratory be established in Europe available to all European physicists (the comparison with Brookhaven is obvious). The resolution passed, and the establishment of CERN (Conseil Européen pour la Recherche Nucléaire) in Geneva, Switzerland, was the eventual result.

Rabi always believed he could have averted the tragic outcome of the Oppenheimer hearing if he, Rabi, had advised Oppenheimer on what to do. But Rabi faced a difficult dilemma. At the time of the Oppenheimer hearing, Rabi was working with President Dwight Eisenhower and Dag Hammarskjöld, the secretary general of the United Nations, to plan the first International Conference on the Peaceful Uses of Atomic Energy to be held in Geneva, Switzerland, in August 1955. Lewis Strauss, the chairman of the AEC, was also actively involved in the planning. It was this same Strauss who provided the principal impetus in the drive to discredit Oppenheimer and bring him down. (Oppenheimer had not only recommended against the development of the hydrogen bomb, but had also embarrassed Strauss in June 1949 during a congressional hearing, and Strauss never forgot it.) As a result, Rabi had to maintain a reasonably cordial working relationship with Strauss while, at the same time, he tried to influence the outcome of the Oppenheimer hearing.

Rabi retired in 1967 as the first university professor at Columbia University; however, he remained active for almost another twenty years. Nine months before he died, he was interviewed on the television program, *The Open Mind.* "Science," Rabi said, "is much closer to something you might call religion. It's something for all humanity. It's a point of view and direction which we've never had before" (1987 inverview).

BIBLIOGRAPHY

Rabi's papers are in the Library of Congress.

WORKS BY RABI

With Victor W. Cohen. "The Nuclear Spin of Sodium." *Physical Review* 43 (1933): 582–583.

With Jerome M. B. Kellogg and Jerrold R. Zacharias. "The Magnetic Moment of the Proton." *Physical Review* 46 (1934): 157–163.

"On the Process of Space Quantization." *Physical Review* 49 (1936): 324–328.

With Jerrold R. Zacharias, Sidney Millman, and Polykarp Kusch. "A New Method of Measuring Nuclear Magnetic Moment." *Physical Review* 53 (1938): 318.

With Jerome M. B. Kellogg and Norman F. Ramsey, Jr. "An Electric Quadruploe Moment of the Deuteron: The Radiofrequency Spectra of HD and D_2 Molecules in a Magnetic Field." *Physical Review* 57 (1940): 677–695.

With John E. Nafe and Edward B. Nelson. "The Hyperfine Structure of Atomic Hydrogen and Deuterium." *Physical Review* 71 (1947): 914–915.

"Rabi: Scientist and Citizen." Interview by Richard Heffner. *The Open Mind* (WPIX, WNET), 12 April 1987. Video and transcript available from http://www.theopenmind.tv/tom/searcharchive_episode_output.asp?id=1112.

OTHER SOURCES

Bernstein, Jeremy. "Profile: Physicist." *The New Yorker,* 13 and 20 October 1975.

Day, Michael A. "I. I. Rabi: The Two Cultures and the Universal Culture of Science." *Physics in Perspective* 6 (2004): 428–476.

Laws, Walter H. C., and Charles A. Thomson. *UNESCO: Purpose, Progress, Prospects.* Bloomington: Indiana University Press, 1957.

"Otto Stern and the Discovery of Space Quantization: I. I. Rabi as Told to John S. Rigden." *Zeitschrift für Physik D – Atoms, Molecules and Clusters* 10 (1988): 119–120.

Pais, Abraham. *The Genius of Science: A Portrait Gallery of Nineteenth-Century Physicists.* Oxford; New York: Oxford University Press, 2000.

Rigden, John S. "Molecular Beam Experiments on the Hydrogens during the 1930s." *Historical Studies in the Physical Sciences* 13 (1983): 335–373.

———. "The Birth of the Magnetic Resonance Method." In *Observation, Experiment, and Hypothesis in Modern Physical Science,* edited by Peter Achinstein and Owen Hannaway. Cambridge, MA: MIT Press, 1985.

———. *Rabi: Scientist and Citizen.* Cambridge, MA: Harvard University Press, 2000.

John S. Rigden

RACKER, EFRAIM (*b.* Neu Sandez, Poland, 28 June 1913; *d.* Ithaca, New York, 9 September 1991) *enzymology, energy metabolism, biomembranes.*

Racker—Ef to his friends and colleagues—contributed significantly to the study of enzymes and energy in the cell in the mid-twentieth century. He developed methods for reconstituting proteins in biological membranes, fundamental to studying their individual effects. Using these methods, he helped assemble artificial vesicles that demonstrated conclusively the chemiosmotic theory as proposed by Peter Mitchell (who subsequently earned a Nobel Prize for his ideas in 1978).

Racker also earns credit for many important particular discoveries: F_o, a major component of the enzyme that generates adenosine triphosphate (ATP), the basic molecule of energy in the cell; CF_1, the central component of ATP synthase in plant chloroplasts; the mechanism of energy transfer to ATP in glycolysis; the first energy-rich thioester; and transketolase and (in parallel with other labs) the pentose phosphate cycle. These reflect Racker's remarkable experimental skills in tinkering with and coaxing unfamiliar cellular enzyme systems into relief. Racker was equally important institutionally, mediating debate, writing advanced textbooks, promoting basic research and a strong work ethic, and buoying the high-stakes field of bioenergetics with good humor. He also became involved in two episodes of misconduct by others. One gained wide renown and eventually became a canonical case of fraud in science, although Racker's role is often misreported. His legacy also includes a series of aphorisms that wittily express experimental know-how.

Pathway to Basic Research Racker was born in a large town in southern Poland to Jewish parents. In his infancy the family moved to Vienna, where the Rackers lived in a poor neighborhood and experienced the anti-Semitism of the era. Young Efraim did not respond well to the formalisms of school. He enjoyed competitive sports and chess. He also liked to draw and paint. Inspired by the work of Viennese native Egon Scheile, and with the encouragement of painter and art educator Victor Löwenfeld, Efraim decided to pursue a career as a painter. At age eighteen he gained admission to the highly selective Akademie der bildenden Künste Wien (Vienna Academy of Art). Again, he became disillusioned with the formal training style, left, and enrolled at the University of Vienna School of Medicine. He passed Sigmund Freud's home on his daily walk to school and, with his older brother Heinrich, shared a fascination with psychiatry and psychoanalysis. He graduated in 1938 when, as Racker described it, a mass psychosis invaded Vienna. As Nazism advanced, he left via Denmark for England.

After reading a 1936 paper, "Biochemistry and Mental Disorder," Racker sought work with its author, J. Hirsh Quastel, in Cardiff, Wales. Racker studied the psychotic effects of amines on brain metabolism with him but began to realize that the background knowledge of normal metabolism was then too limited. When Great Britain entered World War II, Racker was classified as an enemy alien. He emigrated to the United States in 1941, ultimately going to the University of Minnesota. Capitalizing on funds available from the March of Dimes, Racker began research (for a salary of 12,000 dimes a year, he noted). on how the polio virus altered metabolism in the brain. Again, he faced problems due to lack of foundational knowledge about glycolysis, the breakdown of sugar in cells. He later called this a turning point, which led him into basic research on carbohydrate and energy metabolism. Later in his career, in 1979, Racker defended the value of basic research against political critics and began by citing this experience.

Glycolysis. Following two years as a physician at Harlem Hospital (1942–1944), Racker joined the Microbiology Department at New York University Medical School, where he enjoyed support from Severo Ochoa and Colin MacLeod. Racker continued his research on viral inhibition of glycolysis but soon found that his samples had been contaminated with iron. Undeterred, he traced how the iron inhibited the enzyme glyceraldehyde-3-phosphate (GAP) dehydrogenase and then how glutathione reversed the effect. Glutathione was a known co-factor for another enzyme, glyoxalase, and Racker was led to interpret its role as an intermediate in energy transfer. Although glyoxalase itself was relatively obscure, Racker had identified for the first time how energy could be transferred biologically though an energy-rich (sulfur-containing) thioester bond. His 1951 discovery became an important precedent for interpreting this widely occurring energy-transfer mechanism. Racker would also later instruct his students that "Troubles Are Good for You," as he put it in his *A New Look at Mechanisms in Bioenergetics* (1976). He profiled

how, as in this case, a skilled investigator can turn ostensibly disastrous results into an advantage.

Continuing his work with his technician, Isidore Krimsky, Racker returned to the glycolysis enzyme that helped break down and capture energy from GAP. There, he found, GAP reacted with an enzyme-bound sulfhydryl group. This, in turn, produced an energy-rich thioester bond (as in the case of glyoxalase), which was handed off, along with its energy, to phosphate. The energy-rich phosphate was transferred again to adenosine triphosphate, or ATP, the basic molecule of energy in the cell. Racker's findings upset the then widely accepted claims by the renowned biochemist Otto Warburg. More importantly, however, Racker documented the first mechanism for how ATP is generated in cells. This 1952 discovery also set an important precedent, but one that, ironically, misguided biochemists for the next two decades, as described below.

Pentose Phosphate Pathway. In 1952 Racker accepted a position at Yale University, where he shifted his metabolic investigations to a reaction pathway that branches off from glycolysis: the hexomonophosphate shunt. Energy is derived from a six-carbon sugar, which is then broken down into a series of five-carbon sugars, or pentose phosphates. Some of these become important components in synthesizing other molecules, such as the units of DNA. Racker's lab discovered a new enzyme, transketolase, that breaks down the five-carbon sugars further (coincidentally, into GAP as a product). In 1954 Racker returned to New York City, now at the Public Health Research Institute as chief of the Division of Nutrition and Physiology. As he continued work, the successively recrystallized enzyme lost its specific activity. Racker traced the problem to the presence of a second enzyme, an epimerase, that had been extracted along with the first and which partly accounted for the reactions they had been observing. Racker sorted out which enzyme reacted with which pentose, correcting what he and several labs had concluded earlier. Racker found a lasting lesson in his experience, which he later preached to his students: "Don't think, purify first"—and, "Don't waste clean thinking on dirty enzymes" (1979b, p. 572; 1985, p. 26; Hinkle, 1992, p. 517; Miller, 1992, p. 97).

In further work, Racker recognized a chemical analogy that prompted him to test transketolase on another molecule in the pentose phosphate reaction pathway. It worked there as well. The enzyme functioned twice. This helped Racker (aided by students Paul Srere, Dan Couri, and June Fessenden) to reconstruct the whole system. The pathway ultimately recreated the initial hexose; it was a cycle, a conclusion also reached in other labs, notably by Bernard Horecker at the National Institutes of Health. Racker's transketolase experiment had further significance as well. Melvin Calvin had been working to elucidate the steps of photosynthesis, whereby plants fix carbon dioxide from the air, then synthesize glucose. Many of the enzymes and intermediate compounds were shared with the pentose pathway. While having dinner with Calvin in New York in 1954, Racker mentioned his experiments revealing the second function of transketolase, which transformed a six-carbon molecule into a four-carbon molecule. "I see it all now," Calvin replied cryptically (Racker, 1979a, p. 572). He then explained to Racker that he had just provided him the clue for linking his own photosynthetic reactions into a cycle—an achievement that earned Calvin the 1961 Nobel Prize in Chemistry.

ATPase. Racker's new institutional surroundings in New York proved exceptionally fruitful. Maynard Pullman arrived shortly after Racker, and they decided to tackle another major metabolic system, oxidative phosphorylation, or ox phos. These reactions in the mitochondria use the oxygen people breathe to transform the energy from the citric acid cycle (breaking down the food they eat) to the energy-rich adenosine triphosphate, or ATP (by adding the final phosphate). Racker believed that to solve complex problems, such as psychoses of the mind or multienzyme systems of the cell, one needed to resolve them into their parts and reassemble them functionally. Racker apparently exhibited his strategy early in life: at age six he took apart a broken clock and tried (unsuccessfully) to fix it. He now applied this strategy to ox phos.

Racker noted later that reconstituting systems successfully required three things. First, one needed cheap labor. Pullman's skilled new student, Harvey Penefsky, provided that. Second, one needed large quantities of stable material. David Green had pioneered how to prepare mitochondria from beef heart. He invited the team to the University of Wisconsin, where they learned his techniques. Finally, one needed new ideas. Here, that meant a new machine for shaking the cells and proteins apart. Centrifugation then sedimented out submitochondrial particles and the team tested re-adding various soluble fractions to identify functional factors. The first, named F_1, was the main part of the enzyme, ATPase (later called ATP synthase), where ATP was formed. Subsequently, Yasuo Kagawa helped confirm that F_1 units could be seen in electron micrographs as small knobs on the inside of the mitochondrial membrane. Kagawa and Racker then isolated the segment of ATPase, embedded in the membrane, where F_1 attached. It was named F_o for reestablishing a known function: inhibition by oligomycin. Racker tried many other methods of destroying and separating the mitochondria, yielding an array of particle types. More supplemental factors emerged: two factors that held F_1 to F_o (F_6 and part of F_4, later renamed OSCP) and F_2 (also called Factor B), all whose regulatory function was

elucidated much later. (F_3, F_4, and F_5 were later reclassified or abandoned as contaminated extracts.)

As progress stalled, Racker looked for a more easily resolvable system, targeting the ATPase in photosynthesis. Switching from beef heart to the more agreeably smelling spinach, he and Vida Vambutas isolated the chloroplast's analog to F_1: CF_1. Their work helped underscore the strong similarities between ox phos and photophosphorylation (how plants generate ATP from light). Racker summarized his work and the state of the field in a monograph, *Mechanisms in Bioenergetics*, in 1965. The following year his professional contributions were recognized by his election to the National Academy of Sciences.

Reconstituting Membrane-Bound Enzymes. In the mid-1960s, research on ox phos became notoriously frustrating. The system was located in the mitochondrial membrane. Membranes are primarily lipids, chemically more like oil than water, and no one could extract membrane-bound proteins that would still function. Peter Mitchell suggested a possible reason. He contended that energy did not flow through a succession of energy-rich bonds, as modeled in Racker's 1952 account of glycolysis. Mitchell proposed a chemiosmotic mechanism instead, whereby ox phos generated an electrochemical proton gradient across the membrane. Any system would thus require an intact closed vesicle. The membrane was itself viewed as a functional barrier. Racker met with Mitchell in New York City in 1965, and they discussed his ideas, but Racker did not deem them supported by the available evidence.

Racker accepted an opportunity to lead the new Section of Biochemistry and Molecular Biology at Cornell University and moved to Ithaca, New York, in 1966. His investigative focus also shifted. Whether influenced primarily by Mitchell or by experimental exigencies, he began examining the role of the membrane more fully. He showed first how proteins functioned differently on each side of the membrane and then how they were positioned asymmetrically. Eventually, the membrane became part of his reconstitution strategy. Racker's lab recombined the isolated proteins with lipids and a detergent, then gradually removed the excess by either dialysis or dilution. In 1971 Yasuo Kagawa, working with Racker, successfully reconstituted ATPase. Racker and his student Anne Kandrach then did the same for a component of the electron transport chain, cytochrome oxidase. Effective reconstitution had finally begun. Racker's theoretical views changed the following year. Peter Hinkle, a former student then also working at Cornell, was measuring how the reaction rate of reconstituted cytochrome oxidase could be controlled by an electrochemical gradient. Racker, while observing the instrument readings in the lab, seemed to concede that Mitchell was correct, at least about the proton gradient. Soon, Kagawa's ATPase reconstitutions could also pump protons. These liposome vesicles lost function when the membranes "leaked." Persuaded that closed compartments were essential, Racker fully switched his allegiance to chemiosmotic principles.

Adopting a new theoretical framework, Racker soon consolidated his laboratory's findings in a dramatic capstone experiment. In 1973 Dieter Oesterhelt and Walther Stoeckenius isolated a new photosynthetic pigment, bacteriorhodopsin, from halobacteria and showed that when exposed to light, it transported protons across the membrane in accord with chemiosmotic mechanisms. In 1974 Racker collaborated with Stoeckenius to create a thoroughly unnatural vesicle. Introducing sound waves as yet another method of reconstitution, they recombined membrane lipids from soybeans, bacteriorhodopsin from halobacteria, and ATPase from beef mitochondria. Although mixing elements from cells from three kingdoms, the artificial vesicles produced ATP in light. That "unphysiological" chimera epitomized reconstitution for Racker: it integrated the separate parts not just structurally but also functionally. The chimeric vesicles were also an important benchmark in demonstrating chemiosmotic mechanisms for ox phos and photophosphorylation to a wide community of biochemists. By 1975 all the components of ox phos had been isolated and analyzed separately. Racker again summarized the status in the field in a new advanced textbook in 1976, *A New Look at Mechanisms in Bioenergetics*. Racker shared the Warren Triennial Prize with Mitchell in 1974 and received the National Medal of Science in 1976.

Late Work. Racker's methods of lipsome reconstitution opened wide the investigation of membrane-bound proteins. He helped train a whole new generation in membrane biology, including Günter Hauska, Peter Hinkle, Richard Huganir, Baruch Kanner, Ladislav Kovác, Richard McCarty, Chris Miller, Maurice Montal, Nathan Nelson, Michael Newman, Jan Rydstrøm, Dennis Stone, Bernie Trumpower, and Charles Yocum. Having demonstrated that protons were indeed transferred across membranes, Racker turned to study the mechanisms of transport. He considered many ion pumps for clues. In so doing, he reconstituted the first Ca^{2+}-ATPase pump from muscle cells and (with Richard Huganir) the acetylcholine receptor of nerve cells. He showed how the latter functioned through conformational changes, opening a channel for the passage of ions that initiate the nerve impulse. In parallel work, however, he failed with the lactate transporter and with the Na^+-K^+-ATPase in tumor cells. Racker once described the erratic behavior of membrane proteins as molecular psychology. In 1985 Racker wrote one last text, *Reconstitutions of Transporters, Receptors, and Patho-*

logical States, detailing the strategies and methods of reconstitution.

During his career, Racker's interest in pathological states never waned. Much of his late work, far less fruitful than his earlier achievements, was oriented to cancer. A series of minor contributions, tallied over several decades, was accompanied by many stymied efforts, ironically illustrating his own views about the primacy of basic research. Racker never considered his investigations complete. Even at age seventy-three he was retooling, learning the new techniques of recombinant DNA. He even modified his old adage about proteins, "Don't think, purify first," to "Don't think, don't purify: clone!" (1985, p. 26).

Professional Leadership. Racker's stature derived in part from his professional leadership. He served on the editorial boards for the *Journal of Biological Chemistry* in the 1960s and later for the *Journal of Membrane Biology* and *Biochimica et Biophysica Acta*. His posture towards resolving disagreement was especially significant, notably during the highly contentious debates over ox phos. For example, after a disagreement about sequence of elements in the electron transport chain with Britton Chance, Racker and his student went to his lab, where additional tests clarified the results. Racker expressed the moral for students: "When you find something that disagrees with a paper or review, … get in touch with the person with whom you disagree. If the issue is indeed important to you, straighten it out by collaborative experiments rather than by polemics" (1976, p. 52).

His early life experience with politics in Europe seemed to shape his later actions. Racker tried to find the middle ground in theoretical debates on chemiosmotic ideas. In a letter to Peter Mitchell in January 1975, Racker offered one conceptual hybrid, he admitted, as "a gentleman's political compromise. From my early childhood, I had wanted to live in a peaceful world. Although I have always enjoyed friendly controversy and arguments, I have been most uncomfortable during the bitter polemics in our field in the last decade" (Prebble and Weber, 2003, p. 203). Racker endeavored to quell the ox phos tempest. In March 1974 he circulated a letter to ten leading biochemists, appealing for unity and proposing to publish a joint statement that, he hoped, would help stabilize the field and improve its negative image among other scientists and funding agencies. After two and a half years of correspondence and of alliances severed and mended, with Racker personally coaxing Mitchell to rejoin the project on at least two occasions, six researchers published a multi-authored review that, while hardly free of residual conflicts, was nonetheless widely interpreted as resolving the decades-old controversy. In 1975 Peter Mitchell received the Nobel Prize in Chemistry. Given Racker's important work on reconstitution and the chimeric vesicles that helped secure the status for chemiosmotic theory, many colleagues were surprised that the honor did not include him as well. He continued to receive recognition, however, with a Gairdner Award in 1980.

Episodes of Research Misconduct. Racker became involved in two episodes of scientific misconduct. In one case, he was leading critic; in the other, primary victim. The case in Racker's own lab gained wide notoriety and remained in the early 2000s an oft-cited example of scientific fraud. Both cases, however, need to be studied to understand fully Racker's conduct. They are striking complements, yet each illustrates Racker's professional leadership. His responses were considered exemplary by most colleagues.

The first episode occurred during the heyday of conventional chemical approaches to ox phos. George Webster, working with David Green's lab, had published a series of papers from 1962 to 1965 proposing a high-energy intermediate in the reaction series: Reduced Cytochrome *c* Coupling Factor, or RCCF. Racker tried to replicate the findings, hoping to resolve discrepancies with his own findings. At first, he noticed only errors in the methods for measuring ATP. Eventually, Racker went with two colleagues to Green's lab at the University of Wisconsin, where experiments again failed, using Webster's methods on samples they had prepared themselves. Racker asked to consult Webster's laboratory notebooks. Webster acknowledged having fabricated his data. In this episode, Racker was credited for actively pursuing the false claims and for establishing definitive results with his strong experimental skills.

In the second episode, fraudulent data were fabricated in Racker's own lab. Initially, in 1980, Mark Spector was considered a brilliant PhD student with exceptional technical aptitude and promise. At the time, Racker was shifting his research to cancer cells as he returned to puzzles about rates of glycolysis that he had set aside for several decades. Spector was set the task of purifying the membrane-bound ATPase from tumor cells, where it exhibited increased activity. Spector's quick success seemed to confirm the strong recommendations that had accompanied his graduate school application. His remarkable work seemed to continue as he reportedly isolated, in turn, a series of enzymes that sequentially triggered inefficient ATP-dependent membrane transport of sodium (leading further to excess glycolysis). Finally, he announced that the first component in the "kinase cascade" was similar to a protein produced by the Rous sarcoma virus. The events that led to viral cancer seemed dramatically solved. The model generated much excitement when first presented to the Tumor Virus Group in

May 1981. Racker and Spector published the scheme in *Science* on 17 July.

Just one week later, one of Spector's collaborators at Cornell, Volker Vogt, approached Racker. He and his student had earlier encountered problems generating Spector's results. They had secured some of Spector's original electrophoretic gels. The radioactive labels on them were not the telltale phosphorus, but an easily applied iodine. The developed images (autoradiograms) used in data analysis would thus have carried no trace of any manipulation. The original gels were the first substantive clue to doctored results. Racker and Vogt confronted Spector. Racker personally supervised the next set of experimental replications. Some of the original results seemed partly confirmed, others not. By September, Racker had dismissed Spector. The coauthors, led by Racker, retracted all the suspect papers. At the first evidence of fraud, Racker acted decisively. He offered to resign from his various committees and editorial boards until the issue was fully resolved, and he even withdrew an important five-year grant renewal. Consequences continued, however. Earlier that spring, U.S. congressional hearings had stirred up public concerns about scientific misconduct. In addition, the case served as grist for Nicholas Wade, a science journalist for *Nature*, who was actively reporting fraud. Exposure to the Spector episode was thus greatly amplified. Still, colleagues respected Racker for investigating and acknowledging the errors himself, thereby modeling how to manage such problems responsibly. The American Society of Biological Chemists apparently did not find the affair reason against awarding Racker their prestigious Sober Memorial Lectureship the following year, in 1982. Seven years later Racker reflected on his experience, publishing his views on misconduct in science in *Nature*.

Personality in Professional Context. Racker exuded good humor and a dry wit that even enriched his scientific discourse. He made light of the many obstacles that faced chemists working on cell metabolism in the 1960s. For example, "'Nature may be difficult, but she is never malicious,'" he quoted Einstein as saying. Einstein, he then commented, "obviously had never worked on oxidative phosphorylation" (Rowen, 1986, p. 285). At a 1963 conference, Racker remarked slyly that "anyone who is not thoroughly confused just does not understand the situation." He reviewed the complex reactions, then concluded: "I shall not show you a scheme of the topography of the various factors in mitochondria because I promised to keep this presentation simple. But I carry a picture of it in my wallet, together with photos of my wife and daughter and I'll be glad to show all three of them to anyone who cares to see them." The comment, which appeared in the published paper, was not entirely gratuitous. It conveyed in a light-hearted way, the complexity that so deeply and repeatedly frustrated the "family" of biochemists working on the problem. Such comments helped counterbalance the prevailing mood of debate at the time, characterized by other researchers as contentious and often rancorous, even vitriolic.

In a similar spirit, Racker issued to his entering graduate students at Cornell University "Twelve Rules for Graduate Students in Biochemistry," styled tongue-in-cheek after the biblical commandments. For example, "When thou usest isotopes, thou shalt remember that 'not everything that counteth counteth.'" Such pithy lessons also appeared in his advanced textbooks. Examples are "A clean experiment is worth more than a few hundred dirty calculations," and "It doesn't matter if you fall down as long as you pick up something from the floor while you get up" (1976, pp. 6, 9). Many such witticisms, typically encoding bits of professional wisdom, became stock sayings echoed throughout the field.

Racker was an avid artist. He began painting at age thirteen when he received a box of oil paints for his birthday. Later he likened reconstituting liposomes to drawing a portrait: each was a functional but distorted representation. Colleagues recognized how Racker embodied a fruitful combination of creative thinking and rigorous experimental analysis. Racker's paintings included landscapes and seascapes in somber hues and an austere, semi-abstracted German expressionist style. For one colleague, they reflected the darker, and also private, side of Racker's thoughts. He sold many paintings to support scholarships for students. Posthumous sales of others funded an annual lecture in his memory. Racker's artistic interests also extended to music. He played cello with enthusiasm, although he was also apparently incompetent, according to former students.

Racker also modeled the spirit of investigation. "We need to know more," he once said, "about ion fluxes, neurotransmitters, mental diseases, love, hate, crime, and mass psychology. I believe they are all related" (1979b, p. 587). He enjoyed "the game of intellectual domination" (Schatz, 1996, p. 326) and "loved argument for its ability to plow up and ventilate the scientific earth" (Miller, 1992, p. 97). He was not afraid to be wrong, however, and extolled the virtues of learning from error. While sometimes "egocentric, insensitive, even overbearing," Racker was also known to friends and colleagues for his warmth and openness (Schatz, 1996, p. 342). Racker was, above all, a tireless worker. He kept long days in the laboratory, working on Saturdays—and expecting his students and research associates to do likewise. In one of his Twelve Rules, he instructed students: "Every week hath seven days. Six days shalt thou labor for twelve hours of the day. But on the seventh day thou canst stop ONE HOUR EARLIER. And in that hour thou shalt clean thy bench."

The humor was balanced by Racker's own dedication to his labors. Indeed, he died at age seventy-eight, two days after a stroke, which had followed a full Saturday of work in the lab.

BIBLIOGRAPHY

WORKS BY RACKER

"Mechanism of Action of Glyoxalase." *Journal of Biological Chemistry* 190 (1951): 685–696. Documents the first energy-rich thioester.

With Isidore Krimsky. "Mechanism of Oxidation of Aldehydes by Glyceraldehyde-3-phosphate Dehydrogenase." *Journal of Biological Chemistry* 198 (1952): 731–743. First mechanism for transfer of energy to ATP.

With Gabriel de la Haba and I. G. Leder. "Crystalline Transketolase from Baker's Yeast: Isolation and Properties." *Journal of Biological Chemistry* 214 (1955): 409–426. Discovery of enzyme in the pentose phosphate pathway.

With M. E. Pullman, H. S. Penefsky, and A. Datta. "Partial Resolution of the Enzymes Catalyzing Oxidative Phosphorylation. I. Purification and Properties of Soluble Dinitrophenol-stimulated Adenosine Triphosphatase." *Journal of Biological Chemistry* 235 (1960): 3322–3329. Discovery of the F_1 part of ATPase.

"A Mitochondrial Factor Conferring Oligomycin Sensitivity on Soluble Mitochondrial ATPase." *Biochemical Biophysical Research Communications* 10 (1963): 534–439. Discovery of the F_o part of ATPase.

Mechanisms in Bioenergetics. New York: Academic Press, 1965. First in a series of advanced texts.

With Vida K. Vambutas. "Partial Resolution of the Enzymes Catalyzing Photophosphorylation. I. Stimulation of Photophosphorylation by a Preparation of Latent Ca^{++}-dependent Adenosine Triphosphate from Chloroplasts." *Journal of Biological Chemistry* 240 (1965): 2660–2667. Discovery of the CF_1 part of chloroplast ATPase.

With Yasuo Kagawa. "Partial Resolution of the Enzymes Catalyzing Oxidative Phosphorylation. XXV. Reconstitution of Vesicles Catalyzing $^{32}P_i$-adenosine Triphosphate Exchange." *Journal of Biological Chemistry* 246 (1971): 5477–5487. First vesicle-based reconstitution of ATPase.

With Anne Kandrach. "Reconstitution of the Third Site of Oxidative Phosphorylation." *Journal of Biological Chemistry* 246 (1971): 7069–7071. First reconstitution of component of the electron transport chain.

"Reconstitution of a Calcium Pump with Phospholipids and a Purified Ca^{++}adenosine Triphosphatase from Sarcoplasmic Reticulum." *Journal of Biological Chemistry* 247 (1972): 8198–8200.

With Yasuo Kagawa and Anne Kandrach. "Partial Resolution of the Enzymes Catalyzing Oxidative Phosphorylation. XXVI. Specificity of Phospholipids Required for Energy Transfer Reactions." *Journal of Biological Chemistry* 248 (1973): 676–684. First reconstitution of ATPase as demonstrated proton pump.

With Walther Stoeckenius. "Reconstitution of Purple Membrane Vesicles Catalyzing Light-driven Proton Uptake and

Adenosine Triphosphate Formation." *Journal of Biological Chemistry* 229 (1974): 662–663. Chimeric vesicles as capstone demonstration of chemiosmotic theory.

A New Look at Mechanisms in Bioenergetics. New York: Academic Press, 1976. Racker's second text.

With Paul D. Boyer, Britton Chance, Lars Ernster, et al. "Mechanisms of Energy Tranformations." *Annual Review of Biochemistry* 46 (1977): 955–1026. Benchmark in public resolution of ox phos controversy. Multiple authorship initiated by Racker.

Science and the Cure of Diseases: Letters to Members of Congress. Princeton, NJ: Princeton University Press, 1979a.

"Reconstitutions: Past, Present and Future." In *Membrane Bioenergetics*, edited by Chuan-Pu Lee, Gottfried Schatz and Lars Ernster. Reading, MA: Addison-Wesley, 1979b.

With Richard Huganir. "Properties of Proteoliposomes Reconstituted with Acetylcholine Receptor from *Torpedo californica.*" *Journal of Biological Chemistry* 257 (1982): 9372–9378.

Reconstitutions of Transporters, Receptors, and Pathological States. Orlando, FL: Academic Press, 1985.

"Twelve Rules for Graduate Students in Biochemistry," Unpublished, undated, courtesy of William B. Jakoby.

OTHER SOURCES

Lee, C. P., G. Schatz, and L. Ernster, eds. *Membrane Bioenergetics: Based on the International Workshop Held at Cranbrook Schools, Bloomfield Hills, Michigan, July 5–7, 1979 in Honor of Efraim Racker.* Reading, MA: Addison-Wesley, 1979. Contains autobiographical comments by Racker.

Miller, Chris. "Efraim Racker 1913–1991." *Journal of Membrane Biology* 125 (1992): 95–98.

Nelson, Nathan. "Obituary: Efraim Racker (1913–1991)." *Photosynthesis Research* 31 (1992): 165–166.

Prebble, John, and Bruce Weber. *Wandering in the Gardens of the Mind: Peter Mitchell and the Making of Glynn.* Oxford, U.K.: Oxford University Press, 2003.

Rowen, Lee. *Normative Epistemology and Scientific Research: Reflections on the "Ox-Phos" Controversy, A Case History in Biochemistry.* PhD diss., Vanderbilt University, 1986.

Schatz, Gottfried. "Efraim Racker." In *Biographical Memoirs.* Vol. 70. Washington, DC: National Academy Press, 1996.

Douglas Allchin

RaMBaM

SEE **Maimonides, Rabbi Moses Ben Maimon**.

RAMSEY, FRANK PLUMPTON (*b.* Cambridge, England, 22 February 1903; *d.* London, 19 January 1930), *philosophy, logic, mathematics, economics,*

decision theory. For the original article on Ramsey see *DSB*, vol. 11.

Admiration of Ramsey's brilliant career continues to grow. Despite having lived only twenty-six full years, his seminal work in various fields puts him in the top rank of twentieth-century scientists. His contributions to mathematical logic, combinatorics, and economics—which T. A. A. Broadbent describes in his *DSB* article—were quickly appreciated and are still influential. His contributions to decision theory, philosophy of science, semantics, epistemology, and metaphysics—some appearing in posthumous publications as late as 1990—took many years to gain the attention they deserve. They show that he anticipated several currents of thought in twentieth-century philosophy. Ramsey's ideas have lasting significance for many disciplines. The following summary emphasizes components of his work entering the limelight after Broadbent wrote.

Logic and the Foundations of Mathematics. Bertrand Russell and Alfred North Whitehead in *Principia Mathematica* sought to derive mathematics from logic. Ramsey simplified their theory of types and dispensed with their axiom of reducibility. His proposals are in "The Foundations of Mathematics" (1925) and "Mathematical Logic" (1926).

Mathematics. Ramsey's article "On a Problem of Formal Logic" (1928) treats decision procedures in logic. Along the way, it proves two major theorems in combinatorics. The theorems describe structural patterns appearing in groups. For example, any group of six people contains either three who know each other or three who do not know each other. These theorems generated a thriving branch of mathematics known as Ramsey theory. A typical question asks, what is the minimal number of members that ensures a group's having a certain structure? Certain Ramsey numbers, as they are called, exist but are unknown.

Economics. Ramsey's articles "A Contribution to the Theory of Taxation" (1927) and "A Mathematical Theory of Saving" (1928) lay the foundations for the theory of optimal taxation and the theory of the optimal rate of saving for future generations. Ramsey's approach to these topics endures in macroeconomics.

Decision Theory. Ramsey's groundbreaking paper "Truth and Probability" (1926) presents the main ideas of decision theory. It proves a theorem establishing the existence and uniqueness, given a choice of scale, of probability and utility functions representing preferences among gambles. The demonstration uses simple assumptions about structure and coherence to show that preferences may be represented as agreeing with expected utilities. Ramsey also observed that having degrees of belief conforming to the probability axioms is necessary for avoiding Dutch books, that is, systems of bets that guarantee a loss. Later, he established results about the value for decision making of gathering information.

It took decision theorists some time to grasp the significance of Ramsey's results. Theorists such as John von Neumann, Oskar Morgenstern, and Leonard Savage obtained similar results during the middle of the twentieth century. They roused enthusiasm for Ramsey's approach to probability and utility and prompted rediscovery of Ramsey's pioneering work. Representation theorems such as Ramsey's are the foundation of Bayesian methods in decision and game theory.

Philosophy of Science. An interpretation of scientific theories must decide how to understand theoretical entities such as electrons and genes. In "Theories" (1929) Ramsey takes a theory to assert that the roles of its theoretical entities are occupied. The Ramsey sentence for a theory makes this claim explicit. To obtain the Ramsey sentence, begin with a big sentence stating the theory, replace its theoretical terms with variables, then existentially generalize the variables of that open sentence. The resulting sentence asserts that the theory is true under some interpretation of its theoretical entities. Ramsey's treatment of theoretical terms explains, for example, why their meanings may vary as a theory changes.

To distinguish the causal laws of science from accidentally true generalizations, Ramsey takes the laws as rules of inference in a formalization of complete knowledge of the world. David Lewis later advanced a similar view.

Semantics and Philosophy of Language. In "Facts and Propositions" (1927) Ramsey expresses pragmatism concerning truth, belief, and meaning. His aim is a simple, naturalistic account of these subjects. Ramsey's theory of truth observes that an assertion of the truth of a sentence claims no more than the sentence itself. For example, to say that it is true that Caesar was murdered is to say just that Caesar was murdered. His account of acceptance of conditional sentences simplifies their interpretation, too. The Ramsey test says that you accept the conditional, "If p, then q," just in case when you add p to your beliefs, minimally revising to maintain consistency, you also add q. The Ramsey test continues to guide accounts of the semantics and pragmatics of conditionals and also accounts of belief revision.

Analyzing the content of a true belief, Ramsey relied on the belief's effect on behavior. A belief is true if and only if it generates successful acts. For example, a chicken's

belief that a caterpillar is poisonous is a true belief if and only if the chicken benefits from not eating the caterpillar. A true belief's content depends on the type of success holding the belief ensures. This principle, called Ramsey's principle, inspires a field known as "success semantics." Philosophers such as Fred Dretske, Ruth Millikan, and David Papineau have articulated Ramsey's naturalistic account of the contents of beliefs.

Epistemology. In a short note titled "Knowledge" (1929), Ramsey presents an account of knowledge according to which it is defined as true, full belief acquired by a reliable process. Epistemologists, such as Alvin Goldman, who hold similar views, note the advantages of making knowledge depend on a belief's source rather than on evidence supporting the belief. Reliabilism explains, for instance, why a child may acquire knowledge through perception. The child may learn that a ball is red by perceiving its color. No review of the evidence concerning its color is necessary.

Metaphysics. In "Universals" (1925) Ramsey denies the metaphysical significance of the grammatical distinction between subject and predicate. The sentence "Socrates is wise" is equivalent to the sentence "Wisdom is a characteristic of Socrates." Hence, it is arbitrary to take Socrates as a particular and wisdom as a universal.

Besides pursuing lines of thought that Ramsey initiated, scholars have also shown their esteem for Ramsey by naming awards after him. The Decision Analysis Society awards its Ramsey Medal to outstanding decision theorists. The journal *Macroeconomic Dynamics* awards its Ramsey Prize to eminent economists.

SUPPLEMENTARY BIBLIOGRAPHY

WORKS BY RAMSEY

Foundations: Essays in Philosophy, Logic, Mathematics, and Economics. Edited by D. H. Mellor. London: Routledge & Kegan Paul, 1978.

Philosophical Papers. Edited by D. H. Mellor. Cambridge, U.K.: Cambridge University Press, 1990.

On Truth: Original Manuscript Materials (1927–1929) from the Ramsey Collection at the University of Pittsburgh. Edited by Nicholas Rescher and Ulrich Majer. Dordrecht, Netherlands: Kluwer Academic, 1991.

Notes on Philosophy, Probability, and Mathematics. Edited by Maria Carla Galavotti. Naples, Italy: Bibliopolis, 1991.

OTHER SOURCES

Dokic, Jérôme, and Pascal Engel. *Frank Ramsey: Truth and Success.* London: Routledge, 2002. Treats belief, knowledge, truth, probability, decision, and universals.

Frápolli, María J., ed. *F. P. Ramsey: Critical Reassessments.* London: Thoemmes Continuum, 2005. Treats economics, logic, truth, pragmatism, reliabilism, Ramsey sentences, and universals.

Galavotti, Maria Carla, ed. "The Philosophy of F. P. Ramsey." *Theoria* 57 (1991). A special issue of the journal that treats probability and universals.

———, ed. *Cambridge and Vienna: Frank P. Ramsey and the Vienna Circle*. New York: Springer, 2006. Treats logic, belief, the value of knowledge, and Ramsey sentences.

Jeffrey, Richard. "Ramsey." In the *Cambridge Dictionary of Philosophy*. 2nd ed., edited by Robert Audi. Cambridge, U.K.: Cambridge University Press, 1999.

Lillehammer, Hallvard, and D. H. Mellor, eds. *Ramsey's Legacy*. Oxford: Clarendon Press, 2005. Treats logic, metaphysics, and philosophy of mind.

Mellor, D. H., ed. *Prospects for Pragmatism: Essays in Memory of F. P. Ramsey*. Cambridge, U.K.: Cambridge University Press, 1980. Treats belief, probability, and pragmatism.

Sahlin, Nils-Eric. *The Philosophy of F. P. Ramsey*. Cambridge, U.K.: Cambridge University Press, 1990. A comprehensive account of Ramsey's philosophical and scientific research.

Paul Weirich

RAMUS, PETER (*b.* Cuts, Vermandois, France, 1515; *d.* Paris, France, 26 August 1572), *logic and method, pedagogy, mathematics, astronomy, optics, mechanics.* For the original article on Ramus see *DSB,* vol. 11.

Ramus studies up to 1960 were dominated by two works by Father Walter Ong: his *Ramus, Method, and the Decay of Dialogue* (1958) and his exhaustive bibliographical study of the publication of Ramus's texts after his death (the *Ramus and Talon Inventory* of the same year). There were a number of presuppositions in his approach that have since been questioned. Ong's underlying thesis was that the relationship between print culture and oral culture changed over the period of Ramus's life, and that Ramus reflected, rather than instigated, this change. This change meant a shift away from the transmission of learning through oral and broadly discursive means to a visual representation of thought in diagrams and dichotomous tables. Ong argued that the spatialization and quantification of thought in dialectic and logic from the late Middle Ages onward enabled a new state of mind to emerge in print culture representing a real mathematical transformation of thinking associated with the emergence of modern science. According to this thesis, Ramus was characterized not as an original thinker but as a pedagogue responding to this subconscious movement in intellectual life. Ramism was said to be "not a respectable theory but a set of mental habits." Ramus was portrayed as a not very erudite and philistine schoolteacher with an unimpressive grasp of ancient languages, who sacrificed accuracy, sub-

tlety, and depth to ease of exposition. The great popularity of Ramus's writings after his death, and of the method which they exemplify, was said to be due to their simplicity and their applicability to many forms of pedagogy rather than any intrinsic merit.

Ong himself did not devote much space in his work to the biography of Ramus. More work has since been done by Guido Oldrini, Kees Meerhoff, Marc van der Poel, Judith Rice Henderson, and Jean-Eudes Giret to shed light on the Parisian context of his activities, his role in the university, the polemics in which he engaged, and the consistency of the positions adopted by him. From this it emerged that he was a quite exceptionally combative figure both in his attacks on ancient and contemporary thinkers, and his proposal of his own very radical ideas. His plans for syllabus reform, and his attacks on some of the mainstays of the curriculum—Aristotle (or rather, Aristotelianism), Cicero, Euclid, and Quintilian—provoked the wrath of established figures in the university such as Antoine de Gouveia and Joachim Périon, who were as violent in their responses as Ramus had been in his attacks. His positive proposals for syllabus reform, expressed in the *Advertissements sur la reformation de l'université de Paris, au Roy* (also issued in Latin) of 1562, were reflected also in his radical redrawing of the relationship of dialectic to rhetoric, and his promotion of the *quadrivium*, especially mathematics. He remained remarkably consistent in his views on these issues, even though some were not fully spelled out until the late 1560s.

His own method of teaching was practical and direct in style, involving both teacher and pupil: for the study of humanist texts, for instance, an initial brief methodical exposition of texts was followed by direct exposure to them. Ramus expressed the belief that all men possessed a natural capacity for reasoning, which Aristotelian logic disguised rather than helped deploy. This natural faculty should be developed in the briefest and clearest way, and together with a simplified version of rhetoric, it should be applied to human life and actions for the practical benefit of individual and society. His democratic commitment to the natural light of reason led him to extend his teaching to those who had no Latin; although a French translation of his *Dialectica* and a vernacular Ramist version of rhetoric did appear in the 1550s, this part of his educational program was never fully worked out or implemented.

Ramus's radical critique of education did not stop at the arts faculty; his suggestions for reforms in the higher faculties of law, medicine, and theology were as fundamental, and created a different set of enemies for him. In an enterprising biography, James Veazie Skalnik convincingly argues that his proposed reforms were prompted by a vision of university education as a site of social mobility. Ramus, the low-born provincial who suffered the social

Peter Ramus. © BETTMANN/CORBIS.

disdain of his academic colleagues, was a meritocrat whose reason for shortening the arts course was to make it affordable to poorer students, and who openly declared himself the enemy of the self-perpetuating university oligarchies he saw around him. He was also convinced of the sound intellectual basis of his contributions to a new version of the arts course. Studies on the *Dialectica* (his most published work, whether in Latin or in vernacular languages) and his concept of method and logic, notably by Nelly Bruyère, have shown in detail how simplified schema for logic gradually took shape; and Kees Meerhoff revealed the importance of Philipp Melanchthon as one of his major sources, together with Roelof Agricola and Johannes Sturm. The *Rhetorica* of 1548, once ascribed to Omer Talon, has been attributed by James J. Murphy to Ramus himself, and reveals another facet of his general reshaping of the field of logic and rhetoric. His contributions to mathematics, science, grammar, and orthography are also now seen as more important than hitherto, thanks to the work of Reijer Hooykaas, J. J. Verdonk, and Geneviève Clerico.

Religious Aspects. More attention has been paid to Ramus's religious beliefs and thinking, including the difficult question of when he was converted to a Reformed practice of religion. Although his first participation in a Protestant Eucharist did not occur until 1569, in Heidel-

berg, there is some evidence that he was a sympathizer by the 1550s. The characterization of Ramus as a Protestant martyr, which began with Théophile de Banos's biography of 1576, was adopted by Charles Waddington in his nineteenth-century biography: to it, he added a vision of Ramus as the herald of a new age that would cast off the shackles of superstition and the tyranny of ancient authorities. Against this, Ong's work portrayed Ramus as a lukewarm Christian humanist, whose work was taken up by international Calvinism in the years after his death. Ong's view has been shown to be as misleading as Waddington's whiggish hagiographical account. Ramus left one, late, work on religion, the *Commentaria de religione Christiana,* which was published posthumously in 1576. This has been shown to be anything but Calvinist, as it does not espouse the sacramental theology of the Genevan church of Ramus's day, but rather is consistent with the Zwinglian doctrine of the Eucharist as no more than an act of commemoration. In his relations with French Reformed churches, Ramus also made clear his Congregationalist rather than Presbyterian leanings. His dealings with Théodore de Bèze and Geneva were stormy: After his death, both the French Calvinist academies and the Dutch universities with similar sympathies evinced strong resistance to his theological and anti-Aristotelian ideas. What emerged from this is Ramus's independent-mindedness, his uneasy relationship with authority, and his unwillingness to compromise; but these characteristics do not make of him the lukewarm Christian and the slavish passive mirror of underlying forces in intellectual life that Ong portrayed: they rather reveal his energy, courage, determination, clear objectives, and fixed principles, as well as his fiery nature.

Ramus's Legacy. The earlier accounts of the fortunes of Ramism after his death have also attracted criticism for their concentration on his influence in England, Scotland, and seventeenth-century America, and their relative neglect of its European dimension, especially in Germany and farther east. This occurred in spite of the fact that Ong's *Ramus and Talon Inventory* showed the extraordinary extent to which Ramus's works were used as textbooks in precisely those areas. Howard Hotson rejects both technological change and religious ideology as the fundamental explanation of the unique flourishing of Ramist pedagogy in northwestern Germany and focuses instead on the basic geopolitical feature of the region in a major new study. Ramism, Hotson argues, was embraced by rulers and magistrates in many of central Europe's smaller Protestant territories as a means to deliver quasi-university education within states too small to maintain full universities. The streamlined pedagogy developed in these sub-university institutions also appealed strongly to students seeking an efficient, affordable, and readily applicable education.

There is a strong prosopographical patterning to this uptake, which is also not purely Reformed (Calvinist) but also Philippist in nature, confirming the Melanchthonian element in Ramus's thought that his later adherents would have found attractive. A somewhat different reason for the popularity of his method and thinking has been offered by Christian Strom, who argues that an important factor in the appeal of Ramism was its relevance to the anxieties caused by the breakdown of the coherent social, religious, and political world of the later Middle Ages and the desire to reestablish a sense of order. These two views are not inconsistent with each other and are united in seeing the contribution of Ramus to the emerging need for a new overarching intellectual order, which culminates in the encyclopedism of Johann Heinrich Alsted. From all these studies, a more positive representation of Ramus the man and Ramism the philosophy emerged than that which characterized Ramist scholarship up to the 1960s.

SUPPLEMENTARY BIBLIOGRAPHY

WORKS BY RAMUS

Collectaneae praefationes, epistolae, orations. Introduction by Walter J. Ong. Hildesheim, Germany: Georg Olms, 1969.

The logike of the moste excellent philosopher P. Ramus, martyr. Translated by Roland MacIlmaine. Edited by Catherine M. Dunn. Northridge, CA: San Fernando Valley State College, 1969.

Scholae in liberales artes. Edited and with an introduction by Walter J. Ong. Hildesheim, Germany: Georg Olms, 1970.

Rudiments of Latin Grammar. Menston, U.K.: Scolar Press, 1971.

Grammaire. Paris: France Expansion, 1973.

Rami Scholarum metaphysicarum libri quatuordecim, in totidem Metaphysicos libros Aristotelis; recens emendati. Edited by Joan. Piscatorem Argentinensem. Frankfurt am Main, Germany: Minerva, 1974.

Arguments in Rhetoric against Quintilian: Rhetoricae distinctiones in Quintilianum. Translated by Carole Newlands with an introduction by James J. Murphy. DeKalb: Northern Illinois University Press, 1986.

Peter Ramus's Attack on Cicero: Brutinae quaestiones. Translated by Carole Newlands, with an introduction by James J. Murphy. Davis, CA: Hermagoras Press, 1992.

Dialectique. Edited by Michel Dassonville. Geneva, 1964. 2nd ed. Edited by Nelly Bruyère. Paris: Librairie Philosophique J. Vrin, 1996.

OTHER SOURCES

Bruyère, Nelly. *Méthode et dialectique dans l'oeuvre de la Ramée.* Paris: Librairie Philosophique J. Vrin, 1984.

Feingold, Mordechai, Joseph S. Freedman, and Wolfgang Rother, eds. *The Influence of Petrus Ramus: Studies in Sixteenth and Seventeenth Century Philosophy and Sciences.* Basel, Switzerland: Schwabe, 2001.

Hooykaas, Reijer. *Humanisme, science et réforme: Pierre de la Ramée.* Leiden, Netherlands: E.J. Brill, 1958.

Hotson, Howard. *Commonplace Learning: Ramism and Its German Ramifications, 1543–1630.* Oxford: Oxford University Press, 2007.

Meerhoff, Kees, ed. *Ramus et l'université.* Paris: Éditions Rue d'Ulm, 2004.

Meerhoff, Kees, and Jean-Claude Moisan, eds. *Autour de Ramus: texte, théorie, commentaire.* Quebec, Canada: Nuit Blanche, 1997.

Meerhoff, Kees, Jean-Claude Moisan, and Michel Magnien, eds. *Autour de Ramus: le combat.* Paris: Champion, 2005.

Oldrini, Guido. *La disputa del metodo nel Rinascimento: indagini su Ramo e sul ramismo.* Florence, Italy: Le Lettere, 1997.

Robinet, André. *Aux sources de l'esprit cartésien: l'axe La Ramée-Descartes: de la Dialectique des 1555 aux Regulae.* Paris: J. Vrin, 1996.

Schmidt-Biggemann, Wilhelm. *Topica universalis. Eine Modelgeschichte humanistischer und barocker Wissenschaft.* Hamburg, Germany: Meiner, 1983.

Sharratt, Peter. "The Present State of Studies on Ramus." *Studi francese* 47–48 (1972): 201–203.

———. "Recent Work on Peter Ramus (1970–86)." *Rhetorica* 5 (1987): 7–58.

———. "Ramus 2000." *Rhetorica* 18 (2000): 399–455.

Skalnik, James Veazie. *Ramus and Reform: University and Church at the End of the Renaissance.* Kirksville, MO: Truman State University Press, 2002.

Verdonk, J. J. *Petrus Ramus en de Wiskunde.* Assen, Netherlands: Van Gorcum, 1966.

Ian Maclean

RATCLIFFE, FRANCIS NOBLE (*b.* Calcutta, India, 11 January 1904; *d.* Canberra, Australia, 2 December 1970), *zoology.*

Ratcliffe pioneered applied animal ecology and wildlife conservation in Australia. He wrote a best-selling book, *Flying Fox and Drifting Sand: The Adventures of a Biologist in Australia* (1938), and provided the scientific foundations for the Australian Conservation Foundation.

Background and Education. Ratcliffe was born in India, the son of Samuel Kirkham Ratcliffe, editor of the *Calcutta Times,* and his wife, Katie Maria, née Geeves. He was educated in England at Berkhamsted School and Wadham College, Oxford, where he read zoology under (Sir) Julian Huxley. After graduating with first-class honors in zoology in 1925, he was appointed J. E. Proctor Visiting Fellow at Princeton University. His next post was with the Empire Marketing Board (EMB) in London, which led to his invitation in 1929 as a "scientific ambassador" to assist

Australia's Council for Scientific and Industrial Research (CSIR) in a study of flying foxes in Queensland and northern New South Wales. In 1932 he returned to Scotland to lecture in zoology at the University of Aberdeen, but his Australian experiences had made him restless, and when he was offered a second chance to undertake a scientific mission for CSIR in Australia in 1935, he took it and remained in Australia for the rest of his life.

Flying Fox and Drifting Sand. Ratcliffe's first Australian mission was to advise on giant fruit-eating bats (*Pteropus poliocephalus*, grey-headed flying fox), a major pest species for fruit growers. Although "a considerable number of odd facts about the natural history of the Australian species of flying fox had been accumulated," he commented, "an accurate picture of their population as a whole and what might be called their economy was conspicuously lacking" (1938, pp. 4–5). Like others of the generation of applied ecologists trained at Oxford under Julian Huxley in the 1920s, his approach was to consider the biology and behavior of the whole population. Charles Elton, who was part of the same cohort, wrote *Animal Ecology* (1927), a seminal text in this field.

Applied ecology demanded understanding of the migratory patterns of the giant bats; this kept Ratcliffe on the move over large areas, typically in places where his fellow travelers were "bullock-drivers, drovers and possum hunters" (1938, p. 4). He spent much of his time with those whose livelihood was threatened by flying fox invasions. He was interested not in "the animal" but in the intersection between it and the economics of fruit growing. Total destruction of the population would be economically futile, Ratcliffe ultimately argued, because the economic problem rested with "a numerically insignificant minority" (p. 5). The costly elimination of nonoffenders could not be justified.

Consistent with the aspirations of the EMB, Ratcliffe married ecology with economics in his biological research. The EMB, according to David Rivett, the first chief executive officer of the CSIR, was "a brilliant piece of Empire-building" (1934 manuscript). It analyzed markets, publicized empire products, and advocated "a biological outlook" in scientific research. Its secretary, Stephen Tallents, described it as "part of a movement away from a mechanical toward a biological conception of government." It responded organically to circumstance rather than following a preordained path. Tallents reported to Rivett in 1931 that Ratcliffe was "much improved … by his time in Australia" (Tallents papers).

In 1932, at the University of Aberdeen, Ratcliffe took up writing "to lighten the darkness of the northern Scottish winters by calling up memories of antipodean warmth and sunshine" (1947, p. vi). His journalist father encouraged him to write for a popular audience, and writing "adventures of a biologist in Australia" maintained his interest in things Australian. When in 1935 Rivett offered Ratcliffe a new post as a "biological scout" in Australia, he seized the opportunity. This doubled the "adventures" for his book, and it also changed the context of his writing. He was no longer writing as a visitor; he had become an Australian. Agnes Marnoch, daughter of Sir John Marnoch in Aberdeen, agreed to join him, and they were married on 14 January 1936 in Melbourne.

Ratcliffe's new task was to look into the problems of wind erosion affecting the interior from South Australia to Queensland. Even from Melbourne the extent of the problem was apparent, as dust storms darkened the city and mallee topsoil gathered on urban roofs. The snow-capped mountains of New Zealand were stained red. As with his flying fox work, he began by traveling to the people most affected.

"A Creeping Cancer of the Land." The "Dirty Thirties" were nightmare years for pastoralists. Ratcliffe described soil erosion as "a creeping mortal sickness" of the land and inland Australia as "nothing less than a battlefield" (1938, pp. 326, 323). He saw the arid pastoral belt of inland South Australia and southwest Queensland denuded of its natural saltbush by overstocking, in the same years as the Dust Bowl in the Great Plains of the United States. In Australia, as in America, it was a time of extended drought—most of the stations he visited had failed to register average annual rainfall for fourteen consecutive years.

Ratcliffe traveled alone, listening, observing, and asking questions: The people were as much his subject of study as the land. He visited deserted homesteads where the drift sand piled to the top of the windows, where stockyards and even riverbeds were buried. "We breathed sand, drank sand and ate sand; and when we blinked our eyeballs grated. Sand was in the butter, in the sugar, in the cake, and in the vegetables" (1938, p. 280). Dinner was sometimes even served under a tablecloth; Ratcliffe and his hosts ate blind, poking underneath the cloth and snatching mouthfuls before too much sand collected in the food.

The "kingdoms of dust" threatened not just the economy but sanity. Ratcliffe's solution for soil erosion was not about science but rather about Australian society and expectations of the inland. Australians "had every reason to be intensely proud of their record in settling the great spaces of the inland," he commented. "They are only to be blamed in that they seem to have done the job too thoroughly" (1938, p. 332). Australian inland settlement needed a whole landscape solution, with a social as well as natural balance:

The essential features of white pastoral settlement—a stable home, a circumscribed area of land, and a flock or herd maintained on this land year-in and year-out—are a heritage of life in the reliable kindly climate of Europe. In the drought-risky semi-desert Australian inland they tend to make settlement self-destructive. (p. 323)

At a time when populating the inland was regarded as a patriotic duty, Ratcliffe regretfully concluded *Flying Fox and Drifting Sand* with a contrary edict: The only thing that would preserve such country would be "consciously to plan a decrease in the density of pastoral population of the inland." It was, he wrote, "not the answer I wanted or hoped to find" (1938, pp. 331, 326).

The Cost of Inland Settlement. Ratcliffe's report of 1936, *Soil Drift in the Arid Pastoral Areas of South Australia*, was immediately influential. Rivett gave a public lecture that year about the environmental cost of production, noting that "the conservation of our soils is no doubt one of our major obligations as a people" (1937, p. 2). Soil conservation authorities were established in New South Wales in 1938 and Victoria in 1940.

In 1937 Ratcliffe redirected his "applied ecology" skills to insects, particularly the pests of stored wheat, in his work as senior research officer in CSIR's Division of Economic Entomology in Canberra. The imperatives of war drove new research on mosquitoes and mosquito-borne diseases, particularly malaria, scrub typhus, and dengue fever. In 1942–1943 he traveled extensively in the southwest Pacific area. Ratcliffe's research in the postwar reconstruction period focused on termites, a major concern for the development of northern Australia.

Ratcliffe's *Flying Fox and Drifting Sand* had been published in London in 1938 but not in Australia until 1947, and its influence gathered pace in the postwar years. It was reprinted seven times between 1947 and 1976. One reviewer noted that Ratcliffe's writing revealed "an abiding admiration for the qualities of the men and women" he had encountered in his work (*Sydney Morning Herald*, 26 March 1938, p. 6). The review in the London *Spectator* concluded:

The chief impression that remains after reading this book is of the indomitable spirit of the stockmen and boundary riders and drovers (and still more, perhaps, of their wives) who are fighting what may be a losing battle against drought and drifting sand. (28 January 1938, p. 142)

Its celebration of pioneering culture recommended it as a text for Australian high schools. It could also explain Australians and their country to the world: It was one of five books chosen in the late 1950s to be printed for the "Cheap Books Scheme for Asia," a secret plan to combat communism by competing with "the flood of cheap books provided in Asia by Soviet Russia" (R. G. Casey to H. E. Holt, 1959). The plan was not implemented, but the government clearly felt that publicizing the limits of Australia's "empty" lands might protect them from invasion.

Rabbit Research. In 1949 the CSIR expanded to become the Commonwealth Scientific and Industrial Research Organization (CSIRO), and Ratcliffe was appointed officer-in-charge of the new Wildlife Survey Section, established to undertake a comprehensive survey of the nation's biological resources, a recommendation at the 1935 Congress of the Australian and New Zealand Association for the Advancement of Science. The biological survey, however, became second priority for the Wildlife Survey Section behind the scourge of rural politics, the rabbit. The contribution of the exploding rabbit population to soil erosion in inland Australia was described by Ratcliffe in 1959 as "one of the world's significant ecological events" (p. 545). He worked closely with the virologist Frank Fenner on myxomatosis, the rabbit-specific disease that dramatically reduced rabbit populations for many years. The loudest critic of Ratcliffe's cautious approach was the medical scientist Jean Macnamara, who had advocated the introduction of myxoma since first observing it at Princeton University in the 1930s. Ratcliffe commented wryly that he regarded him as "a boil on the bum of progress" (Warhurst, p. 62).

The only way to advance "pure" scientific knowledge in such a pragmatic political climate was to undertake CDK ("Chief Doesn't Know") projects. Ratcliffe ensured that one day per week should be available to "unfundable" projects that gave his section's scientists personal satisfaction. Under Ratcliffe's nurturing expectations, some scientific studies of non-pest wildlife (particularly birds) emerged.

When a directive was issued in 1955 that all research results had to be published by CSIRO, Ratcliffe appealed to the head office to grant him, as officer-in-charge, "a certain amount of discretion" about what might be regarded as "official":

Many of my staff publish, or want to publish a lot of unofficial stuff; and sometimes the line between the official and the unofficial is quite impossible to draw. Sometimes work which started as a purely hobby interest, done in a man's spare time and at weekends, may develop into a piece of official research—the best example of this is Harry Frith's interest in the Mallee Fowl, and the physics of its egg incubation. (National Library of Australia MS 2493, 16 August 1955, p. 1)

Research for Wildlife Conservation Five years later, on 22 July 1960, Ratcliffe wrote to the Australian ornithologist Dominic Serventy of his frustrations about the lack of progress with scientific wildlife research:

> You will probably realize, when you read my Report, that I was deliberately angling for an official blessing on basic research activities. Hitherto my policy has been to "get away with" as much as we could without over-publicizing our academic work. I felt that when we had the results to show the world we could risk seeking an official blessing for this type of study. (MS 2493, 22 July 1960, p. 1)

In fact the committee that reviewed the section's work in 1960 was enthusiastic about its broad program but offered no guidance as to how the section could continue this work alongside "the applied side—our responsibilities to the taxpayer and the land-holder you might say" (1960, p. 2). Ratcliffe trusted his staff, and it annoyed him that he was not granted either the resources or the discretion to develop a quality scientific program. His preferred approach was intense and time-consuming, demanding long immersion in fieldwork. He was convinced by his own earlier work that "the cheapest and most profitable [method] in the long run is to send a good man into the problem area to spend a year or so … making his own on-the-spot assessment of the problem."

Recommendations needed "first-hand local knowledge," Ratcliffe wrote to Hugh Tyndale-Biscoe in 1958, when he was a promising junior mammalogist considering the problems of red kangaroos in Western Australia. "Many field pest problems are half solved when they have been assessed and re-stated by a man combining ecological and commonsense after a fact-collecting survey of six months or so" (24 March 1958). Too busy with management to maintain his personal research projects, Ratcliffe sought to create an environment in which good ecologists with people skills gathered local knowledge and facilitated what was later called "community participation."

Ratcliffe worried constantly about work undone and sought alternative support for a national conservation program. The Wildlife Survey section had not collected or collated even basic "data needed for appraisal of the present situation" or "information on the status and distribution of the more interesting species" or assessed the biological adequacy of reserves. A survey of "the status of marsupials in the State of New South Wales" was the sole achievement of the first eight years of the section's research effort, and that was only achieved with additional funding from the state government, he wrote on 1 May 1957 (AAS, file 1002). Ratcliffe saw the foundation of the new Australian Academy of Science as a possible umbrella for

something "planned, positive and national" for the endangered Australian biota. He recognized that this required "more than a dash of idealism" and appealed for support and sponsorship (p. 1). The academy promoted nature conservation through its committees but did not have the capacity to do more than "point the way."

Australian Conservation Foundation. Ratcliffe had hoped that emerging political enthusiasm for the environment would provide a new source of funds for science. He had stepped aside from the Wildlife Survey in 1961, returning as assistant chief to the Division of Entomology until his full retirement in 1969. This freed him to undertake the position of honorary director of the new Australian Conservation Foundation (ACF) in 1965. He regarded ecological science for nature conservation as a cause worthy of both government and non-government funding, and the academy and the CSIRO supported his "backroom" scientific efforts.

In 1968, at the height of a major minerals boom, Ratcliffe wrote *Conservation and Australia*, bemoaning the fact that "any suggestion of restraint, or request for second thoughts on some local development guaranteed to provide a quick and sure economic pay-off, is only too easily brushed aside as unrealistic or even unpatriotic" (p. 5). Ratcliffe argued that conservation demanded reconciliation between "economic conservation" and "nature conservation." It should include the wise use of economically important natural resources and also the preservation of "the less tangible things … for a full and satisfying life," including wildlife and the natural beauty of the landscape. He separated the intangibles from the commodities, recognizing that natural resource managers often failed to take these into account. *Conservation in Australia*, written before the world had come to hear terms like *green*, foreshadowed the agenda of the 1970s environmental movement. Ratcliffe's "applied ecological" turn of phrase acknowledged the place of species other than humans in nature and the role of the natural in human life.

Ratcliffe's last years, despite ill health, were spent defending scientific nature conservation. He was increasingly worried that the ACF was becoming professionally political rather than providing scientific advice to elected politicians. He died in 1970, still "in harness," working as technical adviser to the House of Representatives Select Committee on Wildlife Conservation. In a large country with very few ecologists and that still lacked baseline surveys for mammals and reptiles, such work laid the foundations for an Australian Biological Resources Study, which tentatively commenced operations in 1973 and was made permanent in 1978.

BIBLIOGRAPHY

The National Library of Australia has almost all archival materials, apart from letters from Ratcliffe in other collections.

WORKS BY RATCLIFFE

Soil Drift in the Arid Pastoral Areas of South Australia. Melbourne: Council for Scientific and Industrial Research (CSIR), 1936.

Flying Fox and Drifting Sand: The Adventures of a Biologist in Australia. London: Chatto and Windus 1938. Sydney: Angus and Robertson, 1947.

Weevil Control: Information for Guidance of Wheatgrowers. Melbourne: Government Printer, 1941.

With F. J. Gay and R. N. McCulloch. *Studies on the Control of Wheat Insects by Dust.* Melbourne: CSIRO, 1947.

The Rabbit Problem: A Survey of Research Needs and Possibilities. Melbourne: CSIRO, 1951.

With F. J. Gay and T. Greaves. *Australian Termites: The Biology, Recognition, and Economic Importance of the Common Species.* Melbourne: CSIRO, 1952.

"The Rabbit in Australia." *Monographiae Biologicae* 8 (1959).

With Frank Fenner. *Myxomatosis.* Cambridge, U.K.: Cambridge University Press, 1965.

Conservation and Australia. Canberra: Australian Conservation Foundation, 1968. Reprinted from *Australian Quarterly* 40, no. 1 (March 1968).

Commercial Hunting of Kangaroos. Parkville, Australia: Australian Conservation Foundation, 1970.

OTHER SOURCES

Casey, R. G., to H. E. Holt. 14 August 1959. Series A1838/283, item 563/6/5. National Archives of Australia.

Dunlap, Tom. "Ecology and Environmentalism in the Anglo Settler Colonies." In *Ecology and Empire: Environmental History of Settler Societies,* edited by Tom Griffiths and Libby Robin. Edinburgh: Keele University Press, 1997.

Griffiths, Tom. "Going with the Flow: *Flying Fox and Drifting Sand.*" In *Storykeepers,* edited by Marion Halligan. Sydney: Duffy & Snellgrove, 2001.

———. "Francis Ratcliffe and Changing Ecological Visions." In *Perspectives on Wildlife Research,* edited by Denis Saunders, David Spratt, and Monica van Wensveen. Sydney: Surrey Beatty & Sons, 2002.

Noble, J. C., and G. H. Pfitzner. "'They Know Not What They Do': On William Rodier and His Mission to Exterminate Rabbits and Other Pests." *Historical Records of Australian Science* 14, no. 4 (2003): 431–457.

Oakman, Daniel. "The Seed of Freedom: Regional Security and the Colombo Plan." *Australian Journal of Politics and History* 46, no. 1 (March 2000): 67–85.

Powell, Stephen. "'Why Misguided Humans Have Attempted to Make Their Homes in It Is More Than I Can Comprehend': Francis Ratcliffe's First Impressions of Australia." *Eras* 1, 2001. Available from http://www.arts.monash.edu.au/eras/edition_1/powell.htm.

Rivett, A. C. David. "The Empire Marketing Board." *Australian Rhodes Review,* Melbourne, 1934.

———. "A Talk about Wool: R. M. Johnston Memorial Lecture," 8 November 1937. MS 83/19, file 1002, National Parks. Australian Academy of Science Archives, Canberra.

Robin, Libby. "Nature Conservation as a National Concern: The Role of the Australian Academy of Science." *Historical Records of Australian Science* 10, no. 1 (1994): 1–24.

———. "Ecology: A Science of Empire?" In *Ecology and Empire: Environmental History of Settler Societies,* edited by Tom Griffiths and Libby Robin. Edinburgh: Keele University Press, 1997.

———. "Collections and the Nation: Science, History, and the National Museum of Australia." *Historical Records of Australian Science* 14, no. 3 (June 2003): 251–289.

Tallents, Sir Stephen G. Papers. ICS 79, file 10. Institute of Commonwealth Studies Archives, London.

Tyndale-Biscoe, C. H. Private archives.

Warhurst, John. "Francis Noble Ratcliffe 1904–1970." In *Australian Dictionary of Biography,* vol. 16, edited by John Ritchie and Diane Langmore. Melbourne: Melbourne University Press, 2002.

Libby Robin
Tom Griffiths

RAYLEIGH, THIRD BARON
SEE **Strutt, John, third Baron Rayleigh**.

RĀZĪ, ABŪ BAKR MUḤAMMAD IBN ZAKARIYYĀʾ AL-,
known in the Latin West as Rhazes (*b.* Rayy, south of today's Teheran, Iran, 1 Šaʿbān 251 / 28 August 865; *d.* Rayy, 5 Šaʿbān 313 / 26 October 925 [or perhaps ten years later, 935?]), *medicine, alchemy, logic and philosophy, religious criticism.* For the original article on Al-Rāzī see *DSB,* vol. 11.

Since Shlomo Pines wrote his entry for the original *Dictionary of Scientific Biography* (1975), only a few new data have emerged about Rāzī's life. The situation that the rich bio-bibliographical share of classical and medieval Arabic literature conspicuously neglects Rāzī has not changed, and the well-known reasons for this—Rāzī's distance from the caliph's capital Baghdād for the greater part of his life, and more saliently, his position as an outsider to the scholarly establishment and as a freethinker—

remain the same. However, the precise dates of his birth and death recorded by al-Bīrūnī in his account of Rāzī's works may well be trusted. The information that the debate between Abū Bakr al-Rāzī and Abū Ḥātim al-Rāzī was conducted before the governor of Rayy, Mardāwīj, who took over the town only in 930 CE, would suggest a later year of death for Rāzī (as later authorities have it), but it has been plausibly argued that the actual governor was not Mardāwīj, but Aḥmad b. ʿAlī who died in 923 or 924 CE. Bīrūnī's precise recording of Rāzī's dates might also serve to credit his family with a certain level of education and affluence, which would also have facilitated his access to the scholarship to which his works amply attest. Rāzī's scholarly relations include two students of the philosopher al-Kindī, al-Sarakhsī and Abū Zayd al-Balkhī, the latter of whom he mentions as his teacher in philosophy and for whom he in turn wrote a recipe—an early example of its kind—against Abū Zayd's rose allergy during spring in Balkh. He exchanged letters on religious-philosophical problems with some other colleagues from Balkh, Abū l-Qāsim al-Kaʿbī and Abū l-Ḥusayn Shahīd. Rāzī's only known disciple is the Christian philosopher Yaḥyā ibn ʿAdī, who later went on to study with the famous philosopher al-Fārābī (d. 950).

Medical Writings. Rāzī's largest medical work, and the work for which he was most famous in the Latin tradition, *K. al-Ḥāwī* (*Continens*), still represents a largely unexploited treasure of medical information, much of it otherwise lost, from Greek, Sanskrit, Syriac, and early Islamic sources, complemented by his own clinical observations (introduced by *lī*, meaning as for myself) on diagnosis and therapy. The complicated manuscript history of the text has not been investigated since 1975 (and will probably remain a desideratum for some time), but a few studies show that the *Ḥāwī* is composed of a series of thematically neighboring, yet independent, monographs. These studies illustrate the method of composition and prove that the choice of quotations (entirely from written sources) and their authenticity have to be examined from instance to instance, and that the ultimate product is not Rāzī's. Rather, it was written after Rāzī's death by his students, who collected works from Rāzī's files before the year 961, in which the dedicatee, the Būyid vizier Abū l-Faḍl Ibn al-ʿAmīd, died. Rāzī's stance toward medical authority can meanwhile be, but has not so far in depth, studied in his *Doubts concerning Galen*. Both Rāzī's ethical works and a number of medico-ethical texts of his, some of them only known by title, show that he sees his entire work, including his medical writing, as belonging to philosophy; medicine and alchemy are considered as natural philosophy, complemented by metaphysics, and both of these as opposed to mathematics (which he depreciates).

In his attempt to promote medicine to a philosophical discipline, Rāzī conspicuously deviates from the traditional framework of the Aristotelian/late-Alexandrian system of the sciences that also shaped Islamic classifications of the sciences. Here, medicine was mostly considered a mere craft, *ṣināʿa*, lacking a theoretical basis. It is from this frame of reference that Rāzī as a physician was denigrated by later colleagues such as Avicenna and Maimonides, and also by the philosopher al-ʿĀmirī, a near contemporary of Rāzī, who said that he heard people ascribe wisdom (*ḥikma*) to Rāzī—or describe him as a philosopher—because of his proficiency in medicine, in spite of his various ravings. On the other hand, Rāzī, in his *Philosopher's Way of Life*, enumerates an impressive number of his works that successfully support his philosophical claims, covering, in rough order, the Aristotelian curriculum: Logic (in particular the *Analytica posteriora*), Metaphysics, Ethics (for example, his *Spiritual Physick*), Physics, Cosmology, Psychology, and ending in Medicine and Alchemy.

Rāzī's interest in the professional ethics and sociology of medical practice is illustrated by titles such as *On Examining the Physician* and *Treatise on the Causes why Most People Turn Away From Excellent Physicians Toward the Worst Ones*. Rāzī's most influential medical work, his *Compendium for* [the Sāmānid governor of Rayy] *al-Manṣūr*, extant in many manuscripts and in Hebrew and Latin translations (the latter done by Gerard of Cremona), and his celebrated monograph *On Smallpox and Measles*, with an equally long afterlife, remain understudied. The same applies to Rāzī's *K. al-Taqsīm wa-l-tashjīr* (*On Division and Ramification*), which is a tool in graphic form to serve the differential diagnosis of illnesses, symptoms, and pains, and which represents one of the numerous monographs of Rāzī that have the practical aim of facilitating the physician's job.

General Philosophical Stance. It has long been noted that Rāzī's open-minded attitude toward all natural phenomena was at the core of both his critique of Galen and his approach to alchemy: He famously points out that the Galenic doctrine that a warming or cooling body is always warmer or cooler than the body on which it acts does not necessarily hold for medicine where Rāzī reports the boosting effects of, for example, a warm beverage that heats up the patient to a much hotter temperature than the beverage itself was. In alchemy (*Secret of Secrets*, and the still-unpublished treatise on the [occult] *Properties* of Mineral, Vegetable and Animal Substances), Rāzī accepts the existence of unexplained phenomena and likewise analyzes his samples by experiment, rather than by ascribing magical qualities to them. Both these approaches, in medicine and in alchemy, had the potential to disintegrate the traditional doctrine of the four humours and the four elemental qualities, and they were taken up as an argument against that doctrine by later religious thinkers such as al-Ghazālī.

Rāzī's ethics, mainly represented in his *Book of Spiritual Physick* (A. J. Arberry's translation) and his *The Philosopher's Way of Life* (Pines), have been discussed extensively since the mid-1970s. As Rāzī himself said, his *Spiritual Physick* serves as a companion to the -*K. al-Manṣūrī*, Rāzī's great systematic handbook (edited in 1987) on the theory and practice of medicine. The definition of ethics as a kind of medicine for the soul may well go back to al-Kindī's views, possibly negotiated by Abū Zayd al-Balkhī's book *Hygienics for Body and Soul*. Rāzī's philosophical asceticism, originally inspired by the example of Socrates, is tempered by the observation that human beings in general, and legitimately, seek pleasure, but are misguided by an irrational fear of death that seduces them to content themselves by gratifying their base appetites for power, food, or sex. The philosopher's role in society is not that of an infallible authority to be followed; rather he is merely expected to demonstrate to his fellow citizens that happiness cannot be accumulated boundlessly and in fact does not exist by itself, but can be achieved only as a release from prior discomfort or irritation, and that fear of death, as well as speculations about the hereafter, have no rational basis. This position, including a kind of temperate hedonism along with a number of other features, may have its origin with Epicurean ethics. Other aspects of Rāzī's ethical thought, such as his notion of the three aspects of the human soul and their equilibrium that should be pursued, as well as his views on death and the afterlife, may be seen as modifications of Galenic ideas.

It must be stressed, however, that as limited as Rāzī sees the philosopher's function as a model for society in general, equally small is his willingness to rely on book learning as opposed to empirically acquired knowledge. One of the most striking examples of this stance is a debate between Rāzī and his compatriot, Abū Hātim ar-Rāzī, an Ismāʿīlī theologian and missionary, about revelation, prophecy, cosmological problems, and about the question of the proper attitude toward scholarly authorities. The so-called debate between the two Razis has been preserved in Abū Hātim al-Rāzī's work *Signs of Prophethood*. (It remains unclear whether it constitutes a straightforward record of the debate and to what degree he distorts Rāzī's argument.) Abū Hātim's authorship causes Rāzī to have the worst of the argument; however, the modern reader's attention lies on what he (Abū Bakr al-Rāzī, the subject of this article) has to say.

"Abū-Hātim: [...] How is it possible, then, that the subject should be higher than the sovereign, and the led a more accomplished philosopher that the leader?

Abū Bakr: On this issue I will now state something to you whereby you will know that the matter is indeed as I have mentioned, and you will (be able to) recognize the true from the false on this subject. Know that when every succeeding philosopher expends his zeal in philosophical investigations, applies himself with perseverance and assiduity to them, and researches issues that are controversial on account of their subtlety and difficulty, he learns from his predecessors their knowledge, retains it, and supplements it with other things through his sagacity and numerous researches and investigations. This is so because, proficient now in the knowledge of his predecessors, he becomes aware of other useful ideas (*fawāʾid*) and learns even more, since research, investigation, and assiduity necessarily result in additional and abundant material." (Translation with references in Gutas 1988)

Gutas describes Razi's position as follows: "Central to Abū-Bakr's argument is the concept of progress in the acquisition of truth. This lies at the root of his disagreement with the theologian Abū-Hātim for whom truth, by the very nature of what he is professing, was revealed complete all at once. (…) Past philosophers, 'the ancients,' discovered Fundamental Principles (*uṣūl*), and each succeeding generation of philosophers, after learning all they had to teach them, added to their store of knowledge and supplemented it" (Gutas, 1988). In addition to Rāzī's remarkable emphasis on the epistemological principles of learning and research, this debate also contains ideas about cosmology, prophecy and revealed religion, and the hereafter, that in their unheard-of audacity must have horrified his opponent. These have led to a kind of *damnatio memoriae* in the Islamic scholarly tradition, and have fascinated and dominated Western scholarship since Paul Kraus' studies, not least in the past three decennia.

Abū Hātim's text itself has been re-edited in 1977, translated in part, summarized and analyzed, and interpreted under the titles of the Iranian background of Rāzī's cosmological ideas, the political context of postcolonialism, and of the concept of heterodoxy.

Writings on Religion. Rāzī uses five formative principles in his cosmological systems, as did many of his Iranian predecessors, most of whom were Dualists or Zoroastrians. Of the many designers of cosmologies that are reported by heresiographers such as al-Shahrastānī and historians such as al-Masʿūdī, one philosopher stands out, Abū l-ʿAbbās al-Īrānshahrī (fl. 873), a contemporary of Rāzī and to all evidence an influence on him in these matters. It is in working with Īrānshahrī's system that Rāzī was compelled to take issue with the question whether the creator has brought into existence the world automatically, that is, by his very nature, or in a special act of volition. Rāzī opts for the latter, because it is only in this option that the creator remains uncreated, as he should be. If this is so, if the creator is older than his creation and the creation came into existence only by his act of volition, then the question arises why he had not taken this decision from the beginning. Meier describes Razi's situation as follows:"[It is at this junction that] Rāzī was confronted with the principal question, and he answered it by jumping into the notorious pentad of uncreated entities, first of all saying that there must have co-existed along with God something else that was uncreated which impelled him to change his intention from not creating anything to creating the world" (Meier, 1992, p. 9). This something else is the soul (*nafs*), alive and unknowing. Another passage shows clearly the accord between Īrānshahrī and Rāzī, where the former is quoted as saying that "time is a sign of God's knowing, as space is a sign of his power (*qudrat*), movement a sign of his activity, and matter/body (*jism*) a sign of his energy (*quwwat*). Every one of these four is unlimited and uncreated. Time is a wandering and restless substance. A statement of [Rāzī] who follows Īrānshahrī amounts to the same: Time is a passing substance" (Meier 1992). The four uncreated principles that in Īrānshahrī's system clearly are subordinated to God while representing him, are counterparts to Rāzī's quartet of time, space, soul, and matter. Īrānshahrī's movement corresponds with Rāzī's soul, which in a kind of echo of Īrānshahrī's notion indeed introduces movement into the static situation prevailing so far by falling in love with matter and moving God in his mercy and power to allow soul to unite with matter and set the world in motion. Mahdi says Rāzī thus

> "[…] seems to be trying to present a coherent and defensible theory of creation that can absolve God of the evils of creation. On the one hand, he tries to resolve some of the difficulties facing *kalām*-theologians who attribute to God everything present in the physical world, including evil and ignorance. His God is pure knowledge and pure goodness, not responsible for the defects of creation. On the other hand, he is trying to argue against the eternalists, all those who held the view that […] the defects of the world below […] do not reflect on the maker of the world, since the world had no 'maker' " (Mahdi 1996).

It is an interesting, though unanswerable question, whether Rāzī himself would have been willing to accept the possibility that his own system of the five eternals might be subject to a better explanation by future thinkers.

Another instance of Rāzī's rootedness in Iranian intellectual tradition, notwithstanding his originality of thought, may be noticed in his stance toward the message of the prophet Muḥammad in particular, and to prophethood in general. Islam was brought by Arabs from the Arabic peninsula to non-Arabs in far-away regions of Asia and Africa, and it served and was perfectly understood as a religion to organize both individual daily life and collective political affairs. Both Abū Hātim and Abū Bakr al-Rāzī belonged to a generation of postcolonialism that was characterized by Arabic conquerors who had long mediated their beliefs and values to the conquered Iranians, nonetheless allowed the Iranians to retain, and accentuate, their cultural identity. In the time of the two Rāzīs, although the Islamic-Arabic empire had long broken up, there remained a close cultural bond between the former rulers and their subjects. When the two Rāzīs conducted their debate, all of Iran was ruled by Iranians. It is only one of the many features of postcolonial Iran that the role of the prophet Muḥammad was seen by both Rāzīs as political, the law he had brought being only about the organization of the community. For the philosopher Rāzī,

> "the so-called revelation was simply politics in disguise: the so-called prophets *claimed* that their warfare and (by implication) the political activities leading to it were ordered by God, but God had nothing to do with mundane affairs. As he saw it, the truth was elevated above such affairs, and accessible through the intellect which all humans shared, not through membership of this or that community, and it was not a prescription for order in this world at all, but on the contrary something that purified your soul of worldly concerns and caused you to be released from this world." (Crone, 2006)

For the religious propagandist Abu-Ḥatim al-Rāzī, on the other hand, although the law of the Prophet was equally temporary, it was practically necessary for the maintenance of communal organization. The inner meaning of the revelation was necessary for salvation, and in order to decipher revelation's symbols one had to take recourse to the authority of the imams, not that of the prophets—one fault as horrible as the other in Abū Bakr al-Rāzī's eyes. Crone summarizes the situation this way:

> "[W]e are now in the period that some call the Iranian intermezzo and others the Renaissance of Islam, with reference to the return of the above-mentioned Iranian rulers plus Persian culture and the Persian language on the one hand and that of Greek science and philosophy (without the rulers) on the other. The debate between the two Rāzīs is symptomatic in that respect, too, for both men were Iranians and most of what they said had long roots in Near Eastern culture." (Crone, 2006, p. 19)

It is difficult to assess Rāzī's exact position in his contemporary society, professional and otherwise. He must have enjoyed a wide reputation as a physician, at court and in the hospitals. His philosophy and worldview were well known, although, to the extent his views were programmatically heretical, they were hushed and do not even figure in his auto-bibliography. It may well be that in the two generations following al-Kindī a greater variety of theological and philosophical views were discussed than the literature of the tenth and eleventh century would suggest, cf. for instance the information collected in van Ess 1997 and the list of works by Kindī's students al-Sarakhsī and Abū Zayd al-Balkhī. "It is thus possible that some views, which would be considered shockingly heretical in the fifth Islamic century, could still have offered a legitimate option a century earlier" (Stroumsa, 1999). However, had it not been for Rāzī's incontestable excellence and integrity of conviction, the Islamic intellectual world would perhaps have regarded freethinking as a dismissible slip of an eccentric; after him it was prepared "to strike pre-emptively against any danger, real or imagined, of the resurgence of this folly" (Stroumsa, 1999).

SUPPLEMENTARY BIBLIOGRAPHY

WORKS BY AL-RĀZĪ

Abū Hātim al-Rāzī. *Aʿlām al-nubuwwa*. Edited by Ṣalāḥ aṣ-Ṣāwī, Ghulāmriḍā Aʿwānī. Tehran, Iran: Imperial Iranian Academy of Philosophy, 1977.

K. al-Mudkhal ilā l-ṭibb. Edited by M. de la Concepción Vazquez de Benito. Salamanca, Spain: Universidad, 1979.

K. Sirr ṣināʿat al-ṭibb. Edited and translated by R. Kuhne. *al-Qantara* 3 (1982), 5 (1984), 6 (1985).

-K. al-Manṣūrī fī l-ṭibb. Edited by Hāzim al-Bakrī al-Ṣiddīqī. al-Kuwayt: Publications of Institute of Arab Manuscripts, 1987.

K. al-Taqsīm wa-l-tašğīr. Edited [under the title *Taqāsīm al-ʿilal*] by Ṣ. M. Hammāmī. Syria: University of Aleppo, Institute for the History of Arabic Science, 1992.

K. al-Šukūk ʿalā Jālīnūs. Edited by M. Mohaghegh. Tehran, Iran: Muʾassasa-i Muṭalaʿāt-i Islāmī, 1372/1993.

OTHER SOURCES

Bar-Asher, Meir M. "Quelques aspects de l'éthique d'Abū Bakr al-Rāzī et ses origins dans l'œuvre de Galien." *Studia Islamica* 69 (1989): 5–38; 70 (1989): 119–147.

Brague, Rémi. *Rhazès. La medicine spirituelle* [*K. al-Ṭibb al-rūḥānī*]. Paris: Garnier-Flammarion, 2003.

Bryson, Jennifer S. *The Kitāb al-Hāwī of Rāzī (ca. 900 AD), Book One of the Hāwī on Brain, Nerve, and Mental Disorders: Studies in the Transmission of Medical Texts from Greek into Arabic into Latin*. PhD diss. Yale University, 2000.

Crone, Patricia. "Post-Colonialism in Tenth-Century Islam." *Der Islam* 83 (2006): 2–38. On Rāzī's debate with Abū Hātim al-Rāzī.

Daiber, Hans. *Bibliography of Islamic Philosophy*. 2 vols. Leiden, Netherlands: Brill, 1999.

Druart, Thérèse-Anne. "Al-Rāzī's Conception of the Soul: Psychological Background to his Ethics." *Medieval Philosophy and Theology* 5 (1996): 245–263.

Goodman, Lenn E. "al-Rāzī, Abū Bakr Muḥammad." *Encyclopaedia of Islam*, Vol. VIII. 2nd ed. Leiden, Netherlands: E. J. Brill, 1952–2005.

———. "The Epicurean Ethic of Muḥammad ibn Zakariyāʾ ar-Rāzī." *Studia Islamica* 34 (1971): 5–26.

———. "Muḥammad ibn Zakariyyāʾ al-Rāzī." In *History of Islamic Philosophy*, vol. I, edited by S. H. Nasr and Oliver Leaman. London: Routledge 1996.

———. "Rāzī vs. Rāzī – Philosophy in the *Majlis*." In *The Majlis. Interreligious Encounters in Medieval Islam*, edited by Hava Lazarus-Yafeh, Marc R. Cohen, Sasson Somekh, and Sidney H. Griffith. Wiesbaden, Germany: Harrassowitz 1999.

Gutas, Dimitri. *Avicenna and the Aristotelian Tradition. Introduction to Reading Avicenna's Philosophical Works*. Leiden, Netherlands: Brill, 1988. On Rāzī's debate with Abū Hātim al-Rāzī.

Gutas, Dimitri. "Notes and Texts from Cairo Mss. I. Addenda to P. Kraus' Edition of Abū Bakr al-Rāzī's *Ṭibb al-Rūḥānī*." *Arabica* 24 (1977): 91–93.

Hau, Friedrun R. "Razis Gutachten über den Rosenschnupfen." *Medizinhistorisches Journal* 10 (1975): 94–102.

Jacquart, Danielle. "Note sur la traduction latine du Kitab al-Mansuri de Rhazès." *Revue d'Histoire des Textes* 24 (1994): 359–374.

Kahl, Oliver. "Fragments of an Anonymous 'Old Dispensatory' in ar-Rāzī's *Kitāb al-Ḥāwī*." *Journal of Semitic Studies* 49 (2004): 289–301.

Mahdi, Muhsin. "Remarks on al-Rāzī's Principles." *Bulletin d'Études Orientales* 48 (1996): 145–153.

Meier, Fritz. "Der 'Urknall' eine Idee des Abū Bakr ar-Rāzī." *Oriens* 33 (1992): 1–21.

Pines, Shlomo. *Studies in Islamic Atomism*. Jerusalem: The Magnes Press, 1997.

Pormann, Peter E., and Emilie Savage-Smith. *Medieval Islamic Medicine*. Edinburgh: University Press 2007.

Rashed, Marwan. "Abū Bakr ar-Rāzī et le *kalām*." *Mélanges de l'Institut Dominicain d'Études Orientales du Caire* 24 (2000): 39–54.

Rāzī, Muḥammad Ibn Zakariyāʾ al-. *Texts and Studies*, vols. I-III, edited by Fuat Sezgin, A. Amawi, C. Ehrig-Eggert, and E. Neubauer. Frankfurt am Main, Germany: Institut für Geschichte der arabisch-islamischen Wissenschaften, 1996.

Richter-Bernburg, Lutz. "Abū Bakr Muḥammad al-Rāzī's (Rhazes) Medical Works." *Medicina nei Secoli Arte et Scienza* 6 (1994): 377–392.

Rosenthal, Franz. "Ar-Rāzī on the Hidden Illness." *Bulletin of the History of Medicine* 52 (1978): 45–56.

Sezgin, Fuat. *Geschichte des arabischen Schrifttums*. Leiden, Netherlands: Brill, 1970, 1974, 1979.

Stroumsa, Sarah. *Freethinkers of Medieval Islam. Ibn al-Rāwandī, Abū Bakr al-Rāzī, and Their Impact on Islamic Thought*. Leiden, Netherlands: Brill, 1999.

Ullmann, Manfred. *Die Medizin im Islam.* Leiden, Netherlands: Brill, 1970.

van Ess, Josef. *Theologie und Gesellschaft im 2. und 3. Jahrhundert Hidschra. Eine Geschichte des religiösen Denkens im frühen Islam*, vol. 4. New York: de Gruyter 1997.

Walker, Paul E. "The Political Implications of al- Rāzī's Philosophy." In *The Political Aspects of Islamic Philosophy. Essays in Honor of Muhsin S. Mahdi*, edited by Charles E. Butterworth. Cambridge, MA: Harvard University Press, 1992.

Weisser, Ursula. "Zur Rezeption der *Methodus medendi* im *Continens* des Rhazes." In *Galen's Method of Healing. Proceedings of the Second International Galen Symposium*, edited by Fridolf Kudlien and Richard J. Durling. Leiden, Netherlands: Brill, 1991.

Hinrich Biesterfeldt

REGIOMONTANUS, JOHANNES (*b.* Königsberg, Franconia, Germany, 6 June 1436; *d.* Rome, Italy, c. 8 July 1476), *astronomy, mathematics.* For the original article on Regiomontanus see *DSB,* vol. 11.

Studies of Regiomontanus since 1975 have enriched scholars' understanding of his antecedents, the contemporary context of his work in astronomy and mathematics, and his significance for the Copernican revolution.

Intellectual Debts. The astronomical manuscripts Regiomontanus owned or copied during his Viennese years (1450–1461) show a greater engagement with the Viennese astronomical tradition and its library holdings than has been heretofore documented. From Paris, Henry of Langenstein (d. 1397) had brought to Vienna his critique of the epicycles and eccentrics of Ptolemaic astronomy (*De reprobatione ecentricorum et epiciclorum,* 1364—see Kren, 1968 and 1969). Regiomontanus not only copied it in the 1450s (Vienna, ÖNB cod. 5203), but also drew upon it. Among other points, Langenstein's treatise criticized Ptolemy's models for the Moon, inferior planets, and Mars for implying large (but unobserved) variations in their areas. This type of argument motivated Regiomontanus's efforts to reform astronomical modeling using concentric (homocentric) spheres and surfaced in such later writings as the *Epitome of the Almagest,* book 5, prop. 22, the correspondence with Bianchini (Swerdlow, 1990, esp. pp. 173–174), and the *Defense of Theon against George of Trebizond.* In Vienna, Regiomontanus also encountered other astronomical alternatives to the *Almagest,* notably al-Bitruji's homocentric *De motibus celorum,* and criticisms of al-Bitruji in the fourteenth-century *Tractatus planitorbii* of Guido de Marchia, who also proposed as the carriers of the planets not spheres, but

eccentric rings moving in a fluid heaven (Shank, 1992, 1998, and 2003).

In a letter of 1460 to Bishop Janós Vitéz of Hungary, Regiomontanus sketched for the Sun and Moon homocentric models that were silent modifications of a flawed model by al-Bitruji, of whose work Regiomontanus was otherwise critical. He also hoped to eliminate the eccentrics and epicycles of all the planets, producing a "fully concentric" astronomy that would yield improved tables (Swerdlow, 1999). Neither the inherent problems with this program nor his mastery of the nonhomocentric *Almagest* prevented him from nurturing this hope into the 1470s.

Controversy with George of Trebizond. Regiomontanus's association with Cardinal Basilius Bessarion (1460–c. 1465) drew him into the latter's controversies with George of Trebizond, which shaped the decade he spent in Italy and Hungary. Bessarion had criticized George of Trebizond's translation of and commentary on the *Almagest* soon after they appeared in 1451, initiating a twenty-year feud that extended most famously to their evaluations of Plato. Regiomontanus played the leading role in the astronomical part of these controversies, which framed both his travels and his writings, including two of his most important theoretical works, the *Epitome of the Almagest* and the *Defense of Theon against George of Trebizond.*

The *Epitome of the Almagest* was not a translation (*pace* DSB XI 349a), but an exposition and updated analysis of Ptolemy's work. Bessarion had urged Georg Peuerbach to write it as an alternative to Trebizond's inadequate commentary. When Peuerbach's death left the *Epitome* half complete, Regiomontanus finished and revised it circa 1462. Recent work has shown that Bessarion was more than a patron and dedicatee, for he worked through portions of the work with some care (Rigo, 1991). In contrast to the *Epitome,* Regiomontanus's *Defensio Theonis contra Georgium Trapezuntium* (1460s–1470s) was a highly polemical work that went well beyond addressing Bessarion's anger at Trebizond's attacks on Theon of Alexandria's *Almagest* commentary, which the cardinal favored highly. This 573-page autograph (St. Petersburg, Archive of the Russian Academy of Sciences) contains a book-by-book attack on George's commentary on the *Almagest,* criticizing errors that range from computation and logic to fundamental assumptions and interpretations of Ptolemy. Regiomontanus's death interrupted his plan of printing both the *Epitome* and the *Defensio* on his own press (only the *Epitome* appeared in print, in 1496). Although these four works—George of Trebizond's translation of the *Almagest* and commentary on it, and Regiomontanus's *Epitome* and *Defensio*—constitute hundreds of folios of controversy about the interpretation of

Ptolemy in the generation before Nicolaus Copernicus, they have scarcely been studied and outline a new research frontier that will enrich substantially scholars' understanding of fifteenth-century Latin astronomy.

Commenting on Ptolemy. Of the astronomers to whom the *Epitome* introduced the *Almagest,* Copernicus is the most famous. The first two propositions from book 12 of the *Epitome* have special significance for the emergence of Copernicus's reorganization of the planets around the mean Sun. Regiomontanus's silent correction of Ptolemy deserves special mention. Ptolemy held that two alternative models could account for the superior planets' second anomaly (that with respect to the Sun, involving their retrograde motion): an epicyclic model (a traditional small epicycle carried by a large deferent) and an eccentric model (in effect, an inversion of the previous model, with a large epicycle carried by a small deferent). In *Almagest,* book 12, chapter 1, Ptolemy denied that the eccentric model worked for the second anomaly of the inferior planets (Toomer, 1984, p. 555), and George of Trebizond repeated this claim in his commentary. In *Epitome,* book 12, proposition 2, however, Regiomontanus proved without comment that an eccentric model could also account for the second anomaly of Mercury and Venus. The corresponding passage in the *Defensio* attacks George of Trebizond for denying this equivalence, which Regiomontanus asserts to be Ptolemy's own obvious intention on the grounds that he had already discussed similar equivalences in books 3 and 4 of the *Almagest* (Shank, 2007). Recent work shows that Regiomontanus was not the first to offer such a proof. The head of the Samarqand observatory, Ali Qushji, had done so before the mid-fifteenth century in explicit criticism of Ptolemy. The strikingly similar orientation of the diagrams of this proof in the Qushji manuscript and in Regiomontanus's *Epitome* tantalizingly raises questions of transmission, even as the antithetical interpretations of Ptolemy point to different, and perhaps independent, motivations and contexts (Ragep, 2005; Shank, 2007).

Whatever its origins, the *Epitome*'s proof in book 12, proposition 2 carries considerable significance for the subsequent history of astronomy, because the eccentric model of the second anomaly of the inferior planets transforms directly into a configuration with Venus and Mercury moving around the mean Sun. The language of Copernicus's manuscript notes shows that he was working with the alternative eccentric model, in which he treated the distance between Earth and the mean Sun as the eccentricity. When Copernicus used this metric to calculate the size of each planet's sphere, their spacing gave him a "necessary" sequence of the planets around the mean Sun (Swerdlow, 1973). The new arrangement thus eliminated the long-standing uncertainties in the order of the Sun, Venus, and

Mercury and yielded the "commensurability" extolled in *De revolutionibus,* I, 10. There is, however, no good reason to suppose that Regiomontanus was a proto-Copernican. Contrary to *DSB* vol. 11, 351b–352a, the claim that "The motion of the stars must vary a tiny bit on account of the motion of the earth," which Georg Hartmann in the sixteenth century ascribed to Regiomontanus, probably refers not to Earth's annual motion, but to the small shifts in the central Earth's center of gravity that some fourteenth-century natural philosophers inferred from the motions of heavy bodies on Earth's surface (Duhem, 1913–1959).

The *Defensio*. Whereas the *Defensio* clarifies some of the motivations behind Regiomontanus's mathematical proofs in the *Epitome,* it also sheds light on Regiomontanus's physical assumptions and the polemical context of his work. Begun in the 1460s, the *Defensio* was at one point to be offered to King Matthias Corvinus of Hungary, for whom Regiomontanus drafted a dedication and to whose court he also moved (c. 1467–1471). The timing of both the dedication and the move follows heightened antagonism between Bessarion and George of Trebizond. The cardinal had prevailed on Pope Paul II to imprison George after discovering that the latter had sought to dedicate his works on the *Almagest* to Mehmed II, the conqueror of Constantinople, in 1466. Upon his release, George attempted to dedicate these works to King Matthias Corvinus in 1467–1468 (Monfasani, 1976, pp. 286–287). Both Regiomontanus's move to Hungary and his *Defensio* were no doubt meant to undercut George of Trebizond's quest for patronage from Matthias. Although Regiomontanus spent several years in Hungary (c. 1467–1471), books 12 and 13 of the *Defensio* were not finished until after he had settled in Nürnberg, where he listed it circa 1474 among the works slated for publication on his own press.

A preliminary examination of the polemical *Defensio* has already offered new insights into Regiomontanus's natural philosophical concerns, physical assumptions, and understandings of the astronomer's role. Regiomontanus was clearly in theoretical turmoil in the early 1460s, as is evident in the fact that his Ptolemaic expositions in the *Epitome* (1462) are bracketed by his homocentric (non-Ptolemaic) astronomical yearnings in both the *Letter to Vitéz* (1460) and his correspondence with Giovanni Bianchini during 1464 (Swerdlow, 1990). The *Defensio* confirms that this was not a temporary phase, but a career-long predicament. The same juxtapositions appear in passages from the *Defensio* that date from the 1470s. Alongside its praise of Ptolemy, the *Defensio* also contains criticisms of the *Almagest* on physical grounds. Regiomontanus assails Ptolemy and his followers for using circles to save the phenomena and to produce numerical results.

Johannes Regiomontanus. © BETTMANN/CORBIS.

But planets, he argues, cannot be moved by mere circles, that is, by two-dimensional models devoid of physical properties. Elsewhere, he rails against such an astronomy as a "fictitious art." Underlying these criticisms was a vision of astronomy as an enterprise that integrated physical considerations (including size, movers, media, etc.) with the task of producing excellent numerical predictions (Shank, 2002).

Sources of Mathematical Results. Recent scholarship on Regiomontanus's mathematics has qualified earlier claims about his originality while tightening his links to the Arabic and late-medieval Latin traditions, the foundation on which his access to Bessarion's rich library later built. His work on the computation of the first five perfect numbers, formerly considered original, was in fact copied from a thirteenth-century manuscript in Bessarion's library (Venice, Biblioteca Marciana, f.a. 332). Likewise, while he was working on solving the general cubic equation algebraically, his solution of a special case of the cubic equation goes back to the fourteenth century (Master Dardi of Pisa and others). The reassessment of his mathematics anchors Regiomontanus firmly in his late-medieval intellectual context, whereas his unusual aim of understanding

fully and capturing the original meaning of Euclid and Archimedes set him apart from it, and led him to collate Greek and Latin manuscripts by these authors. His efforts reveal a deep understanding of the *Elements* and of the Archimedean corpus, both of which he intended to print in corrected versions. He read very carefully Campanus of Novara's recension of Euclid's *Elements,* catching problems in the Latin and in Campanus's attempts to make sense of them. His philological and codicological sensibilities also shaped his mathematics, as they did his astronomy. Thus he disapproved of Campanus's inclusion of the "parallel postulate" among the postulates, believing—probably on the evidence from a Greek manuscript—that it belonged among the axioms (Folkerts, 1996, pp. 94–96, 104–105, 108). His several hundred corrections of and comments on the translations of Archimedes by Jacobus Cremonensis also drew on his study of several Greek manuscripts (Clagett, 1978, pp. 357–365).

The last phase of Regiomontanus's forty-year life focused heavily on his Nürnberg press (Stromer, 1980). He planned to devote it overwhelmingly to significant and philologically correct mathematical, astronomical, and astrological works, including some of his own, and it probably motivated his large personal library (see Kremer, 2004). Although his output was modest, he pioneered the printing of complex astronomical tables and geometrical diagrams imbedded in the text in a single pull of the press. Unpublished research on his output shows Regiomontanus's active involvement in the day-to-day operation. A survey of the twenty-four extant copies of his *Disputationes contra deliramenta cremonensia* (c. 1475) reveals that he stopped the press for aesthetic resettings of pages (the hypercorrect Latin orthography can be only his) and for corrections of typographical errors. He even made systematic pen corrections of errors missed during the press run (as he also did in the *Ephemerides*). This attention to detail illustrates his hopes for the production of texts that would be correct philologically as well as typographically. In terms of diffusion, the most important reader of Regiomontanus's press was Erhard Ratdolt, whose presses in Venice and Augsburg reissued many of Regiomontanus's works and adopted much of his unrealized printing program.

SUPPLEMENTARY BIBLIOGRAPHY

Clagett, Marshall. *Archimedes in the Middle Ages.* Vol. 3. Philadelphia: American Philosophical Society, 1978, pp. 357–365.

Duhem, Pierre. *Le Système du monde: histoire des doctrines cosmologiques de Platon à Copernic.* Vol. 9. Paris: Hermann, 1913–1959, pp. 237–323.

Folkerts, Menso. "Regiomontanus als Mathematiker." *Centaurus* 21 (1977): 214–245.

———. "Regiomontanus's Role in the Transmission and Transformation of Greek Mathematics." In *Tradition, Transmission, Transformation: Proceedings of Two Conferences on Pre-modern Science held at the University of Oklahoma*, edited by F. Jamil Ragep, Sally Ragep, and Steven Livesey, 89–113. Leiden, Netherlands: Brill, 1996.

———. "Regiomontanus's Role in the Transmission of Mathematical Problems." In *From China to Paris: 2000 Years Transmission of Mathematical Ideas*, edited by Yvonne Dold-Samplonius, et al., 411–428. Stuttgart, Germany: Franz Steiner Verlag, 2002.

Gerl, Armin. *Astronomisches Rechnen kurz vor Copernicus: Der Briefwechsel Regiomontanus-Bianchini*. Boethius, vol. 21. Stuttgart, Germany: Franz-Steiner Verlag, 1989.

Grössing, Helmut. *Humanistische Naturwissenschaft: Zur Geschichte der Wiener mathematischen Schulen des 15. und 16. Jahrhunderts*. Saecula Spiritalia, vol. 8. Baden-Baden, Germany: Verlag Valentin Koerner, 1983.

Hamann, Günther, ed. *Regiomontanus-Studien*. Vienna: Verlag der Österreichischen Akademie der Wissenschaften, 1980.

King, David A., and Gerard L'E. Turner. "The Astrolabe Presented by Regiomontanus to Cardinal Bessarion in 1462." *Nuncius* 9 (1994): 165–206.

Kremer, Richard L. "Text to Trophy: Shifting Representations of Regiomontanus's Library." In *Lost Libraries: The Destruction of Great Book Collections since Antiquity*, edited by James Raven, 75–90. London and New York: Palgrave Macmillan, 2004.

Kren, Claudia. "Homocentric Astronomy in the Latin West: The *De reprobatione ecentricorum et epiciclorum* of Henry of Hesse." *Isis* 59 (1968): 269–281.

———. "A Medieval Objection to 'Ptolemy.' " *British Journal of the History of Science* 4 (1969): 378–393.

———. "Planetary Latitudes, the Theorica Gerardi, and Regiomontanus." *Isis* 68 (1977): 194–205.

Monfasani, John. *George of Trebizond: A Biography and a Study of His Rhetoric and Logic*. Leiden, Netherlands: Brill, 1976.

Ragep, F. Jamil. "Ali Qushji and Regiomontanus: Eccentric Transformations and Copernican Revolutions." *Journal for the History of Astronomy* 36 (2005): 359–371.

Rigo, Antonio. "Bessarione, Giovanni Regiomontano e i loro studi su Tolomeo a Venezia e Roma (1462–1464)." *Studi veneziani*, n.s. 21 (1991): 83–95.

Rose, Paul Lawrence. *The Italian Renaissance of Mathematics: Studies on Humanists and Mathematicians from Petrarch to Galileo*. Travaux d'Humanisme et Renaissance, vol. 145. Geneva: Librairie Droz, 1975.

Schmeidler, Felix, ed. *Johannes Regiomontani opera collectanea*. Osnabrück, Germany: O. Zeller Verlag, 1972. Facsimiles of key works, including the *Epitome, Disputationes, De triangulis omnimodis*, etc.

Shank, Michael H., "The 'Notes on al-Bitruji' Attributed to Regiomontanus: Second Thoughts." *Journal for the History of Astronomy* 23 (1992): 15–30.

———. "Regiomontanus and Homocentric Astronomy." *Journal for the History of Astronomy* 29 (1998): 157–166.

———. "Rings in a Fluid Heaven: The Equatorium-Driven Physical Astronomy of Guido de Marchia (fl. 1309)." *Centaurus* 45 (2003): 175–203.

———. "Regiomontanus as a Physical Astronomer: Samplings from the *Defense of Theon against George of Trebizond.*" *Journal for the History of Astronomy* 38 (2007) (forthcoming).

Stromer, Wolfgang von. "Hec opera fient in oppido Nuremberga Germanie ductu Ioannis de Monteregio: Regiomontan und Nuremberg, 1471–1475." In *Regiomontanus-Studien*, edited by Günther Hamann, 271–272. Vienna: Verlag der Österreichischen Akademie der Wissenschaften, 1980.

Swerdlow, Noel. "The Derivation and First Draft of Copernicus's Planetary Theory: A Translation of the *Commentariolus* with Commentary." *Proceedings of the American Philosophical Society* 117 (1973): 423–512.

———. "Regiomontanus on the Critical Problems of Astronomy." In *Nature, Experiment and the Sciences*, edited by Trevor H. Levere and William R. Shea, 165–195. Boston Studies in the Philosophy of Science, vol. 120. Boston and Dordrecht, Netherlands: Kluwer, 1990.

———. "Science and Humanism in the Renaissance: Regiomontanus's Oration on the Dignity and Utility of the Mathematical Sciences." In *World Changes: Thomas Kuhn and the Nature of Science*, edited by Paul Horwich. Cambridge, MA: MIT Press, 1993.

———. "Regiomontanus's Concentric-Sphere Models for the Sun and Moon." *Journal for the History of Astronomy* 30 (1999): 1–23.

Toomer, G. J. *Ptolemy's Almagest*. New York: Springer, 1984.

Wingen-Trennhaus, Angelika. "Regiomontanus als Frühdrucker in Nürnberg." *Mitteilungen des Vereins für Geschichte der Stadt Nürnberg* 78 (1991): 17–87.

Zinner, Ernst. *Regiomontanus: His Life and Work*. Studies in History and Philosophy of Mathematics, vol. 1. Translated by Ezra Brown. Amsterdam: North-Holland 1990.

Michael H. Shank

REICHELDERFER, FRANCIS WILTON
(*b.* Harlan, Indiana, 6 August 1895; *d.* Washington, D.C., 26 January 1983), *meteorology, scientific administration.*

Reichelderfer led the U.S. Weather Bureau between 1938 and 1963. During this period he oversaw the introduction of radar, computer modeling, and satellites to weather forecasting. He promoted American foreign policy through science, serving as the founding president of the World Meteorological Organization and encouraging the open exchange of international weather data. Throughout his career he connected people and facilitated innovative projects, creating institutional spaces where advanced meteorology could flourish, especially by forging connections between military and civilian weather organizations.

Childhood and Early Career. Francis Reichelderfer was the oldest child of Mae Carrington Reichelderfer and Francis R. Reichelderfer, a Methodist pastor. He lived with his parents and his younger sister Janet in northeastern Indiana, where he sailed on the local glacial lakes. In 1913 the family moved to Evanston, Illinois, where his father attended a college for ministers and Reichelderfer studied chemistry at Northwestern University. After graduating in June 1917, Reichelderfer took a job in the Calumet Company's chemistry lab and enrolled in the U.S. Naval Flying Reserve Corps.

Reicheldefer was called to active duty in May 1918. With the expectation that he would be sent to Europe more quickly, Reichelderfer volunteered for aerology training. In connection with its interest in balloons, the navy trained its weathermen in aerology, the study of the free air above Earth's surface, rather than meteorology, which was then more associated with surface weather conditions. Following a short but intensive course under Alexander McAdie, director of the Harvard Blue Hill Meteorological Observatory, Reichelderfer prepared to be deployed to Europe. Instead, a British officer looked at his surname and requested a more English-sounding American; Reichelderfer was sent to Nova Scotia, where he forecast for a squadron that was hunting German submarines.

After the armistice, navy aerology rapidly shrank from about 250 weathermen to twenty. Reichelderfer chose to remain. "Convinced that aviation was on the threshold of an explosive growth," Reichelderfer abandoned chemistry for meteorology (Taba, 1988, p. 89). In 1919 Reichelderfer earned his wings in an accelerated pilot training course before being transferred to Lisbon, where he forecast for the navy transatlantic flying expedition as it completed the first transatlantic flight.

Returning to the United States, Reichelderfer flew as a navy observer on the bombing tests conducted by army general William Mitchell against a captured German battleship in 1921. An unpredicted squall forced Mitchell to make an emergency landing on the beach, and prompted Reichelderfer to explore alternative models of storm formation, particularly the new model of cyclogenesis being developed by Vilhelm and Jacob Bjerknes in Bergen, Norway. These methods offered both a physical explanation for the surprise squall, as well as forecasting techniques that addressed the needs of aviators. Reichelderfer introduced these techniques to the military when he became head of navy aerology in 1922.

In 1926 Reichelderfer's interest in the Bergen techniques brought him into contact with Bjerknes's student, Carl-Gustaf Rossby, who hoped to spread the ideas of the Bergen School to the United States. An American Scandinavian Foundation fellowship had brought Rossby to the U.S. Weather Bureau Headquarters in Washington, but his ambition and confidence soon provoked a conflict with Chief Charles Marvin. Rossby needed a new place to work.

In trying to make careers outside the Weather Bureau hierarchy, Rossby and Reichelderfer had more freedom to act than most American meteorologists in the 1920s. Reichelderfer's most influential contact, Harry Guggenheim, enabled them to use this freedom to connect advances in dynamic meteorology research to the practical concerns of daily forecasting. In the early 1920s, forecasting for the U.S. Navy balloon racing teams, Reichelderfer had met Guggenheim, who managed the Daniel Guggenheim Fund for the Promotion of Aeronautics, and Guggenheim recruited Reichelderfer to the fund's meteorology committee. Reichelderfer's influence with the Guggenheim Fund helped establish a professorship for Rossby at the Massachusetts Institute of Technology (MIT). The first formal American graduate program in meteorology, this course was designed to train navy aerologists in the advanced techniques of the Bergen school.

In 1928 Lieutenant Reichelderfer was transferred to Lakehurst Naval Air Station, New Jersey, to be a pilot and aerological officer for the navy's airship service. He was promoted to executive officer in charge of Lakehurst in 1936. Safe airship operations depended upon accurate weather maps and reliable forecasting. Flights aboard dirigibles counted as "sea duty," crucial for promotion within the navy. Between 1928 and 1931, Reichelderfer met navy qualifications as a pilot for balloons, blimps, and rigid airships. During this period, Reichelderfer noticed disparities between the way in which navy aerologists and Rossby's group at MIT analyzed weather maps. He secured permission to travel to Europe to investigate the methods directly, spending six months in Bergen in 1931–1932 on official assignment from the navy, working with Jacob Bjerknes, Tor Bergeron, and Sverre Petterssen to analyze both American and European weather maps. His final report on the trip, *Report of Norwegian Methods of Weather Analysis*, became an informal manual used by many forecasters. Though marked "Restricted," mimeographed copies circulated among Army and Weather Bureau forecasters in addition to navy officers.

Following his stint in Europe, Lieutenant Reichelderfer gained actual sea experience aboard the battleship *Oklahoma*. While Reichelderfer was at sea, the airship *Akron* crashed in severe thunderstorms. Seventy-three people died, including the head of the Navy Bureau of Aeronautics, Admiral William Moffat. (Moffat had once called Reichelderfer "the best damn meteorologist in the world.") The resulting Congressional hearings uncovered shortcomings in Weather Bureau aviation forecasts. A special committee of the Science Advisory Board, led by university presidents Robert Millikan, Karl Compton, and Isaiah Bowman, recommended Weather Bureau reforms, particularly that forecasters receive university education in the modern Norwegian techniques. Following the committee's report, Chief Charles Marvin retired after fifty years of service in the Weather Bureau, to be replaced by Willis Gregg, head of the bureau's aerology division, and a friend and colleague of Reichelderfer from the Guggenheim Fund committee.

Returned to Lakehurst in 1934, newly promoted Lieutenant Commander Reichelderfer spent more time as an administrator than as a forecaster. His duties with the navy airship program brought him into close contact with the German zeppelin flights. He flew aboard the *Hindenburg* several times, informally observing and assisting with weather forecasting for these flights. On 6 May 1937, Reichelderfer had his luggage packed for a flight to Germany when the *Hindenburg* burned. Transferred back to sea, Reichelderfer was second-in-command of the former battleship *Utah,* by then a target and gunnery-training vessel. Returning to port in late 1938, Reichelderfer received a telegram that informed him of Gregg's death and nominated him chief of the Weather Bureau. He was promoted to navy commander that year.

Chief of the Weather Bureau. Upon his installation as chief of the Weather Bureau, *Time* magazine described Reichelderfer as "quiet, matter-of-fact … [he] likes dancing, music, an occasional cocktail, [and] spends much time reading up on new developments in weather science" (26 December 1938, p. 31). In the years after World War II, three new technological developments would be particularly important to Reichelderfer and the Weather Bureau: radar, computers, and satellites. The effective integration of these military-derived technologies into Weather Bureau practice, however, depended upon a transformation in the bureau's organizational culture guided by Reichelderfer before and during the war.

During the 1930s, many aviation advocates saw the Weather Bureau as an insular and conservative organization unable to adapt to changing circumstances. Few bureau men had higher degrees in science; forecasters advanced through an apprenticeship system that rewarded deference to authority and developed skills in "isobaric geometry," an intuitive, visual process for forecasting surface conditions from synoptic maps. Because individual forecasters used a range of disparate methods, including extrapolation from recent events, analogous historical conditions, and empirically derived rules for local conditions, many people considered weather forecasting more art than science. In 1938 the Civil Aeronautics Administration threatened to create a separate organization for avi-

ation forecasting if a bureau outsider did not succeed Willis Gregg.

Reichelderfer met these challenges by building bridges to universities and supporting research in dynamic meteorology. He hired Rossby as assistant chief for research and education, broadened the Air Mass Analysis Section, and sent the handful of university-educated specialists trained in the Norwegian methods to regional offices to spread the new approach throughout the bureau. He also worked with Secretary of Agriculture Henry Wallace to increase Weather Bureau funding. Some of these appropriations sent bureau employees to universities for advanced meteorological education, notably Harry Wexler, who completed work for his doctorate at MIT in 1937–1938 on assignment from the weather bureau and eventually became the bureau's director of research early in the era of radar, computing and satellites. Other appropriations supported studies of the atmosphere's general circulation, an attempt to develop longer range forecasting capabilities and explain climatic fluctuations such as the drought that contributed to the dust bowl. Reichelderfer described these developments as "The How and Why of Weather Knowledge," in the 1941 Yearbook of Agriculture, *Climate and Man.* Reichelderfer's connections to scientific community led to his tenure as president of the American Meteorological Society in 1940–1941, and as president of the American Geophysical Union during the period 1944–1947.

Reichelderfer also connected the Weather Bureau and the military. Even before U.S. entry into World War II, he participated in a Joint Meteorology Committee (JMC) that brought together the Weather Bureau, army air force, and navy to coordinate weather-related activities. During the war, the JMC organized improved hurricane warning efforts along Caribbean and the eastern seaboard, and established more pilot balloon and radios on the stations to expand the network of upper air observations so important for aviation forecasting. These forecasts were integrated with a national air traffic control system, distributed to pilots and dispatchers through the Civil Aeronautics Administration. This system improved the safety and efficiency of wartime flights, and continued after the war.

The JMC's most pervasive impact upon meteorology was an enormous training program based at five universities and one military base. Funded by the military but taught by the leading academic meteorologists in America, the training program instructed more than seven thousand new forecasters in physics, mathematics, synoptics, and fronts, and the latest in dynamic meteorology. Several of the most influential figures in postwar American atmospheric science were trained in this program (Edward Lorenz, George P. Cressman, and Robert White,

Francis W. Reichelderfer. *Francis W. Reichelderfer operating an experimental close circuit television weather station.* AP IMAGES.

for instance), while many more spent lengthy but little celebrated careers in the Weather Bureau and military weather services after the war. These men became some of the key early operators of the three military-related technologies that substantially improved forecasting during Reichelderfer's tenure as head of the Weather Bureau: radar, electronic computers, and satellites.

Radar enabled meteorologists to see through clouds and detect precipitation at significant distances. Reichelderfer played a minor role in the development of radar before World War II, flying aboard an aluminum-covered dirigible used in testing experimental army radars. He played a more significant role by soliciting twenty-five surplus navy sets in 1946 and having them modified for meteorological use. By the mid-1950s radar had become a key component of the bureau's storm warning system, especially for tornadoes in the Midwest and hurricanes along the East Coast. Reichelderfer oversaw the development of the WSR-57 radar system specifically designed for weather surveillance in the late 1950s.

As part of Reichelderfer's career-long effort to integrate dynamic meteorology research with daily forecasting, he promoted the development of numerical weather prediction and general circulation modeling using electronic computers. In addition to contributing Weather Bureau funds and political support, Reichelderfer delegated assistant chief Wexler to represent the Weather Bureau's stake in the Institute for Advanced Study's meteorology project during the eight years it took to develop operational numerical weather prediction capabilities. Serving the Weather Bureau, air force, and navy, the joint numerical weather prediction unit became operational in Washington in 1954. The bureau emerged as an important purchaser of advanced computers, influencing the development of electronic hardware as well as scientific computing.

Imagined in air force studies almost immediately after World War II, early weather satellites produced images of large-scale weather systems, helping to detect hurricanes earlier, for instance. While Wexler again largely guided the scientific development, Reichelderfer worked with National Aeronautics and Space Administration administrators to ensure efficient collaboration between the two agencies, while speaking publicly about the civilian benefits expected from these expensive new devices.

Weather modification also received a great deal of public attention in the decades after World War II. Using new techniques for seeding clouds with dry ice or silver iodide smoke, weather control was right around the corner in the 1950s, according to outspoken advocates such as chemist Irving Langmuir. Despite the considerable skepticism of many leading meteorologists, support for weather modification research came from the U.S. military as well as the federal and state governments, agricultural interests, and private citizens' groups. Reichelderfer navigated between these parties, working to tone down the claims of the boldest cloud seeders while continuing to fund exploratory work in weather and climate modification through Weather Bureau programs.

International Organizations. International meteorology was part of a larger American foreign policy during the 1930s–1960s. Reichelderfer worked to make meteorology a domain of open international cooperation under benevolent and constrained American leadership. As part of a larger effort to encourage Latin American countries to look to the United States for advanced science and aviation capabilities, the Weather Bureau paid for meteorologists from various Latin American countries to attend the same training programs at American universities that produced thousands of military weather forecasters during World War II.

Reichelderfer helped guide the transformation of the International Meteorological Organization (IMO) into the World Meteorological Organization (WMO) in the late 1940s. As a nongovernmental entity, the IMO had brought together leading meteorologists to promote voluntary exchanges of weather data and standardization of weather observations. In contrast, the WMO was an intergovernmental organization under the auspices of the United Nations. While many of the same people attended WMO meetings as had attended IMO meetings, in the WMO they acted in their official capacities as the heads of national weather services, thus ensuring that WMO decisions had the force of government policy. Serving as the first president of the WMO from 1951 to 1955, Reichelderfer encouraged the organization to help newly independent nations build the technical expertise necessary for economic development, such as planning a modern meteorology service for Libya in 1952. Coordinating the free exchange of weather data around the world also became a central mission of the WMO, first through standardized coding of observations, and later through the development of the World Weather Watch, a system of instruments and data processing facilities for sharing global weather information.

Retirement and Personal Life. Reichelderfer retired in October 1963. He continued to participate in meteorology, serving on National Academy of Sciences committees and testifying as an expert witness in an influential 1964 weather modification trial. Reichelderfer's legacy in meteorology and public service is illustrated by two awards named for him. Each year the National Oceanic and Atmospheric Administration presents the Francis W. Reichelderfer award for distinguished environmental services to the nation, while the American Meteorological Society invokes his name to recognize distinguished contributions to the provision of operational environmental services to the public. He traveled extensively with his wife Beatrice, who died in 1975 after fifty-five years of marriage. Reichelderfer also spent time gardening, though he admitted he had never had "green fingers," and continued to swim and sail well into his seventies. The Reichelderfers were survived by their son, Bruce, who followed his father's footsteps in the U.S. Navy.

BIBLIOGRAPHY

Archival Sources: Library of Congress, NARA (Navy and RG 27 Weather Bureau); there are some insights as well in the Library of Congress Wexler Papers, which include Reichelderfer's comments on many of Wexler's memos.

WORKS BY REICHELDERFER

"Forecasting Thunderstorms by Means of Static Electricity." *Monthly Weather Review* (1921): 152–153.

"The Present Meteorological Needs of Aeronautics." *Monthly Weather Review* (1925): 259.

"Airship Meteorology." In *Aeronautical Meteorology,* edited by Willis R. Gregg. New York: Ronald Press, 1930.

"Report of Norwegian Methods of Weather Analysis." Mimeographed report, U.S. Bureau of Aeronautics, Navy Department, 1932.

"The How and Why of Weather Knowledge." In *Climate and Man: Yearbook of Agriculture,* edited by G. Hambridge, 129–153. Washington, DC: Government Printing Office, 1941.

"Weather's Role in the Fight for Freedom." U.S. Weather Bureau, Office of the Coordinator of Inter-American Affairs, Press Division, April 1943.

"Remarks on Weather Bureau Policy, Plans and Program." *Bulletin of the American Meteorological Society* (1946): 169–171.

"The Science of the Atmosphere." In *The Scientists Speak,* edited by Warren Weaver, 19–23. New York: Boni and Gaer. 1947.

"Hurricanes, Tornadoes, and Other Storms." *Annals of the American Academy of Political and Social Science* (1957): 23–35.

"On the Role of the IUGG in Advancement of Geophysics." *Transaction of the American Geophysical Union* (March 1960): 1–3.

"Meteorological Satellite Systems in Weather Research and Services." *Aerospace Engineering* (1961): 22–23, 91–96.

OTHER SOURCES

Bates, Charles C. "The Formative Rossby-Reichelderfer Years in American Meteorology: 1926–1940." *Weather and Forecasting* 4, no. 12 (1989): 593–603.

Cressman, George P. "Francis W. Reichelderfer, 1895–1983." *Bulletin of the American Meteorological Society* 64, no. 4 (1983): 398–400.

Hughes, Patrick. "Francis W. Reichelderfer, Part I: Aerologists and Airdevils." *Weatherwise* 34, no. 2 (1981): 52–59.

———. "Francis W. Reichelderfer, Part II: Architect of Modern Weather Services." *Weatherwise* 34, no. 4 (1981): 148–157.

Lear, James. "Changing the Guard on Weather. Gentleman of the Guard: Francis Wilton Reichelderfer." *Saturday Review,* 3 August 1963: 35–38.

Namias, Jerome. "Francis W. Reichelderfer, 1895–1983." *Biographical Memoirs of the National Academy of Sciences* 60 (1995): 272–291.

Taba, Hessam. "Dr. F. W. Reichelderfer." In *The 'Bulletin' Interviews,* edited by Hessam Taba. Geneva: World Meteorological Organization, 1988.

Roger Turner

REICHSTEIN, TADEUS (*b.* Wloclawek, Poland, 20 July 1897; *d.* Basel, Switzerland, 1 August 1996), *chemistry, chemical engineering, organic chemistry, pharmacy, corticosteroids, vitamin C.*

Reichstein was amongst the leading scientists in organic chemistry in the twentieth century. With his synthesis of Vitamin C by using microorganisms he combined chemical and biological methods, and thus introduced patterns that became standard in modern biotechnology. In 1950 he received the Nobel Prize for the discovery of the chemical structure of the corticosteroids, opening up an avenue leading to the uses of cortisone and other hormones as pharmaceuticals.

Early Years. Tadeus Reichstein was born on 20 July 1897 in Wloclawek (at that time in the Russian part of Poland) as the oldest of five sons of Jewish parents. His father's name was Isidor Reichstein. His mother, Gustava Brochmann, was descended from a respected Wloclawek family.

Following studies at the Technical Institute in St. Petersburg, which was unusual for a Polish Jew in Tsaristic Russia, Isidor Reichstein moved to Kiev (Ukraine) with his parents where he set up his own business as an engineer specializing in sugar processing plants. In 1904 Reichstein's youngest brother Paul was born, and the small flat in Kiev was becoming too crowded. As a result, Tadeus was sent to live with his aunt who was married to a pharmacist. Even though Tadeus was only eight years old, he took great interest in his uncle's pharmacy. He was allowed to make pills and syrups, mix plasters, and assist in numerous other tasks in the pharmacy. Back in his parents' flat, he converted his bedroom into a laboratory and tried, together with a friend, to transform iron shavings into gold by means of chemical reactions. This was his first (and last!) excursion into the realm of alchemy.

The year 1905 witnessed horrific pogroms against Russia's Jewish population. Reichstein was never to forget this scene of terror. Having never seen blood before, he later remembered that, apart from being shocked, he was also very interested in the wounds and bodily functions that he had seen.

The recurrent eruptions of anti-Semitic violence persuaded Isidor Reichstein that the family had to leave Russia, and so they immigrated to Switzerland. On their way through Germany, the family left Tadeus in a residential school in Jena. Because it was a renowned boy's boarding school, Isidor Reichstein hoped that an education there would secure a good future for his son. The flat in Zurich was too small in any case, all the more so as numerous relatives who were also fleeing from anti-Semitic violence had to be housed.

As Tadeus later said himself, the two years spent in the German boarding school were hell for him. He loathed the military atmosphere of the Prussian institution where flogging even for minor instances of disobedience was commonplace. Being small and thin for his

age—the smallest boy in his class—he was understandably unable to keep up with the others during the daily outdoor hikes. Out of sheer exhaustion, he would often collapse, something that would trigger a fit of Teutonic rage in his teacher who would beat little Tadeus black and blue with a cane until the boy was unable to walk at all.

Tadeus did not tell his parents anything about all that. Although aged only ten, he did not want to burden them even more and decided to endure the hardship until there would be room in Zurich for him too. Fortunately, Isidor Reichstein was able to acquire a house in the countryside just outside Zurich in 1907, and Tadeus was able to return to his beloved family. He reflected later that it was from this moment on that his life was a happy one. Indeed, he was still a cheerful person even in old age.

For the next seven years, the Reichstein children were taught at home. Taking the greatest care, Isidor himself instructed them in mathematics and physics. Visitors taught other subjects, and a young scientist replaced Isidor whenever the latter had to travel to Kiev. It can safely be assumed that it was this excellent private education that led to his enormous thirst for knowledge and his childlike ability to marvel at the wonders of life and nature and especially plants, traits that were to accompany Reichstein throughout his long life.

At the age of seventeen Reichstein entered the upper secondary school in Zurich where he pursued his interest in science subjects with great eagerness. Having become naturalized Swiss citizens, along with his four brothers in 1914, he was conscripted for military service as early as the first month after the outbreak of World War I. The situation in Europe at the time was catastrophic. The family got into major financial difficulties. No longer able to travel to Kiev, Isidor lost his business, his capital, and his savings there. Worse still, his health deteriorated, he became bed-ridden, and was never to recover fully. He died in the year 1931. His wife converted the family's home into a boarding house in order to earn money. One of the guests who stayed with the family was a young woman from the Netherlands, Louise van Ufford, whom Tadeus married in 1927. Their daughter Ruth was born in 1933.

Having been dismissed from the army in 1916, Reichstein was now able to complete his school education at the upper secondary school in Zurich. He then began studying chemistry at the Eidgenössische Technische Hochschule Zürich (ETHZ). After four years, Reichstein passed his degree in chemical engineering with flying colors. Driven by the ardent wish finally to be able to support his family financially, he wanted to find a well-paying job. Having compiled a list of twenty chemical companies, he went all over Zurich and its surrounding areas, visiting one company after another, finally finding a temporary position in a small company in Rorschach. The objective was to improve batteries for flashlights, a problem Reichstein was able to solve and he was delighted to be well enough paid that he could contribute to the family budget.

Research. In 1921 Reichstein began his doctorate under the supervision of Nobel Laureate Hermann Staudinger. He saw his supervisor as a brilliant teacher of organic chemistry who knew how to create a stimulating and entertaining atmosphere for his 200 students. Practical laboratory skills were not Staudinger's forte, however. He is said to have had a predilection for strong reactions that were both fulminant and smelly.

At the same time, however, Reichstein was able to work with Leopold Ruzicka in the cellar laboratory at the ETHZ, and benefit from the great practical skills of this poorly paid assistant of Staudinger's. Although Ruzicka was less gifted as a teacher of theoretical subjects, he developed brilliant working methods for the analysis of natural materials. Reichstein's connection with Ruzicka was to have a profound impact on his entire subsequent career. Whereas Reichstein had originally planned to embark on a career in chemical engineering and certainly did not want to become a university teacher, he increasingly turned his attention to research as a result of Ruzicka's influence.

On the basis of a plan drawn up by Staudinger, Reichstein worked on the isolation of the volatile flavor components of roasted coffee for the German company Frank (Kathreiner's malt coffee) in a small laboratory in Albisrieden, beginning in 1922. Together with his assistant and friend Joseph von Euw, he worked on this project for a total of nine years.

The connection with Joseph von Euw proved productive and developed into a collaboration and friendship that was to last for some fifty years. Von Euw was actually a precision mechanic by training, which meant that he first had to familiarize himself with the ins and outs of chemistry. But he soon grew accustomed to handling the sensitive substances and even constructed most devices and apparatuses himself. Chromatographic methods were still unknown at the time and the analysis of very small quantities of complex mixtures of unstable products posed major problems. However, by means of fractional distillation, isolation of the various pH values, and finally crystallization and derivatization, the required results were ultimately obtained. Although Staudinger used all these findings as part of his own patents, Reichstein was at least able to publish his newly found reactions of heterocyclic components (furans and pyrroles) under his own name in the journal *Helvetica Chimica Acta*.

The goal of the work was to find an artificial aroma of coffee. This was not possible because these natural prod-

ucts have too many components, but they succeeded in the end to find a mixture of about fifty compounds, which could be marketed as artificial coffee flavor. They held several patents on this. Based on this work the German company Haarmann & Reimer in Holzminden was able to produce and market an artificial coffee aroma in 1928.). Upon completion of the works in Albisrieden, Leopold Ruzicka succeeded in persuading Reichstein to become an assistant at the Institute of Organic Chemistry of the ETHZ and to seriously consider an academic career.

Vitamin C. After two years of being a titular professor at the ETH, Reichstein was appointed associate professor. He assembled a group of doctoral and post-doctoral students and was then increasingly enabled to invest his enormous energy in his research. Because he was particularly interested in substances that both played an important role and had great potential in medicine, he chose vitamins as his field of specialization.

The aim at the time was to find a way to synthesize the anti-scorbutic vitamin C artificially. It had been isolated in 1928 by Albert Szent-Gyorgyi, using Hungarian paprika. For artificial synthesis and as a starting material, a sugar, L-sorbose, was to be used. Although this substance was known, it was not available on the market. What to do? It was a known fact that there were strains of bacteria that could transform the readily available sugar alcohol sorbitol into L-sorbose. It was generally assumed that the bacteria in question were the slime-producing microorganisms found in mother of vinegar. Reichstein immediately came up with the idea of trying that route. However, many tests with mold cultures failed. No sorbose was produced. Inspired by a nineteenth-century research dissertation, Reichstein devised a new experiment. Glasses containing a watery sorbitol solution, yeast, and a small quantity of vinegar (the pH value must be around 5 to ensure that no other bacteria grow) were put outdoors for a few days. When the glasses were taken back inside, three of them still contained sorbitol. However, three others contained a deposit of white crystals. As the analysis showed, the deposit consisted of the sugar so urgently needed: pure L-sorbose.

Responsible for the transformation was a strain of bacteria that was later to be called Acetobacter suboxydans. In one of the glasses, a dead fruit fly was floating in the liquid. On one of its legs, L-sorbose crystals had grown. Evidently, a colony of precisely this type of bacteria had been on the fly's leg.

No time was lost in cultivating the bacteria, and after only a few days, a hundred grams of pure sorbose had been produced. The rest of the synthesis went according to plan. Together with his doctoral student R. Oppenauer, Reichstein was able to continue the process of synthesis, acetylation, and oxidation, until it was possible to produce synthetic vitamin C in a way that had great commercial potential.

What seems so simple and elegant in retrospect also involved a great deal of hard work, however. The heavy workload in the laboratory, the unavailability of methods for the analysis and control of intermediate steps that are taken for granted in the early twenty-first century (no chromatography, no spectrometry), and the competition from research teams who were working on the same problem in other countries all meant that Reichstein and his colleagues were under enormous pressure. Reichstein and the company that had supported him for the research, the foodstuff company Haco on Gümligen near Bern, now held the patent for the only commercially profitable method of producing vitamin C. The laboratory's financial future was secure for the next few years because the patent, which Reichstein and Haco had made available to the company Hoffmann-La Roche, yielded substantial revenues, at least after an initial period of low sales.

The interface between chemistry, biology and medicine was Reichstein's great passion. His original idea of including a microbiological component in organic synthesis meant that he was far ahead of his times, and he faced substantial resistance in the chemical company Hoffmann-La Roche to rely on a microbiological production step. But this resistance was overcome, and it is impressive to think that Reichstein's ingenious synthesis technique has not changed to this day and that many thousands of tons of vitamin C are still produced by this method every year.

Basel and the Pharmaceutical Institute in the Totengässlein.

All of a sudden, there were insurmountable administrative obstacles at the ETH in Zurich stemming from the new research direction Reichstein had decided to take, namely, the elucidation of the structures of the hormones of the adrenal cortex. The laboratory director, Leopold Ruzicka, had a contract with the company CIBA, stipulating that the patent rights of research results on steroids in his laboratory had to be assigned to CIBA. Reichstein, having himself a contract with the Dutch company N.V. Organon in Oss, could not do this, as Organon had substantially supported his research on the adrenal cortical hormones.

So, Reichstein had to leave Ruzicka's laboratory in Zurich, and faced the problem that in the late 1930s it was almost impossible for a Polish Jew to be appointed as full professor at a Swiss university despite that he was actually a Swiss citizen who had served in the Swiss army. The only exception, as he soon found out, was to be the University of Basel. There, the combination of a social democratic government and strong liberal forces within the parliament (called red Basel by outsiders and social

Tadeus Reichstein. *Tadeus Reichstein, circa 1940.* HULTON ARCHIVE/GETTY IMAGES.

Basel by insiders) led to a prevailing mood of anti-Fascism and extreme skepticism with regard to the Third Reich, both among the population and in political circles. In part, this political climate was probably due to Basel's geographical proximity to the German border and the news that came across daily. In addition, individual personalities shaped the world of Basel at the time, such as the director of Education, legendary social democrat Fritz Hauser, and the liberal president of the Grand Council (and editor in chief of the *Basler Nachrichten*), Albert Oeri-Preiswerk.

It was thanks to Hauser that Reichstein was offered the chair of Pharmacy at the University of Basel. He accepted and thus became head of the Pharmaceutical Institute of the University of Basel, a position he held from 1938 to 1950. He soon succeeded in his task of modernizing the Institute, located in idyllic Totengässlein in the middle of the old city, in order to bring it up to international standards. He was entirely wrapped up in his research and later reflected that the twelve years spent at the Pharmaceutical Institute were, despite the catastrophe into which the whole of Europe plunged in this time, the most fruitful and the happiest years of his life.

Reichstein had taken his closest research assistant, Joseph von Euw, to Basel with him, and he soon assembled a small group of students and assistants. The new fields of activity were adrenal cortical hormones. Reichstein had begun to study these substances as early as 1934, when he was still at the ETHZ. Together with his new group, Reichstein isolated about thirty chemically similar corticosteroids that were, however, different in terms of their biological effects. The team even succeeded in producing crystalline forms of most of the corticosteroids. The so-called Substance E—universally known as cortisone in the early 2000s—was one of them. These substances perform a wide range of biological functions: they control sugar metabolism, they play an important role in the development of nerve and heart muscle cells, they are sexual hormones, and they influence the entire immune system. It is hardly surprising, then, that their isolation and identification was an extremely important undertaking. Only those experienced in the chemistry of natural products can fully appreciate how incredibly difficult it can be to separate substances of high chemical affinity that exist only in small quantities among a great multitude of organic materials. From more than a ton of slaughter waste (bovine adrenal glands), these substances were eventually extracted in quantities of milligrams.

If it is borne in mind that these substances readily form mixed crystals and is remembered that modern chromatographic methods for their isolation and identification did not exist as yet, one begins to wonder why Reichstein did not despair at the task. Other groups abroad were working on the same problem, and this led to a race against time. However, the aims were achieved: The substances were isolated and the results published. Together with his American rivals (Hench und Kendall), Reichstein was awarded the Nobel Prize for Medicine in 1950. In his speech given on the occasion of the award ceremony, Reichstein expressed his gratitude to his rivals (and co-Laureates) for their mutual support. He said that he owed his Nobel Prize entirely to them, because it was only due to their work that the biological significance of these substances became known and had received —all the public attention that this significance entailed worldwide.

Once again, the possibility of (semi-)synthetic production—of cortisone in particular—was the result of his research. The starting materials were bile pigments and plant material from Africa (so-called Strophantus types). As early as 1947 Reichstein had sent two of his assistants on an expedition to Africa for months on end to look for suitable starting materials, for already during the war, a race for the potential botanic sources of steroids had

begun. It was hoped that industrial production of this new substance class would not only yield huge financial profits but, for a while, even that it might help win the war. There was the hope that steroids could be used to increase the performance of soldiers by reducing their need to sleep. This was most interesting in respect of the lack of pilots in the late years of World War II.

The Institute of Organic Chemistry. In 1948 the head of the Institute of Organic Chemistry at the University of Basel died unexpectedly, and Reichstein was asked whether he would like to take up the position. He did not want to turn down the offer and as a result, he was, for four years, in charge of both institutes at the same time. However, as he later said, he would have much preferred to stay in his old institution in the Totengässlein to continue with his research projects. The chemical institute had to be substantially extended and modernized. For two years, Reichstein had to work particularly hard in order to convince the Grand Council of Basel of the importance and adequacy of the project. He succeeded. His strong conviction that the entire city of Basel would ultimately benefit from the fruits of chemical research eventually prevailed and has, from the point of view of the early twenty-first century, undoubtedly been confirmed.

The Institute of Organic Chemistry was rebuilt from the ground up. It was Reichstein's vision, as well as his energy and effectiveness, that ensured the success of the complete reconstruction and reorganization of the institute. Unlike many of his academic colleagues, he did not shy away from administrative tasks and was determined to create an outstanding teaching and research institution.

Reichstein was far ahead of his time in more than one respect. Thus, he accepted women as scientists and colleagues as a matter of course and without any reservations. His leadership style as the head of both the academic and administrative units was characterized not by dictatorial authority but rather by his great ability to motivate others. His enthusiasm for new possibilities and methods, his curiosity for the processes of nature, and also his cheerful personality were all contagious qualities. He was not only a brilliant teacher but showed great psychological skills as head of his institute and great empathy in his interactions with his subordinates.

Retirement Years: Plants and Butterflies. Throughout his life Reichstein had a great passion for plants. On a practical level he loved cultivating plants, especially ferns, but here too his interests ranged widely. He himself repeatedly said that he had inherited his aptitude for gardening from his mother. His garden on Weissensteinstrasse in the Bruderholz area in Basel is still vividly remembered by many as a botanical paradise as is his garden in Agarone in the Ticino region where he owned a summer cottage. Reichstein combined an emotional attachment to the world of plants with a scientific approach to understanding plant development.

Plant substances always interested Reichstein. Apart from his works on the flavoring substances in coffee, his wine analyses, and his research on vitamins, this interest manifested itself in his botanical and phytochemical work on plant substances, which was to contribute to a semi-synthetic production of corticosteroids, as mentioned above. There were many other subjects to which Reichstein turned his attention, however, for example steroid glycosides that have cardiotonic properties. It was this interest that later led him to an entirely new field of activity, namely the isolation of steroid glycosides from insects. That these substances are found in insects was not known at all until the 1960s. Together with Miriam Rothschild, Reichstein published a series of articles about more than twenty cardenolides that were not only found in the famous monarch butterflies, but also in grasshoppers and many other insects.

Already in the late 1950s, Reichstein began to take an interest in ferns. Following his retirement in 1967, his scientific work, which he was to continue to the end of his life, increasingly focused on this subject. At the age of seventy-five, he said that he wanted to abandon his research in organic chemistry in order to dedicate himself entirely to ferns. He explained that the scientific literature in the field of organic chemistry had become too vast for him, so that he hardly had time to read even the titles of all the publications anymore. He added that he preferred to work with live material only in future.

The systematics, chemotaxonomy, cytology, and micromorphology of ferns: Those were now to become the subjects of his scientific work. Reichstein soon built up yet another international network of scientists and specialists. It was very lucky that Reichstein had found such an ideal field of work for his long retirement. After all, he worked longer as a scientist after he retired than many of his colleagues did all their lives. On the one hand, he had his work in the garden and greenhouse, and on the other hand he had his scientific work. After his retirement, he published more than 100 works on the subject of ferns.

Reichstein died in 1996 at the age of ninety-nine. Also advanced in years, his beloved wife Louise had died a few years before him. When he was ninety-five, he once said that he had the impression of having lived too long already. He also pointed out, however, that he needed at least three more years in order to complete his botanical publications.

In the course of his life, Reichstein worked on many different subjects. He became an internationally renowned authority in all his various fields. Apart from

the Nobel Prize and the Copley Medal, Reichstein received more than fifty honors and prizes, not in one, but in many different fields.

Evidently, it was not only his intellectual capacity and the effectiveness of his scientific approach that led to the astonishing diversity of his work. Reichstein was also an extraordinary human being. He had the ability to immerse himself deeply in a subject without narrowing his horizon in the process. This ability not only gave him rare cognitive powers, but it was also a precondition for his development into a non-fanatic yet highly motivated scientist, as well as a great human being.

BIBLIOGRAPHY

Many personal notes were given to the author by Tadeus Reichstein and Dorothee Ammann.

Bächi, Beat. "'Rein schweizerisches' Vitamin C aus Basel. Zur Kulturgeschichte einer soziotechnischen Innovation." *Basler Zeitschrift für Geschichte und Altertumskunde* 105 (2005): 79–113.

Hürlimann, H. "Prof. Dr. T. Reichstein zum 90. Geburtstag." *Bauhinia* 8/4. (1987): 173.

Rasbach, Helga. "Der Pteridologe Tadeus Reichstein—eine persönliche Würdigung." Basel, Germany. *Bauhinia* 11/4. (1996): 211–219.

Reichstein, Tadeus, and Hermann Staudinger. "Das Aroma des gerösteten Kaffees." *Experientia* VI/7. (1950): 280.

Rothschild, Miriam. "Tadeus Reichstein, 20 July 1897–1 August 1996." *Biographical Memoirs Fell. Royal Society London* 45 (1999): 449–467.

Schneller, J. "Prof. Dr. Tadeus Reichstein (20. Juli 1897–1. August 1996)." *Botanica Helvetica* 107 (1997): 143–145.

Michael Kessler

REPPE, JULIUS WALTER (*b.* Göringen, Germany, 29 July 1892; *d.* Heidelberg, Germany, 27 July 1969), *industrial chemistry, polymer synthesis, acetylene chemistry, ethylene chemistry.*

Reppe was one of the finest industrial chemists of the interwar period. He carried out hazardous research on the reactions of acetylene (ethyne) under pressure and thereby opened up entirely new fields of industrial organic chemistry. Numerous industrial processes have resulted from his work, including acrylic acid (propenoic acid) and 1,4-butynediol from acetylene, propionic acid (propanoic acid) from ethylene (ethene), and acetic acid (ethanoic acid) from methanol; he is also well-known for his remarkable synthesis of cyclooctatetraene. These new areas were soon called "Reppe chemistry." He also developed several polymers, including substitutes for chewing gum and human blood plasma.

After World War II, Reppe was described as making a larger contribution to chemistry than any other employee of the large German chemical firm I. G. Farben. The project to transfer leading German scientists to the United States (Project Paperclip) ranked Reppe as highly as the discoverer of nuclear fission, Otto Hahn. Yet for all his scientific achievements, Reppe never won the Nobel Prize. This was partly the result of bias against industrial chemists (a prejudice that would have been incomprehensible to Reppe's fellow industrial chemist, Alfred Nobel) and partly because of Reppe's research at I. G. Farben, which was closely linked to the Nazi regime in Germany.

Despite his hopes, Reppe's industrial processes never became the basis for the entire organic chemical industry. In the 1950s acetylene was replaced as a major raw material for the chemical industry by cheaper, petroleum-based starting materials, and new processes were developed that made Reppe's work in certain key areas obsolescent. After the Americans failed to persuade him to relocate to the United States after World War II, he was permitted to become research director at BASF, created out of the former I. G. Farben. In that capacity he was a participant in the shift from coal to petroleum, which was spearheaded in Germany by BASF; he had been one the pioneers of ethylene chemistry in the mid-1920s.

Childhood and Early Career. Walter Reppe was born in Göringen, near Eisenach, in Thuringia, Germany, on 29 July 1892, the son of Rudolf Reppe, a schoolteacher, and his wife, Maria Reppe (née Schröder). He went to school in Apolda and Weimar. Reppe studied chemistry at the University of Jena and the University of Munich before serving in the artillery during the World War I. After being wounded three times, he was commissioned as a lieutenant in the reserve in February 1917 and moved from the front line. After the war Reppe returned to the University of Munich where he took his PhD in 1920 on the reduction of aryl derivatives of nitric acid, working under Professor Kurt H. O. Meyer. After a short spell as an assistant to Meyer at the University of Munich, Reppe joined BASF at Ludwigshafen in the Palatinate in 1921. This move was clearly a result of Meyer's impending appointment as the head of BASF's main research laboratory. Reppe's first year at Ludwigshafen was spent in the Hauptlaboratium (Central Research Laboratory) and his second year in the indigo laboratory. Between 1924 and 1933 he carried out research in the new solvents laboratory, but he also helped to manage the industrial plant and carried out the development of processes to the industrial scale. This combination of research, development, and factory management was quite normal in the German chemical industry at this time. Reppe's company, BASF, merged with the other major firms in the German dyestuffs industry—Bayer, Hoechst, Griesheim, and Agfa—in 1925 to form a large combine, I. G. Farbenindustrie AG, headed by Carl Bosch, developer of the

Haber-Bosch ammonia process, and the former chairman of BASF. The Ludwigshafen works became part of the Oberrhein Betriebsgemeinschaft (Upper Rhine works community), but life at the factory level continued much as before.

Reppe's first major project was the industrial synthesis of butyl alcohol (butanol) from acetylene, under the direction of Curt Schumann and Gerhard Steimmig. This effort was linked to the soaring popularity of the automobile, particularly in the United States but also in Germany, where the number of automobiles rose from 4,600 in 1908 to 39,000 in 1925. This growth created a huge demand for several organic chemicals, including butyl alcohol, which was a solvent for the lacquers used to paint automobiles. By 1929 the United States produced nearly 23,000 metric tonnes of butyl alcohol by the fermentation of maize and from petroleum. Fermentation was out of the question, as food was increasingly scarce in Germany, which also lacked any major oil or gas fields. The well-known aldol reaction, which converts acetaldehyde (ethanal) to aldol (3-hydroxybutanal), offered an attractive alternative. The acetaldehyde was made from acetylene and the aldol was easily reduced to butyl alcohol. This process later became the core of I. G. Farben's route to butadiene, a key building block of synthetic rubber.

After the butyl alcohol research was successfully completed, Reppe worked on the manufacture of ethylene oxide. This too was connected with the rise of the automobile and in particular the need to add an antifreeze to the coolant water. The earliest antifreezes were natural glycerol (1,2,3-propanetriol) and methanol, still obtained in America from wood distillation in this period. However, glycerol was replaced by the superior ethylene glycol (1,2-ethanediol), marketed by Union Carbide as Prestone in 1927. Ethylene glycol—one of the first major petrochemical products—was a problematic product for I. G. Farben, as it did not have an abundant source of ethylene apart from expensive fermentation-based ethyl alcohol (ethanol). Even so, the growing demand for antifreeze and the fear of competition from Union Carbide compelled I. G. Farben to develop its own route to ethylene glycol between 1926 and 1928. Ethylene, initially from natural ethyl alcohol and subsequently extracted from coal gas, was reacted with chlorine and water to produced ethylene chlorohydrin (2-chloroethanol), which was then made into ethylene glycol. Glysantin, the German response to Prestone, was launched in the cold winter of 1928–1929. In the course of this research, Reppe discovered a new catalyst for the conversion of ethyl alcohol to ethylene and developed a continuous process for the manufacture of ethylene chlorohydrin.

Research on Butadiene. The increasing demand for rubber created by the automobile, and the attempt by the British government to push up the price of natural rubber by limiting exports from Malaya, encouraged I. G. Farben to resume the synthesis of rubber. An early form of synthetic rubber called methyl rubber (polymethylisoprene) had been developed by Bayer and BASF before World War I, but its manufacture had been abandoned after the end of World War I in November 1918. By this time most chemists agreed that butadiene was the best building block for an economically viable synthetic rubber, as it is cheaper to make than isoprene, the building block of natural rubber. And in I. G. Farben, acetylene was the obvious starting material for butadiene, beginning with the addition of water to acetylene to form acetaldehyde.

The butyl alcohol synthesis of BASF provided the basis for the two middle steps, the conversion of acetaldehyde to aldol and its reduction to 1,3 butylene glycol (1,3-butanediol). This much was clear, but none of the existing catalysts could remove the elements of water from the glycol to make butadiene without producing other unwanted by-products. In 1927 Reppe and Ulrich Hoffmann, his colleague in the solvent laboratory, discovered that sodium hydrogen phosphate was a good catalyst for this dehydration reaction, and they soon improved it by adding a little phosphoric acid. This catalyst paved the way for the industrial production of butadiene (the so-called four-step process, *Vierstufenverfahren* in German), which was later used to make Buna S synthetic rubber, a copolymer of butadiene and styrene invented in 1929 by chemists in I. G. Farben's laboratories in Leverkusen, near Cologne.

Beginning of Reppe Chemistry. When his work on the dehydration of butylene glycol was completed in 1928, Reppe was given the task of finding an industrial process for making vinyl ethers. The polymers of these ethers were regarded as possible alternatives to the hitherto troublesome polyvinyl chloride (PVC), which at that time had a tendency to decompose when worked on hot rollers. The few known routes to vinyl ethers were found to be unsuitable or not to work at all, and Reppe was forced to devise a new synthesis. He discovered that vinyl chloride reacted with sodium ethoxide to form the desired ethyl vinyl ether with very little of the expected (but unwanted) by-product acetylene. Further research revealed that the acetylene formed in the initial reaction was combining with ethyl alcohol under the pressure in the autoclave, and that the sodium ethoxide was acting as a catalyst. When Reppe first tried the reaction between acetylene and ethyl alcohol at 15 atmospheres, he expected an explosion to occur at any moment, as acetylene is very unstable under pressure. As he said in his idiosyncratic English in his report written for the Allies after World War II, "our tension was tops." To use the reaction on the industrial scale, I. G. Farben had to ignore government regulations about the use of acetylene under pressure introduced for the protection of welders. The polyvinyl ethers were not as widely applicable as at first hoped and subsequent improvements in the stability of PVC removed the driving force for the development of these polymers as a substitute for PVC. Nonetheless, the polyvinyl ethers were used for a variety of purposes including adhesives, lacquers, and waxes. During World War II, polyvinyl ethers and polyvinyl amines served as very useful substitutes for chewing gum, human blood plasma, and mica.

The early 1930s saw major changes in the management of research at Ludwigshafen. The Hauptlaboratorium was badly hit by the Great Depression, although the number of chemists working was maintained. Meyer left in January 1932, apparently because of disagreements with the main board of directors. Hermann Mark followed in September, and in his case the worsening political situation (Mark was half-Jewish) was at least part of the reason, although he too may have had policy differences with the firm's leaders. Reppe's outstanding research on butadiene and vinyl ethers was rewarded by his appointment as the head of the intermediates and plastics laboratory at the beginning of 1934. This new laboratory spearheaded the research on the production of synthetic materials at Ludwigshafen and in particular the scaling up of the production of vinyl ethers. I. G. Farben was also doubtlessly attempting to regain some of its momentum in the plastics field, which had been lost with the departure of Meyer and Mark. This promotion also brought Reppe into closer contact with Otto Ambros, a fellow graduate of the University of Munich and a rising star within I. G. Farben who was in charge of the development of organic chemicals at Ludwigshafen and who worked on the planning of the synthetic rubber program under I. G. Farben's powerful technical director, Fritz ter Meer.

The Ethynylation Reaction. The Nazis seized power in 1933 and the new National Socialist regime's desire for self-sufficiency revitalized the synthetic rubber project. Reppe was involved in the search for a better route to butadiene than the four-stage process. The long-desired breakthrough came in September 1937, when Reppe discovered the so-called ethynylation reaction. The most important example of ethynylation was the addition of two molecules of formaldehyde (methanal) to acetylene, under pressure, to form 2-butyne-1,4-diol. If the use of acetylene under pressure was not worrying enough, the catalyst used in this reaction, copper acetylide, had hitherto only been used as a detonator for dynamite. Reppe had in fact originally tried to use inorganic copper salts as catalysts, presumably drawing an analogy with Julius Nieuwland's process for the dimerization of acetylene, a reaction that been intensively investigated elsewhere in I. G. Farben but which was abandoned after two chemists were killed in an explosion. Aware of the dangers of copper acetylide, Reppe took great care to prevent its formation in his experiments. Only after nine months of continuous failure did he suddenly realize that copper acetylide was actually acting as a catalyst.

This ethynylation reaction became the basis of the Reppe process for butadiene, which used only one molecule of expensive acetylene rather than the two consumed by the four-step process. After the initial teething problems were solved, the Reppe process was used to make synthetic rubber at Ludwigshafen in 1943–1944. The operation of a high-pressure acetylene plant that employed a percussive compound as a catalyst in the midst of aerial bombardment was a feat of technical skill and great courage. The sides of the butynediol building were left open to reduce the debris caused by any explosion. After the war, Allied investigators were astounded that the Germans had even considered using this reaction on a large scale. A group of Imperial Chemical Industries (ICI) chemists had made four pounds of butynediol in the early years of the war using Reppe's reaction, and they had naively imagined that they had made the largest-ever batch of this compound. By contrast, Ludwigshafen had produced 30,000 metric tonnes in 1944. Reppe energetically developed new end uses for butynediol in the laboratory, but his intricate pathways to products such as nylon 66 found little favor outside Ludwigshafen.

Carboylation and Cyclooctatetraene. Reppe was once again rewarded for his success with a promotion at the beginning of 1938 to become head of the Hauptlaboratium at Ludwigshafen, the position once held by his old PhD supervisor, Kurt Meyer. But Reppe's view of research was very different from that of Meyer, with Reppe focusing on technical developments of use to I. G. Farben and the German state rather than broadly based basic research with an international outlook. This was largely a result of the times—the National Socialist Four Year Plan to create a self-sufficient Germany was at its height—and also a reflection of Reppe's desire to use highly novel chemical reactions to produce valuable products.

Leaving the scaling up of the ethynylation process to his colleagues, notably Georg Niemann and Franz Reicheneder, Reppe now turned to the reaction between carbon monoxide and acetylene in the presence of alcohols to form acrylate esters. The polymers of the acrylate esters (and the related polymethacrylates) were (and still are) an important group of plastics. Reppe attempted to use nickel carbonyl as the original catalyst, but it was converted during the reaction to a nickel halide. This problem was eventually solved by using the nickel halide (usually

the bromide) as the catalyst; it forms a transient carbonyl compound with carbon monoxide under the conditions of the reaction. While this method of making acrylates was very useful, it suffered from a number of problems—mainly to do with the catalyst—at the pilot plant stages, problems that remained largely unsolved in 1945. Reppe also used nickel carbonyl to add carbon monoxide to methanol to produce acetic acid. This reaction also had problems at the pilot plant stage, and the full-scale plant only came onstream in 1957.

Meanwhile, in the spring of 1940, Reppe became aware of Otto Roehlen's research at Ruhrchemie in Oberhausen on his so-called OXO process, which combined olefins with carbon monoxide to form aldehydes, which were converted into the corresponding alcohols (used, for example, to make detergents). This work was a spin-off of Ruhrchemie's development of the Fischer-Tropsch process for synthetic fuel. During World War II, Reppe and his colleague Hugo Kröper used his carbonylation reaction to make propionic acid from ethylene. Unfortunately, this process suffered greatly from corrosion problems, and a silver-lined reaction vessel had to be used in 1943. Partly because of the French occupation after the war, the full-scale plant was not ready until 1951.

In December 1940 Reppe's colleague, Tim Toepel, tried to make 3-hexyne-1,6-diol by adding ethylene oxide to acetylene using nickel cyanide as a catalyst, presumably with the aim of preparing the monomers of nylon 66 from acetylene. This was unsuccessful but, quite unexpectedly, a mixture of cyclic hydrocarbons was formed. Further investigation revealed that the major product was cyclooctatetraene (COT), a cyclic compound that was at the heart of scientific investigations into the basis of aromaticity. Despite the difficulties created by wartime conditions, particularly air raids and lack of trained staff, Reppe and his group carried out an extensive amount of fundamental research on COT during the war. In 1948 they published their findings, which formed the basis for later academic research on this interesting compound However, Reppe's hopes for industrial end uses for COT have turned out to be ill-founded, partly because acetylene has become too expensive and partly because it has been displaced by the related oligomerization of butadiene patented by Günther Wilke at the Max-Planck-Institut für Kohlenforschung (Max Planck Institute for Coal Research) at Mülheim in the Ruhr in 1956.

The End of I. G. Farben. It has to be emphasised that most of Reppe's processes had not left the laboratory, or at best had reached the pilot plant stage, by 1945. Only the vinyl ethers and the Reppe process (for butadiene) had been transferred to the industrial scale. The chemicals produced of the new Reppe chemistry accounted for a trivial 2.5 percent of all acetylene-based chemicals in Germany in 1943. As Allied bombs rained down on the large chemical complex at Ludwigshafen, Ambros moved on 21 September 1944 to Gendorf—a small factory east of Munich, near the Austrian border—that made ethylene diglycol for explosives. This evacuation was linked to a vain attempt to move synthetic rubber production from Ludwigshafen to an underground factory nearby. Reppe was also transferred to Gendorf with most of his laboratory. He installed himself in one of the factory buildings and attempted to resume his research on chemical reactions under pressure.

On 6 May 1945 the U.S. Army entered Gendorf and encountered Ambros and Reppe. At first they were allowed to remain at Gendorf, but on 10 June they were taken into custody so that they could be interrogated about their work at I. G. Farben, especially the production of nerve gases (with which Reppe had never had any connection). On 6 July the American Chemical Society suggested that Reppe should be questioned about his work on acetylene, and eight days later Reppe was taken to Dustbin, the Allied detention center—at Schloss Kransberg, Hermann Goering's former castle northeast of Frankfurt—run by the British. Reppe insisted he needed more freedom and access to his files if he were to be able to write a report on his pioneering research. He was released from Dustbin in October 1945 into the custody of Lieutenant Colonel Maurice Bigelow of the U.S. Chemical Corps.

For the next five months Reppe worked on his report in the Frankfurt area under the supervision of Bigelow, but after he turned down a contract to work for the U.S. War Department and became uncooperative, he was returned to Dustbin, remaining there from March to November 1946. He was then moved to Nürnberg (possibly with a view to putting him on trial with the board directors of I. G. Farben); to Ludwigsburg; and in the spring of 1947, to Dachau. Reppe was released from Dachau on 5 June 1947 after almost two years in Allied custody. Bigelow claimed in 1949 that it had been necessary to keep Reppe in custody to prevent him being forced to work in a road gang as a former Nazi Party member. The Americans had probably also hoped that this imprisonment would make Reppe eager to go to America, as he was one of the top targets for Project Paperclip. During this period, teams of Allied investigators assiduously gathered documents about Reppe chemistry that they found in I. G. Farben's works and interviewed his colleagues. This was only a small part of a massive effort to collect all possible technical information about German industry and military technology. Reppe chemistry, however, was near the top of the list, alongside rocket technology and chemical warfare. Asked by the U.S. Chemical Corps (on behalf of the American Chemical Society) to write a brief popular report for the layperson on his new chemistry, Reppe—rather unwillingly—wrote a long, sometimes rambling account that was highly technical and not at all suitable for the layperson—but which provided the raw material for most contemporary accounts of Reppe chemistry, even Reppe's own publications.

As soon as the war ended, the Allies dissolved I. G. Farbenindustrie, and its component units came under the control of the occupying power. Ludwigshafen was in the French zone of occupation and came under French control. In 1952, after considerable negotiation, the Western Allies agreed that three successor firms should be set up to take over the former I. G. Farben works in West Germany. Ludwigshafen, along with the neighboring Oppau works, became the nucleus of the new BASF, which considered itself to be the successor of the pre-1925 firm. Meanwhile, the board of directors of I. G. Farben (the *Vorstand*) had faced an American military tribunal at Nürnberg in 1948, charged with war crimes, although the resulting sentences were relatively light and were commuted in 1950.

Research Director at BASF. On his return to Ludwigshafen in September 1947, Reppe worked hard to bring the Hauptlaboratorium back to its prewar peak. He also fought successfully to prevent the dismantlement of the synthetic rubber plant at Ludwigshafen so that the production of butyndiol could continue. In 1949 Reppe became head of research at BASF while also remaining head of the Hauptlaboratorium. When the new company was given legal standing in 1952, he joined the management board of directors. In the 1950s he supervised the transfer of his carbonylation chemistry to the industrial scale and struggled with the corrosion problems. The acetic acid plant came onstream in 1957 and the proprionic acid plant followed two years later. By contrast, the pilot plant for the production of acrylic acid was not replaced by a full-scale plant until 1965. Reppe developed a new way of making butyl alcohol by reacting propylene (propene) with carbon monoxide and hydrogen, using special catalysts to ensure that only the desired n-butyl alcohol was produced. This was the culmination of his early research on butyl alcohol in the solvents laboratory.

General Aniline and Film Corporation (GAF) pioneered the transfer of Reppe chemistry to the United States. GAF was the successor of the I. G. Farben's American subsidiaries, and as such, it held the U.S. patents on Reppe's reactions. One of its chemists, John W. Copenhaver, was a member of the intelligence team that investigated Reppe chemistry after the war. In 1949 he coauthored, with Maurice H. Bigelow, an excellent monograph on Reppe's work titled *Acetylene and Carbon Monoxide Chemistry*. GAF's butyndiol plant at Calvert City, Kentucky, came onstream in 1956, followed by a later plant at Texas City, Texas. By the 1970s the Reppe process was also used by du Pont in Houston, Texas, and BASF-Wyandotte in Geismar, Louisiana.

After his retirement in 1957, Reppe continued to carry out research in his private laboratory. He became interested in vitamin chemistry and was also eager to find a way of making formaldehyde by combining carbon monoxide with hydrogen, but was not successful. He was also a member of the supervisory board of BASF until 1966. Reppe died in Heidelberg on 27 July 1969, two days short of his seventy-seventh birthday.

The Reppe process for butyndiol is still is use in Germany and the United States. It is mainly employed to produce the solvent tetrahydrofuran and in the manufacture of polyurethanes, a new type of plastics that was developed by Otto Bayer, Walter Reppe's counterpart at I. G. Farben's laboratory at Leverkusen, near Cologne. In the 1960s and 1970s, COT was widely used in academic research and was the starting point for several important laboratory syntheses, including cyclobutadiene and bullvalene. Interest in COT declined after BASF withdrew free supplies of it in the early 1970s. The BASF pilot plant was closed in 1988, and COT is no longer the subject of intensive research.

Reppe had a rather outspoken personality and was not known for his social skills. He could also be imprudent, a trait that led to the development of Reppe chemistry but that also had its drawbacks. On one occasion in the early 1950s, he was showing some important Japanese visitors around the laboratory when he threw the stub of his cigar—he was a dedicated cigar smoker—into a sink. As the sink contained traces of flammable solvents, a large flame shot up in front of the shocked visitors, and smoking was subsequently banned in BASF's laboratories. This combination of frankness and recklessness doubtlessly hindered his movement up the corporate ladder, especially in the late 1930s, when diplomatic skills were at a premium when dealing with the Nazi hierarchy. Reppe felt keenly his lack of advancement and honors, at least in 1945. In his I. G. Farben days, Reppe did not travel abroad—international relations were handled by ter Meer and Ambros. However, when Reppe was head of research at BASF in the 1950s, he made successful trips to Spain and Japan in 1953 and to the United States in the following year. This was a sign of the new firm's international outlook and its desire to forge technological alliances with foreign firms and academics.

It was Reppe's misfortune that he was at the peak of his powers during the Depression and then the Third Reich, which prevented him from continuing his promising early work on ethylene and forced him to concentrate on acetylene-based strategic materials. His links with the Third Reich probably cost him the Nobel Prize that he

richly deserved for his courageous research and his path-breaking acetylene chemistry. Although in the early twenty-first century it may appear to be a representative of a bygone era that used coal and sought economic self-sufficiency, his prewar research and his postwar leadership of research at BASF played an important role in the postwar reconstruction of the West German chemical industry.

BIBLIOGRAPHY

WORKS BY REPPE

With O. Schichting, K. Klager, and T. Toepel, "Cyclisierende Polymerisation von Acetylen I: Über Cyclooctatetraen." *Justus Liebigs Annalen der Chemie* 560 (1948): 1–116.

Neue Entwicklungen auf dem Gebiet der Chemie des Acetylens und Kohlenoxyds. Berlin: Springer, 1949. A good overview of Reppe's research based on his report for the Allied investigators, but less informative than the book by Copenhaver and Bigelow (see Other Sources) based on the same report.

Chemie und Technik der Acetylen-Druck-Reactionen. Expanded ed. Weinheim, Germany: Verlag Chemie, 1952.

"Carbonylierung I: Über die Umsetzung von Acetylen mit Kohlenoxyd und Verbindungen mit reaktionsfähigen Wasserstoffatomen." *Annalen* 582 (1953): 1–161.

Polyvinylpyrrolidon. Weinheim, Germany: Verlag Chemie, 1954.

With others. *Annalen* 596 (1955): 1–224 (ethynylation); *Annalen* 601 (1956): 81–138 (vinylation).

OTHER SOURCES

Abelshauser, Werner, Wolfgang von Hippel, Jeffrey Allan Johnson, et al. *German Industry and Global Enterprise: BASF—The History of a Company.* New York: Cambridge University Press, 2004. A history of Reppe's company that puts his career into its corporate context but which surprisingly has little to say about Reppe (and even less about Reppe chemistry).

Baptista, Robert J., and Anthony S. Travis. "I. G. Farben in America: The Technologies of General Aniline & Film." *History and Technology* 22, no. 2 (June 2006): 187–224.

Copenhaver, John W., and Maurice H. Bigelow. *Acetylene and Carbon Monoxide Chemistry.* New York: Reinhold, 1949. The best account of Reppe's research up to 1945, with an often-elegant translation of Reppe's own report.

Hummel, Hans Georg. "Walter Reppe." *Chemische Berichte* 117 (1984): i–xxii. Concentrates on Reppe's chemical achievements.

Morris, Peter J. T. "The Technology-Science Interaction: Walter Reppe and Cyclooctatetraene Chemistry." *British Journal for the History of Science* 25 (1992): 145–167. Places Reppe's research on COT in the context of the history of COT chemistry and the study of aromaticity.

———. "Ambros, Reppe, and the Emergence of Heavy Organic Chemicals in Germany, 1925–1945." In *Determinants in the Evolution of the European Chemical Industry, 1900–1939: New Technologies, Political Frameworks, Markets, and Companies,* edited by Anthony S. Travis, Harm G. Schröter, Ernst Homburg, et al. Dordrecht, Netherlands: Kluwer,

1998. Explores the relationship between Reppe's research and the development of synthetic rubber during the Third Reich.

Stokes, Raymond G. *Opting for Oil: The Political Economy of Technological Change in the West German Chemical Industry, 1945–1961.* Cambridge, U.K.: Cambridge University Press, 1994. Places Reppe's research in the political and corporate context of the post-1945 rebuilding of the West German chemical industry.

Peter J. T. Morris

REPPE, WALTER
SEE **Reppe, Julius Walter**.

REVELLE, ROGER RANDALL DOUGAN
(*b.* Seattle, Washington, 7 March 1909; *d.* San Diego, California, 15 July 1991), *oceanography, climate change, science policy, and public policy.*

Revelle was a leading oceanographer of his generation. The scientific results of his midcentury Pacific expeditions called into question the prevailing view of a fixed and ancient seafloor. He championed measurements of atmospheric carbon dioxide in 1956 and his subsequent work on climate change stimulated worldwide research on the topic. As a naval officer he helped formulate the navy's postwar scientific research program. As an academic he was an institution builder who defined basic research in geophysics in the United States and secured the military and federal dollars to support it. His knowledge of the oceans broadened into an interest in resources and population. He worked internationally to foster policies that might achieve a balance of resources and population, especially in the developing world. His work in support of international cooperation made him a statesman of science.

Youth and Education. Revelle was the son of Ella Robena Dougan Revelle and William Roger Revelle, an attorney and teacher. The family moved to Pasadena in 1917. Revelle was identified as a gifted student and was included in Stanford psychologist Lewis Terman's study. Revelle received an AB from Pomona in 1929 as a student of Alfred O. Woodford. He entered the University of California, Berkeley, in 1930 as a graduate student in geology under George Davis Louderback and worked on problems of sedimentation. He married Ellen Virginia Clark, a member of the philanthropic Scripps newspaper family, on 22 June 1931.

In 1931, John A. Fleming, director of the Department of Terrestrial Magnetism at the Carnegie Institution, contacted Thomas Wayland Vaughan at the Scripps Institution of Oceanography, requesting that Scripps examine sediment cores taken on the seventh cruise of the nonmagnetic brig *Carnegie.* Vaughan consulted Louderback, who recommended Revelle for the work. Revelle moved to La Jolla, California, and registered for graduate work at Scripps.

Revelle's analysis of the sediments in the *Carnegie* cores became the subject of his dissertation. He received a doctorate in oceanography from the University of California–Berkeley on 22 May 1936. Revelle's sediment work was closely associated with studies of calcium carbonate sediments initiated by Vaughan and Haldane Gee and in studies of carbon dioxide and other substances involved in the buffer mechanism of sea water.

The Carnegie Institution funded the visits of many Scandinavian scientists to the Scripps Institution including Kurt Buch, Bjørn Helland-Hansen, and Harald Sverdrup. Revelle spent a postdoctoral year at the Geophysical Institute in Bergen, Norway, in 1936 and was introduced to the world community of geophysicists and oceanographers at the International Union of Geodesy and Geophysics meeting in Edinburgh. These connections were important to Revelle's career, and initiated his subsequent commitment to international science.

Revelle got his first seagoing experience on the small coastal vessels operated by the Scripps Institution. His experience in the deep Pacific began as a guest scientist on vessels of the U.S. Coast and Geodetic Survey and the U.S. Navy before World War II. In 1936 Revelle sought a commission in the naval reserve in order to increase his opportunities to go to sea. Beginning in 1937, he worked closely with Scripps director Sverdrup and led a major oceanographic cruise to the Gulf of California in 1939.

Naval Service. Revelle was called for training duty as a sonar officer in February 1941. He was assigned to active duty at the U.S. Navy Radio and Sound Laboratory in San Diego. He conducted research on sonar performance and served as a liaison officer for the University of California Division of War Research. Revelle participated in surveys of oceanographic conditions in San Francisco Bay, Neah Bay, and in the Straits of Juan de Fuca. In October 1942 he was assigned to the Navy Hydrographic Office with a dual appointment to the Sonar Design Section, Bureau of Ships. He was the principal liaison officer between the navy and the National Defense Research Committee oceanographic division. Rear Admiral Thorvald A. Solberg wrote in a letter to Carl Eckart in 1948 that "it is no exaggeration to say that the large role which oceanography now occupies in the Navy research program is in part due to Dr. Revelle's effectiveness and foresight."

Roger Randall Dougan Revelle. FRITZ GORL/TIME LIFE
PICTURES/GETTY IMAGES.

Revelle was in Manila attached to the group planning
the invasion of Japan when the atomic bomb ended the
war. He returned to Washington and was one of a small
group of officers who formulated the navy's postwar policy with regard to oceanographic research. He planned
and initiated the Oceanographic Section of the Navy
Hydrographic Office and participated in planning for the
Office of Naval Research (ONR). Historian Ronald
Rainger credits Revelle with "fostering a powerful combination of military support and intellectual autonomy"
within ONR (Rainger, 2001, p. 336).

Revelle was assigned to Joint Task Force One in 1946,
the joint command that supervised the first postwar
atomic test on Bikini Atoll, Operation Crossroads. He led
the oceanographic and geophysical components of the
operation. He studied the diffusion of radioactive wastes
and the environmental effects of the bomb at Bikini. Revelle's Crossroads team included Kenneth Emery, Gifford
Ewing, Jeffery Holter, Henry Ladd, Walter Munk, and
Allyn Vine. Revelle organized a second team that resur-

veyed Bikini in 1947. During the survey, cores were
drilled from the atoll to a depth of 800 meters, which verified the theories of the origin of atolls proposed by
Charles Darwin and James Dwight Dana. The resurvey
team found evidence for intermittent submergence of the
central Pacific floor throughout the last epoch of geologic
time. Revelle's experiences on Crossroads were invaluable
in his later work as chair of the National Academy of
Sciences/National Research Council Biological Effects of
Atomic Energy committee.

Scripps. Revelle was an imposing figure, six feet four
inches tall with enormous flat feet that almost kept him
out of the navy. He spoke with a low voice, low intensity,
and low pitch, which commanded attention. He focused
completely on whatever he was doing at the moment and
he took on more than he could handle. These characteristics, combined with his wide-ranging interests and willingness to accept responsibilities did not foster a focused
working environment.

Scripps director Harald Sverdrup was aware of Revelle's shortcomings, but groomed him as his successor.
They shared a vision of the Scripps Institution as a seagoing international oceanographic center and a commitment to international science, and they valued scientific
brilliance over administrative acumen. While still on navy
duty, Revelle helped Scripps acquire two mothballed federal vessels and ONR provided direct funding in support
of seagoing research. When Sverdrup proposed Revelle as
his successor, the senior Scripps faculty rebelled, citing his
poor administrative skills. Revelle returned to Scripps in
1948 as associate professor and associate director for
seagoing activities. He was soon promoted to full professor, but did not become director until 1950.

Under Revelle's leadership Scripps became a large and
powerful oceanographic center. When he left, Scripps had
a fleet larger than that of Costa Rica. Beginning in 1956,
Revelle took the lead to create a new campus of the University of California (UC) on land adjacent to the Scripps
campus. While Revelle prevailed over opposition to a San
Diego campus, it cost him support among university
regents, and weakened his relationship with UC President
Clark Kerr. In 1961, when he was passed over for chancellor of the University of California at San Diego (UCSD),
Revelle left Scripps. He returned briefly in 1963, but left
again in September 1964, to become Richard Saltonstall
Professor of Population Policy and first director of the
Center for Population Studies at Harvard. UCSD named
its first college, Revelle College, in his honor in 1965.

Plate Tectonics. As director of Scripps, Revelle planned
and led a dozen oceanographic expeditions to the Pacific
including MIDPAC (1950), CAPRICORN (1952)

connected with the thermonuclear IVY test, Downwind (1957), one of three Scripps International Geophysical Year (IGY) expeditions, and MONSOON (1960–1961), the first of several International Indian Ocean Expedition cruises. These expeditions yielded surprising results. Among the discoveries was the extreme thinness of deep-sea sediments, the similarity of heat flow on the ocean floor and in the continental region, the young ages of seamounts, and the occurrences of enormous fault zones. Revelle remembered these years as the greatest of his career in an August 1989 speech at Scripps: "In those heady days of the 1950s one could hardly go to sea without making an important, unanticipated discovery."

With hindsight, the evidence was all there for proclaiming the doctrine of plate tectonics. Revelle later reflected, "we were not courageous enough, or perhaps smart enough" to make the leap (1987, p. 18). Scripps geologist Bill Menard agreed that the failure was one of vision, but added that scientists were so busy at sea accumulating data that they did not spend sufficient time analyzing it. "Many of us later had time to kick ourselves when earlier we had not had time to think," Menard concluded (Menard, 1986, p. 298).

Climate Change Research. Initially, Revelle's interest in carbon dioxide was general and emerged from his early study of seawater chemistry and the carbon cycle. Rainger has written that Revelle's interest grew during the postwar period, when he followed the work of Willard Libby and recruited Harmon Craig and Hans Suess at Scripps. In the late 1950s Revelle and Suess proposed that the ongoing industrial revolution should yield a signal detectable within decades with profound implications for climate change. Surprisingly, it was detected within a few years of observation.

During the planning phase for the IGY, Carl-Gustaf Rossby, Harry Wexler, and Roger Revelle advocated measurements of atmospheric carbon dioxide. Revelle recruited Charles David Keeling in July 1956 to begin the first precise long-term measurements. Scripps became the principal center for the program, and Keeling's new data demonstrated an increase in atmospheric carbon dioxide that touched off a cascade of scientific investigation and a debate that continues to animate politicians and the public worldwide. Revelle used intentionally provocative language in the 1957 *Tellus* paper he wrote with Suess, calling it a "large scale geophysical experiment (pp. 19–20)." He was delighted that human activities could lead to measurable modifications which would provide improved understanding of atmospheric and ocean processes.

In 1977, Revelle served as chair of a fifteen-member Energy and Climate Panel convened by the National Academy of Sciences to assess the possible consequences of carbon dioxide buildup on climate and agriculture. In 1979, Revelle and other scientists prepared a report for the Council on Environmental Quality on the greenhouse effect. During these years, Revelle was a key player in climate change research and worked tirelessly to bring the issue to the attention of scientists and science policy bodies. He recalled at the end of his life that his longest continuous involvement with any subject in science had been with oceanic and atmospheric carbon dioxide. It was this work that was recognized by the Tyler Ecology Award and the Prix Balzan.

Environment and Population. In 1961 Revelle chaired a study of soil salinity in West Pakistan at the behest of presidents John F. Kennedy and Mohammad Ayub Khan. The study resulted in an increase in agricultural production in the region. As first science adviser to the secretary of the interior, Revelle counseled Interior Secretary Stewart Udall to back Rachel Carson in her dispute with the chemical industry. Revelle's work on population and resources at Harvard deepened his commitment to the developing world. Al Gore and Benazir Bhutto were his students at Harvard during this period. Revelle was a life-long advocate of the use of earth resources for the benefit of humanity; he focused on the achievement of sustainable development. He advocated nuclear power in lieu of burning of fossil fuels. Thus while Revelle discussed and fostered environmental policy, he was not an environmentalist. He felt that scientists, not the public, should investigate and resolve scientific issues and that the best science policy grew out of consultations between scientists and politicians, not public advocacy groups.

International Science. Revelle contributed to international cooperation in oceanography through service in scientific organizations. In 1946 he became a member of the National Research Council's Pacific Science Board. He served on the Department of the Interior Arctic Research Advisory Board. He was a member of the Joint Chiefs of Staff Joint Commission on Oceanography. In 1950, Revelle served as an officer of the Oceanography Section of the American Geophysical Union. He was chair of the Department of Defense Research and Development Board on Oceanography the following year.

In the late 1950s Revelle and other scientists affiliated with the American Association for the Advancement of Science worked to found the International Oceanographic Congress (IOC). Revelle presided over the first one in 1959. One great project of the IOC was the International Indian Ocean Expedition, which was the genesis of Revelle's great interest in the Indian subcontinent. In 1957, he organized the Special Committee on Oceanic Research (now the Scientific Committee on Oceanic Research) of the International Council of Scientific Unions and became its first president. He worked closely with and through the United Nations Educational, Scientific and Cultural Organization (UNESCO) beginning in 1955 on projects, conferences, and discussions concerned with oceanography, economic development, population, food resources, and technology transfer. When UNESCO formed its International Advisory Committee on Marine Sciences in 1955, Revelle represented the United States. He was one of four oceanographers who fostered UNESCO's Intergovernmental Oceanographic Commission.

Revelle's work on the National Academy of Sciences Committee on Oceanography and his growing reputation in science brought him into contact with Congress after *Sputnik*. He worked on legislation related to the sea, especially with Warren G. Magnuson. He was a member of the Advisory Panel on Science and Technology of the House Committee on Science and Astronautics, later renamed the Committee on Science and Technology.

Revelle was elected to the National Academy of Sciences in 1957 and received the academy's Agassiz Medal. He received the Bowie Award of the American Geophysical Union, and he was elected president of the American Association for the Advancement of Science in 1974. Just before his death, Revelle received the Medal of Freedom from President George H. W. Bush, in recognition of his lifelong achievement in science.

BIBLIOGRAPHY

Revelle's personal papers and records as Scripps director are at Scripps Institution of Oceanography Archives, UCSD. Mandeville Department of Special Collections, UCSD, holds Revelle's records as chief campus officer at UCSD. Bureau of Ships, Record Group 19 and Hydrographic Office, Record Group 37 at the National Archives include material documenting Revelle's naval career.

WORKS BY REVELLE

"Physico-chemical Factors Affecting the Solubility of Calcium Carbonate in Sea Water." *Journal of Sedimentary Petrology* 4, no. 3 (1934): 103–110.

"Marine Bottom Samples Collected in the Pacific Ocean by the *Carnegie* on Its Seventh Cruise." In *Scientific Results of Cruise VII of the* Carnegie *during 1928–1929 under Command of Captain J. P. Ault: Oceanography.* Carnegie Institution of Washington Publication no. 556. Washington, DC: Carnegie Institution, 1944.

With E. C. Bullard and A. E. Maxwell. "Heat Flow through the Deep-Sea Floor." In *Advances in Geophysics*, vol. 3. New York: Academic Press, 1956.

With H. E. Suess. "Carbon Dioxide Exchange between the Atmosphere and Ocean and the Question of an Increase of Atmospheric CO$_2$ during the Past Decades." *Tellus* 9 (1957): 18–27.

"Report of the Committee on Oceanography and Fisheries." In *The Biological Effects of Atomic Radiation: Summary Reports.* Washington, DC: National Academy of Sciences–National Research Council, 1960.

"Carbon Dioxide and the World Climate." *Scientific American* 247, no. 2 (1982): 35–43.

"How I Became an Oceanographer and Other Sea Stories." *Annual Review of Earth and Planetary Science* 15 (1987): 1–23.

OTHER SOURCES

Dorfman, Robert, and Peter P. Rogers. *Science with a Human Face: In Honor of Roger Randall Revelle.* Boston: Harvard School of Public Health, distributed by Harvard University Press, 1997. Appendix 3 includes principal publications of Roger Revelle.

Malone, Thomas F., Edward D. Goldberg, and Walter H. Munk. "Roger Randall Dougan Revelle: March 7, 1909–July 15, 1991." *Biographical Memoirs,* vol. 75. Washington, DC: National Academy of Sciences, 1998. Available from http://www. nap.edu/readingroom/books/biomems/ rrevelle.html.

Menard, H. William. *The Ocean of Truth: A Personal History of Global Tectonics.* Princeton, NJ: Princeton University Press, 1986.

Rainger, Ronald. "Patronage and Science: Roger Revelle, the U.S. Navy, and Oceanography at the Scripps Institution." *Earth Sciences History* 19 (2000): 58–89.

———."Constituting a Landscape for Postwar Science: Roger Revelle, the Scripps Institution and the University of California, San Diego." *Minerva* 39 (2001): 327–352.

———. "'A Wonderful Oceanographic Tool': The Atomic Bomb, Radioactivity and the Development of American Oceanography." In *The Machine in Neptune's Garden: Historical Perspectives on Technology and the Marine Environment*, edited by Helen M. Rozwadowski and David van Keuren. Sagamore Beach, MA: Science History Publications, 2004.

Solberg, Thorvald A., letter to Carl Eckart, 22 March 1948, Records of the SIO Office of the Director (Revelle), Box 1, SIO Archives, UCSD.

United States. President's Science Advisory Committee. Environmental Pollution Panel. *Restoring the Quality of Our Environment: Report of the Environmental Pollution Panel, President's Science Advisory Committee.* Washington, D.C.: White House, 1965.

Weart, Spencer R. "Global Warming, Cold War, and the Evolution of Research Plans." *Historical Studies in the Physical and Biological Sciences* 27 (1997): 319–356.

Deborah Day
Walter H. Munk

RICHARD RUFUS DE CORNUBIA

SEE **Rufus, Richard of Cornwall**.

RICHARDSON, LEWIS FRY (*b.* Newcastle upon Tyne, England, United Kingdom, 11 October 1881; *d.* Kilmun, Scotland, United Kingdom, 30 September 1953), *mathematics, meteorology, psychology, peace research.*

Richardson developed an elegant way for solving differential equations by an approximate numerical method and later applied this to weather prediction. To psychologists he is regarded as a pioneer in the measurement of perception. As a pacifist, he devoted his final years to his seminal work on the objective study of arms races and the causes of war.

Preparation. Both Richardson's father, a successful leather manufacturer, and his mother were devout members of the Society of Friends (Quakers). He was accordingly brought up in the best Quaker traditions and completed his school education at Bootham, a Quaker boarding school in York. Here he was greatly influenced by his science masters, who encouraged him especially to pursue his interest in natural history. He proceeded to Durham College of Science (now part of Newcastle University) from where he was awarded a scholarship to King's College, Cambridge. He graduated with a First in the Natural Sciences Tripos in 1903.

Over the next ten years Richardson held a series of research and teaching posts, twice at the National Physical Laboratory, twice in industry, and twice in university physics departments. During his spell with National Peat Industries from 1906 to 1907 he was asked how best to design drains in a peat moss, taking into account the annual rainfall. As the mathematical equations involved were not solvable by analytical methods, he was led to study approximate methods of solution, first graphical and then numerical. He considered two types of problems, boundary value problems and initial value problems, which he called "jury" and "marching" problems respectively. The results of his efforts were published in 1910 in Richardson's first important paper "The Approximate Solution by Finite Differences of Physical Problems Involving Differential Equations." In it he demonstrated how his methods could be used to obtain rapid and sufficiently accurate solutions to many practical problems by calculating the stresses in a masonry dam. A clear account of Richardson's method of numerical analysis was given by Ernest Gold (1954).

Weather. In the following year Richardson suggested to the director of the British Meteorological Office, Sir Napier Shaw, that his method might be applied to calculate weather forecasts. Shaw was favorably impressed and in 1913 he gave Richardson an opportunity to develop his ideas by appointing him superintendent of Eskdalemuir Observatory in Scotland, where the not too burdensome administrative duties would leave him adequate time for research. Shortly after beginning his study, Richardson came under the influence of the ideas of Vilhelm Bjerknes but continued to use numerical methods rather than graphs. At this stage he was apparently not aware of the work of Felix Exner. By 1916 he had almost completed the first draft of his book *Weather Prediction by Numerical Process* but it still remained to provide a practical example.

At this point Richardson resigned from the Meteorological Office to serve as an ambulance driver in the Friends' Ambulance Unit in France. During his rest periods from his horrific task of transporting wounded soldiers, he calculated a weather forecast for central Europe over a six-hour period on 20 May 1910—the date for which he felt that the best set of weather observations was available. The results of the computation were greatly at variance with the observed changes, the most glaring error being a calculated rise in surface pressure of 145 millibars whereas in fact there had been very little change. The calculations were nevertheless included in his book, which was finally published in 1922. An excellent account of the reasons for the failure of the forecast was given by Peter Lynch (2006).

Richardson's book had no immediate impact on the current practices for weather forecasting, which at that time were largely based on subjective methods and on the experience of the forecasters. Quite apart from the disastrous results of his attempt at numerical weather prediction, the available observing and computing facilities would have been wholly inadequate for the routine application of numerical methods. (The agenda to use electronic computers to calculate the weather started in 1946.) To his contemporary meteorologists, Richardson appeared to be a brilliant theoretician with completely impractical ideas.

This attitude changed dramatically in the 1950s, thanks to better mathematics and understanding of atmospheric dynamics, to the development of electronic computers, and to the great improvements in weather observations, especially in the upper air. In 1965 his book, which in the original edition had sold but a few hundred copies, was reissued as a Dover paperback, recommended as a classroom text in dynamic meteorology. Numerical methods of weather forecasting, similar in many ways to those of Richardson, rapidly became routine all over the world.

By the time of his discharge from the Friends' Ambulance Unit in 1919 Richardson had become passionate about meteorology and he was happy to accept an offer from Shaw of a research post at Benson Observatory in Oxfordshire with William Henry Dines, a pioneer in making upper-air measurements with kites. Richardson devised several ingenious methods of conducting these measurements in such a way that the results would be available quickly, in time for use in weather forecasting, but none proved to be suitable for routine use. He also carried out a series of experiments on atmospheric turbulence, from which he derived a criterion, later to be called the Richardson number, for determining whether the turbulence would increase or decrease. This now ranks as a fundamental parameter in problems of the turbulent motion of the atmosphere.

Richardson's stay at Benson was cut short in 1920 when the Meteorological Office became part of the Air Ministry. He regretfully resigned because his Quaker pacifist convictions made it unacceptable for him to work directly for the armed services. There being no university departments of meteorology in Britain at that time, Richardson accepted a position at Westminster Training College in London as lecturer in physics and mathematics (although he had no formal mathematical qualifications at this stage). He was destined to spend the rest of his career in the educational world, ending up from 1929 to 1940 as principal of Paisley Technical College (now the University of Paisley).

One of the conditions of Richardson's appointment at Westminster was that he would have reasonable time for research work. His main achievement during the first part of his ten-year stay there was in the field of atmospheric diffusion. Hitherto, studies of diffusion had been based on measuring the distances of individual elements from a fixed point. Richardson's novel idea was to measure the distance l between each of a pair of particles and its neighbor. From measurements involving parachuting dandelion seeds, the release of clusters of toy balloons, and puffs of tobacco smoke he determined empirically that the rate of diffusion was roughly proportional to $1\ 4/3$. This same ratio was derived theoretically nearly twenty years later by Andrei N. Kolmogorov and Alexander M. Obukhov.

Psychology. While still a student at Cambridge, Richardson had decided to spend the first half of his life under the strict discipline of physics and then to apply this training to researches on living things. To this end he started to study psychology in 1923 as an external student at University College in London. He obtained a pass degree in 1925 in psychology with pure and applied mathematics, and followed this up with an honor's degree in psychology

in 1929. In the meantime he had in 1926 been awarded a DSc for his work on physics, mathematics, and meteorology and had been elected as a Fellow of the Royal Society. In this same year he finally made a deliberate decision to abandon meteorology for psychology and immediately embarked on a series of experiments on the quantitative estimation of perception, the prevailing view at that time being that such estimates were meaningless.

His first paper on the subject, published in 1928, dealt with the threshold of sensation on the forearm. This was followed in 1929 by two papers on quantitative estimates of light and color. For the latter he invited a wide variety of people to assign a number between 0 (white) and 100 (scarlet) to a shade of pink. Most participants had no difficulty in providing a reasonable estimate. Richardson's most famous paper in this field related to loudness. Observers were asked to estimate the ratio of the loudness of a signal to that of a standard signal, the intensity of the signals being measured independently as a telephone voltage. In 1933 Richardson suffered from cellulitis of his right thumb and experienced various intensities of pain over a period of seven weeks. This led him to propose a quantitative scale for pain from A, a pain that can only be perceived by careful attention, up to E, a pain so intense that it arrests the movement of thought.

From all these experiments Richardson concluded that he had cleared the way toward a more scientific study of quantitativeness in sensations of various kinds but he found it difficult to convince other psychologists of the validity of his measurements. By the 1940s, however, the importance of the quantitative study of sensation had been widely recognized, not only in experimental psychology but also in many practical fields such as clinical psychology and the design of environments where people live.

On moving to Paisley Technical College in 1929, Richardson found that his administrative duties and heavy teaching load, which included giving evening classes in mathematics and physics up to degree level, meant that any serious research work was restricted to his limited spare time at home, mainly weekends and holidays. He soon converted a large room in his official residence into a workshop and laboratory and embarked on some experiments to study the analogies between the way thought occurs and the behavior of a neon lamp. When the voltage applied to the lamp is set just below that required for permanent illumination, the lamp behaves in a variable manner. Richardson found no less than sixteen analogies between this behavior and mental processes. He published several papers on this subject between 1930 and 1937 and urged physicists to develop the equations relating to the theory of sparking, in the belief that they would be of great interest both to physiologists and psychologists.

Peace and Other Studies. While serving in the Friends' Ambulance Unit during World War I, Richardson had turned his thoughts to the causes of war and how to prevent them. He developed two simple differential equations showing that the rate of increase in the warlike activity of one nation related to the current warlike activity of the enemy nation. He published these at his own expense in a fifty-page booklet titled *Mathematical Psychology of War* and sent copies to his colleagues in the Friends' Ambulance Unit, most of whom were perplexed by the mathematics. He returned to this topic in 1934, appalled by the failure of the Geneva disarmament conference. To his great satisfaction he found that his equations showed remarkable success in describing the course of the arms races of 1909–1913 and 1933–1938. These results, together with a further elaboration of his ideas, were published in June 1939 in his substantial monograph *Generalized Foreign Politics*.

When World War II erupted in September 1939, Richardson decided that the time had come for him to retire from his post in Paisley so that he could have more time to devote to his war researches. He wanted to determine if any relationships of practical significance could be found from a statistical analysis of past wars. To this end he undertook the mammoth task of compiling quantitative data, such as the number of casualties, about wars which had occurred since 1820. From this he was able to analyze such features as the distribution of wars in time and the frequency of involvement of individual countries, of different languages, and of different religions. By 1945 Richardson had assembled the results of all this research, together with further material on arms races, in the form of a 500-page book, but no publisher could be found. With great difficulty he succeeded in having some of the main results published in a variety of academic journals. He also divided the book in two and published both parts at his own expense in microfilms.

Among the papers not published until after Richardson's death was one on the problem of contiguity, in which he showed that there is a linear relationship between the logarithm of the measured length of a coastline and the length of the steps used in the measurements. The slope of the line gives a good indication of the wiggliness of the coastline. This result later proved to be important in the development of ideas about fractals.

The breadth of Richardson's original thinking is demonstrated by some of his papers on other topics. For example, in 1913 he advocated a comparison of the development of intelligence of children of well-educated parents with that of children they have adopted from poor families. He also wrote three papers on voting methods in international assemblies, in the last of which he proposed a system whereby the voting strength of each country

would be determined by its international importance, calculated on the basis of several readily ascertainable ingredients. Furthermore, after the sinking of the *Titanic* by an iceberg in 1912, he filed two patents for an echo-sounding system to warn ships of their approach to a large object in a fog. All these papers have been widely cited in the relevant literature.

At the time of their publication, Richardson's papers about the causes of war had received little attention, but in the 1950s, when scientists were becoming more interested in the subject, they were brought to a wide audience in the social sciences largely by his son Stephen, especially in the United States. Edited versions of his two microfilms were published in 1960, under the titles *Arms and Insecurity* and *Statistics of Deadly Quarrels*. They were welcomed by economists, mathematicians, and physicists who had wanted to put the academic discipline of international relations onto a firmer and scientific footing. Richardson had become the founding father of peace research and within a few years more than two hundred institutes of peace research or equivalent had been established all over the world.

Throughout his life, Richardson conducted his varied researches almost entirely on his own. His main source of support and help was his wife Dorothy (daughter of the well-known educationalist William Garnett), whom he had married in 1909. Under his influence she left the Church of England and became an enthusiastic Quaker. As they were unable to have children of their own, they adopted two boys and a girl, Olaf and Stephen in 1920 and Elaine in 1922. Richardson died peacefully in his sleep on 30 September 1953 at their home in Kilmun, Argyll, to which they had moved from Paisley in 1943.

BIBLIOGRAPHY

The most important archival collections are in Cambridge University (UK) Library and the Richardson Institute, University of Lancaster. The Ashford publication (cited below) contains a comprehensive bibliography.

WORKS BY RICHARDSON

Weather Prediction by Numerical Process. Cambridge, U.K.: Cambridge University Press, 1922. Reprinted by Dover Publications, New York, 1965, and by Cambridge University Press, 2006.

Arms and Insecurity. Pittsburgh: Boxwood; Chicago: Quadrangle, 1960.

Statistics of Deadly Quarrels. Pittsburgh: Boxwood; Chicago: Quadrangle, 1960.

Collected Papers of Lewis Fry Richardson. Vol. 1, *Meteorology and Numerical Analysis,* edited by P. G. Drazin. Vol. 2, *Quantitative Psychology and Studies of Conflict,* edited by Ian Sutherland. Cambridge, U.K.: Cambridge University Press, 1993. Includes the titles mentioned in the text.

OTHER SOURCES

Ashford, Oliver Martin. *Prophet or Professor?: The Life and Work of Lewis Fry Richardson.* Bristol, U.K.: Adam Hilger, 1985. Contains a comprehensive bibliography of works by Richardson and of works about Richardson.

Gold, Ernest. "Lewis Fry Richardson: 1881–1953." *Obituary Notices of Fellows of the Royal Society* 9 (1954): 217–235.

Lynch, Peter. *The Emergence of Numerical Weather Prediction: Richardson's Dream.* Cambridge, U.K.: Cambridge University Press, 2006.

Platzman, George. "A Retrospective View of Richardson's Book on Weather Prediction." *Bulletin of the American Meteorological Society* 48 (1967): 514–550.

Rapoport, A. "Lewis F. Richardson's Mathematical Theory of War." *Journal of Conflict Resolution* 1 (1957): 249–299.

Oliver M. Ashford

RICHTER, CHARLES FRANCIS (*b.* Hamilton, Ohio, 26 April 1900; *d.* Altadena, California, 30 September 1985), *geology, seismology.*

Carl Richter was one of the key figures in developing the new field of seismology in the first half of the twentieth century, most notably through inventing the magnitude scale used to describe the size of earthquakes, and in investigating the seismicity of the world, especially of southern California.

Early Years. In 1909 Richter's family (his mother Lillian Richter, his maternal grandfather, and an elder sister) moved to Los Angeles, in southern California, where he was to spend his whole career. Richter later credited his grandfather with being one of the major influences on his upbringing. He began college at the age of sixteen; he began his undergraduate work at the University of Southern California and at Stanford University in chemistry, but changed to physics because of his clumsiness with equipment. After graduation he suffered a breakdown, but, remaining interested in science, later enrolled in the graduate physics program at the California Institute of Technology (Caltech), where he obtained a PhD in theoretical physics, on the quantum theory of electron spin, in 1928. Seeking a job that would keep him around Caltech, in 1927 he became an assistant in H. O. Wood's program to map earthquakes in southern California, which had been set up by the Carnegie Institution of Washington in 1921. In 1927 the earthquake program became a joint one with Caltech, and was housed in the new Seismological Laboratory a few miles from the campus; Richter, along with Wood and instrumentalist Hugo Benioff, became one of the small group who worked there to build

the first network of seismometers in the United States specifically designed to record local earthquakes.

Seismological Survey. A major reason for setting up this network was to detect and locate smaller earthquakes in Southern California, in the expectation that the locations of small earthquakes would be a clue to larger ones. For the resulting list of earthquakes not to be misleading, though, it had to somehow indicate if earthquakes were small or large. Earthquake size had usually been described using the intensity of shaking felt by people, an approach that would not work for earthquakes too small to be felt and those in desert areas or offshore. Seeking a method that would use the instrumental data, Richter took the technique of plotting ground motion against distance, presented by the Japanese seismologist Kiyoo Wadati in 1931, and transformed it to produce the motion at a standard distance from measurements made throughout the network; the logarithm of this standardized value gave the relative sizes of earthquakes, a number which Richter, at Wood's suggestion, called the earthquake magnitude—in part by analogy with the usage of this word in astronomy. Earthquakes were assigned magnitudes starting with the first list produced, in 1932, though the procedure was not published until 1935.

In 1930 Caltech hired Beno Gutenberg, then perhaps the world's leading seismologist, whose academic advancement in Germany had probably been hindered by his Jewish background. One important reason for Caltech to hire Gutenberg was to provide expertise in using the data being collected by the network for more purely local study. Gutenberg and Richter established a working relationship that was to extend over more than two decades. While at the start they were employed by different institutions, this ended in 1937 when the seismological program was taken over by Caltech and Richter was put on the faculty. For more than ten years after Gutenberg's arrival, they pursued the combined problem of improving the estimates of travel times for different seismic waves, and the location of earthquakes throughout the world, particularly deep shocks. They were aided in this by the new and more sensitive seismometers developed by Benioff. A result of this effort was a complete set of travel times for different waves, useful for understanding the structure of Earth.

During this time they also extended the magnitude scale from the local area of Southern California to the whole world, first for shallow earthquakes and later (in work by Gutenberg) for deep ones. This extension was put to use in creating the first global catalog of earthquakes in which the sizes and locations were determined entirely from instrumental data collected worldwide, and so was not biased by population distribution. The first version of

Charles Francis Richter. *Charles Francis Richter studying earthquake tremors in his laboratory.*
AP IMAGES.

this (*The Seismicity of the Earth*) was published in 1941; subsequent extensions appeared in different editions to 1954. These catalogs showed the concentration of large shocks into relatively narrow belts around Earth, and the even tighter concentration of deep earthquakes into a few limited regions: both results were an important element in later discussions leading to plate tectonics. Another result of this analysis, and of the listing of earthquakes in South-ern California, was the Gutenberg-Richter relation between magnitude and rate of earthquake occurrence. This relationship is that as the magnitude of earthquakes decreases by one unit, the number of earthquakes increases by a factor of about ten: small earthquakes are much more numerous than large.

Throughout his career Richter remained active in the regular work of analyzing seismic records from local and distant earthquakes, with a commitment to maintaining the quality of the record of local shocks. This remained true even through World War II, when, after a short period of assisting with weapons work, he returned to seismology, providing advice on seismic hazard and current earthquakes to the U.S. authorities. As it happened, following the war seismic activity in Southern California increased, and Richter studied several larger earthquakes that occurred between 1946 and 1952. His care for the continuity of recording also kept him in California with few interruptions, the longest being a one-year sabbatical in Japan in 1959–1960.

Public Spokesman. After Wood's early retirement in 1934, Richter had become the usual Seismological Laboratory spokesman to the press about current seismic activity, a role he enjoyed. This led him, especially in the late 1950s and the 1960s, to become a persistent advocate for improved seismic safety in California: he spoke to many public organizations, and made efforts to get civil defense authorities to treat natural disasters as part of their remit. This interest in seismic hazard also led to research on how to best describe relative risk. After his retirement in 1970 Richter founded, with other Caltech faculty, a consulting firm to advise on the seismic safety of engineering projects. His encounters with the press also made him a well-known debunker of unwarranted earthquake predictions.

During the 1950s Richter also wrote *Elementary Seismology,* which—despite its title—is a complete description of all aspects of the study of earthquakes, their causes, effects, and geography, as well as an outline of the development of seismology over time. The book reflects both Richter's wide knowledge of the subject, and his preference for keeping inferences close to observations and avoiding undue speculation; it helped to train a generation of American seismologists. Richter's primary professional affiliation was with the Seismological Society of America, of which he was president in 1959; in 1976 he received the Society's Harry Fielding Reid Medal.

While a man of considerable charm and some humor, Richter was often awkward socially: he could be blunt, thin-skinned, and somewhat mercurial. He was devoted to his science, even installing a seismic recorder in his living room; but he also privately maintained wider interests, notably in botany, and wrote fiction and poetry, largely unpublished. He enjoyed the outdoors both alone and with his wife Lillian, whom he married in 1928, and who predeceased him in 1972; they had no children.

Though the magnitude scale was invented to solve a purely local problem, its use expanded far beyond that. As a description of earthquake size it began to be used in newspaper reports in the late 1940s, and has become well embedded in popular consciousness, along with the term

Richter scale. In seismology it also became a standard, or rather multiple standards, as different definitions were developed for different kinds of earthquakes; attempting to make these consistent with Richter's original definition, determining the interrelations between different scales, and finding the reasons for the differences, have all been ongoing research activities.

BIBLIOGRAPHY

WORKS BY RICHTER

"An Instrumental Earthquake Magnitude Scale." *Bulletin of the Seismological Society of America* 25 (1935): 1–32.

With Beno Gutenberg. "Richter Frequency of Earthquakes in California." *Bulletin of the Seismological Society of America* 34 (1944): 185–188.

———. *Seismicity of the Earth and Associated Phenomena,* 2nd edition. Princeton, NJ: Princeton University Press, 1954.

Elementary Seismology. San Francisco: W.H. Freeman, 1958.

OTHER SOURCES

Allen, Clarence. "Charles F. Richter: A Personal Tribute." *Bulletin of the Seismological Society of America* 77 (1987): 2232–2233.

Geschwind, Carl-Henry. *California Earthquakes: Science, Risk, and the Politics of Hazard Mitigation.* Baltimore, MD: Johns Hopkins University Press, 2001.

Goodstein, Judith R. "Waves in the Earth: Seismology Comes to Southern California." *Historical Studies in the Physical and Biological Sciences* 14 (1984): 201–230.

Hough, Susan Elizabeth. *Richter's Scale: Measure of an Earthquake, Measure of a Man.* Princeton, NJ: Princeton University Press, 2007.

Duncan Carr Agnew

RICHTER, CURT P.

(*b.* Denver, Colorado, 20 February 1894; *d.* Baltimore, Maryland, 22 December 1988), *psychobiology, biological clocks, homeostasis.*

Richter's research career began at Harvard University, where he was an undergraduate assistant to Robert M. Yerkes before graduating in 1917. Yerkes, a comparative psychologist, advised him to go to graduate school at the Johns Hopkins University and study under John B. Watson, who was becoming known for his strict behaviorist views.

Early Life and Career. Richter's parents were newly arrived from the Saxony region of Germany when Richter was born. He grew up Denver, Colorado, where they ran a machine factory. Richter's early experience in his parents' factory was an important formative experience for him. As

Richter described in an autobiographical essay, "It's a Long Way to Tipperary," (1985), he learned about tools and machines during the long hours that he spent in the factory. He described the context as "play" and himself as being fascinated with all kinds of gadgets; he began to experiment (e.g., with magnets) at a young age. As Richter recalled his childhood, "I spent a lot of time working on locks and clocks—taking them apart and putting them back together again" (Richter, 1985, p. 359).

Meanwhile, Richter received his formal education in the public schools of Denver, graduating from high school in 1912. Then, following what he remembered from childhood as his father's wish, he enrolled at an engineering school in Germany. For the greater part of the period from 1912 to 1915, he studied at the Technische Hochschulen in Dresden. Reflecting on the experience at the engineering school, Richter said, "looking back on my work at the Hochschule, I have come to realize how much I learned that has helped me in the running of my Laboratory of Psychobiological Biology" (Richter, 1985, p. 365). Next attending Harvard University in Cambridge, Massachusetts, he excelled in no particular subject until he took a course in genetics, followed by one in the philosophy of nature with E. B. Holt, a student of William James. The latter course then "stimulated me to sign up for a short experimental course on insect behavior, given by Professor Robert Yerkes" (p. 369). His research career began at Harvard, where in his senior year he was a student-assistant to Yerkes. Before Richter graduated in 1917, Yerkes, a comparative psychologist, advised him to go to graduate school at Johns Hopkins University and study under John B. Watson, who was becoming known for his strict behaviorist views. In his autobiography, reflecting on his time as an undergraduate at Harvard, Richter recalled that

> Yerkes recommended that I read a book, *Animal Behavior,* by John B. Watson. After having read only snatches here and there, I became convinced that I should try to work with him.... I must point out here that at that time, and for a long time later, I had no idea about what Watson meant by "behaviorism." For me "behaviorism" simply meant "behavioral." (Richter, 1985, p. 369)

After serving in the army in 1917–1918, Richter did as Yerkes had recommended, arriving at Johns Hopkins's Phipps Clinic in Baltimore, Maryland, to begin graduate studies with Watson. Richter recalled Watson uttering these words: "I want you to know that I am only interested in getting a good piece of research. You do not have to take any course or attend any lectures. You are strictly on your own" (Richter, 1985, p. 371). After Watson's departure from Johns Hopkins, Adolf Meyer, who has

been called the father of psychobiology, became the main supporter of Curt Richter's research. Meyer also understood psychobiology as a discipline "that takes life as it is without splitting it into something mental and something physical" and that considers the "organismal function and behavior" (Meyer, 1935, p. 94). Richter's dissertation, accepted in 1921, was titled "The Behavior of the Rat: A Study of General and Specific Activities." An attempt to study spontaneous, self-generated behaviors (see below), the dissertation planted the seed for a career in research.

Richter's subsequent empirical research falls into four overlapping categories: (1) the regulation of spontaneous behaviors; (2) homeostatic and nutrition selection; (3) the effects of domestication; and (4) neurological discovery and invention. These were informed by a strongly biological orientation, a preference for hands-on experiments, and a passion for measurement.

Biological Clocks. During the 1920s Richter began his research career by studying cyclic behavior and what many called "spontaneous behaviors." He understood biological clocks as fundamental to the organization of behavior and physiological adaptation. But a full development of the role of clocks in regulating behavior and physiology, particularly in mammals, would await decades. Richter set about demonstrating the role of clocks and their operation under pathological conditions.

For Richter, cyclic behaviors were internally generated and innate. Two issues stood out for him: regularity and uniformity. Clocks keep time and provide order and coherence, which is required by the outer world to which we are trying to adapt. With the advent of Darwinism, fitness and long-term survival became linked by biologists to cyclical events. In Richter's view, the clocks themselves were fixed. They, of course, reflected the events of nature, the daily and seasonal rhythms.

In his experiments, Richter noted alternating patterns of activity and inactivity. He noted that the patterns of active behavior varied with different animals and with age. In young rats, the rate of alternating between activity and inactivity is much greater than in older rats. Richter noted that this pattern of behavioral alternation was present in the newborn rat and presumably was an innate, hard-wired behavioral pattern that was expressed in a diverse range of animals.

During the 1920s, Richter was also beginning to determine that internal oscillators played an important role in the organization of diverse forms of anticipatory behavioral adaptation. One key feature that facilitates activity-inactivity in diverse animals is the light-dark cycle. Circadian clocks orient and synchronize an animal's adaptive behavioral and physiological responses to periodic changes in the environment. The circadian clock is a fundamental timing device present in a wide variety of species.

Richter discovered that an ablation "somewhere in the hypothalamus" would disrupt circadian rhythmicity. Subsequently, it would become known that Richter indeed was close to localizing the region that is essential for circadian rhythmicity. He had noted that damage within the hypothalamus disrupted circadian rhythmicity. Later it would be discovered that the essential region is the suprachiasmatic region (SCN) of the hypothalamus.

During the 1960s, Richter also suggested two types of sleep regulatory mechanisms, one linked to homeostatic requirements for sleep and the other to circadian rhythmic activity. This distinction has credibility among chronobiologists. He suggested that sleep activity was tied to the reticular formation, perhaps beholden to homeostatic needs.

Richter surmised that there were multiple clocks. A study of individual animals showed some variation in the clocks under normal conditions that was further exaggerated under pathological conditions. Richter documented a long list of clinical syndromes that were periodic and linked to bodily pathology. Some of the examples that he noted were acciosis, periodic bleeding, Hodgkin's disease, Parkinsonian pariesis, peptic ulcer, manic-depressive illness, sleep disturbances, and catatonic schizophrenia.

Behavioral Homeostasis. Building on the work of Claude Bernard and Walter Cannon, Richter added an important element: behavioral regulation of the internal milieu was a fundamental scientific question for Curt Richter. Richter was not alone in his interest, but he certainly was a major force in providing interesting and informative contexts in which to consider the biological adaptation required for bodily health.

Richter's research in this area during the 1930s–1950s centered around the question of adaptive versus nonadaptive nutritional choice behaviors. Richter selected an important way into the study of ingestive behavior: the behavioral regulation of and taste psychophysics of sodium. Richter's insight was to add sources of sodium to the diet and then study the ingestion of sodium by the "appetite method," as he liked to call it. Richter noted a range of ingestive patterns that was heavily biased toward sodium solutes when animals were hungry for sodium, something many other investigators also observed after him.

When Richter and his colleagues turned to the study of calcium homeostasis during the 1930s–1940s, he approached the problem in the same manner as he did that of sodium. First, he demonstrated a calcium appetite, and then he suggested that the behavior was organized by innate behavioral mechanisms, an innate capacity to detect calcium salts triggered by decreased levels of calcium.

Richter and his colleagues demonstrated that a number of substances (e.g., sodium chloride and calcium lactate) are further ingested during pregnancy and lactation, when there is further need for them. They also noted that water intake was particularly elevated during lactation.

Nutrient search and identification are basic features of biological hardware. Richter's studies of laboratory rats in the 1940s and 1950s revealed several instances of specialized systems for water, sodium, calcium, and perhaps phosphate ingestion and some aspects of energy balance. Richter understood the regulation of the internal milieu in the context of whole-body regulatory activity.

Nutrient search and identification are basic features of biological hardware. Richter believed that all ingestive behaviors, except for learned aversions for foods (see below), reflect innate appetites. He asserted that rats (his animal of study for the specific hungers), in response to bodily needs, have special appetites for a wide range of substances, including sodium, carbohydrates, protein, calcium, and phosphorus in addition to diverse vitamins. Richter remained a nativist regarding all the specific hungers, but he was mistaken.

How many innate-instinctive specific appetites are there? Certainly sodium and perhaps calcium. Water seems a likely candidate, and protein remains a possibility. Avoidance of diets that render the animal ill, coupled with a tendency to be cautious of new nutritional options, seem to be operative in food choice, particularly for the omnivorous rat. Ecological adaptations are an essential part of discerning the range of strategies available for an animal to solve its nutritional requirements. Richter's work on nutritional selection was done largely for the rat, an omnivore with several noted specific appetites, along with several more general behavioral strategies, that serve it in the regulation of the internal milieu.

Adaptation and Domestication. Richter's roving experimental eye brought him to a phenomenon that would later have a profound effect on American psychology and the understanding of learning, something called "taste aversion learning." Richter, whose insight was rooted in biological considerations, simply understood that the normal reluctance to ingest unfamiliar foods made the wild rat difficult to trap and that gustation was a primary sensory modality and part of the alimentary canal that included gastrointestinal functions. Taste aversion learning would play an important role in the coming battles in psychology with regard to the biological basis of learning and would alter the conceptual and experimental landscape of psychology.

Richter, the self-dubbed "reluctant rat-catcher," caught many rats in the wilds of Baltimore over a ten-year period. He enjoyed this avenue of research. It consisted of scanning a rough environment for a wild animal and testing modern substances that might be linked to a genetic taste function—one that might underlie the self-selection of diets and the avoidance of possibly harmful substances—in physiological and gustatory studies. This special behavioral adaptation serves the animal well in tagging food sources and, most importantly, in linking specific food ingestion with visceral distress in animals in which taste and olfaction are essentially linked to food regulation.

Richter was close to suggesting something like a form of taste aversion with his emphasis on "bait shyness," food avoidance, and visceral distress from poisoning. For example, as indicated above, in one set of experiments he determined the different concentrations of the toxin that would result in food avoidance. Noticing a relationship between the concentrations of the toxin and food avoidance, he reported in 1946 that, when exposed to various concentrations of the toxins, rats stopped eating the food after it made them ill.

Richter investigated the effects domestication on behavior and physiology and made important contributions to this area of inquiry (e.g., size diverse end organ systems in wild and domesticated animals). The effects of domestication on a variety of behavioral and end organ systems were fairly well-known at the time of Richter's investigations in the 1940s and 1950s. But he added a new and systematic dimension to his research by the range of end organ systems that he investigated. For example, Richter and his colleagues demonstrated changes in adrenal, thyroid, and pituitary glands; gonads; and regions of the brain.

Richter always began his investigations with an adaptationist conception of evolution on the effects of domestication and the use and disuse of morphological and behavioral expression. But he also suggested ways in which devolution and the loss of adaptation occurs.

Neurological Study. Richter noted several facts that implied individual differences and cyclic daily patterns in the grasp reflex. There were two themes in Richter's research. Underlying his research on the grasp reflex was the importance of clinging on to the mother during the neonatal period. As Richter noted, the grasp reflex was an important aid for keeping infants afloat. He also suggested that the grasp reflex appeared to be less prominent in the human than in the monkey. The grasp reflex method he used with the monkey was different from that used with the human neonate, however, and so his comparison was misleading. Nonetheless, Richter built on the common evolutionary theme that the grasping reflex was stronger in the monkey than in the human. He also noted variations in the grasping response from day to day.

In 1919 "A Graphic Application of the Principle of the Equilateral Triangle … ," the very first paper of which Richter was an author, reported on a formal technique suggesting that an equilateral triangle could be used to predict the electrical patterns of the heart. Having developed a small portable dermometer (i.e., galvanometer), Richter and his colleagues subsequently measured skin resistance and, with some continued prodding and instruction, he extended its use both to show the simplicity of this technique and to determine peripheral damage.

Further studies by Richter and his colleagues helped to ascertain the mechanisms of sweating and skin resistance. The legacy of the laboratory Richter inherited, namely Watson's, was the use of the grasping reflex. Richter would use this reflex to investigate the neurology and the pharmacology that made this reflex possible. Unlike Watson, he remained rooted in a neurological tradition in which evolution permeated the conception of the brain.

Research Style. Richter found ingenious ways to study phenomena. His approach was hands-on, dirty, and devoid of pristine logical analysis. He was a scientific scavenger-entrepreneur. The experiment dominated his conception of what it meant to be a psychobiologist. He embodied what can be termed a laboratory state of mind.

A laboratory state of mind is one in which measurement predominates. In interviews with Anne Roe in 1952, for example, Richter tellingly said when asked about his thinking process: "I would say that I think really very little in terms of words. I think largely in terms of moving my hands. I find that I am always about 10 steps behind in my verbalizations." A little later he is quoted as saying: "I have a passion, I suppose, for measuring things" (Roe, interview notes, 1952, Archives, American Philosophical Society, Philadelphia).

Richter considered himself lucky to have worked mostly in an age before "big science," which would come to undermine what he romanticized as "free science." In the 1950s, the era of big grant writing was at hand. Now, Richter lamented, to get a grant one had to know in advance what one was going to find out. Exploration and play, he feared, would be undermined and scientific creativity would be compromised.

Richter prided himself on his surgical abilities. Eliot Vallenstein, a professor of psychology at the University of Michigan, recalled a time when Richter was applying for a grant. He pleaded with the review committee not to let his age (he was then in his late seventies) affect its judgment, that he needed the money for his assistant who had been with him for many years. Moreover, he said, "my eyes are clear, my hands are steady, and I have performed

784 operations this year" (E. Vallenstein, personal communication, July 2002; Schulkin, 2005, p. 128).

Although he was never part of its mainstream, within the field of psychology Richter is typically associated with the concept of drive. One noted historian of psychology in America describes Richter as "a persistent and ingenious experimenter" (Hilgard, 1987).

The biological basis of behavior permeated Richter's work. His lack of interest in the theoretical and intellectual debates of his day is exemplified in the stance he took during an important conference that he attended in 1956, where he remained apart from the debate, instead keeping his focus on his data and experimental results.

Fearless and Free. Richter was a fearless artisan-scientist. An artisan laboratory sensibility ran through his veins, and it is seen in the simplicity of his techniques, the beauty of his laboratory, the devotion to his scientific inventions. His contributions to science in the new field of psychobiology had tremendous range. The one "compleat psychobiologist" would be allowed a free rein. Consequently, he was able to eschew committees and the responsibilities that went with them.

Drawing on material he had presented to a committee at the National Research Council, Richter published in *Science* "Free Research versus Design Research" (1953), which drew heavily on his philosophical side. As the article illustrates, Richter was not of the era of experimental design. In the article he rightly recognized the importance of statistical design but asserted that it "should not substitute for ideas" (p. 92). Most of Richter's contemporaries, whatever their theoretical orientation, did not absorb statistical methods. An important contribution from behavioral psychology would be the logic of experimental design. Experimental design would come to figure in all aspects of the behavioral sciences, along with the use of statistical analysis.

When Richter published the *Science* article, he was only a few years from emeritus status. He would continue doing research for another twenty-five years, but he was already "old school." Richter was fortunate to have received multisource funding. For example, he obtained support from the Rockefeller Foundation (1923–1940, via Adolf Meyer), the National Institutes of Health (1952–1965), the National Science Foundation (1956–1977), the National Research Council (1937–1945), the National Council on Alcoholism (1959–1960), and the Commonwealth Fund (1964–1977).

Richter sought to escape the endless debates taking place within academic psychology. He remained a steadfast experimentalist, while perhaps exaggerating innate behavioral solutions. When this failed, there was always the practical side of knowledge—the clinic, the patient. In these contexts, the engineer could come forward, extending and simplifying devices to measure physiological events that could be used to discern disease and dysfunction. Even at the very end of his life, he published papers on growth hormone ("Growth Hormone 3-6hr Pulsatile Secretion and Feeding Time Have Similar Periods in Rats," 1980) and cortisol secretion in rats, guinea pigs, and monkeys ("Possible Origin of a 90-Min. Cortisol Secretion Cycle in Rats, Guinea Pigs, and Monkeys," 1983) and remained productive, active, and engaged in his scientific pursuits.

One does not get the sense that Richter was changing his mind about core ideas. What would have made him think that perhaps a range of appetitive behaviors required diverse forms of learning? A set of core ideas or metaphors underlies the behavior of scientists, including Richter. His core ideas centered around behavioral adaptation, regulation of the internal milieu, cyclic behavior, and instinctive behavior. Richter set out to demonstrate behavioral competence, physiological signals that orchestrate adaptation to diverse perturbations to the internal milieu.

Richter very much enjoyed both the prestige of and participation in academic societies (e.g., the American Philosophical Society and the National Academy of Sciences). He maintained an active sense of inquiry for over sixty years, all at the Department of Psychiatry at Johns Hopkins University.

Richter was married twice and had three children. He died in Baltimore, Maryland, on 22 December 1988.

BIBLIOGRAPHY

WORKS BY RICHTER

With E. P. Carter and C. H. Greene. "A Graphic Application of the Principle of the Equilateral Triangle for Determining the Direction of the Electrical Axis of the Heart in the Human Electrocardiogram." *Johns Hopkins Hospital Bulletin* 30 (1919): 162–167.

"A Behavioristic Study of the Activity of the Rat." *Comparative Psychology Monographs* 1 (1922): 1–55.

"Nervous Control of the Electrical Resistance of the Skin." *Johns Hopkins Hospital Bulletin* 45 (1929): 56–74.

"The Grasping Reflex in the New-Born Monkey." *Archives of Neurology and Psychiatry* 26 (1931): 784–790.

With Arthur S. Paterson. "On the Pharmacology of the Grasp Reflex." *Brain* 55 (1932): 391–396.

"Total Self Regulatory Functions in Animals and Human Beings." *Harvey Lectures Series* 38 (1942–1943): 63–103.

"Incidence of Rat Bites and Rat Bite Fever in Baltimore." *Journal of the American Medical Association* 128 (1945): 324–326.

"Biological Factors Involved in Poisoning Rats with Alphanaphthyl Thiourea (ANTU)." *Proceedings of the Society of Experimental Biology and Medicine* 63 (1946): 364–372.

"Instructions for Using the Cutaneous Resistance Recorder, or 'Dermometer,' on Peripheral Nerve Injuries, Sympathectomies, and Paravertebral Blocks." *Journal of Neurosurgery* 3 (1946): 181–191.

"Physiology and Endocrinology of the Toxic Thioureas." *Recent Progress in Hormone Research* 11 (1948): 255–276.

"Domestication of the Norway Rat and Its Implication for the Study of Genetics in Man." *American Journal of Human Genetics* 4 (1952): 273–285.

"Free Research versus Design Research." *Science* 118 (1953): 91–93.

"Salt Appetite of Mammals: Its Dependence on Instinct and Metabolism." In *L'instinct dans le comportement des animaux et de l'homme*, edited by P. P. Grasse. Paris: Masson et Cie, 1956.

"Experiences of a Reluctant Rat-Catcher: The Common Norway Rat—Friend or Enemy?" *Proceedings of the American Philosophical Society* 112 (1968): 403–415.

Biological Clocks in Medicine and Psychiatry. 2nd ed. Springfield, IL: C.C. Thomas, 1979.

"Growth Hormone 3-6hr Pulsatile Secretion and Feeding Time Have Similar Periods in Rats." *American Journal of Physiology* 239 (1980): E1–2.

"Possible Origin of a 90-Min. Cortisol Secretion Cycle in Rats, Guinea Pigs, and Monkeys." *American Journal of Physiology* 244 (1983): R514–515.

"It's a Long Way to Tipperary, the Land of My Genes." In *Leaders in the Study of Animal Behavior: Autobiographical Perspectives*, edited by D. A. Dewsbury. Lewisburg, PA: Bucknell University Press, 1985.

OTHER SOURCES

Blass, Elliott M., ed. *The Psychobiology of Curt Richter.* Baltimore, MD: York Press, 1976.

Garcia, J., W. G. Hankins, and K. W. Rusiniak. "Behavioral Regulation of the Milieu Interne in Man and Rat." *Science* 185 (1974): 824–831.

Hilgard, Ernest R. *Psychology in America: A Historical Survey.* San Diego, CA: Harcourt Brace Jovanovich, 1987.

Meyer, A. "Scope and Teaching of Psychobiology." *Journal of the American Medical Association* 10 (1935): 93–98.

Roe, Anne. *The Making of a Scientist.* New York: Dodd, Mead, 1953.

Rozin, Paul. "The Compleat Psychobiologist." In *The Psychobiology of Curt Richter*, edited by Elliott M. Blass. Baltimore, MD: York Press, 1976.

Schulkin, Jay. *Curt Richter: A Life in the Laboratory.* Baltimore, MD: Johns Hopkins University Press, 2005.

Stellar, Eliot. "Curt P. Richter." *American Philosophical Society Biographical Memoirs* (1989): 293–297.

Jay Schulkin

RICHTER, RUDOLF (*b.* Glatz, Silesia, Prussia, 7 November 1881; *d.* Frankfurt, Germany, 5 January 1957), *geology, paleontology, ichnology, sedimentology, taxonomy.*

Richter was considered one of the most influential geologists of the early twentieth century. He founded the Senckenberg Vorschungstelle für Meeresgeologie und Meerespaläontologie (Senckenberg Research Station for Marine Geology and Paleontology) at Wilhelmshaven, Germany, which was subsequently known as Senckenberg am Meer (Senckenberg by the Sea). It was the first institution founded with the specific aim of actively applying the actualistic concepts of Charles Lyell, following the principle "the present is the key to the past." Richter can be considered a founder of actuogeology. He laid important groundwork for modern approaches to sedimentology, stratigraphy, and ichnology.

Early Life. Rudolf Richter was born on 7 November 1881 at Glatz in Silesia. His father was a well-respected medical doctor. Richter studied at the universities of Munich and Marburg and changed his law studies for geology in 1904 after a field excursion with the famous geologist Emanuel Kayser to the Devonian strata in the Eifel area of Germany. Richter completed his doctorate under the supervision of Kayser at Marburg in 1909; his doctoral dissertation was published under the title "Beitraege zur Kenntnis devonischer Trilobiten aus dem Rheinischen Schiefergebirge" (Contributions to the knowledge of Devonian trilobites from the Rheinische Schiefergebirge). Richter's influence reached far beyond the boundaries of Germany.

After leaving Marburg, Richter earned his living as a high school teacher (Lehrer an Einer Schule für Schüler Zwischen) in Frankfurt at the Liebig Senior High School (Liebig Oberscule) while carrying out his scientific work in his spare time. In 1908 he joined the Senckenbergische Naturforschende Gesellschaft (Senckenberg Naturalist Society) and in 1919 he launched the journal *Senckenbergiana* to mark the centenary of the society. Richter was editor of that journal until his death in 1957. He also edited its popular magazine *Natur und Museum* (Nature and the museum), changing the name of the journal in 1931 to *Natur und Volk* (Nature and the people) to reflect his desire to make science accessible to the people. This was a theme that Richter followed throughout his tenure at the Senckenberg Naturalist Society. He was a popularizer of natural history and felt that it was the responsibility of scientists to educate the populace in any way they could, including museum displays, field trips, and popular publications. In 1920 Richter was appointed privatdozent (assistant professor) in geology and paleontology at the Johann-Wolfgang-Goethe University in Frankfurt; in

1925 he became extraordinary professor, and in 1934 ordinary professor and director of the Geological and Paleontological Institute at the Johann-Wolfgang-Goethe University, a position he held until his retirement in 1949. In 1932 Richter took control of the Senckenberg Naturalist Society and in 1933 was named its Leiter (director). In the latter year he also assumed the duties of directorship of the Natur-Museum at Frankfurt.

In 1913 Richter married Emma Hüther, and they enjoyed a remarkable collaboration. She was a skilled artist and was invaluable in their joint work on trilobites and on a series of ichnological papers. During their married life, spanning more than forty years, they wrote seventy coauthored publications. Their papers on animal-sediment relationships were fundamental in establishing basic principles on how organisms affect the substrate. This ichnological work also established the zoological affinities of many trace fossils and became the cornerstone for further work in actuopaleontology and actuoichnology. Emma was not only a wife and trusted colleague, she also assumed Rudolf's duties when he was indisposed. During World War I, Rudolf served as an officer on the front and Emma assumed his duties at the museum. Likewise, she assumed his duties when he was interned in Romania in 1945–1946, just after the World War II. Emma died a few months before Rudolf on 15 November 1956.

Senckenberg am Meer. In 1929, with the support of the Senckenberg Society and the German navy, Richter established the Senckenberg Forschungstelle für Meeresgeologie und Meerespaläontologie (Senckenberg Research Station for Marine Geology and Paleontology) at Wilhelmshaven, which was subsequently known as Senckenberg am Meer (Senckenberg by the Sea). The institute is housed in a building named after him, the Rudolf Richter Haus. Richter's interest in the modern marine environment was apparent as early as 1920, when he gave an inaugural lecture at Frankfurt University titled "Die Erscheinungen des Wattenmeers in ihrer Bedeutung für die Geologie" (The manifestations of the Wadden Sea and their significance for geology). The station was founded with the specific aim of studying animal-sediment relationships in the intertidal environment in the Wadden Sea. It was the first institution founded with the specific aim of actively applying the actualistic concepts of Charles Lyell, following the principle "the present is the key to the past." The Wadden Sea has been the enormously successful hunting grounds of well-known Senckenbergian researchers such as Walther Häntzschel, Wilhelm Schäfer, and Hans-Erich Reineck. It was instrumental in establishing Germany as the home of ichnological research and shallow-water, marine sedimentology. The Senckenberg laboratory has been used as the model for other facilities around the world, including the Sapelo Island Marine

Institute in Georgia in the United States. In fact, these two institutes had very close ties in the 1970s and jointly researched the sedimentology and animal-sediment relationships of modern shoreface and estuarine environments. In the early twenty-first century, the station houses the Marine Science Division of the Senckenberg Institute and the legacy of excellence left by Richter, Häntzschel, Schäfer, and Reineck continues.

Actualistic Paleontology. Richter wrote two key papers in 1928, one on the new field station (Senckenberg am Meer) and a second on the new discipline of *Aktuopaläontologie,* the science of the formation of paleontological objects in the present that are potentially able to become fossil. The new field of study was to consist of three parts: research on traces, "death and embedding," and biofacies. Richter envisaged this work as the "science that brings stones to life." Although this new science was not immediately embraced outside of Germany, it became the cornerstone for direct applications to the petroleum exploration boom during the post–World War II economic boom. In the United States, oil and gas exploration was accompanied by an academic interest in modern-day environments and depositional processes. Major petroleum companies spent millions of dollars to establish research programs studying modern, shallow-water, depositional systems. These studies then served as modern analogues for the interpretation of petroleum-bearing reservoirs throughout the world.

World War II. World War II was a time of great upheaval for both Richter and the Senckenberg laboratory. During the war, Richter took great pains in moving both the museum collections and the extensive Senckenberg library, consisting of some two million volumes, out of the institute to safer areas. In 1943 Richter packed the scientific collections onto two hundred trucks and evacuated them to remote storage depots. This saved most of the holdings from the destruction of the war. Richter also tried to keep the institute safe and the scientists from being conscripted by proposing that research at Senckenberg was essential for work in petroleum and geology. It was concerning petroleum activities that Richter traveled to Romania in 1945. Upon his arrival in Bucharest, he was arrested and interned at the German Embassy because he was a German official. Richter endured immense privation, illness, and malnutrition in the internment camp in Romania and was not freed until 1946. He resumed his duties as a professor in 1947 and continued to supervise graduate students and carry out basic research. Richter was instrumental in resurrecting the Paläontologische Gesellschaft (Paleontology Society).

Publications and Honors. Richter's productivity was prodigious; he published approximately 291 titles, encompassing a wide variety of subjects, including ichnology, trilobite research, Devonian paleogeography, biostratigraphy, micropaleontology, taxonomy and systematics, paleoecology, and constructive morphology. His work was instrumental in establishing the Senckenberg laboratory as the center for actuogeologic and actuopaleontologic studies. Richter was an advocate and interpreter of the international rules of taxonomy and in 1930 was voted onto the International Commission for Zoological Nomenclature. For the next twenty years he worked tirelessly in the verification of types, the development of archival techniques, and the production of collection catalogs.

Richter received many honors. He became an external or corresponding member of the National Research Council of the United States (1929), the Institut royal des Sciences naturelles de Belgique (1930), the Geological Society of London (1950), the Academica delle Scienze in Bologna (1953), and the Instituto de Investigaciones Geológicas "Lucas Mallada" in Madrid (1953). Richter was served as president of the International Union of Paleontology from 1933 to 1937. He was named an honorary member of the Palaeontological Society of America (1926), the International Congress of Geologists in Moscow (1937), and the Société belge de Géologie, de Paléontologie, et d'Hydrologie (1938). He received medals of honor from the Senckenberg Naturalist Society (1951) and also received the Gold Medal of the Paläontologische Gesellschaft (1951) and the Hans Stille Medal given by the Deutsche Geologische Gesellschaft (1951). To celebrate his seventieth birthday, former students and friends put together a special Festschrift volume, published by the Senckenberg Naturalist Society. Rudolf Richter passed away at Frankfurt on 5 January 1957, a few weeks after his wife Emma. At the end he was totally paralyzed but still managed to work with the help of his students and colleagues.

BIBLIOGRAPHY

A complete bibliography of Richter's published works can be found in Herta Schmidt, "Rudolf Richter (1881–1957) in seinen Worten," Aufsätze Reden Senckenbergische Naturforschende Gesellschaft 32 (1982): 1–95. Archives reside at the Senckenberg Institute.

WORKS BY RICHTER

"Beiträge zur Kenntnis devonischer Trilobiten. I. *Dechenella* und einige verwandte Formen." *Senckenbergische Naturforschende Gesellschaft Abhandlungen* 31 (1912): 239–340.

With Emma Richter. "Die Lichadiden des Eifler Devons." *Neues Jahrbuch für Mineralogie, Geologie, und Paläontologie* (1917): 5–72.

"Von Bau und Leben der Trilobiten. I. Das Schwimmen." *Senckenbergiana* 1 (1919): 213–238.

"*Scolithus, Sabellarifex*, und Geflechtquartzite." *Senckenbergiana* 3 (1921): 49–52.

"Flachseebeobachtungen zur Paläontologie und Geologie. VII–XI." *Senckenbergiana* 6 (1924): 119–165.

"Aktuopaläontologie un Paläobiologie, eine Abgrenzung." *Senckenbergiana* 10 (1928): 285–292.

With Emma Richter. *Trilobitae neodevonici.* Fossilium Catalogus, I, Animalia, Pars 37. Berlin: Junk, 1928.

"Tierwelt und Umwelt im Hunsrückschiefer; zur Entstehung eines schwarzen Schlammsteins." *Senckenbergiana* 13 (1931): 299–342.

"Marken und Spuren im Hunsrückschiefer. I. Gefliess-Marken." *Senckenbergiana* 17 (1935): 244–263.

With Emma Richter. "Unterlagen zum Fossilium Catalogus, Trilobitae. VII. Kulm-Trilobiten von Aprath und Herborn." *Senckenbergiana* 19 (1937): 108–115.

"Der nomenklatorische Typus." *Zeitschrift Deutsche Geologische Gesellschaft* 95 (1942): 362–371.

"Taxiologie und Paläotaxiologie zwischen Psychologie und Physiologie." *Senckenbergiana lethaea* 36 (1955): 401–407.

OTHER SOURCES

Flemming, Burghard W. "75 Jahre Senckenberg am Meer: Aktualismus als Forschungsprinzip." *Natur und Museum* 134 (2004): 1–20.

Kegel, W. "Nachruf für Rudolf Richter–Emma Richter." *Zeitschrift Deutsche Geologische Gesellschaft* 110 (1957): 637–642.

Lewis, Ronald D. "Rudolf Richter and Today's Actualistic Paleontology." *Geological Society of America Abstracts with Programs* 35, no. 6 (2003): 206.

Pemberton, S. George. "Rudolf Richter and the Senckenberg Laboratory." In *Encyclopedia of Sediments and Sedimentary Rocks,* edited by G. V. Middleton. Dordrecht, Netherlands: Kluwer Academic Publishers, 2003.

Schmidt, Herta. "Rudolf Richter (1881–1957) in seinen Worten." *Aufsätze Reden Senckenbergische Naturforschende Gesellschaft* 32 (1982): 1–95.

Simon, Wilhelm. "Rudolf und Emma Richter." *Paläontologische Zeitschrift* 31 (1957): 111–115.

Stubblefield, C. J. "Rudolf Richter." *Proceedings of the Geological Society of London* 1554 (1957): 137–138.

Ziegler, Willi. "Rudolf Richter 1881–1957." *Jahre Senckenbergische Naturforschende Gesellschaft, Jubiläumsband* 1. Frankfurt am Main: Kramer, 1992.

S. George Pemberton

RIEMANN, GEORG FRIEDRICH BERNHARD (*b.* Breselenz, near Dannenberg, Germany, 17 September 1826; *d.* Selasca, Italy, 20 July 1866). For the original article on Riemann see *DSB,* vol. 11.

Whereas Georg Friedrich Riemann's scientific results themselves have almost completely been analyzed within the original article in the *DSB,* this postscript emphasizes the mathematical tradition in which he stood, his reception by his contemporaries and in the time shortly after his death, and the shaping influence that he had on mathematics as a scientific discipline.

Academic Teachers. Among mathematicians that influenced Riemann, perhaps the most important was Carl Friedrich Gauss. In fact, the only references in Riemann's doctoral dissertation are to two papers of Gauss; Riemann had studied the writings of Gauss in the university libraries of Göttingen and Berlin. However, Riemann did not write his thesis under what in the early twenty-first century would be called supervision: He apparently informed Gauss about the topic of the dissertation only after he had already finished it. Still, this was the usual procedure at German universities at that time.

Moritz Abraham Stern, Riemann's second academic teacher at Göttingen, is often termed a second-rate mathematician, sometimes even without noting that one is comparing him to Gauss. In any case, Riemann received a profound knowledge of the state of the art of analysis as taught in Germany at that time from Stern's lectures on calculus.

More important was the influence of Peter Gustav Lejeune Dirichlet. Shortly after Riemann arrived at Berlin, Dirichlet recognized his talents and guided his studies of the literature. In particular, he introduced Riemann to the modern techniques in analysis, which had been developed in France in the beginning of the nineteenth century by mathematicians such as Augustin-Louis Cauchy, Siméon-Denis Poisson, and others, and of which many contemporary German mathematicians were unaware. This support with respect to the literature continued even when Riemann was preparing his Habilitation thesis on Fourier series at Göttingen, when Dirichlet sent him the necessary material for the introductory historical section.

One can even speculate that Ferdinand Gotthold Max Eisenstein had a decisive influence on Riemann's mathematics, because Eisenstein found the functional equation for the *L*-series modulo 4 while Riemann was in Berlin, but Riemann was not interested in closer personal contact with Eisenstein. And he had other opportunities for the inspiration for the functional equation of the zeta function and its proof in his 1859 paper on the distribution of primes.

Riemann and the Dirichlet Principle. Riemann's use of the Dirichlet principle was decisive for the advancement of mathematics because of the results that he obtained by

its ingenious, sometimes even bold, use in his doctoral dissertation (1851) and in his paper on Abelian functions (1857). Furthermore, it is one of the landmarks for the change from an algorithmically to a conceptually oriented view of mathematics: The function one is in search of is not given by an explicit formula but implicitly as the solution of a variational problem, even if one can deduce some of the properties that it will necessarily have, for example, that it is harmonic. Resorting to a pure existence statement was clearly ahead of the way of thinking among most mathematicians in the middle of the nineteenth century, and many of Riemann's contemporaries felt uncomfortable with his method.

Sometimes the story of the criticism of the Dirichlet principle is depicted as a battle between the German mathematical centers at Berlin and Göttingen on the highly prestigious theory of Abelian functions in the following way: With his 1857 paper, Riemann took the lead ahead of the Berlin representative Karl Weierstrass. Weierstrass struck back after Riemann's death by showing that variational principles need not have a solution, so that Riemann's proofs were incomplete. But, finally, the Göttingen school under the impetus of Felix Klein vindicated Riemann's visions.

Nevertheless, the situation was a bit more complicated: To be sure, Weierstrass read a note to the Berlin Academy in 1870 that contained a counterexample to a naive use of variational principles. In the terminology of fairy tales, however, Weierstrass was not the stepmother who poisoned Snow White but rather the child who openly said what (almost) everybody knew about the emperor's clothes. In fact, rumors against the liberal use of variational principles had been around as early as the late 1850s and they did not come only from Weierstrass or even Berlin mathematicians—as one learns, for example, from the notes of Felice Casorati from his conversations with Leopold Kronecker in 1864 and from a letter of the Russian mathematician Georg August Thieme to Richard Dedekind on a visit to Riemann at Göttingen in the summer of 1862.

Additionally, because Weierstrass's note was published only in the second volume of his *Mathematische Werke* in 1895, the first *published* counterexample to the Dirichlet principle was in an 1871 article by one of Riemann's own students, Friedrich Emil Prym. Furthermore, Prym directly attacked the specific Dirichlet principle as it had been presented in Dirichlet's lectures, whereas Weierstrass commented on variational principles in general. Also David Hilbert fully acknowledged the justification of Weierstrass's criticism (which was all the easier for him because in 1901 he had contributed to the proof of the Dirichlet principle as used by Riemann). Even Riemann himself knew about the gaps in his reasoning but argued

Mathematician Georg Friedrich Riemann.
© BETTMANN/CORBIS.

in a discussion with Weierstrass in 1859 that he had made use of Dirichlet's principle only as an easy resort that was just at hand. Even if that tool was faulty, his existence theorems still were true.

In fact, not the least influence that Riemann had on mathematics was that he set out a research agenda that was pursued by other mathematicians, most prominently from the Göttingen school: It took more than half a century before Hermann Weyl would be able to transfer Riemann's vision of a "Fläche" (which came to be known as "Riemann surface") into a detailed definition in the language of set theory. At about the same time Richard Courant in his doctoral dissertation also completely vindicated Riemann's use of the Dirichlet principle. But the Berlin school around Weierstrass was also active in this research beginning with Weierstrass himself, who studied Riemann's writings and tried to translate the results into his more algorithmically oriented way of thinking even if he had problems with the Riemann's way of reasoning. Furthermore, Weierstrass's favorite disciple, Hermann Amandus Schwarz, proved explicit formulas that solve the mapping problem of Riemann's doctoral dissertation for the case of polygons and also attacked the general case.

The Distribution of Riemann's Ideas. Riemann exerted his influence mainly through written sources: his own publications; books by his students, themselves prominent, such as Carl Neumann's *Vorlesungen über Riemann's Theorie der Abel'schen Integrale;* and also by handwritten copies of the notes taken during his lectures. These were distributed throughout Europe, in Germany, of course, but to a great extent also in Italy and even in Russia with the Italian mathematicians being extremely receptive to Riemann's ideas. This does not mean that his mathematical standing was not well regarded elsewhere: He was a member of the Gesellschaft der Wissenschaften in Göttingen, of the Preussische Akademie der Wissenschaften (Berlin), of the Bayerische Akademie der Wissenschaften (Munich), of the Académie des Sciences (Paris), and of the Royal Society (London).

Attendance at his lectures personally would have influenced only few mathematicians, the maximal number of thirteen students at a lecture being documented in the Göttingen archives (whereas a few years later Ernst Eduard Kummer (1810–1893) and Weierstrass would have an auditorium of about two hundred students at Berlin).

One of the results that was attributed by hearsay to Riemann is the example $\sum_{n=1}^{\infty} (\sin n^2 x)/n^2$ of a continuous but nondifferentiable function. Neither this example nor any concrete statement about it can be found in Riemann's writings. Although the function is not differentiable at the points of a dense set, there are some points at which it is differentiable, and so it is not nowhere-differentiable. A complete analysis of its differentiability was only given around 1970. What the sources do reveal, however, is that both Kronecker and Weierstrass were interested in the function, that Weierstrass claimed to have a proof that this function is not differentiable at the points of a dense set, and that Riemann himself had studied the boundary behavior of theta functions to such an extent that only an interchange of limit processes was necessary to obtain this result. (In fact, from his lecture notes one learns that Riemann did not care too much about such technical questions.)

Development of Mathematics. Riemann's results and mathematical ideas have had far-reaching consequences, even on the present view of the universe: In his Habilitation lecture on the hypotheses on which geometry is founded Riemann had defined the (differential) geometric structure of space by means of a positive definite differential form, which locally induces a Euclidean structure. Already Hermann Minkowski had studied the generalization to a no longer positive definite but still nondegenerate differential form. So for his theory of general relativity Albert Einstein only had to generalize Riemann's concept from a locally Euclidean to a locally Minkowskian structure. (In fact, Einstein had studied Riemann's Habilitation lecture as early as in his student days.)

If one considers mathematics as a scientific discipline, Riemann's influence on the way in which mathematical objects are conceived in the early 2000s is perhaps even more important. Before his doctoral thesis a function of a complex variable was given as an analytic term that could be used to calculate the values of this function. (Even after the thesis Riemann's older but longer living contemporary Weierstrass followed this approach in the form of power series both successfully and influentially.) Riemann, by contrast, would rather look for a characterization of such a function by its properties, in this case, the Cauchy-Riemann differential equations. As another example, he studied the hypergeometric function not mainly by means of the series by which Gauss had defined it but by means of the differential equation that it fulfills, which would spare him long and tedious calculations. Still more impressive is the advantage that Riemann's approach had in the theory of elliptic and Abelian functions when one compares his results with the pages of long lists of formulas that are typical for the writings of Niels Henrik Abel and, especially, Carl Gustav Jacob Jacobi.

Minkowski attributed to Dirichlet a second mathematical principle besides the one mentioned above, namely to minimize blind calculation and to maximize thoughts led by visions. His close friend Hilbert even brought forth the principle that one should lead proofs by thoughts and not by calculations, in direct connection to Riemann. In this respect, the latter was a turning point in the history of mathematics, one of the lesser examples being the fact that he was the first mathematician who not only defined the notion of an integral but also explicitly defined what it means that a function is integrable. (It is worth noting that Dedekind, Riemann's fellow student and colleague at Göttingen, also deeply influenced by Dirichlet, approached algebra in much the same way as Riemann approached analysis and geometry. And from Dedekind a line of influence runs via Emmy Noether, Emil Artin, and Bartel Leendert van der Waerden to the structuralistic Bourbaki school of the second half of the twentieth century.)

One should stress, however, that Riemann himself was by no means averse to or even afraid of calculations: One learns from the notes of his introductory lectures on complex analysis that he would not hesitate to use besides the nonconstructive Dirichlet principle the more algorithmic and "hands-on" means of power series expansions and even the idea of analytic continuation. Furthermore, his statement that it is probable ("wahrscheinlich") that all zeros of the zeta function have real part 1/2 was based on long explicit calculations of zeros.

This famous Riemann hypothesis was still open in 2007, even though in 2000 the Clay Foundation offered a million-dollar prize for its solution. So Riemann not only opened new, far-leading doors in science, in particular mathematics, but his work continued to show the way to new frontiers.

SUPPLEMENTARY BIBLIOGRAPHY

The 1990 edition of Riemann's collected works includes an overview of the secondary literature; see the bibliographies in Gesammelte mathematische Werke, *pp. 869–895 and 896–910.*

WORKS BY RIEMANN

Narasimhan, Raghavan, ed. *Gesammelte mathematische Werke, wissenschaftilicher Nachlass und Nachträge: Collected Papers.* Berlin: Springer; Leipzig: Teubner, 1990. Third edition of Riemann's collected works, originally edited by Heinrich Weber and Richard Dedekind.

Neuenschwander, Erwin. *Riemann's Einführung in die Funktionentheorie: Eine quellenkritische Edition seiner Vorlesungen mit einer Bibliographie zur Wirkungsgeschichte der Riemannschen Funktionentheorie.* Göttingen: Vandenhoeck & Ruprecht, 1996. This book contains Riemann's notes for his introductory lectures on the theory of functions of a complex variable and a bibliography of the secondary literature on Riemann.

Elstrodt, Jürgen, and Peter Ullrich. "A Real Sheet of Complex Riemannian Function Theory: A Recently Discovered Sketch by Riemann's Own Hand." *Historia Mathematica* 26 (1999): 268–288. Autographic writing of Riemann in which he gives a tour de force through his theory of complex functions, edited with commentary.

OTHER SOURCES

Laugwitz, Detlef. *Bernhard Riemann, 1826–1866: Turning Points in the Conception of Mathematics.* Translated by Abe Shenitzer, with the editorial assistance of the author, Hardy Grant, and Sarah Shenitzer. Basel: Birkhäuser, 1999. First published in 1996. At present the best and most extensive presentation of the life and work of Riemann.

Narasimhan, Raghavan. "Editor's Preface (Together with a Mathematical Commentary on Some of Riemann's Work)." In Riemann, *Gesammelte mathematische Werke,* pp. 1–20. Berlin: Springer; Leipzig: Teubner, 1990.

Neuenschwander, Erwin. "Der Nachlass von Casorati (1835–1890) in Pavia." *Archive for History of Exact Sciences* 19 (1978): 1–89.

———. "Über die Wechselwirkungen zwischen der französischen Schule, Riemann und Weierstrass. Eine Übersicht mit zwei Quellenstudien." *Archive for History of Exact Sciences* 24 (1981): 221–255.

Ullrich, Peter. "Anmerkungen zum 'Riemannschen Beispiel' $\sum_{n=1}^{\infty} (\sin n^2 x)/n^2$ einer stetigen, nicht differenzierbaren Funktion." *Results in Mathematics, Resultate der Mathematik* 31 (1997): 245–265.

Weil, André. "On Eisenstein's Copy of the *Disquisitiones*." In *Algebraic Number Theory in Honor of K. Iwasawa*, edited by J. Coates et al. Advanced Studies in Pure Mathematics 17. Boston: Academic; Tokyo: Kinokuniya, 1989.

Peter Ullrich

RIKER, WILLIAM HARRISON (*b.* Des Moines, Iowa, 22 September 1920; *d.* Rochester, New York, 26 June 1993), *political science, rational choice, positive political theory, federalism.*

Riker did nothing less than revolutionize the study of political science. He introduced the study of game theory and decision theory into the study of politics, moving it away from purely normative and ad hoc descriptions. He coined the term *positive political theory* to describe the effort to develop individual-level, descriptive generalizations about political behavior, often based on axiomatic propositions and always on the supposition that people behave rationally. The term, and the approach, are now accepted parts of political science. A brilliant teacher and a clever administrator, he oversaw the development of the first graduate program in political science devoted to high-level training in quantitative methods, including game theory, decision theory, and econometrics, at the University of Rochester.

Riker's father Ben, a book seller, and his mother Alice, moved his family to Battle Creek and Detroit, Michigan, before settling in Indianapolis, where Riker graduated from high school in 1938. Four years later he graduated from DePauw University and, after a brief hiatus, went to graduate school at Harvard University, where he received a PhD in government 1948.

Research. Riker began his teaching career at Lawrence College (now University) in Wisconsin in 1948. He taught courses in American politics, but he was also called upon to teach other subjects, including an extraordinary course on political philosophy. His early work was traditional. He authored a textbook on American politics that was well received but hardly pathbreaking. He also wrote a book on the National Guard, presaging another topic—federalism—that he studied throughout his career.

In the mid-1950s his thinking and writing changed dramatically. He read Duncan Black's *Theory of Committees and Elections* and was impressed with the insights that the so-called median voter theorem might yield for understanding political behavior. He devoured John von Neumann and Oskar Morgenstern's *The Theory of Games and Economic Behavior*, also thinking that it could provide insights into political behavior. He began thinking of applications of a logical approach to the study of politics. In 1958 he published a paper on the "paradox of voting" (a "cyclical" result, in which voters who have individually transitive preferences over three alternatives, *a, b,* and *c,* might nonetheless vote by majority rule for alternative *a* over alternative *b,* for *b* over *c,* and yet for *c* over *a*) in the U.S. Congress. His first major work was *The Theory of Political Coalitions* (1962). In it he developed what he called the size principle, the idea that political entrepreneurs tend to build support coalitions that are only as large as needed to win (typically a bare majority). To attract a larger coalition is "wasteful" in that the leadership has to make policy or other concessions when they already have enough support to win.

Another signal work was a paper published in 1968 on voter turnout. He and his then-student, Peter Ordeshook, inquired how it was that rational individuals would go to the polls, knowing that the likelihood of their making a difference (being the decisive vote between two candidates) was infinitesimally small. Their formulation—adding consideration of another factor, generally called "citizen duty"—did not solve the problem, but it led to numerous subsequent papers and is still used today to frame the question. A few years later, and also with Ordeshook, he published a text that explained the positive approach to the study of politics and amply demonstrated the kinds of individual and collective behavior to which it could be applied.

Another of Riker's lifelong interests was the role of institutions in politics. This was manifested early on in his work on federalism and in his fascination with "Duverger's law" (the idea that plurality elections in single-member districts promulgate a political system with only two parties). Institutions were at the heart of much of his later work, especially in *Liberalism against Populism,* which dealt with the difficult subject of how to justify democracy in light of the numerous problems and paradoxes associated with the making of social choices. In his later works, he was intrigued with agenda setting broadly conceived, coining the term *heresthetics* to refer to the art of manipulating issue agendas for political advantage and applying it to a study of the campaign to ratify the U.S. Constitution.

Teaching: Building a Graduate Program. On the strength of his new approach, which he called positive political theory, Riker was hired by the University of Rochester to begin a graduate program to complement its newly developed strength in economics. His department-building skills were on par with his teaching skills. He sought out faculty who were sympathetic with his view of political science—sometimes practitioners themselves, but always willing to work with students who would push the bounds of the rational-choice perspective as far as they could take it. Students trained at Rochester were initially outliers, and for a time it was difficult for those using a positive approach to get their work published in the discipline's top journals. Gradually, however, the appeal of this new approach, along with the high quality training his students received, combined to make Rochester PhDs much sought after. In time, the approach he initiated constituted an accepted subfield in political science. More significantly, the game-theoretic and other tools he incorporated into his work, and the assumption of rational actors, infused the study of comparative politics and international relations as well as American politics.

Riker was a charismatic teacher. At times he was a showman, letting his voice rise to a thundering pitch and his face redden as he reached the conclusion of an argument, and at other times speaking so softly one had to strain to hear him. But his showmanship was never a mask for shoddy thinking, illogical arguments, or a dearth of evidence. His knowledge of American political history was legendary. It was this knowledge that led him always to try to apply the abstract theories that he developed to the real world of politics. His undergraduate course on Strategy in Politics was valued for the sometimes surprising but always fruitful perspectives he brought to bear on both historical and contemporary politics. His graduate courses were valued for that same creativity and insight but also for the infusion of a rational-choice approach into all manner of political situations.

Honors. Riker was honored in 1974 by being among the first political scientists to be inducted into the National Academy of Sciences. In 1983 he was elected president of the American Political Science Association. He was awarded honorary degrees by Lawrence University, DePauw University, State University of New York at Stony Brook, and, in 1977, by Uppsala University in Sweden. He died in 1993, leaving behind a vibrant graduate program and a legion of grateful current and former graduate students who knew they had studied with a giant in their chosen profession.

BIBLIOGRAPHY

WORKS BY RIKER

Soldiers of the States: The Role of the National Guard in American Democracy. Washington, DC: Public Affairs Press, 1957.

"The Paradox of Voting and Congressional Rules for Voting on Amendments." *American Political Science Review* 52 (1958): 349–366.

The Theory of Political Coalitions. New Haven, CT: Yale University Press, 1962.

Federalism: Origin, Operation, Significance. Boston: Little Brown, 1964.

With Peter C. Ordeshook. "A Theory of the Calculus of Voting." *American Political Science Review* 62 (1968): 25–42.

———. *An Introduction to Positive Political Theory.* Englewood Cliffs, NJ: Prentice-Hall, 1973.

Liberalism against Populism: A Confrontation between the Theory of Democracy and the Theory of Social Choice. San Francisco: Freeman, 1982.

"The Heresthetics of Constitution-Making: The Presidency in 1787, with Comments on Determinism and Rational Choice." *American Political Science Review* 78 (1984): 1–16.

OTHER SOURCES

Amadae, Sonja M., and Bruce Bueno De Mesquita. "The Rochester School: The Origins of Positive Political Theory." *Annual Review of Political Science* 2 (1999): 269–295.

Black, Duncan. *The Theory of Committees and Elections.* Cambridge, U.K.: Cambridge University Press, 1958.

Bueno De Mesquita, Bruce, and Kenneth Shepsle. "William Harrison Riker, September 22, 1920–June 26, 1993." In *Biographical Memoirs,* vol. 79. Washington, DC: National Academy of Sciences, 2001.

Richard G. Niemi

RILEY, GORDON ARTHUR (*b.* Webb City, Missouri, 11 June 1911; *d.* Halifax, Nova Scotia, Canada, 7 October 1985), *quantitative biological oceanography, ecological modeling.*

Riley introduced quantitative hypothesis testing and modeling to the study of biological oceanography, first using experimental methods and statistics to determine the causes of biological processes in the sea, an approach fostered by his teacher G. Evelyn Hutchinson. In the 1940s, despite the skepticism of the ecological establishment about mathematical techniques, he began the use of differential equations in modeling biological oceanographic processes. Later he made original contributions to regional oceanography, transport and mixing, and particles in seawater, all in a biological context. Late in his career, as an administrator of science, he built a school of oceanography whose graduates carried his influence throughout North America and beyond. He was elected a Fellow of the Royal Society of Canada in 1973, and in 1976 was awarded the American Association for the Advancement of Science's Rosenstiel Award in Marine Sciences for his innovations in biological oceanography.

From Embryology to Limnology. After an undergraduate degree in biology at Drury College (now Drury University), Gordon Riley did research on ascidian (sea squirt) embryology for an MS degree at Washington University, St. Louis, in 1934. He was then accepted at Yale to work toward a PhD with the eminent embryologist Ross G. Harrison. After a few unexciting months with Harrison, Riley was fascinated to discover the world of limnology (study of freshwater lakes), presented in one of his classes by the young Yale faculty member G. Evelyn Hutchinson. Hutchinson soon accepted Riley as his first graduate student and assigned him the problem of investigating the copper cycle of lakes, on the premise that nothing was known of the elements in lakes and their biological effects except for the major nutrients although all might be significant in controlling aquatic production. During his conversion to limnology, Riley also discovered statistics, as taught to him at Yale by the mathematical biologist Oscar W. Richards, and incorporated into his thinking a mathematical, deductive approach to science espoused by Hutchinson and based on the ideas he derived from Harold Jeffreys's book *Scientific Inference* (1931). Stimulated by Richards, and with the encouragement of Hutchinson, Riley applied statistics to his limnological work, also using the newly established technique of light and dark bottle incubations of phytoplankton cells (green unicells at the base of aquatic food webs), culminating in his PhD dissertation in 1937. During postdoctoral research soon after, he began to apply the technique of multiple regression analysis to relate ecological factors to their presumed biological effects.

Making the Study of the Sea Quantitative. During a cruise in the Gulf of Mexico in 1937, Riley first applied multiple regression analysis to marine ecosystems, showing that phytoplankton standing crop was a quantitative function of nutrient levels. Soon thereafter, appointed to the staff of Yale's Bingham Oceanographic Laboratory, he began to study the control of production in Long Island Sound, and, in the summer of 1938 in the Dry Tortugas, Florida, finding in the tropical seas at the Tortugas an unexpectedly high level of phytoplankton production. As he continued to refine and expand these studies during the next few years, he established the light and dark bottle technique as a way of isolating natural systems in a way that allowed manipulation of the interacting factors (such as nutrient supply, light, temperature, and grazing by animals) that affected the abundance and production of the plants, followed by causal analysis using multiple correlations.

Riley's quantitative analyses of the factors influencing marine production extended to the western North Atlantic Ocean, first from his base at Yale, and then as a staff member of the Woods Hole Oceanographic Institution (WHOI) from 1942 to 1948. His attention soon turned too to the fisheries-rich Georges Bank, off Cape Cod, which was becoming a focus of interest at Woods Hole. Until they were ended by the United States's entry into World War II late in 1941, six cruises of the WHOI

ketch *Atlantis* enabled Riley to compare the richness of Georges Bank with the more depauperate western North Atlantic and Gulf of Mexico, focusing especially on the onset of the spring bloom on the bank. Using statistical analyses, he showed that the bloom could be predicted knowing only temperature and nutrient levels. Water motion also played an important role, mixing the cells too deep in the water during the winter to allow net production; only when vertical mixing was limited by surface warming in the spring could the bloom begin. By the middle of 1941, Riley believed that he had developed a sound, quantitative basis for the prediction of seasonally varying production in a wide variety of marine ecosystems ranging from coastal bays to the open oceans.

A Change of Direction to Mathematical Modeling. By the time his active work at sea was curtailed by the onset of war in 1941, Riley believed that he was hot on the trail of a quantitative, ecologically based, predictive theory of plankton growth in the sea. However, after the war years (when he was involved in studies of underwater sound, taught oceanographic techniques to naval officers, studied marine fouling, and was assigned to do follow-up studies of the Bikini Atoll atomic tests in 1946), Riley returned to studies of marine production, but with an enhanced appreciation of the shortcomings of his early work. The immediate stimulus to a new approach was his interest in the effect of grazing animals on the spring phytoplankton bloom, a subject carefully examined by H. W. Harvey and his colleagues at the Plymouth Laboratory in England in a publication in 1935 and characterized mathematically by Richard Fleming of the Scripps Institution of Oceanography in a simple prey–predator equation. This proved to be the stimulus for a wholly new formulation of plankton dynamics, necessary because as the range and number of Riley's multiple regression analyses increased, the results became harder and harder to interpret and were inconsistent from time to time and place to place. Some kind of new approach was necessary. He was ready to turn his methods on their head, for as he said, "the only way to avoid them [the limitations of the multiple correlation method] is by the opposite approach—that of developing the mathematical relationships on theoretical grounds and then testing them statistically by applying them to observed cases of growth in the natural environment" (Riley, 1946, p. 55). This was to be the core of his modeling technique in biological oceanography for nearly twenty years.

The basis of Riley's new approach was to develop predictive equations expressing population changes as a function of a number of simple environmental variables such as, for phytoplankton, light intensity, water transparency, nutrients, the depth of the mixed layer, surface temperature, and the abundance of grazers. Analogous treatments were developed for the herbivorous zooplankton, and eventually, in his last application of the technique in 1963, for fish, the top members of aquatic food chains. The use of differential equations to express the theoretical relationships involved in marine production systems was based on his belief that only a few biological and physical factors interacted in nature. It was greatly stimulated by the work of biological oceanographers at the Plymouth Laboratory in England, especially Hildebrand W. Harvey, who provided precise information on chemical factors, light and grazing in the English Channel. Added to this was the physical oceanographic approach that Riley learned in Woods Hole, and, to a large extent, taught himself.

After his first modeling attempts in 1946 using differential equations, Riley introduced two new modeling studies of considerable complexity and great originality. The first, published in 1949 in collaboration with Henry Stommel and Dean Bumpus, predicted the distribution of populations of phytoplankton in the western North Atlantic Ocean as a result of changes in the physical environment. The second, in 1951, was a study of biological activity in deep water of the Atlantic, predicting the horizontal and vertical distribution of the nonconservative variables (i.e., variables affected by biological activity) oxygen, phosphate, and nitrate as a result of the interaction of biological and physical processes. These models set a new standard for biological oceanographic analysis and firmly lodged physical oceanographic techniques in biological oceanography. Riley's approach, using physical oceanographic techniques with chemical and biological data to solve difficult biological problems, provided the form followed by many later analyses, but was even more important in providing an example of how biological oceanography should be pursued as a quantitative science in which physical analysis was essential.

Yale and Long Island Sound.

Of equal influence was the work that Riley and his graduate students began in Long Island Sound beginning in 1948, when he returned to the Bingham Oceanographic Laboratory from WHOI. The sound became the home sea of Yale oceanography, a testing area for questions dating from the late 1930s about the factors governing levels of production from place to place, the efficiency of material transfers from one group of organisms to another, the relative importance of biological and physical variables, and how to account for variations in fish production. Using quantitative dissection of the biological and physical processes at work, Riley and his students established by the end of the 1950s that Long Island Sound was twice as productive as the English Channel, although less efficient ecologically, and showed a different partition of biological activity than the channel. They noted too that there was a large amount of non-

living particulate matter in the sound, an observation that led into a totally new area of research.

Particulate Organic Matter and a Change of Direction.

In the early 1960s Riley and some of his coworkers began to study the distribution and formation of particulate organic matter, showing that it was widespread in the oceans, was of ecological significance, and could be formed by bubbling seawater. This research came with him from Yale to Dalhousie University in 1965, when, as a result of an administrative decision at Yale to abandon plans for a department of oceanography, Riley left to direct the Institute of Oceanography (founded in 1959) at Dalhousie and to direct its transition into a graduate department of oceanography. This move, along with his program on Long Island Sound at Yale during the 1950s, resulted in a school of oceanographers, some of them initially Yale undergraduates or graduate students, later an active group of graduate students at Dalhousie University. Many of these got their degrees just when oceanography began to expand in the late 1950s and 1960s, and by the 1970s Riley's influence had made the Dalhousie graduate program one of the best on the continent, providing faculty members and scientists to the University of Rhode Island, WHOI, Oregon State University, Dalhousie University, the Bedford Institute of Oceanography, and many other institutions. By the time of his retirement in 1976 he considered himself an administrator, but the effect of his scientific work and graduate teaching was still profound.

Riley's approach to biological oceanography, using physical oceanographic techniques to solve biological problems, provided a new practical and conceptual framework for the field. It was widely influential in providing a new esprit de corps as well as a new modus operandi for biological oceanographers. His approach to scientific investigation recognized that the simpler patterns found in nature could be analyzed or modeled mathematically. The more complex ones required detailed observational or experimental work before mathematical modeling became possible. Modeling was never Riley's only route to understanding: the pattern of nature required a sophistication of approach equal to the varieties of pattern in nature. Working largely alone, and often unappreciated (he was never elected a member of the U.S. National Academy of Sciences), Riley's influence came to pervade biological oceanography when the uniqueness of his work was appreciated and as the influence of his students spread throughout the marine sciences.

BIBLIOGRAPHY

WORKS BY RILEY

"Correlations in Aquatic Ecology." *Journal of Marine Research* 2 (1939): 56–73. Use of the correlation and multiple correlations techniques.

"Factors Controlling Phytoplankton Populations on Georges Bank." *Journal of Marine Research* 6 (1946): 54–73. Introduction of differential equations to modeling in biological oceanography.

With Dean Bumpus and Henry Stommel. "Quantitative Ecology of the Plankton of the Western North Atlantic." *Bulletin of the Bingham Oceanographic Collection* 12, no. 3 (1949): 1–169.

"Oxygen, Phosphate, and Nitrate in the Atlantic Ocean." *Bulletin of the Bingham Oceanographic Collection* 13, no. 1 (1951): 1–126. Innovative physical analysis of the oxygen use and nutrient regeneration in deep ocean waters.

"Review of the Oceanography of Long Island Sound." *Papers in Marine Biology and Oceanography,* supplement to *Deep-Sea Research* 3 (1955): 224–238. Summary of the work of Riley and his students in the home sea of the Yale oceanographers.

"Organic Aggregates in Seawater and the Dynamics of Their Formation and Utilization." *Limnology and Oceanography* 8 (1963): 372–381.

"Theory of Food Chain Relations in the Ocean." In *The Sea,* vol. 2, *The Composition of Sea-Water: Comparative and Descriptive Oceanography,* edited by Maurice Neville Hill. New York: Interscience, 1963. Extension of Riley's modeling technique to the whole food chain.

"Reminiscences of an Oceanographer." Papers. Halifax, NS, Department of Oceanography, Dalhousie University, 1984. The best single source of biographical information and information on the background of Riley's work.

OTHER SOURCES

Hutchinson, G. Evelyn. "Reminiscences and Notes on Some Otherwise Undiscussed Papers." In *Selected Works of Gordon A. Riley,* edited by J. S. Wroblewski. Halifax, NS: Dalhousie University, 1982. Includes information on Riley's student days at Yale.

Jeffreys, Harold. *Scientific Inference.* Cambridge, U.K.: Cambridge University Press, 1931.

Mills, Eric L. *Biological Oceanography: An Early History, 1870–1960.* Ithaca, NY: Cornell University Press, 1989. See especially chapters 10 and 11 for a detailed account of Riley's career and work.

Wroblewski, J. S., ed. *Collected Works of Gordon A. Riley.* Halifax, NS: Dalhousie University, 1982. Reprints of many publications, along with interpretive essays by colleagues.

Eric L. Mills

RINGWOOD, ALFRED EDWARD (TED) (*b.* Melbourne, Victoria, Australia, 19 April 1930; *d.* Canberra, Australian Capital Territory, Australia, 12 November 1993), *geochemistry, mineralogy, geophysics, planetology.*

Ringwood was one of the first scientists to investigate the importance of high-pressure phase transformations for the mineralogy of Earth's mantle. He used experimental high-pressure, high-temperature techniques, and theory from crystal chemical models to make major advances in the study of Earth's interior. He integrated his experimental results with geophysical observations of the deep Earth, and with geochemical information as well, to present influential models of the nature and evolution of Earth and also of the Moon and the solar system. On the return of lunar samples by the Apollo missions in the 1970s, Ringwood conducted experimental studies constraining the petrogenesis of lunar mare and lunar highland basalts, and he was the leading figure in the synthesis of the lunar sampling program into models of origin of the Earth-Moon system. He also applied his theoretical and experimental knowledge of mineral and melt equilibrium in devising suitable mineral hosts for high-level nuclear waste (the SYNROC [synthetic rock] concept).

Ringwood's scientific career was almost entirely in Australia, and he used his physical separation from the scientific centers of Europe and the United States to foster independence and innovation, selecting short visits and attendance at key conferences to influence, while not being constrained by, the scientific mainstream. A very early recruit to the nascent earth sciences in 1960 at the Australian National University (ANU) in Canberra under Professor John Jaeger, he was a key figure in the remarkably rapid rise of the ANU in the 1970s to be one of the world's leading research institutions in geophysics and geochemistry. Ringwood was committed to the ideal of the ANU as a distinctively Australian center of international leadership in research. He was director of the Research School of Earth Sciences at ANU from 1978 to 1983 and acknowledged the role played by the unique support of the ANU given by successive Australian governments from the 1950s to the late 1980s. This support permitted long-term investment in new initiatives of which Ringwood was a powerful supporter, including high-pressure research, the design and construction of the Sensitive High Resolution Ion Microprobe (SHRIMP), the establishment of geophysical fluid dynamics at ANU, and the development of mineral physics, seismology, and geodynamics.

Early Development. Ted Ringwood was born in Kew, an inner Melbourne suburb. He was an only child in a family that strongly identified with Australia, including the tribal and suburban rivalries of Melbourne centered around the distinctive Australian Rules Football and the Victorian Football League. His father, also Alfred, enlisted as an eighteen-year-old in World War I, and his experiences of gas attack, trench feet, and other suffering in the trenches in France impacted heavily on his physical health in and on his outlook in later life. During the 1920s Ted's father held a variety of unskilled jobs and was essentially unemployed from the beginning of the Great Depression. In later years he received a war service pension. Ted's mother, Ena, and the wider family provided stability through difficult financial circumstances and placed a strong emphasis on the value of education.

Ringwood excelled academically through suburban primary school and won a scholarship to attend as a boarder the Geelong Grammar School, Victoria's most prestigious private school. On completion of his secondary education, he won a Trinity College Resident Scholarship at University of Melbourne and began undergraduate studies in 1947. His academic interests were focused on geology and metallurgy and were balanced by a competitive participation in Australian Football in the Melbourne university team. On completion of his BSc degree with award of honors, he proceeded to the two-year MSc degree, based on a field mapping and igneous petrology project on Devonian Snowy River Volcanics in the sparsely populated and physically difficult terrain of eastern Victoria. He completed his MSc with honors in 1953 and immediately embarked on a PhD project at the University of Melbourne.

Influenced by reading the work of Victor M. Goldschmidt on crystal chemical relationships, Ringwood chose a research topic that applied Goldschmidt's ideas to understanding the behavior of elements during magmatic crystallization and that applied this crystal chemical approach from the rock scale to the scale of the structure of Earth. He was particularly interested in the use of crystal chemical concepts to predict the mineralogical constitution of the deep Earth and made a major contribution by using the magnesium germanate system as an analogue for the magnesium silicate system that dominates Earth's interior.

The contextual setting for this work was the advances in seismology revealing internal deep Earth structure—an upper mantle (30–400 km [18–250 mi] below Earth's surface), transition zone (400–900 km [250–560 mi] below the surface), and lower mantle (900–2,900 km [560–1,800 mi] below the surface)—and debate on the cause of the rapid increase in seismic velocities through the transition zone. In "The Olivine-Spinel Transition in the Earth's Mantle" in *Nature* (1956), he attributed the transition zone to polymorphic changes, in particular from monoclinic olivine to cubic spinel structure for $(Mg,Fe)_2 SiO_4$ composition. This work was the beginning of a lifetime of experimental and theoretical study of pressure-induced phase transformations in silicate and oxide minerals involving the major components of Earth's interior (SiO_2, MgO, FeO, CaO, Al_2O_3, Na_2O, NiO). A particular feature of the work was the use of crystal chemical rules based on ionic radii and ionic charge in a systematic way to guide experimental studies of solid solutions in

phases stable at low pressures, but at higher pressure capable of accepting greater proportions of magnesium silicate end-members. The use of germanate phases as low-pressure analogues of high-pressure silicate phases was followed by recognition and experimental study of potential roles for (Mg,Si) substitution for (2Al) in garnet structure and of perovskite ($CaTiO_3$) structure for $CaSiO_3$, ilmenite ($[MgFe]TiO_3$) structure for pyroxenes, and rutile (TiO_2) structure for SiO_2.

High-Pressure Studies. Ringwood worked with a variety of solid media high-pressure apparatuses. From the mid-1980s he collaborated with several Japanese visitors and was very influential among Japanese scientists as he and they led rapid advances in ultra-high-pressure research. Recognition of his pioneering work included the naming of the dense spinel-form of $(Mg,Fe)_2 SiO_4$ composition "ringwoodite" and of the dense garnet-form of the $(Mg,Fe) SiO_3$ composition "majorite" (from Alan Major, Ringwood's technical officer and colleague from 1963 to 1993).

In addition to the experimental studies and their application, Ringwood maintained a strong interest in the interplay between geodynamics, seismology, petrology, and petrophysics so that he applied the experimental constants to models of Earth's behavior. A relatively late convert (in 1968–1969) from "fixist" to continental drift–plate tectonics, Ringwood addressed the interplay of chemical inhomogeneity and phase transformations in the penetration or arrest of subducted lithosphere at transition zone pressures. His 1975 book *Composition and Petrology of the Earth's Mantle* synthesized the experimental work on phase transformations and its geodynamic implications and, equally important, brought together another main theme of Ringwood's research, namely, the chemical composition and evolution of Earth.

Ringwood debated the issue of whole-mantle versus layered-mantle convection and argued that descending slabs (the "engine" of plate tectonics) would be deflected or aggregated within the transition zone due to the interplay between compositional differences and consequent differences in phase assemblages and densities of the downgoing slabs (oceanic crust and lithosphere) and surrounding peridotite mantle. He presented a substantial case that no major compositional difference exists between upper and lower mantle compositions and that the peridotite composition inferred for the upper mantle was consistent with the geophysical constraints on lower mantle properties.

In parallel with his work at very high pressure, he collaborated at ANU with David H. Green, Trevor H. Green, Ian A. Nicholls, and others on investigations using the piston cylinder apparatus (to pressure 4 GPa), complex natural rock compositions, and the newly developed electron microprobe to experimentally investigate petrological processes inferred for the uppermost mantle. Ringwood coined the name *pyrolite* for a model mantle composition of inferred peridotitic character, that is, one dominated by pyroxene and olivine. With his collaborators he experimentally determined the phase relations and the melting behavior of this model composition up to pressures of 4 GPa, that is, equivalent to mantle depths of approximately 130 kilometers (80 miles). Parallel studies of appropriately selected natural volcanic rocks (basalts, andesites) led to interpretations of depths of origin, degrees of melting, and melt-residue relationship for the different types of basaltic magmas occurring at mid-ocean ridges and hot spots, or sites of mantle upwelling. The reactions from low-pressure basaltic or gabbroic mineralogy (rich in plagioclase) to high-pressure eclogite mineralogy (rich in garnet) were studied experimentally, and a major role was ascribed to this transformation in providing a significant driving force for subduction of oceanic crust and lithosphere. For a period of thirty years from the 1960s, Ringwood was thus a leading contributor to the rapidly developing knowledge of Earth's upper mantle, including its melting behavior and melt products, or volcanism, and high-pressure metamorphism. His work on Earth's mantle and crust-mantle relationships was summarized in *Composition and Petrology of the Earth's Mantle.*

Solar System and Lunar Studies. Following completion of his PhD research, Ringwood spent fifteen months as a postdoctoral fellow with Francis Birch at Harvard University. This visit, his longest sojourn outside Australia, introduced Ringwood to experimental high-pressure work, but he also used the opportunity to begin a study of meteorites and to view meteorites in the context of a growing body of knowledge of solar elemental abundances and of the variations in density, moment of inertia, and so on among the planets. In the late 1950s and early 1960s he addressed the chondritic Earth model and discussed the nature and origin of the solar system. He argued that several meteorite classes had formed by auto-reduction processes from parental type I carbonaceous chondrite and emphasized the role of melting and differentiation in precursor bodies in relating suites of meteorite samples. He stressed the importance of differing oxidation states as explanations for different densities among Venus, Earth, and Mars.

In 1960 Ringwood advocated a modified version of Charles Darwin's fission hypothesis, in which Earth's Moon is drawn off from Earth's mantle after core separation (in contrast to models of lunar capture, for example). The lunar samples returned in 1969 provided a field of fertile study in themselves, but their chemical compositions also provided a basis for comparisons with Earth materials and thus prompted vigorous debate on Earth-Moon relationships. Ringwood used the high-pressure laboratory and his experience in studying terrestrial basaltic rocks to test models of petrogenesis of lunar mare basalts and models advocating mare or highland basalt compositions as representative of the lunar interior. Primitive or parental mare basalt compositions were identified and constraints were placed on temperatures and depths of origin as partial melts from a differentiated lunar interior. As the fission hypothesis gathered support with a giant impact as the preferred cause of the detachment of the Earth material, Ringwood remained skeptical on the grounds that a giant impact would have caused catastrophic melting of the core and mantle. He advocated ejection of protolunar material by multiple smaller impacts after separation of Earth's core. The subject remains a debatable one. Ringwood's views on the origin and differentiation of the solar system and of the Earth-Moon system in particular were summarized in his book, *Origin of the Earth and Moon* (1979).

Nuclear Waste and SYNROC. Mineral exploration in Australia through the 1960s and 1970s identified major deposits of uranium mineralization. Growth of the international nuclear power industry, alongside the Nuclear Non-Proliferation Treaty (1968), which attempted to limit the number of states developing nuclear weapons, made the mining and export of uranium a political issue in Australia. Australia, with major coal and natural gas reserves, does not generate power by nuclear means, but environmentalists were strongly opposed to uranium mining and enrichment, and to the use of uranium in thermonuclear reactors whether in Australia or overseas. A principal concern was and remains the disposal of high-level nuclear wastes with high levels of radioactivity, including long-lived radioisotopes. These wastes present a radiological hazard that requires management for timescales of thousands of years, and no nation has yet proceeded to implement permanent disposal of its high-level wastes, whether from military or industrial processes.

In the mid-1970s public debate in Australia about the export of uranium was intensive and divisive. At the same time, most nations with nuclear power programs (which were the potential purchasers of Australia's uranium resources) planned to consolidate and solidify their high-level wastes in glass matrix as the first barrier to mobility of radioactive isotopes. With his experience in geochemistry and background geological knowledge of the behaviors of glass and minerals over geological time scales, along with his knowledge of subsurface conditions of temperature and fluid mobility, Ringwood recognized that the glass matrix strategy was less than ideal. In geological terms, glass is not stable and is readily hydrated or leached by circulating groundwater. Using crystal

260

chemical arguments and knowledge of the behavior of minerals containing radioactive elements over geological time scales, Ringwood developed the concept of crystalline ceramics as hosts to the radio nuclides of nuclear wastes and patented his concept as SYNROC (from synthetic rock). SYNROC is a titania-based ceramic, the constituent minerals of which have the capacity to immobilize, in their crystal lattices, most of the radio nuclides of high-level nuclear wastes. In its further development, the SYNROC concept has developed particular compositions tailored to specific waste forms, and SYNROC remains a significant factor in the planning for military and industrial nuclear waste disposal. It is noteworthy that the launch of the SYNROC concept by Ringwood in 1979 was attacked both by the environmentalist lobby and by the nuclear industry. The latter, in part already committed to the glass waste form, did not welcome the criticism implicit in Ringwood's advocacy of "an improved wasteform." The environmentalist lobby did not welcome any weakening of their case for the total intractability of nuclear waste management.

The development and advocacy of SYNROC was consistent with Ringwood's contributions to science. It was independent; unconstrained by the dominant paradigm, or "establishment" view; insightful; based firmly on basic science principles; and imaginative, "big-picture" science in its applications.

His Methodology and Significance. Ringwood's modus operandi used sound theory to devise an experimental approach, robust experimental data to constrain an hypothesis or hypotheses, and imaginative extension into implications or consequences of favored hypotheses—leading to further testing toward confirmation or rejection. He was not afraid to change his views but preferred to be proved in error by his own efforts rather than by others. In accepting the Feltrinelli International Prize by the National Academy of Italy in 1991, Ringwood said, "Our understanding of the Earth in all her aspects has developed dramatically during the last 25 years. This has been an exhilarating period to have been an Earth Scientist. I feel very fortunate and fulfilled to have been able to participate in some of these developments."

Ted Ringwood was a leader of international stature and distinctively Australian in his independence and selective association. The composition, origin, structure, and dynamics of Earth and the origin and evolution of the solar system were debated and successfully explored in the latter half of the twentieth century, with Ringwood as a major contributor and an influential, articulate, and leading intellect.

Honors and Awards. Ringwood's work was widely honored by medals, distinguished lectures, and election to fellowships of scientific societies. Among others, he received the Bowie Medal of the American Geophysical Union in 1974 and the Goldschmidt Medal Award of the Geochemical Society in 1991; perhaps his most prestigious award was the Feltrinelli International Prize in 1991, granted by the National Academy of Italy. His research contributions remain influential through his more than three hundred scientific articles, and two books, *Composition and Petrology of the Earth's Mantle* and *Origin of the Earth and Moon,* which synthesized many of his investigations and ideas. Ringwood's research was prematurely terminated by his death from lymphoma in 1993.

BIBLIOGRAPHY

WORKS BY RINGWOOD

"The Principles Governing Trace Element Distribution during Magmatic Crystallization. Part I. The Influence of Electronegativity." *Geochemica et Cosmochimica Acta* 7 (1955): 189–202. Application of Goldschmidt's rules on crystal chemical relationships to trace element behaviors in the crystallization of igneous rocks.

"The Principles Governing Trace Element Behaviour during Magmatic Crystallisation. Part II. The Role of Complex Formation." *Geochemica et Cosmochimica Acta* 7 (1955): 242–254. Explores the roles of complex formation in trace element behavior in crystallization of silicate melts.

"The Olivine-Spinel Transition in the Earth's Mantle." *Nature* 178 (1956): 1303–1304. Application of germanate as analogues of silicate crystallization to predict the role of high-pressure phase transformation in Earth's interior.

"The System Mg_2SiO_4-Mg_2GeO_4." *American Journal of Science* 254 (1956): 707–711. Initial study of germanate and silicate melts and crystalline solid solutions.

"On the Chemical Evolution and Densities of the Planets." *Geochemica et Cosmochimica Acta* 15 (1959): 257–283.

"Chemical and Genetic Relationships among Meteorites." *Geochemica et Cosmochimica Acta* 24 (1961): 159–197.

"Present Status of the Chondritic Earth Model." In *Researches on Meteorites,* edited by Carleton B. Moore. New York: Wiley, 1962.

"Chemical Evolution of the Terrestrial Planets." *Geochemica et Cosmochimica Acta* 30 (1966): 41–104.

"Genesis of Chondritic Meteorites." *Reviews of Geophysics* 4 (1966): 113–175.

"Some Comparative Aspects of Lunar Origin." *Physics of the Earth and Planetary Interiors* 6 (1972): 366–376. Exploration of models of lunar origin, based on results from Apollo landings and lunar sampling.

Composition and Petrology of the Earth's Mantle. New York: McGraw-Hill, 1975.

Origin of the Earth and Moon. New York: Springer-Verlag, 1979.

"Immobilization of Radioactive Wastes in SYNROC." *American Scientist* 70 (1982): 201–207. A synthesis of research into the identification of crystalline host minerals for immobilization of high-level nuclear waste.

"Flaws in the Giant Impact Hypothesis of Lunar Origin." *Earth and Planetary Science Letters* 95 (1989): 208–214. A critical look at proposals of lunar origin by a single large impact on Earth.

"Phase Transformations and Their Bearing on the Constitution and Dynamics of the Mantle." *Geochemica et Cosmochimica Acta* 55 (1991): 2083–2110. A review of the applications of high-pressure study of phase transformations to infer the dynamical behaviors and chemical composition of Earth's interior.

With William O. Hibberson. "Solubility of Mantle Oxides in Molten Iron at High Pressures and Temperatures: Implications for Core-Mantle Reaction and the Nature of the D" Layer in the Lower Mantle." *Earth and Planetary Science Letters* 102 (1991): 235–251.

"Volatile and Siderophile Element Geochemistry of the Moon: A Reappraisal." *Earth and Planetary Science Letters* 111 (1992): 537–555.

OTHER SOURCE

Green, David H. "Alfred Edward Ringwood 1930–1993." *Biographical Memoirs of Fellows of the Royal Society of London* 44 (1998): 349–362. Extended obituary and full publication list.

David H. Green

RITTMANN, ALFRED (ALFREDO) FERDINAND

(*b.* Basel, Switzerland, 23 March 1893; *d.* Piazza Armerina, Sicily, 19 September 1980), *volcanology, petrography, mineralogy.*

Rittman was one of the fathers of modern volcanology. Through his long-standing studies in the volcanic areas of Southern Italy, he contributed to the understanding of the geological history of the Italian volcanoes, to the physical chemistry of volcanic processes, and to the petrography of volcanic rocks. His *Volcanoes and Their Activity* became a leading textbook on volcanism for several decades.

Rittmann was born into an old Swiss middleclass family as the sole son of the Basel dentist August Rittmann and his wife Frieda Urech Rittmann. Due particularly to his paternal grandfather, he developed an early interest in mineralogy and petrography. At age fourteen, Rittmann studied the famous textbook on mineralogy by the German mineralogist Friedrich Klockmann. At age fifteen, he had his own collection of minerals, the newest microscopical equipment, and a great number of commercially available sets of thin sections. Within a further year he became a self-taught expert in using the polarizing microscope.

In 1912, Rittman entered the University of Basel to study natural sciences, especially earth sciences, and music. Among his teachers were the Swiss mineralogists and geologists Karl Schmidt and Heinrich Preiswerk-Becker. In 1917 he changed to the University of Geneva, where the geologist Louis Duparc became his teacher. In 1921 he received his PhD with a study of a series of platiniferous rocks from the Urals. In the same year he finished his musical education at the Geneva Conservatoire.

In the following five years Rittmann travelled extensively. He visited the centers of mineralogy and petrology, as well as of music cultivation, studying with, amongst others, Friedrich Becke in Vienna, Alfred Lacroix in Paris, Victor Goldschmidt in Heidelberg, and Rudolf Gross in Hamburg. Gross taught him the new techniques of x-ray crystallography. A later result of early interests was his zonal method for the determination of plagioclase feldspars (1929).

Petrographer at Naples—*Privatdozent* in Basel. In 1926 Rittmann joined the staff of the Volcanological Institute of Immanuel Friedländer at Naples as a petrographer. In these years Mount Vesuvius was in continuous activity, culminating in single spectacular eruptions—an ideal field laboratory for a young volcanologist. Further areas of research became the Campi Flegrei, the Island of Ischia, and the Stromboli volcano—whose crater terrace he entered (Figure 1).

Several reports on volcanological observations and a monograph on the geology of Ischia were first results. From the study of the various emissions of Mount Vesuvius, Rittmann proceeded to a comprehensive discussion of its structures and the magmatological development of the Somma volcano. He proved the assimilation of carbonate rocks as it has been discussed by others, including the American geologist Reginald Aldworth Daly. Thus he explained the anomalous differentiation order of Vesuvian lavas from the original Somma-period to the present Vesuvius (trachyte—orvietite—ottajanite—vesuvite) (Figure 2).

These early studies showed Rittmann's new concept of volcanology, first and foremost, as magmatology. Contrary to the then-prevailing conception of volcanic eruptions as a mere consequence of tectonic movements, he emphasized the active role of magma. Magma's physicochemical characteristics were considered as the key to understanding volcanism, and volcanic activities as the essential source for the composition and the dynamical processes of the Earth's interior.

When the Institute Friedländer was closed in 1934, Rittmann returned to Basel where, from 1935 until 1941, he lectured at the university as a *Privatdozent* for petrography, volcanology, geochemistry, and geophysics. In 1936 he accompanied an expedition to Greenland guided by the

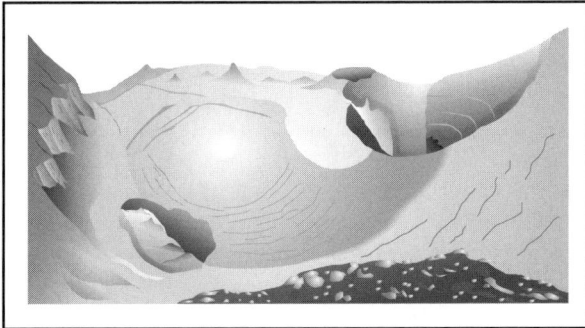

Figure 1. *Perspective view of the crater terrace of the Stromboli volcano, seen from the south-eastern inner slope of the crater ring towards North-West: In the middle there is the lava plug, pushed up and interspersed by faults; at its margins 16 eruption points are currently active (5 July 1931). At the right side the cauldron with a dike wall, where rhythmic jet of ashes take place. In the background spatter cones at the margins of the Sciara del Fuoco.*

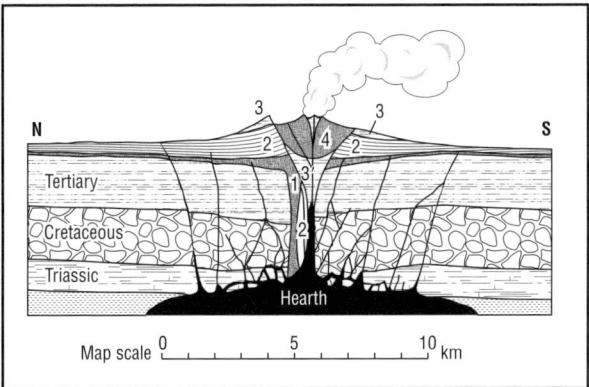

Figure 2. *Section of the Monte Somma-Vesuvius (scale in kilometers, height not increased): The Hauptdolomit of the Triassic forms immediately the roof of the hearth, i.e. the magma chamber, and it is broken and loosened due to settling. On eccentric eruptions the magma emanates immediately from the hearth. In time, the axis of eruption has moved gradually towards south-south-east. 1: Primeval Somma (trachyte). 2: Old Somma (orvietite). 3. Young Somma (ottajanite). 4. Vesuvius (vesuvite). 1', 2', and 3' indicate the relative vents and explosion funnels. Tertiary: sandstone, marl, and clay(stone); Cretaceous: massive/compact lime(stone); Triassic, above mostly dolomite, below marl.*

Danish geologist and polar researcher Lauge Koch. During a short stay in Iceland Rittmann explored the volcanoes at the Myvatn in the north-eastern part of the island. In the same year (1936) the first edition of his textbook *Vulkane und ihre Tätigkeit* was published. The second edition (1960), which was translated into six languages, became an integral part of the study of earth sciences.

Geological Theory—Practical Geology. During the Basel years Rittmann also set forth some more theoretical—and partly controversial—ideas on petrography, geodynamics, and the early geochemical history of the Earth. Together with the German geologist Hans Cloos, he developed a new classification and nomenclature of plutonic rocks (1939). They distinguished five classes of granitic rocks according to origin, that is, first an ultrametamorphic origin, and then four classes for the intrusion and congealing of peculiar types of magma.

A year before, Rittmann suggested a viscous, basic composition of the Earth's primeval congealing crust, instead of a granitic-gneissic one. The incipient sialic crust should have been a product of its decomposition. However, he did not explain where essential remains of this decomposition (such as sodium, or iron) went. In 1941, together with the Swiss physicist Werner Kuhn, he developed a new geochemical theory of the Earth's interior. Instead of the widely accepted iron-nickel core, they assumed a core of solar matter, that is, of highly compressed gaseous hydrogen. In 1942 he explained the process of orogeny as production, or restoration, of a state of thermal equilibrium. This paper included a rough idea of continental drift, caused by convection currents, whereby the mid-Atlantic ridge was seen as a kind of volcanic mountain range.

Because Rittmann's hope for a university career in his native country was not fulfilled—and German universities were out of the question because of the political situation—Rittman, after two years in the service of the Swiss National Defence, went back to Italy in 1941. He directed the national *Centro delle ricerche geominerario* of the *Istituto della Ricostruzione Industriale* (IRI) in Rome. From 1945 to 1949 he also directed the *Centro Geologico Silano* of the *Consiglio Nazionale delle Ricerche* at Naples. There he was mainly engaged in practical geological work. In 1949 he was called as a guest professor to the Institute of Geology and Mineralogy of the University of Alexandria (Egypt), becoming an ordinary professor one year later. In 1953, Rittmann changed to the University of Cairo as professor of petrography, ore geology, and geochemistry. At the same time he directed the Institute of Crystal Optics of the Egyptian National Research Council at Cairo-Dokki. There he produced several papers on crystal optics, most of them in collaboration with his student Essam E. El-Hinnawi (El-Hinnawy).

President of the IAV. In 1957, at age sixty-four, Rittmann returned once more to Italy. He became a professor at the University of Catania, and one year later the director of the *Istituto di Vulcanologia* (which became the *Istituto Nazionale di Geofisica e Vulcanologia*), including the Mount Etna volcanological observatory. Further areas of research became the Iblei Mountains, Pantelleria Island, and—again—Ischia.

Beginning in 1954, he was also the president of the International Association of Volcanology (IAV), which later became the International Association of Volcanology and Chemistry of the Earth's Interior (IAVCEI). He held this post until 1963. He used this position to promote the establishment of an international institute of volcanology at Catania, for instance, by the organization of an international symposium on volcanology, in particular on ignimbrites, at Sicily in 1961. In 1967, the *Istituto Internazionale di Vulcanologia* began its official work, supported by the Italian *Consiglio Nazionale delle Ricerche* and by UNESCO.

In the same year a preliminary report to the mining division of the *Comitato Nazionale dell'Energia Nucleare* on the calculation of stable mineral assemblages in igneous rocks became the initial step for a new method of norm calculation known as the *Rittmann norm*. Rittmann had been engaged in the problem of the interaction between the mode and the chemical composition of volcanic rocks since the early 1940s. Results included new ideas on the nomenclature of volcanic rocks (1952) and the *serial indices* of igneous rocks (1957–1958) designed to order them according to the respective suites, that is, provinces. The Rittmann norm should have produced better results for melanocratic and highly subsilicic rocks than the commonly used CIPW norm. Its application, however, required extensive chemical analyses, and the calculation itself was hardly possible without modern computers. Consequently a comprehensive discussion of the Rittmann norm was not published until 1973.

Altogether, Rittmann wrote more than one hundred fifty monographs and papers on nearly all topics of volcanology, including several popular essays. His last book (*I vulcani*, 1976) was written with Loredana Rittmann, his daughter and only child from his marriage with Clementina Militerni of Naples. Rittmann was appointed an honorary member of the Geological Society of Egypt, and the *Schweizerische naturforschende Gesellschaft*, as well as a foreign correspondent of the Geological Society of America. In 1956 the German *Geologische Vereinigung* awarded him the Gustav Steinmann Medal. In 1959 he became an honorary doctor of the University of Bern, one of the rare acknowledgments which his work found in his native country.

BIBLIOGRAPHY

Rittmann's papers (manuscripts, and correspondence) are held by the manuscript department of the Library of the University of Freiburg (shelf mark: Rittmann GA 47, including a catalogue of the materials); a catalog of the letters can be found at the manuscript database of the Staatsbibliothek Preußischer Kulturbesitz in Berlin, available from http://kalliope.staatsbibliothek-berlin.de.

WORKS BY RITTMANN

Étude pétrographique sur une série de roches des gîtes platinifères de l'Oural. Bad Salzuflen: H. Uekermann, 1922.

"Die Zonenmethode. Ein Beitrag zur Plagioklasbestimmung mit Hilfe des Theodolithtisches." *Schweizerische mineralogische und petrographischeMitteilungen* 9 (1929): 1–46.

Die Geologie der Insel Ischia (including a geological map 1:10.000). *Zeitschrift für Vulkanologie,* Supplement 6. Berlin: Reimer, 1930. Reprinted Amsterdam: Swets and Zeitlinger, 1969; revised edition, together with Violetta Gottini, posthumously, *Bolletino del Servizio Geologico d'Italia* 51 (1980): 131–274.

"Die geologisch bedingte Evolution und Differentiation des Somma-Vesuv Magmas." *Zeitschrift für Vulkanologie* 15 (1933): 8–94.

Vulkane und ihre Tätigkeit. Stuttgart: Ferdinand Enke, 1936. 2nd, enlarged and revised ed., 1960. 3rd, completely revised ed., 1981. Translation of the first edition (revised and enlarged) into Italian by Felice Ippolito (*Vulcani, attività e genesi.* Naples: Ed. Politechnica, 1944). Translations of the second edition into English by Ewart Albert Vincent (*Volcanoes and Their Activity.* New York: Interscience Publishers, 1962); French by Haroun Tazieff (*Les volcans et leur activité.* Paris: Masson, 1963); Russian (*Vulkany i ich dejatel'nost.'* Moskau: Izd. Mir, 1964); Italian, enlarged and revised, by Glauco Gottardi (*I vulcani e la loro attività.* Bologna: Cappelli, 1967; rep., 1972); Romanian (Bucharest, Romania: Ed. Technica, 1967); and Japanese.

"Die Vulkane am Myvatn in Nordost-Island." *Bulletin volcanologique* 4 (1938): 3–38.

With Hans Cloos. "Zur Einteilung und Benennung der Plutone." *Geologische Rundschau* 30 (1939): 600–608.

"Studien an Eruptivgesteinen aus Ost-Grönland." *Meddelelser om Grønland,* udgivne af Kommissionen for videnskabelige undersøgelser i Grønland 115, no. 1 (1940): 1–156.

With Werner Kuhn. "Über den Zustand des Erdinneren und seine Entstehung aus einem homogenen Urzustand." *Geologische Rundschau* 32 (1941): 215–256.

"Zur Thermodynamik der Orogenese." *GeologischeRundschau* 33 (1942): 485–498.

With Felice Ippolito. "Sulla stratigrafia del Somma-Vesuvio." *Atti della fondazione politecnica del mezzogiorno,* 3 (1947): 1–37.

"Origine e differenziazione del magma Ischitano." *Schweizerische mineralogische und petrographische mitteilungen* 28 (1948): 643–698.

"Zur geochemischen Entwicklung der prägeologischen Lithosphäre." *Schweizerische mineralogische und petrographische Mitteilungen* 28 (1948): 36–48.

"Nomenclature of Volcanic Rocks Proposed for the Use in the Catalogue of Volcanoes, and Key-Tables for the Determination of Volcanic Rocks." *Bulletin Volcanologique* 12 (1952), 75–102.

"On the Serial Character of Igneous Rocks." *Egyptian Journal of Geology* 1 (1957): 23–48.

With Essam E. El-Hinnawi. "Optical and Crystallographic Properties of Some Aromatic Disulphides." *Egyptian Journal of Chemistry* 2 (1959): 29–36.

"Die Bimodalität des Vulkanismus und die Herkunft der Magmen." *Geologische Rundschau* 57 (1967): 277–295.

With Lucio Villari, Maria DiRe, and Romolo Romano. "Studio geovulcanologico e magmatologico dell'Isola di Pantelleria, with a geological map 1:50.000." *Rivista Mineraria Siciliana* 18, no. 106–108 (1967): 147–182.

With Violetta Gottini, Wolfgang Hewers, et al. *Stable Mineral Assemblages of Igneous Rocks: A Method of Calculation.* Berlin: Springer, 1973. Translated into Russian (1975) and Chinese.

"Chemistry of Lunar Rocks with Volcanological and Magmatological Considerations and a Model of the 'Hot Moon.'" In *Volcanoes and Impact Craters on the Moon and Mars,* edited by Piero Leonardi. Amsterdam: Elsevier, 1976.

With Loredana Rittmann. *I vulcani.* Novara: Istituto Geografico De Agostini, 1976. Translated into German by Erwin Felkel (*Vulkane in Farbe.* München: Südwest Verlag, 1977); English (*Volcanoes.* London: Orbis Publishing, 1976; rep., 1978); and French (*Les Volcans.* Paris: Atlas, 1976; rep., 1985).

OTHER SOURCES

Cristofolini, Renato. "Ricordo di Alfredo Rittmann." *Rendiconti della Società Italiana di Mineralogia et Petrologia già Società Mineralogica Italiana* 37 (1981): xv–xxii. Most complete available bibliography.

Keller, Jörg, and Ernst Niggli. "Alfred Rittmann (1893–1980)." *Schweizerische mineralogische und petrographische Mitteilungen* 60 (1980): 305–309. With portrait and selected bibliography.

Pichler, Hans. "Alfred Rittmann 23 März 1893–19 September 1980." *Geologische Rundschau* 72 (1983): vii–xi. With portrait.

Bernhard Fritscher

ROBINSON, JULIA BOWMAN (*b.* St. Louis, Missouri, 8 December 1919; *d.* Berkeley, California, 30 July 1985), *mathematics, mathematical logic, number theory, decision problems, definability.*

Robinson's mathematical work exhibits power and charm. She tackled difficult problems and strove for elegant solutions. Her life and work cannot be properly seen without noting that as a woman in a male-dominated field, she was something of a pioneer. Her métier was the interface between two branches of mathematics, logic and the theory of numbers, ordinarily thought to have little to do with one another. She is particularly known for her contributions to the solution of the tenth problem in a famous list of twenty-three proposed by the mathematician David Hilbert in 1900. She was elected to the National Academy of Sciences and also to the presidency

of the American Mathematical Society, in both cases the first female mathematician to be so honored, and was also a recipient of a MacArthur Fellowship.

Early Life. Born Julia Bowman, she suffered two calamities early in life. She was only two when her mother died, leaving her father to cope with Julia and her elder sister Constance. After his remarriage, the family moved west, ultimately to San Diego, where her step-sister Billie was born. When Julia was nine she underwent a devastating illness: scarlet fever followed by rheumatic fever. She missed two years of school and suffered very serious damage to her heart. Academically she excelled and soon made up her lost ground. In high school she was the only girl to take the advanced science and mathematics courses and graduated with a number of honors. In 1936 she entered San Diego State College, majoring in mathematics. Seeking wider vistas, she transferred to the University of California at Berkeley for her senior year. Among the five mathematics courses she took that year was one on the theory of numbers taught by Raphael Robinson. Impressed by her ability, he convinced her to continue her studies as a graduate student. Raphael was a mathematician of broad interests and knowledge and an ideal mentor. But soon their relationship became more personal and they were married in December 1941. Their hopes to begin a family were dashed when Julia suffered a miscarriage and was warned by a doctor that, because of her severely damaged heart, pregnancy would be extremely dangerous. His opinion was that she would likely die before she was forty. In an effort to help Julia overcome the deep depression into which she was flung, Raphael encouraged her to seek solace in mathematics.

Mathematical Background. The 1930s had seen revolutionary developments in the ancient subject of logic, drastically changed from the traditional field originated by Aristotle. Kurt Gödel's famous incompleteness theorem had pointed to the inherent limitations of formal systems of logic in encapsulating mathematical practice. Work by Alonzo Church, Alan Turing, and Emil Post as well as Gödel himself had shown that the question of the existence of algorithmic solutions to specific mathematical problems could be given a precise formulation. This opened the possibility that in specific cases, such algorithmic solutions might not exist, and even that in such cases, this might be proved. Alfred Tarski had explained how to define semantic notions of truth and definability of formal languages. These were the developments that provided the context of Julia Robinson's research.

Any particular branch of mathematics will use symbols to stand for the particular operations and relations that are fundamental to that subject. In addition to such symbols, modern mathematical logic uses the special symbols

$\neg$ (*negation*), $\wedge$ (*and*), $\vee$ (*or*), $\supset$ (*implies*),
$\forall$ (*all*), and $\exists$ (*some*)

along with the familiar = sign. One speaks of these symbols together with those corresponding to a particular branch of mathematics as constituting a language. Julia Robinson's work was largely in the context of the language of arithmetic which uses the two symbols + and × standing for addition and multiplication, respectively, as well as symbols for 0 and 1. Letters of the alphabet are used as variables, and in the case of the language of arithmetic, they are usually understood to vary over the familiar natural numbers 0,1,2 .... So for example, the "sentence"

$$(\forall x, y, u, v)(((x = u + u + 1) \wedge (y = v + v + 1)) \supset (\exists w)(x + y = w + w))$$

expresses the true proposition that adding two odd numbers yields an even number. The formula $(\exists u)(x = u+u+1)>$ by itself defines the set of odd numbers, i.e., if x is replaced by a particular natural number, the resulting sentence will be true if and only if that number is odd. Questions of definability and the existence of algorithms were fundamental to Robinson's work.

A set of natural numbers S is called computable (or recursive) if there is an algorithm that can determine for a given natural number n whether or not n belongs to S. A set of natural numbers is called listable (the term preferred by Julia Robinson) or recursively enumerable if there is an algorithm for systematically making a list of the members of S. All unsolvability results can be thought of as consequences of the key theorem: *There exists a listable set that is not computable.* These matters were also very important in Robinson's work.

Julia Robinson's Dissertation. It was in a seminar led by the charismatic Alfred Tarski, one of the great logicians of the twentieth century, that Robinson found her métier. Tarski had left his native Poland in August 1939 on what was to have been a brief trip to attend a conference in the United States, just before the German invasion of Poland precipitated the Second World War. Tarski posed a number of unsolved questions about definability in the language of arithmetic to which Robinson was attracted. By the 1940s it was well known that there is no algorithm to determine whether a given sentence in the language of arithmetic, with the variables ranging over the natural numbers, is true. As one says, this is an algorithmically unsolvable problem. Tarski wanted to know whether the same is true when in this same language, variables are permitted to range over all rational numbers instead of just the natural numbers. (The rational numbers are those

expressible as fractions m/n or $-m/n$ where m is a natural number and n is a non-zero natural number.) There had been developed techniques for "reducing" one such "decision problem" to another. In this case one would show that if there were an algorithm for testing for truth a sentence of the language of arithmetic with the variables constrained to vary over the rational numbers, such an algorithm could be used to furnish an algorithm to do the same when the variables range over the natural numbers. So, since there is no such algorithm for the latter, it would follow that neither could there be one for the former.

The main result of Robinson's dissertation was an explicit formula in the language of arithmetic, with the variables constrained to vary over the rational numbers, that defines precisely the set of integers (that is, the set of natural numbers and their negatives). It then followed that the problem of determining the truth of a sentence of arithmetic remains unsolvable even when the variables range over the rational numbers. Other unsolvability results followed as well. Robinson's approach was intricate, elegant, and ingenious using some rather deep ideas from number theory.

Elegant Characterizations. Robinson always sought elegance and simplicity in her mathematical work. One of her early papers showed how to characterize, in a particularly simple way, the algorithmically computable functions (also called the recursive functions) that map the natural numbers into themselves. Her beautiful characterization involves two initial functions and three operations for obtaining new functions from given functions. One of the initial functions is just the successor function $S(x) = x+1$. The other, which Robinson calls E, is defined as the difference between a given number and the largest perfect square that does not exceed it. (Thus $E(19) = 19 - 16 = 3$ and $E(25) = 25 - 25 = 0$.) The three operations are as follows: (1) from given functions F and G obtain the function $H(x) = F(G(x))$; (2) from given functions F and G obtain the function $H(x) = F(x) + G(x)$; and (3) from a given function F whose values include all natural numbers obtain the function H where $H(x)$ is the least number t for which $F(t) = x$.

It is truly remarkable that all computable functions (from the natural numbers to the natural numbers) can be obtained by beginning with the two initial functions and applying these three operations over and over again.

Much later Robinson showed the same elegance and verve in finding new characterizations of a domain far removed from the computable. The existence of a listable set K that is not computable has already been mentioned. So there is no algorithm for determining membership in K. By considering sets that can be listed by algorithms having access to membership information about such sets (metaphorically via an "oracle") additional sets can be brought into the fold, and this process can be iterated. By allowing this iteration to occur any finite number of times, the sets obtained turn out to be exactly those called arithmetical, the sets definable in the language of arithmetic with variables ranging over the natural numbers. But there is no need to stop here. One can define a non-arithmetical set, and then use that as an "oracle" to be able list still more sets. There is a natural place where this process does come to an end, and the sets of natural numbers so obtained are called hyperarithmetical. It was this rarefied realm for which Robinson provided a simple and direct characterization.

Existential Definability and Hilbert's Tenth Problem. The work for which Julia Robinson is most remembered originated with an apparently simple problem posed by Alfred Tarski. Tarski wanted to know which sets of natural numbers are definable by formulas of the language of arithmetic if the symbols $\forall$ and $\neg$ are excluded. He called such sets existentially definable and proposed the problem of proving that the set $\{1,2,4,8,16, \ldots\}$ of powers of 2 is *not* existentially definable. This was exactly the sort of problem that Robinson liked. The notion of existential definability could easily be seen to be closely related to problems of a kind that number theorists study, so-called Diophantine problems. These typically have to do with a polynomial equation $p(a,x,y,z,u,v,w,\ldots) = 0$ with integer coefficients where a is a parameter and $x,y,z,u,v,w,\ldots$ are "unknowns." (Recall that such a polynomial is just the sum of terms like $5a^3x^2v^5$ and $-7a^4x^3z^6$.) For particular Diophantine equations of this kind, number theorists try to determine for which natural number values of the parameter a, the equation has natural number solutions in the unknowns. Now by simple standard methods it is easy to see that a set of natural numbers S is existentially definable if and only if there is a polynomial equation of this kind such that S is exactly the set of values of the parameter for which the equation has natural number solutions. For this reason, existentially definable sets are also called *Diophantine,* and this is the term that has been adopted in the later literature.

Not having any success in proving Tarski's conjecture that the set of powers of 2 is not Diophantine, Robinson began to consider the possibility that Tarski's guess might have been wrong. In order to make any progress, she had to assume a certain hypothesis, unproved at the time, that came to be called J.R.; roughly speaking J.R. states that there is a Diophantine equation with two parameters a,b with the property that the pairs (a,b) for which the equation has solutions are such that b grows exponentially as a function of a. By assuming J.R. and carrying out a complex and ingenious analysis, she proved not only that the powers of 2 are Diophantine, but also that the set of prime

numbers as well as many others are also. It is readily seen that all Diophantine sets are listable, but now she wondered whether the converse might be true, whether all listable sets might be Diophantine. This, she knew would have profound consequences.

In 1900, to greet the new century, the great mathematician David Hilbert proposed a list of twenty-three problems to stand as a challenge. The tenth on his list was to provide an algorithm to determine whether a given polynomial Diophantine equation has solutions. If indeed all listable sets were Diophantine, she realized, then in particular there would be a non-computable Diophantine set, implying that there could be no algorithm such as Hilbert had asked for. This would constitute a negative solution of Hilbert's tenth problem.

In the summer of 1959, Robinson received in the mail a preprint of a paper by Martin Davis and Hilary Putnam. The paper contained a proof that, assuming J.R., all listable sets are indeed Diophantine. However, the proof had an important gap. It used the fact that there are arbitrarily long sequences of prime numbers with the special property that the difference between consecutive terms of the sequence is constant. Although this is true, in 1959 it was a mere hypothesis; it was proved only in 2004. Robinson knew the previous work of Davis and Putnam very well and expressed surprise and pleasure at their accomplishment. In very short order, she showed how to do without the extra hypothesis about prime numbers, and even found a short version of the proof. So, to obtain the anticipated negative solution of Hilbert's tenth problem, it only remained to prove J.R.

This was accomplished in January 1970 by the twenty-two-year-old Yuri Matiyasevich using the famous Fibonacci sequence 1,1,2,3,5,8,13,.... He found a Diophantine equation with two parameters a,b that he was able to prove has solutions just in case b is the Fibonacci number in the $2a$-th place in this sequence. Because the Fibonacci numbers do grow exponentially, this did constitute a proof of J.R. Robinson was delighted by Matiyasevich's ingenious proof and traveled to Leningrad where their families met. Their collaboration was fruitful; together they were able to show that Hilbert's tenth problem is unsolvable even for equations in 13 unknowns. (Later Matiyasevich was able to reduce the number to 9.)

Coda. The "nepotism" rules in effect at the University of California would have made a regular faculty appointment for Robinson impossible as long as her husband was on the faculty. In any case it may well be that her health problems would have precluded a full-time position. She did occasionally teach a course as an adjunct, and she served as de facto adviser to two excellent doctoral students, Leonard Adleman and Kenneth Manders. Robinson defied the doctor's prediction that she would not live to be forty, but by her forty-first birthday her damaged heart had brought her close to invalid status. She was rescued by a surgical procedure that had only recently become available and which greatly improved her situation, enabling her to live an active life for an additional twenty-five years.

Her outstanding work was recognized by her election in 1975 to the National Academy of Sciences, the first woman to be elected to the mathematics section. That same year she was finally offered a professorial appointment at the University of California at Berkeley.

At her request it was a quarter-time appointment. A MacArthur Fellowship came in 1983. She was elected president of the American Mathematical Society for 1983–1984, the first woman to hold this office. Tragically, she was unable to complete her term. She was found to be suffering from leukemia during the summer of 1984. After a brief remission, Julia Robinson died of the disease on 30 July 1985.

BIBLIOGRAPHY

WORKS BY ROBINSON

"Definability and Decision Problems in Arithmetic." *Journal of Symbolic Logic* 14 (1949): 98–114. This was Robinson's dissertation.

"General Recursive Functions." *Proceedings of the American Mathematical Society* 1 (1950): 703–718. In addition to the characterization of computable functions of one argument described above, many other interesting results are discussed in this paper.

"Existential Definability in Arithmetic." *Transactions of the American Mathematical Society* 72 (1952): 437–449. A fundamental paper in which what came to be called J.R. was shown to imply the existential definability of the powers of 2, the primes, and actually, the full exponential function.

With Martin Davis and Hilary Putnam. "The Decision Problem for Exponential Diophantine Equations." *Annals of Mathematics* 74 (1961): 425–436. It was in this paper that it was proved that J.R. implies the unsolvability of Hilbert's tenth problem.

"An Introduction to Hyperarithmetical Functions." *Journal of Symbolic Logic* 32 (1967): 325–342. This was Robinson's one excursion to the very uncomputable.

With Yuri Matiyasevich. "Reduction of an Arbitrary Diophantine Equation to One in 13 Unknowns." *Acta Arithmetica* 27 (1975): 521–553. Virtuoso number theory!

With Martin Davis and Yuri Matiyasevich. "Hilbert's Tenth Problem. Diophantine Equations: Positive Aspects of a Negative Solution." In *Mathematical Developments Arising from Hilbert Problems,* edited by Felix Browder. Providence, RI: American Mathematical Society, 1976.

Proceedings of Symposia in Pure Mathematics 28 (1976): 323–378. A survey of the proof of the unsolvability of Hilbert's tenth problem as well as of mathematical developments stemming from it by three of the four mathematicians whose work led to that proof.

The Collected Works of Julia Robinson. Edited by Solomon Feferman. Providence, RI: American Mathematical Society, 1996. All twenty-five of Robinson's publications are reprinted here in full. In addition, there is the fine biographical essay about her written by Feferman for the National Academy of Sciences.

OTHER SOURCES

Davis, Martin. "Hilbert's Tenth Problem Is Unsolvable." *American Mathematical Monthly* 80 (1973): 233–269; reprinted as an appendix in *Computability and Unsolvability,* edited by Martin Davis. New York: Dover, 1983. A Steele-Prize-winning essay that offers the complete proof of the unsolvability of Hilbert's tenth problem. The Dover reprint is of one of the first book-length treatments of computability theory.

———, and Reuben Hersh. "Hilbert's Tenth Problem." *Scientific American* 229 (November 1973): 84–91. Reprinted in *The Chauvenet Papers,* Vol. 2, edited by J. C. Abbott. Washington, DC: Mathematical Association of America, 1978. A Chauvenet-Prize winning article intended for the general educated public.

Matiyasevich, Yuri. "My Collaboration with Julia Robinson." *The Mathematical Intelligencer* 14 (1992): 38–45. His story of how a young Russian and a much older American woman came to produce elegant mathematics together.

———. *Hilbert's Tenth Problem.* Cambridge, MA: MIT Press, 1993. An excellent introduction and survey suitable for undergraduate mathematics majors, with a very inclusive bibliography.

Reid, Constance. *Julia, a Life in Mathematics.* Washington, DC: Mathematical Association of America, 1996. By Robinson's sister, it has photographs, Reid's useful biography, entitled "The Autobiography of Julia Robinson," and a brief note by Martin Davis about his work with Hilary Putnam.

Martin Davis

ROBINSON, ROBERT (*b.* Rufford Farm [near Chesterfield], Derbyshire, United Kingdom, 13 September 1886; *d.* London, United Kingdom, 8 February 1975), *chemistry, electronic theory, natural products, synthesis, structure.*

Robinson was one of the greatest organic chemists of the twentieth century. His outstanding achievements led to both a Nobel Prize and an Order of Merit, particularly for his work on the synthesis and structure of natural products, including alkaloids and plant pigments. He was also one of the founders of the electronic theory of organic chemistry.

Early Years. Robert Robinson was born on 13 September 1886 at Rufford Farm, near Chesterfield in Derbyshire, a thriving market town of great antiquity. His parents were William Bradbury Robinson and William's second wife, Jane Davenport. There had been ten children from William's first marriage, and Robert was the eldest of five by the second wife. The father was an inventive manufacturer whose innovations included the mechanization of cardboard box production and automation in the manufacture of surgical dressings, the latter being the family firm's chief concern.

When Robert was three years old, the family moved to another town near Chesterfield, where he began his education. After attending a kindergarten school he went to Chesterfield Grammar School, whose headmaster seems to have been the first to stimulate his interest in mathematics. Although a weekly boarder, he spent plenty of time at home, and there developed three interests that remained with him for life. One was a general interest in natural phenomena, for the countryside was almost on his doorstep. The second arose from the excursions he often made from home to the hilly country around, not least some rocky outcrops that he climbed with ease and which generated a love for mountains that never left him. The third interest was chess, which he learned from the various Congregational ministers who regularly visited his parents. (They belonged at that time to Brampton Congregational Church.) He did not, however, share their faith and apparently remained a skeptic throughout his life.

At the age of twelve Robert was sent to Fulneck School, near Leeds in West Yorkshire, again as a boarder. The school had been recommended by several people and had a good academic reputation. It was a coeducational establishment run by the Moravians, situated in an area of great natural charm. The years passed fairly uneventfully, and Robert's interest in mathematics was deepened by individual tutoring in his last year from J. H. Blandford, a Cambridge University mathematician on the staff. By this time, at the dawn of the twentieth century, it was not uncommon for comparatively affluent fathers to send their sons to a university, and in Robert's case this seems to have been settled quite early. Robert, however, wanted to study mathematics, but his father saw value in another subject, one that would be more useful to industry, his own in particular. Robert had already won a gold sovereign from his father for designing an automatic lint-cutting machine, thus showing considerable practical inventiveness. Such a flair would be enhanced by scientific knowledge. This had to be in chemistry, for industries using textiles had for long been indebted to chemists for many processes, such as scouring, bleaching, mordanting, dyeing, and testing. Indeed, William Robinson had tried, albeit unsuccessfully, to build a bleachworks on the basis of an encyclopedia article. So chemistry was the choice of subject, the university was Manchester, and there Robert went in 1902.

Manchester. The chemistry department at Manchester was at that time internationally renowned. From the days of Edward Frankland, its first professor, and those of his successor, Henry E. Roscoe, the department had flourished, and at Robinson's arrival it was led by Harold Baily Dixon, famous for his research on explosives and on "dry reactions." The professor of organic chemistry was William H. Perkin Jr. (son of the legendary William H. Perkin, who discovered mauve dye), then at the height of his powers. The two professors were effective lecturers, though it was Perkin who inspired Robert with a lifelong devotion to the chemistry of carbon. His third year included (appropriately enough) special practical work in the chemistry of dyestuffs, directed by Jocelyn Field Thorpe. An interesting comment on his work comes in a laboratory record of 1902: "Robinson, Robert—a good worker but messy." However, he graduated with first class honors in 1905.

Robinson's undergraduate days at Manchester were enlivened by hill walking, cricket, and attendance at the Music Hall, theaters, and operas. Fellow students who later blossomed in chemistry included John Lionel Simonsen and Walter Norman Haworth. At home, vacations offered an opportunity to continue chemical experiments in a small laboratory specially built by his father. One achievement here was a synthesis of terebic acid by the recently discovered Grignard reaction, his first original work in organic synthesis.

Upon graduation Robinson was invited to work in Perkin's private laboratory. After some initial work on the preparation of ethyl piperonylacetate, he was diverted into a study of the natural dyestuff brazilin, a constituent of brazilwood and for some time an interest of Perkin himself. Robinson doubted some of Perkin's conclusions, mainly because brazilinic acid obtained by permanganate oxidation of trimethylbrazilin was assumed to contain $-CH_2-$ groups, rarely found after such oxidations. With Perkin's encouragement he entered the field of brazilin chemistry. A complex molecule, it did not yield up its secrets immediately, and Robinson's last paper on the subject was published in 1974, sixty-eight years after his first. Unhappy with Perkin's tentative structure, he proposed an alternative that later proved to be correct. He went on to examine a number of other natural products with a view to determining their structures. They included hematoxylin and the alkaloids berberine, harmaline, harmine, and strychnine. This last compound fascinated Robinson till the end of his life. This was no doubt partly because of its notoriety as a poison, but also because its structure resisted elucidation till the 1940s. By 1910 his papers had become sufficiently numerous and useful to earn him the degree of DSc. Shortly after this he became residential tutor in chemistry at Dalton Hall, one of the university's halls of residence.

CHO
/
CH₂
|
CH₂   +   H₂NMe   +
\
CHO

CH₂——COOR
\
CO
/
CH₂——COOR

CH————CH₂
/   \   \
CH₂   NMe   CO
| /   /
CH₂   /   \
\   /   \
CH————CH₂

succindialdehyde   methylamine   acetonedicarboxylic ester   **Tropinone**

Robinson's synthesis of tropinone.

During his Manchester years Robinson made many friends in the department, one of whom was Arthur Lapworth, newly arrived in 1909. Trained at the Central Technical College in London, where Henry Edward Armstrong was the professor, he became head of chemistry at Goldsmith's College (owned by the University of London, but not part of it). They shared many interests, including music (Robinson played the piano, Lapworth the violin), identification of wildflowers, walking, and climbing. However, it was Lapworth's ideas on chemical polarity that proved the most important link, and they led directly to Robinson's own speculations on reaction mechanisms.

Another acquaintance in the department was Gertrude Walsh, a young woman student from Cheshire. She and Robert were attracted to each other, and both loved mountains as well as chemistry. They married at Over Parish Church, Cheshire, on 7 August 1912. Shortly after this, life was to take a dramatic new turn as the Robinsons sailed to Australia, where Robert had been appointed to a newly created chair of pure and applied organic chemistry at the University of Sydney. Such a move overseas was by no means unusual for English chemists at that time. He went with Perkin's full support and encouragement and the prospect of a much larger salary, but also for another reason. He himself confessed: "I applied for the post in Sydney, in the first instance, because it would be an excellent base for the exploration of the alpine chain of the New Zealand Alps. This was my primary objective, not, I am afraid at that stage, the advancement of the science of chemistry" (Robinson, 1976, p. 81)

Sydney, Australia. Despite the considerable distance of New Zealand from Australia, the Robinsons managed several trips: "all possible [university] vacations, up to three months at a time," he claimed. They ascended such mountains as Coronet Peak and nearby Mount Neeson in the Southern Alps and Mount Egmont in North Island. He and Gertrude had a full social life in Sydney, she being also a demonstrator in his department. In 1914 the Robinsons had their first child, a daughter who sadly survived for only one day.

During the term there were lectures to give, and Robinson found some difficulty in addressing—and even controlling—classes of medical students and others who were studying chemistry merely because of university regulations. His lectures to aspiring chemists, on the other hand, were well-received, even though they seem to have been largely impromptu romps through the part of the subject that really interested him.

Among the research undertaken at Sydney were studies of C-alkylations of enolates, synthesis of various derivatives of catechol, and an investigation into eudesmin, a component of the oil from the Australian eucalyptus tree. He continued to write up his work from Manchester days and was much encouraged by a visit to Australia by the British Association for the Advancement of Science in 1914. Here he met Nevil V. Sidgwick, H. E. Armstrong, and other British chemists. It turned out that each of these was to give valuable support to an application Robinson was about to make to the University of Liverpool for a chair in organic chemistry. Despite being the youngest candidate at the age of twenty-nine, he was appointed, and after a long and leisurely cruise via the United States, the Robinsons returned to Britain with World War I well underway.

Liverpool. Robinson took up his duties at Liverpool in January 1916. He continued his research on alkaloids and other natural products but by now was beginning to focus on the mechanisms by which such substances are created in nature. He also gave courses of lectures and, as before, used illustrations from his own ongoing research. The Robinsons settled in a house in Warrington, where gardening became a lifelong interest. However, life at that time was overshadowed by the war, and the Liverpool chemists were expected to contribute. The effective head of the department, Edward C. C. Baly, organized attempts to manufacture chemicals vital to the war effort. These included TNT and picric acid, both of which were to receive attention from Robinson. His natural products researches concentrated on the synthesis of alkaloids, then in short supply. Tropinone, a relative of atropine and cocaine, was successfully produced. For some time it had been supposed that tropinone was the first stage in the biosynthesis of both these alkaloids. Robinson's achievement was to discover a very simple synthesis at room temperature, using succindialdehyde, methylamine, and an ester or salt of acetonedicarboxylic acid. Later work concerned the isoquinoline group of alkaloids that include morphine and odeine. He was concerned to ascertain their structural relationships and so to account for their biogenesis. In the ensuing years this work was continued by himself and others, including Richard Wilstätter, Alan Battersby, and Derek H. R. Barton, and was the subject of several major lectures, including his presidential address to the Royal Society in 1947.

Of great long-term importance for Robinson was the Advisory Board set up in 1917 to promote collaboration between academia and industry in northern England, much needed for the development of national resources at that time. It consisted of Baly; Robinson; five other departmental colleagues; and representatives of the local chemical industry, including Brunner Mond, Castner-Kellner Alkali Co., Salt Union, and United Alkali. Another firm was Joseph Crosfield & Co., soap makers in Warrington whose managing director was Edward F. Armstrong, the son of H. E. Armstrong. On their behalf Robinson discovered a new synthesis of octanol, a contribution to Armstrong's program of large-scale catalytic synthesis of simple organic chemicals used in his industry, especially detergents Other industrial contacts included visits to the home of Edmund K. Muspratt, son of James Muspratt, founder of the British alkali industry. An early consultancy project for Robinson was connected to the fact that oil was burning in Liverpool harbor. Robinson established that the problem lay in a combination of oil and floating driftwood. When asked about his fee, he suggested that the harbor authorities give a donation to the university library. He ruefully reported this was the first and last time he was foolish enough to decline a personal fee. Meanwhile, a government-backed company called British Dyes had been established, mainly to protect the industry from a possible revival of its German counterpart. In the absence of many qualified staff the firm approached Perkin, who established small groups of workers in a few university departments, among them Liverpool. Robinson was drawn into this arrangement in 1916, but little seems to have been achieved. In 1919 British Dyes and the rival firm of Levinstein merged to become the British Dyestuffs Corporation (BDC). Robinson resigned his chair and, in January 1920, commenced employment as director of research for BDC at its works in Huddersfield.

Huddersfield. To his colleagues this seemed an astonishing move, initiated by a personal approach from Herbert Levinstein, one of the two new managing directors for the BDC. Robinson's only recorded motive for the change appears to have been that it seemed to him to be "very much in the national interest" for British leadership in the postwar chemical industry, because British firms might well face a threat from German rivals. Patriotism apart, it seems that the new post carried a good salary and conditions.

Not far from the works in Huddersfield, the Robinsons settled in a house where, in 1921, their daughter Marion was born. She became a medical missionary and in 1960 married Mark Way, the bishop of Masasi, Tanganykia (later Tanzania). Robinson had a Liverpool graduate, Wilfred Lawson, to assist him in the laboratory, and their experiments on the azo-dyes led to new products, particularly those derived from coupling diazonium salts with cresols. He gained thereby a deeper insight into the industrial aspects of dyestuffs chemistry. He was elected a Fellow of the Royal Society in 1920 and elected to the council of the Chemical Society in 1921.

However, the years at Huddersfield were marred by fierce antagonism between the two managers, Levinstein and Joseph Turner, and by the existence within the works of a technical chemistry laboratory whose collaboration with Robinson's was minimal. Accordingly, he sought a return to academic life, and when the opportunity arose in 1921, Robinson seized it. The chair of chemistry at St. Andrews had just been vacated by James C. Irvine on his appointment as principal. Robinson successfully applied for the post, and late in 1921 the family moved to Scotland.

St. Andrews. Although at St. Andrews for only a year, the Robinsons enjoyed their new circumstances. Gertrude registered as a research student and Marion began to attend infant school. The opportunities for mountaineering in the Highlands were obvious, and the laboratory occupied by Robert had a spectacular view of the North Sea. In fact, he was able to work in a relatively new laboratory in the oldest university in Scotland (founded in 1410). He did not, however, continue in the carbohydrate tradition inherited from Irvine and his predecessor, Thomas Purdie. That tradition was continued elsewhere, particularly by Walter N. Haworth and by Edmund Langley Hirst, who had been associated with Irvine at St. Andrews before Robinson's time. However, Robinson did suggest to Hirst that the received wisdom that carbohydrates had stable 5-membered rings (like lactones) might be incorrect and that they might instead have 6-membered rings. This speculation was remembered by Hirst, who some years later proved it to be correct.

Robinson continued his work on alkaloids and (with John Mason Gulland) confirmed a new structure for the morphine family.

Robinson's sojourn in St. Andrews was brought to a sharp and unexpected termination by events in Manchester. There, the senior professorship was made vacant by H. B. Dixon's retirement; this was expected, but surprise was occasioned by the elevation to that chair of Arthur Lapworth from his professorship of organic chemistry. Lapworth's chair, therefore, had to be filled; Robinson was approached, made formal application, and was accepted without competition. It is likely that Lapworth's own move, and the subsequent invitation to Robinson, was a deliberate attempt to renew collaboration of the kind they had enjoyed many years earlier. In any event, the move back to Manchester in 1922 proved to be of great importance to chemistry.

Manchester, Again. Now only thirty-six years old but having already occupied two university chairs, Robinson was able to attract many promising workers to his laboratory. Gulland and David Doig Pratt came with him from St. Andrews, the latter continuing work begun on a group of plant pigments known as the anthocyanins, which are responsible for most of the reds and blues in flowers. This work was also followed by Alexander J. Robertson, who was with Robinson from 1924 to 1928. Robinson also collaborated with Arthur George Perkin of the University of Leeds on carajura, a plant material from Venezuela, and with Frank Lee Pyman of the Boots Drug Co. on antimalarials. Among his research students were Tiruvenkata Rajendra Seshadri (who deduced the structure of carajurin, a derivative of carajura) and W. Bradley (who worked on diazo-ketones and anthocyanin synthesis). From 1925 Robinson also worked with his wife, Gertrude, on the synthesis of fatty acids.

Most notable of all his collaborations must surely be his work with Lapworth, whose strong interest in reaction mechanisms had already greatly impressed Robinson in his first Manchester period. Now direct cooperation became a daily possibility, with the two men often seen closeted together at lunch, covering old envelopes with symbols from the new electronic theory that they were developing. Together with James Wilson Armit, he published an idea that was conceived in St. Andrews, a proposal for the electronic structure of benzene. In place of the familiar Kekulé formula with alternating double and single bonds in the ring, he suggested in 1925 that the six "spare" electrons not needed for the three associated with each carbon atom should be regarded as a stable, nonlocalized group. This confers a special kind of stability on the molecule. Since it occurs only in aromatic substances, he called it the "aromatic sextet," which is applicable to

such other systems as pyridine and pyrrole (but not to pyrrole salts, where the electron pair associated with the nitrogen atom is no longer available). This concept proved of great importance in later years and prefigured the use of molecular orbitals.

Also in 1925, Robinson and three coauthors presented a paper about the directive effects of substituents on the course of aromatic substitution. Shortly after this, unfortunately, an acrimonious disagreement arose with Christopher K. Ingold regarding details of the electronic theory. Controversy raged at Chemical Society meetings and elsewhere, and "the absurd game of noughts and crosses [tic tac toe]" was ridiculed by H. E. Armstrong. Robinson remained convinced he was right but soon lost interest in the electronic theory and returned to his first love: natural products. Robinson remarked later in life that he thought his work on the electronic theory was his most important contribution to chemistry. He also believed that Ingold had appropriated his ideas without giving due credit. However, subsequent research has shown the issues were far from simple and the rather distasteful dispute shows neither participant in a very good light.

Robinson came back to the subject in 1932 to deliver two lectures, subsequently published. Also, in 1946 Robinson intended to collaborate with Michael J. S. Dewar on a much larger exposition; in the event, he wrote the foreword to the latter's important *Electronic Theory of Organic Chemistry* (1949).

University College, London. In 1928 Robinson moved yet again after he was invited to become professor of organic chemistry at University College, London. His motives for acceptance are obscure. The family had been unsettled by the birth of a son, Michael, in 1926, who was found to suffer from Down syndrome, and possibly this spurred Robinson to welcome a new sphere of work. After characteristically spending five weeks' holiday in the Alps, the Robinsons settled into a new home in Hendon. Gertrude became known as a generous hostess and Robert drove to the college. Among his friends was Frederick G. Donnan (once a colleague at Liverpool) and his predecessor, J. Norman Collie, who continued as emeritus professor. Like Robinson, Collie delighted in mountains, and they shared many climbing experiences on the Island of Skye, one of whose peaks (Sgurr Thormaid, or Norman's Peak, [926 m., or 3,038 ft., high]) was named after Collie. Robinson's industrial interests were kept alive by a series of consultancy appointments, particularly to Imperial Chemical Industries (ICI) in 1927.

Robinson continued researches from earlier periods, including anthocyanin synthesis and determination of the structure of brazilin. However, he had hardly been in his

Robert Robinson. HULTON ARCHIVE/GETTY IMAGES.

post for a year when, in 1929, his former mentor, W. H. Perkin, died, and his prestigious post at Oxford became vacant. Robinson applied and was soon appointed, though he was not free to leave University College until the following July. Thereafter, he became Waynflete Professor of Chemistry at Oxford, and also head of the Dyson Perrins Laboratory. By a strange irony, his successor at University College was C. K. Ingold.

Oxford. Robinson inherited Perkin's new Dyson Perrins Laboratory, and here he remained for twenty-five years: his wanderings were over. He brought with him about twenty associates from University College and continued to supervise their work. However, he gradually became less involved in working at the laboratory bench and tended to withdraw from the departmental activities. Nor was Robinson greatly interested in the business of his college, Magdalen, and he appears to have made few friends in Oxford during his long stay. One reason was undoubtedly the increase in his outside interests. Robinson continued an enthusiastic gardener, chess player, and mountaineer, and he also engaged in foreign travel to deliver lectures or attend meetings. Much of his time, however, was devoted to deep thought about the chem-

istry of the natural products studied in his laboratory. He tended to avoid detailed experimental work but supervised his research students, who did most of the bench-work. Slightly erratic in his supervision, he gave most attention to the topics that were uppermost in his mind at the time. From 1930 to 1934, colleagues included Bertrie Kennedy Blount and Alexander Todd. His work on plant pigments was drawing to a close, though he still shared his wife's interest in the genetics of color variation in flowers. From the 1930s onward, he concentrated on sterols. This led to, among much else, an industrial synthesis of the female hormone diethylstilbestrol, used for some time in treating prostate cancer. He continued his association with ICI and Boots and joined a research committee set up by Anglo-Persian Oil concerned with the development of a high-octane motor fuel.

By this time Robinson's work was internationally recognized. In 1939 he received a knighthood and became president of the Chemical Society. Six years later he became president of the Royal Society.

With the advent of World War II, Robinson worked on topics of national importance such as chemotherapy and chemical defense, but eventually he concentrated on penicillin studies. Robinson had a well-known dispute with Robert Burns Woodward about the structure of penicillin, with Woodward eventually shown to be correct. This incident is significant because Robinson refused to give much credence to spectroscopic data, while Woodward was a pioneer in using it for organic structure determination. It displays the generational gap between two of the greatest synthetic organic chemists of the twentieth century, and the shift that was taking place at midcentury. Hostilities over, he returned to alkaloid studies (especially brucine and strychnine), and it is these that were named in the citation for his Nobel Prize in Chemistry in 1947. Further distinction came in 1949 with the award of the Order of Merit. He was able to postpone his retirement for four years beyond 1951. He then became president of the British Association for the Advancement of Science in 1955 and a director of Shell Chemical Co., with a small laboratory at Egham, in Surrey, starting that same year.

In 1954 Gertrude Robinson died suddenly. Three years later Robinson married Stearn Hillstrom. He continued to enjoy his lifelong interests of music and chess and climbed his last mountain in 1966. His closing years were marred by failing eyesight, and he became almost completely blind. Nevertheless, his intellect remained active, and he began an autobiography when he was age eighty-five, working at it on the day he died, 8 February 1975.

BIBLIOGRAPHY

Archival material for Robinson is scattered, important collections being at the Royal Society, the Bodleian Library at Oxford, and the Derbyshire County Record Office.

WORKS BY ROBINSON

Outline of an Electrochemical (Electronic) Theory of the Course of Chemical Reactions. London: Royal Institute of Chemistry, 1932.

With E. David Morgan. *An Introduction to Organic Chemistry.* London: Hutchinson, 1975.

Memoirs of a Minor Prophet: 70 Years of Organic Chemistry. New York; Amsterdam, Netherlands: Elsevier, 1976. This was the first and only volume of his autobiography; more had been projected.

OTHER SOURCES

Dewar, Michael James Steuart. *The Electronic Theory of Organic Chemistry.* Oxford: Clarendon Press, 1949. Robinson wrote the foreword.

Eilks, Ingo, and J. Friedrich. "Die Theorie der Reaktionsmechanismen: Ingold oder Robinson?" *Praxis Naturwissenschaft, Chemie* 48 (1999): 29–33.

"Robert Robinson Issue." *Natural Product Reports* 4, no. 1 (1987). Includes articles by Edward P. Abraham, Kenneth W. Bentley, John Cornforth, Robert Livingstone, Colin Russell, Martin D. Saltzman, John Shorter, and Alexander R. Todd.

Saltzman, Martin D. "Sir Robert Robinson—A Centennial Tribute." *Chemistry in Britain* 22 (1986): 543–548.

Slater, L. B. "Woodward, Robinson, and Strychnine: Chemical Structure and Chemists' Challenge." *Ambix* 48 (2001): 161–189.

Todd, Alexander R. "Sir Robert Robinson, 1886–1975." *Chemistry in Britain* 11 (1975): 296.

Todd, Alexander R., and John Cornforth. "Robert Robinson 13 September 1886–8 February 1975." *Biographical Memoirs of Fellows of the Royal Society* 22 (1976): 415–527.

Williams, Trevor I. *Robert Robinson: Chemist Extraordinary.* Oxford: Clarendon Press, 1990.

———. "Robert Robinson." In *Dictionary of National Biography*, edited by Brian Harrison. Oxford and New York: Oxford University Press, 2000.

Colin A. Russell

ROGERS, CARL RANSOM (*b.* Oak Park, Illinois, 8 January 1902; *d.* La Jolla, California, 4 February 1987), *psychology, counseling, psychotherapy.*

Rogers founded the client-centered, or person-centered, approach to psychotherapy. He pioneered techniques for quantifying and analyzing the raw data of psychotherapy that became standards of empirical psychotherapy research in the years following World War II. His views on the therapeutic value of warmth, acceptance, and empathic listening are widely recognized.

At first glance Rogers seems an unusual figure to include in a dictionary of scientific biography. His greatest contribution was not a laboratory discovery or the engineering of intricate machinery but rather an answer to the existential question about whether or not human beings are capable of knowing themselves deeply and of trusting in the intrinsic value of their own experiences. His answer categorically was yes. It was his unusual method for trying to answer this question that inspired the scientific innovations for which he is known. Those innovations led to the formalization of a humanistic system that prized the healing power of individual freedom and self-determination. He achieved this unusual marriage of science and ethics by refashioning the fundamental tenets of scientific inquiry in his field. In 1959 he reminded his colleagues that:

> To observe acutely, to think carefully and creatively—these activities, not the accumulation of laboratory instruments, are the beginnings of science. To observe that a given crop grows better on the rocky hill than in the lush bottom land, and to think about this observation, is the start of science…. To recognize that, when a person's views of himself change, his behavior changes accordingly, and to puzzle over this, is again the beginning of both theory and science. I have raised this conviction in protest against the attitude, which seems too common in American psychology, that science starts in the laboratory or at the calculating machine. (p. 189)

Rogers's career spanned the era of mental hygiene (1930s) through the era of the encounter group and beyond (1980s). This biography emphasizes Rogers's scientific projects, which were concentrated in the years between 1940 and 1964. But his later work on behalf of humanistic causes was of equal if not greater consequence for him and was the primary reason for his international celebrity in the last thirty years of his life.

Early Life. Rogers was born in 1902 in Oak Park, Illinois, a suburb of Chicago, the fourth of six children of strict Protestant parents. He would later write about the "uncompromising religious and ethical atmosphere" of his parents' home, particularly their asceticism, strict work ethic, and daily prayers (1961, p. 5). Rogers's parents later moved the family to a farm outside Chicago in order that the isolation and physical demands of farm life would keep their children out of trouble. Rogers had few friends but felt satisfied in his close relationship with two brothers and in the pursuit of hobbies including reading, cultivating night-flying moths, and scientific agriculture. He

Carl R. Rogers. © ROGER RESSMEYER/CORBIS.

credited his early interest in agriculture with providing a "fundamental feeling for science" (1961, p. 6).

Rogers entered the University of Wisconsin, Madison, in 1919 intending to major in agriculture. He became a leader in the campus YMCA, however, and in 1922 was invited to join a Christian youth missionary expedition to China. The trip inspired him to settle on a vision of Christianity less strict and more compassionate than that of his parents and he decided to become a minister. He graduated in June 1924 and married Helen Elliott, a childhood friend, on 28 August 1924. In September 1924 he entered Union Theological Seminary in New York City. Their son David was born in 1926 and their daughter Natalie in 1928.

This period of Rogers's life exemplifies the trajectory of many young men with missionary zeal in the early 1900s. As Ian Nicholson has shown, he left behind small-town life with a mission to pursue the social gospel—to bring "Christ's way" to the social ills of the big city. Rogers discovered, however, that the life of a minister obliged

him to sustain a fixed belief system, the very thing he had tried to leave behind in Illinois. So after two years he changed direction once again and transferred across the street to Teacher's College, Columbia University, to enroll in the PhD program in clinical psychology.

Clinical psychology in the 1920s would have been a very attractive profession for a lapsed social-gospel seminarian, offering Rogers the mixture of moral purpose and intellectual freedom that the seminary had been unable to provide. Clinical psychologists specialized in psychological tests, and many of them used their expertise to try to improve the lives of the poor and destitute. Rogers's dissertation, under the supervision of Goodwin Watson, was one such test. Clinical psychologists also participated in the child guidance movement, a progressive-era mental-hygiene effort to prevent childhood delinquency by treating children of otherwise normal intelligence who were "maladjusted." Rogers studied with Leta Hollingworth, a leader in the child guidance movement, and interned at the new Institute for Child Guidance in 1927, where he studied with Lawson Lowrey and the psychoanalyst David Levy. Rogers was one of very few clinical psychologists at the time to train in psychotherapy. He completed his doctorate in 1931.

In 1928 Rogers moved to Rochester, New York, where he joined the Child Study Department of the Rochester Society for the Prevention of Cruelty to Children as a child psychologist. Rogers counseled delinquents and their parents with a variety of techniques including suggestion, emotional-release, play therapy, and interpretation. Unsatisfied with his success rate he became "infected" with the *relationship-therapy* of the American disciples of the psychoanalyst Otto Rank. Relationship-therapy suggested that therapeutic success could come simply from establishing a good relationship with the client. In 1939 he published *The Clinical Treatment of the Problem Child,* which brought him to the attention of psychologists at Ohio State University. He and his family moved to Columbus, Ohio, in 1940.

Client-Centered Therapy, 1940–1964. Rogers discovered in Rochester that his clients knew more about what they needed to work on in counseling than he did. So he shifted his clinical focus from advice-giving to listening. The more he listened, the more clients demonstrated repeatedly their capacity to guide themselves effectively in their own treatment. He began to experiment clinically with what he called a "nondirective approach" and first announced this method on 11 December 1940, at the University of Minnesota. Rogers (1942a) called it nondirective in contrast to the directive techniques in which he had been trained: "the nondirective viewpoint places a high value on the right of every individual to be psychologically independent and to maintain his psychological integrity. The directive viewpoint places a high value upon social conformity and the right of the more able to direct the less able" (p. 127). His academic position allowed him to begin studying experimentally these clinical hunches.

Scientific Advances. In the 1940s the quantitative science of psychotherapy was in its infancy. Clinical psychologists had not yet turned their practices toward psychotherapy. Psychiatrists (most of whom were psychoanalysts) disavowed the tools of experimental science, believing that scientific scrutiny of the analytic hour would violate the fundamental conditions of therapeutic success. It was only after World War II, when brief psychoanalytic therapies proved their effectiveness on the battlefield, that scientists in larger numbers began to conduct experimental studies on psychotherapy. Rogers was the first clinical psychologist to apply systematically the tools of psychometrics to the data of psychotherapy.

Rogers recognized that it would be impossible to quantify psychotherapeutic processes without obtaining firsthand accounts of what actually happened. Rogers and his graduate student Bernard Covner devised a way to record and transcribe not merely a single session but full courses of treatment. In 1942 Rogers published the first complete transcript of a counseling relationship—eight unedited interviews with an adult client named "Herbert Bryan." He used a numbering system to label each set of utterances of C (counselor) and S (subject):

C32. When you feel all right—you feel very much all right.

S32. Oh, yes, yes. Very dynamic—my mind works much more rapidly and everything's all right. Anything I try I do successfully.

C33. And what you want is to find ways of increasing the amount of time that you have that dynamic self, is that it?

S33. Oh, yes. Be that way all the time. I don't see any reason why I couldn't be. The whole thing is psychological, and I want to get at it. (1942a pp. 95–96)

Rogers's students William Snyder at Ohio State in 1945 and Julius Seeman at Chicago in 1949 published category systems based on the content and feelings of these client and counselor statements. Simple response categories for the content of the client's statements included, for instance:

YAI—Asking for advice or information

YAQ—Answer to a question

YAC—Simple acceptance or acquiescence to a clarification of feeling

YRS—Rejection of a clarification or interpretation (Seeman, 1949, p. 157)

Although Rogers felt isolated in his early academic career, he nonetheless enjoyed professional success. He was chairman of the clinical section of the American Association for Applied Psychology (AAAP) from 1942 to 1944, and president of the AAAP for the year 1944–1945. He also was president of the American Psychological Association (APA, 1946–1947) during a critical time of reorganization. Rogers's graduate students at Ohio State University went on to successful careers of their own, including the Catholic priest Charles Curran, Arthur Combs, and Nicholas Hobbs. During World War II he trained staff in the United Service Organization (USO) in counseling techniques with armed servicemen. This success led to an invitation from the University of Chicago to establish a new counseling center. Rogers and his family moved to Chicago in 1945.

A Systematic Theory of Client-Centered Therapy. During his twelve years in Chicago, Rogers and his research group transformed the nondirective approach into a formal system, renaming it client-centered therapy. It was his decision to conceptualize his new theory of psychotherapy and personality change in the language of science itself, such that by its very nature it could be tested empirically, that brought Rogers to the attention of many psychologists. In 1956 he won the first Distinguished Scientific Contribution Award from the American Psychological Association for "developing an original method to objectify the description and analysis of the psychotherapeutic process, for formulating a testable theory of psychotherapy and its effects on personality and behavior, and for extensive systematic research to exhibit the value of the method and explore and test the implications of the theory" (Melton, 1957, p. 128).

Rogers built around himself a vibrant and stimulating community of graduate students and colleagues. His students at Chicago developed a wide range of inventories to test even more sophisticated concepts about the process and outcome of client-centered therapy. A particular technique with which his group innovated was the British psychologist William Stephenson's Q-sort. In Rogers's adaptation of the Q-sort, subjects separated a pile of one hundred cards containing self-statements derived from client transcripts (such as "I am successful" or "I am worthless") into a normal distribution based on the degree to which the subject believed the statements applied to themselves. Subjects sorted the cards three times—first as the statements applied to themselves in reality, second as the statements applied to their "ideal" selves, and third

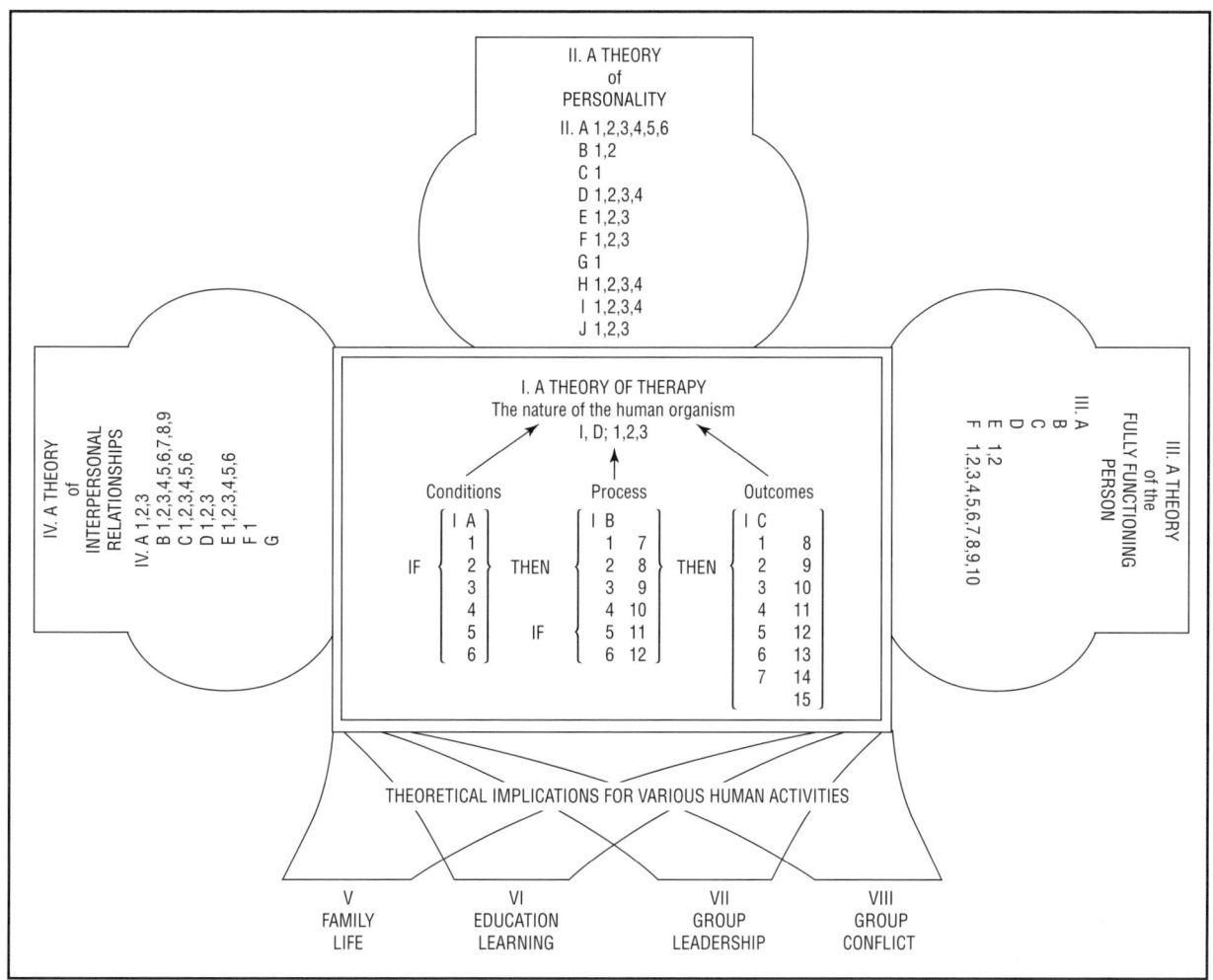

Figure 1. *Rogers's Theories of Therapy, Personality, and Interpersonal Relationships.*

as the statements would apply to an ordinary person. With Q-sorts the researchers tracked changes in how the subjects viewed themselves over the course of therapy, including whether or not their real and ideal selves were coming into *congruence*. They also examined changes in subjects' responses over the course of therapy on other personality inventories including the Rorschach inkblot, the Thematic Apperception Test (TAT), and the Minnesota Multiphasic Personality Inventory (MMPI). In 1949 seven of his students published projects in a special issue of the *Journal of Consulting Psychology* with data from the same ten cases. In 1954 Rogers and Rosalind Dymond edited a larger collection of studies, also conducted on a block of cases, which included a chapter explaining their research designs and two chapters on a successful case and a failed case in their research protocol.

Rogers presented the formal structure of the theory, based on his group's research findings, in a frequently cited 1957 article, "The Necessary and Sufficient Condi-

tions of Therapeutic Personality Change." He proposed that six conditions were necessary and sufficient for therapeutic personality change to occur—conditions that could be achieved regardless of the therapist's theoretical orientation and of the client's diagnosis:

1. Two persons are in psychological contact.

2. The first, whom we shall term the client, is in a state of incongruence, being vulnerable or anxious.

3. The second person, whom we shall term the therapist, is *congruent* or integrated in the relationship.

4. The therapist experiences *unconditional positive regard* for the client.

5. The therapist experiences an *empathic understanding* of the client's internal frame of reference and endeavors to communicate this experience to the client.

6. The communication to the client of the therapist's empathic understanding and unconditional positive regard is to a minimal degree achieved. (p. 96; emphases added)

In other words, Rogers proposed, a person in therapy automatically will move toward a greater integration of his real self and his experiences (congruence) in an environment in which the therapist is fully available (congruent), is accepting and warm (unconditional positive regard), and listens and responds with a desire to understand the client's feelings from the client's point of view (empathic listening).

In 1959 he recast these six conditions in an if-then formula for predicting the outcome of psychotherapy. He posited that if the aforementioned conditions were met then a predictable and automatic set of processes would result, which themselves would lead to a predictable and automatic set of changes in the client's personality (see Figure 1).

He made these statements in formalistic language suitable to empirical investigation. But he also ventured into more conceptually abstract territory, arguing that the human organism has an innate tendency toward growth (organismic valuing process) which is positive and constructive in nature and which automatically will guide the person under the right conditions:

> I believe it is obvious that the basic capacity which is hypothesized is of very decided importance in its psychological and philosophical implications. It means that psychotherapy is the releasing of an already existing capacity in a potentially competent individual, not the expert manipulation of a more or less passive personality. Philosophically it means that the individual has the capacity to guide, regulate, and control himself, providing only that certain definable conditions exist. Only in the absence of these conditions, and not in any basic sense, is it necessary to provide external control and regulation of the individual. (p. 221)

In 1957 Rogers accepted an invitation from the University of Wisconsin to join the psychology faculty with a cross-appointment in psychiatry. Throughout this period and beyond he was intrigued with exploring the limits of his new theory. He conducted a large study on the client-centered approach with schizophrenic inpatients at Mendota State Hospital. Rogers's student Eugene Gendlin joined him at Wisconsin as research director. For this study his student Charles Truax developed a rating scale for unconditional positive regard, and his student Donald Kiesler developed a rating scale for congruence. They published their results in 1967.

During the period from 1957 to 1964 Rogers was recognized with a number of honors and leadership positions including his election as Fellow of the American Academy of Arts and Sciences in 1961. APA Division 12 also honored him with an award for Distinguished Contributions to the Science and Profession of Clinical Psychology in 1962. His work also continued to flourish through the innovations of several former students from Chicago, including Gendlin's work on focusing at Chicago, John Shlien's work in education at Harvard University, and Laura Rice's work on client vocal quality at York University.

Person-Centered Therapy. Rogers moved to La Jolla, California, in 1964 to shift his focus once again. At the Western Behavioral Sciences Institute (WBSI) and after 1968 at the Center for the Study of the Person, which he cofounded, Rogers extended the client-centered approach to the group context. He renamed it the *person-centered approach* to emphasize its applicability not merely to people in therapy but to all human interactions. Rogers's school, along with that of Abraham Maslow, Rollo May, and others, became part of the "humanistic psychology" movement, a "third force" (as Maslow called it) distinct from behaviorism and psychoanalysis. He conducted countless encounter groups and wrote on such subjects as education, encounter groups, marriage, and personal essays on the past and future of client-centered therapy.

Back at Chicago, Rogers had begun to explore the links between his theory and the philosophies of Søren Kierkegaard and Martin Buber. This interest led to a public conversation with Buber on 18 April 1957, in Ann Arbor, Michigan, as well as dialogues with the Christian theologian Paul Tillich on 7 March 1965 and the philosopher of science Michael Polanyi in July 1966 at San Diego State University. He traveled extensively, promoting the person-centered approach as a tool for peace-making, and conducting workshops in the USSR, South Africa, Japan, Austria, and Central America.

Rogers also created a large and influential body of film and video recordings. His interview with a real client named Gloria, one of the *Three Approaches to Psychotherapy* film series, is particularly noteworthy. Rogers's ability to develop an intimate relationship with her in thirty minutes has been the subject of much scholarly discussion. A filmed encounter group he led with Richard Farson and produced by Bill McGaw, titled *Journey into Self,* won the 1968 Academy Award for Best Feature-Length Documentary. In addition Rogers made several films with McGaw for the Public Broadcasting System, including an encounter group with drug addicts, titled *Because That's My Way* (1971) and another with Protestants and

Catholics from Northern Ireland, titled *The Steel Shutter* (1973).

Conclusion. David Cohen has suggested that Rogers's later years, particularly in the years leading up to his wife Helen's death on 29 March 1979, were challenging. He portrays a man eager to loosen the constraints of his marriage at a time when his wife needed constant physical and psychological attention. He also shows, however, the close relationship between Rogers and his children, Rogers's continuing love of gardening, and his ambitious work schedule even up to his death. Rogers died from a heart attack following surgery for a fractured hip on 4 February 1987, at the age of eighty-five.

Rogers's belief in the fundamental trustworthiness of human nature was not just a scientific creed but a strident rejection of oppression wherever it might be found. He upheld it in a famous symposium with the behaviorist B. F. Skinner at the annual convention of the APA on 4 September 1956, and again with Skinner on 11 and 12 June 1962, at the University of Minnesota at Duluth. He also accused adherents of the doctrines of Christianity and psychoanalysis with making it impossible for individuals to reach their own conclusions about human nature:

> One of the most revolutionary concepts to grow out of our clinical experience is the growing recognition that the innermost core of man's nature, the deepest layers of his personality, the base of his "animal nature," is positive in character—is basically socialized, forward-moving, rational and realistic.
>
> This point of view is so foreign to our present culture that I do not expect it to be accepted. Religion, especially the Christian religion, has permeated our culture with the concept that man is basically sinful and that only by something approaching a miracle can his sinful nature be negated. In psychology, Freud and his followers have presented convincing arguments that the id, man's basic and unconscious nature, is primarily made up of instincts which would, if permitted expression, result in incest, murder, and other crimes. (1959, p. 256)

And in 1961 he even asked the general public to face his own theories with a healthy skepticism: "Neither the Bible nor the prophets—neither Freud nor research—neither the revelations of God nor man—can take precedence over my own direct experience" (p. 24). The client-centered approach in the end was a grand realization of his youthful leanings toward both the social gospel and science—a philosophy of self-determination inspired by the methods of scientific inquiry.

Not all psychologists approved of Rogers's unorthodox scientific approach. His critics accused him of mysticism and fanaticism and of hurting the field's efforts to achieve a viable science of psychotherapy research. In the 1970s the rise of experimentally sophisticated behavior therapies drew scientific attention away from those Rogerians who remained in the academy. Nevertheless, Rogers's research techniques and his clinical acumen influenced the practices of a wide variety of disciplines including sociology, social work, counseling psychology, pastoral counseling, education, and business. Client-centered therapy also made its mark on the computer—that most impersonal of technologies. Joseph Weizenbaum of the Massachusetts Institute of Technology emulated Rogerian empathic responses in a 1966 demonstration of natural language processes with an interactive computer program named ELIZA. ELIZA generated such a great demand for computer therapy that Weizenbaum, dismayed at how easily humans anthropomorphized the computer, devoted the rest of his career to critiquing artificial intelligence. If imitation is the best form of flattery, the ELIZA affair made clear that whatever the truth of Rogers's scientific critics, the ubiquity of the Rogerian way in mid-twentieth-century American life could never have been in doubt.

BIBLIOGRAPHY

Archival sources include the Carl R. Rogers Collection, 1902–1990, University of California–Santa Barbara Library, Department of Special Collections, available from http://www.oac.cdlib.org/findaid/ark:/13030/tf2f59n977; and the Papers of Carl R. Rogers, 1913–1989 (bulk 1960–1987), Archival Manuscript Collection, Library of Congress. "Carl Rogers.info" is the best source for comprehensive bibliography as well as Web-streaming videos of Rogers's teaching and research, available from http://www.carlrogers.info/.

WORKS BY ROGERS

The Clinical Treatment of the Problem Child. Boston: Houghton Mifflin, 1939.

Counseling and Psychotherapy: Newer Concepts in Practice. Boston: Houghton Mifflin, 1942a. Includes "The Case of Herbert Bryan."

"The Use of Electrically Recorded Interviews in Improving Psychotherapeutic Techniques." *American Journal of Orthopsychiatry* 12 (1942b): 429–434. Reprinted in *Carl Rogers Reader* (1989), pp. 211–218.

"A Coordinated Research in Psychotherapy: A Non-Objective Introduction." *Journal of Consulting Psychology* 13 (1949): 149–153.

Client-Centered Therapy: Its Current Practice, Implications, and Theory. With chapters contributed by Elaine Dorfman, Thomas Gordon, and Nicholas Hobbs. Boston: Houghton Mifflin, 1951.

With Rosalind F. Dymond, eds. *Psychotherapy and Personality Change: Co-ordinated Research Studies in the Client-Centered*

Approach. Chicago: University of Chicago Press, 1954. Useful collection of studies and explanation of scientific procedures.

"Some Issues Concerning the Control of Human Behavior (Symposium with B. F. Skinner)." *Science* 124 (1956): 1057–1066.

"The Necessary and Sufficient Conditions of Therapeutic Personality Change." *Journal of Consulting Psychology* 21, no. 2 (1957): 95–103. Reprinted in *Carl Rogers Reader* (1989), pp. 219–235.

"A Theory of Therapy, Personality, and Interpersonal Relationships, as Developed in the Client-Centered Framework." In *Psychology: A Study of a Science.* Vol. 3, *Formulations of the Person and the Social Context,* edited by Sigmund Koch, 184–256. New York: McGraw-Hill, 1959. Highly technical but very influential in his field.

"Client-Centered Therapy." In *American Handbook of Psychiatry.* Vol. 3, edited by Silvano Arieti, 183–200. New York: Basic Books, 1959–1966. Reprinted in *Carl Rogers: Dialogues,* (1989) pp. 9–35. Excellent introduction for beginners.

On Becoming a Person: A Therapist's View of Psychotherapy. Boston: Houghton Mifflin, 1961. Collection of essays and talks. Good bibliography through 1960.

Client-Centered Therapy. Film no. 1 in *Three Approaches to Psychotherapy.* Edited by E. Shostrom. Three 16mm color motion pictures. Orange, CA: Psychological Films, 1965. Worth viewing if you can find it.

"Autobiography." In *A History of Psychology in Autobiography.* Vol. 5, edited by Edwin G. Boring and Gardner Lindzey, 343–384. New York: Appleton-Century-Crofts, 1967. Very good introduction to his life.

With Eugene T. Gendlin, Donald J. Kiesler, and Charles B. Truax, eds. *The Therapeutic Relationship and Its Impact: A Study of Psychotherapy with Schizophrenics.* Madison: University of Wisconsin Press, 1967.

A Way of Being. Boston: Houghton Mifflin, 1980. Another excellent collection of essays.

Carl Rogers—Dialogues: Conversations with Martin Buber, Paul Tillich, B. F. Skinner, Gregory Bateson, Michael Polanyi, Rollo May, and Others. Edited by Howard Kirschenbaum and Valerie Land Henderson. Boston: Houghton Mifflin, 1989. Edited collection of Rogers's public conversations with philosophers and theologians. Excellent for beginners.

The Carl Rogers Reader. Edited by Howard Kirschenbaum and Valerie Land Henderson. Boston: Houghton Mifflin, 1989. Edited collection of Rogers's most important essays. Excellent for beginners.

OTHER SOURCES

Cohen, David. *Carl Rogers: A Critical Biography.* London: Constable, 1997. Not suitable for beginners.

DeCarvalho, Roy J. "Otto Rank, the Rankian Circle in Philadelphia, and the Origins of Carl Rogers' Person-Centered Psychotherapy." *History of Psychology* 2 (1999): 132–148.

Hall, Calvin, Gardner Lindzey, John C. Loehlin, et al. *Introduction to Theories of Personality.* New York: Wiley, 1985. Chapter 6, "Holism and Humanism: Abraham Maslow and

Carl Rogers," is an excellent introduction to the science of client-centered therapy.

Hayashi, Sachiko, Toru Kuno, Yoshihiko Morotomi, et al. "Client-Centered Therapy in Japan: Fujio Tomoda and Taoism." *Journal of Humanistic Psychology* 38 (1998): 103–124.

Kirschenbaum, Howard. *On Becoming Carl Rogers.* New York: Delacorte, 1979. Good for beginners but does not include years 1979–1987. Includes photographs.

Melton, Arthur W. "The American Psychological Association Distinguished Scientific Contribution Awards for 1956." *American Psychologist* (1957): 125–133.

Nicholson, Ian. "From the Kingdom of God to the Beloved Community, 1920–1930: Psychology and the Social Gospel in the Work of Goodwin Watson and Carl Rogers." *Journal of Psychology and Theology* 22 (1994): 196–206.

Rice, Laura N., and Leslie S. Greenberg. "Humanistic Approaches to Psychotherapy." In *History of Psychotherapy: A Century of Change,* edited by Donald K. Freedheim, 197–224. Washington, DC: American Psychological Association, 1992. Good summary of Rogers's work in context of humanistic psychology movement.

Seeman, Julius. "A Study of the Process of Nondirective Therapy." *Journal of Consulting Psychology* 13, no. 3 (1949): 157–168.

Sterner, William H. "Symbolic Demeaning: The Loss of Meaning in Human-Computer Communication." Unpublished 1998 essay that is a very informative analysis of ELIZA with actual transcripts of therapy sessions from Rogers and Eugene Gendlin. Available from http://www.billsterner.cs.uchicago.edu/eliza.pdf.

Thorne, Brian. *Carl Rogers.* London: Sage, 1992. Part of the Sage collection of biographies of influential psychotherapists. Straightforward summary of work and influence.

Weizenbaum, Joseph. "ELIZA: A Computer Program for the Study of Natural Language Communication between Man and Machine." 1966 article on ELIZA. Available from http://i5.nyu.edu/~mm64/x52.9265/january1966.html.

Rachael I. Rosner

ROSSI, BRUNO BENEDETTO (*b.* Venice, Italy, 13 April 1905; *d.* Cambridge, Massachusetts, 21 November 1993), *physics, space science.*

Rossi was a pioneer in the experimental investigation of cosmic rays and the properties of the new unstable particles produced in the interactions of cosmic rays with matter. In the early days of space research he initiated the research programs that led to direct measurements of the ionized gas in interplanetary space and to the beginning of extrasolar x-ray astronomy.

Rossi was born in Venice, the eldest of three sons of Lina Minerbi and Rino Rossi. In his autobiography (1990, p. 1) Rossi attributed to his father, an electrical engineer involved in the electrification of Venice, the influence that turned what may have been an "inborn tendency toward science … into a lifelong commitment." After schooling in Venice, Rossi studied for two years at the University of Padua, and another two years at the University of Bologna from which he received the doctoral degree in physics. In 1928 he took up his first appointment as assistant at the University of Florence in the Institute of Physics located on the hill of Arcetri overlooking the city. After a year of searching for a suitable research topic that he could pursue within the limited resources of the Institute, Rossi found it in cosmic rays.

At that time, the only known "fundamental" particles were the negative electron, the positive proton, and the neutral photon. The highest energy particles available for experiments were emitted in the decay of radioactive elements with energies of no more than a few million electron volts. There was also the mysterious "Höhenstrahlung," the "radiation from above" that had been discovered by Viktor Hess in 1912. In the 1920s Robert Millikan took up the study of the radiation from above, which he dubbed "cosmic rays." From extensive measurements with ionization chambers of cosmic ray intensities under water and in the atmosphere, Millikan concluded that cosmic rays were ultrahigh energy gamma rays produced from the energy released in the formation of atoms by fusion of hydrogen in interstellar space.

To the limited extent that Rossi had thought about cosmic rays before 1928 he had accepted the conventional wisdom that they were gamma rays, though he doubted Millikan's theory of their origin. He was apparently not yet aware of the recent discoveries of Jacob Clay and Dmitry Skobelzyn that contradicted Millikan's ideas. However, in 1929 Rossi read the paper of Walther Bothe and Werner Kohlhörster describing an experiment that showed that cosmic rays contain charged particles capable of penetrating large thicknesses of dense matter. The experiment employed two inventions that would transform experimental cosmic-ray and particle physics, namely the "discharge counter," recently invented by Hans Geiger and Wilhelm Müller, and the "coincidence method" invented by Bothe. In their experiment, Bothe and Kohlhörster found that two parallel counters surrounded by thick shielding of lead and iron and separated by several centimeters in a vertical plane were occasionally discharged in coincidence by the passage of a charged particle through the shield and the two counters. They detected such events by attaching the counters to separate fiber electrometers and photographing on a moving film the deflections of the fibers caused by discharges of the counters. They found that the rate of coincidences decreased by only a small fraction when a 4.1 centimeter thick gold brick was inserted between the two counters,

Bruno Rossi. AP IMAGES.

clear proof of the high energy and penetrating power of the detected particles.

In his autobiography (p. 10) Rossi wrote that the Bothe-Kohlhörster paper opened "a field of inquiry rich in mystery and promises. Working in a field of this kind had been my dream." Rossi fabricated Geiger-Müller counters according to the published description and powered them with a bank of batteries. And he invented the electronic "coincidence circuit" to register the occurrence of coincident pulses from two or more counters. His novel circuit could be adapted to register coincidences among any number of counters, and it achieved a much shorter resolving time than the mechanical coincidence method employed by Bothe and Kohlhörster. The coincidence circuit was an essential device in all of Rossi's cosmic-ray experiments, and was rapidly adopted by experimenters around the world.

During a brief visit to Bothe's Berlin laboratory in the summer of 1930, Rossi learned about the mathematical theory of Carl Störmer regarding the motion of charged particles in a dipole magnetic field similar to that of Earth. Rossi perceived in the complex theory a simple and observable consequence that would permit an experimental determination of the sign of the electric charge carried by the primary cosmic rays that arrive from outer space. In a letter to the *Physical Review* he predicted a difference between the intensities of cosmic rays arriving from the east and the west depending on the sign of their charge. Back at Arcetri he attempted to measure the "east-west effect" with a cosmic-ray telescope consisting of two parallel counters mounted several centimeters apart on a swivel base and connected to his coincidence circuit. Failing to obtain a statistically certain difference between the coincidence rates with the telescope pointed east and west, Rossi began plans for an expedition to a mountain site at low geomagnetic latitude where, according to the theory, the east-west difference at ground level would be much larger.

In an introductory talk on cosmic rays at the Rome conference on nuclear physics in the fall of 1931, Rossi explained how recent discoveries had disproved Millikan's theory about the nature and origin of cosmic rays. Both Arthur Compton and Millikan were in the audience. In his autobiography (p. 18) Rossi wrote that Millikan was not pleased by the demolition of his theory and that "from that moment on he refused to recognize my existence." Rossi also wrote that years later Compton told him "his interest in cosmic rays was born from my presentation."

In a series of coincidence experiments with various arrangements of counters and absorbers, Rossi demonstrated that the local cosmic rays contain a component that is rapidly attenuated in dense matter by interactions that produce showers of secondary particles. His report on this phenomenon was so astonishing at the time that it was refused for publication by the first journal to which he submitted it, and accepted by another only after Werner Heisenberg vouched for Rossi's reliability. It was confirmed the following year by Patrick Blackett and Giuseppe Occhialini who published photographs of particle showers in a cloud chamber whose expansions were triggered by the signal from a Rossi coincidence circuit connected to an arrangement of Geiger-Müller counters. The idea for counter control of a cloud chamber had been brought to Blackett's laboratory by Occhialini, who was Rossi's first student at Arcetri. The showers were soon identified as cascades of photons, electrons, and positrons, and Rossi's measurements of their growth and attenuation in matter provided an early test of the cascade shower theory based on the new quantum electrodynamics.

In another experiment, Rossi demonstrated that there are cosmic-ray particles that can penetrate more than one meter of lead with an energy loss by ionization in excess of 2 billion electron volts. In 1936–1937 experiments at the California Institute of Technology and at Harvard proved that these penetrating particles have a mass between the electron and the proton. They were initially called mesotrons, and are now called muons.

In the fall of 1932, having won a competition for a university position, Rossi was called to the University of Padua as professor of experimental physics. There, in addition to research and teaching, he was responsible for planning and supervising the construction of a new Physics Institute of which he became the director. At Padua Rossi finally found time to test his prediction of the east-west effect in an experiment that he carried out in the fall of 1933 near the town of Asmara in the Italian colony of Eritrea. He found the intensity of penetrating particles was about 20 percent greater from the west than the east, which proved that the primary cosmic rays that arrive from outer space are particles with positive charge. Essentially identical results were obtained in two experiments carried out a few months earlier at Mexico City by Thomas Johnson and by Luis Alvarez and Arthur Compton. After World War II, direct observations by various groups, using detectors carried to great altitudes by balloons, proved that the primary cosmic rays are indeed positive and that they consist of protons and the bare nuclei of helium and heavier elements.

During tests of his equipment at Asmara, Rossi discovered particle showers that are initiated high in the atmosphere by ultrahigh energy primary cosmic rays and are spread over wide areas when they arrive at ground level. He wrote about it in his autobiography (p. 36), and provided a translation of a portion of his report on the Eritrean expedition:

> it seems that once in a while the recording equipment is struck by *very extensive showers* of particles, which cause coincidences between counters, even placed at large distances from one another. Unfortunately, I did not have the time to study this phenomenon more closely.

These particle showers came to be called "extensive air showers" to distinguish them from the particle showers produced locally in interactions of cosmic rays with condensed matter. Pierre Auger published the first detailed study of extensive air showers in 1937. Measurements of extensive air showers would eventually provide the means for determining the energies and arrival directions of the highest-energy primary cosmic rays. After the war they were a major topic of research by Rossi's group at the Massachusetts Institute of Technology (MIT) and by others at laboratories around the world.

In April 1938 Rossi married Nora Lombroso, daughter of Silvia Forti and Ugo Lombroso, professor of physiology at the University of Genoa. The following September, Rossi was dismissed from his position as a result of the anti-Jewish decrees of the fascist government. The Rossis managed to obtain passports and left Italy in October. They were welcomed, first by Niels Bohr at his institute in Copenhagen, and then at Manchester University by Patrick Blackett, who had obtained for Rossi a fellowship from the Society for the Preservation of Science and Culture. During this sojourn Rossi began to focus his attention on the experimental problem of testing the stability of mesotrons.

In the spring of 1939 Rossi accepted an invitation from Arthur Compton to attend a July conference on cosmic rays at the University of Chicago. The Rossis arrived in New York in June. After a brief visit with the Fermis, already established at Columbia University, they drove with Hans Bethe to Chicago. The expected instability of mesotrons was a principal topic of the conference. Afterward, during a visit to the Comptons' summer cottage, Rossi presented to Arthur Compton his idea for a definitive experiment on mesotron decay based on a comparison between the attenuation of the intensity of the penetrating component of cosmic rays in air and in an equivalent amount of graphite. With Compton's encouragement and support, Rossi prepared and carried out the experiment on Mount Evans in Colorado before the winter set in. The experiment proved that mesotrons decay in flight with a lifetime of the order of microseconds.

In the fall of 1940, on the recommendation of Bethe, a member of the physics faculty at Cornell University, Rossi was appointed associate professor of physics at Cornell. There, with a graduate student, Norris Nereson, he made a precise measurement of the mean life of mesotrons at rest, the first such measurement of an unstable subatomic particle. For that work they invented an electronic time-to-amplitude converter of which various versions have since been widely used in nuclear and particle physics.

During World War II Rossi worked first as a part-time consultant on instrumentation for radar development at the Radiation Laboratory of the Massachusetts Institute of Technology. Then, in the late spring of 1943, he joined the atomic bomb project at Los Alamos, New Mexico, where he was responsible, with Hans Staub, for development of detectors for nuclear experiments. Among their inventions was the "fast ionization chamber." Rossi used it in various experiments including a series of tests that validated the implosion method for detonating the plutonium bomb and in a measurement of the exponential growth of the chain reaction in the test of the first plutonium bomb at Trinity. Rossi remained at Los Alamos for a year after the end of the war to complete with Staub a treatise on the instruments their group had developed.

In the fall of 1946 Rossi came to MIT where he established the Cosmic Ray Group to carry out research on the greatly increased scale made possible by the new availability of government support and the recent advances in technology. In these new circumstances, as professor of physics responsible for teaching and for leading a large group of students and senior coworkers, Rossi changed his mode of operation. In his autobiography he wrote:

[Previously], working alone or, at most, with the help of a few students, I would build the instruments needed for my experiments, I would take them to the place where they had to be used, I would make the measurements and analyze the results. Now I had the responsibility of an entire group, and what mattered was no longer my own work but the work of the group. In the first place my task was to identify the most promising research programs among those that were within our reach. I had then to help where help was needed in the planning of the instrumentation and evaluation of the experimental results, all of this without discouraging the individual initiative of the researchers. (p. 101)

Under Rossi's leadership, the Cosmic Ray Group carried out a wide variety of investigations aimed at determining the properties of the primary cosmic rays, elucidating the processes involved in their propagation through the atmosphere, and measuring the unstable particles generated in the interactions of cosmic rays with matter. Among these investigations was an experiment carried to a high altitude by a cluster of balloons that placed an upper limit of 1 percent on the proportion of electrons and photons in the primary cosmic rays. Experiments with a multiplate cloud chamber yielded early evidence for the neutral pion and its decay into a pair of gamma rays, measurements of the properties of kaons and hyperons, and the first direct observation of the annihilation of an antiproton. Studies of extensive air showers determined the energy spectrum of the primary cosmic rays in the range from 10^{15} to 10^{20} electron volts.

In 1958, when cosmic-ray phenomena were well understood and experiments at particle accelerators had come to dominate particle physics, Rossi's interests turned to the new opportunities for exploratory investigations made possible by the availability of space vehicles. At MIT he initiated a program aimed at measuring the properties of the ionized gas (plasma) in interplanetary space that would eventually extend to the farthest reaches of the solar system. In 1961, an MIT "plasma probe," carried on the spacecraft *Explorer 10*, yielded the first direct measurement of the density, speed and direction of the solar wind at the boundary of Earth's magnetosphere.

In the same period, Rossi inspired the program in x-ray astronomy at American Science and Engineering, Inc., (AS&E) a small research and development company founded in 1958 by his former student, Martin Annis, and for which Rossi served as scientific consultant and chairman of the board. Riccardo Giacconi, a former student of Occhialini at the University of Milan, had recently been hired by Annis to develop a program in space science at the new company. At Rossi's suggestion, Giacconi began a study of the possibilities for x-ray astronomy that led to a series of AS&E rocket experiments, sponsored by the U.S. Air Force. After two failures, the third experiment, launched in June 1962, discovered the first extrasolar source of x-rays that came to be called Sco X-1. AS&E took the lead for many years in developing x-ray astronomy with the support of the National Aeronautics and Space Administration. This new field of astronomy proved to be an essential source of information about neutron stars, black holes, and the high-energy processes in the universe.

Rossi was an inspiring teacher, speaker, and writer. In 1965 he was appointed Institute Professor, the highest honor given to members of the MIT faculty. Among his many other honors were memberships in the National Academy of Sciences, the American Academy of Arts and Sciences, and the Academia Nazionale dei Lincei of Rome. His awards included the Gold Medal of the Italian Physical Society, the U.S. National Medal of Science and honorary doctorates from the universities of Durham, Palermo, and Chicago. The 1987 Wolf Prize in Physics for the development of x-ray astronomy was awarded jointly to Rossi, Riccardo Giacconi, and Herbert Friedman, the latter having pioneered the study of solar x-rays at the U.S. Naval Research Laboratory in the 1950s. After his official retirement in 1970, Rossi remained active for many years as an advisor and commentator on interplanetary plasma research and x-ray astronomy, and in the preparation of his scientific autobiography.

Bruno Rossi died at his home in Cambridge, Massachusetts, on 21 November 1993. He was survived by his wife; three children, Florence, Frank, and Linda; and three grandchildren. His ashes lie under a monument in the graveyard of the church of San Miniato al Monte, overlooking the city of Florence and across a valley from the hill of Arcetri, where he began his scientific career.

BIBLIOGRAPHY

WORKS BY ROSSI

"Method of Registering Multiple Simultaneous Impulses of Several Geiger Counters." *Nature* 125 (1930): 636.

"On the Magnetic Deflection of Cosmic Rays." Letter. *Physical Review* 36 (1930): 606.

"Uber die Eigenschaften der durchdringenden Korpuskularstrahlung in Meeresniveau." *Zeitschrift für Physik* 82 (1933): 151–178.

"Directional Measurement on the Cosmic Rays near the Geomagnetic Equator." *Physical Review* 45 (1934): 212–214.

"I risultati della Missione scientifica in Eritrea per lo studio della radiazione penetrante." *La Ricerca Scientifica* 5, no. 1 (1934): 559–605.

With L. Pincherle. *Rayons Cosmiques*. Paris: Hermann & Co., 1935.

Lezione di fisica sperimentale elettrologia. Padova, Italy: CEDAM, 1936.

With Norman Hilberry and J. Barton Hoag. "The Variation of the Hard Component of Cosmic Rays with Height and the Disintegration of Mesotrons." *Physical Review* 57 (1940): 461–469.

With Norris Nereson. "Further Measurements on the Disintegration Curve of Mesotrons." *Physical Review* 64 (1 and 15 October 1943): 199–201.

———. "Experimental Arrangement for the Measurement of Small Time Intervals between the Discharges of Geiger-Müller Counters." *Review of Scientific Instruments* 17 (1946): 65–71.

With Robert I. Hulsizer. "Search for Electrons in the Primary Cosmic Radiation." Letter. *Physical Review* 73 (1948): 1402–1403.

With Hans Staub. *Ionization Chambers and Counters*. New York: McGraw-Hill, 1949.

With B. P. Gregory and J. H. Tinlot. "Production of Gamma-Rays in Nuclear Interactions of Cosmic Rays." Letter. *Physical Review* 77 (1950): 299–300.

High-Energy Particles. New York: Prentice-Hall, 1952.

With H. S. Bridge, C. Peyrou, and R. Safford, "Cloud-Chamber Observations of the Heavy Charged Unstable Particles in Cosmic Rays." *Physical Review* 90 (1953): 921–933.

With H. S. Bridge, H. Courant, and H. DeStabler Jr. "Possible Example of the Annihilation of a Heavy Particle." *Physical Review* 95 (1954): 1101–1103.

Optics. Reading, MA: Addison-Wesley, 1957.

With G. Clark, J. Earl, W. Kraushaar, et al. "Cosmic-Ray Air Showers at Sea Level." *Physical Review* 122 (1961): 637–654.

With John Linsley and Livio Scarsi. "Extremely Energetic Cosmic-Ray Event." *Physical Review Letters* 6 (1961): 485–487.

With Riccardo Giacconi, Herbert Gursky, and Frank R. Paolini. "Evidence for X Rays from Sources outside the Solar System." *Physical Review Letters* 9 (1962): 439–443.

With A. Bonetti, H. S. Bridge, A. J. Lazarus, and F. Scherb. "*Explorer 10* Plasma Measurements." *Journal of Geophysical Research* 68 (1963): 4017–4063.

Cosmic Rays. New York: McGraw-Hill, 1964.

With Stanislaw Olbert. *Introduction to the Physics of Space*. New York: McGraw-Hill, 1970.

Moments in the Life of a Scientist. Cambridge, U.K.: Cambridge University Press, 1990. His autobiography.

OTHER SOURCES

Blackett, P. M. S., and G. P. S. Occhialini. "Some Photographs of the Tracks of Penetrating Radiation." *Proceedings of the Royal Society of London. Series A* 139 (1933): 699–726.

Bothe, W., and W. Kohlhörster. "Das Wesen der Höhenstrahlung." *Zeitschrift für Physik* 56 (1929): 751–777.

Brown, Laurie M., and Lillian Hoddeson. *The Birth of Particle Physics*. Cambridge, U.K.: Cambridge University Press, 1983.

Clay, J. "Penetrating Radiation." *Proceedings Royal Academy Amsterdam* 30 (1927): 1115–1127.

Hess, Viktor F. "Uber Beobachtungen der durchdringenden Strahlung bei sieben Freiballonfahrten." *Physikalische Zeitschrift* 13 (1912): 1084–1091.

Hoddeson, Lillian, Paul W. Henriksen, Roger A. Meade, et al. *Critical Assembly: A Technical History of Los Alamos during the Oppenheimer Years, 1943–1945*. New York: Cambridge University Press, 1993.

Millikan, R. A., and G. H. Cameron. "The Origin of the Cosmic Rays." *Physical Review* 32 (1928): 533–557.

Sekido, Y., and H. Elliot, eds. *Early History of Cosmic Ray Studies: Personal Reminiscences with Old Photographs*. Dordrecht, Netherlands: Reidel Publishing Co., 1985.

Skobelzyn, D., "Über eine neue Art sehr schneller b-Strahlen." *Zeitschrift für Physik* 54 (1929): 686–702.

Tucker, Wallace, and Riccardo Giacconi. *The X-Ray Universe*. Cambridge, MA: Harvard University Press, 1985.

George W. Clark

ROTA, GIAN-CARLO (*b.* Vigevano, Italy, 27 April 1932; *d.* Cambridge, Massachusetts, 18 April 1999), *mathematics, combinatorics.*

Rota is widely regarded as the founder of modern combinatorics. He was the spearhead of a movement that transformed combinatorics from a lightly regarded bag of tricks to a unified and deep discipline with profound connections to other areas of mathematics.

Life History. Rota was the son of Giovanni Rota, a civil engineer and architect, and Gina Facsetti Rota. Giovanni Rota was a prominent antifacist who had to flee Italy in 1945 to escape Benito Mussolini's death squads. The remarkable story of his family's escape is recounted by Gian-Carlo Rota's sister Ester Rota Gasperoni in the two books *Orage sur le lac* and *L'arbre des capulies*. Rota ended up completing his secondary school education in Ecuador. As a result of his escape, Rota was fluent in English, Italian, Spanish, and French.

In 1950 Rota entered Princeton University and graduated summa cum laude in 1953. He then attended graduate school at Yale University, receiving a master's degree in mathematics in 1954 and a PhD in 1956 under the supervision of Jacob T. Schwartz. After graduating from Yale, Rota married Teresa Rondón (whom he subsequently divorced in 1980) and received a postdoctoral research fellowship from the Courant Institute at New York University. The next academic year Rota became a Benjamin Peirce Instructor at Harvard University and in 1959 accepted a position at the Massachusetts Institute of Technology (MIT). Except for a two-year hiatus (1965–1967) at Rockefeller University, Rota remained at MIT for the rest of his career. His honors and achievements include the Colloquium Lectures of the American Mathematical Society (1998), election to the National

Academy of Sciences (1982), the Leroy P. Steele Prize for Seminal Contribution to Research (1988), vice president of the American Mathematical Society (1995–1997), four honorary degrees, and the supervision of forty-two PhD students. He held numerous consulting positions, including a fruitful association with Los Alamos Scientific Laboratory beginning in 1966. He died unexpectedly in his sleep at his home in Cambridge on 18 April 1999.

The Foundations of Combinatorics. Rota was originally trained in functional analysis, and his early work was in this area. In the early 1960s he became interested in combinatorics, then a rather seedy and disreputable backwater of mathematics. Combinatorics is concerned with the arrangement of discrete objects and looks at such problems as the existence of an arrangement, the number or approximate number of arrangements, relations among the different arrangements, and the "optimal" arrangement according to given criteria. In general, the definitions involved are easy to understand, and the arrangements have little (obvious) internal structure. For this reason, combinatorics was not regarded by most mathematicians as a serious subject. Rota had the vision to realize that combinatorics had tremendous potential for elucidating and extending other areas of mathematics. He was able to recognize intuitively many problems to which combinatorics could be unexpectedly applied. In doing so, he became the founder of the movement that lifted the subject of combinatorics to its current position as a major branch of mathematics.

Hermann Weyl has described Arthur Cayley's development of invariant theory as "[coming] into existence somewhat like Minerva: a grown-up virgin, mailed in the shining armor of algebra, she sprang forth from Cayley's jovian head." A similar statement could be made about the work of Rota on the foundations of combinatorics. Though led into combinatorics by his work on functional analysis, Rota's work on combinatorics was from the beginning a completely fresh combination of innovation and synthesis. His first paper in this area, published in 1964, had the characteristically audacious title "On the Foundations of Combinatorial Theory I: Theory of Möbius Functions." This paper was the first in a series of ten seminal "Foundations" papers that transformed the field of combinatorics.

The Möbius function of a partially ordered set, the subject of Rota's first "Foundations" papers, was originally defined by Louis Weisner and later Philip Hall as a tool for obtaining inversion formulas. Rota realized that this rather specialized and arcane topic had tremendous potential to unify, clarify, and generalize many apparently disparate combinatorial topics, including the calculus of finite differences, the principle of inclusion-exclusion, set partitions, generating functions, and matroid theory. This paper also inaugurated the burgeoning subject of topological combinatorics.

Subsequent papers in the "Foundations" series, with various coauthors, developed a unified theory of generating functions, a theory of operator calculus, a rigorous foundation of the classical "umbral calculus," and a revival of the nineteenth-century subject of invariant theory. "Foundations" IV and V, written jointly with Jay Goldman and George Andrews, foresaw what is now a thriving cottage industry within mathematics and mathematical physics—the theory of q-analogues (or in more stylish terminology, "quantum mathematics").

Invariant Theory. Invariant theory remained a subject dear to Rota's heart for the remainder of his career. Simply, invariant theory is concerned with properties of mathematical objects, especially polynomials that are preserved by certain transformations. For instance, the polynomial x^2 is preserved by substituting $-x$ for x (a simple example). This preservation of properties is intimately related to an object's symmetry, a major theme in present-day mathematics and the physical sciences. Work of many nineteenth- and twentieth-century mathematicians had shown that invariant theory has deep connections with algebra and geometry. Much ad hoc combinatorics was involved in this work, but the combinatorial aspects of invariant theory had not been adequately developed or systematized.

"Foundations" IX (with Peter Doubilet and Joel Stein) was his first of more than twenty papers in invariant theory. This paper began the development of a simple and powerful method to extend Weyl's work on vector invariants of the classical groups to the characterstic p case. The basis for this work was a symbolism for the product of minors called bitableaux, together with a "straightening algorithm" to express any bitableau in terms of special ones called standard. This work later found a host of applications, such as the proof by Edward Formanek and Claudio Procesi, that the general linear group is geometrically reductive and the proof by Klaus Pommerening that certain rings of invariants are finitely generated. The techniques of straightening were later applied to such topics as resolutions of determinantal ideals in characteristic p (Kaan Akin and David Buchsbaum), the Robinson-Schensted-Knuth algorithm (B. Leclerc and J. Y. Thibon), and the development of the notion of an "algebra with straightening law" (Corrado De Concini and David Eisenbud, and independently Baclawski).

In another direction related to invariant theory, Rota developed the classical "symbolic method" into a powerful tool for doing computations in invariant theory. He extended his methods to the "letterplace (super)algebra" (based on a suggestion by Richard Feynman) and to skew-symmetric tensors. Rota also showed that the use of super-algebras allows Capelli's method of auxiliary variables to be extended to deal with symmetry and skew-symmetry in a uniform way.

Other Activities. Rota had many academic activities not directly related to his research. He had a passionate interest in phenomenology and regularly taught courses and wrote papers in this area. His philosophy courses were the most popular in that subject at MIT, though he taught outside the Department of Linguistics and Philosophy and received no teaching credit for his efforts. He was in general an extremely popular teacher and advisor of undergraduate and graduate students at MIT. This commitment to students was a major factor in his receiving in 1996 the James R. Killian Faculty Achievement Award at MIT. Rota was also a bon vivant who loved to entertain all with whom he came in contact; he was exceptionally generous not only with his pocketbook, but also with his time and his ideas.

Although English was not Rota's native language, he regularly wrote essays and reviews with a masterful ear for English and with a surpassing clarity, incisiveness, and wit. The subjects of these essays ranged from mathematics and philosophy to personal reminisces centering on the human aspects of mathematicians he had known. Many of these essays are collected in the books *Discrete Thoughts* (coauthored with Mark Kac and Jacob Schwartz) and *Indiscrete Thoughts.*

Rota's long and fruitful association with the Los Alamos National Laboratory began after meeting Stan Ulam in 1964. Rota rapidly became a significant member of the Los Alamos community and was appointed Director's Office Fellow in 1971. He was involved in a wide range of activities there, including collaboration, lectures, and politicking. He developed many deep friendships, especially with Ulam, whose strengths and imperfections he understood perfectly.

Rota was a founding editor in 1966 of the *Journal of Combinatorial Theory*, the first journal devoted entirely to combinatorics. Forty years later, there are over a dozen such journals, attesting to the tremendous growth of the field since Rota entered it. In 1967 Rota took over the faltering Academic Press journal *Advances in Mathematics* and remained in charge of the journal until his death. He single-handedly built *Advances* into a leading research journal, known especially for its eclectic content. A popular feature of *Advances* was Rota's book reviews, which managed to convey the essence of a complicated mathematics book in a few trenchant sentences.

BIBLIOGRAPHY

WORKS BY ROTA

"On the Foundations of Combinatorial Theory I: Theory of Möbius Functions." *Zeitschrift für Wahrscheinlichkeitstheorie und Verwandte Gebiete* 2 (1964): 340–368.

With Henry H. Crapo. "On the Foundations of Combinatorial Theory II: Combinatorial Geometries." *Studies in Applied Mathematics* 49 (1970): 109–133.

With D. Kahaner and A. Odlyzko. "On the Foundations of Combinatorial Theory VIII: Finite Operator Calculus." *Journal of Mathematical Analysis and Applications* 42 (1973): 684–760.

With Peter Doubilet and Joel Stein. "On the Foundations of Combinatorial Theory IX: Combinatorial Methods in Invariant Theory." *Studies in Applied Mathematics* 53 (1974): 185–216.

With Mark Kac and Jacob T. Schwartz. *Discrete Thoughts: Essays on Mathematics, Science, and Philosophy*, edited by Harry Newman. Boston: Birkhäuser, 1986.

With F. Bonetti, Domenico Senato, and A. M. Venezia. "On the Foundations of Combinatorial Theory X: A Categorical Setting for Symmetric Functions." *Studies in Applied Mathematics* 86 (1992): 1–29.

Gian-Carlo Rota on Combinatorics, edited by Joseph P. S. Kung. Boston: Birkhäuser, 1995. A collection of Rota's papers on combinatorics with a number of commentaries.

Indiscrete Thoughts, edited by Fabrizio Palombi. Boston: Birkhäuser, 1997.

Gian-Carlo Rota on Analysis and Probability, edited by Jean D. Dhombres, Joseph P. S. Kung, and Norton Starr. Boston: Birkhäuser, 2003. A collection of Rota's papers on analysis and probability theory with a number of commentaries.

OTHER SOURCES

Andrews, George E. "On the Foundations of Combinatorial Theory V: Eulerian Differential Operators." *Studies in Applied Mathematics* 50 (1971): 345–375.

Beschler, Edwin F., David A. Buchsbaum, Jacob T. Schwartz, et al. "Gian-Carlo Rota (1932–1999)." *Notices of the American Mathematical Society* 47 (2000): 203–216. Several essays on Rota's accomplishments, including a discussion of all the "Foundations" papers by Richard P. Stanley and a survey of Rota's work on invariant theory by Buchsbaum and Brian D. Taylor.

Doubilet, Peter. "On the Foundations of Combinatorial Theory VII: Symmetric Functions through the Theory of Distribution and Occupancy." *Studies in Applied Mathematics* 51 (1972): 377–396.

Gasperoni, Ester Rota, *Orage sur le lac*. Paris: Médium, 1995.

———. *L'arbre de capulies*. Paris: Médium, 1996.

Richard Stanley

ROYER, CLÉMENCE-AUGUSTE (*b.* Nantes, France, 21 April 1830; *d.* Paris, France, 5 February 1902), *philosophy of science, evolution, feminism.*

Best known as the first French translator of Charles Darwin's *Origin of Species,* Royer was recognized by members of the French Société d'Anthropologie de Paris as a scientist and philosopher in her own right. In a culture that barred women from most formal education and professional activities, her contributions to the organization's discussions demonstrate the breadth of her learning and span a wide variety of scientific subjects. Elected to membership by this organization in 1870, she was also awarded the Legion of Honor by France for her services as a "woman of letters and scientific writer."

Early Influences. At the time of Royer's birth her parents, Josephine-Gabrielle Andouard and Augustin-Tené Toyer, were not yet married, but her birth was legitimated by their subsequent marriage. Her family was educated, Catholic, royalist, and politically active. Her father resigned his commission in the army in order to participate in the revolution of July 1830 on the side of the Bourbons, for which he was later tried and acquitted of treason. After some idiosyncratic teaching by her parents and some formal teaching in a convent school, Royer's intellect was stimulated by the Revolution of 1848, which caused her to reject her parents' royalist political leanings and become an ardent republican. Following her father's death in 1849, she began to reeducate herself through self-study and courses leading to teaching certificates. In 1854 she taught at a girls' school in Wales, gaining her knowledge of English that would be important for translating Darwin, and encountering a religious diversity that provoked her transition away from Christianity. Returning to France in 1855, she taught in a school possessing a great library of eighteenth-century writers, and upon reading through this library became convinced of two things: (1) she had been deceived by Catholic dogma and therefore should reject it; and (2) she had inherited the French Encyclopédists' love of science and should pursue the study of science and nature.

Royer went to Lausanne, Switzerland, in 1856 and after two years of reading systematically through the library, felt confident enough in her increased knowledge to offer courses for women in logic. She followed these in 1859 by a forty-lesson course on the Philosophy of Nature and History (of which only the first lesson is extant) in which she espoused a Lamarckian evolutionary position. She also began writing articles on economics for two journals established by Pascal DuPrat, who was active in French politics and with whom she would begin living as "wife" in 1865. In 1860, her entry on tax reform in a competition sponsored by the Swiss canton of Vaud earned second place, behind that of the famous socialist/anarchist Pierre Proudhon.

Darwin, Social Darwinism, and Feminism. As a result of her writings, the contacts she made through her relationship with DuPrat, her knowledge of English, and her understanding of Malthusian economics, she was contacted to translate Darwin's *Origin of Species.* Her translation, based on the third English edition, appeared in 1862 and included voluminous notes by Royer and a long preface extending Darwin's theory to human society. Many scholars of this period have accused Royer of distorting Darwin's text to serve her own philosophical and scientific purposes. Yvette Conry accused Royer of "intellectual Jesuitism" and of justifying Jean-Baptiste-Pierre-Antoine de Monet de Lamarck over Darwin. She then accused Royer of willfully destroying the authenticity of the Darwinian text for her own purposes. Some recent scholars, however, have shown Royer to have been more faithful to the text and more critically astute than earlier historians claimed, while acknowledging that her editorial footnotes and lengthy preface did not help the French to accept Darwin's theory (see the works by Blanckaert, Harvey, and Miles cited below). She continued as Darwin's authorized French translator until 1870, when, in the third French edition, she added a preface castigating Darwin for the hereditary theory of pangenesis he had proposed in *Variation of Animals and Plants under Domestication,* while neglecting to include changes he had made in later English editions of the *Origin.* Angered, Darwin withdrew permission and sought another translator.

By this time Royer had published at least twenty-four articles, reviews, and monographs on a variety of topics, the treatise on tax reform, a two-volume novel (*Les Jumeaux d'Hellas*), and a major book applying Darwinian theory to the evolution of humans and human society (*Origine de l'homme et des sociétés*). In 1870 she became the first woman elected to membership in the Société d'Anthropologie, for her scientific contributions as well as her translation of Darwin. She believed her strength in science was taking the facts that male scientists were able to discover (due to their access to laboratories and teaching positions) and forming theories and applications from their detailed findings. Increasingly she used this forum to disseminate her feminist and scientific beliefs concerning women and their roles in society. She argued for increased education and economic freedom for women, a position that many of her colleagues were willing to support. However, some of her proposals, including giving women new social and economic power, granting women the right to have children outside of marriage, and providing education to women that was equal to that of men, were too extreme for them.

Her comments, read before the *société* in 1874 and scheduled for publication as "Sur la natalité" in the organization's journal the following year, were suppressed by the *société*'s leadership in deference to other professional colleagues, clerical leaders in the country, and the new conservative governmental leaders. In 1877 the Paris police denied her request to speak on a related topic in a lecture series organized by the Belgian writer Céline Renooz Muro. Joy Harvey, who has studied Royer extensively, argues that this denial explains why Royer did not participate in the first Congress on the Rights of Women held in Paris in 1878.

During the decade preceding this congress, the French feminist movement had developed a new vigor and had begun to lobby for changes in laws and attitudes, changes that Royer had advocated since her days in Lausanne. She became involved in the International Congress for the Rights of Women sometime in the early 1880s and gradually became more active in the women's movement by joining a mixed Masonic lodge (1893) and by writing for the feminist newspaper *La Fronde* when it was formed in 1897. Royer's participation in the feminist movement and her sensitivity to the plight of women were grounded in the philosophical and scientific systems she had developed over forty years of study and reflection.

Between 1890 and 1900, she published over twenty articles and a book in which she developed her grand theory of nature (*Natura rerum*). In her book, she advocated a monistic theory of matter that rejected the physical descriptions of atoms and their behaviors proposed by Isaac Newton and John Dalton. Her atoms were living, conscious, and dynamic (active), and they repulsed each other. She also attempted to demonstrate a fundamental unity throughout nature, such that everything had life and even the atoms were subject to natural selection. While these ideas seem outrageous to modern readers, they were widely discussed in the nineteenth century. Royer's unique contribution was to develop a theory that addressed criticisms of mechanistic post-Newtonian science and incorporated various ideas proposed largely by the romantic *Naturphilosophers* into one grand unified theory. In 1897 more than 250 celebrated intellectuals, including two political leaders (Georges Clemenceau and Anatole France), the celebrated chemist Marcellin Berthelot, and the writer Émile Zola, attended a banquet organized to honor her life and work. In 1900, *La Fronde* carried a four-part review of *Natura rerum,* predicting that some day Royer would receive the glory due her. On 16 August 1900, the Minister of Public Instruction named Royer a Chevalier of the Legion of Honor for her services as a "woman of letters and scientific writer." She received her certificate and cross on 12 November, and her friends organized a second banquet on 16 November to celebrate what they considered a long overdue honor.

Royer's health continued to decline during the year following this second banquet, with her asthmatic problems increasing and her sight decreasing. She died on 5 February 1902 after lapsing into a coma and was buried on 10 February in the Cemetery of Neuilly in Paris.

BIBLIOGRAPHY

The following places in Paris are rich resources for works by Royer and correspondence from or to her: the Bibliothèque Marguerite Durand, the Bibliothèque Nationale, the Archives Nationales de France, and the Archives of the Société d'Anthropologie located at the Musée de l'Homme.

WORKS BY ROYER

Théorie de l'impôt; ou, La dîme sociale. 2 vols. Paris: Guillaumin, 1862. Tax reform.

L'Origine des espèces; ou, Des lois du progrès chez les êtres organisés. Translation. Paris: Guillaumin et Cie et Victor Masson et Fils, 1862. The infamous "Préface" details Royer's evolutionary views. Later editions with additional notes, Préfaces, and "Avant-propos" by Royer were published in 1866 (2nd ed.), 1869 (3rd ed.), and 1882 (4th ed., published by Flammarion). Fraisse (1985 and 2002) includes Royer's preface to the first French edition.

Les Jumeaux d'Hellas. 2 vols. Paris: A. Lacroix, Verboeckhoven et Cie, 1864.

"Lamarck: Sa vie, ses travaux et son système." *La Philosophie Positive* 3, no. 2 (1868): 173–205; 3, no. 3 (1868): 333–372; 4, no. 1 (1869): 5–30.

Origine de l'homme et des sociétés. Paris: Guillaumin, 1869.

"Remarques sur le transformisme." *Bulletins de la Société d'Anthropologie,* 2nd series, 5 (21 April 1870): 265–312.

"De l'Origine des diverses races humaines, et de la race aryenne en particulier." *Bulletins de la Société d'Anthropologie,* 2nd series, 8 (18 December 1873): 905–936.

"Sur la natalité." *Bulletins de la Société d'Anthropologie,* 2nd series, 9 (16 July 1874): 597–616. Page proofs suppressed by the publications committee and located in the Archives of the Société d'Anthropologie, Carton B, Bibliothèque du Musée de l'Homme, Paris. Translated in Harvey (1997).

"Deux hypothèses sur l'hérédité." *Revue d'Anthropologie* 6 (1877): 443–484, 660–685.

Le Bien et la loi morale: Éthique et téléologie. Paris: Guillaumin, 1881.

"L'instinct social." *Bulletins de la Société d'Anthropologie,* 3rd series, 5 (16 November 1882): 707–727.

"Attraction et gravitation d'après Newton." *La Philosophie Positive* 31 (1883): 206–226.

"L'Evolution mentale dans la série organique." *Revus Scientifique,* 3rd series, 39 (1887): 749–758; 40 (1887): 70–79.

"Discussion sur la dépopulation de la France." *Bulletins de la Société d'Anthropologie,* 4th series, 1 (2 October 1890).

Natura rerum: La Constitution du monde, dynamique des atomes, nouveaux principes de philosophie naturelle. Paris: Schleicher Frères, 1900.

"Introduction à la philosophie des femmes." In *Clémence Royer: Philosophe et femme de sciences,* by Geneviève Fraisse. Paris: Éditions La Découverte, 1985 and 2002. An English translation can be found in Miles (1988).

OTHER SOURCES

Blanckaert, Claude. "L'Anthropologie au féminin: Clémence Royer (1830–1902)." *Revue de Synthèse,* 3rd series, 105 (1982): 23–38.

———. "'Les bas-fonds de la science française': Clémence Royer, *L'Origine de l'homme* et le Darwinisme social." *Bulletin et Mémoires de la Société d'Anthropologie de Paris,* n.s., 3 (1991): 115–130.

Clark, Linda L. *Social Darwinism in France.* Tuscaloosa: University of Alabama Press, 1984.

Conry, Yvette. *L'Introduction du Darwinisme en France au XIXe siècle.* Paris: Vrin, 1974.

Fraisse, Geneviève. *Clémence Royer: Philosophe et femme de sciences.* Paris: Éditions de la Découverte, 1985 and 2002. Fraisse has included the French texts for the first lecture for Philosophy for Women and for the preface of the first French edition of *Origin of Species.*

Harvey, Joy. "'Doubly Revolutionary': Clémence Royer before the Société d'Anthropologie de Paris." In *Proceedings of the 16th International Congress of the History of Science: B. Symposia.* Bucharest: Academy of Socialist Republic of Romania, 1981.

———. "'Strangers to Each Other': Male and Female Relationships in the Life and Work of Clémence Royer, 1830–1902." In *Uneasy Careers and Intimate Lives: Women in Science, 1789–1979,* edited by Pnina G. Abir-Am and Dorinda Outram. New Brunswick, NJ: Rutgers University Press, 1987.

———. *"Almost a Man of Genius": Clémence Royer, Feminism, and Nineteenth-Century Science.* New Brunswick, NJ: Rutgers University Press, 1997. This is undoubtedly the best biography of Royer and includes an English translation of the suppressed "Sur la natalité."

Miles, Sara Joan. "Evolution and Natural Law in the Synthetic Science of Clémence Royer." PhD diss., University of Chicago, 1988. This work contains a transcription of Royer's autobiography and English translations of the first lecture for the course of Philosophy for Women and Royer's prefaces to the first and third French editions of *Origin of Species.*

———. "Clémence Royer et *De l'Origine des espèces:* Traductrice ou traîtresse?" *Revue de Synthèse,* 4th series, no. 1 (January–March 1989): 61–83.

Roger, Jacques. "Les Néo-Lamarckiens français." *Revue de Synthèse* 95–96 (1979): 279–468.

Stebbins, Robert E. "France." In *Comparative Reception of Darwinism,* edited by Thomas F. Glick. Austin: University of Texas Press, 1972.

Sara Joan Miles

RUFUS OF EPHESUS (first century CE),
medicine. For the original article on Rufus of Ephesus see *DSB*, vol. 11.

Research over the last thirty years of the twentieth century has substantially altered historians' understanding of Rufus of Ephesus in two ways. The revival of critical interest in Galen has led to a re-evaluation of his debts to his predecessors, among them Rufus, and, more importantly, many more writings by Rufus have been published for the first time. Most derive from translations made into Arabic that have been preserved in their entirety or in the form of substantial extracts, and more can be expected as major libraries in the Muslim world are made more accessible. Together they have thrown new light on the range of his medicine and on his therapeutic strategies.

Dates. According to a Byzantine encyclopedia, Rufus of Ephesus was a contemporary of Statilius Criton in the time of the emperor Trajan, meaning he would have been active around 100 CE. However, Servilius Damocrates, writing fifty years earlier, cited a pharmacologist called Rufus, and another writer on pharmacology, Asclepiades, writing about 90 CE, gave a recipe composed by a Menius Rufus. That both or either of these citations should be attributed to Rufus of Ephesus is far from clear, and most scholars prefer the later date. He was dead by 140 CE.

Life. This uncertainty about when Rufus lived mirrors the sparse biographical information provided in his writings, which provide little historical or geographical background to the cases he describes. Rufus spent considerable time in Egypt, probably studying at Alexandria and gaining a knowledge of anatomy, for he commented about the general health of the country and some specific diseases found there, such as guinea worm infestation. His other specific references to his patients or to what he saw all relate to the region around his home city of Ephesus (later in southwestern Turkey), and there is no evidence that he ever visited Rome, as did his contemporary, Soranus, or, later, Galen. His medical ideas place him firmly as a follower of Hippocrates and so a believer in the theory that health and disease were largely the result of a disturbance or imbalance in the four humors, or fluids, of the body—blood; bile; phlegm; and black bile, or melancholy—and that treatment should restore the individual's balance. But he could be flexible, even using some ideas more often associated with the Methodist sect of doctors.

Writings. What remains of his writings in Greek, whether in their original form or in quotations appearing in later works, gives only an idea of his enormous range. They include works on therapeutics—*On Diseases of the Bladder and Kidneys* and *On Satyriasis and Gonorrhoea*—as well as a treatise on anatomical nomenclature for those beginning medical study: "for the smith, the cobbler, and the carpenter first learn the words for metal, tools and such like. Why should it be any different in more noble arts?" (*Oeuvres,* p. 133, ed. Daremberg-Ruelle). His short treatise, *Medical Questions,* advising a doctor on how best to gain information from a patient by means of questions, offers a rare glimpse into the bedside skills of an ancient doctor. There are tantalizing fragments of a long botanical poem, in four books of hexameters, and of his views on plague, which may include a very early reference to plague buboes in North Africa. Other works survive only in translation: *On Gout* in Latin, *On Jaundice* in Latin and Arabic, and some of his case histories in Arabic. Even more, however, are known from citations in the medical encyclopedias of Late Antiquity or in the works of Arabic medical writers, for whom Rufus was second only to Galen as an authority.

What is most striking about Rufus's writings as people today have them is that theoretical discussion and argument are almost entirely absent. His emphasis was on therapeutics, buttressed by his own successful treatments. His commitment to the theory of the four humors is justified by the results of his therapies rather than by physiological exposition. The basis of Rufus's medicine can be briefly stated in his own words: "we are not naturally all the same; we differ very greatly from one another" (Brock, 1929, p. 115). Hence follows the need to discover the individuality of each patient by every possible means. A patient's illness could be deduced simply from its external manifestations, but this should be a mere preliminary, for true therapy consists in fitting the remedy exactly to the patient. This takes considerable time and effort, and may involve questions about all aspects of his or her life, from food and drink to habits and dreams. Even when the doctor has found out what is wrong, and can foresee the likely outcome, he must ensure that the treatment is adapted precisely to the patient, for "no substance is so constant in its actions that the physician can place it in a single category" (Brock, 1929, p. 115).

Although Galen applauded Rufus's profound knowledge of the Hippocratic corpus and respectfully referred several times to him as a commentator on Hippocrates, it is not certain whether Rufus wrote formal commentaries on select tracts or merely discussed particular passages in the course of other works. But Rufus's "deep affection for the man and his art" did not mean that he could see no progress beyond Hippocrates. His treatise *On Melancholy,* considered by Galen the best work on the subject before his own, developed the brief sketch in the Hippocratic *On the Nature of Man* into a detailed exposition of the therapeutic consequences of an excess or deficiency of the mysterious "melancholy" humor. Similarly, the final section of *Medical Questions* is an extension, not a criticism, of

Hippocrates's views in *Airs, Waters, and Places*. Rufus argued that local circumstances are likely to provide local remedies as well as local diseases, and that hence, talking with the natives of an area would often lead to discoveries of great value.

Throughout, Rufus adopted a pragmatic rather than a confrontational approach. Criticism of others was muted or avoided. He regretted that internal anatomy was better taught "in the old days," when one could use humans, but contented himself with recommending the dissection of animals closest to humans and the demonstration of surface anatomy on a slave. Although most of his treatises are addressed to his fellow doctors, Arabic authors have preserved a large number of quotations from what was a substantial and comprehensive manual of self-help, *For the Layman,* or, as some authors translated its title, *For Those Who Have No Doctor to Hand.* It covered a wide range of diseases, from headache and failing eyesight to kidney and bladder problems, and it gave advice for health as well as for sickness, for prophylactic dietetics was a Hippocratic speciality. Students wishing to develop a good memory were advised to avoid excessive drinking and eating lettuce, the bromide of antiquity. Rufus also considered groups in society whose particular needs were not always addressed in medical writings: travelers, the elderly, and the very young (with very sound advice on child care and pediatrics, including what the wet nurse should be able to deal with herself and when she must call in a doctor). He wrote a tract *On Buying Slaves,* in which he reported his examination of a slave with a congenital skull defect and warned against the risks of buying a slave with a suppurating discharge from the ear: this portended serious harm to the slave and a loss of investment to his or her owner. His sympathies with the sick are clear from his comments on those with sexual dysfunctions or with chronic conditions, where his stress on what is needed to eliminate their cause in each individual is the closest he came to an attack on the so-called Methodist doctors of his day, who preferred general diagnoses and remedies.

It was the misfortune of Rufus to have fallen under the shadow of Galen, who, while eloquent about his opponents' beliefs, was far more reticent about the amount he appropriated from those with whom he agreed. His general approval scarcely allows us to appreciate all that Rufus did to earn the admiration of the Arabs. The material that has survived the filtration process of the centuries highlights his practicality as a physician in his dealings with patients of all kinds. The learning that lay behind all this, however, can be glimpsed only faintly in his advice in *Medical Questions* or the references (not all of them necessarily his own) he provided to explicate anatomical terminology in *On the Names of Bodily Parts.* Enough remains, however, to show his great strengths as a clinical observer and to make readers regret the loss of so great a proportion of his writings.

Legacy. The fate of Rufus's works and reputation is bound up with Galen and Galenism. Although Galen praised him highly, he never made clear the full extent of his debts to Rufus and took direct issue with him only rarely. That he was an influential figure in the Hippocratic tradition is obvious, but precisely in what that influence consisted can scarcely be gleaned from Galen's self-centered comments. A better idea can be gained from the compilers of later Greek medical encyclopedias, Oribasius, Aetius, and Paul of Aegina, who all often cited him at length. He was, in the eyes of the Byzantines, one of the four great names in their medical literature. But increasingly, his individual voice was subsumed under that of Galen, even to the extent that some of his notions, and indeed experiences and writings, were credited to Galen. Arabic authors were still able to draw extensively on him from the ninth century onwards and possessed far more of his writings than survive today in their original Greek. They regarded his work on childcare highly, and his treatise *On Melancholy* formed the basis for many of their subsequent discussions of this puzzling illness. The medieval West knew much less of his works. Constantine the African quoted some of his ideas on melancholy through an Arabic intermediary, and many citations were to be found in the *Continens,* the Latin translation of the *Kitab al-Hawi* (the *All-embracing Book)*of Rhazes. But Rufus was largely known to the Latin West as the author of a purgative drug, the *hiera Rufi.*

Rufus's rehabilitation was long in coming. Some of his extant Greek works were edited with a Latin translation by Jacques Goupyl in Paris in 1554, and a few other fragments were published in Latin translation in the sixteenth century, but many treatises had to wait until the appearance of the standard edition of Charles Daremberg and Emile Ruelle, published in Paris in 1879. Although this edition also contained many of the fragments preserved in the later Byzantine encyclopedias and, to a lesser extent, the *Continens,* and allowed scholars to see why he was so highly regarded by Galen, it gave only a partial picture. Researches since the 1960s among Arabic writers, notably by Manfred Ullmann, have brought to light many new texts, some of them translated into Arabic in their entirety. They have confirmed Rufus's great strengths as a medical observer and writer who could produce a clear synthesis of abundant information from the past for therapeutic purposes.

SUPPLEMENTARY BIBLIOGRAPHY

WORKS BY RUFUS OF EPHESUS

Oeuvres de Rufus d'Ephèse. Edited by Charles Daremberg and Emile Ruelle. Paris: Imprimerie Nationale, 1879. Reprint,

Amsterdam: Hakkert, 1963. The standard edition of Rufus's writings.

De podagra. Edited by Henning Mørland. *Symbolae Osloenses.* Supplement 6. Oslo: A. W. Brøgger, 1933.

Quaestiones medicinales. Edited by Hans Gärtner. Berlin: Akademie Verlag, 1962. Includes an excellent commentary.

De renum et vesicae morbis. Edited by Alexander Sideras. Berlin: Akademie Verlag, 1977.

Krankenjournal. Edited by Manfred Ullmann. Wiesbaden, Germany: Harrassowitz, 1978. Contains case histories, not all of which may be by Rufus.

De cura icteri. Edited by Manfred Ullmann. *Abhandlungen der Akademie der Wissenschaften in Göttingen.* No. 138. Göttingen: Vandenhoeck & Ruprecht, 1983.

OTHER SOURCES

Aly, Amal Abou. *The Medical Writings of Rufus of Ephesus.* PhD diss., University of London, 1992.

Brock, Arthur J. *Greek Medicine.* London: J. M. Dent, 1929. Includes a partial translation of Rufus's *Quaestiones medicinales.*

Kowalski, Georg. *De corporis humani appellationibus.* PhD diss., University of Göttingen, 1960.

Lloyd, Geoffrey E. R. *Science, Folklore, and Ideology: Studies in the Life Sciences in Ancient Greece.* Cambridge, U.K.: Cambridge University Press, 1983. See the pages on anatomy.

Pormann, Peter E. "Paul of Aegina's Therapy of Children." BPhil diss., Oxford University, 1999.

Sideras, Alexander. "Rufus von Ephesos und sein Werk im Rahmen der antiken Medizin." In *Aufstieg und Niedergang der römischen Welt,* edited by Hildegard Temporini and Wolfgang Haase. Vol. 37. Berlin: W. De Gruyter, 1994.

Smith, Wesley D. *The Hippocratic Tradition.* Ithaca, NY: Cornell University Press, 1979. Discusses Rufus's Hippocratism.

Thomassen, H., and Christian Probst. "Die Medizin des Rufus von Ephesos." In *Aufstieg und Niedergang der römischen Welt,* edited by Hildegard Temporini and Wolfgang Haase. Vol. 37,2. Berlin: W. De Gruyter, 1994.

Ullmann, Manfred. "Neues zu den diätetischen Schriften des Rufus von Ephesos." *Medizinhistorisches Journal* 9 (1974): 23–40.

———. "Die Schrift des Rufus 'De infantium curatione.'" *Medizinhistorisches Journal* 10 (1975): 165–190

———. *Islamic Medicine.* Translated by Jean Watt. Edinburgh, U.K.: Edinburgh University Press, 1978. A short survey in English of the new Arabic material.

———. "Die arabische Überlieferung der Schriften des Rufus von Ephesos." In *Aufstieg und Niedergang der römischen Welt,* edited by Hildegard Temporini and Wolfgang Haase. Vol. 37,2. Berlin: W. De Gruyter, 1994. The best account of the new Arabic material.

Vivian Nutton

RUFUS OF CORNWALL
SEE **Rufus, Richard of Cornwall**.

RUFUS, RICHARD OF CORNWALL
(*b.* c. 1200, *d.* c. 1260), *natural philosophy, physics, matter theory, psychology.*

A founder of the Western tradition of natural philosophy, Rufus was among the first teachers of Aristotelian natural philosophy at the University of Paris in the 1230s, when Paris was the major university. He flourished in the period when Aristotle's physics, chemistry (*On Generation and Corruption* and *Meteorology*), and psychology (*On the Soul*) went from being forbidden subjects to being required courses. Rufus's natural philosophy consisted in the first instance of commentaries on Aristotle. Chiefly indebted to the Islamic philosopher Averroes (Ibn Rushd) for his knowledge of the Aristotelian tradition, Rufus was a critical thinker who supplemented or replaced accounts by Aristotle and Averroes he considered inadequate. Rufus gave up being an arts master, entered the Franciscan order, and left Paris in 1238. Most of the rest of his career was spent at Oxford University. When lecturing on theology at Oxford, Rufus cited views stated in his lectures on Aristotle as the opinions of a secular author; this confirms that these lectures were delivered in Paris before Rufus became a Franciscan.

Rediscovery. As with many medieval thinkers, Rufus was for centuries an author without known works: Some works were lost; others survived only in anonymous copies. The last medieval citation of Rufus by name dates from 1350, and the first of his works to be rediscovered was reported in 1926; the first of his philosophical works, in 1950; the first of his contributions to natural philosophy, in 1996. The attribution of these works to Rufus remained in the early 2000s controversial.

The process of rediscovery was serendipitous. Rufus's lectures on physics, chemistry, and psychology, for example, are known because they are preserved in a collection of his philosophical works copied at Oxford. Sometimes called the "Ave Maria Aristotle Quires," this collection was sold to Amplonius Ratingk de Berka in the fifteenth century not as a collection of Rufus works but of works by Walter Burley (c. 1275–1344), one of Amplonius's favorite authors. This attribution prompted the president of the Burley Society to examine Rufus's *Physics* at Erfurt in 1983. Because the quires were copied in about 1240, and Burley did not publish much before 1300, it was immediately obvious that Burley was not the author.

Establishing the attribution to Rufus took a decade longer. The construction of the quires themselves showed that Rufus's physics and metaphysics belonged together; the metaphysics was copied on folios 1–44, followed by the lectures on physics, chemistry, and psychology on folios 45–87, and the metaphysics and physics were indexed together in the thirteenth century. That connection was fortunate, since the metaphysics lectures were ascribed to Richard Rufus by a rubricator of Vatican lat. 4538, another copy of the same work. Also, two clear references from the metaphysics lectures to the physics lectures were verified. Finally, shared views on substantial change, instantaneous transmutation, and weak identity provided internal evidence for the attribution.

Projectile Motion. Following Aristotle, Rufus equates science (*scientia*) with the conclusion of a logical demonstration. As a science teacher he undertakes first to elucidate the deductive structure of Aristotle's writing, asking and answering questions about such topics as whether Aristotle's claims were consistent, whether his assumptions were justified, and whether the alternatives he enumerated were exhaustive. Rufus also asks whether Aristotle's conclusions are consistent with Christian doctrine and with experience.

Rufus's treatment of projectile motion is an influential example of his methods. Projectile motion poses a challenge for a basic Aristotelian principle (*Physics* 8.4–5.255b30–256a8): everything that moves is moved by something, either naturally by itself or violently by another mover. Aristotle himself poses the question in *Physics* 8, chapter 10: "How can things thrown continue to move when their mover is not in contact with them?" A thrown stone obviously does not move itself, so this is violent motion, but a projectile has no contact with the thrower after motion begins. How can that be? Aristotle explains projectile motion as a result of the action of the thrower on the medium through which the projectile travels (*Physics* 8.4.267a3–4). In air, for example, the thrower moves the first layer of the air, which moves the second layer, and so on, carrying the projectile along with it.

Unless it is assumed that air, and the motion that occurs in it, is discrete not continuous, this explanation is just as inconsistent with the basic Aristotelian principle as the phenomenon it explains, because it suggests that a body, air, moves itself when not in contact with a mover. Averroes glosses this explanation by suggesting that air can move itself on account of its fluidity. Rufus rejects both accounts, because "bodies as bodies cannot essentially move themselves." He substitutes a hylomorphic (form acting on matter) explanation more consistent with the basic principles of Aristotelian natural philosophy (*In Physicam Aristotelis* 8.3.1, pp. 238–241).

Rufus claims that the form of air determines the density of its parts. The violent action of the thrower divides the air's parts unnaturally so that they are farther apart

than their nature (form) dictates. In response to being violently pushed apart, the air's nature moving accidentally reinclines those parts, pushing them back almost as hard as the original mover. Now denser than their nature dictates, the parts are again reinclined so that they are farther apart than their nature dictates, and so on. This successive expansion and compression produces motion in the medium that gradually decreases in amplitude. Similar to that of the strings of a lyre when plucked, this motion partly accounts for the movement of projectiles in the medium, according to Rufus. Because this reinclination is a response to violent motion, it is self-limiting and does not persist.

Rufus cautions, however, that experience (*signa*) shows that the action of the medium cannot by itself account for projectile motion. If the action of the medium were the entire explanation, projectiles could not travel at different speeds in the same medium or pass each other traveling in different directions. So Rufus postulates an action of the thrower on the projectile itself. The thrower produces an impression that acts mechanically by transposing the parts of the projectile such that it moves contrary to its nature for a time. The impression is "some quality, form, or something" else in the projectile itself. Presumably Rufus hesitates about calling this impression a form, because since it results from violent motion, it weakens continuously. Encountering the same problem, Francis of Appignano postulated a third kind of form, intermediate between permanent and successive forms (1968, p.180).

Here Rufus has corrected the account of the action of the medium on the projectile by making it more consistent with the basic principles of Aristotelian natural philosophy, and he has supplemented the account to conform to experience. Roger Bacon responds by accepting the correction but rejecting the supplement (*In Physicam Aristotelis* 8, Opera Hactenus Inedita I 13: 338). He rejects the supplement because he views it as an attempt to substitute virtual contact for substantial contact between mover and moved object. Thomas Aquinas rejects theories such as Rufus's because impressions act internally on the projectile; positing them seems to make projectile motion a case of natural rather than violent motion (*On the Heavens*, 3.7.5–6). Rufus's supplement was more successful later: A similar explanation postulating that the thrower acts both on the medium and on the projectile is advanced in the fourteenth century by Francis of Appignano. Moreover, in the fifteenth century not only were views like Rufus's generally adopted, they were even attributed to Aristotle; Galileo was in the minority when he claimed that Aristotle held the contrary view (Maier, 1968, pp. 298–305).

Theory of Mixture. For Aristotelians, bodies are composed of homoeomeries, like-parted substances such as blood and bone, mercury and sulfur. Homoeomeries in turn may be produced by mixing the four Aristotelian elements (earth, water, air, and fire) directly, but more frequently complex homoeomeries result from combining less complex homoeomeries. In Latin, an Aristotelian homoeomery is called a *mixtum;* here, this entry will speak of a *mixt* and call the process of forming a mixt *mixture.* The modern counterpart of an Aristotelian mixt is a chemical compound, because it is a uniform, stable substance with a nature different from the elements composing it. However, Aristotelian mixture is carefully defined in a manner radically different from modern chemical theory, so it is better to speak of mixture, even though the ingredients in an Aristotelian mixt are bound together rather than physically juxtaposed.

Like many topics in Aristotelian natural philosophy, the science of mixture starts with a puzzle—namely, that mixture seems impossible (*On Generation and Corruption* 1.10.327b1–6). The mixt has to contain at least two ingredients; so if one or more is destroyed in the process, the result is not a mixt. Yet, if the ingredients are not transformed in the process, there is an aggregate, not a unified substance. As if this dilemma were not tough enough, Aristotle also stipulates:

1. The ingredients of the mixt must be in equilibrium;

2. When a mixt is destroyed, its ingredients must be recoverable;

3. The mixt must be uniform, like-parted, however much it is divided;

4. Nonetheless, it must also be less unified than elements;

5. The qualities of the ingredients must be altered in the process of mixture.

Aristotle himself supplies the solution to his puzzle: The ingredients cannot be fully actualized in a mixt; they must exist only in potential. The problem for his successors was to specify what kind of potential would permit mixture and yet satisfy the requirements Aristotle had stipulated.

Avicenna (Ibn Sina) and Averroes proposed the two most famous descriptions of the potential of the substantial forms of the ingredients in a mixt: fixed forms (*formae fixae*) and fractured forms (*formae fractae*). Avicenna's fixed forms retain their substantial identity despite their primary qualities having been altered in the course of mixture. By contrast, when they lose their characteristic primary qualities, such as heat, Averroes's forms are broken or diminished. According to Averroes, elemental forms are like accidental forms, and unlike most substantial forms, can be diminished.

Rufus responds by revising Averroes's views to better account for the Aristotelian distinction between substance and accidents. Rufus begins by criticizing Averroes: Because the forms of the ingredients are lost or broken in the process of mixture, Averroes cannot escape the first horn of the dilemma; also it is difficult to see how the ingredients could be recovered. Focusing on ontology, Rufus also objects that a change in the qualities of a substance cannot cause a change in the substance. Quite the contrary, substantial change produces accidental chance, since Aristotelian substances are prior to Aristotelian accidents. But, of course, fixed forms also will not do, since mixing fixed forms would produce juxtaposition, not a unified mixt.

Rufus's solution is to claim that the ingredients in a mixt are in accidental potential, a kindl of proximate potential. Ingredients in accidental potential have all their essential properties, but an external obstacle prevents them from expressing their full natures. Specifically, each of the ingredients interferes with the actualization of the other ingredients. Because they balance each other, the mixt is stable. But because one element in the mixt, fire, is far removed from its natural place, it is susceptible to weakening, and hence the mixt is less unified than the elements themselves and can be destroyed. In the process of generating or destroying mixts, the qualities of their ingredients are altered. Rufus considers this solution a version of Averroes's account, since he like Averroes supposes that elemental forms in a mixt are diminished in comparison with fully actualized substantial forms.

Perception. Aristotelian psychology describes perception as a process of assimilation. When, for example, one sees something green, one's sense of sight gets to be like the green object perceived. In a famous simile from *On the Soul* (2.12.424a17–24), Aristotle compares perception to the act of pressing a signet ring on wax. The impression made by a gold signet ring is just the same as the impression made by an iron ring with the same pattern. The wax receives not the ring's material, but the pattern on it. Similarly, in perception the sense receives form, not matter. Just how that happens is a subject of debate among interpreters of Aristotelian psychology even in the early twenty-first century. Does the eye jelly, for example, physically turn green when one sees something green? Or is what is received spiritual, so that the eye is altered not by becoming green, but by seeing green?

Rufus considers the physical alternative absurd, since the eye would have to become not just green, but also simultaneously red; there would even be a bathtub in our sensitive soul when we perceived a bathtub (*Contra Averroem* Q312.82va). So Rufus turns to Averroes's great commentary on Aristotle's *On the Soul* (2.67, p. 232). Averroes says that sensible objects in physical bodies are material, but in the medium and the sense they are spiritual; they have to be spiritual in a medium such as air, because air simultaneously transmits many and contrary colors to the senses. Averroes solves the contraries problem two ways: He stipulates that color, for example, as perceived, has a spiritual nature different from its material nature in external objects, and he also stipulates that the recipient of sensory impressions must be barren: a color receptor has to be colorless.

Rufus adopted Averroes's description of "spiritual beings," but eventually he came to prefer the description *species-being*, where a species is a form maximally similar to the external form, an express similitude as defined by Augustine. Also, though Averroes holds that such spiritual beings differ by definition and essence, Rufus argues that they must be essentially the same; otherwise, the proximate objects of perception would differ too much from the distal objections of perception. Since, however, they have a different ontological status or being, they cannot be the same in every respect. According to Rufus, species and the objects they image for people differ by name and definition—a phrase Aristotle uses to describe unambiguous terms in his *Metaphysics* (4.11.1006b18)—though they are the same by essence (*Dissertatio in Metaphysicam Aristotelis* 6, Vatican, lat. 4538, fol. 44ra; *Sententia Oxoniensis*, proem, Balliol College 62, fol. 9vb). Ultimately, Rufus claims that because species-being does not belong to Aristotle's categories of substance and accident, they are not natural forms (*Speculum animae* 2, Erfurt Q312, fol. 108ra-rb). Sensible species are not substances because they are not self-subsistent; neither are they accidents, because they are not found in the substances that give rise to them.

This refinement furnished Rufus with the solution to another problem: self-perception. Self-perception is a problem on account of the so-called barrenness stipulation. Averroes stipulates that the soul lacks all material forms and thus can receive all spiritual forms. But the soul itself is a spiritual not a material form. So how can the soul receive knowledge of itself? Or if it can apprehend itself, how can it be the kind of form Aristotle says it is? According to Aristotle, the soul is assimilated to and so apprehends all things, but what apprehends everything can have no form if people take the barrenness condition seriously (*In De anima Aristotelis* 3.3.Q1, Madrid, BN 3314, fol. 81va; *Speculum animae* 5, Erfurt Q312, fol. 109vb). Having distinguished species-being, Rufus has an answer to that question, albeit a controversial answer: he says that the soul comprehends itself in just the same way it apprehends or perceives other things, by abstracting and subsequently apprehending its own species, which belongs to a different category from its substantial form (*In De anima Aristotelis* 3.3.Q1, Madrid BN 3314, fol. 81va-82ra; *Con-*

tra Averroem 1.12, Erfurt Q312, fol. 83vb, *Speculum animae* 5, Erfurt Q312, fol. 119rb).

Augustine's influence on Rufus's theories of perception was not limited to supplying the definition of species that Rufus employed. Initially, under Augustine's influence, Rufus held that species do not act directly on the soul, but only excite the soul, which responds to that stimulus by considering a preexisting similitude within itself (*In De anima Aristotelis* 2.12.Q2, Madrid BN, fol. 76rb). This is Rufus's first reply to the objection based on the Neoplatonic claim that the less noble cannot act on the more noble. He modifies his reply to this objection subsequently in his *Against Averroes* [*Contra Averroem*] and in his *Dissertation on Aristotle's Metaphysics*. According to the *Dissertation,* the receiver is less noble than the species it receives not in itself, but insofar as it is in potential to receive the species (*Dissertation on Aristotle's Metaphysics* 4, V4538.26vb). Rufus seemingly found this reply adequate, since he did not consider the objection further in subsequent works. Rather, in his theological works and in his *Mirror of the Soul* [*Speculum anima*], he states Aristotle's view that sensible objects act on the soul (*Sententia Oxoniensis* proem, Balliol College 62, fol. 9vb). So this is a case where the influence of Christian theology declined over time.

Intellectual Development. Rufus entered the Franciscan Order in 1238 as a Parisian Master of Arts and moved to Oxford, where he studied theology. He lectured on Peter Lombard's *Sentences* at Oxford around 1250 and at Paris around 1253. He returned to Oxford as the Franciscan Master of Theology around 1256.

As a secular master, Rufus responded creatively to many problems in Aristotelian natural philosophy. As a theologian, he continued to address many of the same problems. He was deeply indebted to Averroes from whom he took not only an interpretative approach to Aristotle but also a set of problems. Rufus criticizes Averroes on both theological and philosophical grounds, most importantly regarding the nature of divine knowledge, the nature of matter, and the cause of individuation. But Rufus was never disrespectful; he considered even Averroes's views on the material intellect to be reasonable (*Contra Averroem* 1, Q312.81vb).

Rufus was fully prepared to revise Aristotle's scientific claims based on the testimony of experience and the demands of Christian belief. His critical approach set an agenda for his successors. When he first encountered Aristotle's natural philosophy, he was confident that there would be no problem reconciling it with Christian belief. Under the influence of Robert Grosseteste, however, Rufus came to see the extent of the disagreement. On the question of the eternity of the world, for example, he condemned those who sought to excuse Aristotle in his *Dissertation*. However, as we have seen in his work on perception, sometimes Rufus preferred a standard Aristotelian to a Christian, Augustinian account.

At Paris, Roger Bacon succeeded Rufus as a lecturer. Bacon often adopted Rufus's approach to problems in Aristotelian science, but equally often he rejected them. Both lecturers exercised considerable influence on the subsequent commentary tradition, and their differences explain in part the richness of the tradition. The excitement of Rufus's approach and Bacon's response was vital to the rapid introduction of Aristotelian natural philosophy in the West.

BIBLIOGRAPHY

A complete list of Rufus's works is available from http://rrp.stanford.edu/works.html.

WORKS BY RUFUS

Contra Averroem. Erfurt: Universitäts Bibliothek, Dep. Erf., CA. Q.312, folios 81va–86rb; Prague: Archiv Prazskeho Hradu, Ms. 1437, fol. 33ra–36vb. An individual folio, for example folio 81va, is cited below as Q312.81va.

De mutatione. Toulouse, Bibl. mun. 737, folio 158ra–va. Edited by R. Plevano. "Richard Rufus of Cornwall and Geoffrey of Aspall: Two Questions on the Instant of Change." *Medioevo* 19 (1993): 167–232. Includes a good discussion of Rufus on the instant of change.

Dissertatio in Metaphysicam Aristotelis. Vatican lat. 4538. Salamanca: Biblioteca Universidad 2322, folios 72rb–129rb; Erfurt: Universitäts Bibliothek, Dep. Erf., CA. Q.290, folios 1ra–40vb. Excerpts published by Donati, 2003, Gál, 1950, and Noone, 1987. Title based on the incipit for a work also known as *Scriptum super Metaphysicam Aristotelis* and *Commentarius in Metaphysicam Aristotelis*. Further discussion of the title is found below in the entry on Noone, 1987.

Expositio libri De anima. Madrid, 1952. In *Obras filosóficas,* vol. 3, edited by Manuel Alonso. Madrid: Consejo Superior de Investigaciones Cientificas, 1952. An incomplete edition based on a single manuscript, frequently mistranscribed. Better partial editions available at the Web site cited above.

In Analytica posteriora Aristotelis, ed. Rega Wood. Erfurt, Universitäts Bibliothek, Dep. Erf., CA. Q312, folios 29va–32vb. Available from rrp.stanford.edu/apos.html.

In De anima Aristotelis. Florence: Biblioteca Nazionale, Conv. Soppr. G.4.853, folios 193ra–222va; Madrid: Biblioteca Nacional 3314, folios 68ra–89rb. Erfurt: Universitäts Bibliothek, Dep. Erf., CA. Q.312, folios 19rb–20va, 22va–28vb. The Erfurt redaction is available from http://rrp.stanford.edu/DAnE1.html, http://rrp.stanford.edu/DAnE2.html, and http://rrp.stanford.edu/DAnE3.html.

In De generatione et corruptione Aristotelis. Erfurt, Universitäts Bibliothek, Dep. Erf., CA. Q.312, folios 14ra–19ra. The texts cited above mostly come from 1.6.2–3 (16va–17ra) and 2.4.3 (18ra–rb), which includes Rufus's comparison of his

views with those of Averroes. The texts are quoted and discussed in greater detail in Wood and Weisberg, 2004.

In Physicam Aristotelis. Edited by Rega Wood. *Auctores britannici medii aevi,* XVI. Oxford: Oxford University Press, 2003. The introduction includes a description of the "Ave Maria Aristotle Quires" and describes the old foliation mentioned in the section on rediscovery. Because Amplonius rebound the "Quires," the modern foliation differs from the thirteenth-century foliation.

Sententia Oxoniensis. Oxford: Balliol College, folio 62 (year unknown).

Speculum animae. Erfurt: Universitäts Bibliothek, Dep. Erf., CA. Q.312, folios 107va–110rb; Assisi, Bibl. Sacro Convento 138, folios 281va–284rb.

OTHER SOURCES

Amerini, Fabrizio. "Utrum inhaerentia sit de essentia accidentis: Francis of Marchia and the Debate on the Nature of Accidents." *Vivarium* 44 (2006): 95–150. Discusses the history of the medieval controversy on the nature of accidents.

Aristotle. *Complete Works of Aristotle: The Revised Oxford Translation,* 2 vols. Edited by Jonathan Barnes. Princeton, NJ: Princeton University Press, 1984. The texts cited for the five Aristotelian stipulations regarding mixture are, respectively: 1 (GC 1.10.328a28–30), 2 (GC 1.10.327b23–30), 3 (GC 1.10.328a9–11), 4 (GC 2.7.334b20–21), and 5 (GC 1.10.328a31–35).

Augustinus. *De diversis quaestionibus octoginta tribus,* edited by Almut Mutzenbecher. In *Corpus Christianorum,* Series Latina, 44A. Turnhout: Brepols, 1975. Published as *Eighty-three Different Questions,* translated by David L. Mosher. Washington, DC: Catholic University of America Press, 1982. An important source for Rufus's definition of sensible and intelligible species.

———. *De trinitate.* Edited by William Mountain and F. Glorie. In *Corpus Christianorum,* Series Latina, 50A. Turnhout: Brepols, 1975. In *The Works of St. Augustine,* translated by Edmund Hill, edited by John E. Rotelle. Brooklyn, NY: New City Press, 1990. Another source for Rufus on sensible species.

Averroes. *Commentarium magnum in Aristotelis De anima.* Edited by F. Stuart Crawford. Cambridge, MA: Medieval Academy of America, 1953.

Bacon, Roger. *Compendium of the Study of Theology.* Edited and translated by Thomas S. Maloney. Leiden: Brill, 1988. Describes Rufus's fame among the foolish multitude, considered mad by the wise, and censured at Paris.

———. *Questiones supra libros octo Physicorum Aristotelis. Opera Hactenus Inedita* 13. Edited by Ferdinand M. Delorme and R. Steele. Oxford: Clarendon Press, 1935. First response to many of Richard Rufus's views.

Brams, Josef. "Le premier commentaire médiéval sur le 'Traité de l'âme' de Aristote?" *Recherches de théologie et philosophie médiévales* 68 (2001): 213–227. Provides information about the Florentine manuscript G.4.853 of *In De anima Aristotelis.* Suggests that we consider a late note in G.4.853 ascribing the work to Alexander.

Brown, Stephen F. "The Eternity of the World Discussion at Early Oxford." In *Mensch und Natur im Mittelalter*, edited by A. Zimmermann and A. Speer. Berlin: Walter de Gruyter, 1991. Includes an excerpt from Rufus's Oxford theology lectures, *Sent.* II d. 1 q. 1, Balliol 62, f. 103–105.

Donati, Silvia. "Un nuovo testimone dello Scriptum super Metaphysicam di Riccardo Rufo di Cornwall (Salamanca, Bibl. Univ. Ms. 2322)." *Bulletin de philosophie médiévale* 45 (2003): 31–60. Reports the discovery of a new manuscript of *Dissertatio in Metaphysicam Aristotelis (DMet)*, also known as *Scriptum super Metaphysicam.*

———. "The Anonymous Commentary on the Physics in Erfurt, Cod. Amplon. Q. 312 and Richard Rufus of Cornwall." *Recherches de philosophie et théologie médiévales* 72 (2005): 232–362. Questions the authenticity of *In Physicam Aristotelis* and *In De anima Aristotelis.*

Francis of Marchia. *In Sent.* In *Zwei Grundprobleme der scholastischen Naturphilosophie: Das Problem der intensiven Grösse; Die Impetustheorie*, edited by Anneliese Maier. 3rd ed. Rome: Edizioni di Storia e Letteratura, 1968. Presents a theory of projectile motion similar to Richard Rufus's. Cites Bonaventure and Richard on a form intermediate between a permanent and successive that lasts for a short time.

Gál, G. "Commentarius in 'Metaphysicam' Aristotelis cod. Vat. lat. 4538 fons doctrinae Richardi Rufi." *Archivum franciscanum historicum* 43 (1950): 209–242. First published discussion of DMet, which Auguste Pelzer discovered. Gál described DMet, using the title *Commentarius,* as an important source for the *Sententia Oxoniensis.* Rufus's references to DMet as the work of a secular author misled Gál. His excellent article provides a useful guide to the commentary and the views expressed in it, lists the titles of the questions, and publishes excerpts.

Hackett, Jeremiah. "Roger Bacon and the Reception of Aristotle in the Thirteenth Century." In *Albertus Magnus und die Anfänge der Aristoteles-Rezeption im lateinischen Mittelalter: Von Richardus Rufus bis zu Franciscus de Mayronis*, edited by Ludger Honnefelder, Rega Wood, Mechthild Dreyer, et al. Münster: Aschendorff Verlag, 2005. Notes Roger Bacon's references to Rufus as an Averroist.

Karger, Elizabeth. "Richard Rufus on Naming Substances." *Medieval Philosophy and Theology* 7 (1998): 51–67. On the development of Rufus's metaphysical views, "a striking example of 'Christian Aristotelianism.'" Shows that Rufus began by carefully reconstructing Aristotelian naming theory in MMet.

———. "Richard Rufus's Account of Substantial Transmutation." *Medioevo* 27 (2002): 165–189. Explains Rufus's theory of substantial transformation, which relies on a notion of active potency and provides a quasi-Aristotelian explanation of Augustine's seminal reasons. Mentions the authors who accepted the view (Bonaventure, Albert the Great, and Roger Marston) and those who rejected it (Aquinas, Henry of Ghent, and John Duns Scotus).

Little, Andrew G. "The Franciscan School at Oxford in the Thirteenth Century." *Archivum franciscanum historicum* 19 (1926): 803–874. Essential historical information.

Lloyd, A. C. "The Principle that the Cause Is Greater than Its Effect." *Phronesis* 21 (1976): 145–156. A discussion of a Neoplatonic principle that strongly influenced thirteenth-century thinkers.

Long, R. J. "The First Oxford Debate on the Eternity of the World." *Recherches de philosophie et théologie médiévales* LXV (1998): 54–98. On Rufus's defense of Robert Grosseteste and his attack on the views stated in Richard Fishacre's theology lectures.

Maier, A. *Zwei Grundprobleme der scholastischen Naturphilosophie: Das Problem der intensiven Grösse; Die Impetustheorie.* Edited by Anneliese Maier. 3rd ed. Rome: Edizioni di Storia e Letteratura, 1968.

Marsh, Adam. "Epistolae." In *Monumenta franciscana*, vol. 2, *Rerum britannicarum medii aevi scriptores.* London: Longman, 1858. Marsh's correspondence describes Rufus and his decision to return to Paris c. 1253.

Needham, Paul. "Duhem's Theory of Mixture in the Light of the Stoic Challenge to the Aristotelian Conception." *Studies in History and Philosophy of Science* 33 (2002): 685–708. Introduces the practice of referring to mixts (p. 687).

Noone, Timothy B. "An Edition and Study of the Scriptum super Metaphysicam, Bk. 12, Dist. 2. A Work Attributed to Richard Rufus of Cornwall." PhD diss., University of Toronto, 1987. Prints excerpts of DMet's commentary on lambda (pp. 167–334) and describes the work as a reportatio "coming from the pen of auditores in a classroom" (p. 64). Note that the term "Scriptum" normally refers not to a reportatio but to a redaction revised and corrected by its author. For this reason a less controversial title based on the work's incipit was chosen.

———. "Richard Rufus of Cornwall and the Authorship of the Scriptum super Metaphysicam." *Franciscan Studies* 49 (1989): 55–91. Reproduces information from the dissertation. Questions the attribution of *Sententia Oxoniensis (SOx)* to Rufus.

———. "Richard Rufus on Creation, Divine Immutability, and Future Contingency in the Scriptum super Metaphysicam." *Documenti e studi sulla tradizione filosofica medievale* 4 (1993): 1–23. A discussion of texts from DMet.

———. "Roger Bacon and Richard Rufus on Aristotle's Metaphysics. A Search for the Grounds of Disagreement." *Vivarium* 35 (1997): 251–265.

———. "Prefatory Note. Richard Rufus, *Scriptum super Metaphysicam.*" *Bulletin de philosophie médiévale* 44 (2002): 95–96. Disputes the use of the title "*Dissertatio in Metaphysicam,*" drawn from the work's incipit, on the grounds that a titulus on the first folio begins with the words: "Scriptum super Metaphysicam magistri ricardi." This titulus, like the colophon at the end of the work that begins "Explicit tractatus metaphysicus magistri" (V4538.102va), is not by the scribe who copied the text itself.

Pelster, Franz F. "Der älteste Sentenzenkommentar aus der Oxforder Franziskanerschule. Ein Beitrag zur Geschichte des theologischen Lehrbetriebs an der Oxforder Universität." *Scholastik* 1 (1926): 50–80. Announces the first major rediscovery, the Oxford theology lectures, SOx. Indicates that Rufus was the first Oxford bachelor to lecture on Lombard's *Sentences.*

———. "Neue Schriften des englischen Franziskaners Richardus Rufus von Cornwall (um 1250)." *Scholastik* 8 (1933):

561–568, 9 (1934): 256–264. Announces the discovery of "De intellectu divino" and other minor works in Assisi 138.

Plevano, R. "Richard Rufus of Cornwall and Geoffrey of Aspall: Two Questions on the Instant of Change." *Medioevo* 19 (1993): 167–232. A good discussion of Rufus on the instant of change, based on a minor work. Edits Toulouse 737 f.158.

———. "Two British Masters and the Instant of Change." In *Aristotle in Britain during the Middle Ages: Proceedings of the International Conference at Cambridge, 8–11 April 1994, Organised by the Société Internationale pour l'Étude de la Philosophie Médiévale*, edited by J. Marenbon. Turnhout: Brepols, 1996. Compares Rufus with Geoffrey of Aspall.

Raedts, Peter. *Richard Rufus of Cornwall and the Tradition of Oxford Theology.* Oxford: Clarendon Press, 1987. Denies the attribution of *Dissertatio in Metaphysicam* to Rufus. Establishes the authenticity of SPar. Compares Rufus with Robert Grosseteste.

Thomas of Eccleston. *Tractatus de adventu fratrum minorum in Angliam.* Edited by Andrew G. Little. Manchester, U.K.: Manchester University Press, 1951. Describes Rufus's entry into the order, the appearance of Francis in a dream warning against scholarly pride, and Rufus's position as the fifth Franciscan Master of Theology at Oxford.

Trifogli, Cecelia. "The Unicity of Time in XIIIth Century Natural Philosophy." In *Was ist Philosophie im Mittelalter? Qu'est-ce que la philosophie au moyen âge? What Is Philosophy in the Middle Ages? Akten des X. internationalen Kongresses für mittelalterliche Philosophie der Société Internationale pour l'Étude de la Philosophie Médiévale, 25. bis 30. August 1997 in Erfurt*, edited by Jan A. Aertsen and Andreas Speer. Berlin: Walter de Gruyter, 1998.

———. *Oxford Physics in the Thirteenth Century (ca. 1250 – 1270): Motion, Infinity, Place and Time.* Leiden: Brill, 2000. First major discussion of Rufus's influence the tradition of natural philosophy.

Weisberg, Michael, and Rega Wood. "Richard Rufus's Theory of Mixture: A Medieval Explanation of Chemical Combination." In *Chemical Explanation: Characteristics, Development, Autonomy*, ed. Joseph E. Earley, Sr. New York: New York Academy of Sciences, 2003.

Wood, Rega. "Richard Rufus of Cornwall and Aristotle's Physics." *Franciscan Studies* 52 (1992): 247–81. Announces the rediscovery of *In Phys.*

———. "Richard Rufus of Cornwall on Creation: The Reception of Aristotelian Physics in the West." *Medieval Philosophy and Theology* 2 (1992): 1–30. Describes the evolution of Rufus's views on the beginning of time. Discusses Rufus's version of the argument Kant presents in his "First Antinomy of Pure Reason."

———. "Richard Rufus: Physics at Paris Before 1240." *Documenti e studi sulla tradizione filosofica medievale* 5 (1994): 87–127. Describes Rufus's views on the place of the world.

———. "Richard Rufus' 'Speculum animae.' Epistemology and the Introduction of Aristotle in the West." In *Die Bibliotheca Amploniana. Ihre Bedeutung im Spannungsfeld von Aristotelismus, Nominalismus und Humanismus*, edited by Andreas Speer. *Miscellanea mediaevalia* 23. Berlin: De Gruyter, 1995. First study of Rufus's epistemology. Describes a new manuscript and a new title for a work on perception,

previously described as part of a theological work on the miserable human condition, *Miserabilia humana condicio.*

———. "Roger Bacon: Richard Rufus' Successor as a Parisian Physics Professor." *Vivarium* 35 (1997): 222–250. Compares Bacon and Rufus.

———. "Richard Rufus's *De anima* Commentary: The Earliest Known, Surviving, Western *De anima* Commentary." *Medieval Philosophy and Theology* 10 (2001): 119–156.

———. "Richard Rufus of Cornwall." In *A Companion to Philosophy in the Middle Ages,* edited by Jorge J. E. Gracia and Timothy B. Noone. Oxford: Blackwell Publishing, 2003.

———. "Richard Rufus of Cornwall's Significance in the Western Scientific Tradition." In *Albertus Magnus und die Anfänge der Aristoteles-Rezeption im lateinischen Mittelalter: Von Richardus Rufus bis zu Franciscus de Mayronis*, edited by Ludger Honnefelder, Rega Wood, Mechthild Dreyer, et al. Münster: Aschendorff Verlag, 2005. Compares the reception of Rufus's views on the beginning of the world, the place of the world, and projectile motion.

———, and Michael Weisberg. "Interpreting Aristotle on Mixture: Problems about Elemental Composition from Philoponus to Cooper." *Studies in History and Philosophy of Science* 35 (2004): 681–706. Compares Rufus with other interpreters of Aristotle on mixture.

———, and Jennifer Ottmanr. "Richard Rufus of Cornwall." In *Medieval Science, Technology, and Medicine,* edited by Thomas Glock, Steven J. Livesey, and Faith Wallis. New York: Routledge, 2005.

Rega Wood

RUNCORN, STANLEY KEITH (*b.* Southport, Lancashire, England, 19 November 1922; *d.* San Diego, California, 5 December 1995), *geophysics, geomagnetism, planetary science.*

Runcorn ranks among the most innovative geophysicists of the late twentieth century, having endeavored to interpret geomagnetic data and its relation to possible movement of Earth's continents over geological time. He also contributed to the elaboration and testing of theories of Earth's main magnetic field and was a pioneer in paleomagnetism and the investigation of the magnetism of the Moon, Mars, and other planets.

Early Years. Keith Runcorn was born in Southport, Lancashire, England. He was the only son of William Henry Runcorn, a monumental mason, and Lily Idena Runcorn (née Roberts). He had one younger sister. Little is known of his childhood. He studied at King George V Grammar School in Southport and entered Gonville and Caius College, Cambridge University, in 1940. There he read electrical engineering; passed the tripos, or final examination, in mechanical sciences in 1943; and received his BA degree in 1944.

In 1943 Runcorn was temporarily transferred to the Royal Radar Research and Development Establishment (RRDE), Malvern, Worcestershire, as an experimental officer. At the end of World War II, Charles W. Oatley, who had been the director of the RRDE, moved to Cambridge as reader in electrical engineering and accepted Runcorn for PhD work. However, the government required Runcorn and other researchers to remain at RRDE for three years, his time ending in September 1946.

Interest in Geomagnetism. Meanwhile, Runcorn realized that his interest was shifting to physics, so he applied for a fellowship in that subject at the University of Manchester. Although he did not get the fellowship, Manchester—where Patrick M. S. Blackett was dean of science and headed the Physics Department—asked him to apply for a position as an assistant lecturer in physics. Runcorn began lecturing there in 1946 and worked with Clifford Butler and George Rochester to recondition Blackett's pre-war cloud chamber for cosmic ray research. Runcorn considered concentrating in this subject.

This interest, however, lasted less than one year. Shortly after Runcorn arrived in Manchester, Blackett presented a colloquium in November 1946 on the magnetic fields of the Earth and Sun. He noted that the ratios of the magnetic dipoles to the respective angular momenta of the two bodies were roughly equal. Following Horace Babcock's discovery that the star 78 Virginis has a magnetic field, Blackett revived the theory that rotating bodies produce a magnetic field because of a fundamental but unknown physics. Runcorn quickly switched to investigations of Earth's magnetic field.

Runcorn noted in a letter to geophysicist Ted Irving in September 1980 that "Blackett's excitement was immense." After Blackett presented his theory to the Royal Society in May 1947, Runcorn and Blackett collaborated on an experimental test of it. Edward Crisp Bullard had noted that if Blackett were correct that all of Earth's rotating mass contributes to its magnetic field, then intensity should decrease with depth in the Earth, whereas if electrical currents in Earth's core produced its magnetism, then the magnetic field should increase with depth.

Runcorn first worked out the theory behind the test and was satisfied that these effects should be measurable. Then he directed a series of magnetic measurements in mines in the United Kingdom from 1947 to 1951. He drew his instrumentation and methods from colleagues in Holland and Scandinavia. Although Runcorn's initial results (and those of others) supported Blackett's theory, later results contradicted it. Runcorn's first research project in geomagnetism demanded significant theoretical

and experimental acumen. While part of the team measured magnetic intensity 900 meters (2,950 feet) down, others observed magnetic diurnal variation at the surface, and still others flew an aeromagnetic survey overhead. This large-scale experimental approach to geophysics came to characterize Runcorn's research. Likewise, following the leads of Blackett and Bullard, Runcorn developed geomagnetic research projects that tested elements of theory against observables. This contrasted sharply with the gulf between physical speculation and magnetic data gathering of previous generations of researchers. Runcorn obtained his PhD from Manchester in 1949 based on this project.

During his time at Manchester from 1946 to 1950, Runcorn also had his first experience measuring the magnetism of sediments and familiarized himself with similar research underway in Europe and at the Department of Terrestrial Magnetism of the Carnegie Institution of Washington in Washington, D.C. He taught the geomagnetism part of a course on geophysics for postgraduate students and attended meetings of the International Union of Geodesy and Geophysics and the Geophysical Section of the Royal Astronomical Society. At the latter in 1949, J. M. Bruckshaw introduced him (and others) to the possible reverse magnetization of some rocks, until then a neglected (though known) phenomenon. Runcorn shifted his interest to paleomagnetism and to questions of deep-Earth processes this ancient record could address.

Move to Cambridge. Meanwhile, Runcorn was elected to a fellowship at his alma mater, Gonville and Caius College, Cambridge University, in 1948 and was also promoted from assistant lecturer to lecturer at Manchester. In 1950 Ben Browne invited him to apply for Bullard's former position as assistant director of research at the Cambridge Department of Geodesy and Geophysics, and he moved to Cambridge, at that time one of the leading research centers in geophysics in the world. As at Manchester, at Cambridge Runcorn included research students in his coordinated research projects. Many of these students later developed significant research careers.

In the 1950s Runcorn investigated paleomagnetism from many perspectives. To measure the weak remanent magnetism of rocks, he borrowed the very sensitive astatic magnetometer Blackett had designed for testing his theory of the rotational origin of magnetism. He had Kenneth Creer, a research student, produce a copy of this instrument for use at Cambridge in 1951, thus beginning a second British paleomagnetic research program. This program began an active collaboration between geologists and geophysicists at Cambridge. Runcorn also strengthened cooperation with the British Geological Survey.

Trained as an engineer and a physicist, Runcorn admitted his limited knowledge of geology.

Given that background, Runcorn directed his attention not to Earth's crust but toward the mantle and core. When Jan Hospers published his paleomagnetic study of Tertiary Icelandic lavas in 1951, Runcorn noted the axial character of the magnetic field at that geological epoch and thought this indicated a connection between the Coriolis force and core motions. He assigned research students to conduct rotating convection experiments as a model of convection in the core and to investigate electrical conductivity of minerals and the paleomagnetism of the Precambrian Torridonian formation. He collected rock samples at the Grand Canyon in Arizona in 1954 and 1955 for the same purpose. Runcorn intended to determine the changing orientation of Earth's magnetic dipole axis through paleomagnetic measurements.

While some other scientists in the early 1950s entertained the possibility of continental drift, Runcorn saw his paleomagnetic work in a different context. Having rejected Blackett's rotational theory of Earth's magnetism, he considered a core dynamo more likely. This led him to assume the alignment of Earth's dipole axis with its rotational axis. He linked magnetic reversals to a dynamo model and to paleomagnetic results. That these results indicated a strongly oblique magnetic axis, differently oriented at different geological periods, led Runcorn to consider the possibility that Earth's rotational axis had "wandered." Polar wander became Runcorn's alternative, overarching theory. Already in 1954, he and colleagues had produced a "polar wander curve" on a globe for a Royal Society soirée.

The idea of polar wander led him and then graduate student Neil Opdyke (at Columbia University in New York City) to investigate paleoclimates correlated against paleomagnetic results. Initial paleomagnetic results from Britain and the Grand Canyon indicated roughly the same axial orientations (erroneously). Wandering poles should mean wandering polar and equatorial climatic zones. Hence, Runcorn and Opdyke investigated paleoclimate, too. New field results in 1955 and 1956 indicated that the "latitude" was wrong. As he, Edward Irving, and others obtained paleomagnetic results from the United States, Australia, and elsewhere, it became clear that results from different continents indicated different dipole axes. That is, Runcorn came to see this as evidence of continental drift. In 1956 Runcorn became enthusiastic about this evidence; it changed the context of paleomagnetic research for him from polar wander to continental drift. Notably, this is several years after Blackett, Ronald A. Fisher, and other British colleagues had begun to consider drift seriously. He did not, however, abandon the idea of polar wander; he now considered how polar wan-

der and drift could both occur and both contribute to the observed phenomena.

Planetary Studies. In January 1956, Runcorn accepted the chair of physics at King's College, University of Newcastle at Newcastle upon Tyne (then the University of Durham). He also served as head of the Physics Department from 1956 until his retirement in 1988. Runcorn brought former research students to Newcastle as junior faculty members and built a strong geophysical research program within the Physics Department. The group contributed to many research areas, including convection in the Earth and Moon, the magnetic fields of the Moon and planets, magnetohydrodynamics of Earth's core, changes in length of day, and various topics in paleogeophysics. He organized many conferences funded by the North Atlantic Treaty Organization, bringing international colleagues together in Newcastle to consider geophysical issues.

During his thirty-two years as head of the Physics Department at Newcastle, Runcorn traveled almost incessantly, lecturing to geophysicists around the world. For example, in 1957 he was visiting professor of geophysics at the California Institute of Technology (Caltech) in Pasadena, California, in 1961 and 1962 a visiting scientist at the Jet Propulsion Laboratory at Caltech, and in 1963 a senior visiting fellow at the Australian Academy of Science. Although most of these visiting posts occurred during summer breaks in the academic schedule, a number were during the academic year. Runcorn also attended a great many scientific meetings. He was sometimes referred to as the "theoretical visiting professor of physics in Newcastle."

Runcorn never abandoned the idea that the core of a planet (or a moon) might display complex interactions with its surface. That is, acceptance of continental drift did not deny the possibilities of polar wander and a slippage between Earth's core and mantle. These just became secondary phenomena. In the 1960s he continued to publish articles such as "Paleomagnetic Methods of Investigating Polar Wandering and Continental Drift" (1953) and many articles on the effects of convection currents in the mantle on continental displacement.

Runcorn also considered possible electromagnetic linkages between the core and mantle and how these could affect the rotation of the planet. He saw Earth as part of a complex system of interacting forces, including these electromagnetic linkages as well as tidal friction interactions with the Moon. He even saw coral growth rings as an independent way to check other means of studying Earth's rotation rate. When Runcorn undertook an empirical study, whether of paleomagnetism, coral growth rings, or predominant climates or wind directions in ages long past, it was never a simple empirical study. It was always part of a deep investigation of possible

Earth-system phenomena. It was always tied to profound, if tentative, theory.

Runcorn received many honors. The Royal Meteorological Society awarded him its Napier Shaw Prize in 1959 for studies of paleoclimate. He became a Fellow of the Royal Society of London in 1965. He received the Charles Chree Medal in 1969 from the Physical Society (which merged the next year with the Institute of Physics) and the most valued prize for earth science, the Vetlesen Prize, in 1971 from Columbia University and the Vetlesen Foundation (known as the Nobel Prize of Geology). In recognition of his research in planetary physics, the Royal Astronomical Society awarded him its Gold Medal in 1984. In 1987 the European Geophysical Society awarded him the Wegener Medal, a most appropriate award given Runcorn's important role in supporting the theory of continental drift. He was a Fellow of the Royal Astronomical Society, the Institute of Physics and the Physics Society, the American Physical Society, and the American Geophysical Union. Lastly, he received honorary doctorates from Utrecht, Ghent, Paris, and Bergen universities and was named Honorary or Foreign Fellow of the Indian National Science Academy, Royal Netherlands Academy of Science, Pontifical Academy of Science, Royal Norwegian Academy of Science and Letters, Academia Europaea, Bavarian Academy of Science, and Royal Society of New South Wales.

Keith Runcorn never married. A homosexual, he did not keep that fact secret, but neither did he make it a topic of conversation. He was murdered in a hotel room in San Diego, California, by a professional kickboxer who claimed he was defending himself from an unwanted sexual advance. The court convicted the kickboxer of first-degree murder and robbery and sentenced him to twenty-five years to life in prison.

Runcorn primarily dedicated himself to promoting geophysics and to his research. When he was murdered he was on his way to a meeting of the American Geophysical Union, which he attended regularly and where he was known for his active discussions with colleagues and students of geophysical theory and research. Keith Runcorn's curiosity and open mind about the deepest processes within Earth's core and mantle, and his broad vision of Earth as one of many planets, are his greatest legacies.

BIBLIOGRAPHY

Runcorn's correspondence, manuscript notebooks, and other papers are at Imperial College, London. The collection of Sir Edward Crisp Bullard at Churchill College, Cambridge, U.K., includes extensive Runcorn correspondence. A bibliography of over four hundred research articles and monographs is available in the database GEOREF.

WORKS BY RUNCORN

"The Radial Variation of the Earth's Magnetic Field." *Proceedings of the Royal Society Series A,* 61 (1948): 373–382.

"Variation of Geomagnetic Intensity with Depth." *Nature* 161 (1948): 52.

With A. C. Benson, D. H. Griffiths, and A. F. Moore. "Measurements of the Variation with Depth of the Main Geomagnetic Field." *Philosophical Transactions of the Royal Society of London Series A,* 244, no. 878 (1951): 113–151.

"The Earth's Core." *Transactions of the American Geophysical Union* 35, no. 1 (February 1954): 49–63.

"Rock Magnetism: Geophysical Aspects." *Advances in Physics* 4 (14) (1955): 244–291.

"The Earth's Magnetism." *Scientific American* 193, no. 3 (September 1955): 152–162. A readable overview.

With D. W. Collinson, K. M. Creer, and E. Irving. "The Measurement of the Permanent Magnetization of Rocks." *Philosophical Transactions of the Royal Society of London Series A,* 250, no. 974 (1957): 73–82.

With Edward Irving. "Analysis of the Palaeomagnetism of the Torridonian Sandstone Series of North-west Scotland." *Philosophical Transactions of the Royal Society of London Series A,* 250, no. 974 (1957): 83–99.

With Kenneth M. Creer. "Palaeomagnetic Results from Different Continents and Their Relation to the Problem of Continental Drift." *Annales de Geophysique* 14 (1959): 492–501.

"Rock Magnetism." *Science* 129, no. 3355 (17 April 1959): 1002–1012.

With D. W. Collinson. "Polar Wandering and Continental Drift—Evidence from Paleomagnetic Observations in the United States." *Geological Society of America Bulletin* 71, no. 7 (1960): 915–958.

With Neil D. Opdyke. "Wind Direction in the Western United States in the Late Paleozoic." *Geological Society of America Bulletin* 71, no. 7 (1960): 959–971.

"Climatic Change through Geological Time in the Light of the Palaeomagnetic Evidence for Polar Wandering and Continental Drift." *Royal Meteorological Society Quarterly Journal* 87, no. 373 (1961): 282–313.

"Palaeomagnet Methor or Investigating Polar Wandering and Continental Drift." *Society of Economic Paleontologists and Mineralogists* 10 (1963): 47–54.

"Palaeomagnetic Comparisons between Europe and North America: Symposium on Continental Drift." *Royal Society of London, Philosophical Transactions Series A,* 258, no. 1088 (1965): 1–11.

"Planetary Magnetic Fields as a Test of the Dynamo Theory." *Geophysical Journal of the Royal Astronomical Society* 15 (1968): 183–189.

"On the Interpretation of Lunar Magnetism." *Physics of the Earth and Planetary Interiors* 10, no. 4 (August 1975): 327–335.

"Mechanism of Plate Tectonics: Mantle Convection Currents, Plumes, Gravity Sliding or Expansion? Orthodoxy and Creativity at the Frontiers of Earth Sciences." *Tectonophysics* 63 (10 March 1980): 297–307.

With Kenneth M. Creer and John A. Jacobs. "The Role of the Core in Irregular Fluctuations of the Earth's Rotation and the Excitation of the Chandler Wobble—The Earth's Core: Its Structure, Evolution, and Magnetic Field: Discussion." *Philosophical Transactions of the Royal Society of London Series A,* no. 306, no. 1492 (1982): 261–270.

"The Moon's Ancient Magnetism." *Scientific American* 257, no. 6 (December 1987): 60–68.

OTHER SOURCES

Collinson, D. W. "Stanley Keith Runcorn." *Biographical Memoirs of the Royal Society of London* 48 (2002): 391–403.

Creer, Kenneth M. "(Stanley) Keith Runcorn." *Oxford Dictionary of National Biography.* Vol. 48. Oxford, U.K.: Oxford University Press, 2004.

Lowes, Frank J. "Keith's Early Work in Geomagnetism." *Physics and Chemistry of the Earth* 23, nos. 7–8 (1998): 703–707.

Nye, Mary Jo. *Blackett: Physics, War, and Politics in the Twentieth Century.* Cambridge, MA: Harvard University Press, 2004.

Gregory A. Good

RYLE, MARTIN (*b.* Brighton, Sussex, United Kingdom, 27 September 1918; *d.* Cambridge, Cambridgeshire, United Kingdom, 14 October 1984), *radio astronomy, aperture synthesis, evolutionary cosmology, radio galaxies, and quasars.*

Ryle was one of the most important pioneers of radio astronomy. His major contributions concerned the practical implementation of the principles of aperture synthesis, resulting in enormous increases in angular resolution and sensitivity for radio astronomical observations. These revealed the detailed radio structures of galactic and extragalactic radio sources for the first time and established the strong evolution of the source population with cosmic epoch. He was awarded the Nobel Prize in Physics, jointly with Antony Hewish, in 1974.

Prewar and War Years. Ryle was the second son and second child in a family of three sons and two daughters of John Alfred Ryle, a professor of medicine, and his wife, Miriam Power, the daughter of William Charles Scully, a civil servant who came from a landowning family in county Tipperary in Ireland. His father, a medical doctor, was to become Regius Professor of Physics at Cambridge University, and after World War II, the first professor of social medicine at Oxford University. His uncle, Gilbert Ryle, was a professor of philosophy at Oxford.

Martin Ryle's early education was entrusted to a governess who taught him and his siblings at the family home on Wimpole Street, London. He then attended Gladstone's preparatory school in Eaton Square, London,

before entering Bradfield College, Berkshire, at age thirteen. His ability with his hands was fostered at home, where regular instruction was provided to him and his elder brother by a professional carpenter. In 1936 he entered Christ Church, Oxford, where he obtained first class honors in physics in 1939. His enthusiasm for radio engineering and electronics was already apparent. By the time he left school, he had built his own radio transmitter and acquired a post office license to operate it. At Oxford, he and E. Cooke-Yarborough, a fellow undergraduate, set up the university amateur radio station.

In 1939, Ryle joined J. A. Ratcliffe's ionospheric research group at the Cavendish Laboratory at Cambridge University. On the outbreak of World War II, Ratcliffe joined the Air Ministry Research Establishment, later to become the Telecommunications Research Establishment (TRE), and Ryle followed in May 1940. For the first two years, he worked mainly on the design of antennae and test equipment. In 1942, he became the leader of Group 5 of the newly formed Radio Countermeasures Division, whose task was to provide jamming transmitters against the German radar defense system and to devise radio-deception operations. Among the latter was the electronic "spoof invasion" on D-day, which led the German High Command to believe that the invasion was to take place across the Straits of Dover, rather than in Normandy.

Radar techniques developed at an astounding pace during these years, and Ryle and his colleagues worked in a frantic atmosphere, constantly having to find immediate practical solutions for the electronic defense of the RAF's bomber fleet. Bernard Lovell remarked, "As head of this group, Ryle's extraordinary inventiveness and scientific understanding soon became evident. Under the stress of urgent operational requirements he became intolerant of those who were not blessed with his immediate insight" (p. 359).

But Ryle also learned how to motivate groups of research workers. In a letter to the present writer, written only two months before his death, he wrote,

> Presumably I knew some physics in 1939—but this evaporated during the six succeeding years— though it was replaced by other things. But six years of designing/installing/flying boxes of electronics gave one "state of the art" electronics, a fair intimacy with aircraft and the ability to talk constructively with Air Vice-Marshals—or radar mechanics—and above all gave one the privilege of flying with the in-between-operational-tours aircrew who flew our aircraft.

According to Francis Graham-Smith, perhaps the greatest achievement of his war years was the discovery of a vulnerable element in the V-2 rocket radio guidance system. The system developed by Ryle and his old college

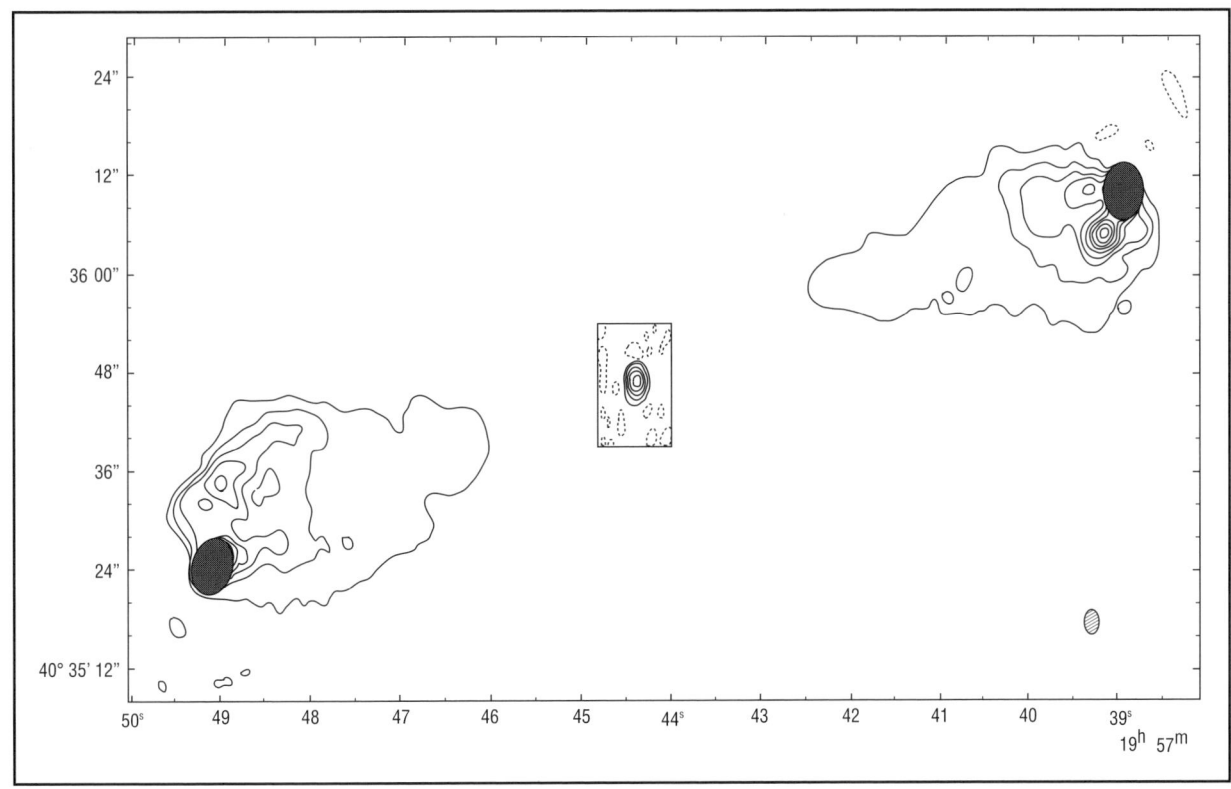

Figure 1. *The first map of the radio source Cygnus A observed with an angular resolution of 2.5 arcsec by the 5-km Telescope.*

friend Cooke-Yarborough successfully disrupted the accurate aim of the V-2 rockets and probably contributed to the abandonment of radio control only a few weeks later.

Development of Radio Astronomy. After the war, Ryle returned to Cambridge on an Imperial Chemical Industries fellowship and soon turned his energies to understanding the nature of the radio emissions from cosmic sources that had interfered with antiaircraft radars. J. S. Hey had found that the jamming was caused by intense radio outbursts from the Sun, apparently associated with large solar flares and sunspot groups. The angular resolving power of the radio antennae available at that time was not sufficient to resolve the disk of the Sun, let alone locate the origin of the radio emission on it. Ryle and D. D. Vonberg adapted surplus radar equipment and developed new receiver techniques for meter wavelengths to create a radio interferometer, the antennae being separated by several hundreds of meters in order to provide high enough angular resolution. Only later was it realized that they had reinvented the radio equivalent of the Michelson interferometer. A massive sunspot occurred in July 1946, and their observations showed conclusively that the radio emission originated from a region on the surface of the Sun similar in size to that of the sunspot region.

In addition to the emission from the Sun, Hey had discovered a discrete source of radio emission in the constellation of Cygnus and Ryle and Francis Graham-Smith, later Sir Francis Graham-Smith, adapted the solar interferometer to observe the radio source, which became known as Cygnus A. In 1947, the source was successfully observed and, in addition, another even more intense discrete source was found in the nearby constellation of Cassiopeia. By 1950, Graham-Smith had measured very precisely the position of Cygnus A, and it was found that the source was associated with a distant, massive galaxy.

As the fledgling radio group began to take shape, Ryle married Ella Rowena Palmer, the youngest sister of Graham-Smith's wife, Elizabeth, in 1947. It was a wonderfully happy marriage and they had three children, Alison, John, and Claire. Somewhat to his surprise, midway through his fellowship, Ryle was appointed a university lecturer at Cambridge in 1948. In 1952, he was elected a Fellow of the Royal Society.

Although trained as a physicist, Ryle was primarily an electrical engineer with a genius for making complex radio receiving systems operate. His contribution of genius was the practical development of the concept of aperture synthesis, the technique by which images of radio sources are created by combining interferometric observations made with modest-sized radio telescopes located at different interferometer spacings. The basic principles of interferometry had been understood since the time of Albert Abraham Michelson and interferometry was used successfully to study the radio emission of the Sun and the very brightest radio sources. Ryle's more ambitious program was to determine both the amplitudes and phases of the incoming radio signals so that, by Fourier inversion, the detailed brightness distribution of the radio emission could be reconstructed. Although understood in principle, the key technical issues concerned whether or not these concepts could be realized in practice, given the problems of receiver sensitivity, the need to preserve phase coherence over long periods, and the stability of overall system performance.

Over the twenty-five-year period starting in 1950, Ryle and his colleagues developed a series of radio interferometers of increasing complexity and ingenuity that made it possible to carry out surveys of the sky and unravel the structures and nature of the radio sources. This program involved a great deal of innovative electronics, such as the phase-switching interferometer, which enabled the full amplitude and phase information to be recovered. The practical development of aperture synthesis was a virtuoso technical achievement that involved a considerable team of researchers and support staff. Ryle put together a tightly knit group of physicists, including Francis Graham-Smith, Antony Hewish, John Baldwin, John Shakeshaft, Bruce Elsmore, Paul Scott, and Sidney Kenderdine, as well as a strong support team of technicians and research students, many of whom were later to become leaders in radio astrophysics. Those of us who were members of the radio astronomy group remember Ryle's inspiring leadership and total involvement in all aspects of our work.

Radio Source Number Counts. Throughout the 1950s and 1960s, one of Ryle's major objectives was to produce reliable catalogs of all the bright radio sources in the northern sky. In "Radio Astronomy," his review of the new science of radio astronomy published in 1950, he expressed his belief that most of the "radio stars" belonged to our own galaxy. As early as 1949, however, the Australian astronomers John Bolton, Gordon Stanley, and Bruce Slee had shown that two of the brightest sources were associated with nearby galaxies with strange optical features, the galaxies M87 and NGC 5128. The first Cambridge survey of radio sources, published in 1950 by Ryle, Graham-Smith, and Bruce Elsmore, showed that the distribution of radio stars was remarkably uniform over the sky.

Ryle and Antony Hewish designed and constructed a large, four-element interferometer on the rifle range site just behind Ryle's house in Herschel Road, Cambridge, to carry out a new survey of the sky at 81.5 MHz, which was also an interferometer and therefore sensitive to small angular diameter sources. The second Cambridge (2C) survey of radio sources was completed in 1954 and the first results published in the following year. Ryle and his colleagues found that the small-diameter radio sources were uniformly distributed over the sky and that the numbers of sources increased enormously as the survey extended to fainter and fainter flux densities. In any uniform Euclidean model, the numbers of sources brighter than a given limiting flux density S are expected to follow the relation $N(\geq S) \propto S^{-3/2}$ In contrast, Ryle found a huge excess of faint radio sources, the slope of the source counts between 20 and 60 Jy being described by $N(\geq S) \propto S^{-3}$ (The Jy, or Jansky, is a unit of radio flux density used in radio astronomy, named in honor of Carl Jansky, who discovered the cosmic radio emission in 1933. In SI units, 1 Jy = 1 Jansky = 10^{-26} W m^{-2} Hz^{-1}.) He concluded that the only reasonable interpretation of these data was that the sources were extragalactic; that they were objects similar in radio luminosity to the radio galaxy Cygnus A; and that the radio sources were very much more numerous at large distances, and hence at earlier cosmological epochs, than there are nearby. As Ryle announced in his Halley Lecture in Oxford in 1955, "This is a most remarkable and important result, but if we accept the conclusion that most of the radio stars are external to the Galaxy, and this conclusion seems hard to avoid, then there seems no way in which the observations can be explained in terms of a Steady-State theory [of the universe]" ("Radio Stars and Their Cosmological Significance," p. 146).

These remarkable conclusions came as a surprise to the astronomical community. There was enthusiasm but also some skepticism that such profound conclusions could be drawn from the counts of radio sources, particularly when their physical nature was not understood and only the brightest twenty or so objects had been associated with relatively nearby galaxies.

The members of the Sydney (Australia) group led by Bernard Mills were carrying out radio surveys of the southern sky at about the same time with the Mills Cross telescope, which was sensitive to sources of large angular sizes; they found that the source counts could be represented by the relation $N(\geq S) \propto S^{-1.65}$ which they argued was not significantly different from the expectation of uniform world models. In 1957 Mills and Bruce Slee stated: "We therefore conclude that discrepancies, in the main, reflect errors in the Cambridge catalogue, and accordingly deductions of cosmological interest derived from its analysis are without foundation. An analysis of our results shows that there is no clear evidence for any effect of cosmological importance in the source counts" (p. 181).

The problem with the Cambridge number counts was that they extended to number densities of radio sources such that the flux densities of the faintest sources were overestimated because of the presence of faint sources in the beam of the telescope, a phenomenon known as "confusion." Peter Scheuer, who was Martin Ryle's research student from 1951 to 1954, devised a statistical procedure for deriving the number counts of sources from the survey records themselves without the need to identify individual sources. The technique that he discovered, which he referred to as the *P(D)* technique and which has since been adopted in many other astronomical contexts, showed that the slope of the source counts was actually −1.8. Ironically, this result, which is exactly the correct answer, was not trusted, partly because the mathematical techniques used by Scheuer were somewhat forbidding and also because his result differed from the preconceived opinions of both Ryle and Mills. The dispute reached its climax at the Paris Symposium on Radio Astronomy in 1958, and the conflicting positions were not resolved at that meeting.

These events had positive and negative impacts upon the work of the Cambridge radio astronomy group. The negative side was that the group became more defensive in its interaction with outside groups. Great care was taken to ensure the reliability and completeness of subsequent catalogs and radio maps and it was some considerable time before they were released to the astronomical community. The positive side was that it was apparent to Cambridge University and the community at large that new astrophysical and cosmological opportunities had been opened up. In 1956, the radio observatory moved to a disused wartime Air Ministry bomb store at Lord's Bridge outside Cambridge, and in acknowledgment of a grant of £100,000 from the electronics company Mullard Ltd., the new observatory was opened in 1957 at Lord's Bridge as the Mullard Radio Astronomy Observatory.

The resolution of the controversy over the number counts of sources came with the construction of the next generation of radio telescopes, which had higher angular resolution and hence were less sensitive to the effects of source confusion. In the revised third Cambridge catalog (3CR) and the 4C catalog, care was taken to understand the effects of confusion, and the accuracy of the radio source positions was improved so that more radio sources could be identified with distant galaxies. A major breakthrough resulting from these studies was the discovery of quasars in the early 1960s through Cyril Hazard's radio occultation observations of the source 3C 273 with the Parkes radio telescope in Australia and the subsequent

Martin Ryle. HULTON ARCHIVE/GETTY IMAGES.

measurement of the large redshift of the starlike object by Maarten Schmidt in 1963. Within a couple of years, over forty quasars were discovered among the 3CR sources.

The radio source counts derived from the 4C survey were continually refined in the period from 1961 to 1966 and showed a significant excess over the expectations of Euclidean world models, the source count slope being found to be −1.8. Ryle's conclusions of 1955 were basically correct, but the magnitude of the excess had been overestimated. By the mid-1960s, there was compelling evidence that there is indeed an excess of sources at large redshifts and that they corresponded to large evolutionary changes with cosmic epoch.

Earth Rotation Aperture Synthesis. In 1959 Ryle was appointed professor of radio astronomy in the Cavendish Laboratory in the Department of Physics of Cambridge University. In the early 1960s, his most ambitious experiment to date was underway: the use of the rotation of Earth to carry telescopes at fixed points on Earth about each other as observed from a point on the celestial sphere. The germ of this idea had already appeared in his notebooks in 1954. By 1959, digital computers were fast enough to cope with the demands of this form of synthesis mapping and, in a classic set of observations, Ryle and

Ann C. Neville created an Earth-rotation aperture synthesis map of a region of sky about the north celestial pole. The angular resolution of the survey was 4.5 arcmin and the sensitivity eight times greater than that of the original antenna system.

The success of this project pointed the way to the future. The succeeding generations of aperture synthesis arrays employed fully steerable antennae—as with the One-Mile Telescope completed in 1965 and the 5-kilometer telescope, later known as the Ryle Telescope, in 1972. The first radio maps made by the One-Mile Telescope revealed the power of radio astronomy to uncover the structures of galactic and extragalactic radio sources and led to new astrophysical challenges concerning the origin of the enormous fluxes of relativistic electrons and magnetic fields present in these sources. In addition, the number counts of sources in the 5C catalogs extended to very small flux densities at which the cosmological convergence expected in all world models was clearly observed. Both the One-Mile and 5-kilometer telescopes were far ahead of the radio astronomical capability of any other telescope system in the world.

The measure of Ryle's achievement was that, over a twenty-five-year period, the sensitivity of radio astronomical observations increased by a factor of about one million and the imaging capability of the telescope system improved from several degrees to a few arcseconds, comparable to that of ground-based optical telescopes. Ryle was personally involved in every aspect of these very complex telescope systems. As remarked by Scheuer, the development of aperture synthesis "was the story of one remarkable man, who not only provided the inspiration and driving force but actually designed most of the bits and pieces, charmed or savaged official persons according to their deserts, wielded shovels and sledgehammers, mended breakdowns, and kept the rest of us on our toes" (Sullivan, 1984, pp. 263–264).

Intellectually, he relied almost completely upon his well-honed intuitive understanding of physical processes as the way to solve any problem, be it in engineering, astrophysics, or cosmology; indeed, he believed this was the only way research should be conducted. These telescopes were central to understanding the nature of the radio sources. Radio astronomy has played a crucial role in the realization that high-energy astrophysical activity involving supermassive black holes and general relativity are part of the large-scale fabric of our universe. Ryle was knighted in 1966.

From the beginning, the Cambridge radio astronomy group developed a remarkably coherent and focused research program, led by the dynamism and vision of Ryle. He was fortunate in being supported by an outstanding group of physicists. Among these, Antony

Hewish had played a central role in the development of aperture synthesis and in 1964 began the study of the twinkling, or scintillation, of radio sources due to irregularities in the outflow of material from the Sun, what is known as the solar wind. A remarkable by-product of these studies was the discovery of pulsating radio sources, subsequently called pulsars, by Hewish and his graduate student, Jocelyn Bell. These objects were soon convincingly identified as rapidly rotating, magnetized neutrons stars, which had been predicted to exist on theoretical grounds. Their serendipitous discovery at long radio wavelengths was a crucial event for all astronomy.

National and International Recognition. In 1974, Ryle and Hewish were jointly awarded the Nobel Prize in Physics, the citation explicitly describing the development of aperture synthesis as Ryle's major contribution. His list of honors was extensive, including foreign memberships in the Royal Danish Academy of Sciences and Letters, (1968), the American Academy of Arts and Sciences (1970), and the U.S.S.R. Academy of Sciences (1971). Among many medals received were the Gold Medal of the Royal Astronomical Society (1964), the Popov Medal of the U.S.S.R. Academy of Sciences (1971), and the Royal Medal of the Royal Society of London (1973).

In 1972 Ryle was appointed Astronomer Royal, the first time the post was separated from the directorship of the Royal Greenwich Observatory. This period coincided with a grave deterioration in his health, at least partly brought on by the stress of telescope construction over many years, but originating from a malfunctioning heart. Exploration for this condition exposed lung cancer, for which he had surgery in 1977. Over the same period, his main preoccupations shifted from radio astronomy. His acute awareness of the dangers of nuclear power fueled a passionate, ethical sense of crusade concerning the potential misuse of science. His conviction was that we violate the natural order at our peril. His deep concern for alternative energy sources led to an enthusiasm for wind energy, a natural outcome of his expertise as a sailboat designer, and he began a successful research and development program at Lord's Bridge involving the construction of wind-powered generators. He was passionately concerned about the proliferation of nuclear weapons and wrote a monograph, *Towards the Nuclear Holocaust*, which, as expressed by Graham-Smith, "is partly a cry of pain and a desperate plea for a halt in the arms race, and partly an indictment of all those concerned with the civil nuclear programme, which he regarded as sustainable only on account of its production of plutonium for military purposes" (1986, pp. 517–518).

Ryle died in 1984 at the family home in Cambridge. His legacy went far beyond the technical brilliance of his contribution to radio astronomy. When he began his career after the war, the United Kingdom could not compete with the United States in observational astronomy. Through his technical and scientific contributions as well as his inspiring leadership, Ryle played a major role in rejuvenating British astronomy and bringing it to a leadership position in world astronomy.

BIBLIOGRAPHY

Ryle's papers and working materials are archived at Churchill College, Cambridge University, Cambridge, U.K. A sample of historical exhibits showing the development of radio astronomy in Cambridge is contained in the Meeting Room at the Lord's Bridge Observatory. A complete list of Ryle's publications is contained in an obituary, Francis Graham-Smith, "Sir Martin Ryle: A Biographical Memoir," Biographical Memoirs of Fellows of the Royal Society *33 (1986): 495–524.*

WORKS BY RYLE

With F. G. Smith. "A New Intense Source of Radio-Frequency Radiation in the Constellation of Cassiopeia." *Nature* 162 (1948): 462–463.

"Radio Astronomy." *Reports on Progress in Physics* 13 (1950): 184–246.

With F. G. Smith and B. Elsmore. "A Preliminary Survey of the Radio Stars in the Northern Hemisphere." *Monthly Notices of the Royal Astronomical Society* 110 (1950): 508–523. This was the first Cambridge survey of radio sources.

"A New Radio Interferometer and Its Application to the Observation of Weak Radio Stars." *Proceedings of the Royal Society of London.* Series A, *Mathematical and Physical Sciences* 211 (1952): 351–375.

With K. E. Machin and D. D. Vonberg. "The Design of an Equipment for Measuring Small Radio-Frequency Noise Powers." *Proceedings of the Institution of Electrical Engineers* 99 (May 1952): 127–134.

"Radio Stars and Their Cosmological Significance." *Observatory* 75 (1955): 137–147. This is the published version of Ryle's Halley Lecture, given at Oxford University.

With J. R. Shakeshaft, J. E. Baldwin, B. Elsmore, et al. "A Survey of Radio Sources between Declinations −38° and +83°." *Memoirs of the Royal Astronomical Society* 67 (1955): 106–154. This is referred to as the 2C survey.

With A. Hewish. "The Synthesis of Large Radio Telescopes." *Monthly Notices of the Royal Astronomical Society* 120 (1960): 220–230.

With A. C. Neville. "A Radio Survey of the North Polar Region with a 4.5 Minute of Arc Pencil-Beam System." *Monthly Notices of the Royal Astronomical Society* 125 (1962): 39–56.

With B. Elsmore and A. C. Neville. "High-Resolution Observations of the Radio Sources in Cygnus and Cassiopeia." *Nature* 205 (1965): 1259–1262.

With G. G. Pooley. "The Extension of the Number-Flux Density Relation for Radio Sources to Very Small Flux Densities." *Monthly Notices of the Royal Astronomical Society* 139 (1968): 515–528.

"The 5-km Radio Telescope at Cambridge." *Nature* 239 (1972): 435–438.

With P. J. Hargrave. "Observations of Cygnus A with the 5km Radio Telescope." *Monthly Notices of the Royal Astronomical Society* 166 (1974): 305–327.

"Radio Telescopes of Large Resolving Power." *Reviews of Modern Physics* 47 (1975): 557–566. This is Ryle's Nobel Prize lecture.

Towards the Nuclear Holocaust. 2nd ed. London: Menard Press, 1981.

OTHER SOURCES

Bertotti, B., R. Balbinot, S. Bergia, et al., eds. *Modern Cosmology in Retrospect.* Cambridge, U.K.: Cambridge University Press, 1990. Among the excellent articles in this volume, those by Peter Scheuer and Woodruff T. Sullivan III are of particular interest in relation to Ryle's scientific achievements.

Graham-Smith, Francis. "Sir Martin Ryle: A Biographical Memoir." *Biographical Memoirs of Fellows of the Royal Society* 33 (1986): 495–524.

Hey, J. S. The *Evolution of Radio Astronomy.* New York: Science History Publications, 1973. He was one of the earliest pioneers of radio astronomy, and this book gives a good picture of how the subject developed.

Kragh, Helge. *Cosmology and Controversy: The Historical Development of Two Theories of the Universe.* Princeton, NJ: Princeton University Press, 1996. This book gives a thorough and readable account of the controversies concerning evolutionary and steady state cosmologies.

Longair, Malcolm S. *The Cosmic Century: A History of Astrophysics and Cosmology.* Cambridge, U.K.: Cambridge University Press, 2006. This volume sets the development of radio astronomy and cosmology in its wider astrophysical and cosmological context.

Lovell, A. C. B. "Martin Ryle." *Quarterly Journal of the Royal Astronomical Society* 26 (1985): 358–368.

Mills, B. Y., and O. B. Slee. "A Preliminary Survey of Radio Sources in a Limited Region of Sky at a Wavelength of 3.5 m." *Australian Journal of Physics* 10 (1957): 162–194.

Pooley, G. G. "Sir Martin Ryle." *Observatory* 104 (1984): 283–284.

Smith, F. G. "Ryle, M. 1918–1984." *Nature* 312 (1984): 18.

———. "Martin Ryle, Pioneer Radio Astronomer." *Sky and Telescope* 69 (1985): 123.

Sullivan, W. T., III. *Classics in Radio Astronomy.* Dordrecht, Netherlands: D. Reidel, 1982. This is a very useful compilation of important early papers on radio astronomy.

———, ed. *The Early Years of Radio Astronomy.* Cambridge, U.K.: Cambridge University Press, 1984. This is an excellent survey of the early history of radio astronomy.

Malcolm S. Longair

S

SAGAN, CARL EDWARD (*b.* Brooklyn, New York, 9 November 1934; *d.* Seattle, Washington, 20 December 1996), *space science, astronomy, astrobiology, biomolecular evolution, atmospheric chemistry, atmospheric radiative transfer, extraterrestrial aeolian dynamics, science journalism, philosophy of science.*

Sagan was one of the best-known planetary scientists and science popularizers of the twentieth century, a winner of the Pulitzer Prize and the Public Welfare Medal of the U.S. National Academy of Sciences. To the general public, he is mainly recalled as a television personality—in particular, as a suave commentator on the possibility of extraterrestrial life and on the robotic exploration of the solar system. Secondarily, and more controversially, he is recalled as a firm secularist who defended the superiority of science and reason against what he depicted as pseudoscience and irrationalism. He is also remembered as an anti–nuclear weapons activist who clashed with the United States's right-wing presidential leadership during the last decade of the Cold War. Diverse in the extreme, Sagan attained fame or notoriety for his imaginative speculations on subjects as different as astronomy, neuroscience, biomolecular evolution, nuclear weapons policy, hypothetical exploration strategies for interstellar spaceships, and the physics of dust transport and radiative transfer in planetary atmospheres. The author or coauthor of numerous books and hundreds of scientific papers, he was an urbane, dryly witty speaker who made many appearances on television and hosted the controversial television science series *Cosmos* (1980). Of his popular books, one won the Pulitzer Prize; another inspired a Hollywood "blockbuster" film that envisioned radio communication with semi-godlike aliens from other worlds.

Origins. Born Carl Edward Sagan in Depression-era Brooklyn, New York, he was the first of two children (and the only son) of a Jewish couple, Samuel Sagan and Rachel Molly Gruber Sagan. Samuel Sagan was a Ukrainian émigré who worked his way up from a job as a garment cutter to factory manager. Born in the United States but raised for several years in Austria, Rachel Sagan was a smart, abrasive woman who pressured her son to think logically and to succeed. Even as an adult, according to some accounts, Carl was neurotically anxious about his relationship with his mother.

When he expressed curiosity about stars at age five, his mother suggested that he go to the library and find a book on the subject. He complied, thereby launching his astronomical career. Carl's parents took him to the New York World's Fair of 1939–1940, where he thrilled to see its "extremely technocratic" vision of the future. As an adolescent he loved reading science-fiction stories in "pulp" books and magazines. He was thrilled by reports of "flying saucers" that, he suspected, might be extraterrestrial spaceships. Also while young he became a religious skeptic at least partly because he discovered contradictions in the Bible. (Throughout his life he seemed to waver between agnosticism and atheism. Even so, he was friendly with theologians and pondered quasi-religious themes in his only novel.)

Education and Interest in Extraterrestrial Life. Carl attended high school in Rahway, New Jersey. He became president of the chemistry club and was voted the male students' "Class Brain" and "Most Likely to Succeed." Graduating in 1951, he entered the University of Chicago just shy of his seventeenth birthday. He imbibed the rich diet of classically based education then offered by the school's controversial "Hutchins program." He was a very good, although not brilliant, student in physics. Also, he ran the astronomy club's "theoretical" section (but he cared little for observing). A budding showman, he worked at the campus radio station, where he scripted a program on spaceflight and flying saucers. Although he later became an aggressive UFO skeptic, as an undergraduate he took the "saucer" phenomenon seriously. He even wrote the U.S. Secretary of State to ask if the nation could defend itself in the "extremely remote" chance of an alien attack.

His fascination with other worlds was strengthened by a famous experiment conducted on campus during his undergraduate years. Stanley Miller, a student of Harold Urey, experimentally simulated a reducing (hydrogen-rich) atmosphere in which methane and ammonia were exposed to electrical discharges. The product was scummy layers of amino acids, the building blocks of proteins. The Miller-Urey experiment had a powerful impact on young Sagan. As a religious skeptic, he welcomed physical explanations for the origins of life, as opposed to biblical or vitalistic ones. Even more appealing to him were the extraterrestrial implications of Miller's experiment: Because amino acids formed readily in the proper chemical environment, the building blocks of life might exist on innumerable worlds. Given enough time, they might evolve into living, even intelligent, creatures.

After a period of decline, scientific openness to the idea of extraterrestrials had slowly revived in the 1940s and 1950s. The Miller-Urey experiment was one reason, which (as noted) implied prebiotic molecules might emerge readily wherever the planetary conditions were right. Another reason was Carl Friedrich von Weizsäcker's wartime revival and updating of the Kant-Laplace nebular hypothesis of solar system formation: In his reformulation of the theory, planets were once again seen as a common byproduct of stellar birth. Meanwhile, recent technological innovations inspired new conjectures about extraterrestrial life. For example, after the postwar construction of large radio telescopes, Giuseppe Cocconi and Philip Morrison (1959) suggested the "dishes" might detect intelligent radio signals from interstellar civilizations. The late 1950s also inaugurated the space age: At last, robotic spaceships could directly visit and explore nearby planets, to determine whether they were inhabited by anything from microbes to "advanced" creatures. (As late as 1962, *Science* magazine ran an article that seriously speculated about the remote possibility of intelligent Martians.)

In this atmosphere of revived interest in alien life, young Sagan felt comfortable exploring the idea. He could be arrogant and abrasive, but he was also capable of great charm, and he knew how to convert older, more powerful scientists into mentors and allies. At his mother's behest, he obtained a summer job in 1952 as a lab aide to the geneticist Hermann J. Muller at Indiana University. A Nobel laureate, Muller was intrigued by the clever, enthusiastic young man, and even patiently listened to his youthful conjectures about UFOs. Thanks to Muller's clout, the twenty-three-year-old Sagan was able to publish his first scientific article, "Radiation and the Origin of the Gene," in the journal *Evolution* in 1957. At Chicago Sagan received an AB degree with general and special honors in 1954, an SB in physics in 1955, and a master's degree in physics in 1956. Then, under the supervision of Gerard P. Kuiper, Sagan began work on a doctoral thesis in the department of astronomy and astrophysics at the University of Chicago's Yerkes Observatory in Williams Bay, Wisconsin, where his distinguished instructors included Subrahmanyan Chandrasekhar. Sagan also gave public lectures at the observatory and hosted a lecture series starring notable scientists. In 1957, he married Lynn Alexander, a fellow student at the university. They had two children, Dorion (later a noted science writer) and Jeremy.

Despite "some faculty opposition" (as Kuiper called it), Sagan's doctoral thesis was accepted in 1960. Titled "Physical Studies of Planets," the unusually speculative dissertation explored three questions: (1) Could Miller-Urey-style processes and subsequent evolution have generated organic molecules and even microbes on the early Moon?; (2) Might complex organic molecules exist at the planet Jupiter, and if so, could their spectral signatures be detected remotely via astronomical spectroscopy?; and (3) What caused the intense microwave radiation from Venus, which was discovered by Cornell H. Mayer and others in 1956? In his dissertation, Sagan suggested that Miller-Urey-type processes might have occurred on the primordial Moon. Thus, he warned, future explorers must avoid ferrying biological contaminants to the surfaces of other worlds. Otherwise those contaminants might harm extant life forms or confuse future generations of researchers, who could have trouble distinguishing between native and imported species.

Thanks to Kuiper, Sagan was able to conduct a secret study for the U.S. Air Force–related Armour Research Foundation on the possibility and effects of detonating nuclear weapons in the Moon. (After his death, a biographer accused Sagan of violating security rules by confiding the existence of the secret study to a limited number of people in order to boost his chances of winning a fellowship in California. For details, see Davidson [1999], Reiffel [2000], and Broad [2000]).

As for the Venusian part of Sagan's dissertation: In 1940, based on spectroscopic evidence of abundant carbon dioxide in the Venusian atmosphere, Rupert Wildt

Carl Edward Sagan. *Carl Sagan standing with Voyager record.* © JP LAFFONT/CORBIS.

argued that the planet's atmosphere was exceedingly hot because the gas trapped infrared radiation (the greenhouse effect). Wildt calculated a high surface temperature, over 400 Kelvin, for Venus; even so, that number was on the low side if Mayer and his collaborators' subsequent microwave observations were correct. After uncovering Wildt's paper, Sagan modified it to account for the temperature discrepancy. He posited an extra ingredient in the Venusian atmosphere—water vapor, which, he proposed, trapped infrared radiation that would have otherwise leaked past the carbon dioxide. Nowadays Sagan's paper is recalled as a landmark in modern Venus studies. Even so, his model seriously overestimated the abundance of water vapor and nitrogen in the Venusian atmosphere, severely underestimated the atmospheric density, and significantly underestimated the surface temperature by about 150 Kelvin; it is nowadays thought to be about 750 Kelvin.

The Sagans' marriage was unhappy and they divorced after several years. His wife later remarried and became Lynn Margulis, a celebrated microbiologist. Although she retained a wry affection for her ex-husband, she recalled him after his death as a man with a "limited capacity for any kind of personal relationship. … He had to have ten thousand people all adulating him to make up for that fear that his mother was going to leave him."

Rise to Fame. In 1960, Sagan won a postdoctoral two-year Miller Fellowship at the University of California at Berkeley. During his time in California (which included a brief stint at Stanford), he helped a scientific team develop an infrared radiometer for NASA's *Mariner 2* robotic probe. The probe flew by Venus in December 1962 and measured a surface temperature of about 800 Kelvin. Also significantly, *Mariner 2*'s data indicated that the microwave radiation came from the planetary surface, as Sagan's greenhouse model implied, rather than from a highly ionized region far above the planet, as skeptics had proposed.

Sagan also won another influential ally in another future Nobelist, genetics professor Joshua Lederberg, who was then at the University of Wisconsin. Sagan and Lederberg coauthored an article, "Microenvironments for Life on Mars," in the *Proceedings of the National Academy of Sciences* in 1962. Lederberg treated Sagan as a kind of protégé. Thanks to the older man, Sagan gained entrée to inner sanctums of scientific influence—for example, to a scientific panel on planetary biocontamination that included some of the most distinguished researchers of the day. Among them were Melvin Calvin, Tommy Gold, Harold Urey, and Norman Horowitz, all of whom would later figure (positively or negatively) in Sagan's career. After Sagan's death, Lederberg recalled how he had acted as Sagan's early protector. He regarded the younger man as a "very bright young guy, full of ideas. … Some of them [were] kooky, but they were well worth listening to. … I was often his protector and defender from folks who thought he was wild" (Davidson, p. 90).

Sagan was fascinated by the possibility of radio communication with alien civilizations many light years from Earth. For a few months in 1960, radio astronomer Frank Drake launched the first space age search for alien signals at a radio telescope in Green Bank, West Virginia. In later years, when numerous similar radio telescope searches were conducted around the world, they became collectively known as the search for extraterrestrial intelligence or SETI. In late 1961, SETI strategies were discussed at a scientific workshop in Green Bank. The attendees included Sagan, Drake, Cocconi, Morrison, Calvin, Otto Struve, and other luminaries. Sagan argued that thousands of technically advanced civilizations might be scattered across the galaxy. Some of these societies might be able to communicate with Earth via radio. The back-and-forth messaging might take centuries because of Albert Einstein's speed limit on electromagnetic waves, but the participants felt the search for such signals was worthwhile anyway.

During Sagan's California period, he, Cyril Ponnamperuma, and Ruth Mariner published in *Nature* their claim to have synthesized adenosine triphosphate (ATP), a major source of cellular energy. They appear to have innocently misinterpreted their results, though. After Sagan and Ponnamperuma died, Mariner told a Sagan biographer that the experiment had produced far less ATP (if any) than was originally reported (Davidson, pp. 157–158).

In the early 1960s, two Sagan admirers, the Harvard astronomers Donald Menzel and Fred Whipple, obtained for him joint postings as an assistant professor of astronomy at Harvard and as a staff member at the nearby Smithsonian Astrophysical Observatory. About the same time, Sagan assumed an editorial post at the planetary science journal *Icarus*. He served as associate editor from 1962 until 1969, after which he served for a decade as editor in chief. True to form, he saw to it that *Icarus* ran articles on highly unusual topics (e.g., Francis Crick and Leslie Orgel's thesis [1973] that terrestrial life evolved from organic materials launched to Earth by alien civilizations).

Many radical young academics mellow as they age and approach tenure review. Not Sagan: In the mid-to-late 1960s he spoke out on issues such as the feasibility of interstellar flight and the chance that aliens visited Earth thousands of years ago. In 1967 he and Harold Morowitz proposed in a joint letter to *Nature* that creatures resembling "gas bags" float high in the atmosphere of Venus. Sagan also publicly discussed the then-headline-making topic of UFOs; he even testified to Congress on the subject. By that time he was an outspoken skeptic of the "saucers," although he evidently was not skeptical enough for Menzel, who privately complained that Sagan expressed his skepticism in artfully convoluted sentences that others might misinterpret. Meanwhile, Urey grumbled that Sagan speculated wildly about the possible molecular constituents of other planets.

Sagan attracted early press attention by proposing to "terraform" Venus into a habitable world. Barely thirty years old, the tall, rail-thin, handsome astronomer dazzled the media with his geniality, his patience with dunderhead questions, and his crystal-clear explanations, which he peppered with jokes and evocative metaphors. Like William F. Buckley and Truman Capote, Sagan owed his public celebrity partly to his memorable style of speech, which television comedians later mimicked; his voice was deep yet honey-smooth, his delivery melodious yet eccentrically enunciated. Not everyone was charmed: Some regarded him as arrogant or rude. When Sagan served briefly as an advisor on the famous 1968 science-fiction film *2001: A Space Odyssey*, his demeanor repelled the director, Stanley Kubrick, who quit communicating with him. In later years, Sagan would fight bitterly with the producer of his television series *Cosmos*, who also stopped talking to him.

His most enduring scientific collaboration was with his first graduate student, James B. Pollack, starting in the mid-1960s when they were both at Harvard. The brightness variations of Mars were a long-standing puzzle: What caused them? Some experts attributed them to vegetation changes. In a 1966 article for *Nature*, Sagan and Pollack prophetically suggested the cause was windblown dust. Ironically, they were right partly for the wrong reason: The proposal was indirectly inspired by their (probably) erroneous thesis that Mars has undergone global-scale horizontal crustal movements akin to terrestrial plate tectonics.

In the 1960s, the Soviet astrophysicist Iosif S. Shklovskii wrote a popular science book, *Universe, Life, Mind*. Sagan learned about the book and contacted Shklovskii to suggest that they republish it in English, along with remarks inserted by Sagan. Shklovskii agreed. As it turned out, Sagan's inserts more than doubled the size of the text; in 1966 it was published in English as

Intelligent Life in the Universe. The cover was striking: It bore no title or authors' names, only a black-and-white photo of a galaxy with the edge of Earth in the foreground. The book was a mix of semitechnical analysis and Saganish ebullience. For example, he described the potential for interstellar flight and radio communication with aliens. He also devoted a chapter to his amusing experience in a California courtroom, where he had provided scientific testimony against an accused embezzler who claimed to have contacted flying saucer pilots.

In 1968 Sagan married the aspiring artist Linda Salzman. They had one son, Nicholas. That same year, Harvard officials denied Sagan tenure, at least partly because Urey had written a harsh anti-Sagan letter to the university. (Urey later apologized to Sagan.) Thomas Gold, the chair of astronomy at Cornell, who was himself a noted controversial theorist, spied a kindred spirit in Sagan and offered him a job. Sagan accepted. Located in a small, quasi-bohemian town in upstate New York, Cornell was Sagan's academic home for the rest of his life.

Sagan never ceased trying to find excuses for regarding seemingly inhabitable planets as potential abodes of life, either now or in the past. In 1972, Sagan and George Mullen theorized that early Earth had been veiled in ammonia gas, which trapped solar infrared radiation; this kept the planet warm enough for life to emerge. Likewise, Sagan reasoned that thanks to greenhouse gases, the Martian atmosphere might have once been warm enough to support the emergence of life. Sagan also believed Martian life might still exist to the present—perhaps even large animals the size of polar bears! To some scientists (Urey among them), Sagan's speculations raised doubts about his rigor as a theorist. Some of his hypotheses were so cagily worded, so well-shielded against falsification, that they offer interesting case studies for those scholars who analyze the flightier forms of scientific rhetoric. For example, Sagan and Mullen wrote in their 1972 paper: "Earlier conditions on Mars may have been much more clement. … It is a debatable but hardly quixotic contention that martian organisms may have been able to adapt to the increasingly rigorous Martian environment and may still be present." Some space scientists, even those who liked Sagan and respected his breadth of technical knowledge, grumbled about his undisciplined mouth. They apparently feared that his public pronouncements about Mars risked raising public hopes which might later be disappointed. (And indeed, they would be disappointed: The *Vikings* landed on Mars in 1976 and failed to detect evidence of life, even of organic molecules.) Perhaps not coincidentally, Sagan was secretly an enthusiastic smoker of marijuana. He argued (in an essay published under a pseudonym, "Mr. X") that the drug enhanced his intellectual, aesthetic, and emotional powers. (His authorship of the essay was revealed after his death.)

Sagan's later books of the 1970s became best sellers, thanks substantially to his appearances on a popular late-night television talk show hosted by Johnny Carson. *The Cosmic Connection* (1973) was a boyish riff on the wonders of the cosmos and the possibility of interstellar travel. *The Dragons of Eden* (1977) was an intellectual high-dive act, a theoretically reckless amateur's speculations on neuroanatomy, hominid evolution, mythology, and dreams that won the Pulitzer Prize.

Scientific Celebrity. Sagan's best-publicized "scientific" stunts had little to do with theoretical or experimental science. Rather, they were flamboyant quasi-artistic gestures (akin to Christo's) guided by a liberal ethic that might be called cosmic cosmopolitanism. His Enlightenment-style faith (no doubt inspired by his youthful love of science-fiction tales in which humans and aliens interacted easily) that symbolic and linguistic systems are universally commensurable is most memorably—and controversially—represented by the *Pioneer* plaques. In the early 1970s, Drake, Carl Sagan, and Linda Sagan designed a plaque for the *Pioneer 10* and *Pioneer 11* space probes that were scheduled to visit the outer planets and (because their speed exceeded solar escape velocity) would eventually leave the solar system. Sagan argued that extraterrestrials might eventually recover the spaceships millions of years from now, though he acknowledged the probability was extremely low. The plaques were covered with various symbols that were cleverly designed to convey basic information about the spaceship's planet of origin. The plaques included a cartoonlike drawing of a naked man and woman: The male raised his hand, as if in greeting. Skeptics (including the art historian Ernst H. Gombrich, who had long emphasized the historical and cultural contingency of aesthetic conventions) pointed out that the lines and dots on the plaque, even the human figures, might be incomprehensible to extraterrestrials. Despite Sagan's liberal political values, other critics complained that both human figures appeared to be white skinned, and feminists demanded to know why the woman was shown deferentially standing behind the man.

The episode exposed Sagan's naïveté. He was determined to do better on his next big stunt: the creation of a phonograph-style disk of acoustically recorded images and music from the world's different cultures and ethnicities—a sort of acoustical version of Edward Steichen's "Family of Man" photographic show of the early Cold War era. Sagan and several friends (including his future wife Ann Druyan) designed the recordings. They placed copies of them aboard two other twin deep-space probes, *Voyager 1* and *Voyager 2*, which were launched in 1977.

Sagan was intrigued by astronomical observations of what appeared to be rust-red materials on the surfaces of other worlds. He wondered: Were these prebiological substances? In experiments with Bishun Khare, Sagan tried to mimic the formation of such substances in simulated planetary atmospheres. One product of this research was a brown, gunky substance that Sagan dubbed "tholins" (after the Greek word for mud). Sagan enjoyed doing back-of-the-envelope-style calculations on the odds of protobiotic molecules emerging on a given world, and his calculations were almost always highly optimistic. For example, writing in 1971 in *Science* magazine, he and Khare proposed that on early Earth, volcanically emitted hydrogen sulfide could have absorbed long-wavelength solar ultraviolet radiation and generated up to 200 kilograms of amino acids per square centimeter over a billion years—"a huge number suggesting congenial conditions for the origin of life."

At a time when many scholars (e.g., Thomas Kuhn and Paul Feyerabend) were reassessing science's traditional claims to epistemic and social authority, Sagan continued to champion a view favored by most science pedagogues—namely, that there are clear-cut logical and methodological distinctions (i.e., lines of demarcation) between science and pseudoscience. Dire social consequences might ensue if society failed to respect these distinctions, Sagan suggested. His brilliant public dismantling of the pseudo-astrophysical theories of psychoanalyst Immanuel Velikovsky destroyed the latter's already shaky credibility. In the 1970s Sagan was a founding member of the Committee for the Scientific Investigation of Claims of the Paranormal (CSICOP), an antioccult, antipseudoscience spin-off of the American Humanist Association that published a puckish magazine, *Skeptical Inquirer.*

Sagan's best-known philosophical principle is his oft-quoted remark that extraordinary claims require extraordinary evidence. His approach to philosophy of science was traditional and polemical, not searching or scholarly. Even so, he was too genial and broad-spirited to rally behind the conservative wing of the unfolding "science wars" of the 1980s and 1990s. He had a strong sense of fairness, even when dealing with cranks. Although he despised astrology, he refused to sign a petition protesting popular interest in astrology because he believed such gestures were futile and appeared repressive. In his last years he complained there was "some degree of truth" to the charge that CSICOP activists "tend to be dismissive, closed-mined [*sic*] and given to ad hominem arguments," as he said in a 1993 letter to an official of the organization (unpublished letter, Sagan to Kendrick Frazier, 5 April 1993).

In 1980, Sagan hosted *Cosmos,* a highly publicized thirteen-part public-television series on science that even-

tually reached several hundred million viewers around the globe. The series used special effects that were highly elaborate for the time—for example, a lifelike simulation of the interior of the Library of Alexandria; through its imaginary hallways, Sagan strolled while reminiscing about its past glories (including the great female scholar Hypatia, whose cruel fate he mentioned at the urging of his feminist wife). The television show also deployed the then-novel computer technique of "morphing" to dramatize the evolution of life-forms. The series also depicted episodes in the history of science, such as Johannes Kepler's theoretical grapplings with the enigmas of the orbit of Mars. *Time* magazine ran a cover story on Sagan that called him "the prince of popularizers, the nation's scientific mentor to the masses." A recurrent theme of the show—and of Sagan's writings in general—was the vastness of space and time and the comparative triviality of life on Earth. All of history's heroes and villains had pontificated and battled on that "pale blue dot," and to what end? Many viewers were thrilled by Sagan's musings, but some critics smirked at his pomposity while the religious fumed at his overt religious skepticism. "Why is Carl Sagan so lonely?" asked the novelist Walker Percy. He answered that to Sagan, the cosmos was nothing but "matter in interaction, [and] there is no one left to talk to except other transcending intelligences from other worlds." Some commentators praised the show for bringing scientific ideas to vivid life; others ridiculed the beatific gaze on Sagan's face as he pretended to pilot a cosmic spaceship.

In 1981, Sagan won a $2 million advance to write a science-fiction novel, *Contact.* The resulting book, published in 1985, was an alternately enthralling and sluggish tome with a central character, radio astronomer Ellie Arroway, whose life, career, and values (including her religious skepticism) resemble Sagan's. In 1997 the book was released as a major Hollywood film starring Jodie Foster.

Anti–Nuclear Weapons Activism. In the late 1970s Sagan left his wife Linda for Druyan, a fledgling writer with leftist political sympathies. The couple had two children, Alexandra and Samuel. During their intellectually intense marriage, he and "Annie" coauthored books including *Shadows of Forgotten Ancestors: A Search for Who We Are* (1992). Inspired by his anti–nuclear weapons activism of the 1980s, *Shadows* mused on the social and evolutionary roots of human self-destructiveness. It is the most mature and elegantly written of his books, and occasionally flirts with experimental narrative styles. Druyan's literary and political influence on Sagan is evident in many passages—for example, a paragraph about the nature–nurture debate: Bigots stress "the primate connection to the veldt and the ghetto, but never, ever, perish the thought, to the boardroom or the military academy or, God forbid, to the

Senate chamber or the House of Lords, to Buckingham Palace or Pennsylvania Avenue" (p. 67).

Sagan's new political outspokenness owed much to the election of Ronald Reagan as U.S. president in 1980. Reagan's administration, critics feared, was favorably oriented to nuclear "first strikes," that is, to preemptive nuclear attacks on the Soviet Union. In reply, Sagan and colleagues developed their famous "nuclear winter" hypothesis. Inspired partly by the early studies of Paul Crutzen and John Birks, Sagan and four other scientists— Richard Turco, Brian Toon, Thomas P. Ackerman, and Pollack (collectively known as TTAPS, with the "S" for Sagan)—calculated that even a "small" nuclear war involving hundreds of warheads might spark gigantic urban fires. The blazes could unleash vast clouds of soot that would darken the sky, blocking solar radiation. The possible result: a planetwide cooling or freeze, which could ravage agriculture and, in a worst-case scenario, might kill billions. Thus, Sagan reasoned, only a foolish nation would start a nuclear war because nuclear winter would quickly spoil any initial tactical advantage that it obtained by launching the first strike. The risk of nuclear winter could be lessened, he stressed, if the United States and Soviet Union radically shrank the size of their nuclear arsenals. (It was never clear how many bombs would have to be detonated in order to trigger a nuclear winter.)

Sagan discussed the topic in a face-to-face meeting with Pope John Paul II; he also debated it before Congress alongside a critic of the nuclear winter hypothesis, the hydrogen-bomb pioneer Edward Teller. At an antinuclear rally at the U.S. nuclear weapons test site in Nevada in 1986, Sagan was arrested for trespassing. In 1990, Sagan and Turco published *A Path Where No Man Thought: Nuclear Winter and the End of the Arms Race,* an engrossing review of the history and science behind the nuclear winter thesis. By then, though, the Soviet Union was disintegrating, and the book sold poorly.

Unwisely, Sagan exploited the nuclear winter thesis as a last-ditch argument against U.S. plans for the Gulf War invasion of Iraq in 1990–1991: He and Turco proposed in *Nature* that if Iraqi leader Saddam Hussein ignited his nation's oil wells, the resulting dark clouds might trigger a regional-scale cooling. The Iraqis did start massive oil fires, but the climatic consequences were negligible. Critics charged that in this and other cases, Sagan allowed personal prejudices to distort his scientific judgment.

In a 1994 book, Sagan returned to the optimistic, futuristic—and, thus, commercially more promising— style of his earlier writing, the lavishly illustrated *Pale Blue Dot: A Vision of the Human Future in Space* (1994). Sagan's last book published in his lifetime was *The Demon-Haunted World* (1996). As another retreat from the sophisticated broodings of *Shadows, Demon-Haunted*

World was a series of middlebrow essays about pseudoscience and irrationalism, ideal for the millions of laypersons who enjoyed Sagan's occasional pieces for *Parade,* a Sunday supplement inserted in many American newspapers. In an attempt to illustrate his lifelong dedication to scientific method, Sagan listed some of his scientific mistakes (for example, his underestimation of the air density on Venus); yet he neglected to cite the most embarrassing ones (for example, his suggestion that animals as big as polar bears might inhabit Mars).

Sagan's fame, political activism and occasionally imperious personal manner upset some members of the scientific community. In 1992, when Stanley Miller tried to persuade the National Academy of Sciences to admit Sagan, the subject was vigorously debated; Sagan was rejected. Ironically, two years later, the Academy gave Sagan its Public Welfare Medal in honor of his popularization of science. The Academy citation declared: "No one has ever succeeded in conveying the wonder, excitement and joy of science as widely as Carl Sagan and few as well."

Sagan suffered for much of his life from achalasia, a swallowing disorder for which he was at times hospitalized. He died from complications of myelodysplasia, a blood disorder, in Seattle, Washington, in December 1996. The scientifically savvy U.S. vice president, Albert Gore Jr., spoke at a funeral service in New York City and cited Sagan's influence on him: "Those of us who were privileged to bask in that light, however briefly, will never, ever forget its brilliance."

At present, Sagan's scientific accomplishments are difficult to assess. He wrote or coauthored more than three hundred scientific articles. His most important research contribution was probably his flawed model for the thermal evolution of the Venusian atmosphere. He taught or inspired a large number of space scientists, and did much to keep popular interest in the National Aeronautical and Space Administration's space missions alive in the uncertain years after the end of the Apollo Moon missions (1972). Whatever the shortcomings of Sagan and his coworkers' nuclear winter hypothesis (which, mercifully, was never tested by a full-scale atomic war), he was an inspiring voice for the scientific conscience in an era when many American scientists remained silent while accepting military money to conduct research of debatable merit.

One scholar ranks Sagan among the so-called visible scientists (Goodell, 1977, p. 20) those researchers who popularize their work among the general public. Yet this dry label hardly suggests Sagan's breadth, complexities, ambitions, and achievements. His showmanship, gaudy surmises, and fascination with intellectually ambiguous figures such as Johannes Kepler and Percival Lowell suggests Sagan belonged to a more discomfiting tradition—

what we might call prophetic science or messianic science. (The elderly Arthur Eddington might fall in the same category.) Despite Sagan's fervent advocacy of "scientific" method, his own methodologies and reasoning at times appeared more reminiscent of Feyerabend's infamous dictum (1975) that in the history of science, "anything goes." At the least, Sagan's colorful career dramatizes a phenomenon emphasized by Kuhn (1962): the disparity between pedagogical idealizations of science and its actual historical practice.

BIBLIOGRAPHY

Sagan's private papers and a copy of his 265-page résumé are in the possession of his widow, Ann Druyan of Ithaca, New York. An extensive and chronological bibliography of Sagan's works is in Poundstone (1999).

WORKS BY SAGAN

"Radiation and The Origin Of The Gene," *Evolution* 11 (1957): 1, 40–55.

"Physical Studies of Planets," PhD Diss. University Of Chicago, June 1960.

With Joshua Lederberg. "Microenvironments for Life on Mars." *Proceedings of the National Academy of Sciences* 48, no. 9, (1962).

With Cyril Ponnamperuma and Ruth Mariner. "Synthesis of Adenosine Triphosphate under Possible Primitive Earth Conditions." *Nature* 199 (1963): 222–226.

With James Pollack. "On Nature of Canals of Mars." *Nature* 212 (1966): 117–121.

With I. S. Shklovskii. *Intelligent Life In The Universe.* San Francisco: Holden-Day, 1966.

With James B. Pollack. "On The Nature Of The Canals Of Mars," *Nature* 212 (1966): 117–121.

With Harold Morowitz. "Life in Clouds of Venus?" *Nature* 215 (1967): 1259–1260.

With Bishun N. Khare. "Long-Wavelength UV Photoproduction Of Amino Acids On The Primitive Earth," *Science* 173, no. 3995 (1971): 417–420.

With George Mullen. "Earth And Mars: Evolution of Atmospheres and Surface Temperatures." *Science* 177, no. 4043 (1972): 52–56.

The Cosmic Connection. Garden City, NY: Anchor Press, 1973.

Other Worlds. New York: Bantam Books, 1975.

The Dragons of Eden: Speculations on the Evolution of Human Intelligence. New York: Random House, 1977.

With Frank Drake, Ann Druyan, Timothy Ferris, et al. *Murmurs of Earth: The* Voyager *Interstellar Record.* New York: Random House, 1978.

Broca's Brain: Reflections on the Romance of Science. New York: Random House, 1979.

Cosmos. New York: Random House, 1980.

Contact. New York: Simon & Schuster, 1985.

With Ann Druyan. *Comet.* New York: Random House, 1985.

With Richard Turco. *A Path Where No Man Thought: Nuclear Winter and the End of the Arms Race.* New York: Random House, 1990. Although commercially unsuccessful, this book is a treasure trove of information on the history of atmospheric science research relevant to its controversial thesis.

With Ann Druyan. *Shadows of Forgotten Ancestors: A Search for Who We Are.* New York: Random House, 1992.

Pale Blue Dot: A Vision of the Human Future in Space. New York: Random House, 1994.

The Demon-Haunted World: Science as a Candle in the Dark. New York: Random House, 1996.

Billions and Billions: Thoughts on Life and Death at the Brink of the Millennium. New York: Random House, 1997.

OTHER SOURCES

Broad, William J. "Even in Death, Carl Sagan's Influence Is Still Cosmic." *New York Times,* 1 December 1998.

———. "U.S. Planned Nuclear Blast on the Moon, Physicist Says." *New York Times,* 16 May 2000.

Cocconi, Giuseppe, and Philip Morrison. "Searching for Interstellar Communications." *Nature* 184 (1959): 844–846.

Cooper, Henry S. F., Jr. "A Resonance with Something Alive." *New Yorker,* 21 June 1976. The first important biographical essay on Sagan after he became famous. A second installment appeared in the same magazine on 28 June 1976.

Davidson, Keay. *Carl Sagan: A Life.* New York City: John Wiley & Sons, 1999. A sometimes-critical biography that analyzes Sagan's life and ideas in their larger historical context.

Goodell, Rae. *The Visible Scientists.* Boston: Little, Brown, 1977.

Head, Tom, ed. *Conversations with Carl Sagan.* Jackson: University Press of Mississippi, 2006. Numerous interviews with Sagan.

Poundstone, William. *Carl Sagan: A Life in the Cosmos.* New York: Henry Holt, 1999. A rich, useful biography.

Reiffel, Leonard. "Sagan Breached Security by Revealing U.S. Work on a Lunar Bomb Project." *Nature* 405 (2000): 13.

Weldon, Stephen P. "The Humanist Enterprise from John Dewey to Carl Sagan: A Study of Science and Religion in American Culture." PhD diss., University of Wisconsin, Madison, 1997.

Keay Davidson

SAGER, RUTH

(*b.* Chicago, Illinois, 7 February 1918; *d.* Brookline, Massachusetts, 29 March 1997), *plant genetics, chloroplast genetics, cytoplasmic inheritance, cancer genetics.*

Sager is known primarily for using classical genetic methods to demonstrate the presence of a hereditary system in the chloroplasts of plants and for establishing *Chlamydomonas reinhardtii* as a model organism for the study of chloroplasts. She is also credited with new techniques in mammalian somatic cell culture and the discovery of maspin, a tumor suppressor.

The Early Years and Education. Ruth Sager was the only child born to Leon and Deborah Borovik Sager of Chicago, Illinois. Her mother died in the influenza epidemic in March 1919. Her father, an advertising executive, remarried (Hannah Shulman) and had two more children, Esther and Naomi. Ruth attended New Trier High School in Winnetka, Illinois, from 1930 to 1934. The Sager family emphasized the importance of the best education for their daughters, and after graduating from high school, Sager entered the University of Chicago in September 1934. Her interests originally lay in the humanities. She had planned to major in English, until she took a physiology course taught by Anton Carlson, where she discovered an interest in biology that would last her entire life. Sager received her BS in biology in December 1938 and was elected to Phi Beta Kappa. Her career, however, took a short detour after college.

As part of their philosophy that their daughters should be broadly educated, Sager's parents took the three girls on a trip through Europe and the Middle East from February to May 1938. The trip delayed Sager's graduation from college, but it exposed her to a way of life with which she would maintain contact for the rest of her life and helped direct her toward plant science.

While in Palestine, Sager visited a kibbutz, where she was impressed with the self-sufficiency of the kibbutzniks in creating a life in the desert. Although she wanted to return to Palestine, by 1938 emigration had been severely restricted. Instead, Ruth spent the next few years working on several training farms of Hashomer Hatzair, one of the Zionist organizations in the United States. While doing so, she became interested in the scientific aspects of desert farming and began studying plant physiology at Rutgers University in New Brunswick, New Jersey. She obtained a master's degree in October 1944 on the mineral nutrition of tomato plants, and then spent the academic year working on the horticulture department farm at the University of Maryland. Although this was a phase of her life known only to a few other people, her interest in the practical applications of science stayed with her throughout her life.

A mutual correspondence during World War II with Seymour Melman, an army officer stationed in California, led to marriage in 1944. (They would divorce in 1960.) Both wanted to obtain graduate degrees and were accepted at Columbia University, where they matriculated in 1945. Sager began studying maize genetics under the direction of Marcus Rhoades, a well-known and widely respected plant geneticist. Another maize geneticist at Columbia was Barbara McClintock, a future Nobel laureate, who served as a reader on Sager's dissertation and for

Ruth Sager. AP IMAGES.

whom Sager occasionally did fieldwork. Sager received her PhD in December 1949 for her work on the *waxy* gene of maize, an attempt at identifying new mutations to help elucidate the role of that locus in starch synthesis. During the course of her graduate studies, she also became familiar with the phenomenon of cytoplasmic inheritance, a subject that had long been of interest to Rhoades, who had written his doctoral dissertation, as well as several additional papers, on the subject.

The presence of hereditary material outside of the nucleus had been suggested shortly after Gregor Mendel's principles of inheritance became widely disseminated in 1900. In 1909, the Germans Edwin Baur and Carl Correns published the results of separate investigations on plants in which the inheritance of certain traits could not be explained by Mendel's laws. Their suggestions that these traits were carried through the agency of the cytoplasm were met with skepticism by most of the genetics community at the time, although several researchers in Germany—including Otto Renner, Peter Michaelis, and Fritz von Wettstein—continued investigating the possibility. In the United States, however, where most geneticists emphasized the primacy of the nucleus's role in heredity, few people conducted research on cytoplasmic inheritance, which was associated by some researchers with the discredited theory of Lamarckism, the inheritance of acquired characteristics. Beside Rhoades's investigations of the phenomenon in maize, the most extensive genetic studies in the United States in the 1940s and 1950s were conducted by Tracy Sonneborn, a professor at Indiana University working with the microorganism *Paramecium.* Sager was very familiar with Sonneborn and his work, but in view of certain technical limitations with his experimental system, she took most of her research leads from the bacterial and viral geneticists.

Sager's First Career. In September 1949, with her dissertation nearly complete, Sager received a Merck Fellowship for a postdoctoral position in the laboratory of Dr. Samuel Granick at the Rockefeller Institute. Granick's work focused on the biochemical pathways for the synthesis of porphyrin compounds, specifically hemoglobin and chlorophyll. Given the recent success of biochemical genetics in elucidating the synthesis pathways of amino acids in *Neurospora* by George Beadle and Edward Tatum, Granick considered that Sager's background in plant physiology and genetics would be advantageous for a similar approach to ascertaining the synthesis pathway of chlorophyll.

Granick had been using the alga *Chlorella* in his biochemical studies, but it was not useful for studies modeled on Beadle and Tatum's approach: *Chlorella* did not have a known sexual phase, a necessary prerequisite for conducting genetic crosses. Sager's first objective was to find a suitable organism. To prepare for her work in Granick's laboratory, Sager spent the summer of 1949 at the Hopkins Marine Station taking Cornelis Bernardus van Niel's renowned summer microbiology course. While there, she learned about and acquired *Chlamydomonas reinhardtii* from Gilbert Morgan Smith, who had elucidated its life cycle, which included a sexual phase. Once back at Rockefeller, Sager and Granick determined the organism's nutritional requirements, which resulted in a defined culture medium and, additionally, in methods for environmentally controlling the various phases of the alga's life cycle.

From the beginning of her tenure in Granick's laboratory, she sought to include cytoplasmic inheritance in the research program, and she began to exploit the *Chlamydomonas* system to that end. Because certain antibiotics were known to bleach chlorophyll, Sager began looking for their effects in *Chlamydomonas.* Following the leads of the recent successes in bacterial and microbial genetics and employing their techniques, she discovered several hereditary factors for streptomycin resistance: one was inherited in a Mendelian manner, but the other was always inherited in a non-Mendelian manner; that is, it

always came from only one of the parents. On the basis of backcross data and their simplest explanation, Sager postulated that the factor was nonchromosomal. Citing the stability of the non-Mendelian resistant and sensitive phenotypes, Sager suggested that these factors represented alleles such as those associated with genes found on chromosomes. Although the material nature and location of these non-Mendelian elements remained unidentified, Sager postulated, on the basis of their behavior as unit factors, that they might be associated with an organelle, most probably the chloroplast.

While at Rockefeller, Sager had been appointed as an assistant of the institute in September 1951 and remained in that position for four years, continuing to work under Granick. Eventually, though, her desire to focus completely on cytoplasmic inheritance rather than on the biosynthesis of chlorophyll led her to leave his laboratory in 1955. She returned to Columbia University, where Francis Ryan, a microbial geneticist in the zoology department, provided her with bench space in his laboratory. Her position was listed as "research associate," a non-tenure-track position, and in 1960 she became senior research scientist. Sager independently funded her research and technicians through grants from the National Science Foundation, the National Institutes of Health, and the American Cancer Society.

Ryan was very interested in the nature of mutation, and soon after Sager arrived at Columbia, she began to investigate the origin of the mutations for resistance to streptomycin, an antibiotic that was known to irreversibly bleach the chloroplasts of *Euglena,* a photosynthetic flagellate. Prior to the 1940s, it was unclear whether mutations were induced by the agent to which the organism was resistant or whether the agent merely selected preexisting mutations for resistance. The question had been answered for most mutations by Max Delbrück and Salvator Luria with their fluctuation test (1943) and by Howard Newcombe with his respreading test (1949). They concluded that agents such as viruses and antibiotics selected for preexisting mutations; they did not induce them. Conducting the same tests on her streptomycin mutants, Sager's results indicated that whereas the mutation on the chromosomal factor was shown to be preexisting, the nonchromosomal mutation for streptomycin resistance appeared to be induced by the antibiotic. Although the latter result would ultimately be explained by standard mechanisms of mutation induction, her interpretation helped to spark two decades of experiments on the nature of antibiotic mutations in organelles.

Up to this point, Sager and her longtime coworker, Zenta Ramanis, had been predominantly using classical genetic crossing and pedigree analysis to follow the behavior of the nonchromosomal factors. Sager remained tentative about their chemical composition and location in the cell. In 1962, Hans Ris and Walter Plaut had shown by specific staining that extranuclear DNA was present in the chloroplast of *Chlamydomonas moewusii*. In 1963, Alexander Rich and his coworkers had shown that whole-cell *Chlamydomonas* DNA contained a small amount of DNA that was lighter than the rest. Sager and her postdoctoral researcher, Masahiro Ishida, wanted to determine whether this satellite DNA might be associated with the nonchromosomal factors she had been investigating. Together they developed a method for isolating intact chloroplasts, from which they then extracted DNA and showed that although the major band of DNA was still present, the chloroplast extract was enriched for the satellite DNA and also RNA. This result suggested that molecules capable of serving as genes were located in the chloroplast.

In July 1963, shortly before this work appeared in the *Proceedings of the National Academy*, Francis Ryan suddenly died. By the end of August, Sager was notified that her appointment would end December 31, 1964. Although it was extended to December 1965, by February 1965 she had been offered and accepted a position as a full professor in the biology department at Hunter College (of the City University of New York). It was her first faculty appointment and began January 1966.

At Hunter, Sager continued her work on *Chlamydomonas*. She used ultraviolet light to increase the frequency of biparental (which she called "exceptional zygotes"). With them, she was able to make crosses and observe recombination and segregation. The results provided further evidence that the factors behaved similarly to nuclear genes, and so were probably located on a structure like a nuclear chromosome, but outside the nucleus. Also, because the factors were affected by ultraviolet light, like nucleic acids, she suggested that they might be composed of DNA.

With results from genetic crossing, Sager proposed a map for the hereditary factors. The first map was linear, and the genetic complement of the chloroplast appeared to be diploid. Further mapping work led her to a circular genome, which was confirmed by others, but who also demonstrated substantially more than two copies per chloroplast, a result Sager then confirmed herself through biochemical analysis.

Extending her molecular work, Sager noted that physical exclusion of the paternal chloroplast was not applicable in the case of *Chlamydomonas* and proposed that the mechanism of maternal inheritance was caused by selective elimination of the paternal DNA based upon a modification-restriction system much like that operating in bacteria. Discovery of differential methylation in maternal and paternal DNA and of a site-specific single-strand endonuclease in *Chlamydomonas* (the first identi-

fied in a eukaryote) provided supporting evidence. Sager did not resolve this question, which remained the subject of research in 2005.

Using classical genetic methods and the techniques of molecular biologists and microbial geneticists, Sager severed cytoplasmic inheritance from its negative Lamarckist and Lysenkoist associations and established the existence of second genetic system in plants. She is acknowledged as having laid the foundations for chloroplast genetics, especially establishing *Chlamydomonas reinhardtii* as a model organism, and her original and provocative explanations continued to stimulate research fifty years after her initial investigations.

For her work in this area, Sager was elected to the National Academy of Sciences in 1977 and received the Gilbert Morgan Smith medal, awarded for work on algae, from the academy in 1988. Sager's pioneering work inspired a new generation, including Nicholas Gillham and Elizabeth Harris of the Chlamydomonas Center at Duke University and Ursula Goodenough at Washington University in St. Louis, among others. Sager's work in chloroplast genetics has also provided additional support for the theory of the endosymbiotic origins of organelles promoted by Lynn Margulis of the University of Massachusetts–Amherst.

Sager's Second Career. Sager had always been concerned that her work should have practical applications, from her research in plant physiology to the genetics of maize. She never discussed the significance that her work on cytoplasmic inheritance held for new ideas about the origin and evolution of complex life-forms. Rather, even while Sager was still working with algae in the early 1960s, she thought about the implications that interactions between the cytoplasm and the nucleus held for cellular regulation and disease. Such interests led her to begin shifting the direction of her research career in the early 1970s toward the genetics of human cancer.

In August 1972, she received a Guggenheim Fellowship to spend a year in the laboratory of Dr. (later Sir) Michael Stoker, at the Imperial Cancer Research Fund in London, learning somatic cell culture. After her fellowship was finished, she returned to the United States, where she remarried in 1973. Her new spouse, Dr. Arthur Pardee, was a biochemist at Princeton University who had worked with François Jacob and Jacques Monod. When it was not possible for Sager to obtain a position at Princeton, she and Pardee moved to the Sidney Farber (later Dana-Farber) Cancer Institute, where they also obtained joint appointments with Harvard Medical School in Boston. In 1975, Sager was appointed professor of cellular genetics at the latter institution, one of the few women full professors, and chief of the Division of Cancer Genetics at Sidney Farber.

Sager began her work in cancer genetics by developing another experimental system. She established cell cultures of normal and tumorigenic Chinese hamster embryo fibroblasts (CHEF cells) that could be fused to show the effects of the different nuclei and cytoplasms on each other. Unlike the oncogene models for carcinogenesis, which postulated that the key step was the mutation of an oncogene that then promoted tumor growth, Sager's work with CHEF cells suggested that the process also involved the loss or inactivation of tumor suppressor genes. Her results in the early 1980s reemphasized the idea of cancer as a two-step process involving tumor suppressor genes—not merely single oncogenes—and provided new hypotheses about the process.

Because of the high incidence of breast cancer in women, in the mid-1980s Sager transferred and extended her work on tumor suppressors to include human mammary epithelial cell cultures, again developing another culture system. She worked out a low-serum medium that supported long-term growth of primary cancer cells and identified markers that distinguished normal from tumor cells. Using CHEF and human cells, Sager identified several related genes called *gro* (growth response), which are members of a family of genes that encode cytokines, proteins that have regulatory, as well as anti-inflammatory, properties. The transcription of the *gro* genes appeared to be well regulated in normal cells but not in tumor cells, and this difference eventually led Sager to coin the term *expression genetics*. By that phrase she meant the investigation of regulatory changes, such as the loss of gene products (rather than loss or inactivation of the gene itself) in cancer cells. Such changes were thought to be additional foci for diagnosis and treatment.

In the early 1990s, Sager and her coworkers isolated more than one hundred possible tumor suppressor genes. One of the most significant of these was the gene for maspin, a serine protease inhibitor (serpin) that was expressed in normal cells but not in advanced breast cancer cells. Its action in inhibiting the spread of tumors became another focus of cancer research.

Even in her late seventies, Sager continued to maintain a laboratory, obtain research grants, and publish papers. In addition to the more than two hundred full scientific papers and fifty abstracts that she published over the course of her career, Sager also wrote two textbooks. The first was a collaboration with Francis Ryan resulting in what was described by some as the first molecular genetics book, *Cell Heredity,* which was published in 1961 to excellent reviews. Her second textbook, *Cytoplasmic Genes and Organelles* (1972), was also very well received,

being the most comprehensive book on the subject at the time.

Sager spent many summers and much time writing at the Marine Biology Laboratory in Woods Hole, Massachusetts, where she maintained a second home so that she could visit as often as possible. In light of her love of Woods Hole, she was interred there after her death on 29 March 1997, of cancer.

Throughout her career, Sager traveled to meetings all over the world, gave talks at numerous universities, and made valuable contacts for her laboratory. In addition to the awards mentioned above, Sager's scientific accomplishments were also recognized by election to Sigma Xi in 1947, a National Cancer Institute Outstanding Investigator Award in 1985, the Princess Takamatsu Award of Merit (Japan) in 1990, election to the Institute of Medicine in 1992, and the Alumni Medal from the University of Chicago in 1994.

BIBLIOGRAPHY

WORKS BY SAGER

"On the Mutability of the *Waxy* Locus in Maize." *Genetics* 36 (1951): 510–540.

With Samuel Granick. "Nutritional Studies with *Chlamydomonas reinhardi.*" *Annals of the New York Academy of Sciences* 56 (1953): 831–838.

"Mendelian and Non-Mendelian Inheritance of Streptomycin Resistance in *Chlamydomonas reinhardi.*" *Proceedings of the National Academy of Sciences of the United States of America* 40 (1954): 356–363.

With Samuel Granick. "Nutritional Control of Sexuality in *Chlamydomonas reinhardi.*" *Journal of General Physiology* 37 (1954): 729–742.

"Inheritance in the Green Alga, *Chlamydomonas reinhardi.*" *Genetics* 40 (1955): 476–489.

"Genetic Systems in *Chlamydomonas.*" *Science* 132 (1960): 1459–1465.

With Francis J. Ryan. *Cell Heredity.* New York: John Wiley and Sons, 1961.

With Masahiro R. Ishida. "Chloroplast DNA in *Chlamydomonas.*" *Proceedings of the National Academy of Sciences of the United States of America* 50 (1963): 725–730.

"Genes outside the Chromosomes." *Scientific American* 212 (1965): 71–79.

With Zenta Ramanis. "Recombination of Nonchromosomal Genes in *Chlamydomonas.*" *Proceedings of the National Academy of Sciences of the United States of America* 53 (1965): 1053–1061.

———. "Biparental Inheritance of Nonchromosomal Genes Induced by Ultraviolet Irradiation." *Proceedings of the National Academy of Sciences of the United States of America* 58 (1967): 931–937.

Cytoplasmic Genes and Organelles. New York: Academic Press. 1972.

With Dorothy Lane. "Molecular Basis of Maternal Inheritance." *Proceedings of the National Academy of Sciences of the United States of America* 69 (1972): 2410–2413.

With Robert Kitchin. "Selective Silencing of Eukaryotic DNA." *Science* 189 (1975): 426–433.

With A. Neil Howell. "Tumorigenicity and Its Suppression in Cybrids of Mouse and Chinese Hamster Cell Lines." *Proceedings of the National Academy of Sciences of the United States of America* 75 (1978): 2358–2362.

With William G. Burton and Constance T. Grabowy. "Role of Methylation in the Modification and Restriction of Chloroplast DNA in *Chlamydomonas*." *Proceedings of the National Academy of Sciences of the United States of America* 76 (1979): 1390–1394.

With Ruth W. Craig. "Suppression of Tumorigenicity in Hybrids of Normal and Oncogene-Transformed CHEF Cells." *Proceedings of the National Academy of Sciences of the United States of America* 82 (1985): 2062–2066.

"Genetic Suppression of Tumor Formation: A New Frontier in Cancer Research." *Cancer Research* 46 (1986): 1573–1580.

With Anthony Anisowicz and Lee Bardwell. "Constitutive Overexpression of a Growth-Related Gene in Transformed Chinese Hamster and Human Cells." *Proceedings of the National Academy of Sciences of the United States of America* 84 (1987): 7188–7192.

"Tumor Suppressor Genes: The Puzzle and the Promise." *Science* 246 (1989): 1406–1412.

With Vimla Band. "Distinctive Traits of Normal and Tumor-Derived Human Mammary Epithelial Cells Expressed in a Medium That Supports Long-Term Growth of Both Cell Types." *Proceedings of the National Academy of Sciences of the United States of America* 86 (1989): 1249–1253.

With Vimla Band, Deborah Zajchowski, and Victoria Kulesa. "Human Papilloma Virus DNAs Immortalize Normal Human Mammary Epithelial Cells and Reduce Their Growth Factor Requirements." *Proceedings of the National Academy of Sciences of the United States of America* 87 (1990): 463–467.

With Stephen Haskill, et al. "Identification of Three Related Human *GRO* Genes Encoding Cytokine Functions." *Proceedings of the National Academy of Sciences of the United States of America* 87 (1990): 7732–7736.

With Douglas K. Trask, et al. "Keratins as Markers That Distinguish Normal and Tumor-Derived Mammary Epithelial Cells." *Proceedings of the National Academy of Sciences of the United States of America* 87 (1990): 2319–2323.

With Peng Liang, Lidia Averboukh, Khandan Keyomarsi, and Arthur B. Pardee. "Differential Display and Cloning of Messenger RNAs from Human Breast Cancer versus Mammary Epithelial Cells." *Cancer Research* 52 (1992): 6966–6968.

With Zou Zhiqiang, et al. "Maspin, a Serpin with Tumor-Suppressing Activity in Human Mammary Epithelial Cells." *Science* 263 (1994): 526–529.

With Shijie Sheng, Juliana Carey, Elisabeth A. Seftor, et al. "Maspin Acts at the Cell Membrane to Inhibit Invasion and Motility of Mammary and Prostatic Cancer Cells."

Proceedings of the National Academy of Sciences of the United States of America 93 (1996): 11669–11674.

"Expression Genetics in Cancer: Shifting the Focus from DNA to RNA." *Proceedings of the National Academy of Sciences of the United States of America* 94 (1997): 952–955.

OTHER SOURCES

Biermann, Carol A. "Ruth Sager." In *Women in the Biological Sciences: A Biobibliographic Sourcebook,* edited by Louise S. Grinstein, Carol A. Biermann, and Rose K. Rose. Westport, CT: Greenwood Press, 1997.

Brown, Patricia Stocking, and Gail K. Schmitt. "Ruth Sager." In *Notable American Women: A Biographical Dictionary,* edited by Susan Ware. Cambridge, MA: Belknap Press of Harvard University Press, 2004.

Pardee, Arthur B. "Ruth Sager, 1918–1997." *Biographical Memoirs,* vol. 80. Washington, DC: National Academy of Sciences, 2001.

———. "Ruth Sager, Geneticist." In *Maspin,* edited by Mary Hendrix. Georgetown, TX: Eurekah Publishing, 2001.

Sapp, Jan. *Beyond the Gene.* New York: Oxford University Press, 1987, pp. 201–206.

Gail K. Schmitt

SAH, PETER P. T. (Sa Bentie; courtesy name: Bide) (*b.* Fuzhou, Fujian Province, China, 3 February 1900; *d.* Davis, California, 19 September 1987), *organic chemistry, physiology, pharmacology.*

Sah gained international recognition for his work on the analysis and synthesis of a wide variety of organic compounds, including vitamins and medicines for leprosy and tuberculosis. During his more than forty years of research career he contributed more scientific papers than other China scientists of his day, assuring his status in the eyes of academic world. Among his nearly 200 treatises published, more than half have continued to be cited since the mid-1950s, even in the early twenty-first century. A prolific researcher, he served as mentor for students who became famous in their own right.

Family Background. Sah was born into the prominent Sa family of government officials in Minhou (the present-day Fuzhou), in Fujian Province. His paternal grandfather was Sa Duowen, and his father was Sa Fusui. Peter, the eldest of four siblings, had one brother and two sisters. His brother, Adam Pen-tung Sah (Sa Bendong), was a physicist, electrical engineer, and educator. Peter and Adam both studied in the United States and both returned to China and took up posts at Tsinghua University, Peter as a professor of chemistry and Adam as a professor of physics. Adam went on to become the president of Xiamen University, chief administrative officer of Academia Sinica, and head of the academy's Institute of Physics.

Overview of Career. In his youth Sah studied in Fuzhou, Fujian Province. There he was taught the Chinese classics, including Confucian philosophy, poetry, and history. He was also a very talented tennis player. In 1920, after he graduated from Tsinghua College (Qinghua Xuetang), he was selected for study in the United States. From 1920 to 1922 he studied at the Worcester Polytechnic Institute, in Worcester, Massachusetts, and then studied chemistry at the University of Wisconsin, obtaining a bachelor's degree in 1923, a master's degree in food chemistry in 1924, and a doctorate in organic chemistry under the guidance of Richard Fischer in June 1926, following which he briefly conducted research at Yale University. In 1928 he returned to China to teach at Peking Union Medical College (1928–1929) and Tsinghua (Qinghua) University (1929–1937). On Academic leave in 1934–1935, he went to Germany for studying sterols and sex hormones in the laboratory of Adolf Windaus, and then to England where he visited Xxford and Cambridge universities. After the outbreak of the Sino-Japanese War in 1937, Tsinghua University relocated in the southwest, but Sah remained in Beiping (now Beijing), teaching at Fu Jen Catholic University and the National Peking University, which was controlled by the Japanese, and for a time serving as the chair of the Chemistry Department at the latter university. (In 1947 Academia Sinica selected its first members, but Sah and another famous chemist were disqualified from the selection process because they performed some university administrative duties under the Japanese occupation.)

In 1946, after the Japanese surrender, the educational ministry of the Chinese government declared that those who had assumed duties at institutions controlled by Japanese during the war would not be in the employ of national institutions for two years. In this situation, Sah and his family emigrated to the United States, where he first worked for the pharmaceutical manufacturer Eli Lilly and Company and later served as a visiting lecturer and research associate in the School of Medicine of the University of California at San Francisco. There, he helped Hamilton H. Anderson to reorganize the university's Department of Pharmacology. Sah then conducted research at the medical schools of both Yale University and Halle University in Germany. In 1953 he was appointed a professor in the School of Veterinary Medicine of the University of California at Davis. He retired as Professor Emeritus of Physiological Sciences there in 1967. Sah continued his research after his retirement; he had a home research laboratory for cancer studies, which principally used tropical fish. His wife was Ethel Tsi Hua Hsia Sah (Xia Zhihua), from Jiangzhen County in Sichuan Province, whom he married in 1932. She died in the United States in 1997. They had four sons and two daughters.

Early Research in China. During his long scientific career of more than forty years, Sah published around 200 papers. His research interests during his academic years in China (1928–1946) were extremely broad, but his primary contributions were in the analysis and synthesis of organic compounds. His work on various types of esters and on reagents for identifying organic compounds proved important in the field of organic chemistry, and his research data have been frequently cited by scientists in Europe and North America. Between 1932 and 1940 Sah and his assistants and students determined the composition of a series of organic compounds and measured their melting points. Soon after these data were published, chemists in the United States and Europe took notice: Ralph L. Shriner and Reynold C. Fuson, in *The Systematic Identification of Organic Compounds: A Laboratory Manual* (1935, 1940, 1948), the most popular U.S. textbook for organic chemical analysis, cited Sah's data numerous times, far more than those of any other chemist. Ernest H. Huntress and Samuel P. Mulliken also extensively cited Sah's work in *Identification of Pure Organic Compounds* (1941). And in the second edition of F. Wild's *Characterisation of Organic Compounds* (1960), Sah is the most cited author.

Research on Vitamins. Sah also did research on pharmaceuticals, hormones, and the composition of vitamins. He did exploratory work on the artificial synthesis of steroid hormones (though the steroid compounds that he manufactured were not biologically active). He proposed the hypothesis that l-ascorbic acid (vitamin C) has the same origin in plants as the sugars to which it is structurally related, and on the basis of this hypothesis he suggested a number of methods for synthesizing l-ascorbic acid in the laboratory, using as the starting materials compounds easily produced in the laboratory in large quantities. He used naphthalene and products readily available in China to synthesize vitamin K (a blood coagulant) and estrone (a female hormone with many pharmacological uses). In addition, Sah also studied nutritional chemistry, biological chemistry, and fermentation chemistry. At Yale University he measured the vitamin content of Chinese lychees, and after returning to China he determined the vitamin content of fruits and vegetables in the Beiping market, measured the vitamin C intake in the diet of Beiping residents, and performed detailed analyses of the nutrients in citrus fruits (such as vitamins A, B, and C, essential oils, sugars, and organic acids).

Syntheses of Medicinals. Late in his career Sah became famous for synthesizing medicines for treating tuberculosis and leprosy. Much of his work in these fields was done during his fifteen years at the University of California at Davis. For example, Sah discovered D-glucuronolactone isonicotinyl hydrazone (INHG), which became one of the leading drugs used (under various trade names) to treat human tuberculosis in France, Germany, England, and Japan. Through his research, Sah found that INHG was more active than streptomycin and less toxic than isoniazid and that INHG successfully treated resistant strains of mycobacterium tuberculosis, H376HV, whereas several other drugs did not. He also made a significant contribution to the treatment of human leprosy and animal paratuberculosis when he synthesized a vitamin C derivative of bis-(4-aminophenyl)-sulfone. This drug became an effective alternative in treating infectious organisms that developed resistance to other drugs.

Sah also developed alternatives to drugs used in agriculture and in medicine. His tetrahalogenated quinones, which include Isochloranil and Isobromanil, proved to be twenty times more effective than the compounds in use for treating fungal infection in plants, and was active against athlete's foot and ringworm as well. In addition, he found that psoriasis could be treated by a 0.5 percent Isochloranil or Isobromanil ointment, instead of the 10 percent chloranil ointment that physicians in the southern United States were using. While at the University of California at Davis and the University of San Francisco, Sah synthesized other drugs that are effective against tuberculosis, leprosy, experimental leukemia, malaria, rheumatoid arthritis in children, and carcinoma in mice.

Role in the Scientific Community. Sah devoted himself to his scientific research even in times of war and, by his wide range of research interests and prodigious number of high-quality papers, he became one of the most productive Chinese chemists of the twentieth century. For example, from 1939 to 1941, during the Sino-Japanese War, he published roughly eighteen papers in *Recueil des travaux chimique des Pays-Bas*, three papers in *Berichte der Deutschen chemischen Gesellschaft*, and one paper in the *Journal of the American Chemical Society*. Of the thirteen papers published in volume 13 (1946) of the *Journal of the Chinese Chemical Society* (also titled *Zhongguo huaxuehui huizhi*), eight were written by Sah, and of the fifteen papers appearing in volume 14 (1946–1947), two-thirds were contributions by Sah.

Moreover, by international chemistry standards, his research was at the forefront of the time. Even after fifty years—in some cases seventy years—researchers still cited many of his nearly 200 papers. Among his cited papers, the earliest concerns the condensation of ortho esters,

excerpted from his doctoral dissertation at the University of Wisconsin and published in the *Journal of the American Chemical Society*, volume 53 (1931), a paper that was still cited seventy years after publication. Another early paper, also widely cited, is one on a method for synthesizing the compound 2-methyl-1,4-naphtho-hydroquinone and its derivatives, published in *Recueil des travaux chimique des Pays-Bas* 59 (1940), a paper still cited some sixty years after publication. One paper, on how to prepare thiosemicarbazone, written with T. C. Daniels and published in *Recueil des travaux chimique des Pays-Bas* 69 (1950) after Sah emigrated to the United States, has been cited 108 times from the inception of the Science Citation Index to 2004, with the latest citation in 2003. The reason for the frequent citations of this paper is that thiosemicarbazone can be used to produce sulfur- and nitrogen-containing heterocyclic compounds—an important result in chemical and pharmacological research.

In his research, Sah maintained good working relationships with other scientists. For example, with Hsi-chün Chang (Zhang Xijun, 1899–1988), professor at Peking Union Medical College, he carried out research on the vitamin C content of various vegetables on the Peiping market. With Hamilton A. Anderson, also professor of Peking Union Medical College, he studied the preparation and properties of three isomeric n-hexyl cresols and their chlorinated derivatives. With Tzu-ching Huang (Huang Ziqing, 1900–1982), professor of chemistry at Tsinghua University, he published research on the parachor of hexamethylenetetramine. With Chung-hsi Kao (Gao Chongxi, 1901–1952), professor of chemistry at Tsinghua University, he carried out research on azides. In this way he not only broadened his individual research horizons but also served as a model for his students.

Among the papers published by Sah are a number that list his students as the primary authors. Many of his students in the 1930s in the Chemistry Department of Tsinghua University later went on to achieve notable results. On the Chinese mainland, several of his students were elected as members of the Chinese Academy of Sciences, including Chen-heng Kao (Gao Zhenheng, class of 1934, former head of the Chemistry Department of Nankai University), Jun Shi (Shi Jun, class of 1934, former head of the Department of Chemical Engineering of Nanjing University), Hsin-min Chen (Chen Xinmin, class of 1935, the first president of Central South College of Mining and Metallurgy), Teh-si Wang (Wang Dexi, class of 1935, former vice director of the China Institute of Atomic Energy), Chi Wu (Wu Chi, class of 1936, former vice director of the Research Institute of Petroleum Processing and chief engineer), and Sing-tuh Voong (Feng Xinde, class of 1937, professor of polymer chemistry of Peking University).

In Taiwan, many prominent scholars and statesmen were once Sah's students, including Ssu-liang Ch'ien (Qian Siliang, class of 1931, former president of Academia Sinica and former president of National Taiwan University), Ming-cheh Chang (Zhang Mingzhe, class of 1935, former president of Tsinghua University and minister of the National Science Council), Kwang-shih Chang (Zhang Guangshi, class of 1935, former minister of economic affairs), and Zhu Shugong (class of 1936, former dean of academic affairs of Tsinghua University). One of the first two students to receive graduate degrees from Tsinghua University in 1934 was Sah's advisee, Tsu Sheng Ma (Ma Zusheng). In 1931 Tsu Sheng Ma finished his bachelor's dissertation and published it in the *Journal of the American Chemical Society*. He then accepted Sah's suggestion to continue his studies at Tsinghua University as a graduate student studying organic chemical analysis. Later he was selected for further study in the United States. At Sah's recommendation he entered the University of Chicago, where he studied the synthesis of pharmaceuticals and began his study of organic microanalysis. He later achieved much renown in the fields of microchemical technology and applied chemistry, becoming a professor at Brooklyn College, City University of New York, and a famous overseas Chinese chemist.

Sah was the recipient of many academic honors and awards. At the launch of the *Journal of the Chinese Chemical Society* (*Zhongguo huaxuehui huizhi*) in 1933, Sah served on its editorial board. In 1937 he was elected to the Deutsche Akademie der Naturforscher (German Academy of Natural Scientists). In the United States he was feted with many honors. In 1951, for example, he was invited to present his work at the Twelfth International Congress of Pure Chemistry, at which he presented eight papers in the division of Medicinal Chemistry. Sah was awarded the American Pharmaceutical Association's Ebert Prize for his work with fungi, yeast, and vitamin K-5.

BIBLIOGRAPHY

WORKS BY SAH

Qinghua Daxue xiao shi bianxie xiaozu, ed. *Qinghua Daxue xiao shi gao* (A Sketch of the History of Tsinghua University). Beijing: Zhonghua Shuju, 1981. Lists representative works of Sah in the fields of organic chemistry and biochemistry.

Zheng Ji, ed. *Zhongguo zaoqi shengwuhuaxue fazhan shi* (A History of the Early Development of Biochemistry in China). Nanjing: Nanjing Daxue Chubanshe, 1989. Lists representative works of Sah in biochemistry.

Zhongguo Huaxue Hui, ed. *Journal of the Chinese Chemical Society; Acta Chimica Sinica: Collective Author and Classified Subject Indices to Vol. 1–20, 1933–1954*. Beijing: Kexue Chubanshe, 1958. Lists all of Sah's papers published in the *Journal of the Chinese Chemical Society*.

OTHER SOURCES

Liu Guangding. "Jian gu yi jin: Cong Sa Bentie xiansheng de xueshu chengjiu tan kexue fazhan" (Viewing the Present through the Lens of the Past: A Discussion of the Development of Science Based on Mr. Sah's Academic Achievements). Paper presented at a symposium on Tsinghua University and the history of Chinese science and technology, April 2004. Available from http://rwxy.tsinghua.edu.cn/xisuo/kjs/thykj.htm. Using citations from the Science Citation Index, the author compiled statistics on the frequency of citations of Sah's published papers. He also summarizes Sah's academic career.

Reardon-Anderson, James. *The Study of Change: Chemistry in China, 1840–1949*. Cambridge: Cambridge University Press, 1991. A brief summary of Sah's life and academic research.

University of California. "In Memoriam: Peter Sah." Available from http://content.cdlib.org.

Zhang Li. "Peter P. T. Sah and the Synthesis of Vitamin C in Europe and China." *East Asian Science, Technology, and Medicine*. 20 (2003): 92–98. The author focuses on Sah's hypothesis of the origin of vitamin C and on its synthesis.

———. "Sa Ben Tie De Qian Ban Sheng, 1912–1946" [Peter Pan Tieh Sah's early career in China: 1912–1946]. *The Chinese Journal for the History of Science and Technology* 27, no.4 (2006): 287–1304. This article, compiled from the archives, periodicals of the 1920–1940s, Sah's published papers, and correspondence between the author and Sah's nephews, draws a closer picture of his studies, research, and teachings in different periods before 1946 and academic achievements after emigrating to the Unite States. It attempts to proceed from societal, personal, and family information to look into decisions that Dr. Sah made during those few critical moments in his life as an initial step; and to construe the mixed feelings that Sah had gone through in his character and religious beliefs.

Li Zhang

SAKHAROV, ANDREI DMITRIYEVICH

(*b.* Moscow, U.S.S.R., 21 May 1921; *d.* Moscow, 14 December 1989), *theoretical physics, thermonuclear design and engineering, cosmology, international security and human rights.*

Devoted to fundamental physics, Sakharov spent two decades designing nuclear weapons before returning to academic research and producing his major scientific accomplishment: In 1966, by combining particle physics and cosmology he provided the first (and the only as of 2007) explanation of baryon asymmetry, the observed drastic disparity in the natural occurrence of matter and antimatter in the universe. Just a few years later, based on his second domain of professional knowledge—strategic weaponry—together with his understanding of the machinery of the Soviet leadership and his feeling of personal responsibility, this "father of the Soviet hydrogen bomb" developed into one of the leading human rights advocates in the Soviet Union. In 1975, he became the first Russian to win the Nobel Peace Prize.

In the Family of Moscow Intelligentsia. Andrei Sakharov was born in Moscow to a family of intelligentsia. His father, Dmitri, a son of a lawyer, taught physics and wrote popular science books. His mother, Ekaterina (nee Sofiano), a daughter of a czarist army officer, was a housewife. His generation was brought up under the confluence of post–Civil War hardships, lofty ideals of social progress, and real advancement of education and science in Soviet Russia. The Stalinist terror missed Andrei's parents, and they tried to shield their child from harsh reality, in particular by affording him the opportunity for six years of home schooling. His father was his first teacher in science. But as to social realities, in Sakharov's words, "My father was afraid that, if I knew too much about Soviet life, I wouldn't be able to get on in this world. This hiding of thoughts from one's son might best characterize the horror of Stalin's era" (Gorelik, 2005, p. 67).

On the eve of World War II, Sakharov entered Moscow University, and, with the period of study shortened by a year, graduated with honors in 1942, when the war was at its height. Having declined an offer to go to graduate school, he was assigned to work in a major munitions factory in Ul'yanovsk on the Volga River. A year later, in 1943, he married Klavdia Vikhireva, a laboratory technician who also worked at the factory. In 1945, their first child was born; two more followed in 1949 and 1957.

A Theorist and Inventor. In Ul'yanovsk, while busy with routine laboratory work, Sakharov authored a few engineering inventions, including devices for testing the quality of bullets. While implementing those inventions based on electromagnetic theory, he started thinking about problems of theoretical physics as such, and as the war was ending, Sakharov sought to do theoretical research in earnest. He returned to Moscow to become a graduate student at the Physical Institute of the Soviet Academy of Sciences (FIAN). He mastered theoretical physics under the prominent theorist Igor Tamm (who would be awarded the 1958 Nobel Prize for the theory of Vavilov-Cherenkov radiation), at a time when the theory of nuclear forces dominated Tamm's research. The topic also provided the subject matter for Sakharov's 1947 dissertation and a few other papers, including the pioneering idea of muon-catalyzed fusion.

This pure physics was put on hold in June 1948, when Tamm was commissioned to head an auxiliary group to explore whether a hydrogen bomb was feasible.

This group was to assist the team of Yakov Zeldovich, then the main theorist of the Soviet nuclear project. Although the first priority was to create an atomic bomb, Zeldovich was also occupied with an H-bomb design. The original H-bomb design was initiated by espionage but lacked promise. In a few months Sakharov suggested a radically new design, named Sloyka (the Russian for a layered pastry). Another student of Tamm, Vitaly Ginzburg, added a second key idea concerning the efficient thermonuclear explosive (lithium deuteride, Li^6D).

In the spring of 1950, Tamm and Sakharov were ordered to move to the "Installation," a secret city in the central Volga region, to implement the Sloyka design. They succeeded, and the first Soviet thermonuclear bomb was tested on 12 August 1953.

Parallel to the bomb effort, in the early 1950s, Sakharov made two major inventions. Together with Tamm he proposed the principle of magnetic confinement of plasma for a controlled thermonuclear (fusion) reactor (the so-called Tokamak, an acronym for the Russian phrase, Toroidal Chamber with Magnetic Coil). Another invention was a way to obtain superstrong magnetic fields created in a magnetic coil compressed by implosion. Both inventions were initially related to weaponry. The thermonuclear reactor, as a powerful neutron generator, was expected to produce plenty of fissile explosive. However, the unforeseen problems of handling plasma made this promise impracticable, and after 1956, when the scientific director of the Soviet nuclear project Igor Kurchatov managed to declassify this research, it was considered as a possibility for a peaceful, practically limitless source of energy.

In 1953, after Tamm returned to Moscow to resume academic work, Sakharov succeeded him at the installation. Sakharov made the key contribution to the fully fledged H-bomb design (of virtually unlimited yield), tested in the U.S.S.R. in 1955, and in 1961 he headed the development of the most powerful bomb ever exploded on Earth (the so-called Czar Bomb, 50 megatons).

In the early 1960s, still at the installation, Sakharov began his return to fundamental physics and, in 1966 and 1967, put forward two highly innovative ideas. The first dealt with a strange cosmological asymmetry. For every kind of particle known in physics there is a kind of antiparticle, its exact opposite in charge and equal in mass. Because the laws of fundamental physics treat particles and antiparticles in exact symmetry, it would be natural to expect these two types of matter to be present in equal quantities. But it is an observational fact that ordinary matter is much more abundant in the universe than antimatter.

Trying to explain this peculiar asymmetry on the cosmological scale, Sakharov connected it to a deviation from symmetry in the submicroscopic world. The so-called CP violation (first proposed by Susumu Okubo in 1958) had indicated a subtle difference between certain kinds of particles and their antiparticles. Sakharov added a hypothesis that protons—commonly assumed to be stable particles—could spontaneously and very slowly decay, converting into other kinds of particles. This decay, combined with the CP violation, would result in an imbalance between matter and antimatter in the swiftly expanding, superdense plasma that made up the very early universe. If the hypothesis were correct, it would then account for the later-observed difference—baryon asymmetry. Experimental attempts to verify "proton decay" continued into the twenty-first century.

Sakharov's second innovative idea attempted to explain gravity as originating from properties of the quantum vacuum. In the words of physicist John Archibald Wheeler, the gravity would be "an elasticity of space that arises from particle physics," like ordinary elasticity that arises from the microphysics of atoms and molecules. It was a brand-new approach in the long quest for unifying gravity with other fundamental forces and, at the same time, in the quest for quantum gravity. This double problem remained a central and exceptionally difficult task of fundamental physics into the twenty-first century.

Sakharov's explanation of the observable baryon asymmetry opened up a new direction for research, sometimes called *cosmomicrophysics, astroparticle physics,* or *particle astrophysics and cosmology*—the combination of particle physics and cosmology. Behind Sakharov's innovations there was a rare combination of talents: those of theorist and inventor. His successful return to theoretical physics strengthened his self-confidence just on the eve of his breakthrough far beyond science.

A Humanitarian Physicist. By 1968, Sakharov's accomplishments in superweaponry had earned him the highest Soviet honors and perks (including membership in the Soviet Academy of Sciences, three Hero of Socialist Labor medals, huge Stalin and Lenin prizes, and a special villa). His theoretical ideas brought the respect of his colleagues, the pure theorists. Moreover, nothing in the public domain portended that this semisecret scientist was about to become a public figure of world stature and—in seven years—a Nobel Peace Prize laureate. Nevertheless Sakharov's humanitarian storyline was tightly intertwined with his storyline as a scientist and expert in strategic high technology.

Most important in Sakharov's background were Igor Tamm, his mentor in science and in life, and the milieu of Leonid Mandelshtam's school at Moscow University and FIAN. Mandelshtam had become a scientist in Strasbourg, under Karl Ferdinand Braun, and returned to Rus-

sia on the eve of World War I. He made important contributions in optics and radiophysics, but his foremost contribution was his Russian school, the group of his disciples, including Tamm, which featured a union of high professionalism and high moral standing, an extraordinary accomplishment at any time, but especially during the years of Stalin's reign.

Tamm's worldview in social life, as well as in science, greatly influenced Sakharov. Tamm was converted to socialism in his teens, before he entered university and well before he became a scientist. Early in 1917, Tamm, a member of a Social Democratic Party of Menshevik internationalists, was elected to the Elizavetgrad Soviet and tasted political life of post-czarist and pre-Bolshevik Russia. Then he "became convinced that Bolshevism in its mass form exists only as demagogic anarchism and unruliness. Of course, this doesn't apply to its leaders, who are simply blind fanatics, dazzled by the genuinely big truth [of socialism] which they are defending, but which prevents them from seeing anything else besides it," as he wrote in his diary "The genuinely big truth" of socialism was the goal of both the Bolsheviks and the Mensheviks. The difference was that for the Bolsheviks, this end justified any means, while Mensheviks were for the evolutionary development by means of parliamentary democracy and in collaboration with other parties. Despite Tamm's personal losses during the Great Terror of 1937, when his brother, close friend, and beloved student had "disappeared," he managed to defend the persecuted and to keep his allegiance to the socialist ideals of his youth.

It was thus under both Tamm's influence and the total control of the media by the Soviet dictatorship, that Sakharov shared the official pro-socialist religion for so long. He felt himself securing peace for the country after a devastating war. "Having given so much to this cause and accomplished so much," Sakharov "unwittingly created an illusory world to justify" himself, in his own harsh self-diagnosis (Gorelik, 2005, p. 165).

It was not merely passive conformism. An ability to provide the Soviet leadership with nuclear weapons secured for physicists the greatest intellectual freedom available in the Soviet land and somewhat emboldened them socially—within the idealistically Soviet, prosocialist mindset. With such a mindset Sakharov consciously and wholeheartedly developed thermonuclear weaponry: "I couldn't ignore how horrible and inhuman our work was. But the world war that had just ended was also inhuman. I wasn't a soldier in that war, but I felt like one in this scientific and technological war" (Gorelik, 2005, p. 141). With the same mindset he declined an invitation to join the party but felt himself serving the same cause the Soviet leaders did. He mourned Stalin's death but, together with other nuclear physicists, defended the true science in physics and in devastated biology.

He grew ashamed of his pop-Stalinism when Stalin's crimes were exposed by the new Soviet leader, Nikita Khrushchev, but his prosocialist ideals remained. With this idealistic mindset, Sakharov was asked to write an article denouncing the new American military development of the so-called clean bomb. He took the matter more seriously than a mere propaganda exercise. Using available biological data, he calculated that the detonation of the one-megaton, "cleanest" H-bomb would produce enough radioactive carbon to result in 6,600 deaths worldwide over the next eight thousand years. "What moral and political conclusions must be drawn from these numbers?" he asked in his 1958 article (Gorelik, 2005, p. 214). For him, the death toll from nuclear testing in the atmosphere—however small compared to other kinds of mortality—was a fact proved by science, with inescapable moral consequences. He considered this paper the start of his growing social awareness.

The next phase of his awareness came in 1961, when Khrushchev decided to revoke the three-year moratorium on nuclear tests. Sakharov was the only one who openly objected to the Soviet leader. He argued that tests would yield little new technical information while threatening international security. But, obeying an order from the head of state, he took part in the development of the most powerful device ever exploded, on 30 October 1961 (the so-called Czar Bomb). Sakharov trusted Khrushchev too much—because the leader had rehabilitated the victims of the Terror, allowed a general cultural "thaw," and called for peaceful coexistence with the West.

Sakharov's illusory world cracked in 1962, when he tried but failed to prevent another test, totally unnecessary from a technical point of view but producing deadly radioactive fallout—the Soviet "military-industrial complex" had defeated him. His feeling of moral responsibility spurred his effort toward the 1963 Test Ban Treaty, which banned all nuclear tests in the atmosphere. In Sakharov's view, the treaty saved the lives of people who would have perished had such tests continued, and also reduced the risk of nuclear war.

Describing the evolution of his social worldview, Sakharov admitted that "it took years" for him "to understand how much substitution, deceit, and lack of correspondence with reality there was" in the Soviet ideals. "At first I thought, despite everything that I saw with my own eyes, that the Soviet state was a breakthrough into the future, a kind of prototype for all countries." Then he came, in his words, to "the theory of symmetry: all governments and regimes to a first approximation are bad, all peoples are oppressed, and all are threatened by common dangers" (Gorelik, 2005, p. 300).

It was at this stage, from 1967 to 1968, that the major change in Sakharov's social worldview took place. It was the time when anti-ballistic missile (ABM) defense became a key issue in U.S.-Soviet relations. Despite the defensive purpose of the new weapons system, Sakharov came to the conclusion that the new kind of strategic arms race would undermine international security and make a world war more likely. He wrote a detailed secret memorandum for the Soviet leaders, advising them to accept a recent American proposal for a moratorium on strategic ABMs. To promote mutual understanding with the West, Sakharov also prepared a nontechnical article on the issue and suggested that its publication in the open press would help "foreign scientific and engineering intelligentsia to restrain their 'hawks.'" (Gorelik, 2005, p. 267) But Soviet leaders rejected Sakharov's advice and did not permit him to initiate a public discussion of the ABM problem in the Soviet press.

Growing aware of the Soviet hawks and the Soviet political machine, Sakharov decided to make his views public and wrote an essay titled "Reflections on Progress, Peaceful Coexistence and Intellectual Freedom" (completed in May 1968). He stated his goal of an "open, sincere discussion" without pretending to be an "expert in social issues." However he started with an issue in which he was a real expert: the threat of nuclear war as a result of the strategic ABM race. And his main conclusion was that "Peace, progress, human rights—these three goals are insolubly linked to one another: it is impossible to achieve one of these goals if the other two are ignored," as he worded his humanitarian discovery seven years later in his Nobel Lecture. In the words of the Nobel Committee's citation: "In a convincing manner Sakharov has emphasised that Man's inviolable rights provide the only safe foundation for genuine and enduring international cooperation."

The essay circulated in typewritten copies before being published by the Western media in July 1968. The secret father of the Soviet H-bomb emerged as an open advocate of peace and human rights. His background in the privileged scientific elite, privy to the regime's top secrets, contributed to his public role.

Just after his humanitarian discovery, Sakharov was banned from all classified research. From then on he combined his work on pure physics with activity in the emerging human rights movement. In 1970, he cofounded the Moscow Human Rights Committee. In the movement he met Elena Bonner, who became his mate and comrade-in-arms; they married in 1972 (his first wife Klavdia had died of cancer in 1969).

As Sakharov's public stature and international support grew, the regime put increasing pressure on him. In 1973 and 1974, the Soviet media campaign targeted both

Andrei Sakharov and Aleksandr Solzhenitsyn, another fearless voice in the Soviet empire. While Sakharov disagreed with Solzhenitsyn's Slavophile vision of Russian revival, he deeply respected the author of *The Gulag Archipelago*. Only a few individuals in the Soviet Union dared to defend "traitors" such as Sakharov and Solzhenitsyn, and those who had dared were inevitably punished.

It was time for Sakharov to realize that his political "theory of symmetry" required amendment, because there is not much

> symmetry between a cancer cell and a normal one. Yet our state is similar to a cancer cell—with its messianism and expansionism, its totalitarian suppression of dissent, the authoritarian structure of power, with a total absence of public control in the most important decisions in domestic and foreign policy, a closed society that does not inform its citizens of anything substantial, closed to the outside world, without freedom of travel or the exchange of information. (Gorelik, 2005, p. 300)

It was time for Sakharov to compare his country to a "gigantic concentration camp" and to find the appropriate name for the system of government: "totalitarian socialism."

In 1975, Sakharov was awarded the Nobel Peace Prize. The Soviet authorities did not allow him to travel to Norway to accept it personally, and he was represented by Elena Bonner (who happened then to be abroad for eye surgery).

After Sakharov's public protest against the 1979 Soviet invasion of Afghanistan, he was extrajudicially exiled to Gorki, a city closed to foreigners. He remained in exile for almost seven years, suffering from the isolation but continuing to promote human rights and international security. During his exile, Sakharov wrote a book of autobiographical memoirs. More than once the KGB stole Sakharov's manuscript, and each time he rewrote his book anew.

Protesting against the persecution he, his wife Elena Bonner, and her children suffered, Sakharov went on hunger strikes. For months he was totally isolated. Most of his friends in the human rights movement failed to appreciate the motivation for his hunger strikes and blamed Bonner for his sufferings. Sakharov was sorry to see such a gap in understanding but claimed his human right to make decisions that he felt to be morally necessary for him personally.

After the new Soviet leader Mikhail Gorbachev had initiated the reforms of perestroika, Sakharov was allowed to return to Moscow. A leading figure in the Russian democratic movement, he became a member of the first really elected parliament. An advocate of constitutional democ-

Andrei Dmitriyevich Sakharov. *Andrei Sakharov speaking to Western journalists, 1988.* CHIRS NIEDENTHAL/TIME LIFE PICTURES/GETTY IMAGES.

racy, he drafted a new constitution. He argued that only quicker and more radical reform could guarantee the peaceful evolution of the country. On 14 December 1989, after a difficult day of discussions in the Parliament, he died of a heart attack.

Free Thinking and Religious Feeling. In 1985, while Sakharov was still in exile, the European Parliament established the Sakharov Prize for Freedom of Thought. Indeed, it was his free thinking based on his professional knowledge and personal responsibility that urged him to connect the world of science with humanitarian politics.

The "father" of the Soviet H-bomb had a good reason to contemplate the lots of his counterparts on the other side of the Iron Curtain—the fathers of the American A- and H-bombs. He saw "striking parallels" between his stand and those of J. Robert Oppenheimer and Edward Teller. While in the view of most American academics, the two were as diametrically opposed as good and evil, Sakharov believed that in this "tragic confrontation of two outstanding people," both deserved respect, because "each of them was certain he had right on his side and was morally obligated to go to the end in the name of truth."

Sakharov never felt that by creating nuclear weapons he had "known sin," in Oppenheimer's haunting expression. Nor did he persuade the Soviet government of the need for an H-bomb, as Teller did the American government. But as far as international security in the early 1950s went, Sakharov believed Teller was right. Sakharov had learned that for Soviet leaders "all steps by the Americans of a temporary or permanent rejection of developing thermonuclear weapons would have been seen either as a clever feint, or as the manifestation of stupidity. In both cases, the reaction would have been the same—avoid the trap and immediately take advantage of the enemy's stupidity" (Gorelik, 2005, p. 349).

So while Sakharov strongly disagreed with Teller over two major issues of "political physics," which were the turning points in his own humanitarian career—nuclear testing in the atmosphere and strategic ABMs (or "Star Wars"), he believed that American academics had been unfair to Teller's resolve to get the H-bomb for the United States.

Have Soviet and American nuclear scientists helped to keep the peace? Sakharov answered this way:

> After more than forty years, we have had no third world war, and the balance of nuclear terror … may have helped to prevent one. But I am not at all sure of this; back then, in those long-gone years, the question didn't even arise. What most troubles me now is the instability of the balance, the extreme peril of the current situation, the appalling waste of the arms race … Each of us has a responsibility to think about this in global terms, with tolerance, trust, and candor, free from ideological dogmatism, parochial interests, or national egotism. (Sakharov, 1990, pp. 97–98)

Sakharov's free thinking went well beyond science and above politics, and that might explain the connection of the two realms he made in the course of his life, as well as his free connection with the spiritual realm. His mother and grandmother were believers and churchgoers, while his father was not. At the age of thirteen, Andrei decided that he, too, was a nonbeliever. However in his sixties he articulated the stance amazing most of his colleagues: "I cannot imagine the Universe and human life without some meaningful element, without a source of spiritual 'warmth,' lying outside matter and its laws. Probably that feeling could be called religious" (Gorelik, 2005, p. 356). Addressing an audience of French physicists and referring to a few centuries when "it seemed that religious thought and scientific thought contradicted each other," he expressed his belief that the apparent contradiction would have "a profound synthetic resolution in the next stage of the development of human consciousness" (Gorelik, 2005, p. 357).

A few lines in his diary reveal his creed: "For me all the religions are equal; I have no affinity to any of them. For me God is not the ruler of the world, not the creator of the world or its laws, but the guarantor of the meaning of existence—despite all the apparent meaninglessness." But in no way did Sakharov consider himself a prophet or the like: "I am no volunteer priest of the idea, but simply a man with an unusual fate. I am against all kinds of self-immolation (for myself and for others, including the people closest to me" (Gorelik, 2005, p. 339).

In defending the human rights of others, together with his own dignity, the humanitarian physicist relied, even if half-jokingly, on fundamental physics itself. In a letter written from his exile, he cheered up a fellow physicist and human rights activist with the words: "Fortunately, the future is unpredictable and also—because of quantum effects—uncertain" (Gorelik, 2005, p. 358). For Sakharov the "uncertainty" of the future held an importance far beyond quantum physics. It supported his belief that he could, and should, take personal responsibility for the future of humanity.

BIBLIOGRAPHY

Andrei Sakharov's Nobel Lecture and other materials are available at the Nobel Foundation Web site: http://nobelprize.org/peace/laureates/1975/.

WORKS BY SAKHAROV

"Radioaktivnyi uglerod iadernykh vzryvov i neporogovye biologicheskie effekty" *Atomnaia energiia* 4, no. 6 (1958): 576–580. English translation: "Radioactive Carbon from Nuclear Explosions and Nonthreshold Biological Effects." *Science & Global Security* 1 (1990a): 175–187; also available at http://www.princeton.edu/%7Eglobsec/publications/pdf/1_3-4Sakharov.pdf. The first of Sakharov's writing involving moral and political issues.

"Thoughts on Progress, Peaceful Coexistence and Intellectual Freedom." In "Text of Essay by Russian Nuclear Physicist Urging Soviet-American Cooperation." *New York Times,* 22 July 1968; available at http://pqasb.pqarchiver.com/nytimes/. Reproduced in: *Progress, Coexistence, and Intellectual Freedom.* New York: Norton, 1968. Sakharov's first writing publicly manifesting his political dissent with the Soviet regime.

Collected Scientific Works. New York: Marcel Dekker, 1982.

Nauchnye trudy [Scientific Works]. Moscow: Tsentrkom, 1995.

Vospominaniya. 2 vols. Moscow: Prava cheloveka, 1996. Available from http://orel.rsl.ru/nettext/russian/saharov/sach_fr/fr_sach1.htm. English: *Memoirs.* Translated by R. Lourie. New York: Knopf, 1990b; *Moscow and Beyond, 1986 to 1989.* Translated by A. Bouis. New York: Knopf, 1991.

"Lecture in Lyons: Science and Freedom." Translated by M. Yankelevich. *Physics Today* 52, no. 7 (July 1999): 22–24. One of the last public talks given at a session of the Société Française de Physique in Lyons, France, 27 September 1989.

OTHER SOURCES

Altshuler, Boris L., et al., eds. *On mezhdu nami zhil. Vospominaniya o Sakharove.* Moscow: Praktika, 1996. *Andrei*

Sakharov: Facets of a Life. Gif-sur-Yvette, France: Editions Frontières, 1991. Recollections of friends and colleagues.

American Institute of Physics. "Andrei Sakharov: Soviet Physics, Nuclear Weapons, and Human Rights." Web exhibit at the American Institute of Physics, Center for History of Physics. Available from http://www.aip.org/history/sakharov/.

Drell, Sydney D., and Sergei P. Kapitza, eds. *Sakharov Remembered: A Tribute by Friends and Colleagues.* New York: American Institute of Physics, 1991.

Ginzburg, Vitaly. *The Physics of a Lifetime: Reflections on the Problems and Personalities of 20th Century Physics.* Berlin: Springer, 2001.

———. *About Science, Myself and Others.* Bristol: IOP Publishing, 2004. Both of Ginzburg's books are recollections of a prominent theoretical physicist, close colleague of A. Sakharov, and cofather of the Soviet H-bomb.

Gorelik, Gennady. "The Metamorphosis of Andrei Sakharov." *Scientific American* 280 (March 1999): 98–101. An explanation of Sakharov's transformation into public and political figure.

———, with Antonina W. Bouis. *The World of Andrei Sakharov: A Russian Physicist's Path to Freedom.* New York: Oxford University Press, 2005. The first authoritative study of Andrei Sakharov as scientist as well as public figure; relies on previously inaccessible documents, archives declassified in the 1990s or later, and personal accounts by Sakharov's friends and colleagues.

Gennady Gorelik

SAKURADA, ICHIRO (*b.* Kyoto, Japan, 1 January 1904; *d.* Kyoto, Japan, 23 June 1986), *polymer chemistry, fiber chemistry.*

Sakurada was the pioneer in polymer chemistry and modern chemical fibers research in Japan. He also was the developer of vinylon, a lightweight, durable, weather-resistant fiber widely used in the agriculture, industrial, and fishing sectors.

Childhood and Education. Sakurada was born, grew up, and spent most of his scientific career in the ancient city of Kyoto. His father, Bungo Sakurada, was a newspaperman and served as a war correspondent for the newspaper *Nihon Shinbun* (literally translated as "Japan newspaper") during the Sino-Japanese War (1894–1895) and the Russo-Japanese War (1904–1905).

In 1920 Sakurada enrolled at the Third High School in Kyoto, a three-year national high school in prewar Japan that prepared elite students for the imperial universities. Influenced by his father, Ichiro Sakurada was fond of writing and thought about majoring in literature. However, his mother, Masa, unhappy with her husband's unsettled occupation and advised her son to enter the engineering field, which he did.

Sakurada's early interest in colloids arose when he was fascinated with the beauty of a red sol of gold in a chemistry class. At this time, when colloid chemistry was reaching at its zenith, the chemistry teacher was eager to include colloids as a subject for high school students.

In April 1923, Sakurada entered the Department of Industrial Chemistry in the Faculty of Engineering at Kyoto Imperial University (the forerunner of Kyoto University). There, he found his lifelong mentor in Gen-itsu Kita, who—holding great administrative power—was running the department and promoting research in such industrially important materials as fibers, petroleum, and rubber. Kita characteristically stressed the importance of basic research in industrial chemistry, a trait that Sakurada inherited.

As a college student, Sakurada became particularly interested in fibers. In the mid-1920s, the rayon industry was booming in Japan. Consequently, fibers and textiles drew much attention from academic chemists as a promising research subject. Kita was one of the active academics who directed research on cellulose acetate fibers. He sent many of his students to rayon companies upon their graduation. For his senior thesis, Sakurada chose to study the synthesis of cellulose derivatives, such as cellulose esters, under Kita's supervision.

Colloids and Macromolecules. After his graduation in 1926, Sakurada spent two years as a research fellow at Kita's laboratory. Impressed by Sakurada's ability, Kita sent him to Germany in 1928 to extend his study of cellulose. Sakurada spent half a year at the University of Leipzig, where he studied the swelling and dissolution of cellulose acetate in organic solvents under the renowned colloid chemist Wolfgang Ostwald. In the summer of 1929, he moved to the Kaiser Wilhelm Institute for Chemistry in Berlin-Dahlem, a suburb of Berlin, to study with the cellulose chemist Kurt Hess.

During the 1920s in Germany, there was a heated debate over the molecular structure of a class of substances called polymers, including cellulose, starch, proteins, rubber, and plastics. Hermann Staudinger proposed his theory that they were made up of enormously large molecules, for which he coined the word *macromolecules.* He argued that the properties of polymers, such as colloidal behaviors in solutions, elasticity of rubber, and the strength of fibers should stem from the largeness and shapes of macromolecules. On the other hand, many chemists supported the aggregate theory that polymers were physical aggregates of molecules of ordinary sizes. The properties of polymers, they insisted, came from physical forces between the aggregates. The debate

Ichiro Sakurada. *Ichiro Sakurada during a meeting.* AP IMAGES.

culminated in a symposium held in 1926 at the Düsseldorf meeting of the Gesellschaft Deutscher Naturforscher und Ärzte (Society of German Natural Scientists and Physicians), in which Staudinger's macromolecular theory was severely criticized by most of the other speakers.

Both Ostwald and Hess were among the leading advocates of the aggregate theory. Ironically, Sakurada, Japan's future leader in macromolecular chemistry, came to their laboratories without knowing about the debate and thus made his German debut as their loyal student. At Hess's laboratory, Sakurada collected data that might support the aggregate structure of cellulose. For the first three months, he attempted to crystallize cellulose in various solvents in order to show that cellulose, like ordinary organic compounds, could be purified by crystallization. After that attempt failed, Sakurada examined how the swelling behavior of cellulose was affected by its impurities. Colloidal properties might be, he and Hess suspected,

due not to the large size of cellulose molecules but to impurities in the cellulose. In his German papers, Sakurada criticized Staudinger's work, a criticism that, Sakurada later recalled, was more or less faultfinding, or criticism for criticism's sake.

While in Germany, Sakurada had an opportunity to attend what became known as a historic symposium on colloid-polymers, titled "Organische Chemie und Kolloidchemie" (Organic chemistry and colloid chemistry), which the Kolloid Gesellschaft (Colloid Society) arranged at its annual meeting in Frankfurt in September 1930. Wolfgang Ostwald, the founder of the society, presided over the meeting. Such notable polymer researchers as Staudinger, Kurt Meyer, Herman Mark, Reginald O. Herzog, Hess, and Rudolf Pummerer were invited as principal speakers. After hearing their presentations, Sakurada sensed that the aggregate theory was now on the verge of falling apart. Nonetheless, Hess would remain as

Staudinger's formidable opponent in German scientific circles until the late 1930s.

Research on Fibers. Back in Japan in 1931, Sakurada received his doctor of engineering degree from his alma mater for his study of cellulose, "Ueber die Cellulose und ihre Substitutionsprodukte" (On cellulose and its substitution products). That year he married Chiyoko Okumura. They had three children, including their only son, Yutaka Sakurada, who would later work on synthetic polymers for medical use at Kuraray Company.

Sakurada was appointed associate professor at Kyoto Imperial University in 1934 and full professor the following year. Although he was reluctant to give up his German teacher's aggregate view for years, he turned into the most active propagator of the macromolecular theory of polymers in Japan's chemical community after the mid-1930s. At that time, he must have thought that the macromolecular theory was definitively gaining significant acceptance in Europe and America. His involvement in the German macromolecular debate no doubt enriched his later scientific career in Japan. All of his fruitful research, which he would carry out in Japan, used the macromolecular theory as its guiding principle.

At Kyoto, Sakurada, together with his colleagues and students, carried out both basic and applied study of cellulose and other polymers. His study on the viscosity of polymer solutions helped to alter the Staudinger law of viscosity, which expressed a linear relationship between viscosity and molecular weight (or degree of polymerization) of polymers in dilute solutions. From this simple linear relationship, Staudinger had drawn a conclusion that macromolecules had a thin, rigid rod shape, like a glass fiber in solution. Sakurada, on the other hand, thought that they should be flexible chain molecules, a concept that gave rise to a new interpretation of the viscosity mechanism. By 1940, refined general formulas had been proposed independently by Werner Kuhn in Switzerland; Herman Mark, then in United States; Roelof Houwink in the Netherlands; and Sakurada. To put the viscosity formula in a general way, consider η_{sp}/c = constant x Pn where η_{sp} = the specific viscosity, c = the concentration, P = the degree of polymerization, and "n" is a characteristic value for a given type of macromolecule. According to Staudinger, "n" should always be 1. Sakurada and others suggested that if the exponent "n" was numerically large, then the molecular chain was less folded; if it was small, the chain was highly folded and did not have a strong influence on viscosity. Sakurada and others assumed different values of "n." Werner Kuhn thought that it should be between 0.6 and 0.9; Mark between two-thirds and three halves; Houwink, 0.6; and Sakurada between 0 and 2.0. They indicated that Staudinger's empirical viscosity-

molecular weight relationship was valid for only a few specific systems and not for many important high polymers such as rubber, polystyrene, and polyamides.

Sakurada proposed his general formula in a Kyoto journal article, "Yoekichu ni okeru itojo-bunshi no katachi narabini yoeki-nendo to bunshiryo no kankei" (The shape of threadlike molecules in solution and the relationship between the solution viscosity and the molecular weight) in 1940, but for years it remained little known to Western scientists. Today, the general formula is often called the Mark-Houwing viscosity formula rather than the Kuhn-Mark-Houwing-Sakurada viscosity formula.

The technique of x-ray diffraction of cellulose, which he had learned from Carl Trogus while in Germany, played an important role in Sakurada's fiber research. Analyzing the structure of cellulose by this technique, he and his student, Keiroku Fuchino, discovered a new crystalline cellulose named "water cellulose," which contained water molecules in the crystal lattice. His other basic research included such topics as the chemical reactions of macromolecules and their mechanism (for example, the mechanism of chain transfer and the relationship between monomer feed ratio and copolymer composition), the permittivity and diffusion of polymers in solutions, and the mechanical properties of fibers.

On the applied side, his work on synthetic fibers was extremely important. Japan's boycott of Australian wool in 1936, which signaled the beginnings of its autarky program, resulted in the establishment of the Nihon Kagaku Sen-i Kenkyusho (Japanese Institute for Chemical Fibers Research) at Kyoto Imperial University. With an ample donation from the mercer and trader Mansuke Ito to the institute, Sakurada and his coworkers, including Seizo Okamura, began to study the synthesis of artificial wool from cellulose acetate. Even though he was aware of some of Wallace Carothers's ongoing research on polymerization at DuPont through the latter's publications and patents, Sakurada predicted that completely synthetic fibers, which would excel existing natural and semisynthetic fibers, would not be feasible. Thus, he focused his investigative efforts on modified natural fibers such as cellulose acetate.

DuPont's announcement of the invention of nylon in October 1938 dashed Sakurada's optimism regarding modified natural fibers and led him to take a hard look at completely synthetic fibers. Japan's industrialists were now concerned that nylon would deal a fatal blow to the Japanese silk industry. Silk was Japan's major export. In 1938 Japan had some 79 percent of the world's export share of silk. The exports depended heavily on the American market: The United States was then buying nearly 80 percent of Japan's silk exports. About 70 percent of the American consumption of silk was for women's stockings. Fabricated into stockings from the outset, nylon appeared ready to replace silk almost immediately in this dominant field of hosiery. A newspaper article reported that the United States intended to shut out silk within ten years, which would be a matter of grave concern to forty million Japanese farmers.

By January 1939, U.S. representatives of two Japanese companies had managed to obtain a few milligrams of nylon, and they immediately sent them to Sakurada and other chemists. Sakurada conducted an x-ray diffraction analysis to determine the starting materials of nylon. Their analyses quickly showed that nylon was a surprisingly good fiber, except that it was too elastic and soft when compared with silk, the only weakness which Sakurada could find—and that one flaw was ameliorated by DuPont by 1940. In February, an emergency symposium on nylon was held in Osaka, the center of Japan's fiber and textile business, where Sakurada and other fiber chemists reported on the properties and possible starting materials of nylon. They also praised Carothers's scientific work as well as DuPont's well-planned fundamental research program, while criticizing the backwardness of Japan's industrial research.

The Development of Vinylon. The "nylon shock" triggered the institutionalization of fiber chemistry in Japan. Owing to the efforts of Kita and Sakurada, Kyoto Imperial University in April 1941 opened the Department of Fiber Chemistry in which Sakurada, Okamura, Masao Horio, and Kiyohisa Fujino began teaching fiber and polymer chemistry. In the same year, government, industry, and academe in Japan joined to create Nihon Gosei Sen'i Kyokai (Japanese Research Association of Synthetic Fibers) to promote research on and the development of synthetic fibers. Under its umbrella, Sakurada's group decided to study polyvinyl alcohol (PVA), while another group at the Tokyo Institute of Technology worked on nylon and polyurethane fibers.

PVA was readily available to Sakurada, as in the previous year he had assigned Seung Ki Li and Hiroshi Kawakami to investigate the hydrolysis rate of poly(vinyl acetate) as a part of his basic research on polymers. Sakurada thought that a cellulose-like fiber could be made from PVA, as it appeared to resemble cellulose in that both had many hydroxyl groups in their macromolecules. Many attempts were needed to solve practical problems. For example, they had to develop the so-called three-step hardening method by using a formalin treatment to make the PVA fiber insoluble in water during its synthesis process. In October 1939, just one year after DuPont's announcement of nylon, Li announced a new PVA fiber, tentatively named the Synthetic No.1.

The Synthetic No. 1 still had a practical flaw for use as a fiber. When wet, its softening point dropped to 50 to 60 degrees centigrade (122°F–140°F). After attempts to solve this problem failed, Sakurada recalled his prior study on water cellulose. Water cellulose was formed by washing alkali cellulose with low-temperature water. It contained water molecules in the crystallization. When it was dried at 100 degrees centigrade (212°F) for a few minutes, it was transformed into cellulose II (mercered cellulose) by losing the water molecules. The drawn PVA fiber, Sakurada reasoned, should contain water, and thus it should be susceptible to water. If water molecules were eliminated by heat, the distance between the PVA molecules would be shortened and the combining power between the PVA macromolecules would increase. Hence, heat resistance would be improved. The result was exactly what he anticipated. In this way, his group was able to establish the process of giving hot-water resistance to the fiber by means of a high temperature treatment.

In January 1941 a pilot plant was constructed in the city of Takatsuki in Osaka Prefecture to produce the Synthetic No. 1. The scale-up work was, however, hampered by the outbreak of war and ended with Japan's surrender in August 1945. It was not until 1950 that a large-scale industrial production of the PVA fiber, named vinylon, started at Kurashiki Rayon Company (later Kuraray Company) in Okayama Prefecture. The industrialization required hard effort by Tsukumo Tomonari (another student of Hess) and his coworkers at Kurashiki Rayon. As Japan's original synthetic fiber, the vinylon fiber has been used for clothes, ropes, and a wide variety of industrial materials. A few years later, Li began the production of vinylon in North Korea.

In retrospect, Sakurada prided himself on the vinylon fiber as an industrial fruit that stemmed from his academic polymer research. After all, the research and development of vinylon was a big project involving several hundred chemists and chemical engineers. With Kita in charge, Sakurada directed a number of eminent academic chemists, including Seung Ki Li, Hiroshi Kawakami, Masakatsu Taniguchi, Keiroku Fuchino, Tetsuro Osugi, Hidenari Toyama, Seizo Okamura, Shoichi Matsumoto, Waichiro Tsuji, Kiyoshi Hirabayashi, Michiharu Negishi, Iwao Tsukahara, Akio Ueno, Masao Hosono, and Takeo Morita. Invented in response to the emergence of America's nylon, the "made-in-Japan" fiber vinylon ignited Japan's polymer research.

Postwar Polymer Chemistry. As has been seen, Japanese polymer research arose first from studies of fibers rather than rubber or plastics. Yet in the midst of war, the activities of the Research Association of Synthetic Fibers were extended to synthetic rubber and plastics. In early 1943, the association was transformed into Kobunshi Kagaku Kyokai (Association of Polymer Chemistry), the world's first independent scholarly society in this field. It published the first issue of its journal, *Kobunshi Kagaku* (Polymer chemistry), in October 1944, one and a half years earlier than the appearance of Mark's *Journal of Polymer Science* and three years before Staudinger's *Die makromolekulare Chemie* (Macromolecular chemistry). In 1951, the association was reorganized as the Kobunshi Gakkai (Society of Polymer Science). One of its founders, Sakurada served as the third president from 1961 to 1968. The society played an indispensable role in the phenomenal growth of the polymer community in postwar Japan.

In 1961 Kyoto's Department of Fiber Chemistry was renamed the Department of Polymer Chemistry, where Sakurada served as a professor until his retirement in 1967. Succeeding Kita's tradition of industrial chemistry, the Kyoto school, to which Sakurada was central, was the major site of Japan's polymer research and education. As an educator, he was charismatic, strict, and punctual, yet he took good care of his students. About 210 students were trained as polymer chemists at his laboratory. Many of them occupied leading academic and industrial positions.

Upon retiring from Kyoto University in 1967, Sakurada assumed a professorship at Doshisha University in the city of Kyoto, which he held until 1974. He played a pivotal role in founding the Nihon Hoshasen Kobunshi Kagaku Kenkyu Kyokai (Japan Radiation Polymer Research Institute) in 1956. He also served as the president of the Chemical Society of Japan from 1968 to 1969. For his work on vinylon and polymers, he was awarded many prizes, including the Japan Academy Award in 1955, the Kun Nito Kyokujitsu Juko-Sho (Gold and Silver Star of the Order of the Rising Sun) in 1974, and the Bunka Kunsho (Order of Culture) in 1977. A prolific writer, Sakurada published over twenty books and some 880 scientific papers and essays. He authored Japan's first textbook on polymer chemistry, *Kobunshi no kagaku* (Chemistry of macromolecules) in 1940. He published a book about his scientific work as an English-language monograph, *Polyvinyl Alcohol Fibers,* in 1985, a year before dying of lung cancer at the age of eighty-two.

BIBLIOGRAPHY

WORK BY SAKURADA

"Yoekichu ni okeru itojo-bunshi no katachi narabini yoeki-nendo to bunshiryo no kankei" [The shape of threadlike molecules in solution and the relationship between the solution viscosity and the molecular weight]. *Nihon Kagaku Sen'i Kenkyusho Koenshu* [Collected lectures of the Japanese Institute for Chemical Fibers Research] 5 (1940): 33–44.

"Kobunshi no kagaku" [Chemistry of polymers]. *Kogyo Kagaku-zasshi* [Journal of industrial chemistry] 22 (March 1940). A special issue comprising 191 pages.

Sen'i kagaku kyoshitsu yori [From laboratory of fiber chemistry]. Kyoto: Bunri-shoin, 1943.

With Seizo Okamura, eds. *Ko-jugo hanno* [The high polymerization reaction]. Kyoto: Sen-i bunken kankokai, 1943.

Senso to kobunshi-kagaku [War and polymer chemistry]. Tokyo: Association of Polymer Chemistry, 1944.

Goseibutu no kagaku [Chemistry of synthetics]. Tokyo: Asahi shinbunsha, 1947.

Sen-i no kagaku [Science of fibers]. Tokyo: Sankyo shuppan, 1948.

Sen'i monogatari [A fiber story]. Kyoto: Maki shoten, 1951.

Dai sanno sen'i [The third fiber]. Kyoto: Kobunshi kankokai, 1955.

With Masakatsu Taniguchi. *Sen'i no kagaku* [Chemistry of fibers]. Kyoto: Sankyo shuppan, 1956.

As editor. *Poribiniru arukoru* [Polyvinyl alcohol]. Kyoto: Kobunshi kankokai, 1956.

Sen-i, hoshasen, kobunshi [Fibers, radiations, and polymers]. Kyoto: Kobunshi kankokai, 1961.

With Hiroshi Sobue and Munenari Kushi, eds. *Gosei sen'i* [Synthetic fibers]. Tokyo: Asakura shoten, 1964.

Kobunshi-kagaku to tomoni [Together with polymer chemistry]. Tokyo: Kinokuniya shoten, 1969. An autobiography.

"Memoirs of My Research, 1–10" (in Japanese). *Kagaku* [Chemistry] 27 (1972): 12–17, 170–177, 284–291, 393–398, 478–483, 571–577, 657–663, 758–764, 867–873, 974–979.

Kagaku no michikusa [Loitering in chemistry]. Kyoto: Kobunshi kankokai, 1979.

Polyvinyl Alcohol Fibers. New York: M. Dekker, 1985. His only English book.

OTHER SOURCES

Furubayashi, Yuka. "The Formation of Polymer Chemistry in Japan: An Analysis of the Contributions of the Japanese Research Association of Synthetic Fibers" (in Japanese). Master's thesis, Tokyo Institute of Technology, 2003.

Furukawa, Yasu. "Ichiro Sakurada" (in Japanese). Available from http://www.civic.ninohe.iwate.jp/100W/03/024/index.htm.

———. *Inventing Polymer Science: Staudinger, Carothers, and the Emergence of Macromolecular Chemistry*. Philadelphia: University of Pennsylvania Press, 1998. See especially pp. 207–210.

Kim, Dong-Won. "Two Chemists in Two Koreas." *Ambix* 52 (2005): 67–84.

Mark, Herman. "In Memory of Ichiro Sakurada (1904–1986)." *Polymer Journal* 19, no. 5 (1987): 439–440.

Morawetz, Herbert. *Polymers: The Origins and Growth of a Science*. 1985. Repr., New York: Dover, 1995. See especially pp. 103–110.

Okamura, Seizo. "Dedication to the Late Professor Ichiro Sakurada." *Polymer Journal* 19, no. 5 (1987): 437–438.

———. "Polymer Chemistry: Ichiro Sakurada, Who Developed Vinylon with Originality" (in Japanese). In *Nihon no sozoryoku: Kindai gendai wo kaika saseta 470 nin* [Creative powers in Japan: 470 people who cultivated the modern age]. Tokyo: Nihon hoso kyokai, 1993.

———. "Professor Ichiro Sakurada and Polymer Chemistry in Japan: A Perspective of Historical Study of Science" (in Japanese). In *Nihon no kobunshi kagaku-gijutsu-shi* [History of Japanese polymer chemistry and technology]. Tokyo: Japan Society of Polymer Science, 1998.

Shibatani, Kyoichiro. "Which Is Beautiful, the Girl or the Flower?" In *The Chemical Society of Japan: A 125-Year Quest for Excellence 1878–2003*, edited by Tadashi Watanabe. Tokyo: Chemical Society of Japan, 2003.

Tsuji, Waichiro. "The Giant in Fiber and Polymer Chemistry: Professor Ichiro Sakurada" (in Japanese). *Sen'i to Kogyo* [Fiber and Industry] 52, no. 6 (1996): 253–257.

———. "An Outline of Professor Ichiro Sakurada's Works in Fiber and Polymer Chemistry" (in Japanese). *Kagakushi* [History of chemistry] 24 (1997): 205–217.

Yoshihara, Kenji. "Vinylon Is the Fiber That Japan Brought Up: Ichiro Sakurada, A Polymer Star" (in Japanese). *Gendai Kagaku* (Modern chemistry) no. 6 (2005): 16–21.

Yasu Furukawa

SALAM, MUHAMMAD ABDUS (ABDUSSALAM)

(*b.* Santokh Das, Punjab, India/Pakistan, 29 January 1926; *d.* Oxford, United Kingdom, 21 November 1996), *theoretical physics, high-energy physics, and particle physics, science in developing countries.*

Abdussalam shared the 1979 Nobel Prize in Physics with Sheldon Glashow and Steven Weinberg for the unification of weak and electromagnetic interactions. Salam, the first professor of theoretical physics at London's Imperial College, directed the International Centre for Theoretical Physics in Trieste, Italy, for nearly thirty years.

Early Years and Education. Abdussalam, a name that means "servant of God, who is Peace," was born in the undivided province of Punjab, then part of British India (after partition in 1947, his birthplace of Santokh Das became part of Pakistan). He came from a devoted Muslim family that cultivated learning and education. His grandfather, who practiced traditional herbal medicine, was an officer in the Department of Government Revenues. Graduating in 1899 from Islamiya College in Lahore, Salam's uncle later worked in the Punjab government's Education Department. His father was a schoolteacher but later became head clerk of the office of the District Inspector of Schools.

The most important influence in Salam's early years was his father, Chaudhri Muhammad Hussain. He trained young Salam through individual coaching and mentoring to become a civil servant. Chaudhri Muhammad, a devout Muslim, made his faith and heritage an integral part of his son's education. Salam's family belonged to an Islamic movement called the Ahmadiyya-Jammat (Ahmadiyya Movement, or Ahmadiyya Society). The tenets of this doctrine are very controversial for mainstream Islam. According to the orthodoxy there is no successor to Muhammad (although it accepts Jesus as a prophet). Ahmad claimed that, according to his interpretation of the Qur'an he could "prove" that Jesus Christ had died a natural death. Then, in 1889, he proclaimed himself the Promised Messiah (*Mahdi*). The Islamic authorities accused Ahmad of heresy and apostasy. It established its headquarters in Qadiyan, near a small village called Faizullah Chak where Salam's mother had been born. From there, it expanded through groups of missionaries to the West African coast; one of Salam's uncles belonged to one of them. Although the movement was tolerated, since the mid-twentieth century it has been fiercely persecuted in Pakistan. After the Ahmadiyya community was officially declared illegal in Pakistan, in 1974, Salam added also "Muhammad" as a sign of his faith and as a political act in support of his movement. Salam did not see any contradiction between religion and science. Citing from the Qur'an, Salam suggested that discovering the fundamental symmetries of the nature of all forces resided at the core Islamic doctrine.

Salam was an outstanding student. In high school, he graduated first in the district, with his marks setting a new record in the Province and, two years later, he placed first once again in mathematics and in English at Government College, Lahore. His first experience in politics started when he was elected president of the College Students Union. In 1946, with a civil service career still in mind, he won a scholarship awarded by a British program aimed at training a small number of Indians at a postgraduate level. Salam was admitted at St. John's College, Cambridge, to read mathematics. In 1948 Salam received a first in the Mathematics Tripos, completing the required cycle in two years instead of three. Then, under the influence of his mentor, mathematician (soon-to-be renowned astrophysicist and cosmologist) Fred Hoyle, and inspired by Paul Dirac's lectures, Salam decided to pursue a career in theoretical physics. Indeed, in many ways, Dirac became Salam's icon of a theoretical physicist, although their epistemological approaches to theoretical physics (and particularly to the normalization program in quantum field theory) were markedly different. In 1949 Salam was awarded a degree from Cambridge University with a double first in mathematics (Wrangler) and physics. That same he underwent an arranged marriage. Much later, in

Muhammad Abdus Salam. HULTON ARCHIVE/GETTY IMAGES.

the 1980s, he would marry again, this time on his own; his second wife was an Oxford professor.

Cambridge extended his fellowship, and Salam undertook a PhD in physics. Salam was chosen to do experimental physics, as were the majority of the students in Cambridge who had a first-class degree in physics. However, after a few months, he transferred to Dirac's department of theoretical physics, where he worked with Nicholas Kemmer and Paul Matthews on the renormalized theory for quantum electrodynamics. Since the 1930s, this branch of quantum field theory applied to electromagnetism had been successful in explaining experimental results, as well as reconceptualizing atomic interactions. Nonetheless, quantum field theory and Dirac's "hole theory" suffered from the same kind of difficulties: Once applied to higher levels of approximation than the first, measurable (and measured) parameters of the theory appeared via the calculations to be infinite, thus in clear contradiction to the experiments. In the late 1940s Richard Feynman and Julian Schwinger, in conjunction with the earlier studies of Sin-itiro Tomonaga and his co-workers in Japan, invented a method to avoid the infinities, the so-called renormalization. After Freeman Dyson unified these three approaches, Feynman,

Schwinger, and Tomonaga were awarded the Nobel Prize in 1965. Although this achievement revived the hope of using quantum field theory effectively to tackle problems relating to the explosion of particles coming from cosmic rays and the new accelerators, the theory could not yet be applied to all varieties. Salam tackled the so-called overlapping divergences problem, a crucial obstacle to know whether meson theory for spin-zero particles was renormalizable. Salam solved the problem and, by doing so, succeeded in applying the new renormalization methods to various meson theories. Abdus Salam became famous practically overnight, and in January 1951 he was invited to join the Institute for Advanced Studies at Princeton. There he continued working on the renormalization program. During this visit, Victor Weisskopf and J. Robert Oppenheimer became very fond of the young Pakistani for his qualities as a physicist and his extraordinary charisma. In autumn 1951 Salam returned to Pakistan. In the meantime, the University of Cambridge awarded him the Smith's Prize for the most outstanding predoctoral contribution to physics.

Exile and the Missing Nobel Prize. On his return to Pakistan, Salam was appointed head of the Mathematics

Department at Punjab University, but this experience proved to be traumatic, as was usually the case for most young scientists who, after carrying out research in elite universities, returned to their precarious university systems. In 1952–1953, a violent anti-Ahmadiyya movement arose in the Punjab Province. After many doubts, Salam decided to leave the country after being threatened by rioters. In January 1954 Salam emigrated to Cambridge. He would never again live in Pakistan, although he maintained his Pakistani citizenship throughout his life. That same year, 1954, the Pakistan Academy of Sciences elected him as a Fellow.

Salam had a great sense for identifying crucial problems in high-energy physics. Among other things, he worked on the so-called parity nonconservation problem. Gauge theory, namely using the mathematical concept of group theory to test if an interaction were "symmetrical"—or "invariant"—under certain transformations, was suggested in 1929 by Hermann Weyl. It was revived in 1954 by Chen Ning Yang and Robert L. Mills and, independently, by Salam's student Ronald Shaw. In the case Salam addressed, the problem was whether or not weak interactions (the nuclear force responsible for radioactivity) were, as was generally accepted, "symmetrical" under transformations such as space inversion, charge conjugation (same charge but with the opposite sign) and time reversal. In particular, if a weak interaction would proceed identically under a space inversion (exchanging right with left), then it would be said to conserve parity. Eventually, the question would be of primary importance because this kind of analysis led to gauge theories as possible means of studying such processes and classifying subatomic particles. In 1956 Yang and Tsung-Dao Lee realized that no previous experiments required the weak force to conserve parity, and that, in fact, parity might not be conserved in those interactions. This revived a two-component neutrino theory discussed by Weyl's pioneering paper, presented by Wolfgang Pauli in his *Handbuch der Physik* in 1933. After Yang presented his results, Salam postulated the so-called γ_5 symmetry, or "chiral" symmetry. This was an alternative, independent, and elegant explanation of why parity might not be conserved in weak interactions. More importantly Salam found a connection between parity conservation and the fact that neutrinos had zero mass. However, the negative reaction of senior physicists such as Pauli to his paper discouraged him from publishing it. When, in early 1957, Columbia University physicist Chien-Shiung Wu presented her experimental results confirming Yang and Lee's hypothesis, Salam's work was still a preprint. In a matter of a few months, parity violation was part of the new physics, but Salam's contribution appeared much later that same year.

Yang's and Lee's Nobel Prize for Physics in 1957 had a great impact on Salam. Several British physicists thought Salam might receive the Nobel Prize for his contribution. Although he did not share the Nobel with his Chinese colleagues, Salam was awarded the Hopkins Prize and the Adams Prize, both from Cambridge University. In 1959 he was elected a Fellow of the Royal Society, becoming the youngest fellow at the time. Yet, for Salam, this episode was also frustrating, and the Nobel Prize became, according to some of his colleagues, "an obsession." After this incident, although Salam continued to seek advice and support from the scientific elite, he adopted a much more aggressive stance toward publishing. His strategy, followed by his students, was that one should never refrain from publishing. It was the role of the scientific community, he argued, to sort out good ideas from bad. Indeed, Salam was one of the most prolific physicists of his generation, publishing 276 scientific papers.

The 1950s were years of a major expansion of Imperial College, London. In 1953 Nobel laureate Patrick M. S. Blackett was appointed professor of physics. Imperial was the largest postgraduate school in the United Kingdom. As part of the planned expansion, there was an increasing interest in reinforcing the basic sciences in the college. Hence, in 1957 physicist Hans Bethe, a close friend of Blackett's who was visiting Cambridge, recommended Abdus Salam for the applied mathematics post. Salam's chief concern at Imperial was to set up a group strongly tied to the international community. Imperial College, he thought, should also be a training center for a new elite of scientists from Third World countries. First the Mathematics Department, and then the Physics Department, would become exceptionally active, thanks to the presence of Salam. The department received an extraordinary number of visitors. Despite his young age, Salam's credibility in scientific circles brought some the most eminent physicists to give seminars at Imperial. At the beginning of the 1960–1961 session, Salam became the first professor of theoretical physics at Imperial College, a post he held until his retirement in 1993.

Political Career. The consolidation of Salam's scientific career and his political activities occurred simultaneously. These seemingly disparate activities were actually two increasingly complementary aspects of Salam's life. As he became part of the international scientific community, his political career encompassed appointments in both international organizations and in Pakistan.

In 1955 and 1958, he was appointed secretary at the Geneva Conference for the Peaceful Uses of Atomic Energy. There he met Swedish physicist Sigvard Eklund. This was the beginning of a long involvement with United Nations politics. Retrospectively, he recalled his first visit to the New York headquarters as "falling in love with all the organization represented—the Family of Man, in all its hues, its diversity, brought together for Peace and Betterment" (1976, pp. 9–15). Salam and Eklund developed a close relationship marked by mutual respect and a common interest in the promotion of science in developing countries. In 1961 Eklund was elected the second director general of the International Atomic Energy Agency (IAEA), an event that was certainly crucial for Salam's career as a scientific diplomat. Between 1964 and 1975, Salam was a member of the United Nations Advisory Committee of Science and Technology and, from 1970 to 1973, he served as a member of the United Nations Panel and Foundation Committee for the United Nations University.

However, it was in Pakistan that Salam spread his wings as a politician of science. In 1958 the tensions between the eastern and western areas of the country led to a coup d'état orchestrated by the former Chief Martial Law Administrator Ayub Khan—the person who had stopped the anti-Ahmadiyya riots. His regime lasted for eleven years and marked the beginning a technocratic era in which the promotion of science was part of the discourse surrounding the ideology and practice of Pakistan's economic and cultural development. Salam's scientific reputation in the West, as well as his youth, humble origins, and determined, but charismatic, personality, made him an ideal symbol of the scientific spirit of modern Pakistan. In 1961 Salam became the chief scientific advisor to the president, a post he held until 1974, when, due to the anti-Ahmadiyya laws decreed by the Pakistani government, he resigned. In collaboration with his friend Cambridge physicist Ishrat H. Usmani, Salam promoted the establishment of the Space and Upper Atmosphere Research Commission (SUPARCO), near Karachi, the creation of the Pakistan Institute of Nuclear Research (Pinstech), and the consolidation of the Pakistan Atomic Energy Commission. After 1958 he became also a member of the following organizations in Pakistan: the Scientific Commission (1959), the National Scientific Council (1963–1975), and the Board of Pakistan Science Foundation (1973–1977). He was advisor to the Education Commission (1959) and chairman of the Pakistan Space and Upper Atmosphere Committee (1961–1964). In 1962 Salam was appointed to the IAEA as a member of the Pakistani delegation.

Meanwhile, a group of scientists, intellectuals and politicians from Trieste (Italy), led by Professor Paolo Budini started a campaign to set up an international center for theoretical physics in that city. The idea had been discussed among a group of physicists, including Salam, during a scientific meeting held in Miramare, near Trieste. As a member of the Pakistani delegation to the IAEA, Salam supported the idea with great resolve. The initiative took four years before the center was formally established under the banner of the IAEA with the financial support

of that agency and the Italian government. Salam's role was crucial in convincing Third World delegations to the IAEA to support the initiative despite the open hostility of both industrialized and communist countries. Budini and the Trieste elite were the main instruments to mobilize Italian diplomats and, consequently, the required financial resources. In 1963 Salam became the first director of the International Centre for Theoretical Physics (ICTP), remaining in office for almost thirty years. In fact, the Budini-Salam alliance determined the double nature of ICTP. The Trieste physicists wanted to reestablish contacts with scientific institutes in central Europe that had been broken off since the end of the Austro-Hungarian Empire, the annexation of Trieste to Italy, and, after 1945, the erection of the Iron Curtain. Salam, politically backed by Eklund, saw the ICTP as an opportunity to promote physics in "developing" countries by establishing a new space for international collaboration with Western physicists.

In a few years, the ICTP became a reference institution for physicists in Africa, Asia, and Latin America. Since 1964, the year the ICTP began operation, it has received more than sixty thousand scientists from 150 countries. This impressive figure is consistent with the ICTP's estimates that at least one physicist from every physics institute in a developing country has made at least one visit to the ICTP. Moreover, the ICTP was the first United Nations institution entirely devoted to scientific training and research, providing a model for several institutions that now play an important role in developing countries in the fields of science, technology, and development policies. Under Salam's directorship, the center was devoted to the general goal of scientific exchange between industrialized and developing countries.

Following a model used at CERN (Conseil Européen pour la Recherche Nucléaire, or European Organization for Nuclear Research), western Europe's premier center for high-energy physics, Salam established the "Associate Membership," exclusively for the benefit of physicists from and working in developing countries. It gave them the possibility of spending six weeks to three months at the ICTP during a five-year period. Salam conceived the aim of the ICTP's associate membership program as a possible solution to the "brain drain" problem. He used his considerable scientific prestige to attract reputed scientists from Europe, the Soviet Union, and the United States to give seminars and participate in the courses organized by the ICTP. He set up small groups that carried out research and organized courses on high-energy physics (under his leadership), solid-state physics, plasma physics, nuclear physics, and mathematics. In the 1970s UNESCO (the United Nations Educational, Scientific, and Cultural Organization) joined IAEA to support the center. UNESCO's instrumentalist view of science forced Salam to include fields beyond theoretical physics. As a result, the ICTP widened its field of action and organized courses on "applicable sciences" such as physics and technology, applied mathematics, and planning models.

The ICTP also became a model for other initiatives in the Third World. In Pakistan, Salam helped to establish the International Schools on Physics and Contemporary Needs in Nathiagali, which sponsored an important annual meeting during the 1970s for scientists in the subcontinent. In the early 1980s, Salam promoted the creation of a twin center of the ICTP in South America. He was instrumental in the establishment of the Centro Internacional de Física in Bogotá, Colombia, which, for several years, received ICTP support to host physics courses attended by scientists from Latin America and the Caribbean. Beginning in 1983 Salam spearheaded the creation of the Third World Academy of Sciences in Trieste, formally launched in 1985 and administered by UNESCO.

Despite ICTP's intensive activity and visibility among physicists around the world, Salam had to struggle throughout his administration to overcome the fragile situation in which the organization found itself due to its financial instability. The ICTP's budget was periodically revised in the General Assemblies of IAEA and UNESCO, following proposals led by the United States and the United Kingdom. Thanks to Salam's political ability and scientific prestige, the center received substantial help from philanthropic foundations such as the Ford Foundation. However, the initial "hard line" adopted by delegations from the industrialized countries concerned about the utility of promoting theoretical physics in poor countries continued for more than thirty years. The ICTP survived thanks both to Salam's ability to neutralize pressures to withdraw United Nations support and to Budini's talent in mobilizing Italian resources.

Salam's Views on Science and Third World Development. As a scientist, Salam carried great weight with politicians in Pakistan. As a Muslim born in poor Pakistan, he seemed to be naturally invested with the authority to speak on behalf of the Third World. Indeed, Salam was a "scientific diplomat," a representative of different communities acting in different social and political settings. After the creation of the ICTP, and especially after being awarded the Nobel Prize, he became one of the most influential participants in the science-for-development discourse. His collected works on science and development, *Ideals and Realities,* became a reference text for Third World politicians of science in the second half of the twentieth century.

Throughout his life, Salam called for international cooperation in science in general, and theoretical physics

in particular, stipulating that such cooperation should take place in an international institution under the banner of the United Nations. Only such an organization could warrant the neutrality in which scientific exchange could occur. It should emulate what had taken place in the eleventh century: the transmission of knowledge from one civilization (Islamic) to another (Christian). The ICTP and other international organizations for science and technology should be the twentieth-century mirrors of Toledo and Gondasipur.

Salam found three main reasons to promote theoretical physics in developing countries. The first reason was that theoretical physics needed no costly apparatus; only, according to him, a good brain, pencil, and paper. This was a stereotype related to the perceived superiority of theory. In contrast to experimentalists, the story goes, theoreticians were able to discover the fundamental laws of nature by purely thinking in the solitude of their offices. The second reason Salam invoked was a metaphysical argument concerning the "fundamentality" of physics. In this view, not only was science above technology in knowledge classification, but, Salam also argued, the question of "fundamentality" of theoretical particle physics had a deeper sense. It involved the transcendental dimension of the search for unity—a central notion in the Islamic tradition. The fourth and last reason to promote theoretical physics was that it had the advantage of being a "glamour subject," which was attracting the majority of young students interested in science.

The Unification Program and the Nobel Prize. Beginning in the late 1950s, Salam's group at Imperial had become perhaps the most active of the groups working in gauge theories during a period in which quantum field theories had been displaced by another approach, the S-matrix model. While many theorists were looking toward this latter method in the hopes of avoiding the seemingly intractable difficulties that had begun to arise with field-theoretic calculations, Salam believed that a more "fundamental" explanation would have to come from invoking the standard perturbation method for quantum field theory. This conviction, shared by his collaborators at Imperial, was transmitted to his students. In 1964 the group started a research program on gauge theories. The aim of this program was to find the mathematical group of transformations that left "invariant" the laws that rule an interaction: The question was whether or not the interaction depended on certain physical properties of the particles, such as electric charge or other "quantum numbers."

The group, led by Salam and Paul Matthews, was working on the search for a relativistic version of a symmetry group called SU(6) to classify those particles ruled by the "strong interactions." Immediately after the establishment of the ICTP, Salam split Imperial's group between London and Trieste. Bringing part the group to Trieste was a strategy to give the new center scientific visibility, and it worked. Salam and his collaborators Bob Delbourgo and John Strathdee, helped by a constellation of PhD students devoted to difficult, long, and tedious calculations, produced a series of papers exploring relativistic versions of SU(6). Although the results turned out to be incompatible with the available experimental results, as two of Salam's students showed, the exercise was crucial to familiarize Salam and his group with a set of techniques necessary to continue working in the "unification program" of subatomic interactions. The aim was to find symmetry groups that showed that interactions that seem essentially different are just manifestations of a more general one, such as in the electromagnetic theory, in which Salam's goal was to unify electromagnetic and weak interactions.

Salam shared the 1979 Nobel Prize for Physics with Glashow and Weinberg for their work on the unification of the weak and electromagnetic interactions. Salam presented his gauge theory for electroweak interactions in a series of seminars at Imperial College in the autumn of 1967. Salam decided not to publish his results in a journal, but in a Nobel symposium the following spring, a widely read publication among physicists, especially the members of the Nobel Committee; the fact that the theory was not "renormalizable" put serious obstacles to empirical verification. Weinberg and Glashow, conversely, did publish their hypotheses. When Gerard t'Hooft proved, in 1971, that gauge theories of the Yang-Mills-Shaw type could be renormalized, the interest of the electroweak unification theories revived. In 1973 the "neutral-currents interactions," predicted by Glashow, Weinberg, and Salam in their works, were observed. The masses of the intermediate bosons (W^+, W^- and Z^0) were not verified until 1983. Salam faced an additional problem: he did not publish his work. However, attendants to Imperial College's seminar and the ICTP courses spoke and wrote on his behalf. His colleagues and students helped to demonstrate to some members of Nobel Committee, whom Salam invited regularly to visit the ICTP, that the Pakistani physicist had obtained the same conclusion independently from his American colleagues.

Beyond the Nobel Prize. In spite of developing progressive supranuclear palsy, a neuronal disease, Salam continued working in science and politics until the end of his life. In the 1970s, Salam and Indian physicist Joghesh Pati struggled to construct the first Great Unified Theory of weak, electromagnetic and strong interactions. Their theory, however, was only partially unified, but it led to further developments in the 1990s. Salam and his lifelong collaborator Strathdee developed a new formalism based on "superspace." This was a significant innovation for the simplification of calculations concerning supersymmetric theories, particularly for supergravity models. In his final years he redirected his research program, tackling problems in condensed-matter physics and biology.

Since 1975, Salam's optimism about the willingness of industrialized countries to contribute actively to scientific progress in developing nations had been dimmed by years of frustration. His efforts thus turned more resolutely toward the promotion of South-South collaboration and self-reliance, focusing particularly on problems regarding science in Islamic countries and the establishment of institutions such as the Third World Academy of Science and the International Centre for Science. In the mid-1980s Salam campaigned to become director-general of UNESCO, but being without the support of a national delegation, due to his having broken with the Pakistani regime in 1974, he failed.

Abdus Salam was one of the most influential scientists of the second half of the twentieth century. He was widely respected as one of the most energetic leaders of the unification program. Among the awards received for his contributions to physics are the J. Robert Oppenheimer Memorial Medal and Prize (University of Miami, 1971), the Royal Medal (1978), and the Copley Medal (1990). He was member of twenty-four academies and received forty-five honorary doctorates. As a scientific diplomat, he was perhaps the best-known politician of international science, and he worked diligently to create and promote new spaces of collaboration between scientists to achieve scientific progress in the developing world. He won the Atoms for Peace Award (1968), the Peace Medal (Charles University, Prague, 1981), the First Edinburgh Medal and Prize (1988), and the "Genoa" International Development of Peoples Prize (1988), among others. Abdus Salam died in 1996 and, following his will, was buried in Pakistan, where his name still produces heated debates: after all, he was a member of a marginalized movement in Pakistan, but also the first Muslim and the only Pakistani to win the Nobel Prize.

BIBLIOGRAPHY

Selected Papers of A. Salam (with Commentary), *edited by Ahmed Ali, C. Isham, Thomas Kibble, and Riazuddin (Singapore: World Scientific, 1994) contains the most important papers by Abdus Salam.*

WORKS BY SALAM

"The Advancement of Science for the Developing Countries." In *The Place of Values in a World of Facts,* edited by Arne Tiselius and Sam Nilsson. New York: Wiley Interscience Division and Almqvist & Wiksell, 1969.

"Ideals and Realities." Lecture given at the University of Stockholm, 23 September 1975. *Bulletin of the Atomic Scientists* 32 (1976): 9–15.

Ideals and Realities: Selected Essays of Abdus Salam. 3rd ed. Edited by C. H. Lai and Azim Kindwai. Singapore: World Scientific Publishing, 1989. This is a selection of Salam's papers on science, technology, and international cooperation between industrialized and developing countries.

"Physics and the Excellences of the Life It Brings." In *Pions to Quarks: Particle Physics in the 1950s: Based on a Fermilab Symposium,* edited by Laurie Brown, Max Dresden, and Lillian Hoddeson. Cambridge, U.K.: Cambridge University Press, 1989.

With Jacques Vauthier. *Abdus Salam un physicien, Prix Nobel de Physique 1979: Entretien avec Jacques Vauthier.* Vol. 3, Scientifiques & Croyants. Paris: Beauchesne Ed., 1990.

Renaissance of Science in Islamic Countries. Singapore and London: World Scientific, 1994.

OTHER SOURCES

Ali, Ahmed, John Ellis, and Seifallah Rabjabar-Daemi. "The Tale of Two Peripheries: The Creation of the International Centre for Theoretical Physics in Trieste." *Historical Studies of Physical and Biological Sciences* (Special Issue, Alexis De Greiff and David Kaiser, eds.) 33, part 1 (2002): 33–60.

———. "The Politics of Non-cooperation: The Boycott of the International Centre for Theoretical Physics," *OSIRIS* ("Science, Technology and International Affairs: Historical Perspectives," John Krige and Kai-Henrik Barth, eds.) 21 (2006): 86–109.

———, eds. *Salamfestschrift. A Collection of Talks from the Conference on Highlights of Particle and Condensed Matter Physics.* Singapore: World Scientific, 1994.

Ellis, John, Faheem Hussain, Thomas Kibble, et al. *The Abdus Salam Memorial Meeting.* Singapore: World Scientific Publishing, 1999.

Hamende, Andre, ed. *From a Vision to a System. The International Centre for Theoretical Physics (1964–1994).* Trieste, Italy: International Foundation Trieste for the Progress and the Freedom of Sciences, 1996.

Hoodbhoy, Pervez. "Abdus Salam: Past and Present." *News International,* 29 January 1996.

Kibble, Thomas. "Abdus Muhammad Salam." *Biographical Memoirs (Royal Society)* 44 (1988): 385–401.

Singh, Jagjit. *Abdus Salam: A Biography.* Kolkata: Penguin Books, 1992.

Alexis De Greiff A.

SALTZMAN, BARRY (*b.* New York, New York, 26 February 1931; *d.* New Haven, Connecticut, 5 February 2001), *meteorology, climatology, paleoclimatology.*

Saltzman was a leading figure in meteorology and climate science research for nearly fifty years. He made significant contributions to both of these fields at their most formative stages. Ahead of his time in many ways, Saltzman contributed to an understanding of the general circulation and the spectral energetics budget of the atmosphere. He also developed a comprehensive theory for climate change across a wide spectrum of time scales, ranging from subannual to millions of years. On his path toward a unified theory of how the climate system works he played a role in the development of energy balance models, statistical dynamical models, and paleoclimate dynamical models. He was a pioneer in developing meteorologically motivated dynamical systems. These included the progenitor of Edward Norton Lorenz's (1963) famous chaos model. In applying his own dynamical-systems approach to long-term climate change, Saltzman recognized the potential for using atmospheric general circulation models in the development of a complete theory. In 1998 he was awarded the Carl-Gustaf Rossby Research Medal, the highest honor of the American Meteorological Society, "for his lifelong contributions to the study of the global circulation and the evolution of the earth's climate."

Early Life and Career. Barry Saltzman was born in New York on 26 February 1931. He grew up in the Bronx, where his parents had settled as immigrants from Eastern Europe in the 1920s. His mother, Bertha Burmil, was from Poland; his father, Benjamin Saltzman, was from Ukraine. They met as workers in the garment district in New York City. Barry had one sibling, his older sister Jean.

As a child Saltzman was interested in history and science. He collected stamps and loved to read the encyclopedia, activities that taught him a lot about these subjects. Saltzman began his academic career at the prestigious Bronx High School of Science. He also loved sports, and spent as much time as he could at the Polo Grounds watching his favorite baseball team, the New York Giants. Saltzman was an outstanding athlete in high school, particularly in track and field.

Saltzman matriculated at City College of New York in 1949. He majored in physics. By his own account, he was significantly influenced by three faculty members during his undergraduate years: Mark Zemansky in physics, Sherburne Barber in math, and later Richard Rommer in meteorology. Actually, Saltzman decided to become a meteorologist one day when visiting the local public library, where he found a book on dynamical meteorology by David Brunt. This experience prompted him to take his first meteorology class in the geology department at City College with Rommer. Saltzman served as president of the City College branch of the American Meteorological

Society. He graduated from City College with a BS degree in meteorology, cum laude, in June 1952.

Later that summer Saltzman started graduate school at the Massachusetts Institute of Technology (MIT). There he specialized in dynamic meteorology, receiving a master's degree in February 1954. His thesis, jointly written with Richard Pfeffer, was titled "Large-Scale Rotational Flow in a Fixed Cylindrical Volume of the Atmosphere." Pfeffer, who first met Saltzman at City College, also arrived at MIT in the summer of 1952. Saltzman and Pfeffer were initially assigned to the "Pressure Change" research project under James M. Austin. After their first semester, Pfeffer asked Victor Starr if he could study for his master's degree with him as major professor. Starr reported this request to the department chairman, Henry Houghton. Houghton, who could not distinguish between the two new students from City College, called Saltzman into his office to ask him if he was the one who wanted to be switched from Austin to Starr. Stating that he did not wish to split "salt and pepper," Houghton moved them both to Victor Starr's research project, where they subsequently did their master's and PhD theses. Saltzman received his PD from MIT in 1957. His thesis was titled "The Energetics of the Larger Scales of Atmospheric Turbulence in the Domain of Wavenumber."

As a graduate student Saltzman established an excellent reputation as a participant in the General Circulation Project at MIT. This project, initiated by Starr in 1948 and funded by the U.S. Air Force through the late 1950s, aimed to collect, archive, and analyze upper-air data on a global scale. From these data, general circulation statistics were generated and used by the MIT scientists to develop theoretical insights into atmospheric dynamics.

Starr served as a mentor to Saltzman, as well as a role model for how to become a complete scholar. Saltzman's keen interest in history was further stimulated and encouraged by the example set by Starr. Later Saltzman's own students would greatly benefit from this early influence on his career. Other participants of the General Circulation Project, including Edward Lorenz and Robert White, also influenced Saltzman.

The MIT General Circulation Project prompted the development of the complex computer models used for nearly all climate and weather prediction studies into the twenty-first century (Phillips, 1956). Saltzman was a pioneer in the use of computers in the geosciences as well as in the use of spectral analysis in the study of atmospheric phenomena. He was the first to use atmospheric energetics rigorously as a key tool in understanding how the atmosphere works, and his methods are still widely used.

Saltzman moved to Connecticut in 1961 to work as a senior research scientist at the Travelers Research Center in Hartford. He married Sheila Eisenberg on 10 June

1962. Pfeffer was the best man at their wedding. Barry and Sheila had two children, Matthew David and Jennifer Ann. The move to Travelers, prompted by Robert White, afforded Saltzman the opportunity to continue his fundamental research on the atmosphere. During the seven years he spent at Travelers, he solidified his reputation as an outstanding atmospheric scientist and climate theoretician. Along the way his work shifted toward developing a quantitative theory that would account for the observed climatic state.

In 1967 the Department of Geology and Geophysics at Yale University decided to hire a meteorology/ climatology faculty member. Karl K. Turekian, who had known White for many years, asked him for his opinion on a good candidate for the job. With no hesitation he said that Saltzman would be a perfect fit. Shortly thereafter George Veronis invited Saltzman to campus for an interview; he was offered and accepted a position at Yale in 1968, and he served as professor of geophysics there for the rest of his life. Saltzman was in large part motivated to move back into the academic world because he felt obligated to train students in addition to doing research.

While at Yale, Saltzman's interests shifted once again, into the realm of climate change and the development of a theory of the ice ages. Beginning in the late 1970s, Saltzman pioneered the development of low-order dynamical system models as a tool for understanding the processes by which climate changes on century to millennial (and longer) time scales. In his pursuit of a theory of climate change, Saltzman employed a hierarchy of models, including complex general circulation models (GCMs).

Meteorology. In his PhD thesis and early publications, Saltzman introduced to the meteorological community the use of spatial Fourier analysis to quantify nonlinear dynamical interactions between zonal scales. This groundbreaking work created a link to meteorology from the contemporary theory of turbulence that relied on Fourier analysis (e.g., Batchelor, 1953; Fjørtoft, 1953; Kolmogorov, 1941a and b). Saltzman generalized the famous Osborne Reynolds (1894) decomposition of an arbitrary spatial field into its domain mean and deviation, to derive a more detailed way to separate weather patterns into their different spatial scales. While previous authors had used the decomposition to analyze interactions between the global and the collection of all smaller scales, Saltzman's "wavenumber energetics" provided detailed interactions among each individual scale, defined by wavelengths.

Saltzman was one of the first to connect the then-recent observation, that atmospheric eddies collectively transfer their kinetic energy to the mean flow (Saltzman, 1957, 1959). Thus, he suggested a physical mechanism for maintaining localized quasi-stationary pressure patterns.

Low-Order Irregular, Nonperiodic Flow. It was in 1962 that Saltzman stumbled upon a low-order system of equations that behaved chaotically. Saltzman (1962) developed a seventh-order system of ordinary differential equations (ODEs) to approximate the classic 2D Oberbeck (1879)–Boussinesq (1903) partial differential equations (PDEs) governing roll convection between two isothermal free surfaces. When this system was numerically integrated, he discovered that for high enough Rayleigh numbers, four of the seven modes tended to zero, while the remaining order-three subsystem underwent irregular, nonperiodic fluctuations. That same year Lorenz (1962) had found nonperiodic solutions of a similar quasi-meteorological ODE system of order 12, and was eager to find a simpler system to demonstrate how this was happening. In his landmark paper "Deterministic Nonperiodic Flow" (Lorenz, 1963), the acknowledgments read that he was "indebted to Dr. Barry Saltzman for bringing to his attention the existence of nonperiodic solutions of the convection equations" (p. 141). With the low-order system provided by Saltzman, Lorenz performed a thorough analysis, obtaining results, including: (1) what would become widely known as a "pitchfork," or subcritical Hopf bifurcation; (2) instability in the sense of what would later be called "chaos"; and (3) the first rough sketch of the complicated structure in 3D-space known as a "butterfly" or "strange attractor."

Climate Theory and Models. Saltzman's work on climate started by distinguishing climatic phenomena from shorter-term weather, or meteorological phenomena emphasizing climate on explicit monthly to seasonal time scales. During the 1960s Saltzman developed parameterizations for energy balance models (EBMs). In the most notable of these (Saltzman, 1967), he attempted to account fully for all processes responsible for determining Earth's surface temperature. Realizing that EBMs, because they lacked dynamics, were severely deficient in describing climate spurred him to develop a class of models called statistical dynamical models (SDMs), which attempted to extend the EBMs by including parameterizations for zonal representations of dry atmospheric dynamics and the hydrologic cycle. To Saltzman the SDM was a "true" climate model in that it solved for relevant quantities directly on monthly to seasonal time scales (as opposed to the widely used GCM, which actually solves for daily weather patterns subsequently averaged to yield climate statistics). His seminal works in this regard were later detailed in two papers written with Anandu Vernekar (Saltzman & Vernekar, 1971, 1972).

He began developing his theory for ice ages using the SDM. Along with Vernekar, he used the newly available Climate: Long-Range Investigation, Mapping, and Prediction (CLIMAP) reconstruction of last glacial maximum boundary conditions to model zonally averaged climate at 18,000 years ago (CLIMAP, 1976; Saltzman & Vernekar, 1975). Others soon followed his lead, using GCMs (e.g., Gates, 1976; Manabe & Hahn, 1977). However, the GCM model experiments provided only an equilibrium "snapshot" of what climate conditions may have been like during the last glacial maximum (LGM). What Saltzman really wanted to understand was the time-dependent behavior of the climate system. Recognizing that GCMs could not feasibly be used as a prognostic tool for the purpose of long-term climate change (because of the small energy fluxes involved), he ultimately turned to developing his own nonequilibrium, time-dependent models. His simpler models were a more useful way to illustrate and explore the many positive feedbacks involved in low-frequency climatic variability. Saltzman called these "paleoclimate dynamics models" (PDMs).

Saltzman was careful in defining climate. Measures of the climate state were separated into a steady equilibrium—or diagnostic—component, and the transient departures from that equilibrium—or the prognostic (time-dependent, predictive)—component. He considered all potentially relevant physical processes (hypothesized by him or others) using explicit representations where possible. After all possible processes were represented, he would then attempt to reduce them to a more manageable number via scale analysis. Two review articles comprehensively summarize this work: "A Survey of Statistical-Dynamical Models of the Terrestrial Climate" and "Climatic Systems Analysis," both published in *Advances in Geophysics* (Salzman, 1978, 1983).

Ice Age Theory. Saltzman spent the better part of the second half of his career attempting to develop an explanation for the origin of the late Cenozoic ice age. He always maintained that a complete theory for ice ages must at a minimum account for the onset of glaciation, and the transitions in the character of glacial-interglacial cycles observed in climate proxy records. In particular, for the Plio-Pleistocene glacial cycles this meant the near-100,000 year cycle and its sudden appearance at around 900,000 years ago. In his endeavor to construct such a complete theory, Saltzman clearly articulated the need for using an inductive approach for the simple reason that the fluxes of energy involved in climate change on these time scales were very small. The amount of energy required to melt Northern Hemisphere ice sheets of the LGM was on the order of 10^{-1} W/m^2. Likewise, the energy flux involved in observed glacial-interglacial change in deep ocean temperature was also only on the order of 10^{-1} W/m^2 (note: the amount of energy reaching the top of Earth's atmosphere from the Sun is 1370 W/m^2).

Saltzman separated the problem of long-term climate change into three basic parts, each requiring a different approach (Saltzman, 1990). He examined the time dependent evolution of global ice volume over the past several million years using a set of equations that formed a closed system linked to shorter-term variables in a GCM. Long-term changes in global climate are the result of dynamical feedbacks between only a few prognostic variables to which the fast-response variables (those governed by a GCM) are equilibrated.

Because of orbital variations on time scales ranging from 20,000 to 100,000 years, Saltzman reasoned that the climate system would not be in equilibrium, and that feedbacks within the climate system could potentially give rise to a rich variety of behavior, including damped oscillations or even auto-oscillations.

At the most fundamental level, Saltzman believed that paleoclimatic variability was due to a complex combination of changes in external forcing and instability of the internal system that arose even in the presence of steady external forcing. However, the concept that instability within the climate system could lead to auto-oscillatory behavior on long time scales met considerable resistance. In the 1980s, however, the vast majority of scientists working on the ice age problem believed that Earth orbital (Milankovitch) forcing was the ultimate cause of glacial-interglacial cycles. On the other hand, Saltzman felt that positive feedbacks within the climate system could drive a near-100,000 year ice age cycle (Saltzman, Sutera, & Hansen, 1982 and 1984; Saltzman & Sutera, 1984). He reasoned that if near-surface air temperature was the critical factor in building an ice sheet, an account was needed of how temperature can vary in high latitude regions not only as a function of changing insolation, but also as related to variations in greenhouse forcing, ocean temperature, and the ice sheets themselves. While Saltzman did not consider Earth orbital forcing a necessary condition for ice age cycles to occur, he did believe that such forcing served as a "pacemaker" (Saltzman, Hansen, & Maasch, 1984).

Inspired by historical ideas concerning the role of CO_2 in climate change (for example, Arrhenius, 1896; Callendar, 1938; Plass, 1956), Saltzman led a revival of the theory that variations of atmospheric CO_2 are a significant driver of ice age cycles. Saltzman's recognition of the importance of greenhouse forcing came prior to the time when direct evidence for variations of CO_2 (and CH_4) became available from ice core records. In his model, many positive feedbacks within the carbon cycle produced an asymmetric, saw-toothed near-100,000-year free solution, with a phase relationship between paleoclimate proxies for global ice mass and atmospheric CO_2 consistent with available paleoclimate records of these variables (Saltzman & Maasch, 1988a and b). The addition of a long-term tec-

tonically forced decrease in atmospheric CO_2 led to a bifurcation of the system from a steady-state to a near-100,000-year auto oscillation (Saltzman & Maasch, 1990a and b and 1991).

Saltzman also made extensive use of GCMs in developing his theory of climate change. Most of these studies involved evaluation of the "fast components" of the climate system, most notably changes in energy balance related to atmospheric carbon dioxide and solar luminosity (Saltzman & Oglesby, 1990a and b, and 1992; Saltzman, Marshall, et al., 1994). These studies explored model sensitivity to a wide range of radiative forcing (e.g., evaluating the climate response to systematic carbon dioxide variations from 100 to 1,000 ppm). Because Saltzman envisioned these models as providing stationary (equilibrium) parameters in a theory of climatic change, he was also very interested in the sensitivity of the GCM to its initial state. He wanted to know if they could be used to obtain a well-defined equilibrium (Saltzman, Oglesby, et al., 1997).

Rapid shifts in global climatic conditions during the last glacial/interglacial cycle occur on two characteristic time scales, roughly 1,000 to 3,000 years and 5,000 to 10,000 years. Saltzman explored what he believed to be the most relevant feedbacks on millennial time scales beginning with his time-dependent SDM of climate change, which contained the fundamental dynamic energy exchanges between the ocean, atmosphere, and sea ice (Saltzman, 1978 and 1982; Saltzman & Moritz, 1980). In this model, the ocean gains or loses heat (and hence changes temperature) through the sea ice, at the sea-ice margin, and across the ocean/air interface. The extent of sea ice varies as a function of the freezing (melting) at its margin, envisioned as a flux of latent heat to (from) the ocean. The model also includes short-wave and long-wave radiation fluxes as a function of solar forcing and atmospheric CO_2. Within the range of plausible solar variability and greenhouse forcing, Saltzman's model predicted the possibility of 1,000- to 2,000-year oscillations. The now well-known millennial scale oscillations, often referred to as abrupt climate change, would not become a mainstream topic of scientific research for at least another decade. In effect, Saltzman had developed a theory for millennial climate oscillations many years before widespread interest in so-called abrupt climate changes developed in the paleoclimate community.

Saltzman also considered other instabilities that have likely contributed to observed climate variability. Through the 1990s he methodically explored the climatic impacts of ice dynamics (Saltzman & Verbitsky, 1992 and 1993). He added to the model bedrock depression and conditional instability due to an ice calving mechanism. He then extended this work to explore systematically the theoretical aspects of millennial scale variations known as "Heinrich events."

During glacial times, climate oscillations also occur about every 5,000 to 12,000 years. These so-called Heinrich events involve massive volumes of ice that discharge from the Laurentide ice sheet into the North Atlantic Ocean. Like most others, Saltzman considered the most likely driving mechanism for Heinrich events to be internal behavior of ice sheets. With their dynamical model based on the fundamental thermomechanical properties of an ice sheet, Mikhail Verbitsky and Saltzman (1994, 1995, 1996) illustrated the essential physical processes governing coupled variations of ice volume, basal water amount, and the surge of ice, clearly exposing the key free parameters likely to be involved in Heinrich oscillations. The instability leading to auto-oscillatory behavior of ice sheets is regulated by both cold advection from the upper ice surface along with the much weaker influence of geo-thermal heating (Saltzman and Verbitsky, 1995, and 1996).

The list of Barry Saltzman's contributions is long. He had a significant impact on many important aspects of the fields of meteorology, climatology, and paleoclimatology. He produced a steady stream of papers across almost five decades. Some of the more outstanding honors bestowed upon Saltzman include membership in Phi Beta Kappa; being a Fellow of the American Meteorological Society (AMS); being a Fellow of the American Association for the Advancement of Science; being elected to membership in the Academy of Sciences of Lisbon (Portugal); serving numerous editorships on prestigious scientific journals, and on numerous visiting and advisory committees. Saltzman was also awarded the Carl-Gustaf Rossby Research Medal in 1998 by the AMS (the highest honor bestowed by the AMS).

Saltzman's ultimate views on a comprehensive theory of climate are detailed in *Dynamical Paleoclimatology* (Saltzman, 2002). This project actually began with an invitation to Saltzman from José Peixoto and Abraham Oort to be a coauthor with them on their planned second edition of the *Physics of Climate* (1992). That book was never finished because Peixoto died of cancer in 1996. Saltzman had so much time and effort invested into summarizing his work on paleoclimate for the section he was to contribute that he decided to write his own book. Ironically, Saltzman was diagnosed with cancer in 2000. He completed *Dynamical Paleoclimatology* during his final year and died of his illness on 5 February 2001. His book was published posthumously.

BIBLIOGRAPHY

WORKS BY SALTZMAN

"Equations Governing the Energetics of the Larger Scales of Atmospheric Turbulence in the Domain of Wave Number." *Journal of Meteorology* 14 (1957): 513–523.

"On the Maintenance of the Large-Scale Quasi-Permanent Disturbances in the Atmosphere." *Tellus* 11, no. 4 (1959): 425–431.

"Finite Amplitude Free Convection as an Initial Value Problem—I." *Journal of the Atmospheric Sciences* 19, no. 4 (1962): 329–341.

"On the Theory of the Mean Temperature of the Earth's Surface." *Tellus* 19, no. 2 (1967): 219–229.

"Large-Scale Atmospheric Energetics in the Wave-Number Domain." *Reviews of Geophysics and Space Physics* 8 (1970): 289–302.

With Anandu Vernekar. "An Equilibrium Solution for the Axially Symmetric Component of the Earth's Macroclimate." *Journal of Geophysical Research* 76 (1971): 1498–1524.

———. "Global Equilibrium Solutions for the Zonally Averaged Macroclimate." *Journal of Geophysical Research* 77, no. 21 (1972): 3936–3945.

———. "A Solution for the Northern Hemisphere Climatic Zonation during a Glacial Maximum." *Quaternary Research* 5 (1975): 307–320.

"A Survey of Statistical-Dynamical Models of the Terrestrial Climate." *Advances in Geophysics* 20 (1978): 183–304.

With Richard E. Moritz. "A Time-Dependent Climatic Feedback System Involving Sea-Ice Extent, Ocean Temperature, and CO." *Tellus* 32 (1980): 93–118.

With Alfonso Sutera and Alan Evenson. "Structural Stochastic Stability of a Simple Auto-Oscillatory Climatic Feedback System." *Journal of the Atmospheric Sciences* 38 (1981): 494–503.

"Stochastically-Driven Climatic Fluctuations in the Sea-Ice, Ocean Temperature, CO_2 Feedback System." *Tellus* 34 (1982): 97–112.

With Alfonso Sutera and Anthony R. Hansen. "A Possible Marine Mechanism for Internally Generated Long-Period Climate Cycles." *Journal of the Atmospheric Sciences* 39 (1982): 2634–2637.

"Climatic Systems Analysis." *Advances in Geophysics* 25 (1983): 173–233.

With Anthony R. Hansen and Kirk A. Maasch. "The Late Quaternary Glaciations as the Response of a Three-Component Feedback System to Earth-Orbital Forcing." *Journal of the Atmospheric Sciences* 41 (1984): 3380–3389.

With Alfonso Sutera. "A Model of the Internal Feedback System Involved in Late Quaternary Climatic Variations." *Journal of the Atmospheric Sciences* 41 (1984): 736–745.

With Alfonso Sutera and Anthony R. Hansen. "Long Period Free Oscillations in a Three-Component Climate Model." In *New Perspectives in Climate Modelling,* edited by Andre L. Berger and Cathy Nicolis. Amsterdam: Elsevier, 1984.

With Kirk A. Maasch. "Carbon Cycle Instability as a Cause of the Late Pleistocene Ice Age Oscillations: Modeling the Asymmetric Response." *Global Biogeochemical Cycles* 2 (1988a): 177–185.

———. "Orbital Forcing and the Vostok Ice Core." *Nature* 333 (1988b): 123–124.

"Three Basic Problems of Paleoclimatic Modeling: A Personal Perspective and Review." *Climate Dynamics* 5 (1990): 67–78.

With Kirk A. Maasch. "A First-Order Global Model of Late Cenozoic Climate Change." *Transactions of the Royal Society of Edinburgh* 81 (1990a): 315–325.

———. "A Low-Order Dynamical Model of Global Climatic Variability over the Full Pleistocene." *Journal of Geophysical Research* 95 (1990b): 1955–1963.

With Robert J. Oglesby. "Extending the EBM: The Effect of Deep Ocean Temperature on Climate with Applications to the Cretaceous." *Paleogeography, Paleoclimatology, Paleoecology (Global and Planetary Change Section)* 82 (1990a): 237–259.

———. "Sensitivity of the Equilibrium Surface Temperature of a GCM to Systematic Changes in Atmospheric Carbon Dioxide." *Geophysical Research Letters* 17 (1990b): 1089–1092.

With Kirk A. Maasch. "A First-Order Global Model of Late Cenozoic Climate Change II: A Simplification of CO_2 Dynamics." *Climate Dynamics* 5 (1991): 201–210.

With Mikhail Verbitsky. "Asthenospheric Ice-Load Effects in a Global Dynamical-System Model of the Pleistocene Climate." *Climate Dynamics* 8 (1992): 1–11.

With Robert J. Oglesby. "Equilibrium Climate Statistics of a General Circulation Model as a Function of Atmospheric Carbon Dioxide. Part I: Geographic Distributions of Primary Variables." *Journal of Climate* 5 (1992): 66–92.

With Mikhail Verbitsky. "Multiple Instabilities and Models of Glacial Rythmicity in the Plio-Pleistocene: A General Theory of Late Cenozoic Climate Change." *Climate Dynamics* 9 (1993): 1–15.

With Susan Marshall, Robert J. Oglesby, and Jay W. Larson. "A Comparison of GCM Sensitivity to Changes in CO_2 and Solar Luminosity." *Geophysical Research Letters* 21 (1994): 2487–2490.

With Mikhail Verbitsky. "Heinrich-Type Glacial Surges in a Low-Order Dynamical Climate Model." *Climate Dynamics* 10 (1994): 39–47.

———. "A Diagnostic Analysis of Heinrich Glacial Surge Events." *Paleoceanography* 10 (1995): 59–65.

———. "Heinrich-Scale Surge Oscillations as an Internal Property of Ice Sheets." *Annals of Glaciology* 23 (1996): 348–351.

With Robert J. Oglesby and Haijun Hu. "Sensitivity of GCM Simulations of Paleoclimate to the Initial State." *Paleoclimates* 2 (1997): 33–45.

Dynamical Paleoclimatology. San Diego, CA: Academic Press, 2002.

OTHER SOURCES

Arrhenius, Svante. "On the Influence of Carbonic Acid in the Air upon the Temperature of the Ground." *Philosophical Magazine* 41 (1896): 237–276.

Batchelor, George Keith. *The Theory of Homogeneous Turbulence.* Cambridge, U.K.: Cambridge University Press, 1953.

Boussinesq, Joseph. *Théorie analytique de la chaleur,* Vol. 2. Paris: Gauthier-Villars, 1903.

Callendar, Guy S. "The Artificial Production of Carbon Dioxide and its Influence on Temperature." *Quarterly Journal of the Royal Meteorological Society* 64 (1938): 223–237.

CLIMAP Project Members. "The Surface of the Ice-Age Earth." *Science,* 191 (1976): 1131–1137.

Fjørtoft, Roger. "On the Changes in the Spectral Distribution of Kinetic Energy for Two-Dimensional, Nondivergent Flow." *Tellus* 5 (1953): 225–230.

Gates, W. Lawrence. "Modeling the Ice-Age Climate." *Science* 191 (1976): 1138–1144.

Kolmogorov, Andrey N. "Dissipation of Energy in Locally Isotropic Turbulence." *Doklady Akademii Nauk SSSR* [Proceedings of the Academy of Sciences USSR] 32 (1941a): 16–18.

———. "The Local Structure of Turbulence in Incompressible Viscous Fluids for Very Large Reynolds Number." *Doklady Akademii Nauk SSSR* [Proceedings of the Academy of Sciences USSR] 32 (1941b): 9–13.

Lorenz, Edward N. "The Statistical Prediction of Solutions of Dynamic Equations." In *Proceedings International Symposium Numerical Weather Prediction.* Tokyo: Meteorological Society of Japan, 1962.

———. "Deterministic Nonperiodic Flow." *Journal of the Atmospheric Sciences* 20 (1963): 130–141.

Maasch, Kirk A., Robert J. Oglesby, and Aime Fournier. "Barry Saltzman and the Theory of Climate." *Journal of Climate* 18, no. 13, (2005): 2141–2150.

Manabe, Syukuro, and D. Hahn. "Simulation of Tropical Climate of an Ice Age." *Journal of Geophysical Research* 82 (1977): 3889–3911.

Oberbeck, A. "Über die wärmeleitung der flüssigkeiten bei berücksichtigung der strömungen infolge von temperaturdifferenzen." *Annalen der Physik und Chemie, Neue Folge* 7 (1879): 271–292.

Oglesby, Robert J., Kirk A. Maasch, and R. B. Smith. "Barry Saltzman, 1931–2001." *Bulletin of the American Meteorological Society* 82 (2001): 1448–1450.

Phillips, Norman A. "The General Circulation of the Atmosphere: A Numerical Experiment." *Quarterly Journal of the Royal Meteorological Society* 82 (1956): 123–164.

Plass, Gilbert N. "The Carbon Dioxide Theory of Climatic Change." *Tellus* 8 (1956): 140–154.

Reynolds, Osborne. "On the Dynamical Theory of Incompressible Viscous Fluids and the Determination of the Criterion." *Philosophical Transactions of the Royal Society of London* A 136 (1894): 123–164.

Kirk Allen Maasch

SAUSSURE, HORACE BÉNÉDICT DE

(*b.* near Geneva [Conches], Switzerland, 17 February 1740; *d.* Geneva, 22 January 1799), *geology, meteorology, botany, education.* For the original article on Saussure see *DSB,* vol. 12.

When Saussure died in 1799, his personal archives were given by the family to the public and university library of Geneva where they were left untouched until

1975 when the author of this postscript decided to study the numerous manuscripts brought to light and discovered astonishing conditions. The only printed version of his work was available under the title *Voyages dans les Alpes…*(1779–1796). The general reader was in a rather strange situation for more than two centuries. It was as if Saussure, the founder of Alpine Geology, had gathered an enormous amount of observations throughout his entire life from which nothing new pertaining to the fundamental mechanisms that built the Alps was extracted.

The Voyages dans les Alpes … The major obstacle originates from the fact that Saussure could not describe all his travels without needless repetitions. Therefore he made the choice of preparing a pastiche consisting of the best descriptions organized into seven ideal voyages dealing with the major massifs, valleys, and structures regardless of the dates of their best original description. Interspersed in the narrative are very short sections dealing with theoretical interpretations, but they are too short and cryptic to give real clues on the evolution of the author's thinking. Consequently, it is not possible to unravel the path of his geological thinking. Not enough appears to have been provided besides the repetition of the statement that more observations were needed and that the major theoretical discussions would be postponed. The main focus was a final *theory of the Earth.* Unfortunately his poor health prevented him from writing, and he died in 1799. Only two abbreviated tables of contents were published in 1786 and in 1796 respectively.

More than two centuries passed during which Saussure fell into oblivion or was designated with the unwarranted label of a simple observer while hundreds of his field-note booklets and other manuscripts were carefully preserved but remained unstudied. These texts contain in perfect chronological order the detailed account of the discovery of a major principle of structural geology as demonstrated by Saussure in the Alps and accepted in the early twenty-first century as fundamental in mountain building in general—*horizontal overthrusting.* From time to time the non-scientific portions of the *Voyages dans les Alpes…* were republished by anonymous editors to satisfy the curiosity of the general public under the title of *Partie Pittoresque des Voyages de M. de Saussure.*

Saussure undertook important field trips outside the Alps and their related manuscripts concerning the basalt in Italy (1772–1773), in Auvergne and Vivarais (1776), and other places in Europe also contain critical data. The same is true for his lecture notes on physical geography at the Academy of Geneva (1775) and many aspects of physics and metaphysics that remain to be evaluated.

The Manuscripts in Chronological Order. Saussure's manuscripts were written mostly in the field in pencil and finalized within at least twenty-four hours in pen every day. This remarkable suite of observations represents a perfect time sequence from which the evolution of his geological interpretations can be obtained. Saussure's notes are in French and occasionally in Latin. The original language was followed by an English translation and footnotes explaining the geological problems in ancient and modern terms and by following his itineraries step by step. Overlapping dates of the manuscripts results from the fact that Saussure investigated various subjects simultaneously during a given period of time.

Early Alpine Structure Concepts. These observations (Ms 1760–1775) pertain to the structural features of the Salève mountain overlooking Geneva, those of the Jura Mountains at the Dôle, and between Pontarlier and Besançon. The problem common to these folds was to understand the cores of the structures made of vertical limestone beds pushed upwards through younger strata leaning against them at variable angles (so-called folds in A). Other parts of the High Calcareous Alps display spectacular S-shaped folds (such as at the Arpenaz Cascade) forming recumbent structures with adjacent cavities in the landscape left open when the limestone beds were folded upon themselves.

Saussure was confused by all this structural complexity. For the time being he proposed a variety of interpretations that cover the whole spectrum of unsupported theories of his time. These included a kind of crystallization on the seafloor generating structures comparable to the microscopic folds of agate concretions or subterranean forces of unknown origin, or even subterranean fires although no traces of their action was visible.

The Cramont and Vallorcine. Saussure proposed a new mechanism (Ms 1774–1778) derived from the panorama as seen from the summit of the Cramont (a peak located immediately south of Mont-Blanc). According to him, the primitive and secondary rock layers were deposited horizontally on the seafloor. The explosion of elastic fluids in subterranean caverns uplifted the primitive rocks in a vertical and contorted position while cutting across the overlying secondary rocks. These secondary rocks remained leaning against the primitive ones at an angle that decreased gradually away from the center of the Alps. The originality of this approach was in the vertical force due to the explosion of the elastic fluids that left no traces. An earlier theory using the action of fire was eliminated from the working hypotheses by Saussure's new theory.

Saussure then tried to characterize his concept of vertical force by investigating the various types of conglomerates, in particular those of Vallorcine (near Chamonix),

Horace Bénédict de Saussure. Horace Bénédict de Saussure, circa 1760. **ROGER VIOLLET COLLECTION/GETTY IMAGES.**

also botany, chemistry, astronomy, physics, mathematics, and philosophy. By wisely using his personal wealth he began to assemble a systematic library. Two catalogs in his own hand (Ms 1788–1797) show holdings of at least 1,202 items, that is 1,143 books and 59 periodicals published by learned societies from all over Europe. Rapidly, it became one of the most diversified collections of the eighteenth century. Related correspondence with major book dealers of Europe reveals an extensive network of purchases and sales. He bought between 1760 and 1768, 1,034 volumes, that is, sixty-five percent of the final library he needed for his research. The major reason for such a collection lies in the fact that Geneva was a relatively isolated city-state and that purchasing books was the only way to keep abreast with scientific development in all fields. However the French Revolution and its turmoil led to the loss of Saussure's fortune, and many precious holdings were sold at auction to his profound chagrin.

Basaltic Volcanism. Saussure wrote a series of manuscripts on the origin of prismatic basalt in Italy, Auvergne, Vivarais, Provence, and Brisgau (Ms 1772–1798). In particular, he wanted to see for himself the examples described in the Massif Central of Auvergne by Nicolas Desmarest who had demonstrated the volcanic origin of basalt by following large prismatic lava flows from the plains up the slopes of scoriaceous cones into the corresponding craters.

Saussure returned from his trip to Auvergne an enthusiastic believer in the volcanic origin of basalt. However, through the years of investigating rather superficially many outcrops, and by accepting the neptunian ideas of Abraham Gottlob Werner, he tempered his position to the extent of assuming two types of basalt: an aqueous deposit and a volcanic lava. Eventually, he believed only in a water-laid origin. In defense of these strange changes of concepts it should be pointed out that Saussure happened to come across many unusual types of basalt that he did not study in sufficient detail. Furthermore he was a famous geologist who had to take a position in the controversy. He took the erroneous one as demonstrated by James Hutton who introduced the modern ideas on the subject at the time of Saussure's death.

Lectures on Physical Geography. The documents pertaining to physical geography (Ms 1775) are of three major types. A first version written in French on index cards that is the most personal document and a second version in Latin also on note cards—now lost—which is the required language of the oral academic presentation. The third version is a complete Latin text, not from Saussure's hand but a manuscript carefully copied in 1786 by one of his students, Jacques-Louis Peschier. Among the references in

that were in the critical intermediate position between the vertical primitive rocks and the tilted, overlying secondary ones. These conglomerates displayed huge and spectacular angular to rounded boulders of granite in a purple, shaly matrix. This unusual rock type was interpreted by Saussure as indicating a powerful process of fragmentation followed by redeposition according to the size of the clasts in a quiet aqueous environment. These depositional events were followed in time by the general uplifting of the beds. The final conclusion reached was that these conglomerates represent the product of violent earthquakes and consequently that mountain building is a seismic process. This interpretation is a theoretical challenge still under consideration by modern geologists. Unquestionably, Saussure was well informed about the spectacular effects of the numerous earthquakes of his century from reading books and periodicals.

Saussure's Scientific Library. From the early part of his career, Saussure had been deeply concerned about being up-to-date with the progress of the various sciences of interest to him, in particular geology and mineralogy, but this unique manuscript two famous works are constantly quoted, criticized, or praised without restrictions, namely George-Louis Buffon's *Théorie de la Terre* (1749) and *The Physikalishe Beschreibung* of Olof Torbern Bergman (1766). Of great interest is the spontaneous presentation of the index cards in French which has a completely informal style with so-called red flags reminding the speaker to attract the attention of the students to important aspects of the presentation. A similar technique is still used by experienced lecturers.

Horizontal Thrusting in Opposite Directions. These manuscripts (Ms 1780–1784) pertain to a large structure of tertiary sandstones (Molasse) of Albi-sur-Chéran: Saussure briefly looked at this structure in 1780. He observed that at this location it could only be formed by horizontal thrusting in opposite directions—a new concept given without any further comments. Returning to the field in 1784 and after detailed studies he presented a speculation of great importance. According to Saussure horizontal thrusting in opposite directions implied not only a detachment (*décollement*) of the Earth's crust from its substratum, but also a general shortening of the seismic system and finally present-day antagonistic stresses that maintain the Alpine structures at their high elevation. The date of this critical observation was 13 October 1784. He even went so far as to suggest laboratory simulations with clay layers, becoming a pioneer of experimental geology.

It is difficult to understand such a concise discussion of a fundamental concept without much consideration, and Saussure's style does not help. It can be better explained by a modern interpretation using a transverse cross-section trending through the Valley of Chamonix and the summit of Mont-Blanc. If overthrusting tilted the rocks from an original horizontal position to their present vertical one and the bottom of the Valley of Chamonix represents the ancient surface of the crust then the horizontal distance between the Chamonix Valley and the top of Mont-Blanc corresponds approximately to the thickness of the crust that has been overthrusted. Therefore, the summit of Mont-Blanc, which reaches in the twenty-first century the elevation of about one league over the present surface of the globe, was originally buried at a depth of more than two leagues (8.8 kilometers) below that surface.

The Alps and World Mountains. In summary, Saussure (Notes of 6 July 1795) considered a worldwide application of his structural ideas to the origin of the great orogenic belts. He stated that it is not at the great depth of coal mines but on the top of mountains consisting of vertical beds uplifted in such a position and maintained in it

by the permanent stresses of earthquakes, that lie the answers of modern tangential tectonics.

SUPPLEMENTARY BIBLIOGRAPHY

Carozzi, Albert V. "Découverte d'une grande découverte:Horace-Bénédict de Saussure et les refoulements en sens contraires dans la formation des Alpes." In *Les Plis du Temps, mythe, science et H.-B. de Saussure*, edited by Albert V. Carozzi, Bernard Crettaz, and David Ripoll. Geneva: Collection Nouveaux Itinéraires Amoudruz, No. 5, Musée d'Ethnographie de Genève, Annexe de Conches, 1998.

———. *Manuscripts and publications of Horace-Bénédict de Saussure on the origin of basalt (1772–1797)*. Bilingual Volume. Geneva: Editions Zoé, 2000.

———. *Horace-Bénédict de Saussure (1740–1799): Un pionnier des sciences de la Terre*. Geneva: Editions Slatkine, 2005. This is the most recent biography.

———, and Gerda Bouvier. *The Scientific Library of Horace-Bénédict de Saussure (1797): Annotated Catalog of an 18th-Century Bibliographic and Historic Treasure*. Mémoires Société de Physique et d'Histoire Naturelle de Genève, vol. 6, 1994.

———, and John C. Newman. *Lectures on Physical Geography Given in 1775 by Horace-Bénédict de Saussure at the Academy of Geneva*. Trilingual volume. Geneva: Editions Zoé, 2003.

Albert V. Carozzi

SAVAGE, LEONARD JAMES (*b.* Detroit, Michigan, 20 November 1917; *d.* New Haven, Connecticut, 1 November 1971), *statistics, mathematics, philosophy.* For the original article on Savage see *DSB* vol.18, Supplement II.

Savage was a founder of twentieth-century Bayesian statistics. Savage's ideas about probability and utility inspired theorists in many fields. Besides advancing his own discipline, statistics, he made significant contributions to philosophy.

Savage's representation theorem for probability and utility is a cornerstone of the theory of subjective probability and utility. It shows that preferences satisfying basic principles of rationality may be represented as maximizing expected utility. Such representation theorems are crucial components of decision theory. Under one interpretation, they ground definitions of probability and utility. Under another interpretation, they demonstrate that probability and utility may be inferred from preferences. Under either interpretation, they form foundations for principles of rational decision making.

Because of the importance of Savage's ideas, scholars continue to analyze and refine them. James M. Joyce's book, *The Foundations of Causal Decision Theory* (1999),

	Ticket numbers		
Gambles	1	2 – 11	12 – 100
A	5	5	5
B	0	25	5
C	5	5	0
D	0	25	0

Figure 1. *Allais's Paradox.*

extends Savage's theory, improving and making more versatile Savage's representation theorem. Joyce's representation theorem offers a choice between causal and evidential decision theory. Its account of conditional probability may make a decision's evaluation depend on either the decision's effect on the future or the evidence it furnishes about the future. Given the first interpretation of conditional probability, the representation theorem grounds a causal decision theory and, given the second interpretation, it grounds an evidential decision theory.

Savage assumes that for any outcome, there is an act that yields that outcome in every case. Some consequences of an act obtain only if the act's outcome is not constant. Savage's assumption therefore puts aside those consequences. In particular, it prevents treating risk as a consequence of an act. Risk arises only from acts that do not yield the same outcome in every case. Joyce's representation theorem gains realism by replacing Savage's assumption of constant acts with structural axioms requiring coherent extensions of preferences.

Furthermore, Joyce attains Savage's goal of streamlining the expected utility principle so that it uses summary "small worlds" instead of "grand worlds" complete in every detail. To accomplish the streamlining, Joyce takes the objects of probabilities and utilities to be propositions and makes calculations of an option's expected utility invariant with respect to partitions of states.

Savage's theory incorporates the sure-thing principle, which he presents in *The Foundations of Statistics* (2nd ed., 1972). That principle states that a rational agent's ranking of a pair of gambles having the same consequence in a state or set of states *S* agrees with the agent's ranking of any other pair of gambles the same as the first pair except for having some other common consequence in *S*. This principle is the target of a number of criticisms. The best known is Allais's paradox, presented by Maurice Allais in an essay, "Foundations of a Positive Theory of Choice

Involving Risk and a Criticism of the Postulates and Axioms of the American School" (1979).

Allais argues that some violations of the sure-thing principle are not irrational. His example presents four gambles involving a 100-ticket lottery. The table (Figure 1) lists in units of $100,000 the prizes the gambles yield for each ticket number. Changing *A*'s and *B*'s common consequence for tickets 12–100 from 5 to 0 yields *C* and *D* respectively. Hence the sure-thing principle prohibits preferring *A* to *B* and simultaneously preferring *D* to *C*. Yet most people have those preferences, which seem coherent. To guarantee a large gain, a typical person prefers gamble *A*, which offers $500,000 for all 100 tickets, to gamble *B*, which yields $0 for ticket number 1. Also, being attracted by the biggest prize, a typical person prefers gamble *D*, which offers $2,500,000 for ten tickets, to gamble *C*, which offers $500,000 for eleven tickets.

The sure-thing principle assumes that if two options have identical consequences in some cases, then a rational agent prefers the first option to the second option if and only if in the remaining cases he prefers the consequences of the first option to the consequences of the second option. The gambles *A* and *B* have the same consequences in 89 cases. So a preference between them indicates a preference concerning their profiles of consequences in the remaining 11 cases. Similarly, the gambles *C* and *D* have the same consequences in 89 cases. So a preference between them indicates a preference concerning their profiles of consequences in the remaining 11 cases. According to the sure-thing principle, preferring *A* to *B* and preferring *D* to *C* each express a preference between the same two 11-case profiles of consequences. However, they express opposite preferences between those profiles. To prevent inconsistency, the sure-thing principle prohibits the typical preferences concerning the gambles.

Theorists disagree about the rationality of the typical preferences concerning Allais's gambles and hence about the sure-thing principle. Moreover, those who defend the rationality of the typical preferences, disagree about the best way of justifying those preferences.

The sure-thing principle is also known as the independence axiom because it makes preferences concerning profiles of consequences independent of the context in which the profiles occur. In response to Allais's paradox, Mark Machina's article, "'Expected Utility' Theory without the Independence Axiom" (1982), relaxes the sure-thing principle. Machina holds that this principle is too demanding to be a requirement of rationality.

Tamara Horowitz's essay, "The Backtracking Fallacy" (2006), analyzes Savage's argument for the sure-thing principle. The argument treats probabilities that depend on evidence and therefore probabilities that depend on what is known. Horowitz distinguishes supposing a proposition true and supposing it to be known true. She contends that Savage's argument inadvertently slips from one form of supposition to the other and, as a result, fails to establish the sure-thing principle. However, the sure-thing principle, in contrast with the argument for it, avoids equivocation, and some guarded formulations of it may succeed.

Many scholars gratefully acknowledge their debt to Savage. The International Society for Bayesian Analysis annually presents the Leonard J. Savage Dissertation Award to two outstanding doctoral dissertations in Bayesian econometrics and statistics, fields that Savage loved and brilliantly advanced.

SUPPLEMENTARY BIBLIOGRAPHY

For a bibliography of Savage's published works, see The Writings of Leonard Jimmie Savage: A Memorial Selection *(Washington, DC American Statistical Association and the Institute of Mathematical Statistics, 1981).*

WORKS BY SAVAGE

With Edwin Hewitt. "Symmetric Measures on Cartesian Products." *Transactions of the American Mathematical Society* 80 (1955): 470–501.

With Lester Dubins. *How to Gamble if You Must: Inequalities for Stochastic Processes.* New York: McGraw-Hill, 1965.

"Implications of Personal Probability for Induction." *Journal of Philosophy* 64 (1967): 593–607.

"Elicitation of Personal Probabilities and Expectations." *Journal of the American Statistical Association* 66 (1971): 783–801.

The Foundations of Statistics. New York: Wiley, 1954. 2nd ed. New York: Dover, 1972.

OTHER SOURCES

Allais, Maurice. "Foundations of a Positive Theory of Choice Involving Risk and a Criticism of the Postulates and Axioms of the American School." In *Expected Utility Hypotheses and the Allais Paradox,* edited by Maurice Allais and Ole Hagen. Dordrecht, Netherlands: Reidel, 1979. The original French version of this essay was written in 1952 in response to Savage's early formulations of his theory.

Gärdenfors, Peter, and Nils-Eric Sahlin, eds. *Decision, Probability, and Utility: Selected Readings.* Cambridge, U.K., and New York: Cambridge University Press, 1988. Besides containing selections from Savage's work, this collection contains many essays appraising Savage's ideas.

Horowitz, Tamara. *The Epistemology of A Priori Knowledge.* Edited by Joseph L. Camp Jr. Oxford, and New York: Oxford University Press, 2006. The principal essay in this collection, "The Backtracking Fallacy," is an accessible and thorough treatment of Savage's sure-thing principle.

Joyce, James M. *The Foundations of Causal Decision Theory.* New York, and Cambridge, U.K.: Cambridge University Press, 1999. Presents Savage's decision theory and extends it to provide foundations for causal decision theory.

Lindley, Dennis V. "L. J. Savage: His Work in Probability and Statistics." *Annals of Statistics* 8 (1980): 1–24.

Machina, Mark. "'Expected Utility' Theory without the Independence Axiom." *Econometrica* 50 (1982): 277–323. Revises Savage's theory in response to Allais's objections.

Weirich, Paul. "Expected Utility and Risk." *British Journal for the Philosophy of Science* 37 (1986): 419–442. Analyzes Allais's objections to Savage's theory.

Paul Weirich

SCHINDEWOLF, OTTO HEINRICH

(*b.* Hanover, Germany, 7 June 1896; *d.* Tübingen, Germany, 10 June 1971), *geology, paleontology, evolutionary theory, philosophy of science.*

"Evolutionary Theory is in a crisis": This assessment was Otto Schindewolf's starting point for his *Paleontology, Development, and Genetics: A Critique and Synthesis* (1936). George Gaylord Simpson, a leading architect of the mid-twentieth-century "modern synthesis" of evolutionary theory, praised Schindewolf as "the first person to attempt a genuine general synthesis of evolutionary genetics and paleontology. For its time that was an original and brilliant achievement ... his initial work in this field was one of the stimuli for the Modern Synthesis, to which he is himself so bitterly opposed" (Simpson, 1952, pp. 388–389). The opposition, according to Simpson, was an old one boldly posed in new terms by Schindewolf as typology versus population concepts. In one of the milestones of the modern synthesis, Ernst Mayr's *Animal Species and Evolution* (1963), Schindewolf earned just one approving citation, which referred to his emphasis on the fact that morphological differences between different "types" of invertebrate animals often originate in early developmental stages. But as the modern synthesis hardened, the time seemed right in 1993 to publish an English translation of Schindewolf's *Grundfragen der Paläontologie* (1950). Called *Basic Questions in Paleontology*, it was introduced by one of the most prominent critics of the modern synthesis, Stephen J. Gould, as "a trenchant and utterly consistent (if spectacularly flawed) account of how an uncompromisingly anti-Darwinian, but fully evolutionary, worldview can operate" (p. xi).

Academic Life. Schindewolf first became exposed to geology and paleontology in his hometown, Hanover, during his high school years through the Geological Society of Lower Saxony (Niedersächsischer Geologischer Verein). In 1914, Schindewolf enrolled in the natural sciences program at the University of Göttingen, where he majored in paleontology under Rudolf Wedekind, a specialist in biostratigraphy (the identification of the relative geological age of successive sedimentary layers by means of index fossils). In 1917, Schindewolf followed Wedekind to the University of Marburg, where he defended his PhD thesis in 1919. The prize-winning thesis on the biostratigraphy of Late Devonian and Early Carboniferous (Paleozoic) ammonites (fossil cephalopods) from northeastern Bavaria and their paleogeographical significance established Schindewolf's reputation as a brilliant biostratigrapher. Expanding his research interests, Schindewolf began publishing on other groups of fossil invertebrates as well, most notably corals. His efforts earned him the Habilitation in 1921 (this required the defense of a second, larger thesis on a different topic resulting in the subsequent title of Privatdozent, a step on the way to full professorship) and the title of honorary professor in 1927. It was within these and subsequent years that Schindewolf developed and consolidated his ideas on macroevolutionary processes, leafing through the fossil-bearing strata, much like through the pages of a book, presenting a literal account of evolutionary history. Gaps in the fossil record on the one hand, and the sudden appearance of new types of organisms on the other, seemed to suggest a saltational mode of macroevolutionary change.

Shortly after his promotion in 1927, Schindewolf moved to Berlin, where he had accepted the post of director of the Prussian Geological Survey. Pursuing his interests in macroevolution, Schindewolf inferred a cyclical pattern of evolution from the fossil record, where evolutionary lineages would go through stages of birth and adolescence, maturity, and senescence and death. The biostratigrapher Karl Beurlen independently developed similar ideas, but Schindewolf rejected Beurlen's vitalism (*Wille zur Macht,* literally will to power), which he felt to be motivated by Beurlen's public sympathy for Nazi ideology. Indeed, Schindewolf probably eschewed contact with Beurlen for political reasons. He preferred not to appear at a workshop, Paleontology and Its Relation to Phylogeny, organized by the German Paleontological Society in 1937 in Göttingen with Beurlen as chair. Schindewolf privately distanced himself from the Nazi regime and refused collaboration, in contrast to Beurlen, who set out to criticize Schindewolf's work during the Third Reich (before choosing to leave for Brazil in 1949). Much later, upon his retirement, Schindewolf would draw parallels between the historical cycles that govern not only evolutionary lineages but also cultures, invoking such authors as Oswald Spengler and Arnold J. Toynbee. This led some to highlight the irony that in his earlier work, Schindewolf used the words "decadence," "abnormal," and "degeneration" in characterizing terminal stages of evolutionary lineages, which were terms that were common in Nazi vocabulary. But Schindewolf's integrity during the Nazi regime is

beyond doubt and earned him national and international respect from colleagues and peers.

In 1947, with the Nazis ousted from power, Schindewolf became associate, and soon thereafter full, professor at the Humboldt University in Berlin. He left Berlin in 1948 to take up the position of chair of geology and paleontology at the Eberhard Karls University in Tübingen. In 1956–1957 he served as president (*Rektor*) of that University, from which he retired in 1964. He continued research on ammonite phylogeny, and in 1969, he published a theoretical paper in which he offered important qualifiers with regards to his magnum opus of 1950, *Grundfragen der Paläontologie.* The 1950 text was written in Berlin under difficult conditions during World War II, and its publication was delayed due to the poor economic conditions that prevailed in Germany after the war. The English translation testifies to the fact that it was the *Grundfragen* above all else that established Schindewolf's reputation as a preeminent if controversial evolutionary theoretician, not only in Germany, but internationally. During his long and active life as a teacher and researcher, Schindewolf served as editor of various professional journals (*Paläontologisches Zentralblatt, Fortschritte der Paläontologie, Palaeontographica,* and *Neues Jahrbuch für Geologie und Paläontologie*), initiated the highly influential book series *Handbuch der Paläozoologie,* and was member of various professional societies and higher academic bodies (*Akademie der Wissenschaften und der Literatur Mainz, Akademie der Naturforscher Leopoldina* in Halle, and the academies of sciences of Heidelberg, Germany; Vienna, Austria; and Lund, Sweden).

Biostratigraphy and Macroevolution. Schindewolf was first and foremost a biostratigrapher. The method of biostratigraphy requires clearly and unequivocally identifiable and re-identifiable species, or taxa, of fossils that by virtue of their distribution through time characterize a certain time horizon line in the column of sedimentary layers of rock laid down during earth's history. Naturally, biostratigraphers look for species, or taxa, that (1) are well demarcated from other fossil taxa, (2) make a relatively sudden appearance in the fossil record, (3) persist relatively unchanged, and (4) disappear relatively suddenly again. In his studies of ammonites and their use as index fossils, Schindewolf took great care to establish the degree of individual variation in order to ensure that the biozones he recognized were delimited by clearly diagnosable species. This required the investigation of the individual development of ammonite fossils, because much variation can potentially be expressed during ontogeny, such that juveniles and adults must not be mistaken for different species. His interest in the ontogeny of ammonites led to inquiries into the causal mechanisms that drive and regulate the developmental process, which through all variation nevertheless preserves the "typical" form of the species. With his *Paläontologie, Entwicklungslehre, und Genetik* (1936), Schindewolf became the first author to attempt a synthesis of (pre–World War II) genetics with the study of the ontogeny and of the morphology of fossil organisms, a synthesis that he naturally pursued against the background of his biostratigraphical research program.

The theories of genetics that best seemed to match the stratigraphic record of fossils—marked by gaps and the sudden appearance of new forms of life, some as startlingly new as the earliest bird *Archaeopteryx*—were those of Richard Goldschmidt. Schindewolf's adviser, Wedekind, was well acquainted with Goldschmidt's work, and in "Über den 'Typus' in morphologischer und phylogenetischer Biologie Schindewolf" (1969), Schindewolf himself reminisced about many discussions he had with Goldschmidt when they both lived and worked in Berlin. Goldschmidt's primary interest was the genetic control of developmental processes, where relatively minor early deviations were thought to potentially result in significant changes at the adult stage. Goldschmidt's claim to fame was accordingly his theory of macromutations, which later developments in genetics proved to be mistaken. Yet the result of Schindewolf's early synthesis, which preceded the spread of population genetics triggered in 1937 by Theodosius Dobzhansky, was accordingly a theory of saltational macroevolution known as typostrophe theory (*typostrophentheorie*). Its central tenets were that (1) internal (structural), not external (natural selection) factors drive macroevolution, which therefore, unlike microevolution, is not adaptive; (2) macroevolution is saltational; and (3) macroevolution is cyclic. During the first phase of an evolutionary cycle, called typogenesis, a "type," or *Bauplan,* is laid down that is adapted only in the sense that it is capable of surviving environmental changes through time. In stage two, called typostasis, the general "type," or *Bauplan,* is maintained as it diversifies through time and space in adaptation to special and varying conditions of life at low taxonomic levels. Stage three, called typolysis, leads to overspecialization and eventual extinction of the evolutionary lineage representing the "type," or *Bauplan.* With his *Der Zeitfaktor in Geologie und Paläontologie* (1950), Schindewolf became the first author in modern times to invoke extraterrestrial causes such as cosmic radiation generated by a supernova (1954, 1963) to explain the mass extinctions at the end of the Paleozoic and Mesozoic periods.

The "Type" Concept. The concept that lies at the core of Schindewolf's typostrophism is that of a "type" of organization, or *Bauplan.* The use of this concept identifies Schindewolf as an exponent of the neo-idealistic morphology that became popular among German-speaking morphologists and paleontologists after World War I. Following the rise of Darwinism, morphological research was caught between "pattern" versus "process" views of nature. The architects of the modern synthesis of evolutionary theory proclaimed "population thinking," with population genetics at its heart, as the only proper way to understand Darwinian evolution. Ever so slight variations and the force of natural selection would result in gradual evolutionary change in a continuous chain of populations extending through time and space. If intermediate populations were absent in the fossil record, their existence had to be inferred on the basis of evolutionary theory. Idealist morphologists, on the other hand, emphasized the primacy of structure, and of the hierarchical pattern that results from the comparative analysis of anatomy, over its historical explanation (evolution). Morphology was to provide the empirical base for the natural system, and if evolutionary theory was to offer a causal-historical explanation of that system, it had to take into account its structure, even if that meant to account for gaps to be bridged by saltational change.

Schindewolf first laid down his views on idealistic morphology as the basis for biosystematics and phylogenetic research in his influential paper of 1928, "Prinzipienfragen der biologischen Systematik," which had its origin in a seminar he presented at Marburg University in 1921. He revisited his type concept in his magnum opus of 1950, and once again returned to its defense in 1969 with his "Über den 'Typus.'" Ernst Mayr, a leading author of the modern synthesis, dismissed the type concept as a Platonic idea (*eidos*), rendering it the hallmark of the worst possible fallacy in evolutionary biology, typological thinking. In "Über den 'Typus,'" Schindewolf naturally rejected Mayr's identification of the type concept as merely a Platonic idea, or a phantasmagoria, as it was called by the botanist Walter Zimmermann. All such arguments Schindewolf considered as resulting from a lack of understanding of the paleontological method. *Ichthyostega* stands for the first tetrapod, *Archaeopteryx* is the first representative of the "type" of birds, and both make a sudden appearance in the fossil record. In that sense, tetrapods, or birds, represent a "type," which is a genuinely scientific concept, and as such objective and real. The sudden appearance of new "types" is what paleontologists observe, and—according to Schindewolf—scientific speculation should not exceed the empirical base to an irresponsible degree. This, however, is exactly what Schindewolf found "population thinking" to be guilty of, as it bridged the gaps between types with hypothetical intermediate populations for which there was no empirical evidence: "I cannot offer up populations," Schindewolf wrote ("Über den 'Typus,'" p. 88).

In his highly influential book on evolutionary theory, *Deszendenzlehre* (1922), Sinai Tschulok sought a compromise between "Machian permissiveness" (a reference to Ernst Mach) and "Millian rigidity" (John Stuart Mill). With reference to evolutionary theory, he distinguished three issues: (1) the "principle issue" (*Grundsatzfrage*), which settles the question that evolution did, in fact, occur; (2) the "phylogenetic tree issue" (*Stammbaumproblem*), which is concerned with the reconstruction of the history of life on Earth; and (3) the "causal issue" (*Faktorenproblem*), which is concerned with the causes that drive the evolutionary process. According to Tschulok, it simply did not make sense either to search for phylogenetic relationships, or to investigate the causes of evolutionary change, without prior acceptance of the fact that evolution as such did occur. The Göttingen workshop of 1937 that Schindewolf had preferred not to attend had concluded that paleontology is the only science that has direct epistemic access to the evolutionary process, that the goal of paleontology therefore must be to reconstruct the history of that process, and that the causes driving this process could at best be inferred from its systematic reconstruction. Regretting his mistake of having accepted Goldschmidt's macromutations in his early theorizing, Schindewolf followed the eminent paleontologist Walter Gross in arguing that the paleontologist has nothing to say about the causal issue. The task of paleontology, Schindewolf wrote in ""Über den 'Typus,'" is simply "the explanatory description of the empirically accessible regularities apparent in the Fossil Record and nothing else" (p. 107). He accordingly distinguished paleontology as a nomographical science, in contradistinction to the idiographic and nomothetical sciences that had been recognized by Wilhelm Windelband. On that account, paleontology comes out as a primarily historical science in the sense of Leopold von Ranke, (1795–1886), who said "to state, how it [actually] was" (Schindewolf, 1969, p. 106). It was not, accordingly, one concerned with the understanding of historically unique situations, as were Windelband's idiographic sciences, nor one concerned with the discovery of universal laws of nature, as were Windelband's nomothetical sciences, but one that seeks the "explanatory description" of regularities from which empirical generalizations can be inferred.

The difficulty of understanding the type concept may have its roots in what appear to be inconsistencies in the idealistic morphological literature. For the early Schindewolf in "Prinzipienfragen der biologischen Systematik" (1928), biosystematics was a purely ordering science and its categories, consequently, are purely conceptual, that is, spatiotemporally unrestricted. These categories are the hierarchically nested and/or stratigraphically stacked "types," or *Baupläne*. In his *Grundfragen*, Schindewolf maintained the need for logical abstraction that is required to conceptualize "types," but he denied that these represent mere mental constructs. Instead, the "types"

marked out by morphology are the result and the expression of the concrete and real phylogenetic process. The hierarchy of "types" must therefore be considered a hierarchy of historical entities, marked out by "typical" characters that have real, indeed vital, significance for the token organisms that exemplify the corresponding "types." In his later reflections, Schindewolf again stressed the "objective biological reality" of the "type," a "scientific reality" that equals the reality of populations. Schindewolf went on to discuss the latest applications of the "type" concept by other authors both in biology and anthropology, and registered his satisfaction that the philosopher Marjorie Grene, in her discussion of "Two Evolutionary Theories" (1958), had come down closer to his own views than to those of George G. Simpson. Indeed, Schindewolf, like most other neo-idealistic morphologists, followed the lead of Adolf Naef, who had called the "type" a concept, or a kind, that is, a natural kind, in his *Idealistische Morphologie und Phylogenetik* (1919). To consider the "type" of neo-idealistic morphology a natural kind raises the question whether these kinds represent immutable and timeless Aristotelian classes of naturally occurring "stuff" or "things," or whether they can also be exemplified by natural historical entities such as species and supraspecific taxa. On a charitable reading, it seems that from 1928 to 1969, Schindewolf progressed from the former to the latter interpretation of types in his writings.

Schindewolf's Legacy. During his long career, Schindewolf published 187 books, book chapters, monographs, and papers and trained more than sixty graduate students. His scientific output, his dedication to teaching and education, and his personal integrity established him as the leading paleontologist of his time in Germany. He was the first author in Germany to attempt a synthesis of genetics, development, morphology, and paleontology, and in so doing developed his own internally coherent but nonselectionist and saltational theory of macroevolution. Naturally, his typostrophism found little acclaim on an international stage that was dominated by the modern synthesis of evolutionary thought. There is good reason to believe that Schindewolf's towering presence delayed the acceptance of the synthetic theory of evolution in German paleontology. In the late twentieth century, however, proponents of the "punctuated equilibria" theory of evolution found in Schindewolf—the man who had famously adopted the statement "the first bird hatched from a reptile's egg" (*Paläontologie, Entwicklungslehre, und Genetik*, p. 59)—a brother in arms, even if only a distant one. Both Schindewolf's typology and the model of punctuated equilibrium of evolution have their roots in a biostratigraphic research program, which, for its successful execution, requires sharp boundaries between taxa.

While biostratigraphy was the main motivating factor for Schindewolf's typostrophe theory, he also found that developmental biology lent support to a typological perspective of organismic diversity. Deviation of developmental pathways during early stages of ontogeny may cause changes in adult morphology that create gaps in the continuity of organic forms. Such gaps in morphospace, at the turn of the twentieth to the twenty-first century the subject matter of the evolution and development research program, were prominently used by Gerry Webster and Brian Goodwin in "The Origin of Species: A Structuralist Approach" (1982), their critique of neo-Darwinism. Their typological perspective is motivated by a field theory of generative mechanisms. In most general terms, a "field is a spatial domain in which every part has a state determined by the state of neighboring parts so that the whole has a specific relational structure" (Goodwin, "What Are the Causes of Morphogenesis?" 1984, p. 228). The result is that any disturbance of the field requires the whole spatial pattern to be reconstituted. Morphogenetic fields that play out during development thus condition "types," that is, they constrain development to typical relations of morphology that mark out empirically discovered natural kinds. The goal is a structuralist morphology that delivers a rational classification of organisms in the form of a hierarchy of "types," which in turn is causally explained by the physico-chemical properties of the underlying morphogenetic fields and their transformations. The answer to Darwinian theories of variation and natural selection is that "no Darwinist has ever understood typology, because he can not possibly understand it" (Webster and Goodwin, "The Origin of Species," p. 26). In Schindewolf's case, the success of applied biostratigraphy may have made it impossible for him to understand the biological processes underlying Darwinian evolutionary theory.

BIBLIOGRAPHY

A complete bibliography of Schindewolf is given in Heinrich K. Erben, "Nachruf auf Otto Heinrich Schindewolf,"Jahrbuch 1971 der Akademie der Wissenschaften und der Literatur in Mainz (1971), pp. 75–86. A selection of Schindewolf's most important publications in biostratigraphy, evolution, and systematics, was compiled by Wolf-Ernst Reif in his "Afterword" for Otto Heinrich Schindewolf, Basic Questions in Paleontology: Geologic Time, Organic Evolution, and Biological Systematics, *translated by Judith Schaefer (Chicago: University of Chicago Press, 1993), pp. 435–453. Universitätsarchiv Tübingen, Wilhelmstrasse 32, D-72074 Tübingen.*

WORKS BY SCHINDEWOLF

"Prinzipienfragen der biologischen Systematik." *Paläontologische Zeitschrift* 9 (1928): 122–166.

"Ontogenie und Phylogenie." *Paläontologische Zeitschrift* 11 (1929): 54–67.

Paläontologie, Entwicklungslehre, und Genetik: Kritik und Synthese [Paleontology, development, and genetics: A critique and synthesis]. Berlin: Gebrüder Bornträger, 1936.

"Beobachtungen und Gedanken zur Deszendenzlehre." *Acta Biotheoretica* 3 (1937): 195–221.

"Zum Kampf um die Gestaltung der Abstammungslehre." *Die Naturwissenschaften* 31 (1944): 269–282.

Grundfragen der Paläontologie: Geologische Zeitmessung, organische Stammesentwicklung, biologische Systematik. Stuttgart, Germany: E. Schweizerbart, 1950.

Der Zeitfaktor in Geologie und Paläontologie. Stuttgart, Germany: E. Schweizerbart, 1950.

"Über die möglichen Ursachen der grossen erdgeschichtlichen Faunenschnitte." *Neues Jahrbuch für Geologie und Paläontlogie, Monatshefte* (1954): 457–465.

"Neue Systematik." *Paläontologische Zeitschrift* 36 (1962): 59–78.

"Neokatastrophismus?" *Zeitschrift der Deutschen Geologischen Gesellschaft* 114 (1963): 430–445.

"Erdgeschichte und Weltgeschichte." *Akademie der Wissenschaften und der Literatur (Mainz), Abhandlungen der Mathematisch-Naturwissenschaftlichen Klasse* 2 (1964): 56–104.

"Über den 'Typus' in morphologischer und phylogenetischer Biologie." *Akademie der Wissenschaften und der Literatur (Mainz), Abhandlungen der Mathematisch-Naturwissenschaftlichen Klasse* 4 (1969): 55–131.

Basic Questions in Paleontology: Geologic Time, Organic Evolution, and Biological Systematics. Translated by Judith Schaefer. Edited by Wolf-Ernst Reif. Foreword by Stephen Jay Gould. Chicago: University of Chicago Press, 1993.

OTHER SOURCES

Beurlen, Karl. "Die gegenwärtige Stellung der Paläontlogie zu den Hauptproblemen der Stammesgeschichte." *Paläontologische Zeitschrift* 20 (1938): 167–176.

Dobzhansky, Theodosius. *Genetics and the Origin of Species.* New York: Columbia University Press, 1937.

Eldredge, Niles. "Genetics and the Origin of Species." *Evolution* 25 (1971): 156–167.

Erben, Heinrich K. "Nachruf auf Otto Heinrich Schindewolf." *Jahrbuch 1971 der Akademie der Wissenschaften und der Literatur in Mainz* (1971): 75–86. Includes a complete bibliography.

Goodwin, Brian C. "What Are the Causes of Morphogenesis?" In *Beyond Neo-Darwinism: An Introduction to the New Evolutionary Paradigm,* edited by Mae-Wan Ho and Peter T. Saunders. London: Academic Press, 1984.

———. "What Are the Causes of Morphogenesis?" *BioEssays* 3 (1985): 32–36.

Grene, Marjorie. "Two Evolutionary Theories." *British Journal for the Philosophy of Science* 9 (1958): 110–127, 185–193.

———."Evolution, 'Typology,' and 'Population Thinking.'" *American Philosophical Quarterly* 27 (1990): 237–244.

Korn, Dieter. "Schindewolf, Otto Heinrich." In *Encyclopedia of Paleontology,* edited by Ronald Singer. Vol. 2. Chicago: Fitzroy-Dearborn Publishers, 1999.

Kullmann, Jürgen, and Jost Wiedmann. "Otto H. Schindewolf." *Neues Jahrbuch für Geologie und Paläontologie, Abhandlungen* 125 (1966): xi–xxvii (Festband Schindewolf).

———. "Otto Heinrich Schindewolf zum Gedächtnis, 7.6.1896–10.6.1971." *Atempto Tübingen* 39–40 (1971): 120–121.

Mayr, Ernst. *Animal Species and Evolution.* Cambridge, MA: Harvard University Press, 1963.

Morris, Simon Conway. "Wonderfully, Gloriously Wrong." *TREE* 9 (1994): 407–408.

Naef, Adolf. *Idealistische Morphologie und Phylogenetik (zur Methodik der systematischen Morphologie).* Jena, Germany: Gustav Fischer, 1919.

Reif, Wolf-Ernst. "Evolutionary Theory in German Paleontology." In *Dimensions of Darwinism: Themes and Counterthemes in Twentieth-Century Evolutionary Theory,* edited by Marjorie Grene. Cambridge, U.K.: Cambridge University Press, 1983.

———. "The Search for a Macroevolutionary Theory in German Paleontology." *Journal of the History of Biology* 19 (1986): 79–130.

———. "Afterword." In *Basic Questions in Paleontology: Geologic Time, Organic Evolution, and Biological Systematics,* by Otto Heinrich Schindewolf, translated by Judith Schaefer. Chicago: University of Chicago Press, 1993.

———. "Typology and the Primacy of Morphology: The Concepts of O. H. Schindewolf." *Neues Jahrbuch für Geologie und Paläontologie, Abhandlungen* 205 (1997): 355–371.

———. "Deutschsprachige Paläontologie im Spannungsfeld zwischen Makroevolutionstheorie und Neo-Darwinismus (1920–1950)." *Verhandlungen Geschichte und Theorie der Biologie* 2 (1999): 151–188.

Seilacher, Adolf. "Otto H. Schindewolf, 7 Juni 1896–10 Juni 1971." *Neues Jahrbuch für Geologie und Paläontologie, Monatshefte* (1972): 69–71.

Simpson, George Gaylord. Obituary. *Quarterly Review of Biology* 27 (1952): 388–389.

Teichert, Curt. "From Karpinsky to Schindewolf—Memories of Some Great Paleontologists." *Journal of Paleontology* 50 (1976): 1–12.

Tschulok, Sinai. *Deszendenzlehre.* Jena, Germany: Gustav Fischer, 1922.

Webster, Gerry. "The Relations of Natural Forms." In *Beyond Neodarwinism. An Introduction to the New Evolutionary Paradigm,* edited by Mae-Wan Ho and Peter T. Saunders. London: Academic Press, 1984.

Webster, Gerry, and Brian C. Goodwin. "The Origin of Species: A Structuralist Approach." *Journal of Social and Biological Structures* 5 (1982): 15–47.

Oliver Rieppel

SCHLEIDEN, MATTHIAS JACOB (*b.* Hamburg, Germany, 5 April 1804; *d.* Frankfurt am Main,

Germany, 23 June 1881), *botany, cell theory, philosophy of science, science popularization, developmental morphology, plant physiology.* For the original article on Schleiden see *DSB,* vol. 12.

Analyses in the late twentieth and early twenty-first centuries reveal that many concepts important to Schleiden's mature cell theory were already present in his earlier work. He would give to cells the same roles that he (and others) earlier assigned to structures such as sprouts, leaves, and pollen. Both before and after he focused on the cell, he was answering questions about generation and morphology by tracing diverse forms and processes back to common origins. Scholars have also unearthed more details about his career and analyzed his other writings, especially his inductive philosophy of science.

Beginnings: Morphology and Generation. While a medical student in Göttingen (1832–1835), Schleiden was initially more interested in physical sciences and their philosophical foundations. A course with Gottlob Bartling got him interested in plant microscopy. In 1835 he continued his studies in Berlin, working chiefly with his uncle Johann Horkel (a former student of Johann Christian Reil), who advocated the study of embryos and denied that plants reproduced by sexual mixture—both key ideas for the nephew as well.

Recent research elucidates how Schleiden's morphology shaped his interpretation of pollen and cells. He began with a critique of Johann Wolfgang Goethe. The poet and other morphologists observed the variety of macroscopic structures such as stamens and leaves (both on the same plant and on different kinds of plants), yet tried to connect those many forms to a few spatial concepts; for instance, they likened a stamen to a contracted version of the basic leaf shape.

Schleiden continued their search for unity underlying diversity, but with different methods and results. Even though Goethe had made many observations, in 1837 Schleiden dismissed his morphology as speculation because Goethe had tried to relate organs by *visualizing in the mind* geometrical variants of mature shapes. Schleiden insisted true inductive morphology must seek a relation *observable in the world*: the developmental continuity between earlier and later structures in the life of a plant.

The first stages of plants were the most important objects of observation. Botanists could see fundamental similarities between plant parts by tracing them back to similar embryonic origins—even if the later forms looked very different. Citing Caspar Friedrich Wolff, Schleiden wrote that everything else developed from the initial sprout which comprised the fundamental organs (*Grundorgane*) stem and leaves.

What, in turn, gave rise to that sprout? The role—or even necessity—of pollen in fertilization had long been controversial. In the eighteenth century, Carl Linnaeus taught that all plants reproduced sexually: higher plants with flowers or other visible sex organs he called phanerogams; lower plants (in which he included ferns, mosses, algae, and fungi) he called cryptogams because their sexuality was hidden. Other botanists attributed sex to phanerogams but thought cryptogams produced only asexual spores. Higher plants were the model, lower ones merely deviant or lacking.

By the 1830s Robert Brown and other botanists had observed pollen tubes extending toward the ovule, but what happened when the pollen arrived was still not clear. Schleiden agreed with Horkel's observation that the pollen tube wall remained intact rather than fusing with anything in the ovule. The nephew defied tradition by using cryptogams as models for phanerogams: spores sprouted and grew by taking up nutrient fluids from the soil; pollen was a spore that needed the special environment and more refined sap in the ovule. Since leaf tissue in some plants directly gave rise to new sprouts, in some became spores, and in some became pollen, all three were equivalent. (Even when he abandoned his pollen theory Schleiden still extrapolated from the simplest cryptogams to phanerogams [1861].) Botanists have rejected details of Schleiden's pollen observations, but the cryptogam model, including the analogy of pollen grains to spores, remains essential to plant physiology and classification.

Schleiden also united the seemingly different processes of development and reproduction. Like leaf tissue that budded directly, a pollen grain or spore was both a continuation of growth and the germ that became the future plant. Schleiden called the pollen/embryo a leaf cell grafted onto the stem (ovule) (1837, p. 313). Reproduction by grafting may have connected Schleiden's understanding of growth to older views of the plant as an aggregate of individuals sprouting within individuals. Some earlier thinkers had interpreted each new sprout on a tree as an individual plant, as if it had been grafted on the stem. Although Schleiden's article on cell theory did not explicitly invoke grafting, he did describe the woody tree trunk "as if it were a mere organized soil" upon which a new generation of sprouts grew (1838, p. 171; 1847 p. 260). He wrote positively of theories that the annual buds on a tree were individuals, even though he said strictly speaking only cells qualified as individuals (1838, pp. 168–174; 1847, pp. 258–263). Development connected these two kinds of individuals: every sprout was traceable back to a cell.

Cells: The New Grundorgane. In the 1837 paper cells were occasionally mentioned but were not yet the star of the show. In 1838 Schleiden put the cell into the role of Grundorgan. He praised Julius Meyen as an observer of mature plant microanatomy, but dismissed his and others' work as irrelevant because it did not study development. In contrast Schleiden considered the crucial prerequisite to his cell theory to have been Robert Brown's calling attention to nuclei. Brown had noted the frequent (not universal) presence of a structure he called the "nucleus of the cell" (Schleiden 1838, p. 139; 1847, p. 233). After meeting with Brown in 1836, Schleiden noticed that nuclei were the *first structures to develop* in the embryo and that cells formed around them. He propounded the first cell theory that gave an essential role to the nucleus.

Schleiden insisted that the same law of cell formation operated in later tissues, even in cases where he had difficulty observing them. The formation of cells within cells became the fundamental process in all development. Like the earlier theories in which new individuals sprouted on trees, Schleiden saw growth as the reiteration of reproduction. Each cell was the first stage in the life of an individual, whether it remained a single cell, or became leaves, spores, or trees. In one sense Schleiden broke the plant into individual cells; in another he asserted an essential similarity among cells, pollen, and whole plants.

The cellular beginnings of organisms would also justify extrapolating cell theory beyond plants. After Schleiden told Theodor Schwann about nuclei forming cells, Schwann recognized a similar process as fundamental to animal development, and compared cell formation to crystallization (1839). Some have suggested Schleiden also based his cell formation theory on crystallization. But the botanist originally said that cell formation made plants *different* from crystals or animals (1838, p. 161; 1847, p. 251). Analogies between crystallization and development are older than Schleiden (e.g., Fries), but only after Schwann suggested cells as the bridge between them did the botanist (in his textbook) praise the analogy, though with emphasis on the differences.

Induction: Key Observations and Extrapolation. The methodological introduction to Schleiden's textbook (1842) went beyond merely denouncing speculation or defending particular observations. It formally connected his emphasis on development and cells to the inductive principles of Jakob Friedrich Fries. Even before becoming a microscopist Schleiden had admired the philosopher Fries, "from whose logic I have learned as much botany as from all botanical writings together" (Lorch, p. xiii, translating Schleiden, 1850, p. 115). Schleiden drew upon Fries not for specifics about plants but for philosophical ideas about unifying physics and physiology, separating spirit from material (e.g., ideas do not cause physical

Matthias Jacob Schleiden. HULTON ARCHIVE/GETTY IMAGES.

phenomena), and "rational induction" guided by regulative "leading principles."

In philosophy of science, *induction* refers to systematic observation leading to general principles based on those observations. As discussed above, Schleiden considered some observations more illuminating than others. Underlying affinities between mature specimens often could not be seen in the specimens themselves; morphologists had to look elsewhere. Goethe used the mind's eye to see the ideal plant form; Schleiden used the microscope to see the embryonic primordia. He pointed to those primordia to defend parallels across different plant taxa. Spores and pollen did not develop into one another within the same plant, but both could be traced back to the same kind of beginning.

Schleiden did refer to development within the same plant when he extrapolated his theory of cell formation from embryos to later tissues. Since pollen, embryos, and leaves were the same object, just at different times, "we may certainly infer" that the formation process observed in embryos also took place in later tissues (1838, p. 164; 1847, p. 254). Here Schleiden made a sort of bootstrapping move: his critique of Goethe had defended the study of development because it was observable, but his cell theory used development to infer beyond what was observable. (In the 1840s Karl Nägeli would overturn

Schleiden's cell formation theory by showing that embryonic tissue in fact displayed cell formation not typical of later tissues.)

In Ulrich Charpa's felicitous phrase, Schleiden's methodological introduction to his textbook prescribed virtues for explorers who needed to rely on the honesty and the theoretical and practical expertise of fellow microscopists and instrument makers. The artisan Carl Zeiss was among those who learned microscopy at the physiology institute that Schleiden cofounded in 1845. Later Schleiden helped Zeiss start his business and endorsed its microscopes. Schleiden directed his textbook remarks about microscopy mainly to warn practitioners about potential pitfalls (including flawed instruments); in brief remarks to skeptics of microscopy, he put the blame for error on the observer, not the tool. Schleiden emphasized skill to justify his new discipline and to exclude other microscopists. Only through long training could one come to understand the optical properties of good (and bad) microscopes, develop dexterity in preparation techniques such as cutting specimens, and learn to convey careful interpretative observation by accurate drawings.

Later Career and Writings. Schleiden proclaimed his developmental morphology, including cell and pollen theories, while a medical student in Berlin in the late 1830s. In 1839 he became (extraordinary) professor of natural history in the philosophical faculty at Jena, where he received his philosophy degree. In 1843 Tübingen granted him an honorary MD. In 1844 he married Bertha Mirus (*d.* 1854), with whom he had three daughters. In 1855 he married Therese Marezoll, who survived him.

Schleiden's most successful course at Jena was originally called comparative physiology. It covered function and development of organisms (including the work of Johannes Müller), physical anthropology (based on Johann Friedrich Blumenbach), and Fries's theory of the human mind. (Schleiden's reading about ethnography would contribute to some of his much later writings.)

The medical faculty complained about a professor in the philosophical faculty encroaching on their prerogative to teach human physiology, so he renamed the course "Anthropologie." Schleiden further offended the medical faculty by teaching pharmacological botany and laboratory practica in physiology. Such turf battles (and other universities' interest in hiring him) led the authorities in Weimar to move Schleiden to the medical faculty in 1846, where he became a full professor in 1849. In 1851 he became director of the botanical garden, but he never held the title professor of botany.

In the 1840s Schleiden also worked on the application of plant chemistry and physiology to agriculture. He rejected vitalism but put limits on the value of chemistry for botany. In 1840 Justus Liebig wrote that a chemistry laboratory was the best place to learn plant physiology. Schleiden retorted that Liebig lacked the philosophical sophistication and the knowledge of cell theory to study plants.

His writings after he left Jena have not as of 2007 been studied in depth, but historians have noted some continuing themes, including anthropology, biological development, and Friesian neo-Kantian philosophy. Already endorsing species transformation in the 1840s, Schleiden was one of the first German scientists to praise Darwinism, and produced books summarizing research on the physical and cultural anthropology of early humans. His last works, monographs on the rose and salt, were intended for scholarly audiences and combined the science and the cultural position of their subjects.

At his death he left an unpublished manuscript on religion. Initially not particularly religious, in 1839 he had adopted orthodox Lutheranism when recovering from a suicidal depression. In botanical lectures in 1840s and his denunciation of materialism in 1863 he insisted that the spiritual and physical worlds both existed but did not causally interact. By his later years he had moved to a unitarianism that he no longer considered Christian.

SUPPLEMENTARY BIBLIOGRAPHY

Almost everything ever written by or about Schleiden or Fries can be found in Glasmacher (1989). Mylott (2002) also has an extensive bibliography. Archival and published sources are listed in Jahn and Schmidt's biography (2006).

WORKS BY SCHLEIDEN

"Einige Blicke auf die Entwicklungsgeschichte des vegetabilischen Organismus bei den Phanerogamen" [A few views of developmental history of the vegetable organism in the phanerogams]. Wiegmann's *Archiv für Naturgschichte* 3, no.1 (1837): 289–320. Morphology, including critique of Goethe, and brief statement of pollen theory.

"Beiträge zur Phytogenesis." Müller's *Archiv für Anatomie, Physiologie, und wissenschaftliche Medicin*, 1838: 137–176. Translated as "Contributions to Our Knowledge of Phytogenesis" in *Scientific Memoirs*, edited by Richard Taylor et al., vol. 2, part 6. London: Taylor, 1841. German version republished with additional notes in Schleiden, *Beiträge zur Botanik*, vol. 1. 1844. The revised version is reprinted in *Klassische Schriften zur Zellenlehre*, edited by Ilse Jahn. Leipzig: Geest & Portig, 1987. Revised version also translated as "Contributions to Phytogenesis" in Smith (1847), which also includes Schwann's book. This article is the classic statement of Schleiden's cell theory.

Grundzüge der Wissenschaftlichen Botanik. 1st ed., 2 vols. Leipzig: Wilhelm Engelmann, 1842 and 1843. Revised ed. 1845 and 1846. First part of 2nd ed. reprinted, edited by Olaf Breidbach. Hildesheim: Georg Olms Verlag, 1998. 3rd ed., 1849 and 1850; 4th ed., 1861. The methodological

introduction from the 4th ed. (virtually unchanged from 2nd ed.) is reprinted in Charpa (1989). Textbook.

Principles of Scientific Botany or Botany as an Inductive Science. Translation of 2nd ed. of *Grundzüge der Wissenschaftlichen Botanik,* by Edwin Lankester, 1849. Reprint, with an introduction by Jacob Lorch. New York: Johnson Reprint Corporation, 1969. This is a translation of the technical botanical content of the *Grundzüge.* As of 2007, no English translation exists of the textbook's "Methodologische Grundlage"; Lankester translated only some remarks on the use of the microscope and a two-page methodological summary from another work by Schleiden.

OTHER SOURCES

Brown, Robert. *Observations on the Organs and Mode of Fecundation in Orchideae and Æsclepiadeae,* 1831. Reprinted with minor revisions as "Observations on the Organs and Mode of Fecundation in Orchideae and Æsclepiadeae." *Transactions of the Linnean Society of London* 16 (1833): 685–742; article reprinted in *The Miscellaneous Botanical Works of Robert Brown,* vol. 1. Edited by John J. Bennett. Includes appendix about the cell nucleus.

Buchdahl, Gerd. "Leading Principles and Induction: The Methodology of Matthias Schleiden." In *Foundations of Scientific Method: The Nineteenth Century,* edited by Ronald N. Giere and Richard S. Westfall. Bloomington: Indiana University Press, 1973. German version in Charpa, 1989. Schleiden's neo-Kantian philosophy.

Charpa, Ulrich, ed. *Wissenschaftsphilosophische Schriften,* by M. J. Schleiden. Cologne: Jürgen Dinter Verlag für Philosophie, 1989. Schleiden's essential philosophical writings, with commentaries.

———. "Matthias Jakob Schleiden (1804–1881): The History of Jewish Interest in Science and the Methodology of Microscopic Botany." *Aleph: Historical Studies in Science and Judaism* 3 (2003): 213–245.

———. "Matthias Jacob Schleiden." In *Naturphilosophie nach Schelling,* edited by Thomas Bach and Olaf Breidbach. Stuttgart: Frommann-Holzboog, 2005.

de Chadarevian, Soraya. "Instruments, Illustrations, Skills, and Laboratories in Nineteenth-Century German Botany." In *Non-verbal Communication in Science Prior to 1900,* edited by Renato G. Mazzolini. Firenze: Olschki, 1993. Schleiden demarcating his discipline.

Duchesneau, François. *Genèse de la théorie cellulaire.* Collections Analytiques 1. Montréal: Bellarmin, 1987. Mainly about situating Schwann with respect to nineteenth-century zoological research programs; one chapter on Schleiden.

Farley, John. *Gametes and Spores: Ideas about Sexual Reproduction, 1750–1914.* Baltimore: Johns Hopkins University Press, 1982. Includes a chapter on Schleiden's pollen theory.

Glasmacher, Thomas. *Fries – Apelt – Schleiden: Verzeichnis der Primär- und Sekundärliteratur, 1798–1988.* Cologne: Jürgen Dinter Verlag für Philosophie, 1989.

Goethe, Johann Wolfgang von. "Die Metamorphose der Pflanzen," 1790. Reprinted in *Die Schriften zur Naturwissenschaft,* vol. 9, *Morphologische Hefte,* edited by Dorothea Kuhn. Weimar: Hermann Bohlaus Nachfolger, 1954. Translated by Bertha Mueller as "The Metamorphosis of Plants" in *Goethe's Botanical Writings*. University Press of Hawaii, 1952. Reprint, Woodbridge, CT: Ox Bow Press, 1989. One of the founding documents of morphology.

Horkel, Johann. "Eine historische Einleitung in die Lehre von den Pollenschläuchen." Summary report of address to the academy. *Bericht über die zur Bekanntmachung geeigneten Verhandlungen der Königlichen Preussischen Akademie der Wissenschaften zu Berlin* 1 (1836): 71–82. Describes and evaluates the observations of various researchers, including Brown and Schleiden.

Jahn, Ilse, and Isolde Schmidt. *Matthias Jacob Schleiden (1804–1881): Sein Leben in Selbstzeugnissen.* Halle: Leopoldina, 2006. Most extensive biography.

Mazumdar, Pauline M. H. *Species and Specificity: An Interpretation of the History of Immunology.* Cambridge, U.K.: Cambridge University Press, 1995. Schleiden emphasized unity rather than diversity of living things.

Mendelsohn, Andrew. "Lives of the Cell." *Journal of the History of Biology* 36 (2003): 1–37. A delight to read; applies many science studies insights to nineteenth-century cell theory and induction from exemplars.

Mylott, Anne. "Cells, Life Force, and Reductionism in the Botany of Matthias Jacob Schleiden." In *Ideengeschichte und Wissenschaftsphilosophie: Festschrift für Lutz Geldsetzer,* edited by Richard Dodel, Esther Seidel, and Larry Steindler. Cologne: Jürgen Dinter Verlag für Philosophie, 1997. Schleiden's Friesian philosophy and his argument with Liebig.

———. "The Roots of Cell Theory in Sap, Spores, and Schleiden." PhD diss., Indiana University, Bloomington, 2002. Analyzes his morphology, pollen, and cell theories, and relates his philosophy to his biology. Also covers some predecessors, including Henri Dutrochet and Franz Julius Ferdinand Meyen.

Nyhart, Lynn. *Biology Takes Form: Animal Morphology and the German Universities, 1800–1900.* Chicago: University of Chicago Press, 1995. Meaning of "Grund" and "Physiologie," as well as morphology.

Ratzeburg, Julius Theodor Christian. *Forstwissenschaftliches Schriftsteller-Lexikon.* Berlin: Nicolai, 1872. Unsympathetic portrait of Schleiden. Most detailed account of Horkel available.

Schickore, Jutta. *The Microscope and the Eye: A History of Reflections, 1740–1870.* Chicago: University of Chicago Press, 2007.

Schwann, Theodor. *Mikroskopische Untersuchungen über die Übereinstimmung in der Struktur und dem Wachsthum der Thiere und Pflanzen,* 1839. Portions reprinted in Jahn (1987). Translated by Henry Smith as *Microscopical Researches into the Accordance in the Structure and Growth of Animals and Plants.* 1847. Classic of the cell theory.

Werner, Petra, and Frederic L. Holmes. "Justus Liebig and the Plant Physiologists." *Journal of the History of Biology* 35 (2002): 421–441.

Anne Mylott

SCHLÜSSEL, CHRISTOPH
SEE **Clavius, Christopher**.

SCHMITT, FRANCIS OTTO (*b.* St. Louis, Missouri, 23 November 1903; *d.* Cambridge, Massachusetts, 3 October 1995), *neuroscience, biophysics, molecular biology, molecular genetics.*

Schmitt was the founder of the field of neuroscience through the Neurosciences Research Program that he established at the Massachusetts Institute of Technology (MIT) in 1962. Earlier, in the 1950s, he was one of the founders of the field of biophysics. Also, along with various colleagues and collaborators, he revolutionized the biological analysis of the fine structure and molecular properties of proteins (collagen, neurofilaments), cells (especially brain cells—neurons and glia), and various body tissues (connective tissue, muscle). Although he focused his own laboratory research at the molecular level, he was more than a reductionist. Rather, he worked to understand molecular structure and function so that tissue and organ function could be elucidated. His was a long and active career and, in a sense, a continuing love affair with science.

In everything he did Schmitt was committed to the belief that the blending and integration of concepts and methodology from different scientific fields was critical to achieving and accelerating advances in solving biological problems, especially in areas as complex as those involving brain, behavior control, and mind. He had the ability to ask good questions and to bring facts and concepts from a broad range of disciplines together in his own mind to address a biological problem. However, he recognized that no one person or discipline could do all that needed to be done, and so he placed a premium on cross-disciplinary scientific exchange and collaboration. With his broad vision and enthusiasm, he was able to bring colleagues from many disciplines together and stimulate effective discussion and collaboration. The lives and careers of many young—and older—scientists were challenged and changed as a result of his efforts.

Early Interdisciplinary Career. Francis O. Schmitt ("Frank," often referred to as "FOS") was the son of second-generation German immigrants and the grandson of a Lutheran minister. Raised in a midwestern home by hardworking, innovative parents, Clara (Senniger) and Otto Franz Schmitt, Frank early on showed a strong interest in science. As a schoolboy he had great curiosity about how things, living and otherwise, worked. With his father's strong encouragement he turned toward medicine;

but it was basic biological science that was to be the focus of his professional academic life.

Schmitt earned his BA degree (1924) at Washington University and PhD in physiology (1927) at Washington University Medical School, both in St. Louis. As an undergraduate he came under the influence of cytologist Caswell Grave, with whom he published his first two papers (1924), both concerned with the coordination and regulation of ciliary movement in a mollusk.

In medical school his first mentor was Joseph Erlanger, under whose influence he moved from cytology to physiology. Working with Herbert Gasser and George Bishop as well, he participated in groundbreaking studies on the structure and function of nerves and the action potential, using newly developed x-ray diffraction and polarization optics methods as well as electrical techniques. But ever-curious and with his penchant for looking into any and all topics that caught his interest—scanning the scientific horizon with his "biological radar," as he sometimes liked to put it—he found time to investigate the structure of the cell membrane and kidney function of the mud puppy, *Necturus maculosus,* with Harvey L. White. White and he published three papers (1925). Schmitt even took a live demonstration of their techniques to the 1926 International Physiological Conference in Stockholm.

In the spring of 1927, after successfully defending his thesis ("The Conduction of the Impulse through Cold-Blooded Heart Muscle") and receiving his PhD, Schmitt married Barbara Hecker, a concert-level pianist from St. Louis. (Frank also played piano, but at a much lower level; he and Barbara often played duets together at home.)

Awarded a National Research Council fellowship, Schmitt did postdoctoral work with Gilbert Newton Lewis in the Chemistry Department at the University of California, Berkeley, on the effect of ultrasound waves on the speed of chemical reactions and on the effect of electric currents on the stability of monomolecular lipid films. He continued researching lipid films with Sir Jack Drummond at University College London. He moved to the Kaiser Wilhelm Institute for Biology in Berlin to study the metabolism of nerve fibers with Otto Warburg, and then to the Kaiser Wilhelm Institute for Medical Research in Heidelberg to continue studies with Otto Meyerhof. Schmitt's creative ideas and interest in new technology, as well as his ability to ask questions going to the heart of theoretical and experimental issues, often brought him to the attention of other top people, such as Otto Loewi and Rudolf Hoeber.

Upon his return to Washington University from Europe in 1930, Schmitt became an assistant professor of zoology and established a highly productive research program devoted to topics ranging from surface chemistry

and neurochemistry to cell ultrastructure and embryology. He and his collaborators (including importantly his younger brother Otto, a brilliant engineer, with whom he developed highly innovative instrumentation techniques) published some one hundred significant papers. Rising through the ranks, Frank eventually became professor and department head. He was an excellent and inspiring teacher who took a real interest in his students—as he always had in everyone with whom he worked.

He maintained his commitment to the importance of interdisciplinary and interpersonal interaction in research, even in informal ways. For example, he founded an informal organization, the "Axonologists," whose members were attendees at the annual American Physiology Society meeting. This group, from various institutions, consisted of scientists (few at the time) who were studying the axon and nervous transmission. He was proud of this private little society. But it did not last too long: it had to disband in 1934 when it became too large—forty-three members—and one of the members was so gauche as to use lantern slides to illustrate his talk!

From Washington to MIT. In 1941, at the invitation of the president of MIT, Karl Compton, Schmitt left Washington University to head MIT's Department of Biology and Biological Engineering. With a vision for the future of twentieth-century life-sciences research, Schmitt emphasized the molecular approach, both in his leadership of his department and in his own research, thus assuring that the 1940s and 1950s would be productive and exciting times for the life sciences at MIT. A "discovery a day" was the rule according to Jerome Gross and Carl Cori (quoted in Worden et al., 1975, p. xvii).

When Schmitt arrived at MIT, World War II had just begun. The application of the lab's findings on collagen for the treatment of burns was a great contribution to the war effort. But far beyond this practical aspect of Schmitt's department's research was the effort to understand the structure and function of biological fibers. For example, collaborating with Gross and John Highberger (1955), he undertook a systematic analysis of the in vitro reconstitution of the cross-striated fibrils from solutions of collagen molecules. Their analysis demonstrated that various supramolecular forms of collagen could be reconstituted by self-assembly; this led to the determination of the dimensions of the collagen molecule (tropocollagen) and also to the quarter-stagger hypothesis, which accounts for the observed 640-angstrom axial periodicity of the molecule. Schmitt and other colleagues (Al Rubin, Donald Pfahl, Paul Speakman, and Peter Davison) went on to isolate and sequence the non-collagen-like peptides (telopeptides) at either end of the molecule, which make it immunogenic and are critical to the process of fibrinogenesis as well as to its pathophysiology.

The work with collagen was indeed important, but much more basic science was going on in Schmitt's MIT laboratories. New techniques of electron microscopy opened new applications of this instrumentation to the life sciences. With Cecil Hall and Marie Jakus, Schmitt (1945) developed heavy-metal stains for use in electron microscopy, and with this new technique he and his colleagues were able to produce some of the earliest electronic micrographs of striated muscle fibers. They correlated this data with data obtained by Richard Bear using x-ray diffraction.

Also in Schmitt's lab during that period Jean Hanson and Hugh Huxley developed their sliding-filament model of muscle fiber contraction, James D. Robertson developed his unit membrane model of the cell membrane, and Betty Geren Uzman, prompted by observations of myelin ultrastructure, proposed the "jelly-roll" model of myelin assembly. Later, Geren and Schmitt (1980) discovered and began to characterize filamentous proteins in the axon.

Schmitt's great talents as a theoretician and a hands-on bench scientist and his ability to inspire collaborative interdisciplinary efforts of colleagues were central factors in the many achievements of the Biology Department he founded at MIT. He made it an exciting place filled with enthusiasm and overflowing with ideas. As one of his colleagues, Norman Geschwind, put it in a conversation with this author, working with Schmitt was like "trying to take a drink from a fire hydrant."

He continued to be acutely aware that the division of science into separate disciplines was an arbitrary administrative convenience that often created barriers to communication. As a trained and experienced physicist/physiologist/chemist he saw the need for a new interdisciplinary perspective that would help to find physical solutions for biological problems. Thus he became a leader in the effort to broaden and reformulate the developing field of biophysics. By its very existence, this new field would encourage the interaction of physics and biology and their ancillary fields and would also encourage the application of the methods and thinking of the physical sciences to the life sciences.

The National Institutes of Health established a Biophysics Study Section in 1955 with Schmitt as its chairman, thus officially recognizing this field. To further review and define "biophysics," Frank and colleagues organized a four-week conference inviting the major players from around with world to come to the Intensive Study Program in Biophysics held in July–August 1958 at the University of Colorado in Boulder. More than two hundred physicists, biologists, chemists, and scientists from related fields came to Boulder and presented and

attended lectures, seminars, and discussions on subjects organized hierarchically from the molecular level to the whole organism. The book that resulted—*Biophysical Science: A Study Program* (1959)—provided a conceptual and research base on which the new field could develop.

Schmitt's involvement throughout the meeting and especially in the planning and harvesting stages was a crucial factor in the success of this cross-disciplinary exchange of information. The power of this kind of program in helping establish a new field made such a strong impression on him that he would use this model again, even more successfully, to found and define the new field of "neuroscience." In 1955, Schmitt was appointed by MIT to be its second "Institute Professor." The appointment allowed him to leave his administrative responsibilities as department head of biology and to pursue his idea of a new interdisciplinary field of brain research.

Neuroscience. The brain and the nervous system had increasingly become Schmitt's primary research interest. His early work with Erlanger and Gasser in St. Louis he continued in a sense by using the giant axon of the squid to study its action potential and nerve conduction. In the Humboldt Current waters off Viña del Mar, Chile, working with the Marine Biology Station there, he found the huge squid, *Dosidicus gigas,* with axons of up to 4 millimeters in diameter. He and his team—investigators from the United States and Chile—studied both the constituents of the axoplasm and the mechanism of the action potential. Back at MIT, he conducted the research with the considerably smaller squid, *Loligo pealii,* which was found in the ocean off Rhode Island and Cape Cod, Massachusetts, and which he had earlier worked on while doing postgraduate work at the Marine Biology Laboratory at Woods Hole in the late 1930s. (He had worked there with the British zoologist John Z. Young, who introduced him to the squid axon preparation.) Bringing the squid back to MIT quickly and in good shape required the use of a refrigerated truck, high speed, and watchfulness for police radar. Stories of adventures en route became legendary.

Other creatures, such as mice, lobsters, and cockroaches; and other topics, such as axonal flow and transport and neurolathyrism, were also part of the lab's activities. But none was more interesting and productive than the squid and its axon.

Schmitt's ultimate goal in studying the neuron was to understand the function of the human brain and higher brain function—the mind itself. The invertebrate nervous system was a good place to start, but it was only a start. How does the human brain not only sense the world and produce appropriate responses to it—sensation, perception, emotion, movement—but also learn, remember, use language, and think? Drawing on his earlier experience with the Biophysics Study Section and the creation and development of the field of biophysics, and sensing that the rapid advances in many fields provided the basis for a new multidisciplinary approach to brain and mind, Schmitt conceived of a goal-oriented effort that would do the same thing for this infinitely more complex area—brain and nervous system—that it did for biophysics.

On a trip to Europe in 1959, Schmitt sounded out two physicists, Manfred Eigen (Göttingen) and Werner Heisenberg (Munich) about his idea for an interdisciplinary group that would look at the "physics of the mind." Eigen was enthusiastic about the idea and expressed interest in being involved. Heisenberg expressed "uncertainty," and urged Frank to examine carefully the "correctness" of his biophysical and biochemical hypotheses about brain structure and function before launching such an organization.

Accordingly, Schmitt organized two seminars in the area at MIT in 1960 and 1961. The first was on fast transfer reactions and stemmed from Eigen's Nobel Prize work. The other, on macromolecular specificity and biological memory, brought together many of the leaders in the field of brain research at that time; this resulted in a book by that name (1962). The "modest" goal of this seminar and book, as quoted from its introduction, was to "help bridge the gap between physical, chemical, and structural studies of the brain on the one hand, and behavioral, psychological, and psychiatric aspects on the other." The talks and discussions raised more questions than answers, of course, but were a rousing success.

Now convinced of the practicality of the interdisciplinary neurobiological research effort he was planning, Frank contacted a small group of outstanding scientists from around the world representing various of the physical and life sciences. These were all people he knew or had worked with, who interacted well, and who were interested in understanding the brain. He arranged an organizing meeting, which was held on 1 February 1962 in New York at the apartment of friends, Louis and Genie Marron. Louis Marron was a wealthy industrialist and sport fisherman who had helped Schmitt gather giant squid in the waters off Chile.

The focus of the informal meeting was to explore the status of the biophysics and biochemistry of "mental processes." Schmitt presented his proposal that, in order to pursue this Promethean quest for understanding the mind/brain, it would be necessary to create a new kind of organization that would enable the productive interaction of many scientists from different disciplines all interacting to achieve this goal. It would be like the program which had defined the new field of biophysics, but on a much larger scale. He explained that the goal of understanding the brain/mind was important for its own sake but also for

improving human abilities, preventing and treating nervous system malfunctions and diseases, and understanding and controlling the human penchant for violence, both on the personal and the broad scale (we were in the midst of the Cold War at the time).

With his great enthusiasm, Schmitt was able to persuade these eminent and productive scientists, accustomed to pursuing their own personal goals and interests, to join together in this idealistic "mission" of solving the most difficult of all mysteries, the workings of the brain and mind. They agreed to form a governing board, the "Associates," to serve as the guiding council of the new organization. First called the Mensa (mind) Program, the group finally decided on the word *neuroscience,* even though some thought the word smacked too much of neurology and did not explicitly bring in other dimensions: mind, behavior, and so forth. But the name stuck. And so began the Neurosciences Research Program (NRP).

NRP officially and administratively remained part of MIT, and Schmitt maintained his institute professorship. But he located the new organization off-campus, joining the American Academy of Arts and Sciences at the lovely Brandegee Estate in Brookline, near Cambridge and MIT. The new headquarters were big enough for several meeting rooms, offices, a library, and a spacious dining room where the notable scientists from around the world who had been invited to present their ideas and findings could be entertained. Schmitt felt that because these invited scientists were the stars of the science world, if one treated them like stars they would perform like stars.

At the first meeting at the new headquarters, August 1962, Schmitt's talk was typical of the way he could present a practical course of action wrapped in his own infectious enthusiasm:

> It is the aim and wish of our group to attempt a synthesis over many interstitial areas of biology and physics and chemistry and neurology and behavioral science … to understand basic matters concerning how the brain functions, questions of mental processes, the mind, if you will.… Much of the functioning will eventually depend on the molecular and macromolecular machinery … and much that has been learned in molecular genetics will apply also to molecular neurology … (excerpted from informal notes taken at the meeting)

So in one brief informal statement, he was able to hint at all manner of new directions brain research might go, touching on an amalgam of recent breakthroughs in physics as well as molecular biology and neurology, which might possibly provide the mechanisms underlying brain function.

To make sure that the "dries" (scientists involved primarily in behavior) would be well represented, Frank recruited Gardner Quarton, an outstanding Harvard and Massachusetts General Hospital psychiatrist, to be program director of the NRP and to help oversee its science programs and administration of science staff.

A major effort of the NRP from 1962 to 1982 became the planning and staging of work sessions, two- or three-day meetings of twenty to twenty-five experts in a particular subject area, a "hot topic" that was judged to be central to brain research and which needed an interdisciplinary information boost. With the assistance of staff scientists, visiting scientists (including such luminaries as John Szentagothai, Eric Lenneberg, Detlev Ploog, Mac Edds, and Bob Galambos), and advice from the NRP associates, many of the hot topics of neuroscience were defined and explored, many to become the subjects of one of the four to six work sessions per year. Many of these work session subjects have now become the day-to-day areas of neuroscience research: the synapse, neurotransmitters, cell receptors, axoplasmic transport, sleep, sensory transduction, schizophrenia, language development, and so forth, but at the time they were underdeveloped areas, relatively unstudied.

The work session results were published in the *Neurosciences Research Program Bulletin,* a 100–150 page monograph series created by Schmitt's new communications director, Ted Melnechuck. It was widely distributed to libraries and laboratories (at no charge for the first ten years) and also helped make this new science a reality.

At the planning sessions and during the work sessions, Frank was indeed, in Gerald Edelman's words, the ultimate "scientist impresario" (quoted in Worden et al., 1975, p. 73). He organized and supervised the NRP staff people working on the planning session; and then, when the decision was finally made to go with the topic as a work session, helped program the coverage of each invited participant so that each presentation would elide with and not interfere with another's presentations. At the work session itself, he helped introduce each section to ensure that the key theoretical and experimental issues would be covered; and then helped the work session chair orchestrate the interactions and discussions at the concluding session.

After the work sessions he worked with the NRP editorial staff who prepared the summaries of presentations and discussions to be sent to the work session chair and participants, and which would be the basis for the eventual *NRP Bulletin* manuscript. He insisted that each *Bulletin* fairly represent each participant, give credit to each, and not allow the work of established "stars" to outshine the work of the less-well known newcomers to the field. There were well over one hundred work sessions from

1963 to 1982, and eighty *NRP Bulletins* were published and widely distributed during those twenty years.

Schmitt was a perfectionist, and his work habits were, to say the least, unusual. He worked, literally, day and night. After a full day at the Biology Department, and, later, at the NRP Center, he would go home for dinner, perhaps relax a bit with music, play duets with Barbara— or maybe just listen to her play—and then retire to bed at 10 or 11. He would be up again at 4 or 5 a.m., work until breakfast, and then off to the NRP. When the staff arrived, the day's work would have been arranged and he would be fully prepared for discussions and program planning. A short nap at lunchtime would revive him for a vigorous afternoon of work.

The other major NRP program involved a concerted effort to describe the contours and content of neuroscience by means of intensive study programs (ISPs). Using the model of the earlier Biophysics Study Program, which had helped create the field of biophysics, Schmitt's NRP staff and NRP associates programmed and staged four, three- to four-week "Neuroscience Intensive Study Programs" from 1967 to 1977. These were also held at the Boulder campus of the University of Colorado and involved a faculty of more than two hundred specially invited scientific experts to cover in lectures, symposia, and discussions the primary areas of neuroscience. Fifty selected junior scientists were also on hand at each ISP to learn more about the elements of neuroscience and to join in the formal and informal discussions.

The goal of these ISPs was to define clearly the parameters of neuroscience and to announce to the world that this new field of neuroscience had arrived, that it was, indeed, an interdisciplinary science, and that it would eventually be able to confront the age-old ultimate question of both philosophy and science, how does the mind/brain work. The four cocktail-table-size books, more than nine hundred pages each (the first two published by Rockefeller University Press, the last two by MIT Press) had an enormous effect on the world of science, especially on newly arriving neuroscientists. They are still in use in schools and colleges around the world in the early twenty-first century.

All this innovation and hard work were worthwhile. The work sessions, *NRP Bulletins,* and the Boulder books—the four massive *Neuroscience Study Programs*— plus the other NRP books and journal articles, did indeed play a significant role in the creation of this important worldwide multi/interdisciplinary science, involving broad basic as well as clinical/medical relevance. Eight years after Schmitt began the Neurosciences Research Program, the Society for Neuroscience was established. It has grown to more than thirty-five thousand members. Of the first twelve presidents of the society, ten were or had been

NRP associates. Frank was justifiably proud of the NRP and of the influence of this "invisible college" that, in the twenty-five years of his involvement, had over three thousand alumni, most of whom were or were later to become the leaders in the field. Several Nobel laureates were in their ranks.

Thus, at the age of fifty-nine, Schmitt had embarked on a new major program, perhaps the most ambitious of his career. With enthusiasm and vision he set the course for the NRP that it followed for the next twenty years: interdisciplinary attacks on neuroscience questions, basic and clinical, staging of interdisciplinary meetings and comprehensive study programs (three-day work sessions and three- to four-week ISPs), recruitment of notable scientists and junior scientists from various fields into neuroscience. An example of one of his recruitment efforts was the neuroanatomy course Schmitt staged at MIT in 1965 for scientists (including several Nobelists) from outside fields who were interested in knowing more about the brain and might even get involved in brain research. The course was taught by such notables as Walle Nauta, Sanford Palay, Robert Galambos, and Jay Angevine.

When Quarton left to become director of the University of Michigan Mental Health Research Institute, Schmitt recruited Fred Worden, psychiatry professor at the University of California, Los Angeles, to be program director. Later, when Schmitt turned seventy and was no longer allowed by MIT and National Institutes of Health rules to be principal investigator, this multitalented neuroscientist took over as the NRP director. But Schmitt stayed on as "foundation scientist," solemnly promising he would not interfere, or at least *try* not to interfere, with Worden's new leadership. He still continued to put in his long work days and nights, perhaps spending more time with staff scientists and the new NRP program directors Mac Edds and Barry Smith.

Other Activities. During his long and active life Schmitt made many important contributions to science, but beyond this he was a husband and father deeply devoted to his wife Barbara, and children David, Robert, and Marian. Music and religion always remained important in his world. Born and brought up a Lutheran, he was a regular churchgoer, active in his later years in the Congregational Church. Through the years he worked to bring the separate worlds of science and religion together and organized gatherings of scientists and theologians to try to reconcile the separate worlds of faith and objective science.

As if all these activities were not enough, Schmitt served for more than forty years as a trustee of the Massachusetts General Hospital and of the McLean Hospital (Harvard Medical School's affiliated mental hospital). At Massachusetts General he was a charter member of the

Committee on Research (from 1947) and organized the Scientific Advisory Committee (from 1948). Although he had turned away from clinical medicine himself to work in the basic biological sciences, he never lost sight of the fact that knowledge gained in basic science should be made available to help sick and suffering human beings as part of what he called the practice of "wholesale medicine." He contributed greatly to medicine, not only with his own discoveries, but also through his training of many MDs at various levels of their careers.

Frank Schmitt was a unique combination of theoretician and experimental scientist plus leader, organizer, inspirer, and helper of others. His practical focus was the molecular and even the submolecular. But his deepest interest was in how the brain worked to produce higher brain function and mind, and, ultimately, human spirit and soul.

BIBLIOGRAPHY

A more complete list may be found in Schmitt's autobiography, The Never-Ceasing Search *(1990).*

WORKS BY SCHMITT

With C. Grave. "A Mechanism for the Coordination and Regulation of the Movement of Cilia of Epithelia." *Science* 60 (1924): 246–248.

With H. L. White. "Observations on Kidney Function in *Necturus maculosus.*" *Science* 62 (1925): 334.

"The Conduction of the Impulse through Cold-Blooded Heart Muscle." PhD diss., Washington University, St. Louis, 1927.

"On the Oxidative Nature of the Nerve Impulse." *Science* 72 (1930): 583–584.

With Otto H. Schmitt. "A Vacuum Tube Method of Temperature Control." *Science* 73 (1931): 289–290.

"The Oxygen Consumption of Stimulated Nerve." *American Journal of Physiology* 104 (1933): 303–319.

With Richard S. Bear and G. L. Clark. "X-ray Diffraction Studies on Nerve." *Radiology* 25 (1935): 131.

With Richard S. Bear and John Z. Young. "Some Physical and Chemical Properties of the Axis Cylinder of the Giant Axons of the Squid, *Loligo pealii.*" *Biological Bulletin* 71 (1936): 402.

———. "The Sheath Components of the Giant Nerve Fibres of the Squid." *Proceedings of the Royal Society of London, Series B, Biological Sciences* 123 (1937): 496–505.

"Optical Studies of the Molecular Organization of Living Systems." *Journal of Applied Physics* 9 (1938): 109–117.

With Otto H. Schmitt. "Partial Excitation and Variable Conduction in the Squid Giant Axon." *Journal of Physiology* 98 (1940): 26–46.

With Cecil E. Hall and Marie A. Jakus. "The Structure of Certain Muscle Fibrils as Revealed by the Use of Electron Stains." *Journal of Applied Physics* 16 (1945): 459–465.

With Richard S. Bear, Cecil E. Hall, and Marie A. Jakus. "Electron Microscope and X-ray Diffraction Studies of

Muscle Structure." *Annals of the New York Academy of Science* 47 (1947): 799.

With Jerome Gross. "The Structure of Human Skin Collagen as Studied with the Electron Microscope." *Journal of Experimental Medicine* 88 (1948): 555–568.

With Betty B. Geren. "The Fibrous Structure of the Nerve Axon in Relation to the Localization of 'Neurotubules.'" *Journal of Experimental Medicine* 91 (1950): 499–504.

With Jerome Gross and John H. Highberger. "Tropocollagen and the Properties of Fibrous Collagen." *Experimental Cell Research,* Supplement 3 (1955): 326–334.

"Macromolecular Interaction Patterns in Biological Systems." *Proceedings of the American Philosophical Society* 100 (1956): 476–486.

With Paul Doty, et al. "Symposium on Biomolecular Organization and Life-Processes." Special Issue, *Proceedings of the National Academy of Sciences of the United States of America* 42 (1956): 780–830.

With Melvin J. Glimcher and Alan J. Hodge. "Macromolecular Aggregation States in Relation to Mineralization: The Collagen-Hydroxyapatite System as Studied in Vitro." *Proceedings of the National Academy of Sciences of the United States of America* 43 (1957): 860–867.

With John Lawrence Oncley, R. C. Williams, M. D. Rosenberg, et al., eds. *Biophysical Science: A Study Program.* New York: J. Wiley & Sons, 1959.

Editor. *Fast Fundamental Transfer Processes in Aqueous Biomolecular Systems.* Cambridge, MA, 1960. Lecture Series. MIT Department of Biology.

Editor. *Macromolecular Specificity and Biological Memory.* Cambridge, MA: MIT Press, 1962.

With Albert L. Rubin, et al. "Tropocollagen: Significance of Protease-Induced Alterations." *Science* 139 (1963): 37–39.

"Molecular and Ultrastructural Correlates of Function in Neurons, Neuronal Nets and the Brain. *Neurosciences Research Program Bulletin (NRP Bulletin)* 2, no. 3 (1964): 43–75.

With P. F. Davison. "Chemical, Structural, and Immunological Studies of Nerve Axon Protein." *Berichte der Bunsen-Gesellschaft für physikalische Chemie* 68 (1964): 887–889.

"The Physical Basis of Life and Learning." *Science* 140 (1965): 931–936.

With Theodore Melnechuk, et al., eds. *Neurosciences Research Symposium Summaries.* Vol. l. Cambridge, MA: MIT Press, 1966.

With Gardner C. Quarton and Theodore Melnechuk, eds. *The Neurosciences: A Study Program.* New York: Rockefeller University Press, 1967.

With Theodore Melnechuk, Gardner C. Quarton, and George Adelman, eds. *Neurosciences Research Symposium Summaries.* Vol. 2. Cambridge, MA: MIT Press, 1967.

"The Divine Spiral: Eternal Verities in a Rapidly Changing World." *Messenger* 7 (1968): 4–10. New England Lutheran Federation.

With Frederick E. Samson Jr., eds. "Neuronal Fibrous Proteins." *Neurosciences Research Program Bulletin* 6 (1968): 113–219.

With F. E. Samson Jr., eds. "Brain Cell Microenvironment." *Neurosciences Research Program Bulletin* 7, no. 4 (1969): 279–417.

"Molecular Neurobiology: An Interpretive Survey." In *The Neurosciences: Second Study Program,* edited by Francis O. Schmitt. New York: Rockefeller University Press, 1970.

With Floyd E. Bloom and Leslie L. Iversen, eds. "Macromolecules in Synaptic Function." *Neurosciences Research Program Bulletin* 8, no. 4 (1970): 325–455.

With L. C. Mokrasch, eds. "Myelin: A Report of a Work Session." *Neurosciences Research Program Bulletin* 9, no. 4 (1970): 439–598.

With Frederick G. Worden, eds. *The Neurosciences: Third Study Program.* New York: Rockefeller University Press, 1973.

With Diane M. Schneider and Donald M. Crothers, eds. *Functional Linkage in Biomolecular Systems.* New York: Raven Press, 1975.

With Parvati Dev and Barry H. Smith. "Electrotonic Processing of Information by Brain Cells." *Science* 193 (1976): 114–120.

With Frederick G. Worden, eds. *The Neurosciences: Fourth Study Program.* Cambridge, MA: MIT Press, 1979.

With Stephanie J. Bird and Floyd E. Bloom, eds. *Molecular Genetic Neuroscience.* New York: Raven Press, 1982.

"Molecular Genetic Neuroscience: A New Hybrid." *IBRO News* 11 (1983): 7–12.

"Molecular Regulators of Brain Function: A New View." *Neuroscience* 13 (1984): 991–1001.

"Adventures in Molecular Biology." *Annual Review of Biophysics and Biophysical Chemistry* 14 (1985): 1–22.

The Never-Ceasing Search. Philadelphia: American Philosophical Society, 1990. Autobiography.

OTHER SOURCES

Adelman, George, and Barry Smith. "Francis Otto Schmitt, November 23, 1903–October 3, 1995." *Biographical Memoirs.* Vol. 75. Washington, DC: National Academy of Sciences, 1998. Available from http://www.nap.edu/ readingroom/books/biomems/fschmitt.pdf.

Worden, Frederick G., Judith P. Swazey, and George Aldelman, eds. *Neurosciences: Paths of Discovery.* Cambridge, MA: MIT Press, 1975.

George Adelman
Barry H. Smith

SCHNEIRLA, THEODORE CHRISTIAN

(*b.* Bay City, Michigan, 23 July 1902; *d.* New York, New York, 20 August 1968), *comparative psychology, ethology, instinct, learning, epigenesis, ants.*

Schneirla was a comparative psychologist who made important empirical and theoretical contributions to the study of animal behavior. His research focused on the behavior of army ants. He was a critic of both behaviorist learning theory and ethological instinct theory, arguing for the necessity of an epigenetic approach to behavioral development, which emphasizes the joint action of genetic and environmental influences, and an appreciation of differences in the levels of organization to be found in the animal kingdom.

Career. T. C. Schneirla grew up in a farming community in Michigan, near Saginaw Bay. He attended public schools, and then the University of Michigan in Ann Arbor. He was musically inclined, playing trumpet in the university band, and maintaining active engagement with music throughout his life. He also became adept at typing and shorthand, a skill he later put to good use as a means of making field notes of behavioral observations.

Schneirla completed his BS degree in 1924, and an MS in psychology the following year. He stayed on at Michigan as a graduate student, working on the behavior of ants under the guidance of John F. Shepard. Thus began the interest that remained the main subject of his research for the rest of his life. In 1926 he married a fellow student, Leone Warner, with whom he fathered two children. The couple spent the summer of 1927 in Oklahoma, where Schneirla had a university teaching job. In 1928 they moved to New York University (NYU), where Schneirla finished his PhD thesis: "Learning and Orientation in Ants."

He taught at NYU for the next three years, and then got a National Research Council fellowship, which enabled him to spend a year working with Karl Lashley in Chicago. There also he began a close friendship with Norman Maier, which eventuated in their writing a book together: *Principles of Animal Psychology* (1935). This text presented a radical approach for its time in that it took the whole animal kingdom, from protozoa to people, as its province, and emphasized how behavioral capacities relate to body design (e.g., symmetry) and the kinds of sensory, neural, and motor equipment possessed. It remains a classic of the animal behavior literature. In 1932 Schneirla returned to NYU, where he continued as a member of the psychology faculty for the rest of his life. In 1932 Schneirla went on a field trip to study ants in the wild on Barro Colorado Island in Panama. This was the first of many such travels to Panama, Mexico, and the southwest United States.

In 1943 Frank Beach, curator of the Department of Animal Behavior at the American Museum of Natural History, invited Schneirla to join him as associate curator. When Beach moved to a professorship at Yale four years later, Schneirla replaced him as curator. However, he continued at NYU as an adjunct professor, teaching courses in comparative psychology, behavioral development, and thinking.

From early on in his career Schneirla involved himself with issues of public concern. For instance he campaigned for support of the government side during the Spanish Civil War and sought to organize relief for out-of-work psychologists during the Depression years of the thirties, activity contributing to the establishment of the Society for the Psychological Study of Social Issues.

For more than twenty years Schneirla suffered from unremitting ringing in the ears (tinnitus), and had to cope with other disabling contingencies. Nevertheless, he maintained a-high level of productivity, both in research and theoretical writing. He also influenced the field of comparative psychology through his teaching, doctoral supervision, and collaborative involvement. Among those he taught or worked with were Lester Aronson, Herbert Birch, Daniel Lehrman, Jay Rosenblatt, William Tavolga, Ethel Tobach, Howard Topoff, and Gerald Turkewitz. One of his last accomplishments was the creation and design of the Behavioral Alcove in the Hall of Invertebrates at the museum.

Research. Unlike many of the animal psychologists of his day, Schneirla can be said to have been truly comparative. His interests ranged over the whole animal kingdom. He also contrasted with the "rat runners" in choosing to concentrate his research efforts on an invertebrate: the army ant *Eciton burchelli*. Of this work a survey of ant biology had this to say: "it was T. C. Schneirla … who, by conducting patient studies over virtually his entire career, first unravelled the complex behavior of … *Eciton*. His results were confirmed and greatly extended in rich studies conducted by C. W. Rettenmeyer" (Hölldobler and Wilson, 1990, p. 573).

These ants live in groups consisting of between 150,000 and 750,000 individuals of different castes. The "armies" alternate between "statary" and "nomadic" phases. During the statary phase the ants form temporary nests or "bivouacs" by having numerous of their number construct an outer shell with their own linked bodies to contain and shelter the single fertile queen and her brood. Every six weeks or so, during the statary phase, the queen lays upwards of 100,000 eggs, which are tended by sterile female worker ants. Hatching of the eggs initiates the nomadic phase, when raiding parties fan out from the colony in search of prey that they can overwhelm by their numbers. The brood and queen are transported as the rest of the colony trails after the host of hunters. Pupation of the larvae, and hence lowering of the food requirements, returns the colony to quiescence.

Schneirla showed how this cycle depends upon an intricate system of reciprocal influences between colony members and the brood, which transcends the limited cognitive capacities of any individual ant, or any simple conception of their collective sum: "The cyclic pattern … is self re-aroused in a feedback fashion, the product of a reciprocal relationship between queen and colony functions, not of a timing mechanism endogenous to the queen" (Schneirla, 1957, p. 129). Nevertheless he eschewed the vague anthropomorphic or supraorganismic explanations of his predecessors. He painstakingly charted a nested hierarchy of feedback loops acting homeostatically to adjust microclimate within a bivouac, and dynamically to meet mounting nutritional needs by launching the hunting frenzy (Schneirla, 1940, 1957, 1971).

Alongside this involvement with cyclicity in the lives of army ants, Schneirla maintained the interest in ant learning that he had inherited from Shepard. For instance he compared the performances of ants and rats when presented with mazes of comparable difficulty. He was able to show that the two species deal with the task quite differently, in accordance with the differences in the kinds of sensory and neural equipment they bring to bear on it. Hence to speak of "learning" here is to label an outcome rather than to refer to a shared mechanism or process, contra the generality of "laws of learning" assumed by most behaviorist learning theory (Schneirla, 1960).

Schneirla made comparable comparisons of the kinds of factors governing social organization in insects and mammals (e.g., Schneirla and Rosenblatt, 1961). In insects, by and large, social interaction is determined by physiological response to stimuli, as in trophallaxis (passing of alimentary fluid between colony members), rather than individual relationships. Such systems can be described as "biosocial." In contrast mammalian social relations involve expectations based on experience, bonding of the sort entailing individual recognition, adjustment according to learned status, a system describable as "psychosocial." Example for the mammalian case was provided by a study of behavioral development in kittens, which Schneirla undertook with Jay Rosenblatt (Schneirla and Rosenblatt, 1961, 1963; Rosenblatt, 1971). They found a succession of phases, intertwining growth changes and experience, constituting an epigenetic progression in which direction was localized neither in an internally situated program, nor in dictation by environmental contingency. This kind of view of development derived from and gave support to Schneirla's theoretical position in comparative psychology.

Theory and Criticism. Fundamental to Schneirla's theorizing was the concept of levels of organization as applying in both evolutionary and developmental contexts. He maintained that there are qualitative differences between animals of different kinds in their morphological design,

Theodore Christian Schneirla. *Ants being tested for their learning ability by Theodore Schneirla at the Museum of Natural History.* NINA LEEN/TIME LIFE PICTURES GETTY IMAGES

neural functioning, and behavioral capacities. So, for example, an understanding of how an animal locates itself in its world (indeed the nature of that world as it exists for the animal) depends upon what sensory capacities it possesses, the manner in which it processes the sensory input, and the means by which it translates the results of the processing into movement or action. Compared with how a ciliate protozoan finds its way about, a planarian flatworm is in another league; but the flatworm, in turn, is put in the shade by comparison with a bee. The radial symmetry and diffuse neural network of a coelenterate polyp confine the creature to a spare behavioral world, which is a mere speck in the universe opened up by the bilateral symmetry and segmented centralized nervous system of an annelid worm (Maier and Schneirla, 1935). The radical contrasts between phyletic (evolutionary) levels of organization oppose the indiscriminate use of terms such as *learning* and *instinct*, and both anthropomorphic and zoomorphic suppositions riding on notions of continuity comparable to the venerable "great chain of Being" (e.g., Lovejoy, 1936).

Similarly Schneirla viewed behavioral development as involving transitions between progressively more sophisticated and qualitatively distinct levels of attainment—such as reflex, motivational drive, trial-and-error learning, intelligence—rather than a seamless continuum of additive assembly. But he also took an epigenetic position that vigorously opposed talk in terms of genetic programs or instinct versus learning. For him developmental processes interweave genetic and environmental contributions so intimately that they cannot be separated in the changes due to growth, maturation, and experience. At any point in behavioral ontogeny the interaction is not between what is innately given and what is externally imposed, but between what has already been jointly synthesized and the new circumstances, which (at least to some extent) are constituted by the achieved capacities of the growing individual.

Another important strand of Schneirla's thinking, woven through the texture of levels of organization in both their phyletic and developmental manifestations, was his notion of "biphasic approach-withdrawal processes." According to this idea animals generally tend to move toward mild stimulation and retreat from strong stimulation. In its simplest form, as exemplified by protozoa, the movements are forced responses, comparable to reflexes. In more advanced forms, both evolutionary and developmental, the movements have come under the control of the animal, so that approach has graduated to seeking, and withdrawal to avoidance. Schneirla deployed this conception liberally. For instance he saw it as exemplified by the vanguard column of his nomadic ants, propelled forward by the intensity of stimulation from the colony, reeled back in when stimulation is lessened by distance.

Sometimes his construals stretched credibility, as when he argued against the claim of Konrad Lorenz and Nikolaas Tinbergen that certain species of ground-nesting birds have a built in "bird of prey" detector which responds to birdlike silhouettes having short necks and long tails. Schneirla (1954) proposed that the short-necked silhouettes presented more abrupt (= intense) stimulus onset than the long-necked shapes, and that could account for the fleeing response. (It turned out that both interpretations were wrong. One of Lorenz's associates showed that familiarity was the key: short-necked birds were rare in the circumstances of the study.) On occasion circular reasoning could creep in, as when intensity of stimulation was judged on the basis of direction of response.

Be that as it may, Schneirla maintained a consistently tough-minded stance, adhering to Lloyd Morgan's canon according to which interpretations of animal behavior should assume the minimal psychological capacity consistent with observation. He was opposed to vitalism in all

its forms, and to failure to appreciate the full variety of behavioral phenomena displayed by the animal kingdom. In this he was a psychologist worthy to be called comparative.

Aftermath. T. C. Schneirla died while still engaged on a number of projects, both in research and on theoretical themes. His contribution to knowledge of the biology of ants is well recognized by experts in the field. His more theoretical writings are not as well known as they should be, partly, perhaps, because they can be hard going for the less dedicated reader. He worked mightily to get down on paper exactly what he had in mind to say, but the results could leave something to be desired in terms of clarity and elegance.

Nevertheless, Schneirla's ideas have been kept alive by a small number of devoted disciples, Ethel Tobach and Gary Greenberg being chief among them. They inaugurated a series of conferences honoring his life and work, the proceedings of which have been published in book form (Greenberg and Tobach, 1984–1990). Among the more widely read of Schneirla's writings is the article he contributed to the 1958 edition of the *Encyclopaedia Britannica*. It brought to a generation of readers the view that "on different levels, comparable biological factors promoting specialization can differ in their developmental consequences, according to phyletic differences."

BIBLIOGRAPHY

A more comprehensive compilation can be found in Aronson et al., 1970.

WORKS BY SCHNEIRLA

With N. R. F. Maier. *Principles of Animal Psychology.* New York: McGraw-Hill, 1935.

"Further Studies on the Army-Ant Behavior Pattern: Mass-Organization in the Swarm Raiders." *Journal of Comparative Psychology* 29 (1940): 401–460.

"The Nature of Ant Learning, II: The Intermediate Stage of Segmental Maze Adjustment." *Journal of Comparative Psychology* 35 (1943): 149–176.

With G. Piel. "The Army Ant." *Scientific American* 178 (1948): 16–23.

"Levels in the Psychological Capacities of Animals." In *Philosophy for the Future: The Quest for Modern Materialism,* edited by R. W. Sellars, V. J. McGill, and M. Farber. New York: Macmillan, 1949. The first full and explicit statement of Schneirla's views on levels of organization.

"Interrelationships of the 'Innate' and the 'Acquired' in Instinctive Behavior." In *L'instinct dans le comportement des animaux et de l'homme,* edited by P.-P. Grasse. Paris: Masson, 1956. A paper delivered at a conference of ethologists and comparative psychologists, sponsored by the Singer-Polignac Foundation in Paris in the wake of D. S. Lehrman's critique of ethological instinct theory.

"The Concept of Development in Comparative Psychology." In *The Concept of Development,* edited by D. B. Harris. Minneapolis: University of Minnesota Press, 1957.

"Psychology, Comparative." *Encyclopaedia Britannica,* vol. 18, edited by Walter Yust. Chicago: William Benton, 1958.

"An Evolutionary and Developmental Theory of Biphasic Processes Underlying Approach and Withdrawal." In *Nebraska Symposium on Motivation 7,* edited by M. R. Jones. Lincoln: University of Nebraska Press, 1959. The major statement of Schneirla's approach-withdrawal theory.

"L'Apprentissage et la Question du Conflit chez la Fourmi: Comparaison avec le Rat." *Journal du Psychologie Normal et Pathologique* 57 (1960): 11–44.

With J. S. Rosenblatt. "Behavioral Organization and Genesis of the Social Bond in Insects and Mammals." *American Journal of Orthopsychiatry* 31 (1961): 223–253.

———. "'Critical Periods' in the Development of Behavior." *Science* 139 (1963): 1110–1115.

"Aspects of Stimulation and Organization in Approach/Withdrawal Processes Underlying Vertebrate Behavioral Development." *Advances in the Study of Behavior* 1 (1965): 1–74. Schneirla's last extended discussion of his approach-withdrawal theory applied to behavioral development.

Army Ants: A Study in Social Organization, edited by Howard Topoff. San Francisco: W.H. Freeman, 1971.

OTHER SOURCES.

Aronson, L. R., E. Tobach, D. S. Lehrman, et al., eds. *Development and Evolution of Behavior: Essays in Memory of T. C. Schneirla.* San Francisco: Freeman, 1970.

Aronson, L. R., E. Tobach, J. S. Rosenblatt, et al., eds. *Selected Writings of T. C. Schneirla.* San Francisco: Freeman, 1972.

Burkhardt, R. W. *Patterns of Behavior: Konrad Lorenz, Niko Tinbergen, and the Founding of Ethology.* Chicago: University of Chicago Press, 2004.

Dewsbury, D. A. *Comparative Psychology in the Twentieth Century.* Stroudsburg, PA: Hutchinson, 1984.

Greenberg, G., and E. Tobach, eds. *T. C. Schneirla Conference Series,* vols. 1–4. Hillsdale, NJ: Erlbaum, 1984–1990.

Hölldobler, Bert, and Edward O. Wilson. *The Ants.* Cambridge, MA: Harvard University Press, 1990.

Lehrman, D. S. "A Critique of Konrad Lorenz's Theory of Instinctive Behavior." *Quarterly Review of Biology* 28 (1953): 337–363.

Lovejoy, A. O. *The Great Chain of Being: A Study of the History of an Idea.* New York: McGraw-Hill, 1936.

Rosenblatt, J. S. "Suckling and Home Orientation in the Kitten: A Comparative Developmental Study." In *The Biopsychology of Development,* edited by E. Tobach, L. R. Aronson, and Evelyn Shaw. New York: Academic Press, 1971.

Colin Beer

SCHOTT, PAUL GERHARD (*b.* Tschirma, Germany, 15 August 1866; *d.* Hamburg, Germany, 15 January 1961), *oceanography.*

Schott devoted his life to the world's oceans. His vast knowledge enabled him to understand the oceans as a unique system with regional distinctions and to communicate his insights to the learned public. For decades he was considered the preeminent German oceanographer, and he was honored by numerous national societies in Europe and abroad.

Education. Schott grew up in a small village, where his father was the schoolmaster. He entered the nearby university in Jena to study geography and history in preparation for a career as a teacher in secondary schools. His mother was a friend of the wife of the famous Ernst Abbe—professor at the university and inventor of optical lenses and cofounder of the company Carl-Zeiss-Jena—so Schott lived with the Abbes during this period. Through this private connection he met important scientists such as Hermann von Helmholtz, philosopher and man of science; and politicians such as August Bebel, founder of the German Social Democratic Party. Such encounters had a lasting influence on him. In 1887 he continued his studies in Berlin with Ferdinand von Richthofen, who later founded the Institut und Museum für Meereskunde (Institute and Museum of Marine Science). He finished his studies in 1891 with a thesis on surface temperature and currents in East Asian waters, for which he had evaluated the data in logbooks of trading vessels collected at the German Hydrographic Office (Deutsche Seewarte) in Hamburg.

Scientific Career. To honor Schott's dissertation, Richthofen and president of the Hydrographic Office, Georg Neumayer, arranged a one-year scholarship funded by the Prussian Ministry of Culture, which included a free ticket for all sailing vessels of the shipping company R. C. Rickmers in Bremen. Schott made extensive use of this offer and conducted observations in the Atlantic, Indian, and Pacific oceans in 1891–1892, choosing different routes to cover as large an area as possible. This voyage took him an entire year. At the age of twenty-seven he moved to Hamburg to take up a permanent position at the Hydrographic Office, where he remained until his retirement in 1931.

Through his considerable publication activity on oceanic matters, Schott soon became a well-known specialist in oceanography. He was asked to participate in the German Deep-Sea Expedition with the steamer *Valdivia* in 1898–1899 to the Atlantic and Indian oceans, initiated by the zoologist Carl Chun from Breslau (who later moved to Leipzig). Schott's volume on the scientific results was honored by the Gesellschaft für Erdkunde zu Berlin (Society of Geography of Berlin), with the Karl Ritter Medal in silver. In the following years he was invited to numerous places in Germany and other European countries to talk about the *Valdivia* Expedition, and he met the leading scientists in this field.

After publishing his book on the geography of the entire Atlantic Ocean, unprecedented in its content, the Hydrographic Office created a special division of marine science for him to supervise. In his new position as chief hydrographer, his obligation was to supervise the oceanographic work of German survey vessels all over the world, including the evaluation of the observations. World War I brought about a complete change in focus of his activities. While he had dealt before with the ocean as a medium of public interest, especially with respect to seafaring, he now was involved in confidential observations to serve German submarine operations. The focus changed back to civilian purposes after the war, when the range of observations was restricted to the North and Baltic seas.

From the start of his official duties in Hamburg, Schott engaged himself in academic teaching, which he continued until his retirement. First he participated in the public program of general lectures in all scientific disciplines, and he taught at the University of Hamburg from the beginning of its founding in 1919. He was appointed a professor there in 1921. As a consequence of his initiative, a chair and an institute of oceanography were established at the new university.

Scientific Reputation. Up to the mid-nineteenth century, knowledge of the world's oceans was very fragmentary. This changed rapidly in 1853, when—following a proposal by U.S. naval officer and hydrographer Matthew Fountain Maury—it was internationally agreed upon to take standardized observations on trading vessels and to collect them at national hydrographic offices. As a student, Schott had been the first in Germany to use these data for his thesis, and during his one-year stay in Hamburg he derived a picture of the surface current system in East Asian waters by calculating the daily drift of ships between their positions at noon. While doing this painstaking work, he soon developed a reliable sense for the processes in the ocean, and he criticized geography scholars of his time, who tended to systematize the view on the ocean too much—a widespread trend in natural science at the time. An example was the search for geographical characteristics to subdivide the ocean into regional areas. This approach had been taken, for example, by the leading oceanographer in Germany, Otto Krümmel of Kiel, who was the first to compile the state of knowledge of oceanic motion in volume 2 of the *Handbuch der Ozeanographie* (Handbook of Oceanography), in

1887. Throughout his life Schott resisted the temptation to develop or accept academic theories, and this was probably the reason for his refusal of a professorship in Berlin.

After completing his university education, Schott had begun to write scientific papers. During his active life he wrote an average of ten papers annually. Beginning with his first journey to East Asia on merchant sailing vessels, he sent reports home, summarizing the results in a monograph in 1893. Six evaluations focusing on specific questions followed. He found pleasure in sailing the seas and describing his observations. He also began at an early stage to report on progress in the field of oceanography in general, with annual updates. He particularly highlighted research results with potential commercial benefits—for example in seafaring or fisheries—and he set out to be read by a wide audience by publishing in different relevant journals. As a result, he became well known even in his early years. In 1898 he published a world map of ocean currents, which was well received by many, though it was criticized by Krümmel, who accused him of inaccuracies in some areas. Schott responded that he preferred to study what nature reveals rather than to follow conceptual models. That same year Schott married Gertrud Tietz; they would have four children.

Soon after the return of the *Valdivia* Expedition, Schott was the first of the scientific crew to deliver the results of his observations in a comprehensive volume and an additional atlas. Krümmel praised this accomplishment as going far beyond the comparable work by Alexander Buchan of the *Challenger* Expedition (1872–1876), which was considered to mark the onset of modern oceanography. By including earlier observations, Schott presented a complete picture of the general temperature distribution in the Atlantic and Indian oceans. His graphs showing the depth of isotherms, from which the large-scale dynamic motion in the oceans may be determined, were unprecedented in oceanography. He furthermore constructed vertical east-west (zonal) and north-south (meridional) sections of the temperature in a way that covered both oceans by large quadratic boxes. This view was not taken up by other scientists until the 1970s in computer-based models of mass transport by the world oceanic circulation.

In 1903 Schott published his book *Physische Meereskunde* (Physical Oceanography) in a scientific popular series, whose third edition was translated into Spanish. Krümmel had written a comparable introduction to oceanography fifteen years earlier, which approximately corresponds to the difference in the age of both men.

Schott emphasized international cooperation and, when the countries of northern Europe had founded the International Council for the Exploration of the Sea (ICES) in 1902, he argued for an exploration of the entire

Atlantic Ocean on an international basis in respect to its physical and biological conditions. He did this together with the Swedish oceanographer Otto Pettersson, who had initiated ICES. Although well supported at international geographic congresses, this plan failed due to the national rivalries preceding World War I.

In 1912 Schott reached the peak of his scientific productivity, publishing a monograph on the Atlantic Ocean. The book starts with a history of the discovery of the Atlantic. This historical introduction was obviously inspired by a similar introduction to the report on the scientific results of the *Challenger* Expedition by John Murray, who had gained an "immortal merit," as Schott put it. The name "Atlantic" originates from antiquity (*mare atlanticum*, for the waters west of the Pillars of Hercules), but it was internationally accepted only in 1845 when the nomenclature of all parts of the world's oceans was clarified. Chapters on geology and geomorphology follow, and Schott enters into the discussion on the origin of the Atlantic Ocean, including the hypothesis by Alfred Wegener on continental drift. The description of physical properties and climatology fills the main part of the book, which is rounded off by information on how humankind avails itself of the Atlantic with respect to shipping, trade, fisheries, and whaling. This book was very well received nationally as well as internationally; for example, a review in *Scientific American* suggested that Schott's book did not have a parallel in the English language.

In the early decades of the twentieth century the development of deep-sea thermometers had reached a precision up to 0.01 degree Celsius, by which it was possible to obtain detailed information on the vertical structure of the oceans—especially from observations in the Atlantic. This increase in accurate data initiated a sharp and sometimes emotional controversy between oceanographers over the correct interpretation of data, as well as the question of who should be credited with first having explained the structure of the internal motion. Schott took the view that German observations had first provided a reliable data base.

In a second edition of his *Geographie des Atlantischen Ozeans* (Geography of the Atlantic Ocean, 1926) Schott included a chapter on marine life, written by the biologist E. Hentschel, and he expanded his section on the Atlantic's commercial value by statements on how this ocean played a geopolitical role. At that time, following World War I, this aspect had been realized as an important driving force for national economic and military development. In a third edition (1944) a further chapter was added on the sediments at the bottom of the Atlantic, written by his son Wolfgang Schott, who later became known as the first scientist postulating that climate

changes at the Earth's surface in geological times are well documented in vertical deep-sea bottom cores.

In the late 1920s Schott was asked to write similar books on the Indian and Pacific oceans. He agreed to do this after his request to finance a one-year exploratory journey around the world was fulfilled by the Notgemeinschaft der deutschen Wissenschaft (German Science Foundation). He boarded sixteen different ships, and he regarded his participation in the Fourth Pacific Science Congress in Java in 1929 as a highlight of his journey. In 1935, four years after his retirement, Schott completed his life's work by publishing *Geographie des Indischen und Stillen Ozeans* (Geography of the Indian and Pacific Oceans). The arrangement of the book follows that of his work on the Atlantic. However, he abandoned chapters on economic geography and geopolitics because these fields were undergoing rapid changes at the time.

Schott continued to write scientific papers—including a longer chapter on the climate of the South Sea Islands for a handbook of climatology—up to 1944, when he was eighty-three years old. The total of his publications exceeded far beyond two hundred. Most of them deal with the hydrography and oceanography of the world's oceans at local, regional, or global scales. The subjects of the other papers include national and international research, measuring instruments, marine meteorology, ocean traffic and its policy, and ocean science and humankind.

Honors and Awards. Schott received numerous awards during his lifetime, including the Karl Ritter Medal, Gesellschaft für Erdkunde, in Berlin (1903); the Medal of the Institut Océanographique from the Prince of Monaco (1911); and the Medal of the Deutsche Seewarte in Hamburg (1912). He was an honorary member of numerous scientific societies, including the Geographic Society in Amsterdam, the Royal Italian Geographical Society, the German Scientific Commission of Marine Research in Berlin, the Geographical Society in Jena, the Geographical Society in Lübeck, and the Challenger Society of the British Museum in London. He was a corresponding member of the Prussian Academy of Science in Göttingen, the Geographic Society in Leningrad, and the Geographical Society in New York. In 1936 he was awarded the Georg Neumayer Medal in gold of the Geographical Society in Berlin.

Preston E. James evaluated Schott's contribution to earth science by comparing it with the work of Eduard Suess regarding geologic structure and surface features and that of Julius Hann regarding climate conditions. "Now once again we are indebted to the genius of the Germans for having produced another compendium to stand with those earlier classics. Henceforth with these other two names we must associate the name of Gerhard Schott, whose monumental work on the oceans completes this trilogy on land, air, and water" (James, 1936, p. 664).

BIBLIOGRAPHY

The article by Bruno Schultz, cited below at the end of the bibliography, includes a nearly complete list of Schott's publications.

WORKS BY SCHOTT

Wissenschaftliche Ergebnisse einer Forschungsreise zur See, ausgeführt in den Jahren 1891 und 1892 [Scientific results of a research trip at sea, conducted in the years 1891 and 1892]. Gotha: Petermanns Geographische Mitteilungen, Ergänzungsheft 109, 1893.

Weltkarte zur Übersicht der Meeresströmungen [General Map of the currents of the world ocean]. Berlin: Dietrich Reimer, 1898 (updated 1905, 1909, 1913, 1917).

Wissenschaftliche Ergebnisse der deutschen Tiefsee-Expedition auf dem Dampfer "Valdivia" 1898 bis 1899. Bd. I. Ozeanographie und Meteorologie. Jena: Verlag von Gustav Fischer, 1902.

Physische Meereskunde [Physical oceanography]. Leipzig: Sammlung Göschen, 1903 (updated 1910, 1924).

With Otto Pettersson. "On the Importance of an International Exploration of the Atlantic Ocean." *Geographical Journal* 33 (1909): 68–71.

Geographie des Atlantischen Ozeans. Hamburg: C. Boysen, 1912 (updated 1926, 1942, 1944).

Geographie des Indischen und Stillen Ozeans. Hamburg: C. Boysen, 1935.

OTHER SOURCES

James, Preston E. "The Geography of the Sea: A Review of the Work of Gerhard Schott." *Geographical Review* 26 (1936): 664–669.

Krümmel, Otto. *Handbuch der Ozeanographie.* Vol. II, *Die Bewegungsformen des Meeres* [The Shapes of Motion in the Sea]. Stuttgart: J. Engelhorn, 1887.

Mills, Eric L. "*Physische Meereskunde*: From Geography to Physical Oceanograpy in the Institute für Meereskunde, Berlin, 1900–1935." *Historisch-meereskundliches Jahrbuch/History of Oceanography Yearbook* 4 (1997): 45–70.

Schulz, Bruno. "Zur Vollendung des 70. Lebensjahres von Gerhard Schott" (On the Accomplishment of the 70th year of life of Gerhard Schott). *Annalen der Hydrographie und Maritimen Meteorologie* 64 (1936): 329–335.

Walter Lenz

SCHOTTKY, WALTER HANS (*b.* Zürich, Switzerland, 23 July 1886; *d.* Forchheim, Germany, 4 March 1976), *physics, vacuum-tube electronics, telecommu-*

nications technology, thermodynamics, defects in crystal lattices, solid-state electronics.

Schottky, although a theorist, was the most important industrial physicist in twentieth-century Germany. Being one of the "outstanding research personalities" of the Siemens company, he was granted scientific freedom to pursue problems of pure physics. Thus his contributions include both technological and scientific achievements: invention of the tetrode electron tube and the superheterodyne principle for receiving wireless signals, discovery of the "small-shot effect" (noise due to the quantum structure of electricity) in electron tubes, theory of crystal defects, and theory of rectification in semiconductor-metal contacts. Unfortunately, Schottky was "a meritorious but unintelligible man," as he would be referred to by his younger Siemens colleagues in the 1950s, and therefore he needed "translators" of his ideas into language that the ordinary industrial researchers and electrical engineers understood.

Education. Walter Hans Schottky was the second son of the German mathematician Friedrich Schottky. After his graduation from the Humanistisches Gymnasium in Berlin-Steglitz in 1904, Walter Schottky enrolled in the Royal Friedrich-Wilhelms-University in Berlin to study physics. Walther Nernst and Max Planck were the teachers who impressed him most. In 1912, Schottky obtained his PhD degree under Planck with an award-winning dissertation on special relativity. Schottky had studied physics twice as long as was usual at the time (sixteen instead of eight semesters), but had acquired an enormously deep and thorough knowledge of physics and physical chemistry. Planck's and Nernst's influence on Schottky later became apparent in his thermodynamic and often also physical-chemistry-based approach to both physical and technological problems.

At Planck's recommendation, Schottky looked for a possibility to be trained in experimental physics as well. He ended up in Jena under Max Wien, inventor of the then-famous Löschfunken (quenched spark) wireless transmitter. Starting out in a lab-work training program for advanced students (experiments on the photoelectric effect), he soon defined his own course of research. During the summer of 1912, he theoretically derived the $V^{3/2}$ law for the dependence of the current on the voltage in a vacuum tube—independently of Irving Langmuir. On 2 December 1913, Schottky was able to prove the $V^{3/2}$ law experimentally.

After having returned to his parents' home in Berlin later in December 1913, Schottky immediately started working up his results for publication. Langmuir's article "The Effect of Space Charge and Residual Gases on Thermionic Currents in High Vacuum" published in

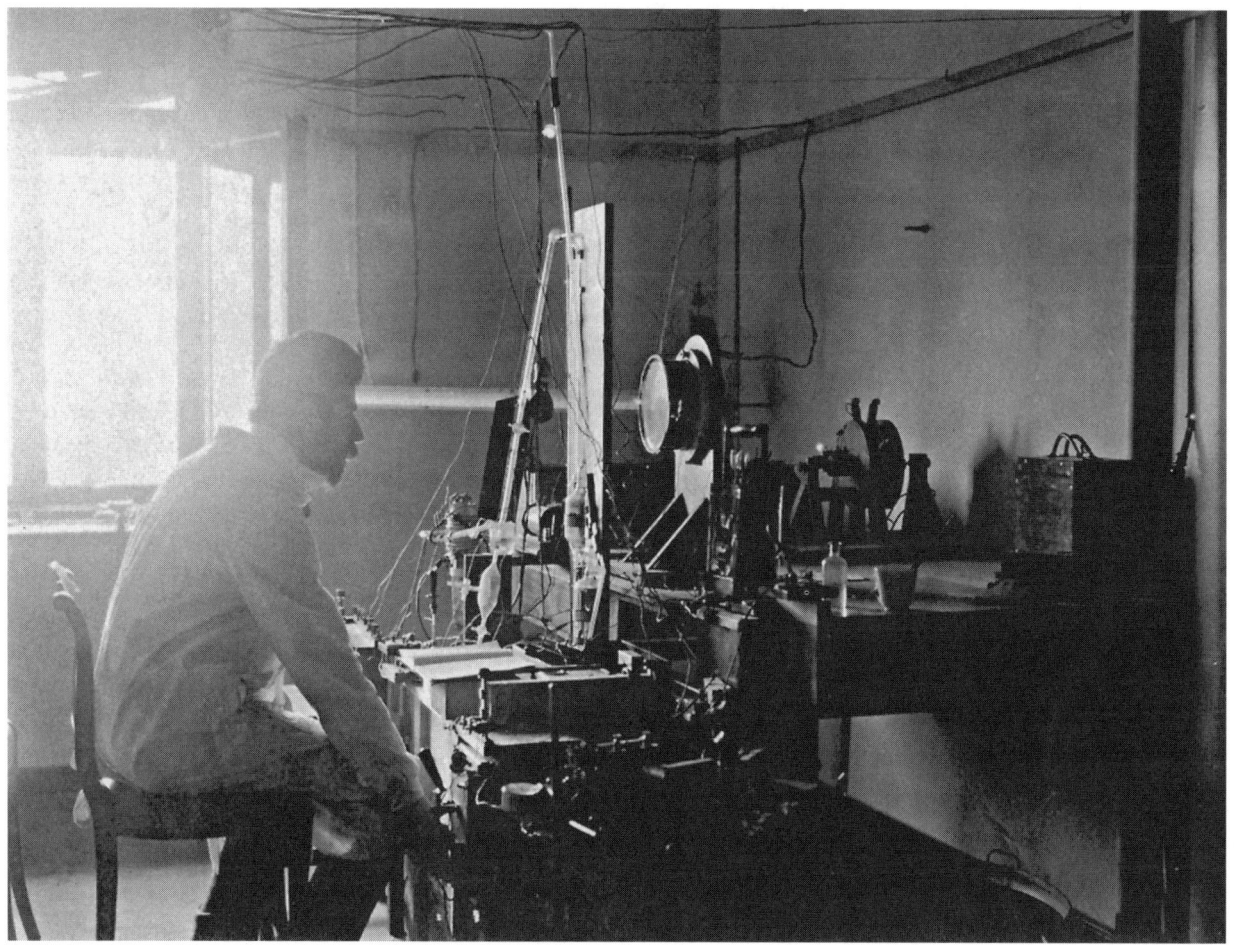

Walter Hans Schottky. COURTESY OF DR. MARTIN SCHOTTKY, M.A.

German translation in *Physikalische Zeitschrift* (Physical journal) in 1914 (the original article had appeared in *Physical Review* in 1913) was like a "blow with a club" for Schottky. Nevertheless, he published some of his findings that went beyond Langmuir's results. In Berlin, he resumed experimental work on electron emission in high vacuum at the Physical Institute of the university and discovered the effect that strong fields increase the emission of electrons from hot filaments—later to be known as the Schottky effect.

Working for Siemens in World War I. Early in 1915, Schottky gave a talk on his work on thermionic emission at Berlin University. The Siemens company was strongly interested in maintaining close contact with university research in order to be able to import new ideas and scientists. Ragnar Holm, a Swedish physicist and Siemens employee, immediately realized the importance of Schottky's work for the problem of electronic amplifier tubes and contacted him after the talk.

When World War I had broken out, Schottky had not been drafted into the army because of his poor health—which he considered to be at least embarrassing, perhaps even a disgrace. By doing research work for Siemens and inventing a war telecommunications device, Schottky wanted "to prove that he, too, could be useful for the fatherland" (Henriette Schottky, 1936); besides, practical work was a chance to escape from the neurotic cage of an extreme introvert in which he lived.

Inspired by Holm, Schottky started working on a vacuum tube that would compensate for the negative effects of space charge. Siemens neither offered Schottky a job nor paid him anything but supported his experimental work at Berlin University by lending him equipment. The company applied for and took out a patent for Schottky's Raumladegitter-Röhre (space-charge-grid tube). On 1 September 1915, Schottky informed Siemens that both the prototype of the space-charge-grid tube (made at the university) and the theory for the design of new vacuum tubes were ready. Despite Holm's backing of Schottky, the

Siemens management failed to understand the importance of Schottky's theory of the vacuum tube. The high amplification factor of the crude prototype tube showed, however, that the strange introvert was more than just another unintelligible theorist.

After Schottky had again been declared unfit for military service, he asked Siemens for a job. He was accepted and took up his work as a regular Siemens employee on 2 March 1916. Schottky's work at Siemens was highly successful. In 1916, he invented the Schutznetz-Röhre (protective-net tube, after further development called screen-grid tetrode). In 1917, he became scientific director of the K-Laboratorium (cable laboratory—the lab where work on Pupin cables, electron tubes, and amplifiers was carried out) of Siemens & Halske. In 1918, he invented the superheterodyne principle for receiving wireless signals and discovered the Schroteffekt (small-shot effect—i.e., noise due to the quantum structure of electricity) in electron tubes.

His work that soon covered all kinds of telecommunications systems brought him into contact with the problem of the crystal detector (point-contact rectifier). The effect of unipolar (i.e., unidirectional, or, as it was later called, rectifying) electricity conduction in metal-on-metal-compound (i.e., metal-semiconductor) contacts had been discovered by Ferdinand Braun as early as 1874. Braun himself had exploited the effect in the crystal detector introduced into wireless telegraphy to replace the unstable coherer. Nevertheless, the physical mechanism responsible for rectification (i.e., conversion of alternating to direct current) was unknown. It was only natural that Schottky's first approach to this problem was based on the theoretical models that had been successfully used to describe the phenomena of thermionic emission.

In 1919 when war restrictions on publications were no longer in effect, Schottky published his theory of the vacuum-tube amplifier. It was not favorably received by engineers because it was difficult to understand, both because of the too mathematical approach and the use of his own symbols (the ones that he had used in his first draft submitted to Siemens in 1915). It was Heinrich Barkhausen who in his famous textbook series *Elektronen-Röhren* (Electron tubes, first editions of volumes I to III, Barkhausen, 1923–1929) translated Schottky's ideas into a language that electrical engineers understood.

In 1936, the Royal Society in London awarded Schottky "the Hughes Medal in recognition of your discovery of the Schrot effect in thermionic emission and your invention of the screen-grid tetrode and superheterodyne method of receiving wireless signals" (Royal Society, 1936).

Academic Interlude. Still in 1919, Schottky left his Siemens post in Berlin and moved to Würzburg in order to work toward his Habilitation degree (in Germany, the completion of a Habilitation thesis and successfully giving a lecture including a discussion afterward was, and in general still is, the precondition for becoming a university lecturer or professor) which he obtained under Wilhelm Wien in 1920. Schottky then became a Privatdozent (lecturer) at Würzburg University. Unfortunately, he was not good at teaching and consequently not enthusiastic about it. Therefore he concentrated on his own scientific interests. In pursuit of problems he had encountered while working on his Habilitation thesis, he investigated the quantum-theoretical implications of Nernst's theorem (third law of thermodynamics). This work, together with his interest in practical applications of thermodynamics, eventually led to his textbook *Thermodynamik,* which was written with the help of coauthors Hermann Ulich and Carl Wagner and published in 1929. This textbook contained several pieces of original work, among them also the roots of Schottky's 1935 discovery of what Wilhelm Jost shortly afterward called SCHOTTKYsche Fehlordnung (literal translation: SCHOTTKYan disorder; *Schottky defect* in the English literature) of a crystal lattice: missing atoms without compensating atoms in interstitial positions because of thermodynamic necessity—above absolute zero the entropy of the crystal is larger than zero, and as entropy is also a measure of disorder, there must be imperfections even in the lattice of a pure substance.

On 19 September 1922, Schottky began to work as a salaried assistant at the Physical State Laboratory in Hamburg, on leave from Würzburg for the whole winter semester of 1922–1923. In Hamburg, Schottky summed up his previous investigations on electron emission and the crystal detector and pursued them further. As an external scientific consultant for Siemens, he kept in touch with the company's technological problems. In 1922, he started working on the problem of arcbacks inside mercury-vapor rectifiers. Siemens soon dropped further development work on these rectifiers since they did not promise big sales at the time. Schottky, however, having been appointed professor of theoretical physics at Rostock University (he assumed this post on 1 January 1923), pursued the problem out of scientific interest. In contrast to Siemens, competitors AEG and BBC continued empirical technological development work because they foresaw future market demands for such rectifiers.

Back to Siemens. The emergence of the cuprous-oxide (Cu_2O) junction rectifier on the market shortly after its announcement in 1926 by its inventor Lars O. Grondahl marks the beginning of modern use of semiconductors. Despite the importance of the new device, its underlying physics were not understood at the time.

When the long-planned electrification of the Berlin S-Bahn (suburban commuter railroad system) finally got under way in 1924, the decision of the state railroads to use direct current supplied via a third rail for this service resulted in a great demand for high-power mercury-vapor rectifiers. AEG and BBC were able to offer units for 1,500 amperes and 1,600 amperes, respectively, whereas the biggest Siemens rectifier at the time had an output of only 600 amperes! Such a mistake was not to be repeated; however, the importance of the Cu_2O rectifier for low-power applications was realized immediately. Both patent and production problems made it imperative to know the physical mechanisms that were responsible for rectification in the boundary layer between Cu_2O and Cu.

Despite a promotion within the academic ranks of Rostock University in 1926, Schottky was not happy there. Theoretical physics led a Cinderella existence, there were few and usually not very talented students, and he still found teaching uncongenial. Schottky wanted to be in closer contact with practical work again and longed for collaboration in a larger context. Driven by an "irresistible inner compulsion [to go] to research centers with optimum conditions" as he later remembered (Schottky, 1960), he contacted Siemens for a job in 1927, just at the time when a heavy research program to catch up with competitors got under way. Fully in line with the prevailing research strategy of the company to put almost all its eggs into the one basket of outstanding research personalities, Siemens hired Schottky to work on the theory of both mercury-vapor and Cu_2O rectifiers. On 1 October 1927, Schottky joined the company as a full-time in-house scientific consultant.

Within the framework of the Siemens corporate research strategy and with full company support, Schottky not only solved the arcback problems in high-power mercury-vapor rectifiers but also worked out the theory of rectification in semiconductor-metal contacts between 1927 and 1939. Eberhard Spenke, who had applied for a job with Siemens and been hired in 1929 at Schottky's recommendation, worked with Schottky to elaborate the new theory mathematically in 1939. The result, titled "Zur quantitativen Durchführung der Raumladungs- und Randschichttheorie der Kristallgleichrichter" (On the quantitative elaboration of the space-charge and boundary-layer theory of crystal rectifiers) and published in the same year in *Wissenschaftliche Veröffentlichungen aus den Siemens-Werken* (Scientific publications from the Siemens-Works), offered for the first time a complete theory of the semiconductor rectifiers known at the time, unraveled "the causes of the most important—wanted and unwanted—properties of the characteristic curves of rectifiers" (Siemens, 1939), and thus gave hints for their improvement. It was a major scientific breakthrough because the effect of rectification in semiconductor-metal

contacts had already been discovered in 1874 and had been used in the form of cat's-whisker detectors (i.e., point-contact rectifiers) in early radio and again since the second half of the 1920s in the form of area (in contrast to point-contact) cuprous-oxide and selenium rectifiers (area rectifiers are called junction rectifiers today).

Spenke became the "translator" of Schottky's ideas, at first only for Siemens research and development (R&D), but after World War II also for the whole semiconductor community in the German-speaking world. Siemens researchers never felt comfortable about developing devices they did not understand—and consequently were not good at it. While competitors had empirically found better production methods than Siemens R&D, a Siemens physicist had worked out the theory of the device and won great renown in the world of physics. Schottky's "Vereinfachte und erweiterte Theorie der Randschichtgleichrichter" (Simplified and extended theory of boundary-layer rectifiers) of 1941, published in 1942, completed his theoretical edifice.

In World War II, Schottky's ideas were taken up by Heinrich J. Welker, who worked on the problem of finding a suitable detector for cm-waves (i.e., radar waves) within the framework of "Aviation Research" at Gräfelfing experimental station. During the second half of the war, parts of production and R&D were evacuated to rural regions in order to escape the ever-increasing Allied air raids on the big cities. In 1943, the Siemens-Schuckertwerke Transformer Works in Nuremberg moved their test lab to Pretzfeld Castle in Upper Franconia. Schottky also moved to Pretzfeld in early 1944 after his house in Berlin had been bombed to pieces and research in Berlin had become impossible.

After World War II. Immediately after World War II, German industry was in a terrible condition. In addition to the war damage, many factories, especially in the east, were dismantled and removed as reparations. The top scientists of the company had been scattered all over Germany during the final stage of the war or had been captured and "convinced" by the Russians to work in the Soviet Union. Schottky, however, was safe in Pretzfeld in the American zone.

He renewed his affiliation with Siemens in 1946 and also lectured on semiconductor theory at Erlangen University during the winter semester of 1947–1948 and the summer semester of 1948. In early 1947, he received an offer from the U.S. War Department to work in the United States, but turned it down; he was sixty at the time and most probably felt too old to adapt to a new language and new surroundings. Besides, in contrast to his attitude in World War I, he did not want to be involved in military research, a commitment that he had been able to evade even during the Nazi regime and what he called the "most criminal and most dilettantish of all wars" (Schottky, 1945). Nevertheless, he worked as a consultant for the Scientific Research Group of the Office of Military Government for Bavaria and then for the Scientific Research Division of the Office of the U.S. High Commissioner for Germany from 1 July 1948 to 2 August 1952.

Despite some patents, Schottky had no influence on technological developments after 1945. His great contribution in the 1950s was of an organizational nature: still on the Siemens payroll, he played a pivotal role in the establishment of solid-state and especially semiconductor physics as a field of research in its own right in postwar Germany.

BIBLIOGRAPHY

A complete list of Schottky's publications can be found in Serchinger, 2007. Collections of Schottky's papers can be found in the following archives:NL 100 Schottky. Archives of the Deutsches Museum, Munich, Germany. SAA 11/Lc 75 and SAA 11–40/Lc 166 Schottky. Siemens Archives, Munich, Germany.

WORKS BY SCHOTTKY

"Vakuumverstärkerröhre mit Glühkathode und Hilfselektrode" [Vacuum amplifier tube with glowing cathode and auxiliary electrode]. DRP [German Reich Patent] 300617, filed 1 June 1916. Schottky's screen-grid tube patent.

"Empfangsanordnung für elektrische Wellensignale" [Receiving array for electric wave signals]. DRP [German Reich Patent] 368937, filed 19 June 1918. Schottky's superheterodyne patent was filed six months before Edwin H. Armstrong's. Old German patents (up to the end of World War II) like these can be found in the library of the Deutsches Museum, Munich, Germany.

"Über spontane Stromschwankungen in verschiedenen Elektritzitätsleitern" [On spontaneous current fluctuations in various electricity conductors]. *Annalen der Physik* 57 (1918): 541–567. The original paper on the "small-shot effect" (shot noise, Schottky noise).

"Über Hochvakuumverstärker" [On high-vacuum amplifiers]. *Archiv für Elektrotechnik* 8 (1920): 1–31, 299–328. Schottky's complete theory of electron tubes and tube amplifiers.

"Small-Shot Effect and Flicker Effect." *Physical Review* 28 (1926): 74–103. Schottky's only publication in English, translated by the discoverer of the flicker effect, J. B. Johnson of the Bell Telephone Laboratories.

With Hermann Ulich and Carl Wagner. *Thermodynamik* [Thermodynamics]. Berlin: Verlag von Julius Springer, 1929. Reprinted Berlin: Springer Verlag, 1973. Schottky's preface gives insights into his ideas about applying theoretical physics to engineering problems.

"Zur Theorie der thermischen Fehlordnung in Kristallen" [On the theory of thermal disorder in crystals]. *Die Naturwissenschaften* 23 (1935): 656–657. Introduced what shortly afterward was called the Schottky defect.

"Über den Mechanismus der Ionenbewegung in festen Elektrolyten" [On the mechanism of ion movement in solid electrolytes]. *Zeitschrift für physikalische Chemie* 29 (1935): 333–355. Elaborated the concept of the Schottky defect.

"Halbleitertheorie der Sperrschicht" [Semiconductor theory of the barrier layer]. *Die Naturwissenschaften* 26 (1938): 843. Short overview published in advance to ensure priority over Nevill F. Mott.

With Eberhard Spenke. "Zur quantitativen Durchführung der Raumladungs- und Randschichttheorie der Kristallgleichrichter" [On the quantitative elaboration of the space-charge and boundary-layer theory of crystal rectifiers]. *Wissenschaftliche Veröffentlichungen aus den Siemens-Werken* 18 (1939): 1–67. Contains detailed derivations of formulas and calculations.

"Vereinfachte und erweitere Theorie der Randschichtgleichrichter" [Simplified and extended theory of boundary-layer rectifiers]. Received 27 September 1941. *Zeitschrift für Physik* 118 (1942): 539–592. Final published version of his theory.

Letter to his mother and his sister Lilly, 17 March 1945. Schottky papers. NL 100 Schottky. Archives of the Deutsches Museum, Munich, Germany. Hitler and his regime were still in power at that time.

Letter to the rector of Berlin Technical University, 18 May 1960. Schottky papers. NL 100 Schottky. Archives of the Deutsches Museum, Munich, Germany. Published in *Physikalische Blätter* 49 (1993): 858–859.

OTHER SOURCES

Barkhausen, Heinrich. *Elektronen-Röhren, I. Elektronentheoretische Grundlagen, II. Verstärkung schwacher Wechselströme* [Electron tubes, I. Electron-rheoretical foundations, II. Amplification of weak alternating currents]. Leipzig, Germany: Verlag von S. Hirzel, 1923. As is usual in textbooks, only the most important original works were cited. Schottky was the author most often cited in the footnotes.

———. *Elektronen-Röhren, 2. Bd., Röhrensender* [Electron tubes, vol. 2, Tube transmitters]. Leipzig, Germany: Verlag von S. Hirzel, 1925.

———. *Elektronen-Röhren, 3. Bd., Empfänger* [Electron tubes, vol. 3, Receivers]. Leipzig, Germany: Verlag von S. Hirzel, 1929. In his explanation of the superheterodyne principle, Barkhausen cited neither Schottky nor Edwin H. Armstrong.

Langmuir, Irving. "The Effect of Space Charge and Residual Gases on Thermionic Currents in High Vacuum." *Physical Review* 2 (1913): 450–486. German translation in *Physikalische Zeitschrift* [Physical journal] 15 (1914): 348–353, 516–526.

Rhoderick, E. H. "Obituary. Walter Schottky." *Nature* 263 (1976): 263. Schottky's affiliation with Siemens incorrectly described, but otherwise correct.

Rothe, Horst, Eberhard Spenke, and Carl Wagner. "Zum 65. Geburtstag von Walter Schottky" [On Walter Schottky's 65th birthday]. *Archiv der elektrischen Übertragung* 5 (1951): 306–313. An excellent overview (including formulas) of his scientific work, written by three outstanding colleagues.

Royal Society, London, to Walter Schottky, 5 November 1936. Schottky papers. NL 100 Schottky. Archives of the Deutsches Museum, Munich, Germany.

Schottky, Henriette. "Vaters Leben vom 24.7.1851–12.8.1935" [Father's life from 24 July 1851 to 12 August 1935]. Schottky papers. NL 100 Schottky. Archives of the Deutsches Museum, Munich, Germany. Published in *Mathematik in Berlin. Geschichte und Dokumentation* [Mathematics in Berlin. History and documentation], edited by Heinrich Begehr. Second half-volume. Aachen, Germany: Shaker Verlag, 1998, pp. 77–102.

Serchinger, Reinhard W. "Walter Schottky und die Forschung bei Siemens" [Walter Schottky and research at Siemens]. In *Oszillationen: Naturwissenschaftler und Ingenieure zwischen Forschung und Markt* [Oscillations: Scientists and engineers between research and the market], edited by Ivo Schneider, Helmuth Trischler, and Ulrich Wengenroth. Munich, Germany: R. Oldenbourg Verlag, 2000, pp. 167–209. Focus is on how Schottky was embedded in the Siemens corporate strategy.

———. "*Wirtschaftswunder* in Pretzfeld, Upper Franconia: Interactions between Science, Technology, and Corporate Strategies in Siemens Semiconductor Rectifier Research & Development, 1945–1956." *History and Technology* 16 (2000): 335–381. Focus is on the transformation of Schottky's theory into technological reality (i.e., products) by Eberhard Spenke.

———. *Walter Schottky—Atomtheoretiker und Elektrotechniker* [Walter Schottky—Atomic theorist and electrical engineer]. Stuttgart, Germany: Franz Steiner Verlag, 2007.

Serchinger, Reinhard W., and Martin Schottky. "Schottky, Walter Hans." In *J. C. Poggendorff Biographisch-literarisches Handwörterbuch der exakten Naturwissenschaften,* vol. 8, part 3, edited by Hans Wussing. Weinheim, Germany: Wiley-VCH Verlag GmbH & Co. KGaA, 2004. Contains a comprehensive list of works about Schottky.

Siemens, Zentralstelle für wissenschaftlich-technische Forschungsarbeiten der Siemens-Werke [Central authority over scientific-technological research work of the Siemens-Works]. Foreword to *Wissenschaftliche Veröffentlichungen aus den Siemens-Werken* 18 (1939).

Teichmann, Jürgen. *Zur Geschichte der Festkörperphysik— Farbzentrenforschung bis 1940* [On the history of solid-state physics—Color-center research up to 1940]. Stuttgart, Germany: Franz Steiner Verlag Wiesbaden, 1988. Although focus is on Robert Wichard Pohl and his school, this book covers Schottky's contributions to color-center research, which are not treated elsewhere.

Reinhard W. Serchinger

SCHTERN, LINA

SEE **Shtern, Lina Solomonovna**.

SCHWARTZ, LAURENT (*b.* Paris, France, 5 March 1915; *d.* Paris, France, 4 July 2002), *mathematics, analysis, probability theory.*

Schwartz is the inventor of distribution theory, now a universally used language of mathematical analysis. He also introduced the concept of radonifying maps, related to both the geometry of Banach spaces and probability theory.

Life and Career. Laurent Schwartz was the first son of Anselme Schwartz, originally an immigrant from Alsatia, at the time under German control, and later a highly successful surgeon. (In 1907 he became the first Jewish surgeon ever officially employed in a Paris hospital.) Through his mother, Claire, Laurent was related to the Debrés, a prominent Jewish French family: his maternal grandfather was the chief rabbi in Neuilly; later, a Debré would be president of the national Academy of Medicine; there have been and still are prominent Gaullist politicians in the Debré family. (These had become Catholic converts.) In 1938 Laurent Schwartz married Marie-Hélène Levy, whose father, Paul Levy, is the initiator of modern probability theory; Marie-Hélène Schwartz was to become a distinguished mathematician in her own right. The eminent mathematician Jacques Hadamard was Laurent's granduncle.

On completing the *lycée* (high school), Laurent Schwartz won, in the Latin category, the Concours Général, the most prestigious nationwide competition in France for high schoolers. But being attracted to geometry as much as to the classics, he applied to and was admitted into the science classes of the École normale supérieure (ENS) of Paris, the most selective and most scholarly oriented of the Grandes écoles, the elite specialized colleges parallel to the universities in the French system of higher education. The ENS students had the privilege of attending the lectures of some the best French mathematicians: Émile Borel, Élie Cartan, Alfred Denjoy, Maurice Fréchet, George Julia, and Paul Montel. At the nearby Collège de France in Paris, they could also hear Henri Lebesgue's lectures and take part in the Hadamard seminar. The enduring love of Laurent Schwartz for probability theory developed through his personal contact with his future father-in-law, Paul Lévy.

In 1937, having completed his studies at the ENS and having secured the *aggrégation,* the diploma required for a teaching position in a lycée, Schwartz was drafted into the military, a three-year term being compulsory in France at that time. War came in 1939, defeat in 1940, and the Schwartzes were forced to move to the south of France to avoid German occupation. For a while and despite the fact that he was Jewish, Laurent Schwartz was paid a stipend by the organization that was to become, after the war, the Centre national de la recherche scientifique (National Center for Scientific Research). After the end of his employment there in 1942, his research was supported until 1944 by the Michelin foundation ARS; he thus circumvented the racial policies of the Vichy government.

A chance encounter with Henri Cartan and Jean Delsarte in Toulouse in 1941 encouraged the Schwartzes to move to the University of Clermont-Ferrand. There they both could work under the guidance of mathematicians who had migrated from the occupied northern zone: Jean Dieudonné, Charles Ehresman, André Lichnerowicz, and Szolem Mandelbrojt, among others. At Clermont-Ferrand, Laurent Schwartz completed his PhD thesis on the approximation of continuous functions on $\mathbf{R}_+=[0,+\infty)$ by sums of exponentials $S = a_0+\Sigma_n a_n \exp(-\lambda_n x)$ where the infinite sequence of real numbers $\lambda_n > 0$ is fixed. A classical theorem of Charles Müntz implies that these sums are dense in $C(\mathbf{R}_+)$ if and only if $\Sigma_n \lambda_n^{-1} = +\infty$. Schwartz proved that when $\Sigma_n \lambda_n^{-1} < +\infty$ the closure in $C(\mathbf{R}_+)$ of the subspace made up of the sums S consists of the functions that can be extended holomorphically to the open half-plane $\mathit{Rz} > 0$.

In Clermont-Ferrand he met and was deeply influenced by several members of the Bourbaki group. Nicholas Bourbaki, the fictitious author of foundational mathematical treatises, was the creation of a small number of French mathematicians (Henri Cartan, Claude Chevalley, Jean Dieudonné, Jean Delsarte, René de Possel, and André Weil) determined to realize the axiomatization of mathematics as envisaged earlier by David Hilbert. The membership in the entity Bourbaki was ever changing, upcoming young mathematicians replacing departing older ones. Schwartz was soon recruited into the elite group.

In November 1944, after the Allies had liberated most of France, Laurent Schwartz made the paramount discovery of his life, distribution theory. After teaching at the University of Grenoble during the academic year 1944–1945, he joined the faculty in Nancy. In 1950 he was awarded the Fields Medal for his discovery of distributions. In 1952 he was named to a professorship at the Sorbonne. Several of Schwartz's PhD students at the Sorbonne have had mathematical careers of great distinction, among them Louis Boutet de Monvel, Alexandre Grothendieck, Jacques-Louis Lions, Bernard Malgrange, and André Martineau. In 1969 he moved to the École polytechnique (Polytechnic School) in Paris (later moved to Palaiseau), the top engineering school in France, where Paul Lévy had taught and where Schwartz embarked on an ambitious, and successful, program of reform. At Polytechnique he organized a very productive seminar on infinite dimensional measure theory, attracting a number of

brilliant students, such as Bernard Maurey and Gilles Pisier (whose PhD thesis he supervised).

During his entire adult life, Schwartz was active in left-wing politics, a follower of Trotsky as a young man before abandoning the movement after World War II, then agitating against France's Algerian war and France's and later America's war in Vietnam. He used his scientific prestige to combat abuses of human rights, especially (but not solely) those of mathematicians and scientists in South America and in the Soviet states.

Schwartz was also well-known among lepidopterists. His collection of tropical butterflies and moths, one of the greatest private collections in the world (with more than twenty-five thousand specimens), was donated in part to the Muséum d'histoire naturelle in Paris, in part to the natural history museum in Cochabamba, Bolivia. His collecting throughout tropical Latin America led to the discovery and description of several new species, now named after him.

Distribution Theory. The start of the twentieth century saw a number of attempts to define derivatives of functions not commonly thought of as differentiable (e.g., step functions), mainly prompted by the need to solve ordinary differential equations (ODEs) or partial differential equations (PDEs). Of such attempts, the two most significant were the symbolic calculus of the British physicist Oliver Heaviside, devised to solve the ODEs of electrical circuits, and Hadamard's finite parts, introduced to make sense of the fundamental solutions (in modern parlance) of the wave equation in higher space-dimensions. Heaviside's calculus transformed convolution into multiplication, but at the price of introducing derivative rules for the convolution $(f * g)(t) = \int_0^t f(t-s) g(s) ds$ of two differentiable functions in the closed half-line $[0,+\infty)$,

$$\frac{d}{dt}(f * g)(t) = f(0)g(t) + (f' * g)(t), \qquad (1)$$

that were hard to understand. Mathematicians who came after Heaviside gave a definition of Heaviside's calculus in terms of the Laplace transform, which, however, was not very convincing. Meanwhile, the first generation of quantum physicists was producing more examples of generalized functions with an impressive array of applications. Among them was the Dirac delta function $\delta(x)$ (known earlier to Heaviside): it was the function with symbol 1, and it was presented as the derivative of what was later called the unit step or Heaviside function, which is equal to zero in $(-\infty,0)$ and to one in $(0,+\infty)$, whose symbol is $1/p$. Paul Dirac did not explicitly connect his intuitive but less than rigorous ideas to Heaviside's calculus, but instead by approximating, defined his "function" with true functions. In the course of this work he introduced multidimensional Dirac measures, for instance, the measure associated to the light-cone $\Gamma \subset \mathbf{R}^4$,

$$\varphi \rightarrow \int \varphi(x)\delta(x_0^2 - x_1^2 - x_2^2 - x_3^2)dx_0 dx_1 dx_2 dx_3$$
$$= \int_\Gamma \varphi(x)\,d\mu \qquad (2)$$

where $d\mu$ is the natural invariant measure on Γ; in (2) φ can be any continuous function in $\mathbf{R}^4$ decaying rapidly at infinity.

Further developments of this highly effective but poorly explained mathematics happened in the late 1920s and the 1930s. In 1926 Norbert Wiener used regularization or smoothing, that is, convolution with compactly supported C^∞ functions, to approximate continuous functions f by smooth ones. Salomon Bochner defined the Fourier transform of finite sums of the form

$$\sum_{n=0}^{N} \frac{d^n}{dx^n}(P_n(x)f_n(x)), \qquad (3)$$

in which P_n is a polynomial and $f_n \in L^2(\mathbf{R}^n)$ ($N \in \mathbf{Z}_+$ can vary). This is essentially the definition of what in Schwartz's later theory was to be called a tempered distribution, but the differences are nonetheless considerable. Bochner considered the derivatives d^n/dx^n purely as formal operations, not as weak derivatives, and although the space of sums (3) is stable by (formal) Fourier transform, which exchanges multiplication and convolution, Bochner did not specify when these operations are defined. Nor did he mention that the Dirac function is of the type (3). Indeed, when in 1946 Bochner defined the generalized (or, as would be said today, the distributional) solution of a linear ODE, he went no further in that direction.

In 1934–1935, Jean Leray gave the prestigious Peccot lectures at the Collège de France, which Schwartz attended. In them, Leray defined the *weak solution* u of a second-order linear PDE in $\mathbf{R}^3$, $P(x,\partial_x)\,u = 0$, by the property that

$$\int_{R^s} u(x)P^\top(x,\partial x)\varphi(x)dx = 0$$

for every compactly supported C^2 function φ; here $P^\top(x,\partial_x)$ denotes the transpose of $P(x,\partial_x)$. The coefficients of $P(x,\partial_x)$ must have some regularity, but u is only required to be locally integrable.

The Soviet mathematician Sergei L'vovich Sobolev came the closest of anyone in the 1930s to the discovering the general concept of a distribution. In his articles "Méthode nouvelle à résoudre le problème de Cauchy" (1936) and "Sur un théorème d'analyse fonctionnelle" (1938), he defined the distributions of a given, arbitrary,

Laurent Schwartz. *In Paris, 1989.* DERRICK CEYRAC/AFP/GETTY IMAGES.

finite order m as the continuous linear functionals on the space C_{comp}^m of compactly supported functions of class C^m. Using transposition, Sobolev defined the multiplication of the functionals belonging to $(C_{\text{comp}}^m)^*$ by the functions belonging to C^m and observed that the differentiation of those functionals maps $(C_{\text{comp}}^m)^*$ into $(C_{\text{comp}}^{\infty+1})^*$. But he made no mention of Dirac's $\delta(x)$, and neither convolution nor the Fourier transform play a role in his theory. At this time he limited himself to applying his new approach to reformulating and solving the Cauchy problem for linear hyperbolic equations. Only after the war did he introduce the *Sobolev spaces* H^m, and then only for integers $m \geq 0$. World War II and the separation between Western and Soviet mathematicians left Schwartz ignorant of Sobolev's papers. No doubt knowing them would have greatly facilitated the final construction of distribution theory. Sobolev also kept the integer m fixed; he never considered the intersection C_{comp}^∞ of the spaces C_{comp}^m for all m, which is surprising since he proved that $C_{\text{comp}}^{\infty+1}$ is dense in C_{comp}^m by Wiener's smoothing method.

In his formulation, Laurent Schwartz used the language and tools of functional analysis, essentially those of the landmark monograph of Stefan Banach, *Théorie des opérations linéaires* (1932): a distribution is a linear functional on the space C^∞_{comp} of test functions in an open subset of Euclidean space or, more generally, in a smooth manifold. The functional must be continuous, in the sense that its value on a sequence of test functions, whose derivatives of all orders converge uniformly and whose supports remain confined to a fixed compact subset, must converge. The basic operations of analysis, differentiation, and multiplication by smooth functions, are defined in the space D' of all distributions by transposition (thus derivative=weak derivative); and so is the convolution of two distributions (under reasonable hypotheses on their decay at infinity). The scale of Sobolev spaces H^s and their variants are seamlessly integrated in the array of distribution spaces (spaces topologically embedded into $\dot{D}'$). On Euclidean space $\mathbf{R^n}$ the interpretation of H^s via Fourier transform is practically self-evident.

A major contribution of the theory was the selection of the Schwartz space S of rapidly decaying C^∞ functions at infinity and of its dual S', the space of tempered distributions (see above), as the proper framework for Fourier analysis (ideas missing from Bochner's earlier analysis). This choice was not preordained: there are many other spaces stable under Fourier transform, spaces of functions that decay much faster at infinity. But other choices would run contrary to the deeper underlying uncertainty principle: the temperedness of tempered distributions ensures the localizability of their Fourier transform (think of analytic functionals whose Fourier transform can grow exponentially and that are not here nor there). Certain spaces of Gevrey ultradistributions are also localizabile, but they are of incomparably narrower usefulness.

Another remarkable feature of distribution theory is the Schwartz kernel theorem. It states a fundamental property of the main distribution spaces: In certain respects they are more like finite-dimensional Euclidean space than infinite-dimensional Banach spaces. Specifically, in any one of them, C^∞, C^∞_{comp}, D', D'_{comp}, S, S', and so on, every closed and bounded set is compact. Moreover, just as the (bounded) linear operators $\mathbf{R^m} \rightarrow \mathbf{R^n}$ are elements of $\mathbf{R^m} \times \mathbf{R^n}$ (i.e., $n \times m$ matrices) so too the bounded linear operators, say $K: C^\infty_{\text{comp}}(M_1) \rightarrow D'(M_2)$ (where M_1 and M_2 are two smooth manifolds) are in one-to-one correspondence with distributions $K(x,y)$ in the product manifold $M_1 \times M_2$. Half a century after its introduction, the Volterra integral was accordingly resuscitated:

$$\forall \varphi \in C^\infty_{\text{comp}}(M_1), \, K\,\varphi(x) = \int K(x,y)\varphi(y)dy$$

using the physicists' integral notation for the duality bracket. Under suitable hypotheses on supports and regularity with respect to x or y, this gives also a rigorous mean-

ing to Volterra composition: the kernel of the composite $K_1 \,\&\hat{x}\, K_2$ is the integral $\int K_1(x,y)K_2(y,z)dy$. The analogy with the finite dimensional situation extends to the fact that this property is equivalent to the isomorphism of $D'(M_1 \times M_2)$ with the tensor product $D'(M_1)\widehat{\otimes}D'(M_2)$ with the hat indicating completion (in the sense of every "natural" topology on the tensor product): distributions $ut(x,y)$ in $M_1 \times M_2$ are equal to "infinite" sums $\sum_{n=0}^\infty v_n(x)\otimes w_n(y)$. In all this, D' can be replaced by any one of the other functional spaces above. Grothendieck took the Schwartz kernel theorem as the starting point for his theory of nuclear spaces (the kernel theorem is true because the spaces under consideration are nuclear), and the theorem now provides a safe base for the study of such special classes of operators as, for example, pseudodifferential operators or Fourier integral operators. One starts by analyzing the corresponding kernel distributions, and there is no real need to know the (relatively simple) proof of the Schwartz kernel theorem.

Distributions can be, and often are, taught at the undergraduate level, without any recourse to functional analysis, using solely sequences of test functions or of distributions. The success of distributions lies in the simplicity of the rules for handling them. It is what mathematical analysis needed at the midpoint of the twentieth century: an easy algorithm allowing the basic operations of, for example, differentiating or integrating under the integral sign, to be carried out without a second thought. With the easy part taken care of, analysts were then free to dig deeper and work on the finer and truly difficult problems. Beyond analysis, distributions provided the language for vast tracks of mathematics, pure and applied. Only three examples will be mentioned here.

In the 1950s and 1960s, François Bruhat and Harish-Chandra showed the role of distributions in noncommutative harmonic analysis. Harish-Chandra defined the natural generalization of the Schwartz space S for semisimple Lie groups and put it to spectacular use in their representation theory.

In the 1940s the theorems of Georges De Rham on Hodge theory indicated that there was a duality between (singular) homology and (De Rham) cohomology on a C^∞ manifold. However, this duality could not be formalized in mathematically acceptable analytic terms until the early 1950s, when De Rham learned of Schwartz's theory of distributions and immediately introduced the necessary concept of currents, which are differential forms with distributional coefficients. The duality of currents with smooth differential forms having compact support is built into their definition, so the concept of currents can be extended to the exterior derivative, to Riemannian manifolds, and to the Hodge operations. In this way, co-cycles and co-boundaries become analytic objects: closed and exact currents, respectively. Chains in singular homology, normally regarded as concrete geometric objects, can also be viewed as currents. During the 1960s and 1970s, what are currents of weak regularity have turned out to be important in the study of minimal surfaces and of analytic varieties.

In general, physicists turned out to have been better prepared than mathematicians to accept distributions, perhaps because of their acquaintance with the work of Dirac. The Heisenberg uncertainty principle had accustomed them to the fact that an observable could not, in general, be evaluated at a point but had to be tested over extended regions. As it turned out, at a deeper level the axiomatic theory of quantum electrodynamics needed a highly sophisticated version of distributions, the distributions with values in the set of unbounded linear operators on a Hilbert space, and this led to serious difficulties, by no means entirely resolved and which are rooted in the impossibility of multiplying arbitrary distributions. Attempts to circumvent these difficulties were made through renormalization.

Probability Theory. At the end of the 1960s, Schwartz redirected his research towards infinite-dimensional measure and probability theory. His approach was through cylindrical Radon probabilities. A cylindrical Radon measure on, say, a separable Banach space $\mathbf{E}$ is the assignment to any pair $(\mathbf{X}, \mathbf{f})$ consisting of a finite-dimensional vector space $\mathbf{X}$ and of a continuous linear map $f: \mathbf{E} \to \mathbf{X}$, of a Radon measure μ_f with the obvious coherence requirements: if $\mathbf{Y}$ is another finite-dimensional vector space, and if $g: \mathbf{X} \to \mathbf{Y}$ is linear, then $\mu_{g \circ f} = g(\mu_f)$ A natural question is whether there is a Radon measure μ on $\mathbf{E}$ such that $\mu_f = (f, \mu)$ for every pair $(\mathbf{X}, \mathbf{f})$. Prokhorov's theorem provides the necessary and sufficient condition for this to be true. Schwartz focused his attention on the linear maps u of $\mathbf{E}$ into another Banach space $\mathbf{F}$ that transform an important class of cylindrical measures on $\mathbf{E}$ into true Radon measures on $\mathbf{F}$, which led him to the concept of p-Radonifying maps ($p > 0$). He proved that for $p > 1$ they are the same as the p-summing maps studied by other mathematicians. The map u is p-summing if it transforms every sequence $\{x_n\}_{n=1,2,...}$ such that $\sup_{\|x^*\|=1} \sum_{n=1}^{\infty} |\langle x^*, x_n \rangle|^p < +\infty$ (x^* an element of the dual $\mathbf{E}^*$ of $\mathbf{E}$) into a sequence such that $\sum_{n=1}^{\infty} \|u(x_n)\|^p < +\infty$. The same equivalence can be proved for $0 < p \le 1$ under some slightly restrictive hypotheses on $\mathbf{E}$ or $\mathbf{F}$. There is also an important Schwartz duality theorem: If $\mathbf{E}^*$ can be embedded into an L^p-space, then the adjoint $u^*: \mathbf{F}^* \to \mathbf{E}^*$ of an arbitrary p-summable map is p-summable. (Later, the embeddability of $\mathbf{E}^*$ into L^p was proved to be necessary.)

In later work Laurent Schwartz turned his attention to random processes and proposed to define semimartingales $\{X_t\}$ valued in a smooth (real or complex) manifold M by the property that $\varphi(X)$ be a real or complex semimartingale for every smooth map $\varphi: M \to \mathbf{R}$ or $\mathbf{C}$ (here "smooth" means C^2 or holomorphic). If M is complex but not Stein, for instance if M is compact, there might not be (enough) holomorphic functions φ for this definition to make sense, which led Schwartz to localize his definition of M-valued semimartingales. Following on his lifelong habit of exploiting duality, he gave a weak definition of dX through stochastic integrals $\int HdX$ in which H plays the role of a test-function. With this approach Schwartz was able to give a new, coordinate-free interpretation of the classical Ito formula as the equation $d(f(X_t)) = (d\underline{X}_t)$ f, where $d\underline{X}_t$ is a special second-order stochastic differential operator on M.

BIBLIOGRAPHY

WORKS BY SCHWARTZ

Théorie des distributions. New ed. Paris, France: Hermann, 1966.

"Applications p-radonifiantes et théorème de dualité." *Studia Mathematica* 38 (1970): 203–213.

"Géométrie différentielle stochastique ...." *Lecture Notes in Mathematics* 780 (1982).

Un mathématicien aux prises avec le siècle. Paris, France: Odile Jacob, 1997.

OTHER SOURCES>

Banach, Stefan. *Théorie des opérations linéaires.* Warsaw, Poland: Monografje Matematyczne, 1932.

Bochner, Salomon. *Vorlesungen über Fouriersche Integrale.* Leipzig, Germany: Akademische Verlagsgesellschaft, 1932.

De Rham, Georges de. *Variétés différentiables.* Paris, France: Hermann, 1955.

Sobolev, S. L. "Méthode nouvelle à résoudre le problème de Cauchy pour les équations hyperboliques linéaires normales." *Mat. Sb.* 1, no. 43 (1936): 39–72.

———. "Sur un théorème d'analyse fonctionnelle." *Mat. Sb.* 1 (46) (1938): 39–68.

Streater, R. F., and A. S. Wightman. *PCT, Spin, Statistics, and All That.* New York: Benjamin, 1964.

Weil, A. *L'intégration dans les groupes topologiques et ses applications.* Paris, France: Hermann, 1940.

François Treves

SCHWARZSCHILD, MARTIN (*b.* Potsdam, Germany, 31 May 1912; *d.* Princeton, New Jersey, 10 April 1997), *astrophysics, galaxy evolution, stellar constitution, interiors, and evolution.*

Schwarzschild, a leading practitioner of the theory of stellar structure and evolution for much of the twentieth century, made enormous contributions not only to astronomical knowledge but to the professional development of the American astronomical community. His mentoring and textbook writing trained generations, and his personality and social sensibilities inspired colleagues and students alike.

Life and Family in Germany. Born to the famed director of the Potsdam Astrophysical Observatory, Karl Schwarzschild, and Else Rosenbach, the daughter of a professor of medicine and surgery at the University of Göttingen, he was the middle of three children. His father died in 1916, and so the family returned to Göttingen, where Martin was raised and trained in astronomy by Hans Kienle, the director at Göttingen. Martin and his siblings grew up in a protected, narrow social stratum surrounded by family and his parents' colleagues and friends. Of them, Martin counted the physicist Carl Runge as one of his earliest influences and mentors in mathematics and physics. Robert Emden, the author of the famous *Gaskugeln*, was an uncle by marriage.

After completing classical secondary school training, Schwarzschild entered the University of Göttingen in 1931, studying mainly mathematics and physics, at Kienle's direction, under Richard Courant and Otto Neugebauer. He also studied in Berlin, and was in fact there when the Reichstag burned and Adolf Hitler became chancellor. At that point, in February 1933, his mother decided that conditions were turning too threatening and called him back to Göttingen, urging him to complete his studies through to the PhD as quickly as possible, which he did, sympathetically encouraged and protected by Kienle through tutorials and directed reading.

Schwarzschild had acquired an interest in the pulsation theory of a class of variable stars called Cepheids, renowned for their utility in calculating distances to stars. But largely through reading Arthur Stanley Eddington's books and learning there that the mechanism through which the stars vary in luminosity was not at all well understood in terms of its varying structure, Schwarzschild set himself the task of understanding how Cepheids pulsate as they do. He was interested in a theoretical study, but Kienle required observational work as well, which took much longer than expected, mainly because of the antiquated equipment and poor weather conditions. In consequence Martin was still at work on his thesis when persons of Jewish descent were barred from any of the university buildings. So Kienle had the janitor of the observatory take the needed measuring equipment each night to Schwarzschild's mother's apartment so that he could finish the work as rapidly and invisibly as possible.

Completing his PhD exam in December 1935, and his thesis soon after, "Zur Pulsationstheorie der delta Cephei-Sterne" (On the pulsation theory of delta Cepheid stars), Schwarzschild still had to finish his observations, and as he was doing this, Kienle searched for a way to get him out of Germany. Svein Rosseland of Oslo quickly offered him a one-year postdoctoral position at his institute starting in the spring of 1936, which allowed him to study pulsation theory, the theory of the stellar interior, and stellar rotation.

Postdoctoral Fellowship in Oslo. Research in Oslo centered around stellar structure calculations aided by one of Vannevar Bush's mechanical analogue computing machine known as a differential analyzer. Rosseland encouraged Schwarzschild and others to use it collectively and even though Schwarzschild was initially skeptical he found it useful enough to do publishable work with it on pulsation, the first astronomical publication to appear based upon its application. During his tenure in Oslo, he also explored observational constraints on possible sources of energy production in stars.

Move to the United States. Schwarzschild was barely in Oslo when Harlow Shapley invited him to a three-year appointment at Harvard University. He arrived at Harvard in the summer of 1937, finding a vibrant company of European refugee scientists and American astronomers and physicists. He continued to work on Cepheid pulsation, analyzing how the pulsation characteristics could be used to determine the phase relationship between the light and velocity variations.

In the summer of 1938, during a visit to Stockholm and the General Assembly of the International Astronomical Union, Schwarzschild argued that pulsations were limited to the outer envelope of stars, and so were not a good indicator of what went on in the stellar core. Thus they were comparatively less interesting as tests or constraints on energy sources. Nevertheless, he carried on with his Cepheid work, all the while becoming more and more involved with problems of the deep stellar interior. His visit to Stockholm also gave him the opportunity to visit his mother in Germany, which was the last time they were together. By then his older sister had moved to England for study, and his younger brother, in deteriorating health, remained behind.

At Harvard Schwarzschild became acquainted with people such as Subrahmanyan Chandrasekhar and Lyman Spitzer. Both would play central roles in the course of Schwarzschild's career. Through Shapley and Bart Bok, he responded to a job offer from Columbia University, and acquired his first permanent position. In a two-person department working for Jan Schilt, Schwarzschild found at his disposal a legacy created by Wallace J. Eckert, who had pioneered the use of punched-card-fed computing machines for astronomy. With support from Thomas J. Watson, Eckert had secured an array of IBM machines and staff in what was called after 1937 the Thomas J. Watson Astronomical Computing Bureau. Schilt's students used the machines for statistical studies of stellar motions, and Schwarzschild applied them to his Cepheid research with the invaluable aid of a machine operator named Lillian Feinstein. She taught Schwarzschild how to use the machines, and then assisted in the actual calculations. These were all mechanical and electrical devices, without logical electronics, but they were so much more capable than Rosseland's Oslo machine that Schwarzschild was able to reevaluate his pulsation models, accurate to far more decimal places. Recent statistical studies of Cepheid periods suggested to Schwarzschild that this class of variable star exhibited the characteristics of harmonic oscillators and so he explored them with this well-known technique.

During his eighteen months at Columbia, Schwarzschild had considerable contact with senior physicists such as Enrico Fermi, as well as Isidor I. Rabi and Harold Urey. He knew that the physicists could not talk about their secret work, so lunches were devoted to astrophysics. Fermi in particular was very helpful and insightful, supplying data that were otherwise difficult to obtain, such as estimates for cross sections for collisions between electrons and hydrogen atoms. These helped Schwarzschild calculate levels of collisional ionization in the hydrogen convection zones in the stellar interiors of red giants, finding them more important than photoionization effects for creating equilibrium conditions.

At Columbia in 1941, following up conversations with Gunnar Randers in Oslo, and continued contact with Chandrasekhar, who was then a visiting professor at Princeton University, Schwarzschild began to look seriously at the importance of stellar rotation, basically to find equilibrium configurations for stars that possessed angular momentum. He was working on this problem as well as teaching when the attack on Pearl Harbor changed his life for he decided then and there to enlist in the army. As a German Jew, he felt he could not avoid active service when the American students he was teaching were all headed that way.

War Service. After basic training and a short assignment to an antiaircraft gunnery unit, Schwarzschild transferred to the Aberdeen Proving Ground in Maryland for ballistics research, but chafed at the assignment, wanting to see action at the front. He was now a citizen, so he applied for Officers' Candidate School, specifically the antiaircraft gunnery officers' school, which brought a special assign-

ment with the Twelfth U.S. Air Force in Italy, performing operations analysis with a front line ordnance unit to assess the types of ordnance needed to carry out such tactical missions as knocking out bridges and railroad lines. With the end of the war, Schwarzschild was discharged as a first lieutenant, receiving the Legion of Merit and a Bronze Star for his services, mainly for producing a simplified fire control system that could be used in the field to operate antiaircraft batteries.

Returning from the war, back at Columbia, Schwarzschild married Barbara Cherry. They had met at Harvard when Barbara, a Radcliffe University student, took graduate astronomy courses. They corresponded throughout the war and married immediately after the war, just as Barbara was finishing her work at the Massachusetts Institution of Technology's Radiation Laboratory. Barbara also became Martin's collaborator and professional associate, engaging in astronomical research, especially the observational aspects, supporting him in his interests, and managing the affairs of the family. They could not have children.

By the time he returned in late 1945 he was already working on stellar rotation again as well as a related study of the solar helium content. As one of the most promising young theorists in America, he soon had offers from major astronomical centers that were reorganizing and strengthening their theoretical expertise in astrophysics. Ultimately Schwarzschild chose Princeton, mainly because Spitzer had been called there as the new director, and his contacts with Spitzer through the Neighbors' meetings, a periodic conference of East Coast astronomers, convinced him that their scientific philosophies and outlook were very similar and that Spitzer would provide just the environment he needed. Both were basically theoreticians, but both knew that they could not work independent of observational constraints, and in fact both wanted to remain active in observational work. Spitzer had, in fact, accepted the directorship with the understanding that a second senior professorship would be provided, and that both would be allowed leaves of absence on a regular basis for observational work. Schwarzschild remained at Princeton for the remainder of his career and life.

Princeton Years. Schwarzschild and Spitzer set about rebuilding Princeton astronomy. They centered their graduate program around a strong theoretical core, creating a two-year cycle of four one-semester graduate astronomy courses, requiring that their students take the rest of their training in physics. Gradually they added staff, mainly through new research programs. In particular Schwarzschild became involved in Spitzer's large project to design and develop a stable fusion reactor called the "Stellerator," an adjunct to Project Matterhorn, John

Martin Schwarzschild. *Schwarzschild adjusting a large telescopic camera.* AP IMAGES.

Wheeler's nuclear weapons program. Both men were stimulated to get involved in such work when the Korean War broke out. Both developed strong connections with staff and graduate students at the combined Mount Wilson and Palomar Observatories. This cross-institutional pattern established one of the most robust programs in stellar astrophysics in the world, which led to, among other things, the modern view of how stars age.

Stellar Structure and Evolution. Schwarzschild had always been interested in stellar structure, as the central theme in stellar astronomy. He was keenly aware of attempts by others to build models of the Sun and stars, based largely upon Eddington's idea that the source of energy causing a star to shine was distributed throughout its interior, and that the energy itself was transported to the stellar surface chiefly by radiation, not by the transfer of matter (convection). By the late 1930s, however, Schwarzschild was among a small but growing circle of theoretical astrophysicists who knew that that Eddington's "standard model" had to be modified in a number of significant ways: first by arguments that thermonuclear energy sources had to lie at the very centers of stars, and

that this created huge temperature gradients and hence convection in stellar cores. Further, the fusion processes would cause chemical inhomogeneities that would change the interior structure. With the appearance and rapid acceptance of Hans Bethe and Karl F. von Weizsäcker's specific nuclear mechanisms, the proton-proton (PP) and the carbon-nitrogen-oxygen (CNO) cycles, which confirmed the need for a high temperature gradient to produce helium from hydrogen, by the early 1940s everyone knew that stratified, composite models would be necessary to explore the evolution of stars. But just at that time, Chandrasekhar and Mario Schönberg had shown that there was an upper limit to the amount of hydrogen within a star available for fusion. Once that fraction was consumed, the core would become isothermal (a single temperature throughout) and beyond that there seemed to be no stable equilibrium configurations for stars. The problem became: how to model stars with varying compositions but isothermal cores, especially at a stage after hydrogen was exhausted in the core? The physicist George Gamow had the idea that increased temperatures in the inner portion of the outer envelope would stimulate a new source called shell burning. Chandrasekhar rejected this idea and Gamow's techniques, arguing that they were not mathematically rigorous.

Chandrasekhar and Gamow's differences destabilized the field somewhat in the 1940s, and Schwarzschild cautiously explored how stars might change in structure in response to chemical and physical changes. Schwarzschild's first stellar model for the Sun in 1946 was homogeneous with a convective core. He adjusted composition to match the solar luminosity and radius and employed the CNO process. He tried for more realism in 1949, collaborating first with Li Hen and later with J. Beverly Oke, constructing red giants that were static and inhomogeneous and at first nonevolving, but soon, with convective cores, they could be made to evolve, through a series of laborious computational exercises. In hindsight, at this time one can see Schwarzschild beginning a series of connected studies leading to a way to overcome the Schönberg-Chandrasekhar limit, and to explore what happens to stars once they exhaust hydrogen in their cores.

The great question at the time was: where do stars "go" on the Hertzsprung-Russell (HR) diagram?, which was then, as now, the heuristic playing field for stellar evolution studies. Since the first elucidation of the HR diagram, a graphical plot of a star's physical characteristics, mainly its temperature against its intrinsic brightness, by Ejnar Hertzsprung and Henry N. Russell independently between 1908 and 1913, astronomers had used the HR diagram to explore how these characteristics of a star change as the star ages. Do they become white dwarfs or red giants? Gamow and almost everyone else had for decades assumed that it had to be toward the white dwarf stages because that was the time-honored direction of gravitational contraction. But observational and theoretical evidence had been mounting since the early 1930s that such was not the case. Schwarzschild's strategy was to test theory against the best observational evidence. The latter was facilitated by his connections with Walter Baade and the Mount Wilson–Palomar–California Institute of Technology staff. Essentially, Schwarzschild and Baade joined forces to solve the stellar evolution problem. The details of this episode are in David H. DeVorkin (2006).

Baade's goal in 1951 was to find, using HR diagrams of globular clusters, just where and how stars in these clusters, all believed to be of the same age, and evolving at rates highly dependent upon their relative masses, ceased being common "main sequence" types and began moving to the red giant range, in other words, where and when in their lives did they "turn off" the main sequence to become giants? Baade coordinated observations in the West, and Schwarzschild the theory in the East, and both visited back and forth, cross-fertilizing students and staff.

Observed cluster "turn-off" points were not fully reconciled with theoretical models of shell burning until Schwarzschild collaborated with Fred Hoyle in the spring of 1953. By then Schwarzschild had the assistance of Richard Härm, who was exceptionally adept at numerical computational techniques. Working also with William Baum and then with Hoyle, who brought in new perspectives from nuclear physics, Schwarzschild had assembled a wealth of talents and insights to combine computational and heuristic techniques to make the final push. Hoyle refined the models Schwarzschild had constructed earlier with Allan Sandage, finding that stellar turnoffs occurred after the envelope of the star went from radiative equilibrium to convective equilibrium with the onset of shell burning. The now-accepted idea of a hydrogen-burning shell migrating outward through the envelope worked sufficiently well to match observations, right up into the giant realm in the upper right-hand corner of the HR diagram. Thus by 1955 the forty-year-old picture of red giants as young stars in formation was finally reversed by Schwarzschild, Baade, and their compatriots, establishing them as old, evolved stars.

Schwarzschild continued on exploring the fine structure of postmain sequence stellar evolution well into the 1970s and to retirement. But a watershed came in 1958 when he published the first advanced textbook that explicitly led students through the process. *Structure and Evolution of the Stars* was considered a central source of instruction and inspiration soon after its publication. It was a straightforward book, designed to be affordable and disposable, and was written in a conversational tone that became an inspiration to generations of advanced students, laying out the processes of stellar evolution on the eve of access to high-speed electronic computers. It described the problems yet to solve, and gave hints on how to solve them. Schwarzschild recalls knowing that it would not be a definitive work; in fact, he intended it to be a stimulus to attract new talent to the field.

Other Lines of Research. Schwarzschild will be most remembered for his contributions to stellar structure and evolution, but he was also keenly interested in the closely related problem of sorting out and interpreting the meaning of Baade's stellar populations and in the nature and importance of convection in the atmospheres of the Sun and stars. There were links between all three.

During the war, at Mount Wilson Baade announced his revolutionary concept that the stellar content of galaxies could be divided into distinct populations with characteristic colors and luminosities. Population I stars were found in the disk of the galaxy, mainly single stars and stars in open galactic clusters, whereas Population II were in the bulge and halo, characteristic of the stars found in globular clusters, the nuclei of spiral galaxies and in elliptical galaxies. He called upon astronomers to figure out why these differences existed. In 1950 Martin and Barbara Schwarzschild made one of their periodic visits to Mount Wilson to take a series of high-dispersion spectra to compare the chemical characteristics of high-velocity and low velocity F-type stars. These velocity classes were thought to be an indicator of age, and indeed, they found a correlation: the metal to hydrogen ratio was higher in the low-velocity Population I stars, and higher in the Population II high-velocity stars. This association between heavy-metal abundance and population helped to establish the evolutionary significance of the populations. Schwarzschild continued this line of work, collaborating with Spitzer and Rupert Wildt, to further explore the origins of these chemical differences in terms of evolutionary differences in the interstellar medium. Again Schwarzschild was most interested in how the stellar populations revealed element-building processes in stellar evolution, whereas Spitzer was more interested in how conditions in the interstellar medium promoted star formation, using his expertise in the physics of plasmas. Schwarzschild continued his interest in stellar populations through the 1950s, in collaboration with students and staff from Mount Wilson.

The second related area he engaged in his postwar career dealt with theories of convection and the importance of element mixing and rotation in an evolving star. After a summer of solar observing at Mount Wilson in 1950 with Robert S. Richardson, trying to examine convective phenomena in the solar photosphere, Schwarzschild became frustrated by limitations of Earth's atmosphere. Back in Princeton, Schwarzschild complained to Spitzer and others about this seemingly insuperable limitation, and, encouraged by Spitzer and James Van Allen, who was then part of Project Matterhorn, decided to pursue building a telescope that could be lofted by balloon into the transparent upper stratospheric layers. Spitzer was thinking about the ultimate use of satellites for astronomy, and even Schwarzschild's father had flown solar instruments on a zeppelin years back. So Martin Schwarzschild, with Spitzer's guidance, eventually created Project Stratoscope, funded by the Office of Naval Research and later by the National Science Foundation (NSF) and finally by the National Aeronautics and Space Administration (NASA).

The first stratoscope was highly successful: a 12-inch photographic reflector on a stabilized platform flew under huge plastic balloons in 1957 and, in an improved form, in 1959 to produce the clearest images of the solar photosphere known to exist at that time. They were in fact sufficiently clear to help Schwarzschild discriminate between competing theories of convection in the outer solar envelope and spurred him to return to convection theory in the 1960s.

In the post-Sputnik era, Spitzer committed his department to building a large spaceborne telescope. Allied with this institutional effort, Schwarzschild continued Project Stratoscope, expanding its scope with NASA funding to build a 36-inch balloon-borne system, Stratoscope 2, capable of performing a range of spectroscopic and visible-range imaging studies requiring precise pointing and stability. As he recalled years later, "We always looked at the balloons as an exercising ground, for scientific results, before the satellites. All of which took more time than we then thought" (Schwarzschild oral history, 19 July 1979, p. 162, American Institute of Physics). It was indeed a time-consuming and deeply frustrating experience for Schwarzschild, who loyally continued with the program well through the 1960s. His mistake, he later felt, was to stick with photographic imaging, which required pointing and stability precision beyond what was feasible at the time.

Beyond his immediate duties of research and teaching, Schwarzschild participated in NSF funding panels and later, as a member of the National Academy of Sciences, was invited to become a member of the Space Science Panel of the President's Science Advisory Committee (PSAC), serving for some eight years during the Apollo era, 1959 through 1967. After that he served on NASA's Astronomy Missions Board from 1967 though 1969. His most active participation on the PSAC panel centered on preparing arguments for the White House, and later for congressional testimony in 1962, regarding a scientific role for Project Apollo. Schwarzschild never felt that science could justify the expense of the Apollo program, but

did testify that good science could be done as a consequence of a human lunar landing. However, he always argued that its real value was to help stimulate and boost science education in the United States, as well as the nation's overall technology capability.

Schwarzschild was active in the International Astronomical Union, serving as a vice president; and in the American Astronomical Society, serving as vice president, president-elect, and president between 1967 and 1972. This was a time of profound change in the society as it formed large specialty-related divisions and managed the transfer of arguably the most important astronomical journal of the time, the *Astrophysical Journal,* to society ownership.

Retirement. Schwarzschild formally retired from Princeton in 1979 but remained active in the profession and in research. Characteristically modest, he later recalled that his retirement was stimulated by the retirement of his longtime associate Richard Härm, who had contributed so much to his effectiveness in stellar structure and evolution calculations. Upon retirement Schwarzschild also switched his research focus from stellar interiors to the study of galactic structure, which had been a longtime interest. Taking a middle course between those interested in the astrophysics of galaxy structure and evolution, and those who examined galaxies dynamically, Schwarzschild decided to perform a series of computational experiments that would create numerical models for the structure of the nuclei of elliptical galaxies that could be tested against observation. His goal was to test an assumption that others had always made: that galaxy nuclei were rotationally symmetric. What he found was that deviations from rotational symmetry fit the observations better than those constrained by symmetry, which, as Jeremiah Ostriker (1997) put it, "revolutionized our understanding of elliptical galaxies," showing them to be triaxial.

Schwarzschild was the recipient of many awards and honors. He was Russell Prize Lecturer of the American Astronomical Society for 1960, and received the Bruce Medal of the Astronomical Society of the Pacific (1965) and the Gold Medal of the Royal Astronomical Society (1969). He was elected a foreign member of the Royal Society in 1996, and was a posthumous recipient of the U.S. National Medal of Science in 1997. Martin and Barbara lived a quiet but full life, on a wooded street between the Princeton campus and the Institute for Advanced Study. They shared many interests beyond astronomy, including skiing, cross-country snowshoe treks, gardening, mineral and rock collecting, and birding. They arranged their backyard to accommodate their interests and there enjoyed being a part of nature.

BIBLIOGRAPHY

Much of the material in this essay is based upon oral histories, Martin Schwarzschild "Oral History" American Institute of Physics Center for History of Physics: 10 March 1977; 3 June 1977; 16 December 1977; 19 July 1977; 18 June 1982; 20 April 1983; 26 August 1991. There is also an interview with Schwarzschild concentrating on computational techniques at the Charles Babbage Institute, University of Minnesota. Martin Schwarzschild's private papers are housed at Princeton University's Firestone Library, Manuscript Division.

WORKS BY SCHWARZSCHILD

"Zur Pulsationstheorie der delta Cephei-Sterne." Veröffentlichungen der Universitäts-Sternwarte Göttingen, Nr. 45. *Zeitschrift für Astrophysik* 11 (1936): 152–180. His thesis.

"Über die Energieerzeugung in den Sternen." *Zeitschrift für Astrophysik* 13 (1937): 126.

"Zur Pulsationstheorie." Mitteilung aus dem Institut für theoretische Astrophysik, Oslo. *Zeitschrift für Astrophysik* 15 (1938): 14–31.

"Overtone Pulsations for the Standard Model." *Astrophysical Journal* 94 (1941): 245–252.

With Lillian Feinstein. "Automatic Integration of Linear Second-Order Differential Equations by Means of Punched-Card Machines." *Review of Scientific Instruments* 12 (1941): 405–408.

With Lyman Spitzer Jr., and Rupert Wildt. "On the Difference in Chemical Composition between High- and Low-Velocity Stars." *Astrophysical Journal* 114 (1951): 398–406.

With I. Rabinowitz, and Richard Härm. "Inhomogeneous Stellar Models. III. Models with Partially Degenerate Isothermal Cores." *Astrophysical Journal* 118 (1953): 326–334.

With Richard Härm. "Inhomogeneous Stellar Models. IV. Models with Continuously Varying Chemical Composition." *Astrophysical Journal* 121 (1955): 445–453.

With Fred Hoyle. "On the Evolution of Type II Stars." *Astrophysical Journal* 121 (1955): 776. Brief summary of the following paper.

———. "On the Evolution of Type II Stars." *Astrophysical Journal Supplement* 2 (1955): 1–40.

With William A. Baum. "A Comparison of Stellar Populations in the Andromeda Galaxy and Its Elliptical Companion." *Astronomical Journal* 60 (1955): 247–253.

Structure and Evolution of the Stars. Princeton, NJ: Princeton University Press, 1958. Reprinted, New York: Dover, 1965.

With John B. Rogerson Jr., and J. W. Evans. "Solar Photographs from 80,000 Feet." *Astronomical Journal* 63 (1958): 313.

With Richard Härm. "Evolution of Very Massive Stars." *Astrophysical Journal* 128 (1958): 348–360.

With J. D. R. Bahng, R. E. Danielson, and J. B. Rogerson Jr. "Sunspot Photographs from the Stratosphere." *Astronomical Journal* 64 (1959): 323.

"Convection in Stars." *Astrophysical Journal* 134 (1961): 1–8. 1960 Henry Norris Russell Prize Lecture.

"Astronomical Photography from the Stratoscope." In *Annual Report of the Smithsonian Institution.* Washington, DC: U.S. Government Printing Office, 1963.

"Prepared Statement on the Space Program." *Publications of the Astronomical Society of the Pacific* 75 (1963): 527. Reprint (from *Congressional Record*) of statement to the Senate Committee on Aeronautical and Space Sciences, 11 June 1963.

"Stellar Evolution in Globular Clusters." *Quarterly Journal of the Royal Astronomical Society* 11 (1970): 12–22. 1969 George Darwin Lecture, RAS.

With E. S. Light and R. E. Danielson. "The Nucleus of M31." *Astrophysical Journal* 194 (1974): 257–263.

"Triaxial Equilibrium Models for Elliptical Galaxies with Slow Figure Rotation." *Astrophysical Journal* 263 (1982): 599–610.

OTHER SOURCES

Arny, Thomas. "The Star Makers: A History of the Theories of Stellar Structure and Evolution." *Vistas in Astronomy* 33, no. 2 (1990): 211–233.

Burbidge, E. Margaret, and Geoffrey Burbidge. "Stellar Evolution." In *Handbuch der Physik.* Vol. 51: *Astrophysik II: Sternaufbau,* edited by S. Flügge. Berlin: Springer, 1958.

DeVorkin, David H. *Henry Norris Russell: Dean of American Astronomers.* Princeton, NJ: Princeton University Press, 2000.

———. "The Changing Place of Red Giants in the Evolutionary Process." *Journal for the History of Astronomy* 37 (2006): 429–469.

Emden, Robert. *Gaskugeln: Anwendungen der mechanischen Wärmetheorie auf kosmologische und meteorologische Probleme.* Leipzig, Germany: B. Teubner, 1907.

Henyey, Louis G. "Award of the Bruce Gold Medal to Martin Schwarzschild." *Publications of the Astronomical Society of the Pacific* 77 (August 1965): 233–236.

Merritt, David. "Martin Schwarzschild's Contribution to Galaxy Dynamics." In *Galaxy Dynamics: A Rutgers Symposium: Proceedings of a Symposium Held at Rutgers University, Piscataway, New Jersey, USA, 8–12 August 1998,* edited by David Merritt, J. A. Sellwood, and Monica Valluri. Astronomical Society of the Pacific conference series, vol. 182. San Francisco: Astronomical Society of the Pacific, 1999.

Mestel, Leon. "Martin Schwarzschild, a Tribute." *Bulletin of the Astronomical Society of India* 25 (1997): 285–287.

Osterbrock, Donald. Chapter 5. In *Walter Baade: A Life in Astrophysics.* Princeton, NJ: Princeton University Press, 2001.

Ostriker, Jeremiah P. "Martin Schwarzschild, (31 May 1912–10 April 1979)." *Nature* 388 (31 July 1997): 430. Reprinted in the *Proceedings of the American Philosophical Society* 143 (September 1999): 487–489.

Sandage, Allan. *Centennial History of the Carnegie Institution of Washington.* Vol. 1, *The Mount Wilson Observatory.* Cambridge, U.K.: Cambridge University Press, 2004.

Tassoul, Jean-Louis, and Monique Tassoul. *A Concise History of Solar and Stellar Physics.* Princeton, NJ: Princeton University Press, 2004.

Trimble, Virginia. "Martin Schwarzschild (1912–1997)." *Publications of the Astronomical Society of the Pacific* 109 (December 1997): 1289–1297.

David H. DeVorkin

SCHWENDENER, SIMON

SCHWENDENER, SIMON (*b.* Buchs, St. Gallen [now Aargau], Switzerland, 10 February 1829; *d.* Berlin, Germany, 27 May 1919), *plant anatomy and physiology.* For the original article on Schwendener, see *DSB,* volume 12.

Recent scholarship has brought two aspects of Schwendener's botanical research to light: his investigations of lichens as component, symbiotic organisms and his mechanical approach to understanding plant anatomy. Though the conclusions he offered in each of these areas drew criticism from his contemporaries, Schwendener was still influential in redirecting investigative botany through his students' studies of biogeography and adaptation.

Since 1990, Schwendener's contributions to nineteenth-century botany have been more closely examined. Whereas in the early 1800s botany was dominated by taxonomic concerns and anatomical research, from the late 1830s onward efforts by a handful of botanists, initially led by Matthias Schleiden at Jena, changed the scope of academic botany from plant anatomy and taxonomy to investigations into the biological processes that controlled plant development, reproduction, growth, and nutrition. Schwendener's research embodies this changing emphasis in two main areas: in his studies of lichens and their implications for symbiosis, and in his physicomechanical approach to plant anatomy.

Study of Lichens. Schwendener's investigations into the physiology of lichens not only changed how botanists classified these puzzling organisms, but also opened new ways into thinking about parasitism and symbiosis. Traditionally, lichens, along with many other newly observed microscopic organisms (including bacteria), had been indiscriminately and inconsistently lumped among the cryptogams—unicellular organisms that lacked differentiated structures (such as algae, fungi, mosses, and some ferns). How to accurately classify and characterize lichens was among the most hotly contested questions in cryptogamic botany in the middle of the century.

During 1868 and 1869 Schwendener published a series of books and papers in which he presented his "dual hypothesis"—that lichens comprised both algae and fungi in a parasitic relationship. Each component of a lichen had a specific physiologic role: the alga contributed carbon dioxide obtained from the air, whereas the fungus contributed water and minerals from soil or other material. From this, Schwendener concluded that lichens were a modified form of fungus. The algae found in lichens, he claimed, were transformed over the course of a few generations of association and were no longer recognizable as individual or distinct organisms. This characterization of fungi drew heavy criticism from some of his colleagues. Cryptogamists who had concentrated their energies upon arguing that lichens were their own distinct group of organisms objected to what they regarded as their reduction to a subdivision of algae or fungi, thus undermining evidence of their distinctiveness from other cryptogams.

In addition, Schwendener had described lichens in social rather than biological terms. Specifically, he regarded the fungi and algae as suspended in a master-slave relationship. The fungi—usually ascomycetes—were predators who enveloped their prey and enslaved them for physiological gain. As Jan Sapp has explained, even botanists who agreed with Schwendener's dual hypothesis took issue with this slavery metaphor; Johannes Reinke, for example, believed lichens were more accurately described as "cooperative" organisms, rather than as modified fungi.

This distinction, along with the idea that lichens might be a dual or composite organism, gained strength among Schwendener's students and the students of Anton de Bary at Strassburg (now Strasbourg, France). As Reinke had insisted, isolating the component organisms destroyed the lichen; while it was possible to isolate the algae from lichens, reintroducing algae to their associated fungi did not consistently produce a lichen. These fungi were not easily cultured, which cryptogamists interpreted as evidence that they had adapted so completely to the presence of algae that they were incapable of surviving when isolated. Lichens were therefore confirmed as double organisms, yet also as sufficiently morphologically and physiologically distinct from algae and fungi. This realization necessitated not only a revision of classificatory schema that saw lichens as fungi or intermediate organisms, but also a revision of Schwendener's conception of the component algae as parasitic "slaves." This, in turn, prompted cryptogamic physiologist Albert Bernhard Frank to coin a new word in 1877 to describe the relationship—*symbiotismus,* later popularized by de Bary as *symbiosis.* Frank used this term to denote the coexistence of organisms without ascribing either a functional role or assuming a parasitic relationship.

Use of the Microscope. Like Schleiden and the first generation of cryptogamic physiologists, Schwendener was dissatisfied with what he regarded as outmoded, traditional approaches to plant anatomy. He, too, turned to microscopy as the best means of tackling unanswered questions, and published a treatise on its proper use in botany: *Das Mikroskop: Theorie und Anwendung desselben* (which he coauthored with Karl von Nägeli), a detailed technical manual for the use of the microscope in botanical investigation. *Das Mikroskop* included an extensive description of physical optics; a comparison (complete with in-text images and a price list at the end of the book) of the different kinds of microscopes then available, the technical and mechanical differences between them, and the different purposes for which they might be used; and instructions for adjusting for optical aberrations and the vagaries of working with different media, before introducing the microscope's use in morphological and anatomical study.

But Schwendener's integration of microscopy into investigative botany was significantly different from that of Schleiden and his colleagues. Whereas the first generation of cryptogamists regarded microscopy as a means of observing physiological processes, Schwendener used microscopy as a means of identifying the principles that regulated the structure and arrangement of plant tissues. He was frustrated with existing morphology and anatomy texts; he dismissed de Bary's comparative morphology textbooks as outdated and descriptive, and criticized them for their lack of analysis.

Schwendener preferred a method that emphasized interpretation over description and was highly derivative of his background in physics and mechanics. He saw in mechanics the analytical tools and methods that could explain multiple traits of plant anatomy and structure. Early in his career, for example, he conducted what Eugene Cittadino has described as a "detailed mathematical study of periodic phenomena" such as the opening of buds. He expanded his mechanical approach into a search for a general principle that could explain the structure and arrangement of plant tissues. His method was rooted in the conviction that plant structures at the cellular level—that is, the shape and arrangement of individual cells—determined the mechanical and structural properties of plants and their component tissues.

Schwendener described this approach as "physicomathematical," that is, a joint physiological and anatomical investigation that could be applied to all tissue systems of a plant and emphasized the relationships between the component tissues of plants and their structural characteristics. The shape and the orientation of cells, he argued, was directly relevant to the mechanical properties of the tissue they constituted—more accurately, the physical properties of the cells determined the physical properties of the tissue. In 1874 Schwendener published *Das mechanische Princip im anatomischen Bau der Monocotylen*, in which he applied this physicomathematical method to his investigations of the relationship between structural tissue

(specifically, sclerenchyma) and responses to physical stress in monocotyledons. he regarded this book as a distinct break from traditional descriptive plant anatomy.

Historical reports of the reception of this volume are somewhat conflicting. De Bary and Julius von Sachs, professor of botany at Würzburg, Germany, supposedly dismissed the volume, yet Cittadino has noted that de Bary declared the book to be "excellent" and was highly complimentary. But Sachs complained that the book was too steeped in mathematics and physics, and that it was not appropriate to describe the tissues on which Schwendener had focused as a "mechanical system." Other criticisms contended that physiological anatomy was too utilitarian and tended toward the teleological or noted that Schwendener's plant anatomy was strictly structural; he limited his discussion to mature plants and did not address development—either as a process or its relationship to anatomy—at all.

Though responses to Schwendener's book may have been mixed, his students—Gottlieb Haberlandt in particular—enthusiastically applied physicomathematical anatomy to research questions in many different areas of botany. Topics such as the mechanical aspects of dissemination of fruits and seeds, the mechanism of coiling in climbing plants, and the effects of exposure to weight on wood growth were among those investigated by his students at the Berlin Botanical Institute.

But the implications of Schwendener's plant anatomy went beyond the properties of specific tissues and extended to questions of structural adaptation and evolution as well. Even so, as Cittadino has noted, this was not as much the result of Darwinian thought as it was a continuation of Schwendener's interest in structure with respect to function. Schwendener was critical of natural selection, and instead argued that internal forces, not environmental pressures, drove evolutionary change. As such, adaptation was a highly individualized, mechanical process, and in the 1880s Schwendener took special interest in the relationship between specific anatomical features of plants and environmental conditions. This interest, in turn, led him to encourage his students to pursue field research.

Schwendener as Educator. At Berlin, Schwendener's students formed a close-knit group of botanists whose enthusiasm for "*physiologische Pflanzenanatomie*" dominated the Botanical Institute in the late 1870s and 1880s. Many of his students faced the same sort of criticisms that Schwendener's own work had drawn, yet remained undaunted in their pursuits. Schwendener's teaching style likely strengthened both his students' sense of camaraderie and their dedication to their work; though he continued writing theoretical papers and books while at Berlin, he conducted no new research, and instead involved himself in his students' investigations. He emphasized inductive, experimental study over rote learning, and often discouraged his students from surveying published literature until they had conducted their own experiments. Schwendener also insisted that fieldwork was essential to understanding adaptation as the product of both structure and function. Only firsthand knowledge of the conditions in which plants lived could support theoretical claims about adaptation, and many of his students undertook field studies within Germany and abroad. Cittadino has examined the importance of Schwendener's students and their field research in the expansion of Darwinian thought in Germany; in addition, such research expanded the scope of biogeography as botanists identified new ways of interpreting the relationship between a region's climate and its vegetation, and also contributed to the development of ecology as a discipline in the late 1870s and 1880s.

SUPPLEMENTARY BIBLIOGRAPHY

WORKS BY SCHWENDENER

With Karl Wilhelm von Nägeli. *Das Mikroskop: Theorie und Anwendung desselben.* Leipzig, Germany: W. Engelmann, 1865.

"Die Flechten als Parasiten der Algen." In *Verhandlungen der Schweizerischen Naturforschenden Gesellschaft* 5 (1869): 527–550. Presents additional information about his interpretation of the nature of lichens and their associated fungi.

Das mechanische Princip im anatomischen Bau der Monocotylen. Leipzig, Germany: W. Engelmann, 1874.

Schwendeners Vorlesungen über mechanische Probleme der Botanik gehalten an der Universität Berlin. Edited by Carl Holtermann. Leipzig, Germany: W. Englemann, 1909. Offers a general overview of Schwendener's physicomathematical botany and illustrates the detailed mathematics he utilized in his physiological investigations.

OTHER SOURCES

Cittadino, Eugene. *Nature as the Laboratory: Darwinian Plant Ecology in the German Empire, 1880–1900.* Cambridge, U.K.: Cambridge University Press, 1990. Examines the significance of Schwendener's physicomathematical plant anatomy in the broader context of Darwinian adaptation and the expansion of German botany in the late nineteenth century.

Haberlandt, Gottlieb. "Das Pflanzenphysiologisches Institut der Universität Berlin, zur Einführung." In *Beiträge zur Allgemeinen Botanik,* vol. 1, edited by Gottlieb Haberlandt. Berlin: Gebrüder Borntraeger1918. Chronicles the development of the Berlin Botanical Institute, in which Schwendener figures prominently.

Jahn, Ilse, and Ulrich Sucker. "Zur Geschichte der Botanik an der Berliner Universität von 1810 bis 1945." *Wissenschaftliche Zeitschrift der Humboldt-Universität zu Berlin, Mathematisch-Naturwissenschaftliche Reihe* 34, nos. 3/4 (1985): 189–202.

Sapp, Jan. *Evolution by Association: A History of Symbiosis.* Oxford: Oxford University Press, 1994. Provides a short but thorough synopsis of Schwendener's research on lichens and their implication for later studies of symbiosis.

Christina Matta

SCHWINGER, JULIAN SEYMOUR

(*b.* New York, New York, 12 February 1918; *d.* Los Angeles, California, 16 July 1994), *electromagnetic theory, quantum mechanics, atomic physics, nuclear theory, quantum field theory, high energy and elementary particle physics.*

On 13 June 1978 the Nobel laureate Chen Ning Yang wrote the following to the chairman of the physics department at the University of California, Los Angeles (UCLA) to support Julian Schwinger's appointment as professor:

> Professor Julian Schwinger is among the great physicists of the contemporary era. His work covers an amazing range, from nuclear physics to elementary particle physics to field theory, from synchrotron radiation to group theory to microwave propagation.… The most important work of Schwinger was his contribution to renormalization, a contribution that stands among the greatest developments in physics in mid-twentieth century. Professor Schwinger is an eminently successful teacher. He probably has graduated more influential theoretical PhD students than any other living physicist.

Early Years. Julian Schwinger was born into a middle-class Jewish family. Schwinger's mother, Belle Rosenfeld, was born in Lodz, a large manufacturing town in eastern Poland, which was then a part of Russia. Her family had emigrated to the United States when she was a very young child. Benjamin Schwinger, Julian's father, was born in Newsandez, a small village in the foothills of the Carpathian Mountains in one of the provinces of the Austrio-Hungarian Empire. He came to the United States around 1880 and eventually became a successful designer of women's clothing.

After they were married, Schwinger's parents lived near Morris Park in Harlem, then a well-to-do Jewish neighborhood. Their first son, Harold, was born in 1911. Some six years later they moved to a large apartment at 640 Riverside Drive near 141st Street. Julian Seymour was born on 12 February 1918. Benjamin Schwinger was a talented couturier, and his business had prospered. Like his elder brother, Julian Schwinger attended Townsend Harris High School, then one of the best secondary

Julian Schwinger. *Schwinger diagramming on a blackboard.* **SPL/PHOTO RESEARCHERS, INC.**

schools in the United States. He graduated in 1934, and entered City College of New York (CCNY) in the fall of that year as a physics major. His precocity and ability in physics were legendary even during his high school years. As a freshman at CCNY, Schwinger had regularly attended the weekly theoretical seminar that Isidor Rabi, Gregory Breit, and Otto Halpern ran at Columbia University on Wednesday evenings. The sixteen-year-old undergraduate clearly must have impressed Halpern, for in 1935 they published a joint paper on the problem of the polarization of electrons in double scattering experiments, the young Julian having done extensive and difficult calculations.

Schwinger, nevertheless, did not do well at CCNY. He spent most of his time in the library, reading advanced physics and mathematical texts, and rarely went to his classes. His grades reflected his erratic attendance. Although he had no difficulty getting As in mathematics and physics courses (even though he rarely attended), the same was not the case in his other courses. The matter became serious enough for Lloyd Motz, one of his physics instructors at CCNY who was studying for his PhD at Columbia University, to bring Schwinger's problems to the attention of Rabi. Rabi was influential in obtaining a

scholarship for Schwinger to come to Columbia. He did well there, though some of the previous problems remained. During his senior year, Schwinger worked on the problem of the magnetic scattering of slow neutrons by atoms. He formulated a fully quantum mechanical treatment of the problem and found that neutrons scattered from an unpolarized beam would be partially polarized by virtue of the magnetic interaction—and that the polarization thus produced could be detected by a second scattering. In early January 1937 Schwinger sent a manuscript describing his research, titled "The Magnetic Scattering of Neutrons," to the *Physical Review*.

All the characteristics that Schwinger exhibited in his subsequent works were present in this paper: an important physical problem was addressed; the solution was elegant; the methods used were powerful; contact was made with experimental data; and suggestions for empirical tests were given. Edward Teller, who was visiting Columbia during the spring term of 1937, suggested that Schwinger's research on the scattering of neutrons could be submitted as a PhD thesis if he developed them further. Schwinger worked with Teller and showed that the scattering of neutrons by ortho- and para-hydrogen could yield information about the spin dependence and the range of the neutron-proton interaction. The fact that Schwinger had written his PhD dissertation before receiving his bachelor's degree is indicative of his remarkable talents.

Columbia and Berkeley. After receiving his BS from Columbia in 1936, Schwinger continued his graduate studies there. Shortly after becoming a graduate student, Schwinger received a traveling fellowship from Columbia for the academic year 1937–1938. The plans were for him to spend six months at Wisconsin to study with Gregory Breit and Eugene Wigner, and then to go on to the University of California, Berkeley, for another six months to work with J. Robert Oppenheimer. He remained at Wisconsin for the year and there developed his characteristic working habits: staying up at night and sleeping during the day. In private, Schwinger indicated that he started staying up at night because of a strong feeling of not wanting to be "dominated" by Wigner and Breit.

Rabi characterized Schwinger "a changed man" when he returned to Columbia after his year at Wisconsin. He became deeply involved in the experimental activities in Rabi's laboratory. Even before going to Wisconsin, stimulated by Rabi's atomic beam experiments, Schwinger had written a paper on the behavior of an arbitrary magnetic moment in a harmonically time-varying magnetic field that has become a classic. This association with Rabi and his atomic beam experiments resulted in Schwinger's protracted fascination with atomic and nuclear moments, and more generally, with the quantum theory of angular momentum. Schwinger also became the "house theorist" for the experiments in nuclear physics being carried out at Columbia at the time. Schwinger's papers from that period reflect not only his wide interests—for example, the scattering of neutrons by hydrogen molecules and by deuterons, the quadrupole moment of the deuteron, the effect of tensor forces on the scattering of neutrons by protons, the widths of nuclear energy levels—but also attest to his talents as a superb phenomenologist.

In the fall of 1939 Schwinger went to Berkeley. By his own admission, Oppenheimer's influence on him was enormous. Oppenheimer steered Schwinger into areas of physics in which he had not yet worked: cosmic rays, meson spin assignments, quantum electrodynamics, and the quantum field theory (QFT) of nuclear forces. Schwinger stayed in Berkeley for two years, the first as a National Research Council Fellow, the second as a research associate to Oppenheimer. His stay was extremely productive. Oppenheimer, as well as the large number of doctoral students and postdoctoral fellows working under his tutelage—Sidney Dancoff, Hartland Snyder, George Volkoff, Leonard Schiff, David Bohm, Philip Morrison, and Robert Serber—made for a very stimulating and congenial atmosphere. Schwinger collaborated extensively—

with Bert Corben, Edward Gerjouy, Oppenheimer, and William Rarita—and worked on a wide range of subjects. The investigations ranged from phenomenological analyses of the empirical data on the deuteron and light nuclei to extensive field theoretic calculations using differing spin and charge assignments for the "mesotrons" involved.

A paper by Nicholas Kemmer in 1938 on a meson field theoretical model of the nuclear forces had made Schwinger aware, before his arrival at Berkeley, of the possibility of the presence of tensor forces in the neutron-proton interaction. An analysis of the electromagnetic properties of the deuteron when tensor forces are present led him to predict the existence of the deuteron's quadrupole moment—before it had been measured by Jerome Kellogg, Norman Ramsey, Rabi, and Jerrold Zacharias in 1939. Tensor forces, and the kind of mesotrons and meson-nucleon couplings that could give rise to them, became a central focus of the investigations Schwinger carried out during the Berkeley period. All his researches from that period have one feature in common: no matter how theoretical or abstract the starting point, whether formulating the QFT of spin 3/2 particles, or investigating the solutions of the Proca equations for a charged spin 1 particle moving in a Coulomb field, contact was always made with "numbers" and with experiments. And in each case Schwinger mastered the intricate details of the experiments that had provided the data he was comparing his numbers to—the apparatus involved as well as the analysis and reduction of the data.

Two pieces of research carried out in Berkeley were later of great importance, when Schwinger worked on quantum electrodynamics in the post–World War II period. The first was a collaboration with Oppenheimer in 1939 that used quantum electrodynamics (QED) to describe electron-positron emission from an excited oxygen nucleus. This calculation brought home to him the physical reality of virtual photon processes. The second was his work on strong-coupling mesotron theory, through which he gained experience in using canonical transformations to extract the physical consequences of a field theory.

Wartime Research. Schwinger left Berkeley in the summer of 1941 to accept an instructorship at Purdue University. His subsequent contributions to the war effort were determined by his presence at Purdue. An active program in semiconductor research was being carried out there for the Radiation Laboratory (Rad Lab) of the Massachusetts Institute of Technology (MIT) by Karl Lark-Horowitz in order to develop better rectifiers for the detection of radar. In 1942 Schwinger and several other theorists were asked to join a Rad Lab project at Purdue under Hans Bethe's direction on the propagation of microwave radiation in microwave cavities.

When in early 1943 the Los Alamos Scientific Laboratory was organized to build an atomic bomb, Oppenheimer invited Schwinger to join the laboratory, but he declined. However, because many of the leading theorists at the Rad Lab were leaving it to go to Los Alamos, Schwinger was asked to come to MIT. This he did in the fall of 1943. In his work there, Schwinger solved a wide variety of microwave problems. Using an integral equation formulation of field problems, he introduced and deployed powerful mathematical techniques that became characteristic features of many of his subsequent inquiries: Green's functions and variational methods. These researches resulted in a rigorous and general theory of microwave structures in which conventional low-frequency electrical theory appeared as a special case. While at the Rad Lab, Schwinger gave lectures on the theory of wave guides that were attended by a small group of colleagues. An abbreviated set of notes—the war ended before the series had finished—were eventually published in 1968 under the title *Discontinuities in Waveguides,* with Schwinger and David Saxon as authors. The lectures exhibited Schwinger's formidable analytical powers and gave proof of his remarkable ability to be equally at home in the worlds of physics, applied science, engineering, and applied mathematics. In a memorial lecture for Sin-Itiro Tomonaga, delivered in 1980, Schwinger commented that his waveguide investigations showed the utility of organizing a theory to isolate those inner structural aspects that are not probed under the given experimental circumstances. That lesson was subsequently applied to the effective-range description of nuclear forces. And it was this viewpoint that would lead to the quantum electrodynamic concept of self-consistent subtraction or renormalization. While at the Rad Lab, Schwinger also worked on the problem of the radiation emitted by fast electrons traveling in synchrotron orbits. The formulation of this problem taught him the importance of describing relativistic situations covariantly, that is, without specialization to any particular coordinate system.

Harvard. When in 1944 universities began competing with one another for outstanding figures in physics, Schwinger was courted by a number of them, and in particular by Harvard University. In the fall of 1945 Schwinger accepted an appointment there as an associate professor. A year later he was offered a full professorship at Berkeley, and Harvard promptly promoted him. Harvard provided him with outstanding graduate students, and he became thesis advisor to many of them. They, together with many of MIT's graduate students and postdoctoral fellows and a fair fraction of the Harvard and MIT physics faculty, formed the audience for Schwinger's brilliant lectures. The impact and influence of these lectures—and of the widely circulated notes based on them—on the generation of physics graduate students of the late 1940s and 1950s cannot be exaggerated. Many of the later textbooks on nuclear physics, electromagnetic theory, quantum mechanics, QFT, and statistical mechanics incorporated the approaches, techniques, and examples that Schwinger had discussed in his lectures.

Shelter Island. At a famous meeting held in June 1947 on Shelter Island, at the tip of Long Island, New York, reliable experimental data were presented by Willis Lamb and Robert Retherford that indicated that, contrary to the prediction of the Dirac equation, the $2S_{1/2}$ and $2P_{j2}$ levels of the hydrogen atom were not degenerate, with the $2S_{1/2}$ state lying some 1,000 megahertz above the $2P_{j2}$. In addition, Rabi reported that he, John E. Nafe, and Edward B. Nelson had made hyperfine measurements in hydrogen and deuterium that indicated that the g value of the magnetic moment of the electron, g (e/2m) 1/2(h/2π) differed from the predicted Dirac value g = 2. Rumors about the Lamb shift had circulated before the meeting. Victor Weisskopf and Schwinger talked about it as they traveled together by train to Shelter Island. Both of them knew that the self-energy of an electron in QED was logarithmically divergent and therefore that if one took the difference of the energies of two fine structure levels, the result would be finite. In fact, Weisskopf had a graduate student, Bruce French, doing such a calculation at MIT. Because he had gotten married to Clarice Carrol shortly after the conference it was only in September 1947 that Schwinger set out on the trail of relativistic QED. He recognized that explaining the anomalous value of the electron's magnetic moment was the crucial calculation, for it did not involve the complications associated with bound states. Making use of the ideas of mass renormalization—that the (divergent) self-energy, δm, generated by the interaction of the electron-positron field with the (quantized) electromagnetic field must be added to the mass m_0 attributed to an electron (as specified by the Lagrangian for the electron-positron field) and that the sum m_0 + δm is to be identified with the experimentally determined mass of the electron—Schwinger obtained in December 1947 the result

$$g/2 = 1 + (\alpha/2\pi),\ \alpha = e^2/hc\ \hbar\ 1/137$$

in agreement with the data of Rabi, Nelson, and Nafe. He then proceeded to calculate the Lamb shift, a much more difficult calculation requiring that, in addition to mass renormalization, a charge renormalization be carried out. Charge renormalization reflects the fact that to parameter e_0 in the Lagrangian that represents the bare charge of an electron must be added the screening effect of virtual pair production in the vacuum (vacuum polarization effects) and that it is their sum that is to be identified with the experimentally determined charge of an electron. Though he obtained a finite answer in close agreement with the Lamb-Retherford value, Schwinger's calculation was plagued with inconsistencies due to the lack of Lorentz covariance. Schwinger thereafter proceeded to formulate an explicitly covariant approach to QED and to field theory in general. Tomonaga in Japan had developed the same formalism and had written down the same generalization of the Schrödinger equation to an arbitrary spacelike surface σ

$$i\hbar c \frac{\delta \Psi[\sigma(x)]}{\delta \sigma(x)} = H(x)\Psi[\sigma(x)] \qquad (1)$$

which equation has become known as the Tomonaga-Schwinger equation. (A spacelike surface is one on which every two points, x, x' are separated by a spacelike distance, i.e., $(x_i - x'_i)^2 > 0$.) In (1) $H(x)$ is the Hamiltonian density of the field system which for quantum electrodynamics is given by

$$H(x) = -(1/c) j_\mu(x) A^\mu(x) \qquad (2)$$

where $j_\mu(x)$ is the electric current operator of the electron-positron field and $A^\mu(x)$ the operator representing the electromagnetic potential.

By the time of the Pocono conference in April 1948, Schwinger had worked out the implications of his new formalism. His covariant formulation, when supplemented with the notions of mass and charge renormalization, was the first self-consistent framework in QFT from which physical consequences could be extracted and checked with experiments. For this work he shared the Nobel Prize in 1965 with Richard Feynman and Tomonaga.

Quantum Field Theory and Green's Functions. Schwinger's covariant approach was communicated to the community at large in a series of papers titled *Quantum Electrodynamics* (Parts I, II, and III) that were submitted to the *Physical Review* in 1948 and 1949. Parts I and II served as the notes for the lectures that Schwinger delivered at the Michigan Summer School in Ann Arbor from 19 July to 7 August 1948. Freeman Dyson, who had just completed a year of graduate studies at Cornell University, was one of the students in Schwinger's course. During the course of that year he had interacted with Feynman and knew the details of Feynman's diagrammatic and calculational approach to QED. That fall Dyson proved the equivalence of the two approaches and proceeded to formulate a proof that the S-matrix for QED can be rendered finite to all orders of perturbation theory by mass and charge renormalization. Thereafter Feynman and Dyson's graphical approach to field theory became the preferred

method for the analysis of field theoretic problems, and Schwinger felt that he had to respond.

The challenge for Schwinger became how to formulate local quantum field theories based ab initio on a quantum action principle. He wanted to get away from quantization procedures that were expressed as a set of operator prescriptions imposed on a classical description based upon a Hamiltonian. This approach produced an asymmetry in the treatment of time and space and resulted in a formulation that was noncovariant. Additionally, it placed the existence of anticommuting Fermi-Dirac fields on a purely empirical basis to be introduced into the formalism on an ad hoc basis.

Schwinger's point of departure were the papers of Feynman in which he had formulated quantum mechanics by exhibiting the probability amplitude connecting the state of a system at one time to that at a later time as a sum of complex unit amplitudes—one for each possible trajectory of the system connecting the initial and final state—the phase of each amplitude being determined by the value of the action, (L dt, for that trajectory. Because action is a relativistic invariant, the formulation could be made covariant. But whereas Feynman gave a global solution, for Schwinger the idea was not, as Feynman had done, to write down the solution, but to continue in the tradition of classical mechanics as a historical model, to find a differential action principle formulation.

In 1951, in eight pages of the *Proceedings of the National Academy of Sciences,* he gave a concise presentation of his formulation of the equations for the Green's functions of quantum fields based on this novel approach to field quantization. Schwinger there introduced the use of "sources"—classical sources for Bosonic fields and Grassman anticommuting sources for Fermionic fields—as functional variables. Schwinger's formulation was the functional differential equation version that in its integral form is called functional integration. The power of the approach stems from the fact that the symmetry properties of the Green's functions can readily be exhibited, and approximation schemes can be devised that preserve these symmetry properties. Dating from the same period are his publication of the Schwinger action principle and, with Paul Martin, the use of temperature-dependent many-particle Green's functions for addressing equilibrium and nonequilibrium problems in condensed matter physics. These contributions by Schwinger were widely appreciated and recognized. He was awarded the National Medal of Science in 1964. In 1951 he had already shared the first Albert Einstein Prize with Kurt Gödel.

Source Theory. In the mid-1960s Schwinger started reformulating the foundations of fundamental physics and expressing them in a new framework: source theory.

Source theory represented Schwinger's efforts to replace the prevailing operator field theory by a philosophy and methodology that eliminated all infinite quantities. Schwinger's objections to operator field theory stemmed at the pragmatic level from the fact that it seemed impossible to incorporate the strong interactions within its framework, and at the philosophical level that it made implicit assumptions about unknown phenomena at inaccessible, very high energies to make predictions at lower energies.

When the interactions are weak, as in the case of QED, it had been possible to go from a quantum field theoretic description to a particle description using the notions of renormalization. These can be interpreted as separating the effects of the experimentally inaccessible very high-energy dynamics from the effects that are experimentally accessible, and incorporating the former into a finite number of parameters values that are to be determined experimentally. However, when the interactions are strong, one has to deal with a possibly unlimited number of entities interacting with one another in a complicated manner, and it becomes nigh impossible to establish a correspondence between the observable particles and the fundamental fields. This failure indicated the need for new approaches to the strong interactions. However, the alternatives that were advanced were not acceptable to Schwinger. He found the S-matrix theory of Geoffrey Chew unacceptable because it lacked the specification of the dynamics involved; and he found the current algebra approach unsatisfactory because he was skeptical that one could obtain dynamical consequences from group theoretical kinematic assumptions. Encouraged by his success in using phenomenological "effective" Lagrangians in reproducing some of the low energy results of current algebra, Schwinger undertook to develop a phenomenological approach that would begin with robust knowledge about known phenomena at accessible energies and proceed to make predictions of physical phenomena at higher energies. The result was source theory.

For Schwinger, source theory was a mathematical description of laboratory practice that is conceptually sound and mathematically simple, a description that did not have any of the difficulties encountered in the quantum field theoretical operator formalism. It contained no divergent quantities, and thus there was no need for any renormalization procedures. And because all the parameters that appeared in the formulation were fixed initially, there were no new constants appearing when the class of phenomena under examination was enlarged. Despite its merits, Schwinger's source theory fell on deaf ears. The attractive features of the quark model of hadrons; of the electroweak theory of Sheldon Glashow, Steven Weinberg, and Abdus Salam; and of quantum chromodynamics (QCD), and most importantly their predictions and exper-

imental corroboration; had removed the appeal of the phenomenological aspects of source theory. Schwinger's insistence on basing his theories on phenomenology had led him to reject both the quark model of hadrons and QCD. The notion of a "particle," such as a quark, which was not describable by asymptotic states, was distasteful to him. His pursuit of source theory in the early 1970s—at the very time of the resurgence of QFT in the aftermath of the successes of the Glashow-Salam-Weinberg electroweak theory and of the proof by Gerard't Hooft that the Yang-Mills theory with a Higgs mechanism for breaking symmetry and giving masses to the particles is renormalizable—alienated him from the community and drove him out of the mainstream of modern physics.

Quantum Field Theory. Schwinger's alienation was aggravated by the fact that in February 1971 he left Harvard to accept a position at UCLA and had to establish ties to a new community with interests somewhat different from those of Cambridge, Massachusetts.

The chasm between Schwinger's views and those of the community at large as set by the younger men who had achieved the breakthroughs (Glashow, Weinberg, Sidney Coleman, David Gross, Hooft) was too deep to be easily bridged. Schwinger was more modest in his approach. In 1965 in his contribution titled "The Future of Fundamental Physics," to the volume *Nature of Matter: Purpose of High Energy Physics* that Luke Yuan edited, Schwinger had written that he believed that "the scientific level of any period is epitomized by the current attitude toward the fundamental properties of matter. The world view of the physicist sets the style of the technology and the culture of the society and gives direction to future progress." For Schwinger fundamental physics was a way to understand human intervention into the physical world; therefore, the way in which it was formulated mattered deeply. For Schwinger quantum mechanics was only the mathematical symbolical representation of measurements in atomic physics, and similarly, source theory was the mathematical symbolism of human manipulations in high-energy physics.

When Schwinger left the mainstream of particle physics and challenged the foundations upon which the theoretical investigations were being carried out, his new endeavors were disdainfully set aside by the community as mistaken or irrelevant. Several of his research papers were rejected dismissively by *Physical Review Letters*. His response was to resign both as a member and as a Fellow of the American Physical Society. These experiences probably contributed to his involvement in unconventional projects such as cold fusion and sonoluminescence.

Starting in the 1980s, after teaching a course in quantum mechanics, Schwinger began a series of papers on the

Thomas-Fermi model of atoms and, together with Berthold-Georg Englert, elaborated the approach. These contributions have been deemed important by the atomic physics community. His last scientific endeavor before his death in 1994 was attempting an explanation of sonoluminescence, the emission of light by bubbles in a liquid excited by acoustic waves. Schwinger died on 16 July 1994 of pancreatic cancer.

Schwinger's lifetime work extends to almost every frontier of modern theoretical physics. He made far reaching contributions to nuclear, particle, and atomic physics; to statistical mechanics; to classical electrodynamics; to general relativity; and to the mathematical formulation of quantum theory. Many of the mathematical techniques that he developed are to be found in the tool kit of every theorist. He was one of the prophets and pioneers in the uses of gauge theories. His name is associated with many concepts and techniques in physics: the Tomonaga-Schwinger equation, the Lippmann-Schwinger equation, the Dyson-Schwinger equation, the Schwinger model, the Schwinger term, and the Kubo-Martin-Schwinger condition on finite-temperature Green's functions. He was the advisor to some seventy-four doctoral students and over twenty postdoctoral fellows, many of whom became the outstanding theorists of their generation. The influence of Julian Schwinger on the physics of his time was profound.

BIBLIOGRAPHY

Schwinger's Nachlass has been deposited in the Department of Special Collections at the University Research Library, University of California, Los Angeles. Kimball A. Milton's introduction to the volume of seminal papers of Julian Schwinger that he edited, A Quantum Legacy, Singapore: World Scientific, 2000, is a concise, valuable overview of Schwinger's works. It also contains informative comments on Schwinger's papers. A list of Schwinger's publications can be found in that volume, as well as in Jack Y. Ng's Julian Schwinger: The Physicist, the Teacher, and the Man, Singapore: World Scientific, 1996. An earlier selection of Schwinger's papers is to be found in Moshe Flato, Christian Fronsdal, and Kimball A. Milton, eds., Selected Papers (1937–1976) of Julian Schwinger, Dordrecht, Netherlands: Reidel, 1979.

WORKS BY SCHWINGER

Quantum Dynamics. Part I. *Cours professé à l'École d'été de physique théorique, Les Houches.* Grenoble, France: Université de Grenoble, 1955.

Quantum Electrodynamics. New York: Dover Press, 1958.

With David Saxon. *Discontinuities in Waveguides.* New York: Gordon and Breach, 1968.

Quantum Kinematics and Dynamics. New York: Benjamin, 1970.

Einstein's Legacy: The Unity of Space and Time. Scientific American Library, vol. 16. New York: W.H. Freeman, 1986.

Particles, Sources and Fields. 3 vols. Redwood City, CA: Addison-Wesley, 1989.

Quantum Mechanics: Symbolism of Atomic Measurements. Edited by Berthold-Georg Englert. Berlin: Springer Verlag, 2001.

OTHER SOURCES

Mehra, Jagdish, and Kimball A. Milton. *Climbing the Mountain: The Scientific Biography of Julian Schwinger.* New York: Oxford University Press, 2000.

Ng, Y. Jack. *Julian Schwinger: The Physicist, the Teacher, and the Man.* Singapore: World Scientific, 1996.

Schweber, Silvan S. *QED and the Men Who Made It.* Princeton, NJ: Princeton University Press, 1994.

Silvan S. Schweber

SCIAMA, DENNIS WILLIAM (*b.* Manchester, England, 18 November 1926; *d.* Oxford, England, 19 December 1999), *cosmology, steady state theory, general relativity, astrophysics, quantum gravity.*

Sciama was one of the key figures in the renaissance of cosmology in the 1960s, and his contributions spanned a broad array of topics in general relativity, astrophysics, and cosmology. The influence of Sciama's own research, however, has not been as great as the influence on the development of relativity and astrophysics he exerted as an inspiring mentor and research leader. He supervised more than seventy doctoral students, many of whom became leading figures in relativistic astrophysics, and conveyed his enthusiasm for the field to many more through his lucid review articles and popular books.

Early Years. Sciama spent his early years in Manchester, the younger of two sons in a nonreligious Jewish family. Both sides of the family had roots in the Middle East: his paternal great grandfather emigrated to Manchester from Aleppo, Syria, and his mother was born and raised in Cairo. Sciama attended Malvern College, a public boarding school in rural Worcestershire, where he discovered an interest in and aptitude for science and mathematics that lead to a minor scholarship at Trinity College, Cambridge.

Sciama went up to Trinity in 1944, and studied mathematics for one year before switching to the natural sciences tripos (focusing on physics) as a condition for a continued wartime deferment. His enrollment in one of Ludwig Wittgenstein's seminars gives an indication of Sciama's broad interests. Because of mediocre exam results (a lower second) on the BA degree, completed in 1947, he could no longer avoid conscription. Thanks to the intervention of the Cambridge physicist Douglas Hartree, most of his two-year stint in the army was devoted to research in solid-state physics (photoconductive materials, in particular) at the Telecommunications Research

Establishment. Reports he wrote on the subject earned him a second chance in academia, and he returned to Trinity in 1949 in an unpaid research position. Initially Sciama planned to write a thesis under Neville Temperley in statistical mechanics regarding cooperative phenomena, but his interests soon shifted to relativity and cosmology. As a result Paul Dirac was assigned to be his advisor, although two young Cambridge fellows, Herman Bondi and Thomas Gold, had much more influence on Sciama's research. Upon completing his thesis, Sciama made a bold wager with his father: if he won a fellowship at Trinity he would continue to pursue physics, and if not he would return to the family business in Manchester.

Influence of Mach's Principle. Sciama's thesis focused on the origins of inertia and Mach's principle. Ernst Mach's influential criticism of Isaac Newton purported to show that the inertia of a given body could be explained in terms of interactions with other bodies without any appeal to "absolute space." Despite the ambiguity of Mach's formulation of these ideas, they were an inspiration for Albert Einstein's theory of general relativity. In 1918 Einstein included Mach's principle—which he formulated as the requirement that the gravitational field is fully determined by the distribution of matter—on a list of three fundamental physical principles of his new theory. However, he eventually realized that his theory did not satisfy Mach's principle so formulated and no longer took it to be a fundamental principle of general relativity. Sciama had the opposite response: he found Mach's principle so appealing that he sought to formulate an alternative gravitational theory in which it holds. His thesis developed a simple theory with a vector potential based on the Machian idea that inertia and gravitation are entirely determined by the distribution of matter. This was intended as a first step toward a fully Machian theory; in the published version (1953) Sciama promised to develop a more sophisticated, relativistic theory with a tensor potential (as in Einstein's theory) in a second paper.

The second paper did not appear until 1969, and it marked a substantial shift in Sciama's approach rather than a completion of the original program. Sciama and his coauthors (his student Peter Waylen and Robert Gilman, a student of John Wheeler) gave an integral formulation of Einstein's theory rather than developing an alternative Machian theory. The gravitational field at a point was expressed as an integral over physical sources in the surrounding volume plus a boundary term. Mach's principle could then be formulated as a selection criteria for acceptable solutions; roughly, in the limit as the volume under consideration grows to include the entire universe, the boundary term should vanish, so that the gravitational field is entirely determined by the distribution of matter. Derek Raine, a later student of Sciama's, further refined

the definition of Mach's principle in this approach by showing how to handle this rather subtle limit. This approach differs from that taken by other advocates of Mach's principle; in particular, Julian Barbour (with various collaborators) has given a Machian reformulation of mechanics based on a "best-matching procedure," a way of defining spatial position and motion intrinsically without appeal to background geometry. Mach's principle continues to be controversial, partly because of the lack of consensus regarding its proper formulation, but Sciama and his collaborators clarified one prominent approach.

Sciama's interest in Mach's principle reflected the philosophical orientation of his mentors Bondi and Gold. Along with their slightly older colleague Fred Hoyle, Bondi and Gold introduced the steady state theory in 1948. Unlike the standard "big bang" models of relativistic cosmology, which describe a universe that evolves with time, the steady state theory was based on the idea that the global properties of the universe do not vary with time. Bondi and Gold defended the theory on explicitly methodological grounds: In their view, the steady state theory was the only possible scientific cosmology. A theory that allowed for variation of the global properties of the universe could not rule out concomitant variation of local physical laws, hence undercutting any attempt to extrapolate physical laws that hold at present to earlier epochs. For Bondi and Gold as well as Sciama, Mach's principle exemplified "interaction" between global properties and local laws, because it holds that the global distribution of matter determines the local inertial properties of a body. In his vector theory of gravity, Sciama derived a relation between the gravitational constant, the average mass density of the universe, and Hubble's constant that illustrated such interconnections between parameters appearing in physical laws (the gravitational constant) and global properties of the universe (Hubble's constant and average density). Sciama was clearly fascinated with global-to-local connections of this kind, which he made the focus of his lucid popular book *The Unity of the Universe* (1959).

Cosmology. Until 1965 Sciama was actively involved in developing and defending the steady state theory. With Bondi and Gold he wrote a paper aptly criticizing the Stebbins-Whitford effect. This effect was initially thought to indicate a correlation between the age and distance of galaxies incompatible with the steady state theory, but it was later withdrawn. Sciama's most important contribution was an ingenious account of galaxy formation published in 1955. At the time there were competing accounts of how the transition from a homogeneous early state to a clumpy state with galaxies and other structures could occur in the big bang models. In the steady state theory, the problem was to maintain an unchanging average density of galaxies as the universe expands. Sciama argued that new galaxies would be created in the gravitational "wake" of existing galaxies, and the requirement of maintaining "equilibrium" put tight constraints on the theory. The theory led to a variety of results in rough agreement with observations, and it was in many ways superior to the speculative accounts of galaxy formation then available for the big bang models.

In the early 1960s Sciama's focus shifted to assessing the implications of radio astronomy for the steady state theory. Martin Ryle and others had measured the relationship between the number of radio sources and flux density in the 2C and 3C surveys. (These surveys are similar to astronomical catalogs of visible objects; they list the properties of radio sources observed using the Cambridge Interferometer. The 2C survey, published in 1955, includes 1,936 sources, and the 3C survey includes 471 sources.) The steady state theory made a very specific prediction that was apparently incompatible with these results, although their interpretation of the results was not without controversy. Sciama proposed that many of the radio sources were galactic rather than extragalactic in nature, and that the apparent discrepancy resulted from a local deficit of galactic sources. The discovery of quasars in 1963 made the situation more difficult for advocates of the steady state theory. Initially Sciama extended his idea of a mixed population to quasars: If some quasars are local rather than extragalactic, then it would again be possible to save the theory. However, unlike Geoffrey Burbidge and Hoyle, Sciama accepted that quasars with measurable redshifts were at cosmological distances rather than within the galaxy. Sciama and his student Martin Rees then showed that the redshift–flux density relation for thirty-five quasars was clearly incompatible with the steady state theory. This result led Sciama to abandon the steady state theory, although he clearly regretted the demise of a theory he found philosophically and aesthetically appealing. Sciama's conversion was complete; the steady state theory merited only a brief dismissal in his book *Modern Cosmology* (1971), whereas the big bang models took center stage.

General Relativity. Sciama also explored Einstein's general relativity throughout the 1950s and 1960s. Following his Trinity fellowship, which was interspersed with two years abroad at Princeton University and Harvard University, Sciama briefly held posts at King's College, London (funded by Bondi's U.S. Air Force research grant), and Cornell University (on an invitation from Gold). He returned to Cambridge in 1961 as a lecturer and later fellow in Peterhouse. Before his return to Cambridge he discovered that spin angular momentum could be introduced as a source of the gravitational field by modifying Einstein's theory to allow for nonzero torsion and

emphasized the formal analogies between this approach and a geometrical treatment of electromagnetism. The resulting theory—called the Einstein-Cartan-Sciama-Kibble theory to acknowledge its sources in work of Einstein and Élie-Joseph Cartan and its independent discovery by Thomas Kibble—inspired further research based on the hope that it would be easier to combine this generalization of general relativity with other field theories.

At Cambridge, Sciama inspired a group of exceptional students to study the then mostly neglected subject of general relativity. Sciama's research group in the Department of Applied Mathematics and Theoretical Physics was one of the world's best relativity groups, comparable to those led by Yakov Zel'dovich in Moscow, and Wheeler at Princeton. Sciama's students, including George Ellis, Stephen Hawking, and Brandon Carter, played an active part in the renaissance of relativity in the 1960s. One of the main contributors to this dramatic upswing in productive research was Roger Penrose; although Penrose was never Sciama's student, Sciama inspired him to change fields from mathematics to physics. Penrose introduced mathematical techniques that allowed theorists to study stellar collapse and cosmology without relying on specific, artificially simple solutions. One of his most important results was a proof that a collapsing star with sufficient mass will inevitably lead to a physical singularity. Hawking extended Penrose's techniques to cosmology, and he proved that cosmological models satisfying a number of plausible requirements must likewise include an initial singularity. Ellis and Hawking wrote the definitive monograph on the subject, *The Large Scale Structure of Space-Time* (1973), which concisely presented the Hawking-Penrose singularity theorems and the new mathematical techniques. Sciama encouraged Carter to study the Kerr solution, which describes a spinning black hole. Carter discovered a number of the properties of the solution, and contributed to proving the black hole uniqueness theorems. Although Sciama himself did not actively contribute to this line of research, his students clearly benefited from his support, guidance, and ability to identify important problems.

Sciama's research interests also extended into a variety of topics in observational astronomy and astrophysics. He continued research regarding quasars and other observational results that he had initiated as an advocate of the steady state theory. After abandoning that theory, he turned to detailed studies of the big bang models, focusing on the interaction of matter and radiation in the expanding universe, the formation of galaxies via gravitational clumping, and other topics. He advised a number of students in astrophysics, including most prominently Rees. With Rees he discovered that time-variation in the gravitational potential of a lump of matter would produce a characteristic temperature variation in radiation passing through the region, which is called the Rees-Sciama effect. Sciama's masterful review articles on observational cosmology convey his excitement at the prospects for new observations across the electromagnetic spectrum to constrain and guide theorists.

In 1970 Sciama moved to Oxford as a senior research fellow at All Souls. He built a theoretical astrophysics group at Oxford and continued to support and train an impressive crop of students, including John Barrow, James Binney, Philip Candelas, and David Deutsch. In 1974 Oxford hosted a conference on quantum gravity, where Hawking announced his discovery that black holes emit black body radiation with a temperature proportional to their surface gravity. This discovery generated a great deal of interest, because it completed the analogy between "black hole mechanics" and the laws of thermodynamics. Sciama and his students contributed to the study of the thermodynamics of black holes following on the heels of Hawking's work. In particular, Sciama and Candelas argued that the dissipation of energy by a radiating black hole could be understood physically based on the fluctuation-dissipation theorem from statistical mechanics. This work was closely tied to Sciama's study of the vacuum in quantum field theory.

Sciama retained ties to Oxford for the rest of his life, but he also held a number of visiting positions. The most important of these were a part-time position at the University of Texas, Austin, from 1978 to 1982, and his appointment as the director of the astrophysics group at the International School for Advanced Study (SISSA), in Trieste in 1983. From 1982 until the end of his life, Sciama's research efforts were mainly devoted to the decaying neutrino hypothesis. Sciama proposed that much of the elusive dark matter detected indirectly by astronomers consists of neutrinos left over from the early universe. If the three neutrino species have different masses, then more massive neutrinos decay into less massive neutrinos and emit light at a characteristic frequency. According to Sciama's theory, the photons emitted by this process serve to ionize the interstellar medium within our galaxy and also explain a number of other puzzling phenomena. Particle physics and astronomical observations both placed tight constraints on the idea, and in 1998 satellite observations failed to detect an emission line predicted by the hypothesis.

Among numerous honors, Sciama was elected a foreign member of the American Academy of Arts and Sciences in 1982, and a Fellow of the Royal Society in 1983. In 1959 he married Lidia Dina, a social anthropologist, and they had two daughters, Susan (b. 1962) and Sonia (b. 1964).

BIBLIOGRAPHY

WORKS BY SCIAMA

"On the Origin of Inertia." *Monthly Notices of the Royal Astronomical Society* 113 (1953): 34–42.

With Herman Bondi and Thomas Gold. "A Note on the Reported Color-Index Effect of Distant Galaxies." *Astrophysical Journal* 120 (1954): 597–599. Critical discussion of the Stebbins-Whitford effect.

"On the Formation of Galaxies in a Steady State Universe." *Monthly Notices of the Royal Astronomical Society* 115 (1955): 3–14.

The Unity of the Universe. London: Faber and Faber, 1959. Popular review of observational astronomy and steady state theory, including discussions of Mach's principle and galaxy formation.

The Physical Foundations of General Relativity. Garden City, NY: Doubleday, 1969. Brief popular account of general relativity.

With Peter C. Waylen and Robert C. Gilman. "Generally Covariant Integral Formulation of Einstein's Field Equations." *Physical Review* 187 (1969): 1762–1766.

Modern Cosmology. Cambridge, U.K.: Cambridge University Press, 1971.

"The Recent Renaissance of Observational Cosmology." In *Relativity and Gravitation,* edited by Charles G. Kuiper and Asher Peres. New York: Gordon and Breach Science, 1971.

With George Ellis. "Global and Non-global Problems in Cosmology." In *General Relativity: Papers in Honour of J. L. Synge,* edited by Lochlainn O'Raifeartaigh. Oxford: Clarendon Press, 1972.

With Chris J. Isham and Roger Penrose, eds. *Quantum Gravity: An Oxford Symposium.* Oxford: Clarendon Press, 1975.

"Black Holes and Their Thermodynamics." *Vistas in Astronomy* 19 (1976): 385–401. Useful introductory survey of black hole thermodynamics.

Oral history interview conducted by Spencer Weart, in April 1978. Transcript available at the Niels Bohr Library, American Institute of Physics, College Park, MD.

With Philip Candelas and David Deutsch. "Quantum Field Theory, Horizons, and Thermodynamics." *Advances in Physics* 30 (1981): 327–366.

With Chris J. Isham and Roger Penrose, eds. *Quantum Gravity 2: A Second Oxford Symposium.* Oxford: Clarendon Press; New York: Oxford University Press, 1981.

Modern Cosmology and the Dark Matter Problem. Cambridge, U.K.: Cambridge University Press, 1993.

OTHER SOURCES

Ellis, George, Antonio Lanza, and John Miller, eds. *The Renaissance of General Relativity and Cosmology: A Survey to Celebrate the 65th Birthday of Dennis Sciama.* Cambridge, U.K.: Cambridge University Press, 1993. Includes a complete bibliography of Sciama's publications (up to 1993), academic family tree (nearly complete list of students), brief biography, and many former students' reflections on their work with him.

Kragh, Helge. *Cosmology and Controversy: The Historical Development of Two Theories of the Universe.* Princeton, NJ:

Princeton University Press, 1996. Definitive historical account of steady state theory, includes detailed discussions of Sciama's contributions to the theory and reasons for abandoning it.

Lightman, Alan, and Roberta Brawer. *Origins: The Lives and Worlds of Modern Cosmologists.* Cambridge, MA: Harvard University Press, 1990. Interviews with Sciama and many of his colleagues.

Thorne, Kip. *Black Holes and Time Warps: Einstein's Outrageous Legacy.* New York: Norton, 1994. Description of research in general relativity throughout the 1960s and 1970s by a leading physicist, at a popular level.

Chris Smeenk

SCOTTUS, IONNES

SEE **Eriugena, Johannes Scottus**.

SEABORG, GLENN (GLEN) THE-ODORE

(*b.* Ishpeming, Michigan, 19 April 1912; *d.* Lafayette, California, 25 February 1999), *discovery of plutonium and nine more transuranium elements, actinide concept, science policy, nuclear energy, nonproliferation, international safeguards, science and math education.*

Seaborg, a world-renowned nuclear chemist, Nobel laureate in chemistry (1951), professor and educator, and scientific advisor to ten U.S. presidents, is probably best known for the discovery of plutonium (1941) and for his leadership of the team that developed plant processes for its purification for use in the U.S. World War II atomic bomb program (1942–1945), and his "revolutionary" actinide concept (1944–1945), which led to the discovery of elements 95 and 96 between 1944 and 1945. He was codiscoverer of elements 97 and 98 (1949–1950) and in 1951 he and Professor Edwin M. McMillan shared the Nobel Prize in Chemistry for their research on the transuranium elements. Subsequently, Seaborg was codiscoverer of elements 99–102 (1952–1958), and in 1974 of element 106, officially named seaborgium in his honor in 1997. From 1961 to 1971 he chaired the U.S. Atomic Energy Commission, strongly supporting peaceful uses of atomic energy, including as a source of electricity. He supervised the PhD research of sixty-eight students before retiring from full-time teaching in 1979. He was also well known as the author of many books, as an educator, and for his tireless efforts to improve U.S. science education at all levels, as well as a hiker, environmentalist, and sports enthusiast.

Family and Early Education (1912–1934). Glen Theodore, the son of Selma Olivia (Erickson) and Her-man Theodore Seaborg, was born in 1912 in the small iron-mining town of Ishpeming on the Upper Peninsula of Michigan. His mother was born in Sweden and his father was born in the United States to Swedish immigrants, and Glen learned Swedish before English. Glen attended kindergarten through fifth grade in Ishpeming. In 1922 the family moved to Home Gardens, near Los Angeles, California, primarily because his mother was seeking better educational and career opportunities for her children. About this time he changed the spelling of his name from "Glen" to "Glenn." He never forgot his roots in Ishpeming nor his Swedish heritage and when he won the Nobel Prize in 1951, he delivered his acceptance speech in Stockholm in Swedish.

His father was never able to obtain permanent employment in California as a machinist (his former trade) and the family was very poor. Early on, Glenn had to earn his own spending money by taking on odd jobs. The first year he was bussed to the Wilmington Avenue Grammar School in the Watts District of Los Angeles, but later transferred to a newly constructed school in Home Gardens where he received his eighth grade diploma and entered David Starr Jordan High School in (Watts) Los Angeles in 1925. He attributed an inspiring high school teacher, Dwight Logan Reid, with sparking his early interest in chemistry and physics. Glenn graduated in 1929 as valedictorian of his class. By working in the summer as a stevedore and night laboratory assistant he earned enough money to attend the University of California, Los Angeles (UCLA), a tuition-free public university, because he could live at home and ride with friends to UCLA about twenty miles away. Seaborg majored in chemistry rather than physics as he thought it would provide him with more job opportunities in the event that he could not find a university position as a teacher, his ultimate goal. After receiving his AB in chemistry in 1933, he stayed on another year in order to take additional physics courses that had just been started at the graduate level in 1934.

Early Berkeley Period (1934–1942). Graduate work in the Department of Chemistry at UCLA had not yet been instituted, so Seaborg went to the University of California at Berkeley (UCB) to start graduate work in chemistry. He hoped to work near the great Professor Gilbert Newton Lewis, dean of the College of Chemistry, and the rising young nuclear physicist Ernest Orlando Lawrence, inventor of the cyclotron in the early 1930s, for which he received the 1939 Nobel Prize in Physics. Seaborg described the atmosphere at Berkeley when he began in August 1934 as "exciting and glamorous" (Seaborg, Hoffman, and Ghiorso, 2000, p. lxxix). He began his graduate research in 1937 on inelastic scattering of neutrons, first under the guidance of physics professor Robert D. Fowler, and then under chemistry professor George Ernest

Gibson, obtaining his PhD in May 1937 in less than three years. The United States was still in the depth of the Depression, but he was soon asked by Professor Lewis to stay on as his personal research assistant and they published many papers together. Between 1936 and 1939 he was a collaborator in experiments that used the newly completed 37-inch cyclotron to produce many new isotopes, for instance, iodine-131 and technetium-99 that have been widely used in diagnostic and therapeutic procedures in nuclear medicine. Seaborg became an instructor in the UCB Chemistry Department in 1939 and was promoted to assistant professor in 1941.

After news of the discovery of nuclear fission reached Berkeley in January 1939, Professor Edwin M. McMillan and recent PhD Philip H. Abelson began investigations of this new phenomenon in bombardments of uranium with neutrons at the newly completed 60-inch cyclotron at Berkeley. Most unexpectedly, they produced and identified the first "real" transuranium element (93), (previously reported erroneously in 1934 by Enrico Fermi and others. Hoffman, Seaborg, and Ghiorso, 2000, p. 2), which they chemically separated and identified in spring 1940. They proposed that it be named neptunium after the planet Neptune because it is just beyond the planet Uranus for which uranium (92) was named.

McMillan then began a search for the next heavier element (atomic number 94), but was called away for wartime radar research at the Massachusetts Institute of Technology (MIT) in November 1940 before he could finish the project. Upon learning of his sudden departure, Seaborg wrote him proposing to continue the search for element 94 and received his ready assent. The team, consisting of Seaborg, fellow instructor Dr. Joseph W. Kennedy, and Seaborg's first graduate student, Arthur C. Wahl, continued with deuteron bombardments of uranium and by late January 1941 had preliminary evidence for the new element. A brief letter describing these results was sent to Washington, D.C., on 28 January 1941, but publication was voluntarily withheld until 1946.

They continued to work on the chemical separation to obtain unequivocal proof that a new element had been discovered. As described by Seaborg, "On the stormy night of February 23, 1941, in an experiment that ran well into the next morning, Wahl performed the oxidation that gave them proof that what they had made was chemically different from all other known elements" (Seaborg, Hoffman, and Ghiorso, 2000, p. 341). This experiment showed that the chemical properties of element 94 were similar to those of uranium and not to osmium (element 76) as suggested by the periodic tables before World War II. Twenty five years later, Room 307 of Gilman Hall on the UCB campus where these experiments were performed was dedicated as a national historic landmark.

Plutonium was first produced in these experiments as the isotope with mass 238, but almost concurrently, Seaborg and Emilio Segrè began irradiations of kilogram quantities of uranyl nitrate with neutrons to produce uranium-239 which quickly decayed to neptunium-239 (half-life ~2.2 days). The neptunium was then purified and allowed to beta decay to the new, longer-lived plutonium isotope of mass 239 (~30,000 years) in order to measure its fissionability with slow neutrons. The experiments were successful in producing sufficient quantities for making the measurement and it was found to be comparable to that of uranium-235, a measurement that changed the course of history. A communication describing this experiment was sent to Washington, D.C., on 7 March 1941. Again, these results were voluntarily withheld from publication until after World War II because of potential military applications. A secret report describing the chemical properties of elements 94 and 93 was also sent to Washington, D.C., on 21 March 1942 by Seaborg and Wahl. The name plutonium (Pu) was proposed for element 94 because the planet Pluto is just beyond the planets Neptune and Uranus. (Pluto lost planetary status in 2006.)

These discoveries led to the U.S. decision to undertake a crash program to develop nuclear reactors to produce plutonium for use in the atomic bomb project, and formed the basis for the secret wartime Plutonium Project at the Metallurgical ("Met") Laboratory of the University of Chicago. Seaborg was asked to direct the group in the chemistry division working on the chemical extraction and purification of plutonium and the decision was made in March 1942 that he should move to Chicago.

He immediately proposed to Helen Lucille Griggs (then E. O. Lawrence's secretary) whom he had been dating since 1941, and she accepted. In April 1942 he took leave of absence from Berkeley to go to Chicago with the understanding that he would return to Berkeley to visit as soon as possible and then he and Helen would be married. In June 1942 Seaborg did return to Berkeley and took Helen to visit his parents in Southgate, California. In the interest of saving time, he persuaded her to return with him immediately to Chicago by train, promising they would be married en route in Nevada, at that time known as the "fast marriage" state. They disembarked from the train at Caliente, Nevada, and were finally married at Pioche, Nevada, on 6 June 1942. Helen and Glenn's marriage was to last until his death in February 1999, more than fifty-six years. Seaborg was fond of pointing out "that I consider her my greatest discovery" (Seaborg and Seaborg, 2001, p. 182). Glenn and Helen had seven children.

University of Chicago, Met Lab (1942–1946). Seaborg joined the Chemistry Division of the Metallurgical

1945 arrangement of periodic table by Glenn T. Seaborg

Actinides placed as members of separate series below lanthanides

1945 Periodic Table Showing Separate Actinide Series.

Laboratory at the University of Chicago in June 1942, to direct the group responsible for devising plant processes for chemical purification of plutonium for the Manhattan Project to develop an atomic bomb. In August 1942 members of the group succeeded in isolating the first "pure" (no other elements present as carriers) sample of a plutonium compound. It contained about one microgram of plutonium and was visible to the naked eye.

The early investigations (1940–1942) of precipitation processes and the oxidation states of plutonium that the chemistry group at UCB had performed using only tracer (submicrogram) quantities of plutonium were the basis for the later development of the large plant processes for separating plutonium from uranium irradiated in reactors. Uranium was irradiated (1943) in the low power reactor in Clinton, Tennessee, and by March 1944 several grams of plutonium had been isolated. The reactors and huge chemical separation plant at Hanford, Washington, were constructed in 1943–1944, and the first production runs to separate plutonium on the kilogram scale began in December 1944. This represented a scale-up factor of more than a billion over the initial Berkeley tracer experiments.

By early 1944, Seaborg felt that the process chemistry for plutonium had progressed to the point where he and his coworkers could devote some effort to the production and identification of the next transuranium elements of atomic numbers 95 and 96. These attempts were at first unsuccessful until Seaborg proposed his actinide concept of heavy element electronic structure in which the fourteen elements heavier than actinium (atomic number 89) are placed in the periodic table as a 5f-transition series under the lanthanide 4f-transition series. Seaborg's new periodic table incorporating this concept was published in *Chemical & Engineering News* in 1945. This was viewed as a "wild" hypothesis because at the time it was commonly believed that thorium, protactinium, uranium, neptunium, plutonium, and the following elements should be placed as the heaviest members of groups 4 through 10. But Seaborg postulated that the heavier actinides, like their lanthanide counterparts, would be extremely difficult to oxidize above the trivalent oxidation state. This concept was verified when chemical separations based on separating elements 95 and 96 as trivalent homologues of the lanthanides were successfully used in 1944–1945 to separate and identify these new elements, subsequently named americium (Am) and curium (Cm) by analogy to their lanthanide homologues, europium and gadolinium.

Glenn Theodore Seaborg. *Seaborg, April 1946.* FRITZ GORO/TIME LIFE PICTURES/GETTY IMAGES.

Berkeley (1946–1961): Elements 97–102 and Administration. After the end of World War II, in May 1946 Glenn Seaborg returned from Chicago to Berkeley as full professor of chemistry, bringing with him some of his associates, including Isadore Perlman, Burris B. Cunningham, Stanley G. Thompson, and Albert Ghiorso. In the following years up to 1958, Seaborg, Thompson, Ghiorso, and coworkers, including many graduate students and postdoctoral fellows, went on to synthesize and identify the next six transuranium elements with atomic numbers 97 through 102. The first of these, berkelium (97) and californium (98), were produced at the Berkeley 60-inch cyclotron in 1949–1950. Shortly thereafter, in 1951, Seaborg and McMillan shared the Nobel Prize in Chemistry for their research on the transuranium elements.

Elements 99 and 100 were most unexpectedly produced in the debris from the first thermonuclear device, which was designed and tested by the Los Alamos Scientific Laboratory on Enewetak Atoll in the South Pacific on 1 November 1952. Its huge yield of some 10 megatons created such an instantaneous high neutron flux that at least seventeen neutrons were captured by the uranium-238 in the device. Seaborg's group at Berkeley was the first to separate and obtain evidence for these new elements, working together with scientists from Argonne National Laboratory and Los Alamos to confirm these results. The group proposed the names einsteinium and fermium for these elements in honor of the great scientists Albert Einstein and Enrico Fermi. Seaborg and coworkers then produced mendelevium (101) in 1956 using the 60-inch cyclotron, and nobelium (102) in 1958 using the Heavy Ion Linear Accelerator at the Berkeley Radiation Laboratory. According to the actinide hypothesis, it was expected that nobelium should have a relatively stable 2+ state by analogy to ytterbium, which can be reduced from 3+ to 2+ with strong reducing agents. However, it was found that not only is the 2+ state of nobelium achievable, it is the most stable oxidation state of nobelium in aqueous solution.

During this period (1946–1958), Seaborg served as director of the Nuclear Chemistry Division. He became an associate director of the Berkeley Radiation Laboratory in 1954. In addition to research on the production and chemical properties of transuranium elements, division scientists discovered dozens of new isotopes and furnished much data on alpha-particle radioactivity and nuclear energy levels needed for evolution of modern theories of nuclear structure.

Seaborg began to broaden his horizons to national public service and served from 1947 to 1950 on the first general advisory committee to the U.S. Atomic Energy Commission (AEC). Consistent with his lifelong interest in athletics, he served as faculty athletic representative for UCB from 1953 to 1958 and played a leading role in organizing the Athletic Association of Western Universities. He was appointed chancellor of UCB in 1958, a position in which he thrived. The athletic teams were unusually successful, and many new facilities, research centers, departments, and museums, including the Lawrence Hall of Science, were established during his short tenure of only two and a half years. He held this position until 1961 when president-elect John F. Kennedy asked him to come to Washington, D.C., to chair the AEC.

AEC Chairman (1961–1971). Seaborg and his family moved to Washington, D.C., when he became chairman of the AEC. His tenure from 1961 to 1971 was longer than that of any other chairman and spanned the presidencies of Kennedy, Lyndon B. Johnson, and Richard M. Nixon. Seaborg led the negotiations resulting in the limited nuclear test ban treaty prohibiting the testing of nuclear devices in the atmosphere or under the sea, which was approved by the U.S. Senate in 1963. He strongly supported the use of nuclear energy as a source of electricity, and led delegations to some sixty countries, including the U.S.S.R., to promote the peaceful uses of atomic energy. During the Johnson and Nixon administrations, the AEC played a significant role in the negotiation of the Non-Proliferation Treaty, took the lead in instituting national and international safeguards to ensure that nuclear materials were not diverted from peaceful uses to weapons purposes, and implemented a cutback in the production of fissionable materials. Seaborg was a strong advocate of a Comprehensive Test Ban Treaty. The AEC was also in charge of the nuclear weapons testing program, and the Plowshare Program.

Seaborg continued his interest in transuranium element research and the National Transplutonium Production Program was established at the High Flux Isotope Reactor (HFIR), commissioned at the Oak Ridge National Laboratory in the mid-1960s. The HFIR and the associated transuranium processing facility were essential in producing rare heavy-element isotopes used in synthesis of new heavy elements and in heat sources for space exploration. Other radioactive isotopes for applications in biology, nuclear medicine, and industry were also produced. Among the many new projects established were: Los Alamos Meson Facility, Lawrence Berkeley Laboratory 200-billion-electron-volt accelerator, civilian nuclear power reactor program, gas centrifuge program, nuclear power in space program, and controlled thermonuclear research program.

Under Seaborg's leadership, the support for basic research in the physical sciences, biology, and medicine nearly doubled. He was instrumental in implementing awards to scientists in the United States and abroad. He was keenly interested in the improvement of teaching in science and mathematics and in attracting young people to careers in science, and the Nuclear Education and Training and Technical Information and Exhibits Programs were initiated.

Return to Berkeley (1971–1999). Seaborg returned to Berkeley in 1971 and was appointed university professor of chemistry by the regents of the University of California. He continued to teach until 1979, and was advisor for sixty-eight PhD, thirteen masters, and fifty-four undergraduate students over his career. After his return to Berkeley, he became more actively involved with the Lawrence Hall of Science (LHS), which he was instrumental in founding while he was chancellor at Berkeley. He played an active role in establishing the LHS as the public science, curriculum development, teacher education, and school outreach center of UCB. He was the principal investigator for the Great Explorations in Math and Science program and helped establish standards for science education. He served as acting director from 1982 to 1984. When a new director was chosen, Seaborg took the new position of founding chairman of LHS and served actively in this capacity until just before his final illness.

He served as associate director-at-large of the Lawrence Berkeley National Laboratory until his death in 1999. He was active in many international organizations for fostering the application of chemistry to world economic, social, and scientific needs. He spoke out for better education in science and mathematics and was a member of the National Commission on Excellence in Education (1983) which issued the influential report "A Nation at Risk: The Imperative for Educational Reform." Seaborg later reiterated that "we have in effect been committing an act of unthinking, unilateral educational disarmament" (Seaborg, 1991). In October 1989, together with then Secretary of Energy, Admiral James D. Watkins, he cochaired the Math/Science Education Action Conference at the Lawrence Hall of Science. Watkins stated that the aim of the conference and its report was to ensure that the history books of the twenty-first century will not tell of a once great nation that declined and fell because it lost its passion for science. In 1998 Seaborg was appointed to the Commission for the Establishment of Academic Content and Performance Standards appointed by California Governor Pete Wilson to chair the committee for the establishment of K–12 science standards. Seaborg guided the committee in formulating the concise and controversial statements of the science standards to be taught in California high schools.

In addition to the 1951 Nobel Prize for Chemistry, he received a host of other honors and awards. These include: selection in 1947 as one of "America's Ten Outstanding Young Men" by the U.S. Junior Chamber of Commerce; election to the National Academy of Sciences in 1948; American Society of Swedish Engineers John Ericsson Gold Medal in 1948; AEC 1959 Enrico Fermi Award; 1971 Nuclear Pioneer Award of the Society of Nuclear Medicine; Order of the Legion of Honor of the Republic of France, Decoration, 1973; Swedish Council of America 1984; Great Swedish Heritage Award; University of California's 1986 Clark Kerr Medal; National Science Board's 1988 Vannevar Bush Award; 1991 National Medal of Science; 1997 Priestley Medal; and many other major awards from the American Chemical Society, fifty honorary degrees from various universities, and election to a dozen foreign national academies of science. Seaborg is listed in the *Guinness Book of World Records* for having the longest entry in *Who's Who in America*.

The name *seaborgium* for element 106 was officially approved by the International Union of Pure and Applied Chemistry in 1997, an honor that Seaborg said he cherished more highly than the Nobel Prize. Seaborg held more than forty patents, authored or coauthored more than 550 articles and 30 books, including editing his daily journal entries that he began at age fourteen and meticulously continued throughout his career. These formed the basis for a number of his books including the autobiography titled *A Chemist in the White House: From the Manhattan Project to the End of the Cold War* (1998).

Glenn loved to hike and he and Helen laid out an interconnected network of twelve-mile trails in the East Bay Hills above Berkeley that extended to the California-Nevada border and forms a link in a cross-country trek of the American Hiking Society. He was also a strong supporter of the athletic program at UCB. He was an avid golfer and considered it excellent therapy under times of stress. Football was his favorite spectator sport and he liked to point out that during his tenure as chancellor the UCB football team went to the Rose Bowl.

Seaborg contributed to a host of professional societies. He was active in the American Chemical Society

throughout his career, serving as its president during its centennial year of 1976. Among his last accolades was being voted one of the "Top 75 Distinguished Contributors to the Chemical Enterprise" over the last seventy-five years by the readers of *Chemical & Engineering News.* The award was presented to him at a huge ceremony and reception on Sunday, 23 August, during the 1998 National ACS meeting in Boston—the evening before he suffered the stroke and fall that ultimately claimed his life on 25 February 1999.

BIBLIOGRAPHY

WORKS BY SEABORG

With G. E. Gibson and D. C. Grahame. "Inelastic Scattering of Fast Neutrons." *Physical Review* 52 (1937): 408–414. Discussion of thesis results.

"A Nation at Risk: The Imperative for Educational Reform." Washington, D.C.: Superintendent of Documents, U.S. Govt. Printing. Office, 1983.

"A Nation at Risk Revisited." *Daedalus* (Fall 1984): 127. Lawrence Berkeley Laboratory, LBL Preprint 31126.

With Joseph J. Katz and Lester R. Morss, eds. *The Chemistry of the Actinide Elements.* 2nd ed. 2 vols. New York: Chapman and Hall, 1986.

Journals of Glenn T. Seaborg: Entire Collection Spanning Years from 1927–1990. Library of Congress, 1990.

Rebuilding American Education for the 21st Century. Industry Education Council of California. San Francisco: Golden Gate University Press, 1991.

Modern Alchemy: The Selected Papers of Glenn T. Seaborg, edited by Glenn T. Seaborg. Singapore: World Scientific Publishing, 1994. Seaborg's selection of representative 100 out of his more than 500 papers, with appendix listing all his students.

The Plutonium Story: The Journals of Professor Glenn T. Seaborg, 1939–1946, edited by Jerry B. Gough, Ronald L. Kathren, and Gary T. Benefiel. Columbus, OH: Battelle Press, 1994.

A Chemist in the White House: From the Manhattan Project to the End of the Cold War. Washington, DC: American Chemical Society, 1998.

With Darleane C. Hoffman and Albert Ghiorso. *The Transuranium People: The Inside Story.* London: Imperial College Press, 2000. Chapters on each of the transuranium elements from 93 (neptunium) through element 112, and searches for superheavy elements, with detailed personal, scientific accounts, and many photos.

With Eric Seaborg. *Adventures in the Atomic Age: From Watts to Washington.* New York: Farrar, Straus and Giroux, 2001. Autobiography taped, transcribed, and edited by son Eric Seaborg giving complete detailed information on personal and scientific life.

OTHER SOURCES

Berkeley Lab Image Library. Images related to Seaborg (including cartoons) available by following Seaborg Archive link from http://www.lbl.gov/image-gallery/image-library.html.

Creative Services Office, Lawrence Berkeley National Laboratory. "Images of Glenn T. Seaborg." Available from http://cso.lbl. gov/photo/gallery/Seaborg. Extensive collection.

"Glenn T. Seaborg: The Nobel Prize in Chemistry 1951." Biography available from the Nobel Web site: http:// nobelprize.org/chemistry/laureates/1951/seaborg-bio.html.

Hoffman, Darleane C. "In Memory of Glenn Theodore Seaborg [19 April 1912–25 February 1999]: Glenn T. Seaborg's Multi-Faceted Career." *Journal of Nuclear Science & Technology,* supp. 3 (2002): 1–7.

Darleane Hoffman

SEGRÈ, EMILIO GINO (*b.* Tivoli, Italy, 30 January 1905; *d.* Lafayette, California, 22 April 1989), *nuclear and particle physics, history of science.*

Segrè opened the world of antimatter to physical investigation with his discovery of the antiproton, discovered the first of the elements produced by a particle accelerator, provided the critical measurements that established the need for implosion in the ignition of nuclear weapons, and provided important resources for the historical understanding of modern physics. Born Jewish in Italy, he fled because of the Fascist anti-Semitic legislation as did his mentor, Enrico Fermi, whose papers he edited.

Education. Born into an industrial family, Emilio Segrè had an early interest in mathematics and physics that was nurtured by his uncle, Claudio Segrè, who was a mining engineer. He was privately educated in addition to attending public school in Tivoli and Rome. After beginning engineering studies in the University of Rome at his father's behest, he switched to physics after meeting Fermi and sneaking into an International Physics Conference at Como in September 1927. He became part of Fermi's group at Rome, working with Franco Rasetti, Edoardo Amaldi, and Ettore Majorana, whom Segrè recruited from the engineering school. After completing his military obligation in 1930 he studied transition lines in the atomic spectra of alkaline metals, which should have been forbidden by the laws of quantum mechanics. At Peter Debye's suggestion, he continued these studies with the Dutch physicist Pieter Zeeman in Amsterdam, which offered superior facilities to those he had in Rome. Perhaps as a result of Zeeman's intervention, he won a Rockefeller Foundation fellowship that allowed him to study with Otto Stern at the University of Hamburg, who set him to finish an experiment on the dynamics of space quantization and schooled him in the precise experimental techniques that had established Stern's reputation in molecular beams. Segrè returned to Rome where he worked with Fermi on the explanation of hyperfine structures in spectra, which they demonstrated resulted

from the nuclear magnetic moment as expressed in the Fermi-Segrè formula.

Nuclear Physics. Segrè's generation entered physics at the time quantum mechanics was consolidating thirty years of discovery in atomic physics and the new field of nuclear physics was opening up. Fermi regarded this as a great opportunity to establish a leading school on the frontiers of theoretical and experimental physics. After the Rome group acquired Geiger-Müller counters, a gamma ray spectrograph, a cloud chamber for experimental nuclear studies, and a source of radium, they held an international congress on nuclear physics in Rome in October 1931, which attracted the leading European nuclear physicists. Fermi soon joined them at subsequent international congresses. He quickly made an important contribution to nuclear theory with his theory of beta decay, which explained how some elements transform into others by emitting an electron from the nucleus.

After the discovery of artificial radioactivity by Irène and Frédéric Joliot-Curie, Fermi realized that low-energy neutrons would be an effective tool of nuclear physics. Discovered in 1932 by James Chadwick, neutrons could easily penetrate atomic nuclei since they were not repelled by the positively charged protons, having no charge of their own. Using neutrons produced when alpha particles struck beryllium, the Fermi group began to activate all the elements. Segrè noticed that paraffin, which was used in experiments bombarding silver with neutrons, greatly increased the activity produced. Fermi deduced from this observation that hydrogen atoms, which were abundant in paraffin, had been struck by neutrons, slowing the neutrons down, and that the slower neutrons, contrary to accepted opinion, actually interacted more effectively with the silver atoms. Further experiments showed this to be the case in a number of elements, and a search began for effective moderators of neutrons that would slow them down to increase their effect. At the same time, a patent application was made on the process of slow-neutron activation.

In the fall of 1935, Segrè was appointed to the physics chair at the University of Palermo in Sicily. The following summer, he and his bride, Elfriede, traveled to the United States, where Segrè had spent part of the summer of 1934 at Columbia University in New York City, and visited Ernest Lawrence's Radiation Laboratory at the University of California, Berkeley. Lawrence had used high-energy neutrons to bombard elements in a program similar to the Fermi group. Returning from Berkeley with discarded fragments of Lawrence's early cyclotrons, Segrè investigated the radioactive substances produced in them by accelerated deuterons and found them "a true mine of radioactive substances" (Segrè, 1993). More followed from Berkeley, leading Segrè to discover a new

Emilio Gino Segrè. © BETTMANN/CORBIS.

element, technetium, which filled the empty space in the periodic table at atomic number 43, using a molybdenum foil that had been incorporated in a beam deflector. It was the first element created artificially.

Refugee. During his second visit to Berkeley in the summer of 1938, he learned that, because of his Jewish origins, his professorship at Palermo had been revoked by Benito Mussolini's government. At Lawrence's invitation, he became a research associate at the Radiation Laboratory. There, he worked with Glenn Seaborg to develop the field of nuclear chemistry, and participated in the discovery of plutonium and the determination of its fissile properties.

Segrè's work with Seaborg began with a search for short-lived technetium-isotopes that resulted in the observation of a nuclear isomerism that produced technicium-99, which is used millions of times annually in medical imaging research and diagnosis. Of the many isotopes that were the object of the Radiation Laboratory's systematic search for medically useful radiopharmaceuticals, it remains the most effective. Segrè also collaborated with

Chien-Shiung Wu in a search for another element missing in the periodic table, element 61. With Robert Cornog, Dale Corson, and K. R. McKenzie, he found element 85, astatine, in 1940.

Fission and Plutonium. Although Fermi and his group had supposed that the slow-neutron bombardment of uranium had produced previously unknown elements of greater atomic weight and number, for which Fermi received the Nobel Prize in 1938, the discovery of nuclear fission by Otto Hahn and Fritz Strassmann in Berlin with help from the exiled Lise Meitner at the end of 1938 made it clear that fission had produced the results: elements of approximately half the atomic weight of uranium. The discovery was quickly verified around the world, which alarmed many refugees like Fermi (who had also emigrated to the United States at about this time) and Segrè. Edwin M. McMillan at the Radiation Laboratory found that fission in uranium foils bombarded by the cyclotron produced a true transuranium element, neptunium, and this launched a search for others, led by Segrè and Seaborg. At Fermi's suggestion, Lawrence gave priority for the project on the 60-inch cyclotron. Assisted by Arthur Wahl and Joseph Kennedy, Segrè and Seaborg found element 94, plutonium, and subsequently showed that it was fissionable with both slow and fast neutrons, making it a potential source of nuclear energy. This work, completed in May 1941, stimulated Lawrence to urge the Briggs Committee, which had been founded as a result of Albert Einstein's letter to President Franklin Delano Roosevelt, to accelerate research leading to the making of nuclear weapons. Plutonium would supply a nuclear fuel similar to the uranium isotope U^{235} for such weapons, and it could be made in a nuclear reactor, which Fermi and Leo Szilard were then developing at Columbia University. This project was subsequently transferred to the University of Chicago, where the first chain-reacting nuclear pile was completed in December 1942, after Roosevelt endorsed a full-scale, top secret program to develop nuclear weapons, which became the Manhattan Project.

Lawrence's role in the project was to develop giant mass spectrographs based on cyclotron technology to separate uranium-235 from uranium-238. Segrè set up an analytical laboratory to perform isotopic analyses of the process. In addition, he began systematic studies of spontaneous fission in uranium and plutonium and, in the summer of 1942, of fission cross sections as well. This information was vital to the success of the atomic bomb program, since an explosive chain reaction would have to be instantaneous: if the chain reaction began too early, the material would be dispersed by the explosion before it could achieve significant energy. This required several generations of fission, each new generation producing exponentially more energy. Any stray neutron could thus predetonate the material and create a "dud" rather than a bomb.

Los Alamos. When Seaborg went to the University of Chicago at the end of 1941 to develop means of refining plutonium for the Manhattan Project, Segrè and his associates Owen Chamberlain and Clyde Wiegand went to Los Alamos National Laboratory at the invitation of laboratory leader J. Robert Oppenheimer to continue their investigation of spontaneous fission in uranium and plutonium. They conducted exceedingly sensitive measurements in a Pajarito canyon cabin, remote from the main technical area at Los Alamos, where other experiments produced electric fields and stray neutrons that would spoil them. The higher altitude of Los Alamos allowed more cosmic rays to initiate spontaneous fission than had been the case at Berkeley, but it still occurred only a few times a month. Unfortunately, as additional supplies of plutonium arrived from Chicago, Oak Ridge, and Hanford, the count went up.

Painstaking studies established plutonium-239 had too high a spontaneous fission rate to be assembled by firing one fraction of the critical mass into another, as was done in the uranium bomb. Segrè's group determined this to be the result of an isotopic impurity, plutonium-240, which had not been observed in accelerator-produced plutonium but which was created in nuclear reactors by neutron bombarded plutonium-239. Since plutonium could not be purified of this contaminant in time to be of use, panic struck, and the entire laboratory was reorganized to develop a new technique for igniting the plutonium bomb, the implosion technique. Ironically, the compartmentalization of the Manhattan Project kept this news from reaching Chicago, where DuPont engineers and scientists at the Metallurgical Laboratory were designing reactors to produce plutonium at Hanford, an effort that would have been in vain had the implosion technique not been perfected at Los Alamos.

Oppenheimer seems to have appreciated the dogged determination exhibited by Segrè in measuring spontaneous fission, and sent him to the Oak Ridge laboratory where Lawrence's calutrons had been installed to investigate the DA atomic electrons NG atomic electrons ER of accruing enough enriched uranium in one spot to set off a fission reaction unintentionally. Segrè was able to prevent a possible catastrophe by correcting the situation, which had not been anticipated in the design and construction of the plant. He also undertook a study of the effects to be expected from a nuclear explosion.

After the implosion technique was developed, it was decided that a test must be made of the resulting device at an army bombing range in central New Mexico on the Jornada del Muerto, a bleak desert between the Oscura Mountains and the Rio Grande, near the birthplace of Conrad Hilton at San Antonio, New Mexico. Segrè's group designed a variety of instruments to diagnose the effect of the blast from the neutron and gamma radiation it produced. He observed the test with Fermi, who was able to estimate the force of the blast by dropping confetti as it passed them at a distance of 10 miles.

Berkeley Professor. Offered positions at the University of Chicago, where Fermi headed a new Institute for Nuclear Studies, and Washington University, St. Louis, where many of the nuclear chemists with whom he had worked took jobs after the war, Segrè elected to negotiate a full professorship at the University of California and to return to his studies of elementary nuclear processes using the new generation of accelerators built after the war. McMillan's principle of phase stability made possible the completion of the Radiation Laboratory's 184-inch cyclotron as a synchrocyclotron, the building of a new electron-synchrotron opened up new areas of exploration at high energies, and Luis Alvarez's linear accelerator, based on techniques he conceived after working on radar during the war, provided high-energy protons for studies of proton-proton interactions. Frustrated in his efforts to continue research in spontaneous fission and nuclear chemistry by the growing influence of Seaborg, who had convinced Lawrence to support a major effort in nuclear chemistry under his direction, Segrè chose to study high-energy interactions of nuclear constituents instead. This was to lead him to his most important discovery.

Segrè also resumed his efforts, begun with C. S. Wu before the war, to measure the effect of atomic electrons nuclear K-capture by beta decay. This work was completed in 1947 and was the last of the unfinished work that he was able to complete, because many of the radioactive materials needed for studies of heavy elements were now controlled by the newly formed Atomic Energy Commission and rationed to workers like Seaborg, whom Segrè believed would not collaborate with him as an equal.

The field of nucleon interactions seemed to offer opportunities to revive Ernest Rutherford's studies of nuclear scattering at much higher energies. Segrè's group spent several years studying interactions between neutrons and protons and between protons and protons. Polarized proton beams from the 184-inch synchrocyclotron supplemented these data, which were also used to compute the wave phase shifts in nuclear interactions with the Los Alamos computer, MANIAC. In order to make it widely available, along with other unclassified work in the field of nuclear physics, Segrè edited *Experimental Nuclear Physics* and beginning in 1952, the *Annual Review of Nuclear Science.*

The death of his mentor Fermi in 1954 sundered the last significant connection with his prewar work, and Segrè paid homage to him by editing Fermi's *Collected Papers* (1958) and by writing a scientific biography, *Enrico Fermi, Physicist* (1970).

William M. Brobeck, with whom Segrè had collaborated in the magnet design of the 184-inch cyclotron before the war, designed a proton synchrotron in 1946, and after the completion of the postwar accelerators, Ernest Lawrence succeeded in winning Atomic Energy Commission funding to build a 6.2-billion-electron-volt (BeV) proton synchrotron at the Radiation Laboratory in 1948. Although the accelerator was delayed by the construction of a one-quarter-scale model (used to test the aperature required) and the laboratory's involvement in the race for the hydrogen bomb, which led to a second laboratory in Livermore, California, the 6.2 BeV machine finally became operational in 1954.

The energy of the machine had been designed to make antiprotons, which had been predicted by nuclear theorists in the 1930s, through proton-proton interactions. Several groups in the Radiation Laboratory competed to develop the appropriate experiment to identify the particle, which would be concealed in a beam of fifty thousand other particles of negative charge produced by the interaction. The new machine was surrounded by their experimental setups, all of which represented variants on two themes: (1) electromagnetic detection and (2) photographic detection of the rare particles.

Segrè's group, which now included Tom Ypsilantis as well as Chamberlain and Wiegand, won the competition. The experimental setup included a mass spectrograph, which used a magnetic field to separate negatively charged protons from other particles, and time-of-flight detectors and a Cerenkov counter, which measured the velocity of the particles thus separated. These detectors had been used in different configurations by other groups involved in the search. Arranging them in sequence with quadrupole focusing magnets allowed the Segrè-Chamberlain group to deduce the mass of the particle from the momentum and velocity. They found their first evidence for antiprotons in September 1955.

Another branch of Segrè's group, led by Gerson Goldhaber, sought to detect antiprotons in a different way, through the use of photographic emulsions, which had long been employed in cosmic-ray physics in the search for antiprotons. Amaldi's group at the University of Rome collaborated with this group in processing the resulting films, and in November 1955 the Amaldi group found a single event in their film corresponding to the theoretical mass of the antiproton. Other Radiation Laboratory groups confirmed the discovery within a month, when a complete track of an antiproton ending in an annihilation by collision with a proton was found in a stack of emulsions. These results were collectively published: thirty-five events by eighteen authors! Segrè and Chamberlain were awarded the Nobel Prize in Physics for the discovery in 1959.

Oreste Piccioni, a Brookhaven physicist who had discussed his plans for an antiproton experiment with Segrè and Chamberlain in December 1954, subsequently filed a lawsuit alleging that they had used those plans in the design of their experiment, from which he had been excluded. Because he filed his suit after the relevant statute of limitations permitted, the suit was never heard. Although many scientists claim credit for work done by others who receive the Nobel Prize, this was the first such claim ever filed in a court of law, and continued to cast a shadow on the discovery for many years. Piccioni was a member of the group that subsequently discovered the antineutron, and Segrè's group confirmed that it resulted from a process called charge exchange whereby the two particles switch identity.

Antiprotons have become important research tools in high-energy particle physics since the invention of stochastic cooling, which makes it possible to store, concentrate, and direct antiproton beams. The Center for European Research in Nuclear Physics (CERN) built a 300 BeV proton-antiproton colliding-beam accelerator, the Super Proton Synchrotron, in the early 1980s. Fermilab's colliding-beam accelerator has energies over 1 trillion electron volts (TeV) produced in the collision of beams of protons and antiprotons. CERN plans a 14 TeV machine. Slowing down antiprotons has also been accomplished and has led to the assembly of antiatoms.

Antiprotons have also figured prominently in cosmology. Although speculation that galaxies made up of antiprotons, antineutrons, and positrons might exist followed the particles' original discovery, this has not been supported either by observations of antiprotons in cosmic rays or by any convincing theory. Nevertheless, the search goes on since the big bang theory accepted by most cosmologists indicates that, at least in the first few seconds of the universe, the number of particles and antiparticles was equivalent. Proposed experiments using magnetic spectrometers placed in orbit around the earth seek to solve the mystery of antimatter.

The Segrè group lost much of its collegiality after their success, as Chamberlain and Wiegand sought greater independence. Although the group held together for another decade, Segrè no longer figured as the intellectual leader. He wrote a treatise on the field in 1964, and continued to provide professional leadership through his editorship of *Annual Review.* He became a senior statesman in science rather than the experimentalist he had been since the 1930s. He gave lectures all around the world, served as a trustee to the National Accelerator Laboratory (later called Fermilab) during its formative period, and received a number of honorary degrees and appointments. After reaching retirement age he returned to Rome where he was given a chair in physics for one year—when he reached Italy's retirement age.

The premature death of Fermi in 1954 and Segrès' subsequent involvement in preserving and recounting Fermi's life and work reinforced Segrè's interest in history of physics. In addition to publishing a two-volume history of twentieth-century physics, Segrè taught courses in history of physics at the University of California annually before and after his retirement and was an active participant in the field. In addition to his participation in Berkeley's hiring the soon-to-be-world-famous historian of science Thomas Kuhn in 1956 and assisting Kuhn in the preparation of the Archive for the History of Quantum Physics, Segrè was the Sarton Lecturer at the Tenth International Congress of the History of Science. He was one of the initiators of the Lawrence Berkeley Laboratory history project, and welcomed opportunities to advise, as well as criticize, the work of historians of modern physics.

Segrè was a man of strong views and seldom hesitated to express them. Early in his career, he earned the title of "Basilisk" because, like the mythical beast, his glance made a deep, if not lethal, impression. Segrè's wife thought him a careful judge of character, although he was not always cautious in expressing his judgments. His eldest son, Claudio, wrote a memoir of his life with his father, which captured Segrè's difficulty in communicating with him. Although not abusive, he was often remote, preoccupied with work and critical rather than encouraging of his children.

In 1993 his autobiography, *A Mind Always in Motion,* provided a candid personal view of physics in Rome and Berkeley. Segrè regarded himself as an outsider at the Radiation Laboratory throughout his career, although his use of its accelerators was among the most fruitful for high-energy physics. This detachment not only made him among the more successful physicist-historians of his age, it allowed him to remain aloof from the exigencies of big science and to avoid being captured by the research programs that subsume hundreds of physicists in huge collaborative experiments. It also reflected his perspective, forged in Rome in his work with Fermi, on the human importance and intellectual elegance of doing physics.

Segrè married Rosa Mines in 1972 after the death of his first wife, Elfriede, and remained in good health, living in Lafayette, California, until 1989, when on 22 April he collapsed and died while walking with her, leaving his son, two daughters, and five grandchildren.

BIBLIOGRAPHY

WORKS BY SEGRÈ

"Some Chemical Properties of Element 43." *Journal of Chemical Physics* 5 (1937): 712–716.

With Glenn T. Seaborg. "Nuclear Isomerism in Element 43." *Physical Review* 54 (1938): 772.

With Joseph W. Kennedy, Glenn T. Seaborg, and Arthur C. Wahl. "Properties of 94^{239}." *Physical Review* 70 (1946): 555–556.

Editor. *Annual Review of Nuclear Science* 1–27 (1952–1977).

Editor. *Experimental Nuclear Physics.* 3 vols. New York: Wiley, 1953–1959.

With Owen Chamberlain, Clyde Wiegand, and Thomas Ypsilantis. "Observation of Antiprotons." *Physical Review* 100 (1955): 947–950.

Nuclei and Particles: An Introduction to Nuclear and Subnuclear Physics. New York: W. A. Benjamin, 1964. Rev. ed. Menlo Park, CA: Benjamin/Cummings Pub. Co., 1977.

Enrico Fermi, Physicist. Chicago: University of Chicago Press, 1970.

From X-rays to Quarks: Modern Physicists and Their Discoveries. New York: W.H. Freeman, 1980.

From Falling Bodies to Radio Waves: Classical Physicists and Their Discoveries. New York: W.H. Freeman, 1984.

A Mind Always in Motion: The Autobiography of Emilio Segrè. Berkeley: University of California Press, 1993.

OTHER SOURCES

Segrè, Claudio G. *Atoms, Bombs & Eskimo Kisses: A Memoir of Father and Son.* New York: Viking, 1995.

Seidel, Robert. "Accelerating Science: The Postwar Transformation of the Lawrence Radiation Laboratory." *Historical Studies in the Physical Sciences* 13, part 2 (1983): 375–400.

Robert Seidel

SEMENOV, NIKOLAĬ NIKOLAE-VICH

(*b.* Saratov, Russia, 15 April 1896, *d.* Moscow, Russia, 25 September 1986), *molecular physics, physical chemistry, chemical physics.*

Semenov is credited with the discovery of a new type of chemical process: the so-called branched chain reaction. He determined the mechanisms of chain processes and developed a general theory for them. Semenov also created theories of chain and thermal explosions and developed the understanding of flame spreading, detonation, and burning of explosives. His theoretical models foreshadowed the discovery of nuclear chain reactions. Together with his colleagues, Semenov made a considerable contribution to the realization of nuclear projects in the Soviet Union. In 1956, he became the first Soviet scientist to be awarded a Nobel Prize in Chemistry.

Early Life. Semenov was born into a middle-class family: his father, Nikolaĭ Aleksandrovich Semenov, served as a clerk in Saratov Appanage District. As a reward for his long service, he was granted a rank of state advisor and life nobleman. His mother, Elena Aleksandrovna (born Dmitrieva), was from a medical assistant's family. In 1913 Nikolai Semenov graduated from a professional secondary school in Samara. He entered the Physical Department of the Physical-Mathematical Faculty of St. Petersburg in 1913. (The name was changed to Petrograd University in 1914). Semenov graduated with honors in 1917, on the eve of Bolshevik Revolution, and was immediately granted a bursary that allowed him to prepare for the title of professor.

During his second year of study at the university, he engaged in experimental scientific work under the direction of Abram F. Ioffe. He studied the electron impact ionization of atoms and molecules in gas discharges. In 1918 Semenov went on vacation to visit his parents, who were living in Samara, and found himself in the vortex of civil war. He served several months in the White Army, in the troops of Aleksandr Vasiliyevich Kolchak—the head of internal counterrevolution in Russia, who organized anti-Bolshevik government in Siberia and Far East in autumn of 1918.

Scientific Career. During 1918–1920 he taught at Tomsk University and at the Tomsk Technological Institute (Siberia). In 1920 he received an invitation to continue his research from Ioffe, who had just been elected as a full member of the Academy of Sciences to come to Petrograd (known as Leningrad since 1924). Semenov became head of the Electronic Phenomena Laboratory of the Petrograd Physical-Technical Radiological Institute. Beginning in 1927 he directed the Physical-Chemical Sector of the Institute. In 1931 on its basis there was established the Institute of Chemical Physics (*Institut khimicheskoĭ fiziki* , IKhF, Leningrad, after 1943 located in Moscow). Semenov headed it for some fifty-five years. The major mission of the institute was to introduce physical theories and methods to academic chemistry and to the chemical industry. In 1929 Semenov was elected a corresponding member of the Academy of Sciences (AS) of the USSR; in 1932 he became a full member of the AS. Having become a member of USSR AS Presidium (in 1957), Semenov held from 1957–1963 the position of secretary of its Department of Chemical Sciences and in 1963–1971 served as USSR AS vice-president. In 1963 he organized the Section of Chemical-Technological and Biological Sciences within the academy. In the Moscow suburb of

Chernogolovka he established in 1955 a division of the IKhF that played an important role in the development of the Noginsk Scientific Center of USSR AS, a large complex of institutes. Several years later he founded within that center the Institute of New Chemical Problems. These reorganizations within the academy's framework made it possible to concentrate the attention of scientists on the solution of scientific tasks necessary for the development of the country's economy.

During all his life Semenov gave much attention to the training of new specialists. In 1920–1931 he taught in Petrograd (Leningrad) Polytechnic Institute, after 1928 as professor, and later as the dean's deputy (1929) and the dean of the Physical-Mechanical Faculty of the Polytechnic Institute. In 1944 he became a professor at Moscow State University, at the Chemical Faculty, where he organized the Chair of Chemical Kinetics, remaining its head until the end of his life. Semenov also taught at the Moscow Mechanical Institute of Ammunition (later Moscow Engineer-Physical Institute), where in 1951 he founded and headed the Chair of Physics of Fast-proceeding Processes (1951–1957). He was also one of initiators and organizers of the Moscow Physical-Technical Institute (1951). Semenov created his own scientific school, having trained a brilliant pleiad of scholars, including V. V. Voevodskiĭ, V. I. Gol'danskiĭ, N. S. Enikopolov, Ia. B. Zel'dovich, D. G. Knorre, V. N. Kondrat'ev, M. A. Sadovskiĭ, Iu. B. Khariton, A. I. Shal'nikov, A. E. Shilov, N. M. Ėmanuêl' (all of whom became full members of USSR AS); A. B. Nalbandian (full member of Armenian SSR AS); A. F. Walther, F. I. Dubovitskiĭ, A. A. Koval'skiĭ, K. I. Shchelkin (USSR AS corresponding members); and others.

Semenov gave a good deal of attention to communication within the scientific physical-chemical community. He actively participated in holding scientific conferences (in particular, as an active organizer of the First Physical-Chemical Conference in the USSR held in 1927), and was an initiator of the establishment of *Zhurnal fisicheskoĭ khimii* (Journal of physical chemistry; 1930) and the journal *Khimicheskaia fizika* (Chemical physics; 1981). With his direct assistance, a number of new educational establishments and research institutes were organized in the Soviet Union.

The Creative Path. Having returned to Petrograd in 1918, Semenov worked on problems in molecular physics and studied the nature of electronic phenomena. He focused his attention on the processes of molecular dissociation under the action of electron impact, and he studied changes in the reactivity of atoms and molecules as a function of their electron excitation. This work laid the groundwork for the molecular beam methods that later became widespread in chemical physics. He researched the interaction of molecular beams of metal atoms with a chemically inert surface, which led to a model for the dependence of two-dimensional gas condensation on the temperature of the condensation surface. In 1925 Semenov, in collaboration with the theoretical physicist Iakov Frenkel, worked out a universal theory of this phenomenon.

Another sphere of Semenov's interest in 1920s was the research of electric fields. He developed two new methods of experimental research of electrostatic fields (1920–1924), which were applied to a number of technically important cases (high-voltage isolators, cables and cable joints, and others). Studying the nature of electric breakdown of dielectrics in collaboration with A. F. Walther and L. D. Inge (1925–1929), he discovered the phenomenon of thermal dielectric breakdown (see *Die physikalischen Grundlagen der elektrischen Festigkeitlehre*, 1928; *Teoriia i praktika proboia dĭelektrikov*, 1929). His research on what appeared to be purely physical problems later led Semenov to develop a thermal theory of spontaneous ignition of a combustible gas.

Creation of a Theory of Chain Reactions. The results of experiments carried out in Semenov's laboratory in 1926–1927 heightened his interest in chemistry. One of the reactions under study was the vapor phase oxidation of phosphorus. The rate of reaction was observed to be marked by unexpected discontinuities. He discovered critical phenomena, consisting in sudden change from an almost absence of reaction to great increases in rate, these abrupt changes were in response to only slight changes in reaction conditions. For example, it was determined that at low pressures the reaction does not proceed at all. But when the pressure of oxygen was increased, at a certain point the combination reaction with phosphorus vapor occurs with ignition. Experiments showed the existence of a lowest limit of oxygen pressure, below which the reaction is very slow, but above which it runs quite rapidly, eventually resulting in the ignition of the mixture of reacting substances. Experiments with inert gas admixtures produced unexpected results. For example, the addition of argon caused ignition at pressures below the critical value observed in the absence of added argon. To explain such critical phenomena, Semenov put forward the idea of branched chain reactions, the theory of which he formulated for the first time in 1930–1934 and showed its wide occurrence. Experiments with oxidation reactions of sulfur vapor, hydrogen, carbon monoxide, carbon bisulfide, and other substances completely confirmed the results that were achieved in course of this work.

Semenov's general theory of chain reactions eventually included consideration of both branched and unbranched chain processes. It represents a series of self-initiating stages of chemical reactions, which, once started, continue until the process halts for lack of reactant. The key to a chain reaction is an initial formation of a so-called active center—an atom or a group of atoms that has a free (unpaired) electron, that is, a free radical. Once formed, the free radical interacts with another molecule in such a way that a new free radical (continuation of chain) is formed as one of reaction's products. The reaction continues until free radicals are somehow prevented from continuing to form similar particles (e.g., by destruction at the flask's walls), that is, until a termination of the chain occurs. In a branched chain reaction, free radicals do not only regenerate active centers, but also actively multiply, creating new chains and constantly accelerating the reaction.

Semenov's model was sufficiently general to explain many regularities of chain processes even without an identification of the precise nature of the active centers. His theory of chain reactions gave an explanation of chemically unusual facts such as a sharp dependence of rate reaction on minor changes of pressure, the effects of the additions of inert gas or a dependence on the diameter of the reaction flask and the condition of its walls. Semenov did not confine the role of the reaction vessel walls to the break of chains. He considered that on solid surfaces there can also occur reactions of origination and branching of chains, and the appearance of free radicals that which initiate a volumetric chain reaction when entering the gas phase from the surface. He established that among chain processes there is prevalence of heterogeneous-homogeneous reactions that begin on the surface of the flask and then pass to the volume. Experiments by Semenov and his colleagues during 1928 and 1929 established the existence of upper and lower ranges of ignition, that is, pressures, above and below which the explosive character of reaction's progress disappears.

According to the theory developed by Semenov, and independently by the English chemist Sir Cyril Norman Hinshelwood, the concentration of active centers in a chain reaction increases exponentially with time. If branching of the chain prevails over breaks, then the speed of the reaction progressively grows in time, and the reaction ends with an explosion. Such a process is characterized as an "isothermal explosion"; there is nearly no heat generation. The origin of the ignition (or chain explosion) in this case is a progressive increase of the number of active centers, and as a consequence, the rate of reaction grows. The existence of an upper range of ignition in this theory is connected with the formation of low-activity radicals or molecules due to "triple concussion" (stabilization of a low-activity radical by a third particle), a result of increasing the system's pressure. A lower range of ignition is caused by an increasing possibility of the loss of active centers (radicals or atoms) on the flask walls (the lower the pressure and the smaller the flask's diameter, the faster the wall is reached by active particles). Though Hinshelwood and his colleagues were satisfied by this variant of the theory, Semenov extended it considerably.

Semenov substantiated important peculiarities of conducting chain processes especially connected with the interaction of active centers between each other (a so-called interaction of chains). In 1930–1932 he showed that the cases when chain self-acceleration occurs over a long period of time without chain ignition happening are quite widespread (for example, for oxidation of hydrocarbons in gas and liquid phases). In such reactions quite substantial periods of induction are typical, sometimes reaching many minutes or even hours. Semenov called these processes reactions of "degenerate explosion." Regularities of development of degenerate explosion reactions are similar to kinetics laws of usual chain ignition, but these processes are developed quite slowly. As a rule, such reactions cannot reach explosive speeds due to a burnout of the initial substances. In cases when these reactions terminate in an explosion, the latter turns out to be connected not with a progressive increase of the number of active centers, but with the predominance of heat generation speed over the rate of heat rejection from the zone of reaction. Slow behavior of acceleration processes of reactions is connected with existence of special kind of "degenerate bifurcation." Active centers are formed as a result of comparatively rare processing reactions of labile molecular intermediate substances.

Academician A. F. Ioffe noted in 1932 that Semenov's studies of chain reactions "have revised the classic study of rates of chemical reactions, [they] created basis of new kinetics" (*Zapiska ob uchenykh trudakh N. N. Semenova*, p. 242). The major theories of chain reactions were expounded by Semenov in his monograph *Tsepnye reaktsii* (1934; published in English as *Chemical Kinetics and Chain Reactions,* 1935). This fundamental work became a classic reference of the chemical physics literature.

The Development of Chain Theory. While making experimental verification of the main postulates of chain reactions theory, Semenov began to think in terms of a chemical substantiation of the chain mechanism. Though in *Chemical Kinetics and Chain Reactions* numerous examples of chain mechanisms were mentioned, they were mostly more or less possible schemes. In 1934–1958 Semenov began a series of researches designed to more concretely define the mechanisms of elementary stages of complicated chain reactions. He developed concepts of the reactionary ability of active particles (atoms and radicals)—participators of this process. These ideas led to the creation of new physical methods of investigation that

allowed him to begin the study of the active particles themselves (atoms and radicals), the existence of which in the end of 1930s could be only surmised.

In this connection Semenov completed a large cycle of works relating to the study of a model reaction of hydrogen oxidation. Experiments confirmed that up to 20 percent of the initial hydrogen converts to the atomic form in the course of reaction. Semenov and his collaborators, using special methods of research involving hydrogen flames, also discovered the free hydroxide radical, the concentration of which was found to reach rather large values. A bit later, in 1960, using electronic paramagnetic resonance, they managed to detect considerable quantities of oxygen atoms and also free hydroxide radicals in a rarefied hydrogen flame.

An important aspect of the research conducted by Semenov was establishing a quantitative link between the structure of reacting substances and their reactivity from the position of chemical kinetics. In his monograph titled *O nekotorykh problemakh khimicheskoi kinetiki i reaktsionnoi sposobnosti* (1954; published in English as *Some Problems of Chemical Kinetics and Reactivity*, 1958), he summarized experimental material on the chemical mechanisms of chain processes. It covered various radical reactions, including those with biradicals. Specific attention was paid to the competition between chain, molecular, and ionic reactions. Semenov also formulated a semiquantitative theory of reactivity of free radicals, which was a generalization of a famous rule of Polanyi. The Polanyi-Semenov rule found broad application in the kinetics of radical reactions, especially in the analysis of complicated chain reactions with a large number of elementary stages. It is used for approximate estimates of activation energy values of any stage.

While researching the mechanisms of degenerate-branched reactions, Semenov also investigated processes of chain oxidation of hydrocarbons in liquid phase. These works had a large practical importance. By direct oxidation of natural and industrial hydrocarbon gases and by oxidation of liquid hydrocarbons and their mixtures (oil stock), it was possible to develop methods of production of aldehydes (in particular, formaldehyde), ketones, organic acids, peroxides, and compound esters, all of industrial importance.

By 1929, in the course of his research on chain processes, Semenov concluded that excited molecules, forming in exothermic elementary steps, can cause branched chains due to excitation energy. But there was no experimental confirmation of that for some time. In the early 1960s Semenov's colleagues showed experimentally for the first time that many fluoridation reactions—in particular, hygrogen fluoridation—are typical chain reaction with energetic branching. During such reactions, products are formed in excited states. In the course of destruction they give rise to free radicals, initiating new chains of chemical transformations. The phenomena of energetic branching were reported as a discovery of Semenov in 1962; his colleagues followed up in 1976. The results served as a stimulus for creating chemical lasers, and the first such laser (on the basis of reaction of fluorine with hydrogen) was created in the Institute of Chemical Physics.

The Theory of Burning and Explosion. Semenov and his school (1930–1950s) laid the foundation of the contemporary theory of burning and detonation of gas mixtures, explosives, and gunpowder. The theory of flame spreading, which received a wide international acknowledgment, a theory of detonation, and a theory of turbulent burning were developed in his institute. A quantitative theory of thermal explosion (the formation of thermal self-accelerating avalanche) was put forward by Semenov in 1928. In the following decade he developed a mathematical formulation for such types of spontaneous ignition. At the same time he established regularities of flame and explosive wave propagation. Thus, along with chain ignition, thermal spontaneous ignition (or thermal explosion) is possible in reactions. The cause of explosion in this case is that heat escaping in the course of the reaction does not have time to be distributed to the surrounding environment; a progressively increasing temperature continually accelerates the speed of the chemical process. Self-heating of the mixture and self-acceleration of the reaction lead to thermal auto-ignition (or explosion). The theory of thermal auto-ignition permits a calculation of the temperature of spontaneous inflammation, if the thermal characteristics of the flammable gas mixture (e.g., thermal conductivity) and the kinetics of burning reactions (rate constants, energy of activation) are known.

In addition to the laws of thermal explosion for simple types of reactions, Semenov and his colleagues determined regularities of explosion for autocatalytic reactions, established criteria of thermal explosion as a function of the time of chemical reaction and the time of thermal relaxation, reviewed thermal explosions for cases of convectional transmission, and solved many other theoretic problems concerning thermal explosion in gases. In the IkhF, under Semenov's direction, a contemporary theory of detonation phenomena was also developed.

The Nuclear Project. Being the author of a theory of branched chain reactions, burning, and explosions, Semenov perfectly understood the meaning of works on the uses of nuclear energy for peaceful and military purposes. Towards the end of 1930s classic researches on the kinetics of chain decay of uranium (Ia. B. Zel'dovich, Iu.

Nikolaĭ Nikolaevich Semenov. Semenov at Congress on chemistry held at University of Moscow. **HOWARD SOCHUREK/TIME LIFE PICTURES/GETTY IMAGES.**

B. Khariton) were accomplished within IKhF. Simultaneously, pioneering estimations of early variants of thermonuclear weapons were conducted. V. N. Kondrat'ev, together with his colleagues, investigated functions of reaction excitation of light nuclei, which were of interest for the realization of nuclear explosions. By the end of 1940 Semenov made an effort to stimulate research in this direction. He addressed the corresponding department (Narkomnefteprom of USSR, to which the institute was subordinated at that time) with a request to support such research, noting the potential for creating a nuclear bomb, but the decision to begin such work was not made.

The beginning of World War II stimulated research on explosives considerably. At the end of 1945, Semenov again submitted to the government a proposal for research on the creation of a nuclear weapon to be carried out within his institute. He formulated a number of objectives that the IKhF could reach theoretically and experimentally by his own efforts, and through collaborations with employees from other organizations. By a Resolution of the USSR Council of Ministers of 9 April 1946, the Institute was charged with the development of a nuclear weapon. IKhF was commissioned to perform calculations connected with the construction of atomic bombs, measurements of necessary constants, preparation of a training ground, and design of equipment for the assessment of the damage resulting from a nuclear weapon. A special sector, with a number of departments and laboratories, was established in the institute for implementation of this work.

Under Semenov's direction, the institute made a substantial contribution to building the nuclear power of the Soviet Union, creating the scientific bases of exploding an atomic bomb and the principles of protection from it. Semenov was the originator of the electronuclear breeding method, which remains one of most promising and safest directions in nuclear power engineering. The first nuclear test was carried out (1949, Semipalatinsk) at a training ground prepared under the aegis of the institute.

Solutions in the Sphere of Catalysis. Processes of homogeneous and heterogeneous catalysis also came within the scope of Semenov's scientific interest. As early as the 1930s, works on heterogeneous catalysis (S. Z. Roginskiĭ, then O. V. Krylov and others) were begun in the IKhF under Semenov's direction. Starting from concepts of an electronic theory of catalysis that had been developed by S. Z. Roginskiĭ and F. F. Vol'kenshteĭn (1948), Semenov, together with V. V. Voevodskiĭ and F. F. Vol'kenshteĭn (1955), formulated a model for heterogeneous chain processes. Under Semenov's guidance, research began in 1947 on a new type of catalysis: ionic-heterogeneous catalysis in thin films of acid. The mechanism of this catalysis was revealed, and the effectiveness of industrial catalysts of the acid type was substantially improved. In the 1970s at his initiative there began research in the USSR on the possibility of developing new fermentation catalytic processes that would be similar to photosynthesis or the fixation of nitrogen and which would utilize solar energy.

At his initiative, research on application of major approaches of fermentation catalysis to the elaboration of new catalytic processes with the usage of solar energy (similar to photosynthesis, fixation of nitrogen) opened in the 1970s. It was at this time that Semenov called attention of his scholars to the problems of searching new ways of conducting purely chemical reaction on the principle of biochemical processes, occurring in live organisms. Semenov considered the solution of this problem, which also relates to photochemical usage of solar energy, as a very important area in the future of chemistry.

Awards and Honors. Semenov's contribution to the development of science was honored, in addition to the Nobel Prize (shared with Hinshelwood), with state prizes: he was twice Hero of Socialist Labor (1966 and 1976) and the recipient of Lenin (1976) and State (Stalin) Prizes (1941 and 1949), and was awarded the order of Labor Red Banner (1946) and the order of the October Revolution (1986). He was awarded seven Lenin Orders (1945, 1953, 1956, 1966, 1971, 1976, 1981), the minor D. I. Mendeleev Prize (USSR AS 1936), and eleven medals.

Semenov's works have received a distinguished assessment in the world. He was elected an honorary member of foreign academies and scientific societies of England, India, Hungary, the United States, Romania, Czechoslovakia, Bulgaria, and was a foreign member of six academies (United States, Czechoslovakia, GDR, Bulgaria, Poland, and France) and of the Royal Society of London (1958). Semenov was granted the title Dr. Honorius Causa by universities of the following cities: Oxford, Brussels, Milan, Budapest, London, Prague, Berlin, and Wrocław.

Semenov was married three times: in 1921 to Mariia Isidorovna Boreĭsha-Liverovskaia, who died in 1923; in 1924 to Natal'ia Nikolaevna Burtseva (this marriage led to the birth of a son, Iuriĭ, and a daughter, Liudmila); and after their divorce, to Shcherbakova Lidiia Grigor'evna in 1971.

BIBLIOGRAPHY

Semenov's creative and scientific heritage, correspondence, and other documents are located in the RAS Archive. In 1989, with a view of preservation and preparation for the publication of archive documents and other materials, the Resolution of USSR AS Presidium established the Commission for Semenov's Scientific Heritage (chairman-academician Aleksandr E. Shilov; deputy chairman-professor Gleb B. Sergeev). A full list of works by Semenov is published in the book Nikolaĭ Nikolaevich Semenov, 1896–1986. Materialy k biobibliografii uchenykh SSSR, *3rd ed. Moscow: Nauka, 1990 (see Other Sources). Executive editors Aleksandr E. Shilov and Gleb. B. Sergeev with the assistance of Russian Foundation for Basic Research published his selected works in 4 volumes: Semenov N.N. Izbrannye trudy (Selected works). Moscow: Nauka, 2004–2006.*

WORKS BY SEMENOV

"K teorii protsessov goreniia. Soobshchenie 1" (To the theory of burning processes. 1st report). *Zhurnal Russkogo Fiziko-khimicheskogo obshchestva* (Journal of Russian Physical-Chemical Society) 60, no. 3, (1928): 247–250.

"Zur Theorie des Verbrennungsprozesses." *Zeitschrift f. Physikalische Chemie* 48, no. 8, (1928): 571–582.

With A. Walther. *Die physikalischen Grundlagen der elektrischen Festigkeitlehre.* Berlin: Springer, 1928.

With S. M. Bragin and A. F. Walther. *Teoriia i praktika proboia diêlektrikov* (Theory and practice of dielectric breakdown). Moscow and Leningrad: Gosizdat, 1929.

Sovremennoe uchenie o skorosti gazovykh khimicheskikh reaktsiĭ (Contemporary studies of speed of gas chemical reactions). Moscow and Leningrad: Gosizdat, 1929.

"Tsepnye reaktsii" (Chain reactions). *Uspekhi fizicheskikh nauk* (Progress of physical sciences) 10, no. 3 (1930): 347–365.

"Gazovye vzryvy i teoriia tsepnykh reaktsii" (Gas explosions and theory of chain reactions). *Uspekhi fizicheskikh nauk* (Progress of physical sciences) 1, no. 2 (1931): 250–275.

"Tsepnaia teoriia i okislitel'nye protsessy" (Chain theory and oxidation processes). *Uspekhi khimii* (Progress of chemistry) 2, no. 5 (1933): 590–621.

Tsepnye reaktsii (Chain reactions). Leningrad: ONTI-Gosizdat, 1934; 2nd ed., revised and complemented. Moscow: Nauka, 1986.

Chemical Kinetics and Chain Reactions. London: Oxford University Press, 1935.

"Teplovaia teoriia goreniia i vzryvov. Vvedenie. Ch. 1, 2" (Thermal theory of burning and explosions. Introduction. Parts 1, 2). *Uspekhi fizicheskikh nauk* (Progress of physical sciences) 23, no. 3 (1940): 251–292; "Teplovaia teorii goreniia i vzryvov. Vvedenie. Ch. 3" (Thermal theory of burning and explosions. Introduction. Part 3). *Uspekhi fizicheskikh nauk* (Progress of physical sciences) 24, no. 4 (1940): 433–486.

"K voprosu o trekh predelakh vosplameneniia" (To the issue of three ranges of inflammation). *Doklady AN SSSR* (USSR AS Reports) 81, no. 6 (1951): 645–648.

O nekotorykh problemakh khimicheskoĭ kinetiki i reaktsionnoĭ sposobnosti (Some problems in chemical kinetics and reactivity). Moscow: Izdatel'stvo AN SSSR, 1954, 2nd ed.; Moscow: Izdatel'stvo AN SSSR, 1958.

Some Problems in Chemical Kinetics and Reactivity. Princeton, NJ: Princeton University Press, 1958.

"Energeticheskoe razvetvlenie tsepeĭ "(Energy branching of chains). *Vestnik AN SSSR* (USSR AS Bulletin), 5 (1970): 38–48.

Khimicheskaia fizika (Chemical physics). Chernogolovka: Institut Chemicheskoi Fiziki AN SSSR, 1975; Moscow: Znanie, 1978.

Nauka i obshchestvo: stat'i i rechi (Science and society: Articles and speeches). Moscow: Nauka, 1981.

OTHER SOURCES

Dainton, F. S. "Nikolaĭ Nikolaevich Semenov (16 April 1896– 25 Sept. 1986)." *Biographical Memoirs of Fellows of the Royal Society London* 36 (1990): 527–545.

Ioffe, Abram F. "Zapiska ob uchenykh trudakh N. N. Semenova" (Notes on the scientific works of N. N. Semenov). In *Khimiki o sebe* (Chemists about themselves), complied by I. Solov'ev. Moscow: Vladmo UMIZ Graf-Press, 2001.

Khimichaskaia kinetika i tsepnye reaktsii: sbornik stateĭ. K 70-letiiu akademika N. N. Semenova (Chemical kinetics and chain reactions: Collected articles. For the seventieth anniversary of academician N. N. Semenov). Moscow: Nauka, 1966.

Kritsman, Viktor.A., Zaikov Gennadiĭ E., and Ĕmanuĕl Nikolaĭ M. *Chemical Kinetics and Chain Reactions: Historical Aspects.* New York: Nova Science Publishers, 1995. The role of Semenov in the creation of chain reactions theory is described in detail, and an analysis of his work *Chain Reactions* is given.

Nikolaĭ Nikolaevich Semenov 1896–1986: Materialy k biobibliografii uchenykh SSSR (Materials for the bibliography of USSR scientists). Seriia khimicheskikh nauk; Vyp. 84, 3rd ed., revised and complemented. Moscow: Nauka, 1990.

Shilov, Aleksandr E., Gleb B. Sergeev, Lidiia G. Shcherbakova-Semenova, et al., compilers. *Semenov, N. N.: Ia ne mysliu drugoĭ zhizni, kak zhizn' vmeste s naukoĭ* (Semenov, N. N.: I do not see any other life, but a life with science). Moscow: Konva, 2001. The book is for a wide readership and includes many documentary photographs. It is a bilingual edition (in Russian and English).

Solov'ev, Iuriĭ I., comp. *Akademik Nikolaĭ Nikolaevich Semenov: Vitse-prezident Akademii Nauk SSSR* (Academician Nikolaĭ Nikolaevich Semenov: The vice-president of USSR Academy of Sciences). Moscow: Vlladmo, UMIZ Graf-Press, 2002. The book includes archive materials (RAS Archive), characterizing the scientific and organizational activity of the scientist, including reports and appearances of Semenov at general meetings of USSR AS and of USSR AS Presidium (1957–1971), and documents concerning the organization of new scientific centers.

Vardugin, Vladimir I. *Taĭna ognia: Povest' o N. N. Semenove* (Mystery of the flame: Narrative about N. N. Semenov). Saratov: Privolzhskoe knizhnoe izdatel'stvo, 1986.

Vospominaniia ob akademike Nikolae Nikolaeviche Semenove (Reminiscences about academician Nikolaĭ Nikolaevich Semenov). Seriia "Uchenye Rossii. Ocherki, Vospominaniia, Materialy," composed by N. V. Gorbunova, preface by Aleksandr E. Shilov. Moscow: Nauka, 1993. For a wide readership; Semenov's colleagues, friends, and relatives tell about his life and activity.

Elena Zaitseva

SENNERT, DANIEL (*b.* Breslau, Germany [now Wrocław, Poland], 25 November 1572; *d.* Wittenberg, Germany, 21 July 1637), *medicine, chemistry.* For the original entry on Sennert see *DSB*, vol. 12.

Since Hans Kangro wrote his entry for the original *Dictionary of Scientific Biography*, a number of new facts have emerged about Daniel Sennert that both nuance his biography and add substantially to the knowledge of his influence in the early modern scientific community. First, Sennert seems to have received virtually his entire education at the University of Wittenberg. His multiple publications stemming from Wittenberg in the period between 1596 and 1601 show the unlikelihood of Sennert's having spent three years attending the Universities of Leipzig,

Daniel Sennert. SPL/PHOTO RESEARCHERS, INC.

Jena, and Frankfurt during this period, as has been claimed. This fact is interesting in that it underscores the high degree to which Sennert was a hothouse product of the University of Wittenberg, molded and encouraged in his scientific interests by his mentor, the professor of anatomy Johann Jessenius.

Second, it is now clear that Sennert was already a self-styled atomist by 1619, the year that he published his *De chymicorum cum Aristotelicis et Galenicis consensu ac dissensu*. Kangro, along with various other scholars, was misled by Sennert's publication of his non-atomistic *Epitome naturalis scientiae* only the year before. But Sennert explicitly ranked the *Epitome* among his juvenilia in the preface, and pointed out that he was publishing it only as an introductory school text. Most scholars have overlooked Sennert's clear alliance with Democritean atomism already in the *De chymicorum* and in private communications with Michael Döring from the early 1620s. Despite his self-styled Democritean allegiances, however, Sennert's atomism was a combination of alchemical corpuscular theory derived from the medieval writer Geber and his followers, more modern Paracelsian notions transmitted by the chymical polemicist Andreas Libavius, Aristotelian meteorological theory culled mainly from Book 4 of the Stagirite's *Meterology*, and neo-Aristotelian currents stemming largely from the extraordinarily influential

work of Julius Caesar Scaliger. This is not to say that Sennert was an eclectic, however, as is often claimed in the secondary literature. Sennert's atomism reveals a striking coherence and integration with laboratory practice. His habit of citing multiple sources is both a diplomatic attempt to arrive at consensus and an example of the early modern need to ground novelty in tradition.

Perhaps the most significant component of Sennert's atomism was its experimental basis. Developing ideas that were already present in earlier alchemy, Sennert argued that the *tria prima* of Paracelsian chymistry, mercury, sulfur, and salt, were principles (literally, beginnings) precisely in the sense that they were the products revealed by fire analysis. Because they were the final results of analysis, they could be viewed as *prima mixta* (first mixts), the primitive bodies out of which nature ordinarily composes more complex mixtures. This analytical ideal was based on a negative-empirical concept that located the physical principles of more complex materials in the limits of the technical analysis that could be carried out in a chymical laboratory. The *a posteriori* approach that Sennert applied to the determination of material components was adopted by subsequent chymists such as Joan Baptista Van Helmont and Robert Boyle, who would transmit this methodology to the chemical reformers of the eighteenth century even as they expressed their doubts about the universality and simplicity of the three principles.

A particularly important feature of Sennert's atomism lay in his polyvalent use of the so-called reduction to the pristine state (*reductio in pristinum statum*), a type of experimental demonstration that he used to combat the theories of perfect Aristotelian mixture advocated by the followers of Thomas Aquinas and John Duns Scotus. The Thomistic and Scotist mixture theories prevalent in early modern universities denied the persistence of the substantial forms of the initial ingredients in a mixture. This meant that if two substances were to undergo Aristotelian *mixis*, it should not be possible to recapture them intact, because their forms had been destroyed in the process of mixing them. The imposition of the new substantial form of the mixture was supposed to replace the individual forms of the ingredients. But what if an opponent could show that seemingly homogeneous mixtures that appeared to be so-called perfect mixts actually retained their ingredients unchanged, though hidden to the senses? Such a demonstration would forcibly throw doubt on the theory of perfect mixture itself, because the criterion of visual homogeneity could no longer be trusted to reveal the composition of materials.

Sennert exploited this possibility with great zeal, showing that mixtures of metals dissolved in strong acids could be made to yield up their ingredients intact, despite their apparent homogeneity. Employing well established metallurgical and chymical processes, Sennert was able to show that, in the case of silver dissolved in aqua fortis (nitric acid), the original silver could indeed be regained intact, merely by adding salt of tartar to the solution. An intermediate step where the metal-acid solution was filtered added additional force to the demonstration by revealing that the silver had to have been broken into particles small enough to pass through the pores of the filter paper. That these corpuscles were sufficiently robust to resist the analytical power of the acid, coupled with their small size, fulfilled the canonic requirements of atomism and showed that even a combination as seemingly homogeneous as a metal dissolved in acid could not really be a perfect mixture in the Aristotelian sense.

Sennert's reductions to the pristine state would have great influence on the following generation. Boyle, whose name is synonymous with the mechanical philosophy, used Sennertian reductions to the pristine state to demonstrate the existence of atoms in his juvenile, unpublished *Essay Of the Atomical Philosophy*, whereas his mature *Sceptical Chymist* elaborated on these demonstrations to argue for the reality of robust, complex corpuscles. Boyle also reinterpreted the reduction to the pristine state so that it became a demonstration of the mechanical origin of qualities, hence obviating the need for substantial forms. Because Boyle did not acknowledge his considerable debt to Sennert, his use of the German academic's atomism has until recently gone largely unnoticed. Sennert's other areas of contribution, particularly in the realms of medicine and theology, require further study, but it is likely that here too his influence has been undervalued.

SUPPLEMENTARY BIBLIOGRAPHY

WORKS BY SENNERT

Epitome naturalis scientiae, comprehensa disputationibus viginti sex. Wittenberg, Germany: Simon Gronenberg, 1600. Although Kangro knew of this text, he had not seen it; since then most of the twenty-six disputations, which were published separately and then collected under a separately printed title-page, have been located in the Bibliothèque nationale (Paris). Despite the similarity in title of the 1600 *Epitome* and that of 1618, the two works are very different. The 1600 *Epitome* consists of Dissertations printed for oral defense, written before Sennert developed any significant interest in chymistry.

De chymicorum cum Aristotelicis et Galenicis consensu ac dissensu. Wittenberg, Germany: Zacharias Schurer, 1619.

OTHER SOURCES

Lüthy, Christoph, and William R. Newman. "Daniel Sennert's Earliest Writings (1599–1600) and their Debt to Giordano Bruno." *Bruniana & Campanelliana* 6 (2000): 263–279.

Lüthy, Christoph. "Daniel Sennert's Slow Conversion from Hylemorphism to Atomism." *Graduate Faculty Philosophy Journal* 26 (2005): 99–121.

Meinel, Christoph. "Early Seventeenth-Century Atomism: Theory, Epistemology, and the Insufficiency of Experiment." *Isis* 79 (1988): 68–103.

Michael, Emily. "Daniel Sennert on Matter and Form: At the Juncture of the Old and the New." *Early Science and Medicine* 2 (1997): 272–299.

———. "Sennert's Sea Change: Atoms and Causes." In *Late Medieval and Early Modern Corpuscular Matter Theories*, edited by Christoph Lüthy, John E. Murdoch, and William R. Newman. Leiden, The Netherlands: E.J. Brill, 2001.

Newman, William R. "The Alchemical Sources of Robert Boyle's Corpuscular Philosophy." *Annals of Science* 53 (1996): 567–585.

———. "Art, Nature, and Experiment Among Some Aristotelian Alchemists." In *Texts and Contexts in Ancient and Medieval Science: Studies on the Occasion of John E. Murdoch's Seventieth Birthday,* edited by Edith Sylla and Michael McVaugh. Leiden, the Netherlands: Brill, 1997.

———. "Corpuscular Alchemy and the Tradition of Aristotle's *Meteorology*, With Special Reference to Daniel Sennert." *International Studies in the Philosophy of Science* 15 (2001): 145–153.

———.. "Experimental Corpuscular Theory in Aristotelian Alchemy: From Geber to Sennert." In *Late Medieval and Early Modern Corpuscular Matter Theories*, edited by Christoph Lüthy, John E. Murdoch, and William R. Newman. Leiden, The Netherlands: E.J. Brill, 2001.

———. "Robert Boyle's Debt to Corpuscular Alchemy." In *Robert Boyle Reconsidered*, eds. Michael Hunter. Cambridge, U.K.: Cambridge University Press, 1994.

———, and Lawrence M. Principe. *Alchemy Tried in the Fire: Starkey, Boyle, and the Fate of Helmontian Chymistry.* Chicago: University of Chicago Press, 2002.

Stolberg, Michael. "Particles of the Soul: The Medical and Lutheran Context of Daniel Sennert's Atomism." *Medicina nei secoli* 15 (2003): 177–203.

William R. Newman

SERBER, ROBERT

(*b.* Philadelphia, Pennsylvania, 14 March 1909; *d.* New York, New York, 1 June 1997), *nuclear and particle physics.*

Serber's long and distinguished career will probably be best remembered for the important contributions he made in producing the world's first nuclear weapons. For two years he served as a group leader at the secret Los Alamos Laboratory, working in Hans Bethe's Theoretical Division. On Tinian Island he prepared the bombs for delivery against Japan. Only a few weeks later he would travel to Hiroshima and Nagasaki, witnessing the destruction firsthand. But Serber's interesting life and productive scientific career transcend the short time he spent at Los Alamos. Foreshadowing the fate of his close friend and mentor J. Robert Oppenheimer, he endured the injustices

Robert Serber. AP IMAGES.

of McCarthy-era America by having a security clearance request rejected by Naval Intelligence. Despite this, he would serve as a consultant to the Brookhaven National Laboratory for nearly two decades. Serber also mentored a myriad of scientists during his years at Columbia University, including 1972 Nobel laureate Leon Cooper. His imprints on Los Alamos, Columbia University, and the field of theoretical physics remain visible over a decade after his passing.

Youth. On 14 March 1909, Robert Serber was born in Philadelphia to David and Rose Frankel Serber. His paternal grandfather had immigrated to the United States from Russia in the mid-1880s. David Serber, a native of Russia, was only a toddler at the time. Robert's mother, Rose Frankel, was born in Philadelphia to Polish immigrants a few years later.

Rose died when Robert was very young, leaving David a widower. Several years later, during Robert's high school years, David married Frances Leof. Frances's uncle, Morris Leof, was a well-known physician who owned a large house in a nearby neighborhood. The house, located

at 322 South Sixteenth Street, was a favorite haunt for Jewish artisans and intellectuals, and soon it would become a refuge for Robert. Here he developed friendships with Dr. Leof's children, Madelin, Milton, and Charlotte, and was introduced to the family's socialist politics. This close connection with his stepmother's family would shape Robert's life for years to come.

Robert's father David, a liberal Democrat, became a wealthy lawyer, which afforded the family a life of comfort. Robert enjoyed gymnastics, swimming, and school, where his curriculum included the study of chemistry, math, and physics. An interesting passage in his Central High Yearbook states: "His wonderful inventive brain has invented inventions galore. The trouble is that none is practical … (Edison must step fast or else he will soon have a strong rival)." Robert graduated in 1926 and went on to Lehigh University in nearby Bethlehem, Pennsylvania, where he earned a BS in engineering physics.

After receiving his degree in 1930, Robert decided to take the advice of his Lehigh professors and left Pennsylvania to attend graduate school at the University of Wisconsin. He earned an $800-per-year salary (a considerable sum, considering the declining economic state of the country) as a teaching assistant and gained valuable experience as a lecturer. Robert was fortunate enough to study under John Van Vleck, one of the nation's leading physicists and a future Nobel laureate. Van Vleck introduced him to the new field of quantum mechanics. To his professor's delight, Robert delivered his first lecture to the American Physical Society in December 1931 and published his first *Physical Review* article the following spring.

While attending Lehigh, Robert had maintained close ties to the Leofs. He started to lose contact with the family until Charlotte, Morris Leof's daughter, decided to write him a letter in late 1931. On a trip home the following summer, Robert and Charlotte started dating. The two were married in Philadelphia less than a year later, in spring 1933, and took up residence in an apartment back in Madison.

Oppenheimer. In 1934, Serber was awarded his doctorate in theoretical physics as well as a National Research Council Fellowship. At Van Vleck's suggestion, he decided to work with Eugene Wigner at Princeton. The twelve hundred dollar prize that accompanied the award would easily support him and Charlotte for the following year, so the couple packed for the journey to New Jersey. The trip included a stop at the University of Michigan where the Serbers attended the annual physics summer school and met a young professor from Berkeley named J. Robert Oppenheimer. "His mind was so quick and his speech so fluent," Serber states in his memoir, "that he dominated nearly every gathering. He was generous and could be very charming. At Ann Arbor that summer I soon became fascinated by him" (Serber, 1998, p. 25) Serber was so impressed that he decided to spend his fellowship working with "Oppie" at Berkeley instead of going to Princeton.

At Berkeley, Serber quickly fell under Oppenheimer's "spell." The two became very close friends, and spent a great deal of time with each other. Not only was Serber introduced to nuclear physics, but also fine foods, wine, and art. This complete education included access to Oppenheimer's colleagues at Caltech, Stanford, and Ernest O. Lawrence's Radiation Laboratory. Only a year later, the Serbers even started joining Oppenheimer on his vacations. During one of these trips, they visited a small ranch Oppenheimer had acquired in northern New Mexico, not too far from a place called Los Alamos. Each year, from 1935 to 1941, this pilgrimage to New Mexico was repeated by the trio.

When Serber's fellowship ran out in 1936, Oppenheimer secured a position for him as a research assistant. In these years Oppenheimer began taking an interest in left-wing politics at the behest of his girlfriend, Jean Tatlock. With help from Oppenheimer, Charlotte established a local chapter of the Medical Aid Committee for the Spanish Loyalists, a communist-sponsored organization set up to aid the Spanish government in the civil war being fought against the fascist forces of Francisco Franco. Activities such as this would haunt the Serbers, and especially Oppenheimer, years later.

In 1938 Serber became an assistant professor at the University of Illinois. He was not anxious to leave Berkeley, but Charlotte convinced him to take advantage of the opportunity. During his years at Illinois he continued to refine his skills as a lecturer, though he often failed to return papers to his students on time. Another deficiency was his inability to recall the names of his students, and as a result Serber was prohibited from teaching the larger undergraduate classes. This period was also marked by his publication of several outstanding scientific articles, many of which were coauthored by Oppenheimer. The productive collaboration between the two would continue into the 1940s. Ironically, events thousands of miles away were about to result in a reunification at Berkeley.

The 1938 discovery of fission in Germany made atomic bombs possible. The public announcement of this discovery, made by Niels Bohr at a theoretical physics conference being held in Washington, D.C., both excited and alarmed physicists. Though an important scientific discovery, it came as Nazi Germany, Imperial Japan, and Fascist Italy were stepping up their territorial conquests. A potential enemy armed with an atomic bomb would be formidable. Despite the significance of this discovery, the United States initially failed to respond in a vigorous manner. Albert Einstein's famous letter to President Franklin Roosevelt stimulated some research, but it was not until the Japanese attack on Pearl Harbor and Enrico Fermi's successful production of a fission chain reaction that work on atomic matters accelerated in the United States.

Shortly after Pearl Harbor, Oppenheimer asked Serber to return to Berkeley. Oppenheimer had been given the task of developing an atomic bomb and wanted Serber to handle major portions of the undertaking. At Berkeley, Serber worked on the general properties of atomic bombs including questions of the masses of material needed and the energy release expected. He also directed studies of fissionable material, the behavior of neutrons in a chain reaction, as well as the hydrodynamics of a nuclear explosion. Also at Berkeley, Serber made estimates of the properties and amounts of material for the planned Water Boiler reactor, so named because it used an aqueous solution. In 1944, the Water Boiler became the first reactor in the world to go critical using enriched uranium. After his year at Berkeley, Serber knew more about atomic bomb design than anyone else in the world.

In the summer of 1942, at the request of the National Bureau of Standards, Oppenheimer convened a conference at the University of California with Hans Bethe, Edward Teller, and others to analyze existing research on fission. During a discussion of how to make a fission bomb, Teller, out of the blue, proposed a hydrogen bomb. As Serber recalled in 1993, "And then a really remarkable thing happened. Edward brought up the super, a detonation wave in liquid deuterium heated by an atomic bomb. Everybody turned eagerly to discuss the super forgetting all about the atomic bomb as if that was an accomplished fact already!" (Serber, 1994, p. 60). Teller, before anyone else, understood that an atomic bomb could produce the stellar temperatures needed to ignite a hydrogen bomb. With further debate, however, the excitement over the "super" quickly died. Even if an atomic bomb could ignite deuterium, radiation cooling, known as the inverse Compton effect, would stop the thermonuclear process. The conference went on to decide that an atomic bomb was achievable and could be developed in a relatively short period. As Serber noted many years later, there seemed to be an implicit assumption "that I had the fission bomb under control, that there was nothing to worry about" (Serber, 1992, p. xxxi).

In early 1943 Serber moved to New Mexico to assist Oppenheimer in setting up the Los Alamos laboratory. Since most of the incoming scientists knew very little, if anything, about atomic bombs, Oppenheimer asked Serber to hold a series of indoctrination lectures. Over the course of two weeks, Serber gave five lectures that shared his extensive knowledge (in reality the sum of known knowledge) of nuclear weapons physics. The first lecture began with a bald statement of the purpose of the Los

Alamos Project: "The object of the project is to produce a *practical military weapon* in the form of a bomb in which the energy is released by a fast neutron chain reaction in one or more of the materials known to show nuclear fission." Edward Condon took notes at each lecture that he and Serber would edit for internal publication. These notes became LA-1, the first technical report produced at Los Alamos. LA-1 served as the research blueprint for subsequent work at Los Alamos. In 1992 the University of California Press published Serber's lectures under the title *The Los Alamos Primer: The First Lectures on How to Build an Atomic Bomb.*

After delivering the five primer lectures, Serber became a group leader in Bethe's Theoretical Division. Serber's group, T-2, had the responsibility of accurately predicting the critical mass of an atomic bomb by developing an understanding of the behavior of neutrons. Serber also assumed responsibility for the theoretical design of the gun-type weapon known as Little Boy. In addition to these two major tasks, Serber worked on implosion bomb physics. Implosion, the use of high explosives to create supersonic shockwaves to compress plutonium, required a great deal of instrumentation, much of which Serber had responsibility for. As part of his implosion work, Serber invented the RaLa (radio-lanthanum) method of analyzing the implosion process. The RaLa method proved valuable and would be used by Los Alamos until 1962.

On 16 July 1945 Serber witnessed the first detonation of an atomic bomb, the Trinity Test, which was conducted in the desert of southern New Mexico. Standing about twenty miles from ground zero, Serber looked directly at the detonation without eye protection and was momentarily blinded by the bright flash of light. He later wrote that "The grandeur and magnitude of the phenomenon were completely breathtaking" (Serber, 1998, p. 79).

Following the Trinity test, Serber traveled to Tinian Island in the Pacific to join the 509th Composite Group, which was making preparations for the combat use of the atomic bombs against Japan. The 509th commander, Paul Tibbets, asked Serber to verify that the strike aircraft would survive the detonation of an atomic bomb. He did so. Slated to fly on the Nagasaki mission, Serber was thrown off the photo plane at the last minute because the supply sergeant had not given him a parachute. As Serber wryly noted, it did not matter in the long run, because the pilot of the photo plane did not make contact with the strike craft and missed the drop completely.

After the surrender of Japan, Serber was chosen to assess bomb damage at Hiroshima and Nagasaki, where he and several others took photographs, collected bomb debris, and made initial estimates of the yields of Little Boy and Fat Man. Although the mission was plagued by logistical problems, it was completed without incident.

Serber was back in Los Alamos on 15 October, one day before Oppenheimer resigned as director of the laboratory.

Cold War Physics and Politics. After the war, professional opportunities abounded for physicists for the first time in Serber's career. Illinois offered him a full professorship, but future Nobel laureates Luis Alvarez and Edwin McMillan (new friends made at Los Alamos) secured the position of Theoretical Division leader for him at Lawrence's Berkeley Radiation Laboratory. Serber did not sever his ties with Los Alamos, however, and agreed to serve on a committee to assess the feasibility of building the hydrogen bomb.

Oppenheimer spent less and less time at Berkeley because of duties as an advisor on atomic energy. Serber often lectured in his stead, and eventually inherited his post in the Physics Department after Oppenheimer agreed to lead Princeton's Institute for Advanced Study. Despite his responsibilities to the Physics Department and the Radiation Laboratory, Serber still managed to publish more articles in 1947 than in any other year of his career. In the classroom he focused on theoretical physics, while his work at the laboratory offered him the opportunity to pursue experimental work using particle accelerators, cyclotrons, and synchrotrons. But Serber was about to face challenges outside the laboratory.

By the late 1940s, the country was changing. The Cold War was beginning to set in and security requirements were being reexamined; a prelude to the "Red Scare." In 1948, the Atomic Energy Commission (AEC) launched an investigation into Serber's background due to his previous associations with several known and suspected members of the Communist Party. Oppenheimer, who had access to the final report as a member of the AEC's General Advisory Committee (GAC), informed his friend that he had "passed with glowing praise." "But," Serber later wrote, "I ... found the experience humiliating and frightening, and resented having been put through it" (Serber, 1998, p. 165).

Others would endure similar hearings, especially after Senator Joseph McCarthy's reign of political terror began. McCarthy fed off the hysteria created by Communist victories in China, the Soviet Union's first successful nuclear test in August 1949, and stalemate on the Korean Peninsula. Many in the scientific community, including Lawrence, Alvarez, and Teller, favored initiating a crash program to build the "super," but Serber felt such an effort was not necessary and that such a device could probably not be built anyway. The GAC recommended that thermonuclear weapons research should not go forward, but President Harry Truman felt otherwise and ordered the development program to proceed rapidly.

Serber found himself in the middle of other controversies as well. The University of California (UC) regents chose to require all UC employees to take an oath of loyalty to the United States or face termination. Though Serber agreed to sign the oath, other top scientists chose to leave the university. Others still, who refused to sign, were fired.

Meanwhile, scientists from around the country were divided over the explosive political issues of the time. The informal leaders of these groups were Oppenheimer, representing the liberals, and Lawrence, who harbored a much more conservative outlook. Serber remained loyal to his very close friend Oppenheimer, though he had developed a deep respect for Lawrence during his years at the Radiation Laboratory. But if Serber had to choose, there was no question that he felt more comfortable in the Oppenheimer camp. Isidor Rabi, a good friend and former consultant to Los Alamos, helped persuade Serber to come to Columbia University and work with him. After struggling to make a decision, the Serbers agreed to leave California and much of its controversy for New York in mid-1951.

Upon arriving at Columbia, Serber inherited George Pegram's office in the university's famous Pupin Laboratory. He settled into his new academic life by teaching a graduate course in quantum mechanics, working on atomic beam measurements for Rabi and taking on his first PhD candidate at Columbia, future Nobelist Leon Cooper. During his Columbia years, Serber collaborated with Abraham Pais on meson studies and developed the Serber-Dancoff method, a more accurate technique for analyzing strong coupling.

Unfortunately, Serber would not be able to escape the Cold War politics of the era. In early 1953, Naval Intelligence denied his request for a security clearance needed to attend a physics conference in Japan. Serber still had his AEC clearance and neither he nor Charlotte had been politically active since World War II, yet the navy was unwilling to accept responsibility for granting a clearance. Serber recalls, "I was really offended, and my resentment played a significant part in my later refusal to become a consultant to the Department of Defense during the Vietnam War" (Serber, 1998, p. 175). Only a year later, Oppenheimer's AEC security clearance would be revoked on similarly baseless grounds, infuriating Serber and rocking the scientific community.

Later Activities. Although the navy rejected his request for a clearance to visit Japan, his AEC clearance enabled Serber to work at Brookhaven National Laboratory, just up the highway from New York City. Once a week, for the better part of two decades, he would make the trip to Brookhaven where he served as a consultant. This position allowed him to contribute to many of the institution's projects, including the construction of the Cosmotron, the world's first billion-electron-volt accelerator.

The Serbers enjoyed the next several years in New York, but made time to journey around the world. Their travels took them to England, France, Italy, Turkey, Israel, India, Cambodia, Hong Kong, and Japan. In 1959 the couple went to Kiev, in the Soviet Union, for an international physics conference; times had clearly changed. Back in New York, the Serbers often sailed off Long Island Sound and even made a voyage to the Virgin Islands. It would be the first of many trips to the Caribbean for Serber.

In 1963, the Oppenheimers went to Brookhaven where Oppie would give the annual Pegram Lecture. By this time his physical state was rapidly deteriorating due to the loss of his clearance, which most agree broke his spirit, and years of heavy smoking. Only a few years later, in February 1967, Oppenheimer would die of throat cancer. Unfortunately for Serber, another tragedy came only months later. Charlotte was suffering from Parkinson's disease, and soon fell into a deep depression brought on by her symptoms. That May, she ended her own life.

After Charlotte's death, Serber's life took on a new direction. At the urging of Kitty Oppenheimer, Robert's widow, Serber organized the first of several annual theoretical physics conferences in honor of Oppenheimer. Serber also became the president of the American Physical Society (APS) in 1971. Serving at the height of social and campus protests against the Vietnam War, he had the unenviable duty of steering the society through treacherous waters. Serber firmly believed that the APS should concern itself solely with matters of science and leave politics to others. As a member of the APS nominating committee, Serber took the lead in nominating the first woman to be president of the society, Chien-Shiung Wu. Her selection ultimately led to the promotion of women in science both as teachers and as science administrators.

Serber's work with Kitty on the annual physics conference led to a renewal of their friendship. In 1972, while on sabbatical, he began an extended sailing expedition with Kitty. While off the coast of Panama, Kitty became ill and was hospitalized in Panama City. She died on 27 October. Serber helped the two Oppenheimer children, Peter and Toni, with funeral arrangements. He remained close to Toni and spent many vacation days with her at the Oppenheimer cottage on St. John.

In 1975 Serber became chair of the Physics Department at Columbia, a post he held until his retirement at the end of the 1978 academic year. He married Fiona St. Clair, a longtime friend from St. John, in 1979. A son, William, was born in November 1980, joining Fiona's son Zachary as part of the family.

After his retirement from Columbia, Serber returned twice to Los Alamos. His 1983 visit was part of the laboratory's fortieth anniversary, where he and many of his colleagues gave talks and lectures related to the scientific work of the wartime laboratory. Serber returned again for the laboratory's fiftieth anniversary in 1993, accompanied by his son William.

Robert Serber died 1 June 1997 following surgery for brain cancer. He was eighty-eight. As his longtime colleague Wolfgang Panofsky said in Serber's *New York Times* obituary, "Serber's talent was being able to comprehend a theory at its widest and narrowest points and to communicate that information to others." This ability enabled Serber to play an important role in the advancement of physics during one of its most exciting periods.

BIBLIOGRAPHY

The Niels Bohr Institute at the Center for the History of Physics, American Institute of Physics, has several oral history interviews of Serber.

WORKS BY SERBER

"The Theory of the Faraday Effect in Molecules." *Physical Review* 41 (1932): 489–506.

With J. Robert Oppenheimer. "On the Stability of Stellar Neutron Cores." *Physical Review* 54 (1938): 540L.

With S. M. Dancoff. "Nuclear Forces in Strong Coupling Theory." *Physical Review* 61 (1941): 53–58.

"The Spins of Mesons." *Physical Review* 75 (1949): 1459A.

With A. Pais. "Interaction between k-Particles and Nucleons." *Physical Review* 99 (1955):1551–55.

With R. P. Feynman and F. de Hoffmann. "Dispersion of the Neutron Emission in U-235 Fission." *Journal of Nuclear Energy* 3 (1956): 64-69.

Serber Says: About Nuclear Physics. Singapore: World Scientific, 1987.

The Los Alamos Primer: The First Lectures on How to Build an Atomic Bomb. Berkeley: University of California Press, 1992.

"Peaceful Pastimes: 1930–1950." *Annual Review of Nuclear and Particle Science* 44 (1994): 1–26.

With Robert Crease. *Peace and War: Reminiscences of a Life on the Frontiers of Science.* New York: Columbia University Press, 1998.

OTHER SOURCES

Bird, Kai, and Martin J. Sherwin. *American Prometheus: The Triumph and Tragedy of J. Robert Oppenheimer.* New York: Knopf, 2006.

Conant, Jennet. *109 East Palace: Robert Oppenheimer and the Secret City of Los Alamos.* New York: Simon & Schuster, 2005.

Crease, Robert. *Making Physics: A Biography of Brookhaven National Laboratory, 1946–1972.* Chicago: University of Chicago Press, 1999.

Hawkins, David, Edith C. Truslow, and Ralph Carlisle Smith. *Project Y: The Los Alamos Story.* New York: Tomash Publishers, 1983.

Hewlett, Richard G., and Oscar E. Anderson Jr. *The New World: A History of the United States Atomic Energy Commission Volume I, 1939–1946.* Berkeley: University of California Press, 1990.

Hoddeson, Lillian, et al. *Critical Assembly: A Technical History of Los Alamos during the Oppenheimer Years, 1943–1945.* New York: Cambridge University Press, 1993.

Alan B. Carr
Roger A. Meade

SHANNON, CLAUDE ELWOOD (*b.* Petoskey, Michigan, 30 April 1916, *d.* Medford, Massachusetts, 24 February 2001), *engineering sciences, communication sciences, cryptography, information theory.*

Shannon is first and foremost known as a pioneer of the information age, ever since he demonstrated in his seminal paper "A Mathematical Theory of Communication" (1948) that information could be defined and measured as a scientific notion. The paper gave rise to "information theory," which includes metaphorical applications in very different disciplines, ranging from biology to linguistics via thermodynamics or quantum physics on the one hand, and a technical discipline of mathematical essence, based on crucial concepts like that of channel capacity, on the other. Shannon never showed much enthusiasm for the first kind of informal applications. He focused on the technical aspects and also contributed significantly to other fields such as cryptography, artificial intelligence, and domains where his ideas had their roots and could be readily applied in a strict fashion, that is, telecommunications and coding theory.

Formative Years. Claude Elwood Shannon was the son of Claude Shannon Sr. (1862–1934), a businessman who was also a judge of probate, and Mabel Wolf Shannon (1880–1945), a high school principal. Until the age of sixteen, he lived in Gaylord, Michigan, where his mother worked. His youth was to prove a decisive influence on his life as a scientist: his grandfather was a tinkerer, possessed a patent on a washing machine, and created various— sometimes nonsensical—objects. By the time he graduated from high school, the young Shannon had already built a radio-controlled boat and a telegraphic system to communicate with a friend nearly a mile away, using barbed wires. He made some pocket money by fixing various electrical devices, such as radios, and he admired Edison, with whom he discovered later that he shared a common ancestor.

Shannon left Gaylord in 1932 for the University of Michigan, where he studied both electrical engineering and mathematics, obtaining in 1936 a bachelor of science degree in both fields. He then found a way to match his tinkering capacities with his knowledge in electrical engineering, working in the Department of Electrical Engineering at the Massachusetts Institute of Technology (MIT) on the maintenance of the differential analyzer that had been constructed by Vannevar Bush (1890–1974). Bush was to become his mentor over the next decades. It was in Bush's department that Shannon wrote his master's thesis, titled "Symbolic Analysis of Relay and Switching Circuits," which he submitted on 10 August 1937. In an interview, Shannon recalled in 1987:

> The main machine was mechanical with spinning disks and integrators, and there was a complicated control circuit with relays. I had to understand both of these. The relay part got me interested. I knew about symbolic logic at the time from a course at Michigan, and I realized that Boolean algebra was just the thing to take care of relay circuits and switching circuits. I went to the library and got all the books I could on symbolic logic and Boolean algebra, started interplaying the two, and wrote my Master's thesis on it. That was the beginning of my great career! (Sloane and Wyner, eds., 1993, p. xxv)

The insight was decisive: It constituted "a landmark in that it helped to change digital circuit design from an art to a science" (Goldstine, 1972, p. 119). His study dealt with the circuits based on relays and switching units, such as automatic telephone exchange systems or industrial motor equipment. He developed rigorous methods for both analysis and synthesis of circuits, showing how they could be simplified. At this time, he probably had his first intuitions on the relations between redundancy and reliability, which he was to deepen later. That his stance was both theoretical and practical becomes clear at the end of his master's thesis, where he illustrated his approach with five circuits: a selective circuit, an electronic combination lock, a vote counting circuit, a base-two adder, and a factor table machine.

This dual approach was also revealed in an important letter that Shannon sent to Bush in February 1939. He wrote that "Off and on [he had] been working on an analysis of some of the fundamental properties of general systems for the transmission of intelligence, including telephony, radio, television, telegraphy, etc." He stated that "Practically all systems of communication may be thrown into the following form: $f_1(t) \rightarrow \boxed{T} \rightarrow F(t) \rightarrow \boxed{R} \rightarrow f_2(t)$ $f_1(t)$ is a general function of time (arbitrary except for certain frequency limitations) representing the intelligence to be transmitted. It

represents for example, the pressure-time function in radio and telephony, or the voltage-time curve output of an iconoscope in television."

Shannon was awarded the Alfred Noble Prize of the American Society of Civil Engineers for his master's thesis in 1940. He continued to work on the use of algebra to deepen analogies and began his doctoral studies in mathematics, with the same supervisor, the algebraist Frank L. Hitchcock. The topic, however, stemmed from Bush, who suggested that Shannon apply Boolean algebra to genetics, as he had to circuits. The result of his research was submitted in the spring of 1940 in his thesis "An Algebra for Theoretical Genetics." Meanwhile, Shannon had also published his "Mathematical Theory of the Differential Analyzer" (1941) and during the summer of 1940 had started working at the Bell Laboratories, where he applied the ideas contained in his master's thesis. He also spent a few months at the Institute for Advanced Study in Princeton working under Hermann Weyl thanks to a National Research Fellowship, and he then returned to the Bell Labs, where he worked from 1941 to 1956.

The Impact of World War II. Any scientist who worked in public institutions, private companies, or universities at this time became increasingly engaged in the war effort. From 1940 onward, interdisciplinary organizations were founded: first the National Defense Research Committee (NDRC, June 1940), under the supervision of Vannevar Bush, and later the Office of Scientific Research and Development (May 1941), which included the NDRC and medical research. Shannon soon became involved in this war-related research, mainly with two projects.

The first project focused on anti-aircraft guns, which were so important in defending Great Britain under the V1 bombs and V2 rockets and more generally for air defense. Because World War II planes flew twice as high and twice as fast as those of World War I, the fire control parameters had to be automatically determined by means of radar data. Shannon was hired by Warren Weaver, at the time also head of the Natural Sciences Division of the Rockefeller Foundation. He worked with Richard B. Blackman and Hendrik Bode, also from Bell Labs. Their report, "Data Smoothing and Prediction in Fire-Control Systems," pointed in the direction of generality in signal processing. Fire control was seen as "a special case of the transmission, manipulation, and utilization of intelligence." They stated that there was "an obvious analogy between the problem of smoothing the data to eliminate or reduce the effect of tracking errors and the problem of separating a signal from interfering noise in communications systems" (Mindell, Gerovitch, and Segal, 2003, p. 73).

The second project was in the field of cryptography. At the outbreak of the war, communications could be easily intercepted. The main transatlantic communication meant for confidential messages was the A3 telephone system developed at Bell Labs, which simply inverted parts of the bandwidth and was easily deciphered by the Germans. Shannon worked on the X-System, which solved this problem, and met British mathematician Alan Turing during this time. Turing had come to Bell Labs to coordinate British and American research on jamming, but the "need-to-know" rule that prevailed prevented them from engaging in a real exchange on these issues. The quintessence of Shannon's contribution to war cryptography can be found in a 1945 report (declassified in 1957) titled "A Mathematical Theory of Cryptography," which outlined the first theory, relying on both algebraic and probabilistic theories. Shannon explained that he was interested in discrete information consisting of sequences of discrete symbols chosen from a finite set. He gave definitions of redundancy and equivocation, and also of "information." Trying to quantify the uncertainty related to the realization of an event chosen among n events for which a probability p_i is known, he proposed the formula

$$H = \sum_{i=1}^{n} p_i \log p_i$$ where H was at first merely a measure

of uncertainty. He then showed that this formula verified eleven properties such as additivity (information brought by two selections of an outcome equals the sum of the information brought by each event) or the fact that H was maximum when all the events had the same probability (which corresponds to the worst case for deciphering). For the choice of the letter H, obviously referring to Boltzmann's H-Theorem, he explained that "most of the entropy formulas contain terms of this type" (Sloane and Wyner, 1993, pp. 84–142). According to some authors, it might have been John von Neumann who gave Shannon the following hint:

> You should call it entropy, for two reasons. In the first place your uncertainty function has been used in statistical mechanics under that name, so it already has a name. In the second place, and more important, no one really knows what entropy really is, so in a debate you will always have the advantage. (Tribus, 1971, p. 179)

From Cryptography to Communication Theory. In his 1945 memorandum, Shannon also developed a general schema for a secured communication. The key source was represented as a disturbing element conceptualize as a "noise," similar to the message, but apart from that, the schema was similar to the one he described in 1939 in his letter to Bush. Shannon always kept this goal in mind, even when he worked in cryptology. In 1985, Shannon declared to Price "My first getting at that was information theory, and I used cryptography as a way of legitimizing

the work. ... For cryptography you could write up anything in any shape, which I did" (Price, 1985, p. 169).

Relying on his experience in Bell Laboratories, where he had become acquainted with the work of other telecommunication engineers such as Harry Nyquist and Ralph Hartley, Shannon published in two issues of the *Bell System Technical Journal* his paper "A Mathematical Theory of Communication." The general approach was pragmatic; he wanted to study "the savings due to statistical structure of the original message" (1948, p. 379), and for that purpose, he had to neglect the semantic aspects of information, as Hartley did for "intelligence" twenty years before (Hartley, 1928, p. 1). For Shannon, the communication process was stochastic in nature, and the great impact of his work, which accounts for the applications in other fields, was due to the schematic diagram of a general communication system that he proposed. An "information source" outputs a "message," which is encoded by a "transmitter" into the transmitted "signal." The received signal is the sum of the transmitted signal and unavoidable "noise." It is recovered as a decoded message, which is delivered to the "destination." The received signal, which is the sum between the signal and the "noise," is decoded in the "receiver" that gives the message to destination. His theory showed that choosing a good combination of transmitter and receiver makes it possible to send the message with arbitrarily high accuracy and reliability, provided the information rate does not exceed a fundamental limit, named the "channel capacity." The proof of this result was, however, nonconstructive, leaving open the problem of designing codes and decoding means that were able to approach this limit.

The paper was presented as an ensemble of twenty-three theorems that were mostly rigorously proven (but not always, hence the work of A. I. Khinchin and later A. N. Kolmogorov, who based a new probability theory on the information concept). Shannon's paper was divided into four parts, differentiating between discrete or continuous sources of information and the presence or absence of noise. In the simplest case (discrete source without noise), Shannon presented the H formula he had already defined in his mathematical theory of cryptography, which in fact can be reduced to a logarithmic mean. He defined the bit, the contraction of "binary digit" (as suggested by John W. Tukey, his colleague at Bell Labs) as the unit for information. Concepts such as "redundancy," "equivocation," or channel "capacity," which existed as common notions, were defined as scientific concepts. Shannon stated a fundamental source-coding theorem, showing that the mean length of a message has a lower limit proportional to the entropy of the source. When noise is introduced, the channel-coding theorem stated that when the entropy of the source is less than the capacity of the channel, a code exists that allows one to transmit a message "so that the output of the source can be transmitted over the channel with an arbitrarily small frequency of errors." This programmatic part of Shannon's work explains the success and impact it had in telecommunications engineering. The turbo codes (error correction codes) achieved a low error probability at information rates close to the channel capacity, with reasonable complexity of implementation, thus providing for the first time experimental evidence of the channel capacity theorem (Berrou and Glavieux, 1996).

Another important result of the mathematical theory of communication was, in the case of a continuous source, the definition of the capacity of a channel of band W perturbed by white thermal noise power N when the average transmitter power is limited to P, given by $C = W \log \dfrac{P+N}{N}$ which is the formula reproduced on Shannon's gravestone. The 1948 paper rapidly became very famous; it was published one year later as a book, with a postscript by Warren Weaver regarding the semantic aspects of information.

Entropy and Information. There were two different readings of this book. Some engineers became interested in the programmatic value of Shannon's writings, mostly to develop new coding techniques, whereas other scientists used the mathematical theory of communication for two reasons: on one hand, a general model of communication; and on the other, the mathematical definition of information, called "entropy" by Shannon. Those ideas coalesced with other theoretical results that appeared during the war effort, namely the idea of a general theory for "Control and Communication in the Animal and the Machine," which is the subtitle of *Cybernetics*, a book Norbert Wiener published in 1948. Shannon, von Neumann, Wiener, and others were later called "cyberneticians" during the ten meetings sponsored by the Macy Foundation, which took place between 1946 and 1953. Shannon and Weaver's 1949 book, along with the work by Wiener, brought forth a so-called "information theory."

Rapidly, connections were made between information theory and various fields, for instance in linguistics, where influences went in both directions. In order to be able to consider "natural written languages such as English, German, Chinese" as stochastic processes defined by a set of selection probabilities, Shannon relied on the work of linguists, who, in turn, were vitally interested in the calculus of the entropy of a language to gain a better understanding of concepts like that of redundancy (Shannon, 1951). Roman Jakobson was among the most enthusiastic linguists; he had participated in one of the Macy meetings in March 1948. At the very beginning of the 1950s, in most disciplines, new works were presented as "applications" of information theory, even if sometimes the appli-

cation only consisted of the use of logarithmic mean. Trying to understand the connections between molecular structure and genetic information—a couple of months before the discovery of the double helix for the structure of DNA—Herman Branson calculated, in a symposium entitled "The Use of Information Theory in Biology," the information quantity (H) contained in a human. He gave the expression "H(food and environment) = H(biological function) + H(maintenance and repair) + H(growth, differentiation, memory)" (Quastler, 1953, p. 39). Henry Quastler came to the conclusion, as did Sidney Dancoff, that "H(man)" was about 2×10^{28} bits (p. 167).

Taking issue with these different kinds of applications, Shannon in 1956 wrote a famous editorial, published in the *Transactions of the Institute of Radio Engineers*, with the title "The Bandwagon." As he stated, referring to his 1948 paper, "Starting as a technical tool for the communication engineer, it has received an extraordinary amount of publicity in the popular as well as the scientific press. In part, this has been due to connections with such fashionable fields as computing machines, cybernetics, and automation; and in part, to the novelty of its subject matter. As a consequence, it has perhaps been ballooned to an importance beyond its actual accomplishments." At this time, some applications of information theory already reflected a mood, essentially based on a loose, rather than a scientific definition of information. Forty years later, the project of "information highways," presented to promote the Internet, partly relied on the same idea.

Shannon as a Pioneer in Artificial Intelligence. At the time Shannon published his relatively pessimistic editorial, he was already engaged in other research, typically related to his ability to combine mathematical theories, electrical engineering, and "tinkering," namely, artificial intelligence. Shannon coauthored the 1955 "Proposal for the Dartmouth Summer Research Project on Artificial Intelligence," which marked the debut of the term "artificial intelligence." Together with Nathaniel Rochester, John McCarthy, and Marvin L. Minsky, he obtained support from the Rockefeller Foundation to "proceed on the basis of the conjecture that every aspect of learning or any other feature of intelligence can in principle be so precisely described that a machine can be made to simulate it." In explaining his own goal, Shannon named two topics.

The first topic, presented as an "application of information theory," was based on an analogy: in the same way that information theory was concerned with the reliable transmission of information over a noisy channel, he wanted to tackle the structure of computing machines in which reliable computing is supposed to be achieved using some unreliable elements, a problem to which John von Neumann devoted considerable attention. Starting from

Claude Shannon. *Claude Shannon with an electronic mouse which has a "super" memory and can learn its way round a maze without a mistake after only one "training" run.* HULTON ARCHIVE/GETTY IMAGES.

this parallel, notions such as redundancy and channel capacity were to be used to improve the architecture of computing machines.

The second topic dealt with the way in which a "brain model" can adapt to its environment. This had no direct link with information theory but was more related to the work Shannon had presented during the eighth Macy meeting, in March 1951, where he gathered with other cyberneticians. Shannon demonstrated an electromechanical mouse he called Theseus, which would be "taught" to find its way in a labyrinth. In his Dartmouth proposal, Shannon put the emphasis on "clarifying the environmental model, and representing it as a mathematical structure." He had already noticed that "in discussing mechanized intelligence, we think of machines perform-

ing the most advanced human thought activities—proving theorems, writing music, or playing chess." He posited a bottom-up approach in the "direction of these advanced activities," starting with simpler models, as he had done in his 1950 paper entitled "Programming a Computer for Playing Chess." In this first published article on computer chess, Shannon offered the key elements for writing a "program," such as an "evaluation function" or a "minimax procedure."

A Complex Legacy. Shannon's contributions to artificial intelligence have often been neglected because of the enormous aura. He is so well known for his work on information theory that his credit for AI is often ignored. Most history of AI does not even mention his presence at the

Dartmouth meeting of information theory. None of the works he wrote after the 1950s received such recognition. He left Bell Labs for the Massachusetts Institute of Technology (MIT) in 1956, first as a visiting professor; he was a permanent member of the Research Laboratory of Electronics at MIT for twenty years, starting in 1958, after he had spent a year as a fellow at the Center for Advanced Study in the Behavioral Sciences in Palo Alto.

Most of his scientific work was devoted to the promotion and deepening of information theory. Shannon was invited to many countries, including the Soviet Union in 1965. While there, giving a lecture at an engineering conference, he had an opportunity to play a chess match against Mikhail Botvinik. He tackled the case of transmission with a memoryless channel (a noisy channel where the noise acts independently on each symbol transmitted through the channel). It is on this topic that he published his last paper related to information theory, as early as 1967, with Robert G. Gallager and Elwyn R. Berlekamp.

In the late 1960s and 1970s, Shannon became interested in portfolio management and, more generally, investment theory. One of his colleagues at Bell Labs, John L. Kelly, had shown in 1956 how information theory could be applied to gambling. Together with Ed Thorp, Shannon went to Las Vegas to test their ideas. In 1966 they also invented the first wearable computer at MIT that was able to predict roulette wheels.

Shannon never gave up constructing eccentric machines, like the THROBAC (THrifty ROman-numeral BAckward-looking Computer) he built in the 1950s, the rocket-powered Frisbee, or a device that could solve the Rubik's Cube puzzle. He developed many automata, many of which he kept at his home: among others, a tiny stage on which three clowns could juggle with eleven rings, seven balls, and five clubs, all driven by an invisible mechanism of clockwork and rods. Juggling was one of his passions, which also included playing chess, riding a unicycle, and playing to clarinet. In the early 1980s Shannon began writing an article for *Scientific American* called "Scientific Aspects of Juggling," which he never finished (Sloane and Wyner, 1993, pp. 850–864).

At the dawn of the twenty-first century, Shannon's contributions are manifold. Whereas there are still applications that only consist of using the logarithmic mean or the schematic diagram of a general communication system (applications he condemned in his 1956 editorial, "The Bandwagon"), there are also numerous new fields that could not be defined without referring to his work. In the field of technology, coding theories that are applied to compact discs or deep-space communication are merely developments of information theory. In mathematics, entire parts of algorithmic complexity theory can be seen as resulting from the development of Shannon's theory. In

biology, the protean use made of the expression "genetic information" explains the development of molecular biology (Fox Keller, Kay and Yockey). From the 1990s onward, in physics, the domain of "quantum information" took off around the definition of *qubits,* which extended the *bit* initially used by Shannon to measure information. Shannon unfortunately could not take part in these developments nor take them into account; from the mid-1990s he struggled with Alzheimer's disease, to which he succumbed in February 2001.

BIBLIOGRAPHY

A comprehensive bibliography appears in Neil J. A. Sloane and Aaaron D. Wyner, eds., Claude Elwood Shannon: Collected Papers, *Piscataway, NJ: IEEE Press, 1993. These collected papers include the 1937 master's thesis (http://libraries.mit.edu/); the "Letter to Vannevar Bush, Feb. 16, 1939"; and the 1940 PhD dissertation (http://libraries.mit.edu/). The master's and PhD essays are also available at the MIT's online institutional repository http://dspace.mit.edu/handle/1721.1/11173 and http://dspace.mit.edu/handle/1721.1/11174;the 1939 letter was first reproduced in Hagmeyer's doctoral dissertation (see below). Shannon's archives are at the Bell Laboratories Archives and at the National Archives in Washington, DC*

WORKS BY SHANNON

"A Mathematical Theory of Communication." *Bell System Technical Journal* 27 (1948): 379–423, 623–656.

"Communication in the Presence of Noise." *Proceedings of the Institute of Radio Engineers* 37 (1949): 10–21.

"Communication Theory of Secrecy Systems." *Bell System Technical Journal* 28 (1949): 656–715.

With Warren Weaver. *The Mathematical Theory of Communication.* Urbana: University of Illinois Press, 1949.

"Programming a Computer for Playing Chess." *Philosophical Magazine* 41 (1950): 256–275.

"Prediction and Entropy in Printed English." *Bell System Technical Journal* 30 (1951): 50–64.

"The Bandwagon." *IRE Transactions on Information Theory* 2 (1956): 3.

With Robert G. Gallager and Elwyn R. Berlekamp. "Lower Bounds to Error Probability for Coding on Discrete Memoryless Channels." *Information and Control* 10 (1967): 65-103.

OTHER SOURCES

Berrou, Claude, and Alain Glavieux. "Near Optimum Error Correcting Coding and Decoding: Turbo-Codes." *IEEE Transactions on Communications* 44 (1996): 1261–1271.

Foerster, Heinz von. *Cybernetics, Circular Causal and Feedback Mechanisms in Biological and Social Systems.* New York: Macy Foundation, 1952.

Fox Keller, Evelyn. *The Century of the Gene.* Cambridge, MA: Harvard University Press, 2000.

Goldstine, Herman H. *The Computer from Pascal to von Neumann.* Princeton, NJ: Princeton University Press, 1972.

Hagemeyer, Friedrich W. *Die Entstehung von Informationskonzepten in der Nachrichtentechnik.* Doktorarbeit an der Freie Universität Berlin (PhD), FB 11 Philosophie und Sozialwissenschaften, 1979.

Hartley, Ralph V. L. "Transmission of Information." *Bell System Technical Journal* 7 (1928): 535–563.

Hodges, Andrew. *Alan Turing: The Enigma.* London: Burnett Books, 1983.

Horgan, John. "Claude E. Shannon: Unicyclist, Juggler and Father of Information Theory." *Scientific American* 242 (1990): 20–22B.

Kay, Lily E. *Who Wrote the Book of Life? A History of the Genetic Code.* Chicago: University of Chicago Press, 2000.

Kelly, John L. "A New Interpretation of the Information Rate." *Bell System Technical Journal* 35 (1956): 917–925.

Mindell, D., S. Gerovitch, and J. Segal. "From Communications Engineering to Communications Science: Cybernetics and Information Theory in the United States, France, and the Soviet Union." In *Science and Ideology: A Comparative History*, edited by Mark Walker, pp. 66–96. London: Routledge, 2003.

Pias, Claus. *Cybernetics/Kybernetik. The Macy-Conferences, 1946–1953. Transactions/Protokolle.* 2 vol. Fernwald, Germany: Diaphanes, 2003 and 2004.

Price, Robert. "A Conversation with Claude Shannon: One Man's Approach to Problem Solving." *Cryptologia* 9 (1985): 167–175.

Quastler, Henry, ed. *Essays on the Use of Information Theory in Biology.* Urbana: University of Illinois Press, 1953.

Segal, Jérôme. *Le Zéro et le un: Histoire de la notion scientifique d'information.* Paris: Syllepse, 2003.

Tribus, Myron, and E. C. McIrvine. "Energy and Information." *Scientific American* 224 (1971): 178–184.

Verdu, Sergio. "Fifty Years of Shannon Theory." *IEEE Transactions on Information Theory* 44 (1998): 2057–2078.

Wiener, Norbert. *Cybernetics , or Control and Communication in the Animal and the Machine.* Paris, France: Hermann et Cie, 1948.

Yockey, Hubert P. *Information Theory and Molecular Biology.* Cambridge, U.K.: Cambridge University Press, 1992.

———. *Information Theory, Evolution, and the Origin of Life.* Cambridge, U.K.: Cambridge University Press, 2005.

Jérôme Segal

SHATSKIY, NIKOLAY SERGEYE-VICH (*b.* Moscow, USSR, 28 August 1895; *d.* Moscow, 1 August 1960), *geology, geotectonics, history of geology.*

Shatskiy was born in Moscow on 28 August 1895. At an early age he showed great interest in and a natural flair for earth sciences. In his early twenties he was already a prominent geologist, leading geological investigations into the Southern Volga regions, the geography around Moscow, the northern Donets Basin, the Caucasus and the Cisbaikal and Transbaikal regions. Shatskiy developed the method of comparative tectonic maps, led geological investigations into, and contributed to the history of geology.

Early Years. Established as an academic, Shatskiy published his first paper in 1922 and went on to become one of the foremost authorities on geotectonics in the USSR.

His career path was as an academic, though he retained an enthusiasm for practical fieldwork throughout his life. From 1922 to 1932 he was an exploration geologist before joining the Moscow Geological Exploration Institute as a lecturer. By the end of the 1940s he was head of the Tectonic Department at the Geological Institute of the USSR Academy of Sciences. From 1940 onward, supervising a team of geologists, he guided the compilation of all USSR and related tectonic maps, including the maps of USSR and neighboring countries, the International Tectonic Map of Europe, which was only completed after his death, the Tectonic Map of Eurasia, and the Tectonic Map of the Artic Regions, edited by Shatskiy and again published after his death.

However, as committed as he was to the practical observation and study of geology in the field, he was one of the school of geologists who felt that the study of the history of geology was equally important to the understanding of the subject. This enabled him to take a broad view of geological interpretation, crossing the more specialist subject boundaries, and led him to make many incisive deductions that stood the test of time. Unlike many of his generation throughout the world who became progressively more specialized, Shatskiy's method of studying geological problems predated the rise of the much wider studies now termed Earth Systems Science.

Shatskiy established theories and techniques new to the study of geology in USSR in the 1930s and 1940s in the areas of stratigraphy, lithology, and tectonics, believing that tectonics almost always related to all areas of geological investigations. For this reason, the investigations he led were often large and comprehensive affairs, crossing specialist boundaries and often were at odds with more focused studies undertaken by his contemporaries. However, on many occasions the more specific studies often yielded results that linked them directly into the broader interpretations defined by Shatskiy's work.

Work on Geotechtonics. A strong leader in the field of geotectonics, Shatskiy's ideas and notations became standard and generally were accepted in the USSR from the 1930s through to 1960, when he died. However, the development of new instruments and hence new techniques during the 1960s enabled new types of data, in particular geophysical data, to be gathered both on landmasses and on the ocean floor. This resulted in allowing later studies to develop different concepts of structures in the lithosphere and to develop a clearer understanding of their formation. Most significantly, the new hypothesis of horizontal motion of lithospheric plates over long distances giving rise to the generation of tectonic structures replaced the global concept of vertical motion as the explanation for dislocation in the earth's crust and with it, the need to re-examine and re-evaluate Shatskiy's findings.

However, many of Shatskiy's scientific findings did provide a valuable base for future studies. In his early works during the 1920s and 1930s he correctly identified the formation of fold structures, indicated their relationship to basement faults, gave convincing proofs of the regional tectonic stratification of the crust, revealed in fold regions tectonic breccias accompanying large formational overthrusts, and showed the importance and need for their study. At the same time he was the first in Russia to use the method of comparative tectonics in studying structures. This was a significant step forward in bringing together formerly incompatible theories of horizontal and vertical plate movement, as global geological findings helped to inform the development of geological concepts.

In his later works Shatskiy elaborated successfully and more broadly on the methodology of combined tectonic investigations. In Russia he is credited with the introduction into practice of this method of tectonic mapping and the method of comparative tectonics. All this allowed him to perform a tectonic zoning of the vast area of Russia and its contiguous regions, and revealed and substantiated the transformation of geosynclinal regions into platform ones and showed the dynamics of this process.

Regarding morphotectonic and geohistoric concepts, Shatskiy's comparative methods enabled him to identify a number of new, earlier unknown structural forms on ancient and young platforms. He gave exact names to these forms and they became the basis of a fairly large body of tectonic terminology on platforms in the USSR. For example, he was the first to elaborate on the idea of inherited development of many platform structures and to reveal in them the lower stages of the Riphean group of deposits, corresponding to a long cycle of tectonic development, which terminated in a structure that he termed the Baikal folding.

Shatskiy's generic concepts were determined in many respects by the regional morphology and tectonic position of the investigated structures. Following on from the specifics of their structure and development, and resting on purely geologic methods of investigation, he made conclusions that those methods available at the time

allowed for. In fold regions he explained the origin of deformations by tangential stresses and horizontal displacements of appreciable amplitude. In platform regions, to the study of which he devoted the greater part of his life, he explained the origin of structures by vertical movements appearing either on mantle compaction or on the migration of matter from below upward. In the last days of his life Shatskiy did not exclude horizontal displacements along large fractures from controlling the subsidence of the crust, a particularly enlightened view considering that the means to substantiate these insights did not become available to Russian geologists until after his death.

The passion Shatskiy had for the subject, together with his belief that historical study was critical in the understanding of geological development, meant that his extensive reading allowed him to apply a broad perspective to observations in the field. This meant that, where findings from individual specialist studies when applied globally would be contradictory, Shatskiy would appreciate their significance as regional findings within a global development.

For example, the hypothesis of the tectonics of lithospheric plates, being originally global, finally grew into individual geodynamic models with differing degrees of accuracy, depending on the factual bases and the ideas used in treating the kinematics and dynamics of tectogenesis in certain regions.

The contradictions between fixism and mobilism were smoothed owing to the increased understanding and awareness of the various tectonic pressures at platform boundaries, which allowed for acceptance of both horizontal and vertical movement resulting variously in upthrusts, folding, and magma intrusions, depending on the particular geography and the directional movement of the masses.

Ahead of his time, Shatskiy was correct when, with foresight as a first-class specialist in platforms, he developed for platform regions diverse relations between vertical movements and structures and in fold regions, when explaining their origins did not exclude either major horizontal displacements or tangential stresses.

Shatskiy contributed greatly to the history of geological knowledge in the USSR by his vivid descriptions of the life and scientific activities of his internationally renowned contemporaries; natural scientists and prominent geologists such as Charles Lyell, Charles Darwin, R. I. Murchison, A. Gressly, A. P. Karpinskiy, A. D. Arkhangelskiy, and V. A. Obruchev. His descriptions are noted for their profundity and depict both the image of the scientists, their propensities and aspirations, and the state of the art as they made remarkable discoveries that both corroborated or contradicted accepted knowledge in Russia at the time.

Well respected in his lifetime, Shatskiy on 29 September 1943 was admitted as a corresponding member of the Russian Academy of Sciences, becoming an academician of the Society ten years later in the Division of Geological and Geographical Sciences. From 1994 to the present, a prize in his name is awarded by the Division of Geology, Geography, Geochemistry, and Mining Sciences for the best research works in tectonics each year.

In recognition of his life's work, the Soviet Antarctic Expedition named a 2,705 meter hill in the Weyprecht Mountains in Queen Maud Land, Antarctica after Shatskiy—Shatskiy Hill—during the remapping of the area in 1960 and 1961. There is also a crater on Mars named in Shatskiy's honor.

BIBLIOGRAPHY

WORKS BY SHATSKIY

"A Contribution to the Problem of the Origin of the Romanian Gypsum and Rocks of the Isachkovskiy Hill in the Ukraine." *Byul. MOIP Otd.Geol.* 9, nos. 3–4 (1931): 136–349.

"Notes on the Tectonics of the Tertiary Piedmont of the Northeastern Caucasus." *Byul. MOIP Otd.Geol.* 5, nos. 3–4 (1927): 321–369.

"On Comparative Tectonics of North America and East Europe." *Izv. Acad. Sci. USSR Ser. Geol.* no. 4 (1945a): 10–20.

"On Neocatastrophism: A Contribution to the Problem of Organic Phases and on Folding." *Probl. Sov. Geol.* 7, no. 7 (1937a): 532–551.

"On the Oldest Deposits of the Sedimentary Cover of the Russian Platform and Its Structure in the Late Paleozoic." *Izv. Acad. Sci. USSR Ser. Geol.* no. 1 (1952): 17–32.

"On the Tectonics of Central Kazakhstan." *Izv. Acad. Sci. USSR Ser. Geol.* no. 5–6 (1938): 737–765.

"On the Tectonics of the East European Platform." *Byul. MOIP Otd. Geol.* 15, no. 1 (1937b): 4–27.

Outlines of the Tectonics of the Volga-Ural Oil-Bearing Region and the Adjacent Part of the Western Slope of the Southern Urals. Moscow: Moscow Society of Naturalists (MOIP), 1945b.

"Principal Features of the Tectonics of the Siberian Platform." *Byul. MOIP Otd.Geol.* 10, nos. 3–4 (1932): 476–509.

Selected Works in 4 Volumes, vol. 1. Moscow: Nauka, 1963.

Selected Works in 4 Volumes, vol. 2. Moscow: Nauka, 1964.

Selected Works in 4 Volumes, vol. 3. *Geologic Formations and Sedimentary Mineral Deposits.* Moscow: Nauka, 1965a.

Selected Works in 4 Volumes, vol. 4. *History and Methodology of Geology.* Moscow: Nauka, 1965b.

OTHER SOURCES

Poliakova, N.B., with Pushcharovskii, and Iurii Mikhailovich. *Nikolay Sergeyevich Shatskii, 1895–1960.* Moscow: Nauka, 1991.

Suvorov, A. I. "Nikolay Sergeyevich Shatskiy and the Present Time (In Commemoration of his Centennial Birthday)." *Geotectonics, English Translation* 29, no. 4 (1996): 271–280.

J. R. Cribb

SHKLOVSKII, IOSIF SAMUILOVICH (*b.* Glukhov, Ukraine (then Russia), 1 July 1916; *d.* Moscow, USSR, 3 March 1985), *theoretical astrophysics.*

Shklovskii's major scientific achievement was to show that both the radio and optical emissions from the Crab Nebula can be explained as synchrotron radiation. He is also known for his book *Intelligent Life in the Universe* (1966), co-authored with Carl Sagan. Shklovskii organized the radio astronomy department at Moscow University and later served as chief of the astrophysics department of the new Institute of Space Research in Moscow, having overcome many of the obstacles confronting Soviet scientists of his generation.

Youth. The son of a rabbi, Shklovskii (Josif Shklovsky is an alternative transliteration) grew up in a traditional Jewish environment in Glukhov, a small Ukrainian town. He regarded himself as an October Revolution baby, fortunate to have survived famine during World War I, the October Revolution of 1917, and the Russian Civil War from 1918 to 1920. His family was desperately poor, especially after his father died. Conditions worsened with the forced collectivization of agriculture beginning in 1929, and in 1930 Shklovskii's family migrated to Kazakhstan. Leaving behind his Jewish childhood, Shklovskii became, he later said, a modern Soviet youth. Though henceforth never a practicing Jew, on travel outside the Soviet Union he would visit Jewish memorials.

In 1931 Shklovskii graduated from secondary school in Akmolinsk (now Astana). Students then attended seven years of school before entering a factory-plant school for further education and training as workers. Shklovskii worked as a foreman in railroad construction. In 1933 he began studies in physics and mathematics at the Far-Eastern State University in Vladivostok, and in 1935 transferred to the physics department of the Moscow State University. Open competition in entrance examinations had begun two years earlier, though preference was still given to those with better biographical particulars. Students lived in wooden barracks on the northern edge of Moscow, an hour by tram when slowed by winter snow and ice. Trenches served as latrines, with frozen stalagmites of repulsive composition. Nonetheless, many of the students were carefree. They ate meat at the beginnings of months, and bread, sugar, and hot water when their monthly stipends ran low.

Not so pleasant were what Shklovskii later called in his autobiographical *Five Billion Vodka Bottles to the Moon: Tales of a Soviet Scientist* (1991) the "mass psychoses" that "rolled over us like tidal waves." A roommate envious of Shklovskii's easy academic success denounced him for Trotskyite agitation, but the matter was quickly dropped. More worrisome was a summons to the Lubyanka. There Shklovskii was asked about another student, answered that he knew nothing incriminating, and was dismissed, though not before seeing a man escorted with his hands behind his back and blood streaming down his face.

Back in the student quarter, Shklovskii was making an impression. He challenged history students to present him with ten questions, all of which he would answer, while their champion would answer only one of Shklovskii's ten history questions. He later claimed to have won decisively all the monthly tournaments; he focused his reading in history rather than physics during this period. Shklovskii was also an artist, having begun drawing at the age of three with a piece of chalk, or a brick, or anything else at hand, and he drew wonderful portraits of fellow students.

Shternberg Astronomical Institute. Upon graduation in 1938, Shklovskii received a two-year work assignment to swamp forests in Siberia. With a wife and a newborn daughter, he was reluctant to go. The physics department would not admit him for graduate work, and he didn't like the atmosphere at the Physical Chemistry Institute. He saw a notice in a newspaper about the P. K. Shternberg State Astronomical Institute, the astronomy department of Moscow University. Astrophysics was becoming recognized as an important branch of astronomy, and the Moscow astronomy department, eager to bring in physics students, admitted Shklovskii.

The department survived the great purge of the late 1930s, in contrast to the Pulkovo Observatory, outside Leningrad (now St. Petersburg). There a disgruntled graduate student, after failing an examination, denounced his adviser for possessing foreign scientific correspondence. Arrested and beaten, the professor confessed to being the leader of a Fascist-Trotskyite-Zinovievite terrorist organization in league with German intelligence to establish a fascist dictatorship in the Soviet Union, and also named fellow conspirators. In the chain reaction and conflagration that followed, approximately 80 percent of the Pulkovo staff were repressed and a majority perished. In the 1950s the Office of the Military Procurator, finding no evidence of any crimes having been committed, would fully rehabilitate the victims, in most cases posthumously.

At Shternberg a student also failed an examination and denounced his advisor, as a nonproletarian scientist blocking the entry of workers into science. The astronomer was also accused of collaborating with an arrested enemy of the people: the director of the Pulkovo Observatory. Other students in the red graduate student organization rebuffed the provocation, the complaining student was expelled, and no one was repressed. (Many years later, during the Cold War, Soviet scientists dared send only published papers and standard new year's greetings to foreign colleagues.)

Following the German invasion in 1941, Shklovskii lived briefly in one of a score of freight cars very slowly evacuating students to Ashkhabad. He lent Andrei Sakharov, a fellow inhabitant, a physics book. Once in Central Asia, many of the students were sent to military schools and then as junior lieutenants to the front, where fewer than 5 percent would survive. Myopia disqualified Shklovskii from military service. He was in Ashkhabad for ten months, and then Sverdlovsk, where he rejoined the Astronomical Institute in September 1942.

In April 1943 Shklovskii and the institute were back in Moscow. He wrote his candidate thesis (nearly equivalent to a PhD thesis in the West) in 1944, on the concept of the electron temperature in astronomy, and his doctoral thesis (usually by someone over thirty years old and the author of dozens of papers; and conferring the right to hold a professor's post) in 1949, on the physics of the solar corona, including its confinement by magnetic fields, its extraordinarily high temperature, of more than a million Kelvin, and its radio emission. Holding the only doctorate in his subfaculty at the Astronomical Institute, Shklovskii was nicknamed the Doctor.

In the summer of 1946, Shklovskii learned from a fragment of a review report he heard by accident at a scientific meeting, that during the war the British Royal Air Force had detected radio emissions from the Sun. Already working for the past three years on the physics of the solar corona, Shklovskii realized immediately that the emission must be from the corona. Another Soviet scientist, Vitaly Ginzburg, came to the same realization independently, from his work on a project to bounce radio waves off the Sun and the Moon. The leader of this project, a favorite of Joseph Stalin, obtained (out of a country ravished by war) funding for a complicated and expensive solar eclipse expedition to Brazil in 1947. Shklovskii was assigned to the optical part of the expedition, whose efforts were frustrated by cloudy conditions. But radio observations found the radio diameter of the Sun larger than its optical diameter, confirming Shklovskii's hypothesis.

Accompanying the expedition was an individual assigned to ensure ideological restraint by the real scientists. At a public celebration, Shklovskii induced this comrade to sing a particular Russian song, some of whose words sounded like obscene Portuguese words. The women walked out while the men yelled and applauded. Shklovskii was not permitted to travel abroad again for eighteen years, though probably more as a matter of general Soviet policy restricting contact with the rest of the world than in reprisal for his Brazilian linguistic escapade. The time in Brazil, contrasted with a poverty-stricken boyhood and wartime privations, was the happiest period of Shklovskii's life.

In 1951 Shklovskii and other Jews were dismissed from Shternberg. He was reinstated two weeks later by the rector of the university, who appreciated Shklovskii as a star in the Soviet astronomical firmament. Still, Shklovskii was a Jew. In 1953 Jewish doctors at a Kremlin hospital were accused of poisoning Soviet elite; the pending pogrom was forestalled only by Stalin's death.

Crab Nebula. In 1953 Shklovskii made his most significant scientific achievement. Waiting for the tram to the student barracks, he was thinking about the Crab Nebula and its emissions. In the radio range they were too strong to be an extension of thermal optical emissions. Why not, he wondered, instead try to explain the optical radiation as an extension of nonthermal radio emissions. He hypothesized that the light emitted by the Crab Nebula was synchrotron radiation from charged particles spiraling at nearly the speed of light through a large and well-ordered magnetic field, and then during the 45-minute trolley ride he did in his head the entire theoretical calculation establishing that, rather than a dense plasma, only a small number of relativistic electrons of sufficiently high energy could produce optical radiation of the observed intensity. Then he wrote it up, with no revisions.

The impossibility of reconciling the optical and radio emissions as thermal in origin was discussed by American astronomers Jesse Greenstein and Rudolph Minkowski in a 1953 paper in the *Astrophysical Journal,* but seemingly this paper was not known to Shklovskii; he did not cite it in his paper. He did cite Minkowski's 1942 paper on the optical emission and a 1949 paper reporting that that the radio emission was a thousand times more intense than the optical emission. Also, in 1950 the Swedish physicist Hannes Alfrén had proposed the general idea of synchrotron radiation. Shklovskii's breakthrough achievement was to link these phenomena, quantitatively as well as suggestively; he connected the dots. It was a major step in the transformation of astronomy from optical to all-wave studies and to high-energy astrophysics with magnetic fields and high-energy particles. Ginzburg had also thought to apply synchrotron radiation to astronomy, and would later claim priority.

Shklovskii did not note in his paper that, if the emissions from the Crab Nebula were synchrotron radiation, they must be polarized. Other Soviet astronomers realized this and quickly reported finding polarization. Few astronomers in the west believed the initial claims, but Jan Oort in the Netherlands convinced his friend Greenstein to use the Mount Palomar telescope, the largest optical telescope in the world, to search for polarization, which he found. Continuing this line of research, Shklovskii suggested in a paper for a 1955 symposium that emission from the galaxy M 87 (NGC 4486) likely was similar to that from the Crab Nebula. A note added in proof in 1957 reported confirmation. Another test of Shklovskii's theory occurred in the 1960s, when he predicted that a young supernova remnant with its rapid expansion would have a correspondingly rapid decrease in the strength of its magnetic field and also its synchrotron radiation. This was confirmed within a year.

Honors and Promotions. In 1954 Shklovskii was appointed a professor and he organized a radio astronomy department. The previous year he had given a series of lectures on radio astronomy. He now moved out of the single room in the student barracks which he and his family had occupied for nineteen years, and into a relatively luxurious three-room apartment in another Moscow University building; and his son was admitted to the university.

Shklovskii received the Order of Lenin, his country's highest civil order, in 1960. The Soviet Union was ready in 1959 to send a rocket to the Moon, after the Americans had failed four times in 1958, but had no radio telescope capable of tracking a lunar rocket. Shklovskii proposed turning the rocket into an "artificial comet" by vaporizing on board several kilograms of sodium, which would scatter the yellow rays of the Sun, resulting in a cloud of resonance fluorescence bright enough to be observed optically. The successful *Lunik 2* was so observed.

Not until 1966, however, was this outspoken Jew elected to the Soviet Academy of Sciences, as a corresponding member, on his fifth try, and he was never elected a full member, failing in some dozen elections. Corresponding members of the Soviet Academy of Sciences received, in addition to regular salaries, a 250 ruble monthly stipend, and full members 500 rubles, when the monthly salary of a young scientist was 150 to 200 rubles and heads of departments were paid 500 rubles. Membership could be the difference between life and death; in 1967 Shklovskii was treated in the academy's hospital for a heart attack.

Shklovskii was highly honored abroad. He was elected a foreign member of the Royal Astronomical Society in 1964, of the American Academy of Arts and Sciences in 1966, an honorary member of the U.S. National

Academy of Sciences in 1972, and also a foreign member of the American Astronomical Society and the Royal Astronomical Society of Canada. He received the Jansky Prize of the U.S. National Radio Astronomy Observatory in 1968 and the prestigious Bruce Medal of the Astronomical Society of the Pacific in 1972. And asteroid 2849 Shklovskij [*sic*] is named in his honor.

Travel and Publications Abroad. After the Brazil expedition in 1947, Shklovskii applied for travel visas dozens of times, and in 1965 in the university dining hall talking to someone he hardly knew, Shklovskii remarked that he was busy with his hobby of hopelessly filling out travel forms. The person worked in the foreign section of the university, and three days later Shklovskii was on a train to Prague, having accepted a repeated invitation to give a talk there. He had attained, so he later recounted in his *Five Billion Vodka Bottles,* the "first cosmic velocity." A year later, with his election to the Soviet Academy of Sciences, he attained the "second cosmic velocity," which made possible trips to capitalist countries. In 1967 he traveled to the United States and France, and Prague again, for the International Astronomical Union meeting there. He impressed foreign colleagues as a very smart, quick-thinking, talkative, and amusing guy, with a sound knowledge of astronomy and astrophysics. For the meeting in Paris, his visa was so late that he only made the last day of the conference. He stayed on, wandering the streets and living on not much more than a kilo of bread a day until his pitifully meager travel funds and his visa expired a week later. At the conference in the United States, he mentioned an interest in visiting several observatories, and his hosts immediately supplied him with airplane tickets and money; Edward Teller was among those eager to talk with Shklovskii. In 1973, after forty Soviet academicians signed a document condemning Andrei Sakharov, Shklovskii signed a letter in Sakharov's defense, and lost his travel privileges. Foreign colleagues were informed that he was ill. When restrictions on his travel were later eased, Shklovskii explained that he had had diabetes from too much Sakharov (the Russian word for sugar is *sakhar*).

Only he who does nothing makes no mistakes, Shklovskii often said. Measurements of the position of Mars's moon Phobos suggested that it was spiraling inward toward Mars. In 1959 Shklovskii hypothesized that friction with the outer atmosphere of Mars was producing a drag on the satellite. However, to explain the inward spiraling quantitatively, Phobos had to be hollow. Perhaps it was an artificial space station launched long ago by a now-extinct Martian civilization. The resulting furor was great fun for Shklovskii and a needed distraction from his mother's death. (Later studies have found the acceleration to be only half as much, and explainable with a solid satellite affected by forces due to tides it raises in Mars.

Phobos will crash into Mars in 40 million years.) Carl Sagan, recognizing a fellow spirit, mailed Shklovskii a preprint of his paper on direct contact among galactic civilizations by relativistic interstellar space flight.

Shklovskii next wrote a book on the possible existence of life elsewhere in the universe. Reasoning that censors would not have time to do much in the rush to meet a deadline set by authorities, he had volunteered at a meeting of Soviet space scientists to write a book to celebrate the fifth anniversary of *Sputnik* the following year. (Actually, he was on safe ideological ground, in as much as members of the Soviet Institute of Astrobotany had concluded that the existence of extraterrestrial life was required by dialectical materialism, and its absence would be clear disproof of the philosophical basis of communism.)

Shklovskii's book sold out fifty thousand copies in a few hours; went through five editions in his lifetime; a sixth, posthumously, in 1987; and many translations, including one into Braille. Sagan, now on the board of a new book publisher hoping to profit from public interest in science fueled by *Sputnik*, wanted to reprint Shklovskii's book in English. Shklovskii agreed, and invited Sagan to add material. Shklovskii thought his invitation applied to biological issues, on which Sagan was more knowledgeable; Sagan added as he saw fit. His travel still restricted, Shklovskii wrote to Sagan that "The probability of our meeting [to cooperate on the book] is unlikely to be smaller than the probability of a visit to the Earth by an extraterrestrial cosmonaut" (Davidson, 1999, p. 150). The resulting book, *Intelligent Life in the Universe*, appeared in 1966. To Shklovskii's surprise, it contained more than twice as many words as he had written, not just on biology, and Sagan's name on the title page as coauthor. At least their respective contributions were delineated. Absent any U.S.-Soviet copyright convention then, Shklovskii received only a token one thousand dollars from the publisher and no share of Sagan's royalties. The first edition was twenty-five thousand copies in hardback, and a paperback edition appeared in the same year. In Sagan's 1985 novel *Contact*, the Russian scientist Vaygay is modeled after Shklovskii, including the episode of the Russian scientist picking up a campaign button in Berkeley with the slogan "Pray for Sex" and commenting that it only offended for one reason in the United States, but for two reasons in his country.

In 1965 Shklovskii joined the newly formed Institute of Space Research in Moscow, and from 1972 until his death in 1985 he was chief of its astrophysics department. He trained some thirty graduate students, and directed the first successful Soviet astrophysical experiments in space. In 1967 he hypothesized that x-ray stars are close binary systems, including an accreting neutron star. Near the end of his life, Shklovskii despaired of success in the search for extraterrestrial intelligence. If there were many other civilizations, some of them would be more advanced than ours, and if so, why had not they contacted us yet? Shklovskii observed that he was the only male of his high school graduating class to survive World War II, and in the subsequent Cold War with its doctrine of mutually assured destruction he perhaps came to worry that intelligent civilizations tend to self-destruct. Surgery for a blood clot in his leg released another blood clot to his brain, and Shklovskii died of a stroke on 3 March 1985.

BIBLIOGRAPHY

For additional scientific papers by Shklovskii see the Web site for Bruce Medalists of the Astronomical Society of the Pacific: http://www.phys-astro.sonoma.edu/BruceMedalists/.

WORKS BY SHKLOVSKII

"O prirode svecheniia krabovidnai tumannosti." *Doklady Akademii Nauk SSSR 90* (1953): 983–986. Shklovskii's most significant scientific paper. English translation with commentary: "The Nature of the Crab Nebula's Optical Emission." In *A Source Book in Astronomy and Astrophysics, 1900–1975,* edited by Kenneth R. Lang and Owen Gingerich. Cambridge, MA: Harvard University Press, 1979.

"On the Nature of Planetary Nebulae." In *Non-Stable Stars,* edited by George H. Herbig. International Astronomical Union Symposium, no. 3. Cambridge, U.K.: Cambridge University Press, 1957.

"On the Nature of the Emission from the Galaxy NGC4486." In *Radio Astronomy,* edited by H. C. van de Hulst. International Astronomical Union Symposium, no. 4. Cambridge, U.K.: Cambridge University Press, 1957.

"Optical Emission from the Crab Nebula in the Continuous Spectrum." In *Radio Astronomy,* edited by H. C. van de Hulst. International Astronomical Union Symposium, no. 4. Cambridge, U.K.: Cambridge University Press, 1957.

"Some Problems of Meta-Galactic Radio-Emission." In *Radio Astronomy,* edited by H. C. van de Hulst. International Astronomical Union Symposium, no. 4. Cambridge, U.K.: Cambridge University Press, 1957.

Cosmic Radio Waves. Translated by Richard B. Rodman and Carlos M. Varsavsky. Cambridge, MA: Harvard University Press, 1960.

Physics of the Solar Corona. International Series of Monographs in Natural Philosophy, vol. 6. Oxford: Pergamon Press, 1965.

"Possible Secular Variation of the Flux and Spectrum of Radio Emissions of Source 1934–63." *Nature* 206 (1965): 176–177.

Vselennaia, Zhizn, Razum. Moscow: Izd-vo Nauka, 1965.

With Carl Sagan. *Intelligent Life in the Universe.* Translation by Paula Fern. San Francisco: Holden-Day, 1966, and New York: Dell, 1966. A translation, extension, and revision of Shklovskii's *Vselennaia, Zhizn, Razum* (Universe, life, mind.)

Supernovae. Translated from the original manuscript by Literaturprojekt, Innsbruck, Austria. Interscience

Monographs and Texts in Physics and Astronomy, vol. 21. New York: Wiley, 1968. 2nd ed. Princeton, NJ: Princeton University Press, 1979.

Stars: Their Birth, Life, and Death. Translated by Richard B. Rodman, foreword by Carl Sagan, prologue by J. P. Ostriker. San Francisco: W. H. Freeman, 1978.

"The Relationship between Supernovae and Their Remnants." *Publications of the Astronomical Society of the Pacific* 92 (1980): 125–126.

"Cosmological Estimate of the Age of Stars Exploding as Type I Supernovae." *Nature* 304 (1983): 513.

With I. G. Mitrofanov. "On the Astronomical Nature of the Sources of Gamma-Ray Bursts." *Monthly Notices of the Royal Astronomical Society* 212 (1985): 545–551.

Five Billion Vodka Bottles to the Moon: Tales of a Soviet Scientist. Translated and adapted by Mary Fleming Zirin and Harold Zirin. New York: W. W. Norton, 1991. Autobiographical tales from Shklovskii's life, written between 1981 and 1984, circulated in typescript within the Soviet scientific community. Twenty-four of the thirty-five samizdat chapters, rearranged in somewhat chronological order and with some digressions eliminated, but charming nonetheless, are presented in English translation in this book. Also, the introduction includes extensive personal reminiscences by the American radio astronomer Herbert Friedman. Parts of some of Shklovskii's tales are quoted, in English translation, in N. S. Kardashev and L. S. Marochnik, "The Shklovsky Phenomenon." In *Astrophysics on the Threshold of the 21st Century,* edited by N. S. Kardashev. Philadelphia: Gordon & Breach, 1992.

OTHER SOURCES

Davidson, Keay. *Carl Sagan: A Life.* New York: John Wiley & Sons, 1999. Thoroughly details Shklovskii's collaboration with Sagan.

Dick, Steven J. *The Biological Universe: The Twentieth-Century Extraterrestrial Life Debate and the Limits of Science.* Cambridge, U.K.: Cambridge University Press, 1966. Discusses the search for extraterrestrial intelligence by Shklovskii and others in the Soviet Union and compatibility with communist ideology.

Eremeeva, A. I. "Political Repression and Personality: The History of Political Repression against Soviet Astronomers." *Journal for the History of Astronomy* 26 (1995): 297–324. Describes the purge of Soviet astronomers.

Friedman, Herbert. "Joseph Shklovsky and X-ray Astronomy." In *Astrophysics on the Threshold of the 21st Century,* edited by N. S. Kardashev. Philadelphia: Gordon & Breach, 1992.

Ginzburg, V. L. "Remarks on My Work in Radio Astronomy." In *The Early Years of Radio Astronomy: Reflections Fifty Years after Jansky's Discovery,* edited by W. T. Sullivan. Cambridge, U.K.: Cambridge University Press, 1984. On a career running parallel to Shklovskii's, including graduate study at the Shternberg State Astronomical Institute and participation in the Brazil eclipse expedition. See also next item.

———. "Notes of an Amateur Astrophysicist." *Annual Review of Astronomy and Astrophysics* 28 (1990): 1–36.

Goldberg, Leo. "Josif Shklovsky: A Personal Reflection." *Sky & Telescope* 70, no. 2 (August 1985): 109.

Greenstein, Jesse, and Rudolph Minkowski. "The Crab Nebula as a Radio Source." *Astrophysical Journal* 118 (1953): 1–15.

McCutcheon, Robert A. "Stalin's Purge of Soviet Astronomers." *Sky & Telescope* 78, no. 4 (October 1989): 352–357.

Minkowski, Rudolph. "The Crab Nebula." *Astrophysical Journal* 96 (1942): 199–213. Reprinted with commentary in *A Source Book in Astronomy & Astrophysics*, edited by Kenneth R. Lang and Owen Gingerich. Cambridge, MA: Harvard University Press, 1979.

Moroz, Vasilii I. "A Short Story about the Doctor." *Astrophysics & Space Science* B252 (1997): 1–2, 5–14.

Oort, Jan H. "The Crab Nebula." *Scientific American* 196, no. 3 (March 1957): 52–60. On Shklovskii's hypothesis of synchrotron radiation as the source of its emission.

Salomonovich, A. E. "The First Steps of Soviet Radio Astronomy." In *The Early Years of Radio Astronomy: Reflections Fifty Years after Jansky's Discovery*, edited by W. T. Sullivan. Cambridge, U.K.: Cambridge University Press, 1984. Comments on Shklovskii and the Brazil expedition.

Shcheglov, P. V. "Iosif Samuilovich Shklovskii." *Quarterly Journal of the Royal Astronomical Society* 27, no. 4 (1986): 700–702. Translated from the Soviet astronomical journal *Astronomicheskii Vestnik* 19, no. 4 (1985): 359–361. This and other Soviet obituaries of Shklovskii, from *Soviet Astronomical Letters* 11, 2 (March–April 1985): 131–132, and *Astronomicheskii Zhurnal* 62 (May–June 1985): 618–619, are available in English translation in the NASA Astrophysics Data System (http://adswww.harvard.edu/). The Soviet obituaries are less informative and revealing of human character.

Strelnitski, Vladimir S. "The Early Post-War History of Soviet Radio Astronomy." *Journal for the History of Astronomy* 26 (1985): 349–362. Comments on Shklovskii and the Brazil expedition.

Sullivan, Walter. "Iosif S. Shklovosky [*sic*], Astronomer, Dies." *New York Times*, 6 March 1985. Herbert Friedman was the source for this brief obituary notice.

van de Hulst, H. C. "Two Great Astrophysicists: Some Personal Reflections." In *Astrophysics on the Threshold of the 21st Century*, edited by N. S. Kardashev. Philadelphia: Gordon & Breach, 1992.

Weaver, Harold. "The Award of the Bruce Gold Medal for 1972 to Professor J. S. Shklovsky." *Mercury* 1 (July–August 1972): 6–7.

Norriss Hetherington

SHOCKLEY, WILLIAM BRADFORD

(*b.* London, United Kingdom, 13 February 1910; *d.* Stanford, California, 12 August 1989), *solid-state physics, invention of the transistor, operations research, eugenics.*

Shockley was one of the most innovative scientists of the twentieth century and a principal figure in establishing the discipline of solid-state physics. Together with John Bardeen and Walter Brattain, he invented the transistor, sharing the 1956 Nobel Prize in Physics with them for this achievement. In particular, he conceived the junction transistor, a solid-state amplifier and switch that was commercialized during the 1950s and eventually led to the microelectronics revolution. In founding the Shockley Semiconductor Laboratory in California, he catalyzed the emergence of Silicon Valley as the epicenter of the global semiconductor industry. As a Stanford University professor during the last two decades of his life, he espoused controversial views on race and intelligence that brought him substantial public attention and notoriety.

Early Years. Shockley was born in London on 13 February 1910, the only son of William Hillman Shockley, a Massachusetts Institute of Technology (MIT)–educated mining engineer and consultant, and Cora May Shockley (née Bradford), who had graduated from Stanford with degrees in art and mathematics. Both Americans, they returned to the United States in 1913 and lived in Palo Alto, California, while the elder Shockley taught mining engineering part time at Stanford. Young William was schooled at home until he was eight, after which he attended private grammar schools. A major influence during this period was Perley Ross, a professor of physics at Stanford and a neighbor, who stimulated his interest in science. In 1923 the family moved to Hollywood, where he attended Hollywood High School for the next four years, graduating in 1927. During his high school years, he began to demonstrate great proficiency in mathematics and science, especially physics.

After a year at the University of California, Southern Branch (now known as UCLA), Shockley transferred in 1928 to the new California Institute of Technology (Caltech) in nearby Pasadena. Under Nobel laureate Robert Millikan, Caltech was then becoming established as one of the premier American institutions of science and technology. There Shockley was exposed to the revolutionary ideas of quantum mechanics by such professors as William Houston, Linus Pauling, and Richard Tolman. In 1932 he drove east to begin graduate study in physics at MIT, doing theoretical research on solid-state physics under John Slater, one of the acknowledged founders of the new discipline. In his PhD dissertation, submitted in early 1936, Shockley calculated the energy-band structure of sodium chloride—the quantum-mechanical energy levels at which electrons can (or cannot) flow through a crystal lattice of this compound. It was among the first attempts to do such calculations for a compound rather than a chemical element.

As a graduate student at MIT, Shockley had met and married Jean Alberta Bailey of Los Angeles while home for the summer of 1933. The couple had their first child,

Alison, the following year. In the summer of 1936, the family relocated from Cambridge, Massachusetts, to New York City. Shockley began his first professional job there as a physicist at Bell Telephone Laboratories, then located in Manhattan. He had been hired by Bell Labs research director Mervin Kelly, who impressed him with the Bell System's need for some kind of solid-state switch to replace the slow, unreliable electromechanical switches then in wide use. The key to Kelly's ultimate vision of electronic switching systems, this device became one of Shockley's major research goals for the next quarter century. He proposed at least two ideas for such a device during the next five years, both based on the compound semiconductor material copper oxide, but neither of them worked as he had hoped.

As it did for almost all U.S. physicists, the onset of World War II interrupted Shockley's research. At first he worked on radar systems at Bell Labs and Western Electric, the manufacturing arm of parent company AT&T. But in the spring of 1942 he was recruited by Philip Morse (under whom he had studied quantum mechanics at MIT) to become the research director of the U.S. Navy's new Anti-Submarine Warfare Operations Research Group. Headquartered initially at Columbia University, this team of scientists and mathematicians applied probability, statistics, and scientific methods to the analysis and improvement of military operations—in particular the naval campaign against German U-boats in the Atlantic Ocean. Operations research and airborne radar systems effectively eliminated this threat by 1943. Following that, Shockley began working in Washington as a special consultant in the office of the secretary of war. Using operations-research methods, he planned and implemented a training program for B-29 crews employing an advanced short-wavelength, high-altitude radar bombing system manufactured by Western Electric. The program proved so effective in the air war against Japan that in October 1946 Shockley was awarded the National Medal of Merit, the nation's highest civilian honor for wartime activities.

The Invention of the Transistor. In early 1945 Shockley returned part time to Bell Labs, which had moved to Murray Hill, New Jersey, and began organizing a solid-state physics research group. Experimental physicists Walter Brattain and Gerald Pearson joined it at the outset; that fall theorist John Bardeen was lured away from the University of Minnesota, where he had planned to return after war ended. Shockley also revived his prewar research on solid-state devices.

In April 1945 he conceived a solid-state switch based on the semiconductor materials silicon and germanium; the technology of these elements had advanced tremendously during wartime radar research. In what is now

called a field-effect transistor, Shockley suggested that a strong electric field applied by a metal plate just above the semiconductor surface would penetrate into the bulk material and dramatically increase the population there of charge carriers—in this case free electrons. A voltage across the semiconductor chip would thus lead to a proportional increase in the current through it. Therefore an electrical signal on the plate could be used to modulate the current flowing through this semiconductor device, which should then act as an amplifier or switch.

But attempts by Brattain and others to make such a device failed miserably in the spring of 1945, and Shockley turned to other research, including the theory of crystalline defects. When Bardeen joined the group that fall, Shockley assigned him the task of trying to understand why, based on the existing semiconductor theory, almost no effect had been observed. In March 1946 Bardeen proposed his surface-state theory: that a layer of electrons drawn to the semiconductor surface by the electric field was blocking penetration of the field into the bulk material, so that no increase in charge carriers could occur.

Based on this hypothesis, Bardeen and Brattain then pursued a long series of experiments that eventually led to their successful invention of the point-contact transistor in December 1947. By a combination of experimental ingenuity, theoretical insight, and plain old serendipity, they stumbled across a technique to overcome the barrier layer by using two closely spaced metal points that contacted the surface of a germanium sliver. As Shockley and Bell Labs executives watched on 23 December 1947, the rickety device amplified 1 KHz AC signals by a factor of forty.

In a memoir written twenty-five years later, Shockley dubbed this breakthrough "a magnificent Christmas present for Bell Labs," which had staunchly supported his group's program of basic research on solid-state physics. But, he continued, "My elation with the group's success was tempered by not being one of the inventors. I experienced frustration that my personal efforts, started more than eight years before, had not resulted in a significant inventive contribution of my own" (Shockley, 1976, p. 612). Shockley also recognized that this fragile, "proof-of-principle" device would be almost impossible to manufacture with stable, reproducible characteristics. Thus only a month later, on 23 January 1948, he conceived his own particular variety of transistor, called the junction transistor. It was a three-layer sandwich of *n*-type and *p*-type germanium or silicon; *n*-type semiconductors have a slight excess—and *p*-type a slight deficit—of electrons. Electrical action at the interfaces, known as *p-n* junctions, between two dissimilar layers perform the same physical function as the point contacts in Bardeen and Brattain's device. In Shockley's junction transistor, a small electrical

William Bradford Shockley. *Shockley in his laboratory with transistor.* AP IMAGES.

signal on the inner, or "base," layer—the meat in the sandwich—would modulate the current flowing from end to end through the device.

But the successful operation of the junction transistor depended upon a new, hypothetical process that Shockley called "minority carrier injection," which was not initially obvious. Quantum mechanical entities called "holes"— which correspond to the electron deficits in a crystal lattice and respond like positively charged entities to an electric field—had to be able to survive at least briefly in the presence of an excess of electrons. Or vice versa. Normally an electron and a hole will "recombine" to produce light when they meet, but Shockley guessed that they

might last long enough in close proximity for his junction transistor to work. After a February 1948 experiment at Bell Labs showed that minority carrier injection did indeed occur, he boldly announced his invention to Bardeen, Brattain, and other surprised colleagues.

Shockley published his detailed theory of this device as "The Theory of *p-n* Junctions in Semiconductors and *p-n* Junction Transistors" in the January 1949 issue of the *Bell System Technical Journal.* When it appeared, no successful demonstration of such a device had yet occurred. But that April Morgan Sparks, a physical chemist in Shockley's group, fabricated a crude junction transistor from germanium that amplified signals by up to sixteen times. Shockley was then busy writing up this research for a book, *Electrons and Holes in Semiconductors*. Published by Van Nostrand in 1950, it quickly became the bible of the emerging semiconductor industry.

The successful development of a commercial junction transistor took another two years, prodded by military requirements for proximity fuses in the Korean War. A crucial enabling technology was the growth of large single crystals of germanium by Bell Labs chemist Gordon Teal; electrons and holes can drift faster and therefore farther in crystalline semiconductor materials under the influence of an electric field. In the spring of 1951, Sparks and Teal succeeded in fabricating germanium junction transistors with narrow base layers less than 50 micrometers thick that amplified electrical signals above 1 megahertz. Consuming only microwatts of power, these transistors exceeded the performance of point-contact transistors in every respect. News of this breakthrough was announced by Bell Labs on 4 July 1951; that same month it was published in a *Physical Review* article by Shockley, Sparks, and Teal.

Shockley continued to invent, patent, and publish at a feverish rate for the next few years. One of his most noteworthy inventions was the junction field-effect transistor, which combined features of these two approaches to transistor design. Another important conception was the four-layer *npnp* diode, or "avalanche" diode, a bistable device with potential applications in electronic switching systems. In a 1954 reorganization, he became the head of a new transistor physics group at Bell Labs responsible for spearheading research on these kinds of advanced devices.

During the decade after World War II, Shockley also maintained the close connections with the military that he had developed during wartime. Beginning in 1947, he served on the policy committee of the Joint Research and Development Board of the armed services, specializing in electronics. With Vannevar Bush, who had led the U.S. Office of Scientific Research and Development during the war, he helped establish the Weapons Systems Evaluation Group at the Defense Department in 1948. This operations-research-style group brought civilian researchers into the Pentagon from industry and academia; they worked closely with military analysts, advising the armed services on highly sophisticated Cold War weaponry such as the hydrogen bomb, intercontinental ballistic missiles, and anti-ballistic-missile systems. Shockley finally stepped in as deputy director of this group for a year, in 1954 to 1955.

He also began to get increasingly widespread recognition in the scientific community for his achievements. In April 1951 he became a member of the National Academy of Sciences, one of the youngest scientists ever to attain this honor. In 1953 the American Physical Society

awarded Shockley its first Oliver E. Buckley Prize for advancements in solid-state and condensed-matter physics. And in 1954 he received the National Academy's prestigious Comstock Prize, awarded every five years for major advances in electricity and magnetism.

But these achievements and honors came at the cost of mounting disaffection from his family. Although close to his daughter Alison, Shockley grew distant from his two sons William and Richard, born in 1942 and 1947, because of the amount of time he spent away from home. This deterioration culminated in a 1955 divorce from his wife Jean, at the time recovering from uterine cancer. That November he remarried, to Emmy Lanning, a psychiatric nurse he had met in Washington while working at the Pentagon.

Shockley Semiconductor Laboratory. Shockley also was increasingly dissatisfied with his employment at Bell Labs. Under his leadership, the transistor physics group had spearheaded development of high-frequency junction transistors based on the diffusion of chemical impurities to form extremely narrow base layers in crystalline silicon. These transistors are able to amplify and switch electrical signals at frequencies above 100 MHz, typical in FM radio and television transmission. But he felt his advancement at the labs was blocked, and he wanted to make his fortune in the emerging semiconductor industry.

Thus in the summer of 1955, with Mervin Kelly's blessings, he began to seek outside financial support to found his own semiconductor Research & Development company. That September he met with fellow Caltech alumnus Arnold Beckman, a successful chemist and businessman who had founded Beckman Industries; they agreed to set up Shockley Semiconductor Laboratory in California as a division of Beckman Industries. Their agreement stated that "the development of automatic means for the production of diffused-base transistors" was to be one of its principal projects.

Shockley began recruiting scientists and engineers for the new firm, which in February 1956 formally began operations near Palo Alto in Mountain View. Among his early recruits were Robert Noyce, who had earned his PhD in physics from MIT and was working on transistors at Philco, and Gordon Moore, a Caltech-educated physical chemist. With about a dozen other scientists and engineers, they toasted their leader that November, after it was announced that he would share the 1956 Nobel Prize in Physics with Bardeen and Brattain for the invention of the transistor.

But all was not well at the fledgling semiconductor firm, the first of its kind in northern California. Shockley repeatedly took his talented recruits off work related to the main goal of developing diffused-base transistors from silicon and reassigned them to research on the junction field-effect transistor, the four-layer diode, and other more challenging projects that were far from commercialization. Add to that his extremely difficult management style, and the seeds of a revolt began to take root among his technical staff.

In September 1957 eight of his best scientists and engineers including Noyce and Moore resigned to form the Fairchild Semiconductor Corporation with funding from the Fairchild Camera and Instrument Company of Syosset, New York. Within a year this renegade firm had manufactured silicon diffused-base transistors for sale to IBM Corporation and was operating profitably. In March 1961 Fairchild began to market its Micrologic series of integrated circuits built around silicon transistors, the first microelectronic circuits to be commercialized. During the early 1960s, these and successive microcircuits found quick application in the Minuteman ballistic missile system and the Apollo Moon-landing project. Later that decade, Noyce and Moore left Fairchild to found the Intel Corporation.

The Shockley Semiconductor Laboratory struggled on under Shockley's leadership. He hired another group of scientists and engineers, which concentrated most of its efforts on the four-layer diode, called the Shockley diode, which he viewed as the key to Kelly's vision of electronic telephone switching systems. But it proved far too difficult to manufacture in quantity with reliable, reproducible characteristics. The company was reorganized into the Shockley Transistor Corporation in 1958 and sold to the Clevite Corporation in 1960, never having realized a profit.

During these Mountain View and Palo Alto years, Shockley kept on making valuable contributions to the literature on semiconductor physics. With Noyce and another scientist, he wrote an important 1957 article on electron-hole recombination in *p-n* junctions, and in 1961 coauthored a theoretical paper on the efficiency of photovoltaic cells. But his creative scientific and technological career essentially ended in 1961 after a disastrous head-on automobile collision that almost killed him and left him and Emmy hospitalized for months. Afterward his scientific productivity slowed to a crawl.

The Stanford Years. In 1963 Stanford University invited Shockley to join its faculty as the new Alexander M. Poniatoff Professor of Engineering and Applied Science. At first it was a part-time position, as he still had ongoing responsibilities directing the company. He taught seminars and advised graduate students in semiconductor physics and electronics. Then he branched out into the study of human creativity, especially as applied to science and mathematics, lecturing a freshman course on what is now known as conceptual blockbusting. He began publishing on the subject, advocating his own "try simplest cases first" approach to problem solving. In 1965, after Clevite sold the company to International Telephone and Telegraph, Shockley returned to Bell Labs part time as a special consultant on scientific training, while continuing to teach at Stanford. He retired from Stanford in 1972 and from Bell Labs in 1975.

About this time Shockley also began to espouse controversial ideas on race and intelligence, initially in connection with two Nobel symposia at the Gustavus Adolphus College in Minnesota in 1963 and 1965. He argued that people of lesser intelligence (as determined by IQ tests) appeared to have more children and that intelligence was a genetically inheritable trait. Thus a kind of reverse evolution or "dysgenics," as he termed it, is unwittingly at play in advanced societies because almost everyone survives today thanks to modern medicine. The fact that he was a Nobel laureate and a Stanford professor meant that these observations attracted major media attention, helping to stoke raging fires of controversy in the mid-1960s. Interviews in *U.S. News and World Report* (1965) and *Playboy* (1980) brought Shockley widespread notoriety and charges of racism after he noted that African Americans generally scored well below average on IQ tests. He began advocating a version of eugenics, based on his operations-research approach to improving human quality, as he viewed it. He never abandoned this topic, pursuing nearly every opportunity to expound his views on it for the rest of his life. Because of his obsession with the subject, his friends and colleagues increasingly avoided contact with him as he aged.

In 1987 Shockley learned that he had prostate cancer but did not choose to undergo surgery. Within a year it had metastasized to his bones and he began receiving x-ray treatments, to little avail. He died at home on the morning of 12 August 1989, age 79.

At the time of his death, Shockley had over one hundred publications in scientific and technical journals, as well as more than ninety patents awarded him, including the crucial U.S. Patent 2,569,347 (issued 25 September 1951) on the junction transistor. In addition to being a member of the National Academy of Sciences, he was a Fellow of the American Academy of Arts and Sciences, the American Physical Society, and the Institute of Electrical and Electronics Engineers. His colleagues recall his intellectual brilliance, especially how quickly he could dig down to the core issues of a scientific or technological problem, reducing it to fundamentals that could be readily tested by experimental or theoretical means. The physics he pursued was usually closely related to practical devices that could have significant impacts on our lives.

He was also adept at explaining physics to nonspecialists, in both his writings and lectures.

In addition to all his scientific and technological achievements, Shockley was an accomplished rock climber and mountaineer, credited with several first ascents. In the 1960s he began pursuing the sport of sailing, especially after his 1961 accident, and soon became skilled at it, winning local competitions. He was also an excellent amateur magician, often using parlor tricks to enhance his scientific presentations.

Shockley's greatest legacies are the transistor, arguably the most important invention of the twentieth century, and the rise of Silicon Valley as the epicenter of the global semiconductor industry. Far more than any other person, he relentlessly pursued the goal of a solid-state amplifier and switch from a hazy conception to its eventual realization as the commercial product that has become ubiquitous in daily life. Shockley also brought the technologies of silicon and diffusion from Bell Labs to the San Francisco Bay area, while gathering together the team of talented scientists and engineers who extended these technologies at Fairchild Semiconductor and took the next step of commercializing integrated circuits. To knowledgeable observers, he deserves to be recognized as the "father of Silicon Valley." Few, if any, people have had a greater impact on what it means to be modern.

BIBLIOGRAPHY

The Department of Special Collections in the Green Library at Stanford University has an extensive collection of documents left by Shockley and his parents.

WORKS BY SHOCKLEY

"Electronic Energy Bands in Sodium Chloride." *Physical Review* 50 (1936): 754–759. Published version of Shockley's MIT PhD dissertation.

"The Theory of *p-n* Junctions in Semiconductors and *p-n* Junction Transistors." *Bell System Technical Journal* 28 (1949): 435–489. First detailed theory of *p-n* junctions.

Electrons and Holes in Semiconductors. Princeton, NJ: Van Nostrand, 1950. Shockley's best-known book, which became a bible of the semiconductor industry in the 1950s.

With M. Sparks and G. K. Teal. "*p-n* Junction Transistors." *Physical Review* 83 (1951): 151–162. Describes the fabrication and operation of microwatt junction transistors.

"Transistor Electronics: Imperfections, Unipolar and Analog Transistors." *Proceedings of the Institute of Radio Engineers* 40 (1952): 1289–1313. On the behavior of electrons and holes in nearly perfect crystalline semiconductors.

With C.-T. Sah and R. N. Noyce, "Carrier Generation and Recombination in *p-n* Junctions and *p-n* Junction Characteristics." *Proceedings of the Institute of Radio Engineers* 45 (1957): 1228–1243. Detailed theory of electron-hole recombination in *p-n* junctions.

With H. J. Queisser. "Detailed Balance Limit of Efficiency of *p-n* Junction Solar Cells." *Journal of Applied Physics* 32 (1961): 510–519. Theory of solar-cell efficiency.

"The Path to the Conception of the Junction Transistor." *IEEE Transactions on Electron Devices* 23 (1976): 597–620. Historical recollection of influences and events that led Shockley to his invention of the junction transistor.

OTHER SOURCES

Golson, G. Barry, ed., *William Shockley: The* Playboy *Interviews*. New York: Perigee Books (Putnam Publishing Group), 1983. Shockley's views on race, intelligence, eugenics and dysgenics, with the editor's interpretations.

Moll, John. "William Bradford Shockley: February 13, 1910—August 12, 1989." In *Biographical Memoirs*, vol. 68. Washington, DC: National Academy of Sciences, 1996. Available from http://www.nap.edu/readingroom/books/biomems/wshockley.html. The official National Academy of Sciences biography of Shockley, by a scientist who worked closely with him at Bell Labs.

Riordan, Michael, and Lillian Hoddeson. *Crystal Fire: The Birth of the Information Age*. New York: W. W. Norton, 1997. The definitive history of the transistor's invention and development, with emphasis on the lives and scientific activities of Bardeen, Brattain, and Shockley.

Shurkin, Joel. *Broken Genius: The Rise and Fall of William Shockley, Creator of the Electronic Age*. London: Macmillan, 2006. A complete biography, especially strong on Shockley's early years, wartime activities, and views on eugenics.

Michael Riordan

SHOEMAKER, EUGENE MERLE (*b.* Los Angeles, California, 28 April, 1928; *d.* near Alice Springs, Australia, 18 July 1997), *space science, astrogeology, studies of the populations of comets and asteroids, specifically those that could strike the Earth.*

Shoemaker began a new science—the history of the solar system and the often violent interactions among the planets—called astrogeology. His early studies of lunar craters suggested that these features were the result of impacts, and that the crater record could provide an indication of the level of risk by impact to the Earth. These studies led to his training of astronauts for the Apollo program in the 1960s. Shoemaker's interests then turned from the effects of impact to the objects themselves, the comets and asteroids that do the impacting. This phase of his career reached its climax in July 1994, when the comet he helped to discover, Shoemaker-Levy 9, collided with Jupiter in a cosmic and forceful demonstration of his ideas.

Early Life. Gene Shoemaker's interest in geology began with the gift of a set of marbles from his mother in 1935, when he was seven years old. These small toys contained some unusual stones like agate, and they set him off to his first geological field trips searching his family neighborhood collecting interesting rocks. The next summer Shoemaker traveled with his father to South Dakota's Black Hills. The boy was so taken with the rose quartz and other minerals in the area that he gathered many samples. By the time the young Shoemaker entered fifth grade, he was being educated in Buffalo, NY, whose Museum of Science had a program that involved evening classes in sciences as diverse as mineralogy and biology. The course even used college-level textbooks. Shoemaker's group went on field trips to a place south of Buffalo called Eighteen Mile Creek, where Shoemaker reveled in the rich trilobite collections in the Devonian rocks there.

After completing high school in Los Angeles, Shoemaker was accepted at Caltech, where he completed his undergraduate degree and where he also tried his hand as a cheerleader. He went on to Princeton for his PhD and continued with fieldwork with a search for uranium in a Northern Arizona field of old volcanoes called the Hopi Buttes. His earliest major discoveries as a geologist were deposits of uranium in the eroded volcanic vents of those long-extinct volcanoes. But it was the ancient volcanism itself that really captured the young geologist's attention. The surrounding craters seemed similar to what he had seen in pictures of the Moon. Was it possible, he thought, that lunar craters were the result of a similar process?

In 1948, Shoemaker decided to go to the Moon. His dream began on the evening of 28 April, his twentieth birthday, as the Moon rose in the southeastern sky. A few days past full, it shone beautifully on the Colorado plateau near West Vancoram, where he was helping prepare for the diamond-drilling project that would search for a badly needed supply of uranium ore. As he drove the five miles from West Vacoram to Naturita, at the headquarters of the Vanadium Corporation of America, for his breakfast, he stared at the rising gibbous Moon and decided, then and there, that he wanted to go to the Moon. "I want to be one of the first people on the Moon. Why will we go to the Moon? To explore it, of course! And who is the best person to do that? A geologist, of course!" (quoted in Levy, p. 27). On that particular morning, the planet Jupiter, which would play a critical role in Shoemaker's later life, shone just three degrees to the west of the Moon.

That same spring Shoemaker met Carolyn Spellman, the sister of his college roommate. Impressed with his passion, Carolyn listened to his explanations of the Earth that filled her with wonder. The couple was married in 1951 and in their early years together, Carolyn often joined Shoemaker in his field work. They were not married long

before getting their first view of meteor crater in Arizona, the crater that would mark the first part of Shoemaker's career. At the end of a long day of fieldwork the young couple drove quickly toward the site, but since they could not afford the admission fee, they drove up an access road on the west side of the crater. They left their jeep and crawled up the hill to the top of the butte. The sun was already setting over the structure, and the long shadows offered a magnificent view. Although they stayed just a few minutes, their first view of the crater was never forgotten.

Shoemaker's early career was creative and filled with work in the field. The studies that he did on the Hopi Buttes would later prove useful in planning for the Apollo missions. Shoemaker thought that it was a good idea to look for a lunar site, like the Davy catena, that was thought at the time to be a structurally controlled string of volcanic craters. If that was true, then the astronauts might find xenoliths, or rock fragments blown out from beneath the lunar surface that might show the deeper structure of the Moon. The Davy Catena was not selected, but in 1993, the discovery of the chain of comets called Shoemaker-Levy 9 demonstrated that the catena was formed not from volcanoes but from an ancient comet that grazed the atmosphere of the Earth, broke apart, and then went on, in multiple pieces, to strike the Moon.

Two years after the young geologist's visit to Meteor Crater, Shoemaker considered the formation again. His new research focused attention on small structures called evaporites dug up by an oil company a few dozen miles east of the crater. Evaporites are the signature of salt flats, and they led to a suggestion by geologist Dorsey Hager that the crater was the result of one that collapsed. Although Shoemaker doubted that theory, he decided to return to the crater and try to test the conclusion of a geologist, Grove Karl Gilbert, from several decades earlier. Gilbert's idea was that the crater was the remains of a volcanic steam explosion. Shoemaker's work led to an unexpected find: The glass was Coconino sandstone, the same rock that is present in such quantities in the Grand Canyon, but its quartz was fused somehow, the end result of a process that involves temperatures of about 1,500 degrees Celsius, some 300 degrees higher than the hottest lava flow. Meteor Crater could not be the result of volcanism, nor could the dynamics of a collapsing salt dome explain temperatures as hot as this. Shoemaker began to suspect that the only mechanism that could generate this much heat was the explosive impact of an asteroid from space as it struck the Earth.

On their way to the 1960 Geological Congress in Copenhagen, he and his wife stopped to explore Bavaria's Rieskessel, a 24-kilometer diameter basin surrounding the town of Nördlingen. "I took one look at these rocks with a hand lens" Shoemaker recalled; "and there was no question these were impact rocks!" (Shoemaker, interview with author, 1993). The next morning the couple made their way to the St. George's Cathedral, which dominated the village. As they looked up at the tall spires, Shoemaker took out his field lens and studied the stone of the cathedral. The building was made of rock that included suevite, a mineral that he believed had been shocked and partially melted by the Ries impact. This was a major discovery, the first find of a major impact on Earth: The object that fell there was not a stadium-sized rock but something the size of a village.

At the Dawn of the Space Age. In the early 1960s, Shoemaker joined Gerard Kuiper and Harold Urey to build the scientific part of NASA's Ranger program, designed as the first unmanned Moon landing. Then in 1963, Shoemaker was offered a highly coveted position as Principal Investigator of Surveyor's television experiment. Where Ranger was a quick slam into the Moon, Surveyor would landing softly to begin a weeklong exploration. But first the Ranger craft had to show some success. After multiple failures, *Ranger 7* was launched to the Moon in 1964. The Atlas launch vehicle performed flawlessly, and the Agena successfully put the Ranger craft into a trajectory to the Moon. For the next three days the group waited as the spacecraft approached 600 miles from the Moon. At that distance the cameras should turn on; cautiously, nervously, an engineer dispatched the signal to turn on the cameras.

"We have video!" came the excited announcement. It was an incredible moment. "Everyone was jumping up and down," Shoemaker raved. "We didn't even know what the pictures were yet, but that didn't matter. There were pictures!" (Shoemaker, interview with author, 1992). On a very small scale, little Ranger was repeating a kind of episode that the Moon was very familiar with, an impact.

Ranger impacted near a ray from the giant crater Tycho, one of the Moon's most recent large impact craters. Formed some 100 million years ago, the crater is the remains of an impact event of some long-gone comet or asteroid. As the incoming object struck, lunar rock shot out in all directions, landing again in a series of ray structures that stretch halfway around the Moon. *Ranger 7* provided the scientists with a view of innumerable secondary craterlets that range in size from doors to rooms.

After two more successful Rangers, it was time to let the first Surveyor craft loose on the Moon's prehistoric surface. On 30 May 1966, Surveyor soared aloft aboard an Atlas-Centaur rocket. As the craft approached a critical distance of sixty miles from the Moon's Oceanus Procellarum, it was still racing along at 6,000 miles per hour. The retrofiring engine turned on exactly as scheduled, slowing the craft to 250 miles per hour. It shut off exactly

on schedule. Surveyor was now using an onboard altimeter to check its progress. After the retrorockets fell away, three smaller rockets took over, firing until the craft slowed almost to a stop just thirteen feet above the surface of the Moon. To leave the surface below as pristine as possible, these rockets then shut down. Surveyor fell to a landing near the crater Flamsteed, the strong shock absorbers in its landing legs absorbing much of the shock. The spacecraft was on the Moon, its systems operating perfectly. In Mission control, the Shoemaker team was astounded. "It was the most surprised bunch of people you ever saw!" he recalled that incredible week as he watched the Sun climb over the craft's landing site. (Shoemaker, interview with author, 1993).

To the Moon. Almost seven years after this challenge, the United States was finally ready to send humans to the Moon, and Shoemaker played a major part of that effort. His prime hope, to go personally to the Moon, was dashed when he was diagnosed with Addison's disease. His dream to go there ended during the summer of 1963, but not his role in the program. In 1965, he was appointed principal investigator for the field geology experiments for Project Apollo. It was a grand challenge, and put him in direct involvement with the astronauts and at the center of one of the most prestigious national scientific efforts in the history of the United States.

As training proceeded, Shoemaker and his team at the U.S. Geological Survey modeled a landing site on the Moon. Standing on the crater-strewn surface was a full-size mockup of the Lunar Excursion Module, or LEM, all arranged so that the geologists could practice good field techniques. "Some of those test pilots were very good observers," Shoemaker remembers, adding how their flight training and alertness gave them the potential to be ideal field geologists—if they could get sufficient training. Under the direction of Gordon Swann, the astronauts also trained in places as diverse as Meteor Crater, Grand Canyon, and the volcanic islands of Hawaii and Iceland.

On 16 July 1969, three of Shoemaker's field geology students—Neil Armstrong, Buzz Aldrin, and Michael Collins—waited to begin a field excursion of their own. In a roar of millions of gallons of burning kerosene, the Saturn 5 rocket beneath them surged to life and bore the three men away from Earth. Shoemaker and his wife were at Cape Kennedy watching. Armstrong and Aldrin remained on the surface at Tranquility Base for more than two hours. Armstrong noted big boulders more than two feet across. He thought they were basaltic, and added that they have probably 2 percent white minerals in them, white crystals. Armstrong's 90-minute moon walk, in Shoemaker's view, was one of the best of the entire Apollo program: "He saw more stuff, and he made more pertinent observations, in the precious little time he had on the surface, than some of the astronauts who followed him. Armstrong's descriptions were lucid and accurate." (Shoemaker, interview with author, 1992).

Even as the astronauts returned from man's first visit to the Moon, Shoemaker's interest in NASA's program was declining. On 8 October 1969, thinking that he was talking off the record to a friendly Caltech audience, he announced his resignation from his work with Project Apollo. It was a sharp rebuke of NASA for considering the astronauts as passengers on a trip to the Moon, their tasks largely limited to setting up and switching on experiments. He believed that NASA wanted to get the men there and back without any mishaps, as cheaply and as safely as possible. His conclusion was that the space agency had no desire to improve Apollo so that the project would teach something about the Moon's geology. Although he was somewhat correct in his assessment, he admitted later that Apollo's geological yield was impressive, resulting in annual Apollo lunar science conferences that continued into the twenty-first century.

A Search for Cosmic Threats to Earth. Shoemaker rejoined his alma mater, the California Institute of Technology, as a research associate in 1968, and shortly after became chairman of its Division of Geological and Planetary Sciences. During the last years of the 1960s, virtually all of his time was spent, vicariously at least, on the Moon, with the exception of some field trips to Meteor Crater with Caltech undergrads. The chairmanship of the division, however, was not a task that he could do by remote. It would require his full attention, and his moving from Flagstaff to California at least while the institute was in session.

It was during these busy days as chairman that Shoemaker's research sights made a ninety-degree turn. His goal to study impacts in the solar system would remain the same, but the strategy would shift. Instead of studying the Moon's record of impacts, he now turned to the impacting objects themselves, the comets and asteroids that threatened every world in the solar system. The beginning of this search for asteroids and comets dates from his seminal 1963 paper on "Interplanetary Correlation of Geologic Time." The code in which these planetary histories are recorded, Shoemaker noted, consists of bodies of rock and rock debris. This code will be cracked by geologic mapping, for it is the spatial relationship of different bodies of rock that tells the sequence of events.

Shoemaker knew that in order for a statistical history of the Earth's encounters with these bodies to make sense, many more Earth-approaching asteroids had to be found. He planned to apply for telescope time and conduct the science, but at this early stage he expected to do little

Eugene Merle Shoemaker. *Shoemaker looking through a telescope.* © **ROGER RESSMEYER.**

direct observing. It turned out that Caltech's Palomar Observatory, home of the 200-inch reflector, then the world's largest telescope, had a small 18-inch diameter Schmidt telescope that was only used occasionally. Shoemaker jumped at the prospect of putting this beautiful instrument to regular use. With funds still remaining from his role in the Apollo project, Shoemaker and his colleague Eleanor Helin drew up a proposal in 1972 for a preliminary search for asteroids in the vicinity of the Earth. At the time, he suspected that about two thousand asteroids two kilometers or larger, could be in orbits that could cross that of the Earth and hence be a threat to this planet, each one packing the wallop of a multimegaton bomb. Shoemaker calculated that by photographing 250 different fields of the sky each year, they would perhaps find some four collision candidates.

Despite slow progress at first, Shoemaker's team doubled the count of Earth-crossing asteroids observed over the last century in just five years. He brought the tools of the geologist, including a stereomicroscope, to the program's task of looking for rocks in the sky. The amazing aspect about Shoemaker during this period was that he could divide his time among many different projects and yet remain centered on his favorite theme of impact geology.

The program was immensely successful, especially after 1980, when Carolyn joined it. Her sharp eye led to the program's many finds: During its run, which ended in June 1996, it yielded hundreds of asteroids, many of them on Earth-crossing orbits, and thirty-two comets. But all those successes paled before the events of March 1993.

Comet Shoemaker-Levy 9 and Jupiter. On the partly clouded evening of March 23, Shoemaker, his wife, and David Levy took two photographs of an area of the sky on which, two days later, the comet Shoemaker-Levy 9 was found. At least as far back as 1929, the comet was in orbit about Jupiter. In July 1992 it passed so close to the giant planet that tidal forces tore it apart into twenty-one separate fragments. Two years later, in July 1994 the comet collided with Jupiter, for the first time ever giving people an idea of what happens when a comet hits a planet.

The discovery began a period that utterly dominated Levy's and the Shoemakers' lives for the next sixteen months. Carl Sagan paid his greatest tribute to the man whose vision made possible its discovery: "This is a most extraordinary find," he said at a Colorado meeting in the fall of 1993. "There are those whose idea of a good time is to stay up on cold nights taking pictures. They get enormous pleasure out of it: [This team] has been at this before—Shoemaker-Levy 9 means that this is their ninth periodic comet find... ."

If the discovery of a comet that was split into twenty-one pieces because of a close encounter with Jupiter was unusual, the course of that comet after its discovery was extraordinary. On 22 May, the International astronomical Union's Central Bureau for Astronomical Telegrams announced that a collision of the comet with Jupiter in July 1994 was likely. The events which followed proved the strength of Shoemaker's ideas about the importance of impacts for a full week on media outlets around the world.

During the week of the comet impacts, Shoemaker was asked to lead a commission designed to set in motion a new era of automated comet and asteroid searches, a set of searches which would completely shut down the photographic technology that had led to his great success. During this period he and Carolyn continued their annual crater surveys they did each July and August in Australia. On 18 July 1997, three years to the day after the largest fragment of Shoemaker-Levy 9 collided with Jupiter, Shoemaker was killed in an auto accident in Australia.

Perhaps the best summary of Shoemaker's own career comes from a lecture he gave a few weeks before his death,

at Queen's University in Canada. Shoemaker's lecture was a beautiful summary of his life's work, and it emphasized his research in cratering on the Moon, in Australia, young features like Meteor Crater and Wabar, and comets. He ended by suggesting that every 26- to 35-million-years, comets in the outer solar system are perturbed, or jostled, when the solar system crosses the densely populated plane of the Milky Way galaxy, and that people are very close to a plane crossing now. The isotope helium-3, once thought to be the product of volcanic eruptions, may actually be of interplanetary origin, having been brought to Earth by dust particles from comets. What caused this periodic flux in the numbers of comets blanketing the sky? Shoemaker suspected that as the solar system pushes its way, like a sine wave, up and down in the galaxy, it encounters the dense plane of this galaxy every thirty million years. The increased gravitational disturbances that are related to the plane crossing may increase the chances that Earth, and the other planets, get struck by comets that have been perturbed into the inner part of the solar system. Ending his presentation with his typical grand flourish, Shoemaker concluded that the study of the impact history of Earth is in reality a way to study the history of the motion of the Earth in the galaxy.

BIBLIOGRAPHY

WORKS BY SHOEMAKER

With R. J. Hackman and R. E. Eggleton. "Interplanetary Correlation of Geologic Time." In *Proceedings of the Seventh Annual Meeting of the American Astronautical Society, Dallas, Texas, January 16-18, 1961*. Advances in the Astronautical Sciences, vol. 8: New York, Plenum Press, 1963.

Ruth Northcott Lecture, Royal Astronomical Society of Canada, Queen's University, June 1997.

"Impact Cratering through Geologic Time." *Journal of the Royal Astronomical Society of Canada* 92 (1998) 297–309.

OTHER SOURCES

Gilbert, Grove Karl. "The Origin of Hypotheses: Illustrated by the Discussion of a Topographic Problem." Presidential Address, The Geological Society of Washington, March 1895. See also "The Origin of Hypotheses, Illustrated by the Discussion of a Topographic Problem." *Science*, new series, 3 (1896): 1–13.

Levy, David H. *Shoemaker by Levy: The Man Who Made an Impact*. Princeton, NJ: Princeton University Press, 2000. Contains a complete Shoemaker bibliography.

Marsden, Brian. *International Astronomical Union Circulars* 5800 and 5801, 22 May 1993. Collision of Shoemaker-Levy 9 with Jupiter was probable.

Sagan, Carl. Lecture to the Division of Planetary Sciences, American Astronomical Society, October 1993.

David Levy

SHTERN, LINA SOLOMONOVNA

(also Stern, Schtern) (*b.* Libava [Libau, Liepaja], Latvia, 14 [26] August 1878; *d.* Moscow, 7 March 1968), *biochemistry, chemical physiology.*

Shtern made important contributions to biochemistry and chemical physiology. She was one of the founders of modern chemical physiology in the USSR. She did pioneering work on the hematoencephalic barrier, that is, the frontier between the blood and the cerebrospinal fluid around the brain (the blood-brain barrier). During her long life she published more than 500 scientific articles. She was the founder and chief editor (until her arrest) of the *Bulletin of Experimental Biology and Medicine,* and she was in the editorial board of several other scientific journals.

Early Life. Born in a Jewish family in czarist Russia, educated and employed in Switzerland, later a professor in the Soviet Union, Lina S. Shtern was a cosmopolitan long before the Soviet Union's anti-Semitic instigators denounced people such as her as (bad) Jews using the word *cosmopolitan* instead of *Jew.*

Shtern was born in the family of a successful merchant, and her grandfather was a rabbi. Because of the discrimination against Jews in czarist Russia, Jewish students had to study mostly in foreign countries, among others in Germany. Like many Jewish women from Russia, Lina Shtern after school went to Switzerland and became one of the Russian women students at the University of Geneva. Shtern studied medicine, and in 1903 she received her doctoral degree. Because of the hopeless job situation for women scientists, and especially women Jews, in Russia, Shtern stayed in Switzerland. After completing her dissertation she got an assistant position; in 1906 she received the *venia legendi* (privatdozent); and finally, in 1917, she became professor of physiological chemistry at the University of Geneva. She was a disciple of Jean-Louis Prevost Jr. (1838–1927) and worked together with his successor Federico Battelli (1867–1941). Until 1925 she succeeded in a remarkable scientific career as one of the first famous women scientists in Europe. In a short autobiographical sketch Shtern described herself as a feminist (Shtern, 1930, p. 140).

Move to Moscow. Attracted by the socialist experiment in the Soviet Union, Shtern decided in the middle of 1920s to move to the Soviet Union. From 1925 onward she lived and worked in Moscow. She became a full professor of physiology at the second Moscow University (the University for Medicine), and in 1929 she became director of her own scientific research institute, the Institute for Physiology. Her institute first belonged to the ministry (commis-sariat) for higher education; later it was one of the academic institutes of the Academy of Science of the USSR. She described the aim of her institute in some letters to the neuroscientists Ce'cile (1875–1962) and Oskar (1870–1959) Vogt in Berlin: she wanted to establish a research program to investigate physiology from the different perspectives of medicine, biology, and chemistry. And she wanted to create an international research institute, where scientists from all countries could work and publish together. This aim she could not fully realize because of the Stalinist policy, yet for more than ten years, she and her team had many scientific successes.

In 1939 Shtern was elected a full member of the Academy of Science of the USSR, the first woman scientist of the USSR to be thus honored. Furthermore, in 1944 she became a member of the newly established Academy of Medical Sciences of the USSR. Already in 1932 she had become a member of the oldest German Academy of Science (Deutsche Akademie der Naturforscher), the Leopoldina; but because of the Nazi regime and its racist policy, she was stricken from the membership list soon after the nomination. After 1945 she was again a member of the Leopoldina.

Although she had been a member of the Communist Party since 1939, Shtern began to act in politics only when the German troops overtook the Soviet Union in June 1941. Asked to participate in antifascist committees, Shtern accepted and became member of several such committees. In 1941–1942 she joined the most important one: she became member of the presidium of the Jewish Anti-Fascist Committee (JAC), headed by the famous Yiddish actor Solomon Michoels (Mikhoels; 1890–1948). During World War II (the "great patriotic war," as it was named in the USSR), Shtern worked on war medicine.

Persecution by the Soviets. In 1948 the tragic part of her life began. Because of the anti-Semitic policy of the Soviet State—the government and the leaders of the Communist Party—a campaign was started against "cosmopolitism," which led soon to arrests and deaths, and new discriminations against Jews were established in all spheres of life. Officially stopped in 1953 (after the death of Joseph Stalin), the anti-Semitic discrimination policy in reality never was ended in the Soviet Union, with fewer arrests after 1953, but with strong barriers against Jews in several professions, including scientific ones.

On 27 January 1948, Shtern was arrested by the MVD. (The secret service in Russia/USSR/Russia was renamed several times: first it was Cheka, then GPU, later OGPU, then NKVD, after 1945 MVD and MGB, then KGB; in the early twenty-first century it is FSB.) She was taken to the notorious Lubjanka prison in Moscow, later to the awful prison Lefortovo. She was interrogated, beaten, and tortured several times. From 1949 to 1952 she was in prison, together with fourteen comrades from the JAC. The trial was planned and prepared at the highest level of the state, under Stalin's leadership. And the end was already fixed: the death penalty. Because some of the prisoners, including Lina Shtern, fought very courageously, the trial was secret, from 8 May to 18 July 1952 (Naumov, 1994; Rubinstein & Naumov, 2001). Although the accused prisoners defended themselves during this trial for several weeks and openly spoke about the tortures and the falsification of testimony by the prosecutors, Stalin and his close circle decided to kill them. In August 1952 in Moscow, thirteen comrades were killed (one died in the prison). But a wonder happened to Lina Shtern: the dictator Stalin himself struck out her name from the list of the death candidates. More than half a century later there are only rumors about the reason for that; most probably Stalin believed in her capacity as a scientist and hoped she would obtain new medical results that would allow him to live longer.

Thus, Shtern survived the trial and was sent in 1952 by the MVD into exile in Jambul (Central Asia). Fortunately, she was still a member of the Academy of Science of the USSR, therefore, her salary helped her to survive the difficult living conditions of her exile in a small village. After Stalin's death and the first rehabilitations of his victims, Shtern was allowed to come back to Moscow in June 1953. She never got back her own institute, which had been closed in 1948. She got only a position as head of the physiological department in the Institute for Biophysics of the academy. This important institute became a niche for many political victims of the regime, and it was the ovum of modern molecular biology in the USSR after 1955. In this institute she worked again, and was honored again. But until the end of the USSR, nothing was published about her fate and the fate of the JAC. The obituary of the Academy of Science (1968) was a brief one without any biographical details. Even her successful career in Switzerland was "forgotten." She got an entry in the *Great Soviet Encyclopedia,* but the years between 1948 and 1955 are missing, and this gap shows informed readers that "something happened" to her in these years. In 1987 a biography about her was published in Moscow with the same gap.

Research. Shtern worked in two important fields: first biochemistry, especially physiological chemistry, until about 1917. She studied metabolism, and she studied in vitro the respiration in special tissues. Furthermore, she worked on the characterization of enzymes involved in substrate metabolism. Between 1904 and 1914, Shtern together with Battelli published about thirty articles on oxidation, mostly in the famous biochemical journal *Bio-*

chemische Zeitschrift of Carl Neuberg (1877–1956). In 1912, Battelli and Shtern published their main results about oxidation and ferments in a long article (Shtern & Batteli, 1912). Starting in 1917, Shtern studied the effects of certain drugs and organ extracts in organisms. Her new scientific field became the blood-brain barrier. From 1919 to 1923, still in Geneva, she studied the permeability of the blood-brain barrier. Because of her work, she came in close contacts with the brain researchers the Vogts at the Kaiser Wilhelm Institute for Brain Research in Berlin. Between 1925 and 1929, after she moved to the Soviet Union and had to struggle for her own research institute, she could publish nothing. Then another decade of important research began. Between 1930 and 1940, she investigated new studies on the blood-brain barrier and published, together with Soviet and foreign coauthors, some important papers. During World War II, Shtern worked on war medicine, helping thousands of wounded soldiers; in 1943 she received the Stalin Prize for the practical applications of her medical studies.

Already in 1947, accusations were made against her scientific work and the research program of her institute (Rapoport, 1991). She was denounced for having cooperated "too much" with foreigners and employed "too many" Jews in her institute, as well as in the medical journal which she edited. During the years in prison and exile, from 1949 to 1953–1955, she had no opportunity for any scientific research. Perhaps she was able (and was allowed) to read some scientific literature in her exile. Less is known about her scientific work in the Institute for Biophysics.

Lina Shtern is best known as a scientist for her work on the blood-brain barrier. She was one of the first woman scientists in Switzerland (as a professor) and in the USSR (as the first woman member of the Academy of Science); a member of the German academy of science, the Deutsche Akademie der Naturforscher Leopoldina (1932); a full member of the Academy of Science of the USSR (1939); a member of the Academy of Medical Sciences of the USSR (1944); and an honorary doctor at the University of Geneva (1960).

BIBLIOGRAPHY

WORKS BY SHTERN

With Federico Battelli. "Die Oxydationsfermente." *Ergebnisse der Physiologie* 12 (1912): 96–268.

"Selbstdarstellung (Autobiographical Sketch)." In *Führende Frauen Europas,* edited by Elga Kern, 137–140. Neue Folge. Munich, Germany: Verlag Ernst Reinhardt, 1930. Republished, edited by Bettina Conrad and Ulrike Leuschner, 1999. Pp. 206–210, remarks 270–271. Contains mistakes.

OTHER SOURCES

Borschtschagowski, Alexander. *Orden für einen Mord. Die Judenverfolgung unter Stalin.* Berlin: Propyläen Verlag, 1997, pp. 125–137.

Dreifuss, Jean Jacques, and Natalja Tikhonov. "Lina Stern (1878–1968): Physiologin und Biochemikerin, erste Professorin an der Universität Genf und Opfer stalinistischer Prozesse." *Schweizerische Ärztezeitung* 86 (2005): 1594–1597.

Hoffer, Gerda. "Lina Stern—Mitglied der sowjetischen Akademie der Wissenschaften (1878–1968)." In *Zeit der Heldinnen. Lebensbilder außergewöhnlicher jüdischer Frauen,* edited by Gerda Hoffler, 159–184. Munich, Germany: Deutscher Taschenbuch Verlag, 1999.

Jaenicke, Lothar. "Lina Stern (1878–1968). Die biologische Oxydation. Die Schranken und die Erstickung der Forschung." *BIOspektrum* 8 (2002): 374–377.

"Lina & the Brain." *Time,* 3 March 1947.

Lustiger, Arno. "Die Geschichte des Jüdischen Antifaschistischen Komitees der Sowjetunion" (Nachwort). In *Das Schwarzbuch. Der Genozid an den sowjetischen Juden,* edited by Wassili Grossmann and Ilja Ehrenburg, 1093–1101. Hamburg, Germany: Reinbek, Rowohlt, 1994.

———. *Rotbuch: Stalin und die Juden. Die tragische Geschichte des Jüdischen Antifaschistischen Komitees und der sowjetischen Juden.* Berlin: Aufbau Verlag, 1998, pp. 371–372. English edition, *Stalin and the Jews: The Red Book. The Tragedy of the Jewish Anti-Fascist Committee and the Soviet Jews.* New York: Enigma, 2003.

Naumov, Vladimir P., ed. *Nepravednyj sud. Poslednij stalinskij rasstrel. Stenogramma sudebnogo processa nad chlenami Evrejskogo Antifashistskogo Komiteta.* Moscow: Nauka, 1994, pp. 311–321, 332–333.

Rapoport, Yakov. "Lina Stern. Persecution of an Academician." In *The Doctors' Plot of 1953.* Cambridge, MA: Harvard University Press, 1991, pp. 234–253. This book is dedicated to Rapoport's wife, Sophia Rapoport, who was a student and associate of Lina Shtern; it was published in Russian in Moscow in 1988.

Rubinstein, Joshua, and Vladimir P. Naumov, eds. *Stalin's Secret Pogro: The Postwar Inquisition of the Jewish Anti-Fascist Committee.* New Haven, CT, and London: Yale University Press, 2001, pp. 400–416; 469. (Contains two photos of Lina Shtern in 1946, the photocopy of the order to arrest Lina Shtern from 27 January 1949, and a photo of her in the prison.

"Shtern, Lina S." In *The Biographical Dictionary of Women in Science.* Vol. 2, edited by Marilyn Ogilvie and Joy Harvey, 1189–1190. New York and London: Routledge, 2000.

"Shtern, Lina S. (Obituary)." *Vestnik AN SSSR* 5 (1968): 118.

Annette B. Vogt

SIMON, HERBERT ALEXANDER (*b.* Milwaukee, Wisconsin, 15 June 1916; *d.* Pittsburgh,

Pennsylvania, 9 February 2001), *administration, artificial intelligence, cognitive psychology, economics.*

Simon's lifelong passion was the study of decision-making and problem-solving. He examined these processes rigorously to advance the social sciences. Computer technology enabled him to investigate human cognition by simulating it. He was a pioneer in the field of artificial intelligence. His creative work in several disciplines led to many prestigious awards, including the 1978 Nobel Prize in economics.

Simon's goal as a student was to become a mathematical social scientist. He earned a BA (1936) and a PhD (1943) in political science at the University of Chicago. His dissertation examined administrative decision-making was later published in book form, *Administrative Behavior* ([1947] 1997). He wrote his dissertation while directing a research group at the University of California, Berkeley. After completing his dissertation, he joined the faculty at the Illinois Institute of Technology. During his appointment he also worked with the Cowles Commission of Research Economics at the University of Chicago. In 1949 he moved to Carnegie Mellon University where he was appointed the Richard King Mellon University professor of computer science and psychology. He was a prolific scholar there for more than fifty years.

Simon's father, an electrical engineer, came to the United States from Germany in 1903. His mother, whose maiden name was Merkel, was a third generation American. Her ancestors immigrated from Prague and Köln. During his childhood Simon become fond of books, music, and the outdoors. From his uncle, Harold Merkel, an economist, he learned about the social sciences. Simon married Dorothea Pye in 1937. They had three children, Katherine, Barbara, and Peter.

Decision-Making. Mid-twentieth accounts of decision-making relied heavily on idealizations about a decision-maker's informational and cognitive resources. Standard idealizations gave agents unlimited cognitive capacity and ample data about their decision problems. Simon relaxed these idealizations to make progress toward a realistic theory of decision-making. His theory accommodated a decision-maker's limited ability to analyze options. Taking rationality as a capacity for reasoning, Simon recognized that people have only bounded rationality. His theory also accommodated a decision-maker's limited information about a decision problem. A person often does not know all the options available or have enough data for a careful analysis of options. Because gathering information is costly and because the time for resolving a decision problem is limited, becoming fully informed is impractical. Simon recommended not seeking an optimal decision but instead seeking a satisfactory decision. He called the

Herbert Alexander Simon. © BETTMANN/CORBIS.

recommended decision procedure satisficing to contrast it with optimizing.

An agent with bounded rationality does not have all logical and mathematical truths at his or her fingertips to assist analysis of a decision problem. The agent's inferential skills are imperfect, and a lack of analytical skill makes selecting an optimal option an unrealistic goal, as there are too many options to analyze and compare. Because requirements of rationality adjust to circumstances, a person may nevertheless decide rationally, despite these handicaps. Cognitive limits lower rationality's requirements. Optimization is a goal of rationality, but a person with good excuses for not attaining that goal may still decide rationally.

Problems requiring a decision do not come with a tidy list of options and a precise assessment of options' prospects. In a typical decision-requiring problem an agent has more options than he or she can grasp. For instance, the number of strategies for playing a chess game is enormous. A player cannot comprehend and review all strategies before making an opening move. Time and resources do not permit thorough analysis and comparison of strategies. Instead of following a decision procedure that yields an optimal decision, Simon held that a limited

agent should adopt the first satisfactory option discovered. That is, the agent should satisfice. Someone selling a house may reasonably accept the first satisfactory offer. Drumming up an optimal offer would take a prohibitively large amount of time and other resources. What counts as a satisfactory decision depends on an agent's aspiration level, that is, the agent's realistic expectation. That level may change as an agent acquires information and assesses the results of past decisions.

Sometimes theorists distinguish between optimizing and maximizing utility. Optimization evaluates options with respect to full information and, according to some theorists, with respect to the agent's objective interests. Utility is a measure of desirability, and utility maximization evaluates options with respect to information in hand and with respect to the agent's subjective goals. To emphasize utility maximization's reliance on probabilities of options' outcomes, instead of certainty of their outcomes, theorists also call it expected utility maximization. According to a common principle, an option's utility equals its expected utility—a probability-weighted average of the utilities of its possible outcomes. Utility maximization takes account of a decision-maker's limited information about options' consequences. It does not require an optimal decision but instead a decision expected to be optimal. In many cases such a decision is rational. A person may rationally make a decision after reasonable efforts to gather information even if he or she still lacks full information. A decision made without full information may nonetheless be fully rational. For example, a businessman makes a rational decision about traveling to an appointment if he takes a train scheduled to bring him to the meeting place on time, even if an unexpected delay on the rails causes him to miss his appointment.

For agents with limited information, utility maximization is attainable. For agents with additional limitations, are other types of maximization in reach? One interpretation of satisficing takes it as utility maximization under constraints. For example, a chess player with a limited amount of time for a move must make a decision before he or she can thoroughly assess all possible moves. The decision the player makes may maximize utility given the cost of delay, although it does not maximize utility in the absence of time constraints. Given more time, the player may have made a decision with better prospects. Perhaps a decision that satisfices is also a decision that maximizes utility under constraints concerning time and the like. The maximization may occur within the set of options the agent actually considers instead of within the set of all options, considered or not. Several theorists have explored this topic. Some, such as Sydney Winter (1964), conclude that satisficing is not equivalent to utility maximization under constraints.

A comparison of satisficing and maximizing utility requires distinguishing two types of decision principles. One type formulates a procedure that an agent may follow to reach a decision. Another type presents a standard for evaluating a decision. An observer may apply the standard of evaluation after the agent reaches a decision. Simon advanced satisficing as a decision-making procedure. Maximizing utility may also be taken as a procedure [in] for making decisions. Taken as a procedure, it has comparative steps that satisficing lacks and so is distinct from satisficing.

Simon distinguished procedural and substantive rationality. A decision meets procedural standards of rationality if the method of making the decision was rational and so, for example, employed sufficient deliberation. A decision meets substantive standards of rationality if its content fits the agent's circumstances and so, for example, selects an act reasonable to perform in the agent's situation. The procedure that generated the decision is irrelevant.

A rational decision procedure may yield a decision that is not substantively rational. The decision reached may be defective because of its content. Satisficing may be a rational decision procedure although it may yield a decision that falls short of a standard of substantive rationality. The first satisfactory option discovered may not maximize utility, for example. An agent may have good reasons to follow a shortcut procedure such as satisficing despite the risk of reaching a decision with a substantive defect. For example, a driver may have to make a snap decision about taking a freeway exit despite the risk that the decision does not maximize utility.

Conversely, an irrational decision procedure may yield a decision that is rational because of its content. Possibly a decision reached in irrational haste is by good fortune the same as the decision careful deliberation would have generated. Perhaps a student picks a career without deliberation but chooses the same career he or she would have chosen after thoughtful reflection and information gathering. Then the student violates a standard of procedural rationality but nonetheless meets a standard of substantive rationality.

Satisficing may be taken as a substantive standard of rationality. A decision meets that standard if it is satisfactory, regardless of the procedure that led to the decision. Utility maximization under constraints, taken as a substantive standard of evaluation, may be equivalent in some cases to satisficing, also taken as a substantive standard of rationality. The aspiration level a decision must reach to be satisfactory may adjust so that only options maximizing utility given the constraints count as satisfactory.

Although treating satisficing and utility maximizing as standards of substantive rationality brings them closer together, their applications still have different informational requirements. Discovering whether an option maximizes utility requires an account of the probabilities and utilities of options' possible consequences. Discovering whether an option satisfices requires only a classification of options. Suppose that an agent does not make quantitative probability and utility assignments to options' possible consequences, but still classifies options as satisfactory or unsatisfactory. Then the substantive standard of satisficing, but not the substantive standard of utility maximizing, applies to the agent's decision.

Simon's term bounded rationality is the rubric for many current research programs in the decision sciences. Theorists consider how cognitively limited agents may reasonably cope with decision problems. A good example is Ariel Rubinstein's book, *Modeling Bounded Rationality* (1998).

Economics. Simon specialized in decision-making within administrative organizations. He recognized that reasonable executives of corporations may fail to maximize profits because they do not access all information, not even all available information, and so misjudge the effects, especially the long-term effects, of their decisions. His models of administrative decision-making gained credibility by acknowledging an administrator's limited time for deliberation and limited capacity to discover options and to acquire information about their consequences. Simon looked for efficient, time-preserving methods of achieving acceptable economic objectives while at the same time, reducing risks. He also recognized that factors independent of an organization's goals contribute to decision-making within the organization. Whether an administrator makes a decision that advances the organization's goals often depends on whether he or she identifies with the organization. Promoting that identification makes an important contribution to successful decisions within an organization.

Herbert Simon's ideas are also influential in behavioral economics, which examines methods people use to make economic decisions. Their methods may result in systematic errors. They may, given a certain triggering event, apply a heuristic outside its successful range of application. That is, they may follow a shortcut procedure for making a decision in a context where the shortcut is unreliable. For example, a person may follow an expert's advice on a topic outside the expert's area of specialization. Although Simon's decision principles are normative, their attempt to set realistic standards draws attention to actual decision processes, which in some cases yield decisions falling short of the appropriate norm.

Drawing on his prodigious mathematical skills, Simon also made major contributions to mathematical economics, especially general equilibrium theory and econometrics. With David Hawkins, he proved the Hawkins-Simon Theorem. It states conditions for the existence of positive solution vectors for matrices representing the input and the output of an economic system.

Artificial Intelligence. To study problem solving, Simon turned to computer simulations of human cognition. His path-breaking work stimulated research in the field of artificial intelligence. With Allen Newell, he produced in 1956 a machine capable of proving theorems of formal logic. The following year, he and Newell invented a general problem-solving machine. His program BACON simulates the process of scientific discovery. It proposes a law governing a phenomenon, compares its proposal with reality, and makes adjustments. His book *Scientific Discovery* (1987) describes the program's operation. In Simon's eyes, computers running problem-solving programs are thinking machines. His book with Newell, *Human Problem Solving* (1972), is a classic in the literature on artificial intelligence. The Association of Computing Machines awarded Simon the Turing Medal in 1975.

The breadth and depth of Simon's research is astonishing. He won top honors in a variety of disciplines. Besides awards already mentioned, he was a member of the National Academy of Sciences, received the National Medal of Science (1986), and won the American Psychological Association's Award for Outstanding Lifetime Contributions to Psychology (1993). He was a brilliant twentieth-century scientist.

BIBLIOGRAPHY

WORKS BY SIMON

Models of Man: Social and Rational; Mathematical Essays on Rational Human Behavior in a Social Setting. New York: Wiley, 1957. Essays presenting mathematical models of human behavior.

The Sciences of the Artificial, 3rd ed. Cambridge, Massachusetts: MIT Press, 1997.

With Allen Newell. *Human Problem Solving.* Written with Allen Newell. Englewood Cliffs, NJ: Prentice-Hall, 1972.

Models of Discovery: And Other Topics in the Methods of Science. Boston: D. Reidel Publishing Company, 1977.

Models of Thought. 2 vols. New Haven, CT: Yale University Press, 1979. Essays on psychology, human information-processing, and problem-solving.

Models of Bounded Rationality. Volumes 1 and 2. Cambridge, MA: MIT Press, 1982. Essays on decision-making.

With Pat Langley, Gary Bradshaw, and Jan Zytkow. *Scientific Discovery: Computational Explorations of the Creative Process.* Cambridge, MA: MIT Press, 1987.

Administrative Behavior: A Study of Decision-Making in Administrative Organizations, 4th ed. New York: The Free Press, 1997.

Models of Bounded Rationality, volume 3. Cambridge, MA: MIT Press, 1997.

The Carnegie Mellon University Herbert A. Simon Collection has the complete corpus of Simon's work.

OTHER SOURCES

Augier, Mie, and James March, eds. *Models of Man: Essays in Memory of Herbert A. Simon.* Cambridge, MA: MIT Press, 2004.

Byron, Michael, ed. *Satisficing and Maximizing.* Cambridge, MA: Cambridge University Press, 2004. A collection of essays reviewing Simon's ideas about satisficing.

Courtois, Pierre Jacques. *Decomposability: Queuing and Computer Systems Applications.* New York: Academic Press, 1977. Continues the work of Simon and Albert Ando on decomposable computer systems.

McCorduck, Pamela. *Machines Who Think.* San Francisco: W. H. Freeman, 1979. Presents Simon's contributions to artificial intelligence.

Rubinstein, Ariel. *Modeling Bounded Rationality.* Cambridge, MA: MIT Press, 1998.

Weirich, Paul. *Realistic Decision Theory: Rules for Nonideal Agents in Nonideal Circumstances.* New York: Oxford University Press, 2004. Pursues Simon's program of making decision principles realistic.

Winter, Sydney. "Economic 'Natural Selection' and the Theory of the Firm." *Yale Economic Essays* 4 (1964): 225–272. Compares satisficing and optimizing.

Paul Weirich

SIMPSON, GEORGE GAYLORD (*b.* Chicago, Illinois, 16 June 1902; *d.* Tucson, Arizona, 6 October 1984), *paleontology, vertebrate paleontology.*

Simpson was an empirical paleontologist specializing in mammals; he led numerous expeditions to discover new fossils. These were described and analyzed in hundreds of technical publications. However, Simpson is best known for incorporation of evidence from fossils and earth history in understanding biological systematics and evolution. Simpson was a principal architect of the "modern synthesis" of evolutionary thought emerging in the 1940s.

Early Life and Education. Simpson's father, Joseph Alexander Simpson, was a successful attorney, first in Chicago and then in the frontier mining and railway city of Denver, Colorado. There he took advantage of opportunities for land development and then mining. Simpson's mother, Helen Kinney, lost her own mother at a young age and was raised in Hawaii by grandparents who were Presbyterian missionaries there. George Gaylord Simpson was the third of three children. He had two sisters,

Margaret and Martha, who were seven and four years older, respectively. The family was Presbyterian, but Simpson himself was never particularly religious.

Simpson grew up in Denver, in a Rocky Mountain environment where he enjoyed nature with family and friends. He credited camping, mountain climbing, and mining with his father for inspiring an interest in geology. These experiences made him comfortable outdoors, where he was to spend many months of his adult life. Looking back as an adult, Simpson felt that certain of his boyhood characteristics—his intelligence, shortness of stature, red hair, and visual impairment that limited ball playing—combined to foster antagonism from his peers. Serious and studious, Simpson advanced rapidly through school in spite of occasional setbacks due to health. He entered the University of Colorado at Boulder when he was age sixteen.

At the University of Colorado, Simpson was influenced by Arthur J. Tieje, who introduced him to the excitement and mystery of historical geology and paleontology, subjects that would inspire a lifetime of intensely focused scholarship. When Tieje left Colorado, he advised Simpson to transfer to Yale University as the best place to study paleontology. Simpson transferred in 1922, finished his AB degree in 1923 at Yale, and entered graduate school there to pursue a career in paleontology.

Soon after moving east, Simpson secretly married Lydia Petroja while he was still an undergraduate. Four daughters, Helen, Patricia (Gay), Joan, and Elizabeth, were born in the next six years, but the marriage ended in separation and divorce. In 1938 Simpson married again, this time to psychologist Anne Roe, a childhood friend from Denver. Simpson and Roe remained married until Simpson's death forty-six years later.

At Yale, Simpson found a large and little-studied collection of North American Mesozoic mammals that he analyzed for his PhD. The Mesozoic Era in Earth history is popularly known as the age of dinosaurs, but it is also the time when mammals began their early diversification. Humanity's history as mammals is deeply rooted in the Mesozoic, and it was natural that Simpson would seek to learn all he could of Mesozoic mammals. The dissertation was completed and the degree awarded in 1926. Simpson immediately moved to the British Museum of Natural History in London as a postdoctoral scholar to undertake a similar study of European Mesozoic mammals. The two resulting monographs—*A Catalogue of the Mesozoic Mammalia in the Geological Department of the British Museum* (1928) and "American Mesozoic Mammalia" (1929) established Simpson as a precocious but surprisingly mature authority on early mammal diversification and evolution.

Museum Work. Returning from Europe in 1927, Simpson joined the American Museum of Natural History in New York as an assistant curator. He continued research on early mammals but moved up stratigraphically and forward in time to study the beginning of the major Cenozoic diversification of mammals. He worked first on North American faunas and in 1932 was invited to study a major collection of Paleocene mammals at the National Museum of Natural History in Washington, D.C. This required fieldwork in the Crazy Mountains Basin of central Montana to collect more specimens and determine their stratigraphic context. Samples for some species were large, requiring statistical characterization for diagnosis and comparison as once-living populations. The Crazy Mountains study, more than any of his previous works, enabled Simpson to quantify and compare evolutionary change through time, and it required implementation of a rational taxonomic framework capable of encompassing history. Simpson emphasized quantification and stratigraphy in a way that soon led to introduction of chronoclines as a way of quantifying how morphology changes through time (analogous to the spatial clines that quantify how morphology changes geographically).

Simpson's curiosity about extinct mammals went beyond those known from North America, and in the 1930s he initiated two major paleontological field expeditions to Patagonia, the first in 1930–1931 and the second in 1933–1934. The purpose was to characterize the history of South American mammals evolving in isolation from the rest of the world. His popular journal of these expeditions, *Attending Marvels* (1934), has been read by many and reprinted several times. Research in Patagonia led to many publications summarized in a major systematic review, *Beginning of the Age of Mammals in South America* (1948), published in two parts over the course of two decades (part 2 appeared in 1967). Fieldwork in Patagonia initiated a lifelong interest in penguins, with a parallel series of publications on penguin fossils and evolution.

At the American Museum, Simpson worked tirelessly, publishing hundreds of technical reports and monographs documenting the morphologies and stratigraphic occurrences of North and South American mammals. But a decade into his career, he started to publish more synthetic works as well. Simpson collaborated with his wife, Anne Roe, on a classic 1939 book, *Quantitative Zoology*, that introduced statistical methods and population thinking to evolutionary disciplines that make little sense without them. It was eventually expanded and republished in 1960, with Richard Lewontin added as third author.

Modern Synthesis. The late 1930s and early 1940s were pivotal for evolutionary thought as a broader understanding of genetics, biogeography, morphology, and paleontology coalesced into a "modern synthesis" in which gradual, step-by-step morphological evolution is understood to reflect the additive effects of small mutations, while larger-scale speciation and macroevolution are explained in the broader context of geography and environmental change. The conclusion was that small-scale mutation and selection are sufficient to explain what is seen today and in the evolutionary past, and macromutations are not required. The principal architects of the modern synthesis were Theodosius Dobzhansky (*Genetics and the Origin of Species* [1937]), Julian Huxley (*Evolution: The Modern Synthesis* [1942]), Ernst Mayr (*Systematics and the Origin of Species* [1942]), Simpson (*Tempo and Mode of Evolution* [1944]), and Bernard Rensch (*Neuere Probleme der Abstammungslehre: Die Transspezifische Evolution* [1947; New problems of phylogenetic systematics: Transspecfic evolution.]).

Simpson's contribution to the modern synthesis was powerful because it combined his empirical paleontological, quantitative, and systematic experience and brought time on a macroevolutionary and geological scale to the subject. *Tempo and Mode of Evolution* is widely regarded not only as paleontology's principal contribution to the modern synthesis, but as a capstone for the synthesis as a whole that integrated all of the relevant disciplines. Simpson developed methods to analyze rates of evolution through time and showed that these were variable. Another innovation was the introduction of the term *quantum evolution* in an attempt to explain the sudden appearance of new lineages and higher taxonomic groups that were otherwise unexplained. In the preface to a 1984 reissue of *Tempo and Mode,* Simpson noted that the "punctuation," or sudden appearance of new species, that is part of current "punctuated equilibrium" theory is essentially a restatement of "quantum evolution" first proposed in *Tempo and Mode:* "origin of a species or other taxon by exceptionally rapid evolution."

War Years and After. Simpson served a two-year tour of duty in the U.S. Army during World War II from 1942 to 1944. He was a captain and major in the Mediterranean theater in Algeria, Tunisia, and Italy. Simpson was not greatly interested by war and even less enamored of authority. At one point he was attached to General George Patton's headquarters in Sicily. Simpson wore a short, "pink" beard that displeased Patton, who sent an aide to tell Simpson to remove it. Simpson replied that his commanding officer was General Dwight Eisenhower, who had given him permission to have a beard, and that if Patton wanted it removed, he should take the matter up with Eisenhower (who was also Patton's commanding officer). Simpson kept the beard.

Following the war Simpson published "Principles of Classification and a Classification of Mammals" (1945). It has served as a standard reference for more than fifty years, and it is still his most-cited work. Simpson's experience with phylogeny and classification led eventually to his book *Principles of Animal Taxonomy* (1961). After the war Simpson was appointed chairman of the American Museum's Department of Geology and Paleontology; simultaneously, he accepted a professorship of vertebrate paleontology at Columbia University.

Simpson was the first president of the Society for the Study of Evolution, founded in 1946, and he helped Glenn L. Jepsen and Mayr organize a pivotal 1947 symposium, Genetics, Paleontology, and Evolution at Princeton, New Jersey. He also set to work at this time revising *Tempo and Mode,* which was reissued in 1953 as an expanded *Major Features of Evolution.* Both of these books, classics as they are, remain widely cited.

In 1953 Simpson took his writing in a different direction when he signed a contract to develop a major new university-level biology textbook. This was titled *Life: An Introduction to Biology,* which appeared in 1957. This first edition was written with Colin S. Pittendrigh and Lewis H. Tiffney, and a revised edition of 1965 was written with William S. Beck. The book reflected the original authors' strong conviction that there is a unified science of life—a science of biology—which is larger than the then often-separate disciplines of botany and zoology. It is a measure of the authors' foresight, and to some extent the influence of the new text itself, that botany and zoology departments were subsequently merged in many universities across the United States.

Amazon Expedition. Simpson was not always lucky. In 1956 he participated in a joint Brazilian-American Museum expedition to the Rio Alto Juruá at the headwaters of the Amazon. There, while clearing a campsite on 24 August, a tree fell on the fifty-four-year-old Simpson, giving him a concussion, dislocating a shoulder, and shattering a lower leg. It was a week before Simpson could receive adequate medical care, and he was unable to return to work full time at the American Museum of Natural History until 1958. The stress and strain of this long absence led to a series of administrative confrontations, and in 1959 Simpson resigned from the American Museum to accept an Agassiz professorship at Harvard University. Simpson retained his Agassiz professorship at Harvard through 1969, but he suffered a heart attack in 1964 and moved to Tucson and the University of Arizona in 1967 for the sake of his and Roe's health. Simpson wrote many scientific articles, an autobiography titled *Concession to the Improbable* (1978), and numerous popular books during his remaining years in Arizona. One of these, *Fossils and the History of Life* (1983), is a semipopular extension of *Major Features of Evolution.*

Simpson died in 1984 of pneumonia and complications following a South Pacific cruise. His body was cremated and his ashes scattered in the Arizona desert. A short, introspective novel by Simpson, *The Dechronization of Sam Magruder,* was discovered and published posthumously. It is interesting for the insight it gives of an exceptional scientist struggling to understand and explain himself.

In retrospect, Simpson is seen as a disciplined and intensely focused scholar, known both for his commitment to observation and for his ability to organize ideas and synthesize interpretations. He was a prolific writer, but a gifted writer, too, able to convey ideas simply and clearly to a wide audience throughout his career. Simpson has been called the greatest paleontologist since Georges Cuvier and the most influential natural historian of the twentieth century. He received many honors, including election to the National Academy of Sciences of the United States in 1941, at the age of thirty-nine. Simpson was awarded the National Medal of Science in 1966 by President Lyndon B. Johnson.

BIBLIOGRAPHY

An extensive Simpson bibliography is included in Max K. Hecht, Bobb Schaeffer, Bryan Patterson, et al., "George Gaylord Simpson: His Life and His Works to the Present," in Evolutionary Biology, *vol. 6, edited by Theodosius Dobzhansky, Max K. Hecht, and William C. Steere. New York: Appleton-Century-Crofts, 1972. Simpson's personal papers and correspondence are archived in the Library of the American Philosophical Society, Philadelphia, available from http://www.amphilsoc.org/library/mole/s/simpson.htm.*

WORKS BY SIMPSON

A Catalogue of the Mesozoic Mammalia in the Geological Department of the British Museum. London: British Museum (Natural History), 1928.

"American Mesozoic Mammalia." *Memoirs of the Peabody Museum of Natural History, Yale University, New Haven* 3 (1929): 1–235.

Attending Marvels: A Patagonian Journal. New York: Macmillan, 1934.

Tempo and Mode in Evolution. New York: Columbia University Press, 1944.

Beginning of the Age of Mammals. New York: American Museum of Natural History, 1948.

With Glenn L. Jepsen and Ernst Mayr, eds. *Genetics, Paleontology, and Evolution.* Princeton, NJ: Princeton University Press, 1949. The proceedings of the International Symposium on Genetics, Paleontology, and Evolution held in Princeton, New Jersey, in 1947.

The Major Features of Evolution. New York: Columbia University Press, 1953. An expanded version of Simpson's *Tempo and Mode of Evolution.*

With Colin S. Pittendrigh and Lewis H. Tiffney. *Life: An Introduction to Biology.* New York: Harcourt, Brace, 1957.

With Anne Roe and Richard C. Lewontin. *Quantitative Zoology.* Rev. ed. New York: Harcourt, Brace, 1960.

"The Beginning of the Age of Mammals in South America. Part 2, Systematics: Notoungulata, Concluded (Typotheria, Hegetotheria, Toxodonta, Notoungulata incertae sedis), Astrapotheria, Trigonostylopoidea, Pyrotheria, Xenungulata, Mammalia incertae sedis." *Bulletin of the American Museum of Natural History* 137 (1967): 1–259.

Concession to the Improbable: An Unconventional Autobiography. New Haven, CT: Yale University Press, 1978.

Fossils and the History of Life. New York: Scientific American Library, 1983. A semipopular extension of *Major Features of Evolution.*

The Dechronization of Sam Magruder. New York: St. Martin's Press, 1996. A posthumously published novel based on Simpson's self-reflections.

OTHER SOURCES

Dobzhansky, Theodosius. *Genetics and the Origin of Species.* New York: Columbia University Press, 1937.

Gingerich, Philip D. "George Gaylord Simpson: Empirical Theoretician." In *Vertebrates, Phylogeny, and Philosophy,* edited by Kathryn M. Flanagan and Jason A. Lillegraven. Laramie: Department of Geology and Geophysics, University of Wyoming, 1986.

Gould, Stephen J. "G. G. Simpson, Paleontology, and the Modern Synthesis." In *The Evolutionary Synthesis: Perspectives on the Unification of Biology,* edited by William B. Provine and Ernst Mayr. Cambridge, MA: Harvard University Press, 1980.

Huxley, Julian. *Evolution: The Modern Synthesis.* London: G. Allen and Unwin, 1942.

LaPorte, Léo F., ed. *Simple Curiosity: Letters from George Gaylord Simpson to His Family, 1921–1970.* Berkeley: University of California Press, 1987.

———. *George Gaylord Simpson: Paleontologist and Evolutionist.* New York: Columbia University Press, 2000.

Mayr, Ernst. *Systematics and the Origin of Species from the Viewpoint of a Zoologist.* New York: Columbia University Press, 1942.

Rensch, Bernard. *Neuere Probleme der Abstammungslehre: Die Transspezifische Evolution* [New problems of phylogenetic systematics: Transspecfic evolution]. Stuttgart, Germany: Enke, 1947.

Philip D. Gingerich

SITTER, WILLEM DE (*b.* Sneek, Netherlands, 6 May 1872; *d.* Leiden, Netherlands, 20 November

1934), *astronomy, cosmology*. For the original article on de Sitter see *DSB,* vol. 12.

This supplement to Adriaan Blaauw's article in the *Dictionary of Scientific Biography* focuses on de Sitter's important contributions to relativistic cosmology and also calls attention to his views on the methods and nature of science. The bibliography includes only works not mentioned in Blaauw's article.

Theories of Gravitation. About 1910, after he had become professor of astronomy in Leiden, de Sitter's main occupation was with celestial mechanics, but this was only one of his research fields. He had an interest in alternatives to Newton's theory of gravitation even before Einstein's theory of general relativity. In 1905 Henri Poincaré had suggested a special-relativistic (and non-Einsteinian) theory of gravitation that five years later was formulated in a different way by H. A. Lorentz. In a paper of 1911 de Sitter examined in detail this kind of theory and its astronomical consequences, concluding that Poincaré's theory predicted an additional perihelion advance, which in the case of Mercury amounted to 7'15" per century. He showed that although the special-relativistic force law could be brought to agree with observations, because of its flexibility (it contained several free parameters) it could not be refuted. At any rate, with the advent of general relativity the Mercury anomaly was fully explained without special hypotheses, and de Sitter immediately turned his interest to the new theory.

As a foreign member of the Royal Astronomical Society, he was invited by Arthur Stanley Eddington (who then served as the society's secretary) to produce an account of the new theory, which he did in three articles in the *Monthly Notices*. These articles introduced Einstein's theory to the English-speaking world, and it was on the basis of them that Eddington wrote his important *Report on the Relativity Theory of Gravitation* in 1918. In the fall of 1916 de Sitter discussed the theory with Einstein, and the discussions led Einstein to attempt to apply his theory to the universe at large. The result was Einstein's closed or spherical model of 1917, incorporating the cosmological constant (Λ). Einstein originally believed that his static, matter-filled model was the only solution to the cosmological field equations. However, in his third report to the Royal Astronomical Society of 1917, de Sitter showed that there exists another solution, corresponding to an empty universe with $\Lambda = 3/R^2$ and spatially closed in spite of its lack of matter (R denotes the radius of curvature). De Sitter termed his new model solution B, to distinguish it from Einstein's solution A. Compared with Einstein's model, de Sitter's was complex and difficult to conceptualize, in particular because it was unclear how to distinguish the properties of the model itself from those

properties that merely reflected a particular coordinate representation of it. Although the de Sitter model would eventually be seen as representing an expanding universe, to de Sitter and his contemporaries it represented a static space-time.

When Einstein was confronted with de Sitter's alternative, he was forced to accept it as a mathematical solution to the field equations, but he considered it a toy model with no physical significance. In his third paper to the *Monthly Notices*, de Sitter showed that if a particle was introduced at some distance from the origin of a system of coordinates, it would appear as moving away from the observer. Moreover, he showed that clocks would appear to run more slowly the farther away they were from the observer. Because frequencies are inverse time-intervals, light would therefore be more redshifted the larger the distance between source and observer. De Sitter was careful to point out that although the redshift corresponded to a Doppler shift, it was not caused by a recession but by the particular space-time metric he used. In spite of the redshift built into de Sitter's model, it was thought of as static.

Keeping abreast of recent astronomical observations in spite of the war, de Sitter suggested that the predicted effect might be related to the measurements of (apparent) radial nebular velocities reported by Vesto Slipher at the Lowell Observatory. This was the first suggestion that Einstein's theory might have connections to the observations of nebular redshifts. With a mean radial velocity of 600 km/s and an average distance of 10 parsecs, he found $R \cong 3 \times 10^{11}$ astronomical units. At the end of his 1917 paper de Sitter compared the two rival world models with available astronomical data. Adopting Jacobus Kapteyn's estimate of a density of about 80 stars per 1000 cubic parsecs, he found that on Einstein's model the radius R would be about 10^{12} astronomical units and the total mass of the universe about 10^{12} sun masses.

Although de Sitter's model, being devoid of matter, may seem a very artificial candidate for the real world, it soon became a foundation for further theoretical work, both among astronomers and mathematicians. It was seen as particularly interesting because of its connection with the redshift observations of spiral nebulae, which by the early 1920s left little doubt that there was a systematic recession. In an examination in 1925 of de Sitter's line element, Georges Lemaître transformed it in such a way that the space part increased with time, yet without concluding that the model described an expanding universe. When, in spring 1929, Edwin Hubble published the celebrated paper in which he demonstrated the linear redshift-distance relationship, he suggested that the relation might represent "the de Sitter effect." However, at that time Hubble did not interpret the redshifts as Doppler shifts caused by the recession of the galaxies.

Willem de Sitter. AP IMAGES.

The Expanding Universe. At a meeting of the Royal Astronomical Society on 10 January 1930, Eddington and de Sitter reached the conclusion that because neither of the solutions A and B had proved adequate, interest should focus on nonstatic solutions. Shortly thereafter the two astronomers "rediscovered" a paper Lemaître had published in 1927 and in which he had derived a model for an expanding universe. In the light of Hubble's new measurements, Lemaître's theory appeared as convincing evidence that the universe is indeed in a state of expansion. De Sitter now abandoned his solution B and immediately began to develop expanding models of the type suggested by Lemaître. In June 1930 he presented his own version of the expanding universe, including a derivation of the Hubble law ($v = Hr$) and a recession constant of H = 490 km/s/Mpc, not far from Hubble's value. One month later he presented a full investigation of Lemaître's theory which he extended to cover also dynamical solutions that had not been considered by Lemaître. Interestingly, he included among his models big-bang solutions corresponding to $R(t = 0) = 0$, the same kind of model that Lemaître would propose in 1931. However, whereas Lemaître considered it a model of the real universe, to de Sitter it was just a mathematical solution of no particular physical importance.

In his work on Lemaître-like expanding models, de Sitter kept to the cosmological constant, which he found

to be a useful quantity, although one whose physical meaning was admittedly unclear. Back in 1917 he had shared Einstein's opinion that it was "somewhat artificial," but he had no strong feelings about the constant and tended to consider it as no stranger than other constants of nature. It is also worth recalling that de Sitter was the first to estimate the value of the cosmological constant: In a letter to Einstein of 18 April 1917 he stated that the constant was certainly smaller than 10^{-45} cm^{-2} and probably smaller than 10^{-50} cm^{-2}.

Although de Sitter was an enthusiastic advocate of the expanding universe, his advocacy did not extend to cosmological models of a finite age. Given his doubts with respect to such models it is noteworthy that he contributed significantly to the early history of big-bang theory, namely in a brief paper of 1932 written jointly with Einstein. The Einstein–de Sitter model made no use of the cosmological constant and assumed space curvature to be zero. It follows that the matter density is given by $\rho_c = 3H^2/8\pi G$, what in later literature became known as the critical density (corresponding to $\Omega \equiv \rho/\rho_c = 1$). The expansion of the Einstein–de Sitter universe follows $R(t) \sim t^{2/3}$, which means that the age is finite and given by $2/3H$. However, Einstein and de Sitter did not write down the variation of $R(t)$, and neither did they note that it implies an abrupt beginning of the world. The Einstein–de Sitter model came to be seen as a typical big-bang model, but in 1932 neither Einstein nor de Sitter seems to have considered it important. With the value of the Hubble constant accepted at the time, the age of their model universe would be 1.2 billion years, which was much less than the age of the stars (and even less than the age of the Earth).

Worried about the age paradox, de Sitter never felt at home with the big-bang theory. He briefly considered the idea in a 1931 paper in the Italian journal *Scientia*, but only to conclude that it was implausible. At a meeting of the British Association for the Advancement of Science in the fall of 1931 he emphasized that the age paradox was a genuine dilemma that somehow might mean that the expansion of the universe and the evolutionary changes of stars were unconnected processes, to be understood in different ways. He apparently preferred two kinds of models at the time, neither of them being the Einstein–de Sitter model. As one possibility he considered a universe of the Lemaître-Eddington type, that is, a model slowly starting its expansion from a stationary state. The other possibility was a model in which the universe had contracted during an infinite time and then, after having passed a minimum, started to expand and would continue to do so indefinitely. In a paper of 1933 he discussed the contraction-expansion scenario, which, he argued, might provide a solution to the paradox of stars being much older than the universe.

An Empiricist Astronomer. De Sitter's mind was not of the philosophical kind, but on several occasions, especially in connection with cosmology, he nevertheless expressed his views about the methods and philosophical foundation of science. These views were decidedly empiricist and inductivist in the sense that he stressed that physical theory must begin and end in observation. If a theory was based on a priori principles or went outside the observational realm it was metaphysical, and de Sitter strongly disliked metaphysics. Now cosmology is concerned with the universe as a whole, something which is not observable, and it relies on tremendous extrapolations. De Sitter realized that this was a problem, but of course without drawing the conclusion that cosmology is therefore nonscientific or metaphysical. He always emphasized the danger of extrapolating beyond the observable part of the universe, yet he found it to be acceptable so long as it was understood that models of the entire universe inevitably depend on "our philosophical taste." In *Kosmos*, a book published 1932, he stated that the concept of the universe was after all a hypothesis, and he suggested that it might have properties that would be contradictory and impossible for a finite material structure.

In agreement with his preference for the inductive-empirical method, de Sitter tended to reject theories based on hypotheses and deductions. He believed Einstein's general theory of relativity belonged to the first class, that it was essentially an empirical theory, uncontaminated by metaphysics. At the same time, he found Eddington's ambitious attempt to connect cosmology with microphysics to be objectionable because it rested on speculations and unverifiable hypotheses. It was also for philosophical reasons that he rejected Edward Arthur Milne's alternative world model without examining it closely. Not only was this model deduced from a priori assumption, it also had no observable consequences—hence from de Sitter's point of view it was hardly a scientific theory. Willem de Sitter died in the fall of 1934 and was thus spared the experience of seeing how popular (and controversial) Milne's system of kinematic relativity became in British cosmological circles.

De Sitter's greatest contribution to cosmology was probably his theory of 1917 which in modernized versions continued to play a role many years after his death, understood in the early twenty-first century as a model of an exponentially expanding universe. For example, the steady-state universe of the 1950s was geometrically described by de Sitter's metric, which was also used in the inflation theories of the very early universe that were developed in the 1980s. In the inflationary model, de Sitter's solution relates to a universe dominated by vacuum energy or, equivalently, the cosmological constant.

SUPPLEMENTARY BIBLIOGRAPHY

De Sitter's unpublished papers and correspondence are in the Collectie-De Sitter, Archive of the Leiden Observatory, Huygens Laboratory.

WORKS BY DE SITTER

"On the Bearing of the Principle of Relativity on Gravitational Astronomy." *Monthly Notices of the Royal Astronomical Society* 71 (1911): 388–415.

"On Einstein's Theory of Gravitation and Its Astronomical Consequences: Third Paper." *Monthly Notices of the Royal Astronomical Society* 78 (1917): 3–28.

"The Expanding Universe: Discussion of Lemaître's Solution of the Inertial Field." *Bulletin of the Astronomical Institutes of the Netherlands* 5 (1930): 211–218.

"The Expanding Universe." *Scientia* 49 (1931): 1–10.

With Albert Einstein. "On the Relation between the Expansion and the Mean Density of the Universe." *Proceedings of the National Academy of Sciences* 18 (1932): 213–214.

"On the Expanding Universe and the Time-Scale." *Monthly Notices of the Royal Astronomical Society* 93 (1933): 628–634.

OTHER SOURCES

Eddington, Arthur S. "Obituary: Prof. Willem de Sitter." *Nature* 134 (1934): 924–925.

Gale, George. "Dingle and de Sitter against the Metaphysicians; or, Two Ways to Keep Modern Cosmology Physical." In *The Universe of General Relativity*, edited by A. J. Kox and Jean Eisenstaedt. Boston: Birkhäuser, 2005.

Kerzberg, Pierre. *The Invented Universe: The Einstein–de Sitter Controversy (1916–17) and the Rise of Relativistic Cosmology.* Oxford: Clarendon Press, 1992.

Kragh, Helge. *Cosmology and Controversy: The Historical Development of Two Theories of the Universe.* Princeton, NJ: Princeton University Press, 1996.

Schulmann, Robert, et al., eds. *The Collected Papers of Albert Einstein.* Vol. 8, part A. Princeton, NJ: Princeton University Press, 1998.

Helge Kragh

SKINNER, BURRHUS FREDERIC (B. F.) (*b.* Susquehanna, Pennsylvania, 20 March 1904; *d.* Cambridge, Massachusetts, 18 August 1990), *psychology, radical behaviorism, reinforcement, behavior analysis.*

Skinner, the most eminent psychologist of the twentieth century, founded a science of behavior and its philosophy. He criticized the construct of mind and offered naturalized accounts of cognition, and he invented and promoted applications that later led to better practices. Among his awards were the National Medal of Science and the first citation from the American Psychological Association for Outstanding Lifetime Contribution.

As Skinner assumed of others, so he assumed of himself: He was a locus for a confluence of variables. Some were encompassing (Western scientific traditions); others were part of his generation (a cultural background); still others he shared with a cohort (social circumstances); and some were unique to him (the individuating contingencies of his life). In the beginning, naturalized tendencies in philosophy and science were a basis for his contributions. As a youth, his familial, social, and cultural context differentially strengthened those influences, as did his life in college. In graduate school, though, the individuating contingencies became as critical as their context, yet the two pulled him in different directions: He sought to advance normal science in psychology, yet at the same time to revolutionize it. In the end, the contingencies were the figure and their context the ground for his contributions—a naturalized psychology. This distinguished his work from mainstream psychology, even as he remained within it, where he became an intellectual provocateur.

Naturalized psychology was not original in science, but Skinner uniquely and vigorously advanced it. In the 1930s he established a science of behavior: the experimental analysis of behavior. In the 1940s he formulated its philosophy: radical behaviorism. In the 1950s he provided behavioral interpretations of psychology's key content domains and considered the ethical implications of determinism: naturalized ethics. In the 1960s he reflected on the social implications of his science, as he advocated its application: applied behavior analysis. In the 1970s he addressed the cultural implications of his science, which made him a public intellectual, as his work became the basis of a new system of psychology: behavior analysis. In the 1980s he promoted the system, admonished psychology for not having adopted it, and reproached his culture for not applying it more widely. In psychology, his contributions were profound and disturbing. In the United States, they were controversial and unsettling. The modern history of psychology, in part, reveals why.

Historical Context. Modern psychology was rooted in René Descartes's dualism of mind and body, the former incorporal, the latter corporal. Philosophers afterward sought rational accounts of the mind, while scientists sought empirical accounts of biology. In the 1800s some of the accounts merged into German experimental psychology: the introspective analysis of mental structures and objective inferences about mental processes. In the United States this became psychology's first system, structuralism, one of two systems that were in place when Skinner was born.

Evolutionary biology led to comparative psychology and the psychology of adaptation. The former inquired into the phylogenetic basis of mind and behavior, the lat-

ter into the ontogenetic basis of psychological processes. Edward Thorndike's studies of cats learning to escape from boxes exemplified both. He discovered that their latencies decreased over trials, which he explained in terms of the law of effect—the satisfactions produced by escape. This was the first quantitative account of instrumental or voluntary behavior, which would be the primary content of Skinner's science. Thorndike's explanation, though, was not Skinner's. For Skinner, satisfactions were explanatory constructs or the consequences of escape, not its cause. From the foregoing psychologies emerged the field's second system, functionalism, which was concerned with the use of mind and behavior, not their structure. In Skinner's youth, functionalists struggled over whether their subject matter was mind, behavior, or both. For Skinner, it was behavior—public and private behavior.

The first systematic research on basic behavioral processes lay in early-twentieth-century experimental physiology: Russian reflexology and general physiology. The former dismissed mind and introspection as unscientific. Psychology was objective; the brain was its subject matter; its actions were reflexive or involuntary. Ivan Pavlov experimentally analyzed reflexive behavior and the conditioning of its eliciting stimuli (e.g., tones paired with food elicit salivation in dogs), which he explained neurologically. Founded by Jacques Loeb, general physiology studied the directed behavior of organisms as a whole, mainly tropisms, not isolated reflexes. Reflexes and tropisms were among the secondary content of Skinner's science. However, he did not explain them neurologically: Behavior was a subject matter in its own right, with its own laws. Skinner did, though, emulate Pavlov's methods: By carefully controlling his experimental conditions, he pioneered in revealing the lawfulness of instrumental behavior.

Given these antecedents, psychology's third system, behaviorism, was almost inevitable. Its classical form was founded by John Watson in 1913: Psychology's subject matter was behavior, not mind; its methods were objective, not introspective; its basic processes were associations among stimuli and responses, not associations in the mind; its goal was the prediction and control of behavior, not a theory of mind; and mind was either a fiction or an incorporal entity unsuited to science. By the time Skinner entered graduate school, classical behaviorism was faltering, in part, because it could not account for variability in behavior with mere stimulus-response associations. From this arose two forms of neobehaviorism.

The first was learning theory, which dominated psychology for the next forty years. Initially, it was consistent with a new philosophy of science, logical positivism, which operationally and exhaustively defined its concepts as observable relations. Learning, for example, was defined as reductions in the time that it took rats to run a maze. Reductions in run-time were *instances* of learning. Unexplained variability, though, remained a problem. It might have been solved with better experimental control, but instead was resolved through logical empiricism: Explanatory constructs explained within- and between-organism variations in behavior. The constructs were also operationally defined, yet had surplus meaning. On this account, reductions in run-time were an *index* of learning, not just instances of it. This was methodological behaviorism: It studied behavior, but behavior was no longer its subject matter. Its subject matter was hypothetical organismic mediators between stimuli and responses (e.g., drives, cognitive maps). The second form of neobehaviorism was Skinner's. It accounted for variations in behavior with variations in biological and behavioral contingencies and context.

In 1904, when Skinner was born, the United States was struggling with internal tensions between a rural, agricultural, and religious culture and an urban, industrial, and scientific society. At the turn of the century, social progressivism sought to resolve these tensions through professionalization and self-improvement, often through science. In the 1920s modernism came to characterize American intellectual life, promoting progress through science and technology. Of the sciences, psychology held great promise because the tensions concerned mental and behavioral adaptation. Skinner was socially progressive and modernist, and he became a psychologist.

Family, Social, and Cultural Context. Burrhus Frederic Skinner—Fred to his family and friends—was born to Grace Burrhus and William A. Skinner on 20 March 1904 in Susquehanna, a small railroad town in northeast Pennsylvania. His sole sibling, Edward (Ebbe), was born in 1906. Skinner's parents embodied the progressive ideal, striving toward middle-class respectability and self-improvement. His father was a self-made lawyer who sought to instill in Skinner the Protestant ethic, civic boosterism, and Kiwanis fraternity. His mother was from a social class above his father's and sought to instill a concern for social propriety. Overall, though, his home was warm and stable, and he was a dutiful son, even as he grew critical of his parents' values and began to challenge authority.

Skinner's childhood was distinguished in ways reflected in his contributions. He had a strong penchant for exploring, inventing, and experimenting, and he was a keen observer of behavior and biology. Mary Graves, a beloved teacher, broadened his intellectual and cultural horizons, leading him to engage in art and literature. He also played the piano for most of his life. While reading Shakespeare in eighth-grade English, he came upon the theory that the seventeenth-century British philosopher,

Francis Bacon, was Shakespeare. He challenged Graves on this point, but she chided him and so he read Bacon, whose natural philosophy would characterize Skinner's approach to the history of science, which lay in artisanry and craft, not disembodied ideas; it also reflected his approach to science, in which he emphasized experimentation, not contemplation, and regarding theory, which for Skinner was empirically induced, not accepted a priori. He also lost his belief in God.

In the fall of 1922 Skinner entered Hamilton College (in Clinton, New York) with an emerging intellectual independence and socially progressive, modernist aspirations. The transition, though, was not seamless. He was self-conscious of his social background, disappointed by his peers' lack of intellectual interest, disdainful of extracurricular requirements such as physical education and chapel, and unlucky in love. At home over Easter, he watched Ebbe die unexpectedly. Eventually, Skinner found his way in college through supportive faculty members, notably the chemist Percy Saunders, and friends, among them John Hutchens, later a *New York Times* editor. Emboldened, he rebelled against convention in campus publications and opposed authority with pranks. He graduated with a major in English, but took only one course related to his science of behavior, a biology course in which he read Loeb.

Skinner had been writing since grade school, was published in his youth, and, with personal encouragement in college from the poet Robert Frost, decided to become a writer. For his parents, this was not the most respectable choice, but they agreed to support him at home for a year. It was, however, a dark year. Although Skinner honed an objective style of writing, he failed to make a difference in the progressive, modernist United States. He wrote: "A writer might portray human behavior accurately, but he did not therefore understand it. I was to remain interested in human behavior, but the literary method failed me; I would turn to the scientific" (1967, p. 395). Becoming a skilled writer, of course, helped Skinner advance his work.

As Skinner was writing, he was also reading. Sinclair Lewis was extolling a career in the biological sciences over that in conventional medicine. Bertrand Russell was praising the epistemological implications of Watson's *Behaviorism*. When Skinner sought advice about psychology and higher education from his Hamilton professors, they directed him to Pavlov's *Conditioned Reflexes* and Harvard University. Deciding on graduate school at Harvard brought him and his parents relief: his career would be useful and respectable. His choice was affirmed as he continued to read. H. G. Wells was promoting Pavlov's science over the humanities for understanding human behavior, and Russell was offering behavioral accounts of mental terms. Before meeting his parents in Europe for summer travel in 1928, Skinner moved to Greenwich Village, in New York City, where he adopted a bohemian lifestyle, worked in a bookstore, and read *Conditioned Reflexes* and Watson's *Psychological Care of Infant and Child.* Watson promoted behaviorism in ways that appealed to Skinner's emerging iconoclasm.

Early Studies of Behavior. When Skinner arrived at Harvard, the Psychology Department was more allied with structuralism than behaviorism, so he supplemented its curriculum with readings and courses in physiology and found support from William Crozier, a devotee of Loeb and chair of the Department of General Physiology. With encouragement from his friend and colleague Fred Keller, Skinner undertook research to demonstrate the lawfulness of behavior on which the environment acted, mainly locomotion. Through trial and error and some serendipity, he devised measures (e.g., cumulative records), invented apparatus (e.g., the Skinner box), and demonstrated lawfulness in behavior that operated on the environment and was strengthened by its consequences in a process that Skinner called reinforcement. He was also influenced by reading the philosopher-physicists Henri Poincaré, Percy Bridgman, and especially Ernst Mach, for whom the meaning of concepts lay in their history, causation was a functional relation between dependent and independent variables, and science was the behavior of scientists maintained by its consequences. The last was a form of Charles Peirce's pragmatism, whose work Skinner read, but rarely acknowledged, although their theories of truth were allied.

Skinner received his doctorate in 1931 for a dissertation titled "The Concept of the Reflex in the Description of Behavior." In it, he argued from history that behavior was no more and no less than an unmediated functional relation between a stimulus and a response. He then demonstrated quantitative order in the rates at which rats pressed panels that gave them access to food (behavioral contingencies) during the course of food satiation (their context).

He remained at Harvard until 1936, notably as a junior fellow in Harvard's Society of Fellows, where he became friends with the philosopher Willard van Orman Quine, whose naturalistic epistemology complemented his own. With continued support from Crozier, he addressed the effects of context on behavior: conditioning (i.e., behavioral history), drive (e.g., food deprivation), emotion (e.g., by eliciting stimuli), and biology (e.g., the nervous system). Eventually, though, he turned to contingencies, where he distinguished between reflexive and instrumental behavior or what he called respondent and operant behavior and made a science of the latter. In thereafter investigating only operant contingencies, though, he was criticized for ignoring their context—his-

B. F. Skinner *B. F. Skinner at Harvard University training brown rat in a Skinner Box to press lever and be rewarded with food.* NINA LEEN/TIME LIFE PICTURES/GETTY IMAGES.

tory, motivation, emotion, and biology. He did not ignore them, however; he controlled for them.

In 1928 Skinner wrote to Saunders that his interests lay in psychology, adding in mild conceit: "even, if necessary, by making over the entire field to suit myself" (1979, p. 38). He never made the field over, but by the late-1930s he had established a new professional persona, no longer as Fred, but as "B. F." Skinner; and a new style of psychological science. In the latter, knowledge was based on experimental control, not contemplation. Experimental control was established through the discovery and demonstration of functional relations, not correlations. The discovery and demonstration of those relations were the process and product of within-individual experimental control, not statistical control of between-group differences. Irreducible functional relations were basic behavioral processes. Theory was their integration. Although these characteristics were not exceptional in natural science, Skinner uniquely extended them to the behavioral, social, and cognitive sciences.

With this style, Skinner founded a psychological science whose basic processes were, like Pavlov's, universal; they transcended individuals and cultures (e.g., reinforcement). Their products, though, were situated, that is, dependent on time and place, and thereby the province of natural history (e.g., reinforcers). Except in later simulation research, Skinner never systematically analyzed behavior's natural history, but instead offered interpretations of it based on and constrained by the basic processes. Where experimental control is not possible in science, for instance, in explaining plate tectonics and tidal forces, interpretation is a common form of explanation. Skinner's most famous and infamous interpretation was of verbal behavior, which he began in 1934 on a challenge from the British philosopher Alfred North Whitehead. Within a year, he offered his first interpretation—"Has Gertrude Stein a Secret?"—arguing that her secret was automatic writing. Appearing in the *Atlantic Monthly*, this was the first of his popular press publications. They made him a visible scientist.

In 1936 Skinner moved to the University of Minnesota as an instructor of psychology and married Yvonne (Eve) Blue, who had majored in English at the University of Chicago. A year later, he was promoted to assistant professor and, in two more years, to associate professor. In 1938 his first daughter, Julie, was born, and he published his seminal text, *The Behavior of Organisms*. The text integrated the style and content of his science, reported new findings (e.g., stimulus generalization, response differentiation, periodic reconditioning), and formalized a generic unit of analysis: a "three-term contingency" comprised of operant behavior, its reinforcing consequences, and antecedent discriminative stimuli that set the occasion for previously reinforced responding. Because the unit was generic, it elided the multiple controls and multiple effects of its constituents, and thus had the appearance of being impoverished, even as it encompassed deeper complexities, as all generic units do in science. For his research Skinner was awarded the Howard Crosby Warren Medal in 1942 by the Society of Experimental Psychologists.

War Years. Skinner then began to extending his science. With William Heron, he conducted arguably the first research in behavioral pharmacology. With William Estes, he simulated anxiety through the suppression of responding by pre-aversive stimuli in an experimental preparation that became a means for assessing the effects of pharmaceuticals on emotion. As for verbal behavior, he taught courses on the psychology of literature and language and, in 1942, received a Guggenheim Fellowship to work on what would become his book, *Verbal Behavior*. However,

he delayed the fellowship until after World War II, during which time he pursued his first sustained program of applied research. This was "Project Pigeon," in which he trained pigeons to peck images on screens that then guided simulated missiles to precise destinations. Although he never overcame the military's objections to engineering through behavior, Skinner did discover how to shape new behavior through differential reinforcement. This led to Marian and Keller Breland's Animal Behavior Enterprises (1943–1990), training programs for the chimpanzees on the unmanned Project Mercury space flights (1959–1961), as well as behaviorally based robotics at the turn of the millennium.

Skinner's next invention was social—an "air crib"—which he built for Eve as a convenience in caring for their second daughter, Deborah (b. 1944). As described in the *Ladies' Home Journal*, the crib was a raised, enclosed, sound-attenuated mobile space with a full front window and shade, air filters, controls for heat and humidity, and a role of sheets for the bedding. Its purpose was to aid maternal care and ensure infant comfort and health. The article's title, however—"Baby in a Box"—led to speculation that Skinner was conducting research with Deborah, which led to later rumors that she had become psychotic. In fact, Skinner manipulated nothing more than the crib's heat and humidity to keep Deborah comfortable. He did attempt to market the cribs, but business was not his forte. Still, many parents built cribs of their own, based on his design.

As for Deborah, she married Barry Buzan, an economist at the University of London, in 1973, and became a restaurant and hotel reviewer in England and an accomplished artist. Julie married Ernest Vargas, a sociologist, in 1962; they were the parents of Skinner's two granddaughters, Lisa (b. 1966) and Justine (b. 1970). With a doctorate in educational research from the University of Pittsburgh, Julie applied her father's science to education as a professor at West Virginia University. After she retired in 2003, she and Ernest promoted Skinner's work through the B. F. Skinner Foundation (est. 1987). Skinner was remembered as an adoring father and grandfather.

As World War II drew to a close, Skinner began reflecting on his dissatisfactions with social conventions and developed an interest in cultural design. The result was his utopian novel, *Walden Two*, which described a community that used his science to improve its practices, for instance, in childrearing, education, and labor. Misunderstood as a blueprint for intentional communities, the book appalled critics who aligned it with fascist regimes. Skinner, however, proposed no blueprint, but rather suggested that communities take an experimental approach to discovering practices that worked. Experimentation was constant; practices were contingent. Although *Walden*

Two was not influential until later, in it, Skinner articulated a key implication of his science: "The organism is always right" in the sense that its behavior was lawful. Individuals were not autonomous agents, even when conscious of their behavior. Consciousness was also behavior. However, Skinner was not suggesting that "anything goes." Cultures have an interest in controlling behavior in the short term to serve social justice and in the long term to assure cultural survival. Skinner's stance, nonetheless, disconcerted those who believed in free will and moral culpability. They charged him with scientism, even as "the organism is always right" was rife with moral values.

Rethinking Operationalism. Skinner took a philosophical turn in his 1945 article "The Operational Analysis of Psychological Terms," where he critiqued two conventional forms of operationalism and offered one of his own. He argued against the operationalism in logical positivism. It led to descriptive concepts so narrowly defined that they belied the richness of psychology's subject matter, for instance, that intelligence quotients defined intelligence. He also inveighed against the operationalism in logical empiricism. It promoted explanatory constructs that were reified descriptions of behavior or mental fictions, for instance, that intelligence quotients were an index of some *thing* called intelligence. In their place, he proposed that psychological terms be operationalized as behavioral relations that were discriminative for using those terms. For instance, giving correct answers to difficult questions is an occasion for calling someone "intelligent." Intelligence is an attribute of behavior, not an entity behind it.

Skinner also extended his analysis to private events, that is, to stimuli and responses within the organism, because they, too, are discriminative for psychological terms. Like the terms for public events, terms for private events are acquired socially, but less reliably, for lack of common public referents. They have to be acquired, for instance, on the basis of public accompaniments of private events (e.g., on seeing their children succeed in the face of adversity, parents ask, "don't you feel proud?") or on the basis of collateral public behavior (e.g., on hearing students give answers to arithmetic problems solved in their heads, teachers say "good thinking"). This led Skinner to call his philosophy of science "radical behaviorism." By radical, though, he did not mean extreme, but instead, thoroughgoing, in the sense that behavior was the basis for everything psychological. This was akin to Gilbert Ryle's concept of mind and Ludwig Wittgenstein's ordinary-language conception of mental terms.

Also in 1945, Skinner moved to Indiana University as a full professor and chairperson of the Department of Psychology. He continued his program of research, for

instance, on the differential reinforcement of response rates and conditional discriminative stimuli, and moved to clarify the meaning of "control" in his work. Control—experimental control—was the goal of research. The goal of science, in contrast, was understanding, by which he meant an empirically derived theory. In science, control was a means for deriving a theory and then for testing it, but not an end in itself. By 1947, Skinner's students and colleagues were establishing their own programs of experimental research, notably, Nat Schoenfeld and Keller at Columbia University, and organizing conferences to present their finding. Also that year, Skinner accepted an invitation from Harvard's Department of Psychology to deliver its William James Lectures, which he titled "Verbal Behavior: A Psychological Analysis." Afterward, he was invited to join the department and again he accepted.

Harvard University. Back at Harvard, Skinner reached the high point of his career. He established a long-standing pigeon laboratory and analyzed how scheduling reinforcers according to, for instance, the number of responses, time, and their interrelations, alone and in sequence, signaled and unsignaled, produced distinctive and reliable patterns of responding. This work resulted in his book with Charles Ferster, *Schedules of Reinforcement* (1957). In addition, Skinner played a significant role in founding behavioral pharmacology, as well as the field of human operant behavior. In the latter, he and Ogden Lindsley replicated the style and content of his science with psychiatric patients. In the 1950s, he also conducted simulation research on superstition and, in the 1960s, on cooperation, competition, and aggression. Overall, several generations of experimental psychologists were trained in his Harvard laboratory, contributing fundamental knowledge on myriad topics, among them, conditioned reinforcement, stimulus control, escape and avoidance, punishment, and concurrent schedules of reinforcement, the last for studying choice as behavior.

By the late 1940s, psychology was fully engaged in testing theories of explanatory constructs, which Skinner criticized in a 1950 article, "Are Theories of Learning Necessary?" He argued that the theories of mediating structures and processes (e.g., learning) were too underdetermined to be confirmed in a hypothetical-deductive manner. For this, he was called anti-theory, but he was criticizing theories of mind, not of behavior. He was not, however, criticizing cognition, emotion, and personality as descriptive concepts. Captured in analogies such as "the climate is to the weather as personality is to behavior," personality was not a psychological structure that mediated between behavior and the environment, but a situated product of behavior's natural history, constrained by biology. It was one of psychology's content domains.

In 1953 Skinner published *Science and Human Behavior,* which integrated his science and philosophy into a system. Reviewed by biologists, philosophers, psychologists, and sociologists, and assigned as an introductory textbook, it reached a wide audience. It was also replete with interpretations of everyday behavior—individual (e.g., emotion, self-control, thinking), social (e.g., personal and group control), and cultural (e.g., education, psychotherapy)—and with descriptions of how his science could be applied to them. This made the book foundational for applied behavior analysis a decade later.

According to Skinner, his most important book was *Verbal Behavior.* Published in 1957, it offered an interpretation of why people say what they say, not how they say it, that is, of the function of verbal behavior, not its structure. The latter is an orthogonal province of knowledge, not an incompatible one (viz. physiology and anatomy). The book was controversial, though: Many of Skinner's colleagues set it aside as pure theory, embarrassed by its lack of data. The psycholinguist Noam Chomsky notably criticized it for not being a mediational neurological-genetic theory, setting the grounds for a longstanding debate. Although the book had little immediate impact, Skinner continued to develop his interpretation, addressing the evolutionary basis of verbal behavior, and then consciousness, generativity, and listener behavior (e.g., rule-governed behavior). By 1982 enough research was being conducted to support a modest journal, *The Analysis of Verbal Behavior.*

In the late 1950s Skinner's contributions became the basis of several institutional developments and further awards. In 1958 the first journal for his science was founded: the *Journal of the Experimental Analysis of Behavior.* This led to better-informed reviews and a more knowledgeable readership, but at the cost of isolation. Also, he was elected that year to the National Academy of Sciences, was given the American Psychological Association's (APA) Award for Distinguished Scientific Contributions, and was named the Edgar Pierce Professor of Psychology at Harvard. In 1964 his colleagues founded APA Division 25 for the Experimental Analysis of Behavior (later, Behavior Analysis), but its modest membership limited its influence. In 1968 he received the National Medal of Science.

Applications of Behaviorism. Although Skinner urged that his science be applied to human behavior, he himself undertook only one direct application. Its impetus was a 1953 visit to Deborah's classroom, where he found the teacher ignoring the basic behavioral processes (e.g., immediate reinforcement). Within a year, he invented teaching machines and programmed instruction; demonstrated their effectiveness and efficiency; and published

the first of more than twenty-five related works. The Soviet Union's launch of Sputnik I in 1957 abetted these developments: Professional societies were formed; conferences were held; journals were founded; and research was funded.

Skinner also tried to market his inventions, but by the time he published his text, *The Technology of Teaching,* in 1968, the teaching machine movement was languishing. Poor programs had flooded the market, tainting the technology, and, in Skinner's view, educators were more inclined to select students who learned and grade them on a curve than to use evidence-based practices to assure that all students achieved mastery. His relationship with educators was not harmonious. His technology survived mainly where teaching had to be effective: in industry, the armed forces, and, in particular, special education, where his work led to a 1971 award from the Joseph P. Kennedy Foundation for Mental Retardation and a 1978 award from the National Association for Retarded Persons. By the end of the millennium, higher education's embrace of the scholarship of teaching brought renewed interest in evidence-based practices, making Skinner's technology again relevant (e.g., Keller's personalized system of instruction), but by then his name was rarely associated with it.

The influence of *Science and Human Behavior* and the effectiveness of teaching machines notwithstanding, or perhaps because of them, Americans were growing wary of the unintended effects of behavioral technology and the intended effects of social control. These dangers made the ethical implications of Skinner's science salient, leading him to address them. In a 1955–1956 article, "Freedom and the Control of Men," he pointed out that control is assumed in science; it was determinism. Basic science discovers control; applied science uses it. The danger lies in failing to discover or modify the extant control to improve the human condition. Skinner also argued that aversive control—what is usually meant by "control"—be replaced with positive reinforcement. The latter worked better in the long run, did not have negative side effects, and yielded feelings of freedom and dignity. In a debate, the client-centered psychotherapist Carl Rogers argued that values and free choice were the basis of behavior. Skinner countered: Values were not the basis of behavior, they specified reinforcers; and choice was not free, it was lawful. Later he addressed the naturalistic fallacy, that is, the fallacy that individuals can derive values about how the world ought to be from how it is. In his view, a science of human behavior could address "ought" statements: They are verbal behavior about values; values concern short-term and long-term positive and negative reinforcers; and reinforcers are the consequences of action. Skinner's science was a science of action, reinforcers, and verbal behavior. It offered an empirical basis for determining what

PUNISHMENT	
Positive punishment	**Negative punishment**
When the subject—a person or animal—engages in a behavior and something negative is applied as a result, the behavior is less likely to be repeated.	When the subject—a person or animal—engages in a behavior and something positive is taken away, that behavior is less likely to be repeated.

B. F. Skinner's table of positive and negative punishment.

practices might (not must) produce valued consequences for individuals and the culture at large. Skinner's naturalized ethics, though, was never fully developed.

In the 1960s the ethical implications of Skinner's contributions expanded into social implications, especially as *Walden Two* became the basis for intentional communities (e.g., Twin Oaks in1967; Los Horcones in 1973). For this, Skinner turned to topics in the design of intentional communities, especially their controls and counter-controls. By the 1970s the social implications expanded into cultural implications, which Skinner addressed in a 1964–1974 Career Award from the National Institute of Mental Health for "A Behavioral Analysis of Cultural Practices." The result was his book, *Beyond Freedom and Dignity* (1971), in which he argued that Western culture must move beyond these concepts. They were not the basis of behavior, but attributes of behavior that needed explaining. Moreover, cultures that supported a science of human behavior were the ones most likely to survive. The book was unsettling in the American culture, but it made Skinner a public intellectual or, to his detractors, an anti-intellectual. Given his overarching concern for humanity, though, the American Humanist Society gave him its 1972 Humanist of the Year Award to underscore this shared goals, albeit amid controversy over differences in their philosophies. By then, Skinner was no less inclined to enjoin controversy, nor would he be in the future, but his youthful conceit, while always cleverly engaged, was giving way to a more colleagial and congenial style, for which he was remembered.

By the late 1950s a new generation of Skinner's colleagues and students began applying his science to human behavior and, in 1968, founded what became its leading journal, the *Journal of Applied Behavior Analysis*. At the turn of the millennium, it was one of more than twenty related journals. Indeed, by then, more applied and inter-

vention research was being published than basic research, and applied behavior analysis becoming a profession.

Retirement. Skinner retired from Harvard as a professor emeritus in 1974, the same year he published *About Behaviorism*, a summary and defense of his science and system. Afterward, he remained engaged as a scholar and intellectual, publishing more than one hundred additional works. His contributions also became the basis of new journals: *Behaviorism* in 1972 (later, *Behavior and Philosophy*), *The Behavior Analyst* in 1978, and *Social Action and Behavior* in 1982 (later, *Behavior and Social Issues*). *The Behavior Analyst* was the house journal of the Association for Behavior Analysis (ABA). Founded in 1974, ABA defined an independent system of psychology or, possibly, a separate discipline. In the first decade of new millennium, its membership had grown to more than 5,000, in addition to 6,000 members in thirty U.S. affiliated chapters and 7,000 in thirty chapters abroad. ABA was international. Other organizations followed, among them the Cambridge Center for Behavioral Studies in 1981.

After a hiatus of several decades, Skinner returned briefly to research, conducting simulation research with Robert Epstein on problem solving, remembering, and self-awareness. He also extended his science to self-management, of which he had always been a master, publishing *Enjoy Old Age*, with Margaret Vaughan in 1983. He engaged ethics again: the ethics of helping people, when help fostered dependence, not independence, and the ethics of aversive control, whose utility he acknowledged in special cases, but whose use was often flawed. The topics he addressed most systematically, though, were biological and cognitive psychology. They were eclipsing his science and system.

Skinner had begun integrating biology into his system in the 1960s, in particular, evolutionary biology. Natural selection and reinforcement shared a mode of causation—selection by consequences. In retirement, though, he had to defend his science against charges of environmentalism. It was environmentalistic in the sense of being a science of behavior-environment relations, in which biology was controlled for. Otherwise, Skinner took the middle ground on nature and nurture, but in doing so, he retained the problematic dichotomy between them, as did mainstream psychology. Earlier attempts notwithstanding, the dichotomy was not systematically challenged until the end of the millennium by developmental systems theory, at that time itself a minority view.

As for reductionism, Skinner held two complementary positions. First, he rejected explanatory reductionism: In a natural science, behavioral processes were not reducible to biological processes. In fact, biology should first look to behavior for what it has to explain. Second, he accepted constituative reductionism: In a natural history of behavior, biology is an independent variable. Skinner's views were largely consistent with behavioral neuroscience, but opposed to cognitive neuroscience, which he considered a reductive program that sought to escape literal dualism by instantiating the mind as brain.

By the time Skinner retired, a putative cognitive revolution was in full force. In his view, though, the revolution only changed the field's surface structure, not its deep structure. It changed psychology's terminology from stimulus-and-response to input-and-output, but left psychology's explanatory practices unaltered. Cognitivism was but another instantiation of mediational behaviorism, now couched in a computational metaphor. In a constructive mode, though, he described how behavior analysis could rescue psychology: The origins of cognitive terms lay in behavior, and their operational analysis showed how cognition could be explained by biological and behavioral contingencies and context. Cognition was an *explanandum*, not an *explanans*. Skinner was not alone in these views, but the other like-minded programs in psychology rarely saw or they denied any affinity; moreover, they too were minority programs unable to wield much authority (e.g., ecological approaches to perception and memory). As the new millennium dawned, the APA still described psychology as the science of mind *and* behavior—not the science of mind as behavior.

Skinner died of leukemia on 18 August 1990, at the age of eighty-six, the day after he completed the manuscript version of an invited APA address he had delivered nine days earlier, "Can Psychology Be a Science of Mind?" This was the occasion of the APA's first award for Outstanding Lifetime Contribution. His answer to the rhetorical question was of course no, but he was optimistic, in principle, about psychology's naturalization. In practice, though, he worried. He worried about the fate of the Earth, especially of humanity, expressing concerns about daily life in Western culture, international conflict and peace, and why people were not acting to save the world. The solutions he proffered lay in a science of human behavior, but the science may have evolved too late in history to ensure a human and humane future. If, however, as Skinner avowed, cultures were experiments in nature, then he might have viewed the increased internationalization of his science and system with some hope for the future.

BIBLIOGRAPHY

The Harvard University archives is the main repository of Skinner's unpublished works and correspondence. Still others are housed at his home in Cambridge, Massachusetts, under the oversight of the B. F. Skinner foundation (www.bfskinner.org). The foundation also maintains an updated, on-line bibliography of Skinner's published works.

WORKS BY SKINNER

"Has Gertrude Stein a Secret?" *Atlantic Monthly* 153 (January 1934): 50–57. His first popular press article and the one that made him a visible scientist.

The Behavior of Organisms. New York: Appleton-Century, 1938. The seminal presentation of his science.

"Baby in a Box." *Ladies' Home Journal* 62 (October 1945): 30–31, 135–136, 138. His first popular press article to spawn an urban legend.

"The Operational Analysis of Psychological Terms." *Psychological Review* 52 (1945): 270–277, 291–294. His differentiation of radical behaviorism from other behaviorisms.

Walden Two. New York: Macmillan, 1948. His break with social convention in utopian genre.

"Are Theories of Learning Necessary?" *Psychological Review* 57 (1950): 193–216. The cause of his being called "anti-theory," when he was only questioning hypothetical constructs.

Science and Human Behavior. New York: Macmillan, 1953. His first systematic text.

"Freedom and the Control of Men." *The American Scholar* 25 (1955–1956): 47–65. A well-written essay and thoughtful grappling with issues.

"A Case History in Scientific Method." *American Psychologist* 11 (1956): 221–233. A retrospective and bemused look at how his science started.

With Charles B. Ferster. *Schedules of Reinforcement.* New York: Appleton-Century-Crofts, 1957. His last great contribution to his science.

Verbal Behavior. New York: Appleton-Century-Crofts, 1957. What he said was his most important work, which would be his most controversial book in psychology.

"B. F. Skinner." In *A History of Psychology in Autobiography*, edited by Edwin. G. Boring and Gardner Lindzey. New York: Appleton-Century-Crofts, 1967. His first autobiography.

The Technology of Teaching. New York: Appleton-Century-Crofts, 1968. An overview of his major applied endeavor.

Beyond Freedom and Dignity. New York: Knopf, 1971. The far-ranging implications of his science for the human condition.

About Behaviorism. New York: Knopf, 1974. The last statement and defense of his science and system.

Particulars of My Life. New York: Knopf, 1976. The first of three autobiographical volumes.

The Shaping of a Behaviorist. New York: Knopf, 1979.

A Matter of Consequences. New York: Knopf, 1983.

With Margaret E. Vaughan. *Enjoy Old Age.* New York: Norton, 1983. Skinner's self-management at its best.

"Can Psychology Be a Science of the Mind?" *American Psychologist* 45 (1990): 1206–1210.

Cumulative Record. Cambridge, MA: B. F. Skinner Foundation, 1999. A collection of his important publications.

OTHER SOURCES

Andresen, J. T. "Skinner and Chomsky: 30 Years Later. *Historiographica Linquisitica* 17 (1990): 145–165. Places Chomsky's and Skinner's work in historical and contemporary context.

Bjork, Daniel. W. *B. F. Skinner: A Life*. New York: Basic Books, 1993. An accurate and accessible biography.

Boakes, Robert. *From Darwin to Behaviourism: Psychology and the Minds of Animals*. Chicago: University of Chicago Press, 1984. Describes the origins of a science of behavior.

Maccorquodale, K. "On Chomsky's Review of Skinner's *Verbal Behavior*." *Journal of the Experimental Analysis of Behavior* 13 (1970): 83–99. The most detailed response to Chomsky's review of *Verbal Behavior*.

Morris, Edward K., and James T. Todd, eds. *Modern Perspectives on B. F. Skinner and Contemporary Behaviorism*. Westport, CT: Greenwood, 1985. Studies of Skinner's science and system.

O'Donnell, John. M. *The Origins of Behaviorism: American Psychology, 1870–1920*. New York: New York University Press, 1985. Places behaviorism in social and cultural context—progressivism and modernism.

Pavlov, Ivan P. *Conditioned Reflexes*. London: Oxford University Press, 1927. The science of involuntary behavior on which Skinner modeled his science of voluntary behavior.

———. "B. F. Skinner's Technology of Behavior in American Life: From Consumer Culture to Counterculture." *Journal of the History of the Behavioral Sciences* 39 (2003): 1–23.

Rutherford, Alexandra. "A 'Visible Scientist': B. F. Skinner Writes for the Popular Press." *European Journal of Behavior Analysis* 5 (2004): 109–129.

Smith, Laurence D. *Behaviorism and Logical Positivism: A Reassessment of the Alliance*. Stanford, CA: University of California Press, 1986. A definitive treatment of Skinner's science of science.

———, and William R. Woodward, eds. *B. F. Skinner and Behaviorism in American Culture*. Bethlehem, PA: Lehigh University Press, 1996. Studies of Skinner and his science in context.

Smith, Nathaniel G., and Edward. K. Morris. "A Tribute to B. F. Skinner at 100: A Review and Chronology of His Awards and Honors." *European Journal of Behavior Analysis* 5 (2004): 121–128.

Todd, James T., and Edward K. Morris. "Case Studies in the Great Power of Steady Misrepresentation." *American Psychologist* 47 (1992): 1441–1453. Review and analysis of the misrepresentations of Skinner's work, published in a special issue in honor of Skinner.

Watson, John B. *Behaviorism*. New York: Norton, 1925. The first behaviorist's last statement of behaviorism.

Zuriff, Gerald E. *Behaviorism: A Conceptual Reconstruction*. New York: Columbia University Press, 1985. A systematic review of the bases of the behaviorisms.

Edward K. Morris

SLOSS, LAURENCE LOUIS (*b*. Mountain View, California, 26 August 1913; *d*. Evanston, Illinois, 2 November 1996), *stratigraphic geology.*

The science of stratigraphy is focused on the layered sedimentary rocks of Earth's crust, which provide the primary evidence for the physical history of the planet and for the history of life. Sloss was the preeminent American stratigrapher of the twentieth century. His work reorganized the discipline and gave rise to the concept of sequence stratigraphy.

Career Overview. Laurence L. Sloss was a California native, the son of Joseph and Edith (Esberg) Sloss. He stayed in California long enough to attend Stanford University (AB, 1934) and then departed for the heartland, which was to be his permanent base of operations. He studied paleontology at the University of Chicago, completing a dissertation on Devonian corals under the direction of Professor Carey Croneis.

Sloss finished his PhD in 1937 and began teaching as an instructor at the Montana School of Mines, in Butte. He held a concurrent position as geologist with the State Bureau of Mines and Geology, which gave him access to stratigraphic data from across the huge area of the state of Montana. He began to compile information on the distribution of sedimentary rocks, utilizing drilling records from the petroleum industry to supplement the natural exposures in the mountain ranges. His summary paper on the Devonian System (with Wilson M. Laird) was published in 1947, in the *Bulletin of the American Association of Petroleum Geologists*, and won the AAPG President's Award, as the best article of the year. That same year, Sloss moved to Northwestern University, where he remained for the rest of his life. At Northwestern he was part of a famous triumvirate (with William C. Krumbein and Edward C. Dapples) that modernized and quantified the study of sedimentary rocks. Krumbein and Sloss's textbook, *Stratigraphy and Sedimentation* (1951) became the standard classroom work for the next generation.

Sequence Stratigraphy. Sloss's primary accomplishment was the recognition that the rock record of the North American continent was naturally subdivided. Throughout much of the past 500 million years or so, the continent has lain below sea level; marine strata accumulated during these times. Sporadically there have been intervals of relative sea-level fall, each of which ended deposition and exposed the previously deposited rocks to erosion. The resulting erosion surface was covered by renewed deposition when relative sea level rose again. Such an ancient erosion surface is called an unconformity. Beginning in the 1940s in Montana, Sloss recognized the existence of several such unconformities that could be traced laterally, first on a regional basis and eventually all the way across the stable central nucleus (craton) of North America. The assemblage of strata lying between successive unconformities was

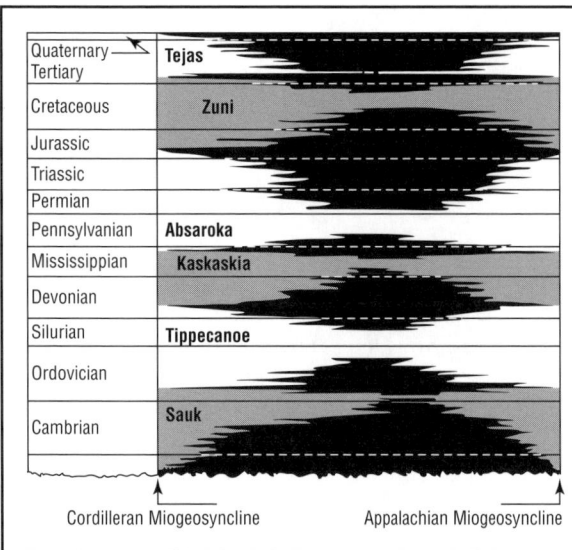

Figure 1. *Diagram of Sloss sequences from his 1963 paper. Horizontal scale is cross-section across North American craton, with bounding mountain belts on west and east. Vertical scale is geologic time, with the standard names of the periods. The six Indian-name rock sequences are shown as white or gray (alternating to clarify individual sequences). Black shows missing time encompassed by non-deposition and erosion at each unconformity surface.*

termed by Sloss to be a stratigraphic *sequence*. He named the sequences (see figure) using geographic terms for areas where the particular rocks were exposed; the names were derived from American Indian words, for terminological uniformity and to emphasize that the sequences derive from the study of North America, rather than Europe, the source of most previous stratigraphic concepts and terms. Sloss announced his basic concept and named the lower four sequences in 1949. In 1963 he published his most important paper, "Sequences in the Cratonic Interior of North America," in which he added the final two sequences and documented the stratigraphic details for all six.

Significance. The six cratonic sequences record the depositional and erosive history of the continent over a time span of half a billion years. Each sequence involves sedimentary accumulation lasting tens of millions to more than 100 million years (the sequences are not of equal duration). The intervals of emergence and erosion are shorter, a few million to a few tens of millions of years. The individual rock formations that make up the sequences record much shorter time intervals, and as a rule they are products of deposition in a local setting. Hence the formations cannot be traced far laterally, and the age relations between all the various formations in dif-

ferent regions are commonly obscure. That is, in one area the order of events is recoverable by studying the formation column, but in a second area, different events took place and the formations are not the same as in the first area. Matching the two orders of events (stratigraphic correlation) is very difficult. Sloss's sequences, because they are based on (usually) unambiguous unconformity surfaces, surfaces evident even in geologic well cores and geophysical logs, allow geologists to trace them from one region to another. Each sequence is roughly equivalent in time. Thus the sequences provided a new method of correlation.

Although the data used by Sloss were largely based on subsurface records generated by the petroleum industry, Sloss's concept was developed in academia, and for more than a decade his six sequences remained an academic curiosity. Some geologists adopted his terminology as a parallel system to the traditional geologic time scale terms (Cambrian, Ordovician, and so forth). The concept was not built upon, though, for two reasons: (1) the sequences were too thick to be useful in detailed stratigraphy in a small area; and (2) no one, including Sloss, knew what the cause of the sea-level fluctuations was. Sloss was determined, in his original paper and afterward, to show that the sequences were a function of dynamic movements of the craton, independent of movements in the mountain belts marginal to the continent (the Cordilleran and Appalachian chains). The craton-wide unconformities cannot be traced into the stratigraphy of the mountain belts; there, more localized upheavals generated a series of local unconformities, not synchronous with the breaks on the craton. In 1963, Sloss's uncertainty as to cause was simply part of the larger uncertainty all geologists experienced in trying to explain structural movements of the earth (tectonics). In the ensuing decade, the new theory of plate tectonics revolutionized geologic thought. Mountains came to be understood in terms of plate margin collisions; the structures and uplifts of ancient mountain belts were shown to have detailed analogues in active plate settings in the early twenty-first century. However, vertical movements of the cratonic interiors of the continents proved more difficult to fit into the plate theory. Sloss's ongoing assertion, which continued his entire life, that the sequences are fundamentally tectonic in origin was, and continued to be, regarded in 2007 as unproven.

Seismic Stratigraphy. The sequence concept was eventually developed further by geologists in the petroleum industry, using subsurface information from the modern continental margins, especially seismic reflection profiling. Artificial seismic (sound) waves are capable of penetrating kilometers down into the thick piles of sediment that accumulate to form the continental shelves and slopes. The seismic waves reflect from subsurface structures back to the surface where they are recorded. The echoes reveal the buried patterns of stratification, especially the unconformities. Sloss's former PhD student, Peter Vail at Exxon Production Research Laboratories, realized that these subsurface unconformities could be used to define sequences on the continental margins. These sequences were of short duration, orders of magnitude shorter than Sloss's original sequences. By comparing the relative sea-level fluctuations on separate continental shelves, industry geologists were able to recognize a worldwide pattern of sea-level rise and fall extending back to Triassic time, more than 200 million years ago ("Vail curve"). Very short-term fluctuations on the sea-level curve (10^4–10^5 year duration) probably represent glaciers waxing and waning. Longer cycles (10^6–10^7 year) are probably plate tectonic in origin. In principle, the short sequences provide geologists with a global method of time correlation as precise as that based on fossils. Sloss's concept of subdividing the rock record based on its internal breaks led to a new field in geology, sequence stratigraphy.

Honors. Sloss's new approach to stratigraphic geology made him one of the best-known geologists of his generation. He was called upon for service and given awards by the profession. After beginning as a lecturer at Northwestern in 1947, he progressed rapidly through the ranks, reaching professor status in 1954. In 1971 he was named William Deering Professor of Geological Sciences, the position he held until his retirement from teaching in 1981. Sloss was elected president of SEPM (Society for Sedimentary Geology) in 1961 and president of the American Geological Institute in 1968. In 1974 SEPM made him an honorary member, and in 1980 it conferred upon him its highest honor, the Twenhofel Medal. That same year he was elected president of the Geological Society of America. In 1986 he was the recipient of GSA's top award, the Penrose Medal. Finally, he was memorialized in 1999, when the Sedimentary Geology Division of GSA instituted an annual medal, the Sloss Award.

Sloss was active during his retirement, editing the craton volume in the Geology of North America series and participating vigorously in the controversies over seismic stratigraphy and the sea-level curve. He continued to work until the very end of his life. In 1996 he attended the Geological Society of America meeting in late October. He died following surgery in Evanston a few days later.

BIBLIOGRAPHY

WORKS BY SLOSS

With Wilson M. Laird. "Devonian System in Central and Northwestern Montana." *American Association of Petroleum Geologists Bulletin* 31 (1947): 1404–1430.

With William C. Krumbein and Edward C. Dapples. "Integrated Facies Analysis." In *Sedimentary Facies in Geologic History,* Memoir 39, edited by Chester R. Longwell. New York: Geological Society of America, 1949.

With William C. Krumbein. *Stratigraphy and Sedimentation.* San Francisco: Freeman, 1951.

"Sequences in the Cratonic Interior of North America." *Geological Society of America Bulletin* 74 (1963): 93–114.

"Areas and Volumes of Cratonic Sediments, Western North America and Eastern Europe." *Geology* 4 (1976): 272–276.

"Tectonic Evolution of the Craton in Phanerozoic Time." In *Sedimentary Cover—North American Craton: U. S.,* edited by Laurence L. Sloss. Geology of North America, vol. D-2. Boulder, CO: Geological Society of America, 1988.

"Forty Years of Sequence Stratigraphy." *Geological Society of America Bulletin* 100 (1988): 1661–1665.

OTHER SOURCE

"Memorial to Laurence L. Sloss, 1913–1996." *Geological Society of America Memorials* 30 (1999): 79–82. This short summary includes Sloss's acceptance remarks at his Twenhofel Medal ceremony. There is also a selected bibliography of his publications.

Charles W. Byers

SMAGORINSKY, JOSEPH

(*b.* New York, New York, 29 January 1924; *d.* Skillman, New Jersey, 21 September 2005), *dynamic meteorology, numerical modeling.*

Smagorinsky was the founder and director of the Geophysical Fluid Dynamics Laboratory, Princeton, New Jersey—an outgrowth of work on theoretical and operational numerical weather prediction in the late 1940s and early 1950s. Under his leadership the laboratory considered problems related to the general circulation of the atmosphere, pioneering collaborative research and expanding its reach to include numerical modeling of the oceans and a variety of atmospheric phenomena.

Early Years. Smagorinsky was born in New York City to Byelorussian immigrants Nathan and Dinah (Azaroff) Smagorinsky, the youngest of five sons. Intrigued by meteorology at an early age, during the thirties he would visit the top of the New York *Daily News* building to look at the weather instruments and see what was happening at their weather observatory as forecasters prepared the latest information for the newspaper. Extremely interested and talented in science and mathematics, Smagorinsky took and passed the entrance examination for one of New York's three science high schools, Stuyvesant High. As a student there, he received an enriched education in mathematics and science, and further indulged his interest in meteorology.

However, his true passion was naval architecture. Smagorinsky designed and built model boats that he would race on the lake in Central Park. When he was unable to pursue naval architecture in college due to financial considerations, he turned to his second love: meteorology.

Meteorological Education. Smagorinsky entered New York University (NYU) in 1941 as a student in its recently formed Meteorology Department. Within a few months, the United States entered World War II, and by 1943 he found himself in the Army Air Corps.

The United States had been woefully short on meteorologists at the beginning of the war. The military services needed thousands of forecasters to support aviation, land, and sea missions, but there were only four hundred professional meteorologists in the country. A training program, hastily assembled by Swedish American meteorologist Carl-Gustaf Rossby of the University of Chicago, had started training young college graduates with degrees in mathematics and physics to be meteorologists, and then turned to students who did not have degrees in hand. Those handpicked students were sent to the "B" course, offered at universities around the country, and then sent on to the final "A" course at one of the "Big Five" meteorology programs (University of Chicago; New York University; Massachusetts Institute of Technology (MIT); University of California, Los Angeles; or California Institute of Technology).

Smagorinsky, selected to attend the "B" course at Brown University, was one of the very few of these young men and women who had ever entertained the idea of being a meteorologist before the war. Successfully completing the course at Brown, he finished up the "A" course at MIT and was commissioned in 1944 the day before the D-day invasion. As an Army Air Corps weather officer, Smagorinsky provided flight forecasts for B-29 squadrons in Nebraska, and then concluded his military service as a weather reconnaissance officer in the North Atlantic.

Returning to NYU at the end of the war, Smagorinsky finished his BS in 1947, and his MS in 1948. While finishing his undergraduate degree, he met U.S. Weather Bureau statistician Margaret Knoepfel. One of the few women who had ever worked for the Weather Bureau, Knoepfel had been sent to NYU for graduate meteorology training. She had to return to headquarters in Washington, D.C., in 1947. A year later Smagorinsky moved south to join her and they were married. (The Smagorinskys would later have five children.) He had no intention of working for the Weather Bureau, but his other job options did not work out, and he soon found himself

working in the scientific services division—the bureau's research arm.

Numerical Weather Prediction. When he first entered meteorology, Smagorinsky was under the mistaken impression that it was a rational, scientific discipline whose forecasts were based on numerical calculations and the laws of physics. Inquiring as to why that was not the case, he was told by one of his professors that it had been suggested by Bergen School of Meteorology founder Vilhelm Bjerknes in 1904, and unsuccessfully tried during World War I by British meteorologist Lewis Fry Richardson. Calculating the weather was still a possibility; it just had not happened yet.

While at NYU, Smagorinsky heard dynamic meteorologist Jule Charney speak on the scale properties of the equations of motion—the early work that would lead to numerical weather prediction. Smagorinsky was fascinated by the possibilities of this rational approach to weather forecasting. He had the opportunity to hear Charney again when the latter spoke at the Weather Bureau in Washington, D.C. On that occasion Smagorinsky had several questions ready for Charney, who responded by inviting him to join the Meteorology Project at the Institute for Advanced Study in Princeton, New Jersey, where his team was developing numerical weather prediction models. Gaining a release from the Weather Bureau, Smagorinsky moved to Princeton to help with the one-dimensional linear barotropic model calculations while he simultaneously worked on his PhD at NYU. Margaret Smagorinsky joined the project also, working to program John von Neumann's new computer that would solve the atmospheric models being prepared by Charney's team.

Having completed his PhD in 1953, Smagorinsky was unsure of his next move. That was settled for him when Weather Bureau chief Francis W. Reichelderfer asked him to return to Washington, D.C., to head up the new numerical weather prediction unit. Reichelderfer, anticipating that numerical weather prediction would become an operational reality within a short period of time, realized the bureau needed to train people and procure equipment. The job went to Smagorinsky, who was given plenty of guidance, and a long list of things to do, by Charney. The Joint Numerical Weather Prediction Unit, an effort funded and staffed by the Weather Bureau, navy, and air force, opened its doors in 1954 and issued its first operational forecast in 1955. Smagorinsky had been responsible for evaluating and obtaining the unit's computer, determining efficient ways to handle data, and ensuring that Weather Bureau employees were trained in numerical techniques. Once the unit was operational, he turned his attention from operational modeling (prediction) to theoretical modeling.

General Circulation Research. The new joint unit was concerned with operational numerical weather prediction—the issuance of short-term forecasts. Von Neumann and Charney encouraged Reichelderfer to establish a separate group that would continue research on the general circulation of the atmosphere, work that had been started by meteorologist Norman A. Phillips. With funding from the navy and air force, Reichelderfer agreed and the Weather Bureau established the General Circulation Research Section in 1955 to conduct basic research on the general circulation of the atmosphere and on climate. Smagorinsky became the director in October 1955, and through three name changes for the section remained its director until his retirement in 1983.

At first, the small group (five people at the end of 1955) worked on general atmospheric circulation (i.e., the overall global movement of air), a complex problem for which there would be no quick solution. Smagorinsky realized, however, that if they were to extend their atmospheric circulation modeling to climate modeling they would need to incorporate ocean modeling, which they did in 1960. Until that time, the ocean had been held static. Indeed, early models did not include surface interactions because they were too difficult to model. Smagorinsky also realized the importance of modeling individual meteorological processes and taking the lessons learned from those virtual experiments and applying them to weather forecasting and climate models. His work with G. O. Collins in 1955 on numerically predicting precipitation was a forerunner of all later efforts on specific processes. Smagorinsky pioneered interdisciplinary interactions in meteorological modeling, and his team gradually included radiation, condensation, boundary layer processes, and ocean surface interactions into their increasingly complicated models.

By 1963, Smagorinsky's group had changed its name along with its mission, becoming known as the Geophysical Fluid Dynamics Laboratory (GFDL). Five years later the laboratory moved from Washington, D.C., to Princeton, New Jersey, to become associated with, but remain independent of, Princeton University. Princeton had a strong interest in fluid dynamics and the arrival of the laboratory provided them with a ready-made graduate program in the subject.

However, the laboratory was not tied to a specific department. It had formal ties to the civil engineering, aerospace and mechanical sciences, and geology and geophysical sciences departments, and unofficial ties to astrophysics, chemical engineering, and statistics. These ties were important to Smagorinsky, who looked upon the modeling work being done by the laboratory as being at the intersection of a variety of disciplines. By the mid-1970s, however, the laboratory became administratively part of the Geology and Geophysical Sciences Department even though it maintained a separate identity as a national weather service-funded activity.

The laboratory tested circulation models by using real initial condition data and then considering it as a forecast run, that is, as if the model were predicting the weather instead of providing insight into the atmosphere's behavior, to check the results. In 1963, Smagorinsky published his primitive equation model of the general circulation. The so-called primitive equations of the atmosphere—equations of motions, continuity equation, equation of state, and the first law of thermodynamics—had been proposed as the way to calculate the weather by Norwegian Vilhelm Bjerknes in 1904, and had been taken up by Lewis Fry Richardson in his failed World War I–era attempt to produce a numerical forecast. However, the early numerical weather prediction modeling led by Jule Charney in the late forties and early fifties had opted for simpler models that would run on extant computers. By the 1960s, the primitive equations became viable modeling options due to advances in computing power. Smagorinsky's model was a significant breakthrough in model sophistication. Over time, the GFDL team increased the model run times, and turned its attention to modeling wind- and heat-driven ocean circulation, convection, hurricanes, mesoscale features, and climate. The weather and climate models developed by the laboratory since its inception have significantly increased meteorologists' understanding of atmospheric circulation, including heat and moisture transport, and human impact on Earth's changing climate.

Observational Experiments. The GFDL consistently needed large amounts of data to feed into its models, so Smagorinsky was always on the lookout for additional observation sources. He was extremely enthusiastic when Charney—mulling over ways to increase international cooperation for this most global of sciences—proposed a major observational data-gathering experiment. Later known as the Global Atmospheric Research Program (GARP), Charney's grand scheme for pulling together massive amounts of observational data from every conceivable direct and remote sensing platform got started in the late 1960s. Smagorinsky was asked by the National Academy of Sciences to be a member of the U.S. National Committee for GARP, and later served from 1967 to 1975 as one of twelve members of the Joint GARP Organizing Committee assembled under the auspices of the World Meteorological Organization and the International Council of Scientific Unions. He was chair of the organizing committee from 1976 to 1979, playing an important role in coordinating GARP's main event: the five-hundred-million-dollar, year long Global Weather Experiment of 1978 that involved scientists from 147 nations gathering data from satellites, buoys, ships, and constant-level balloons.

Awards. Smagorinsky received many awards during his distinguished career. He was elected as an American Meteorological Society (AMS) fellow in 1967 and selected as an honorary member—the highest distinction bestowed by the society—in 1992. Smagorinsky received several other awards from the AMS, including the Clarence Leroy Meisinger Award given for distinguished work by a scientists under age forty when nominated (1967), the Carl-Gustaf Rossby Research Medal for outstanding research leading to understanding of atmospheric behavior or structure (1972), the Cleveland Abbe Award for distinguished service to the atmospheric sciences by an individual (1980), and the Charles Franklin Brooks Award for outstanding services to the society (1991).

Smagorinsky was also recognized internationally. He received the Royal Netherlands Academy of Sciences' Buys Ballot Medal (1973), the World Meteorological Organization's IMO Prize—the most important international meteorological award—in 1974, and the Royal Meteorological Society's Symons Memorial Medal in 1981.

In 2003, Smagorinsky and longtime colleague and general circulation model creator Norman A. Phillips received the prestigious Benjamin Franklin Award in Earth Science given by the Franklin Institute of Philadelphia, for their work in computer modeling and Smagorinsky's role in establishing the global observational network.

Retirement. Smagorinsky retired from federal service in 1983 after leading the GFDL for twenty-eight years. Having survived a heart attack some ten years before, he had decided that it was time to leave the stress of running the laboratory to someone else. Although he had told the World Meteorological Organization's Hessam Taba that he had no specific plans, he did anticipate spending a considerable amount of time of on non-meteorology-related projects. However, he remained professionally active into the 1990s.

In 1986 he served as president of the American Meteorological Society, and remained on the executive committee until 1988. He also was chair of the National Research Council's Climate Research Committee from 1981 until 1987, and was an officer on the National Research Council's Board on Atmospheric Sciences and Climate. Smagorinsky continued his academic affiliations as a visiting senior fellow with Princeton University's Department of Geological and Geophysical Sciences, and

served as the Brittingham Visiting Professor at the University of Wisconsin in 1986. Although Smagorinsky had spent almost his entire career with GFDL, through his ties with Princeton he came to influence many graduate students in meteorology, encouraging them to pursue a broad range of interests within the field instead of becoming too specialized.

Smagorinsky died in 2005 after a long struggle with Parkinson's disease.

BIBLIOGRAPHY

WORKS BY SMAGORINSKY

"The Dynamical Influence of Large-Scale Heat Sources and Sinks on the Quasi-Stationary Mean Motions of the Atmosphere." *Quarterly Journal of the Royal Meteorological Society* 79 (1953): 342–366.

With G. O. Collins. "On the Numerical Prediction of Precipitation." *Monthly Weather Review* 83 (1955): 53–68.

"General Circulation Experiments with Primitive Equations: I. The Basic Experiment." *Monthly Weather Review* 91 (1963): 99–164.

Interview by Richard R. Mertz. Tape recording. 19 May 1971. National Museum of American History, Smithsonian Institution, Washington, DC.

"GARP—An Interim Retrospection." *WMO Bulletin* 29 (1980): 92–100.

Interview by John Young. Tape recording. 16 May 1986 and 21 May 1986. National Center for Atmospheric Research, Boulder, Colorado.

OTHER SOURCES

Smagorinsky, Margaret. Interview by Kristine C. Harper, Ronald E. Doel, and Terry Smagorinsky Thompson. Tape recording. 2 January 2006. National Center for Atmospheric Research, Boulder, Colorado.

Taba, Hessam. "Professor J. Smagorinsky." In *The "Bulletin" Interviews: Reprints of the 32 Interviews with Eminent Personalities in Meteorology and Hydrology That Appeared in the* WMO Bulletin *between 1981 and 1988.* Geneva: World Meteorological Organization, 1988.

Kristine C. Harper

SMALLEY, RICHARD ERRETT (*b.* Akron, Ohio, 6 June 1943; *d.* Houston, Texas, 28 October 2005), *chemistry, nanotechnology, fullerenes.*

Smalley was widely known as one of the three major influences in the beginning of the nanotechnology revolution. He was equally well known in the United States for his advocacy for strong science support at the federal level, for exciting children toward a career in science, and for awakening the world to impending energy problems. In only forty short years he created several fields of science, and he won the Nobel Prize in Chemistry in 1996 for the discovery of Carbon-60, identifying a new form of carbon, popularly known as "buckyballs."

Early Life and Career. Smalley, the youngest of four children of Frank Dudley Smalley Jr. and Esther Virginia Rhoads, was born into an upper-middle-class family that valued both education and mechanical and electrical handiwork. His interest in science began in his early teens with his mother showing him the ideas and beauty of nature with a microscope, but the impetus for his career in science came from the launch of *Sputnik* in 1957. After his junior year in high school, he knew he could be a serious student of science, and he began his love for chemistry, exemplified by his drawing the complete periodic table on the rafters of his attic in Kansas City, Missouri, where he set up his own private study for reading and reflection.

He began his academic career at Hope College in Holland, Michigan, and later transferred to the University of Michigan, where he earned a BSc in chemistry in 1965. Deciding to take time to work in the real world, he joined Shell Chemical Company in Woodbury, New Jersey, as a chemist in the quality control laboratory for the polypropylene plant. Smalley learned about industrial-scale processes and the critical importance of efficient catalysts in polymerization (which would prove useful much later in life when he began to scale-up carbon nanotube synthesis), and working with chemical engineers, he learned that chemists can do anything. After two years, he transferred to the Plastics Technical Center, where he developed analytical methods for studying the olefins. He married Judith Grace Sampieri in 1968 and their son, Chad Richard Smalley, was born in 1969.

Smalley moved his family to Princeton and began graduate studies at Princeton University in the fall of 1969. He joined the new research group of assistant professor Elliott Bernstein and began work on the chemical physics of condensed phase and molecular systems, using optical and microwave spectroscopy, a field stimulating Smalley's theoretical and experimental curiosities. Although not particularly fruitful, his study of sym-triazine gave him the tools and insight he needed for future studies. He began preparations for a postdoctoral fellowship in Chicago, and while preparing for his final dissertation defense, he seized on the idea of using supersonic expansion to cool molecules in order to slow their rotations, and to study the now simplified single-rotational-state molecules by laser spectroscopy. The experiment could be performed at the University of Chicago, and so, after receiving his PhD degree from Princeton University in 1973, he moved to Chicago.

Supersonic Beam Laser Spectroscopy. During his post-doctoral period with Lennard Wharton and Donald Levy at the University of Chicago, Smalley pioneered what has become one of the most powerful techniques in chemical physics, supersonic beam laser spectroscopy. The team achieved record low temperatures through clever improvements and soon could study polyatomic molecules, and then medium-sized molecules such as benzene, and finally van der Waals complexes and metal atom–rare earth gas complexes. In 1976 Smalley accepted an assistant professor position at Rice University in Houston, Texas, where he was eager to work with Robert Curl, a laser spectroscopist. Smalley immediately began building an elegant apparatus, modified to use pulsed ultraviolet dye lasers to look at even larger molecules. That was followed by a larger system to use pulsed nozzles for the cooling jet, synchronized with pulsed visible and ultraviolet lasers to study large molecules and clusters. Following his powerful pattern of building even larger machines with new capabilities, he continued to open up new fields of chemical physics, and his next generation machine used a pulsed laser to vaporize any material into the cold jet—opening up the entire periodic table to form clusters of controllable nanometer size of any element, and creating the science of metal and semiconductor cluster beams.

The Discovery of Fullerenes. Building a version of his apparatus for the Exxon laboratories, Smalley began a collaboration with Andrew Kaldor that led the Exxon group to study carbon clusters, and in 1983 they noted some strange, even-numbered clusters of carbon atoms, but did not follow up on their interpretation. In the summer of 1985, the British chemist Harold Kroto from Sussex University (later Sir Harold Kroto) visited Rice to perform experiments with Smalley's and Curl's research groups on carbon long-chain molecules predicted to have been formed in interstellar clouds from carbon-rich stars. Smalley's apparatus was used to vaporize carbon and, indeed, long-chain carbons were observed, along with the even-numbered carbon clusters previously noted by Kaldor. The high abundance of the C-60 cluster among clusters from 40 to 80 carbon atoms could only be explained by a stable, closed cage structure comprised of 12 pentagon and 20 hexagon faces, resembling a soccer ball, and named Buckminsterfullerene in honor of the famous architect and his geometrically similar geodesic domes.

Thus was created another new science—fullerenes, which has been recognized as one of the key discoveries leading to the nanotechnology revolution which began in earnest in the 1990s. The "buckyball" described in their two-page paper in *Nature*—coauthored by James Heath and Sean O'Brien, graduate students on the project—was recognized in 1996 by the award of the Nobel Prize in Chemistry to Smalley, Curl, and Kroto.

Richard E. Smalley *Prof. Smalley on campus.*
AP IMAGES.

Smalley, Curl, and Kroto spent the next several years after the publication of the fullerene paper defending their work and the concepts embodied in the series of fullerenes of varying sizes. Smalley and Curl continued to work closely together as colleagues and collaborators, whereas Kroto returned to England to pursue his own research directions. By 1990 fullerenes could be produced in sufficient quantity to permit unequivocal verification of their chemical existence and their remarkable properties. Smalley then turned toward the "big brother" of the buckyball, the carbon nanotube, which was reported initially by Sumio Iijima in Japan and others in 1991, and which Smalley had predicted from chemical geometrical arguments in the late 1980s. He redirected his research yet again into this new field with great enthusiasm, whereas Curl chose to resume a broader interest in spectroscopy, and by 1995 Smalley had succeeded in developing two efficient synthesis methods for making single-wall carbon nanotubes.

The properties of single-wall carbon nanotubes were predicted by Smalley and his collaborators to exceed any known materials in several respects. With the density of carbon, and a theoretical strength many times that of steel, carbon nanotubes will enable very strong, light-weight structures, and will make cars, trucks, airplanes

and spacecraft stronger, yet require less fuel. Nanotubes can be made to be much better conductors of electricity than copper or aluminum, which will enable much more efficient wiring for power cables, motors, and generators. They can also be made to be better semiconductors than silicon, to enable smaller and more powerful computers and electrical and optical devices. Their ability to conduct heat is better than any other material, which will allow smaller radiators and more powerful laptop computers. For these beneficial applications and many other revolutionary implications, such as in medicine, Smalley became the leading advocate for new funding and more extensive research in this particular form of nanotechnology.

Furthering Nanotechnology. In addition to being the most widely cited author in nanotechnology in the 1990s, Smalley was recognized as one of the leaders in establishing the U.S. National Nanotechnology Initiative (NNI), leading to greatly expanded federal funding, and creating a groundswell of research across the world. Smalley made samples of carbon nanotubes readily available to all researchers, and he founded a company to help promote commercialization. He was the only academic representative invited to the White House for the signing of the law in 2003 that ensured continuation of the NNI funding.

Smalley's strong advocacy for nanoscience and nanoengineering brought him into conflict with another of nanotechnology's early advocates, Eric Drexler. Smalley's objections to Drexler's ideas of molecular manufacturing and nanobots were raised in very public forums, particularly in *Scientific American*'s September 2001 issue. Smalley and other nanoscientists (especially Harvard's George Whitesides) suggested that atoms could not be simply moved around at will to be assembled into nanoscopic machines that resembled larger machines, and that chemical and physical laws dictated more collective approaches to molecular assembly "from the bottom up." The arguments provided much discussion and spurred research in both technical camps, and after several years the molecular manufacturing ideas were discredited to the extent of moving most of the proponents, including Drexler, into the more scientific nanochemistry mode.

Smalley advanced an extraordinary vision for using nanotechnology to solve the world's energy problems, including accelerating climate change, using carbon nanotubes to wire an intercontinental electrical grid capable of carrying all the world's energy needs in the form of electricity, instead of transporting masses of oil, gas, or coal. For the last four years of his life, his research group was dedicated to solving the scientific problems remaining in the manufacture of industrial-scale amounts of pure, metallic-conductivity, single-walled carbon nanotubes. Smalley tirelessly advanced his vision not only to the technical community, but also to the political and policy communities, and its capacity to include all the possible forms of renewable energy as well as fossil fuel (cleaned of greenhouse gas emissions) was recognized as unique. After his death, many in the field of energy and nanotechnology continued to advocate and advance his vision.

Smalley's vision for nanotechnology to transform the practice of medicine was as powerful as his energy vision, and he was the driving force to establish an Alliance for NanoHealth in the Houston, Texas, region. He believed that nanotechnology could enable the detection of disease at its earliest possible stages of only a few errant cells, by simple blood tests, and then analyzing the hundreds of thousands of protein fragments to indicate the presence of problems as they arise in the body. Only by coupling micro and nanotechnology with systems biology can the incredible complexities be managed. This vision continued to be advanced by many researchers in the early 2000s, with the potential to save many lives and to prolong life expectancy.

Honors. Smalley was named to the Gene and Norman Hackerman Chair in Chemistry in 1981, and became a university professor (highest rank) in 2002. Realizing the importance of collaborative research, especially in a small university, he was a founder of the Rice Quantum Institute in 1979, and in 1993 he established the Center for Nanoscale Science and Technology at Rice, the first organized institute or center for nanotechnology in the world. He was a member of the National Academy of Sciences and the American Academy of Arts and Sciences. He was the recipient of many national and international awards but was proudest of his election as "homecoming queen" by the students of Rice University in 1996. He received eight honorary academic degrees.

Smalley eventually married four times, having a second son Preston Reed Smalley with his third wife, and marrying his fourth wife, Deborah Sheffield Smalley, a science teacher, in June of 2005. Being married to a science teacher expanded his great love for teaching science to everyone he encountered. His passion for learning about nature through science was shared by his fellow Nobelists, and the world is fortunate that Robert Curl and Sir Harry Kroto also continued Smalley's passion for teaching.

Richard Smalley fought a seven-year battle with leukemia and died at the age of sixty-two in October of 2005. Remembered especially for his Nobel Prize–winning research, he left a legacy of many students and collaborators that he inspired to do meaningful, important work on the toughest problems, for the betterment of all humanity. "Be a Scientist–Save the World," Smalley's motto, continues to inspire.

BIBLIOGRAPHY

More than three hundred scientific papers, many newspaper and magazine articles, congressional testimony, and lectures have as of 2007 yet to be cataloged. A partial list of publications is available from Rice University (at http://smalley.rice.edu/index.cfm) and a complete listing was planned by 2010 (publications continue to appear based on his many collaborations). Video of his energy vision presentation is also included on the Internet site. A collection of Smalley's extensive laboratory notebooks, original manuscripts, and various pieces of experimental equipment are at the Chemical Heritage Foundation in Philadelphia, Pennsylvania, and an online archive was planned.

WORKS BY SMALLEY

With Harold W. Kroto, James R. Heath, Sean C. O'Brien, et al. "C-60—Buckminsterfullerene." *Nature* 318 (1985): 162–163.

"Discovering the Fullerenes." In *Chemistry, 1996–2000*, edited by Ingmar Grenthe. Nobel Lectures. Singapore: World Scientific, 2003.

OTHER SOURCES

Adams, W. Wade, and Ray H. Baughman. "Retrospective: Richard E. Smalley (1943–2005)." *Science* 310, no. 5756 (2005): 1916.

Aldersey-Williams, Hugh. *The Most Beautiful Molecule: The Discovery of the Buckyball.* New York: Wiley, 1995.

Baum, Rudy. "Nanotechnology: Drexler and Smalley Make the Case for and against 'Molecular Assemblers.'" *Chemical and Engineering News* 81, no. 48 (1 December 2003): 37–42. Available from hhtp://pubs.acs.org/cen/coverstory/8148/8148counterpoint.html. After publication of this debate Smalley refused to discuss this topic further as a waste of his time, considering the matter to be settled in his favor.

Curl, Robert F. "Obituary: Richard E. Smalley (1943–2005); Chemist and Champion of Nanotechnology." *Nature* 438, no. 7071 (2005): 1094.

Dagani, Ron. "Nobel Laureate Richard Smalley Dead at 62." *Chemical and Engineering News* 83, no. 45 (2005): 7.

Halford, Bethany. "The World According to Rick." *Chemical and Engineering News* 84, no. 41 (2006): 13–19. Includes Web site supplemental information.

Wade Adams

SMITH, JAMES LEONARD BRIERLEY
(*b.* Graaff-Reinet, Cape Province (now South Africa), 26 September 1897; *d.* Grahamstown, South Africa, 8 January 1968) *ichthyology, fishes of the Western Indian Ocean, discovery and identification of the coelacanth.*

The most eminent ichthyologist that South Africa has produced, Smith is particularly notable for his seminal role in the discovery, identification, and description of the

Coelacanth. *Prof. J. L. B. Smith poses with hand on Coelacanth surrounded by sailors and natives.* **AP IMAGES.**

first two coelacanths, a "living fossil" fish believed to have died out some 70 million years ago. He was also an unrivaled authority on the fishes of the western Indian Ocean.

Early Life. Born of English parents in the small Karoo town of Graaff-Reinet, where his father was postmaster, Smith did undergraduate studies in chemistry at the Victoria College, Stellenbosch, which were interrupted by World War I service in East Africa as a machine gunner in the 12th South African Infantry regiment. Invalided out of the army after contracting malaria, Malta fever, and dysentery, he completed his BA (1917) and MSc (cum laude; 1918) at the Victoria College before proceeding to Selwyn College, Cambridge, on an Ebden Scholarship.

There he worked on mustard gas under Sir William Pope and photosensitizing dyestuffs under William Hobson Mills, obtaining a PhD in 1922.

On his return to South Africa, Smith joined the Department of Chemistry at Rhodes University College, Grahamstown, where over the years his work resulted in some dozen research papers and three undergraduate textbooks. However, his deep lifelong interest in fishes was competing ever more strongly with his work in chemistry, and in 1931 he published his first of more than two hundred papers on ichthyology, a field in which he had received no formal training and in which he had few collaborators other than his wife Margaret (née Macdonald). In 1946 Smith received a research fellowship in ichthyology from the South African Council for Scientific and Industrial Research while in 1947 a research Department of Ichthyology was founded at Rhodes University enabling Smith, who was still officially a member of the Department of Chemistry, to devote all his time and energy to Ichthyology.

Discovery of the Coelacanth. On 22 December 1938 Smith's life changed dramatically. When a local trawler, the *Nerine* (see note following entry), caught an unknown fish of curious appearance near the mouth of the Chalumna River, some thirty kilometers (nineteen miles) southwest of East London, South Africa, the captain, Hendrik Goosen, handed it to Marjorie Courtenay-Latimer of the East London Museum. Strongly suspecting its importance, she requested Smith, who was well known to her as a leading South African ichthyologist, to identify it. He was incredulous for, to his utter astonishment, it turned out to be a living coelacanth, a member of a group of fishes that had first appeared some 300 million years ago but were long believed to be extinct as none of the numerous fossil specimens that had been found were later than about 70 million years.

The coelacanth discovery was announced at a meeting of the Royal Society of South Africa in Cape Town on 15 March 1939, followed by a note in *Nature* three days later and a more detailed description in the next issue of the *Transactions* of the society. An event without parallel in the history of the life sciences, the discovery was at first greeted with disbelief but very soon aroused the utmost excitement throughout the scientific world. Smith named the fish *Latimeria chalumnae,* in honor of Courtenay-Latimer and the place of its discovery. He concluded that this was a stray that had been carried far from its natural home, probably by the Mozambique current.

To Smith's dismay the soft parts of the fish had not been saved, and he was determined to find a second, intact, specimen, which he believed would be found far to the north in the western Indian Ocean, where, in his own words, he could imagine "natives feasting on succulent coelacanth steaks on a remote Madagascar shore" (1971, p. 292). Thus after an inevitable delay caused by World War II, he had thousands of copies of a leaflet printed in English, French, and Portuguese and systematically distributed throughout the coastal regions of the western Indian Ocean. This not only included a photograph of the first coelacanth but also the offer of a reward of £100 for each of the first two specimens caught—then half the price of a small car! To his great joy, late in December 1952 Smith received a cable from Eric Hunt, the English captain of a trading schooner that undertook regular voyages in the area, informing him that Hunt had found a coelacanth off Anjouan, one of the Comoros, a group of

French-controlled islands located east of northern Madagascar.

Desperate to bring the coelacanth back to South Africa for preservation and detailed study before it deteriorated, Smith managed to contact Daniel François Malan, the newly elected South African prime minister, who was recuperating at the Cape. To his great credit Malan (a trained, conservative theologian) at once authorized the use of a South African Air Force (SAAF) Dakota aircraft in order to bring the fish back to South Africa. The discovery of a second coelacanth was once more the cause of worldwide excitement, particularly as its internal structure could now be studied in detail. While on the Comoros, Smith discovered that coelacanths had been known to the native fishermen for centuries—although not to the French authorities. They were not in fact regarded locally as good eating!

Since that time numerous further specimens have been discovered in the western Indian Ocean stretching from Malindi, off the coast of Kenya (2001), to substantial numbers at Sodwana, in the Greater St. Lucia Wetland National Park in Kwazulu-Natal, South Africa (2000). Thus hopefully Smith's early fears of the extinction of the coelacanth as a result of it being limited to the Comoros have become significantly less likely.

Other Work. Throughout his professional life Smith was closely assisted by his wife Margaret, an accomplished artist who illustrated his works. He traveled widely in the western Indian Ocean, becoming a world authority on the fishes of that area as well as the principal authority on southern African marine fishes. His major work, *The Sea Fishes of Southern Africa* (1949), was reprinted a number of times. The publication of this substantial work was so eagerly awaited that the first edition of five thousand copies sold out in three weeks and it has been said that "There is probably no other ichthyologist who can claim to have queues forming outside bookshops on the day his regional monograph was published" (Greenwood, 1968, p. 690). In 1963 Smith and his wife jointly published *Fishes of Seychelles.*

Always sympathetic to the needs of both laymen and anglers, and more than happy to share his knowledge with them, Smith published well over 400 popular and semiscientific articles, as well as describing more than 375 fishes new to science. His health was never robust and, fearing that he would become a burden to others, he died by his own hand in Grahamstown in January 1968.

Note: *On the outbreak of war in 1939 the* Nerine *was commandeered by the South African Navy and, after being painted grey and fitted with a 3-inch gun, assumed duty as a minesweeper. In November 1941 she played a key role in the rescue from the remote and desolate South West African (later*

Namibian) shore of the survivors of the wrecked liner the Dunedin Star.

BIBLIOGRAPHY

WORKS BY SMITH

"A Living Fish of the Mesozoic Type." *Nature* 143 (1939): 455–456.

"A Surviving Fish of the Order Actinistia." *Transactions of the Royal Society of South Africa* 27, no. 1 (1939): 47–50. Reprinted in *Transactions of the Royal Society of South Africa* 47, no. 1 (1989): 9–17.

"A Living Coelacanthid Fish from South Africa." *Transactions of the Royal Society of South Africa* 28 (1940): 1–106.

The Sea Fishes of Southern Africa. Johannesburg: Central News Agency, 1949.

"The Second Coelacanth." *Nature* 171 (1953): 99–101.

Old Fourlegs: The Story of the Coelacanth. London: Longmans, Green, 1956.

With Margaret M. Smith. *Fishes of Seychelles.* Grahamstown, South Africa: Department of Ichthyology, Rhodes University, 1963.

OTHER SOURCES

Bruton, Michael N. "The Living Coelacanth Fifty Years Later." *Transactions of the Royal Society of South Africa* 47, no. 1 (1989): 19–28.

"Coelacanth." *Standard Encyclopaedia of Southern Africa*, vol. 3, pp. 292–294. Cape Town: Nasou. 12 vols., 1970–1976.

De Vos, Luc, and Dalmas Oyugi. "First Capture of a Coelacanth, *Latimeria chalumnae* Smith, 1939 (Pisces: Latimeridae), off Kenya." *South African Journal of Science* 98 (2002): 345–347.

Greenwood, Peter Humphry. "Professor J. L. B Smith [Obituary]." *Nature* 217 (1968): 690–691.

Smith, Margaret M. "J. L. B. Smith: His Life, Work, Bibliography, and List of New Species." Rhodes University Department of Ichthyology Occasional Paper 16, pp. 173–214. Grahamstown: South African Institute for Aquatic Biodiversity, 1969. Includes a complete bibliography of Smith's publications, both scientific and popular.

Weinberg, Samantha. *A Fish Caught in Time: The Search for the Coelacanth.* London: Fourth Estate, 2000.

P. E. Spargo

SMITH, MICHAEL (*b.* Blackpool, Lancashire, England, 26 April 1932; *d.* Vancouver, British Columbia, Canada, 4 October 2000), *biochemistry, molecular biology, biotechnology, organic chemistry.*

Michael Smith's invention of a technique for introducing mutations at specific sites in genes made it possible to identify DNA sequences responsible for regulating expression of genes and amino acid sequences responsible for functional properties of proteins. Site-directed mutagenesis also raised the possibility of curing hereditable diseases of humans by correcting the defective DNA sequence in somatic or germ cells. For his achievements as DNA's "mutagenius," Smith shared the 1993 Nobel Prize in Chemistry.

Early Years. Rowland Smith was a market gardener in Marton Moss, near Blackpool in Lancashire. He married Mary Armstead (known as "Molly"), who worked as a bookkeeper, in 1926. Michael Smith was their first child. He was educated at the local Church of England school, St. Nicholas, then at the private Arnold School for Boys, where he excelled in mathematics and science. On graduating from the Arnold School in 1950, Smith won a scholarship from the local education authority that enabled him to study chemistry at the University of Manchester. He obtained an upper-second-class degree in 1953 and began studies toward a PhD under the supervision of Dr. H. Bernard Henbest. Smith's project involved studies on the synthesis of steroids and cyclohexane diols.

On completing his PhD in 1956 Smith took up a National Research Council postdoctoral fellowship and moved to the British Columbia Research Council Laboratories in Vancouver, Canada, to work with Har Gobind Khorana. This opportunity only became available when the award was declined by the student to whom it had originally been offered. Khorana, Smith's postdoctoral supervisor, had trained with the nucleic acid chemist Alexander Todd at Cambridge. In the late 1940s Todd's laboratory had achieved the complete chemical synthesis of nucleotides, the building blocks of nucleic acids. In Vancouver, Khorana was trying to develop the means of synthesizing oligonucleotides—short artificial nucleic acids—and Smith was put to work on this project.

Synthesizing DNA. Phoebus Levene in the 1930s conclusively demonstrated that DNA is a deoxyribonucleotide polymer in which the bases—adenine, cytosine, guanine, and thymine—are attached to the 1' position of deoxyribose and the sugars are linked to one another by phosphodiester bonds. As the furanose (5-membered ring) form of deoxyribose only has hydroxyl groups at the 1', 3', and 5' positions, it was clear that the phosphodiester bonds must involve the 3' hydroxyl of one nucleotide and the 5' hydroxyl of the adjacent one. In RNA, however, the sugar is ribose, which has an additional 2' hydroxyl group. Not until 1952 did Todd show that 3', 5' bonds also join the ribonucleotides in RNA.

The double-helix model of DNA structure proposed by James Watson and Francis Crick in 1953 consists of two antiparallel polynucleotide chains joined by hydrogen

Michael Smith. AP IMAGES.

bonds between the bases. Specifically, guanine forms hydrogen bonds with cytosine, and adenine with thymine. This feature means that the two polynucleotide chains are complementary—the sequence of one specifies the sequence of the other.

This absence of a 2' hydroxyl group on deoxyribose meant that it was easier to synthesize oligodeoxyribonucleotides than it was to synthesize oligoribonucleotides. Even in this case, however, the functional groups attached to the purine and pyrimidine bases had to be protected (made chemically unreactive) in order to prevent side reactions with the hydroxyl groups of deoxyribose. To make a phosphodiester bond between the 3' hydroxyl group of one nucleotide and the 5' group of another, the 5' hydroxyl group of the former and the 3' group of the latter also had to be protected. In the 1956–1960 period, Smith and Khorana achieved the first synthesis of oligoribonucleotides (Smith and Khorana, 1959). They also developed a technique for synthesizing 3', 5' cyclic nucleotide monophosphates, which had been shown to be

important intracellular regulators of glycogen metabolism.

In 1960 Smith married Helen Christie. The marriage produced three children: Tom, Ian, and Wendy. Smith and his wife separated in 1983 but never divorced.

Also in 1960 Khorana moved to the University of Wisconsin–Madison, taking Smith with him. Only a few months later, Smith returned to British Columbia to become head of the Chemistry Division at the Vancouver Technological Station of the Fisheries Board of Canada. There he initiated a research program on the pituitary hormones of salmon, but he also obtained external funding to continue his work on oligonucleotide synthesis. The Technological Station was situated on the campus of the University of British Columbia, and Smith formed links with members of the Department of Biochemistry, to which he was appointed as an associate professor in 1964. When Smith came into conflict with his superiors at the Fisheries Research Board concerning his research on nucleic acids, the head of the Department of Biochemistry successfully sponsored him for a research associate award from the Medical Research Council of Canada. In 1966 Smith took up his new position and moved into a laboratory in the Medical Sciences Building. He was promoted to the rank of professor in 1970 and awarded tenure the following year. Despite his falling-out with the Fisheries Board, Smith continued to work on the physiology and biochemistry of sexual maturation of salmon.

By the mid-1960s it was known that the DNA of genes was transcribed into messenger RNA, and the mRNA was then translated into protein. The genetic code—the relationship between the nucleotide sequences of DNA and RNA and the amino acid sequences of proteins—had also been elucidated. In recognition of the large part his synthetic oligoribonucleotides had played in solving the genetic code, Khorana shared the 1968 Nobel Prize in Physiology or Medicine. Smith realized that, because the nucleotide sequence of a gene is complementary to that of the corresponding mRNA, synthetic oligonucleotides might be used to bind to and thereby isolate specific mRNA molecules. He asked a PhD student, Caroline Astell, to determine the conditions under which synthetic deoxyribonucleotides could hybridize (form stable hydrogen-bonded duplex molecules).

In a series of studies published in the early 1970s, Astell and Smith showed that short oligonucleotides were capable of forming duplexes, the stabilities of which could be characterized by the temperature at which the two oligonucleotides dissociate, or "melt" (Astell and Smith, 1971). These melting temperatures were directly correlated with the length of the oligonucleotides and the amount of guanine and cytosine present. Two additional observations were critical for future developments. First, the melting temperatures of duplexes consisting of two oligodeoxyribonucleotides were much higher than those of duplexes containing one oligoribonucleotide and one oligodeoxyribonucleotide. From this Smith concluded that synthetic oligonucleotides would be more useful for isolating genes than for isolating RNAs. Second, stable duplexes could be formed between oligonucleotides containing a mismatched base, although the presence of such mismatches lowered the melting temperatures by approximately five degrees.

Chemical synthesis of oligonucleotides was time-consuming and inefficient. For this reason, Khorana had used a combination of chemical and enzymatic methods to produce polynucleotides large enough to function as templates for protein synthesis. The enzyme Khorana had used, DNA polymerase, was not suitable for making oligonucleotides of defined sequence. However, another enzyme, polynucleotide phosphorylase, had been shown to be capable of making oligoribonucleotides from ribonucleotide diphosphates. Studies involving Smith's

research associate, Shirley Gillam, established that, in the presence of the manganese ion, polynucleotide phosphorylase could be used to synthesize oligodeoxyribonucleotides (Gillam and Smith, 1972). As in Khorana's studies, a combination of chemistry and biology produced the best results: chemical methods were used to make a short oligonucleotide which was then elongated by the enzyme. The elongation reactions were carried out in aqueous solution, and no protecting groups were required.

Synthetic oligonucleotides could only be used to isolate genes if the nucleotide sequence of the gene were known. In the early 1970s such information was extremely limited. Frederick Sanger of Cambridge University was developing a technique for the sequencing of genes, using the single-stranded DNA virus NX174 as a model. Sanger's "plus-minus" method used enzymes to either extend or digest "primer" pieces of DNA. Following a visit to Smith's laboratory in 1973, Sanger received some oligonucleotides, made using the method developed by Gillam, for use in the sequencing of the NX174 genome.

Motivated by a desire to learn DNA-sequencing methods, Smith spent the 1975–1976 academic year on sabbatical in Sanger's laboratory. In what he later described as "the most fruitful and enjoyable scientific experience of my life" (Damer and Astell, 2004, p. 112), Smith was part of the team that determined the sequence of the 5,386 nucleotides in the NX174 genome (Brown and Smith, 1977). Another participant was Clyde Hutchison III, a virologist who was on sabbatical leave from the University of North Carolina. Hutchison had shown that if the bacterium *Escherichia coli* were infected with NX174 plus a fragment of NX174 DNA containing a mutation, a very small percentage of progeny viruses would "inherit" the mutation. As the replication of the virus involves a double-stranded DNA intermediate, this was interpreted to mean that occasionally the mutation-bearing DNA fragment would be incorporated into the new polynucleotide strand, and thereby into a progeny virus. In discussing this experiment, Smith and Hutchison came up with the idea of using synthetic oligonucleotides to introduce mutations into the DNA of NX174. The attraction of this approach was that it would allow any DNA sequence to be mutated.

Mutating DNA. Back in Vancouver, Smith sent Gillam to Hutchison's laboratory in Chapel Hill to learn how to handle *E. coli* and NX174. On her return, Smith attempted to utilize his group's expertise in nucleic acid synthesis and hybridization to generate a specific mutation. The general idea was to synthesize an oligodeoxyribonucleotide that was complementary to part of a viral gene except for one mismatched base. Using the oligonucleotide as primer and single-stranded NX174 DNA as

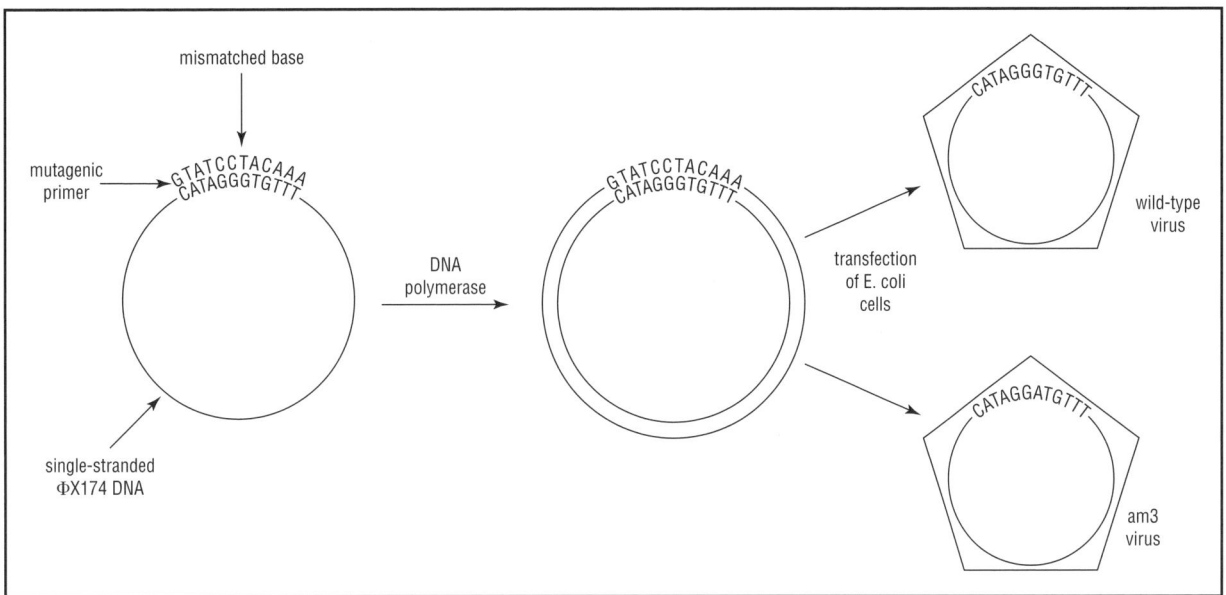

Figure 1. *Smith's 1978 demonstration of site-directed mutagenesis. A synthetic oligonucleotide complementary to part of the single-stranded DNA of bacteriophage phiX174 except for a single-base mismatch was used as a primer for enzymatic synthesis of a second DNA strand. Following infection of E. coli with the double-stranded DNA, some of the progeny viruses contained the mismatched sequence, as shown by their inability to grow in certain strains of bacteria.*

template, DNA polymerase, he could then synthesize a polynucleotide complementary to the template strand except for the substitution of one base. If the resultant double-stranded DNA were used to infect *E. coli*, half the progeny viruses should carry the mutation. In order to screen for mutant viruses, Smith designed the synthetic oligonucleotide so that it was complementary to a known mutation, *am*3, which causes premature chain termination of a protein required for NX174 replication and is thus normally lethal. However, certain strains of *E. coli* were known to contain suppressor mutations allowing replication of viruses bearing this mutation. If Smith's experiment worked perfectly, half the viruses produced would have acquired the *am*3 mutation, and thus would grow in the suppressor strain but not the wild-type strain of the bacterium (see Figure 1).

In fact, only a small percentage of progeny viruses was found to have the mutation. By treating the DNA to remove incomplete second strands, however, Smith and his colleagues were able to raise the efficiency of mutation to 15 percent. In an elegant additional experiment, they showed that synthetic oligonucleotides could also be used to revert mutant viruses back to wild type.

The paper describing these findings was published in the *Journal of Biological Chemistry* in September 1978—having first been rejected by *Proceedings of the National Academy of Sciences* and *Cell.* Clyde Hutchison was the

first author, having won a coin toss to decide the priority of authorship (Hutchison et al., 1978).

The significance of site-specific mutagenesis—or site-directed mutagenesis, as it later became known—was not immediately recognized, perhaps because the initial method was only applicable to genes in certain viruses. In order to make it possible to mutate nonviral genes, Smith switched from NX174 to another bacteriophage, M13. NX174 is an icosahedral virus, with no room in the viral capsid for additional DNA, but M13 is filamentous, and a large amount of nonviral DNA can be incorporated into its filament. Therefore it was now possible to introduce a nonviral gene into M13 and then create a specific mutation using the appropriate oligonucleotide. Within five years of the first description of the technique, site-directed mutagenesis had been used to induce a variety of point mutations and deletions in genes isolated from organisms from bacteria to humans.

A paper published in *Nature* in 1982, describing a collaboration involving Smith and the enzymologist Alan Fersht, provided an early example of the power of site-directed mutagenesis in the genetic engineering of proteins (Winter et al., 1982). Fersht, Smith, and coworkers cloned the gene encoding the enzyme tyrosyl tRNA synthetase of the bacterium *Bacillus stearothermophilus* into M13, then used a synthetic oligonucleotide to create a mutation that changed a single amino acid at the active site of the enzyme. The mutant protein was then expressed, purified, and shown to have decreased catalytic activity. Automated methods of oligonucleotide synthesis, mutagenesis strategies based on the polymerase chain reaction, and other technological developments soon made site-directed mutagenesis a standard approach for correlating protein structure and function.

As noted above, Smith had concluded from Astell's hybridization studies that synthetic oligonucleotides might be better suited to the isolation of genes than to the isolation of mRNAs. Contemporaneously with the development of site-directed mutagenesis, Smith collaborated with Benjamin Hall of the University of Washington to isolate the cytochrome c gene of yeast. Yeast was used because of the relatively small size of its genome; cytochrome c was chosen because partial sequence data were available. Using an oligodeoxyribonucleotide "13-mer" radiolabeled with phosphorus-32 to probe enzymatically generated fragments of yeast DNA, Hall, Smith, and coworkers were able to identify DNA fragments containing parts of the cytochrome c gene (Montgomery et al., 1978). In a subsequent study, the complete nucleotide sequence of the gene was determined. Continuation of the collaboration between Smith's and Hall's laboratories led to the elucidation of the three-dimensional structure of yeast cytochrome c and played an important role in the first identification of a factor controlling gene transcription in eukaryotes.

In 1981 Smith joined Hall and Earl Davie in founding the Seattle-based biotechnology company Zymos (later ZymoGenetics), with the aim of producing protein therapeutics such as recombinant human insulin. For several years Smith received a substantial consultancy fee from Zymos. He held stock in the company until 1988, when he sold his shares for a large sum that made him financially independent.

Honors. Smith was increasingly recognized as a founder of molecular biology and biotechnology. He became a career investigator of the Medical Research Council of Canada in 1978 and received many awards for his research achievements. These included a Gairdner Foundation International Award and election as a fellow of the Royal Society, both in 1986. In his fifties, Smith started to devote more time to administrative activities and less to his own research program, although his laboratory remained highly productive. His administrative positions included director of the Centre for Molecular Genetics at UBC (1986–1987); director of the Biotechnology Laboratory, a center of excellence funded by the province of British Columbia (1987–1997); first scientific director of the federally funded Protein Engineering Network of Centres of Excellence (1990–1995); and interim scientific

director of the Biomedical Research Centre at UBC (1991–1992).

The ultimate scientific accolade came in 1993, when Smith shared the Nobel Prize in Chemistry with Kary Mullis, inventor of the polymerase chain reaction. Already a wealthy man, Smith donated his share of the prize money to agencies supporting schizophrenia research, the training of women scientists, and the communication of science to the public. Shrewdly exploiting the publicity accompanying the Nobel award, he persuaded the governments of Canada and British Columbia to match his donations. The Canadian government also established the Michael Smith Award for Excellence, first awarded in 1994. In addition to the promotion of biomedical research, Smith used the prestige of his Nobel Prize to advance other causes in which he believed strongly, including peace and environmentalism.

The University of British Columbia recognized Smith's Nobel award by granting him the honorary title of University Professor. In 1994 he was appointment Peter Wall Distinguished Professor of Biotechnology. By this time Smith was preparing to shed his administrative positions and was winding down his research program (he closed his laboratory in 1996). He used his freedom to go back to the bench, spending parts of 1996 and 1997 working in Maynard Olson's laboratory at the University of Washington on the sequencing of human chromosome 7 and the genome of the bacterium *Pseudomonas aeruginosa*. Following this "sabbatical," however, Smith was persuaded to take another administrative position, this time with the British Columbia Cancer Agency, which had launched a large-scale gene-sequencing program.

In 1998 Smith was diagnosed with myelodysplastic syndrome, an incurable form of cancer. Two years later this had developed into leukemia. After a brief period of hospitalization he died in October 2000.

BIBLIOGRAPHY

Smith's papers are held at the University of British Columbia Archives.

WORKS BY SMITH

With Har Gobind Khorana. "Specific Synthesis of the C5'-C3' Inter-Ribonucleotide Linkage: the Synthesis of Uridylyl-(5'-3')-Uridine." *Journal of the American Chemical Society* 81 (1959): 2911–2912.

With Caroline Astell. "Thermal Elution of Complementary Sequences of Nucleic Acids from Cellulose Columns with Covalently Attached Oligonucleotides of Known Length and Sequence." *Journal of Biological Chemistry* 246 (1971): 1944–1946.

With Shirley Gillam. "Enzymatic Synthesis of Deoxyribo-oligonucleotides of Defined Sequence." *Nature New Biology* 238 (1972): 233–234.

With Nigel L. Brown. "The Sequence of a Region of Bacteriophage NX174 DNA Coding for Parts of Genes *A* and *B*." *Journal of Molecular Biology* 116 (1977): 1–30.

With Donna L. Montgomery, Benjamin D. Hall, and Shirley Gillam. "Identification and Isolation of the Yeast Cytochrome c Gene." *Cell* 14 (1978): 673–680.

With Clyde A. Hutchison, Sandra Phillips, Marshall H. Edgell, et al. "Mutagenesis at a Specific Position in a DNA Sequence." *Journal of Biological Chemistry* 253 (1978): 6551–6560.

With Greg Winter, Alan R. Fersht, Anthony J. Wilkinson, and Mark Zoller. "Redesigning Enzyme Structure by Site-Directed Mutagenesis: Tyrosyl tRNA Synthetase and ATP Binding." *Nature* 299 (1982): 756–758.

"In Vitro Mutagenesis." *Annual Review of Genetics* 19 (1985): 423–462.

OTHER SOURCES

Astell, Caroline. "Michael Smith." *Biographical Memoirs of Fellows of the Royal Society* 47 (2001): 429–441.

Damer, Eric, and Caroline Astell. *No Ordinary Mike: Michael Smith, Nobel Laureate.* Vancouver, BC: Ronsdale Press, 2004.

Graeme K. Hunter

Jan Christian Smuts. © HULTON-DEUTSCH COLLECTION/CORBIS.

SMUTS, JAN CHRISTIAN (CHRISTIAAN)

(*b.* Bovenplaats near Riebeeck West, Cape Colony (now South Africa), 24 May 1870; *d.* Irene, near Pretoria, South Africa, 11 September 1950), *lawyer, politician, general, prime minister, scientist, philosopher.*

Smuts was a South African statesman, an idealist philosopher, and a botanist who coined the word *holism.* Smuts enjoyed respect in the South African scientific community as one of the world's leading experts on savanna grass. One type, *Digitaria smutsii*, was named in his honor. His botanical library was the largest in the country, and Smuts participated in various botanical expeditions. He also took personal interest in who should be hired in the biological sciences at the South African universities, in the social and economic welfare of botany professors, in generating research funds, and in supervising scientific publications.

He grew up in the district of Swartland, known for its fertility, beautiful scenery, vineyards, traditional Dutch country life, and its conservative and largely religious population of farmers. His interest in the agricultural sciences and religious views emerged in this context. He participated in Rudolf Marloth's flora expeditions and read Asa Gray's work while he was a student at Victoria College in Stellenbosch, where he ranked first in the class.

In 1891 he went to study for the Law Tripos at Christ's College, Cambridge University, where he wrote a small treatise titled "Law, a Liberal Study." To Smuts legal rights were a result of a gradual evolutionary liberation from the biological realm, hence the word *liberal* in the title. He placed civil rights on a Darwinian ladder with inanimate nature at one end of the scale of nature, and human society at the other, sanctioned by an all-embracing divine law given by God. He argued that there was a governing principle or natural law behind the evolutionary development of civil rights. Civic law evolved from the primitive family to the modern state by analogy with the growth of a human being, and civil rights gradually progressed historically toward more and more respect for individual freedom and greater unity within humanity. Through the rest of his life Smuts modified and elaborated on this student thesis.

He entered the Middle Temple University Research Society with an honorary grant in 1894, which he used, to everybody's surprise, to write a book about Walt Whitman (published posthumously). Here he explored the biological evolution of Whitman's personality, since he believed his mental evolution had reached the highest possible development, a point of evolution that only men but no women or nonwhites could reach.

Smuts returned to Cape Town in 1895 where he started to practice as a lawyer, and he soon became involved in politics as an admirer of Cecil Rhodes. Smuts followed the reasoning from his student thesis, and argued that native Africans and Indians should be placed socially within the natural hierarchy of evolution, which placed white men at the top of the ladder followed by white women, Asians, and Africans at the bottom. As state attorney and general of the Transvaal Army he was first a nationalist believing in separation from Britain, while his political views shifted with World War I toward a defense of the British Empire as a union of states and protectorates. Smuts was devoted to uniting the Orange Free State, Transvaal, Natal, and the Cape Province under the British Crown, a vision he helped to realize with Louis Botha with the establishment of the Union of South Africa in 1910.

Inspired by the unification of his country, Smuts wrote a book titled *Holism and Evolution* (1926). Here he expanded his Whitman thesis to the entire biological realm, arguing that the ontogeny of a human being should be extended to a phylogeny of the living world. These were ideas held by many scientists of the period, most notable by the German evolutionary biologist Ernst Haeckel. The book was a blend of science and philosophy, leading to a new vision of a global ecology based on the human ability to experience a greater harmonious "whole" in nature. By analogy to the growth of a human being, Smuts argued that only white men had reached the stage of grown-ups who understood how everything was connected. They were thus most suited to organize and govern aspects of the whole; as the whole city of Pretoria, the whole Cape Town Province, the whole Union of South Africa, the whole British Empire, or the whole world through the League of Nation. The book was a public success, and the new word *holism* became a catchword in debates between idealists such as Smuts and mechanist biologists and philosophers of the 1930s. Smuts was hailed as a moral and political example to follow among the idealists, who secured the election of him as Fellow of the Royal Society, president of the British Association for the Advancement of Science, chancellor of Cambridge University, among various other prizes and honors.

As prime minister (1919–1924, 1939–1948), Smuts became known for his gradualist politics toward South African peoples based on their imagined levels of evolutionary development. He had many encounters with Mahatma Gandhi, and the two men clashed over the social and legal status of Asian minorities and the constant flow of immigrants from India to South Africa, which Smuts tried to impede. Smuts's racist views were, at his time, a moderate position because he thought natives in the far future, at least theoretically, could evolve into higher or more advanced levels. Business leaders in the mining companies thought it was a good idea to help native evolution on its way by employing them in the

industry, and were thus some of Smuts's most important allies.

As a statesman-philosopher Smuts tried to place his country's civic constitution on a scientific basis. In this effort he was guided by South African ecologists such as John William Bews and John Phillips, who provided him with updates on the latest scientific advances through correspondence and friendship. Two aspects of their ecological research were particularly important to Smuts's politics of holism: the gradual ascendancy of human personalities from native Africans to white people of the Nordic kind, and the holistically informed notion of an ecological biotic community. Smuts transformed ecological research into a policy of racial gradualism meant to respect local ways of life by separating different communities. He tried to morally sanctify and promote this racial policy as author of the 1945 preamble of the United Nations Charter about human rights.

BIBLIOGRAPHY

WORKS BY SMUTS

Holism and Evolution. London: Macmillan, 1926.

Africa and Some World Problems. Oxford: Clarendon Press, 1930.

Greater South Africa: Plans for a Better World: The Speeches of General the Right Honorable J. C. Smuts. Johannesburg: Truth Legion, 1940.

Selections from the Smuts Papers, vols. 1–4, edited by William Keith Hancock and Jean van der Poel. Cambridge, U.K.: Cambridge University Press, 1966.

Selections from the Smuts Papers, vols. 5–7, edited by Jean van der Poel. Cambridge, U.K.: Cambridge University Press, 1973.

Walt Whitman: A Study in the Evolution of Personality. Detroit: Wayne State University Press, 1973.

OTHER SOURCES

Anker, Peder. *Imperial Ecology: Environmental Order in the British Empire.* Cambridge, MA: Harvard University Press, 2001.

Hancock, William Keith. *Smuts: The Sanguine Years 1870–1919.* Cambridge, U.K.: Cambridge University Press, 1962.

———. *Smuts: The Fields of Force 1919–1950.* Cambridge, U.K.: Cambridge University Press, 1968.

Peder Anker

SOFFEN, GERALD ALAN (*b.* Cleveland, Ohio, 7 February 1926; *d.* Washington, D.C. 22 November 2000), *astrobiology, biochemistry, biology, space science.*

Soffen was a thirty-year veteran of the National Aeronautics and Space Administration (NASA), between 1961 and his death. He is best known for his service as chief scientist of the Viking missions to Mars in 1976. This project took as its centerpiece the search for life on the Red Planet, but found none. In addition, Soffen managed the development of biological instruments for NASA's Jet Propulsion Laboratory in the 1960s, the NASA Earth science program in the early 1980s, and served as the director of Life Sciences at NASA Headquarters, where he oversaw the biomedical, space biology, and astrobiology programs.

Early Professional Experiences. Gerald Soffen, known to all as "Gerry," was born on 7 February 1926 in Cleveland, Ohio. Educated in the local public schools, when Soffen completed high school in 1944 he was drafted into the U.S. Army, went to basic training, and then served in George S. Patton's Third Army in western Europe in late 1944 and early 1945. He saw combat as a rifleman and, as related by longtime friend James Tucker of NASA's Goddard Space Flight Center, Greenbelt, Maryland,

> he decided he didn't like shooting people, so he became a combat medic. Being a combat medic is very dangerous, because combat medics administer medical attention to wounded soldiers while the battle is still raging. It didn't matter if the wounded soldiers were German or American. That was Gerry Soffen—always trying to help others, even at great risk to himself." (Tucker Web site)

Soffen was sent with a message to another unit along with two other soldiers just as the war was ending and found themselves surrounded by about fifteen German infantrymen when they rounded a bend in the road. Soffen spoke some German since members of his family had emigrated from Germany, and he persuaded them to surrender despite their larger numbers. He explained that the war was virtually over, that Germany had lost, and that Soviet troops were in the area. He promised that if they surrendered the American army would keep them from the Russians. So he and his comrades returned to their unit to a heroes' welcome.

When Soffen returned from military service he attended Wayne State University in Detroit for three years and earned a bachelor of arts degree in zoology from the University of California, Los Angeles, in 1949. He then worked his way through graduate school, earning a master of science degree in biology from the University of Southern California in 1956 and a PhD in biophysics from Princeton University in 1960. He had gone to Princeton to study with Harold F. Blum, whose book, *Time's Arrow and Evolution*, had excited his imagination. Soffen came to believe that evolution was related to the second law of thermodynamics. As later explained in the official NASA history of the Mars exploration program, Blum theorized:

The universe's supply of energy is slowly diminishing, and all biological forms must adapt to lower, less satisfactory energy sources. Simple organisms present in a more primitive age when the oceans supplied them with a very rich nutrient broth had to develop more specialized and complex mechanisms for gathering energy (nutrients) as the ocean environment became less rich. Evolution is not a random process, since organisms must make orderly changes to survive in a changing world. This process leads to more complex, not simpler, organisms. (1984, p. 58)

Soffen wanted to pursue the search for life beyond Earth, convinced that experience on this planet must be but one small part of a much larger and diverse evolutionary history. At the same time, he participated as a fellow in the U.S. Public Health Survey. From there he journeyed to Washington, D.C., to work on a postdoctoral fellowship at the National Institutes of Health. In 1960 he accepted a position in biochemistry at the New York University Medical School.

While in graduate school, Soffen met Hoshi Irakiri, a second-generation Japanese American born in Salinas, California. One of nine children in the family of a farmer, seven of whom were girls, she spent some of her childhood in Japan but returned to the United States before World War II. She had completed a BA degree in journalism from Park College, Kansas City, Missouri, in 1950, and was studying English literature at the University of Southern California when she met Soffen. They married in 1956. When he began his PhD program at Princeton, she worked as a reporter on the local newspaper. Later, while Soffen pursued his postdoctoral work at New York University, she worked for the weekly *Suburbia Today*. When the couple lived in California in the 1960s, she worked as an editor for the Japanese-language newspaper, *Shin Nichi Bei*. She continued to work in various journalistic positions until her death from a drowning in the couple's pool in 1978.

In a 1990 interview published in *Goddard News*, Gerry Soffen recalled that he had taken seriously President John F. Kennedy's 1961 call to "Ask not what your country can do for you, but what you can do for your country," and his answer was "out of this world." He moved from New York University to NASA's Jet Propulsion Laboratory (JPL) in Pasadena, California. At JPL, Soffen held the title of senior scientist but spent most of his time managing biological instrument development, especially his pet project, a Mars Microscope. He viewed it as a possible life detector on the Red Planet. He argued incessantly for it throughout his JPL years, unsuccessfully urging its adoption by the Mariner program that sent four probes to Mars between 1965 and 1971. Soffen viewed the discovery of life on another planet as the critical scientific question of the space program, if not the entire space age, and dedicated himself to furthering that investigation. He also worked on the early Voyager program, a JPL lander for Mars, but it was canceled for budgetary reasons in 1967.

The Viking Program. As early as 1964 Soffen had become an exponent of the search for life in the universe, known as exobiology at the time (now usually called astrobiology). He participated in a 1964 summer study at Stanford University that gave the field intellectual respectability and drew bright young scientists to it. The participants were all advocates of the search for extraterrestrial life and they quickly decided that Mars was the most Earthlike of all the planets, and therefore a likely abode of life. The summer study did not endorse a position that argued for advanced life on Mars, as had astronomer Percival Lowell at the turn of the twentieth century, but it noted a

> kind of seasonal change one would expect were they due so the presence of organisms absent in the "bright" (desert) areas. In spring, the recession of the ice cap is accompanied by development of a dark collar as its border, and as the spring advances a wave of darkening proceeds through the dark areas toward the equator and, in fact, overshoots it 20° into the opposite hemisphere. (Pittendrigh, et al., 1966, p. 7)

It was also during that 1964 summer study that Soffen first drew the attention of James Martin, the future project director for the Viking program to Mars. He was impressed with the slightly-built and goateed young scientist's thoughtful perspective, his skills of persuasion, and his ability to keep a notoriously individualistic group of scientists on the same track. Those were the skills necessary in conducting the Viking program and Martin called on Soffen in 1969 to serve as the project's chief scientist for just those reasons.

Soffen's hopes of finding something on Mars were dashed by *Mariner 4,* which reached Mars on 15 July 1965 and took twenty-one close-up pictures. All of these images showed a cratered lunarlike surface. *U.S. News and World Report* announced that "Mars is dead." *Mariner*s 6 and 7, launched in February and March 1969, each passed Mars in August 1969, studying its atmosphere and surface to lay the groundwork for an eventual landing on the planet. Their pictures verified the Moonlike appearance of Mars, but they also found that volcanoes had once been active on the planet, that some of the frost observed seasonally on the poles was made of carbon dioxide and that huge plates indicated considerable tectonic activity in the planet's past. Suddenly, Mars fascinated scientists, reporters, and the public once again, largely because of the possibility of past life that might have emerged because of the evidence of flowing water.

In 1969 Soffen moved from JPL to NASA's Langley Research Center, Hampton, Virginia, where he became chief scientist on the Viking program, a combination Mars orbiter and lander. For him, it was a dream job. He oversaw the process of decision making for the vehicle's experiments, and by extension the appointment of the science team for the program. He was responsible for all scientific investigations to be accomplished by Viking, and directed the activities of more than seventy scientists from throughout the United States and one foreign country. Under his direction thirteen science teams conducted a wide range of scientific investigations.

Soffen ensured that Viking was specifically designed to find the answer to Mars's origins and development. Very clearly, the search for signs of life prompted this emphasis on the exploration of Mars. NASA administrator James C. Fletcher, for example, supported the Viking mission because of his belief that life was present in the universe and that greater knowledge of this might probability might be found on Mars. As Fletcher said in 1975:

> Although the discoveries we shall make on our neighboring worlds will revolutionize our knowledge of the Universe, and probably transform human society, it is unlikely that we will find intelligent life on the other planets of our Sun. Yet, it is likely we would find it among the stars of the galaxy, and that is reason enough to initiate the quest....We should begin to listen to other civilizations in the galaxy. It must be full of voices, calling from star to star in a myriad of tongues. Though we are separate from this cosmic conversation by light years, we can certainly listen ten million times further than we can travel.

The Viking mission consisted of two identical spacecraft, a lander and an orbiter. Launched in 1975 from the Kennedy Space Center, Florida, *Viking 1* spent nearly a year cruising to Mars, placed an orbiter in operation around the planet, and landed on 20 July 1976, on the Chryse Planitia (Golden Plains), with *Viking 2* following in September 1976. While one of the most important scientific activities of this project involved an attempt to determine whether there was life on Mars, the scientific data returned militated against the possibility of life. The two landers continuously monitored weather at the landing sites and found both exciting cyclical variations and an exceptionally harsh climate. Atmospheric temperatures at the more southern *Viking 1* landing site, for instance, were only as high as +7 degrees Fahrenheit at midday, but the predawn summer temperature was –107 degrees Fahrenheit. And the lowest predawn temperature was –184 degrees Fahrenheit, about the frost point of carbon dioxide.

Although the three biology experiments discovered unexpected and enigmatic chemical activity in the Martian soil, they provided no clear evidence for the presence of living microorganisms in soil near the landing sites. According to Soffen, Mars was self-sterilizing. They concluded that the combination of solar ultraviolet radiation that saturates the surface, the extreme dryness of the soil, and the oxidizing nature of the soil chemistry had prevented the formation of living organisms in the Martian soil. Moreover, and perhaps most importantly, the gas chromatograph gas spectrometer found no organic molecules to parts per billion, and life cannot form without organic molecules. The uncertainty of the conclusions from Viking haunted Soffen thereafter, He was known to second guess his judgment; perhaps he should have installed a microscope on the lander. But, he also believed he did the best he could. "I think what we did was ahead of our time. We were young enough not to know that it couldn't be done," he recalled in 1992.

The failure to find any evidence of life on Mars, past or present, devastated the optimism of Soffen and others involved in exobiology. Collectively, these missions led to the development of two essential reactions. The first was an abandonment by most scientists of the hope that life might exist elsewhere in the solar system. Planetary scientist and JPL director Bruce Murray complained at the time of Viking about the lander being ballyhooed as a definite means of ascertaining whether or not life existed on Mars. The public expected to find it, and so did Soffen and many of the other scientists involved in the project. Murray later argued that "the extraordinarily hostile environment revealed by the Mariner flybys made life there so unlikely that public expectations should not be raised" (1989, p. 61). Murray believed that the legacy of failure to detect life, despite the billions spent and a succession of overoptimistic statements, would spark public disappointment and perhaps a public outrage. Murray was right. The immediate result was that NASA did not return to Mars for two decades. As Soffen commented in 1992, "If somebody back then had given me 100 to 1 odds that we wouldn't go back to Mars for 17 years, I would've said, 'You're crazy.'"

A second reaction, never accepted by scientists, took hold among the public. Some asserted that a corrupt federal government, and its mandarins of science, had found evidence of life beyond Earth but was keeping it from the public for reasons ranging from stupidity to diabolical plots. Soffen had to respond to these charges repeatedly throughout the remainder of his life. This issue first arose on 25 July 1976 when the *Viking 1* orbiter took an image of the Cydonia region of Mars that looked like a human face. All evidence suggests that this was the result of shadows on the hills, and Gerry Soffen said so at a press conference, but some refused to accept this position. The

"face" remains a sore point to the present, with Soffen being asked about it many times over the years. Always, he stated it was not the remnant of some ancient civilization but was a natural feature lit oddly in this one image but not in any others. As NASA stated officially in 2001,

> The "Face on Mars" has since become a pop icon. It has starred in a Hollywood film, appeared in books, magazines, radio talk shows—even haunted grocery store checkout lines for 25 years! Some people think the Face is *bona fide* evidence of life on Mars—evidence that NASA would rather hide, say conspiracy theorists. Meanwhile, defenders of the NASA budget wish there *was* an ancient civilization on Mars." ("Unmasking the Face on Mars," 2001)

Without question, during the bicentennial of the Declaration of Independence in 1976 Soffen had been in the center in the media. That attention helped to damage Soffen's reputation among the more staid scientists working with NASA. He was viewed by some as little more than a NASA public relations flak. Soffen overcame this with time, but the immediate result was that some viewed him with suspicion. He transferred to a new position at the Langley Research Center, serving as chief environmental scientist. It was not a bad job, but it was a far cry from working as chief scientist for an $850 million program. To make matters worse, on 28 July 1978 his wife of more than twenty years drowned in their swimming pool. She had been swimming about 10:15 P.M. when Soffen went into the house to answer a telephone call. When he returned he discovered her body in the pool. Later, Soffen would marry another Japanese American, Kazuko, who survived him. Soffen never had any children.

Later Years. In 1979 NASA administrator Robert Frosch named Soffen the director of Life Sciences at NASA Headquarters. He moved to Washington, D.C., to direct biomedical programs ensuring the well-being of space shuttle astronauts. Soffen held this position for five years, and then moved to the Goddard Space Flight Center, in suburban Maryland, to help establish the Earth science program, then called Mission to Planet Earth. Goddard had the core of this mission for NASA, and Soffen worked tirelessly to mold a discipline containing numerous scientists of different fields to explore the nuances of the Earth system and the effects of natural and human-induced changes on the global environment. He was quite proud of his accomplishments in this regard. Bonding together into a cohesive program scientists focused on climatology, oceanography, geology, volcanism, biology, and a host of other fields into a cooperative working relationship required superior leadership. "In the past," said Soffen in 1990,

Earth was studied by looking at its parts: oceanographers studied the oceans, geologists studied the land. But planetologists have a global perspective, and one goal of EOS [the Earth Observing System] is to bring that global perspective to Earth Science and use it to answer the question of how the interacting parts of Earth operate together. (Soffen and Nelson, 1990)

Soffen demonstrated in this regard the skills he had first displayed more than twenty years earlier in leading unruly scientists toward a useful purpose. The NASA Earth science program eventually launched more than ten satellites providing data to this community and had notable successes in helping to understand global climate change.

Soffen formed the University Programs Office at Goddard in 1990, and for the next ten years he directed activities and programs designed to maintain and broaden the center's interaction with the university community. One of his lasting contributions was the establishment in 1993 of the NASA Academy. This summer institute brought together undergraduates from all over the United States to explain NASA efforts and to recruit future scientists and engineers. He guided this organization until his death and many of its graduates went on to careers in the space agency. In 1995 Soffen returned briefly to NASA Headquarters to develop an Astrobiology Institute, a renewed interest at the space agency. This virtual organization sought to bring together scientists interested in the search for extraterrestrial life.

Soffen developed heart problems several years before his death, and it was myocardial infarction that finally led to his death. On 22 November 2000 he was rushed to the George Washington University Medical Center in Washington, D.C., but died soon after his arrival.

BIBLIOGRAPHY

WORKS BY SOFFEN

With A. Thomas Young. "The Viking Missions to Mars." *Icarus* 16 (February 1972): 1–16.

"The Viking Project." *Journal of Geophysical Research* 82 (September 1977): 3959–3970.

With Gerald L. Burdett, editors. *Human Quest in Space: 24th Goddard Memorial Symposium: Proceedings of a Conference Held March 20–21, 1986.* American Astronautical Society Science and Technology Series, vol. 65. San Diego, CA: Univelt, 1987.

Editor. *Visions of Tomorrow: A Focus on National Space Transportation Issues.* American Astronautical Society Science and Technology Series, vol. 69. San Diego, CA: Univelt, 1988.

With Mark Nelson, eds. *Biological Life Support Technologies— Commercial Opportunities: Proceedings of a Workshop Sponsored by the NASA Office of Commercial Programs and Held at the Biosphere 2 Project Site near Tucson, Arizona,* *October 30–November 1, 1989.* Washington, DC: NASA Office of Management, Scientific and Technical Information Division, 1990.

"Life in the Universe." In *The New Solar System,* edited by J. Kelly Beatty, Carolyn Collins Peterson, and Andrew Chaikin. Cambridge, U.K.: Cambridge University Press, 1999.

OTHER SOURCES

Blum, Harold Francis. *Time's Arrow and Evolution.* Princeton, NJ: Princeton University Press, 1951.

Cox, Billy. "Mars Pioneer Remembered." *Florida Today* (Orlando), 6 December 2000.

"An End to the Myths about Men on Mars." *U.S. News and World Report,* 9 August 1965, p. 4.

Ezell, Edward Clinton, and Linda Neuman Ezell. *On Mars: Exploration of the Red Planet, 1958–1978.* NASA Special Publication 4212. Washington, DC: Scientific and Technical Information Branch, National Aeronautics and Space Administration, 1984.

Fletcher, James C. "NASA and the 'Now' Syndrome." Washington, DC: National Aeronautics and Space Administration, 1975. From an address delivered at the National Academy of Engineering in November 1975, printed by NASA.

"From Mars to Earth: A Conversation with Gerald Soffen." *Space World,* July 1986.

Garvin, James B. "The Emerging Face of Mars: A Synthesis from Viking to Mars Global Surveyor." *Astrobiology* 1, no. 4 (2001): 513–521.

Meyer, Michael A. "A Lasting Legacy—Gerald Soffen (1926–2000)." *Astrobiology* 1, no. 1 (2001): 1.

Murray, Bruce. *Journey into Space.* New York: W.W. Norton, 1989.

"NASA Astrobiology Architect, Dr. Gerald Soffen, Dies." NASA Press Release 00-186, 24 November 2000. Available from NASA Historical Reference Collection, NASA History Office, Washington, DC.

Pittendrigh, Colin S., Wolf Vishniac, and J. P. T. Pearman, eds. *Biology and the Exploration of Mars: Report of a Study Held under the Auspices of the Space Science Board, National Academy of Sciences–National Research Council, 1964–1965.* National Research Council publication, 1296. Washington, DC: National Academy of Sciences, 1966.

"Rites Set for Mrs. Soffen, Apparent Drowning Victim." *Daily-Press* (Newport News–Hampton, VA), 29 July 1978.

Tucker, James. "As Told by Jerry's Friends." *Dr. Gerald A. Soffen Memorial.* Available from http://www.nasa-academy.org/ soffen/stories.html.

"Unmasking the Face on Mars." 24 May 2001. *Science@NASA.* Available from http://science.nasa.gov/headlines/y2001/ ast24may_1.htm.

White, Carolynne. "Dr. Gerald Soffen: A Renaissance Man with a Global Perspective." *Goddard News,* April 1990.

Roger D. Launius

SOMMERFELD, ARNOLD JO-HANNES WILHELM (*b.* Königsberg, Prussia [later Kaliningrad, Russia], 5 December 1868; *d.* Munich, Germany, 26 April 1951), *theoretical physics, quantum theory.* For the original article on Sommerfeld see *DSB*, vol. 12.

Paul Forman's and Armin Hermann's thoughtful and detailed portrayal of Sommerfeld's career does not need major revisions (see *DSB*). However, the historical research since that essay has resulted in a deeper understanding of the boundary zones between physics and mathematics at the turn from the nineteenth to the twentieth century, so that Sommerfeld's case may be better evaluated in larger contexts. New source material concerning his early career displays in great detail the contingent and fragile nature of the nascent discipline of theoretical physics; for the later period, Sommerfeld's scientific correspondence reveals his dominant role for the spread of this discipline.

Although best known for the relativistic extension of Niels Bohr's atomic model, Sommerfeld's career should not be regarded with a focus on relativity and quantum theory alone. Physics was not his initial calling. For more than a decade of his beginning academic life, Sommerfeld traversed disciplinary boundaries between mathematics, physics, and technology: During his study at the university of his home town, Königsberg, his favorite discipline was mathematics; he graduated with a doctoral dissertation in mathematics and a state examination that qualified him to teach mathematics, physics, chemistry, and mineralogy at the high school (Gymnasium) level. During a five-year sojourn at the University of Göttingen, from 1892 to 1897, he acquired the qualification to present lectures at universities (*venia legendi*) with a dissertation on the "mathematical theory of diffraction." In 1897 he became professor of mathematics at the mining academy (Bergakademie) in Clausthal. Three years later he accepted a position as professor of mechanics at the technical university (Technische Hochschule) in Aachen. In 1906 he became a professor of theoretical physics at the University of Munich, which became his lifelong academic home.

Work at Göttingen. The emergence of theoretical physics has been largely perceived as a specialization from its mother-discipline, physics, pursued by low-ranking professors as a transient activity in the beginning of their career. However, Sommerfeld's approach to theoretical physics, as well as the early career of other theorists, such as Max Born, and the physical work of mathematicians such as David Hilbert, Henri Poincaré, and Hermann Minkowski—all among Sommerfeld's frequent correspondents—indicate a stronger role for mathematics in

this process of disciplinary formation during the crucial period between the 1890s and World War I. Local traditions, such as those at Cambridge and Göttingen, have been described in great detail with regard to the enticements and constraints of developing new research agendas. From this perspective, Sommerfeld's academic maturation in Göttingen deserves a renewed interest. While he was Felix Klein's assistant in the mathematics institute at Göttingen University, Sommerfeld's specialty was designated as "physical mathematics"—a mathematical subfield that used physics as a tool for mathematics rather than the other way around. With this orientation, Sommerfeld became an expert in physical differential equations and complex functions (potential theory). He regarded Klein as his role model.

Although his early scientific papers appear disparate from the perspective of physics, because they addressed phenomena in such diverse areas as optics, electromagnetism, and x-rays, they are coherent with respect to their underlying mathematical approach. When Sommerfeld was called as professor of mechanics to Aachen in 1900, he embraced technology in addition to physics as an opportunity to display and interpret Klein's tendencies. At the same time, another Kleinian legacy brought him into closer contact with physics: As an editor of the physics volumes of the *Encyclopedia of Mathematical Sciences*, Sommerfeld traveled together with Klein to England, for example, in order to invite leading representatives of contemporary physics to review their field for the encyclopedia. His correspondence with encyclopedia authors reveals how he occasionally developed new research problems based on contemporary themes from a wide range of subjects. Thus, he combined mathematical versatility with an awareness of the actual research front in physics. When he was considered as a candidate for the chair of theoretical physics at the university in Munich, the committee found Sommerfeld's approach attractive because it attempted to bring to bear "the new knowledges of the theory of functions to solve various physical problems" (Eckert and Pricha, 1984, p. 112).

Years at Munich. In Munich, mathematics, technical mechanics, and physics finally merged into theoretical physics as his lifelong profession. Traversing disciplinary boundaries, however, entailed problems. Mathematicians, such as Sommerfeld's Königsberg professor Ferdinand von Lindemann, and physicists, like those at the University of Leipzig, where Sommerfeld was considered and turned down in 1902 as successor to Ludwig Boltzmann, had mixed feelings about Sommerfeld's qualification as a theoretical physicist. During his first years in Munich, where he became director of a new institute of theoretical physics, Sommerfeld struggled hard for recognition among physicists. At the same time, during a period when

Arnold Sommerfeld. SPL/PHOTO RESEARCHERS, INC.

there were few ordinary chairs for theoretical physics, Sommerfeld's Munich institute naturally attracted the interest of aspiring theory-minded students. Sommerfeld had to find his own way of teaching theoretical physics. He often chose contemporary problems as subject matter for lecture courses. It took several years before Sommerfeld's haphazard lectures gradually turned into a regular six-semester sequence of lectures, which was later considered as canonical for teaching theoretical physics. He also granted considerable freedom to his students to pursue their own research interests for doctoral theses. The topics ranged from turbulence in a river to wireless telegraphy and often involved both experimental and theoretical investigations with uncertain prospects of success. Those who mastered the difficulties spread the renown of Sommerfeld's "nursery" (Pflanzstätte), as he himself called his institute, but at least in one case he was criticized for not caring enough for his doctoral student.

Sommerfeld's approach in theoretical physics has been described as a "physics of problems"—in contrast to the "physics of principles" of Max Planck, for example (Seth, 2003, p. 8). Sommerfeld's eagerness to demonstrate

the mathematical accessibility of physical problems from many areas made him aware of new challenges and brought him into close contact with contemporary experimental investigations. Shortly before his call to Munich, for example, he exchanged long letters with the experimental physicist Friedrich Paschen, whose recent experiments on gamma rays seemed to verify his ideas on the electron theory. Although this effort of "theoretically experimenting" failed in 1905 (Eckert and Märker, 2000), it was successfully renewed a decade later, when Sommerfeld and Paschen focused their interest on atomic spectra. Sommerfeld made Bohr's atomic model a subject of his own research not for theoretical reasons but because of its success in determining a spectroscopic quantity (Rydberg's constant); by extending Bohr's model Sommerfeld hoped to break new ground in the field of atomic spectroscopy. This time, Paschen's measurements indeed confirmed Sommerfeld's theoretical results, which in turn motivated further spectroscopic investigations. During World War I, Sommerfeld and Paschen opened a new chapter of atomic theory by exploring the fine structure of atomic spectra. After the war, a similar collaboration with Manne Siegbahn on x-ray spectroscopy further consolidated the success of this approach.

Barriers to the Nobel Prize. It has long been a subject of debate why Sommerfeld was not awarded the Nobel Prize. For more than a decade after he had published his monumental paper "On the Quantum Theory of Spectral Lines" in 1916, Sommerfeld was nominated almost regularly for the Nobel Prize. There were rumors that he was turned down because of "rivalry with Bohr," as Sommerfeld confided in a letter to a close colleague; he felt hurt by this neglect and argued that "it would have been the only correct and sincere manner to award me in 1923, after Bohr had received the prize in 1922." ("Jedenfalls wäre es das einzig Richtige u. Anständige gewesen, nachdem Bohr den Preis 1922 erhalten hatte, mir ihn 1923 zu geben"; quoted in Eckert and Märker, 2004, p. 292). As is apparent now from the files of the Nobel archives, he had no chance for the award because the representative of physics on the Nobel committee, Carl Wilhelm Oseen, regarded Sommerfeld's style of theorizing as not fundamental enough.

Research Program. Sommerfeld's versatile approach toward a variety of physical problems makes it difficult to discern a favorite specialty. Following atomic theory, to which he focused his own and his students' research for about a decade after 1915, the electron theory of metals became a major object of study. Just as Sommerfeld's extension of Bohr's model had opened a route toward quantum mechanics, his semiclassical electron theory (1927) paved the way for the quantum theory of solids.

However, it would be misleading to sum up his contributions only as a hinge between classical and modern physics—a transition that deserves critical analysis on its own. The editors of Sommerfeld's collected works sorted his published articles into thirteen categories: mathematics, mechanics, electrodynamics, electron theory and relativity, statistical mechanics, electron theory of metals, electromagnetic waves, atomic structure and spectral lines, quantum mechanics, elementary processes, x-ray diffraction, x-ray Bremsstrahlung-spectrum, and popular writings. The same versatility is mirrored by those who grew up in the "Sommerfeld school," a lineage that was regarded with high esteem among the first generations of twentieth-century theoretical physicists. By comparison with Planck and Albert Einstein, who have been characterized as the authority and the genius, respectively, of German theoretical physics in the first decades of the twentieth century, Sommerfeld was labeled as the teacher of the discipline. "Schools" in science, often called "research schools," "thought collectives," "invisible colleges," or otherwise, have been discerned as crucial for the formation of new specialties. The "Sommerfeld school" played such a role for the emergence of theoretical physics. However, the character of Sommerfeld's school differs from that of a thought collective: Versatility rather than a common style or focus on a specific subject matter was characteristic for the pupils as much as for their teacher. Peter Debye and Werner Heisenberg, for example, represented rather different styles of theorizing, although they were both Sommerfeld pupils and later even colleagues at the same university in Leipzig. During World War II, when some of Sommerfeld's pupils were involved in the German and in the British-American atomic bomb and radar projects, little hinted at their common descent from the Munich "nursery."

It is worth mentioning, however, that not only in Germany but all around the world theoretical physicists felt connected in one way or another with Sommerfeld's school. Sommerfeld was an ambitious missionary of his discipline and spread the gospel of new research results throughout the world. His book *Atombau und Spektrallinien* went through many editions and was translated in many languages. He was invited as a guest lecturer to many countries and welcomed foreign students in his institute. His ties with physics in the United States were confirmed in 1949, when the American Association of Physics Teachers chose Sommerfeld as the recipient of its Oersted Medal "in recognition of your contribution to the broad field of the teaching of physics both directly here and elsewhere and through students who have worked with you" (Eckert and Märker, 2004, p. 632). To award this distinction to a German so shortly after World War II also shows that American physicists counted Sommerfeld among the few German scientists who were untainted

with regard to Nazi affiliations. Sommerfeld was known for his strong national feelings during and after World War I, but he was cured from nationalism when he experienced the National Socialists' rise to power. After his retirement in 1935, the succession of Sommerfeld's chair turned into a tug-of-war with an anti-Semitic faction of fanatics, who regarded modern theoretical physics as Jewish. Although recent historical research calls for a more refined view of what is generally labeled as the "German Physics movement"—the fanatics did not act as one group and did not represent the regime's views on science policy—the tug-of-war ended with a victory for Sommerfeld's enemies and ruined the reputation of his former institute within a few years.

In order to overcome his depression about this decline, in the 1940s Sommerfeld actualized his long-held intent to edit his lecture courses. Like *Atombau und Spektrallinien*, which was celebrated as the "bible of atomic physics," Sommerfeld's six volumes of *Vorlesungen über theoretische Physik* became a textbook classic of his discipline. "We are proud that we can do our share to distribute your 'Lebenswerk' throughout English-speaking countries," his American publisher announced in December 1948, referring to the forthcoming appearance of the English translation of volume 6, *Partial Differential Equations in Physics*, Sommerfeld's favorite lecture course. It must have been a great relief for the eighty-year-old theorist to see his life's work thus acknowledged worldwide—when his Munich "nursery" was in ruins, physically as much as intellectually.

SUPPLEMENTARY BIBLIOGRAPHY

Most of Sommerfeld's publications have been reprinted (see original DSB article). A selection of Sommerfeld's scientific correspondence has been edited in two volumes.

WORKS BY SOMMERFELD

Arnold Sommerfeld: Wissenschaftlicher Briefwechsel, Band 1: 1892–1918. Edited by Michael Eckert and Karl Märker. Berlin, Diepholz, Munich: Deutsches Museum, GNT-Verlag, 2000.

Arnold Sommerfeld: Wissenschaftlicher Briefwechsel, Band 2: 1919–1951. Edited by Michael Eckert and Karl Märker. Berlin, Diepholz, Munich: Deutsches Museum, GNT-Verlag, 2004.

"Arnold Sommerfeld (1868–1951), Wissenschaftlicher Briefwechsel." Leibniz Computing Centre of the Bavarian Academy of Sciences and Humanities. Available from http://www.lrz-muenchen.de/~Sommerfeld/. A survey of Sommerfeld's correspondence.

OTHER SOURCES

Corry, Leo. "David Hilbert and the Axiomatization of Physics." *Archive for the History of Exact Science* 51 (1997): 83–198.

Eckert, Michael. "Propaganda in Science: Sommerfeld and the Spread of the Electron Theory of Metals." *Historical Studies in the Physical and Biological Sciences* 17, no. 2 (1987): 191–233.

———. "Theoretical Physicists at War: Sommerfeld Students in Germany and as Emigrants." In *National Military Establishments and the Advancement of Science and Technology: Studies in the 20th Century History*, edited by Paul Forman and José M. Sánchez-Ron. Boston: Kluwer Academic, 1996.

———. "Mathematik auf Abwegen: Ferdinand Lindemann und die Elektronentheorie." *Centaurus* 39 (1997): 121–140.

———. "Mathematics, Experiments, and Theoretical Physics: The Early Days of the Sommerfeld School." *Physics in Perspective* 1 (1999): 238–252.

———. "The Emergence of Quantum Schools: Munich, Göttingen, and Copenhagen as New Centers of Atomic Theory." *Annalen der Physik* 10, no. 1–2 (2001): 151–162.

———. "The Practical Theorist: Sommerfeld at the Crossroads of Mathematics, Physics, and Technology." *Philosophiae Scientiae* 7, no. 2 (2003): 165–188.

———. "Die Deutsche Physikalische Gesellschaft und die 'Deutsche Physik.'" In *Physiker zwischen Autonomie und Anpassung: Die Deutsche Physikalische Gesellschaft im Dritten Reich*, edited by Dieter Hoffmann and Mark Walker. Berlin/Weinheim: Wiley-VCH, 2007.

———, and Willibald Pricha. "Boltzmann, Sommerfeld und die Berufungen auf die Lehrstühle für theoretische Physik in Wien und München, 1890–1917." *Mitteilungen der Österreichischen Gesellschaft für Geschichte der Naturwissenschaften* 4 (1984): 101–119.

Eckert, Michael, et al. *Geheimrat Sommerfeld: Theoretischer Physiker; Eine Dokumentation aus seinem Nachlass.* Munich: Deutsches Museum, 1984.

Friedman, Robert Marc. *The Politics of Excellence: Behind the Nobel Prize in Science.* New York: Times Books, 2001.

Geison, Gerald L. "Scientific Change, Emerging Specialties, and Research Schools." *History of Science* 19 (1981): 20–40.

Greenspan, Nancy Thorndyke. *The End of the Certain World: The Life and Science of Max Born; The Nobel Physicist Who Ignited the Quantum Revolution.* New York: Basic Books, 2005.

Hoddeson, Lillian, Gordon Baym, and Michael Eckert. "The Development of the Quantum-Mechanical Electron Theory of Metals: 1928–1933." *Reviews of Modern Physics* 59 (1987): 287–327.

Jungnickel, Christa, and Russell McCormmach. *Intellectual Mastery of Nature.* 2 vols. Chicago: University of Chicago Press, 1986.

Litten, Freddy. *Mechanik und Antisemitismus: Wilhelm Müller (1880—1968).* Munich: Institut für Geschichte der Naturwissenschaften, 2000.

Rowe, David E. "Klein, Hilbert, and the Göttingen Mathematical Tradition." *Osiris* 5 (1989): 189–213.

———. "Mathematical Schools, Communities, and Networks." In *The Cambridge History of Science*, vol. 5, *The Modern Physical and Mathematical Sciences*, edited by Mary Jo Nye. Cambridge, U.K.: Cambridge University Press, 2003.

Servos, John W. "Research Schools and Their Histories." *Osiris* 8 (1993): 2–15.

Seth, Suman. "Principles and Problems: Constructions of Theoretical Physics in Germany, 1890–1918." Ph.D. diss., Princeton University, Princeton, 2003.

Staley, Richard. "Max Born and the German Physics Community: The Education of a Physicist." Ph.D. diss., Cambridge University, Cambridge, U.K., 1992.

———. "On the Co-Creation of Classical and Modern Physics." *Isis* 96 (2005): 530–558.

Walter, Scott. "Minkowski, Mathematicians, and the Mathematical Theory of Relativity." In *The Expanding Worlds of General Relativity*, edited by Hubert Goenner, et al. Einstein Studies, no. 7. Boston: Birkäuser, 1999.

———. "Henri Poincaré and the Theory of Relativity." In *Albert Einstein: Chief Engineer of the Universe*, edited by Jürgen Renn. Weinheim, Germany: Wiley-VCH, 2005.

Warwick, Andrew. *Masters of Theory: Cambridge and the Rise of Mathematical Physics.* Chicago: University of Chicago Press, 2003.

Michael Eckert

SONNEBORN, TRACY MORTON (*b.* Baltimore, Maryland, 19 October 1905; *d.* Bloomington, Indiana, 26 January 1981); *genetics, evolution, protozoology, education.* For the original article on Sonneborn see *DSB*, vol. 18.

Sonneborn was an early and visionary leader in microbial genetics. He was widely regarded for the sophistication of his experimental designs, which he used to explore a range of largely non-Mendelian hereditary phenomena in the ciliated protozoan *Paramecium aurelia*. Sonneborn also stood out among geneticists as a highly successful teacher, writer, and public speaker. He was a well-known critic of radical reductionism at a time, during the middle decades of the twentieth century, when studies of the simplest phenomena in the simplest organisms such as viruses and bacteria dominated the experimental life sciences. Since the original *DSB* article was published, new light has been shed on the philosophical tenets that guided his research and his role in the reaction to the politicization of genetics under Lysenko in the Soviet Union.

Sonneborn's experimental mastery with *P. aurelia* can be traced to his relentless and painstaking efforts throughout the 1930s to achieve experimental control of cytological events in the single-celled organism for the purpose of Mendelian analysis. As a research associate to his mentor Herbert Spencer Jennings at Johns Hopkins, he pursued the development of methods for inducing breeding among diverse types of *P. aurelia*, leading to his groundbreaking discovery of mating types in the organism in 1937. From roughly 1937 to 1947 Sonneborn worked out much of the basic genetics of the organism. Beginning in 1939 this work was carried out in Sonneborn's laboratory at Indiana University, where he remained for the balance of his career.

Although an avid experimentalist, Sonneborn's experimental style was characterized by a natural-history-like approach to the understanding of the research organism. In particular, he capitalized on the existence of two functionally distinct nuclei in *Paramecium,* the macronucleus and the micronucleus. Sonneborn demonstrated that the former was the nuclear locus of phenotypic expression and that the latter controlled the regeneration of the macronucleus. Furthermore, he aimed to gain extensive control over the onset of life cycle events associated with conjugation (reduction division and cross-fertilization followed by macronuclear regeneration) and autogamy (reduction division and self-fertilization also followed by macronuclear regeneration). Such control was achieved through the manipulation of environmental conditions such as food supply, which when changed trigger certain cytological responses in the organism. The control of conjugation enabled both Mendelian analysis and the control of Mendelian phenomena. Control of autogamy enabled the production of a homozygous macronucleus comparable to the production of homozygosity through inbreeding in higher organisms.

The wealth of experimental tools arising from his knowledge of the natural history of the organism yielded Sonneborn a high level of control over both nuclear and nonnuclear sources of hereditary phenomena; these circumstances led him to explore and emphasize the interaction between the two in his genetics research. It likewise made possible his 1955 critique of the biological species concept as championed by the evolutionary biologist Ernst Mayr at a symposium sponsored by the American Association for the Advancement of Science. Although a strong proponent of a population-genetic conception of species, Sonneborn criticized Mayr's biological species concept for its failure to incorporate asexual and obligatory inbreeding organisms, which represent a considerable portion of the living world. Mayr defined species as groups of actually or potentially interbreeding natural populations that are reproductively isolated from other such groups. In an effort to foster the development of a fully comprehensive species concept, in 1957 Sonneborn published a massive survey of the protozoa spanning from obligatory outbreeding to obligatory inbreeding and asexual organisms, which rejected the fundamental break in nature between sexual and asexual organisms maintained by many leading biologists.

Sonneborn's discovery of mating types and subsequent research helped to launch a new era of genetics during the middle decades of the twentieth century, in which microorganisms became the favored tools of genetics research. Microorganisms were embraced largely due to their physiological simplicity, rapid rates of reproduction, and the ease and exactitude with which their environmental conditions could be controlled. Unlike other researchers, however, Sonneborn never migrated to genetics research with even simpler microorganisms such as bacteria and viruses that became popular shortly later, nor did he incorporate into his research program the molecular biology techniques that developed in concert with the use of these organisms.

Sonneborn stood at a crossroads then as a pioneer of microbial genetics who nonetheless remained throughout his career a classical geneticist in the tradition of such programs as *Drosophila* and maize genetics. At the same time, he aimed to modify the largely reductionist, nucleocentric legacy of classical genetics, by employing classical genetics techniques to explore non-Mendelian phenomena in *Paramecium.* Unlike the fruit fly *Drosophila*, the bacterium *E. coli*, or phage virus, *Paramecium* never became a widely employed model for genetics research. It nonetheless was appreciated by an active network of researchers that circulated around Sonneborn's laboratory. Like Jennings, Sonneborn considered the protozoa biologically important due to their dual status as organisms and complex single cells comparable to those found in higher organisms. Throughout his career he promoted their value as models for the study of cellular heredity.

Sonneborn's focus on the role of the cytoplasm and on the interaction between genic and nongenic sources in inheritance was counter to the hierarchical model held by most geneticists circa 1950 of the nuclear genes as the sole locus of heredity. As a skilled writer and public speaker as well as a respected experimentalist, Sonneborn became the effective spokesperson during the 1940s and 1950s for research in cytoplasmic inheritance. In his popular article "Beyond the Gene" published in 1949, for example, Sonneborn argued for a revision of what he referred to as the "general gene theory" to include not only nuclear genes but cytoplasmic genes as well (p. 58). In "Partner of the Genes," published a year later, he maintained that the cellular material outside the nucleus should no longer be considered a "silent partner" but rather an "active partner with the nucleus in the control of inheritance" (p. 30).

During the same period, Sonneborn played a lead role in a major defense of classical genetics, when reports began to surface both inside and outside the Soviet Union that his research supported Lysenkoism. In 1948, Trofim D. Lysenko won the official support of Joseph Stalin and the Communist Party to lead efforts to improve Soviet agricultural output through the use of techniques predicated on the inheritance of acquired characteristics. Soviet policy and propaganda associated with these events proclaimed the invalidity of classical gene theory and labeled it as reactionary and idealist. These events nourished Cold War fears among scientists in the United States and Europe related to the suppression of scientific freedom in the Soviet Union. Sonneborn joined forces with leading geneticists including Hermann J. Muller and Theodosius Dobzhansky in attacking Lysenkoism on both scientific and political grounds. In defense of his own work, Sonneborn maintained that his research was an extension of classical genetics rather than a rejection of it, as had been suggested by Lysenkoists.

At both the undergraduate and graduate level and in the laboratory, Sonneborn's infectious enthusiasm for the study of life fueled the interest of many in the study of genetics. In informal weekly seminars held at his home, Sonneborn attracted the faithful participation of not only his own students, but many from the laboratories of other university biologists. Sonneborn's Bloomington laboratory was considered an international mecca for "Paramecium workers," including many advanced researchers, postdocs, and more than forty students who earned their PhDs under his guidance.

Many biologists feel that Sonneborn's work anticipated, when others had not, the late-twentieth-century preoccupation with genetic systems and biological complexity brought about by the use of molecular biology tools and techniques beginning in the 1960s. Sonneborn represented his philosophy of biology not as the antithesis of reductionism, but as a centrist position similar to that held a generation earlier by Jennings, who was also both a critic of reductionism and a champion of the principle of emergent evolution. Sonneborn maintained that genetic understanding would not arise from the study of the simplest biological models alone, but from the investigation of evolutionary innovation from the simplest to the highest organisms. In addition to those honors listed in the original *DSB* article, Sonneborn was elected to the American Philosophical Society in 1952.

SUPPLEMENTARY BIBLIOGRAPHY

WORKS BY SONNEBORN

"Sex, Sex Inheritance and Sex Determination in *Paramecium aurelia*." *Proceedings of the National Academy of Sciences of the United States of America* 23 (1937): 378–385.

"Recent Advances in the Genetics of Paramecium and Euplotes." *Advances in Genetics* 1 (1947): 263–358.

"Beyond the Gene." *American Scientist* 37 (1949): 33–59.

"Partner of the Genes." *Scientific American* 183 (November 1950): 30–39.

"Heredity, Environment, and Politics." *Science,* n.s., 111 (1950): 529–539.

"The Role of the Genes in Cytoplasmic Inheritance." In *Genetics in the 20th Century,* edited by Leslie Clarence Dunn. New York: Macmillan, 1951.

"Breeding Systems, Reproductive Methods, and Species Problems in Protozoa." In *The Species Problem,* edited by Ernst Mayr. Washington, DC: American Association for the Advancement of Science, 1957.

"Does Preformed Cell Structure Play an Essential Role in Cell Heredity?" In *The Nature of Biological Diversity,* edited by John M. Allen. New York: McGraw-Hill, 1963.

With Janine Beisson. "Cytoplasmic Inheritance of the Organization of the Cell Cortex in *Paramecium aurelia*." *Proceedings of the National Academy of Sciences of the United States of America* 53 (1965): 275–282.

"The Evolutionary Integration of the Genetic Material into Genetic Systems." In *Heritage from Mendel,* edited by R. Alexander Brink. Madison: University of Wisconsin Press, 1967.

OTHER SOURCES

Nanney, D. L. "Tracy M. Sonneborn (1905–1981)." *Genetics* 102 (1982): 1–7.

———. "T. M. Sonneborn: Reluctant Protozoologist." *Progress in Protozoology: Proceedings of VI International Congress of Protozoology,* Special Congress Volume of *Acta Protozoologica.* Part I. Warsaw: Panstowwe Wydawn. Nauk., 1982.

Preer, John R. Jr. "Tracy Morton Sonneborn, October 19, 1905–January 26, 1981." *Biographical Memoirs,* vol. 69. Washington, DC: National Academy of Sciences, 1996. Available at http://www.nap.edu/readingroom/books/biomems/.

Sapp, Jan. "Concepts of Organization: The Leverage of Ciliate Protozoa." In *A Conceptual History of Modern Embryology,* edited by Scott F. Gilbert. Baltimore: Johns Hopkins University Press, 1991.

Schloegel, Judith Johns. "From Anomaly to Unification: Tracy Sonneborn and the Species Problem in Protozoa, 1954–1957." *Journal of the History of Biology* 32 (1999): 93–132.

———. "Intimate Biology: Herbert Spencer Jennings, Tracy Sonneborn, and the Career of American Protozoan Genetics." PhD diss., Indiana University, Bloomington, 2006.

Judith Johns Schloegel

SPERRY, ROGER WOLCOTT (*b.* Hartford, Connecticut, 20 August 1913; *d.* Pasadena, California, 17 April 1994), *psychobiology, functions of the hemispheres of the human brain, chemoaffinity hypothesis of neuron growth, cognitive neuroscience.*

Sperry shared the Nobel Prize in the category of Physiology or Medicine in 1981 for clarifying the functions of the two hemispheres of the human brain. Before Sperry's time, the brain's left hemisphere was generally seen as dominant and the right hemisphere as making relatively minor contributions. Sperry's research involving patients with "split" brains—brains with surgical division of the corpus callosum and frontal commisures—showed instead that the hemispheres have complementary functions, with the left hemisphere specializing in language and the right hemisphere excelling in visual perception and related processes. This research contributed to the development of a new field of cognitive neuroscience and to the cognitive revolution in psychology in the 1960s. Sperry also advocated a new perspective on the mind–brain relationship in which the mind was conceived as an emergent phenomenon that exerted causal influence on the brain. (He denied that this view implied any dualism.) In this way Sperry's work built a bridge between the formerly separate "two cultures" of science and the humanities. His earlier research on neurophysiology elaborated a chemoaffinity hypothesis in which the growth and function of neurons was viewed as largely prewired and under genetic control rather than being mechanical and somewhat random with connections functionally determined.

Early Development. Roger Sperry grew up as a relatively shy child in rural Connecticut with an early interest in biological topics. In grade school he collected and raised moths. At junior high school age, he showed a continued interest in animals, including trapping and acquiring wild animals as pets. These interests prefigured his later research activities, many of which involved fish, frogs, lizards, rats, cats, and monkeys, as well as humans. As an adult he continued pursuing his youthful interests in boating, fishing, diving, and collecting fossils. In his brief Nobel autobiographical sketch, Sperry mentioned that he had been a letterman in three sports in high school and college—his skills in baseball, basketball, and track perhaps showing not only a concern for high achievement but also an intense focus on the potentialities of the human body. He attended Oberlin College in Ohio on an athletic scholarship.

At Oberlin, Sperry majored in English literature and received his bachelor of arts degree in 1935. His choice of a major was related to his lifelong concern with clarity of written expression. (During the rest of his life he spent much time writing, revising, and editing his scientific manuscripts and those of his students.) His undergraduate major also represented a commitment to the arts and humanities, and as an adult Sperry continued to engage in such activities as sculpture, ceramics, drawing, water colors, and folk dancing. He continued his studies at Oberlin and received a master's degree in psychology in 1937

under R. H. Stetson; for the rest of his career he identified to some extent with the field of psychology.

Sperry went on to the University of Chicago, where he completed a PhD in 1941 in zoology under Paul Weiss, a scientist well-known for research on the nervous system of amphibians. This time—the late 1930s and early 1940s—was an era of behaviorism in American psychology and related areas of neurology. It was thought that the growth of neurons was controlled mainly by mechanical factors and was a somewhat random process. The ultimate function of a nerve was supposed to be influenced functionally by whatever end structures it happened to innervate. For example, Weiss implanted a supernumerary leg onto the body of a salamander and showed that it functioned normally despite the fact that it was innervated by nerves that did not normally connect to a leg.

Sperry's own research often seemed to have the opposite implications. If he implanted motor nerves into the "wrong" muscles of a rat's leg, the leg continued to function incorrectly throughout the animal's life, with no functional adaptation. The same was true of sensory nerves. Many years later, Sperry transferred skin from a frog's belly (together with its nerve supply) to the animal's back, and skin from the back to the belly. From that time onward, whenever the animal's belly was stimulated, it scratched its back, and vice versa, with no readjustment of function resulting from experience. In other subsequent research Sperry cut the optic nerve of a goldfish and reimplanted the eye rotated 180 degrees. The parts of the nerve grew back into the brain of this fish (its optic tectum) in precisely the same locations as before, even though they had to cross over other possible sites to do so. It was as if the nerves were guided by some kind of precise chemical markers directly to their destinations (though the exact chemicals hypothesized to do this have still not been identified). After the fish recovered from this surgery, its visual orientation to prey remained 180 degrees out of phase. When a morsel of food was located on the left, the fish would swim to the right, and vice versa. No functional readaptation of this response occurred during the remainder of the life of the fish, and if it had not been fed artificially, it would have starved.

Postdoctoral Work. After completing his PhD in 1941, Sperry did a year of postdoctoral work under psychologist Karl S. Lashley of Harvard University. He continued to work with Lashley from 1942 to 1946 as a biology research fellow at the Yerkes Laboratories of Primate Biology in Orange Park, Florida. In 1942–1945 he also met his military obligations by working on the government's Medical Research Project on Nerve Injuries. Much like his doctoral supervisor, Weiss, Sperry's postdoctoral mentor Lashley was known as a behaviorist who endorsed functional views of the central nervous system. Lashley had carried out extensive studies of the effects of brain lesions on rats' maze performance, searching for the location of the neurophysiological substrate of memory (the engram). Lashley's work had found little evidence that the location of such brain lesions was significant. Instead, what seemed to be important was simply the amount of brain tissue destroyed. Once more, Sperry's work seemed to have somewhat the opposite implications, strongly supporting the importance of hard-wired, specific neurological connections. For example, when Sperry attached the neurons of monkeys to the "wrong" muscles of their arms, their motor activities with these limbs became permanently abnormal. However, unlike fish, frogs, or rats, these monkeys seemed to be aware that something was wrong with their arms and tried their best to correct their movements by conscious efforts. At first, these efforts simply took the form of suppressing the abnormal movements caused by the incorrect neurological connections that had been surgically imposed.

University of Chicago. After completing his postdoctoral work, Sperry returned to the University of Chicago as an assistant professor of anatomy from 1946 to 1952. At Chicago his research continued to address "big" issues, leaving minor technical matters to other scientists. Sometime before 1950, Sperry's career was disrupted by tuberculosis. In an attempt to recover from the disease, he spent time in a sanitorium at Saranac, New York, and in the warmer climates of the Bahamas. It was in this latter location that he met a fellow biologist, Norma G. Deupree; they married in Wichita, Kansas, in 1949.

When Sperry attempted to return to the University of Chicago in 1952 after a leave of absence, the Department of Anatomy was reluctant to reappoint him because with tuberculosis, he was not likely to live very long. Under these circumstances, he took an alternative appointment offered by James Grier Miller, head of the Department of Psychology and Psychiatry, as a tenured associate professor. In 1952–1953, Sperry served as section chief, Neurological Diseases and Blindness, at the National Institutes of Health in Bethesda, Maryland.

California Institute of Technology. In 1954 Sperry moved to the California Institute of Technology (Caltech) in Pasadena, where Sperry was appointed the Hixon Professor of Psychobiology. Sperry continued in this position for several decades until his retirement. One topic he addressed during these years was the question of "field" effects in the brain, as hypothesized by Gestalt psychology. Sperry approached this question quite directly. If the brain functions through creating magnetic or other electrical fields (rather than, as conventionally believed, simply by

the transmission of impulses by neurons), it should be possible to disrupt such field effects. Sperry introduced various wires and mica chips into the surface of the cerebral cortex to disrupt any such electrical fields but found no effects on neurological function. The burden of proof concerning such electrical fields and their effects was thus placed on Gestalt theorists. To this date they have not tried to counter these findings, and thus their "field" hypothesis remains weakened.

At this time Sperry began the research on "split-brain" animals that eventually led to his Nobel Prize. He began with cats, examining the effect of cutting the optic chiasm and the corpus callosum on their ability to transfer their learning of certain visual patterns from one visual field to another. The split-brain animals were deficient in such transfers. In fact, they could now learn incompatible responses using the separated hemispheres of the brain. The cat might learn to prefer a triangle to a circle in the left visual field but to prefer a circle to a triangle in the right visual field. Sperry continued his work on other split-brain animals, now with monkeys. Research under way at this time by others, such as Robert Patton and his colleagues, went further than simply cutting the corpus callosum and other frontal commisures of primates and actually carried out hemicerebrectomies. Such animals, with only one cerebral hemisphere, were surprisingly normal in their functioning. Of course, they had the expected effects of such massive lesions, such as hemiparesis (paralysis of the arm and leg opposite the hemisphere that was removed) and visual field defects on the side of space opposite to the lesion. But such hemicerebrectomized monkeys performed about as well on discrimination problems as control animals without such surgery. They simply turned their heads to use their "good" visual field and their nonparalyzed hand to pick up the object that was correlated with reward in the experimental problem.

It was at this point that the opportunity to do research with human "split-brain" patients arose for Sperry. Neurosurgeon Joseph E. Bogen cooperated in this work. The patients involved each suffered from intractable epilepsy, so resistant to the usual medical treatments that a procedure as drastic as cutting the corpus callosum and frontal commisures seemed to offer a reasonable hope of limiting the spread of seizures. At the same time, graduate students sophisticated in psychological testing methods, such as Michael Gazzaniga, were available at Caltech to work under Sperry's direction.

To casual observers, the patients who had their corpus callosum and commisures cut showed remarkably few effects of the procedure. More refined testing procedures were necessary to show its full results. The usual testing procedure was to seat the patient in front of a screen, with a slot in which the hands could be placed underneath it.

Roger Wolcott Sperry. *Sperry collects his Nobel Prize in Medicine in Stockholm, for his work on the functional specialization of the cerebral hemispheres, December 10, 1981.* HULTON ARCHIVE/GETTY IMAGES.

The patient was asked to fixate on the midline while visual displays were projected to either the left or the right visual field (or both), but too briefly to permit any visual scanning. Under these conditions, it was apparent that the left hemisphere was in charge of speaking. It could name objects projected to the right visual field or presented to the right hand beneath the screen. It was also able to read and interpret sentences presented to the right visual field or to do mathematical calculations with numbers presented there. In contrast, the right hemisphere was mute, unable to understand connected verbal expressions and unable to do arithmetic. However, the right hemisphere was not as helpless as it at first appeared to be. It could direct the behavior of the left hand beneath the screen to indicate in nonverbal ways what it had experienced. In this way the right hemisphere could demonstrate an ability to read and understand single words. Moreover, the right hemisphere was considerably superior to the left in carrying out various visual perceptual tasks with respect to materials presented to the left visual field or to the left hand. Thus, the right hemisphere was better able to copy geometrical figures, to recognize faces, or to build or copy

structures with three-dimensional wooden blocks. In interpreting these and other such results, it became evident to researchers that there were essentially two separate conscious beings within one head. (The two hemispheres could function independently of one another, but there is no evidence regarding consciousness in this fact.) This was evidently the type of scientific breakthrough that most impressed the Nobel Committee.

The results of these split-brain studies of Sperry and his colleagues were consistent with and clarified the large existing literature concerning hemisphere differences in the human brain, and they revolutionized scientific views on this topic. For example, studies of dichotic listening with normal subjects had long shown right-ear (and thus left-hemisphere) superiority in repeating words and left-ear (right-hemisphere) superiority in the perception of musical tones. Studies of unilateral cerebral lesions dating back to the time of Paul Broca and Hughlings Jackson in the nineteenth century had long since shown left-hemisphere damage to be associated with aphasia or alexia, while right-hemisphere damage was associated with prosopagnosia (difficulty recognizing faces) and constructional apraxia (difficulty in drawing or building block structures, for example).

During his career at both Chicago and Caltech, Sperry served as a mentor to many doctoral students and postdoctoral fellows. Although he had the reputation of being a lecturer of outstanding scientific clarity, he was always less comfortable in dealing with large groups than in one-to-one conversations with students. As a professor he continued to be a shy, even dour man, albeit one with a twinkle in his eye and a sly grin. He was never one to tell his students what experiments they should run but stood ready with a trenchant critique of any detailed plans they might devise on their own initiative. As stated already, Sperry preferred to work on the "big" issues and let others do the detailed, technical mopping up. He always cautioned students against spending their time on scientific trivia.

Already by the 1960s, Sperry had rejected the idea that brain activity can be accounted for strictly on the basis of physical, chemical, and physiological concepts, with the mind being some kind of epiphenomenon that can safely be disregarded by science. Although he rejected dualism, Sperry came to believe that the mind is an emergent entity that exerts its own causal force downward on the central nervous system and is important in the process of deciding how to act in the world. He used the analogy of a television, where although the concepts of electronics are necessary to understand how it works, they fail utterly to deal with the overarching content of news, drama, or artistic activity seen by viewers. In his view, a baseball game on television is not an activity played to empty benches but one with human purpose, meaning, and value. Science must take such factors into consideration to render an adequate account of brain activity. Providing such an account is one purpose of many researchers in the new field of cognitive neuroscience that Sperry helped to create. Sperry's views of the mind-brain relationship were controversial when he first voiced them but are less so today. Many researchers in cognitive neuroscience (including the late Francis Crick, who moved into this area as a follow-up to his work on the double helix model of DNA) take the issue of consciousness very seriously.

Roger Sperry died in 1994 at the age of eighty of aspiration pneumonia, a complication of a long-term neuromuscular disease that had made it impossible in his later years for him to attend the numerous symbolic occasions to which he was invited. He was survived by his wife, Norma, his son, Tad, and his daughter, Jan.

BIBLIOGRAPHY

Appendix A of Colwyn Trevarthen, ed., Brain Circuits and Functions of the Mind: Essays in Honor of Roger W. Sperry *(Cambridge, U.K.: Cambridge University Press, 1990), contains a list of Sperry's publications. Archives of his papers exist at the California Institute of Technology and at Oberlin College.*

WORKS BY SPERRY

"The Problem of Central Nervous Reorganization after Nerve Regeneration and Muscle Transposition." *Quarterly Review of Biology* 20 (1945): 311–369.

"Regulative Factors in the Orderly Growth of Neural Circuits." *Growth Symposium* 10 (1951): 63–67.

"Cerebral Organization and Behavior." *Science* 133 (1961): 1749–1757.

"Chemoaffinity in the Orderly Growth of Nerve Fiber Patterns and Connections." *Proceedings of the National Academy of Sciences of the U.S.A.* 50 (1963): 703–710.

With Michael S. Gazzaniga and J. E. Bogen. "Interhemispheric Relationships: The Neocortical Commisures: Syndromes of Hemisphere Disconnection." In *Handbook of Clinical Neurology,* edited by P. J. Vinken and G. W. Bruyn. Vol. 4. Amsterdam: North-Holland Publishing, 1969.

"Lateral Specialization in the Surgically Separated Hemispheres." In *Neurosciences: Third Study Program,* edited by Francis O. Schmitt and Frederic G. Worden. Vol. 3. Cambridge, MA: MIT Press, 1974.

"Mind-Brain Interaction: Mentalism, Yes; Dualism, No." *Neuroscience* 5 (1980): 651–662.

Science and Moral Priority: Merging Mind, Brain, and Human Values. New York: Columbia University Press, 1982.

OTHER SOURCES

Bogen, Joseph E. "My Developing Understanding of Roger Wolcott Sperry's Philosophy." *Neuropsychologia* 36 (1998): 1089–1096. Bogen, a neurosurgeon, collaborated with Sperry in the split-brain studies on humans.

Meyer, Ronald L. "Roger Sperry and His Chemoaffinity Hypothesis." *Neuropsychologia* 36 (1998): 957–980.

Sperry, Norma D. "In Memoriam—Roger Sperry." *Neuropsychologia* 36 (1998): 955–956. This article by Roger Sperry's widow was part of a memorial issue of a scientific journal containing articles by a group of his former students and associates.

Trevarthen, Colwyn, ed. *Brain Circuits and Functions of the Mind: Essays in Honor of Roger W. Sperry.* Cambridge, U.K.: Cambridge University Press, 1990.

Voneida, Theodore J. "Sperry's Concept of Mind as an Emergent Property of Brain Function and Its Implications for the Future of Humankind." *Neuropsychologia* 36 (1998): 1077–1082.

Donald K. Routh

SPITZER, LYMAN JR.

SPITZER, LYMAN JR. (*b.* Toledo, Ohio, 26 June 1914; *d.* Princeton, New Jersey, 31 March 1997), *theoretical astrophysics, physics of the interstellar medium, stellar dynamics, space astronomy, plasma physics, and controlled fusion.*

Spitzer was one of the leaders of mid- to late-twentieth-century American theoretical astrophysics, specializing in the physics of the interstellar medium, broadly based studies in stellar dynamics, large-scale applied studies in plasma physics and ultraviolet space astronomy. He will be remembered by generations of astronomers as a gifted teacher, chairman of Princeton's Department of Astrophysical Sciences and director of the Princeton Observatory, and by the science-aware public as the inspirational force advocating what became the Hubble Space Telescope.

Early Life and Training. Born 26 June 1914 into a seventh-generation American family, Spitzer was one of four children (two older sisters and a younger brother) of a prosperous manufacturer of paper boxes and paper products in Toledo, Ohio, who had previously been in the municipal bond trade. His father, Lyman Spitzer, had trained at Phillips Academy Andover and Yale, and his mother, Blanche Brumback, at Vassar, and the family was actively interested in fine arts and intellectual pursuits. The family attended the First Congregational Church in Toledo, where the father was an active board member. Spitzer remembered his father encouraging him to pursue a college career as a professor.

Spitzer attended public schools in Toledo and then followed in his father's footsteps to Andover, where he came under the guidance of the physics professor Frederick M. Boyce. Spitzer and a classmate, Max Millikan, convinced Boyce to add a course in astronomy after they had read popular texts by Arthur Stanley Eddington and James Jeans. Spitzer was especially attracted to physical problems because at Andover he found, much to his satisfaction, that he had "an ability to visualize what goes on physically in terms of physical models … I can see how things fit together, and sort of understand the physical process." ("Oral History Interview with Lyman Spitzer Jr." [hereinafter OHI], p. 8; all quotes are from the 1977 interview). While Spitzer was at Andover, Boyce took his class on a field trip to Boston to hear the astronomer Henry Norris Russell talk about stellar evolution. Also during his Andover years, the family took extended trips to Europe, spending six months in Rome and four months in Paris as well as extended trips to California, England, and Switzerland, where he gained a lifelong passion for mountain climbing.

Yale was Spitzer's choice for college after considering alternatives to the family tradition. He was supported by his family, but also by prizes won at Andover that covered tuition at Yale. He chose Yale for its social atmosphere and concentrated in physics, where he came under the supervision of Alan T. Waterman and under the influence of Leigh Page. Spitzer excelled, managing to be excused from formal course requirements in favor of independent study. In his junior year he reunited with Max Millikan as a roommate. The two had kept in touch after Max attended his famous father's school, the California Institute of Technology (Caltech); Spitzer traveled to California, visited Max in Pasadena, and they climbed the San Gabriel range. During these trips, stimulated by the serials he was reading in *Amazing Stories* and Hugo Gernsbach's *Astounding Science Fiction,* Spitzer mused on ways to create regional and even global subterranean transportation systems using diversification and branching concepts found in telephone network models, where small cars suspended in frictionless electromagnetic fields were subject only to gravity.

Under Waterman, Spitzer took a passing interest in schemes for particle accelerators, but managed only rudimentary experiments concentrating more on theoretical analysis and modeling. He was active in campus life, becoming chairman of the Yale *Daily News.* He took part in various informal discussion circles and came to know Richard Bissell, Walt Rostow, Bill Hull, and Charles Seymour. These contacts stimulated an interest in theoretical economics for a while as he pondered how he might apply his passion for modeling to both physics and economic theory. Advised by his father that in economics it is "very difficult to establish the correctness of any viewpoint" (OHI, p. 16) Spitzer opted for physics, graduating in 1935.

After Yale, Spitzer spent a year at St. John's College, Cambridge University, on a Lady Julia Henry Fellowship

to study nuclear physics. He was assigned to Ralph Fowler, who disregarded his interests and directed him to read a recent Bengt Strömgren paper on electron capture and Fraunhofer line intensities, which Spitzer enjoyed. At a subsequent tutorial session, however, Fowler announced he was taking a leave of absence to be at Princeton, and suggested he read under Eddington on noncoherent scattering theory. Spitzer did so, meeting Eddington less than five times during the year, once again finding satisfaction in his ability to physically visualize the scattering processes he was modeling. During his Cambridge year Spitzer came to know Fred Hoyle and Max Krook, and often attended evening seminars and discussions of modern topics led by Subramanyan Chandrasekhar (known informally to colleagues as Chandra), who was then a Trinity Fellow. Spitzer greatly enjoyed Chandra's lectures in stellar structure, "a wonderful aesthetic experience" (OHI, p. 20). During his year at Cambridge, Spitzer decided to enroll at Princeton, entering the graduate school intending to combine theoretical physics with astronomy under Russell.

Spitzer's plan was to enroll in courses taught by Eugene Wigner, Edward Uhler Condon, and Howard Percy Robertson among other strong theorists at Princeton; take the general examinations in theoretical physics; and then perhaps do a thesis informed by Russell's interests. Russell knew some excellent spectroscopic plates were available at Mount Wilson Observatory and suggested Spitzer visit Pasadena in the summer of 1937 and use them to analyze the spectra of M supergiant stars.

During his graduate years at Princeton, Spitzer attended Albert Einstein's occasional lectures, but spent more and more time with Russell, informally at first in the astronomy library, and eventually in more structured sessions as Russell revised his famous textbook and engaged students and postdoctoral fellows in discussions that would inform the revisions. These discussions, which included the visiting Cambridge theorist Ray Lyttleton, mainly dealt with Russell's passion at the time: the origin of the solar system. This led Spitzer to explore what would happen if the Sun were to encounter another star and suffer a tidal collision. Would material drawn off the two stars condense into planetary bodies or dissipate? This was a major question in that day before nebular condensation theories were successfully placed on a physically plausible basis. Spitzer had been interested in stellar atmosphere theory at Cambridge, and believed he could apply it to answer this question, which held the key to accepting or rejecting the idea that the solar system arose from a chance collision of the Sun with a passing star. Eventually, during his postdoctoral year at Harvard, Spitzer would show conclusively that the tidal filaments would not coalesce, but would dissipate. His work proved to be a watershed study in the history of that subject.

Lyman Spitzer Jr. AL FENN/TIME LIFE PICTURES/GETTY
IMAGES

Postdoctoral Years and War Work. After a summer in
Switzerland with his family, Spitzer, supported by a
National Research Council postdoctoral fellowship,
moved to Harvard, where he completed and published his
study of filament dissipation. At the time, the question
had become a contentious topic of debate between Lyttleton and Willem J. Luyten, and Spitzer distinguished himself by soberly and diplomatically offering conclusive
evidence of his findings, avoiding the ad hominem debate,
and settling the matter. Spitzer found Harvard very stimulating; his office mate was Leo Goldberg and he came in
contact with Theodore Sterne, Lawrence Aller, Donald
Menzel, Fred Whipple, and Cecilia Payne-Gaposchkin.
He was most impressed with Martin Schwarzschild's colloquia and his always-prescient questions and commentary. Harvard astronomy was distinguished by social
interaction, personified by Shapley's "Hollow Squares."
Bart Bok followed Shapley's style, offering "social seminars" that graduate students and postdocs attended.
Spitzer recalls some of his most fruitful ideas flowing from
these occasions, such as his interest in the dynamics of
globular clusters as isothermal gas spheres.

During his postdoctoral year, Spitzer was invited to
join the Harvard Society of Fellows but chose instead to
accept an offer from the Yale physics department in the
fall of 1939 as an instructor. Spitzer engaged in undergraduate physics teaching and studied the dynamics of
galaxies and what circumstances favored spirals and ellip-
ticals, finding important influences from the presence or
absence of rotation and of the existence of an interstellar
medium of gas and dust. He maintained this interest
while at Yale, where he had a little contact with Yale
astronomers, mainly Frank Schlesinger, but remained
wholly in physics. As the war intensified in Europe in
early 1941, Spitzer volunteered to give a graduate course
in aerodynamic theory as a means to acquaint himself
with physics useful for wartime research.

In June 1940 he and Doreen Canaday were married.
Both from Toledo, they had known each other for some
time, enjoyed dancing together, and saw each other in the
summers during and after graduate school. She had been
active in archaeology but did not continue this interest
professionally after marriage. Eventually they had four
children: a son, Nicholas, and three daughters, Dionis,
Sarah, and Lydia.

Spitzer left Yale in January 1942 for war work in an
National Defense Research Committee (NDRC) Division
6 contract office connected with Columbia University
devoted to undersea warfare. He had aligned with the
"America First Committee" created within the Yale Law
School, resisting involvement in the war, but after Pearl
Harbor, all that vanished. The invitation was by telephone
and Spitzer was asked to assist in the scientific administration and evaluation of underwater sound research, acting
as liaison with navy personnel such as Roger Revelle.
Offices were set up in the Empire State Building and in
the later years of the war, Spitzer moved to Washington,
DC, to head up a Sonar Analysis Group. His primary
responsibility was to manage research, perform evaluative
studies of underwater sound propagation, and eventually
act as general editor of a major report, *The Physics of
Sound in the Sea.* His wartime activities, especially with
Revelle, sensitized him to new ways to conduct large-scale
research and its management, including the creation of
synergistic arrangements between universities and the military services.

Yale and Princeton. Spitzer briefly considered an offer
from the University of Pittsburgh to head the astronomy
department, but at the end of the war returned to Yale,
where President Seymour had promised he could set up an
interdisciplinary "astrophysical unit" with a foot in both
astronomy and physics. He was given an additional faculty slot to fill, and first asked Schwarzschild, then at
Columbia, to join him. When Schwarzschild deferred,
thinking the "unit" was an administrative oddity, he asked
Rupert Wildt, who took the position.

Postwar Yale astronomy was experiencing small changes. Longtime director Schlesinger died in 1944, and was replaced by the mathematical astronomer Dirk Brouwer, who maintained Yale's traditions in astrometry and celestial mechanics. Spitzer did what he could to establish new astrophysical programs, including a small consulting unit funded by the navy to analyze the data that were expected to flow from V-2 rocket flights of ultraviolet solar spectrographs. In mid-1946 he secured the funds and made plans, trying to attract Leo Goldberg to Yale. But the early data returns were woefully inadequate, promising no great improvements soon. Even so he consulted for Project RAND, producing a seminal and initially classified study on "Astronomical Advantages of an Extra-Terrestrial Observatory," which outlined the astronomy that could be done with telescopes of various apertures in earth orbit, and notably offered his vision of how new technologies such as space telescopes would reveal new and unanticipated questions that would lead to new areas of exploration and knowledge. Although the physics department was indifferent to these activities, Brouwer chafed somewhat, especially at the creation of the consultant group.

Spitzer's rekindled research activities now centered more and more on the physics of the interstellar medium although he was still contributing to stellar atmosphere theory, including a study of noncoherent scattering mechanisms in stellar atmospheres. Extending a set of three studies that were published in 1941 on the "Dynamics of the Interstellar Medium," after the war Spitzer examined the temperature of the interstellar medium, the galactic magnetic field, and the formation and evolution of interstellar clouds.

His return to Yale, however, was brief. He had quietly always hoped to return to Princeton to replace Russell, and the opportunity came in 1947. The process from Princeton's side, however, was protracted and far from straightforward, and included offers to Svein Rosseland and Chandrasekhar. The goal had been to replace Russell with someone equally prominent. But the problem was that Russell had so neglected the astronomical infrastructure of the observatory, there was not much to offer in his wake. Finally Princeton, realizing this, turned to Spitzer and offered him virtually a blank slate. When Spitzer responded with a very well received plan of action that included federal funding schemes, hiring Schwarzschild and maintaining formal connections to west coast observatories for periodic observing visits, Princeton happily accepted.

Spitzer and Schwarzschild together were a formidable team, one of the great astronomical teams of the second half of the twentieth century. Both were theorists, but with strong interests in observational work, and both labored to create a strong graduate program in modern astrophysics. Both believed in broadly based collaborative and inclusive styles of research, and both sought out expertise and interests in mainstream physical science, and Spitzer wholly supported Schwarzschild's attention to computational mathematics and high-speed computing. Spitzer continued to pursue a coherent set of studies exploring the temperature and abundances of the elements in the interstellar medium, including studies of physical mechanisms in the interstellar medium that could produce the recently observed polarization in starlight. In a 1950 collaboration with Walter Baade, Spitzer suggested that the absence of interstellar material in some galaxies was caused by prior collisions between galaxies.

Plasma Physics at Princeton. Spitzer's interests in the physics of the interstellar medium directed his attention to problems in plasma physics and magnetohydrodynamics, partly aided by a visit of Hannes Alfvèn to Princeton. A few months prior, returning to Princeton from Pasadena, Spitzer had stopped in Los Alamos to confer with John Wheeler about matters relating to the development of the H-Bomb. Stanislaw Ulam and Edward Teller had just announced that they had a solution to the problem of energy losses through rapid cooling using radiation coupling for fuel compression, and Spitzer was intrigued by it. The two agreed to continue fusion research somehow at Princeton. Then, in the spring of 1951, after a spectacular but bogus announcement that Argentine scientists had succeeded in creating controlled nuclear fusion, Spitzer once again consulted Wheeler, who would have the last word on the matter. Together, they decided to develop a multifaceted government-funded program at Princeton to explore practical methods of controlled fusion as well as continue theoretical research on bomb development. Spitzer led the former effort, called "Matterhorn-S," developing a magnetically confined plasma device, a "Stellerator" that would fuse hydrogen into helium in a slow controlled process, creating energy to drive electricity generators. Wheeler would manage "Matterhorn-B" to perform calculations predicting the characteristics of thermonuclear reactions. "Matterhorn," coined by Spitzer in the spirit of climbing a great mountain, achieved notoriety when it faithfully predicted the characteristics for the thermonuclear stage of the first H-Bomb tests in November 1952. In fact, the test worked better than predicted, but very much along the theoretical lines established at Princeton. This achievement, classified of course, led to optimism for controlled fusion, and so Spitzer's group grew rapidly. After a year of theoretical studies, he created a small experimental group, headed for a while by James Van Allen, and this grew exponentially, especially after it was declassified in 1958 as a result of the

Geneva "Atoms for Peace" Conference. In 1958 it was renamed the Princeton Plasma Physics Laboratory. Early hopes for success, from evidence of neutron emission, soon were dashed because the emission came from instabilities in the plasma caused by turbulence. The problem of overcoming turbulence became the driving force beyond achieving the extreme temperatures needed for fusion. Spitzer remained director of the project until 1961, and left it only in 1966.

Space Astronomy. Spitzer's 1946 study for Project RAND was not stillborn in him, even though it remained classified for some time. He promoted his ideas to colleagues but in the early years knew there was too much frustration associated with such efforts to attract a wide interest base. Yet he contributed to related studies, such as a 1947 report on the nature of the Earth's atmosphere at 300 kilometers (186 miles), a 1950 report on satellite perturbations, and in 1952, for the *Journal of the American Rocket Society*, on interplanetary travel. This led to a televised speech in Princeton in 1954 that was translated by the French popular journal *Ciel et Terre* in 1955. He contributed a paper "On the Determination of Air Density from a Satellite" to a symposium organized by Van Allen on the *Scientific Uses of Earth Satellites* in 1956, and in the wake of Sputnik described observations of the interstellar medium that could be made from a satellite, as well as options for optical space telescopes. Starting in the mid- to late 1950s, he avidly supported and facilitated Schwarzschild's program of building and flying a series of balloon-borne telescopes to study the Sun and then nonsolar objects, "Project Stratoscope." Always taking the long view, he regarded this as a step in the direction of a true space telescope capability.

Spitzer will be remembered for his advocacy of a large orbiting optical telescope, and his name is central to the history of the Hubble Space Telescope. By the time he resigned from Matterhorn, his planned payload for an Orbiting Astronomical Observatory (OAO) mission was well underway, having started after Spitzer's initial response to queries ranging from the Air Force to Lloyd Berkner of the National Academy in 1958 asking what astronomers would do if they had access to space. Spitzer was one of several who immediately proposed some form of space telescope, and this led to the National Aeronautics and Space Administration (NASA) OAO series, which by the early 1960s included a 81-centimeter (32-inch) reflecting telescope for high-resolution nonsolar ultraviolet spectroscopic studies. This eventually came to be called the "Princeton Experiment Package" aboard OAO-III, *Copernicus*, launched in 1972. By then, Princeton under Spitzer had been vigorously exploring space astronomy, including Schwarzschild's "Project Stratoscope" and a sounding rocket program, and Spitzer himself was a lead-

ing voice articulating what a true optical space telescope might look like, first at a summer study in Iowa in 1962, and then more formally in 1965 after a study at Wood's Hole that called for a 305-centimeter (120-inch) optical reflector. Spitzer chaired an ad hoc committee arising from the proposal.

Even though Spitzer and Princeton remained central to the definition of the telescope, and Spitzer was no doubt among its most passionate and effective advocates in both astronomy and in Washington, their successive proposals, first to build a wide-field camera and then to host the scientific headquarters for the facility, were not successful. What would become the Wide Field–Planetary Camera was decided on the basis of the promise of new technologies (charge-coupled devices [CCDs] over traditional Secondary Electron Conduction [SEC] Vidicons proposed by Princeton) and the Space Telescope Science Institute's more favorable and effective administrative and political circumstances offered by a coherent proposal from the Association of Universities for Research in Astronomy (AURA) consortia that selected Johns Hopkins University as the site. These were both disappointments, of course, both to the institution and for Spitzer, but both managed to maintain positive leading roles in the Hubble mission and space astronomy generally.

Spitzer was an active member of policymaking and oversight groups in astronomy, including the National Academy of Sciences Decadal survey led by Jesse Greenstein in the 1970s. He held membership on the Astronomy Missions Board, the editorial board of the *Astrophysical Journal*, and many other posts of similar importance. He was one of the first (1953) incumbents of the Henry Norris Russell Lectureship of the American Astronomical Society (AAS), and starting in the 1970s received virtually every major prize given to astronomers, as well as the National Medal of Science in 1979 and the Crafoord Prize in 1985. He was president of the AAS from 1960 to 1962. He has an asteroid named in his honor as well as a major NASA infrared satellite, and to recognize his support for mountain climbing, the American Alpine Club created the Lyman Spitzer Climbing Grants Program, known also as the Lyman Spitzer Cutting Edge Award.

Spitzer maintained active research and publishing until his death, contributing to understanding the physics of the interstellar medium. His latest papers remained in the early 2000s highly cited works, and his collaboration with Ed Fitzpatrick as a guaranteed time observer on the Hubble Space Telescope resulted in the recognition of the existence of a new class of objects called "proplyds"—protoplanetary disks encapsulating stars still forming in dense interstellar clouds. Spitzer died suddenly at home after a normal working day. Appreciations by his colleagues attest to his great humanity.

BIBLIOGRAPHY

Archives held at Princeton University include a collection of Spitzer's papers (1936–1997) and Records of the Department of Astrophysical Sciences (1835–1988), both available at the Princeton University Department of Special Collections, Princeton, New Jersey. Project Matterhorn publications and reports (1951–1958) are available at the Furth Plasma Physics Laboratory, Forrestal Campus of Princeton University, Princeton, New Jersey. A number of interviews with Spitzer are available at the American Institute of Physics, Center for History of Physics, Niels Bohr Library, College Park, Maryland, and as part of the Space Astronomy Oral History Project of the National Air and Space Museum Archives, Smithsonian Institution, Washington, DC.

WORKS BY SPITZER

"The Stability of Isolated Clusters." *Monthly Notices of the Royal Astronomical Society* 100 (1940): 396–413.

"The Dynamics of the Interstellar Medium. III. Galactic Distribution." *Astrophysical Journal* 95 (1942): 329–344.

"The Temperature of Interstellar Matter. I." *Astrophysical Journal* 107 (1948): 6–33.

With Walter Baade. "Stellar Populations and Collisions of Galaxies." *Astrophysical Journal* 113 (1951): 413–418.

With David R. Bates. "The Density of Molecules in Interstellar Space." *Astrophysical Journal* 113 (1951): 441–463.

With Martin Schwarzschild. "The Possible Influence of Interstellar Clouds on Stellar Velocities." *Astrophysical Journal* 114 (1951): 385–397.

With Paul McRae Routly. "A Comparison of the Components in Interstellar Sodium and Calcium." *Astrophysical Journal* 115 (1952): 227–243.

"On a Possible Interstellar Galactic Corona." *Astrophysical Journal* 124 (1956): 20–34.

Physics of Fully Ionized Gases. New York: Interscience, 1956.

With Leon Mestel. "Star Formation in Magnetic Dust Clouds." *Monthly Notices of the Royal Astronomical Society* 116 (1956): 503–514.

"Distribution of Galactic Clusters." *Astrophysical Journal* 127 (1958): 17–27.

With William C. Saslaw. "On the Evolution of Galactic Nuclei." *Astrophysical Journal* 143 (1966): 400–419.

"Astronomical Research with the Large Space Telescope." *Science* 161, no. 3838 (1968): 225–229.

Diffuse Matter in Space. New York: Interscience, 1968.

With Michael H. Hart. "Random Gravitational Encounters and the Evolution of Spherical Systems. I. Method." *Astrophysical Journal* 164 (1971): 399–409.

With Jeremiah P. Ostriker and Roger Chevalier. "On the Evolution of Globular Clusters." *Astrophysical Journal* 176, part 2 (1972): L51–L56.

With J. B. Rogerson, J. F. Drake, et al. "Spectrophotometric Results from the Copernicus Satellite. I. Instrumentation and Performance." *Astrophysical Journal* 181, part 2 (1973): L97–L102.

———. "Spectrophotometric Results from the Copernicus Satellite. IV. Molecular Hydrogen in Interstellar Space." *Astrophysical Journal* 181, part 2 (1973): L116–L121.

———. "Spectrophotometric Results from the Copernicus Satellite. VI. Extinction by Grains at Wavelengths between 1200 and 1000 Å." *Astrophysical Journal* 182 (1973): L1–L6.

With Edward B. Jenkins. "Ultraviolet Studies of the Interstellar Gas." In *Annual Review of Astronomy and Astrophysics* 13 (1975): 133–164.

With Scott D. Tremaine and Jeremiah P. Ostriker. "The Formation of the Nuclei of Galaxies. I - M31." *Astrophysical Journal* 196, part 1 (1975): 407–411.

"Oral History Interview with Lyman Spitzer, Jr., 8 April 1977 and 10 May 1978." Interview by David DeVorkin. College Park, Maryland: American Institute of Physics, Center for History of Physics, Niels Bohr Library, 1977–1978. All quotes are from the 1977 interview.

Physical Processes in the Interstellar Medium. New York: J. Wiley, 1978.

Searching between the Stars. New Haven, CT: Yale University Press, 1982.

With Ralph C. Bohlin, Edward B. Jenkins, Blair D. Savage, et al. "A Survey of Ultraviolet Interstellar Absorption Lines." *Astrophysical Journal Supplement Series* 51 (1983): 277–308.

Dynamical Evolution of Globular Clusters. Princeton, NJ, Princeton University Press, 1987.

"Dreams, Stars, and Electrons." *Annual Review of Astronomy and Astrophysics* 27 (1989): 1–17.

With Edward Fitzpatrick. "Composition of Interstellar Clouds in the Disk and Halo. IV. HD 215733." *Astrophysical Journal* 475, part 1 (1997): 623–641.

With Jeremiah P. Ostriker, eds. *Dreams, Stars, and Electrons: Selected Writings of Lyman Spitzer, Jr.* Princeton, NJ: Princeton University Press, 1997. Includes detailed annotations by Spitzer of some thirty-two works he felt best describe his career accomplishments and interests.

———. "Hubble Space Telescope Observations of Orion Nebula, Helix Nebula, and NGC 6822." Technical Report, Princeton University. NASA STI/Recon Technical Report N. (1999).

OTHER SOURCES

Bahcall, John N., and Jeremiah P. Ostriker. "Lyman Spitzer Jr." *Physics Today* 50, no. 10 (1997): 123–124.

Bromberg, Joan Lisa. *Fusion: Science, Politics, and the Invention of a New Energy Source.* Cambridge, MA: MIT Press, 1982.

DeVorkin, David H. *Henry Norris Russell: Dean of American Astronomers.* Princeton, NJ: Princeton University Press, 2000.

Field, George B. "Lyman Spitzer, Jr. (1914–1997)." *Publications of the Astronomical Society of the Pacific* 110, no. 745 (1998): 215–222.

King, Ivan R. "Obituary: Lyman Spitzer, 1914-1997." *Bulletin of the American Astronomical Society* 29, no. 4 (1997): 1489–1491.

Smith, Robert W., with contributions by Paul A. Hanle, Robert H. Kargon, and Joseph N. Tatarewicz. *The Space Telescope: A Study of NASA, Science, Technology, and Politics.* New York: Cambridge University Press, 1989.

David DeVorkin

Georg Ernst Stahl. **PHOTO RESEARCHERS.**

STAHL, GEORG ERNST (*b.* Ansbach, Germany, 20 October 1659; *d.* Berlin, 14 May 1734), *chemistry, animism, vitalism, combustion, alchemy, medicine.* For original article on Stahl see *DSB,* vol. 12.

Stahl has a prominent place in the histories of both chemistry and medicine, and had a successful career in court service and medical practice. His attempt to account for the inflammability of matter and reduction of metals was developed in the eighteenth century by his followers into a phlogistic paradigm preceding the modern chemistry of combustion that Antoine-Laurent Lavoisier (1743–1794) and his colleagues established. His medicine stressed the fundamental difference between the organism and the machine, and was thus opposed to a medical orientation of his time that sought to reduce medicine into mere mechanics and hydraulics of body parts and fluids.

Much new work has been done or come to light since the publication of Lester S. King's biography of Stahl in the original *DSB.* Stahl's year of birth, long held by historians as 1660, was found to be 1659 based on a birth certificate found in his parents' parish church in Ansbach. His formulation of life has been under rigorous analysis by philosophers and historians alike. There have been fine studies on his relationship with the Pietsts in Weimar and Halle. And very importantly, scholars have come to a better understanding of Stahl's chemistry, matter theory, and alchemy, subjects that King neglected to a large degree in his biography.

Career and Life. Stahl was born into a Lutheran family in Ansbach, Germany in 1659. His father Johann Lorenz, an MA, worked in different times as a secretary to the council of the court (*Hofrat*) of Brandenburg-Ansbach, the Lutheran church consistory, and the local marriage court; his mother Maria Sophia Meelführer was the daughter of a local deacon. He went to the local gymnasium and thereafter studied medicine at Jena, then a stronghold of chemical medicine. Stahl received his MD at Jena in 1684, and taught there as an unsalaried lecturer until he began in 1687 to serve as personal physician (*Leibmedicus*) to the Duke of Saxon-Weimar. In 1694 he accepted the offer of the professorship of medicine at the newly opened University of Halle. He and Friedrich Hoffmann (1660–1742), also a Jena MD and an advocate of mecha-

nistic medicine, soon made their faculty one of the most flourishing in Germany, although they before long developed an intense rivalry. Also on the faculty upon the inauguration of Halle were Christian Thomasius (1655–1728), famous jurist representative of the Early Enlightenment in Germany; August Hermann Francke (1663–1727), theologian and leader of German Pietism; and Johann Franz Buddeus (1667–1729), professor of moral philosopher and Lutheran theologian. Christian Wolff (1679–1754) joined the faculty later, in 1706.

Although he thrived as a professor of medicine, Stahl also enjoyed a distinguished career as a clinician and a courtier. He practiced medicine from the time that he received his MD, if not earlier, and renewed his courtier career when he was called in 1715 to serve as first physician to King Friedrich Wilhelm I of Prussia (r. 1713–1740). Compared with Hoffmann's dismissal from the same position in 1712 after a mere three years, Stahl's continual service at court in Berlin until his death was a significant success, and doubtless it was owed to the king's trust in his medical care. His fame as a clinician transcended national borders so that the ailing Russian Tsar Peter the Great tried twice to invite him to his sickbed in St. Petersburg. Besides attending to the health of the king and his family, Stahl was a court councilor (*Hofrat*) and was entrusted with the presidency of the medical board that regulated issues related to medicine, pharmacy, and public health in Berlin and later over all of Prussia. He was also instrumental in the founding of a college of medicine and surgery (inferior to the university in status) in Berlin in 1724.

Scientific Work in Chemistry. Stahl's chemical work demonstrates the width and depth of his knowledge of chemical practitioners' work, as well as of his own empirical observations and experimentations. His first book, *Zymotehnia Fundamentalis* (1697), showed his acquaintance with brewers' and bakers' practical knowledge of fermentation. His works on metallurgy, inflammable materials, and salts recorded his familiarity with miners' and smelters' practice and beliefs and with chemical literature, in addition to his rich observations on minerals and often elaborate laboratory experiments.

Stahl had a corpuscularian, and largely mechanistic, interpretation of matter and chemical processes. Though agnostic about the number of the most fundamental particles, which he at times identified as indivisible atoms, he postulated that natural substances resulted from the aggregation or compounding (*mixtio*) of composite corpuscles of different orders. Chemical processes were the recombinations of the constituent corpuscles of starting materials. Because the primary qualities of the fundamental particles were unknown, Stahl proposed to examine the changes of physical and chemical qualities at the phenomenal level. He nevertheless was certain that particles were by nature passive, and their motion was transported by other particles in motion and ultimately came from heat. His rather mechanistic interpretation of fermentation, basically as the release of sulphurous particles in the fermentable materials, quietly rejected the theories of fermentation prevalent prior to his time that stressed the ferment as a somewhat magic agent that accounted for material changes in all the three kingdoms of animal, vegetable, and mineral. It also left no room for the Aristotelian form in the explanation of material constitution and changes.

Stahl himself did not seem to see phlogiston as his invention. Following Johann Joachim Becher (1635–1682), he denoted the substance underlying all inflammable matters with the term phlogiston, although the roots of this notion can be traced at least back to the Paracelsian notion of sulphur as the principle of inflammability. This trace is evident in Stahl's regular references to inflammable or oily substances as sulphurs and his frequent substitution of "phlogiston" with *Schwefelswesen* (essence of sulphur or sulphurous being). What distinguished his *Schwefelswesen* from the previous Paracelsian principle of sulphur was its material identity. The Paracelsian principle worked like the Aristotelian element to the extent that it showed no material consistency in the different substances

of which it was said to form a part. Robert Boyle especially ridiculed this material inconsistency of the Paracelsian principle and Aristotelian element in his *Sceptical Chymist*. As Boyle's criticism was absorbed by the following generations, Stahl postulated, and tried to demonstrate, that the material composition of phlogiston remained uniform in all bodies that contained it, even though it did not exist in nature as a pure uncompounded substance. Phlogiston could be released into the air from inflamed sulphurous minerals, from vegetable substances in fermentation, or from animal parts in putrefaction. It could come into the corporeal constitution of animals by their digestion of vegetables, or into the vegetable constitution by the absorption of the air. Thus phlogiston circulated across the three kingdoms of nature and around the globe in air streams. It was nutrition for plants, especially for resinous trees. It reduced calxes into their metallic forms, restoring their luster, tinkling sound, and fusibility; when losing their phlogiston, metals were reversed into calxes. Thus phlogiston played a key part in the reduction of metals.

Conception of Vital Principle. Stahl's conception of material constitution dictated his theory of life. He observed that organic bodies decomposed almost immediately when deprived of life, and reasoned that the strong corruptibility of organic matter resulted from its chemical nature. He thus postulated that there must be a reason or a vital principle that kept the living body from its natural decomposition, and that this reason of life could only derive from something other than matter. Meanwhile the delicacy and complexity of life seemed to require that this vital principle worked with alacrity, precision, and spontaneity in response to the organism's real-time needs to maintain health and ward off threats. Thus Stahl assumed that this principle must be an immaterial agent, which he sometimes called *natura* (nature), and sometimes *anima* (the soul). Galen and his early modern followers in medicine also taught that each organ had its natural "reason" so that it knew to perform its natural faculty at the right time, in the right way, and under the right circumstance. For Stahl, this spiritual agent, *anima*, usually exercised natural reason (*ratio*) in the conservation of the body or its parts, rather than performed the logical reasoning (*ratiocinatio*) of the rational soul (often identified as *animus* by Stahl and his contemporaries). Because *anima* guided and regulated physiological processes in the living body, once misled, by emotions, for example, it produced illnesses. In this sense it became a pathological agent. The participation of *anima* in physiology and pathology in accordance with reason and the purpose of life thus made the living organism distinct from a machine made of dead material parts. Medicine, the science of life, therefore must never be a mere application of mechanical principles.

Such a formulation of life ascribed much to the healing power of nature, a doctrine that dates back at least to the Hippocratic authors. For Stahl, the fact that very often the organism healed itself without resorting to medicine served as a proof of *natura* or *anima* at work, employing natural measures such as fever, hemorrhages, vomiting and diarrhea when necessary. The aim of the physician's therapeutics was to facilitate this natural healing power based on attentive observation. Reckless interventions or crude applications of mechanical principles would cause disastrous effects.

It must not be thought that Stahl ignored the importance of mechanism in medicine. The material body was an indispensable instrument of the soul, and its operation basically followed mechanical principles. He assigned a great place to what he called tonic motion (*motus tonicus*), a contractive and relaxative movement of body parts or tissues. In his theoretical formulation that took almost a decade to complete, the contraction and relaxation of the tissues regulated the passage of the circulatory blood, and, thanks to the porous structure of the tissues, filtered out waste and harmful particles in the capillary blood flow into excretive ducts, thus playing as a key devise of metabolism. All these functions of tonic motion were achieved through corporeal mechanisms, although, as always, *anima* as the agent directed the motion.

Critique of Alchemy. Stahl was an interested investigator of alchemy in the first few decades of his career but later turned into a critic. He examined as a believer the theories and experiments on the philosopher's stone in the first chemistry course he taught in 1684, and still wrote approvingly, though also cautiously, on transmutation in the 1700s. In works published in the late 1710s and 1720s, he came to criticize Becher's alchemical belief and the general Renaissance alchemical assumptions, although he retained his allegiance to Becher's theory of material composition. In his well-known "Bedancken von der Gold-macherey," he distinguished between chemistry (*chemie*) and alchemy (*alchemie*), seeing the former as useful, practical work as opposed to the latter as fruitless, and often fraudulent, effort.

A deeper significance of Stahl's criticism is his departure from the vitalist cosmography that the alchemy of Becher and many Renaissance authors relied on. Renaissance vitalism often assumed an animating principle that originated in the heavens and permeated the celestial and terrestrial space alike, or a vital principle that was immanent to the most fundamental unit of matter, the monad or *semina*. In contrast, Stahl's formulation of life and matter deprived organic substance of any form in the Aristotelian sense, of the animal and vital spirits in Galenic medicine, and of the cosmic spirits or immanent seminal principles. This formulation broke with the unity of heaven and earth, and of life and matter in Renaissance vitalism, and came to emphasize the difference between the living organism and dead matter, and indeed between the bio-medical and the physico-chemical.

It is often suggested that Stahl's medicine had a natural bond with Pietism. It is true that Stahl had a long relationship with the Pietists, which began at least at the court of Saxon-Weimar, ran through his tenure at Halle, and continued even at court in Berlin. He was on good terms with Francke and served a king who, though Calvinist himself, was a patron of the Pietists. Some of Stahl's students either played important parts in the pharmacy of the *Weisenhaus* (as Fracncke's institution of charities was known) or became devout Pietists. Yet these relations were not enough to confirm that Stahl's sympathy with Pietism shaped his medicine or that Pietism was by nature opposed to mechanistic medicine. Stahl's rival, the mechanist Hoffmann, for example, befriended and was befriended by the Halle Pietists, and also supported some programs of the *Weisenhaus*. Robert Boyle, probably the best-known mechanical philosopher, was held in high regard by the Pietists. Although Stahl shared with the Pietists' criticism of excessive mechanistic reductionism, it must be remembered that Boyle and Hoffmann, as good Christians, were careful to avoid the danger of atheist materialism. By contrast, Stahl's physiology, pathology, and therapeutics showed few elements that were distinctly characteristic of Pietism (spiritual rebirth, for example), or that proposed religious causation of illnesses (such as the effects of sin on health).

Influence. The influence of Stahl's medical and chemical teachings was enormous over Europe throughout the eighteenth century. His students Johann Juncker (1679–1759) and Michael Alberti (1682–1757) carried on his chemical and medical teachings at Halle. Alberti especially incorporated Pietist ideas into his medicine. Stahl's emphasis on the irreducibility of biomedical phenomena to mechanical laws inspired the doctrines of the so-called Montpellier vitalists, including François Boissier de la Croix de Sauvages, Théophile de Bordeu (1722–1776), and Paul-Joseph Barthez (1734–1806), although the eighteenth-century vitalists, finding it increasingly difficult to defend the place of *anima* in medicine for theoretical and empirical reasons, later differentiated themselves, "the vitalists," from Stahl, "the animist." Although Albrecht von Haller, perhaps the most influential medical figure in mid-century Germany, was critical of Stahl, eminent late eighteenth-century figures in life sciences such as Johann Friedrich Blumenbach (1752–1840) and Pierre Jean Georges Cabanis (1757–1808) hailed him as a genius in medicine. Stahl's chemistry was introduced to Paris largely thanks to Guillaume François Rouelle (1703–1770), and found among his followers Pierre-Joseph Macquer (1718–1784) and Gabriel-François Venel (1723–1775). His teaching of phlogiston was developed in the 1780s and 1790s into a theory of combustion that tried to incorporate new findings in pneumatic chemistry by Joseph Black (1728–1799), Joseph Priestley (1733–1804), Henry Cavendish (1731–1810), Carl Wilhelm Scheele (1742–1786), and others. Stahl's formulation of tonic motion is discernible in the discussion of tonic motion in the lectures of John Thomson (1756–1846) published as late as 1813.

SUPPLEMENTARY BIBLIOGRAPHY

Stahl published most of his works in Latin, the academic language of his age, prior to 1715, the year of his departure for Berlin. Then gradually his works were translated into German, and in the 1720s especially, his dissertations were translated in large numbers. Stahl supervised more than a hundred and forty dissertations, and wrote a great majority of them on his students' behalf. In Halle he experimented with new forms of publication of his age: for example, a personal periodical, Observationes physico-chymico-medicae curiosae *(monthly from July 1697 to June 1698, apparently imitating his colleague Thomasius' well-known precedence* Monatsgespräche*), and a learned journal,* Observationvm selectarvm ad rem litterariam spectantivm *(1700–1705), co-edited with Thomasius and Buddeus. In Berlin he began to write and publish directly in German, which met with the new trend of learned German chemico-medical authors' publication practice.*

WORKS BY STAHL

Dissertatio epistolica ad Tit. Dominum Johannem Adrianum Slevogt … De motu tonico vitali, & hinc inde pendente motu sanguinis particulari. Jenae, Germany: Sumtibus Joh. Jacob Ehrten, 1692. The first of Stahl's publications on tonic motion.

Zymotechnia fundamentalis, seu Fermentationis theoria generalis … Halle, Germany: Typis & sumptibus Christoph. Salfeldii, 1697. A theory of fermentation, where Stahl's matter theory was first laid out.

Propempticon inaugurale de differentia rationis et ratiocinationis … Halle, Germany: 1701. A dissertation program on the difference between natural reason (*ratio*) and logical, reflective thinking (*ratiocinatio*).

Dissertatio medica inauguralis de vita. Halae Magdeburgicae: Typis Johannis Jacobi Krebsii, 1701. One of Stahl's first treatises that formulated what life was.

"Specimen Beccherianum …" In *Physica Subterranea* by Johann Joachim Becher. Lipsiae: Apud Joh. Ludov. Gleditschium, 1703. Stahl republished Becher's work in order to append this commentary.

Opusculum chymico-physico-medicum curiosorum. Halae Magdeburgicae: Typis & Impensis Orphanotrophei, 1715. A collection of Stahl's early works, including *Zymotechnia Fundamentalis* and articles published in his personal periodical and in the journal *Observationvm selectarvm.*

G. E. Stahls zufällige Gedancken und nützliche Bedencken über den Streit von dem so genannten Svlphvre … Halle, Germany: In Verlegung des Wäysenhauses, 1718. Stahl's study on inflammable bodies and their material base.

Georgii Ernesti Stahlii Negotium otiosum, seu, Skiamachia: adversus positiones aliquas fundamentales, theoriae verae medicae à viro quodam celeberrimo intentata … Halae: Litteris et Impensis Orphanotrophei, 1720. A collection of the polemic epistolary exchanges between Stahl and Leibniz on the nature of life.

Herrn George Ernst Stahls, … Chymia rationalis et experimentalis: oder, gründliche, der Natur und Vernunfft gemässe und mit Experimenten erwiesene Einleitung zur Chymie … Leipzig, Germany: bey Caspar Jacob Eysseln, 1720. A chemical textbook based on the notes of his lectures given in 1684. It was translated into English by Peter Shaw as *Philosophical Principles of Universal Chemistry …* (London: Printed for J. Osborn and T. Longman, 1730), which is one of the very few works by Stahl available in English.

Ausführliche Betrachtung und zulänglicher Beweiss von den Saltzen … Halle, Germany: In Verlegung des Wäysenhauses, 1723. A treatise on salts.

Billig Bedencken, Erinnerung und Erläuterung uber D. J. Bechers Natur-Kündigung der Metallen. Frankfurt & Leipzig, Germany: W. C. Multz, 1723. A commentary of Becher's *Natur-Kündigung der Metallen* (1661), in which Stahl criticized alchemical theories and beliefs on the nature of metals.

Ausfürliche Abhandlung von den Zufällen und Kranckheiten des Frauenzimmers. Leipzig, Germany: C. J. Eyssel, 1724. A collection of Stahl's gynecological dissertations, translated into German.

"Gedancken von der Gold-Macherey." In Johann Joachim Becher, *Chymischer Glücks-Hafen, oder, Grosse Chymische Concordantz und Collection …* Halle, Germany: Verlegts Ernst Gottlieb Krug, 1726. Stahl's relatively well-known critique of alchemy.

Praxis Stahliana, das ist … Collegium practicum … Leipzig, Germany: Eyssel, 1728. A collection of Stahl's medical cases.

OTHER SOURCES

Chang, Ku-ming (Kevin). "Fermentation, Phlogiston, and Matter Theory: Chemistry and Natural Philosophy in Georg Ernst Stahl's *Zymotechnia Fundamentalis.*" *Early Science and Medicine* 7 (2002): 31–64. An analysis of Stahl's largely mechanistic matter theory that places his formulation of fermentation in the intellectual context of his age and his own conceptual development.

———. "The Matter of Life: Georg Ernst Stahl and the Reconceptualizations of Matter, Body, and Life in Early Modern Europe." PhD diss., University of Chicago, 2002.

———. "*Motus Tonicus*: Georg Ernst Stahl's Formulation of Tonic Motion and Early Modern Medical Thought." *Bulletin of the History of Medicine* 78 (2004): 767–803. An analysis of the formulation and development of Stahl's theory of tonic motion.

———. "Georg Ernst Stahl's Alchemical Publications: Anachronism, Reading Market, and a Scientific Lineage Redefined." In *New Narratives in Eighteenth-Century*

Chemistry: Contributions from the First Francis Bacon Workshop 21-23 April 2005, 23-43. Dordrecht: Springer, 2007.

———. "From Vitalistic Cosmos to Materialistic World: The Lineage of Johann Joachim Becher and Georg Ernst Stahl and the Shift of Early Modern Chymical Cosmology" In *Chymists and Chymistry: Studies in the History of Alchemy and Early Modern Chemistry*, edited by Lawrence M. Principe, 215-225. Segamore Beach, MA: Science History Publications, 2007.

Coleby, L. J. M. "Studies in the Chemical Work of Stahl." PhD diss., University College, University of London, 1938. A very good study of Stahl's chemistry, unfortunately never published, and thus very rare.

De Ceglia, Francesco Paolo. *Introduzione alla fisiologia di Georg Ernst Stahl*. Lecce: Pensa, 2000. A survey of Stahl's physiology.

———. "The Blood, the Worm, the Moon, the Witch: Epilepsy in Georg Ernst Stahl's Pathological Architecture." *Perspectives on Science* 12 (2004): 1–28. A study of Stahl's conception of epilepsy and pathology in general.

Duchesneau, François. "G. E. Stahl: Antimécanisme et Physiologie." *Archives internationale d'histoire des sciences* 26 (1976): 3–26. Duchesneau, a philosopher and an intellectual historian, analyzes Stahl's medical thought with philosophical rigor.

———. "Leibniz et Stahl: divergences sur le concept d'organisme." *Studia Leibnitiana* 27 (1995): 185–212.

———. "Stahl, Leibniz, and the Territories of Soul and Body." In *Psyche and Soma: Physicians and Metaphysicians on the Mind-Body Problem from Antiquity to Enlightenment*, edited by John P. Wright and Paul Potter. Oxford: Clarendon Press, 2000.

Engelhardt, Dietrich von, and Alfred Gierer, eds. *Georg Ernst Stahl (1659–1734) in wissenschaftshistorischer Sicht: Leopoldina-Meeting am 29. und 30. Oktober 1998 in Halle (S.)*. Halle (Saale): Deutsche Akademie der Naturforscher Leopoldina, 2000. The proceedings of a conference on Stahl.

Geyer-Kordesch, Johanna. "Georg Ernst Stahl's Radical Pietist Medicine and its Influence on the German Enlightenment." In *The Medical Enlightenment of the Eighteenth Century*, edited by Andrew Cunningham and Roger French. Cambridge, U.K.: Cambridge University Press, 1990. A very influential article that suggests Stahl's strong ties to the Pietists.

———. *Pietismus, Medizin und Aufklärung in Preussen im 18. Jahrhundert: das Leben und Werk Georg Ernst Stahls*. Tübingen: Niemeyer, 2000. A fundamental work that elucidates the Pietist background for Stahl's life and work. Includes an updated, though selective, bibliography, of works by and on Stahl, limited to his medical works.

Goetze, Johann Christoph. *Scripta D. Georg. Ern. Stahlii ..., aliorumque ad ejus mentem disserentium, serie chronologica ...* Norimbergae: Apud Petr. Conr. Monath, 1726. A contemporary, annotated bibliography of Stahl's publications, albeit not complete.

Helm, Jürgen. "Das Medizinkonzept Georg Ernst Stahls und seine Rezeption im Halleschen Pietismus und in der Zeit der Romantik." *Berichte zur Wissenschaftsgeschichte* 23 (2000):

167–190. A study of the reception of Stahl's influence in Halle Pietism and German Romanticism.

———. "'Quod naturae ipsae sint morborum medicatrices.' Der Hippokratismus Georg Ernst Stahls." *Medizinhistorisches Journal* 35 (2000): 251–262.

———. *Krankheit, Bekehrung und Reform: Medizin und Krankenfürsorge im Halleschen Pietismus*. Habilitationschrift, Universität Halle-Wittenberg, 2004. A section of this fine work reconsiders the place of Pietism in Stahl's medicine work.

Hoffmann, Paul. "La controverse entre Leibniz et Stahl sur la nature de l'âme." *Studies on Voltaire and the Eighteenth Century* 199 (1981), 237-49.

———. "L'âme et les passions dans la philosophie medicale de Georg-Ernst Stahl." *Dix-Huitiènme Siècle* 23 (1991): 31–43.

Metzger, Hélène. "La Philosophie de la matière chez Stahl et ses disciples." *Isis* 8 (1926): 427–464.

———. "La théorie de la composition des sels et la théorie de la combustion." *Isis* 9 (1927): 294–325. These two outstanding articles form the basis of the part on Stahl in her *Newton, Stahl, Boerhaave et la doctrine chimique* (Paris: Alcan, 1930).

Partington, J. R., and Douglas McKie. "Historical Studies on the Phlogiston Theory." *Annals of Science* 2 (1937): 361–404; 3 (1938): 1–58, 337–371. A series of papers that traces the development and fall of the phlogiston theory in the works of the late eighteenth-century pneumatic chemists.

Rather, Lelland J. "G. E. Stahl's Psychological Physiology." *Bulletin of the History of Medicine* 35 (1961), 37–49.

Rather, Lelland J., and John B. Frerichs. "The Leibniz-Stahl Controversy—I: Leibniz' Opening Objections to the *Theoria Medica Vera*." & "The Leibniz-Stahl Controversy—II: Stahl's Survey of the Principal Points of Doubts." *Clio Medica* 3 (1968): 21–40; 5 (1970): 53–67. An English translation of part of the polemics between Stahl and Leibniz, with a concise analysis.

Strube, Irene. *Georg Ernst Stahl*. Leipzig, Germany: B. G. Teubner, 1984. A book that is based on her dissertation, "Der Beitrag Georg Ernst Stahls, 1659–1734: zur Entwicklung der Chemie," University of Leipzig, 1961. It is in her dissertation that Stahl's birth certificate was first presented, and it corrected the received knowledge of the year of his birth.

Völker, Arina, and Wolfram Kaiser, eds. *Georg Ernst Stahl (1659–1734): Hallesches Symposium 1984*. Halle (Saale): Martin-Luther-Universität Halle-Wittenberg, 1985. The proceedings of a conference held in the 250th anniversary of Stahl's death.

Völker, Arina. "Bei Durchsicht der Stahlschen Disputatioslisten." In *Georg Ernst Stahl*, edited by Arina Völker and Wolfram Kaiser. Halle (Saale): Martin-Luther-Universität Halle-Wittenberg, 1985. A list of Stahl's dissertations. It does not include the prefaces (called programs or *propempticons*) he wrote for a selected number of the dissertations. These dissertations and programs are very important for understanding Stahl's medical teaching.

Ku-Ming (Kevin) Chang

STANCHINSKIY, VLADIMIR VLADI-MIROVICH

(*b.* Moscow, Russia, 20 April 1882; *d.* Vologda, Russia, 29 March 1942), *ecological energetics, biocenology.*

One of several talented Soviet biologists whose full potential was not realized, Vladimir Stanchinskiy nevertheless pioneered the study of energy flow through natural communities. This new approach to ecology arose from the application of Vladimir Ivanovich Vernadskiy's biosphere theory to field biology. Stanchinskiy's other important contributions to ecology were his move away from the rigid biocenosis concept to the idea known today as the ecosystem, and his emphasis on long-term in-depth studies of how individual ecosystems work. He was twice arrested and charges with political offenses; he died during his second imprisonment.

Early Life. Stanchinskiy's father was a chemical engineer and factory inspector. The family moved from place to place, and as a result Stanchinskiy, although born in Moscow, finished his schooling in Smolensk in 1901, 350 kilometers west of Moscow. His university education was no more settled than his schooling: having enrolled at Moscow University to study under the ornithologist Mikhail Aleksandrovich Menzbir, he was expelled in 1902 for political activity. He moved to Heidelberg University in Germany and gained his doctorate there in 1906. Since this degree was not recognized in Moscow, he had to enroll at Moscow University once more, where he soon passed his exams. He was then employed in various teaching posts, and from 1915 to 1917 saw service in the army. For a time he was a member of the Menshevik Party, but gave up politics late in 1917 when the Bolsheviks came to power.

Subsequently, during the civil war, Stanchinskiy was back in the Smolensk area, working in the Education Commissariat (Ministry). He quickly became prominent locally, setting up the Smolensk Society of Physicians and Naturalists, and also participating in the foundation of Smolensk University, where he became professor and head of the Zoology Department. Much of his published work up to 1926 concerned ornithology, beavers, and the other fauna of the Smolensk area.

Steppe Studies. It was at about this time that Stanchinskiy's interests appear to have changed direction. Nineteen twenty-six is notable as the year when Vernadskiy's book *Biosfera* was published. Although some of his ideas had appeared in print earlier, the book was the first comprehensive presentation of the biosphere theory. Vernadskiy emphasized the transfer and transformations of energy and chemical substances between the various component parts of the planet, and the importance of living organ-

isms in these geological processes. As a biologist Stanchinskiy responded enthusiastically, and determined to apply Vernadskiy's ideas to ecological fieldwork, particularly regarding energy transfer. Vernadskiy took a holistic view of the biosphere, and this too is reflected in Stanchinskiy's understanding of natural communities.

Much of Stanchinskiy's early ecological fieldwork was conducted in the Smolensk area with his students from Smolensk University. The main natural habitat in that part of Russia is forest, but forest was not ideal for applying Vernadskiy's ideas. In 1926 Stanchinskiy participated in a commission charged with guiding scientific research at the famous Askaniya-Nova estate in southern Ukraine, a short distance north of the Crimea. Private owners had developed this as a botanic garden, animal reserve, experimental farm, and gigantic sheep ranch before the 1917 revolution, and it still contained about 40,000 hectares of virgin steppe (prairie). Stanchinskiy was soon convinced that grassland was much more suitable than forest for research into ecological energetics since all the organisms, both plants and animals, could be collected whole and their energy content measured. Part of the steppe had been withdrawn from agriculture in 1888, and an official *zapovednik* (nonintervention nature reserve for scientific research) was set up in the 1920s.

In 1929 he was appointed science director of the *zapovednik*. He soon also became head of the Department of Vertebrates at Kharkov University in southern Ukraine. During the summers his colleagues and students from both Kharkov and Smolensk universities would come to Askaniya-Nova to carry out ecological fieldwork. Meanwhile Stanchinskiy set up and directed a Steppe Institute at the *zapovednik*.

Ecological Energetics and Biocenology. The field studies conducted at Askaniya-Nova from 1930 to 1933 aimed to describe as fully as possible the energy content of each trophic level (green plants, herbivores, carnivores, and so on) in the steppe community, how these contents varied through the year, and how energy flowed between the trophic levels. In fact the entomologist Sergey Medvedev was already making similar measurements there from 1927. A variety of steppe types was studied, both at Askaniya-Nova and in other parts of southern Ukraine. The wet and dry weights of the different plants were measured weekly, invertebrates were collected and weighed in a special device (called a biocenometer) invented by Stanchinskiy, the microclimate was measured, and the soils studied. A permanent transect was set up. The aim was to measure the primary and secondary productivity of each natural community.

Stanchinskiy's other main contribution to theoretical ecology concerned the concept of the biocenosis. At a time when ecologists were still mostly working in the separate areas of animal, plant, freshwater, and marine ecology, the classification of natural terrestrial communities tended to be undertaken by botanists (phytosociologists) applying a taxonomic approach, in other words, with the assumption that there exist distinct communities (biocenoses) that can be described, named, and classified much as species of plants and animals can be.

Along with his conviction that natural communities should be studied holistically, giving equal emphasis to all groups of organisms at all trophic levels, Stanchinskiy began to question the traditional concept of the biocenosis. Not all natural communities could be fitted easily into a biocenotic classification: there was too much variation within each biocenosis, and too many intermediates between them. In a paper published in 1933 Stanchinskiy developed a more flexible concept of the biocenosis that was similar to what Arthur Tansley was to term the *ecosystem* two years later.

In the early twentieth century, ecology in Russia was making the important transition from the expeditionary to the stationary approach. Much useful information, especially concerning the geographical distribution of species, was being collected by expeditions, but this was not a suitable way of gathering the long-term monitoring data necessary for understanding how natural communities function. Research stations in *zapovedniks* were first set up in Russia in the years around 1900, but it was Stanchinskiy's Steppe Institute that clearly demonstrated the tremendous scientific benefits, especially for ecology, to be derived from long-term stationary studies. He also made use of the comparative principle implicit in the *zapovednik* system: the *zapovedniks* were intended to contain self-sustaining samples of virgin nature, serving as a baseline with which to compare the artificial communities created by farmers and foresters. By this means it was hoped to improve the efficiency of agriculture and forestry by maximizing the conversion of solar energy to useful products. So Stanchinskiy included both natural vegetation and managed areas in his studies.

First and Second Arrests. At this very productive stage in his career, Stanchinskiy began to face opposition from Trofim Denisovich Lysenko and Isay Izraylovich Prezent, who were later to inflict much damage on Soviet genetics. The first branch of biology they interfered in was ecology, and at a conference in Kiev in 1930 Prezent publicly criticized Stanchinskiy and expressed doubt as to whether ecology deserved to be called a science at all.

In the following year a commission, including Nikolay Ivanovich Vavilov, visited Askaniya-Nova, and within a few days it had been decided to use the site for an Institute of Acclimatization & Hybridization. Lysenko and

Prezent themselves visited Askaniya-Nova in 1933. Although the results of three years' study of ecological energetics had been analyzed and were ready for publication, this was canceled on the grounds of being "not relevant." Stanchinskiy's Steppe Institute was closed down and he was assigned the task of developing the theory of acclimatization of animals. So ended the study of ecological energetics at Askaniya-Nova, and it was only in the 1950s that the subject was resumed seriously in the Soviet Union, thanks to Vladimir Nikolayevich Sukachev.

The pressure on Stanchinskiy's group intensified in August 1933 when several of them, including Sergey Medvedev, were arrested. Some of those detained admitted to counterrevolutionary activities, and fingers were pointed at Stanchinskiy. Anticipating what was likely to happen next, he resigned, but was arrested in November. He made a "confession," probably to protect his family. In February 1934 he was sentenced to five years corrective labor. He also lost his academic posts, and resigned as editor of the *Zhurnal ekologii i biotsenologii* (Journal of ecology and biocenology). It is likely that at least part of the motivation for his persecution was the official view that his scientific research did not support communist plans holding out rather unrealistic prospects for agriculture and particularly the role to be played in it by acclimatization of alien plants and animals. Lysenko and Prezent were also against the use of mathematics in biology, and one of Stanchinskiy's groundbreaking innovations was to show how a complete natural community could be described and explained in terms of mathematical regularities in the energy flows between trophic levels.

Stanchinskiy's "imprisonment" was not in fact so harsh, since his detention was at a collective farm where he worked as a veterinarian. Here he was allowed to continue scientific work and write books. He was released prematurely in 1936. For some time unable to find employment, in 1937 he was eventually found a suitable post by his old acquaintance Grigoriy Leonidovich Grave as science director at the Central-Forest Zapovednik near Nelidovo, 300 kilometers west of Moscow.

No longer allowed to teach, Stanchinskiy now devoted his energies to research, concentrating on the role of decomposers in soil. An important publication at this time was an article on the organization of scientific research in the *zapovedniks*—a form of institution that the Russians had been developing since the 1890s.

By August 1940 he was once more attracting suspicion, and his second arrest followed in June 1941. He was taken to Nelidovo and accused of spying and making anti-Soviet remarks to colleagues at the *zapovednik*. It may not have helped his case that he was a former Menshevik and had also studied in Germany. The sentence was eight years in corrective labor camps. The following year he died at

Vologda. With respect to both his sentences Stanchinskiy was rehabilitated in 1956 and 1957.

A Missed Opportunity. Stanchinskiy's scientific talents, drive, and administrative abilities are undoubted, and it is tragic that his scientific output was disproportionately small, owing to political interference. There are parallels with Vavilov, who had similar skills and was arrested shortly before Stanchinskiy on similar charges. Both men died after about a year in imprisonment. In terms of scientific and administrative skills Stanchinskiy and Vavilov were of comparable stature.

Had Stanchinskiy been given full rein, there is little doubt that he would have established the foundations of ecological energetics and built up an impressive body of measurements in the 1930s. He might also have been given more credit for developing the ecosystem concept. It is a moot point how independent were the developments in both fields in the Soviet Union and in the West. Certainly several Soviet ecologists visited the West at this time, and Stanchinskiy was acquainted with work in the West; moreover British and American ecologists were receiving Russian ecological publications and citing Russian work—including Stanchinskiy's (in 1939). Energy capture by crops was already being measured in the United States by Edgar Nelson Transeau in the mid-1920s, and ecological energetics was developed again in the United States by ecologists such as G. Evelyn Hutchinson, Raymond L. Lindeman, and Chancey Juday around 1940. They too acknowledged Vernadskiy as the inspiration for their work, but appear not to have known about Stanchinskiy.

BIBLIOGRAPHY

WORKS BY STANCHINSKIY

"K metodike kolichestvennogo izucheniya biotsenozov travyanistykh assotsiatsiy." *Zhurnal ekologii i biotsenologii* 1 (1931): 133–137. On quantitative methods for studying steppe biocenoses (including the biocenometer).

"O nekotorykh osnovnykh ponyatiakh zoologii v svete sovremennoy ekologii." In *Trudy chetvertogo Vsesoyuznogo c"ezda zoologov, anatomov i gistologov* [Proceedings of the Fourth Congress of the zoologists, anatomists, and histologists], edited by Ivan Ivanovich Shmal'gauzen. Kiev and Kharkov: Gosmedizdat USSR, 1931. On certain fundamental zoological concepts in contemporary ecology (including ecological energetics).

"O znachenii massy vidovogo veshchestva v dinamicheskom ravnovesii biotsenozov." *Zhurnal ekologii i biotsenologii* 1 (1931): 88–98. On the importance of biomass for the dynamic equilibrium in biocenoses.

"K ponimaniyu biotsenoza." *Trudy Sektora ekologii Zool.-biologicheskogo instituta pri Khar'kovskom universitete* 1 (1933): 20–37. On the biocenosis concept (anticipating Tansley's "ecosystem").

"Teoreticheskiye osnovy akklimatizatsii zhivotnykh." *Trudy Instituta sel'sko-khozyaystvennoy gibridizatsii i akklimatizatsii zhivotnykh v Askanii-Nova* 1 (1933): 33–66. The theory of animal acclimatization.

"Zadachi, soderzhaniye, organizatsiya i metody kompleksnykh issledovaniy v goszapovednikakh." *Nauchno-metodicheskiye zapiski Komiteta po zapovednikam* 1 (1938): 28–50. Aims and methods of multidisciplinary research in state *zapovedniks*.

OTHER SOURCES

Bailes, Kendall E. *Science and Russian Culture in an Age of Revolution: V. I. Vernadsky and His Scientific School, 1863–1945.* Bloomington: Indiana University Press, 1990.

Boreyko, Vladimir Evgen'evich. *Don Kikhoty: istoriya, lyudi, zapovedniki.* Moscow: Logata, 1998. Biographical sketches of prominent ecologists and nature conservationists.

Mirzoyan, Eduard Nikolaevich. *Etyudy po istorii teoreticheskoy biologii.* Kiev, 2001. One chapter on Stanchinskiy.

Nechaeva, N. T., and Sergey Ivanovich Medvedev. "Pamyati Vladimira Vladimirovicha Stanchinskogo (k istorii biotsenologii v SSSR)." *Byulleten' Moskovskogo obshchestva ispytateley prirody, Otdel biologicheskiy* 82 (1977): 109–117. Stanchinskiy's life and work, especially at Askaniya-Nova, by two biologists who worked with him there; with a list of Stanchinskiy's works.

Shtil'mark, Feliks Robertovich. *History of the Russian Zapovedniks, 1895–1995.* Edinburgh: Russian Nature Press, 2003.

Weiner, Douglas R. *A Little Corner of Freedom: Russian Nature Protection from Stalin to Gorbachev.* Berkeley: University of California Press, 1999.

———. *Models of Nature: Ecology, Conservation and Cultural Revolution in Soviet Russia.* 2nd ed. Pittsburgh: University of Pittsburgh Press, 2000. The best source in English on Stanchinskiy.

Geoffrey H. Harper

STARKEY, GEORGE

(*b.* Bermuda, 1628; *d.* London, England, 1665), *medicine, alchemy.* For the original article on Starkey see *DSB,* vol. 12.

The original *DSB* entry on George Starkey suggested that he was the "probable author" of the highly popular alchemical treatises ascribed to Eirenaeus Philalethes. This rather provisional claim can now be affirmed with much greater certainty, thanks to extensive research done on Starkey's correspondence and laboratory notebooks.

Starkey as Philalethes. The central processes concealed in the highly allusive Philalethes treatises are expressed in plain language in a letter composed by Starkey, probably in 1651, and sent by him to his patron Robert Boyle. Most of these processes are also laid out in Starkey's laboratory notebooks, especially the important document British Library Sloane MS 3750, where Starkey identifies his major source as the Prussian chymist Alexander von Suchten. Starkey's claim that he received the secret of chrysopoeia (alchemical gold-making) from an anonymous friend still living in New England, the putative author of the Philalethes tracts, was clearly a mystification that he promulgated in order to increase his standing in the technical and scientific circle centered on Samuel Hartlib in Interregnum London. Although Starkey himself was the author behind the pseudonym of Philalethes, the young American did in fact receive important information on chymistry from a variety of sources while he was still living in New England. His education at Harvard College introduced him to important components of alchemical theory, as found in contemporary natural philosophy treatises such as those of Jonathan Mitchell and William Ames. Along with his classmate John Alcocke, Starkey was initiated into the practice of alchemy by the obscure Richard Palgrave, a physician of Charlestown. Equally important, Starkey learned valuable metallurgical secrets from investors and employees of the Hammersmith ironworks at Saugus, which was in full operation during his time in New England. Among these figures were William White, Robert Child, Richard Leader, and John Winthrop Jr. The unique combination of Starkey's Harvard education and the technical and medical knowledge acquired in New England allowed the young immigrant to be received as a sort of wunderkind upon his arrival in London in 1650.

Influence on Boyle and Newton. Despite the fact that Boyle is nowhere mentioned in the original *DSB* article on Starkey, the young American in fact had a direct and immediate impact on the British "naturalist." Considerable evidence has emerged to support the claim first made by William Newman in *Gehennical Fire* (1994) that Starkey was Boyle's chymical tutor. Manuscripts kept in the Royal Society and the Bodleian Library reveal that Boyle was copying entries from Starkey's notebooks under the direct supervision of the latter. One manuscript even contains entries by Starkey that are overlaid in Boyle's early hand (Bodleian Library, MS Locke c. 29). The relationship of the two youthful researchers is further clarified by Boyle's comments in his *Usefulness of Natural Philosophy* to the effect that Boyle was subsidizing Starkey's experimentation on *ens veneris,* a medicament described allusively by the Belgian chymist Joan Baptista van Helmont. Starkey was undoubtedly the most influential of Boyle's various Helmontian contacts, and significant traces of the training that the latter received from the New England chymist can still be found in Boyle's mature oeuvre. Boyle's work on the classification of salts into the three categories of urinous, alkalizate, and acid owes a par-

ticular debt to the Helmontian chymistry reformulated and transmitted by Starkey.

Perhaps an even more striking testament to the unsuspected degree of Starkey's influence in the seventeenth century has emerged as a result of the scholarship devoted over the last generation to Isaac Newton's alchemy. Unlike Boyle, Newton seems never to have met Starkey in person. Nonetheless, under the guise of Eirenaeus Philalethes, Starkey exercised a remarkable influence on Newton over a period of some thirty years. Newton's cross-referencing tool, the *Index chemicus,* is filled with references to Philaelethes—by Richard Westfall's count, Starkey's pseudonym gets more billing in the *Index chemicus* than any other author. Even Newton's published comments on chymistry, such as Query 31 of the *Opticks* and the short *De natura acidorum,* contain significant signs of Starkey's influence, especially in the area of Newton's corpuscular matter theory. Like Newton in his chymical writings, Starkey espoused a theory that matter at the micro level is made up of complex corpuscles forming shells around a simpler nucleus; both Newton and Starkey associate these shells with the mercury and sulfur of traditional alchemy. Although Newton exercised significant modifications on the chrysopoetic practice that he derived from Starkey, one can also clearly make out the heavy influence of the Philalethes treatises in Newton's experimental laboratory notebooks as well (Cambridge University MSS Add. 3973 and 3975).

Reputation. It is ironic that despite Starkey's literary, medical, and scientific attainments, his reputation suffered as the fame of Philalethes grew. Starkey himself had written numerous polemical writings under his own name, such as the Helmontian diatribes *Natures Explication and Helmont's Vindication* (1657) and *Pyrotechny Asserted and Illustrated* (1658). It was in these works as well as in shorter pamphlets that Starkey railed against the "piss-pot prophets" of orthodox medical practice. As a result of his invective, as well as his apparently immoderate drinking, Starkey developed an unsavory reputation in some circles. This allowed his detractors to capitalize on the very story that Starkey himself had created about Philalethes, namely that Starkey was only the intermediary, rather than the author, of the Philalethan corpus. Hence Johann Heinrich Cohausen, the author of *Hermippus redivivus* (1742), described Starkey as a "vicious and extravagant man," unlike Philalethes, who was "a Man of remarkable Piety," while the chymical chronicler Olaus Borrichius described Starkey in his *De ortu et progressu chemiae: Dissertatio* (1668) as a drunkard and liar who had merely exploited Philalethes for his own sophistical purposes. Despite these unflattering and misleading comments, Starkey clearly deserves to be accorded a high position among the seventeenth-century practitioners of chymistry. His work displays a keen gravimetric awareness, in accordance with the principle of mass balance, which had received its first clear enunciation in the works of Starkey's avatar van Helmont. In Starkey's work one can find unequivocal adumbrations of the gravimetric "balance-sheet" method immortalized by Antoine-Laurent Lavoisier. Under his Philalethan guise, Starkey would exercise considerable influence in the environs of the French Académie des Sciences, where writers such as Wilhelm Homberg would refine and transmit his innovative quantitative analyses to a subsequent generation of scientists who had divested themselves of the dream of chrysopoeia but in every other respect remained the heirs of early modern chymistry

SUPPLEMENTARY BIBLIOGRAPHY

WORK BY STARKEY

Alchemical Laboratory Notebooks and Correspondence. Edited by William R. Newman and Lawrence M. Principe. Chicago: University of Chicago Press, 2004. Starkey's previously unpublished correspondence and laboratory notebooks.

OTHER SOURCES

Newman, William R. "Newton's Clavis as Starkey's 'Key.'" *Isis* 78 (1987): 564–574.

———. "The Authorship of the *Introitus apertus ad occlusum Regis palatium*." In *Alchemy Revisited,* edited by Z. R. W. M. von Martels, 139–144. Leiden, Netherlands and New York: E.J. Brill, 1990.

———. "The Corpuscular Transmutational Theory of Eirenaeus Philalethes." In *Alchemy and Chemistry in the 16th and 17th Centuries,* edited by Piyo Rattansi and Antonio Clericuzio, 161–182. Dordrecht, Netherlands and Boston: Kluwer, 1994.

———. *Gehennical Fire: The Lives of George Starkey, an American Alchemist in the Scientific Revolution.* Cambridge, MA: Harvard University Press, 1994; republished with a new foreword, Chicago: University of Chicago Press, 2003.

———. "George Starkey and the Selling of Secrets." In *Samuel Hartlib and Universal Reformation,* edited by Mark Greengrass, Michael Leslie, and Timothy Raylor, 193–210. Cambridge, U.K., and New York: Cambridge University Press, 1994.

———. " '*Decknamen* or Pseudochemical Language'? Eirenaeus Philalethes and Carl Jung." *Revue d'Histoire des Sciences* 49 (1996): 159–188.

Newman, William R., and Lawrence M. Principe. *Alchemy Tried in the Fire: Starkey, Boyle, and the Fate of Helmontian Chymistry.* Chicago: University of Chicago Press, 2002.

———. "The Chymical Laboratory Notebooks of George Starkey." In *Reworking the Bench: Research Notebooks in the History of Science,* edited by Frederic L. Holmes, Jürgen Renn, and Hans-Jörg Rheinberger, 25–41. Dordrecht, Netherlands and Boston: Kluwer, 2003.

Principe, Lawrence M. "Apparatus and Reproducibility in Alchemy." In *Instruments and Experimentation in the History*

of Chemistry, edited by Frederic L. Holmes and Trevor H. Levere, 55–74. Cambridge, MA: MIT Press, 2000.

William R. Newman

STEBBINS, GEORGE LEDYARD, JR.

(*b.* Lawrence, New York, 6 January 1906; *d.* Davis, California, 19 January 2000), *botany, genetics, evolutionary biology.*

Stebbins is best known as one of the architects of the "evolutionary synthesis" of the 1930s and 1940s. His primary contribution to the incorporation of Mendelian genetics with Darwinian evolutionary theory was the publication of his 1950 book, *Variation and Evolution in Plants,* which brought understanding of plant evolution in line with understanding of animal evolution as it was being formulated during the period of synthesis. Stebbins is also known for his varied contributions in areas of systematic botany, plant geography, cytogenetics, plant breeding, and plant developmental biology, but is generally recognized as the pioneer of the field of plant evolutionary biology, which incorporated elements from all these areas. He was the master of the synthetic review article and is especially remembered for his contributions to general understanding of phenomena such as polyploidy, apomixis (a form of asexual fertilization), and hybridization, especially as they played out in the pattern and process of evolution in the plant world.

Family Background and Education. George Ledyard Stebbins Jr. was born in Lawrence, New York, the son of George Ledyard Stebbins of Cazenovia, New York, and Edith Alden Candler of Brooklyn, New York. His father was a wealthy New York financier and real estate developer who was responsible for developing the resort town of Seal Harbor, Maine. He was also instrumental in helping to create Acadia National Park on Mount Desert Island, Maine. His mother was a New York socialite whose brother Duncan was a popular architect known for his connections with New York elites. Ledyard (as he preferred to be called) Stebbins was named after his father, and until shortly after his father's death in 1950 used "junior" after his surname. He was the third offspring in the family. His older brother Henry became a popular physician in Seal Harbor and his older sister Marcia became an artist.

Stebbins showed an early interest in natural history generally, and plant life in particular, which his family encouraged. Both of his parents took their children out for nature walks, canoe rides, and hikes along the shorelines, mountains, and tide pools in Maine. The resort life of Seal Harbor, which was popular with northeastern intellectuals, also brought the Stebbins children in contact with scientists such as Edgar T. Wherry, an expert on ferns. Stebbins later credited Wherry with his initial interest in the plants of Maine.

In 1914 the entire family relocated to the West Coast when Edith Stebbins contracted tuberculosis. Ledyard Stebbins was enrolled at the Polytechnic School in Pasadena, California. His early educational career was undistinguished, though he did excel at outdoor activities such as hiking, mountaineering, and horseback riding. In 1917 the family was forced to move to Colorado Springs, Colorado, so that Edith Stebbins could be treated at Cragmore Sanitarium. Ledyard and his brother Henry enrolled in St. Stephen's school for boys, a school known for its outdoors activities; there his interests in natural history were further nurtured. In 1920 the family returned to California and settled in Santa Barbara, where Ledyard was enrolled at the Cate School in Carpinteria.

In 1924 Stebbins followed his older brother to Harvard University, with loose plans to major in political science in the hope of obtaining a law degree. He changed his mind after a summer of botanizing on Mount Desert Island and after he had fallen under the influence of the distinguished plant taxonomist at Harvard, Merritt Lyndon Fernald, who was then preparing the eighth, or "centennial edition" of *Gray's Manual of Botany*. Taking Fernald's "Botany 7" course, the Flora of New England and the Maritime Provinces of Canada, Stebbins accompanied him on field trips, became an expert on floristics, and fell under the influence of Fernald's controversial "nunatak theory," a biogeographic theory based on the distribution of glacial relics, popular at the time. Despite some initial parental disapproval (they were concerned about his employment prospects and financial hardship), Stebbins enrolled formally in Harvard's graduate program in 1928 with the intention of training in botany. From approximately 1926 until 1929, Stebbins worked closely with Fernald on the taxonomy of the New England flora. He completed several taxonomic studies but switched his emphasis—and his advisor—when he turned to the newer area of plant cytology, working closely with the Harvard morphologist and anatomist Edward Charles Jeffrey.

His dissertation topic focused on the cytology (cellular structure and function) of geographic variants of the plant *Antennaria*. Toward the end of his dissertation research, he sought the aid of Karl Sax, the new geneticist hired at the Arnold Arboretum. Sax, trained in the most recent genetics techniques, made a number of important suggestions to the research on *Antennaria* and included at least one important correction on the orientation of the chromosomes, which Stebbins had incorrectly interpreted. Sax's last minute intervention in the dissertation

was not well taken by Jeffrey, however, and the dissertation committee nearly fell apart but for the well-timed intervention of the chair of the department, Oakes Ames, and the mediation skills of the developmental morphologist, Ralph Wetmore. Only after the dissertation was rewritten a number of times was it finally accepted and the degree granted in 1931. The completed dissertation, which drew on a disparate set of approaches that were uncommon for a systematic project at the time, formed the backbone of Stebbins's subsequent cytologic and systematic studies. It also demonstrated what became a lifelong tendency to cross barriers in discipline, methodology, and even interpersonal relationships in the spirit of synthesis.

Scientific Career: Botanist, Geneticist, and Evolutionist. In 1932 Stebbins took a position as teacher of biology at Colgate University in Hamilton, New York. Though he did not have much time for research, he continued to refine his expertise in cytogenetics, the new science that concentrated on chromosomes and integrated cytology with genetics. He collaborated closely with Percy Saunders, of the famous Canadian family of wheat breeders, at nearby Hamilton College. Saunders's passion was breeding hybrid peonies, which he grew in his backyard and which were used for his cytological studies conducted out of his home laboratory. With Saunders, Stebbins attended the 1932 International Congress of Genetics in nearby Ithaca, New York, which exposed him to the work of geneticists such as Cyril Dean Darlington and Barbara McClintock as well as evolutionists such as Sewall Wright.

In 1935 the opportunity to pursue scientific research in genetics full-time was realized when Stebbins accepted a position as junior geneticist to the botanist Ernest Brown Babcock, at the University of California, Berkeley. At that time, Babcock was working on an ambitious project to understand the genetics of the evolutionary process in the genus *Crepis*. It was Babcock's hope that *Crepis* would function much as *Drosophila* had in serving as a model organism that lent itself to study in evolutionary genetics. Working as Babcock's assistant, Stebbins applied much of what he had learned in cytogenetics and systematics to the new genus. Together, Babcock and Stebbins published a series of important articles and a monograph titled *The American Species of* Crepis: *Their Interrelationships and Distribution as Affected by Polyploidy and Apomixis* in 1938. Their most notable contribution was in articulating the notion of "the polyploid complex" (sometimes also called "the agamic complex"), a geographic complex of reproductive forms that centered on diploids fringed by apomictic or asexual forms. It was the most complete analysis of the interplay of polyploidy, apomixis, and hybridization with geographic and systematic considerations for any plant genus known at the time. It also offered insights into species formation, polymorphy in apomictic forms, and knowledge of how all these complex processes could inform an accurate phylogenetic history of the genus. Stebbins later extended these ideas further with subsequent breeding in forage grasses and published a series of important articles in 1940, 1941, and 1947. The latter article, "Types of Polyploids: Their Classification and Significance," became a widely read review that synthesized knowledge of polyploidy; it is still regarded as a major contribution to understanding of plant evolutionary biology.

Stebbins worked with Babcock for some six years and in 1939, with Babcock's support, he was hired as full-time assistant professor in the department of genetics at the University of California, Berkeley. He also took over teaching the general course in evolution when the opportunity arose. In preparation for this course, Stebbins read the evolution literature widely and was quickly exposed to the exciting new literature incorporating genetics and evolutionary studies. He was part of a fortnightly journal club in genetics, called Genetics Associated, that included the émigré geneticist Isadore Michael Lerner. Lerner, in turn, introduced him to his Russian colleague Theodosius Dobzhansky, who was then working with Thomas Hunt Morgan at the California Institute of Technology. Stebbins interacted with Lerner and Dobzhansky, but also with a small but growing circle of systematists in the San Francisco Bay Area who were turning their interests to what they hailed as the "new" systematics, built on current ideas that drew on genetics and evolution; they later called themselves the Biosystematists. The group included leading botanists in the Bay Area such as the Danish genecologist Jens Clausen but also visitors such as the botanists Edgar Anderson from the Missouri Botanical Garden and Carl Epling from the University of California at Los Angeles. With their encouragement, Stebbins pursued evolutionary research closely and incorporated their insights into plant evolution, but he also read widely on the animal side of evolution. By the early 1940s he was one of the few botanists easily conversant with the disparate literature in genetics, ecology, systematics, cytology, and paleontology in both the animal and the plant world. His growing friendship with Dobzhansky, which was reinforced by collecting trips at Mather, California, also proved to be especially important.

The opportunity to draw all the disparate branches together in a synthesis in understanding mechanisms and patterns of plant evolution came in 1946, when Stebbins was invited on the recommendation of Dobzhansky to deliver Columbia University's prestigious Jesup Lectures. In 1950 the lectures were published in book form as *Variation and Evolution in Plants,* which proved to be one of the most important books published in twentieth-century American botany because of its synthetic breadth; it also

led to a virtual revolution in understanding plant evolution so that it became the foundational text of the field that was eventually known as plant evolutionary biology. It became part of the canon of biological works written between 1936 and 1950 that formed the backbone of the "modern synthesis of evolution" or the historical event known as the "evolutionary synthesis." From 1950 on, Stebbins became one of the most visible experts on the science of modern evolutionary biology and the person generally credited with founding the science of evolutionary botany or plant evolutionary biology.

In 1950 Stebbins moved to the newer campus of the University of California, Davis, where he was assigned the task of building a new Department of Genetics. His own research interests shifted appreciably to areas associated with development biology and developmental genetics, eventually incorporating newer techniques from plant molecular biology into his research program. Through the 1950s and 1960s he trained more than thirty graduate students, most of whom were in genetics, developmental biology, or agricultural science.

Throughout the course of his scientific career, Stebbins showed a remarkable ability to understand new problems and to apply new techniques. Unlike most botanists, Stebbins worked on a staggering range of plant organisms, from grasses to peonies to members of the daisy family. He published extensively in systematics, morphology, cytology, genetics, plant geography, and developmental biology. Neither fish nor fowl, Stebbins frequently failed to receive credit for work in some of these areas, however, usually at the hands of narrower colleagues. Systematists felt that he concentrated too heavily on genetics and too lightly on taxonomic studies of a special set of organisms; geneticists, in contrast, felt that his work was too evolutionary and natural history–oriented and that it did not concentrate sufficiently on understanding mechanisms of gene action. Few, however, have challenged his contributions to plant evolutionary biology, nor questioned his ability to synthesize disparate literature that he could place into a coherent framework, a feat he achieved repeatedly over the course of his long career. His publication list includes a staggering number of review articles that reflect his ability to command new literature and to synthesize disparate information. In 1965, for example, he and the Berkeley botanist Herbert Baker edited *Genetics of Colonizing Species.* This was to prove a pioneering work in what would later be called the science of "invasion biology." In 1974 he brought much of his life-long knowledge of plant evolution to bear on the complex problem of angiosperm evolution in his influential *Flowering Plants: Evolution above the Species Level.* Stebbins continued to read widely and to publish such synthetic works, though in a diminished capacity, up until the time of his death.

His influence increasingly extended outside research science, especially after the publication of his 1950 book. He became active in organizations such as the International Union of Biological Sciences. He served as president of the American Society of Naturalists, the Western Society of Naturalists, the Botanical Society of America, and the Society for the Study of Evolution. He was a member of the National Academy of Sciences and in 1980 received the National Medal of Science from President Jimmy Carter. Throughout the 1960s and the 1970s he was an active defender of evolution against creationist assaults of varied types. He worked closely with the Biological Sciences and Curriculum Study (BSCS) to develop curricula at the high school level built on evolution as the central unifying principle in biology. Stebbins contributed to the teaching of evolution even more heavily by writing textbooks and semipopular books of science, and through many public lectures.

Yet another area of interest was in conservation, which proved a lifelong passion. In the 1960s Stebbins was instrumental in helping to create the California Native Plant Society, for which he served as president in 1967. He organized numerous field trips that included amateurs and students, and fought tirelessly to protect ecologically sensitive areas such as a well-known strip of raised beach on the Monterey Peninsula. For his work in conservation and in evolutionary science the University of California, Davis, paid him a rare honor, naming a 227-acre preserve near Lake Beryessa, California, the Stebbins Cold Canyon Reserve.

Stebbins was married twice. His first marriage ended in divorce but produced three children, Edith, Robert, and George. Stebbins remarried in the 1950s. His second wife, Barbara, had one son by a previous marriage; she died suddenly in 1993 while accompanying Stebbins on a lecture tour.

Stebbins became emeritus professor of genetics in 1973 but continued to lecture, publish, and travel widely until a series of debilitating diseases in the 1990s bound him to Davis. He died there as a result of cancer.

BIBLIOGRAPHY

WORKS BY STEBBINS

With Ernest B. Babcock. *The American Species of Crepis: Their Interrelationships and Distribution as Affected by Polyploidy and Apomixis.* Washington, DC: Carnegie Institution of Washington, 1938.

"The Significance of Polyploidy in Plant Evolution." *American Naturalist* 74 (1940): 54–66.

"Apomixis in the Angiosperms." *Botanical Review* 7 (1941): 507–542.

"Types of Polyploids: Their Classification and Significance." *Advances in Genetics* 1 (1947): 403–429.

Variation and Evolution in Plants. New York: Columbia University Press, 1950.

With Herbert G. Baker, eds. *Genetics of Colonizing Species: Proceedings of the First International Union of Biological Sciences Symposia on General Biology.* New York: Academic Press, 1965.

Flowering Plants: Evolution above the Species Level. Cambridge, MA: Belknap Press, 1974.

The Scientific Papers of G. Ledyard Stebbins: (1929–2000). Edited by Daniel J. Crawford and Vassiliki Betty Smocovitis. Regnum Vegetabile, vol. 142. Ruggell, Liechtenstein: Gantner, 2004. A complete list of publications by G. Ledyard Stebbins is included here.

The Lady Slipper and I. Edited by Vassiliki Betty Smocovitis, Victoria Hollowell, and Eileen Duggan. St. Louis: Missouri Botanical Garden Press, 2007. This is an autobiography left uncompleted at the time of his death.

OTHER SOURCES

Bradshaw, Anthony, and Vassiliki Betty Smocovitis. "G. Ledyard Stebbins." *Biographical Memoirs of Fellows of the Royal Society* 51 (2005): 397–408.

Faber, Phyllis M. "G. Ledyard Stebbins Jr., 1906–2000." *Fremontia* 28 (2000): 69–70.

Smocovitis, Vassiliki Betty. "Botany and the Evolutionary Synthesis: The Life and Work of G. Ledyard Stebbins Jr." PhD diss., Cornell University, 1988.

———. "G. Ledyard Stebbins Jr. and the Evolutionary Synthesis (1924–1950)." *American Journal of Botany* 84 (1997): 1625–1637.

———. "Living with Your Biographical Subject: Problems of Distance, Privacy, and Trust in the Writing of the Biography of G. Ledyard Stebbins, Jr." *Journal of the History of Biology* 32 (1999): 421–438.

———. "G. Ledyard Stebbins and the Evolutionary Synthesis." *Annual Review of Genetics* 35 (2001): 803–814.

———. "Keeping up with Dobzhansky: G. Ledyard Stebbins, Plant Evolution, and the Evolutionary Synthesis." *History and Philosophy of the Life Sciences* 28 (2006): 11–50.

Smocovitis, Vassiliki Betty, and Francisco Ayala. "G. Ledyard Stebbins (1906–2000)." *Biographical Memoirs of the National Academy of Sciences* 85 (2004): 3–24.

Solbrig, Otto. "George Ledyard Stebbins." In *Topics in Plant Population Biology,* edited by Otto Solbrig, Subodh Jain, George B. Johnson, et al., 1–17. New York: Columbia University Press, 1979.

Vassiliki Betty Smocovitis

STEPHANUS OF ALEXANDRIA. (*b.* Athens, c. 550–555; *d.* Constantinople, c. 622), *philosophy, astronomy, astrology, alchemy, medicine, mathematics.* For the original article on Stephanus of Alexandria see *DSB,* vol. 13.

During the last quarter of the twentieth century the research regarding Stephanus of Alexandria focused on the identification of his personality and the authorship of the works attributed to him, as well as to the edition of his unpublished works. Firstly, Wanda Wolska-Conus (1989, 1992, 1994) has shown that Stephanus of Athens should be identified with Stephanus of Alexandria. The designation *Alexandrian* does not indicate that this was his native city. It indicates only that, in moving his place of residence and activity to Constantinople, he did so from Alexandria. She has discussed his authorship of several works that we know by title or because they still survive, including his commentaries on Porphyry's *Eisagoge* and treatises of the Aristotelian, Hippocratic, and Galenic corpus. According to her, Stephanus's involvement in the doctrinal politics of his time and the serial transfer of his loyalties between the Caledonians, Monothelites, and Monophysites, cost him his reputation in posterity. Regarded as a traitor by all, he was embraced by none.

Secondly, in their *Thèses de Licence* Elisabeth Chauvon (1979) and Marie-Chantal Hugo (1987) have edited parts of the unpublished astronomical work of Stephanus of Alexandria, namely his "Commentary on the Handy Tables of Ptolemy." Thus they have shown both Stephanus's excellent astronomical knowledge and his virtues as a teacher, which reinforce the tradition of his great reputation as a teacher, especially of the mathematical sciences, the quadrivium.

Finally, Maria Papathanassiou (1990, 1991, 1992, 1996, 1997, 2005, 2006) has focused her research on the authorship of the alchemical and the astrological works traditionally attributed to Stephanus of Alexandria. Based on the analysis of their content she has attempted to elucidate his personality and to reveal his deep philosophical and scientific knowledge, which contributed to his great reputation as "oecumenic teacher."

According to tradition, Stephanus of Alexandria was the author of the work *On the Great and Sacred Art of Making Gold.* Many scholars misunderstood and underestimated its importance, criticizing it on account of its rhetorical style and the absence of original scientific ideas. However, as commentary on selected passages of earlier alchemical texts, the work in fact presented its author with an opportunity to demonstrate wide rhetorical prowess, extensive learning, and a significant breadth of philosophical understanding. Its loose structure was the result of Stephanus's effort to synthesize various ideas from different philosophical theories into a logical sequence and fashion them into a whole, into a single theory able to account for all phenomena.

Leendert G. Westerink's view (1962, Introd. p. xxiv) that a lack of clarity and logical sequence in combining ideas characterizes Stephanus's *Commentary on the Book 3*

of Aristotle's *De anima* (published as the third book of Philoponus, *De anima, Commentaria in Aristotelem Graeca* 15, 446–607). Henry Blumenthal's statement that "a curious mixture of Neoplatonic aims and Aristotelian content emerges from Stephanus's theoria" in the same commentary (Blumenthal, 1982, pp. 56, 244 note 11), and the study of the author of this entry, according to which Stephanus's alchemical work is deeply influenced by Neoplatonism and especially Damascius's *De principiis* (Papathanassiou, 2005), offer additional arguments in favor of Stephanus's authorship of this work corpus.

The manuscript tradition of the alchemical work clearly indicates that it was greatly appreciated. It survives in fifty-three manuscripts. Six manuscripts were produced between the eleventh and the fifteenth centuries, and the rest were copied between the sixteenth and the nineteenth centuries. This work greatly influenced the so-called poet-alchemists. The Arabic alchemical corpus attributed to Jābir ibn Hayyān cites passages from Stephanus's work or uses analogous terminology without making direct reference to the Greek source. Moreover the *Rosarium philosophicum* (a mid-fourteenth-century compilation in Latin), cites and comments on Stephanus.

Stephanus's alchemical work was edited in 1842 by Julius L. Ideler. The text stops actually on page 247,23 (and not on page 253,26), corresponding to the final line of f. 39v of *Cod. Marc. gr.* 299 (tenth to eleventh centuries). As shown by H. D. Saffrey (1995), this codex suffered both a loss of folios and a gap in its binding which resulted in losing the end of Stephanus's work. Moreover, study of the work (Papathanassiou, 1996) reveals that, some time earlier than the date of *Marc. gr.* 299 the text was technically divided into nine lectures and a short letter to Theodorus; the proposed original division is the following:

First Lesson (MSS and Ideler: Lectures 1 and 2),

Letter to Theodorus (: Letter to Theodorus and Lecture 3),

Second Lesson (: Lecture 4),

Third Lesson (: Lecture 5),

Fourth Lesson (: Lecture 6),

Fifth Lesson (: Lecture 7),

Sixth Lesson (: Lecture 8),

Seventh Lesson (: Lecture 9).

Astronomical Evidence. The observation of a particular planetary phenomenon at the time that Stephanus was writing his alchemical work and the known correspondence between planets and metals inspired him to include its description in his text (p. 225,25–32 ed. Ideler). This passage can be understood as describing Constantinople's (the Byzantine) eastern sky near the horizon at dawn and may be used as a clue to aid in the identification of its author and the date of the composition. If our interpretation of this passage is correct, the only viable celestial phenomenon it could be describing between the seventh and the eleventh centuries would be the one visible from Constantinople and evolving between 26 May and 3 June 617.

It is well known that Stephanus of Alexandria was the author of a commentary on Ptolemy's *Handy Tables,* in which he gave his own examples for the calculation of the solar, lunar, and planetary positions, as well as solar and lunar eclipses calculated for the coordinates of Constantinople. As shown by Otto Neugebauer and H. B. Van Hoesen (1959), the dates of calculated examples in the commentary fall in the years 617 to 619. This suggests that during this period Stephanus was in Constantinople and consistently observed and calculated the position of the Sun, the Moon, and the other planets. Had he not been in Constantinople but Alexandria, he would have used the data of Ptolemy's tables as they are given for the geographical coordinates of Alexandria without converting them into Constantinople's coordinates. Consequently, the authorship of Stephanus for the alchemical work should be considered genuine.

According to tradition, Stephanus cast the horoscope of the emperor Heraclius and was the author of the *Apotelesmatike Pragmateia* (astrological treatise) (ed. H. Usener, 1914, pp. 266–289), referring to the *Horoscope of Islam.* This treatise can be divided into three parts; in the first part (p. 266,5–271,22) the author shows his piousness, explaining that astrological predictions do not contradict God's omnipotence and asserts firmly that "perfect and true knowledge belongs to god, while men, forming their conjectures on the ground of elements and stars, in part know and in part predict" (271,19–21). In the second part (p. 271, 23–279,13) he explains for what reason and when he cast the horoscope of Islam and he proceeds in a general astrological analysis of it. The third part (p. 279,14–289) includes the predictions about the events that will take place "during the dominion of this nation" (p. 279,15–17). The main argument against the authorship of Stephanus is that the author demonstrated accurate knowledge of the events that transpired during the reign of the successive Arab caliphs from the beginning of Islam until the end of the eighth century. From that point on the predictions are all wrong. Some scholars consider the surviving *Apotelesmatike Pragmateia* might be the reinvention of a preexisting work by Stephanus on the same topic that is no longer extant. However, if these arguments (based on literary tradition, astrological practice, and relations between the alchemical work and the astrological treatise) are correct, the first and the second parts of the treatise should be considered a genuine work of

Stephanus's, whereas the original third part (apart from its end [p. 286, 22–289]) was thoroughly rewritten at the end of the eighth century to fit the events that had already occurred in Islam (Papathanassiou, 1992, 1997, 2006).

SUPPLEMENTARY BIBLIOGRAPHY

WORKS BY STEPHANUS OF ALEXANDRIA

Edited by Elisabeth Chauvon. "Étude sur le Commentaire astronomique de Stephanos d' Alexandrie." Louvain, France: Université Catholique de Louvain, 1979–1980.

Edited by Marie-Chantal Hugo. "Stéphane d'Alexandrie: Calcul de l'éclipse de Soleil du 4 novembre 617." Louvain, France: Université Catholique de Louvain, 1987.

Stephani Alexandrini. *De Sacra et Magna Arte, de Chrysopoeia.* Edited by Julius L. Ideler. *Physici et Medici Graeci Minores,* II, Leipzig 1842, (Reprint, Hakkert, Amsterdam 1963): 199–253.

Stephanus Philosophus. *Lectio prima Peri chrysopoieias.* Graece et latine cum notis crit. primus ed. Ch. Gf. Gruner, Jenae 1777, in J. G. Th. Graesse, *Trésor de livres rares et précieux,* 8 vols. (Kuntze-Dresde, 1859–1869). 6 (1865) 492.

Edited by Hermann Usener. *Kleine Schriften,* Band III, Teubner, Leipzig 1914, 247–321 (Xiv. *De Stephano Alexandrino,* 1879): 266–289. In Greek.

OTHER SOURCES

Blumenthal, Henry. "John Philoponus and Stephanus of Alexandria: Two Neoplatonic Christian Commentators on Aristotle?" *Studies in Neoplatonism Ancient and Modern.* Vol. 3: *Neoplatonism and Christian Thought.* Edited by D. J. O'Meara. International Society for Neoplatonic Studies (1982): 54–63, 244–246 (notes).

Jensen, Ingeborg Hammer. "Die älteste Alchymie." *Kgl. Danske Vidensk. Selsk., Hist.-filol. Medd.* (Copenhagen) 4, no. 2 (1921): 8–9, 146–159.

Lumpe, Adolf. "Stephanos von Alexandrien und Kaiser Heraclius." *Classical and Mediaeval Dissertationes* 9 (1973): 150–159.

———. "Stephanos von Alexandria (Stephanus Philosophus)." *Biographisch-Bibliographisches Kirchenlexikon,* Band X (1995): Spalten 1406–1409.

Neugebauer, Otto. *A History of Ancient Mathematical Astronomy.* 3 vols. Berlin: Springer, 1975. Vol. 2: 1045–1051.

Neugebauer, Otto, and H. B. Van Hoesen. "Greek Horoscopes." *Memoirs of the American Philosophical Society* 48 (1959): 158–160, 190.

Papathanassiou, Maria. "Stephanus of Alexandria: Pharmaceutical Notions and Cosmology in His Alchemical work." *Ambix* 37, no. 3 (1990): 121–133; 38, no. 2 (1991): 112 (addenda).

———. *Stephanus von Alexandreia und sein alchemistisches Werk.* PhD diss., Humboldt Universität zu Berlin, 1992.

———. "Stephanus of Alexandria: On the Structure and Date of His Alchemical Work." *Medicina nei secoli* 8, no. 2 (1996): 247–266.

———. "Stephanus of Alexandria: Apotelesmatike pragmateia, or The Horoscope of Islam." In *Oi epistimes ston helliniko khoro*. Athens: Kentro Neoellinikon Ereunon, Ethniko Idryma Ereunon, 1997, 107–117. In Greek.

———. "L'œuvre alchimique de Stéphanos d'Alexandrie: Structure et transformations de la matière, unité et pluralité, l'énigme des philosophes." In *L'alchimie et ses racines philosophiques. La tradition grecque et la tradition arabe,* edited by Cristina Viano, 113–133. Collection Histoire des Idées et des Doctrines 32. Paris: Vrin, 2005.

———. "Stephanos of Alexandria: A Famous Byzantine Scholar, Alchemist and Astrologer." In *The Occult Sciences in Byzantium,* edited by Paul Magdalino and Maria Mavroudi, 163–203. Geneva: La Pomme d'Or, 2006.

Pingree, David. "Classical und Byzantine Astrology in Sassanian Persia." *Dunbarton Oaks Papers* 43 (1989): 227–239.

Saffrey, H. D. "Historique et description du manuscrit alchimique de Venise Marcianus Graecus 299." In *Alchimie: art, histoire et mythes,* edited by Didier Kahn and Sylvain Matton, 1–10. Paris: S.E.H.A., 1995.

Tihon, Anne. "L'astronomie Byzantine (du Ve au XVe siècle)." *Byzantion* 51 (1981): 603–624.

Ullmann, Manfred. *Die Natur- und Geheimwissenschaften im Islam*. Leiden, Netherlands: Brill, 1972, pp. 189–190.

Vancourt, Raymond. *Les derniers commentateurs Alexandrins d' Aristote: L' École d' Olympiodore, Étienne d' Alexandrie*. Lille, France: Thèse, 1941.

Westerink, Leendert G. *Anonymous Prolegomena to Platonic Philosophy*. Amsterdam: North Holland, 1962, pp. xxiv–xxv.

———. "The Greek Commentaries on Plato's Phaedo." Vol. 1 on Olympiodorus *Verhandelingen der Koninklijke Nederlandse Akademie* 92. Amsterdam: North Holland, 1976, pp. 20–23.

Wolska-Conus, Wanda. "Stéphanos d'Athènes et Stéphanos d'Alexandrie. Essai d'identification et de biographie." *Revue des études byzantines* 47 (1989): 5–89.

———. "Les Commentaires de Stéphanos d'Athènes au Prognosticon et aux Aphorismes d'Hippocrate: De Galien à la pratique scolaire alexandrine." *Revue des études byzantines* 50 (1992): 5–86.

———. "Stéphanos d'Athènes (Stéphanos d'Alexandrie) et Théophile le Prôtospathaire, commentateurs des Aphorismes d'Hippocrate sont-ils indépendants l'un de l'autre?" *Revue des études byzantines* 52 (1994): 5–68.

Maria K. Papathanassiou

STEPHANUS OF ATHENS

SEE **Stephanus of Alexandria**.

STEPHENSON, MARJORY (*b.* Burwell, near Cambridge, United Kingdom, 24 January 1885; *d.* Cambridge, 12 December 1948), *microbiology, biochemistry.* For the original article on Stephenson see *DSB,* vol. 18, Supplement II.

Stephenson belongs among the founders of new interdisciplinary fields known under various names—chemical microbiology, microbial biochemistry, or general microbiology, which are considered predecessors of molecular biology. Late twentieth- and early twenty-first century research into her life and work has highlighted her key position in forming the conceptual and methodical principles of these fields and her leadership, exceptional for a woman scholar of her time.

Archives disclose that Frederick Gowland Hopkins had followed with interest the career of the young Stephenson since 1913. That was a momentous year for Hopkins, when his interest in nutrition chemistry was at its peak and simultaneously he formulated his strategic program of "dynamic biochemistry," which guided not only his Cambridge Biochemical Laboratory, but also biochemistry development in Europe in the forty years to come. Therefore, when Stephenson joined the Hopkins group in 1919, she did not take up her prewar nutrition research but, on the contrary, launched an entirely new field of "general" biochemistry corresponding to Hopkins's vision. At Hopkins's instigation, she turned her attention to bacterial metabolism, in which she became a leading specialist in the 1930s.

It is important to add a few details about Stephenson's institutional position in Cambridge. In 1924 Hopkins's department became the Dunn Institute of Biochemistry, where Stephenson held her research appointment, which had been subsidized by the Medical Research Council (MRC) since 1922. She was appointed a permanent member of the MRC's staff on 1 April 1929, but remained in her research post at the Dunn Institute in an independent position thanks to the MRC funding. Without ever being appointed its director, she eventually succeeded in putting into practice the MRC's plan to establish in Cambridge a permanent research unit in bacterial chemistry. She stayed with the MRC and the Dunn Institute for the rest of her life.

The focus of Stephenson's laboratory was investigation of various manifestations of metabolic activities in microorganisms, especially the actions of bacterial enzymes. Research into hydrogen-activating enzymes and identification of several new enzymes in the 1930s ensured her high reputation both in Britain and abroad. This applies even more to her monograph *Bacterial Metabolism,* published first in 1930 and then in two revised editions in 1939 and 1949. Written in a "lucid and forceful style" (Elsden and Pirie, 1949, p. 335), it became a reference work for several generations of biochemists and microbiologists all over the world.

For Stephenson, microorganisms represented not only research objects but also general models of the cell whose investigation provided for deeper understanding of cellular biochemistry and its organization. As early as 1930, in the preface to the first edition of her monograph, Stephenson stressed the importance of data

> on the chemical activities of bacteria which may help us to gain an insight into the essential chemical processes accompanying the life of the organisms concerned.

She further stated that

> it is time that an attempt should be made to arrange the scattered data in order to appraise our knowledge of bacteria as living organisms apart from their role as disease germs or the bearers of commercially important catalysts.

Her experiments demonstrating that bacterial enzymes behave similarly to enzymes in higher organisms and that metabolism in bacteria is governed by regularities analogous to those in higher organisms, contributed to the acceptance of the principle of unity in biochemistry in the 1930s.

These concepts also prompted her involvement with cellular metabolic adaptation phenomena. In 1930, Stephenson and Leonard Stickland discovered a new enzyme, formic hydrogenlyase, produced by various coliform organisms including *Escherichia coli*. Experiments performed in the years 1932 to 1936 with John Yudkin and Ernest F. Gale proved that this and several other enzymes are formed in *E. coli* and yeast as a "direct response of the enzymic composition of the cell to the constituents of the growth medium."

It had been known long before Stephenson, that cultures of bacteria can adapt themselves to various nutrients in their growth medium. For instance, as early as 1900, F. Dienert reported that yeast that usually grows on glucose may acquire the ability to grow on galactose if this other sugar is present in the growth medium. Such adaptation to a new nutrient was usually accompanied by the production of a specific "adaptive" enzyme. In the first two decades of the twentieth century, various instances of such adaptive enzyme formation in multiplying cultures were investigated, but Stephenson and her collaborators were first to prove that also nongrowing bacterial cultures and individual cells are capable of fast adaptive formation of substrate-specific enzymes. Such observations enabled Stephenson and Yudkin to define in 1936 the enzymic type of adaptation as a "direct a response of the enzymic composition of the cell to the constituents of the growth

medium," independent of mutant formation or cell division, that "is definitely temporary and does not affect the heredity mechanism of the cell, which reverts to normal …when the organism is grown without the specific stimulus" (both quotes from *Bacterial Metabolism*, 1949, p. 296).

The first relevant so-called mass action theory of adaptive enzyme formation was advanced in the years 1936 to 1938 by Yudkin. He anticipated that the cells contain a small, sometimes immeasurable amount of the adaptive enzyme which normally is in equilibrium with its precursor. If substrate is added, the preexisting enzyme combines with the substrate and upsets the equilibrium. In consequence, more enzyme is formed until the equilibrium is restored.

Enzymatic adaptation (later known as enzymatic induction) was taken up by Jacques Monod in the 1940s to become a point of departure for the theories of cellular regulatory mechanisms and protein synthesis developed in the 1950s and 1960s.

From the 1930s on, Stephenson was an indisputable authority in her field and attracted many people to work with her. A list compiled from various sources names about sixty persons who cooperated with Stephenson in the years 1922–1948 (staff paid by MRC, graduate students, informal collaborators, local and foreign visitors), among them people who later became prominent scientists including two Nobel Prize winners, Hans Krebs and Peter Mitchell.

During World War II Stephenson coordinated teams of microbiologists, biochemists, and pathologists in fighting acute neonatal diarrhea in Britain. In the years 1941 to 1943 a group composed of specialists from the National Institute for Medical Research, the Royal College of Surgeons, the Lister Institute, and Cornell University participated under Stephenson's guidance in exploring active immunization against gas gangrene. Other projects led by Stephenson investigated strategically important biotechnological production of organic compounds. Even this specialized wartime research led to discoveries of new bacterial enzymes and coenzymes. The invitation of Stephenson to become a member of the MRC's Committee on Chemical Microbiology was the recognition of her efficient supervision of this interdisciplinary wartime network.

After the Nazis came to power in Germany, Stephenson assisted persecuted European scholars in finding adequate positions in Cambridge. A letter from Stephenson to the prominent German biochemist Otto Warburg written in early 1933 indicates that she was involved in the escape of the biochemist Krebs from Germany and his placement at the Biochemistry Department. Two refugee scholars from Czechoslovakia worked with Stephenson:

Arnošt Kleinzeller, who became a leading biochemist in postwar Czechoslovakia, and Heinrich Waelsch.

In 1945 Stephenson returned to her prewar research and organizing the Society for General Microbiology. In her plenary lecture, "Levels of Microbiological Investigation," at the inaugural meeting of the Society for General Microbiology in 1945, Stephenson presented a strategic vision of general microbiology as a new field. She defined five equipotent levels of bacterial cultures at which interdisciplinary research in microbiology should be undertaken to arrive at a complex knowledge of the cell's chemical activities.

Stephenson's profile would not be complete without considering her experience as a woman playing an unusually important role in the scientific community of her time. Before and during World War II she belonged without question to the few women in the world who pioneered a new field of science and managed a research team. However, her position at the MRC was inconsistent with her indisputable scientific authority, competence, and leadership. On the one hand, MRC trusted her decisions and provided her with adequate salary and laboratory equipment; on the other she was faced with practices of undeclared discrimination: She was allowed and expected to do first-rate research but not to hold an executive appointment. The MRC's plans of the 1920s to establish in Cambridge a permanent research unit in bacterial chemistry consisting of a director and a small team of researchers did not materialize in Stephenson's lifetime; she was charged with the task without being assigned director. Most women in her position would have accepted reality, unlike Stephenson who from 1944 led a persistent campaign for the official acknowledgment of her "directorship" and recognition of the laboratory as an independent "Unit." Her struggle reflected itself among other things in her annual reports to the MRC, submitted with the heading of a nonexistent "M.R.C. Research Unit for Microbiological Chemistry, The Biochemical Laboratory Cambridge" and Stephenson's signature over the title "Director of the Unit." Another issue that also became a permanent source of argument with the MRC's authorities was Stephenson's deliberate attempt to retain her scientific autonomy in choosing general topics to be investigated, compared with the MRC's scheme of focusing on practical medical issues. Especially thanks to Stephenson's wartime responsibilities, the MRC authorities eventually surrendered by tolerating Stephenson's obstinate routine in using the terms *Unit* and *Director*, and her independence in research, but never recognized her status officially and did not give her sufficient technical assistance. In spite of that, Stephenson with her groundbreaking work and steadfast effort to crack the glass ceiling in a male-dominated field became a role model for other women scientists and as such was also remembered by her collaborators, among them Dorothy Needham.

In 1949, the Society for General Microbiology created the Marjory Stephenson Memorial Fund and agreed that the "most suitable memorial would be a Lecture, to be given at regular intervals … and to be known as the Marjory Stephenson Memorial Lecture."

SUPPLEMENTARY BIBLIOGRAPHY

WORKS BY STEPHENSON

With Leonard H. Stickland. "Hydrogenlyases: Bacterial Enzymes Liberating Molecular Hydrogen." *Biochemical Journal* 36 (1932): 712–724.

With Ernest Frederick Gale. "The Adaptability of Glucozymase and Galactozymase in *Bacterium coli*." *Biochemical Journal* 31 (1937): 1311–1315.

"Enzyme Variation and Adaptation." In *Bacterial Metabolism*. 3rd ed. London: Longmans Green, 1949.

OTHER SOURCES

Elsden, Sidney R., and Norman W. Pirie. "Marjory Stephenson 1885–1948." *Journal of General Microbiology* 3 (1949): 329–339.

Mason, Joan. "The Admission of the First Women to the Royal Society of London." *Notes and Records of the Royal Society* 46 (1992): 272–300.

———. "Marjory Stephenson 1885–1948." In *Cambridge Women: Twelve Portraits*, edited by Edward Shils and Carmen Blacker. New York: Cambridge University Press, 1996.

Needham, Dorothy. "Dr. Marjory Stephenson, M.B.E., F.R.S." *Nature* 163 (1949): 201–202.

———. "Women in Cambridge Biochemistry." In *Women Scientists: The Road to Liberation*, edited by Derek Richter. London: Macmillan, 1982.

Štrbáňová, Soňa. "Enzyme Adaptation—The Road to Its Understanding: Early Theoretical Explanation." In *Biology Integrating Scientific Fundamentals: Contributions to the History of Interrelations between Biology, Chemistry, and Physics from the 18th to the 20th Centuries*, edited by Brigitte Hoppe. Algorismus 21. Munich: Institut für Geschichte der Naturwissenschaften, 1997.

———. "Marjory Stephenson and the Medical Research Council—A New Managing Role for a Woman Scholar." In *Women Scholars and Institutions: Proceedings of the International Conference, Prague, June 8–11, 2003*, edited by Soňa Štrbáňová, Ida H. Stamhuis, and Kateřina Mojsejová. Studies in the History of Sciences and Humanities, vol. 13 A and 13 B. Prague: Research Centre for the History of Sciences and Humanities, 2004.

———. "Stephenson, Marjory." In *Lexikon der Bedeutenden Naturwissenschaftler*, edited by Deter Hoffmann, Hubert Laitko, and Staffan Müller-Wille. Munich: Elsevier Spektrum Akademischer Verlag, 2004.

Soňa Štrbáňová

STERN, LINA

SEE **Shtern, Lina Solomonovna**.

STERN, LOUIS WILLIAM (*b.* Berlin, Germany, 29 April 1871; *d.* Durham, North Carolina, 27 March 1938), *philosophy, psychology.*

Stern is known primarily as the inventor of the intelligence quotient (IQ), since it was he who originally suggested that a child's level of intellectual functioning be indexed not as the *difference* between mental age (MA) and chronological age (CA), that is, as [MA – CA], but instead as the *ratio* of the former to the latter, that is, as [MA/CA]. However, Stern made notable contributions to many other areas of psychology, including child psychology and differential psychology, and from his own perspective his most important contribution was a comprehensive system of thought he called *critical personalism.* The conceptual foundation of that system is the irreducible distinction between *persons* and *things,* and it was this distinction that guided virtually all of Stern's many contributions to psychology over the course of his illustrious and highly productive career.

Youth and Student Years. Stern was the only child of Sigismund Stern and his wife Rosa Stern (whose maiden name was also Stern; indeed she and Sigismund Stern were cousins). Throughout his life, Stern preferred the name William to his given first name, Louis. In some of his early publications, authorship was attributed to L. William Stern, but from 1906 on he identified himself simply as William Stern.

Sigismund Stern operated a small studio specializing in wallpaper sketches, and though the income from this business usually sufficed, the family's financial resources were nevertheless often quite limited. As a schoolboy young William had to earn spending money by tutoring other pupils, and at times he also had to make do with secondhand books.

We learn something about Stern as an adolescent from *Anfänge der Reifezeit: Ein Knabentagebuch in psychologischer Bearbeitung* (1925; Coming of age: A psychological analysis of a boy's diary). Written when Stern was fifty-four, the book did not reveal that the author and the subject were one and the same. Especially salient in *Anfänge der Reifezeit* are Stern's revelations about his struggles with arrogance—his own as well as that of others. For example, following several previous diary entries in 1885 in which Stern had mentioned his concerns in this regard, he wrote the following on 15 May 1886:

Nothing was settled today except that the leaders of the club would be elected, and that there would be three. S., R., and F. were elected. I voted for the first two and for K. I got only one vote, … because, I must admit, I behaved rather badly as a result of my damned arrogance. If only I could overcome that! (p. 73)

Many years later, Stern's daughter, Eva Michaelis-Stern, wrote in "Erinnerung an meine Eltern" (1991; Recollections of my parents) that her father was "completely free of vanity" (p. 136). If this was true of Stern as an adult, that was only because, years earlier, he had prevailed in his youthful struggle against his own inclinations toward arrogance.

In schoolwork, Stern's talents were manifest early on, and these are the gifts he quite deliberately cultivated as he matured. His model here was not his father but his maternal grandfather, also named Sigismund Stern. The scion of a cultured Jewish family, grandfather Sigismund studied philology and philosophy at the Friedrich-Wilhelm University of Berlin (today the Humboldt University), and concluded his doctoral studies in 1834 with a dissertation titled "Grundlegung zur Sprachphilosophie" (Foundations of a philosophy of language) (Bühring, 1996b). At the tender age of fourteen, William Stern wrote admiringly in his diary about his grandfather, and resolved to follow in his footsteps.

In 1888 Stern began his studies at the Friedrich-Wilhelm University of Berlin. He soon lost interest in philology, however, and shifted his attention to philosophy and its new subspecialty, psychology. In this latter connection, Stern was especially intrigued by the work of the young experimental psychologist Hermann Ebbinghaus, who was teaching and conducting research at the University of Berlin at just the time that Stern was pursuing his studies there. What most captured Stern's imagination as a student was the possibility of combining his philosophical interests with concrete, empirical work of the sort being carried out by Ebbinghaus and other prominent practitioners of the so-called New Science. So, sometime during the third or fourth semester of his university studies, Stern wrote (rather melodramatically) in his personal diary: "Now it is done. All the bridges are burned, and there is no turning back. I will find my way in philosophy or not at all. It is a consolation that a scientific subspecialty of philosophy, psychology, is open to me" (*Selbstdarstellung* 1927, p. 134).

The Breslau Years. After completing his doctoral dissertation, "Die Analogie im volkstümlichen Denken" (Analogy in popular thought), in 1893 under the direction of Moritz Lazarus, Stern remained in Berlin, conducting independent experimental research at the university and hoping eventually to secure a faculty position there. The prospects for this were not good, however, and in 1897 he accepted the offer of a position as Privatdozent in the Institute of Philosophy, with a specialization in psychology, at the University of Breslau (present-day Wrocław, Poland). This offer was arranged by Ebbinghaus, who had moved from Berlin to Breslau a few years earlier.

On 7 April 1900, Stern and his new wife Clara welcomed their first child, daughter Hilde, into the world, and immediately started keeping a diary on the child's development. The diary project continued through the births of two other children, Günther (1902), and Eva (1904), for a total of eighteen years. In the more than five thousand handwritten pages that eventually accumulated, the Sterns recorded observations on virtually all aspects of the psychological development of their children.

In 1907 Clara and William Stern published the first of six planned monographs based on the diaries, *Die Kindersprache* (1907; Children's speech). Two years later, the couple published *Erinnerung, Aussage und Lüge in der ersten Kindheit* (1909; Recollection, testimony, and lying in early childhood). The other four planned monographs never materialized. In 1914, however, William Stern published, as sole author, *Psychologie der frühen Kindheit, bis zum sechsten Lebensjahr* (The psychology of early childhood up to the sixth year of life), and in this project he drew extensively on the diary material. Georg Eckardt (1989) referred to *Psychologie der frühen Kindheit* as "the unchallenged standard work in scientific child psychology in the German-speaking world" (p. 11) and indeed seven editions of the work eventually appeared.

In his 1927 intellectual autobiography (*Selbstdarstellung*), Stern made explicit his sense of the significance of the diary work for the larger undertaking that centered his entire scholarly life. In particular he explained how the material accumulated in the diaries provided him with "a perspectival foundation for the philosophical theory I was gradually developing" (1927, p. 145). The philosophical theory to which Stern was referring is that comprehensive system of thought that he called *critical personalism*, a comprehensive worldview (*Weltanschauung*) predicated on the incontrovertible distinction between *persons* and *things*.

"Ich werte, also bin ich ... Wert" (I evaluate, therefore I am ... valu[able]), Stern wrote in the *Wertphilosophie* (Philosophy of value; p. 34), and though that work was not published until 1924, Stern had embraced its essential principles many years earlier. To e-valuate is to project value outward onto some entity or state of affairs. Persons do this; things do not. Things can be evaluated, passively, but cannot themselves actively evaluate. Moreover, since persons can and do e-valuate, it follows that value must somehow inhere within them, for an entity

cannot project outward something that is not in some sense "within" to begin with. Persons are thus *inherently* valuable, whereas things are not.

Stern's thinking in this regard took shape against the background of an experimental psychology that, already by 1900, was embracing what he took to be a far too mechanistic view of human mental life and behavior. The ascendant view, embodied for Stern most vividly though by no means exclusively in the works of his own one-time mentor and senior colleague Ebbinghaus, was an essentially Newtonian one according to which persons, like any other objects of scientific investigation, could properly be regarded as units of matter in motion. This view effaces the distinction between persons and things, and this, Stern steadfastly maintained, was both scientifically unwarranted and morally problematic. In this light, Stern's efforts to secure a place for critical personalism within psychology can be seen as part of a larger effort within German intellectual circles during the first three decades of the twentieth century to "reenchant" (Harrington, 1996) the scientific worldview through an appreciation for organismic wholeness, meaningfulness, and genuine purposefulness of human thought and action, both individual and collective. In all of this, Stern's views were much closer to those of such scholars as Wilhelm Dilthey and Wilhelm Windelband than to those of prominent experimental psychologists of the era, such as Ebbinghaus, Edward Lee Thorndike, and Hugo Münsterberg. Already in 1900, Stern wrote to his philosopher friend and colleague at the University of Freiburg:

> What we need above all is a comprehensive worldview, one that relates the psychological and the physical, that is antimechanistic, that is vitalistic-teleological; one in which modern natural science dogma is reduced to its true—that is, relatively inferior—value. This is a huge task, but I will work on it as I can. (Stern letter to Jonas Cohn, 31 July 1900; 1994, p. 33)

A particularly noteworthy feature of Stern's oeuvre is the fact that even as he sustained his efforts on the theoretical and philosophical aspects of this "huge task" over the entirety of his scholarly life, he was also a leading figure in the establishment and proliferation of psychology as an empirical—and applied—science. In collaboration with Otto Lipmann, Stern founded the Institute for Applied Psychology in 1906 and, two years later, the *Zeitschrift für angewandte Psychologie* (Journal of applied psychology). Until 1930, when financial pressures forced the cessation of publication, this journal served as a primary outlet for articles in the areas of differential psychology, forensic psychology, social and anthropological psychology, and experimental pedagogy.

By Stern's own account, his ultimate scholarly objective was to achieve a philosophically sound and scientifically defensible conception of human individuality (1927, p. 142). Indeed, in the first sentence of the foreword to his 1900 book *Über Psychologie der individuellen Differenzen* (On the psychology of individual differences), a work that effectively founded the subdiscipline of differential psychology, Stern identified the problem of understanding individuality as the single greatest challenge to twentieth-century scientific psychology. He followed this preliminary work followed a decade later with the much more extensive and thoroughly developed *Die Differentielle Psychologie in ihren methodischen Grundlagen* (1911; Methodological foundations of differential psychology).

Consistent with his vision of this latter work as, essentially, a methods handbook, Stern explicitly relegated his theoretical ideas to a secondary role. On the other hand, reflecting his convictions regarding the indispensability of theoretical and philosophical considerations to a viable psychology, he urged readers of the 1911 book to consult his "philosophical book," referring to the first volume of *Person und Sache* (1906). It was in that work, Stern noted, where he had developed his "conception of the structure of the human individual"—that is, *the person*—and in the process elaborated a set of "philosophical assumptions which on many points deviate in non-trivial ways from the currently prevailing opinions" (1911, p. v).

As it happened, the other "prevailing opinions" to which Stern alluded in this passage were the ones to win widest favor among his contemporaries. Highly influential in this regard was a perspective on the scientific study of individuality set forth by Thorndike. In a monograph titled *Individuality* and published in 1911 (coincidentally, the same year in which Stern's *Die Differentielle Psychologie in ihren methodischen Grundlagen* appeared), Thorndike argued that any given individual's personality could be represented quantitatively in terms of his or her standing, measured relative to others, on each of some presumably small number of basic dimensions applicable to all individuals. The essential task of a scientific psychology of personality would thus consist of (1) establishing the basic dimensions empirically (relying largely on a statistical analysis technique known as factor analysis), and then (2) determining through further empirical investigation the statistical relationships between measures of individual differences along those dimensions and measures of individual differences in whatever domains of human behavior might be deemed worthy of investigation.

In Thorndike's approach to scientific personality studies, persons are properly regarded simply as instances of measurement categories, in principle substitutable for all other persons identified as instances of the same measurement categories. In effect, this approach to one of the

two major knowledge objectives of psychology, which Stern called *Menschenkenntnis* or the *understanding* of human persons, entails the reduction of those persons to things, in diametric opposition to the fundamental tenet of critical personalism. Further complicating matters were the initiatives of Stern's colleague and countryman Münsterberg in the applied domain of *Menschenbehandlung,* or the *treatment* of human persons. In his *Psychology and Industrial Efficiency* (1913), Münsterberg explicitly advocated the systematic assessment and study of individual differences in talents, preferences, and personality characteristics as a basis for deploying workers in ways maximally beneficial, in the long run, to employers. In effect, this entailed regarding certain individuals simply in terms of their usefulness to others. This commitment ran counter to the Kantian moral imperative, which Stern embraced within critical personalism, to always regard persons as ends in and of themselves, and never simply as a means for achieving others' ends.

It is for just these reasons that, as the ideas of Thorndike and Münsterberg won favor among Stern's contemporaries, the founder of differential psychology became increasingly critical of the discipline as a framework for advancing the scientific understanding of persons.

The Hamburg Years. In 1916, in the midst of World War I, Stern accepted an offer to succeed Ernst Meumann (1862–1915) as director of the research laboratory for educational psychology in Hamburg, a vibrant and cosmopolitan port city in northern Germany. There was no university in Hamburg at that time, but the efforts of Stern and a number of other academics and influential civic figures soon changed that. In 1919 the University of Hamburg formally opened its doors, with Stern as director of the Philosophical Seminar and the Psychological Laboratory. In this capacity, Stern also continued as editor of the *Zeitschrift für Pädagogische Psychologie und experimentelle Pädagogik* (Journal of pedagogical psychology and experimental pedagogy), a job he had inherited from Meumann.

If Stern's time in Breslau can properly be characterized as "foundational years," then his time in Hamburg was certainly a time of fruition. Stern carried out dozens of empirical investigations in the Psychological Laboratory either by himself or in collaboration with others under his direction. He also continued to write significant philosophical and theoretical works, including *Die Psychologie und der Personalismus* (1917; Psychology and personalism), *Grundgedanken der personalistischen Philosophie* (1918; Foundations of personalistic philosophy), volumes two and three of *Person und Sache, Die menschliche Persönlichkeit* (1918; The human personality) and *Wertphilosophie*

(1924; Philosophy of value). Still another programmatic work, *Studien zur Personwissenschaft* (Studies in personalistic science) appeared in 1930.

These works give clear evidence of Stern's enduring convictions about the necessity of maintaining close intellectual ties between the disciplines of philosophy and psychology, which already by then were becoming estranged from one another. It was, moreover, largely in consideration of his philosophical commitment to the irreducible distinction between persons and things that, as noted earlier, Stern became critical of developments within the mainstream of differential psychology. During his Hamburg years Stern authored several works sharply critical of the exclusive commitment of many investigators to quantitative measurement procedures and statistical analysis techniques at the expense of sustained and penetrating—but nonstandardized—probing of individual cases. To cite just one example, in a lecture delivered at the Fourth International Congress for Psychotechnics in Paris in 1927, Stern criticized the increasingly widespread practice of trying to represent persons strictly in terms of multiattribute personality "profiles" based on standardized assessment instruments. He argued, "the person is a unified whole, and has depth.... A human being is not a mosaic, and therefore cannot be described as a mosaic. All attempts to represent a person simply in terms of a sequence of test scores are fundamentally false" (1929, pp. 63–64). Later in the same lecture, Stern directed his remarks at psychotechnicians engaged primarily in applied work in industrial and organizational settings: "Psychotechnicians using their test results for various selection purposes must remember that they are not dealing with machines or materials, whose quality and economic significance for the company is in fact expressible through test scores, but rather with human beings, whose occupation is a part—and indeed a very essential part—of their entire personal life" (p. 72).

Influence during and after His Lifetime. In his 1927 *Selbstdarstellung* Stern could write with evident satisfaction that although the worldview that had grounded all of his other scholarly contributions had at first not commanded much attention, he could speak of seeing "many signs that in my personalistic convictions I was no longer so alone ... as I have been two for the past two decades" (p. 152). Indeed, by the late 1920s his works were earning wide and overwhelmingly favorable commentary not only in German-speaking countries but also with substantial frequency in France and the United States. Without doubt, Stern had become one of the most well known and highly regarded scientific psychologists of his time, a development confirmed by his election in 1931 as president of the German Psychological Society.

Two years later, Stern's star was still rising. In *Die Hauptrichtungen der gegenwärtigen Psychologie* (1933; Major trends in contemporary psychology), the prominent philosopher Richard Müller-Freienfels (1882–1949) devoted substantial space to a discussion of Stern's work. To be sure, Müller-Freienfels expressed concern that Stern viewed both the world and the psychological lives of the persons living in that world as "less in conflict than in reality they are." In the main, however, Müller-Freienfels expressed not only high admiration for Stern's extraordinarily multifaceted contributions to psychology but also great optimism about the future of his personalistic worldview. After mentioning Stern's pioneering work in differential psychology, Müller-Freienfels continued:

> One cannot do justice to the wealth of Stern's contributions without taking into consideration the valuable results of his investigations in child psychology, the psychology of testimony, and countless other areas of psychological research. In any case, Stern's personalistics offers an impressive program in which the decisive directions of contemporary research are formulated with great clarity. Admittedly, this clarity overly simplifies certain complexities that will have to be accommodated by future research within the system. Yet even here, especially in his [1930 publication], "Studies in Personalistic Science," Stern himself has pointed us in the right direction. (p. 93)

The Final Years. Alas, even as the ink was drying on this positive appraisal of Stern's work, the scientific edifice that he had so painstakingly constructed over his scholarly lifetime was beginning to collapse around him. On 30 January 1933, Adolf Hitler ascended to power in Germany. Less than three months later Stern, as a Jew, was barred from all academic and administrative activities at the University of Hamburg, and his scholarly life was thus effectively ended. Two of his closest associates, Lipmann and Martha Muchow, committed suicide within a month of each other in the fall of that same year. Finally persuaded by his daughter Eva in 1935 that he needed to flee Germany, he lived briefly in the Netherlands, where he managed to complete *Allgemeine Psychologie auf personalistischer Grundlage* (1935; General psychology from the personalistic standpoint), his last major work. Together with Clara, he then emigrated to the United States, where he served on the faculty at Duke University in Durham, North Carolina, until his death due to heart failure on 27 March 1938.

Of course, no appreciation of Stern appeared in Nazi Germany. However, the American psychologist Gordon Allport (1897–1967), who was a personal friend as well as professional associate of Stern's, honored his departed colleague in words reminiscent of those of Müller-Freien-fels cited above:

> William Stern was both a pioneer and a system-atizer in psychology.... He will be remembered ... for his sure-footed explorations in differential psy-chology, forensic psychology, psychotechnics, child psychology, and intelligence testing. But he will be remembered likewise and, I think, with increasing renown for his theoretical system of personalistic psychology.... It troubled him rela-tively little that his formulations ran counter to the trend of the times, particularly in American thought.... [H]e believed so intensely in the liber-ating powers of personalistic thought that he had faith in its ultimate acceptability to others. Think-ing [personalistically], Stern became a monumen-tal defender of an unpopular cause. [But] the personalistic way of thought will yet have its day, and its day will be long and bright. (1938, pp. 770, 773)

To date, developments within the mainstream of sci-entific psychology cannot be said to have repaid either Stern's unwavering personalistic convictions or Allport's confident prognostication. On the contrary, throughout the twentieth century mainstream thinking about what Stern called the "problem of individuality" has been thor-oughly dominated by concepts and—above all—statistical research methods conforming closely to those ideas first explicitly set forth by Thorndike and roundly criticized by Stern. At a more general, perspectival level, critical person-alism long ago vanished from a landscape defined prima-rily by the literature of a highly positivistic-empiricistic psychology, and to this day critical personalism remains all but completely unknown among contemporary scholars. Whether the twenty-first century will host any conse-quential revival of Stern's estimable contributions to psy-chology remains to be seen.

BIBLIOGRAPHY

WORKS BY STERN

Über Psychologie der individuellen Differenzen (Ideen zu einer "Differentiellen Psychologie"). Leipzig, Germany: Barth, 1900. With this book, Stern effectively founded the discipline of differential psychology.

Person und Sache: System der philosophischen Weltanschauung von William Stern. Vol. 1, *Ableitung und Grundlehre (des kritischen personalismus).* Leipzig, Germany: Barth, 1906. The first of the three volumes comprising *Person and Thing,* this work lays out the philosophical foundations of critical personalism.

With Clara Stern. *Die Kindersprache.* Leipzig, Germany: Barth, 1907.

With Clara Stern. *Erinnerung, Aussage und Lüge in der ersten Kindheit.* Leipzig, Germany: Barth, 1909. Translated by

James T. Lamiell as *Recollection, Testimony, and Lying in Early Childhood* (Washington, DC: American Psychological Association, 1999).

Die Differentielle Psychologie in ihren methodischen Grundlagen. Leipzig, Germany: Barth, 1911. By Stern's own account, this book was written "in place" of a second edition of the 1900 book, and solidified differential psychology's place as a major subdiscipline within scientific psychology.

Psychologie der frühen Kindheit, bis zum sechsten Lebensjahr. Leipzig, Germany: Quelle and Meyer, 1914. The first of what would eventually be seven editions of a child psychology textbook. Translated from the 1923 edition by Anna Barwell as *The Psychology of Early Childhood up to the Sixth Year of Age* (London: Allen and Unwin, 1924).

Vorgedanken zur Weltanschauung (niedergeschrieben im Jahre 1901). Leipzig, Germany: Barth, 1915. This text was actually written in 1901, and clearly establishes that, already by that early date, Stern was formulating the foundational ideas of critical personalism.

Die Psychologie und der Personalismus. Leipzig, Germany: Barth, 1917. A highly condensed presentation of the central ideas of critical personalism.

Grundgedanken der personalistischen Philosophie. Philosophische Vorträge 20. Berlin: Reuther and Reichard, 1918. This work is similar in its content to the 1917 work *Die Psychologie und der Personalismus,* but was written for a readership constituted primarily of philosophers rather than of psychologists.

Person und Sache: System der philosophischen Weltanschauung. Vol. 2, *Die menschliche Persönlichkeit.* Leipzig, Germany: Barth, 1918.

"Richtlinien für die Methodik der psychologischen Praxis." *Beihefte zur Zeitschrift für angewandte Psychologie* 29 (1921): 1–16.

"Selbstdarstellung." In *Die Philosophie der Gegenwart in Selbstdarstellungen,* edited by Raymond Schmidt, vol. 6, 128–184. Leipzig, Germany: Meiner, 1922–1929. This is an intellectual autobiography. Translated by Susanne Langer as "William Stern" in *A History of Psychology in Autobiography,* vol. 1, edited by Carl Murchison, pp. 335–388 (Worcester, MA: Clark University Press, 1930).

Person und Sache: System der philosophischen weltanschuung von William Stern. Vol. 3, *Wertphilosophie.* Leipzig, Germany: Barth, 1924.

Anfänge der Reifezeit: Ein Knabentagebuch in psychologischer Bearbeitung. Leipzig, Germany: Quelle and Meyer, 1925.

"Aus dreijähriger Arbeit des Hamburger Psychologischen Laboratoriums." *Zeitschrift für pädagogische Psychologie* 26 (1925): 289–307.

"Persönlichkeitsforschung und Testmethode." *Jahrbuch der Charakterologie* 6 (1929): 63–72. One of several articles published between 1920 and 1933 in which Stern is sharply critical of the increasingly exclusive reliance of differential psychologists on standardized tests and statistical analysis procedures.

Studien zur Personwissenschaft: Personalistik als Wissenschaft. Leipzig, Germany: Barth, 1930.

"Der personale Faktor in Psychotechnik und praktischer Psychologie." *Zeitschrift für angewandte Psychologie* 44 (1933): 52–63.

Allgemeine Psychologie auf personalistischer Grundlage. The Hague: Nijhoff, 1935. Stern's last major work. Translated by Howard Davis Spoerl as *General Psychology from the Personalistic Standpoint* (New York: Macmillan, 1938).

Der Briefwechsel zwischen William Stern und Jonas Cohn: Dokumente einer Freundschaft zwischen zwei Wissenschaftlern. Edited by Helmut E. Lück and Dieter-Jürgen Löwisch. Frankfurt am Main, Germany: Peter Lang, 1994. This book offers an extensive compilation of nearly all of the letters sent by William Stern to his friend and philosopher colleague Jonas Cohn over a period extending from 1893 to 1938.

OTHER SOURCES

Allport, Gordon W. "The Personalistic Psychology of William Stern." *Character and Personality* 5 (1937): 231–246. Offers a concise exposition of Stern's conception of the human personality.

———. "William Stern: 1871–1938." *American Journal of Psychology* 51 (1938): 770–773. Allport's appreciation of Stern, published in the year of Stern's death.

Ash, Mitchell G. *Gestalt Psychology in German Culture, 1890–1967: Holism and the Quest for Objectivity.* Cambridge, U.K.: Cambridge University Press, 1995.

Bühring, Gerald. *Titelbibliographie zu und über William Stern.* 1996a. This is an unpublished bibliography of Stern's works compiled by his biographer.

———. *William Stern, oder, Streben nach Einheit.* Frankfurt am Main, Germany: Peter Lang, 1996b. To date, the only published biography of Stern.

———. "Zur Rezeption William Sterns im Spiegel der Rezensionen." *Psychologie und Geschichte* 8 (2000): 189–199.

Deutsch, Werner, ed. *Über die verborgene Aktualität von William Stern.* Frankfurt am Main, Germany: Peter Lang, 1991. A collection of essays originally prepared for a conference held in Berlin in 1988 to commemorate the fiftieth anniversary of Stern's death.

Ebbinghaus, Hermann. *Psychology: An Elementary Text-Book.* Translated and edited by Max Meyer. Boston: D.C. Heath, 1908.

Eckardt, Georg. "William Stern—Aspekte seines wissenschaftlichen Lebenswerkes." *Psychologie für die Praxis* 7 (1989): 3–27.

Harrington, Anne. *Reenchanted Science: Holism in German Culture from Wilhelm II to Hitler.* Princeton, NJ: Princeton University Press, 1996.

Lamiell, James T. *Beyond Individual and Group Differences: Human Individuality, Scientific Psychology, and William Stern's Critical Personalism.* Thousand Oaks, CA: Sage, 2003. This work situates a renewal and extension of the author's long-running critique of mainstream thinking in twentieth-century personality psychology.

———. "William Stern und der 'Ursprungsmythos' der Differentiellen Psychologie." *Journal für Psychologie* 14 (2006): 253–273. This work documents Stern's mounting criticism, during the 1920s and early 1930s, of psychologists'

ever-increasing reliance on standardized measurement operations and statistical analysis techniques.

Lamiell, James T., and Werner Deutsch. "In the Light of a Star: An Introduction to William Stern's Critical Personalism." *Theory and Psychology* 10 (2000): 715–730. This is the lead article in a special issue of *Theory and Psychology* containing nine additional articles discussing the relevance of Stern's thinking to a variety of contemporary topics.

McCrae, R. R., and P. T. Costa Jr. "Trait Explanations in Personality Psychology." *European Journal of Personality* 9 (1995): 231–252.

———. "Toward a New Generation of Personality Theories: Theoretical Contexts for the Five-Factor Model." In *The Five-Factor Model of Personality: Theoretical Perspectives,* edited by Jerry S. Wiggins, 51–87. New York: Guilford, 1996.

———. "A Five-Factor Theory of Personality." In *Handbook of Personality: Theory and Research,* edited by Lawrence A. Pervin and Oliver P. John, 2nd ed., 139–153. New York: Guilford, 1999.

Michaelis-Stern, Eva. "Erinnerung an meine Eltern." In *Über die Verborgene Aktualität von William Stern,* edited by Werner Deutsch, 131–141. Frankfurt am Main, Germany: Peter Lang, 1991. Eva Michaelis-Stern was the youngest of the three children born to Clara and William Stern.

Müller-Freienfels, Richard. *Die Hauptrichtungen der gegenwärtigen Psychologie.* Leipzig, Germany: Quelle and Meyer, 1933.

Münsterberg, Hugo. *Psychology and Industrial Efficiency.* Boston: Mifflin, 1913. This book firmly established the subdiscipline of psychotechnics in industrial and organizational psychology, even though it was Stern who had coined the term *psychotechnics* in 1903.

Ringer, Fritz. *The Decline of the German Mandarins: The German Academic Community, 1890–1933.* Cambridge, MA: Harvard University Press, 1969.

Thorndike, Edward L. *Individuality.* Boston: Houghton, Mifflin, 1911. In this work, Thorndike sketched a perspective on the scientific study of individuality that in important respects runs contrary to the views of Stern.

Toulmin, S., and D. E. Leary. "The Cult of Empiricism in Psychology, and Beyond." In *A Century of Psychology as Science,* edited by Sigmund Koch and David E. Leary, 594–617. New York: McGraw-Hill, 1985.

James T. Lamiell

STERN, LOUIS WILLIAM

SEE **Stern, William**.

STOMMEL, HENRY MELSON (*b.* Wilmington, Delaware, 27 September 1920; *d.* Boston, Massachusetts, 17 January 1992), *oceanography.*

Until the second half of the twentieth century, most oceanographers believed that ocean currents were driven by winds and limited to the oceans' upper, mixed layer. Deeper circulation, driven by density gradients induced by temperature or salinity differences, was intermittently advocated, notably by the German naturalist Alexander von Humboldt, the American hydrographer Matthew Fontaine Maury, and the British naturalist William B. Carpenter. In the 1870s, however, there was an acrimonious debate in Britain between Carpenter and James Croll over the role of wind vs. density in driving ocean currents density. When it was settled largely in Croll's favor, most Anglophone oceanographers abandoned serious consideration of thermo-haline effects.

Deep density-driven currents gained credence in the late 1920s–1930s with the results of the German *Meteor* expedition of 1925, which demonstrated the existence of cold, dense, mid-layer waters apparently derived from polar regions, and with the development of a method to calculate the effects of density gradients caused by variations in temperature and salinity. But data from the abyssal ocean remained scarce, and absent evidence, most oceanographers presumed that the abyssal ocean was essentially still. For example, the leading textbook of the mid-twentieth century, *The Oceans, Their Physics, Chemistry, and General Biology*, held that below depths of 2,000 meters [6,600 feet], currents were likely to be "so weak that they are negligible" (Sverdrup et al., 1942, p. 392).

This presumption was refuted when Henry Stommel constructed the first widely accepted mathematical model of abyssal circulation. His model, which demonstrated that density- and wind-driven gradients could be understood as a coupled system that explained the observed surface circulation, predicted significant mid-layer and abyssal currents and demonstrated that the ocean had two potentially stable states.

Personal History and Early Career. Brilliant, original, funny, and unpretentious, "Hank" Stommel was the son of a chemist, Walter Stommel, born in Germany, and Marian Melson Stommel. Hank built his scientific career on modest formal education. Growing up with his mother and his sister, Anne, in Brooklyn, New York, where his mother settled after divorcing his father, Stommel attended public schools populated by the children of Jewish and Scandinavian immigrants, where he saw "that application to school work was our only escape from uncertain employment" (Stommel Papers 1, Royal Society, London). He spent a year at the prestigious Townsend Harris High School, a competitive public school in the Bronx (the precursor of the Bronx High School of Science), before the family moved to Long Island. Stommel received a scholarship to Yale University, receiving his B.S.

degree in astronomy in 1942, and then worked at the Yale Observatory while taking courses at the Divinity School, considering a career dedicated either literally or figuratively to the heavens.

In 1944 Stommel was offered a position at the Woods Hole Oceanographic Institution at Woods Hole, Massachusetts, where wartime funding was abundant for oceanographic research sponsored by the National Defense Research Committee (NDRC). Stommel joined as a research associate working with geophysicist Maurice Ewing, analyzing temperature-depth profiles taken during sound transmission exercises as part of the NDRC program in sub-surface warfare. Stommel remained at Woods Hole for the next sixteen years, his research largely sponsored by the newly established Office of Naval Research (ONR).

In 1948—at the age of twenty-eight and with no graduate training, save for his Divinity School experience—Stommel wrote the article that would establish his reputation. "On the Westward Intensification of Wind-driven Currents," published in the *Transactions of the American Geophysical Union* in 1948, demonstrated that strengthening of currents along the western sides of ocean basins was a direct consequence of the variation of the Coriolis effect with latitude. This both explained the

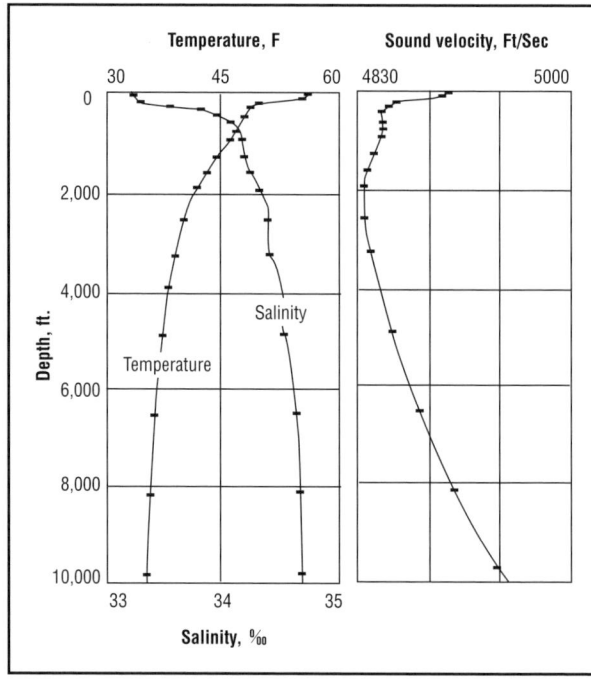

Figure 1. *A typical temperature-salinity profile with computed sound velocities, showing a steep temperature drop just below the surface layer and corresponding drop in velocity. Note the thermocline at 20-200 feet, and the velocity minimum at 2000 feet; the sound channel is focused around this velocity minimum.*

strength and location of the Gulf Stream and predicted a deep countercurrent traveling towards the equator below it. This prediction was confirmed in 1957 by oceanographers John Swallow and Valentine Worthington and is often cited as a rare example of a successful prediction in the field of oceanography. Meanwhile, Stommel had extended his work into a full-fledged theory of ocean circulation. It began with a simple observational fact: the existence of the ocean thermocline.

The Ocean Thermocline. The thermocline—the zone of rapid temperature transition between the ocean's warm surface layer and frigid deeps—was studied in great detail during World War II for its importance to submarine warfare. As the temperature drops through the thermocline, the density of water increases and sound waves are refracted, creating acoustic shadow zones where submarines may hide. Moreover, while temperature falls with depth, salinity generally increases (because surface layers are diluted by rainfall), and these countervailing effects produce a velocity minimum zone—the "sound channel"—in which sound waves travel with little attenuation, a phenomenon exploited as the basis of cold war submarine surveillance systems. (See Figure 1.)

Stommel argued that any theory of ocean circulation had to account for the thermocline and the global presence of deep cold water. German oceanographers, including Alfred Merz, Albert Defant, and Georg Wüst, had argued that this cold water was transported from polar regions. But how? In a characteristic pattern, Stommel presented the answer qualitatively first, based on a physical insight, and then developed it quantitatively. The insight was that upward diffusion of deep water throughout the abyssal ocean could permit cold, dense waters to sink in the polar regions, while preventing warm surface waters from sinking. This suggested a picture of abyssal circulation dramatically different from the earlier models dating back to Humboldt: not a conveyor belt on which coherent water parcels sank at the poles, maintained their identity, and rose at the equator, but rather water that lost its identity as it diffused throughout the ocean.

Figure 2, published in 1959, contains all the conceptual elements of Stommel's insight but lacked mathematical development.

"The above presentation is in the nature of a tour-de-force," Stommel wrote. "One cannot pretend that it describes the abyssal circulation accurately in detail" (Stommel, 1959, p. 82). For that, Stommel turned to Arnold Arons.

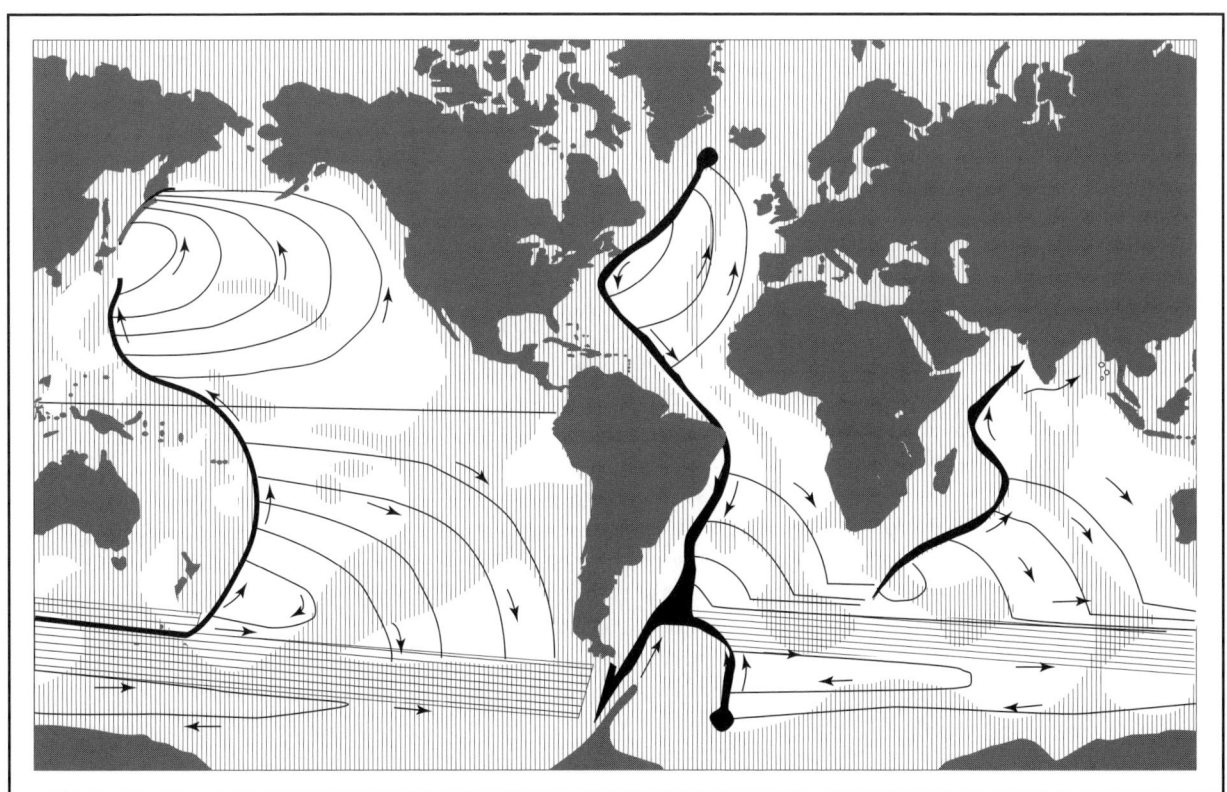

Figure 2. *Henry Stommel's conceptual model of ocean circulation.*

Arons was a physicist who had been drawn into oceanography by Cold War–related issues, including the dispersal of nuclear fallout in the oceans and the base surge produced by large explosions in shallow water harbors. In 1954 he was invited to a meeting organized by the U.S. Atomic Energy Commission (AEC) at Woods Hole on ocean disposal of civilian nuclear waste. One issue raised at the meeting was the potential effects of radiogenic heat from waste packages on the thermohaline circulation. Arons recalled:

> The AEC people pointed with concern to the mounting volume of wastes being stored [at power plants] but no oceanographer was sanguine about [oceanic] disposal. … On the other hand, no one was prepared to make categorical predictions. … It was about this time that Stommel and I had begun thinking about abyssal circulation and … the work that led to what is now usually called the Stommel-Arons model. (Arons, personal communication, 16 October 2000)

The model was laid out in a five-part paper published over the course of twelve years. Most critical were the first two, published in *Deep-Sea Research* in 1960 by Stommel and Arons. They concluded that it was wrong to think of the ocean as having two different forms of circulation: one wind-driven and the other density-driven. It was better, they said, to envisage a single system in which the surface effects were in part dependent on vertical transport and vice versa. Wind could be viewed as a source or a sink, no more or less than sinking or upwelling of water masses. Moreover the requirements of geostrophy and the conservation of mass led to western boundary currents irrespective of the location of sources and sinks, a conclusion that had important consequences for the stability of earth's climate. Stommel and Arons wrote: "The exact location of the sources is … more or less a climatological accident. One could disappear and another appear somewhere else … with changing climatic conditions, but these would be accompanied by no major modifications of the interior region of the abyssal circulation, and with no major change of the amplitude of the overall abyssal circulation." This perspective was odds with the conventional wisdom, which held that the magnitude of the abyssal circulation would be controlled by the amount of winter cooling in polar regions and "that a warming of polar regions of only a few degrees would largely stop the abyssal flow." Instead, they concluded, "warming of polar regions of one or two degrees would not affect deep transports except possibly to shift the location of the sources, and to reshuffle the western boundary currents" ("On the Abyssal Circulation of the World Ocean II," 1960, p. 225).

There was, however, another factor to consider. Because heat transfer tends to be faster and more efficient than the processes that change salinity—mainly evaporation, but also mixing, diffusion, and sea ice formation—in the natural world temperature effects tend to dominate. But one could imagine a situation in which salinity differences predominate, and to determine how likely that would be, one could calculate the relative effects of temperature and salinity on density.

In "Thermohaline Convection with Two Stable Regimes of Flow" (1961), Stommel imagined two adjacent idealized basins with different temperature and salinity conditions and solved the equations for heat and salinity transfer between them. In the case where two vessels were connected by a capillary tube at the bottom (through which more dense water could move) and an overflow connector at the top (through which less dense water could move), there were two stable solutions to the equations: one in which temperature effects dominated and one in which salinity effects dominated. This implied that two stable regimes might exist in nature. Stommel wrote:

> The fact that even in a very simple convective system … two distinct stable regimes can occur … suggests that a similar situation may exist somewhere in nature. One wonders whether other, quite different states of flow are permissible in the ocean or some estuaries and if such a system might jump into one of these with a sufficient perturbation. If so, the system is inherently fraught with possibilities for speculation about climatic change. (1961, p. 228)

In the context of anthropogenic global warming, these possibilities are a topic of heightened concern in the early twenty-first century, and their recognition is part of Stommel's lasting legacy.

Rise of "Big Oceanography." Stommel's life spanned a period in which American oceanography was transformed in size and scope by the influx of financial and logistical support from the U.S. Navy, and his feelings about this transformation were ambivalent. Although his fame rested on work funded by the navy, Stommel repeatedly expressed misgivings over the application of science to warfare. Reflecting back on his early career, Stommel later recalled: "I was troubled by the morality of killing in war, and it seemed to me that antisubmarine warfare was the least immoral of any military application of science that I could do. At any rate, it did not involve civilian targets" (Stommel Papers 1, Royal Society, London). In 1960 he helped to lead a rebellion of faculty at Woods Hole—the "palace revolt"—over the question of military funding and direction of research, feeling that the director, Paul Fye, was pushing the institution too far in the direction of "mission-driven" research and leaving insufficient opportunities for individual initiative and creativity. When Fye dismissed this as nostalgic "pastoralism," Stommel responded with a memo in which he suggested that if the director did not want his scientists to be shepherds, evidently he wanted them to be sheep. The revolt culminated in a faculty vote of no confidence, but when the trustees backed Fye, many of the faculty involved left. Stommel was among them, working for the next sixteen years as a university professor—briefly at Harvard, then at MIT—and returning to Woods Hole on the retirement of Paul Fye in 1977.

Stommel was also ambivalent about the growth of "big oceanography"—viewing it, like the military largesse that enabled much of it—as a threat to individual curiosity and creativity. Yet he became involved in several highly political, even bureaucratic, big-science projects of the 1970s, including the Global Atmospheric Research Program (GARP), the GARP Atlantic Tropical Experiment (GATE), the Mid-Ocean Dynamics Experiment (MODE), and the World Ocean Circulation Experiment (WOCE). While referred to as "experiments," these were for the most part large-scale data gathering efforts, which Stommel accepted as necessary to advance oceanography even as he worried that they were risky to the autonomy and creativity of the individuals involved with them. His own scientific hero was John Swallow, the gentle and modest inventor of the neutrally buoyant float, whom Stommel admired to the end of his life for being a "full sized observer in the old-fashioned one-man way" (Stommel Papers 4: Correspondence 1990).

Honors and Awards. Stommel married Elizabeth Brown on December 6, 1950. They had three children, two boys and a girl. He had a dynamic personality that graduate students and colleagues found highly appealing. His success as a scientist was based on his wide-ranging curiosity, prodigious powers of intuition and visualization, and a wry sense of humor. Stommel's many honors and awards included the (U.S.) National Medal of Science, the Craaford Prize of the Royal Swedish Academy, the Huntsman Award of the Bedford Institution of Oceanography, his election to the (U.S.) National Academy of Sciences in 1959, and his foreign membership in the Royal Society of London, the Soviet Academy of Sciences, and the Académie des Sciences de Paris.

BIBLIOGRAPHY

WORKS BY STOMMEL

"On the Westward Intensification of Wind-driven Currents." *Transactions of the American Geophysical Union* 29 (1948): 202–206.

"The Abyssal Circulation of the Ocean." *Nature* 180, no. 4589 (1957): 733–734.

"A Survey of Ocean Current Theory." *Deep-Sea Research* 4 (1957): 149–184.

The Gulf Stream: A Physical and Dynamical Description. Berkeley: University of California Press, 1958.

"The Abyssal Circulation." *Deep-Sea Research* 5 (1958): 80–82.

With Arnold Arons and A. J. Faller. "Some Examples of Stationary Planetary Flow Patterns in Bounded Basins." *Tellus* 10 no. 2 (1958): 179–187.

With Allan R. Robinson. "The Oceanic Thermocline and the Associated Thermohaline Circulation." *Tellus* 3 (1959): 295–308.

With Arnold B. Arons. "On the Abyssal Circulation of the World Ocean I. Stationary Planetary Flow Patterns on a Sphere." *Deep-Sea Research* 6 (1960): 140–154.

With Arnold B. Arons. "On the Abyssal Circulation of the World Ocean II. An Idealized Model of the Circulation Pattern and Amplitude in Oceanic Basins." *Deep-Sea Research* 6 (1960): 217–233.

"Thermohaline Convection with Two Stable Regimes of Flow." *Tellus* 13 (1961): 131–149.

"The Large-Scale Oceanic Circulation." In *Advances in Earth Science,* edited by Patrick M. Hurley. Cambridge, MA: MIT Press, 1966.

With Arnold B. Arons. "On the Abyssal Circulation of the World Ocean: III. An Advection–lateral Mixing Model of the Distribution of a Tracer Property in an Ocean Basin." *Deep-Sea Research* 14 (1967): 441–457.

With Arnold B. Arons. "On the Abyssal Circulation of the World Ocean: V. The Influence of Bottom Slope on the Broadening of Inertial Boundary Currents." *Deep-Sea Research* 19 (1972): 707–718.

Collected Works of Henry M. Stommel. Edited by Nelson G. Hogg and Rui Xin Huang. 3 vols. Boston: American Meteorological Society, 1995.

OTHER SOURCES

Arons, Arnold. "The Scientific Work of Henry Stommel." In *Evolution of Physical Oceanography: Scientific Surveys in Honor of Henry Stommel,* edited by Bruce A. Warren and Carl Wunsch. Cambridge, MA: The MIT Press, 1981.

Sverdrup, Harald; Martin W. Johnson; and Richard H. Fleming. *The Oceans, Their Physics, Chemistry, and General Biology.* Fleming, NY: Prentice-Hall, 1942.

Swallow, John C., and L. Valentine Worthington. "Measurements of Deep Currents in the Western North Atlantic." *Nature* 179, no. 4571 (1957): 1183–1184.

Veronis, George. "A Theoretical Model of Henry Stommel." In *Evolution of Physical Oceanography,* edited by Bruce A. Warren and Carl Wunsch. Cambridge, MA: The MIT Press, 1981.

Warren, Bruce A. "Arnold B. Arons (1916–2001)." *EOS: Transactions of the American Geophysical Union* 82, no. 30 (2001): 328.

———, and Carl Wunsch, eds. *Evolution of Physical Oceanography: Scientific Surveys in Honor of Henry Stommel.* Cambridge, MA: The MIT Press, 1981.

Wunsch, Carl. "Henry Melson Stommel: September 27, 1920–January 17, 1992." *National Academy of Sciences Biographical Memoir* 72 (1997): 331–350.

Naomi Oreskes

STRACHEY, CHRISTOPHER (*b.* London, United Kingdom, 16 November 1916; *d.* Oxford, United Kingdom, 18 May 1975), *computer science, computer programming languages and semantics.*

Strachey was one of the most original computer scientists of his generation, making important contributions to computer design and to programming practice and theory. After some exposure to computing instruments during World War II, in the 1950s and 1960s he held several wide-ranging appointments and consultancies. In 1969 he established the Programming Research Group at Oxford University, and was professor of computer science from 1971 until his death in 1975.

Family Background and Education. Born in Hampstead, London, Strachey was the only son and the second of the two children of Oliver Strachey and Ray Costelloe. Oliver was born into a distinguished British literary and political dynasty, and his relations included Lytton Strachey, the biographer, and John Strachey, who became secretary of state for war in the Clement Atlee government. Inheriting the Strachey family's passion for puzzles and games, Oliver served as a cryptographer in the War Office Code and Cypher School during World War I. Christopher's mother, Ray, was the daughter of an American Quaker family. Trained as a mathematician and engineer, she was a pioneer of the women's movement, and the author of one of its most influential books (*The Cause*, 1928).

In 1919 the family moved to Gordon Square, Bloomsbury, London, the center of an intellectual circle known as the Bloomsbury Group. The family's neighbors included some of Britain's leading intellectuals, such as Clive and Vanessa Bell, Virginia and Leonard Woolf, and John Maynard Keynes. Exposure to this well-born intellectual clique left an indelible stamp on Strachey. He was brilliant in conversation, musically accomplished, and held strong opinions on all subjects. He could be charming and witty, but also arrogant with a woundingly sarcastic tongue.

Although he was a precocious child, Strachey's educational achievements were undistinguished. At the age of thirteen he was sent to Gresham's School, Norfolk, an establishment selected for its reputation in science teaching. Although showing occasional flashes of brilliance, his mediocre examination results enabled him to secure only

a "minor exhibition" to Kings College, Cambridge University. He went up to Kings College in October 1935, and initially studied mathematics, but he quickly fell behind and then switched to physics, which he found less demanding. He graduated in 1939 with a disappointing "lower second" in the natural science tripos, a result that dashed his hopes of a research studentship. He therefore obtained a post as a physicist with Standard Telephones and Cables Limited (STC). He took up his appointment in August 1939, just a month before Britain declared war on Germany.

War Service and Schoolmastering. Strachey was employed in the Valve Development Laboratory of STC in London, but the laboratory was shortly evacuated to Ilminster, in the southwest of England. There he was a member of a small team led by John H. Fremlin (later professor of physics at Birmingham University) investigating the theoretical design of centimetric radar valves ("valve" was the United Kingdom term for what was known as a "tube" in the United States). Strachey worked on the derivation of analytical formulae for valve characteristics and their experimental verification. This required him to integrate differential equations numerically, for which he used a differential analyzer, the most important prewar computing instrument. Strachey became fascinated by computing problems and computing machinery; he read widely on the subject, and became a local expert in STC. Thereafter he took every opportunity to work on computing problems for both his own research and that of colleagues.

Strachey had a long-standing intention of becoming a schoolmaster, and at the end of the war he left STC to become a teacher of physics and mathematics at St Edmund's School, Canterbury, a minor public school (that is, a private, fee-paying school—British terminology is confusing on this point). He proved an inspirational teacher and reveled in school life—he revived societies moribund since the start of the war, sang in the school choir, and played in the orchestra. In 1949, in order to advance his career, he sought and obtained a position at Harrow School, one of Britain's top half-dozen public schools. There he further honed his teaching skills and he was known as a spellbinding instructor. He never lost this gift, though it sometimes crossed over into a schoolmasterish manner that could grate on colleagues.

Strachey's interest in computing had been dormant since leaving STC, but was reawakened by press and radio reports of "electronic brains" in the late 1940s. He bought a copy of Norbert Weiner's classic *Cybernetics* (1948) and from that time on he never looked back. During 1949–1951 the first British experimental computers came into service—at Cambridge University, Manchester

University, and the National Physical Laboratory (NPL—the British equivalent of the U.S. National Bureau of Standards, now the National Institute of Standards and Technology). In spring 1951 Strachey was given an opportunity—through the introduction of a well-placed friend—to use the Pilot ACE computer at the NPL. He wrote a program to enable the computer to play the game of draughts (checkers). It was typical of Strachey that he should write a program that explored machine logic and reasoning rather than one for mathematical computing, for which the machine was designed.

Early in 1951 Manchester University installed the Ferranti Mark I, the world's first commercially available computing machine, built to the university's own design. This was a much bigger machine than that at the NPL, and therefore much more suitable for Strachey's kind of programming. At that time Alan Turing was the assistant director of the computer laboratory, and Strachey knew him just well enough to be allowed to use the machine—they had both been at Kings College, when Strachey was a lowly student and Turing a research fellow with a growing reputation. At Turing's suggestion, Strachey wrote a machine-simulation program to enable the computer to monitor the execution of its own programs. This was an esoteric program for its day and, at more than one thousand instructions long, considerably the longest so far written for the machine. Strachey was given overnight use of the machine, and by the following morning the program was working. It was a programming tour de force that established his reputation, which rapidly diffused through the small British computing community.

A few months later, Strachey was approached by Lord Halsbury (John Giffard), managing director of the National Research and Development Corporation (NRDC). The corporation had been established by the government in 1949 to exploit and patent British inventions in developing areas of technology—of which computing was seen as that with the most potential. Strachey accepted a post as a technical officer in the computer division of the corporation, at a salary of double his schoolmaster's pay.

At the National Research and Development Corporation. Strachey began work at the NRDC in June 1952, with the remit to work on computer applications and computer design. He initially worked on computer applications. The most important of these was the calculations for the St. Lawrence Seaway project for the Hydro-Electric Board of Canada. For this program he used the Ferranti FERUT computer—a copy of the Manchester University machine—installed at the University of Toronto. Besides being a feat of programming virtuosity—some two thousand instructions altogether—the experience heightened

Strachey's awareness of the requirements of programmers. Strachey became convinced that computer designers who were not also programmers could not empathize sufficiently with users to create effective designs. In 1953–1954 he redesigned the instruction set—the programmer's primary computer interface—for a prototype computer known as the Elliott 401, and the revised machine was subsequently marketed as the model 402. During 1954–1956 he undertook the design of a new computer, the Ferranti Pegasus, from the ground up.

The Pegasus was a pathbreaking design, with many large and small innovations. One of the most important inventions was the elimination of the "optimum coding" technique. Optimum coding was first used by Turing in his design for the NPL ACE computer. In this design, every instruction nominated the address of its successor in order to minimize the waiting time between successive instructions. Optimum coding could improve machine performance by a factor of five, but at the cost of such programming complexity that in practice few users could get the best out of the machine. Using elegant hardware design, Strachey achieved an acceptable level of optimization in a way that was transparent to the user and required no special programming techniques. This made the Pegasus both very usable and price competitive, and it was one of the best-selling British computing machines of its era. As well as the overall system design, Strachey designed the instruction set and the programming system. Perhaps no machine, before or since, has borne the stamp of its principal designer to such a degree. Strachey's design style influenced British computer architecture for the next decade.

Strachey is credited as being the first individual to propose computer "time sharing," although the first practical system was developed by the Massachusetts Institute of Technology (MIT). In a time-sharing computer of the period, a large expensive computer was shared between many simultaneous users, each of whom was given a fraction of the machine's power. In this way users had the illusion of having a full computer (though one of reduced power) to themselves—it was the nearest that era came to a personal computing experience. Strachey described his ideas at the UNESCO Conference on Information Processing in Paris, June 1959, and a patent application was also filed. Strachey's scheme was far more than a blue-sky proposal; it was worked out in practical detail. The user experience in the Strachey scheme was somewhat different to that which subsequently evolved in practical time-sharing computers. Strachey envisaged users having a traditional input-output console consisting of a paper-tape reader and a printer. His scheme would thus have used a large computer to replicate the typical 1950s computing experience for many simultaneous users. In part this was a limited vision, but it was also one that was grounded in computing practice as he knew and understood it. In the event, practical time-sharing systems came to use teletypes and CRT-based visual display units as the standard user interface. This superior interface owed much to J. C. R. (Joseph Carl Robnett) Liklider, the visionary head of the Advanced Research Project Agency's Information Processing Techniques Office, which provided funding for MIT's time-sharing computer projects.

In 1959 Strachey resigned from the NRDC to work as a freelance computer consultant. During his time at the NRDC he had served as the corporation's representative on numerous national committees; he had become something of a pundit, frequently lecturing on computer topics and making occasional broadcasts; and his reputation as a computer designer and programming expert was unrivaled. He was therefore exceptionally well placed to operate as an independent consultant.

Private Consulting and Cambridge University. Strachey opened his consulting business from an office in his home in Bedford Gardens, Kensington, London, in June 1959. The next few years were perhaps the most productive of his life; certainly the most remunerative. His primary consulting engagements were in computer design, applications programming, and programming language implementation. His computer-design commissions included work on the Elliott 502, a military computer for Decca Radar, and the EMI 2400 and the EMI 3400 computers—the latter a giant machine that never came to market.

Strachey's most important programming-language contract was for a scientific "autocode" for the Ferranti Orion computer. To assist in this work he hired a young researcher, Peter Landin (subsequently a professor at Queen Mary College, University of London). Landin spent much of his time trying to specify the semantics (what the language *did*) as opposed to the syntax (how to form grammatically correct statements); at that time the latter had attracted much more academic interest. Landin's work opened a new research window for Strachey, and programming language semantics would be his primary research interest for the remainder of his life. Strachey was at the center of programming language research in the United Kingdom, actively participating in committees of the British Computer Society and International Federation for Information Processing (IFIP), as well as organizing research colloquia at his London residence in Bedford Gardens.

Maurice V. Wilkes, head of the Cambridge University Computer Laboratory, invited Strachey to design and implement a programming language for the Titan computer that was then under construction. Despite a considerable financial sacrifice, Strachey accepted a part-time research fellowship in the laboratory in June 1962. He collaborated with David Barron and David Hartley, and

within two months they had produced a preliminary specification for the Combined Programming Language (CPL). Stylistically, CPL was similar to the international Algol language, but it had many additional features for the efficient implementation of programs in different problem domains—scientific computation, business data processing, and systems programming. The following autumn, Eric Nixon and John Buxton of the London University Computing Unit joined in the development, and a complete specification was published in the *Computer Journal* in February 1963.

CPL never became a mainstream language, in part because Strachey never completed the Cambridge implementation, instead being diverted to the study of programming language semantics. He delivered a paper, "Towards a Formal Semantics," at an IFIP conference in 1965, which was published the following year. Strachey regarded this paper as the most important outcome of his CPL work. A less important paper on programming, though more widely read for sure, appeared in *Scientific American* in a special edition on computers and information in September 1966. Although little used, CPL had an important influence on programming language design. In 1966 Martin Richards, a research assistant on the CPL project, moved to MIT, where he developed the BCPL (Basic CPL) language. In its turn, BCPL was a key influence on the design of the C programming language introduced in the early 1970s; C was to become the most important systems implementation language until it began to be superseded by C++ in the 1990s.

Another outcome of the CPL project was Strachey's General Purpose Macrogenerator (GPM). This tiny programming system was intended as an implementation tool for CPL, but it soon took on a life of its own. The macrogenerator used a small set of programming primitives to transform text. It was designed to make program transformations and extensions, but it could also be used for less serious purposes—in one case it was used to compute nursery rhymes. GPM was implemented in almost every country where computing was a research subject. Although Strachey described GPM as a beguiling timewaster, in the mid-1960s its economy and elegance captured the hearts and minds of many academic computer scientists. Although largely forgotten in the early twenty-first century, it was the most complete and self-contained piece of work he produced.

Strachey was strident in his belief that too much university computer science research was directed to numerical applications, whereas he believed that far more interesting problems lay in nonnumerical applications—such as artificial intelligence and systems programming. His outspoken comments—some made with Professor Stanley Gill of Imperial College—led the numerical analyst Leslie Fox, who was director of the Oxford University Computing Laboratory, to invite the pair to organize a summer school on nonnumerical computing at Oxford in 1963. The publication of the proceedings of the summer school *Advances in Programming and Non-Numerical Computation* (1966) marked a shift in the cultural landscape away from scientific applications to real computer science.

Strachey had always had a hankering for the academic life, and with the help of Fox, he obtained funding from the Department of Scientific and Industrial Research to establish a Programming Research Group (PRG) at Oxford University. Located in a Victorian house in Banbury Road, Oxford, the organization was to become the most prestigious center for programming research in the United Kingdom, a distinction it still holds at the time of writing.

The Programming Research Group, Oxford University. Strachey took up residence in Oxford in April 1966. The PRG initially consisted of just himself and a research fellow, David Park (subsequently professor of computer science at Warwick University). The first several months were spent cleaning up the CPL activity of the previous years and producing a reference manual that was issued, not so much with a roar as a whimper, as a mimeographed report *The CPL Working Papers.* Strachey was notoriously reluctant to publish, seemingly intimidated by the stellar literary talents of the Bloomsbury Group. In speech he was voluble and loquacious, even overbearing, but he was reluctant to publish anything he felt was less than perfect. Just 150 copies of the *CPL Working Papers* were circulated within the programming language research community. The following year he wrote "Fundamental Concepts of Programming Languages," another influential paper, but less influential than it could have been because of its limited circulation as an unpublished research report.

In 1967 Strachey was appointed a university reader in computer science, and was made a fellow of the newly created Wolfson College. Strachey threw himself into college life with an enthusiasm not seen since his days as a schoolmaster. The PRG had also begun to take off, having attracted several research students and was offering courses in computing to final year undergraduate and postgraduate students.

In 1969 the PRG acquired a British-manufactured minicomputer, the Computer Technology Limited (CTL) Mod 1, for which Strachey and his research assistant J. E. (Joe) Stoy wrote a single-user operating system. It was a programming tour de force, Strachey's first in many years. After a number of iterations, the operating system was named OS6 and a two-paper account was published in the *Computer Journal.* The project had some parallels with the Unix operating system developed at Bell Labs at the same time. Sadly, very few CTL computers were sold, so

the Strachey-Stoy operating system was little used outside Oxford. By contrast, Unix had been developed for a very popular Digital Equipment Corporation minicomputer that was used by hundreds of U.S. universities, and it spread like wildfire.

The last five years of Strachey's life were dominated by a single-minded effort to write a definitive account of his theory of programming language semantics—subsequently known as "denotational semantics." He gave up most of his consultancies and speaking engagements, only occasionally being induced to speak at high-profile events such as political committees or on the famous BBC television debate on the future of artificial intelligence in July 1973. During this period he entered on the most important academic collaboration of his life with Dana Scott, a Princeton mathematical logician. Scott visited Strachey for a sabbatical term in fall 1969 and helped him to put his semantics on a sound mathematical footing, which had previously been lacking. At the same time that denotational semantics was taking shape, the PRG was gaining an international reputation, and Strachey's personal reputation was soaring with his appointment to a personal chair and a Distinguished Fellowship of the British Computer Society, both in 1971.

Strachey decided to submit an essay on programming language semantics for the 1973–1974 Adams Prize of Cambridge University, with the aim of perhaps winning but also of using the deadline to force his normal writing pace. He collaborated with a research visitor from Cambridge University, Robert Milne. The essay did not win, and Strachey was exhausted by the effort. In early 1975 he began revising the essay for publication in book form, but a few weeks later he contracted what was diagnosed as jaundice. He made an apparent recovery, but then relapsed. He died of infectious hepatitis on 18 May 1975. The book was published posthumously in 1976 in two formidable volumes as *A Theory of Programming Language Semantics.* Strachey's protégé and collaborator Stoy published a more accessible textbook *Denotational Semantics* the following year, and programming language semantics firmly entered the computer science curriculum.

As with many computer scientists of his generation, Strachey's projects and publications do not amount to a coherent body of work. He lived at a time when computing was being shaped—the theories, practices, and technologies were all advancing rapidly. For example, one of his triumphs, the Pegasus computer, was rendered obsolete within a few years and is only of historical interest in the twenty-first century. Likewise his application programs, although brilliantly executed, were frankly ephemeral. Their ingenuity was dictated by the constraints of the technology; once those constraints were removed for the next generation of programmers, such ingenuity was unnecessary. In the study of programming languages and their semantics, however, Strachey produced work of permanent value. The "DNA" of CPL runs right through modern programming languages, and denotational semantics is likely to be a permanent strand of computer science.

BIBLIOGRAPHY

WORKS BY STRACHEY

"Time Sharing in Large Fast Computers." *Proceedings of the International Conference on Information Processing, UNESCO* (Paris, June 1959): B336–B341.

With David W. Barron, John N. Buxton, et al. "The Main Features of CPL." *Computer Journal* 6, no. 2 (1963): 134–143.

"A General Purpose Macrogenerator." *Computer Journal* 8, no. 3 (1965): 225–241.

"Systems Analysis and Programming." *Scientific American* 215 (March 1966): 112–124.

"Towards a Formal Semantics." In *Formal Language Description Languages for Computer Programming; Proceedings,* edited by Thomas B. Steel, 198–220. Amsterdam: North-Holland, 1966.

With David W. Barron. "Programming." In *Advances in Programming and Non-Numerical Computation,* edited by Leslie Fox, 49–82. Oxford and New York: Symposium Publications Division, Pergamon, 1966.

With Joseph E. Stoy. "OS6—An Experimental Operating System for a Small Computer. Part 1: General Principles and Structure." *Computer Journal* 15, no. 2 (1972): 117–124.

———. "OS6—An Experimental Operating System for a Small Computer. Part 2: Input/Output and Filing System." *Computer Journal* 15, no. 3 (1972): 195–203.

With Robert E. Milne. *A Theory of Programming Language Semantics.* London: Chapman & Hall; New York: Wiley, 1976.

OTHER SOURCES

Alton, Jeannine, Harriot Weiskittel, and Julia Latham-Jackson, comps. *Report on Correspondence and Papers of Christopher Strachey, Computer Scientist, 1934–1975.* London: Reproduced for the Contemporary Scientific Archives Centre by the Royal Commission on Historical Manuscripts, 1980. Strachey's extensive personal papers are located in the Bodleian Library, Oxford. The catalog provides valuable biographical context.

Campbell-Kelly, Martin. "Christopher Strachey 1916–1975: A Biographical Note." *Annals of the History of Computing* 7 (January 1985): 19–42. The most comprehensive biographical account of Strachey.

Higher-Order and Symbolic Computation 13 (April 2000). A special issue of the journal commemorating the 25th anniversary of Strachey's death and surveying his intellectual legacy.

Martin Campbell-Kelly

STRAHLER, ARTHUR NEWELL (*b.* Kolhapur, India, 20 February 1918; *d.* New York, New York, 6 December 2002), *geology, physical geography, quantitative-dynamic approach to geomorphology, slopes, drainage basins.*

In the middle of the twentieth century, Strahler spearheaded the campaign to fundamentally change how geologists and physical geographers pursue the study of landforms, which is called geomorphology. He challenged geomorphologists to move away from the traditional qualitative and descriptive Davisian approach to landform studies (named for William Morris Davis) that had been developed in the late nineteenth century and which emphasizes the long-term evolution of landscapes. In its place, Strahler advocated a quantitative, dynamic, process-oriented approach to the study of landforms that relies on detailed field observation, numerical measurements of form and process, mathematical representations, statistical methods, and systems analysis. Strahler's conception of geomorphology was widely adopted in the second half of the twentieth century, and it remained the foundation of geomorphic research and education into the early 2000s.

Early Life and Education. Strahler was born in Kolhapur, India, to parents who were Presbyterian missionaries. Back in the United States he went to school in the Chicago area before attending the College of Wooster in Ohio, where he met his future wife, Margaret (Marge) Strahler. At Wooster he majored in geology and became most interested in structural geology and geomorphology as taught by Charles B. Moke and Karl Ver Steeg, respectively. The study of landforms in the United States at that time was almost completely dominated by the qualitative, descriptive approach developed by the prominent Harvard University professor William Morris Davis. Davis's deductive theory of landscape development, called the geographical cycle, considered landforms to be the result of geologic structure, landforming processes, and time, the latter of which was referred to as stage. The emphasis in Davisian geomorphology was on the stage factor, rather than structure or process. Davis's most influential contribution was in positing how a landscape of given initial geological structure, such as an uplifted fault block, subjected to processes of weathering, erosion, transportation, and deposition in a humid climate, would evolve over long periods of time. Davis outlined qualitatively and with detailed drawings what a landscape would look like relatively soon after the initial structural relief came into existence (youthful stage of development), after a significant passage of time (mature stage of development), and long after the initial uplift (old age). In the Davisian approach to landform analysis, geomorphologists interpreted the landforms or landform assemblages in a region according to (1) their inferred stage of development; (2) whether it appeared that an erosional cycle had been interrupted (rejuvenation); and (3) if the features had been subjected to multiple erosion cycles. Against this traditional backdrop, as a college junior, Strahler attended summer geology field camp in Wisconsin under the then-controversial geomorphologist J Harlen Bretz. Mainstream geomorphologists and geologists at the time considered Bretz's claim that field evidence in the Channeled Scabland region of the Pacific Northwest revealed the occurrence of a cataclysmic flood, which he called the Spokane Flood, to be outlandish. Much of Strahler's own later field studies consisted of similar collections of detailed field evidence accompanied by interpretation in terms of landforming processes.

Graduate Education and Early Career. After receiving his BA from the College of Wooster in 1938, Strahler moved to New York City to begin graduate study in the Department of Geology at Columbia University supported by a Britton scholarship and later a university fellowship. He soon decided to emphasize geomorphology in his graduate studies and was directed in his work by Professor Douglas Johnson.

For his master's research, Strahler studied landslides along the Vermilion and Echo Cliffs in the Grand Canyon region of northern Arizona. He conducted this work completely within the Davisian paradigm of the geographical cycle, and his resulting paper includes an outline of the ideal cycle of erosion that Strahler inferred must account for the landslides. Nevertheless, because of his careful field observations on the correlation of the slope failures with the occurrence of weak shale rocks, that is, on elements of the geomorphic structure and process, Strahler concluded that Davis's temporal explanation of the features as the result of two erosion cycles was incorrect.

Strahler conducted considerable additional fieldwork throughout the Grand Canyon region, in part as field assistant to a fellow graduate student. In a series of resulting publications in the 1940s, Strahler continued to use fundamental field observations to challenge the Davisian two-erosion cycle interpretation of the recent geologic history of the Grand Canyon region. Although Strahler never explicitly stated so, the implication was that if the Davisian explanations are not correct for a region as important as the Grand Canyon area, they might be incorrect in other regions as well. In a separate 1946 publication, "Geomorphic Terminology and Classification of Land Masses," Strahler also criticized Davis's use of some specific landform terms (e.g., mountains, plains, plateaus) as being inconsistent. Despite these criticisms of some of the work of Davis and Davisian geomorphologists, in his publications Strahler continued to use the basic life-cycle terminology of youth, maturity, and old age, and to make his criticisms from within the Davisian paradigm.

For his dissertation research, Strahler tackled another large, important field area, the Appalachian Mountains. Strahler focused his efforts in Pennsylvania, testing multiple hypotheses that had been postulated previously by Davisian geomorphologists to explain the development of the present drainage system there. Once again, Strahler used extensive primary field observations, detailed map interpretation, a thorough review of the literature, and his knowledge of stream processes to assess the various explanations. Although he was already drifting from the established approach by focusing on detailed, site-specific field evidence and stream processes, his conclusions remained couched within the Davisian paradigm of landscape evolution. Strahler relied even more on the crucial role of force and resistance, that is, geomorphic processes, in explaining the unusual form of meanders in a Pennsylvania river in a subsequent, related paper.

Strahler had been appointed to the Columbia University faculty as a lecturer in 1941 while still a graduate student. Despite the demands of being a lecturer while also a graduate student, his publication record of the 1940s shows tremendous enthusiasm for tackling large-scale problems as well as great respect for previous researchers. That record, however, reveals an even greater respect for the field evidence and for invoking the best explanation for that evidence, even if it disagrees with explanations of eminent predecessors.

Professional Maturity: The 1950s. Strahler had been deeply impressed by the quantitative approach to drainage-system analysis detailed in a 1945 paper that was published in the *Geological Society of America Bulletin* by the civil engineer Robert Elmer Horton. Recognizing, in contrast to Horton's contributions, the severe limitations of working solely within the qualitative confines of the Davisian geographical cycle, Strahler began the decade of the 1950s by unleashing a blunt, but effective, criticism of Davis's stage approach to geomorphology while advocating what he termed the dynamic-quantitative system of landform analysis. In what was one of the most influential papers in twentieth-century geomorphology, Strahler (1950a) used the opportunity of writing a paper for an issue of the *Annals of the Association of American Geographers* published in honor of the anniversary of Davis's birth to characterize the scientific value of Davis's qualitative, descriptive approach to geomorphology as inadequate and superficial. He argued that a meaningful understanding of landforms instead requires quantitative measurements and numerical analyses of processes and forms, as well as the general application to landform studies of methods and techniques used in the other sciences. Only in this way, according to

Strahler, would geomorphologists be able to solve real-world problems in which landforms and landforming processes were involved. Strahler also advocated employing the concepts of open systems and steady state, as used in thermodynamics and biological science, to bring geomorphology into line with current advances in other sciences. Strahler warned, moreover, that if geomorphologists failed to make this methodological shift, they risked forfeiting their field of study to engineers and hydrologists. With a separate paper, Strahler (1950b) provided a detailed example of how to apply the quantitative-dynamic approach to studying slopes using statistical methods. Strahler's fullest statement of what modern geomorphology should encompass was published in 1952 as "Dynamic Basis of Geomorphology." In that paper Strahler outlined in detail how geomorphic processes are essentially chemistry and physics applied to the variety of earth materials.

Strahler's view of the direction in which the field should move resonated with the new generation of geomorphologists in the postwar era, and the movement grew to dominate geomorphology in the second half of the twentieth century. His logical and straightforward arguments for and examples of the quantitative-dynamic approach to geomorphology changed the direction of the discipline in the mid-twentieth century and enabled its practitioners to communicate more effectively with scientists in other disciplines.

Throughout the 1950s, Strahler published a steady stream of methodological papers: (1) encouraging geomorphologists in geology and geography to use various quantitative and statistical methods; and (2) demonstrating how these methods could be applied in analyzing geomorphic systems. He repeatedly credited Horton for his early application of such techniques to stream and drainage basin analysis. Among other things, Horton had advanced the fundamental concept of stream ordering, that is, of quantitatively describing where a given stream segment lies in the hierarchy of a drainage basin's tributaries. Strahler found it useful to modify Horton's stream ordering technique slightly to enhance the ease with which stream orders are subjected to further numerical assessment. In Strahler's version, streams without tributaries are first-order channels, two first-order channels must meet to form a second-order channel, two second-order channels join to create a third-order channel, and so forth. Strahler's version of stream ordering remains an important, fundamental element in the study of streams and drainage systems.

The professional journal articles that Strahler published in the 1950s contain a strong instructional aspect. They inform readers about the quantitative-dynamic approach to geomorphology and on various ways to implement it. The instructional aspect of these papers reflects one of Strahler's most significant professional attributes—his ability to educate others.

The Educator. Strahler's influence reached far beyond the mid-twentieth-century geomorphologists who read his published articles. Strahler enthusiastically involved his graduate students at Columbia in the paradigm shift to the process approach to geomorphology. Several of his graduate students went on to become among the most successful practitioners of process geomorphology in the second half of the twentieth century. Students with whom he worked at Columbia University included Richard Chorley, Donald Coates, Mark Melton, Marie Morisawa, Stanley Schumm, and Michael Woldenberg. Although Strahler was a faculty member of the Columbia University Geology Department, achieving the rank of professor in 1958 and serving as department chair from 1959 to 1962, he also served the university by representing physical geography on the committee overseeing instruction and advanced degrees in geography. Because in the United States geomorphology is a subfield of both geology and physical geography, Strahler's role in championing the paradigm change from Davisian to process geomorphology is equally well known in both disciplines.

Beyond the subfield of geomorphology, Strahler is a well-known name to geologists and physical geographers of all specialties in part because of the extensive list of thorough, well-organized, and well-illustrated textbooks that he authored and coauthored, especially in physical geography but also in physical geology and other aspects of the earth and environmental geosciences. Beginning with publication of his first physical geography textbook in 1951, Strahler authored at least eighteen different textbooks, many through multiple editions. In 1966, he published the popular book *A Geologist's View of Cape Cod* for the lay reader. His powerful incorporation of systems concepts into physical geography textbooks set the standard for the rest of the century and continued to be emulated into the early 2000s.

Strahler's research, productivity, and influence did not end when he retired from formal university teaching. He moved in 1973 to Santa Barbara, where he continued to work on his existing book projects and develop new ones, some of which he coauthored with his son, the geographer Alan H. Strahler. Strahler's enduring importance to the field of physical geography is illustrated by the fact that the first paper published in the journal *Physical Geography* is a contribution by Strahler (1980) on systems theory. During this period he also wrote an informative retrospective article on his days at Columbia University and authored books on the evolution-creationism controversy, the philosophy of science, and plate tectonics.

Strahler died in New York on 6 December 2002, survived by his son Alan, daughter Elaine, and their respective families. During his long, influential, and productive career, Strahler had been affiliated with the Geological Society of America, the Association of American Geographers, the American Geographical Society, the American Association for the Advancement of Science, the American Geophysical Union, the American Meteorological Society, the National Association of Geology Teachers, Sigma Xi, and Phi Beta Kappa. He received a distinguished service award from the Geographic Society of Chicago and had conducted important contract research for the U.S. Office of Naval Research. Among his most enduring contributions to the science of geomorphology is his redirection of the discipline away from Davisian geomorphology and toward the measurement, numerical assessment, and systematic analysis of landforms and landforming processes.

BIBLIOGRAPHY

WORKS BY STRAHLER

"Landslides of the Vermilion and Echo Cliffs, Northern Arizona." *Journal of Geomorphology* 3 (1940): 285–301.

"Geomorphic Significance of Valleys and Parks of the Kaibab and Coconino Plateaus, Arizona." *Science* 100 (8 September 1944): 219–220.

"Valleys and Parks of the Kaibab and Coconino Plateaus, Arizona." *Journal of Geology* 52 (1944): 361–387.

With Donald L. Babenroth. "Geomorphology and Structure of the East Kaibab Monocline, Arizona and Utah." *Geological Society of America Bulletin* 56 (1945): 107–150.

"Hypotheses of Stream Development in the Folded Appalachians of Pennsylvania." *Geological Society of America Bulletin* 56 (1945): 45–87.

"Elongate Intrenched Meanders of Conodoguinet Creek, PA." *American Journal of Science* 244 (1946): 31–40.

"Geomorphic Terminology and Classification of Land Masses." *Journal of Geology* 54 (1946): 32–42.

"Geomorphology and Structure of the West Kaibab Fault Zone and Kaibab Plateau, Arizona." *Geological Society of America Bulletin* 59 (1948): 513–540.

"Davis' Concepts of Slope Development Viewed in the Light of Recent Quantitative Investigations." *Annals of the Association of American Geographers* 40 (1950a): 209–213.

"Equilibrium Theory of Erosional Slopes Approached by Frequency Distribution Analysis." *American Journal of Science* 248 (1950b): 673–696, 800–814.

"Dynamic Basis of Geomorphology." *Geological Society of America Bulletin* 63 (1952): 923–938.

"Hypsometric (Area-Altitude) Analysis of Erosional Topography." *Geological Society of America Bulletin* 63 (1952): 1117–1141.

"Statistical Analysis in Geomorphic Research." *Journal of Geology* 62 (1954): 1–25.

"Quantitative Slope Analysis." *Geological Society of America Bulletin* 67 (1956): 571–596.

"The Nature of Induced Erosion and Aggradation." In *Man's Role in Changing the Face of the Earth*, edited by William L. Thomas Jr., with the collaboration of Carl O. Sauer, Marston Bates, and Lewis Mumford. Chicago: University of Chicago Press, 1956.

"Quantitative Analysis of Watershed Geomorphology." *Transactions, American Geophysical Union* 38 (1957): 913–920.

"Dimensional Analysis Applied to Fluvially Eroded Landforms." *Geological Society of America Bulletin* 69 (1958): 279–299.

With E. Donaldson Koons. *Objective and Quantitative Field Methods of Terrain Analysis*. U.S. Office of Naval Research Final Report of Contract 266-50, 1960.

Final Report of Project NR 388-057. U.S. Office of Naval Research Final Report of Contract 266-68, 1964.

A Geologist's View of Cape Cod. Garden City, NY: American Museum of Natural History [by] Natural History Press, 1966.

"Systems Theory in Physical Geography." *Physical Geography* 1 (1980): 1–27.

Science and Earth History: The Evolution/Creation Controversy. Buffalo, NY: Prometheus, 1987.

"Quantitative/Dynamic Geomorphology at Columbia 1945–60: A Retrospective." *Progress in Physical Geography* 16 (1992): 65–84.

Understanding Science: An Introduction to Concepts and Issues. Buffalo, NY: Prometheus, 1992.

Plate Tectonics. Cambridge, MA: Geo-Books, 1998.

OTHER SOURCES

Baker, Victor R. "The Spokane Flood Controversy and the Martian Outflow Channels." *Science* 202 (1978): 1249–1256.

Bretz, J Harlen. "The Channeled Scablands of the Columbia Plateau." *Journal of Geology* 31 (1923): 617–649.

Davis, William M. "The Rivers and Valleys of Pennsylvania." *National Geographic Magazine* 1 (1889): 183–253.

———. "The Geographical Cycle." *Geographical Journal* 14 (1899): 481–504.

———. "An Excursion to the Grand Canyon of the Colorado." *Harvard College Museum of Comparative Zoology Bulletin* 38 (1901): 107–203.

Horton, Robert E. "Erosional Development of Streams and Their Drainage Basins: Hydrophysical Approach to Quantitative Morphology." *Geological Society of America Bulletin* 56 (1945): 275–370.

Sack, Dorothy. "New Wine in Old Bottles: The Historiography of a Paradigm Change." *Geomorphology* 5 (1992): 251–263.

Santa Barbara News-Press, Obituary of "Strahler, Arthur Newell," 29 December 2002.

Schumm, Stanley A. "Arthur Newell Strahler (1918–2002)." *Annals of the Association of American Geographers* 94 (2004): 671–673.

Tinkler, Keith J. *A Short History of Geomorphology*. London: Croom Helm, 1985.

Dorothy Sack

STRATO OF LAMPSACUS

STRATO OF LAMPSACUS (*b.* [?] Lampsacus, Mysia; *d.* Athens, 271/268 BCE) *natural philosophy*. For the original article on Strato of Lampsacus see *DSB,* vol. 13.

Scholarship on the work of Strato of Lampsacus continues to show interest in his reputation for scientific pursuits, and to have little regard for the view that he was an atomist of sorts. Scholars have examined the possible biases of ancient reporters who have an interest in dismissing Strato's views and implicating him in the story of the decline of the Peripatos. They also emphasize that his views may not be as un-Aristotelian as was once thought. But the paucity of surviving material makes definitive interpretation of this intriguing figure problematic.

Scholarly treatment has become more cautious with regard to including Greek texts not referring directly to Strato of Lampsacus within his corpus. Following Hermann Diels, it was once widely thought that virtually the whole of the introduction to Hero's *Pneumatica* could be regarded as Strato's work. This position has encountered much criticism. The new edition of the fragments of Strato of Lampsacus by R. W. Sharples is more cautious in accepting Hero's work as evidence for Strato's views. The idea of a "law of *horror vacui* " also comes under scrutiny, because a number of different explanations of the tendency for void or emptier spaces to refill seem to have been advanced by Strato's day. The reconstruction of Strato's theory of matter, without the Heronian material, is less certain, because the quantity of surviving evidence is considerably reduced.

The work of the Hellenistic doctors Erasistratus and Herophilus has attracted more scholarly attention. They may have been important as a source for some of Strato's ideas, especially given that he was known to have spent time in the Alexandrian court.

Not only does the location of the "psychic center" near the brain owe something to the discovery of the nervous system; but the idea that the soul's activity is carried out by a physical substance, pneuma, dispersed through manifold passageways, may also owe its origins to the theory of the *neura* in Hellenistic medicine. Strato refers to the idea that cutting off the transmission of impact with ligatures prevents us from referring pain to its source. His willingness to countenance a two-seed theory of reproduction may also stem from Herophilus's discovery of the ovaries, rather than to a theory of competing forces.

The received view of Strato's scientific contributions includes a tendency for producing physical evidence in support of Aristotle's theories. Most famously, he attempted to provide a quantifiable demonstration of the downward acceleration of falling bodies. He argued that a falling stream of water becomes discontinuous as it falls farther, and also compared the impacts made by bodies falling from different heights, to demonstrate the greater speed of fall. On methodological grounds, he also stressed the importance of demonstrative methods in his criticisms of Plato's theory of recollection.

Speculation continues as to Strato's authorship of some texts in the Aristotelian corpus. In particular, he is often proposed as a possible author of Book Four of the Aristotelian *Mechanica,* although—apart from the existence of a book title suggesting this—the attribution is based on circumstantial evidence.

SUPPLEMENTARY BIBLIOGRAPHY

WORKS BY STRATO OF LAMPSACUS

Strato of Lampsacus. Edited by William W. Fortenbaugh and Marie-Laurence Desclose. Rutgers University Studies in Classical Humanities, 2008. A new edition and translation of the fragments of Strato of Lampsacus by R. W. Sharples, with a collection of interpretative essays.

OTHER SOURCES

Diels, Hermann. "Über Das Physikalische System Des Straton." *Sitzungsberichte der Preussischen Akademie der Wissenschaften* (1893): 101–127.

Furley, David. "Strato's Theory of Void." In *Cosmic Problems: Essays on Greek and Roman Philosophy of Nature,* edited by R. E. Allen and David Furley. Cambridge, U.K.: Cambridge University Press, 1989.

Parente, Margherita Isnardi. "Le obiezioni di Stratone al Fedone e l'epistemologia peripatetica nel primo ellenismo." *Rivista di Filologia e di Istruzione Classica* 105 (1977): 285–306.

Repici, Luciana. *La natura de l'anima: Saggi su Stratone de Lampsaco.* Turin, Italy: Tirrenia Stampatori, 1988.

Von Staden, Heinrich. *Herophilus: The Art of Medicine in Early Alexandria.* Cambridge, U.K.: Cambridge University Press, 1989. An excellent source on new medical discoveries.

Sylvia A. Berryman

STRICKLAND, CATHARINE PARR

SEE **Traill, Catharine Parr.**

STRÖMGREN, BENGT GEORG DANIEL (*b.* Göteborg, Sweden, 21 January 1908; *d.* Copenhagen, Denmark, 4 July 1987), *astronomy, astrophysics, stellar structure, interstellar gas, photoelectric photometry.*

Strömgren has been highlighted as one of the most prominent astrophysicists of the twentieth century. Born and educated in Denmark, he spent more than sixteen years as director at Yerkes and McDonald observatories and as professor of astrophysics at the Institute of Advanced Study at Princeton. Strömgren's scientific contributions can be separated into three main topics: problems of chemical composition of stellar structure and stellar interiors (1930–1940), the physics of interstellar gas (1938–1953), and photoelectric photometry of stellar spectra (from 1948). His contributions to the internationalization of astronomy were also considerable.

Origins. The son of Svante Elis and dentist Hedvig, née Lidforss, Strömgren was brought up in Denmark into a life of science, as was his brother Erik (later professor of psychiatry at Aarhus University, Denmark). Elis Strömgren was professor of astronomy at Copenhagen University and director of the Copenhagen Observatory. He secured Bengt's education at the best schools of Copenhagen and promoted his academic and practical training in astronomy. The son grew up surrounded by scientists: observers, assistants, and visiting international researchers in his father's official observatory residence. Bengt's scientific career began at a very early age: He published his first joint paper at the age of fourteen. After graduating from high school, he enrolled at Copenhagen University in 1925 to study astronomy and atomic physics.

In Germany, the commitment to advancing science led in 1863 to the founding of the international society Astronomische Gesellschaft (AG). Even before World War I, more than 400 members from mainly the Western world joined the AG, which was of significant importance to astronomical research, not least through the international astronomical periodical *Astronomische Nachrichten,* originally founded by H. C. Schumacher in 1821. German astronomers played important roles in the development of early twentieth century astrophysics. Being the national cradle of the observation of the photoelectric effect—and hence of practical photometry, i.e. the methods of studying stellar light—Germany fostered a series of important astrophysicists working with observational technology at a series of German observatories.

Already in 1921 and 1922, Strömgren's father brought Bengt to visit the Bonn Observatory and Neubabelsberg Observatory in Berlin, directed by Frank Küstner and Paul Guthnick respectively. There he learned the theory and practice of photographic photometry. He joined his father at meetings of the AG and the International Astronomical Union and thus was introduced to international aspects of science at a very early age.

Bengt Strömgren was one of the first to use the photocell for astrometry, by which he managed to record accurate times of meridian transits (passages of a star through the observer's meridian) by monitoring the image of a star while it crossed a grid of parallel wires in the focal plane of a telescope. His technological innovation of automated photocell-astrometry occurred when he was eighteen, and the national newspapers soon portrayed the young man as a genius destined to enter the world of science.

At Niels Bohr's Institute of Theoretical Physics, the cradle of the quantum revolution, Strömgren was taught quantum physics by figures such as Bohr, Hendrik A. Kramers, Werner Heisenberg, and Oskar Klein. Thus in the right place at the right time, Strömgren graduated in 1927, already appointed assistant at his father's observatory the year before—despite allegations of nepotism. In 1929, after working as observatory assistant and doctoral student for two years, Strömgren received his doctoral degree. He was just twenty-one years old.

In his dissertation, "Formulas and Tables for Determinations of Parabolic Orbits," Strömgren presented extensive calculations using a so-called numerical Archimedes calculator. The advent of the electromechanical calculators in the 1920s made it possible for astronomers to carry out numerical calculations of the novel astrophysical equations. The handling of numerical calculations became a necessity in the 1930s, and the Copenhagen Observatory had to purchase electromechanical calculators for this purpose. On the basis of recent work by the astronomer Gerald Merton on modified Gaussian methods for determinations of orbits, Strömgren devised a new method for calculating comet trajectories.

The technological development of Danish astronomy, however, went slowly and was predominantly focused on classical celestial astronomy and numerical calculations. He was educated in classical astronomy, but owing to the spirit and stimulating environment at Bohr's institute, Strömgren realized his professional future program: the application of the new quantum mechanics to astrophysics.

Chemical Composition of Stellar Interiors. Strömgren was instrumental in transferring his inspiration and theoretical knowledge from Bohr's institute to his father's observatory. In 1930, Strömgren entered fully into the field of stellar models and chemical composition of stellar interiors. The year of his appointment as lecturer at Copenhagen University (1932), Strömgren published his landmark article, "The Opacity of Stellar Matter and the Hydrogen Content of the Stars," in which he revised existing theory of the internal structure of stars, which had hitherto been formulated mainly by the British astronomer, Arthur S. Eddington.

In the paper Strömgren concluded that the main constituent of a star was hydrogen and not the heavier elements as was generally assumed in the late 1920s. The rapid development of physics in the mid-1920s had triggered Strömgren's idea of large hydrogen abundances inside stars. As the first steps in determining the hydrogen content, the work of the Cambridge physicists John A. Gaunt and the Japanese physicist Yoshikatse Sugiura played an important qualitative role for astronomy because they set in motion the development of novel astrophysical theories. Detailed quantum mechanical calculations undertaken by Gaunt and Sugiura indicated very clearly to Strömgren that there were some fundamental complications in the basic theoretical assumptions about stellar interiors.

Strömgren's hydrogen hypothesis was not quite novel in itself, but he made its basis more clear owing to improved calculation methods. The proposal of a large hydrogen abundance was advanced by Arthur Eddington at about the same time, although his reasoning was based on mathematical-analytical methods. Eddington's classic *The Internal Constitution of the Stars* (*ICS*) (1926) is one of the great masterpieces of astronomical literature. Stellar interior theories had made great progress during the preceding years, and Eddington's renowned monograph was long-awaited because of its all-embracing exposition of relevant subjects. *ICS* was also admired owing to its clear exposition of the theory of radiative equilibrium, and also because it emphasized two serious difficulties within the framework of Eddington's "'standard model." The first of these was a persistence of an order-of-magnitude discrepancy between observed and deduced opacities of stellar matter. The other was the so-called stellar-energy problem of finding the source of energy-generation processes, which remained unsolved until specialists in nuclear physics entered the field in the late 1930s. In *ICS*, Eddington wrote that the order-of-magnitude opacity discrepancy could be removed by assuming a high hydrogen abundance in the stars, but he did not regard this a proper way out of the problem. Consequently he would wait for the discovery of either new absorption mechanisms, or some further development of Heisenberg's quantum mechanics.

The methodological differences between the works of Eddington and Strömgren were manifest in this connection: Strömgren adopted the mixture of elements found earlier by the American astronomer Henry N. Russell in the solar atmosphere and calculated its so-called opacity (a

property of matter that prevents light from passing through it). Eddington instead employed a general theory, which he claimed should apply to any likely mixture of chemical elements (hydrogen, helium, and heavier elements).

With Strömgren's paper, the abundance of the light elements in stars—and hence in the entire universe—was closer to being determined. The hypothesis of hydrogen preponderance provided the missing link in the understanding of the values of stellar luminosities and radii. In addition, Strömgren's paper furthered the knowledge of the temperatures inside stars—which had far-reaching consequences, as it meant a radical change of the prevailing views upon the physical conditions inside stars. Strömgren's numerical style turned out to be essential for the new astrophysics owing to the empirical-inductive character and, contrary to hypothetical-deductive methods as undertaken by Eddington, James Jeans, and Edward A. Milne, it has remained so ever since. At the same time, Strömgren's efforts secured Denmark a significant position on the international scene of theoretical astrophysics.

American Astronomy. The shift in focus of Danish astronomy toward the United States became apparent in the 1930s. There were political-economic motives as well as techno-scientific reasons for the Western orientation of Scandinavian astronomy. One reason was the boycott of German astronomy after World War I, which hampered international contact between astronomers inside and outside Germany. Internal issues also characterized the problems of German astronomers: lack of resources, dismissals of Jewish scientists, and the shut-down of projects. At the same time, numerous ideas and astronomers from foreign countries, the Netherlands in particular, made their way to the United States between the wars and in so doing furthered the development of American astronomy and to laid the foundations of many new theories.

One of the foreigners to visit the United States was Strömgren. His first visit lasted from 1936 to 1938 and was at the invitation of the director of Yerkes Observatory—and colleague through many years—Otto Struve (Strömgren left Denmark again to the benefit of the United States in 1951–1967). Work that was not possible to carry out in Denmark but possible in the States was multifarious: close cooperation between theoretical and observational astronomy; spectral photometry requiring comparisons between theory and practical astronomy; scientific confirmations and refinement of both theory and experiment; and practical work in geometrical optics. Had Strömgren stayed in Denmark, mainly pure theoretical astronomy of all sorts would have constituted the outcome of his research activities—predominantly due to lack of financial resources and modern observational technology.

In the United States, Strömgren followed up his work on hydrogen abundance. He wrote an important paper on the theory of stellar interiors and development (1937). In this paper, Strömgren sought to answer how the addition of helium would change his stellar model. The only observational basis to support a helium hypothesis was estimates of relative amounts of hydrogen and helium, but determinations were rather weak. The final result was a model comparatively close to the present relative chemical composition by weight, which Strömgren found to be 60 to 70 percent hydrogen, 26 to 36 percent helium, and 4 percent heavier elements.

As it was also a survey article, accumulating existing knowledge in one place, it opened the problem of stellar interiors and energy production for investigation not only by astrophysicists but also by theoretical physicists. Strömgren was accustomed to collaboration between astronomers and physicists already from the early 1930s and naturally he welcomed their views on the riddle of the time: What sources of energy powered the radiation output of stars?

Solar Energy Production Strömgren's hydrogen hypothesis—later improved by his helium assertion—paved the way for Bethe's and Weizsäcker's 1938 theories of stellar energy loss through the conversion of hydrogen into helium in nuclear reactions. It was thus a central step in a fruitful line of reasoning in the understanding of nuclear physicists of stellar energy sources at the end of the 1930s.

Before leaving the United States in 1938, Strömgren was invited by George Gamow to participate in a Washington conference attended by a select group of theoretical physicists and astronomers. The theme of the 1938 Washington conference was the sources of stellar energy. Strömgren attended along with figures such as Edward Teller, Donald H. Menzel, Merle Tuve, George Gamow, and the Nobel laureates Hans Bethe and Strömgren's lifelong friend, Subrahmanyan Chandrasekhar.

Strömgren opened the conference by outlining the present status of the problem of temperature and density distribution in the interior of stars. For the theory of internal structure of stars, he argued that two issues were of particular importance, namely, the calculation of opacities and the rate of energy production. In a subsequent publication by Chandrasekhar, Gamow, and Tuve, the results of the Washington conference were issued in *Nature*, in which Carl Friedrich von Weizsäcker's so-called "Aufbauhypothese" was presented. The key point of the hypothesis was that stellar interiors continually build up heavier elements from hydrogen and that such processes liberate sufficient amounts of energy to account for the radiation of the stars. But Weizsäcker's model schemes of transmutations of helium into lithium and back to

another helium isotope, while emitting radiation and positrons, were contradicted by experimental evidence. It was uncertain which processes accounted for the stellar energy production.

Strömgren's experience of the first part of the conference was that no solution was in sight. However, input from Hans Bethe gave hope, as the Washington conference occasioned Bethe's interest in the nuclear aspects of the energy problem.

The ideas of Weizsäcker, Bethe, and Gamow about nuclear energy production in stars were later also discussed with Strömgren at the 1938 International Astronomical Union's General Assembly in Stockholm. Bethe managed to calculate the energy production in the interior of the Sun by the proton-proton chain in which part of the matter involved is converted into electromagnetic energy by hydrogen fusion. Moreover, Strömgren believed that Bethe used better empirical data than Weizsäcker. From the new knowledge about stellar temperatures, densities, and chemical composition, Bethe looked systematically for the possibilities of reactions under those conditions. Until 1950, it was thought that the so-called carbon cycle was the main process of stellar energy production (in stars with central temperatures greater than 15 million Kelvin, the carbon cycle takes over the dominant role of energy production from hydrogen fusion). In 1950, however, it became clear that the proton-proton process was the primary process for the Sun.

It is somewhat striking, but not atypical, that it was theoretical physicists, and not astrophysicists, who eventually solved the problem of nuclear reactions in stellar interiors. Even though Strömgren and the community of astronomers were very familiar with nuclear reactions, Strömgren found it "so difficult to sort out what was going on in nuclear physics at the time that it took nuclear physicists who had devoted all their time to the field to sort it out" (quoted in Rebsdorf, 2005, p. 301).

Interstellar Gas. Bethe's nuclear energy results had important consequences for the astronomers' estimates of stellar age. The lifetime of solar-type stars was anticipated to be about 10^{10} years, but at the same time it was evident that massive main-sequence stars had much shorter lifetimes, of about 10^7 years in extreme cases. This led the astronomical community to conclude that star formation must occur under conditions such as those observed in the earth's neighborhood of the galaxy at the present epoch. A compelling question naturally arose from this conclusion: Is there a sufficient amount of matter in interstellar space to allow for such processes?

It was well known that particles existed in interstellar space and that they caused the absorption and reddening of starlight travelling through space, but the amounts observed were rather modest. Strömgren investigated theoretically the photoionization of interstellar gas and discovered the great importance of the radiation from the relatively rare, hot O stars in fixing the physical conditions in space. As an important result he published "The Physical State of Interstellar Hydrogen" (1939). In the paper he showed that homogeneously distributed interstellar atomic hydrogen was ionized by ultraviolet light from hot O and B stars in particular, out to certain sharply determined radial distances from these stars. These shells of ionized hydrogen, such as the diffuse Orion Nebula, later became known as *Strömgren spheres*.

The paper was based on relatively simple methods, considerations, and calculations. Strömgren's theoretical calculations also turned out to match the intensities of hydrogen emission lines in extended areas of the Milky Way, observed by Otto Struve at the McDonald Observatory on Mount Locke in Texas. The match was evident when the hydrogen density in interstellar space was of the order of magnitude of one atom per cubic centimeter. The crucial conclusion reached by Strömgren was that the galaxy contains very large amounts of hydrogen outside of the hydrogen observed in ionised regions.

Strömgren's interest in the interstellar medium and the problem of the formation of these so-called H II regions around stars was triggered by Struve's development of a new technique for observing very faint stars. In fact, in 1936 Struve had made the important discovery of Balmer line glow in extensive regions of the galaxy, and this triggered Strömgren's interest in questions of the interstellar medium. Until that time it was known that a number of diffuse nebulae emitted an emission spectrum of strong Balmer lines, arising from $n = 2$ transitions of the hydrogen atom. What Struve found, in addition to these well-known areas, was that even large regions of hundreds of square degrees on the sky had a faint glow. At the McDonald Observatory Struve developed what was called the Centipede: a device pointed toward the celestial Pole, which could record faint spectra of extended areas and had a focal length of one hundred meters. By use of this instrument, Struve and the American astrophysicist Christian T. Elvey were able to measure this glow. They found emission lines in eight out of fifteen fields, immediately challenging Strömgren to develop a theoretical model to match the observations.

Strömgren constructed a stellar model of a luminous star with high temperature embedded in a uniform medium of hydrogen. The salient result of his investigation was a sharp transition. Despite numerous efforts at Mount Wilson Observatory to identify more absorption lines, the general assumption had been that the density of interstellar gas was very low. It was not possible to conclude that the amount of mass was distinctly high or that

there was a large amount of hydrogen. In his 1939 paper, Strömgren attributed to Struve and Elvey the discovery of extended areas in the Milky Way in which the Balmer lines were observed.

Strömgren's investigations revealed that high-temperature stars and clusters of such stars in particular were found to be capable of ionizing interstellar hydrogen in regions large enough to be of importance in problems of interstellar space. Strömgren's sought to arrive at a picture of the actual physical state of interstellar hydrogen, and he calculated that the Balmer-line emission should be limited to certain rather sharply bounded regions in space surrounding O-type stars or clusters. Moreover, Strömgren found relations between the gas density, the luminosity of the star, and the size of the sphere of ionized hydrogen around it. He found that such regions should have diameters of about 200 parsecs, or c. 650 light-years, which was found to be in general agreement with Struve and Elvey's observations. Strömgren calculated the density of hydrogen in these areas, later to be denoted H II regions, or Strömgren spheres, namely 3 per cubic centimeter.

Strömgren's paper ushered in a new line of research for him, one that he would follow until about 1953, when his photoelectric photometry research on spectra took over. In fact, Strömgren's last paper on interstellar emission was published in 1951.

Photoelectric Photometry. In 1952, the year after he succeeded Struve as director of Yerkes and McDonald Observatories, Strömgren pioneered a new photometric system to succeed the supplement of an existing photometric system, the so-called *UVBGRI system* invented in 1943 by Joel Stebbins and Albert Whitford at the Washburn Observatory, Wisconsin. Strömgren's novel narrow-band system made use of a photomultiplier (converting light into an electric signal), the so-called *abcdef* system, which was a six-color system like the *UVBGRI*. The *abcdef* system was not very practical for photometric work when dealing with very faint stars, though.

Then Strömgren investigated the possibilities of spectral classification (the classification of stars according to their spectra; each major spectral classification is given a letter, with additional numbers providing further subdivisions) through photoelectric photometry with interference filters. The first observations were made in 1950 at the McDonald Observatory, and by 1951, he had published a paper on his ideas of the system. In collaboration with Danish astronomer Kjeld Gyldenkerne, Strömgren made photoelectric measures with the 32-inch reflector of the Observatoire Haute Provence in France, using a set of twenty-six filters covering the wavelength region from 3350 to 5500 Å. The American astronomer William W. Morgan helped determine spectral and luminosity classes